人 → ihjk (p 1176-1177)

Design Concepts in Programming Languages

Design Concepts in Programming Languages

Franklyn Turbak and David Gifford
with Mark A. Sheldon

The MIT Press
Cambridge, Massachusetts
London, England

MIT Press books may be purchased at special quantity discounts for business or sales promotional use. For information, please email special_sales@mitpress.mit.edu or write to Special Sales Department, The MIT Press, 55 Hayward Street, Cambridge, MA 02142.

This book was set in LaTeX by the authors, and was printed and bound in the United States of America.

Library of Congress Cataloging-in-Publication Data

Turbak, Franklyn A.
Design concepts in programming languages / Franklyn A. Turbak and David K. Gifford, with Mark A. Sheldon.
   p. cm.
Includes bibliographical references and index.
ISBN 978-0-262-20175-9 (hardcover : alk. paper)
1. Programming languages (Electronic computers). I. Gifford, David K., 1954–. II. Sheldon, Mark A. III. Title.
QA76.7.T845   2008
005.1—dc22   2008013841

10 9 8 7 6 5 4 3 2 1

Brief Contents

Preface   xix

Acknowledgments   xxi

I   Foundations   1

   1   Introduction   3

   2   Syntax   19

   3   Operational Semantics   45

   4   Denotational Semantics   113

   5   Fixed Points   163

II   Dynamic Semantics   205

   6   FL: A Functional Language   207

   7   Naming   307

   8   State   383

   9   Control   443

   10 Data   539

III   Static Semantics   615

   11 Simple Types   617

   12 Polymorphism and Higher-order Types   701

   13 Type Reconstruction   769

   14 Abstract Types   839

   15 Modules   889

   16 Effects Describe Program Behavior   943

IV   Pragmatics   1003

   17 Compilation   1005

   18 Garbage Collection   1119

A   A Metalanguage   1147

B   Our Pedagogical Languages   1197

References   1199

Index   1227

Contents

Preface   xix

Acknowledgments   xxi

I   Foundations   1

1   Introduction   3
  1.1   Programming Languages   3
  1.2   Syntax, Semantics, and Pragmatics   4
  1.3   Goals   6
  1.4   PostFix: A Simple Stack Language   8
    1.4.1   Syntax   8
    1.4.2   Semantics   9
    1.4.3   The Pitfalls of Informal Descriptions   14
  1.5   Overview of the Book   15

2   Syntax   19
  2.1   Abstract Syntax   20
  2.2   Concrete Syntax   22
  2.3   S-Expression Grammars Specify ASTs   23
    2.3.1   S-Expressions   23
    2.3.2   The Structure of S-Expression Grammars   24
    2.3.3   Phrase Tags   30
    2.3.4   Sequence Patterns   30
    2.3.5   Notational Conventions   32
    2.3.6   Mathematical Foundation of Syntactic Domains   36
  2.4   The Syntax of PostFix   39

3   Operational Semantics   45
  3.1   The Operational Semantics Game   45
  3.2   Small-step Operational Semantics (SOS)   49
    3.2.1   Formal Framework   49
    3.2.2   Example: An SOS for PostFix   52
    3.2.3   Rewrite Rules   54
    3.2.4   Operational Execution   58

       3.2.5   Progress Rules 62

       3.2.6   Context-based Semantics 71

  3.3   Big-step Operational Semantics 75

  3.4   Operational Reasoning 79

  3.5   Deterministic Behavior of EL 80

  3.6   Termination of PostFix Programs 84

       3.6.1   Energy 84

       3.6.2   The Proof of Termination 86

       3.6.3   Structural Induction 88

  3.7   Safe PostFix Transformations 89

       3.7.1   Observational Equivalence 89

       3.7.2   Transform Equivalence 92

       3.7.3   Transform Equivalence Implies Observational Equivalence 96

  3.8   Extending PostFix 100

4 Denotational Semantics 113

  4.1   The Denotational Semantics Game 113

  4.2   A Denotational Semantics for EL 117

       4.2.1   Step 1: Restricted ELMM 117

       4.2.2   Step 2: Full ELMM 120

       4.2.3   Step 3: ELM 124

       4.2.4   Step 4: EL 127

       4.2.5   A Denotational Semantics Is Not a Program 128

  4.3   A Denotational Semantics for PostFix 131

       4.3.1   A Semantic Algebra for PostFix 131

       4.3.2   A Meaning Function for PostFix 134

       4.3.3   Semantic Functions for PostFix: the Details 142

  4.4   Denotational Reasoning 145

       4.4.1   Program Equality 145

       4.4.2   Safe Transformations: A Denotational Approach 147

       4.4.3   Technical Difficulties 150

  4.5   Relating Operational and Denotational Semantics 150

       4.5.1   Soundness 151

       4.5.2   Adequacy 157

       4.5.3   Full Abstraction 159

       4.5.4   Operational versus Denotational: A Comparison 161

5 Fixed Points 163
> 5.1 The Fixed Point Game 163
>> 5.1.1 Recursive Definitions 163
>> 5.1.2 Fixed Points 166
>> 5.1.3 The Iterative Fixed Point Technique 168
> 5.2 Fixed Point Machinery 174
>> 5.2.1 Partial Orders 174
>> 5.2.2 Complete Partial Orders (CPOs) 182
>> 5.2.3 Pointedness 185
>> 5.2.4 Monotonicity and Continuity 187
>> 5.2.5 The Least Fixed Point Theorem 190
>> 5.2.6 Fixed Point Examples 191
>> 5.2.7 Continuity and Strictness 197
> 5.3 Reflexive Domains 201
> 5.4 Summary 203

II Dynamic Semantics 205

6 FL: A Functional Language 207
> 6.1 Decomposing Language Descriptions 207
> 6.2 The Structure of FL 208
>> 6.2.1 FLK: The Kernel of the FL Language 209
>> 6.2.2 FL Syntactic Sugar 218
>> 6.2.3 The FL Standard Library 235
>> 6.2.4 Examples 239
> 6.3 Variables and Substitution 244
>> 6.3.1 Terminology 244
>> 6.3.2 Abstract Syntax DAGs and Stoy Diagrams 248
>> 6.3.3 Alpha-Equivalence 250
>> 6.3.4 Renaming and Variable Capture 251
>> 6.3.5 Substitution 253
> 6.4 An Operational Semantics for FLK 258
>> 6.4.1 FLK Evaluation 258
>> 6.4.2 FLK Simplification 270
> 6.5 A Denotational Semantics for FLK 275
>> 6.5.1 Semantic Algebra 275
>> 6.5.2 Valuation Functions 280
> 6.6 The Lambda Calculus 290

6.6.1   Syntax of the Lambda Calculus   291
6.6.2   Operational Semantics of the Lambda Calculus   291
6.6.3   Denotational Semantics of the Lambda Calculus   296
6.6.4   Representational Games   297

7   Naming   307
7.1   Parameter Passing   309
   7.1.1   Call-by-Name vs. Call-by-Value: The Operational View   310
   7.1.2   Call-by-Name vs. Call-by-Value: The Denotational View   316
   7.1.3   Nonstrict versus Strict Pairs   318
   7.1.4   Handling `rec` in a CBV Language   320
   7.1.5   Thunking   324
   7.1.6   Call-by-Denotation   328
7.2   Name Control   332
   7.2.1   Hierarchical Scoping: Static and Dynamic   334
   7.2.2   Multiple Namespaces   347
   7.2.3   Nonhierarchical Scope   352
7.3   Object-oriented Programming   362
   7.3.1   HOOK: An Object-oriented Kernel   362
   7.3.2   HOOPLA   368
   7.3.3   Semantics of HOOK   370

8   State   383
8.1   FL Is a Stateless Language   384
8.2   Simulating State in FL   390
   8.2.1   Iteration   390
   8.2.2   Single-Threaded Data Flow   392
   8.2.3   Monadic Style   394
   8.2.4   Imperative Programming   397
8.3   Mutable Data: FLIC   397
   8.3.1   Mutable Cells   397
   8.3.2   Examples of Imperative Programming   400
   8.3.3   An Operational Semantics for FLICK   405
   8.3.4   A Denotational Semantics for FLICK   411
   8.3.5   Call-by-Name versus Call-by-Value Revisited   425
   8.3.6   Referential Transparency, Interference, and Purity   427
8.4   Mutable Variables: FLAVAR   429
   8.4.1   Mutable Variables   429
   8.4.2   FLAVAR   430
   8.4.3   Parameter-passing Mechanisms for FLAVAR   432

9 Control 443

9.1   Motivation: Control Contexts and Continuations   443

9.2   Using Procedures to Model Control   446

    9.2.1   Representing Continuations as Procedures   446

    9.2.2   Continuation-Passing Style (CPS)   449

    9.2.3   Multiple-value Returns   450

    9.2.4   Nonlocal Exits   455

    9.2.5   Coroutines   457

    9.2.6   Error Handling   461

    9.2.7   Backtracking   465

9.3   Continuation-based Semantics of FLICK   471

    9.3.1   A Standard Semantics of FLICK   472

    9.3.2   A Computation-based Continuation Semantics of FLICK   482

9.4   Nonlocal Exits   493

    9.4.1   `label` and `jump`   494

    9.4.2   A Denotational Semantics for `label` and `jump`   497

    9.4.3   An Operational Semantics for `label` and `jump`   503

    9.4.4   `call-with-current-continuation` (`cwcc`)   505

9.5   Iterators: A Simple Coroutining Mechanism   506

9.6   Exception Handling   513

    9.6.1   `raise`, `handle`, and `trap`   515

    9.6.2   A Standard Semantics for Exceptions   519

    9.6.3   A Computation-based Semantics for Exceptions   524

    9.6.4   A Desugaring-based Implementation of Exceptions   527

    9.6.5   Examples Revisited   530

10 Data 539

10.1   Products   539

    10.1.1   Positional Products   541

    10.1.2   Named Products   549

    10.1.3   Nonstrict Products   551

    10.1.4   Mutable Products   561

10.2   Sums   567

10.3   Sum of Products   577

10.4   Data Declarations   583

10.5   Pattern Matching   590

    10.5.1   Introduction to Pattern Matching   590

    10.5.2   A Desugaring-based Semantics of `match`   594

    10.5.3   Views   605

III   Static Semantics   615

11 Simple Types   617
   11.1   Static Semantics   617
   11.2   What Is a Type?   620
   11.3   Dimensions of Types   622
       11.3.1   Dynamic versus Static Types   623
       11.3.2   Explicit versus Implicit Types   625
       11.3.3   Simple versus Expressive Types   627
   11.4 μFLEX: A Language with Explicit Types   628
       11.4.1   Types   629
       11.4.2   Expressions   631
       11.4.3   Programs and Syntactic Sugar   634
       11.4.4   Free Identifiers and Substitution   636
   11.5   Type Checking in μFLEX   640
       11.5.1   Introduction to Type Checking   640
       11.5.2   Type Environments   643
       11.5.3   Type Rules for μFLEX   645
       11.5.4   Type Derivations   648
       11.5.5   Monomorphism   655
   11.6   Type Soundness   661
       11.6.1   What Is Type Soundness?   661
       11.6.2   An Operational Semantics for μFLEX   662
       11.6.3   Type Soundness of μFLEX   667
   11.7   Types and Strong Normalization   673
   11.8   Full FLEX: Typed Data and Recursive Types   675
       11.8.1   Typed Products   675
       11.8.2   Type Equivalence   679
       11.8.3   Typed Mutable Data   681
       11.8.4   Typed Sums   682
       11.8.5   Typed Lists   685
       11.8.6   Recursive Types   688
       11.8.7   Full FLEX Summary   696

12 Polymorphism and Higher-order Types   701
   12.1   Subtyping   701
       12.1.1   FLEX/S: FLEX with Subtyping   702
       12.1.2   Dimensions of Subtyping   713
       12.1.3   Subtyping and Inheritance   723
   12.2   Polymorphic Types   725

12.2.1 Monomorphic Types Are Not Expressive   725

12.2.2 Universal Polymorphism: FLEX/SP   727

12.2.3 Deconstructible Data Types   738

12.2.4 Bounded Quantification   745

12.2.5 Ad Hoc Polymorphism   748

12.3 Higher-order Types: Descriptions and Kinds   750

12.3.1 Descriptions: FLEX/SPD   750

12.3.2 Kinds and Kind Checking: FLEX/SPDK   758

12.3.3 Discussion   764

13 Type Reconstruction   769

13.1 Introduction   769

13.2 μFLARE: A Language with Implicit Types   772

13.2.1 μFLARE Syntax and Type Erasure   772

13.2.2 Static Semantics of μFLARE   774

13.2.3 Dynamic Semantics and Type Soundness of μFLARE   778

13.3 Type Reconstruction for μFLARE   781

13.3.1 Type Substitutions   781

13.3.2 Unification   783

13.3.3 The Type-Constraint-Set Abstraction   787

13.3.4 A Reconstruction Algorithm for μFLARE   790

13.4 Let Polymorphism   801

13.4.1 Motivation   801

13.4.2 A μFLARE Type System with Let Polymorphism   803

13.4.3 μFLARE Type Reconstruction with Let Polymorphism   808

13.5 Extensions   813

13.5.1 The Full FLARE Language   813

13.5.2 Mutable Variables   820

13.5.3 Products and Sums   821

13.5.4 Sum-of-products Data Types   826

14 Abstract Types   839

14.1 Data Abstraction   839

14.1.1 A Point Abstraction   840

14.1.2 Procedural Abstraction Is Not Enough   841

14.2 Dynamic Locks and Keys   843

14.3 Existential Types   847

14.4 Nonce Types   859

14.5 Dependent Types   869

14.5.1 A Dependent Package System   870

14.5.2 Design Issues with Dependent Types   877

15 Modules   889
15.1 An Overview of Modules and Linking   889
15.2 An Introduction to FLEX/M   891
15.3 Module Examples: Environments and Tables   901
15.4 Static Semantics of FLEX/M Modules   910
15.4.1 Scoping   910
15.4.2 Type Equivalence   911
15.4.3 Subtyping   912
15.4.4 Type Rules   912
15.4.5 Implicit Projection   918
15.4.6 Typed Pattern Matching   921
15.5 Dynamic Semantics of FLEX/M Modules   923
15.6 Loading Modules   925
15.6.1 Type Soundness of load via a Load-Time Check   927
15.6.2 Type Soundness of load via a Compile-Time Check   928
15.6.3 Referential Transparency of load for File-Value Coherence   930
15.7 Discussion   932
15.7.1 Scoping Limitations   932
15.7.2 Lack of Transparent and Translucent Types   933
15.7.3 The Coherence Problem   934
15.7.4 Purity Issues   937

16 Effects Describe Program Behavior   943
16.1 Types, Effects, and Regions: What, How, and Where   943
16.2 A Language with a Simple Effect System   945
16.2.1 Types, Effects, and Regions   945
16.2.2 Type and Effect Rules   951
16.2.3 Reconstructing Types and Effects: Algorithm Z 959
16.2.4 Effect Masking Hides Unobservable Effects   972
16.2.5 Effect-based Purity for Generalization   974
16.3 Using Effects to Analyze Program Behavior   978
16.3.1 Control Transfers   978
16.3.2 Dynamic Variables   983
16.3.3 Exceptions   985
16.3.4 Execution Cost Analysis   988
16.3.5 Storage Deallocation and Lifetime Analysis   991
16.3.6 Control Flow Analysis   995
16.3.7 Concurrent Behavior   996

16.3.8 Mobile Code Security   999

IV Pragmatics   1003

17 Compilation   1005

17.1 Why Do We Study Compilation?   1005
17.2 TORTOISE Architecture   1007
    17.2.1 Overview of TORTOISE   1007
    17.2.2 The Compiler Source Language: FLARE/V   1009
    17.2.3 Purely Structural Transformations   1012
17.3 Transformation 1: Desugaring   1013
17.4 Transformation 2: Globalization   1014
17.5 Transformation 3: Assignment Conversion   1019
17.6 Transformation 4: Type/Effect Reconstruction   1025
    17.6.1 Propagating Type and Effect Information   1026
    17.6.2 Effect-based Code Optimization   1026
17.7 Transformation 5: Translation   1030
    17.7.1 The Compiler Intermediate Language: FIL   1030
    17.7.2 Translating FLARE to FIL   1036
17.8 Transformation 6: Renaming   1038
17.9 Transformation 7: CPS Conversion   1042
    17.9.1 The Structure of TORTOISE CPS Code   1044
    17.9.2 A Simple CPS Transformation   1049
    17.9.3 A More Efficient CPS Transformation   1058
    17.9.4 CPS-Converting Control Constructs   1070
17.10 Transformation 8: Closure Conversion   1075
    17.10.1 Flat Closures   1076
    17.10.2 Variations on Flat Closure Conversion   1085
    17.10.3 Linked Environments   1090
17.11 Transformation 9: Lifting   1094
17.12 Transformation 10: Register Allocation   1098
    17.12.1 The FIL_{reg} Language   1098
    17.12.2 A Register Allocation Algorithm   1102
    17.12.3 The Expansion Phase   1104
    17.12.4 The Register Conversion Phase   1104
    17.12.5 The Spilling Phase   1112

18 Garbage Collection   1119

18.1   Why Garbage Collection?   1119

18.2   FRM: The FIL Register Machine   1122

    18.2.1   The FRM Architecture   1122

    18.2.2   FRM Descriptors   1123

    18.2.3   FRM Blocks   1127

18.3   A Block Is Dead if It Is Unreachable   1130

    18.3.1   Reference Counting   1131

    18.3.2   Memory Tracing   1132

18.4   Stop-and-copy GC   1133

18.5   Garbage Collection Variants   1141

    18.5.1   Mark-sweep GC   1141

    18.5.2   Tag-free GC   1141

    18.5.3   Conservative GC   1142

    18.5.4   Other Variations   1142

18.6   Static Approaches to Automatic Deallocation   1144

A   A Metalanguage   1147

A.1   The Basics   1147

    A.1.1   Sets   1148

    A.1.2   Boolean Operators and Predicates   1151

    A.1.3   Tuples   1152

    A.1.4   Relations   1153

A.2   Functions   1155

    A.2.1   What Is a Function?   1156

    A.2.2   Application   1158

    A.2.3   More Function Terminology   1159

    A.2.4   Higher-order Functions   1160

    A.2.5   Multiple Arguments and Results   1161

    A.2.6   Lambda Notation   1165

    A.2.7   Recursion   1168

    A.2.8   Lambda Notation Is Not Lisp!   1169

A.3   Domains   1171

    A.3.1   Motivation   1171

    A.3.2   Types   1172

    A.3.3   Product Domains   1173

    A.3.4   Sum Domains   1176

    A.3.5   Sequence Domains   1181

    A.3.6   Function Domains   1184

A.4   Metalanguage Summary   1186
        A.4.1   The Metalanguage Kernel   1186
        A.4.2   The Metalanguage Sugar   1188

B Our Pedagogical Languages   1197

References   1199

Index   1227

Preface

This book is the text for 6.821 *Programming Languages*, an entry-level, single-semester, graduate-level course at the Massachusetts Institute of Technology. The students that take our course know how to program and are mathematically inclined, but they typically have not had an introduction to programming language design or its mathematical foundations. We assume a reader with similar preparation, and we include an appendix that completely explains the mathematical metalanguage we use. Many of the exercises are taken directly from our problem sets and examination questions, and have been specifically designed to cause students to apply their newfound knowledge to practical (and sometimes impractical!) extensions to the foundational ideas taught in the course.

Our fundamental goal for *Programming Languages* is to use a simple and concise framework to teach key ideas in programming language design and implementation. We specifically eschewed an approach based on a tour of the great programming languages. Instead, we have adopted a family of syntactically simple pedagogical languages that systematically explore programming language concepts (see Appendix B). Contemporary concerns about safety and security have caused programmers to migrate to languages that embrace many of the key ideas that we explain. Where appropriate, we discuss how the ideas we introduce have been incorporated into contemporary programming languages that are in wide use.

We use an s-expression syntax for programs because this syntactic form is easy to parse and to directly manipulate, key attributes that support our desire to make everything explicit in our descriptions of language semantics and pragmatics. While you may find s-expression syntax unfamiliar at first, it permits the unambiguous and complete articulation of ideas in a simple framework.

Programming languages are a plastic and expressive medium, and we are hopeful that we will communicate our passion for these computational canvases that are an important underpinning for computer science.

Web Supplement

Specialized topics and code that implements many of the algorithms and compilation methods can be found on our accompanying Web site:

dcpl.mit.edu

The Web Supplement also includes additional material, such as a section on concurrency and proofs of the theorems stated in the book.

To the Student

The book is full of examples, and a good way to approach the material is to study the examples first. Then review the figures that capture key rules or algorithms. Skip over details that bog you down at first, and return to them later once you have additional context.

Using and implementing novel programming language concepts will further enhance your understanding. The Web Supplement contains interpreters for various pedagogical languages used in the book, and there are many implementation-based exercises that will help forge connections between theory and practice.

To the Teacher

We teach the highlights of the material in this book in 24 lectures over a 14-week period. Each lecture is 1.5 hours long, and students also attend a one-hour recitation every week. With this amount of contact time it is not possible to cover all of the detail in the book. The Web Supplement contains an example lecture schedule, reading assignments, and problem sets. In addition, the MIT OpenCourseWare site at `ocw.mit.edu` contains material from previous versions of 6.821.

This book can be used to teach many different kinds of courses, including an introduction to semantics (Chapters 1–5), essential concepts of programming languages (Chapters 1–13), and types and effects (Chapters 6 and 11–16).

We hope you enjoy teaching this material as much as we have!

Acknowledgments

This book owes its existence to many people. We are grateful to the following individuals for their contributions:

- Jonathan Rees profoundly influenced the content of this book when he was a teaching assistant. Many of the mini-languages, examples, exercises, and software implementations, as well as some of the sections of text, had their origins with Jonathan. Jonathan was also the author of an early data type and pattern matching facility used in course software that strongly influenced the facilities described in the book.

- Brian Reistad and Trevor Jim greatly improved the quality of the book. As teaching assistants, they unearthed and fixed innumerable bugs, improved the presentation and content of the material, and created many new exercises. Brian also played a major role in implementing software for testing the mini-languages in the book.

- In addition to his contributions as a teaching assistant, Alex Salcianu also collected and edited homework and exam problems from fifteen years of the course for inclusion in the book.

- Valuable contributions and improvements to this book were made by other teaching assistants: Aaron Adler, Alexandra Andersson, Arnab Bhattacharyya, Michael (Ziggy) Blair, Barbara Cutler, Timothy Danford, Joshua Glazer, Robert Grimm, Alex Hartemink, David Huynh, Adam Kiezun, Eddie Kohler, Gary Leavens, Ravi Nanavati, Jim O'Toole, Dennis Quan, Alex Snoeren, Patrick Sobalvarro, Peter Szilagyi, Bienvenido Velez-Rivera, Earl Waldin, and Qian Wang.

- In Fall 2002 and Fall 2004, Michael Ernst taught 6.821 based on an earlier version of this book, and his detailed comments resulted in many improvements.

- Based on teaching 6.821 at MIT and using the course materials at Hong Kong University and Georgia Tech, Olin Shivers made many excellent suggestions on how to improve the content and presentation of the material.

- While using the course materials at other universities, Gary Leavens, Andrew Myers, Randy Osborne, and Kathy Yelick provided helpful feedback.

- Early versions of the pragmatics system were written by Doug Grundman, with major extensions by Raymie Stata and Brian Reistad.

- Pierre Jouvelot did the lion's share of the implementation of FX (a language upon which early versions of 6.821 were based) with help from Mark Sheldon and Jim O'Toole.

- David Espinosa introduced us to embedded interpreters and helped us to improve our presentation of dynamic semantics, effects, and compilation.

- Guillermo Rozas taught us many nifty pragmatics tricks. Our pragmatics coverage is heavily influenced by his source-to-source front end to the MIT SCHEME compiler.

- Ken Moody provided helpful feedback on the course material, especially on the POSTFIX Equivalence Theorem.

- Numerous students have improved this book in various ways, from correcting bugs to suggesting major reorganizations. In this regard, we are especially grateful to: Atul Adya, Kavita Bala, Ron Bodkin, Philip Bogle, Miguel Castro, Anna Chefter, Natalya Cohen, Brooke Cowan, Richard Davis, Andre deHon, Michael Frank, Robert Grimm, Yevgeny Gurevich, Viktor Kuncak, Mark Lillibridge, Greg Little, Andrew Myers, Michael Noakes, Heidi Pan, John Pezaris, Matt Power, Roberto Segala, Emily Shen, Mark Torrance, Michael Walfish, Amy Williams, and Carl Witty.

- Tim Chevalier and Jue Wang uncovered numerous typos and inconsistencies in their careful proofreading of book drafts.

- Special thanks to Jeanne Darling, who has been the 6.821 course administrator for over ten years. Her administrative, editing, and technical skills, as well as her can-do spirit and cheerful demeanor, were critical in keeping both the course and the book project afloat.

- We bow before David Jones, whose TeX wizardry is so magical we are sure he has a wand hidden in his sleeve.

- Kudos go to Julie Sussman, PPA, for her excellent work as a technical editor on the book. Julie's amazing ability to find and fix uncountably many technical bugs, inconsistencies, ambiguities, and poor explanations in every chapter we thought was "done" has improved the quality of the book tremendously. Of course, Julie cannot be held responsible for remaining erorrs, especially them what we introducd after she fixished the editos.

- We are grateful to the MIT Press for their patience with us over the years we worked on this book.

We also have some personal dedications and acknowledgments:

Franklyn: I dedicate this book to my parents, Dr. Albin F. Turbak and Irene J. Turbak, who taught me (1) how to think and (2) never to give up, traits without which this book would not exist.

I owe my love of programming languages to Hal Abelson and Jerry Sussman, whose *Structure and Interpretation of Computer Programs* book and class changed the course my life, and to Dave Gifford, whose 6.821 class inspired an odyssey of programming language exploration that is still ongoing. My understanding of programming languages matured greatly through my interactions with members of the Church Project, especially Assaf Kfoury, Torben Amtoft, Anindya Banerjee, Alan Bawden, Chiyan Chen, Allyn Dimock, Glenn Holloway, Trevor Jim, Elena Machkasova, Harry Mairson, Bob Muller, Peter Møller Neergaard, Santiago Pericas, Joe Wells, Ian Westmacott, Hongwei Xi, and Dengping Zhu.

I am grateful to Wellesley College for providing me with a sabbatical during the 2005-06 academic year, which I devoted largely to work on this book.

Finally, I thank my wife, Lisa, and daughters, Ohana and Kalani, who have never known my life without "the book" but have been waiting oh-so-long to find out what it will be like. Their love keeps me going!

Dave: Heidi, Ariella, and Talia — thanks for your support and love; this book is dedicated to you.

To my parents, for providing me with opportunities that enabled my successes.

Thanks Franklyn, for your labors on this book, and the chance to share your passion for programming languages.

Thanks Julie. You are a beacon of quality.

Thanks Mark, for all your help on this project.

And finally, thanks to all of the 6.821 students. Your enthusiasm, intelligence, and questions provided the wonderful context that motivated this book and made it fun.

Mark: I am grateful to my coauthors for bringing me into this project. The task was initially to be a few weeks of technical editing but blossomed into a rewarding and educational five-year coauthoring journey.

I thank my colleagues and students at Wellesley. My students were patient beyond all reason when told their work hadn't been graded because I was working on "the book."

I am fortunate to have the love and support of my family: my wife, Ishrat Chaudhuri, my daughters, Raina and Maya, and my parents, Beverly Sheldon and Frank Sheldon.

I would also like to thank my dance partner, Mercedes von Deck, my coaches (especially Stephen and Jennifer Hillier and Charlotte Jorgensen), and my dance students.

Part I

Foundations

1

Introduction

Order and simplification are the first steps toward the mastery of a subject — the actual enemy is the unknown.

— Thomas Mann, *The Magic Mountain*

1.1 Programming Languages

Programming is a lot of fun. As you have no doubt experienced, clarity and simplicity are the keys to good programming. When you have a tangle of code that is difficult to understand, your confidence in its behavior wavers, and the code is no longer any fun to read or update.

Designing a new programming language is a kind of metalevel programming activity that is just as much fun as programming in a regular language (if not more so). You will discover that clarity and simplicity are even more important in language design than they are in ordinary programming. Today hundreds of programming languages are in use — whether they be scripting languages for Internet commerce, user interface programming tools, spreadsheet macros, or page format specification languages that when executed can produce formatted documents. Inspired application design often requires a programmer to provide a new programming language or to extend an existing one. This is because flexible and extensible applications need to provide some sort of programming capability to their end users.

Elements of programming language design are even found in "ordinary" programming. For instance, consider designing the interface to a collection data structure. What is a good way to encapsulate an iteration idiom over the elements of such a collection? The issues faced in this problem are similar to those in adding a looping construct to a programming language.

The goal of this book is to teach you the great ideas in programming languages in a simple framework that strips them of complexity. You will learn several ways to specify the meaning of programming language constructs and will see that small changes in these specifications can have dramatic consequences for program behavior. You will explore many dimensions of the programming

language design space, study decisions to be made along each dimension, and
consider how decisions from different dimensions can interact. We will teach you
about a wide variety of neat tricks for extending programing languages with interesting features like undoable state changes, exitable loops, and pattern matching.
Our approach for teaching you this material is based on the premise that when
language behaviors become incredibly complex, the descriptions of the behaviors
must be incredibly simple. It is the only hope.

1.2   Syntax, Semantics, and Pragmatics

Programming languages are traditionally viewed in terms of three facets:

1. **Syntax** — the *form* of programming languages.

2. **Semantics** — the *meaning* of programming languages.

3. **Pragmatics** — the *implementation* of programming languages.

Here we briefly describe these facets.

Syntax

Syntax focuses on the concrete notations used to encode programming language
phrases. Consider a phrase that indicates the sum of the product of v and w and
the quotient of y and z. Such a phrase can be written in many different notations
— as a traditional mathematical expression:

$$vw + y/z$$

or as a LISP parenthesized prefix expression:

$$(+ (* v w) (/ y z))$$

or as a sequence of keystrokes on a postfix calculator:

$$\boxed{V}\ \boxed{\text{ENTER}}\ \boxed{W}\ \boxed{\text{ENTER}}\ \boxed{\times}\ \boxed{Y}\ \boxed{\text{ENTER}}\ \boxed{Z}\ \boxed{\text{ENTER}}\ \boxed{\div}\ \boxed{+}$$

or as a layout of cells and formulas in a spreadsheet:

	1	2	3	4
A	v=		v*w =	*A2 * B2*
B	w=		y/z =	*C2 / D2*
C	y=		ans =	*A4 + B4*
D	z=			

or as a graphical tree:

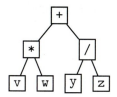

Although these concrete notations are superficially different, they all designate the same abstract phrase structure (the sum of a product and a quotient). The syntax of a programming language specifies which concrete notations (strings of characters, lines on a page) in the language are legal and which tree-shaped abstract phrase structure is denoted by each legal notation.

Semantics

Semantics specifies the mapping between the structure of a programming language phrase and what the phrase means. Such phrases have no inherent meaning: their meaning is determined only in the context of a system for interpreting their structure. For example, consider the following expression tree:

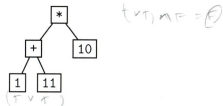

Suppose we interpret the nodes labeled 1, 10, and 11 as the usual decimal notation for numbers, and the nodes labeled + and * as the sum and product of the values of their subnodes. Then the root of the tree stands for $(1+11) \cdot 10 = 120$. But there are many other possible meanings for this tree. If * stands for exponentiation rather than multiplication, the meaning of the tree could be 12^{10}. If the numerals are in binary notation rather than decimal notation, the tree could stand for (in decimal notation) $(1+3) \cdot 2 = 8$. Alternatively, suppose that odd integers stand for the truth value *true*, even integers stand for the truth value *false*, and + and * stand for, respectively, the logical disjunction ($\lor$) and conjunction ($\land$) operators on truth values; then the meaning of the tree is *false*. Perhaps the tree does not indicate an evaluation at all, and only stands for a property intrinsic to the tree, such as its height (3), its number of nodes (5), or its shape (perhaps it describes a simple corporate hierarchy). Or maybe the tree is an arbitrary encoding for a particular object of interest, such as a person or a book.

This example illustrates how a single program phrase can have many possible meanings. Semantics describes the relationship between the abstract structure of a phrase and its meaning.

Pragmatics

Whereas semantics deals with *what* a phrase means, pragmatics focuses on the details of *how* that meaning is computed. Of particular interest is the effective use of various resources, such as time, space, and access to shared physical devices (storage devices, network connections, video monitors, printers, speakers, etc.).

As a simple example of pragmatics, consider the evaluation of the following expression tree (under the first semantic interpretation described above):

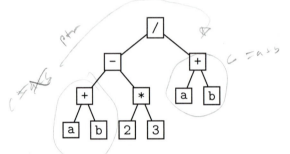

Suppose that a and b stand for particular numeric values. Because the phrase (+ a b) appears twice, a naive evaluation strategy will compute the same sum twice. An alternative strategy is to compute the sum once, save the result, and use the saved result the next time the phrase is encountered. The alternative strategy does not change the meaning of the program, but does change its use of resources; it reduces the number of additions performed, but may require extra storage for the saved result. Is the alternative strategy better? The answer depends on the details of the evaluation model and the relative importance of time and space.

Another potential improvement in the example involves the phrase (* 2 3), which always stands for the number 6. If the sample expression is to be evaluated many times (for different values of a and b), it may be worthwhile to replace (* 2 3) by 6 to avoid unnecessary multiplications. Again, this is a purely pragmatic concern that does not change the meaning of the expression.

1.3   Goals

The goals of this book are to explore the semantics of a comprehensive set of programming language design idioms, show how they can be combined into complete practical programming languages, and discuss the interplay between semantics and pragmatics.

Because syntactic issues are so well covered in standard compiler texts, we won't say much about syntax except for establishing a few syntactic conventions at the outset. We will introduce a number of tools for describing the semantics of programming languages, and will use these tools to build intuitions about programming language features and study many of the dimensions along which languages can vary. Our coverage of pragmatics is mainly at a high level. We will study some simple programming language implementation techniques and program improvement strategies rather than focus on squeezing the last ounce of performance out of a particular computer architecture.

We will discuss programming language features in the context of several **mini-languages**. Each of these is a simple programming language that captures the essential features of a class of existing programming languages. In many cases, the mini-languages are so pared down that they are hardly suitable for serious programming activities. Nevertheless, these languages embody all of the key ideas in programming languages. Their simplicity saves us from getting bogged down in needless complexity in our explorations of semantics and pragmatics. And like good modular building blocks, the components of the mini-languages are designed to be "snapped together" to create practical languages.

Issues of semantics and pragmatics are important for reasoning about properties of programming languages and about particular programs in these languages. We will also discuss them in the context of two fundamental strategies for programming language implementation: **interpretation** and **translation**. In the interpretation approach, a program written in a **source language** S is directly executed by an S-**interpreter**, which is a program written in an **implementation language**. In the translation approach, an S program is translated to a program in the **target language** T, which can be executed by a T-interpreter. The translation itself is performed by a **translator** program written in an implementation language. A translator is also called a **compiler**, especially when it translates from a high-level language to a low-level one. We will use mini-languages for our source and target languages. For our implementation language, we will use the mathematical **metalanguage** described in Appendix A. However, we strongly encourage readers to build working interpreters and translators for the mini-languages in their favorite real-world programming languages. **Metaprogramming** — writing programs that manipulate other programs — is perhaps the most exciting form of programming!

1.4   PostFix: A Simple Stack Language

We will introduce the tools for syntax, semantics, and pragmatics in the context of a mini-language called POSTFIX. POSTFIX is a simple stack-based language inspired by the POSTSCRIPT graphics language, the FORTH programming language, and Hewlett Packard calculators. Here we give an informal introduction to POSTFIX in order to build some intuitions about the language. In subsequent chapters, we will introduce tools that allow us to study POSTFIX in more depth.

1.4.1   Syntax

The basic syntactic unit of a POSTFIX program is the **command**. Commands are of the following form:

- Any integer numeral. E.g., 17, 0, -3.

- One of the following special command tokens: add, div, eq, exec, gt, lt, mul, nget, pop, rem, sel, sub, swap.

- An **executable sequence** — a single command that serves as a subroutine. It is written as a parenthesized list of subcommands separated by whitespace (any contiguous sequence of characters that leave no mark on the page, such as spaces, tabs, and newlines). E.g., (7 add 3 swap) or (2 (5 mul) exec add).

Since executable sequences contain other commands (including other executable sequences), they can be arbitrarily nested. An executable sequence counts as a single command despite its hierarchical structure.

A POSTFIX **program** is a parenthesized sequence consisting of (1) the token postfix followed by (2) a natural number (i.e., nonnegative integer) indicating the number of program parameters followed by (3) zero or more POSTFIX commands. Here are some sample POSTFIX programs:

```
(postfix 0 4 7 sub)
(postfix 2 add 2 div)
(postfix 4 4 nget 5 nget mul mul swap 4 nget mul add add)
(postfix 1 ((3 nget swap exec) (2 mul swap exec) swap)
         (5 sub) swap exec exec)
```

In POSTFIX, as in all the languages we'll be studying, all parentheses are required and none are optional. Moving parentheses around changes the structure of the program and most likely changes its behavior. Thus, while the following

POSTFIX executable sequences use the same numerals and command tokens in the same order, they are distinguished by their parenthesization, which, as we shall see below, makes them behave differently.

```
((1) (2 3 4) swap exec)
((1 2) (3 4) swap exec)
((1 2) (3 4 swap) exec)
```

1.4.2   Semantics

The meaning of a POSTFIX program is determined by executing its commands in left-to-right order. Each command manipulates an implicit stack of values that initially contains the integer arguments of the program (where the first argument is at the top of the stack and the last argument is at the bottom). A value on the stack is either (1) an integer numeral or (2) an executable sequence. The result of a program is the integer value at the top of the stack after its command sequence has been completely executed. A program signals an error if (1) the final stack is empty, (2) the value at the top of the final stack is not an integer, or (3) an inappropriate stack of values is encountered when one of its commands is executed.

The behavior of POSTFIX commands is summarized in Figure 1.1. Each command is specified in terms of how it manipulates the implicit stack. We use the notation $P \xrightarrow{args} v$ to mean that executing the POSTFIX program P on the integer argument sequence $args$ returns the value v. The notation $P \xrightarrow{args}$ error means that executing the POSTFIX program P on the arguments $args$ signals an error. Errors are caused by inappropriate stack values or an insufficient number of stack values. In practice, it is desirable for an implementation to indicate the type of error. We will use comments (delimited by braces) to explain errors and other situations.

To illustrate the meanings of various commands, we show the results of some simple program executions. For example, numerals are pushed onto the stack, while pop and swap are the usual stack operations.

(postfix 0 1 2 3) $\xrightarrow{[]}$ 3   {*Only the top stack value is returned.*}
(postfix 0 1 2 3 pop) $\xrightarrow{[]}$ 2
(postfix 0 1 2 swap 3 pop) $\xrightarrow{[]}$ 1
(postfix 0 1 swap) $\xrightarrow{[]}$ error   {*Not enough values to swap.*}
(postfix 0 1 pop pop) $\xrightarrow{[]}$ error   {*Empty stack on second pop.*}

Program arguments are pushed onto the stack (from last to first) before the execution of the program commands.

N: Push the numeral N onto the stack.

sub: Call the top stack value v_1 and the next-to-top stack value v_2. Pop these two values off the stack and push the result of $v_2 - v_1$ onto the stack. If there are fewer than two values on the stack or the top two values aren't both numerals, signal an error. The other binary arithmetic operators — add (addition), mul (multiplication), div (integer division[a]), and rem (remainder of integer division) — behave similarly. Both div and rem signal an error if v_1 is zero.

lt: Call the top stack value v_1 and the next-to-top stack value v_2. Pop these two values off the stack. If $v_2 < v_1$, then push a 1 (a true value) on the stack, otherwise push a 0 (false). The other binary comparison operators — eq (equals) and gt (greater than) — behave similarly. If there are fewer than two values on the stack or the top two values aren't both numerals, signal an error.

pop: Pop the top element off the stack and discard it. Signal an error if the stack is empty.

swap: Swap the top two elements of the stack. Signal an error if the stack has fewer than two values.

sel: Call the top three stack values (from top down) v_1, v_2, and v_3. Pop these three values off the stack. If v_3 is the numeral 0, push v_1 onto the stack; if v_3 is a nonzero numeral, push v_2 onto the stack. Signal an error if the stack does not contain three values, or if v_3 is not a numeral.

nget: Call the top stack value v_{index} and the remaining stack values (from top down) v_1, v_2, ..., v_n. Pop v_{index} off the stack. If v_{index} is a numeral i such that $1 \leq i \leq n$ and v_i is a numeral, push v_i onto the stack. Signal an error if the stack does not contain at least one value, if v_{index} is not a numeral, if i is not in the range $[1..n]$, or if v_i is not a numeral.

$(C_1 \ldots C_n)$: Push the *executable sequence* $(C_1 \ldots C_n)$ as a single value onto the stack. Executable sequences are used in conjunction with exec.

exec: Pop the executable sequence from the top of the stack, and prepend its component commands onto the sequence of currently executing commands. Signal an error if the stack is empty or the top stack value isn't an executable sequence.

---

[a]The integer division of n and d returns the integer quotient q such that $n = qd + r$, where r (the remainder) is such that $0 \leq r < |d|$ if $n \geq 0$ and $-|d| < r \leq 0$ if $n < 0$.

Figure 1.1   English semantics of POSTFIX commands.

(postfix 2) $\xrightarrow{[3,4]}$ 3   {*Initial stack has 3 on top with 4 below.*}

(postfix 2 swap) $\xrightarrow{[3,4]}$ 4

(postfix 3 pop swap) $\xrightarrow{[3,4,5]}$ 5

It is an error if the actual number of arguments does not match the number of parameters specified in the program.

(postfix 2 swap) $\xrightarrow{[3]}$ error {*Wrong number of arguments.*}

(postfix 1 pop) $\xrightarrow{[4,5]}$ error {*Wrong number of arguments.*}

Note that program arguments must be integers — they cannot be executable sequences.

Numerical operations are expressed in postfix notation, in which each operator comes after the commands that compute its operands. add, sub, mul, and div are binary integer operators. lt, eq, and gt are binary integer predicates returning either 1 (true) or 0 (false).

(postfix 1 4 sub) $\xrightarrow{[3]}$ -1

(postfix 1 4 add 5 mul 6 sub 7 div) $\xrightarrow{[3]}$ 4

(postfix 5 add mul sub swap div) $\xrightarrow{[7,6,5,4,3]}$ -20

(postfix 3 4000 swap pop add) $\xrightarrow{[300,20,1]}$ 4020

(postfix 2 add 2 div) $\xrightarrow{[3,7]}$ 5 {*An averaging program.*}

(postfix 1 3 div) $\xrightarrow{[17]}$ 5

(postfix 1 3 rem) $\xrightarrow{[17]}$ 2

(postfix 1 4 lt) $\xrightarrow{[3]}$ 1

(postfix 1 4 lt) $\xrightarrow{[5]}$ 0

(postfix 1 4 lt 10 add) $\xrightarrow{[3]}$ 11

(postfix 1 4 mul add) $\xrightarrow{[3]}$ error {*Not enough numbers to add.*}

(postfix 2 4 sub div) $\xrightarrow{[4,5]}$ error {*Divide by zero.*}

In all the above examples, each stack value is used at most once. Sometimes it is desirable to use a number two or more times or to access a number that is not near the top of the stack. The nget command is useful in these situations; it puts at the top of the stack a copy of a number located on the stack at a specified index. The index is 1-based, from the top of the stack down, not counting the index value itself.

(postfix 2 1 nget) $\xrightarrow{[4,5]}$ 4 {*4 is at index 1, 5 at index 2.*}

(postfix 2 2 nget) $\xrightarrow{[4,5]}$ 5

It is an error to use an index that is out of bounds or to access a nonnumeric stack value (i.e., an executable sequence) with nget.

(postfix 2 3 nget) $\xrightarrow{[4,5]}$ error {*Index 3 is too large.*}

(postfix 2 0 nget) $\xrightarrow{[4,5]}$ error {*Index 0 is too small.*}

(postfix 1 (2 mul) 1 nget) $\xrightarrow{[3]}$ error
{*Value at index 1 is not a number but an executable sequence.*}

The `nget` command is particularly useful for numerical programs, where it is common to reference arbitrary parameter values and use them multiple times.

(postfix 1 1 nget mul) $\xrightarrow{[5]}$ 25   {*A squaring program.*}

(postfix 4 4 nget 5 nget mul mul swap 4 nget mul add add) $\xrightarrow{[3,4,5,2]}$ 25
{*Given a, b, c, x, calculates* $ax^2 + bx + c$.}

As illustrated in the last example, the index of a given value increases every time a new value is pushed onto the stack. The final stack in this example contains (from top down) 25 and 2, showing that the program may end with more than one value on the stack.

Executable sequences are compound commands like (2 mul) that are pushed onto the stack as a single value. They can be executed later by the `exec` command. Executable sequences act like subroutines in other languages; execution of an executable sequence is similar to a subroutine call, except that transmission of arguments and results is accomplished via the stack.

(postfix 1 (2 mul) exec) $\xrightarrow{[7]}$ 14   {(2 mul) *is a doubling subroutine.*}

(postfix 0 (0 swap sub) 7 swap exec) $\xrightarrow{[]}$ -7
{(0 swap sub) *is a negation subroutine.*}

(postfix 0 (2 mul)) $\xrightarrow{[]}$ error   {*Final top of stack is not an integer.*}

(postfix 0 3 (2 mul) gt) $\xrightarrow{[]}$ error
{*Executable sequence where number expected.*}

(postfix 0 3 exec) $\xrightarrow{[]}$ error   {*Number where executable sequence expected.*}

(postfix 0 (7 swap exec) (0 swap sub) swap exec) $\xrightarrow{[]}$ -7

(postfix 2 (mul sub) (1 nget mul) 4 nget swap exec swap exec)
$\xrightarrow{\frac{[-10,2]}{a,b}}$ 42   {*Given a and b, calculates* $b - a \cdot b^2$.}

The last two examples illustrate that evaluations involving executable sequences can be rather contorted.

The `sel` command selects between two values based on a test value, where zero is treated as false and any nonzero integer is treated as true. It can be used in conjunction with `exec` to conditionally execute one of two executable sequences.

(postfix 1 2 3 sel) $\xrightarrow{[1]}$ 2

(postfix 1 2 3 sel) $\xrightarrow{[0]}$ 3

(postfix 1 2 3 sel) $\xrightarrow{[17]}$ 2   {*Any nonzero number is "true."*}

(postfix 0 (2 mul) 3 4 sel) $\xrightarrow{[]}$ error   {*Test not a number.*}

(postfix 4 lt (add) (mul) sel exec) $\xrightarrow{[3,4,5,6]}$ 30

(postfix 4 lt (add) (mul) sel exec) $\xrightarrow{[4,3,5,6]}$ 11

(postfix 1 1 nget 0 lt (0 swap sub) () sel exec) $\xrightarrow{[-7]}$ 7
{*An absolute value program.*}

(postfix 1 1 nget 0 lt (0 swap sub) () sel exec) $\xrightarrow{[6]}$ 6

Exercise 1.1 Determine the value of the following PostFix programs on an empty stack.

a. (postfix 0 10 (swap 2 mul sub) 1 swap exec)

b. (postfix 0 (5 (2 mul) exec) 3 swap)

c. (postfix 0 (() exec) exec)

d. (postfix 0 2 3 1 add mul sel)

e. (postfix 0 2 3 1 (add) (mul) sel)

f. (postfix 0 2 3 1 (add) (mul) sel exec)

g. (postfix 0 0 (2 3 add) 4 sel exec)

h. (postfix 0 1 (2 3 add) 4 sel exec)

i. (postfix 0 (5 6 lt) (2 3 add) 4 sel exec)

j. (postfix 0 (swap exec swap exec) (1 sub) swap (2 mul)
              swap 3 swap exec)

Exercise 1.2

a. What function of its argument does the following PostFix program calculate?

        (postfix 1 ((3 nget swap exec) (2 mul swap exec) swap)
                (5 sub) swap exec exec)

b. Write a simpler PostFix program that performs the same calculation.

Exercise 1.3 Recall that executable sequences are effectively subroutines that, when invoked (by the exec command), take their arguments from the top of the stack. Write executable sequences that compute the following logical operations. Recall that 0 stands for false and all other numerals are treated as true.

a. *not*: return the logical negation of a single argument.

b. *and*: given two numeric arguments, return 1 if their logical conjunction is true, and 0 otherwise.

c. *short-circuit-and*: return 0 if the first argument is false; otherwise return the second argument.

d. Demonstrate the difference between *and* and *short-circuit-and* by writing a PostFix program with zero arguments that has a different result if *and* is replaced by *short-circuit-and*.

Exercise 1.4

a. Without nget, is it possible to write a PostFix program that squares its single argument? If so, write it; if not, explain.

b. Is it possible to write a PostFix program that takes three integers and returns the smallest of the three? If so, write it; if not, explain.

c. Is it possible to write a PostFix program that calculates the factorial of its single argument (assume it's nonnegative)? If so, write it; if not, explain.

1.4.3   The Pitfalls of Informal Descriptions

The "by-example" and English descriptions of PostFix given above are typical of the way that programming languages are described in manuals, textbooks, courses, and conversations. That is, a syntax for the language is presented, and the semantics of each of the language constructs is specified using English prose and examples. The utility of this method for specifying semantics is apparent from the fact that the vast majority of programmers learn to read and write programs via this approach.

But there are many situations in which informal descriptions of programming languages are inadequate. Suppose that we want to improve a program by transforming complex phrases into phrases that are simpler and more efficient. How can we be sure that the transformation process preserves the meaning of the program?

Or suppose that we want to prove that the language as a whole has a particular property. For instance, it turns out that every PostFix program is guaranteed to terminate (i.e., a PostFix program cannot enter an infinite loop). How would we go about proving this property based on the informal description? Natural language does not provide any rigorous framework for reasoning about programs or programming languages. Without the aid of some formal reasoning tools, we can only give hand-waving arguments that are not likely to be very convincing.

Or suppose that we wish to extend PostFix with features that make it easier to use. For example, it would be nice to name values, to collect values into arrays, to query the user for input, and to loop over sequences of values. With each new feature, the specification of the language becomes more complex, and it becomes more difficult to reason about the interaction between various features. We'd like techniques that help to highlight which features are orthogonal and which can interact in subtle ways.

Or suppose that a software vendor wants to develop PostFix into a product that runs on several different machines. The vendor wants any given PostFix program to have exactly the same behavior on all of the supported machines. But how do the development teams for the different machines guarantee that they're all implementing the "same" language? If there are any ambiguities in the PostFix specification that they're implementing, different development teams might resolve the ambiguity in incompatible ways. What's needed in this case is an unambiguous specification of the language as well as a means of proving that an implementation meets that specification.

The problem with informal descriptions of a programming language is that they're neither concise nor precise enough for these kinds of situations. English is often verbose, and even relatively simple ideas can be unduly complicated to explain. Moreover, it's easy for the writer of an informal specification to underspecify a language by forgetting to cover all the special cases (e.g., error situations in POSTFIX). It isn't that covering all the special cases is impossible; it's just that the natural-language framework doesn't help much in pointing out what the special cases are.

It is possible to overspecify a language in English as well. Consider the POST-FIX programming model introduced above. The current state of a program is captured in two entities: the stack and the current command sequence. To programmers and implementers alike, this might imply that a language implementation *must* have explicit stack and command sequence elements in it. Although these would indeed appear in a straightforward implementation, they are not in any way *required*; there are alternative models and implementations for POSTFIX (e.g., see Exercise 3.12 on page 70). It would be desirable to have a more abstract definition of what constitutes a legal POSTFIX implementation so that a would-be implementer could be sure that an implementation was faithful to the language definition regardless of the representations and algorithms employed.

1.5   Overview of the Book

The remainder of Part I introduces a number of tools that address the inadequacies outlined above and that form an essential foundation for the study of programming language design. Chapter 2 presents **s-expression grammars**, a simple specification for syntax that we will use to describe the structure of all of the mini-languages we will explore. Then, using POSTFIX and a simple expression language as our objects of study, we introduce two approaches to formal semantics:

- An **operational semantics** (Chapter 3) explains the meaning of programming language constructs in terms of the step-by-step process of an abstract machine.

- A **denotational semantics** (Chapter 4) explains the meaning of programming language constructs in terms of the meaning of their subparts.

These approaches support the unambiguous specification of programming languages and provide a framework in which to reason about properties of programs and languages. Our discussion of tools concludes in Chapter 5 with a presentation of a technique for determining the meaning of recursive specifications. Throughout the book, and especially in these early chapters, we formalize concepts in terms of a mathematical **metalanguage** described in Appendix A. Readers are encouraged to familiarize themselves with this language by skimming this appendix early on and later referring to it in more detail on an "as needed" basis.

Part II focuses on **dynamic semantics**, the meaning of programming language constructs and the run-time behavior of programs. In Chapter 6, we introduce FL, a mini-language we use as a basis for investigating dimensions of programming language design. By extending FL in various ways, we then explore programming language features along key dimensions: naming (Chapter 7), state (Chapter 8), control (Chapter 9), and data (Chapter 10). Along the way, we will encounter several **programming paradigms**, high-level approaches for viewing computation: function-oriented programming, imperative programming, and object-oriented programming.

In Part III, we shift our focus to **static semantics**, properties of programs that can be determined without executing them. In Chapter 11, we introduce the notion of type — a description of what an expression computes — and develop a simple type-checking system for a dialect of FL such that "well-typed" programs cannot encounter certain kinds of run-time errors. In Chapter 12, we study some more advanced features of typed languages: subtyping, universal polymorphism, bounded quantification, and kind systems. A major drawback to many of our typed mini-languages is that programmers are required to annotate programs with significant amounts of explicit type information. In some languages, many of these annotations can be eliminated via type reconstruction, a technique we study in Chapter 13. Types can be used as a mechanism for enforcing data abstraction, a notion that we explore in Chapter 14. In Chapter 15, we show how many of the dynamic and static semantics features we have studied can be combined to yield a mini-language in which program modules with both value and type components can be independently type-checked and then linked together in a type-safe way. We wrap up our discussion of static semantics in Chapter 16 with a study of effect systems, which describe *how* expressions compute rather than *what* they compute.

The book culminates, in Part IV, in a pragmatics segment that illustrates how concepts from dynamic and static semantics play an important role in the implementation of a programming language. Chapter 17 presents a compiler that translates from a typed dialect of FL to a low-level language that resembles assembly code. The compiler is organized as a sequence of meaning-preserving translation steps that construct explicit representations for the naming, state, control, and data aspects of programs. In order to automatically reclaim memory in a type-safe way, the run-time system for executing the low-level code generated by the compiler uses garbage collection, a topic that is explored in Chapter 18.

While we will emphasize formal tools throughout this book, we do not imply that formal tools are a panacea or that formal approaches are superior to informal ones in an absolute sense. In fact, informal explanations of language features are usually the simplest way to learn about a language. In addition, it's very easy for formal approaches to get out of control, to the point where they are overly obscure, or require too much mathematical machinery to be of any practical use on a day-to-day basis. For this reason, we won't cover material as a dry sequence of definitions, theorems, and proofs. Instead, our goal is to show that the *concepts* underlying the formal approaches are indispensable for understanding particular programming languages as well as the dimensions of language design. The tools, techniques, and features introduced in this book should be in any serious computer scientist's bag of tricks.

2

Syntax

since feeling is first
who pays any attention
to the syntax of things
will never wholly kiss you;
...
for life's not a paragraph

And death i think is no parenthesis

— e. e. cummings, "since feeling is first"

In the area of programming languages, syntax refers to the form of programs
— how they are constructed from symbolic parts. A number of theoretical and
practical tools — including grammars, lexical analyzers, and parsers — have been
developed to aid in the study of syntax. By and large we will downplay syntactic
issues and tools. Instead, we will emphasize the semantics of programs; we will
study the meaning of language constructs rather than their form.

We are not claiming that syntactic issues and tools are unimportant in the
analysis, design, and implementation of programming languages. In actual programming language implementations, syntactic issues are very important and a
number of standard tools (like Lex and Yacc) are available for addressing them.
But we do believe that syntax has traditionally garnered much more than its fair
share of attention, largely because its problems were more amenable to solution
with familiar tools. This state of affairs is reminiscent of the popular tale of the
person who searches all night long under a street lamp for a lost item not because
the item was lost there but because the light was better. Luckily, many investiga-
tors strayed away from the street lamp of parsing theory in order to explore the
much dimmer area of semantics. Along the way, they developed many new tools
for understanding semantics, some of which we will focus on in later chapters.

Despite our emphasis on semantics, however, we can't ignore syntax completely. Programs must be expressed in *some* form, preferably one that elucidates
the fundamental structure of the program and is easy to read, write, and reason

about. In this chapter, we introduce a set of syntactic conventions for describing our mini-languages.

2.1   Abstract Syntax

We will motivate various syntactic issues in the context of EL, a mini-language of expressions. EL expressions have a tree-like structure that is more typical of program phrases than the mostly linear structure of POSTFIX command sequences. EL describes functions that map any number of numerical inputs to a single numerical output. Such a language might be useful on a calculator, say, for automating the evaluation of commonly used mathematical formulas.

Figure 2.1 describes (in English) the abstract structure of a legal EL program. EL programs contain numerical expressions, where a numerical expression can be constructed out of various kinds of components. Some of the components, like numerals, references to input values, and various kinds of operators, are **primitive** — they cannot be broken down into subparts.[1] Other components are **compound** — they are constructed out of constituent components. The components have names; e.g., the subparts of an arithmetic operation are the **rator** (short for "operator") and two **rands** (short for "operands"), while the subexpressions of the conditional expression are the **test** expression, the **then** expression, and the **else** expression.

There are three major classes of phrases in an EL program: whole programs that designate calculations on a given number of inputs, numerical expressions that designate numbers, and boolean expressions that designate truth values (i.e., true or false). The structural description in Figure 2.1 constrains the ways in which these expressions may be "wired together." For instance, the test component of a conditional must be a boolean expression, while the then and else components must be numerical expressions.

A specification of the allowed wiring patterns for the syntactic entities of a language is called a **grammar**. Figure 2.1 is said to be an **abstract grammar** because it specifies the logical structure of the syntax but does not give any indication how individual expressions in the language are actually written.

Parsing a program phrase with an abstract grammar results in a value called an **abstract syntax tree (AST)**. As we will see in Section 2.3, abstract syntax trees are easy to inspect and disassemble, making them ideal substrates for defining the meaning of program phrases in terms of their parts.

Consider an EL program that returns zero if its first input is between 1 and 10 (exclusive) and otherwise returns the product of the second and third inputs.

---

[1]Numerals can be broken down into digits, but we will ignore this detail.

A legal EL program is a pair of (1) a *numargs* numeral specifying the number of parameters and (2) a *body* that is a *numerical expression*, where a numerical expression is one of:

- an *intval* — an integer literal *num*;

- an *input* — a reference to one of the program inputs specified by an *index* numeral;

- an *arithmetic operation* — an application of a *rator*, in this case a binary *arithmetic operator*, to two numerical *rand* expressions, where an arithmetic operator is one of:

  - addition,

  - subtraction,

  - multiplication,

  - division,

  - remainder;

- a *conditional* — a choice between numerical *then* and *else* expressions determined by a boolean *test* expression, where a *boolean expression* is one of:

  - a *boolval* — a boolean literal *bool*;

  - a *relational operation* — an application of *rator*, in this case a binary *relational operator*, to two numerical *rand* expressions, where a relational operator is one of:

    - less-than,

    - equal-to,

    - greater-than;

  - a *logical operation* — an application of a *rator*, in this case a binary *logical operator*, to two boolean *rand* expressions, where a logical operator is one of:

    - and,

    - or.

Figure 2.1 An abstract grammar for EL programs.

The abstract syntax tree for this program appears in Figure 2.2. Each node of the tree except the root corresponds to a numerical or boolean expression. The leaves of the tree stand for primitive phrases, while the intermediate nodes represent compound phrases. The labeled edges from a parent node to its children show the relationship between a compound phrase and its components. The AST is defined purely in terms of these relationships; the particular way that the nodes and edges of a tree are arranged on the page is immaterial.

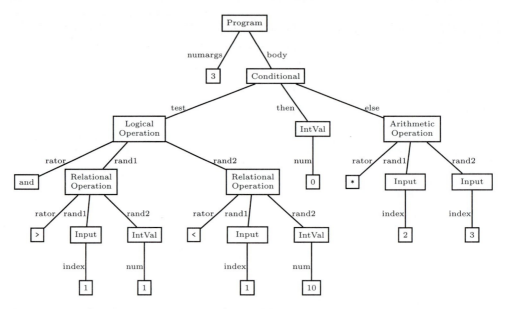

Figure 2.2   An abstract syntax tree for an EL program.

2.2   Concrete Syntax

Abstract grammars and ASTs aren't very helpful when it comes to representing programs in a textual fashion.[2] The same abstract structure can be expressed in many different concrete forms. The sample EL conditional expression in Figure 2.2, for instance, could be written down in some strikingly different textual forms. Here are three examples:

```
if $1 > 1 && $1 < 10 then 0 else $2 * $3 endif
(cond ((and (> (arg 1) 1) (< (arg 1) 10)) 0)
      (else (* (arg 2) (arg 3))))
1 input 1 gt 1 input 10 lt and {0} {2 input 3 input mul} choose
```

The above forms differ along a variety of dimensions:

- *Keywords and operation names.* The keywords if, cond, and choose all indicate a conditional expression, while multiplication is represented by the names

---

[2]It is also possible to represent programs more pictorially, and visual programming languages are an active area of research. But textual representations enjoy certain advantages over visual ones: they tend to be more compact than visual representations; the technology for processing them and communicating them is well established; and, most important, they can effectively make use of our familiarity with natural language.

* and `mul`. Accessing the *i*th input to the program is written in three different ways: $i, (`arg` *i*), and *i* `input`.

- *Operand order.* The example forms use infix, prefix, and postfix operations, respectively.

- *Means of grouping.* Grouping can be determined by precedence (`&&` has a lower precedence than `>` and `<` in the first example), keywords (`then`, `else`, and `endif` delimit the test, then, and else parts of the first conditional), or explicit matched delimiter pairs (such as the parentheses and braces in the last two examples).

These are only some of the possible dimensions. Many more are imaginable. For instance, numbers could be written in many different numeral formats such as decimal, binary, or octal numerals, scientific notation, or even Roman numerals!

2.3 S-Expression Grammars Specify ASTs

The examples in Section 2.2 illustrate that the nature of concrete syntax necessitates making representational choices that are arbitrary with respect to the abstract syntactic structure. While we will dispense with many of the complexities of concrete syntax, we still need *some* concrete notation for representing abstract syntax trees. Such a representation should be simple, yet permit us to precisely describe abstract syntax trees and operations on such trees. Throughout this book, we need to operate on abstract syntax trees to determine the meaning of a phrase, the type of a phrase, the translation of a phrase, and so on. To perform such operations, we need a far more compact representation for abstract syntax trees than the English description in Figure 2.1 or the graphical one in Figure 2.2.

We have chosen to represent abstract syntax trees using **s-expression grammars**. An s-expression grammar unites LISP's fully parenthesized prefix notation with traditional grammar notations to describe the structure of abstract syntax trees via parenthesized sequences of symbols and metavariables. Not only are these grammars very flexible for defining unambiguous program language syntax, but it is easy to construct programs that process s-expression notation. This facilitates writing interpreters and translators for the mini-languages we will study.

2.3.1 S-Expressions

An **s-expression** (short for **symbolic expression**) is a notation for representing trees by parenthesized linear text strings. The leaves of the trees are **sym-**

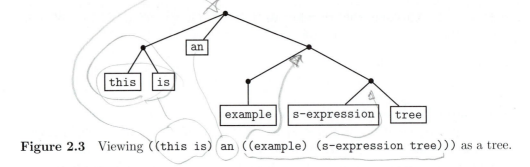

Figure 2.3   Viewing `((this is) an ((example) (s-expression tree)))` as a tree.

bolic tokens, where (to first approximation) a symbolic token is any sequence of characters that does not contain a left parenthesis ('('), a right parenthesis (')'), or a whitespace character. Examples of symbolic tokens include `x`, `foo`, `this-is-a-token`, `17`, `6.821`, and `4/3*pi*r^2`. We always write s-expressions in `teletype font`.

An intermediate node in a tree is represented by a pair of parentheses surrounding the s-expressions that represent the subtrees. Thus, the s-expression

`((this is) an ((example) (s-expression tree)))`

designates the structure depicted in Figure 2.3. Whitespace is necessary for separating tokens that appear next to each other, but can be used liberally to enhance the readability of the structure. Thus, the above s-expression could also be written as

```
((this is)
 an
 ((example)
  (s-expression
   tree)))
```

without changing the structure of the tree.

2.3.2   The Structure of S-Expression Grammars

An s-expression grammar combines the domain notation of Appendix A with s-expressions to specify the syntactic structure of a language. It has two parts:

1. A list of **syntactic domains**, one for each kind of phrase.

2. A set of **production rules** that define the structure of compound phrases.

Figure 2.4 presents a sample s-expression grammar for EL.

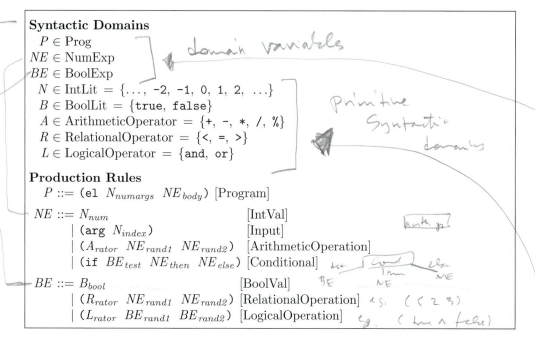

Syntactic Domains

$P \in$ Prog
$NE \in$ NumExp
$BE \in$ BoolExp
$N \in$ IntLit $= \{\dots,$ -2, -1, 0, 1, 2, $\dots\}$
$B \in$ BoolLit $= \{$true, false$\}$
$A \in$ ArithmeticOperator $= \{$+, -, *, /, %$\}$
$R \in$ RelationalOperator $= \{$<, =, >$\}$
$L \in$ LogicalOperator $= \{$and, or$\}$

Production Rules

$P ::= ($el $N_{numargs}$ $NE_{body})$ [Program]

$NE ::= N_{num}$ [IntVal]
    $|$ $($arg $N_{index})$ [Input]
    $|$ $(A_{rator}$ NE_{rand1} $NE_{rand2})$ [ArithmeticOperation]
    $|$ $($if BE_{test} NE_{then} $NE_{else})$ [Conditional]

$BE ::= B_{bool}$ [BoolVal]
    $|$ $(R_{rator}$ NE_{rand1} $NE_{rand2})$ [RelationalOperation]
    $|$ $(L_{rator}$ BE_{rand1} $BE_{rand2})$ [LogicalOperation]

Figure 2.4 An s-expression grammar for EL.

A syntactic domain is a collection of program phrases. **Primitive syntactic domains** are collections of phrases with no substructure. The primitive syntactic domains of EL are IntLit, BoolLit, ArithmeticOperator, RelationalOperator, and LogicalOperator. Primitive syntactic domains are specified by an enumeration of their elements or by an informal description with examples. For instance, the details of what constitutes a numeral in EL are left to the reader's intuition.

Compound syntactic domains are collections of phrases built out of other phrases. Because compound syntactic domains are defined by a grammar's production rules, the list of syntactic domains does not explicitly indicate their structure. All syntactic domains are annotated with **domain variables** (such as NE, BE, and N) that range over their elements; these play an important role in the production rules.

The production rules specify the structure of compound domains. There is one rule for each compound domain. A production rule has the form

$domain\text{-}variable ::=$ **pattern** [*phrase-type*]
                  $|$ **pattern** [*phrase-type*]
                  $\dots$
                  $|$ **pattern** [*phrase-type*]

where

- *domain-variable* is the domain variable for the compound syntactic domain being defined,

- *pattern* is an s-expression pattern (defined below), and

- *phrase-type* is a mnemonic name for the subclass of phrases in the domain that match the pattern. The phrase types correspond to the labels of intermediate nodes in an AST.

Each line of the rule is called a **production**; it specifies a collection of phrases that are considered to belong to the compound syntactic domain being defined. The second production rule in Figure 2.4, for instance, has four productions, specifying that a NumExp can be an integer literal, an indexed input, an arithmetic operation, or a conditional.

S-expression grammars are specialized versions of *context-free grammars*, the standard way to define programming language syntax. Domain variables play the role of *nonterminals* in such grammars. Our grammars are context-free because each production specifies the expansion of a single nonterminal in a way that does not depend on the context in which that nonterminal appears. The *terminals* of an s-expression grammar are tokens written in `teletype font`, such as parentheses, keywords, and literals. For certain elementary domains, we gloss over the details of how their elements are constructed from more basic parts, and instead provide a set-based description. For example, we use the description {..., -2, -1, 0, 1, 2, ...} to define integer literals rather than using productions to specify how they can be constructed from digits and an optional minus sign.

An s-expression pattern appearing in a production stands for all s-expressions that have the form of the pattern. An s-expression pattern may include symbolic tokens (such as `el`, `arg`, `if`) to differentiate it from other kinds of s-expression patterns. Domain variables may appear as tokens in s-expression patterns. For example, the pattern (`if` BE_{test} NE_{then} NE_{else}) contains a symbolic token (`if`) and the domain variables BE_{test}, NE_{then}, and NE_{else}. Such a pattern specifies the structure of a **compound phrase** — a phrase that is built from other phrases. Subscripts on the domain variables indicate their role in the phrase. This helps to distinguish positions within a phrase that have the same domain variable — e.g., the then and else parts of a conditional, which are both numerical expressions. This subscript appears as an edge label in the AST node corresponding to the pattern, while the phrase type of the production appears as the node label. So the `if` pattern denotes an AST node pattern of the form:

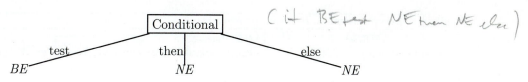

An s-expression pattern PT is said to **match** an s-expression SX if PT's domain variables $d_1, \ldots, d_n$ can be replaced by matching s-expressions $SX_1, \ldots, SX_n$ to yield SX. Each SX_i must be an element of the domain over which d_i ranges. A compound syntactic domain contains exactly those s-expressions that match the patterns of its productions in an s-expression grammar.

For example, Figure 2.5 shows the steps by which the NumExp production

$$\text{(if } BE_{test} \ NE_{then} \ NE_{else})$$

matches the s-expression

$$\text{(if (= (arg 1) 3) (arg 2) 4)}$$

Matching is a recursive process: BE_{test} matches (= (arg 1) 3), NE_{then} matches (arg 2), and NE_{else} matches 4. The recursion bottoms out at primitive syntactic domain elements (in this case, elements of the domain IntLit). Figure 2.5 shows how an AST for the sample if expression is constructed as the recursive matching process backs out of the recursion.

Note that the pattern (if BE_{test} NE_{then} NE_{else}) would not match any of the s-expressions (if 1 2 3), (if (arg 2) 2 3), or (if (+ (arg 1) 1) 2 3), because none of the test expressions 1, (arg 2), or (+ (arg 1) 1) match any of the patterns in the productions for BoolExp.

More formally, the rules for matching s-expression patterns to s-expressions are as follows:

- A pattern $(PT_1 \ \ldots \ PT_n)$ matches an s-expression $(SX_1 \ \ldots \ SX_n)$ if each subpattern PT_i matches the corresponding subexpression SX_i.

- A symbolic token T as a pattern matches only itself.

- A domain variable for a primitive syntactic domain D matches an s-expression SX if SX is an element of D.

- A domain variable for a compound syntactic domain D matches an s-expression SX if one of the patterns in the rule for D matches SX.

If SX is an s-expression, we shall use the notation SX_D to designate the domain element in D that SX designates. When D is a compound domain, SX_D

s-expression	domain	production	AST
(arg 1)	NE	(arg N_{index})	
3	NE	N_{num}	
(= (arg 1) 3)	BE	(R_{rator} NE_{rand1} NE_{rand2})	
(arg 2)	NE	(arg N_{index})	
4	NE	N_{num}	
(if (= (arg 1) 3) (arg 2) 4)	NE	(if BE_{test} NE_{then} NE_{else})	

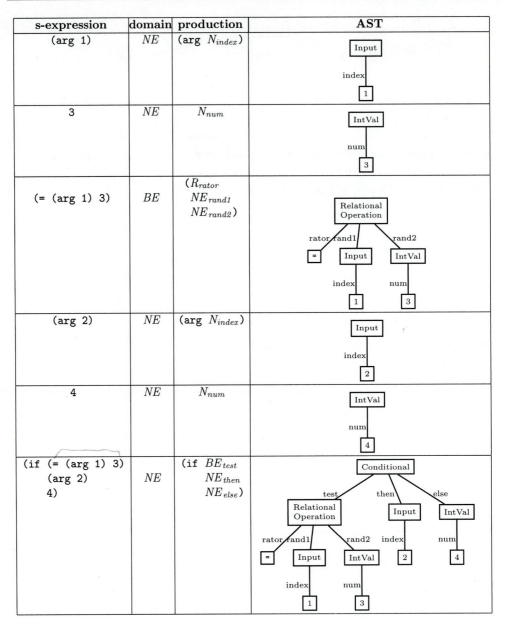

Figure 2.5   The steps by which (if (= (arg 1) 3) (arg 2) 4) is determined to be a member of the syntactic domain NumExp. In each row, an s-expression matches a domain by a production to yield an abstract syntax tree.

$P \in \text{Prog} ::= (\texttt{el}\ N_{numargs}\ NE_{body})\ [\text{Program}]$

$NE \in \text{NumExp} ::= N_{num}$ [IntVal]

     $| \ (\texttt{arg}\ N_{index})$ [Input]

     $| \ (A_{rator}\ NE_{rand1}\ NE_{rand2})$ [ArithmeticOperation]

     $| \ (\texttt{if}\ BE_{test}\ NE_{then}\ NE_{else})$ [Conditional]

$BE \in \text{BoolExp} ::= B_{bool}$ [BoolVal]

     $| \ (R_{rator}\ NE_{rand1}\ NE_{rand2})$ [RelationalOperation]

     $| \ (L_{rator}\ BE_{rand1}\ BE_{rand2})$ [LogicalOperation]

$N \in \text{IntLit} = \{\ldots,\ \texttt{-2},\ \texttt{-1},\ \texttt{0},\ \texttt{1},\ \texttt{2},\ \ldots\}$

$B \in \text{BoolLit} = \{\texttt{true},\ \texttt{false}\}$

$A \in \text{ArithmeticOperator} = \{\texttt{+},\ \texttt{-},\ \texttt{*},\ \texttt{/},\ \texttt{\%}\}$

$R \in \text{RelationalOperator} = \{\texttt{<},\ \texttt{=},\ \texttt{>}\}$

$L \in \text{LogicalOperator} = \{\texttt{and},\ \texttt{or}\}$

Figure 2.6 A more concise rendering of the s-expression grammar for EL.

corresponds to an abstract syntax tree that indicates *how SX* matches one of the rule patterns for the domain. For example,

$$(\texttt{if}\ (\texttt{=}\ (\texttt{arg}\ \texttt{1})\ \texttt{3})\ (\texttt{arg}\ \texttt{2})\ \texttt{4})_{\text{NumExp}}$$

can be viewed as the abstract syntax tree depicted in Figure 2.5 on page 28. Each node of the AST indicates the production that successfully matches the corresponding s-expression, and each edge indicates a domain variable that appeared in the production pattern.

In the notation SX_D, domain subscript D serves to disambiguate cases where SX belongs to more than one syntactic domain. For example, 1_{IntLit} is 1 as a primitive numeral, while 1_{NumExp} is 1 as a numerical expression. The subscript will be omitted when the domain is clear from context.

Using the s-expression grammar specified in Figure 2.4, the abstract syntax tree in Figure 2.2 can be expressed as:

```
(el 3 (if (and (> (arg 1) 1) (< (arg 1) 10))
          0
          (* (arg 2) (arg 3)))))
```

To make s-expression grammars more concise, we will often combine the specification of a compound syntactic domain with its production rules. Figure 2.6 shows the EL s-expression grammar written in this more concise style.

Exercise 2.1

a. Write an EL program that takes three integers and returns the largest one.

b. Draw an AST for your program.

(handwritten notes)
(ef (> (arg1) (arg2))
(if (> (arg 1) (arg3))
(arg1)
(arg3)
(if (> (arg 2)(arg 3)) (arg2) (arg3)))

2.3.3   Phrase Tags

S-expression grammars for our mini-languages will generally follow the LISP-style convention that compound phrases begin with a **phrase tag** that unambiguously indicates the phrase type. In EL, if is an example of a phrase tag. The fact that all compound phrases are delimited by explicit parentheses eliminates the need for syntactic keywords in the middle of or at the end of phrases (e.g., then, else, and endif in a conditional).

Because phrase tags can be cumbersome, we will often omit them when no ambiguity results. Figure 2.7 shows an alternative syntax for EL in which every production pattern is marked with a distinct phrase tag. In this alternative syntax, the addition of 1 and 2 would be written (arith + (num 1) (num 2)) — quite a bit more verbose than (+ 1 2)! But most of the phrase tags can be removed without introducing ambiguity. Because numerals are clearly distinguished from other s-expressions, there is no need for the num tag. Likewise, we can dispense with the bool tag. Since the arithmetic operators are disjoint from the other operators, the arith tag is superfluous as are the rel and log tags. The result of these optimizations is the original EL syntax in Figure 2.4.

2.3.4   Sequence Patterns

As defined above, each component of an s-expression pattern matches only a single s-expression. But sometimes it is desirable for a pattern component to match a *sequence* of s-expressions. For example, suppose we want to extend the + operator of EL to accept an arbitrary number of numeric operands, making (+ 1 2 3 4) and (+ 2 (+ 3 4 5) (+ 6 7)) legal numerical expressions in EL. Using the simple patterns introduced above, this extension requires an infinite number of productions:

$$NE ::= \ldots$$
$$| \ (+) \qquad\qquad\qquad\qquad\qquad \text{[Addition-0]}$$
$$| \ (+ \ NE_{rand1}) \qquad\qquad\qquad \text{[Addition-1]}$$
$$| \ (+ \ NE_{rand1} \ \ NE_{rand2}) \qquad\quad \text{[Addition-2]}$$
$$| \ (+ \ NE_{rand1} \ \ NE_{rand2} \ \ NE_{rand3}) \ \text{[Addition-3]}$$
$$| \ \ldots$$

$$P ::= \text{(el } N_{numargs} \text{ } NE_{body}) \text{ [Program]}$$

$$
\begin{aligned}
NE ::= &\text{ (num } N_{num}) &&\text{[IntVal]}\\
&| \text{ (arg } N_{index}) &&\text{[Input]}\\
&| \text{ (arith } A_{rator} \text{ } NE_{rand1} \text{ } NE_{rand2}) &&\text{[ArithmeticOperation]}\\
&| \text{ (if } BE_{test} \text{ } NE_{then} \text{ } NE_{else}) &&\text{[Conditional]}
\end{aligned}
$$

$$
\begin{aligned}
BE ::= &\text{ (bool } B_{bool}) &&\text{[BoolVal]}\\
&| \text{ (rel } R_{rator} \text{ } NE_{rand1} \text{ } NE_{rand2}) &&\text{[RelationalOperation]}\\
&| \text{ (log } L_{rator} \text{ } BE_{rand1} \text{ } BE_{rand2}) &&\text{[LogicalOperation]}
\end{aligned}
$$

Figure 2.7 An alternative syntax for EL in which every production pattern has a phrase tag.

Here we introduce a concise way of handling this kind of syntactic flexibility within s-expression grammars. We extend s-expression patterns so that any pattern can be annotated with a postfix $*$ character. Such a pattern is called a **sequence pattern**. A sequence pattern PT^* matches any consecutive sequence of zero or more s-expressions $SX_1 \ldots SX_n$ such that each SX_i matches the pattern PT.

For instance, the extended addition expression can be specified concisely by the pattern (+ NE^*_{rand}). Here are some phrases that match this new pattern, along with the sequence matched by NE^*_{rand} in each case:[3]

$$
\begin{aligned}
&\text{(+ 6 8 2 1)} &&NE^*_{rand} = [6, 8, 2, 1]_{\text{NumExp}}\\
&\text{(+ 7 (+ 5 8 4) (+ 9 6))} &&NE^*_{rand} = [7, (+ 5\ 8\ 4), (+ 9\ 6)]_{\text{NumExp}}\\
&\text{(+ 3)} &&NE^*_{rand} = [3]_{\text{NumExp}}\\
&\text{(+)} &&NE^*_{rand} = [\,]_{\text{NumExp}}
\end{aligned}
$$

In graphical depictions of ASTs, a sequence node will be drawn as a solid circle whose components (indexed starting at 1) branch out from the node. E.g., Figure 2.8 shows the AST for (+ 7 (+ 5 8 4) (+ 9 6)) in EL with extended addition expressions.

Note that a sequence pattern can match any number of elements, including zero or one. To specify that an addition should have a minimum of two operands, we could use the following production pattern:

$$(+ \text{ } NE_{rand1} \text{ } NE_{rand2} \text{ } NE^*_{rest})$$

A postfix $^+$ is similar to $*$, except that the pattern matches only a sequence with at least one element. Thus, the pattern (+ NE^+_{rand}) is an alternative way

---

[3] $[\,]_{\text{NumExp}}$ denotes the empty sequence of numerical expressions, as explained in Section A.3.5.

of expressing the essence of the pattern (+ NE_{rand} NE^*_{rest}). However, the two patterns are subtly different: (+ NE^+_{rand}) denotes an AST node with a single component that is a sequence of numerical expressions, while (+ NE_{rand} NE^*_{rest}) denotes an AST node with two components — a numerical expression (its rand) and a sequence of numerical expressions (its rest).

A postfix $^?$ indicates a sequence of either zero or one elements of a domain. It is used to specify optional syntactic elements. For example, (- E_1 $E_2^?$) describes the syntax for a - operator that designates subtraction (in the two-element case) or unary negation (in the one-element case).

A postfix *, $^+$, or $^?$ can be attached to any s-expression pattern, not just a domain variable. For example, in the s-expression pattern

$$(\text{cond } (BE_{test}\ NE_{then})^*\ (\text{else } NE_{default})^?)$$

the subpattern $(BE_{test}\ NE_{then})^*$ matches any sequence of parenthesized clauses containing a boolean expression followed by a numerical expression, and the subpattern $(\text{else } NE_{default})^?$ matches an optional else clause.

To avoid ambiguity, s-expression grammars are not allowed to use s-expression patterns in which multiple sequence patterns enable a single s-expression to match a pattern in more than one way. As an example of a disallowed pattern, consider (op NE^*_{rand1} NE^*_{rand2}), which could match the s-expression (op 1 2) in three different ways:

- NE^*_{rand1} = $[1,\ 2]_{\text{NumExp}}$ and NE^*_{rand2} = $[\ ]_{\text{NumExp}}$

- NE^*_{rand1} = $[1]_{\text{NumExp}}$ and NE^*_{rand2} = $[2]_{\text{NumExp}}$

- NE^*_{rand1} = $[\ ]_{\text{NumExp}}$ and NE^*_{rand2} = $[1,\ 2]_{\text{NumExp}}$

A disallowed pattern can always be transformed into a legal pattern by inserting explicit parentheses to demarcate components. For instance, the following are all unambiguous legal patterns:

$$(\text{op } (NE^*_{rand1})\ (NE^*_{rand2}))$$
$$(\text{op } (NE^*_{rand1})\ NE^*_{rand2})$$
$$(\text{op } NE^*_{rand1}\ (NE^*_{rand2}))$$

2.3.5   Notational Conventions

In addition to the s-expression patterns described above, we will employ a few other notational conventions for syntax.

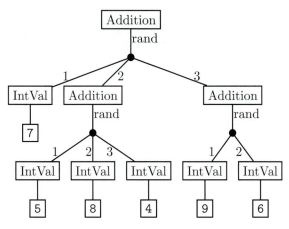

Figure 2.8 AST notation for (+ 7 (+ 5 8 4) (+ 9 6)) in EL with extended addition expressions.

Domain Variables

In addition to being used in s-expression patterns, domain variables can appear inside s-expressions when they denote particular s-expressions. For example, if NE_1 is the s-expression (+ 1 2) and NE_2 is the s-expression (- 3 4), then (* NE_1 NE_2) is the same syntactic entity as (* (+ 1 2) (- 3 4)).

Ellipsis Notation

If SX is an s-expression pattern denoting an element of a syntactic domain D, then the ellipsis notation SX_j ... SX_k specifies a sequence with $(k - j + 1)$ elements from D^*. For example, (+ NE_1 ... NE_5) designates an EL extended addition expression with 5 operands, and

$$(\texttt{cond}\ (BE_1\ NE_1)\ \ldots\ (BE_m\ NE_m)\ (\texttt{else}\ NE_{default}))$$

stands for an expression containing m pairs of the form $(BE_i\ NE_i)$. The pattern

$$(\texttt{+}\ N_1\ \ldots\ N_{i-1}\ NE_i\ \ldots\ NE_n)$$

designates an EL extended addition expression with n operands in which the first $i-1$ operands are numeric literals (a specific kind of numeric expression) and the remaining operands are arbitrary numeric expressions.

Note that ellipsis notation can denote sequences with zero elements or one element: SX_j ... SX_k denotes a sequence with one element if $k = j$ and a sequence with zero elements if $k = (j - 1)$.

Index Notation

To abbreviate ellipsis notation further, we will sometimes employ the indexed notation $SX_{i=j}^{k}$ to stand for $SX_j \ldots SX_k$, where SX_i refers to a particular element of this sequence. Here are the ellipsis notation examples from above expressed with index notation:

$$(+ \ NE_{i=1}^{5})$$
$$(\texttt{cond} \ (BE_j \ NE_j)_{j=1}^{m} \ (\texttt{else} \ NE_{default}))$$
$$(+ \ N_{j=1}^{i-1} \ NE_{k=i}^{n})$$

Note that $SX_{i=j}^{k}$ denotes a sequence with one element if $k = j$ and a sequence with zero elements if $k = (j - 1)$.

Sequence Notation

Sequence notation, including the infix notations for the *cons* (".") and *append* ("@") sequence functions (see Section A.3.5), can be intermixed with s-expression notation to designate sequence elements of compound syntactic domains. For example, all of the following are alternative ways of writing the same extended EL addition expression:

$$(+ \ 1 \ 2 \ 3)$$
$$(+ \ [1, \ 2, \ 3])$$
$$(+ \ [1, \ 2] \ @ \ [3])$$
$$(+ \ 1 . [2, \ 3])$$

Similarly, if $NE_1 = 1$, $NE_2^* = [2, (+\ 3\ 4)]$, and $NE_3^* = [(*\ 5\ 6), (-\ 7\ 8)]$, then $(+\ NE_1 . NE_2^*)$ designates the same syntactic entity as

$$(+ \ 1 \ 2 \ (+ \ 3 \ 4))$$

and $(+\ NE_2^* \ @ \ NE_3^*)$ designates the same syntactic entity as

$$(+ \ 2 \ (+ \ 3 \ 4) \ (* \ 5 \ 6) \ (- \ 7 \ 8))$$

The sequence notation is legal only in positions where a production for a compound syntactic domain contains a sequence pattern. For example, the following notations are illegal because `if` expressions do not contain any component sequences:

$$(\texttt{if} \ [(< \ (\texttt{arg} \ 1) \ 1), \ 2, \ 3])$$
$$(\texttt{if} \ [(< \ (\texttt{arg} \ 1) \ 1), \ 2] \ @ \ [3])$$
$$(\texttt{if} \ (< \ (\texttt{arg} \ 1) \ 1) . [2, \ 3])$$

$nheight : \text{NumExp} \rightarrow Nat$

$nheight[\![N]\!] = 0$

$nheight[\![(\texttt{arg}\ N)]\!] = 0$

$nheight[\![(A\ NE_1\ NE_2)]\!] = (1 +_{Nat} (\max\ nheight[\![NE_1]\!]\ nheight[\![NE_2]\!]))$

$nheight[\![(\texttt{if}\ BE_{test}\ NE_{then}\ NE_{else})]\!]$
$\quad = (1 +_{Nat} (\max\ bheight[\![BE_{test}]\!]\ (\max\ nheight[\![NE_{then}]\!]\ nheight[\![NE_{else}]\!])))$

$bheight : \text{BoolExp} \rightarrow Nat$

$bheight[\![B]\!] = 0$

$bheight[\![(R\ NE_1\ NE_2)]\!] = (1 +_{Nat} (\max\ nheight[\![NE_1]\!]\ nheight[\![NE_2]\!]))$

$bheight[\![(L\ BE_1\ BE_2)]\!] = (1 +_{Nat} (\max\ bheight[\![BE_1]\!]\ bheight[\![BE_2]\!]))$

Figure 2.9 Two examples illustrating the form of function definitions on syntactic domains.

Similarly, the notation (+ 1 [2, 3]) is not legal for an EL extended addition expression, because the production pattern (+ NE^*_{rand}) requires a single sequence component, not two components (a numerical expression and a sequence of numerical expressions). If the production pattern were instead (+ NE_{rand} NE^*_{rest}), then the expression (+ 1 [2, 3]) *would* match the pattern, but (+ [1, 2, 3]), (+ [1, 2] @ [3]), and (+ 1 . [2, 3]) would not. However, according to our conventions, (+ 1 2 3) would match either of these production patterns.

Sequence notation can be used in s-expression patterns as well. For example, the pattern (+ NE_{rand1} . NE^*_{rest}) matches any extended addition expression with at least one operand, while the pattern (+ [4, 7] @ NE^*_{rest}) matches any extended addition expression whose first two operands are 4 and 7.

Syntactic Functions

We will follow a convention (standard in the semantics literature) that functions on compound syntactic domains are defined by a series of clauses, one for each production. Figure 2.9 illustrates this style of definition for two functions on EL expressions: *nheight* specifies the height of a numerical expression, while *bheight* specifies the height of a boolean expression. Each clause consists of two parts: a *head* that specifies an s-expression pattern from a production; and a *body* defining the meaning of the function for s-expressions that match the head.

The double brackets, $[\![\,]\!]$, are often used in syntactic functions to demarcate a syntactic operand. They help to visually distinguish phrases in the programing language being processed from phrases in the metalanguage defining the function. These brackets may be viewed as part of the name of the syntactic function. In function applications involving bracket notation, the function is assumed to bind tightly with the syntactic argument. For instance, the application *max nheight*$[\![NE_1]\!]$ *nheight*$[\![NE_2]\!]$ is parsed as if it were written (*max* (*nheight*$[\![NE_1]\!]$) (*nheight*$[\![NE_2]\!]$)).

2.3.6   Mathematical Foundation of Syntactic Domains

Exactly what kinds of entities are defined by s-expression grammars? The answer to this question is important, because we will spend the rest of this book manipulating such entities. Intuitively, each compound syntactic domain in an s-expression grammar is defined to be the set of trees whose structure is determined by the productions for that domain. But can we define these trees in a more formal way?

Yes! Using the domain concepts introduced in Section A.3, we can precisely define the mathematical structures specified by an s-expression grammar via what we will call the **sum-of-products interpretation**. An s-expression grammar defines a (potentially mutually recursive) collection of syntactic domains. In the sum-of-products interpretation we define:

- the primitive syntactic domains mentioned in the s-expression grammar, each simply containing the elements specified for that domain;

- a new domain for each production, which we name with the phrase type of that production and define to be the product of the domains associated with the domain-variable occurrences in the production pattern;

- the compound syntactic domains mentioned in the s-expression grammar, each defined as a sum of domains, one for each production for that domain.

Note these special cases:

- The domain for a production containing exactly one domain-variable occurrence turns out to be a synonym for the domain associated with that domain variable.

- A compound domain with just one production turns out to be a synonym for the domain associated with that production.

- A production containing no domain-variable occurrences represents the *Unit* domain.

Prog = Program
Program = IntLit × NumExp
NumExp = IntVal + Input + ArithmeticOperation + Conditional
IntLit = {..., -2, -1, 0, 1, 2, ...}
IntVal = IntLit
Input = IntLit
ArithmeticOperation = ArithmeticOperator × NumExp × NumExp
ArithmeticOperator = {+, -, *, /, %}
Conditional = BoolExp × NumExp × NumExp
BoolExp = BoolVal + RelationalOperation + LogicalOperation
BoolLit = {true, false}
BoolVal = BoolLit
RelationalOperation = RelationalOperator × NumExp × NumExp
RelationalOperator = {<, =, >}
LogicalOperation = LogicalOperator × BoolExp × BoolExp
LogicalOperator = {and, or}

Figure 2.10 Syntactic domains for sum-of-products interpretation of the s-expression grammar for EL.

Any occurrence of a sequence pattern PT^* in a production represents a sequence domain whose elements are described by the pattern PT.

For example, Figure 2.10 shows the complete domain definitions implied by the s-expression grammar for EL in Figure 2.4. Recall that the Prog domain is defined by the single production pattern (el $N_{numargs}$ NE_{body}), with phrase type Prog. So Prog is a synonym for Program, a product domain of IntLit (the domain associated with the domain variable N) and NumExp (the domain associated with the domain variable NE). In the s-expression grammar, the NumExp domain is defined by the following four productions:

$$
\begin{aligned}
NE ::= \; & N_{num} & & [\text{IntVal}] \\
\mid \; & (\texttt{arg } N_{index}) & & [\text{Input}] \\
\mid \; & (A_{rator} \; NE_{rand1} \; NE_{rand2}) & & [\text{ArithmeticOperation}] \\
\mid \; & (\texttt{if } BE_{test} \; NE_{then} \; NE_{else}) & & [\text{Conditional}]
\end{aligned}
$$

So NumExp is interpreted as a sum of four domains:

1. the IntVal domain, a synonym for IntLit, representing an integer literal;

2. the Input domain, a synonym for IntLit, representing the index of a reference to a program input;

⟨3,
  Conditional ↣→NumExp
    ⟨LogicalOperation ↣→BoolExp⟨**and**,
                              RelationalOperation ↣→BoolExp
                                ⟨**>**, (Input ↣→NumExp 1), (IntVal ↣→NumExp 1)⟩,
                              RelationalOperation ↣→BoolExp
                                ⟨**<**, (Input ↣→NumExp 1), (IntVal ↣→NumExp 10)⟩
                              ⟩,
    (IntVal ↣→NumExp 0),
    (ArithmeticOperation ↣→NumExp ⟨*****, (Input ↣→NumExp 2), (Input ↣→NumExp 3)⟩)
    ⟩
⟩

Figure 2.11   Sample EL program from Figure 2.2 expressed in syntactic-domain notation.

3. the ArithmeticOperation domain, whose elements are triples of an arithmetic operator in ArithmeticOperator and two operands from NumExp; and

4. the Conditional domain, whose elements are triples of a test expression from BoolExp and two branch expressions from NumExp.

The structure of BoolExp is similarly determined from its productions. Figure 2.11 shows how the EL program AST from Figure 2.2 can be expressed in this domain notation.

   In the sum-of-products interpretation, the tag on an AST node indicates the summand domain to which it belongs, and the subtrees of that node are the product components of that summand domain. Throughout the rest of this book, we will assume that any syntactic phrase constructed from an s-expression grammar is really an element of a syntactic domain defined via the sum-of-products interpretation. E.g., the EL expression (+ 1 (* 2 3)) is not a sequence of characters, nor is it an s-expression tree; it is an element of the NumExp domain.

Exercise 2.2

a. Define two syntactic functions

$$nrange : \text{NumExp} \rightarrow (\text{IntLit} \times \text{IntLit})$$
$$brange : \text{BoolExp} \rightarrow (\text{IntLit} \times \text{IntLit})$$

such that *nrange* returns a pair of the smallest and largest argument index referenced in an EL numerical expression and *brange* does the same for a boolean expression. E.g., for the conditional expression in Figure 2.2, *nrange* should return ⟨1, 3⟩.

b. Define a function *argcheck* : Prog → *Bool* that returns *true* if all argument indices referenced within an EL program are between 1 and the declared number of arguments; otherwise, it returns *false*. *argcheck* performs a simple **static analysis** — determining a property of the program (might it encounter an out-of-bounds argument index?) without executing it.

(To complete this exercise, you may need to review some of the metalanguage notation in Appendix A.)

2.4 The Syntax of PostFix

Equipped with our syntactic tools, we are now ready to formally specify the syntactic structure of PostFix, the stack language introduced in Section 1.4, and to explore some variations on this structure. Figure 2.12 presents an s-expression grammar for PostFix. Top-level programs are represented as s-expressions of the form (postfix $N_{numargs}$ Q_{body}), where $N_{numargs}$ is a numeral specifying the number of arguments and Q_{body} is the command sequence executed by the program. The sequence pattern C^* in the production for CommandSeq (Q) indicates that CommandSeq is a sequence domain over elements from the Command domain. All of the elements of Command (C) are single tokens (e.g., add and sel), except for executable sequences, which are parenthesized elements of the CommandSeq domain. The mutually recursive structure of Command and CommandSeq permits arbitrary nesting of executable sequences.

The concrete details specified by Figure 2.12 are only one way of capturing the underlying abstract syntactic structure of the language. Figure 2.13 presents an alternative s-expression grammar for PostFix. In order to avoid confusion, we will refer to the language defined in Figure 2.13 as PostFix2.

There are two main differences between the grammars of PostFix and Post-Fix2.

1. The PostFix2 grammar strictly adheres to the phrase tag convention introduced in Section 2.3.3. That is, every element of a compound syntactic domain appears as a parenthesized structure introduced by a unique tag. For example, 1 becomes (int 1), pop becomes (pop), and add becomes (arithop add).[4]

2. Rather than representing command sequences as a sequence domain, Post-Fix2 uses the : and (skip) commands to encode such sequences. (skip) is intended to be a "no op" command that leaves the stack unchanged, while

---

[4]The arithop keyword underscores that the arithmetic operators are related; similarly for relop.

$P \in \text{Prog} ::= (\texttt{postfix} \ N_{numargs} \ Q_{body}) \ [\text{Program}]$

$Q \in \text{CommandSeq} ::= C^* \ [\text{CommandSequence}]$

$$
\begin{array}{lll}
C \in \text{Command} ::= & N_{num} & [\text{IntVal}] \\
& | \ \texttt{pop} & [\text{Pop}] \\
& | \ \texttt{swap} & [\text{Swap}] \\
& | \ A_{op} & [\text{ArithOp}] \\
& | \ R_{op} & [\text{RelOp}] \\
& | \ \texttt{nget} & [\text{NumGet}] \\
& | \ \texttt{sel} & [\text{Select}] \\
& | \ \texttt{exec} & [\text{Execute}] \\
& | \ (Q_{coms}) & [\text{ExecutableSequence}]
\end{array}
$$

$A \in \text{ArithmeticOperator} = \{\texttt{add, sub, mul, div, rem}\}$

$R \in \text{RelationalOperator} = \{\texttt{lt, eq, gt}\}$

$N \in \text{IntLit} = \{\ldots, \texttt{-2, -1, 0, 1, 2}, \ldots\}$

Figure 2.12   An s-expression grammar for POSTFIX.

$(: \ C_1 \ C_2)$ is intended first to perform C_1 on the current stack and then to perform C_2 on the stack resulting from C_1. The : and (skip) commands in POSTFIX2 serve the roles of *cons* and [] for command sequences in POSTFIX. For example, the POSTFIX command sequence

$$[8, 9, \text{add}]_{\text{Command}} = (cons \ 8 \ (cons \ 9 \ (cons \ \text{add} \ []_{\text{Command}})))$$

can be encoded in POSTFIX2 as a single command:

$$(: \ (\text{int } 8) \ (: \ (\text{int } 9) \ (: \ (\text{arithop add}) \ (\text{skip}))))$$

The difference in phrase tags is a surface variation in concrete syntax that does not affect the structure of abstract syntax trees. Whether sequences are explicit (the original grammar) or implicit (the alternative grammar) is a deeper variation because the abstract syntax trees differ in these two cases (see Figure 2.14).

Although the tree structures are similar, it is not *a priori* possible to determine that the second tree encodes a sequence without knowing more about the semantics of compositions and skips. In particular, : and (skip) must satisfy two behavioral properties in order for them to encode sequences:

- (skip) must be an **identity** for the command :
  I.e., $(: \ C \ (\text{skip}))$ and $(: \ (\text{skip}) \ C)$ must behave like C.

$P \in \mathrm{Prog} ::= (\texttt{postfix}\ N_{numargs}\ C_{body})$ [Program]

$C \in \mathrm{Command} ::= (\texttt{int}\ N_{num})$ [IntVal]

               $|$ (pop)   [Pop]

               $|$ (swap)   [Swap]

               $|$ (arithop A_{op})   [ArithOp]

               $|$ (relop R_{op})   [RelOp]

               $|$ (nget)   [NumGet]

               $|$ (sel)   [Select]

               $|$ (exec)   [Execute]

               $|$ (seq C_{com})   [ExecutableSequence]

               $|$ (: C_{com1} C_{com2}) [Compose]

               $|$ (skip)   [Skip]

$A \in \mathrm{ArithmeticOperator} = \{\texttt{add}, \texttt{sub}, \texttt{mul}, \texttt{div}, \texttt{rem}\}$

$R \in \mathrm{RelationalOperator} = \{\texttt{lt}, \texttt{eq}, \texttt{gt}\}$

$N \in \mathrm{IntLit} = \{\ldots, \texttt{-2}, \texttt{-1}, \texttt{0}, \texttt{1}, \texttt{2}, \ldots\}$

Figure 2.13 An s-expression grammar for PostFix2, an alternative syntax for Post-Fix.

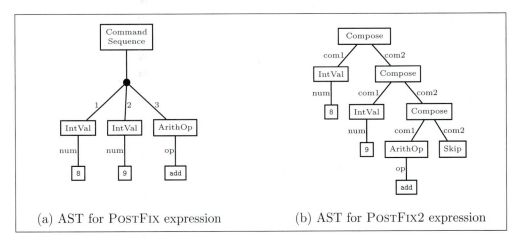

(a) AST for PostFix expression   (b) AST for PostFix2 expression

Figure 2.14 A comparison of the abstract syntax trees for two encodings of an expression.

- The command : must be **associative**

  I.e., (: C_1 (: C_2 C_3)) must behave the same as (: (: C_1 C_2) C_3).

These two properties amount to saying that (1) skips can be ignored and (2) in a tree of compositions, only the order of the leaves matters. With these properties, any tree of compositions is isomorphic to a sequence of the non-skip leaves. The informal semantics of : and (skip) given above satisfies these two properties.

Is one of the two grammars presented above "better" than the other? It depends on the context in which they are used. As the following example indicates, the POSTFIX grammar certainly leads to programs that are more concise than those generated by the POSTFIX2 grammar:

```
(postfix 1 (1 2 add) (3 4 mul) sel exec)
```

```
(postfix2 1
  (: (seq (: (int 1) (: (int 2) (: (arithop add) (skip)))))
    (: (seq (: (int 3) (: (int 4) (: (arithop mul) (skip)))))
      (: (sel) (: (exec) (skip)))))))
```

Additionally, we shall see that the explicit sequences of POSTFIX make it more amenable to certain kinds of semantic analysis. On the other hand, other semantic and pragmatic tools are easier to apply to POSTFIX2 programs. Though we will focus on the POSTFIX grammar, we will consider POSTFIX2 when it is instructive to do so. In any event, the reader should be aware that even the fairly constrained boundaries of s-expression grammars leave some room for design decisions.

Exercise 2.3

a. Consider a subset of POSTFIX that has the following commands: integer literals, executable sequences, arithmetic operators, and exec. Using the sum-of-products interpretation described in Section 2.3.6, give definitions for all the syntactic domains implied by the s-expression grammar for this subset. Your domain definitions may be recursive.

b. Express the POSTFIX program (postfix 1 (2 mul) exec) as an element of your syntactic domains.

c. Repeat the above two parts for the corresponding subset of POSTFIX2.

(To complete this exercise, you may need to review some of the metalanguage notation in Appendix A.)

Notes

Early proponents of abstract syntax were McCarthy [McC62] and Landin [Lan66]. This notion is commonly used in operational and denotational semantics to ignore unimportant syntactic details. Interpreters and compilers often have a "front-end" stage that converts concrete syntax into data structures representing abstract syntax trees.

The concrete syntax for programming languages is usually specified via a *context-free grammar*, a formalism covered in any automata theory text (e.g, [Min67, HU79, Sip06]). In the programming language literature, a standard notation for such grammars is *Backus-Naur form (BNF)*, which was used in the report defining ALGOL 60 [BBG⁺63].

Our s-expression grammars are based on McCarthy's LISP s-expression notation [McC60], which is a trivially parsable generic and extensible concrete syntax for programming languages.

Many tools — most notably the scanner generator Lex [Les75] and the parser generator Yacc [Joh75] — are available for converting concrete syntactic notations that satisfy more complex grammatical specifications into abstract syntax trees. A discussion of these tools, the scanning and parsing theory behind them, and the grammatical specifications they use can be found in almost any compiler textbook. For a particularly concise account, consult one of Appel's textbooks [App98b, App98a, AP02].

3

Operational Semantics

And now I see with eye serene
The very pulse of the machine.
　　　　　　— William Wordsworth, "She Was a Phantom of Delight"

3.1　The Operational Semantics Game

Consider executing the following PostFix program on the arguments [4, 5]:

```
(postfix 2 (2 (3 mul add) exec) 1 swap exec sub)
```

It helps to have a bookkeeping notation that represents the process of applying the informal rules presented in Chapter 1. For example, the table in Figure 3.1 illustrates one way to represent the execution of the above program. The table has two columns: the first column in each row holds the current command sequence; the second holds the current stack. The execution process begins by filling the first row of the table with the command sequence of the given program and a stack consisting of the program arguments. Execution proceeds in a step-by-step fashion by using the rule for the first command of the current row to generate the next row. Each execution step removes the first command from the sequence and updates the stack. In the case of **exec**, new commands may also be prepended to the command sequence. The execution process terminates as soon as a row with an empty command sequence is generated. The result of the execution is the top stack element of the final row (**-3** in the example).

　　The table-based technique for executing PostFix programs exemplifies an **operational semantics**. Operational semantics formalizes the common intuition that program execution can be understood as a step-by-step process that evolves by the mechanical application of a fixed set of rules. Sometimes the rules describe how the state of some physical machine is changed by executing an instruction. For example, assembly code instructions are defined in terms of the effect that they have on the architectural elements of a computer: registers, stack, memory, instruction stream, etc. But the rules may also describe how

Commands	Stack
(2 (3 mul add) exec) 1 swap exec sub	4
	5
1 swap exec sub	(2 (3 mul add) exec)
	4
	5
swap exec sub	1
	(2 (3 mul add) exec)
	4
	5
exec sub	(2 (3 mul add) exec)
	1
	4
	5
2 (3 mul add) exec sub	1
	4
	5
(3 mul add) exec sub	2
	1
	4
	5
exec sub	(3 mul add)
	2
	1
	4
	5
3 mul add sub	2
	1
	4
	5
mul add sub	3
	2
	1
	4
	5
add sub	6
	1
	4
	5
sub	7
	4
	5
	-3
	5

Figure 3.1   A table showing the step-by-step execution of a POSTFIX program.

language constructs affect the state of some **abstract machine** that provides a mathematical model for program execution. Each state of the abstract machine is called a **configuration**.

For example, in the POSTFIX abstract machine implied by the table in Figure 3.1, each configuration is modeled by one row of the execution table: a pair of a program and a stack. The next configuration of the machine is determined from the current one based on the first command in the current program. The behavior of each command can be specified in terms of how it transforms the current configuration into the next one. For example, executing the add command removes it from the command sequence and replaces the top two elements of the stack by their sum. Executing the exec command pops an executable sequence from the top of the stack and prepends its commands in front of the commands following exec.

The general structure of an operational semantics execution is illustrated in Figure 3.2. An abstract machine accepts a program to be executed along with its inputs and then chugs away until it emits an answer. Internally, the abstract machine typically manipulates configurations with two kinds of parts:

1. The **code component**: a program phrase that controls the rest of the computation.

2. The **state components**: entities that are manipulated by the program during its execution. In the case of POSTFIX, the single state component is a stack, but configurations for other languages might include state components modeling random-access memory, a set of name/object bindings, a file system, a graphics state, various kinds of control information, etc. Sometimes there are no state components, in which case a configuration is just code.

The stages of the operational execution are as follows:

- The program and its inputs are first mapped by an **input function** into an **initial configuration** of the abstract machine. The code component of the initial configuration is usually some part of the given program, and the state components are appropriately initialized from the inputs. For instance, in an initial configuration for POSTFIX, the code component is the command sequence body of the program and the single state component is a stack containing the integer arguments in order with the first argument at the top of the stack.

- After an initial configuration has been constructed, it's time to "turn the crank" of the abstract machine. During this phase, the rules governing the abstract machine are applied in an iterative fashion to yield a sequence of intermediate configurations. Each configuration is the result of one step in the step-by-step

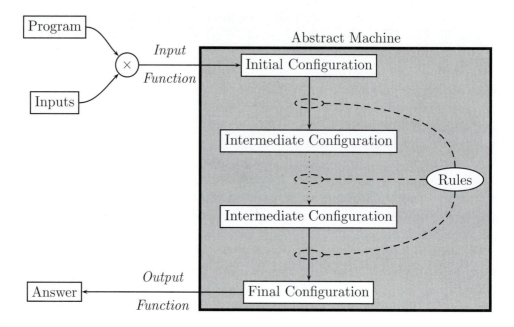

Figure 3.2   The operational semantics "game board."

execution of the program. This stage continues until a configuration is reached
that is deemed to be a **final configuration**. What counts as a final configuration varies widely between abstract machines. In the case of POSTFIX, a
configuration is final when the code component is an empty command sequence.

- The last step of execution is mapping the final configuration to an **answer** via
  an **output function**. What is considered to be an answer differs greatly from
  language to language. For POSTFIX, the answer is the top stack value in a final
  configuration, if it's an integer. If the stack is empty or the top value is an
  executable sequence, the answer is an error token. In other systems, the answer
  might also include elements like the final state of the memory, file system, or
  graphics screen.

  Sometimes an abstract machine never reaches a final configuration. This can
happen for one of two reasons:

1. The abstract machine may reach a nonfinal configuration to which no rules
   apply. Such a configuration is said to be a **stuck state**. Stuck states often
   model error situations.

2. The rule-applying process of the abstract machine might not terminate. In any **universal** programming language (a programming language that can express all computable functions) it is possible to write programs that loop forever. For such programs, the execution process of the abstract machine never terminates. As a consequence of the **halting theorem** — which states that there is no program that can decide for all programs P and all inputs A whether P terminates on A — we can't do better than this: there's no general way to tweak the abstract machine of a universal language so that it always indicates when it is in an infinite loop.

We show in Section 3.6 that all PostFix programs must terminate. This implies that PostFix is not universal.

3.2 Small-step Operational Semantics (SOS)

3.2.1 Formal Framework

Above, we presented a high-level introduction to operational semantics. Here, we iron out all the details necessary to turn this approach into a formal framework known as **small-step operational semantics** (SOS[1]). An SOS is characterized by the use of **rewrite rules** to specify the step-by-step transformation of configurations in an abstract machine.

To express this framework formally, we will employ the mathematical metalanguage described in Appendix A. Before reading further, you should at least skim this appendix to familiarize yourself with the notational conventions of the metalanguage. Later, when you encounter an unfamiliar notation or concept, consult the relevant section of this appendix for a detailed explanation.

Consider a programming language L with legal programs $P \in \text{Prog}$, inputs $I \in \text{Inputs}$, and elements $A \in \text{AnsExp}$ that are considered to be valid answers to programs. Then an SOS for L is a five-tuple $S = \langle CF, \Rightarrow, FC, IF, OF \rangle$, where:

- CF is the domain of configurations for an abstract machine for L. The domain variable cf ranges over configurations.

- $\Rightarrow$, the **transition relation**, is a binary relation on configurations that defines the allowable transitions between configurations. The notation $cf \Rightarrow cf'$ means that there is a **(one step) transition** from the configuration cf to the configuration cf'. This notation, which is shorthand for $\langle cf, cf' \rangle \in \Rightarrow$, is

---

[1]This framework, due to Plotkin [Plo81], was originally called **structural operational semantics**. It later became known as the small-step approach to distinguish it from — you guessed it — a big-step approach (see Section 3.3).

pronounced "cf rewrites to cf prime in one step." The two parts of a transition have names: cf is called the **left-hand side (LHS)** and cf' is called the **right-hand side (RHS)**. The transition relation is usually specified by rewrite rules, as described below in Section 3.2.3.

The reflexive, transitive closure of $\Rightarrow$ is written $\overset{*}{\Rightarrow}$. So $cf \overset{*}{\Rightarrow} cf'$ means that cf rewrites to cf' in zero or more steps. The sequence of transitions between cf and cf' is called a **transition path**. The **length** of a transition path is the number of transitions in the path. The notation $cf \overset{n}{\Rightarrow} cf'$ means that cf rewrites to cf' in n steps, i.e., via a transition path of length n. The notation $cf \overset{\infty}{\Rightarrow}$ means that there is an infinitely long transition path beginning with cf.

A configuration cf is **reducible** if there is some cf' such that $cf \Rightarrow cf'$. If there is no such cf', then we write $cf \nRightarrow$ and say that cf is **irreducible**. An irreducible configuration (or its code component) is often called a **normal form**. CF can be partitioned into two sets, $Reducible_S$ (containing all reducible configurations) and $Irreducible_S$ (containing all irreducible ones). We omit the subscript when it is clear from context. A transition relation $\Rightarrow$ is **deterministic** if for every $cf \in Reducible_S$ there is exactly one cf' such that $cf \Rightarrow cf'$. Otherwise, $\Rightarrow$ is said to be **nondeterministic**.

- FC, the set of **final configurations**, is a subset of $Irreducible_S$ containing all configurations that are considered to be final states in the execution of a program. The set $Stuck_S$ of stuck states is defined to be ($Irreducible_S - FC$) — i.e., the nonfinal irreducible configurations.

- $IF : (\text{Prog} \times \text{Inputs}) \to CF$ is an **input function** that maps a program and its inputs to an initial configuration.

- $OF : FC \to \text{AnsExp}$ is an **output function** that maps a final configuration to an appropriate answer domain.

An SOS defines the behavior of a program in a way that we shall now make precise. What are the possible behaviors of a program? As discussed in Section 3.1, a program either (1) returns an answer, (2) gets stuck in a nonfinal irreducible configuration, or (3) loops infinitely. We model these via the following Outcome domain, where `stuckout` designates a stuck program and `loopout` designates an infinitely looping program:

$$
\begin{aligned}
&\text{StuckOut} = \{\texttt{stuckout}\} \\
&\text{LoopOut} = \{\texttt{loopout}\} \\
o \in &\text{ Outcome} = \text{AnsExp} + \text{StuckOut} + \text{LoopOut} \\
&\texttt{stuck} = (\text{StuckOut} \rightarrowtail \text{Outcome } \texttt{stuckout}) \\
&\infty = (\text{LoopOut} \rightarrowtail \text{Outcome } \texttt{loopout})
\end{aligned}
$$

Suppose that an SOS has a deterministic transition relation. Then we can define the **behavior** of a program P on inputs I as follows:

$$beh_{det} : (\text{Prog} \times \text{Inputs}) \to \text{Outcome}$$

$$beh_{det}\ \langle P, I \rangle = \begin{cases} (\text{AnsExp} \rightarrowtail \text{Outcome}\ (OF\ cf)) & \text{if } (IF\ \langle P, I \rangle) \overset{*}{\Rightarrow} cf \in FC \\ \texttt{stuck} & \text{if } (IF\ \langle P, I \rangle) \overset{*}{\Rightarrow} cf \in Stuck \\ \infty & \text{if } (IF\ \langle P, I \rangle) \overset{\infty}{\Rightarrow} \end{cases}$$

In the first case, an execution starting at the initial configuration eventually reaches a final configuration, whose answer is returned. In the second case, an execution starting at the initial configuration eventually gets stuck at a nonfinal configuration. In the last case, there is an infinite transition path starting at the initial configuration, so the program never halts.[2] We call this behavior **deterministic** because a deterministic translation relation guarantees a unique outcome.

What if the transition relation is not deterministic? In this case, it is possible that there are multiple transition paths starting at the initial configuration. Some of these might end at final configurations with different answers. Others might be infinitely long or end at stuck states. In general, we must allow for the possibility that there are many outcomes, so the signature of the behavior function beh in this case must return a *set* of outcomes — i.e., an element of the powerset domain $\mathcal{P}(\text{Outcome})$.[3]

$$beh : (\text{Prog} \times \text{Inputs}) \to \mathcal{P}(\text{Outcome})$$

$$o \in (beh\ \langle P, I \rangle) \text{ if } \begin{cases} o = (\text{AnsExp} \rightarrowtail \text{Outcome}\ (OF\ cf)) \\ \quad \text{and } (IF\ \langle P, I \rangle) \overset{*}{\Rightarrow} cf \in FC \\ o = \texttt{stuck and } (IF\ \langle P, I \rangle) \overset{*}{\Rightarrow} cf \in Stuck \\ o = \infty \text{ and } (IF\ \langle P, I \rangle) \overset{\infty}{\Rightarrow} \end{cases}$$

An SOS with a nondeterministic transition relation won't necessarily give rise to results that contain multiple outcomes. Indeed, we will see later (in Section 3.5) that some systems with nondeterministic transition relations can still have a behavior that is deterministic — i.e., the resulting set of outcomes is always a singleton.

---

[2]Though mathematically well defined, the beh_{det} function is uncomputable because the ∞ symbol cannot actually be returned by a nonterminating process. However, if we instead view ∞ as indicating that beh_{det} is undefined for a given program and inputs, then beh_{det} is a partial recursive function and is therefore computable [HU79]. This idea reappears in Chapter 5, where we use the $\bot$ symbol to stand for nonterminating computations.

[3]The result of beh must in fact be a *nonempty* set of outcomes, since every program will have at least one outcome.

An SOS (as well as the language defined by an SOS) is said to be **strongly normalizing**, or **terminating**, if there are no infinitely long transition paths starting with an initial configuration. In a strongly normalizing SOS, all program executions terminate: for all programs P and inputs I, $\infty \notin (\mathit{beh} \langle P, I \rangle)$. As we will see in Section 3.6, both PostFix and EL are strongly normalizing.

3.2.2   Example: An SOS for PostFix

We can now formalize the elements of the PostFix SOS described informally in Section 3.1 (except for the transition relation, which will be formalized in Section 3.2.3). The details are presented in Figure 3.3, which uses domains and domain variables defined in the s-expression grammar for PostFix defined in Figure 2.12 on page 40.

A stack is a sequence of values that are either integer numerals (from domain IntLit) or executable sequences (from domain CommandSeq). PostFix programs take a sequence of integer numerals as their inputs, and, when no error is encountered, return an integer numeral as an answer. A configuration is a pair of a command sequence and a stack. A final configuration is one whose command sequence is empty and whose stack is nonempty with an integer numeral on top (i.e., an element of FinalStack). The input function IF maps a program and its numeric inputs to a configuration consisting of the body command sequence and an initial stack with the inputs arranged from top down. If the number of arguments N expected by the program does not match the actual number n of arguments supplied, then IF returns a stuck configuration $\langle [\,]_{\mathrm{Command}}, [\,]_{\mathrm{Value}} \rangle$ that represents an error. The output function OF returns the top integer numeral from the stack of a final configuration.

The PostFix SOS in Figure 3.3 models errors using stuck states. By definition, stuck states are exactly those irreducible configurations that are nonfinal. In PostFix, stuck states are irreducible configurations whose command sequence is nonempty or those that pair an empty command sequence with a stack that is empty or has an executable sequence on top. The outcome of a program that reaches such a configuration will be stuck.

Although it is convenient to use stuck states to model errors, it is not strictly necessary. With some extra work, it is always possible to modify the final configuration set FC and the output function OF so that such programs instead have as their outcome some error token in AnsExp. Using PostFix as an example, we can use a modified answer domain AnsExp$'$ that includes an error token, a modified final configuration set FC' that includes all irreducible configurations, and the modified OF' shown below:

$CF = $ config. *(handwritten note at top)*

Domains

$V \in \text{Value} = \text{IntLit} + \text{CommandSeq}$

$S \in \text{Stack} = \text{Value*}$

  $\text{FinalStack} = \{S \mid (length\ S) \geq 1$
  $\qquad\qquad\qquad\text{and } (nth\ 1\ S) = (\text{IntLit} \rightarrowtail \text{Value } N) \text{ for some } N \in \text{IntLit}\}$

  $\text{Inputs} = \text{IntLit*}$

  $\text{AnsExp} = \text{IntLit}$

SOS

Suppose that the POSTFIX SOS has the form $PFSOS = \langle CF, \Rightarrow, FC, IF, OF \rangle$. Then the SOS components are:

  $CF = \text{CommandSeq} \times \text{Stack}$

  $\Rightarrow$ is a deterministic transition relation defined in Section 3.2.3

  $FC = \{[\,]_{\text{Command}}\} \times \text{FinalStack}$

  $IF : (\text{Prog} \times \text{Inputs}) \to CF$
  $= \lambda \langle (\texttt{postfix } N\ Q), [N_1, \ldots, N_n] \rangle\ .$
     if $N = \overline{n}$; *for* $n \in Int, \overline{n}$ *stands for the IntLit* N *that denotes* n.
     then $\langle Q, [(\text{IntLit} \rightarrowtail \text{Value } N_1), \ldots, (\text{IntLit} \rightarrowtail \text{Value } N_n)] \rangle$
     else $\langle [\,]_{\text{Command}}, [\,]_{\text{Value}} \rangle$ **end**

  $OF : FC \to \text{AnsExp}$
  $= \lambda \langle [\,]_{\text{Command}}, (\text{IntLit} \rightarrowtail \text{Value } N)\ .\ S' \rangle\ .\ (\text{IntLit} \rightarrowtail \text{AnsExp } N)$

Figure 3.3 An SOS for POSTFIX.

  $\text{Error} = \{\texttt{error}\}$
  $\text{AnsExp}' = \text{IntLit} + \text{Error}$

  $FC' = Irreducible_{PFSOS}$

  $OF' : FC' \to \text{AnsExp}'$
  $= \lambda \langle Q, V^* \rangle\ .\ \textbf{match } \langle Q, V^* \rangle$
          $\triangleright \langle [\,]_{\text{Command}}, (\text{IntLit} \rightarrowtail \text{Value } N)\ .\ S' \rangle \parallel (\text{IntLit} \rightarrowtail \text{AnsExp}' N)$
          $\triangleright \textbf{else } (\text{Error} \rightarrowtail \text{AnsExp}' \texttt{ error})$
          end

(Here the pattern-matching capabilities of the metalanguage construct **match**, defined in Section A.4, are used to distinguish the cases in which $\langle Q, V^* \rangle$ is and is not a final configuration.) With these modifications, the outcome of a POSTFIX program that encounters an error will be $(\text{AnsExp}' \rightarrowtail \text{Outcome } (\text{Error} \rightarrowtail \text{AnsExp}' \texttt{ error}))$ rather than `stuck`.

Exercise 3.1 Look up definitions of the following kinds of automata and express each of them in the SOS framework: deterministic finite automata, nondeterministic finite automata, deterministic pushdown automata, and Turing machines. Represent strings, stacks, and tapes as sequences of symbols.

3.2.3   Rewrite Rules

The transition relation, $\Rightarrow$, for an SOS is often specified by a set of **rewrite rules**. A rewrite rule has the form

$$\frac{antecedents}{consequent} \qquad\qquad [rule\text{-}name]$$

where the antecedents and the consequent contain transition patterns (described below). Informally, the rule asserts: "If the transitions specified by the *antecedents* are valid, then the transition specified by the consequent is valid." The label [*rule-name*] on the rule is just a handy name for referring to the rule, and is not a part of the rule structure. A rewrite rule with no antecedents is an **axiom**; otherwise it is a **progress rule**. The horizontal bar is often omitted in an axiom.

A complete set of rewrite rules for POSTFIX appears in Figure 3.4. All of the rules are axioms. Together with the definitions of *CF*, *FC*, *IF*, and *OF*, these rules constitute a formal SOS version of the informal POSTFIX semantics originally presented in Figure 1.1. We will spend the rest of Section 3.2 studying the meaning of these rules and considering alternative rules.

Since an axiom has no antecedents, it is determined solely by its consequent. As noted above, the consequent must be a **transition pattern**. A transition pattern looks like a transition except that the LHS and RHS may contain domain variables interspersed with the usual notation for configurations. Informally, a transition pattern is a schema that stands for all the transitions that match the pattern. An axiom stands for the collection of all configuration pairs that match the LHS and RHS of the transition pattern, respectively.

As an example, let's consider in detail the axiom that defines the behavior of POSTFIX numerals:

$$\langle N \cdot Q, S \rangle \Rightarrow \langle Q, N \cdot S \rangle \qquad\qquad [num]$$

This axiom stands for an infinite number of pairs of configurations of the form $\langle cf, cf' \rangle$. It says that if cf is a configuration in which the command sequence is a numeral N followed by a command sequence Q and the stack is S, then there is a transition from cf to a configuration cf' whose command sequence is Q, and whose stack holds N followed by S.

$$\langle N \cdot Q, \, S \rangle \Rightarrow \langle Q, \, N \cdot S \rangle \qquad \text{[num]}$$

$$\langle (Q_{exec}) \cdot Q_{rest}, \, S \rangle \Rightarrow \langle Q_{rest}, \, (Q_{exec}) \cdot S \rangle \qquad \text{[seq]}$$

$$\langle \texttt{pop} \cdot Q, \, V_{top} \cdot S \rangle \Rightarrow \langle Q, \, S \rangle \qquad \text{[pop]}$$

$$\langle \texttt{nget} \cdot Q, \, N_{index} \cdot [\, V_1, \ldots, V_{N_{size}}]\rangle \Rightarrow \langle Q, \, V_{N_{index}} \cdot [\, V_1, \ldots, V_{N_{size}}]\rangle \qquad \text{[nget]}$$
$$\text{where } (compare \; \texttt{gt} \; N_{index} \; 0) \wedge \neg (compare \; \texttt{gt} \; N_{index} \; N_{size})$$
$$\wedge \; (V_{N_{index}} \in \text{IntLit})$$

$$\langle \texttt{swap} \cdot Q, \, V_1 \cdot V_2 \cdot S \rangle \Rightarrow \langle Q, \, V_2 \cdot V_1 \cdot S \rangle \qquad \text{[swap]}$$

$$\langle \texttt{sel} \cdot Q_{rest}, \, V_{false} \cdot V_{true} \cdot 0 \cdot S \rangle \Rightarrow \langle Q_{rest}, \, V_{false} \cdot S \rangle \qquad \text{[sel-false]}$$

$$\langle \texttt{sel} \cdot Q_{rest}, \, V_{false} \cdot V_{true} \cdot N_{test} \cdot S \rangle \Rightarrow \langle Q_{rest}, \, V_{true} \cdot S \rangle \qquad \text{[sel-true]}$$
$$\text{where } N_{test} \neq 0$$

$$\langle \texttt{exec} \cdot Q_{rest}, \, (Q_{exec}) \cdot S \rangle \Rightarrow \langle Q_{exec} \,@\, Q_{rest}, \, S \rangle \qquad \text{[execute]}$$

$$\langle A \cdot Q, \, N_1 \cdot N_2 \cdot S \rangle \Rightarrow \langle Q, \, N_{ans} \cdot S \rangle \qquad \text{[arithop]}$$
$$\text{where } N_{ans} = (calculate \; A \; N_2 \; N_1)$$

$$\langle R \cdot Q, \, N_1 \cdot N_2 \cdot S \rangle \Rightarrow \langle Q, \, 1 \cdot S \rangle \qquad \text{[relop-true]}$$
$$\text{where } (compare \; R \; N_2 \; N_1)$$

$$\langle R \cdot Q, \, N_1 \cdot N_2 \cdot S \rangle \Rightarrow \langle Q, \, 0 \cdot S \rangle \qquad \text{[relop-false]}$$
$$\text{where } \neg (compare \; R \; N_2 \; N_1)$$

Figure 3.4 Rewrite rules defining the transition relation ($\Rightarrow$) for POSTFIX.

In the [num] rule, N, Q, and S are domain variables that act as patterns that can match any element in the domain over which the variable ranges. Thus, N matches any integer numeral, Q matches any command sequence, and S matches any stack. When the same pattern variable occurs more than once within a rule, all occurrences must denote the same element; this constrains the class of transitions specified by the rule. Thus, the [num] rule matches the transition

$$\langle (\texttt{17 add swap}), \, [\texttt{19, (2 mul)}]\rangle \Rightarrow \langle (\texttt{add swap}), \, [\texttt{17, 19, (2 mul)}]\rangle$$

with $N = \texttt{17}$, $Q = [\texttt{add, swap}]$, and $S = [\texttt{19, (2 mul)}]$. On the other hand, the rule does not match the transition

$$\langle (\texttt{17 add swap}), \, [\texttt{19, (2 mul)}]\rangle \Rightarrow \langle (\texttt{add swap}), \, [\texttt{17, 19, (2 mul), 23}]\rangle$$

because there is no consistent interpretation for the pattern variable S — it is [19, (2 mul)] in the LHS of the transition, and [19, (2 mul), 23] in the RHS. As another example, the configuration pattern $\langle Q, \, N \cdot N \cdot S \rangle$ would match only configurations with stacks in which the top two values are the same integer numeral. If the RHS of the [*num*] rule consequent were replaced with this configuration pattern, then the rule would indicate that two copies of the integer numeral should be pushed onto the stack.

At this point, the meticulous reader may have noticed that in the rewrite rules and sample transitions we have taken many liberties with our notation. If we had strictly adhered to our metalanguage notation, then we would have written the [*num*] rule as

$$\langle (\text{IntLit} \rightarrowtail \text{Command } N) \,.\, Q, S \rangle \Rightarrow \langle Q, (\text{IntLit} \rightarrowtail \text{Value } N) \,.\, S \rangle \qquad [num]$$

and we would have written the matching transition as

$$\langle [17, \text{add}, \text{swap}]_{\text{Command}}, \; [(\text{IntLit} \rightarrowtail \text{Value } 17),$$
$$(\text{CommandSeq} \rightarrowtail \text{Value } [2, \text{mul}]_{\text{Command}}) \;] \rangle$$
$$\Rightarrow \langle [\text{add}, \text{swap}]_{\text{Command}}, \; [(\text{IntLit} \rightarrowtail \text{Value } 17),$$
$$(\text{IntLit} \rightarrowtail \text{Value } 19),$$
$$(\text{CommandSeq} \rightarrowtail \text{Value } [2, \text{mul}]_{\text{Command}}) \;] \rangle$$

However, we believe that the more rigorous notation severely impedes the readability of the rules and examples. For this reason, we will stick with our stylized notation when it is unlikely to cause confusion. In particular, in operational semantics rules and sample transitions, we adopt the following conventions:

- Injections will be elided when they are clear from context. For example, if N appears as a command, then it stands for $(\text{IntLit} \rightarrowtail \text{Command } N)$, while if it appears as a stack element, then it stands for $(\text{IntLit} \rightarrowtail \text{Value } N)$.

- Sequences of syntactic elements may be written as parenthesized s-expressions. For example, the POSTFIX command sequence

$$[3, \; [2, \text{ mul}]_{\text{Command}}, \; \text{swap}]_{\text{Command}}$$

will often be abbreviated as

$$(3 \; (2 \text{ mul}) \text{ swap})$$

The former is more precise, but the latter is easier to read. In POSTFIX examples, we have chosen to keep the sequence notation for stacks to visually distinguish the two components of a configuration.

- For POSTFIX, the explicit parentheses in the notation (Q) are syntactic markers that abbreviate an underlying injection. If this notation appears where an element of Command is expected, it stands for $(\text{CommandSeq} \rightarrowtail \text{Command } Q)$. If it appears where an element of Value is expected, it stands for $(\text{CommandSeq} \rightarrowtail \text{Value } Q)$.

Despite these notational acrobatics, keep in mind that we are manipulating well-defined mathematical structures. So it is always possible to add the appropriate decorations to make the notation completely rigorous.[4]

Some of the POSTFIX rules ([*arithop*], [*relop-true*], [*relop-false*], [*sel-true*], and [*nget*]) include **side conditions** that specify additional restrictions on the domain variables. For example, consider the axiom that handles a conditional whose test is true:

$$\langle \texttt{sel} \cdot Q_{rest},\ V_{false} \cdot V_{true} \cdot N_{test} \cdot S \rangle \Rightarrow \langle Q_{rest},\ V_{true} \cdot S \rangle \qquad \text{[\textit{sel-true}]}$$
$$\text{where } N_{test} \neq 0$$

This axiom says that $\texttt{sel}$ treats any nonzero integer numeral as true. As long as the test numeral N_{test} (the third element on the stack) is not the same syntactic object as 0, then the next configuration is obtained by removing $\texttt{sel}$ from the command sequence and pushing the second stack element onto the result of popping the top three elements off the stack. The domain variable N_{test} that appears in the side condition $N_{test} \neq 0$ stands for the same entity that N_{test} denotes in the LHS of the consequent, providing the link between the transition pattern and the side condition. Note how the domain variables and the structure of the components are used to constrain the pairs of configurations that satisfy this rule. This rule represents only pairs $\langle cf, cf' \rangle$ in which the stack of cf contains at least three elements, the third of which is a nonzero integer numeral. The rule does not apply to configurations whose stacks have fewer than three elements, or whose third element is an executable sequence or the numeral 0.

The side conditions in the [*arithop*], [*relop-true*], [*relop-false*], and [*nget*] rules deserve some explanation. The *calculate* function used in the side condition of [*arithop*] returns the numeral N_{ans} resulting from the application of the operator A to the operands N_2 and N_1; it abstracts away the details of such computations.[5] We assume that *calculate* is a partial function that is undefined when A is $\texttt{div}$ or $\texttt{rem}$ and N_1 is 0, so division or remainder by zero yields a stuck state. The [*relop-true*] and [*relop-false*] rules are similar to [*arithop*]; here the auxiliary *compare* function is assumed to return the truth value resulting from the associated comparison. The rules then convert this truth value into a POSTFIX value of 1 (true) or 0 (false). In the [*nget*] rule, the *compare* function is used to ensure

---

[4]But those who pay too much attention to rigor may develop rigor mortis! — HEY-oh!

[5]Note that *calculate* manipulates *numerals* (i.e., names for integers) rather than the *integers* that they name. This may seem pedantic, but we haven't described yet how the meaning of an integer numeral is determined. If we had instead defined the syntax of POSTFIX to use integers rather than integer numerals, then we could have used the usual integer addition operation here. But we chose integer numerals to emphasize the syntactic nature of operational semantics.

that the numeral N_{index} is a valid index for one of the values on the stack. If not, the configuration is stuck. In the side conditions, the symbol $\neg$ stands for logical negation and $\wedge$ stands for logical conjunction.

You should now know enough about the rule notation to understand all of the rewrite rules in Figure 3.4. The [*num*] and [*seq*] rules push the two different kinds of values onto the stack. The [*swap*], [*pop*], [*sel-true*], and [*sel-false*] rules all perform straightforward stack manipulations. The [*exec*] rule prepends an executable sequence from the stack onto the command sequence following the current command.

It is easy to see that the transition relation defined in Figure 3.4 is deterministic. The first command in the command sequence of a configuration uniquely determines which transition pattern might match, except for the case of sel, where the third stack value distinguishes whether [*sel-true*] or [*sel-false*] matches, and the relational operators, where the side condition distinguishes whether [*relop-true*] or [*relop-false*] matches. The LHS of each transition pattern can match a given configuration in at most one way. So for any given POSTFIX configuration cf, there is at most one cf' such that $cf \Rightarrow cf'$.

3.2.4   Operational Execution

The operational semantics can be used to execute a POSTFIX program in a way similar to the table-based method presented earlier. For example, the execution of the POSTFIX program shown earlier in Figure 3.1 is illustrated in Figure 3.5. The input function is applied to the program to yield an initial configuration, and then a series of transitions specified by the rewrite rules are applied. In the figure, the configuration resulting from each transition appears on a separate line and is labeled by the applied rule. When a final configuration is reached, the output function is applied to this configuration to yield -3, which is the result computed by the program. We can summarize the transition path from the initial to the final configuration as

$$\langle((2\ (3\ \text{mul}\ \text{add})\ \text{exec})\ 1\ \text{swap}\ \text{exec}\ \text{sub}),\ [4,\ 5]\rangle \overset{11}{\Longrightarrow} \langle(),\ [\text{-3},\ 5]\rangle$$

where 11 is the number of transitions. If we don't care about this number, we write $*$ in its place.

Not all POSTFIX executions lead to a final configuration. For example, executing the program (postfix 2 add mul 3 4 sub) on the inputs [5, 6] leads to the configuration $\langle(\text{mul}\ 3\ 4\ \text{sub}),\ [11]\rangle$. This configuration is not final because there are still commands to be executed. But it does not match the LHS of any rewrite rule consequent. In particular, the [*arithop*] rule requires the stack to

```
(IF ⟨(postfix 2 (2 (3 mul add) exec) 1 swap exec sub), [4, 5]⟩)
= ⟨((2 (3 mul add) exec) 1 swap exec sub), [4, 5]⟩
⇒ ⟨(1 swap exec sub), [(2 (3 mul add) exec), 4, 5]⟩      [seq]
⇒ ⟨(swap exec sub), [1, (2 (3 mul add) exec), 4, 5]⟩     [num]
⇒ ⟨(exec sub), [(2 (3 mul add) exec), 1, 4, 5]⟩          [swap]
⇒ ⟨(2 (3 mul add) exec sub), [1, 4, 5]⟩                  [execute]
⇒ ⟨((3 mul add) exec sub), [2, 1, 4, 5]⟩                 [num]
⇒ ⟨(exec sub), [(3 mul add), 2, 1, 4, 5]⟩                [seq]
⇒ ⟨(3 mul add sub), [2, 1, 4, 5]⟩                        [execute]
⇒ ⟨(mul add sub), [3, 2, 1, 4, 5]⟩                       [num]
⇒ ⟨(add sub), [6, 1, 4, 5]⟩                              [arithop]
⇒ ⟨(sub), [7, 4, 5]⟩                                     [arithop]
⇒ ⟨(), [-3, 5]⟩ ∈ FC                                     [arithop]
(OF ⟨(), [-3, 5]⟩) = -3
```

Figure 3.5   An SOS-based execution of a POSTFIX program.

have two integers at the top, and here there is only one. This is an example of a stuck state. As discussed earlier, a program reaching a stuck state is considered to signal an error. In this case the error is due to an insufficient number of arguments on the stack.

Exercise 3.2 Use the SOS for POSTFIX to determine the values of the POSTFIX programs in Exercise 1.1 on page 13.

Exercise 3.3 Consider extending POSTFIX with a `rot` command defined by the following rewrite rule:

$$⟨\text{rot} . Q, N . V_1 \ldots . V_N . S⟩ ⇒ ⟨Q, V_2 \ldots . V_N . V_1 . S⟩ \qquad [rot]$$
$$\text{where } (compare \text{ gt } N \text{ 1})$$

a. Give an informal English description of the behavior of `rot`.

b. What is the contents of the stack after executing the following program on zero arguments?

$$\text{(postfix 0 2 3 4 2 3 4 rot rot rot)}$$

c. Using `rot`, write a POSTFIX executable sequence that serves as subroutine for reversing the top three elements of a given stack.

d. List the kinds of situations in which `rot` can lead to a stuck state, and give a sample program illustrating each one.

Exercise 3.4 The SOS for POSTFIX specifies that a configuration is stuck when the stack contains an insufficient number of values for a command. For example, $\langle(\texttt{mul}), [2]\rangle$ is stuck because multiplication requires two stack values.

a. Modify the semantics of POSTFIX so that, rather than becoming stuck, it uses sensible defaults for the missing values when the stack contains an insufficient number of values. For example, the default value(s) for $\texttt{mul}$ would be 1:

$$\langle(\texttt{mul}), [2]\rangle \Rightarrow \langle(), [2]\rangle$$
$$\langle(\texttt{mul}), []\rangle \Rightarrow \langle(), [1]\rangle$$

b. Do you think this modification is a good idea? Why or why not?

Exercise 3.5 Suppose the Value domain in the POSTFIX SOS is augmented with a distinguished error value. Modify the rewrite rules for POSTFIX so that error configurations push this error value onto the stack. The error value should be "contagious" in the sense that any operation attempting to act on it should also push an error value onto the stack. Under the revised semantics, a program may return a non-error value even though it encounters an error along the way. E.g., (postfix 0 1 2 add mul 3 4 sub) should return -1 rather than signaling an error when called on zero inputs.

Exercise 3.6 An operational semantics for POSTFIX2 (the alternative POSTFIX syntax introduced in Figure 2.13) can be defined by making minor tweaks to the operational semantics for POSTFIX. Consider the following domains:

$$Q \in \text{CommandSeq}_{PostFix2} = \text{Command}^*_{PostFix2}$$
$$V \in \text{Value}_{PostFix2} = \text{IntLit} + \text{Command}_{PostFix2}$$
$$S \in \text{Stack}_{PostFix2} = \text{Value}^*_{PostFix2}$$

Then $\text{CommandSeq}_{PostFix2} \times \text{Stack}_{PostFix2}$ can be used as the configuration domain for a POSTFIX2 SOS. Using this approach, most POSTFIX2 rewrite rules differ only cosmetically from the corresponding POSTFIX rewrite rules. For example, here is the rewrite rule for a POSTFIX2 numeral command:

$$\langle(\texttt{int}\ N)\,.\,Q, S\rangle \Rightarrow \langle Q, N\,.\,S\rangle \qquad\qquad [num']$$

a. Define an input function that maps POSTFIX2 programs (postfix2 N C) into an initial configuration.

b. Give rewrite axioms for the POSTFIX2 commands (exec), (: C_{com1} C_{com2}), and (skip).

(See Exercise 3.7 for another approach to defining the semantics of POSTFIX2.)

Exercise 3.7 A distinguishing feature of POSTFIX2 (the alternative POSTFIX syntax introduced in Figure 2.13) is that its grammar makes no use of sequence domains. It is reasonable to expect that its operational semantics can be modeled by configurations in which the code component is a single command rather than a command sequence. Based on this idea, design an SOS for POSTFIX2 in which $CF = \text{Command} \times \text{Stack}$. (Note: do not modify the Command domain.)

Exercise 3.8 The Hugely Profitable Calculator Company has hired you to design a calculator language called RPN that is based on POSTFIX. RPN has the same syntax as POSTFIX command sequences (an RPN program is just a command sequence that is assumed to take zero arguments) and the operations are intended to work in basically the same manner. However, instead of providing an arbitrarily large stack, RPN limits the size of the stack to four values. Additionally, the stack is always *full* in the sense that it contains four values at all times. Initially, the stack contains four 0 values. Pushing a value onto a full stack causes the bottommost stack value to be forgotten. Popping the topmost value from a full stack has the effect of duplicating the bottommost element (i.e., it appears in the last two stack positions after the pop).

a. Develop a complete SOS for the RPN language.

b. Use your SOS to find the results of the following RPN programs:

  i.   (mul 1 add)

  ii.   (1 20 300 4000 50000 add add add add)

c. Although POSTFIX programs are guaranteed to terminate, as we will see in Section 3.6, RPN programs are not. Demonstrate this fact by writing an RPN program that loops infinitely.

Exercise 3.9 A class of calculators known as *four-function* calculators support the four usual binary arithmetic operators (+, −, *, /) in an infix notation.[6] Here we consider a language FF based on four-function calculators. The programs of FF are any parenthesized sequence of numbers and commands, where commands are +, −, *, /, and =. The = command is used to compute the result of an expression, which may be used as the first argument to another binary operator. The = may be elided in a string of operations.

$$(1 + 20 =) \xrightarrow[FF]{} 21$$
$$(1 + 20 = + 300 =) \xrightarrow[FF]{} 321$$
$$(1 + 20 + 300 =) \xrightarrow[FF]{} 321 \ \{\textit{Note elision of first} =.\}$$
$$(1 + 20) \xrightarrow[FF]{} 20 \ \{\textit{Last number is returned when no final} =.\}$$

Other features supported by FF include:

- *Calculation with a constant.* Typing a number followed by = uses the number as the first operand in a calculation with the previous operator and previous second operand.

  $$(2 * 5 =) \xrightarrow[FF]{} 10 \ (2 * 5 = 7 =) \xrightarrow[FF]{} 35 \ (2 * 5 = 7 = 11 =) \xrightarrow[FF]{} 55$$

- *Implied second argument.* If no second argument is specified, the value of the second argument defaults to the first.

  $$(5 * =) \xrightarrow[FF]{} 25$$

- *Operator correction.* An operator key can be corrected by typing the correct one after (any number of) unintentional operators.

  $$(1 * - + 2 \ ) \xrightarrow[FF]{} 3$$

---

[6]The one described here is based on the TI-1025. See [You81] for more details.

a. Design an SOS for FF that is consistent with the informal description given above.

b. Use your SOS to find the final values of the following command sequences. (Note: some of the values may be floating point numbers.) Comment on the intended meaning of the unconventional command sequences.

    i.   `(8 - 3 + * 4 =)`

    ii.   `(3 + 5 / = =)`

    iii.   `(3 + 5 / = 6 =)`

3.2.5 Progress Rules

The commands of POSTFIX programs are interpreted in a highly linear fashion in Figure 3.4. Even though executable sequences give the code a kind of tree structure, the contents of an executable sequence can be used only when they are prepended to the single stream of commands that is executed by the abstract machine. The fact that the next command to execute is always at the front of this command stream leads to a very simple structure for the rewrite rules in Figure 3.4. Transitions, which appear only in rule consequents, are all of the form

$$\langle C_{first} \cdot Q, S \rangle \Rightarrow \langle Q', S' \rangle$$

where Q' is either the same as Q or is the result of prepending some commands onto the front of Q. In all rules, the command C_{first} at the head of the current command sequence is consumed by the application of the rule.

These simple kinds of rules are not adequate for programming languages exhibiting a more general tree structure. Evaluating a node in an arbitrary syntax tree usually requires the recursive evaluation of its subnodes. For example, consider the evaluation of a sample numerical expression written in the EL language described in Section 2.3:

$$(+ (* (- 5\ 1)\ 2)\ (/ 21\ 7))$$

Before the sum can be performed, the results of the multiplication and division must be computed; before the multiplication can be performed, the subtraction must be computed. If the values of operand expressions are computed in left-to-right order, we expect the evaluation of the expression to occur via the following transition path:

$$
\begin{aligned}
&(+ (* (- 5\ 1)\ 2)\ (/ 21\ 7)) \\
\Rightarrow\ &(+ (* 4\ 2)\ (/ 21\ 7)) \\
\Rightarrow\ &(+ 8\ (/ 21\ 7)) \\
\Rightarrow\ &(+ 8\ 3) \\
\Rightarrow\ &11
\end{aligned}
$$

$P \in \text{Prog} ::= (\texttt{elmm}\ NE_{body})\ [\text{Program}]$

$NE \in \text{NumExp} ::= N_{num}$ $[\text{IntLit}]$

                $|\ (A_{rator}\ NE_{rand1}\ NE_{rand2})\ [\text{ArithmeticOperation}]$

$N \in \text{IntLit} = \{\ldots,\ \texttt{-2},\ \texttt{-1},\ \texttt{0},\ \texttt{1},\ \texttt{2},\ \ldots\}$

$A \in \text{ArithmeticOperator} = \{\texttt{+},\ \texttt{-},\ \texttt{*},\ \texttt{/},\ \texttt{\%}\}$

Figure 3.6 An s-expression grammar for ELMM.

In each transition, the structure of the expression tree remains unchanged except at the node where the computation is being performed. Rewrite rules for expressing such transitions need to be able to express a transition from tree to tree in terms of transitions between the subtrees. That is, the transition

$$(\texttt{+ (* (- 5 1) 2) (/ 21 7))} \Rightarrow (\texttt{+ (* 4 2) (/ 21 7))}$$

is implied by the transition

$$(\texttt{* (- 5 1) 2}) \Rightarrow (\texttt{* 4 2})$$

which in turn is implied by the transition

$$(\texttt{- 5 1}) \Rightarrow 4$$

In some sense, "real work" is done only by the last of these transitions; the other transitions just inherit the change because they define the surrounding context in which the change is embedded.

These kinds of transitions on tree-structured programs are expressed using **progress rules**, which are rules with antecedents. Progress rules effectively allow an evaluation process to reach inside a complicated expression to evaluate one of its subexpressions. A one-step transition in the subexpression is then reflected as a one-step transition of the expression in which it is embedded.

Example: ELMM

To illustrate progress rules, we will develop an operational semantics for an extremely simple subset of the EL language that we will call ELMM (which stands for EL Minus Minus). As shown in Figure 3.6, an ELMM program is just a numerical expression, where a numerical expression is either (1) an integer numeral or (2) an arithmetic operation. There are no arguments, no conditional expressions, and no boolean expressions in ELMM.

In an SOS for ELMM, configurations are just numerical expressions themselves; there are no state components. Numerical literals are the only final configurations. The input and output functions are straightforward. The interesting aspect of the ELMM SOS is the specification of the transition relation $\Rightarrow$, which is shown in Figure 3.7. The ELMM [*arithop*] axiom is similar to the same-named axiom in the POSTFIX SOS; it performs a calculation on integer numerals.

To evaluate expressions with nested subexpressions in left-to-right order, the rules [*prog-left*] and [*prog-right*] are needed. The [*prog-left*] rule says that if the ELMM abstract machine would make a transition from NE_1 to NE'_1, it should also allow a transition from $(A\ NE_1\ NE_2)$ to $(A\ NE'_1\ NE_2)$. This rule permits evaluation of the left operand of the operation while leaving the right operand unchanged. The [*prog-right*] rule is similar, except that it permits evaluation of the right operand only once the left operand has been fully evaluated to an integer numeral. This forces the operands to be evaluated in left-to-right order. Rules like [*prog-left*] and [*prog-right*] are called "progress rules" because an evaluation step performed on a subexpression allows progress to be made on the evaluation of the whole expression.

In the case of axioms, it is easy to determine if a transition is justified by an axiom. But how do we determine if a transition is justfied by a progress rule? A transition is justified by a progress rule if it matches the consequent of the rule and it is possible to show that the antecedent transition patterns are also justified. For example, since the ELMM transition (- 7 4) $\Rightarrow$ 3 is justified by the [*arithop*] rule, the transition (* (- 7 4) (+ 5 6)) $\Rightarrow$ (* 3 (+ 5 6)) is justified by the [*prog-left*] rule, and the transition (* 2 (- 7 4)) $\Rightarrow$ (* 2 3) is justified by the [*prog-right*] rule. Furthermore, since the above transitions themselves match the antecedents of the [*prog-left*] and [*prog-right*] rules, it is possible to use these rules again to justify the following transitions:

$$(/ \ (* \ (- \ 7 \ 4) \ (+ \ 5 \ 6)) \ (\% \ 9 \ 2)) \Rightarrow (/ \ (* \ 3 \ (+ \ 5 \ 6)) \ (\% \ 9 \ 2))$$
$$(/ \ (* \ 2 \ (- \ 7 \ 4)) \ (\% \ 9 \ 2)) \Rightarrow (/ \ (* \ 2 \ 3) \ (\% \ 9 \ 2))$$
$$(/ \ 100 \ (* \ (- \ 7 \ 4) \ (+ \ 5 \ 6))) \Rightarrow (/ \ 100 \ (* \ 3 \ (+ \ 5 \ 6)))$$
$$(/ \ 100 \ (* \ 2 \ (- \ 7 \ 4))) \Rightarrow (/ \ 100 \ (* \ 2 \ 3))$$

These examples suggest that we can justify any transition as long as we can give a proof of the transition based upon the rewrite rules. Such a proof can be visualized as a so-called **proof tree** (also known as a **derivation**) that grows upward from the bottom of the page. The root of a proof tree is the transition we are trying to prove, its intermediate nodes are instantiated progress rules, and its leaves are instantiated axioms. A proof tree is structured so that the consequent of each instantiated rule is one antecedent of its parent (below) in the tree. For example, the proof tree associated with the transition of (/ 100 (* (- 7 4) (+ 5 6))) appears in Figure 3.8.

$$(A \ N_1 \ N_2) \Rightarrow N_{ans}, \quad \text{where } N_{ans} = (calculate \ A \ N_1 \ N_2) \qquad [arithop]$$

$$\frac{NE_1 \Rightarrow NE'_1}{(A \ NE_1 \ NE_2) \Rightarrow (A \ NE'_1 \ NE_2)} \qquad [prog\text{-}left]$$

$$\frac{NE_2 \Rightarrow NE'_2}{(A \ N \ NE_2) \Rightarrow (A \ N \ NE'_2)} \qquad [prog\text{-}right]$$

Figure 3.7   Rewrite rules defining the transition relation ($\Rightarrow$) for ELMM.

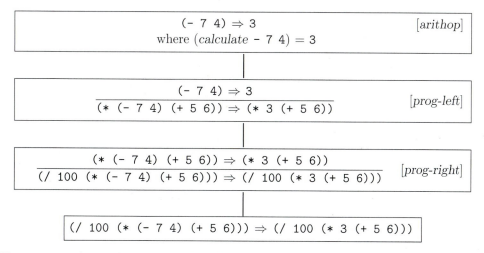

Figure 3.8   A proof tree for an ELMM transition involving nested expressions. The root of the tree is at the bottom of the page; the leaf is at the top.

We can represent the proof tree in the figure much more concisely by displaying each transition only once, as shown below:

$$\cfrac{\cfrac{\rule{2cm}{0.4pt}}{(-\ 7\ 4) \Rightarrow 3} \ [arithop]}{\cfrac{(*\ (-\ 7\ 4)\ (+\ 5\ 6)) \Rightarrow (*\ 3\ (+\ 5\ 6))}{(/\ 100\ (*\ (-\ 7\ 4)\ (+\ 5\ 6))) \Rightarrow (/\ 100\ (*\ 3\ (+\ 5\ 6)))} \ [prog\text{-}right]} \ [prog\text{-}left]$$

The proof tree in this particular example is linear because each of the progress rules involved has only one antecedent transition pattern. A progress rule with n antecedent transition patterns would correspond to a tree node with a branching factor of n. For example, suppose we added the following progress rule to the ELMM SOS:

$$\frac{NE_1 \Rightarrow NE'_1 \quad ; \quad NE_2 \Rightarrow NE'_2}{(A \ NE_1 \ NE_2) \Rightarrow (A \ NE'_1 \ NE'_2)} \qquad [prog\text{-}both]$$

This rule allows simultaneous evaluation of both operands. It leads to proof trees that have branching, such as the following tree in which three arithmetic operations are performed simultaneously:

$$\frac{}{(+ \ 25 \ 75) \Rightarrow 100} [arithop] \quad \frac{\dfrac{}{(- \ 7 \ 4) \Rightarrow 3}[arithop] \quad \dfrac{}{(+ \ 5 \ 6) \Rightarrow 11}[arithop]}{(* \ (- \ 7 \ 4) \ (+ \ 5 \ 6)) \Rightarrow (* \ 3 \ 11)}[prog\text{-}both]}{(/ \ (+ \ 25 \ 75) \ (* \ (- \ 7 \ 4) \ (+ \ 5 \ 6))) \Rightarrow (/ \ 100 \ (* \ 3 \ 11))}[prog\text{-}both]$$

It is possible to express any proof tree (even one with branches) in the more traditional linear textual style for a proof. In this style, a proof of a transition is a sequence of transitions where each transition is justified either by an axiom or by a progress rule whose antecedent transitions are justified by transitions earlier in the sequence. A linear textual version of the branching proof tree above is:

#	Transition	Justification
[1]	(+ 25 75) $\Rightarrow$ 100	[arithop]
[2]	(- 7 4) $\Rightarrow$ 3	[arithop]
[3]	(+ 5 6) $\Rightarrow$ 11	[arithop]
[4]	(* (- 7 4) (+ 5 6)) $\Rightarrow$ (* 3 11)	[prog-both] & [2] & [3]
[5]	(/ (+ 25 75) (* (- 7 4) (+ 5 6)))	
	$\Rightarrow$ (/ 100 (* 3 11))	[prog-both] & [1] & [4]

The elements of the linear textual proof sequence have been numbered, and justifications involving progress rules include the numbers of the transitions matched by their antecedents. There are many alternative proof sequences for this example that differ in the ordering of the elements. Indeed, the legal linear textual proof sequences for this example are just topological sorts of the original proof tree. Because such linearizations involve making arbitrary choices, we prefer to use the tree-based notation, whose structure highlights the essential dependencies in the proof.

When writing down a transition sequence to show the evaluation of an ELMM expression we will not explicitly justify every transition with a proof tree, even though such a proof tree must exist. However, if we are listing justifications for transitions, then we will list the names of the rules that would be needed to perform the proof. See Figure 3.9 for an example. (This example uses the original SOS, which does not include the [prog-both] rule.)

We shall see in Section 3.6.3 that the fact that each transition has a proof tree is key to proving properties about transitions. Transition properties are often proven by structural induction on the structure of the proof tree for the transition.

```
(/ (+ 25 75) (* (- 7 4) (+ 5 6)))
⇒ (/ 100 (* (- 7 4) (+ 5 6)))      [prog-left] & [arithop]
⇒ (/ 100 (* 3 (+ 5 6)))            [prog-right] & [prog-left] & [arithop]
⇒ (/ 100 (* 3 11))                 [prog-right] (twice) & [arithop]
⇒ (/ 100 33)                       [prog-right] & [arithop]
⇒ 3                                [arithop]
```

Figure 3.9   An example illustrating evaluation of ELMM expressions.

Exercise 3.10

a. Consider a language ELM (short for EL MINUS) that extends ELMM with indexed references to program inputs. That is, ELM is EL without conditionals and boolean expressions. The syntax for ELM is like that of ELMM except that (1) ELM programs have the form (elm $N_{numargs}$ NE_{body}), where $N_{numargs}$ specifies the number of expected program arguments and (2) numerical expressions are extended with EL's (arg N_{index}) construct, which gives the value of the argument whose index is given by N_{index} (assume indices start at 1).

   Write a complete SOS for ELM. Your configurations will need to include a state component representing the program arguments.

b. Write a complete SOS for the full EL language described in Section 2.3.2. You will need to define two kinds of configurations: one to handle numeric expressions and one to handle boolean expressions. Each kind of configuration will be a pair of an expression and a sequence of numeric arguments and will have its own transition relation.

Example: PostFix

For another example of progress rules, we will consider an alternative approach for describing the exec command of POSTFIX. The [execute] axiom in Figure 3.4 handled exec by popping an executable sequence Q_{exec} off the stack and prepending it to the command sequence Q_{rest} following the exec command. Figure 3.10 presents a progress rule, [exec-prog], that, together with the axiom [exec-done], can replace the [execute] rule. Rather than prepending the commands in Q_{exec} to Q_{rest}, the [exec-prog] rule effectively executes the commands in Q_{exec} while it remains on the stack.

   The [exec-prog] rule says that if the abstract machine would make a transition from $\langle Q_{exec}, S \rangle$ to $\langle Q'_{exec}, S' \rangle$ then it should also allow a transition from $\langle$exec . Q_{rest}, (Q_{exec}) . $S\rangle$ to $\langle$exec . Q_{rest}, (Q'_{exec}) . $S'\rangle$. Note that, unlike all the rules that we have seen before, this rule does *not* remove the exec command from the current command sequence. Instead, the exec command is left in place so that the execution of the command sequence at the top of the stack will continue during the next transition. Since the commands are removed from Q_{exec} after being executed, the executable sequence at the top of the stack will eventually become empty. At this point, the [*exec-done*] rule takes over, and removes both the completed `exec` command and its associated empty executable sequence.

Figure 3.11 shows how the example considered earlier in Figure 3.1 and Figure 3.5 would be handled using the [*exec-prog*] and [*exec-done*] rules. Each transition is justified by a proof tree that uses the rules listed as a justification. For example, the transition

$$\langle(\text{exec sub}), [(\text{exec}), (\text{mul add}), 3, 2, 1, 4, 5]\rangle$$
$$\Rightarrow \langle(\text{exec sub}), [(\text{exec}), (\text{add}), 6, 1, 4, 5]\rangle$$

is justified by the following proof tree:

$$\cfrac{\cfrac{\cfrac{}{\langle(\text{mul add}), [3, 2, 1, 4, 5]\rangle \Rightarrow \langle(\text{add}), [6, 1, 4, 5]\rangle}\ [\textit{arithop}]}{\langle(\text{exec}), [(\text{mul add}), 3, 2, 1, 4, 5]\rangle \Rightarrow \langle(\text{exec}), [(\text{add}), 6, 1, 4, 5]\rangle}\ [\textit{exec-prog}]}{\begin{array}{c}\langle(\text{exec sub}), [(\text{exec}), (\text{mul add}), 3, 2, 1, 4, 5]\rangle \\ \Rightarrow \langle(\text{exec sub}), [(\text{exec}), (\text{add}), 6, 1, 4, 5]\rangle\end{array}}\ [\textit{exec-prog}]$$

The Meaning of Progress Rules

There are some technical details about progress rules that we glossed over earlier. When we introduced progress rules, we blindly assumed that they were always reasonable. But not all progress rules make sense.

For example, suppose we extend POSTFIX with a `loop` command defined by the following progress rule:

$$\cfrac{\langle\text{loop}\,.\,Q,\,S\rangle \Rightarrow \langle Q,\,S\rangle}{\langle\text{loop}\,.\,Q,\,S\rangle \Rightarrow \langle Q,\,S\rangle} \qquad [\textit{loop}]$$

Any attempt to prove a transition involving `loop` will fail because there are no axioms involving `loop` with which to terminate the proof tree. Thus, this rule stands for no transitions whatsoever!

We'd like to ensure that all progress rules we consider make sense. We can guarantee this by restricting the form of allowable progress rules to outlaw nonsensical rules like [*loop*]. This so-called **structure restriction** guarantees that any attempt to prove a transition from a given configuration will eventually terminate. The standard structure restriction for an SOS requires rules that are

$$\frac{\langle Q_{exec}, S \rangle \Rightarrow \langle Q'_{exec}, S' \rangle}{\langle \text{exec} . Q_{rest}, (Q_{exec}) . S \rangle \Rightarrow \langle \text{exec} . Q_{rest}, (Q'_{exec}) . S' \rangle} \qquad [\textit{exec-prog}]$$

$$\langle \text{exec} . Q_{rest}, () . S \rangle \Rightarrow \langle Q_{rest}, S \rangle \qquad [\textit{exec-done}]$$

Figure 3.10 A pair of rules that could replace the [*execute*] axiom.

```
(IF ⟨(postfix 2 (2 (3 mul add) exec) 1 swap exec sub), [4, 5]⟩)
  = ⟨((2 (3 mul add) exec) 1 swap exec sub), [4, 5]⟩
  ⇒ ⟨(1 swap exec sub), [(2 (3 mul add) exec), 4, 5]⟩        [seq]
  ⇒ ⟨(swap exec sub), [1, (2 (3 mul add) exec), 4, 5]⟩       [num]
  ⇒ ⟨(exec sub), [(2 (3 mul add) exec), 1, 4, 5]⟩            [swap]
  ⇒ ⟨(exec sub), [((3 mul add) exec), 2, 1, 4, 5]⟩           [exec-prog] & [num]
  ⇒ ⟨(exec sub), [(exec), (3 mul add), 2, 1, 4, 5]⟩          [exec-prog] & [seq]
  ⇒ ⟨(exec sub), [(exec), (mul add), 3, 2, 1, 4, 5]⟩         [exec-prog] (twice)
                                                             & [num]
  ⇒ ⟨(exec sub), [(exec), (add), 6, 1, 4, 5]⟩                [exec-prog] (twice)
                                                             & [arithop]
  ⇒ ⟨(exec sub), [(exec), (), 7, 4, 5]⟩                      [exec-prog] (twice)
                                                             & [arithop]
  ⇒ ⟨(exec sub), [(), 7, 4, 5]⟩                              [exec-prog]
                                                             & [exec-done]
  ⇒ ⟨(sub), [7, 4, 5]⟩                                       [exec-done]
  ⇒ ⟨(), [-3, 5]⟩ ∈ FC                                       [arithop]
(OF ⟨(), [-3, 5]⟩) = -3
```

Figure 3.11 An example illustrating the alternative rules for `exec`.

purely structural in the sense that the code component of the LHS of each antecedent transition is a subphrase of the code component of the LHS of the consequent transition. Since program ASTs are necessarily finite, this guarantees that all attempts to prove a transition will have a finite proof.[7]

While simple to follow, the standard structure restriction prohibits many reasonable rules. For example, the [*exec-prog*] rule does not obey this restriction, because the code component of the LHS of the antecedent is unrelated to the code component of the LHS of the consequent. Yet, by considering the entire configuration rather than just the code component, it is possible to design a

---

[7]This restriction accounts for the term "Structural" in Plotkin's Structural Operational Semantics [Plo81].

metric in which the LHS of the antecedent is "smaller" than the LHS of the consequent (see Exercise 3.11). Although it is sometimes necessary to extend the standard structure restriction in this fashion, most of our rules will be purely structural.

Exercise 3.11 To guarantee that a progress rule is well defined, we must show that the antecedent configurations are smaller than the consequent configurations. Here we explore a notion of "smaller than" for the POSTFIX configurations that establishes the well-definedness of the [*exec-prog*] rule. (Since [*exec-prog*] is the only progress rule for POSTFIX, it is the only one we need to consider.)

Suppose that we define a relation $<$ on POSTFIX configurations such that

$$\langle Q_1, \ S\rangle < \langle \texttt{exec} \, . \, Q_2, \ Q_1 \, . \, S\rangle$$

for any command sequences Q_1 and Q_2 and any stack S. This is the *only* relation on POSTFIX configurations; two configurations not satisfying this relation are simply incomparable.

a. A sequence $[a_1, a_2, \ldots]$ is **strictly decreasing** if $a_{i+1} < a_i$ for all i. Using the relation $<$ defined above for configurations, show that every strictly decreasing sequence $[cf_1, cf_2, \ldots]$ of POSTFIX configurations must be finite.

b. Explain how the result of the previous part implies the well-definedness of the [*exec-prog*] rule.

Exercise 3.12 The abstract machine for POSTFIX described thus far employs configurations with two components: a command sequence and a stack. It is possible to construct an alternative abstract machine for POSTFIX in which configurations consist only of a command sequence. The essence of such a machine is suggested by the transition sequence in Figure 3.12, where the primed rule names are the names of rules for the new abstract machine, not the abstract machine presented earlier.

a. The above example shows that an explicit stack component is not necessary to model POSTFIX evaluation. Explain how this is possible. (Is there an implicit stack somewhere?)

b. Write an SOS for POSTFIX in which a configuration is just a command sequence. The SOS should have the behavior exhibited above on the given example. Recall that an SOS has five components; describe all five. Use only axioms to specify your transition relation.

c. In the above example, the `exec` command is handled by replacing it and the executable sequence Q to its left by the contents of Q. This mirrors the prepending behavior of [*execute*] in the original abstract machine. Write rules for the new abstract machine that instead mirror the behavior of [*exec-prog*] and [*exec-done*].

```
((swap exec swap exec) (1 sub) swap (2 mul) swap 3 swap exec)
⇒ ((1 sub) (swap exec swap exec) (2 mul) swap 3 swap exec)      [swap']
⇒ ((1 sub) (2 mul) (swap exec swap exec) 3 swap exec)           [swap']
⇒ ((1 sub) (2 mul) 3 (swap exec swap exec) exec)                [swap']
⇒ ((1 sub) (2 mul) 3 swap exec swap exec)                       [exec']
⇒ ((1 sub) 3 (2 mul) exec swap exec)                            [swap']
⇒ ((1 sub) 3 2 mul swap exec)                                   [exec']
⇒ ((1 sub) 6 swap exec)                                         [arithop']
⇒ (6 (1 sub) exec)                                              [swap']
⇒ (6 1 sub)                                                     [exec']
⇒ 5                                                             [arithop']
```

Figure 3.12 Sample transition sequence for an alternative POSTFIX abstract machine whose configurations are command sequences.

d. Develop an appropriate notion of "smaller than" that establishes the well-definedness of your new [exec-prog] rule. (See Exercise 3.11.)

e. Sketch how you might prove that the new SOS and the original SOS define the behavior.

3.2.6   Context-based Semantics

Rewrite rules are not the only way to specify the transition relation of a small-step operational semantics. Here we introduce another approach to specifying transitions that is popular in the literature. This approach is based on a notion of **context** that specifies the position of a subphrase in a larger program phrase. Here we will explain this notion and show how it can be used to specify transitions.

In general, a context is a phrase with a single **hole** node in the abstract syntax tree for the phrase. A sample context $\mathbb{C}$ in the ELMM language is (+ 1 (- □ 2)), where □ denotes the hole in the context. "Filling" this hole with any ELMM numerical expression yields another numerical expression. For example, filling $\mathbb{C}$ with (/ (* 4 5) 3), written $\mathbb{C}\{$(/ (* 4 5) 3)$\}$, yields the numerical expression (+ 1 (- (/ (* 4 5) 3) 2)).

Contexts are useful for specifying a particular occurrence of a phrase that occurs more than once in an expression. For example, (+ 3 4) appears twice in (* (+ 3 4) (/ (+ 3 4) 2)). The leftmost occurrence is specified by the context (* □ (/ (+ 3 4) 2)), while (* (+ 3 4) (/ □ 2)) specifies the rightmost one. Contexts are also useful for specifying the part of a phrase that remains unchanged (the **evaluation context**) when a basic computation (known as a re-

Redexes
$\mathcal{R} \in$ ElmmRedex ::= $(A\ N_1\ N_2)$ [ArithmeticOperation]

Reduction Relation $(\leadsto)$
   $(A\ N_1\ N_2) \leadsto N_{ans}$, where $N_{ans} = (calculate\ A\ N_1\ N_2)$

Evaluation Contexts
$\mathbb{E} \in$ ElmmEvalContext ::= $\square$ [Hole]
                          | $(A\ \mathbb{E}\ NE)$ [EvalLeft]
                          | $(A\ N\ \mathbb{E})$ [EvalRight]

Transition Relation $(\Rightarrow)$
   $\mathbb{E}\{\mathcal{R}\} \Rightarrow \mathbb{E}\{\mathcal{R}'\}$, where $\mathcal{R} \leadsto \mathcal{R}'$

Figure 3.13   A context-based specification of the ELMM transition relation.

dex, short for "reducible expression") is performed. E.g., consider the evaluation
of the ELMM expression (/ 100 (* (- 7 4) (+ 5 6))). If operands are evaluated in left-to-right order, the next redex to be performed is (- 7 4). The
evaluation context for this redex is $\mathbb{E} = $ (/ 100 (* $\square$ (+ 5 6))). The result
(3 in this case) of performing the redex is plugged into the evaluation context
to yield the result of the transition: $\mathbb{E}\{3\} = $ (/ 100 (* 3 (+ 5 6))). This
transition can also be written as:

$$
\begin{aligned}
&\text{(/ 100 (* (- 7 4) (+ 5 6)))}\\
&= \text{(/ 100 (* } \square \text{ (+ 5 6)))}\{\text{(- 7 4)}\}\\
&\Rightarrow \text{(/ 100 (* } \square \text{ (+ 5 6)))}\{3\}\\
&= \text{(/ 100 (* 3 (+ 5 6)))}
\end{aligned}
$$

Evaluation contexts and redexes can be defined via grammars, such as the
ones for ELMM in Figure 3.13. In ELMM, a redex is an arithmetic operator
applied to two integer numerals. An ELMM evaluation context is either a hole
or an arithmetic operation one of whose two operands is an evaluation context.
If the evaluation context is in the left operand position (*[Eval Left]*) the right
operand can be an arbitrary numerical expression. But if the evaluation context
is in the right operand position (*[Eval Right]*), the left operand *must* be a numeral.
This structure enforces left-to-right evaluation in ELMM in a way similar to the
[prog-left] and *[prog-right]* progress rules. Indeed, evaluation contexts are just
another way of expressing the information in progress rules — namely, how to
find the redex (i.e., where an axiom can be applied).

   Associated with redexes is a **reduction relation** $(\leadsto)$ that corresponds to
the basic computation axioms we have seen before. In the simplest case, the left-

hand side of the relation is the redex, while the right-hand side is the **reduct**. The transition relation ($\Rightarrow$) is defined in terms of the reduction relation using evaluation contexts: the expression $\mathbb{E}\{\mathcal{R}\}$ rewrites to $\mathbb{E}\{\mathcal{R}'\}$ as long as there is a reduction $\mathcal{R} \rightsquigarrow \mathcal{R}'$. The transition relation is deterministic if there is at most one way to parse an expression into an evaluation context filled with a redex (which is the case in ELMM). The following table shows the context-based evaluation of an ELMM expression:

Expression	Evaluation Context	Redex	Reduct
(/ (+ 25 75) (* (- 7 4) (+ 5 6)))	(/ □ (* (- 7 4) (+ 5 6)))	(+ 25 75)	100
$\Rightarrow$ (/ 100 (* (- 7 4) (+ 5 6)))	(/ 100 (* □ (+ 5 6)))	(- 7 4)	3
$\Rightarrow$ (/ 100 (* 3 (+ 5 6)))	(/ 100 (* 3 □))	(+ 5 6)	11
$\Rightarrow$ (/ 100 (* 3 11))	(/ 100 □)	(* 3 11)	33
$\Rightarrow$ (/ 100 33)	□	(/ 100 33)	3
$\Rightarrow$ 3			

Context-based semantics are most convenient in an SOS where the configurations consist solely of a code component. But they can also be adapted to configurations that have state components. For example, Figure 3.14 is a context-based semantics for ELM, the extension to ELMM that includes indexed input via the form ($\textbf{arg}$ N_{index}) (see Exercise 3.10). An ELM configuration is a pair of (1) an ELM numerical expression and (2) a sequence of numerals representing the program arguments. Both the ELM reduction relation and transition relation must include the program arguments so that the $\textbf{arg}$ form can access them.

When the reduction relation involves additional components, such as program arguments in the case of ELM, there is some ambiguity in the terms "redex" and "reduct." Sometimes they refer to the left-hand and right-hand sides of the reduction rule, but often they refer to just the expression components of these sides. E.g., in ELM, both ($\textbf{arg}$ 2) and $\langle(\textbf{arg}\ 2), [7, 4, 5]\rangle$ can be called a redex.

Exercise 3.13 Starting with Figure 3.14, develop a context-based semantics for the full EL language.

Exercise 3.14 The most natural context-based semantics for POSTFIX is based on the approach sketched in Exercise 3.12, where configurations consist only of a command sequence. Figure 3.15 is the skeleton of a context-based semantics that defines the transition relation for these configurations. It uses a command sequence context $\mathbb{EQ}$ whose hole can be filled with a command sequence that is internally appended to other command sequences. For example, if $\mathbb{EQ} = [1, 2, \square, \texttt{sub}]$, then $\mathbb{EQ}\{[3, \texttt{swap}]\} = [1, 2, 3, \texttt{swap}, \texttt{sub}]$. Complete the semantics in Figure 3.15 by fleshing out the missing details.

Redexes

$\mathcal{R} \in \text{ElmRedex} ::= (A \ N_1 \ N_2) \quad [\text{ArithmeticOperation}]$
$\qquad\qquad\qquad | \ (\text{arg} \ N_{index}) \ [\text{IndexedInput}]$

Reduction Relation ($\rightsquigarrow$)

$\langle (A \ N_1 \ N_2), N^* \rangle \rightsquigarrow N_{ans}$ where $N_{ans} = (calculate \ A \ N_1 \ N_2)$
$\langle (\text{arg} \ N_{index}), [N_1, \ldots, N_{N_{size}}] \rangle \rightsquigarrow N_{N_{index}}$
$\quad$ where $(compare > N_{index} \ 0) \wedge \neg(compare > N_{index} \ N_{size})$

Evaluation Contexts

$\mathbb{E} \in \text{ElmEvalContext} ::= \square \qquad\qquad [\text{Hole}]$
$\qquad\qquad\qquad\qquad | \ (A \ \mathbb{E} \ NE) \ [\text{EvalLeft}]$
$\qquad\qquad\qquad\qquad | \ (A \ N \ \mathbb{E}) \quad [\text{EvalRight}]$

Transition Relation ($\Rightarrow$)

$\langle \mathbb{E}\{\mathcal{R}\}, N^* \rangle \Rightarrow \langle \mathbb{E}\{\mathcal{R}'\}, N^* \rangle$ where $\langle \mathcal{R}, N^* \rangle \rightsquigarrow \mathcal{R}'$

Figure 3.14   A context-based specification of the ELM transition relation.

Redexes

$\mathcal{R} \in \text{PostFixRedex} ::= [V, \text{pop}] \qquad [\text{Pop}]$
$\qquad\qquad\qquad | \ [V_1, V_2, \text{swap}] \ [\text{Swap}]$
$\qquad\qquad\qquad | \ [N_1, N_2, A] \qquad [\text{ArithmeticOperation}]$
$\qquad\qquad\qquad | \ \ldots \ other \ redexes \ left \ as \ an \ exercise \ \ldots$

Reduction Relation ($\rightsquigarrow$)

$[V, \text{pop}] \rightsquigarrow [\,]$
$[V_1, V_2, \text{swap}] \rightsquigarrow [V_2, V_1]$
$[N_1, N_2, A] \rightsquigarrow [N_{ans}]$ where $N_{ans} = (calculate \ A \ N_1 \ N_2)$
$\ldots \ other \ reduction \ rules \ left \ as \ an \ exercise \ \ldots$

Evaluation Contexts

$\mathbb{E}\mathbb{Q} \in \text{PostfixEvalSequenceContext} ::= V^* @ \square @ Q$

Transition Relation ($\Rightarrow$)

$\mathbb{E}\mathbb{Q}\{\mathcal{R}\} \Rightarrow \mathbb{E}\mathbb{Q}\{\mathcal{R}'\}$, where $\mathcal{R} \rightsquigarrow \mathcal{R}'$

Figure 3.15   A context-based specification of the transition relation for a subset of POSTFIX.

$$\frac{NE \;\twoheadrightarrow_{NE}\; N_{ans}}{(\texttt{elmm}\;\; NE)\;\twoheadrightarrow_P\; N_{ans}} \qquad\qquad [prog]$$

$$N \;\twoheadrightarrow_{NE}\; N \qquad\qquad [num]$$

$$\frac{NE_1 \;\twoheadrightarrow_{NE}\; N_1 \quad;\quad NE_2 \;\twoheadrightarrow_{NE}\; N_2}{(A\;\; NE_1\;\; NE_2)\;\twoheadrightarrow_{NE}\; N_{ans}} \qquad\qquad [arithop]$$
$$\text{where } N_{ans} = (calculate\;\; A\;\; N_1\;\; N_2)$$

Figure 3.16 Big-step operational semantics for ELMM.

3.3 Big-step Operational Semantics

A small-step operational semantics is a framework for describing program execution as an iterative sequence of small computational steps. But this is not always the most natural way to view execution. We often want to evaluate a phrase by recursively evaluating its subphrases and then combining the results. This is the key idea of denotational semantics, which we shall study in Chapter 4. However, this idea also underlies an alternative form of operational semantics, called **big-step operational semantics (BOS)** (also known as **natural semantics**). Here we briefly introduce big-step semantics in the context of a few examples.

Let's begin by defining a BOS for the simple expression language ELMM, in which programs are numerical expressions that are either numerals or arithmetic operations. A BOS typically has an **evaluation relation** for each nontrivial syntactic domain that directly specifies a result for a given program phrase or configuration. The BOS in Figure 3.16 defines two evaluation relations:

1. $\twoheadrightarrow_{NE}\, \in$ NumExp $\times$ IntLit specifies the evaluation of an ELMM numerical expression; and

2. $\twoheadrightarrow_P\, \in$ Prog $\times$ IntLit specifies the evaluation of an ELMM program.

There are two rules specifying $\twoheadrightarrow_{NE}$. The [num] rule says that numerals evaluate to themselves. The [arithop] rule says that evaluating an arithmetic operation $(A\;\; NE_1\;\; NE_2)$ yields the result (N_{ans}) of applying the operator to the results (N_1 and N_2) of evaluating the operands. The single [prog] rule specifying $\twoheadrightarrow_P$ just says that the result of an ELMM program is the result of evaluating its numerical expression.

As with SOS transitions, each instantiation of a BOS evaluation rule is justified by a proof tree, which we shall call an **evaluation tree**. Below is the proof tree for the evaluation of the program (elmm (* (- 7 4) (+ 5 6))):

$$\cfrac{\cfrac{}{7 \longrightarrow_{NE} 7}\ [num] \qquad \cfrac{}{4 \longrightarrow_{NE} 4}\ [num]}{(\text{-}\ 7\ 4) \longrightarrow_{NE} 3}\ [arithop] \qquad \cfrac{\cfrac{}{5 \longrightarrow_{NE} 5}\ [num] \qquad \cfrac{}{6 \longrightarrow_{NE} 6}\ [num]}{(\text{+}\ 5\ 6) \longrightarrow_{NE} 11}\ [arithop]$$

$$\cfrac{(\text{*}\ (\text{-}\ 7\ 4)\ (\text{+}\ 5\ 6)) \longrightarrow_{NE} 33}{(\text{elmm}\ (\text{*}\ (\text{-}\ 7\ 4)\ (\text{+}\ 5\ 6))) \longrightarrow_{P} 33}\ [prog]$$

Unlike the proof tree for an SOS transition, which justifies a single computational step, the proof tree for a BOS transition justifies the entire evaluation! This is the sense in which the steps of a BOS are "big"; they tell how to go from a phrase to an answer (or something close to an answer). In the case of ELMM, the leaves of the proof tree are always trivial evaluations of numerals to themselves.

With BOS evaluations there is no notion of a stuck state. In the ELMM BOS, there is no proof tree for an expression like (* (/ 7 0) (+ 5 6)) that contains an error. However, we can extend the BOS to include an explicit error token as a possible result and modify the rules to generate and propagate such a token. Since all ELMM programs terminate, a BOS with this extension completely specifies the behavior of a program. But in general, the top-level evaluation rule for a program only partially specifies its behavior, since there is no tree (not even an infinite one) asserting that a program loops. What would the answer A of such a program be in the relation $P \longrightarrow_{P} A$?

The ELMM BOS rules also do not specify the order in which operands are evaluated, but this is irrelevant since there is no way in ELMM to detect whether one operation is performed before another. The ELMM BOS rules happen to specify a function, which implies that ELMM evaluation is deterministic. In general, a BOS may specify a relation, so it can describe nondeterministic evaluation as well.

In ELMM, the evaluation relation maps a code phrase to its result. In general, the LHS (and RHS) of an evaluation relation can be more complex, containing state components in addition to a code component. This is illustrated in the BOS for ELM, which extends ELMM with an indexed input construct (Figure 3.17). Here, the two evaluation relations have different domains than before: they include an integer numeral sequence to model the program arguments.

1. $\longrightarrow_{NE}\ \in (\text{NumExp} \times \text{IntLit}^{*}) \times \text{IntLit}$ specifies the evaluation of an ELM numerical expression; and

2. $\longrightarrow_{P}\ \in (\text{Prog} \times \text{IntLit}^{*}) \times \text{IntLit}$ specifies the evaluation of an ELM program.

Each of these relations can be read as "evaluating a program phrase relative to the program arguments to yield a result." As a notational convenience, we abbreviate

$$\frac{NE \xrightarrow{[N_1,\ldots,N_n]}_{NE} N_{ans}}{(\text{elm } N_{numargs} \ NE) \xrightarrow{[N_1,\ldots,N_n]}_{P} N_{ans}} \quad [prog]$$

$$\text{where } (compare = N_{numargs} \ \overline{n})$$
$$\text{and } \overline{n} \text{ stands for the IntLit } N \text{ that denotes } n \in Int$$

$$N \xrightarrow{N^*}_{NE} N \quad [num]$$

$$\frac{NE_1 \xrightarrow{N^*}_{NE} N_1 \quad ; \quad NE_2 \xrightarrow{N^*}_{NE} N_2}{(A \ NE_1 \ NE_2) \xrightarrow{N^*}_{NE} N_{ans}} \quad [arithop]$$

$$\text{where } N_{ans} = (calculate \ A \ N_1 \ N_2)$$

$$(\text{arg } N_{index}) \xrightarrow{[N_1,\ldots,N_n]}_{NE} N_{N_{index}} \quad [input]$$

$$\text{where } (compare > N_{index} \ 0) \wedge \neg(compare > N_{index} \ \overline{n})$$

Figure 3.17   Big-step operational semantics for ELM.

$\langle X, N^*_{args} \rangle \rightarrow_X N_{ans}$ as $X \xrightarrow{N^*_{args}}_X N_{ans}$, where X ranges over P and NE. The [*prog*] rule is as in ELMM, except that it checks that the number of arguments is as expected and passes them to the body for its evaluation. These arguments are ignored by the [*num*] and [*arithop*] rules, but are used by the [*input*] rule to return the specified argument.

Here is a sample ELM proof tree showing the evaluation of the program (elm 2 (* (arg 1) (+ 1 (arg 2)))) on the two arguments 7 and 5:

$$\frac{(\text{arg } 1) \xrightarrow{[7,5]}_{NE} 7 \ [input] \quad \dfrac{1 \xrightarrow{[7,5]}_{NE} 1 \ [num] \quad (\text{arg } 2) \xrightarrow{[7,5]}_{NE} 5 \ [input]}{(+ \ 1 \ (\text{arg } 2)) \xrightarrow{[7,5]}_{NE} 6} [arithop]}{(\text{elm } 2 \ (* \ (\text{arg } 1) \ (+ \ 1 \ (\text{arg } 2)))) \xrightarrow{[7,5]}_{P} 42} \ [prog]$$

Can we describe POSTFIX execution in terms of a BOS? Yes — via the evaluation relations $\rightarrow_P$ (for programs) and $\rightarrow_Q$ (for command sequences) in Figure 3.18. The $\rightarrow_Q$ relation $\in$ (CommandSeq × Stack) × Stack treats command sequences as "stack transformers" that map an input stack to an output stack. We abbreviate $\langle Q, S \rangle \rightarrow_Q S'$ as $Q \xrightarrow{S}_Q S'$. The [*non-exec*] rule "cheats" by using the SOS transition relation $\Rightarrow$ to specify how a non-exec command C transforms the stack to S'. Then $\rightarrow_Q$ specifies how the rest of the commands transform S' into S''. The [*exec*] rule is more interesting because it uses $\rightarrow_Q$ in both antecedents. The executable sequence commands Q_{exec} transform S to S', while the remaining commands Q_{rest} transform S' to S''. The [*exec*] and [*nonexec*] rules illustrate how evaluation order (in this case, executing Q_{exec} before Q_{rest}

$$\frac{Q \xrightarrow{[N_1,\ldots,N_n]}_Q N_{ans} . S}{(\texttt{postfix } N_{numargs} \ Q) \xrightarrow{[N_1,\ldots,N_n]}_P N_{ans}} \qquad [prog]$$

where $(compare = N_{numargs} \ \overline{n})$
and $\overline{n}$ stands for the IntLit N that denotes $n \in Int$

$$\frac{\langle C . Q, S \rangle \Rightarrow \langle Q, S' \rangle \quad ; \quad Q \xrightarrow{S'}_Q S''}{C . Q \xrightarrow{S}_Q S''} \qquad [non\text{-}exec]$$

where $C \neq \texttt{exec}$

$$\frac{Q_{exec} \xrightarrow{S}_Q S' \quad ; \quad Q_{rest} \xrightarrow{S'}_Q S''}{\texttt{exec} . Q_{rest} \xrightarrow{(Q_{exec}) . S}_Q S''} \qquad [exec]$$

Figure 3.18   Big-step operational semantics for POSTFIX.

or C before Q) can be specified in a BOS by "threading" a state component (in this case, the stack) through an evaluation.

It is convenient to define $\rightarrow\!\!\!\rightarrow_Q$ so that it returns a stack, but stacks are not the final answer we desire. The [prog] rule $\in$ (Prog $\times$ IntLit*) $\times$ Stack takes care of creating the initial stack from the arguments and extracting the top integer numeral (if it exists) from the final stack.

How do small-step and big-step semantics stack up against each other? Each has its advantages and limitations. A big-step semantics is often more concise than a small-step semantics, and one of its proof trees can summarize the entire execution of a program. The recursive nature of a big-step semantics also corresponds more closely to the structure of interpreters for high-level languages than a small-step semantics does. On the other hand, the iterative step-by-step nature of a small-step semantics corresponds more closely to the way low-level languages are implemented, and it is often a better framework for reasoning about computational resources, errors, and termination. Furthemore, infinite loops are easy to model in a small-step semantics but not in a big-step semantics.

We will use small-step semantics as our default form of operational semantics throughout the rest of this book. This is not because the big-step semantics approach is not useful — it is — but because we will tend to use denotational semantics rather than big-step operational semantics for language specifications that compose the meanings of whole phrases from subphrases.

Exercise 3.15 Construct a BOS evaluation tree that shows the evaluation of

$$(\texttt{postfix 2 (2 (3 mul add) exec) 1 swap exec sub})$$

on arguments 4 and 5.

Exercise 3.16 Extend the BOS in Figure 3.16 to handle the full EL language. You will need a new evaluation relation, $\twoheadrightarrow_{BE}$, to handle boolean expressions.

Exercise 3.17 Modify each of the BOS specifications in Figures 3.16–3.18 to generate and propagate an error token that models signaling an error. Be careful to handle all error situations.

3.4 Operational Reasoning

The suitability of a programming language for a given purpose largely depends on many high-level properties of the language. Important global properties of a programming language include:

- **universality**: the language can express all computable programs;

- **determinism**: the set of possible outcomes from executing a program on any particular inputs is a singleton;

- **strong normalization**: all programs are guaranteed to terminate on all inputs (i.e., it is not possible to express an infinite loop);

- **static checkability**: a class of program errors can be found by static analysis without resorting to execution;

- **referential transparency**: different occurrences of an expression within the same context always have the same meaning.

Languages often exhibit equivalence properties that allow **safe transformations**: systematic substitutions of one program phrase for another that are guaranteed not to change the behavior of the program. Finally, properties of *particular* programs are often of interest. For instance, we might want to show that a given program terminates, that it uses only bounded resources, or that it is equivalent to some other program. For these sorts of purposes, an important characteristic of a language is how easy it is to prove properties of particular programs written in a language.

A language exhibiting a desired list of properties may not always exist. For example, no language can be both universal and terminating, because a universal language must be able to express infinite loops. (But it is often possible to carve a terminating sublanguage out of a universal language.)

The properties of a programming language are important to language designers, implementers, and programmers alike. The features included in a language strongly depend on what properties the designers want the language to have. For example, designers of a language in which all programs are intended to terminate cannot include general looping constructs, while designers of a universal language must include features that allow nontermination. Compiler writers extensively use safe transformations to automatically improve the efficiency of programs. The properties of a language influence which language a programmer chooses for a task as well as what style of code the programmer writes.

An important benefit of a formal semantics is that it provides a framework that facilitates proving properties both about the entire language and about particular programs written in the language. Without a formal semantics, our understanding of such properties would be limited to intuitions and informal (and possibly incorrect) arguments. A formal semantics is a shared language for convincing both ourselves and others that some intuition that we have about a program or a language is really true. It can also help us develop new intuitions. It is useful not only to the extent that it helps us construct proofs but also to the extent that it helps us find holes in our arguments. After all, some of the things we think we can prove simply aren't true. The process of constructing a proof can give us important insight into *why* they aren't true.

In the next three sections, we use operational semantics to reason about EL and POSTFIX. In Section 3.5, we discuss the deterministic behavior of EL under various conditions. Then we show in Section 3.6 that all POSTFIX programs are guaranteed to terminate. In Section 3.7, we consider conditions under which we can transform one POSTFIX command sequence to another without changing the behavior of a program.

3.5   Deterministic Behavior of EL

A programming language is **deterministic** if there is exactly one possible outcome for any pair of program and inputs. In Section 3.2.1, we saw that a deterministic SOS transition relation implies that programs behave deterministically. In Section 3.2.3, we argued that the POSTFIX transition relation is deterministic, so POSTFIX is a deterministic language.

We can similarly argue that EL is deterministic. We will give the argument for the sublanguage ELMM, but it can be extended to full EL. There are only three SOS rewrite rules for ELMM (Figure 3.7 on page 65): [*arithop*], [*prog-left*], and [*prog-right*]. For a given ELMM numerical expression *NE*, we argue that there is at most one proof tree using these three rules that justifies a transition for *NE*. The proof is by structural induction on the AST for *NE*.

- (Base cases) If *NE* is a numeral, it matches no rules, so there is no transition. If *NE* has the form $(A\ N_1\ N_2)$, it can match only the [*arithop*] rule, since there are no transitions involving numerals.

- (Induction cases) *NE* must have the form $(A\ NE_1\ NE_2)$, where at least one of NE_1 and NE_2 is not a numeral. If NE_1 is not a numeral, then *NE* can match only the [*prog-left*] rule, and only in the case where there is a proof tree justifying the transition $NE_1 \Rightarrow NE'_1$. By induction, there is at most one such proof tree, so there is at most one proof tree for a transition of *NE*. If NE_1 is a numeral, then NE_2 must not be a numeral, in which case *NE* can match only the [*prog-right*] rule, and similar reasoning applies.

Alternatively, we can prove the determinism of the ELMM transition relation using the context semantics in Figure 3.13. In this case, we need to show that each ELMM numerical expression can be parsed into an evaluation context and redex in at most one way. Such a proof is essentially the same as the one given above, so we omit it.

The ELMM SOS specifies that operations are performed in left-to-right order. Why does the order of evaluation matter? It turns out that it doesn't — there is no way in ELMM to detect the order in which operations are performed! Intuitively, either the evaluation is successful, in which case all operations are performed anyway, leading to the same answer, or a division or remainder by zero is encountered somewhere along the way, in which case the evaluation is unsuccessful. Note that if we could distinguish between different kinds of errors, the story would be different. For instance, if divide-by-zero gave a different error from remainder-by-zero, then evaluating the expression (+ (/ 1 0) (% 2 0)) would indicate which of the two subexpressions was evaluated first. The issue of evaluation order is important to implementers, because they sometimes can make programs execute more efficiently by reordering operations.

How can we formally show that evaluation order in ELMM does not matter? We begin by replacing the [*prog-right*] rule in the SOS by the following [*prog-right'*] rule to yield a modified ELMM transition relation $\Rightarrow'$.

$$\frac{NE_2 \Rightarrow' NE'_2}{(A\ NE_1\ NE_2) \Rightarrow' (A\ NE_1\ NE'_2)} \qquad [\textit{prog-right'}]$$

Now operands can be evaluated in either order, so the transition relation is no longer deterministic. For example, the expression (* (- 7 4) (+ 5 6)) now has two transitions:

$$(* \ (-\ 7\ 4)\ (+\ 5\ 6)) \Rightarrow' (*\ 3\ (+\ 5\ 6))$$
$$(* \ (-\ 7\ 4)\ (+\ 5\ 6)) \Rightarrow' (*\ (-\ 7\ 4)\ 11)$$

Nevertheless, we would like to argue that the behavior of programs is still deterministic even though the transition relation is not.

A handy property for this purpose is called **confluence**. Informally, confluence says that if two transition paths from a configuration diverge, there must be a way to bring them back together. The formal definition is as follows:

Definition 3.1 (Confluence)   *A relation $\rightarrow \; \in X \times X$ is confluent if and only if for every $x_1, x_2, x_3 \in X$ such that $x_1 \xrightarrow{*} x_2$ and $x_1 \xrightarrow{*} x_3$, there exists an x_4 such that $x_2 \xrightarrow{*} x_4$ and $x_3 \xrightarrow{*} x_4$. Confluence is usually displayed via the following diagram, in which solid lines are the given relations and the dashed lines are assumed to exist when the property holds.*

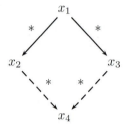

Because of the shape of the diagram, $\xrightarrow{*}$ is said to satisfy the **diamond property**. *Saying that a relation is* **Church-Rosser** *(CR for short) is the same as saying it is confluent.*

Suppose that a transition relation $\Rightarrow$ is confluent. Then if an initial configuration cf_i has transition paths to two final configurations cf_{f_1} and cf_{f_2}, these are necessarily the same configuration! Why? By confluence, there must be a configuration cf such that $cf_{f_1} \xrightarrow{*} cf$ and $cf_{f_2} \xrightarrow{*} cf$. But cf_{f_1} and cf_{f_2} are elements of *Irreducible*, so the only transition paths leaving them have length 0. This means $cf_{f_1} = cf = cf_{f_2}$. Thus, a confluent transition relation guarantees a unique final configuration. Indeed, it guarantees a unique irreducible configuration: it is not possible to get stuck on one path and reach a final configuration on another.

Confluence by itself does not guarantee a single outcome. It is still possible for a confluent transition relation to have some infinite paths, in which case there is a second outcome (∞). This possibility must be ruled out to prove deterministic behavior. In the case of ELMM — and even EL — it is easy to prove there are no loops (see Exercise 3.27 on page 89).

We can now show that ELMM has deterministic behavior under $\Rightarrow'$ by arguing that $\Rightarrow'$ is confluent. We will actually show a stronger property, known as **one-step confluence**, in which the transitive closure stars in the diamond diagram are removed; confluence easily follows from one-step confluence.

Suppose that $NE_1 \Rightarrow' NE_2$ and $NE_1 \Rightarrow' NE_3$. Any such ELMM transition is justified by a linear derivation (like the one depicted in Figure 3.8 on page 65) whose single leaf is an instance of the [arithop] rule. As in context-based semantics, we will call the LHS of the basic arithmetic transition justified by this [arithop] rule a redex. Call the redex reduced in $NE_1 \Rightarrow' NE_2$ the "red" redex and the one reduced in $NE_1 \Rightarrow' NE_3$ the "blue" redex. Either these are the same redex, in which case $NE_2 = NE_3$ trivially joins the paths, or the redexes are disjoint, i.e., one does not occur as a subexpression of another. (A redex has the form $(A\ N_1\ N_2)$, and the integer numerals N_1 and N_2 cannot contain another redex.) In the latter case, there must be an expression NE_4 that is a copy of NE_1 in which both the red and blue redexes have been reduced. Then $NE_2 \Rightarrow' NE_4$ by reducing the blue redex and $NE_3 \Rightarrow' NE_4$ by reducing the red redex. So NE_4 joins the diverging transitions.

We have shown that ELMM has deterministic behavior even when its operations are performed in a nondeterministic order. A similar approach can be used to show that ELM and EL have the same property (see Exercise 3.20). Confluence in these languages is fairly straightforward. It becomes much trickier in languages where redexes overlap or performing one redex can copy another.

We emphasize that confluence is a sufficient but not necessary condition for a nondeterministic transition relation to give rise to deterministic behavior. That is, confluence implies deterministic behavior, but deterministic behavior can exist without confluence. In general, many distinct final configurations might map to the same outcome.

Exercise 3.18 Suppose that in addition to replacing [prog-right] with [prog-right'] in the ELMM SOS, we add the rule [prog-both] introduced on page 65 to the SOS.

a. In this modified SOS, how many different transition paths lead from the expression (/ (+ 25 75) (* (- 7 4) (+ 5 6))) to the result 3?

b. Does the modified SOS still have deterministic behavior? Explain your answer.

Exercise 3.19 Consider extending ELMM with a construct (either NE_1 NE_2) that returns the result of evaluating either NE_1 or NE_2.

a. What are the possible behaviors of the following program?

    (elmm (* (- (either 1 2) (either 3 4)) (either 5 6)))

b. The informal specification of either given above is ambiguous. For example, must the expression (+ (either 1 (/ 2 0)) (either (% 3 0) 4)) return the result 5, or can it get stuck? The semantics of either can be defined either way. Give a formal specification for each interpretation of either that is consistent with the informal description.

Exercise 3.20

a. Show that the two transition relations (one for NumExp, one for BoolExp) in an EL
   SOS can be deterministic.

b. Suppose that both transition relations in an EL SOS allow operations to be performed
   in any order, so that they are nondeterministic. Argue that the behavior of EL
   programs is still deterministic.

3.6   Termination of PostFix Programs

The strong normalization property of PostFix is expressed by the following
theorem:

> **Theorem 3.2 (PostFix Termination)** *All* PostFix *programs are guar-*
> *anteed to terminate. That is, executing a* PostFix *program on any inputs*
> *always either returns a numeral or signals an error.*

This theorem is based on the following intuition: existing commands are consumed by execution, but no new commands are ever created, so the commands
must eventually "run out." This intuition is essentially correct, but an intuition
does not a proof make. After all, PostFix is complex enough to harbor a subtlety that invalidates the intuition. The `nget` command allows the duplication
of numerals — is this problematic with regard to termination? Executable sequences are moved to the stack, but their contents can later be prepended to the
command sequence. How can we be certain that this shuffling between command
sequence and stack doesn't go on forever? And how do we deal with the fact
that executable sequences can be arbitrarily nested? In fact, the termination
theorem can fail to hold if PostFix is extended with new commands, such as a
`dup` command that duplicates the top stack value (see Section 3.8 for details).

These questions indicate the need for a more convincing argument that termination is guaranteed. This is the kind of situation in which formal semantics
comes in handy. Below we present a proof for termination based on the SOS for
PostFix.

3.6.1   Energy

Associate with each PostFix configuration a natural number called its *energy*
(so called to suggest the potential energy of a dynamical system). By considering
each rewrite rule of the semantics in turn, we will prove that the energy strictly
decreases with each transition. The energy of an initial configuration must then

be an upper bound on the length of any path of transitions leading from the initial configuration. Since the initial energy is finite, there can be no unbounded transition sequences from the initial configuration, so the execution of a program must terminate.

The energy of a configuration is defined by the following energy functions:

$$\text{E}_{config}[\![\langle Q,\, S \rangle]\!] \;=\; \text{E}_{seq}[\![Q]\!] + \text{E}_{stack}[\![S]\!] \tag{3.1}$$

$$\text{E}_{seq}[\![\,[\,]\,\text{Command}]\!] \;=\; 0 \tag{3.2}$$

$$\text{E}_{seq}[\![C \,.\, Q]\!] \;=\; 1 + \text{E}_{com}[\![C]\!] + \text{E}_{seq}[\![Q]\!] \tag{3.3}$$

$$\text{E}_{stack}[\![\,[\,]\,\text{Value}]\!] \;=\; 0 \tag{3.4}$$

$$\text{E}_{stack}[\![V \,.\, S]\!] \;=\; \text{E}_{com}[\![V]\!] + \text{E}_{stack}[\![S]\!] \tag{3.5}$$

$$\text{E}_{com}[\![(Q)]\!] \;=\; \text{E}_{seq}[\![Q]\!] \tag{3.6}$$

$$\text{E}_{com}[\![C]\!] \;=\; 1, \quad C \text{ not an executable sequence.} \tag{3.7}$$

These definitions embody the following intuitions:

- The energy of a configuration, sequence, or stack is greater than or equal to the sum of the energy of its components.

- Executing a command consumes at least one unit of energy (the 1 that appears in 3.3). This is true even for commands that are transferred from the code component to the stack component (i.e., numerals and executable sequences); such commands are worth one more unit of energy in the command sequence than on the stack.[8]

- Since the commands in an executable sequence may eventually be executed, an executable sequence on the stack must have at least as much energy as its component command sequence. This is the essence of 3.6, where $\text{E}_{com}[\![(Q)]\!]$ is interpreted as the energy of a command sequence on the stack (by 3.5).

The following lemmas are handy for reasoning about the energy of sequences:

$$\text{E}_{com}[\![C]\!] \;\geq\; 0 \tag{3.8}$$

$$\text{E}_{seq}[\![Q_1 \,@\, Q_2]\!] \;=\; \text{E}_{seq}[\![Q_1]\!] + \text{E}_{seq}[\![Q_2]\!] \tag{3.9}$$

These can be derived from the energy definitions above. Their derivations are left as an exercise.

Equipped with the energy definitions and lemmas 3.8 and 3.9, we are ready to prove the POSTFIX Termination Theorem.

---

[8]The invocation $\text{E}_{com}[\![V]\!]$ that appears in 3.5 may seem questionable because $\text{E}_{com}[\![\,]\!]$ should be called on elements of Command, not elements of Value. But since every stack value is also a command, the invocation is well defined.

3.6.2   The Proof of Termination

Proof: We show that every transition reduces the energy of a configuration. Recall that every transition in an SOS has a proof in terms of the rewrite rules. In the case of POSTFIX, where all the rules are axioms, the proof is trivial: every POSTFIX transition is justified by one rewrite axiom. To prove a property about POSTFIX transitions, we just need to show that it holds for each rewrite axiom in the SOS. Here's the case analysis for the energy reduction property:

- [num]: $\langle N \, . \, Q, \, S \rangle \Rightarrow \langle Q, \, N \, . \, S \rangle$

$$
\begin{aligned}
\mathrm{E}_{config}&[\![\langle N \, . \, Q, \, S \rangle]\!] \\
&= \; \mathrm{E}_{seq}[\![N \, . \, Q]\!] + \mathrm{E}_{stack}[\![S]\!] & \text{by 3.1} \\
&= \; 1 + \mathrm{E}_{com}[\![N]\!] + \mathrm{E}_{seq}[\![Q]\!] + \mathrm{E}_{stack}[\![S]\!] & \text{by 3.3} \\
&= \; 1 + \mathrm{E}_{seq}[\![Q]\!] + \mathrm{E}_{stack}[\![N \, . \, S]\!] & \text{by 3.5} \\
&= \; 1 + \mathrm{E}_{config}[\![\langle Q, \, N \, . \, S \rangle]\!] & \text{by 3.1}
\end{aligned}
$$

The LHS has one more unit of energy than the RHS, so moving a numeral to the stack reduces the configuration energy by one unit.

- [seq]: $\langle (Q_{exec}) \, . \, Q_{rest}, \, S \rangle \Rightarrow \langle Q_{rest}, \, (Q_{exec}) \, . \, S \rangle$

Moving an executable sequence to the stack also consumes one energy unit by exactly the same argument as for [num].

- [pop]: $\langle \text{pop} \, . \, Q, \, V_{top} \, . \, S \rangle \Rightarrow \langle Q, \, S \rangle$

Popping V_{top} off a stack takes at least two energy units:

$$
\begin{aligned}
\mathrm{E}_{config}&[\![\langle \text{pop} \, . \, Q, \, V_{top} \, . \, S \rangle]\!] \\
&= \; \mathrm{E}_{seq}[\![\text{pop} \, . \, Q]\!] + \mathrm{E}_{stack}[\![V_{top} \, . \, S]\!] & \text{by 3.1} \\
&= \; 1 + \mathrm{E}_{com}[\![\text{pop}]\!] + \mathrm{E}_{seq}[\![Q]\!] + \mathrm{E}_{com}[\![V_{top}]\!] + \mathrm{E}_{stack}[\![S]\!] & \text{by 3.3 and 3.5} \\
&= \; 2 + \mathrm{E}_{com}[\![V_{top}]\!] + \mathrm{E}_{seq}[\![Q]\!] + \mathrm{E}_{stack}[\![S]\!] & \text{by 3.7} \\
&\geq \; 2 + \mathrm{E}_{config}[\![\langle Q, \, S \rangle]\!] & \text{by 3.1 and 3.8}
\end{aligned}
$$

- [swap]: $\langle \text{swap} \, . \, Q, \, V_1 \, . \, V_2 \, . \, S \rangle \Rightarrow \langle Q, \, V_2 \, . \, V_1 \, . \, S \rangle$

Swapping the top two elements of a stack consumes two energy units:

$$
\begin{aligned}
\mathrm{E}_{config}&[\![\langle \text{swap} \, . \, Q, \, V_1 \, . \, V_2 \, . \, S \rangle]\!] \\
&= \; \mathrm{E}_{seq}[\![\text{swap} \, . \, Q]\!] + \mathrm{E}_{stack}[\![V_1 \, . \, V_2 \, . \, S]\!] & \text{by 3.1} \\
&= \; 1 + \mathrm{E}_{com}[\![\text{swap}]\!] + \mathrm{E}_{seq}[\![Q]\!] \\
&\quad\; + \mathrm{E}_{com}[\![V_1]\!] + \mathrm{E}_{com}[\![V_2]\!] + \mathrm{E}_{stack}[\![S]\!] & \text{by 3.3 and 3.5} \\
&= \; 2 + \mathrm{E}_{seq}[\![Q]\!] + \mathrm{E}_{stack}[\![V_2 \, . \, V_1 \, . \, S]\!] & \text{by 3.7 and 3.5} \\
&= \; 2 + \mathrm{E}_{config}[\![\langle Q, \, V_2 \, . \, V_1 \, . \, S \rangle]\!] & \text{by 3.1}
\end{aligned}
$$

- *[execute]:* $\langle \texttt{exec} . Q_{rest}, (Q_{exec}) . S \rangle \Rightarrow \langle Q_{exec} @ Q_{rest}, S \rangle$

  Executing the $\texttt{exec}$ command consumes two energy units:

$$
\begin{aligned}
&\mathrm{E}_{config}[\![\langle \texttt{exec} . Q_{rest}, (Q_{exec}) . S \rangle]\!] \\
&= \ \mathrm{E}_{seq}[\![\texttt{exec} . Q_{rest}]\!] + \mathrm{E}_{stack}[\![(Q_{exec}) . S]\!] && \text{by 3.1} \\
&= \ 1 + \mathrm{E}_{com}[\![\texttt{exec}]\!] + \mathrm{E}_{seq}[\![Q_{rest}]\!] && \\
&\quad + \ \mathrm{E}_{com}[\![(Q_{exec})]\!] + \mathrm{E}_{stack}[\![S]\!] && \text{by 3.3 and 3.5} \\
&= \ 2 + \mathrm{E}_{seq}[\![Q_{exec}]\!] + \mathrm{E}_{seq}[\![Q_{rest}]\!] + \mathrm{E}_{stack}[\![S]\!] && \text{by 3.6 and 3.7} \\
&= \ 2 + \mathrm{E}_{seq}[\![Q_{exec} @ Q_{rest}]\!] + \mathrm{E}_{stack}[\![S]\!] && \text{by 3.9} \\
&= \ 2 + \mathrm{E}_{config}[\![\langle Q_{exec} @ Q_{rest}, S \rangle]\!] && \text{by 3.1}
\end{aligned}
$$

- *[nget], [arithop], [relop-true], [relop-false], [sel-true], [sel-false]:* These cases are similar to those above and are left as exercises for the reader. $\diamond$

The approach of defining a natural number function that decreases on every iteration of a process is a common technique for proving termination. However, inventing the function can sometimes be tricky. In the case of POSTFIX, we have to get the relative weights of components just right to handle movements between the program and stack.

The termination proof presented above is rather complex. The difficulty is not inherent to POSTFIX, but is due to the particular way we have chosen to formulate its semantics. There are alternative formulations in which the termination proof is simpler (see Exercise 3.25 on page 89).

Exercise 3.21 Show that lemmas 3.8 and 3.9 hold.

Exercise 3.22 Complete the proof of the POSTFIX termination theorem by showing that the following axioms reduce configuration energy: *[nget]*, *[arithop]*, *[relop-true]*, *[relop-false]*, *[sel-true]*, *[sel-false]*.

Exercise 3.23 Bud "eagle-eye" Lojack notices that Definitions 3.2 and 3.4 do not appear as the justification for any steps in the POSTFIX Termination Theorem. He reasons that these definitions are arbitrary, so he could just as well use the following definitions instead:

$$
\begin{aligned}
\mathrm{E}_{seq}[\![[\,]]\!] &= 17 &&(\ 3.2') \\
\mathrm{E}_{stack}[\![[\,]]\!] &= 23 &&(\ 3.4')
\end{aligned}
$$

Is Bud correct? Explain your answer.

Exercise 3.24 Prove the termination property of POSTFIX based on the SOS for POSTFIX2 from Exercise 3.7.

a. Define an appropriate energy function on configurations in the alternative SOS.

b. Show that each transition in the alternative SOS reduces energy.

3.6.3   Structural Induction

The above proof is based on a POSTFIX SOS that uses only axioms. But what if the SOS contained progress rules, like [exec-prog] from Figure 3.10 in Section 3.2.5? How do we prove a property like reduction in configuration energy when progress rules are involved?

Here's where we can take advantage of the fact that every transition of an SOS must be justified by a finite proof tree based on the rewrite rules. Recall that there are two types of nodes in the proof tree: the leaves, which correspond to axioms, and the intermediate nodes, which correspond to progress rules. Suppose we can show that

- the property holds at each leaf — i.e., it is true for (the consequent of) every axiom; and

- the property holds at each intermediate node — i.e., for every progress rule, if the property holds for all of the antecedents, then it also holds for the consequent.

Then, by induction on the height of its proof tree, the property must hold for each transition specified by the rewrite rules. This method for proving a property based on the structure of a tree (in this case the proof tree of a transition relation) is called **structural induction**.

As an example of a proof by structural induction, we consider how the previous proof of the termination property for POSTFIX would be modified for an SOS that uses the [exec-done] and [exec-prog] rules in place of the [exec] rule. It is straightforward to show that the [exec-done] axiom reduces configuration energy; this is left as an exercise for the reader. To show that the [exec-prog] rule satisfies the property, we must show that *if* its single antecedent transition reduces configuration energy, *then* its consequent transition reduces configuration energy as well.

Recall that the [exec-prog] rule has the form:

$$\frac{\langle Q_{exec}, S \rangle \Rightarrow \langle Q'_{exec}, S' \rangle}{\langle \texttt{exec} . Q_{rest}, (Q_{exec}) . S \rangle \Rightarrow \langle \texttt{exec} . Q_{rest}, (Q'_{exec}) . S' \rangle} \qquad \text{[exec-prog]}$$

We assume that the antecedent transition,

$$\langle Q_{exec}, S \rangle \Rightarrow \langle Q'_{exec}, S' \rangle$$

reduces configuration energy, so that the following inequality holds:

$$\mathrm{E}_{config}[\![\langle Q_{exec}, S \rangle]\!] > \mathrm{E}_{config}[\![\langle Q'_{exec}, S' \rangle]\!]$$

Then we show that the consequent transition also reduces configuration energy:

$$
\begin{aligned}
& \mathrm{E}_{config}[\![\langle \mathtt{exec} . \, Q_{rest}, \, (Q_{exec}) . \, S \rangle]\!] \\
&= \mathrm{E}_{seq}[\![\mathtt{exec} . \, Q_{rest}]\!] + \mathrm{E}_{stack}[\![(Q_{exec}) . \, S]\!] && \text{by 3.1} \\
&= \mathrm{E}_{seq}[\![\mathtt{exec} . \, Q_{rest}]\!] + \mathrm{E}_{com}[\![(Q_{exec})]\!] + \mathrm{E}_{stack}[\![S]\!] && \text{by 3.5} \\
&= \mathrm{E}_{seq}[\![\mathtt{exec} . \, Q_{rest}]\!] + \mathrm{E}_{seq}[\![Q_{exec}]\!] + \mathrm{E}_{stack}[\![S]\!] && \text{by 3.6} \\
&= \mathrm{E}_{seq}[\![\mathtt{exec} . \, Q_{rest}]\!] + \mathrm{E}_{config}[\![\langle Q_{exec}, \, S \rangle]\!] && \text{by 3.1} \\
&> \mathrm{E}_{seq}[\![\mathtt{exec} . \, Q_{rest}]\!] + \mathrm{E}_{config}[\![\langle Q'_{exec}, \, S' \rangle]\!] && \text{by assumption} \\
&= \mathrm{E}_{seq}[\![\mathtt{exec} . \, Q_{rest}]\!] + \mathrm{E}_{seq}[\![Q'_{exec}]\!] + \mathrm{E}_{stack}[\![S']\!] && \text{by 3.1} \\
&= \mathrm{E}_{seq}[\![\mathtt{exec} . \, Q_{rest}]\!] + \mathrm{E}_{com}[\![(Q'_{exec})]\!] + \mathrm{E}_{stack}[\![S']\!] && \text{by 3.6} \\
&= \mathrm{E}_{seq}[\![\mathtt{exec} . \, Q_{rest}]\!] + \mathrm{E}_{stack}[\![(Q'_{exec}) . \, S']\!] && \text{by 3.5} \\
&= \mathrm{E}_{config}[\![\langle \mathtt{exec} . \, Q_{rest}, \, (Q'_{exec}) . \, S' \rangle]\!] && \text{by 3.1}
\end{aligned}
$$

The $>$ appearing in the derivation sequence guarantees that the energy specified by the first line is strictly greater than the energy specified by the last line. This completes the proof that the [exec-prog] rule reduces configuration energy. Together with the proofs that the axioms reduce configuration energy, this provides an alternative proof of POSTFIX's termination property.

Exercise 3.25 Prove the termination property of POSTFIX based on the alternative POSTFIX SOS suggested in Exercise 3.12 on page 70:

a. Define an appropriate energy function on configurations in the alternative SOS.

b. Show that each transition in the alternative SOS reduces energy.

c. The termination proof for the alternative semantics should be more straightforward than the termination proofs in the text and in Exercise 3.24. What characteristic(s) of the alternative SOS simplify the proof? Does this mean the alternative SOS is a "better" one?

Exercise 3.26 Prove that the rewrite rules [exec-prog] and [exec-done] presented in the text specify the same behavior as the [execute] rule. That is, show that for any configuration cf of the form $\langle \mathtt{exec} . \, Q, \, S \rangle$, both sets of rules eventually rewrite cf into either (1) a stuck state or (2) the same configuration.

Exercise 3.27 As in POSTFIX, every program in the EL language terminates. Prove this fact based on an operational semantics for EL (see Exercise 3.10 on page 67).

3.7 Safe PostFix Transformations

3.7.1 Observational Equivalence

One of the most important aspects of reasoning about programs is knowing when it is safe to replace one program phrase by another. Two phrases are said to be

observationally equivalent (or **behaviorally equivalent**) if an instance of one can be replaced by the other in any program without changing the behavior of the program.

Observational equivalence is important because it is the basis for a wide range of program transformation techniques. It is often possible to improve a pragmatic aspect of a program by replacing a phrase by one that is equivalent but more efficient. For example, we expect that the POSTFIX sequence $[1, \mathtt{add}, 2, \mathtt{add}]$ can always be replaced by $[3, \mathtt{add}]$ without changing the behavior of the surrounding program. The latter may be more desirable in practice because it performs fewer additions.

A series of simple transformations can sometimes lead to dramatic improvements in performance. Consider the following three transformations on POSTFIX command sequences, just three of the many safe POSTFIX transformations:

Before	After	Name
$[V_1, V_2, \mathtt{swap}]$	$[V_2, V_1]$	[swap-trans]
$[(Q), \mathtt{exec}]$	Q	[exec-trans]
$[N_1, N_2, A]$	$[N_{ans}]$ where $N_{ans} = (calculate\ A\ N_1\ N_2)$	[arith-trans]

Applying these to our example of a POSTFIX command sequence yields the following sequence of simplifications:

```
((2 (3 mul add) exec) 1 swap exec sub)
```
$\xrightarrow{simp}$ `((2 3 mul add) 1 swap exec sub)`   [exec-trans]
$\xrightarrow{simp}$ `((6 add) 1 swap exec sub)`   [arith-trans]
$\xrightarrow{simp}$ `(1 (6 add) exec sub)`   [swap-trans]
$\xrightarrow{simp}$ `(1 6 add sub)`   [exec-trans]
$\xrightarrow{simp}$ `(7 sub)`   [arith-trans]

Thus, the original command sequence is a "subtract 7" subroutine. The transformations essentially perform operations at compile time that otherwise would be performed at run time.

It is often tricky to determine whether two phrases are observationally equivalent. For example, at first glance it might seem that the POSTFIX sequence [swap, swap] can always be replaced by the empty sequence []. While this transformation is valid in many situations, these two sequences are not observationally equivalent because they behave differently when the stack contains fewer than two elements. For instance, the POSTFIX program (postfix 0 1) returns 1 as a final answer, but the program (postfix 0 1 swap swap) generates an error. Two phrases are observationally equivalent only if they are interchangeable in *all* programs.

$\mathbb{P} \in$ PostfixProgContext ::= (postfix $N_{numargs}$ $\mathbb{Q}$) [ProgramContext]

$\mathbb{Q} \in$ PostfixSequenceContext ::= $\square$ [Hole]

        | Q @ $\mathbb{Q}$ [Prefix]

        | $\mathbb{Q}$ @ Q [Suffix]

        | $[(\mathbb{Q})]$ [Nesting]

Figure 3.19 Definition of POSTFIX contexts.

Observational equivalence can be formalized in terms of the notions of **behavior** and **context** presented earlier. Recall that the behavior of a program (see Section 3.2.1) is specified by a function *beh* that maps a program and its inputs to a set of possible outcomes:

$$beh : (\text{Prog} \times \text{Inputs}) \rightarrow \mathcal{P}(\text{Outcome})$$

The behavior is deterministic when the resulting set is guaranteed to be a singleton. A program context is a program with a hole in it (see Section 3.2.6).

Definition 3.3 (Observational Equivalence) *Suppose that $\mathbb{P}$ ranges over program contexts and H ranges over the kinds of phrases that fill the holes in program contexts. Then H_1 and H_2 are defined to be observationally equivalent (written $H_1 =_{obs} H_2$) if and only if for all program contexts $\mathbb{P}$ and all inputs I, beh $\langle \mathbb{P}\{H_1\}, I \rangle = beh \langle \mathbb{P}\{H_2\}, I \rangle$.*

We will consider POSTFIX as an example. An appropriate notion of program contexts for POSTFIX is defined in Figure 3.19. A command sequence context $\mathbb{Q}$ is one that can be filled with a sequence of commands to yield another sequence of commands. For example, if $\mathbb{Q} = [(2 \text{ mul}), 3] @ \square @ [\text{exec}]$, then $\mathbb{Q}\{[4, \text{add}, \text{swap}]\} = [(2 \text{ mul}), 3, 4, \text{add}, \text{swap}, \text{exec}]$. The [*Prefix*] and [*Suffix*] productions allow the hole to be surrounded by arbitrary command sequences, while the [*Nesting*] production allows the hole to be nested within an executable sequence command. (The notation $[(\mathbb{Q})]$ designates a sequence containing a single element. That element is an executable sequence that contains a single hole.) Because of the presence of @, the grammar for PostfixSequenceContext is ambiguous, but that will not affect our presentation, since filling the hole for any parsing of a sequence context yields exactly the same sequence.

The possible outcomes of a program must be carefully defined to lead to a satisfactory notion of observational equivalence. The outcomes for POSTFIX defined in Section 3.2.1 are fine, but small changes can sometimes lead to surprising results. For example, suppose we allow POSTFIX programs to return the top value

of a nonempty stack, even if the top value is an executable sequence. If we can
observe the structure of a returned executable sequence, then this change invalidates all nontrivial program transformations! To see why, take any two sequences
we expect to be equivalent (say, $[1, \mathtt{add}, 2, \mathtt{add}]$ and $[3, \mathtt{add}]$) and plug them into
the context $(\mathtt{postfix}\ 0\ (\square))$. In the modified semantics, the two outcomes are
the executable sequences $(\mathtt{1\ add\ 2\ add})$ and $(\mathtt{3\ add})$, which are clearly not the
same, and so the two sequences are not observationally equivalent.

The problem is that the modified SOS makes distinctions between executable
sequence outcomes that are too fine-grained for our purposes. We can fix the
problem by instead adopting a coarser-grained notion of behavior in which there
is no observable difference between outcomes that are executable sequences. For
example, the outcome in this case could be the token $\mathtt{executable}$, indicating
that the outcome *is* an executable sequence without divulging *which* particular
executable sequence it is. With this change, all the expected program transformations become valid again.

3.7.2   Transform Equivalence

It is possible to show the observational equivalence of two particular POSTFIX
command sequences according to the definition on page 91. However, we will follow another route. First, we will develop an easier-to-prove notion of equivalence
for POSTFIX sequences called **transform equivalence**. Then, after giving an
example of transform equivalence, we will prove a theorem that transform equivalence implies observational equivalence for POSTFIX programs. This approach
has the advantage that the structural induction proof on contexts needed to show
observational equivalence need be proved only once (for the theorem) rather than
for every pair of POSTFIX command sequences.

Transform equivalence is based on the intuition that POSTFIX command sequences can be viewed as a means of transforming one stack to another. Informally, transform equivalence is defined as follows:

> **Definition 3.4 (Transform Equivalence)** *Two* POSTFIX *command se-
> quences are* **transform equivalent** *if they always transform equivalent
> input stacks to equivalent output stacks.*

This definition is informal in that it doesn't say how command sequences can be
viewed as transformers or pin down what it means for two stacks to be equivalent.
We will now flesh out these notions.

Our approach to transform equivalence depends on a notion of the last stack
reached when all commands are executed in a POSTFIX program. We model

the possibility of executions stuck at a command by introducing a StackAnswer domain that contains the usual POSTFIX stacks (Figure 3.3 on page 53) along with a distinguished error stack element SA_{error}:

$$\text{ErrorStack} = \{\texttt{errorStack}\}$$
$$SA \in \text{StackAnswer} = \text{Stack} + \text{ErrorStack}$$

$$SA_{error} : \text{StackAnswer} = (\text{ErrorStack} \rightarrowtail \text{StackAnswer } \texttt{errorStack})$$

We now define a *lastStack* function that returns the last stack reached for a given initial command sequence and stack when all commands are executed:

$$lastStack : \text{CommandSeq} \rightarrow \text{Stack} \rightarrow \text{StackAnswer}$$

$$(lastStack \; Q \; S) = \begin{cases} (\text{Stack} \rightarrowtail \text{StackAnswer } S') & \text{if } \langle Q, S \rangle \overset{*}{\Rightarrow} \langle [\,], S' \rangle \\ SA_{error} & \text{otherwise} \end{cases}$$

The *lastStack* function is well defined because POSTFIX is deterministic. The longest transition path starting with an initial configuration $\langle Q, S \rangle$ ends in a unique configuration that either has an empty command sequence or doesn't. Because it handles the nonempty command sequence case by returning SA_{error}, *lastStack* is also a total function. For example, $(lastStack \; [\texttt{add}, \texttt{mul}] \; [4, 3, 2, 1])$ = $[14, 1]$ and $(lastStack \; [\texttt{add}, \texttt{exec}] \; [4, 3, 2, 1]) = SA_{error}$. It easily follows from the definition of *lastStack* that if $\langle Q, S \rangle \Rightarrow \langle Q', S' \rangle$ then $(lastStack \; Q \; S) = (lastStack \; Q' \; S')$. Note that a stack returned by *lastStack* may be empty or have an empty command sequence at the top, so it may not be an element of FinalStack (defined in Figure 3.3 on page 53).

The simplest notion of "stack equivalence" is that two stacks are equivalent if they are identical sequences of values. But this notion has problems similar to those discussed above with regard to outcomes in the context of observational equivalence. For example, suppose we are able to show that (1 add 2 add) and (3 add) are transform equivalent. Then we'd also like the transform equivalence of ((1 add 2 add)) and ((3 add)) to follow as a corollary. But given identical input stacks, these two sequences do *not* yield identical output stacks — the top values of the output stacks are different executable sequences!

To finesse this problem, we need a notion of stack equivalence that treats two executable sequence elements as being the same if they are transform equivalent. The recursive nature of these notions prompts us to define *four* mutually recursive equivalence relations that formalize this approach: one between command sequences (transform equivalence), one between stack answers (stack-answer equivalence), one between stacks (stack equivalence), and one between stack elements (value equivalence).

1. Command sequences Q_1 and Q_2 are said to be **transform equivalent** (written $Q_1 \sim_Q Q_2$) if, for all stack-equivalent stacks S_1 and S_2, it is the case that ($lastStack$ Q_1 S_1) is stack-answer equivalent to ($lastStack$ Q_2 S_2).

2. Stack answers SA_1 and SA_2 are said to be **stack-answer equivalent** (written $SA_1 \sim_{SA} SA_2$) if

   - both SA_1 and SA_2 are the distinguished error stack, SA_{error}; or

   - $SA_1 = (\text{Stack} \rightarrowtail \text{StackAnswer } S_1)$, $SA_2 = (\text{Stack} \rightarrowtail \text{StackAnswer } S_2)$, and S_1 is stack equivalent to S_2.

3. Stacks S_1 and S_2 are **stack equivalent** (written $S_1 \sim_S S_2$) if they are equal-length sequences of values that are elementwise value equivalent. I.e., $S_1 = [V_1, \ldots, V_n]$, $S_2 = [V_1', \ldots, V_n']$, and $V_i \sim_V V_i'$ for all i such that $1 \leq i \leq n$. Equivalently, S_1 and S_2 are stack equivalent if

   - both S_1 and S_2 are the empty stack; or

   - $S_1 = V_1 . S_1'$, $S_2 = V_2 . S_2'$, $V_1 \sim_V V_2$, and $S_1' \sim_S S_2'$.

4. Stack elements V_1 and V_2 are **value equivalent** (written $V_1 \sim_V V_2$) if V_1 and V_2 are the same integer numeral (i.e., $V_1 = N = V_2$) or if V_1 and V_2 are executable sequences whose contents are transform equivalent (i.e., $V_1 = (Q_1)$, $V_2 = (Q_2)$, and $Q_1 \sim_Q Q_2$).

Despite the mutually recursive nature of these definitions, we claim that all four are well-defined equivalence relations as long as we choose the largest relations satisfying the descriptions.

Two POSTFIX command sequences can be proved transform equivalent by case analysis on the structure of input stacks. This is much easier than the case analysis on the structure of contexts that is implied by observational equivalence. Since (as we shall show below) observational equivalence follows from transform equivalence, transform equivalence is a practical technique for demonstrating observational equivalence.

As a simple example of transform equivalence, we show that $[1, \mathsf{add}, 2, \mathsf{add}]$ $\sim_Q [3, \mathsf{add}]$. Consider two stacks S_1 and S_2 such that $S_1 \sim_S S_2$. We proceed by case analysis on the structure of the stacks:

1. S_1 and S_2 are both $[\,]$, in which case

   $(lastStack\ [3, \mathsf{add}]\ [\,])$
   $= (lastStack\ [\mathsf{add}]\ [3])$
   $= SA_{error}$
   $= (lastStack\ [\mathsf{add}, 2, \mathsf{add}]\ [1])$
   $= (lastStack\ [1, \mathsf{add}, 2, \mathsf{add}]\ [\,])$

2. S_1 and S_2 are nonempty sequences whose heads are the same numeric literal and whose tails are stack equivalent. I.e., $S_1 = N \cdot S_1'$, $S_2 = N \cdot S_2'$, and $S_1' \sim_S S_2'$. We use the abbreviation $\overline{N_1 + N_2}$ for $(calculate\ +\ N_1\ N_2)$.

$(lastStack\ [3, \mathsf{add}]\ N \cdot S_1')$
$= (lastStack\ [\mathsf{add}]\ 3 \cdot N \cdot S_1')$
$= (lastStack\ []\ \overline{N+3} \cdot S_1')$
$= (Stack \rightarrowtail StackAnswer\ \overline{N+3} \cdot S_1')$
$\sim_{SA} (Stack \rightarrowtail StackAnswer\ \overline{N+3} \cdot S_2')$
$= (lastStack\ []\ \overline{N+3} \cdot S_2')$
$= (lastStack\ [\mathsf{add}]\ 2 \cdot \overline{N+1} \cdot S_2')$
$= (lastStack\ [2, \mathsf{add}]\ \overline{N+1} \cdot S_2')$
$= (lastStack\ [\mathsf{add}, 2, \mathsf{add}]\ 1 \cdot N \cdot S_2')$
$= (lastStack\ [1, \mathsf{add}, 2, \mathsf{add}]\ N \cdot S_2')$

3. S_1 and S_2 are nonempty sequences whose heads are transform-equivalent executable sequences and whose tails are stack equivalent. I.e., $S_1 = Q_1 \cdot S_1'$, $S_2 = Q_2 \cdot S_2'$, $Q_1 \sim_Q Q_2$, and $S_1' \sim_S S_2'$.

$(lastStack\ [3, \mathsf{add}]\ Q_1 \cdot S_1')$
$= (lastStack\ [\mathsf{add}]\ 3 \cdot Q_1 \cdot S_1')$
$= SA_{error}$
$= (lastStack\ [\mathsf{add}, 2, \mathsf{add}]\ 1 \cdot Q_2 \cdot S_2')$
$= (lastStack\ [1, \mathsf{add}, 2, \mathsf{add}]\ Q_2 \cdot S_2')$

In all three cases,

$$(lastStack\ [1, \mathsf{add}, 2, \mathsf{add}]\ S_1) \sim_{SA} (lastStack\ [3, \mathsf{add}]\ S_2)$$

so the transform equivalence of the sequences follows by definition of $\sim_Q$.

We emphasize that stacks can be equivalent without being identical. For instance, given the result of the above example, it is easy to construct two stacks that are stack equivalent but not identical:

$$[(1\ \mathsf{add}\ 2\ \mathsf{add}), 5] \sim_S [(3\ \mathsf{add}), 5]$$

Intuitively, these stacks are equivalent because they cannot be distinguished by any POSTFIX command sequence. Any such sequence must either ignore both sequence elements (e.g., [pop]), attempt an illegal operation on both sequence elements (e.g., [mul]), or execute both sequence elements on equivalent stacks (via exec). But because the sequence elements are transform equivalent, executing them cannot distinguish them.

3.7.3   Transform Equivalence Implies Observational Equivalence

We wrap up the discussion of observational equivalence by showing that transform equivalence of POSTFIX command sequences implies observational equivalence. This result is useful because it is generally easier to show that two command sequences are transform equivalent than to construct a proof based directly on the definition of observational equivalence.

The fact that transform equivalence implies observational equivalence can be explained informally as follows. Every POSTFIX program context has a top-level command-sequence context with two parts: the commands performed before the hole and the commands performed after the hole. The commands before the hole transform the initial stack into S_{pre}. Suppose the hole is filled by one of two executable sequences, Q_1 and Q_2, that are transform equivalent. Then the stacks S_{post1} and S_{post2} that result from executing these sequences, respectively, on S_{pre} must be stack equivalent. The commands performed after the hole must transform S_{post1} and S_{post2} into stack-equivalent stacks S_{final1} and S_{final2}. Since behavior depends only on the equivalence class of the final stack, it is impossible to construct a context that distinguishes Q_1 and Q_2. Therefore, they are observationally equivalent.

We will need the following lemma for the formal argument:

Lemma 3.5 *For any command-sequence context $\mathbb{Q}$, $Q_1 \sim_Q Q_2$ implies $\mathbb{Q}\{Q_1\} \sim_Q \mathbb{Q}\{Q_2\}$.*

Proof of Lemma 3.5:   We will employ the following properties of transform equivalence, which are left as exercises for the reader:

$$Q_1 \sim_Q Q_1' \text{ and } Q_2 \sim_Q Q_2' \quad \text{implies} \quad Q_1 @ Q_2 \sim_Q Q_1' @ Q_2' \qquad (3.10)$$

$$Q_1 \sim_Q Q_2 \quad \text{implies} \quad [(Q_1)] \sim_Q [(Q_2)] \qquad (3.11)$$

Property 3.11 is tricky to read; it says that if Q_1 and Q_2 are transform equivalent, then the singleton command sequences containing the exectuable sequences made up of the commands of Q_1 and Q_2 are also transform equivalent.

We proceed by structural induction on the grammar of the PostfixSequence-Context domain (Figure 3.19 on page 91):

- (Base case) For sequence contexts of the form $\Box$, $Q_1 \sim_Q Q_2$ trivially implies $\Box\{Q_1\} \sim_Q \Box\{Q_2\}$.

- (Induction cases) For each of the compound sequence contexts — $Q @ \mathbb{Q}$, $\mathbb{Q} @ Q$, $[(\mathbb{Q})]$ — assume that $Q_1 \sim_Q Q_2$ implies $\mathbb{Q}\{Q_1\} \sim_Q \mathbb{Q}\{Q_2\}$ for any $\mathbb{Q}$.

  - For sequence contexts of the form $Q @ \mathbb{Q}$,

    $Q_1 \sim_Q Q_2$
    | implies | $\mathbb{Q}\{Q_1\} \sim_Q \mathbb{Q}\{Q_2\}$ | by assumption |
    | implies | $Q @ (\mathbb{Q}\{Q_1\}) \sim_Q Q @ (\mathbb{Q}\{Q_2\})$ | by reflexivity of $\sim_Q$ and 3.10 |
    | implies | $(Q @ \mathbb{Q})\{Q_1\} \sim_Q (Q @ \mathbb{Q})\{Q_2\}$ | by definition of $\mathbb{Q}$ |

  - Sequence contexts of the form $\mathbb{Q} @ Q$ are handled similarly to those of the form $Q @ \mathbb{Q}$.

  - For sequence contexts of the form $[(\mathbb{Q})]$,

    $Q_1 \sim_Q Q_2$
    | implies | $\mathbb{Q}\{Q_1\} \sim_Q \mathbb{Q}\{Q_2\}$ | by assumption |
    | implies | $[(\mathbb{Q}\{Q_1\})] \sim_Q [(\mathbb{Q}\{Q_2\})]$ | by 3.11 |
    | implies | $[(\mathbb{Q})]\{Q_1\} \sim_Q [(\mathbb{Q})]\{Q_2\}$ | by definition of $\mathbb{Q}$ | $\diamond$

Now we are ready to present a formal proof that transform equivalence implies observational equivalence.

Theorem 3.6 (PostFix Transform Equivalence)
$Q_1 \sim_Q Q_2$ *implies* $Q_1 =_{obs} Q_2$.

Proof of Theorem 3.6:   Assume that $Q_1 \sim_Q Q_2$. By the definition of $Q_1 =_{obs} Q_2$, we need to show that for any POSTFIX program context of the form (`postfix` N_n $\mathbb{Q}$) and any integer numeral argument sequence N^*_{args}

$$beh_{det} \langle (\text{postfix } N_n \ \mathbb{Q}\{Q_1\}), N^*_{args} \rangle = beh_{det} \langle (\text{postfix } N_n \ \mathbb{Q}\{Q_2\}), N^*_{args} \rangle$$

Here we use beh_{det} (defined for a generic SOS on page 51) because we know that POSTFIX has a deterministic behavior function.

By Lemma 3.5, $Q_1 \sim_Q Q_2$ implies $\mathbb{Q}\{Q_1\} \sim_Q \mathbb{Q}\{Q_2\}$. Let S_{init} be a stack consisting of the elements of N^*_{args}. Then by the definition of $\sim_Q$, we have

$$(lastStack \ \mathbb{Q}\{Q_1\} \ S_{init}) \sim_{SA} (lastStack \ \mathbb{Q}\{Q_2\} \ S_{init})$$

By the definition of $lastStack$ and $\sim_{SA}$, there are two cases:

1. $\langle \mathbb{Q}\{Q_1\}, S_{init} \rangle \overset{*}{\Rightarrow} cf_1$ and $\langle \mathbb{Q}\{Q_2\}, S_{init} \rangle \overset{*}{\Rightarrow} cf_2$, where both cf_1 and cf_2 are irreducible POSTFIX configurations with a nonempty command sequence component. In this case, both executions are stuck, so

   $beh_{det} \langle (\text{postfix } N_n \ \mathbb{Q}\{Q_1\}), N^*_{args} \rangle$
   $= \text{stuck}$
   $= beh_{det} \langle (\text{postfix } N_n \ \mathbb{Q}\{Q_2\}), N^*_{args} \rangle$

2. $\langle \mathbb{Q}\{Q_1\}, S_{init}\rangle \stackrel{*}{\Rightarrow} \langle [\,], S_1\rangle$, $\langle \mathbb{Q}\{Q_2\}, S_{init}\rangle \stackrel{*}{\Rightarrow} \langle [\,], S_2\rangle$, and $S_1 \sim_S S_2$. In this case, there are two subcases:

   (a) S_1 and S_2 are both nonempty stacks with the same integer numeral N on top. In this subcase,

$$beh_{det} \;\langle(\texttt{postfix } N_n \;\; \mathbb{Q}\{Q_1\}), N^*_{args}\rangle$$
$$= (\text{IntLit} \rightarrowtail \text{Outcome } N)$$
$$= beh_{det} \;\langle(\texttt{postfix } N_n \;\; \mathbb{Q}\{Q_2\}), N^*_{args}\rangle$$

   (b) S_1 and S_2 either (1) are both the empty stack or (2) are both nonempty stacks with executable sequences on top. In this subcase,

$$beh_{det} \;\langle(\texttt{postfix } N_n \;\; \mathbb{Q}\{Q_1\}), N^*_{args}\rangle$$
$$= \texttt{stuck}$$
$$= beh_{det} \;\langle(\texttt{postfix } N_n \;\; \mathbb{Q}\{Q_2\}), N^*_{args}\rangle \qquad\qquad \diamond$$

Exercise 3.28 For each of the following purported observational equivalences, either prove that the observational equivalence is valid (via transform equivalence), or give a counterexample to show that it is not.

a. $[N, \texttt{pop}] =_{obs} [\,]$

b. $[\texttt{add}, N, \texttt{add}] =_{obs} [N, \texttt{add}, \texttt{add}]$

c. $[N_1, N_2, A] =_{obs} [N_{ans}]$, where $N_{ans} = (calculate \; A \; N_1 \; N_2)$

d. $[(Q), \texttt{exec}] =_{obs} Q$

e. $[(Q), (Q), \texttt{sel}, \texttt{exec}] =_{obs} \texttt{pop} . Q$

f. $[N_1, (N_2 \; (Q_a) \; (Q_b) \; \texttt{sel exec}), (N_2 \; (Q_c) \; (Q_d) \; \texttt{sel exec}), \texttt{sel}, \texttt{exec}]$
   $=_{obs} [N_2, (N_1 \; (Q_a) \; (Q_c) \; \texttt{sel exec}), (N_1 \; (Q_b) \; (Q_d) \; \texttt{sel exec}), \texttt{sel}, \texttt{exec}]$

g. $[C_1, C_2, \texttt{swap}] =_{obs} [C_2, C_1]$

h. $[\texttt{swap}, \texttt{swap}, \texttt{swap}] =_{obs} [\texttt{swap}]$

Exercise 3.29 Prove Lemmas 3.10 and 3.11, which are used to show that transform equivalence implies operational equivalence.

Exercise 3.30 Transform equivalence ($\sim_Q$) is defined in terms of *lastStack*, where *lastStack* is defined on page 93. Below we consider two alternative definitions of *lastStack*.

$$lastStack_1 : \text{CommandSeq} \to \text{Stack} \to \text{StackAnswer}$$

$$(lastStack_1 \; Q \; S) = \begin{cases} (\text{Stack} \rightarrowtail \text{StackAnswer } S') & \text{if } \langle Q, S\rangle \stackrel{*}{\Rightarrow} \langle [\,], S'\rangle \\ & \text{and } S' \in \text{FinalStack} \\ SA_{error} & \text{otherwise} \end{cases}$$

$$lastStack_2 : \text{CommandSeq} \to \text{Stack} \to \text{StackAnswer}$$
$(lastStack_2 \; Q \; S) = (\text{Stack} \rightarrowtail \text{StackAnswer } S')$ if $\langle Q, S\rangle \stackrel{*}{\Rightarrow} \langle Q', S'\rangle \not\Rightarrow$
   (Recall that $cf \not\Rightarrow$ means that configuration cf is irreducible.)

a. Give an example of two sequences that are transform equivalent using the original definition of *lastStack* but not using *lastStack$_1$*.

b. Show that property (3.10) does not hold if transform equivalence is defined using *lastStack$_2$*.

Exercise 3.31

a. Modify the POSTFIX semantics in Figure 3.3 so that the outcome of a POSTFIX program whose final configuration has an executable sequence at the top is the token `executable`.

b. In your modified semantics, show that transform equivalence still implies observational equivalence.

Exercise 3.32 Prove the following composition theorem for observationally equivalent POSTFIX sequences:

$$Q_1 =_{obs} Q_1' \text{ and } Q_2 =_{obs} Q_2' \text{ implies } Q_1 @ Q_2 =_{obs} Q_1' @ Q_2'$$

Exercise 3.33 Which of the following transformations on EL numerical expressions are safe? Explain your answers. Be sure to consider stuck expressions like `(/ 1 0)`.

a. `(+ 1 2)` $\xrightarrow{simp}$ `3`

b. `(+ 0 NE)` $\xrightarrow{simp}$ `NE`

c. `(* 0 NE)` $\xrightarrow{simp}$ `0`

d. `(+ 1 (+ 2 NE))` $\xrightarrow{simp}$ `(+ 3 NE)`

e. `(+ NE NE)` $\xrightarrow{simp}$ `(* 2 NE)`

f. `(if (= N N) NE`$_1$` NE`$_2$`)` $\xrightarrow{simp}$ `NE`$_1$

g. `(if (= NE`$_1$` NE`$_1$`) NE`$_2$` NE`$_3$`)` $\xrightarrow{simp}$ `NE`$_2$

h. `(if BE NE NE)` $\xrightarrow{simp}$ `NE`

Exercise 3.34 Develop a notion of transform equivalence for EL that is powerful enough to formally prove that the transformations in Exercise 3.33 that you think are safe are really safe. You will need to design appropriate contexts for EL programs, numerical expressions, and boolean expressions.

Exercise 3.35 Given that transform equivalence implies observational equivalence in POSTFIX, it is natural to wonder whether the converse is true. That is, does the following implication hold?

$$Q_1 =_{obs} Q_2 \text{ implies } Q_1 \sim_Q Q_2$$

If so, prove it; if not, explain why.

Exercise 3.36 Consider the following $\mathcal{T}_\mathcal{P}$ function, which translates an ELMM program to a POSTFIX program:

$$\mathcal{T}_\mathcal{P} : \text{Prog}_{ELMM} \rightarrow \text{Prog}_{PostFix}$$
$$\mathcal{T}_\mathcal{P}[\![(\text{elmm } NE_{body})]\!] = (\text{postfix } 0 \ \mathcal{T}_{\mathcal{NE}}[\![NE_{body}]\!])$$

$$\mathcal{T}_{\mathcal{NE}} : \text{NumExp} \rightarrow \text{CommandSeq}$$
$$\mathcal{T}_{\mathcal{NE}}[\![N]\!] = [N]$$
$$\mathcal{T}_{\mathcal{NE}}[\![(A \ NE_1 \ NE_2)]\!] = \mathcal{T}_{\mathcal{NE}}[\![NE_1]\!] @ \mathcal{T}_{\mathcal{NE}}[\![NE_2]\!] @ [\mathcal{T}_\mathcal{A}[\![A]\!]]$$

$$\mathcal{T}_\mathcal{A} : \text{ArithmeticOperator}_{ELMM} \rightarrow \text{ArithmeticOperator}_{PostFix}$$
$$\mathcal{T}_\mathcal{A}[\![+]\!] = \text{add}$$
$$\mathcal{T}_\mathcal{A}[\![-]\!] = \text{sub}, \textit{etc.}$$

a. What is $\mathcal{T}_\mathcal{P}[\![(\text{elmm } (/ \ (+ \ 25 \ 75) \ (* \ (- \ 7 \ 4) \ (+ \ 5 \ 6))))]\!]$?

b. Intuitively, $\mathcal{T}_\mathcal{P}$ maps an ELMM program to a POSTFIX program with the same behavior. Develop a proof that formalizes this intuition. As part of your proof, show that the following diagram commutes:

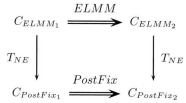

The nodes C_{ELMM_1} and C_{ELMM_2} represent ELMM configurations, and the nodes $C_{PostFix_1}$ and $C_{PostFix_2}$ represent POSTFIX configurations of the form introduced in Exercise 3.12 on page 70. The horizontal arrows are transitions in the respective systems, while the vertical arrows are applications of $\mathcal{T}_{\mathcal{NE}}$. It may help to think in terms of a context-based semantics.

c. Extend the translator to translate (1) ELM programs and (2) EL programs. In each case, prove that the program resulting from your translation has the same behavior as the original program.

3.8   Extending PostFix

We close this chapter on operational semantics by illustrating that slight perturbations to a language can have extensive repercussions for the properties of the language.

You have probably noticed that POSTFIX has a very limited expressive power. The fact that all programs terminate gives us a hint why. Any language in which all programs terminate can't be universal, because any universal language must allow nonterminating computations to be expressed. Even if we don't care about universality (maybe we just want a good calculator language), POSTFIX suffers from numerous drawbacks. For example, nget allows us to "name" numerals by their position relative to the top of the stack, but these positions change as values are pushed and popped, leading to programs that are challenging to read and write. It would be preferable to give unchanging names to values. Furthermore, nget accesses only numerals, and there are situations where we need to access executable sequences and use them more than once.

We could address these problems by allowing executable sequences to be copied from any position on the stack and by introducing a general way to name any value; these extensions are explored in exercises. For now, we will consider extending POSTFIX with a command that just copies the top value on a stack. Since the top value might be an executable sequence, this at least gives us a way to copy executable sequences — something we could not do before.

Consider a new command, dup, which duplicates the value at the top of the stack. After execution of this command, the top two values of the stack will be the same. The rewrite rule for dup is given below:

$$\langle \text{dup} . Q, V . S \rangle \Rightarrow \langle Q, V . V . S \rangle \qquad\qquad [dup]$$

As a simple example of using dup, consider the executable sequence (dup mul), which behaves as a squaring subroutine:

(postfix 1 (dup mul) exec) $\xrightarrow{[12]}$ 144
(postfix 2 (dup mul) dup 3 nget swap exec swap 4 nget swap exec add)
$\xrightarrow{[5,12]}$ 169

The introduction of dup clearly enhances the expressive power of POST-FIX. But adding this innocent little command has a tremendous consequence for the language: it destroys the termination property! Consider the program (postfix 0 (dup exec) dup exec). Executing this program on zero arguments yields the following transition sequence:

$$\langle ((\text{dup exec}) \ \text{dup exec}), [\,] \rangle$$
$$\Rightarrow \langle (\text{dup exec}), [(\text{dup exec})] \rangle$$
$$\Rightarrow \langle (\text{exec}), [(\text{dup exec}), (\text{dup exec})] \rangle$$
$$\Rightarrow \langle (\text{dup exec}), [(\text{dup exec})] \rangle$$
$$\Rightarrow \dots$$

Because the rewrite process returns to a previously visited configuration, it is clear that the execution of this program never terminates.

It is not difficult to see why dup invalidates the termination proof from Section 3.6. The problem is that dup can increase the energy of a configuration in the case where the top element of the stack is an executable sequence. Because **dup** effectively creates new commands in this situation, the number of commands executed can be unbounded.

It turns out that extending POSTFIX with **dup** not only invalidates the termination property, but also results in a language that is universal![9] (See Exercise 3.48 on page 112.) That is, any computable function can be expressed in POSTFIX+{**dup**}.

This simple example underscores that minor changes to a language can have major consequences. Without careful thought, it is never safe to assume that adding or removing a simple feature or tweaking a rewrite rule will change a language in only minor ways.

We conclude this chapter with numerous exercises that explore various extensions to the POSTFIX language.

Exercise 3.37 Extend the POSTFIX SOS so that it handles the following commands:

pair: Let v_1 be the top value on the stack and v_2 be the next-to-top value. Pop both values off the stack and push onto the stack a pair object $\langle v_2, v_1 \rangle$.

fst: If the top stack value is a pair $\langle v_{fst}, v_{snd} \rangle$, then replace it with v_{fst} (the *first* value in the pair). Otherwise signal an error.

snd: If the top stack value is a pair $\langle v_{fst}, v_{snd} \rangle$, then replace it with v_{snd} (the *second* value in the pair). Otherwise signal an error.

Exercise 3.38 Extend the POSTFIX SOS so that it handles the following commands:

get: Call the top stack value v_{index} and the remaining stack values (from top down) v_1, v_2, ..., v_n. Pop v_{index} off the stack. If v_{index} is a numeral i such that $1 \leq i \leq n$, push v_i onto the stack. Signal an error if the stack does not contain at least one value, if v_{index} is not a numeral, or if i is not in the range $[1..n]$. (**get** is like **nget** except that it can copy any value, not just a numeral.)

put: Call the top stack value v_{index}, the next-to-top stack value v_{val}, the remaining stack values (from top down) v_1, v_2, ..., v_n. Pop v_{index} and v_{val} off the stack. If v_{index} is a numeral i such that $1 \leq i \leq n$, change the slot holding v_i on the stack to hold v_{val}. Signal an error if the stack does not contain at least two values, if v_{index} is not a numeral, or if i is not in the range $[1..n]$.

Exercise 3.39 Write the following programs in POSTFIX+{**dup**}. You may also use the pair commands from Exercise 3.37 and/or the **get**/**put** commands from Exercise 3.38 in

---

[9]We are indebted to Carl Witty and Michael Frank for showing us that POSTFIX+{**dup**} is universal.

your solution, but they are not necessary — for an extra challenge, program purely in POSTFIX+{dup}.

a. A program that takes a single argument (call it n) and returns the factorial of n. The factorial function f of an integer is defined so that $(f\ 0) = 1$ and $(f\ n) = (n \times_{Int} (f\ (n -_{Int} 1)))$ for $n \geq 1$.

b. A program that takes a single argument (call it n) and returns the nth Fibonacci number. The Fibonacci function f of an integer is defined so that $(f\ 0) = 0$, $(f\ 1) = 1$, and $(f\ n) = ((f\ (n -_{Int} 1)) +_{Int} (f\ (n -_{Int} 2)))$ for $n \geq 2$.

Exercise 3.40 Abby Stracksen wishes to extend POSTFIX with a simple means of iteration. She suggests adding a command of the form (for N (Q)). Abby describes the behavior of her command with the following rewrite axioms:

$$\langle (\text{for}\ N\ (Q_{for})) \cdot Q_{rest},\ S \rangle \qquad\qquad [\textit{for-once}]$$
$$\Rightarrow \langle N \cdot Q_{for}\ @\ [(\text{for}\ N_{dec}\ (Q_{for}))]\ @\ Q_{rest},\ S \rangle$$
$$\text{where}\ (N_{dec} = (\text{calculate sub}\ N\ 1)) \wedge (\textit{compare}\ \text{gt}\ N\ 0)$$

$$\langle (\text{for}\ N\ (Q_{for})) \cdot Q_{rest},\ S \rangle \Rightarrow \langle Q_{rest},\ S \rangle \qquad [\textit{for-done}]$$
$$\text{where}\ \neg(\textit{compare}\ \text{gt}\ N\ 0)$$

Abby calls her extended language POSTLOOP.

a. Give an informal specification of Abby's for command that would be appropriate for a reference manual.

b. Using Abby's for semantics, what are the results of executing the following POST-LOOP programs when called on zero arguments?

   i.   (postloop 0 1 (for 5 (mul)))

   ii.   (postloop 0 1 (for 5 (2 mul)))

   iii. (postloop 0 1 (for 5 (add mul)))

   iv.   (postloop 0 0 (for 17 (pop 2 add)))

   v.   (postloop 0 0 (for 6 (pop (for 7 (pop 1 add)))))

c. Extending POSTFIX with the for command does not change its termination property. Show this by extending the termination proof described in Section 3.6.2 in the following way:

   i.   Define the energy of the for command.

   ii.   Show that the transitions in the [*for-once*] and [*for-done*] rules decrease configuration energy.

d. Bud Lojack has developed a **repeat** command of the form (repeat N (Q)) that is similar to Abby's for command. Bud defines the semantics of his command by the following rewrite rules:

$$\langle(\texttt{repeat } N \ (Q_{rpt})) \, . \, Q_{rest}, \ S\rangle \qquad\qquad \textit{[repeat-once]}$$
$$\Rightarrow \langle N \, . \, (\texttt{repeat } N_{dec} \ (Q_{rpt})) \, . \, Q_{rpt} \ @ \ Q_{rest}, \ S\rangle$$
$$\text{where } (N_{dec} = (\textit{calculate } \texttt{sub } N \ 1)) \wedge (\textit{compare } \texttt{gt } N \ 0)$$

$$\langle(\texttt{repeat } N \ (Q_{rpt})) \, . \, Q_{rest}, \ S\rangle \Rightarrow \langle Q_{rest}, \ S\rangle \qquad\qquad \textit{[repeat-done]}$$
$$\text{where } \neg(\textit{compare } \texttt{gt } N \ 0)$$

Does Bud's `repeat` command have the same behavior as Abby's `for` command? That is, does the following observational equivalence hold?

$$[(\texttt{repeat } N \ (Q))] =_{obs} [(\texttt{for } N \ (Q))]$$

Justify your answer.

Exercise 3.41 Alyssa P. Hacker has created POSTSAFE, an extension to POSTFIX with a new command called `sdup`: safe `dup`. The `sdup` command is a restricted form of `dup` that does not violate the termination property of POSTFIX. The informal semantics for `sdup` is as follows: if the top of the stack is a number or a command sequence that doesn't contain `sdup`, duplicate it; otherwise, signal an error.

As a new graduate student in Alyssa's ARGH (Advanced Research Group for Hacking), you are assigned to give an operational semantics for `sdup`, and a proof that all POSTSAFE programs terminate. Alyssa set up several intermediate steps to make your life easier.

a. Write the operational semantics rules that describe the behavior of `sdup`. Model the errors through stuck states. You can use the auxiliary function

$$contains\_sdup : \text{CommandSeq} \rightarrow \textit{Bool}$$

that takes a sequence of commands and checks whether it contains `sdup` or not.

b. Consider the product domain $P = \mathbb{N} \times \mathbb{N}$ (recall that $\mathbb{N}$ is the set of natural numbers, starting with 0). On this domain, Alyssa defined the ordering $<_P$ as follows:

Definition 1 (lexicographic order) $\langle a_1, b_1 \rangle <_P \langle a_2, b_2 \rangle$ *iff* $((a_1 <_{Nat} a_2) \vee ((a_1 =_{Nat} a_2) \wedge (b_1 <_{Nat} b_2)))$. *E.g.,* $\langle 3, 10000 \rangle <_P \langle 4, 0 \rangle <_P \langle 4, 6 \rangle <_P \langle 5, 2 \rangle$.

Definition 2 *A* **strictly decreasing chain** *in P is a series of elements $p_1, p_2, \ldots$ such that $\forall i \, . \, p_i \in P$ and $\forall i \, . \, p_{i+1} <_P p_i$.*

  i.   Consider a finite strictly decreasing chain $\langle a_1, b_1 \rangle, \langle a_2, b_2 \rangle, \ldots, \langle a_k, b_k \rangle$, where $\langle a_i, b_i \rangle \in P$, such that $k > b_1 + 1$ (i.e., the chain has more than $b_1 + 1$ elements). Prove that $a_k < a_1$.

  ii. Show that there is no infinite strictly decreasing chain in P.

c. Prove that each POSTSAFE program terminates by defining an appropriate energy function $\mathcal{ES}_{config}$. *Note:* If you need to use some helper functions that are intuitively easy to describe but tedious to define (e.g., $contains\_sdup$), just give an informal description of them.

Exercise 3.42 Sam Antics extends the PostFix language to allow programmers to directly manipulate stacks as first-class values. He calls the resulting language StackFix. StackFix adds three commands to PostFix:

package: This command packages a copy of the stack as a first-class value, S. It then clears the stack, leaving S as the only value on the stack.

unpackage: This command pops the top of the stack, which must be a stack-value S, and replaces the stack with an "unpackaged" version of S.

switch: This command pops the top of the stack, which must be a stack-value, S. Then the rest of the stack is packaged (as if by the package command); this results in a new stack-value, S_{rest}. Finally, the stack is completely replaced with an "unpackaged" version of S, and the stack-value S_{rest} is pushed on top of the resulting stack. Thus, switch effectively switches the roles of the stack-value on top of the stack and the rest of the stack.

As a warm-up, Sam has written some simple StackFix programs. First-class stack values may be returned as the final result of a program execution; in that case, the outcome is the token stack-value, which hides the details of the stack value.

$$(\text{stackfix 0 1 2 package}) \xrightarrow{\|} \text{stack-value}$$
$$(\text{stackfix 0 1 2 package unpackage}) \xrightarrow{\|} 2$$
$$(\text{stackfix 0 1 2 package 3 switch}) \xrightarrow{\|} \text{error } \{top\ of\ stack\ not\ stack\text{-}value\}$$
$$(\text{stackfix 0 1 2 package 3 swap switch}) \xrightarrow{\|} \text{stack-value}$$
$$(\text{stackfix 0 2 package 3 swap switch pop}) \xrightarrow{\|} 2$$
$$(\text{stackfix 0 1 2 package 3 swap switch unpackage}) \xrightarrow{\|} 3$$

a. Write a definition of the Value domain for the StackFix language.

b. Give rewrite rules for the package, unpackage, and switch commands.

c. Does unpackage add new expressive power to StackFix, beyond that provided by package and switch? If yes, argue why. If no, provide an equivalent sequence of commands from PostFix+{package,switch}.

d. Does every StackFix program terminate? Give a short, intuitive description of your reasoning.

Exercise 3.43 Rhea Storr introduces a new PostFix command called execs that permits executing a sequence of commands while saving the old stack. She calls her extended language PostSave.

Rhea asks you to help her define rewrite rules for PostSave that in several steps move $\langle \text{execs} . Q, (Q_{exec}) . S \rangle$ to the configuration $\langle Q, V . S \rangle$. This sequence of transformations assumes that the configuration $\langle Q_{exec}, S \rangle$ will eventually result in a final configuration $\langle []_{\text{Command}}, V . S' \rangle$.

Here are some examples that contrast exec with execs:

```
(postsave 0 1 2 (3 mul) exec add) ⊔↦ 7
(postsave 0 1 2 (3 mul) execs add) ⊔↦ 8
(postsave 0 (1) execs) ⊔↦ 1
(postsave 0 2 3 (mul) execs add add) ⊔↦ 11
```

To implement the SOS for PostSave, Rhea modifies the configuration space:

$$cf \in CF = \text{Layer*}$$
$$L \in \text{Layer} = \text{CommandSeq} \times \text{Stack}$$

Rhea's rewrite rule for **execs** is:

$$\langle \text{execs} . Q, (Q_{exec}) . S \rangle . L^* \Rightarrow \langle Q_{exec}, S \rangle . \langle Q, S \rangle . L^* \qquad \text{[execs]}$$

Note that the entire stack is copied into the new layer!

a. If $\langle Q, S \rangle \xRightarrow{PF} \langle Q', S' \rangle$ is a rewrite rule in PostFix, provide the corresponding rule in PostSave.

b. Provide the rule for an empty command sequence in the top layer.

c. Show that programs in PostSave are no longer guaranteed to terminate by giving a command sequence that is equivalent to **dup**.

Exercise 3.44 One of the chief limitations of the PostFix language is that there is no way to name values. In this problem, we consider extending PostFix with a simple naming system. We will call the resulting language PostText.

   The grammar for PostText is the same as that for PostFix except that there are three new commands:

$$C ::= \dots \mid I \mid \text{def} \mid \text{ref}$$

Here, I is an element of the syntactic domain Ident, which includes all alphabetic names except for the PostText command names (**pop**, **exec**, **def**, etc.), which are treated as reserved words of the language.

   The model of the PostText language extends the model of PostFix by including a current dictionary as well as a current stack. A dictionary is an object that maintains bindings between names and values. The commands inherited from PostFix have no effect on the dictionary. The informal behavior of the new commands is as follows:

I: I is a literal name that is similar to an immutable string literal in other languages. Executing this command simply pushes I on the stack. The Value domain must be extended to include identifiers in addition to numerals and executable sequences.

def: Let v_1 be the top stack value and v_2 be the next-to-top value. The **def** command pops both values off the stack and updates the current dictionary to include a binding between v_2 and v_1. v_2 should be a name, but v_1 can be any value (including an executable sequence or name literal). It is an error if v_2 is not a name.

ref: The ref command pops the top element v_{name} off of the stack, where v_{name} should be a name. It looks up the value v_{val} associated with v_{name} in the current dictionary and pushes v_{val} on top of the stack. It is an error if there is no binding for v_{name} in the current dictionary or if v_{name} is not a name.

For example:

```
(posttext 0 average (add 2 div) def 3 7 average ref exec) ⟶ 5
(posttext 0 a 3 def dbl (2 mul) def a ref
    dbl ref exec 4 dbl ref exec add) ⟶ 14
(posttext 0 a b def a ref 7 def b ref) ⟶ 7
(posttext 0 a 5 def a ref 7 def b ref) ⟶ error {5 is not a name.}
(posttext 0 c 4 def d ref 1 add) ⟶ error {d is unbound.}
```

In an SOS for PostText, the usual PostFix configuration space must be extended to include a dictionary object as a new state component:

$$CF_{PostText} = \text{CommandSeq} \times \text{Stack} \times \text{Dictionary}$$

a. Suppose that a dictionary is represented as a sequence of identifier/value pairs:

$$D \in \text{Dictionary} = (\text{Ident} \times \text{Value})^*$$

   i. Define the final configurations, input function, and output function for the Post-Text SOS.

   ii. Give the rewrite rules for the I, def, and ref commands.

b. Redo part **a**, assuming that dictionaries are instead represented as functions from identifiers to values, i.e., $D \in \text{Dictionary} = \text{Ident} \rightarrow (\text{Value} + \{\text{unbound}\})$ where unbound is a distinguished token indicating that an identifier is unbound in the dictionary.

You may find the following *bind* function helpful:

$$bind : \text{Ident} \rightarrow \text{Value} \rightarrow \text{Dictionary} \rightarrow \text{Dictionary}$$
$$= \lambda I_{bind} V D . \ \lambda I_{ref} . \ \textbf{if } I_{bind} = I_{ref} \ \textbf{then } V \ \textbf{else } (D \ I_{ref}) \ \textbf{end}$$

bind takes a name, a value, and a dictionary, and returns a new dictionary in which there is a binding between the name and value in addition to the existing bindings. (If the name was already bound in the given dictionary, the new binding effectively replaces the old.)

Exercise 3.45 After several focus-group studies, Ben Bitdiddle has decided that Post-Fix needs a macro facility. Below is Ben's sketch of the informal semantics of the facility for his extended language, which he dubs PostMac.

Macros are specified at the beginning of a PostMac program, as follows:

$$(\texttt{postmac } N_{numargs} \ ((I_1 \ V_1) \ \dots \ (I_n \ V_n)) \ Q)$$

Each macro $(I_i \ V_i)$ creates a command, called $I_i \in \text{Ident}$, that, when executed, pushes the value V_i (which can be an integer numeral or an executable sequence) onto the stack. It is illegal to give macros the names of existing POSTFIX commands, or to use an identifier more than once in a list of macros. The behavior of programs that do so is undefined. Here are some examples Ben has come up with:

(postmac 0 ((inc (1 add))) (0 inc exec inc exec)) $\xrightarrow{\parallel}$ 2

(postmac 0 ((A 1) (B (2 mul))) (A B exec)) $\xrightarrow{\parallel}$ 2

(postmac 0 ((A 1) (B (2 mul))) (A C exec)) $\xrightarrow{\parallel}$ error
    {undefined macro C}

(postmac 0 ((A 1) (B (C mul)) (C 2)) (A B exec)) $\xrightarrow{\parallel}$ 2

(postmac 0 ((A pop)) (1 A)) $\xrightarrow{\parallel}$ error
    {Ill-formed program: macro bodies must be values, not commands}

Ben started writing an SOS for POSTMAC, but had to go make a presentation for some venture capitalists. It is your job to complete the SOS.

Before leaving, Ben made the following changes/additions to the domain definitions:

$P \in \text{Prog} ::= (\texttt{postmac } N_{numargs} \; M_{macros} \; Q_{body})$ [Program]

$M \in \text{MacroList} ::= (\text{Ident Value})^{*}$

$C \in \text{Command} ::= \ldots \mid I$ [Macro Reference]

$cf \in CF_{PostMac} = \text{CommandSeq} \times \text{Stack} \times \text{MacroList}$

He also introduced an auxiliary partial function, *lookup*, with the following signature:

$$lookup : (\text{Ident} \times \text{MacroList}) \rightharpoonup \text{Value}$$

If *lookup* is given an identifier and a macro list, it returns the value that the identifier is bound to in the macro list. If there is no such value, *lookup* gets stuck.

a. Ben's notes begin the SOS rewrite rules for POSTMAC as follows:

$$\frac{\langle Q, S \rangle \xrightarrow{PF} \langle Q', S' \rangle}{\langle Q, S, M \rangle \xrightarrow{PM} \langle Q', S', M \rangle} \qquad \text{[POSTFIX commands]}$$

where $\xrightarrow{PF}$ is the original transition relation for POSTFIX and $\xrightarrow{PM}$ is the new transition relation for POSTMAC. Complete the SOS for POSTMAC. Your completed SOS should handle the first four of Ben's examples. Don't worry about ill-formed programs. Model errors as stuck states.

b. Louis Reasoner finds out that your SOS handles macros that depend on other macros. He wants to launch a new advertising campaign with the slogan: "Guaranteed to terminate: POSTFIX with mutually recursive macros!" Show that Louis's new campaign is a bad idea by writing a nonterminating program in POSTMAC.

c. When Ben returns from his presentation, he finds out that you've written a nonterminating program in POSTMAC. He decides to restrict the language so that nonterminating programs are no longer possible. Ben's restriction is that the body (or value) of a macro cannot use any macros. Ben wants you to prove that this restricted language terminates.

i. Extend the PostFix energy function so that it assigns an energy to configurations that include macros. Fill in the blanks in Ben's definitions of the functions $E_{com}[\![I, M]\!]$, $E_{seq}[\![Q, M]\!]$ and $E_{stack}[\![S, M]\!]$ and use these functions to define the configuration energy function $E_{config}[\![\langle Q, S, M \rangle]\!]$.

$$E_{com}[\![(Q), M]\!] = E_{seq}[\![Q, M]\!]$$

$$E_{com}[\![C, M]\!] = 1 \ (\text{C is not an identifier or an executable sequence})$$

$$E_{com}[\![I, M]\!] = $$

$$E_{seq}[\![[\,]_{\text{Command}}, M]\!] = 0$$

$$E_{seq}[\![C \cdot Q, M]\!] = $$

$$E_{stack}[\![[\,]_{\text{Value}}, M]\!] = 0$$

$$E_{stack}[\![V \cdot S, M]\!] = $$

$$E_{config}[\![\langle Q, S, M \rangle]\!] = $$

ii. Use the extended energy function (for the restricted form of PostMac) to show that executing a macro decreases the energy of a configuration. Since it is possible to show that all the other commands decrease the energy of a configuration (by adapting the termination proof for PostFix without macros), this will show that the restricted form of PostMac terminates.

Exercise 3.46 Dinah McScoop, a Lisp hacker, is unsatisfied with PostText, the name-binding extension of PostFix introduced in Exercise 3.44. She claims that there is a better way to add name binding to PostFix, and creates a brand-new language, PostLisp, to test out her ideas.

The grammar for PostLisp is the same as that for PostFix except that there are four new commands:

$C ::= \ldots \mid I \mid \texttt{bind} \mid \texttt{unbind} \mid \texttt{lookup}$

Here, I is an element of the syntactic domain Ident, which includes all alphabetic names except for the PostLisp command names (pop, exec, bind, etc.), which are treated as reserved words of the language.

The model of the PostLisp language extends the model of PostFix by including a *name stack* for each name. A name stack is a stack of values associated with a name that can be manipulated with the bind, unbind, and lookup commands as described below. The commands inherited from PostFix have no effect on the name stacks. The informal behavior of the new commands is as follows:

I: I is a literal name that is similar to an immutable string literal in other languages. Executing this command simply pushes I onto the stack. The Value domain is extended to include names in addition to numerals and executable sequences.

bind: Let v_1 be the top stack value and v_2 be the next-to-top value. The bind command pops both values off the stack and pushes v_1 onto the name stack associated with v_2. Thus v_2 is required to be a name, but v_1 can be any value (including an executable sequence or name literal). It is an error if v_2 is not a name.

lookup: The command `lookup` pops the top element v_{name} off the stack, where v_{name} should be a name. If v_{val} is the value at the top of the name stack associated with v_{name}, then v_{val} is pushed onto the stack. (v_{val} is *not* popped off the name stack.) It is an error if the name stack of v_{name} is empty, or if v_{name} is not a name.

unbind: The command `unbind` pops the top element v_{name} off the stack, where v_{name} should be a name. It then pops the top value off the name stack associated with v_{name}. It is an error if the name stack of v_{name} is empty, or if v_{name} is not a name.

Initially each name is associated with the empty name stack. Here are some PostLisp examples:

(postlisp 0 a 3 bind a lookup) $\overset{\mathbb{ll}}{\longrightarrow}$ 3

(postlisp 0 a 8 bind a lookup a lookup add) $\overset{\mathbb{ll}}{\longrightarrow}$ 16

(postlisp 0 a 4 bind a 9 bind a lookup a unbind a lookup add) $\overset{\mathbb{ll}}{\longrightarrow}$ 13

(postlisp 0 19 a bind a lookup) $\overset{\mathbb{ll}}{\longrightarrow}$ error   {19 *is not a name.*}

(postlisp 0 average (add 2 div) bind 3 7 average lookup exec) $\overset{\mathbb{ll}}{\longrightarrow}$ 5

(postlisp 0 a b bind a lookup 23 bind b lookup) $\overset{\mathbb{ll}}{\longrightarrow}$ 23

(postlisp 0 c 4 bind d lookup 1 add) $\overset{\mathbb{ll}}{\longrightarrow}$ error   {d *name stack is empty.*}

(postlisp 0 b unbind) $\overset{\mathbb{ll}}{\longrightarrow}$ error {b *name stack is empty*}

In an SOS for PostLisp, the usual PostFix configuration space must be extended to include the name stacks as a new state component. Name stacks are bundled up into an object called a *name file*.

$$CF_{PostLisp} = \text{CommandSeq} \times \text{Stack} \times \text{NameFile}$$
$$F \in \text{NameFile} = \text{Name} \rightarrow \text{Stack}$$

A NameFile is a function mapping a name to the stack of values bound to the name. If F is a name file, then $(F\ I)$ is the stack associated with I in F. The notation $F[I = S]$ denotes a name file that is identical to F except that I is mapped to S.

a. Define the final configurations, input function, and output function for the PostLisp SOS.

b. Give the rewrite rules for the I, `bind`, `unbind`, and `lookup` commands.

Exercise 3.47 Abby Stracksen is bored with vanilla PostFix (it's not even universal!) and decides to add a new feature, which she calls the *heap*. A heap maps locations to elements from the Value domain, where locations are simply integer numerals:

Location = IntLit

Note that a location can be any integer numeral, including a negative one. Furthermore, integer numerals and locations can be used interchangeably in Abby's language, very much like pointers in pre-ANSI C.

Abby christens her new language PostHeap. The grammar for PostHeap is the same as that for PostFix except that there are three new commands:

$C ::= \ldots \mid$ allocate $\mid$ store $\mid$ access

The commands inherited from POSTFIX have no effect on the heap. The informal behavior of the new commands is as follows:

allocate: Executing this command pushes onto the stack a location that is not used in the heap.

store: Let v_1 be the top stack value and v_2 be the next-to-top value. The store command pops v_1 off the stack and writes it into the heap at location v_2. Thus v_1 can be any element from the Value domain and v_2 has to be an IntLit. It is an error if v_2 is not an IntLit. Note that v_2 remains on the stack.

access: Let v_1 be the top stack value. The access command reads from the heap at location v_1 and pushes the result onto the stack. Thus v_1 has to be an IntLit. It is an error if v_1 is not an IntLit or if the heap at location v_1 has not been written with store before. Note that v_1 remains on the stack.

For example:

(postheap 0 allocate) $\xrightarrow{\text{IL}}$ N {*implementation dependent*}

(postheap 0 allocate 5 store access) $\xrightarrow{\text{IL}}$ 5

(postheap 0 allocate 5 store 4 swap access swap pop add) $\xrightarrow{\text{IL}}$ 9

(postheap 0 4 5 store) $\xrightarrow{\text{IL}}$ 4

(postheap 0 4 5 store access) $\xrightarrow{\text{IL}}$ 5

(postheap 0 access) $\xrightarrow{\text{IL}}$ error {*no location given*}

(postheap 0 allocate access) $\xrightarrow{\text{IL}}$ error {*location has not been written*}

(postheap 0 5 store) $\xrightarrow{\text{IL}}$ error {*no location given*}

After sketching this initial description of the heap, Abby asks you to flesh out her initial draft.

a. Give the definition of the Heap domain and the configuration domain CF.

b. Let *access-from-heap* be a partial function that, given a Location and a Heap in which Location has been bound, returns an element from the Value domain. In other words, *access-from-heap* has the following signature and definition:

$access\text{-}from\text{-}heap : \text{Location} \rightarrow \text{Heap} \rightarrow \text{Value}$

$(access\text{-}from\text{-}heap\ N\ \langle N, V \rangle . H) = V$

$(access\text{-}from\text{-}heap\ N_1\ \langle N_2, V \rangle . H) = (access\text{-}from\text{-}heap\ N_1\ H),\ \text{where}\ N_1 \neq N_2$

Give the rewrite rules for the allocate, store, and access commands. You may use *access-from-heap*.

c. Is POSTHEAP a universal programming language? Explain your answer.

d. Abby is concerned about security because POSTHEAP treats integer numerals and locations interchangeably. Since her programs don't use this "feature," she decides to restrict the language by disallowing pointer arithmetic. She wants to use *tags* to distinguish locations from integer numerals. Abby redefines the Value domain as follows:

$$V \in \text{Value} = (\text{IntLit} \times \text{Tag}) + \text{CommandSeq}$$
$$\text{Tag} = \{\texttt{integer}, \texttt{pointer}\}$$

Informally, integer numerals and locations are represented as pairs on the stack: integer numerals are paired with the `integer` tag, while locations are paired with the `pointer` tag.

Give the revised rewrite rules for integer numerals, `add`, `allocate`, `store`, and `access`.

Exercise 3.48 Prove that POSTFIX+{`dup`} is universal. This can be done by showing how to translate any Turing machine program into a POSTFIX+{`dup`} program. Assume that integer numerals may be arbitrarily large in magnitude.

Notes

Early approaches to operational semantics defined the semantics of programming languages by translating them to standard abstract machines. Landin's SECD machine [Lan64] is a classic example of such an abstract machine. Plotkin [Plo75] used it to study the semantics of the lambda calculus. Along the way, Plotkin developed a notion of observational equivalence that he called both "operational equality" and "contextual equality."

Later, Plotkin introduced structural operational semantics [Plo81] as a more direct approach to specifying an operational semantics. The context-based approach to specifying transition relations for small-step operational semantics was invented by Felleisen and Friedman in [FF86] and explored in a series of papers culminating in [FH92] that explored state and control features of programming languages. There is a forthcoming textbook [FFF] based on this material that covers both expression-based models and machine-based models of program execution.

Big-step (natural) semantics was introduced by Kahn in [Kah87].

A concise overview of various approaches to semantics, including several forms of operational semantics, can be found in the first chapter of [Gun92]. The early chapters of [Win93] present an introduction to operational semantics in the context of a simple imperative language.

Many forms of operational semantics are examples of *term rewriting systems* [DJ90, BN98]. Properties like termination and confluence are key objects of study in these systems. *Graph rewriting systems* [Cou90] extend term rewriting systems by modeling sharing.

For a discussion of universal languages and the halting problem, consult a theory of computation text, such as [Sip06].

4

Denotational Semantics

First learn the meaning of what you say, and then speak.

— Epictetus

4.1 The Denotational Semantics Game

We have seen how an operational semantics is a natural tool for evaluating programs and proving properties like termination. However, it is less than ideal for many purposes. A framework based on transitions between configurations of an abstract machine is usually better suited for reasoning about complete programs than program fragments. In POSTFIX, for instance, we had to extend the operational semantics with elaborate notions of observational equivalence and transform equivalence in order to effectively demonstrate the interchangeability of command sequences. Additionally, the emphasis on syntactic entities in an operational semantics can complicate reasoning. For example, in a version of POSTFIX that allows executable sequences as answers, syntactically distinct executable sequence answers in POSTFIX must be treated as the same observable value in order to support a nontrivial notion of observational equivalence for command sequences. Finally, the step-by-step nature of an operational semantics can suggest notions of time and dependency that are not essential to the language being defined. For example, an operational semantics for the expression language EL might specify that the left operand of a binary operator is evaluated before the right even though this order may be impossible to detect in practice.

An alternative framework for reasoning about programs is suggested by the notion of transform equivalence developed for POSTFIX. According to this notion, each POSTFIX command sequence is associated with a **stack transform** that describes how the sequence maps an input stack to an output stack. It is natural to view these stack transforms as functions. For example, the stack transform associated with the command sequence $[3, \mathtt{add}]$ would be an *add3* function with the following graph:[1]

$$\{\langle errorStack, errorStack\rangle,\ \ \langle[\,], errorStack\rangle,\ \ldots,$$
$$\langle[-1], [2]\rangle,\ \ \langle[0], [3]\rangle,\ \ \langle[1], [4]\rangle,\ \ldots,$$
$$\langle[add3], errorStack\rangle,\ \ \langle[mul2], errorStack\rangle,\ \ldots,$$
$$\langle[5,\ 23], [8,\ 23]\rangle,\ \ \langle[5,\ mul2,\ 17,\ add3], [8,\ mul2,\ 17,\ add3]\rangle,\ \ldots\,\}$$

Here, *errorStack* stands for a distinguished error stack analogous to SA_{error} in the extended POSTFIX SOS. Stack elements that are executable sequences are represented by their stack transforms (e.g., *add3* and *mul2*) rather than by some syntactic phrase.

Associating stack transform functions with command sequences has several benefits. First, this perspective directly supports a notion of equivalence for program phrases. For example, the *add3* function is the stack transform associated with the sequence $[1, \mathtt{add}, 2, \mathtt{add}]$ as well as the sequence $[3, \mathtt{add}]$. This implies that the two sequences are behaviorally indistinguishable and can be safely interchanged in any POSTFIX context. The fact that stack elements that are executable sequences are represented by functions rather than syntactic entities greatly simplifies this kind of reasoning.

The other major benefit of this approach is that the stack transform associated with the concatenation of two sequences is easily composed from the stack transforms of the component sequences. For example, suppose that the sequence $[2, \mathtt{mul}]$ is modeled by the *mul2* function, whose graph is:

$$\{\langle errorStack, errorStack\rangle,\ \ \langle[\,], errorStack\rangle,\ \ldots,$$
$$\langle[-1], [-2]\rangle,\ \ \langle[0], [0]\rangle,\ \ \langle[1], [2]\rangle,\ \ldots,$$
$$\langle[add3], errorStack\rangle,\ \ \langle[mul2], errorStack\rangle,\ \ldots,$$
$$\langle[5,\ 23], [10,\ 23]\rangle,\ \ \langle[5,\ mul2,\ 17,\ add3], [10,\ mul2,\ 17,\ add3]\rangle,\ \ldots\,\}$$

Then the stack transform of $[3, \mathtt{add}, 2, \mathtt{mul}] = [3, \mathtt{add}] @ [2, \mathtt{mul}]$ is simply the function $mul2 \circ add3$, whose graph is:

$$\{\langle errorStack, errorStack\rangle,\ \ \langle[\,], errorStack\rangle,\ \ldots,$$
$$\langle[-1], [4]\rangle,\ \ \langle[0], [6]\rangle,\ \ \langle[1], [8]\rangle,\ \ldots,$$
$$\langle[add3], errorStack\rangle,\ \ \langle[mul2], errorStack\rangle,\ \ldots,$$
$$\langle[5,\ 23], [16,\ 23]\rangle,\ \ \langle[5,\ mul2,\ 17,\ add3], [16,\ mul2,\ 17,\ add3]\rangle,\ \ldots\,\}$$

Similarly the stack transform of $[2, \mathtt{mul}, 3, \mathtt{add}] = [2, \mathtt{mul}] @ [3, \mathtt{add}]$ is the function $add3 \circ mul2$, whose graph is:

---

[1]Here, and for the rest of this chapter, we rely heavily on the metalanguage concepts and notations described in Appendix A. Consult this appendix as necessary to unravel the formalism.

$$\{\langle errorStack, errorStack \rangle, \ \langle [\,], errorStack \rangle, \ \ldots, $$
$$\langle [-1], [1] \rangle, \ \langle [0], [3] \rangle, \ \langle [1], [5] \rangle, \ \ldots, $$
$$\langle [add3], errorStack \rangle, \ \langle [mul2], errorStack \rangle, \ \ldots, $$
$$\langle [5, \ 23], [13, \ 23] \rangle, \ \langle [5, \ mul2, \ 17, \ add3], [13, \ mul2, \ 17, \ add3] \rangle, \ \ldots \}$$

The notion that the meaning of a program phrase can be determined from the meaning of its parts is the essence of a framework called **denotational semantics**. A denotational semantics determines the meaning of a phrase in a compositional way based on its static structure rather than on some sort of dynamically changing configuration. Unlike an operational semantics, a denotational semantics emphasizes *what* the meaning of a phrase is, not *how* the phrase is evaluated. The name "denotational semantics" is derived from its focus on the mathematical values that phrases "denote."

The basic structure of the denotational framework is illustrated in Figure 4.1. A denotational semantics consists of three parts:

1. A **syntactic algebra** that describes the abstract syntax of the language under study. This can be specified by the s-expression grammar approach introduced in Chapter 2.

2. A **semantic algebra** that models the meaning of program phrases. A semantic algebra consists of a collection of **semantic domains** along with functions that manipulate these domains. The meaning of a program may be something as simple as an element of a primitive semantic domain like *Int*, the domain of integers. More typically, the meaning of a program is an element of a function domain that maps **context domains** to an **answer domain**, where

   - Context domains are the denotational analogue of state components in an SOS configuration. They model such entities as name/value associations, the current contents of memory, and control information.

   - An answer domain represents the possible meanings of programs. In addition to a component that models what we normally think of as the result of a program phrase, the answer domain may also include components that model context information that was transformed by the program.

3. A **meaning function** that maps elements of the syntactic algebra (i.e., nodes in the abstract syntax trees) to their meanings in the semantic algebra. Each phrase is said to **denote** its image under the meaning function. In practice, the meaning function is specified by a collection of so-called **valuation functions**, one for each syntactic domain defined by the abstract syntax for the language.

   Not any function can serve as a meaning function; the function must be a **homomorphism** between the syntactic algebra and the semantic algebra.

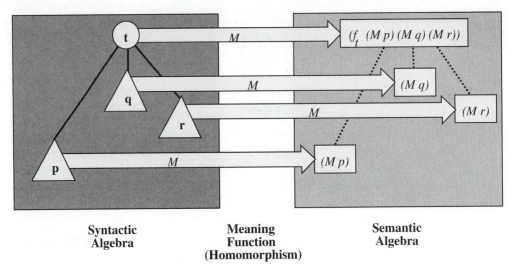

Syntactic   **Meaning**   **Semantic**
Algebra   **Function**   **Algebra**
                   (Homomorphism)

Figure 4.1   The denotational semantics "game board."

This is just the technical condition that constrains the meaning of an abstract
syntax tree node to be determined from the meaning of its subnodes. It can
be stated more formally as follows:

Suppose M is a meaning function and t is a node in an abstract syntax
tree, with children $t_1, \ldots, t_k$. Then

$$(M \; t) \text{ must equal } (f_t \; (M \; t_1) \; \ldots \; (M \; t_k))$$

where f_t is a function that is determined by the syntactic class of t.

The reason to restrict meaning functions to homomorphisms is that their
structure-preserving behavior greatly simplifies reasoning. This design choice
accounts for a property of denotational semantics we call **compositionality**
that is summarized by the motto "the meaning of the whole is composed out
of the meaning of the parts." A key consequence of compositionality is that the
meaning of a program remains the same when one of its phrases is replaced by
another phrase with the same meaning.

Compositionality also facilitates the implementation of programming languages. The core syntactic processing procedures of interpreters and translators
based on denotational semantics have a natural recursive structure that mimics
the recursive structure of the valuation functions and the abstract syntax trees
they manipulate. For example, parser generators like Yacc [Joh75] allow grammar
descriptions to specify **semantic actions** that are performed when an abstract
syntax tree node is recognized during the parsing of a program. Typically, these

actions are used to construct a data structure representing the abstract syntax tree, but the compositional nature of denotational semantics enables using semantic actions to directly define interpreters and translators for the language being parsed. So denotational semantics has practical applications as well as theoretical ones.

4.2 A Denotational Semantics for EL

As our first example, we will develop a denotational semantics for the EL expression language. We begin with a pared-down version of the language and show how the semantics changes when we add features to yield full EL.

4.2.1 Step 1: Restricted ELMM

Recall that ELMM (Figure 3.6, page 63) is a simple expression language in which programs are just expressions, and expressions are trees of binary operations using the operators (+, -, *, /, %) whose leaves are integer numerals. For the moment, let's ignore the / and % operations, because removing the possibility of divide-by-zero and remainder-by-zero errors simplifies the semantics. We shall use the name **restricted ELMM** to refer to the version of ELMM without / and %.

In restricted ELMM, the meaning of each numeral, expression, and program is an integer. This meaning is formalized in Figure 4.2, which presents a denotational semantics for restricted ELMM. The syntactic algebra is defined as a restricted version of the s-expression grammar for EL from Figure 2.4 on page 25. The semantic algebra consists of a single semantic domain (the domain Int of integers) and some operations ($+_{Int}$, $-_{Int}$, $\times_{Int}$) on this domain. The meaning function of an ELMM program is specified by a collection of valuation functions, one for each syntactic domain in the s-expression grammar. For each syntactic domain, the name of the associated valuation function is usually a script version of the metavariable that ranges over that domain. For example, $\mathcal{P}$ is the valuation function for $P \in \text{Prog}$, $\mathcal{NE}$ is the valuation function for $NE \in \text{NumExp}$, and so on.

The signature of $\mathcal{P}$, Prog $\rightarrow$ Int, indicates that the meaning of a restricted ELMM program is an integer. The restricted ELMM language is so simple that it has only an answer domain (Int) and no context domains (these notions were introduced on page 115). The meaning $\mathcal{P}[\![(\texttt{elmm } NE_{body})]\!]$ of an ELMM program (elmm NE_{body}) is simply the integer $\mathcal{NE}[\![NE_{body}]\!]$ denoted by its body expression NE_{body}. Since an ELMM numerical expression may be either an integer numeral or an arithmetic operation, the definition of $\mathcal{NE}$ has a clause

---

Syntactic Algebra

The syntactic algebra for restricted ELMM is a version of the s-expression grammar for EL from Figure 2.4 on page 25 in which ArithmeticOperator contains only +, -, and *, and in which the only productions for NE are the ones with phrase types IntVal and ArithmeticOperation.

Semantic Algebra

$i \in Int = \{\ldots, -2, -1, 0, 1, 2, \ldots\}$

Operations on Int: $+_{Int}$, $-_{Int}$, $\times_{Int}$

Valuation Functions

$\mathcal{P} : \text{Prog} \to Int$

$\mathcal{P}[\![(\text{elmm } NE_{body})]\!] = \mathcal{NE}[\![NE_{body}]\!]$

$\mathcal{NE} : \text{NumExp} \to Int$

$\mathcal{NE}[\![N]\!] = \mathcal{N}[\![N]\!]$

$\mathcal{NE}[\![(A \ NE_1 \ NE_2)]\!] = (\mathcal{A}[\![A]\!] \ \mathcal{NE}[\![NE_1]\!] \ \mathcal{NE}[\![NE_2]\!])$

$\mathcal{A} : \text{ArithmeticOperator} \to (Int \to Int \to Int)$

$\mathcal{A}[\![\text{+}]\!] = +_{Int}$
$\mathcal{A}[\![\text{-}]\!] = -_{Int}$
$\mathcal{A}[\![\text{*}]\!] = \times_{Int}$

$\mathcal{N} : \text{IntLit} \to Int$

$\mathcal{N}$ maps integer numerals to the integer numbers they denote.

Figure 4.2   Denotational semantics for a version of ELMM without / and %.

for each of these two cases. In the integer numeral case, the $\mathcal{N}$ function maps the syntactic representation of an integer numeral into a mathematical integer. We will treat integer numerals as atomic entities, but their meaning could be determined in a denotational fashion from their component signs and digits (see Exercise 4.1). In the arithmetic operation case, the $\mathcal{A}$ function maps the operator name (one of +, -, and *) into a binary integer function with signature $Int \to Int \to Int$ that determines the meaning of the operation from the meanings of the operands. As explained on page 36, in applications of a function to a first argument delimited by double square brackets, we assume that the function binds tightly with the argument. So $(\mathcal{A}[\![A]\!] \ \mathcal{NE}[\![NE_1]\!] \ \mathcal{NE}[\![NE_2]\!])$ is parsed as if it were written $(\mathcal{A}[\![A]\!] \ (\mathcal{NE}[\![NE_1]\!]) \ (\mathcal{NE}[\![NE_2]\!]))$.

Figure 4.3 illustrates how the denotational semantics for the restricted version of ELMM can be used to determine the meaning of the sample ELMM program (elmm (* (+ 1 2) (- 9 5))). Because $\mathcal{P}$ maps programs to their meanings,

$\mathcal{P}[\![$(elmm (* (+ 1 2) (- 9 5)))$]\!]$

$= \mathcal{NE}[\![$(* (+ 1 2) (- 9 5))$]\!]$, by definition of $\mathcal{P}$

$= (\mathcal{A}[\![*]\!] \ \mathcal{NE}[\![$(+ 1 2)$]\!] \ \mathcal{NE}[\![$(- 9 5)$]\!])$, by definition of $\mathcal{NE}$ on arithmetic operations

$= \mathcal{NE}[\![$(+ 1 2)$]\!] \times_{Int} \mathcal{NE}[\![$(- 9 5)$]\!]$, by definition of $\mathcal{A}$

$= (\mathcal{A}[\![+]\!] \ \mathcal{NE}[\![1]\!] \ \mathcal{NE}[\![2]\!]) \times_{Int} (\mathcal{A}[\![-]\!] \ \mathcal{NE}[\![9]\!] \ \mathcal{NE}[\![5]\!])$,
   by definition of $\mathcal{NE}$ on arithmetic operations

$= (1 +_{Int} 2) \times_{Int} (9 -_{Int} 5)$, by definition of $\mathcal{NE}$ on integer literals and of $\mathcal{A}$

$= 3 \times_{Int} 4$, by definitions of $+_{Int}$ and $-_{Int}$

$= 12$, by definition of $\times_{Int}$

Figure 4.3 Meaning of a sample program in restricted ELMM.

$\mathcal{P}[\![$(elmm (* (+ 1 2) (- 9 5)))$]\!]$ *is* the meaning of this program. However, this fact is not very useful as stated, because the element of *Int* denoted by the program is not immediately apparent from the form of the metalanguage expression $\mathcal{P}[\![$(elmm (* (+ 1 2) (- 9 5)))$]\!]$. We would like to massage the metalanguage expression for the meaning of a program into another metalanguage expression more recognizable as an element of the answer domain. We do this by using **equational reasoning** to simplify the metalanguage expression. That is, we are allowed to make any simplifications that are permitted by usual mathematical reasoning about the entities denoted by the metalanguage expressions. Equational reasoning allows such manipulations as:

- substituting equals for equals;

- applying functions to arguments;

- equating two function-denoting expressions when, for each argument, they map that argument to the same result (this is called **extensionality**).

Instances of equational reasoning are organized into **equational proofs** that contain a series of equalities. Figure 4.3 presents an equational proof that the metalanguage expression $\mathcal{P}[\![$(elmm (* (+ 1 2) (- 9 5)))$]\!]$ is equal to the integer 12. Each equality in the proof is justified by familiar mathematical rules. For example, the equality

$$\mathcal{NE}[\![$(* (+ 1 2) (- 9 5))$]\!] = (\mathcal{A}[\![*]\!] \ \mathcal{NE}[\![$(+ 1 2)$]\!] \ \mathcal{NE}[\![$(- 9 5)$]\!])$$

is justified by the arithmetic operation clause in the definition of $\mathcal{NE}$, while the equality

$$(1 +_{Int} 2) \times_{Int} (9 -_{Int} 5) = 3 \times_{Int} 4$$

is justified by algebraic rules for manipulating integers. As we explained in Section A.2.5, for applications of standard numerical and logical functions, we often use infix notations like $(1 +_{Int} 2) \times_{Int} (9 -_{Int} 5)$ instead of prefix notations like $(\times_{Int} (+_{Int} 1\ 2)\ (-_{Int} 9\ 5))$ because the former are more familiar. We emphasize that every line in Figure 4.3 denotes exactly the same integer. The whole purpose of the equational proof is to simplify the original expression into another metalanguage expression whose form more directly expresses the meaning of the program.

4.2.2   Step 2: Full ELMM

What happens to the denotational semantics for ELMM if we add back in the / and % operators? We now have to worry about the meaning of expressions like (/ 1 0) and (% 2 0). We will model the meaning of such expressions by the distinguished token *error*. Since ELMM programs, numerical expressions, and arithmetic operators can now return errors in addition to integers, we represent their meanings using elements of an *Answer* domain that is a sum domain (Section A.3.4) including both of these kinds of entities (Figure 4.4).

We must also change the valuation functions $\mathcal{P}$, $\mathcal{NE}$, and $\mathcal{A}$ accordingly. The integer numeral clause for $\mathcal{NE}$ now needs the injection $Int \rightarrowtail Answer$. The arithmetic operation clause for $\mathcal{NE}$ must now propagate any errors found in the operands. This is done using the pattern-matching capabilities of the metalanguage construct **match**, which is defined in Section A.4. The expression

$$\textbf{match}\ \langle \mathcal{NE}[\![NE_1]\!], \mathcal{NE}[\![NE_2]\!] \rangle$$
$$\triangleright\ \langle (Int \rightarrowtail Answer\ i_1), (Int \rightarrowtail Answer\ i_2) \rangle\ [\!]\ (\mathcal{A}[\![A]\!]\ i_1\ i_2)$$
$$\triangleright\ \textbf{else}\ (Error \rightarrowtail Answer\ error)\ \textbf{end}$$

can be read as

> If the pair of answers $\langle \mathcal{NE}[\![NE_1]\!], \mathcal{NE}[\![NE_2]\!] \rangle$ can be created via the expression $\langle (Int \rightarrowtail Answer\ i_1), (Int \rightarrowtail Answer\ i_2) \rangle$ by substituting particular integers for i_1 and i_2, then return the integer answer that results from substituting the same integers for i_1 and i_2 in the expression $(\mathcal{A}[\![A]\!]\ i_1\ i_2)$. Otherwise, return the error answer $(Error \rightarrowtail Answer\ error)$.

The $\mathcal{A}$ clauses for / and % handle specially the case where the second operand is zero, and $Int \rightarrowtail Answer$ injections must be used in the "regular" cases for all operators.

In full ELMM, the sample program (elmm (* (+ 1 2) (- 9 5))) has the meaning $(Int \rightarrowtail Answer\ 12)$. Figure 4.5 presents an equational proof of this fact. All the pattern-matching clauses appearing in the proof are there to handle the propagation of errors.

Semantic Algebra

$i \in Int = \{\ldots, -2, -1, 0, 1, 2, \ldots\}$
  $Error = \{error\}$
$a \in Answer = Int + Error$

Operations on Int: $+_{Int}$, $-_{Int}$, $\times_{Int}$, $\div_{Int}$ (integer quotient), $\%_{Int}$ (remainder)

Valuation Functions

$\mathcal{P} : \text{Prog} \rightarrow Answer$

$\mathcal{P}[\![(\texttt{elmm } NE)]\!] = \mathcal{NE}[\![NE]\!]$

$\mathcal{NE} : \text{NumExp} \rightarrow Answer$

$\mathcal{NE}[\![N]\!] = (Int \rightarrowtail Answer \; \mathcal{N}[\![N]\!])$

$\mathcal{NE}[\![(A \; NE_1 \; NE_2)]\!] = \textbf{match } \langle \mathcal{NE}[\![NE_1]\!], \mathcal{NE}[\![NE_2]\!] \rangle$
$\qquad\qquad\qquad \triangleright \langle (Int \rightarrowtail Answer \; i_1), (Int \rightarrowtail Answer \; i_2) \rangle \; [\!] \; (\mathcal{A}[\![A]\!] \; i_1 \; i_2)$
$\qquad\qquad\qquad \triangleright \textbf{else } (Error \rightarrowtail Answer \; error) \textbf{ end}$

$\mathcal{A} : \text{ArithmeticOperator} \rightarrow (Int \rightarrow Int \rightarrow Answer)$

$\mathcal{A}[\![+]\!] = \lambda i_1 i_2 \; . \; (Int \rightarrowtail Answer \; (i_1 +_{Int} i_2))$
- and * are handled similarly.

$\mathcal{A}[\![/]\!] = \lambda i_1 i_2 \; . \; \textbf{if } i_2 = 0$
$\qquad\qquad\qquad \textbf{then } (Error \rightarrowtail Answer \; error)$
$\qquad\qquad\qquad \textbf{else } (Int \rightarrowtail Answer \; (i_1 \div_{Int} i_2)) \textbf{ end}$
% is handled similarly.

$\mathcal{N} : \text{IntLit} \rightarrow Int$

$\mathcal{N}$ maps integer numerals to the integer numbers they denote.

Figure 4.4 Denotational semantics for full ELMM (including / and %).

The sample program has no errors, but we could introduce one by replacing the subexpression (- 9 5) by (/ 9 0). Then the part of the proof beginning

$\quad = \textbf{match } \langle (\mathcal{A}[\![+]\!] \; 1 \; 2), (\mathcal{A}[\![-]\!] \; 9 \; 5) \rangle \ldots$

would become:

$\quad = \textbf{match } \langle (\mathcal{A}[\![+]\!] \; 1 \; 2), (\mathcal{A}[\![/]\!] \; 9 \; 0) \rangle$
$\qquad \triangleright \langle (Int \rightarrowtail Answer \; i_1), (Int \rightarrowtail Answer \; i_2) \rangle \; [\!] \; (\mathcal{A}[\![*]\!] \; i_1 \; i_2)$
$\qquad \triangleright \textbf{else } (Error \rightarrowtail Answer \; error) \textbf{ end}$

$\quad = \textbf{match } \langle (Int \rightarrowtail Answer \; (1 +_{Int} 2)), (Error \rightarrowtail Answer \; error) \rangle$
$\qquad \triangleright \langle (Int \rightarrowtail Answer \; i_1), (Int \rightarrowtail Answer \; i_2) \rangle \; [\!] \; (\mathcal{A}[\![*]\!] \; i_1 \; i_2)$
$\qquad \triangleright \textbf{else } (Error \rightarrowtail Answer \; error) \textbf{ end}$

$\quad = (Error \rightarrowtail Answer \; error)$

The final equality is justified by the fact that there is no integer i_2 for which $(Int \rightarrowtail Answer\ i_2)$ matches $(Error \rightarrowtail Answer\ error)$ in the second component of the pair of answers that is the discriminant of the **match** expression.

Expressing error propagation via explicit pattern matching makes the equational proof in Figure 4.5 rather messy. As in programming, in denotational semantics it is good practice to create abstractions that capture common patterns of behavior and hide messy details. This can improve the clarity of the definitions and proofs while at the same time making them more compact.

We illustrate this kind of abstraction by extending the semantic algebra to include the following higher-order function for simplifying error handling in ELMM:

$$with\text{-}int : Answer \rightarrow (Int \rightarrow Answer) \rightarrow Answer$$
$$= \lambda af \text{ . } \textbf{match } a$$
$$\triangleright (Int \rightarrowtail Answer\ i) \parallel (f\ i)$$
$$\triangleright \textbf{else } (Error \rightarrowtail Answer\ error) \textbf{ end}$$

with-int takes an answer a and a function f from integers to answers and returns an answer. It automatically propagates errors, in the sense that it maps an input error answer to an output error answer. The function f specifies what is done for inputs that are integer answers. Thus, *with-int* hides details of error handling and extracting integers from integer answers.

A metalanguage expression of the form $(with\text{-}int\ a\ (\lambda i \text{ . } E))$ serves as a kind of binding construct, i.e., a construct that introduces a name (in this case, i) for a value (in this case, the integer supplied to the injection function $Int \rightarrowtail Answer$ to create a). One way to read $(with\text{-}int\ a\ (\lambda i \text{ . } E))$ is:

If a can be expressed as $(Int \rightarrowtail Answer\ i)$ for a particular integer i, return the value of the expression that results from substituting this integer for every occurrence of i in E. Otherwise, a must be an error, in which case an error should be returned.

For example, the expression $(with\text{-}int\ (Int \rightarrowtail Answer\ 3)\ (\lambda i \text{ . } (i \times_{Int} i)))$ is equivalent to $3 \times_{Int} 3 = 9$, while $(with\text{-}int\ (Error \rightarrowtail Answer\ error)\ (\lambda i \text{ . } (i \times_{Int} i)))$ is equivalent to $(Error \rightarrowtail Answer\ error)$. The following equalities involving *with-int* are useful:

$$(with\text{-}int\ (Int \rightarrowtail Answer\ i)\ f) = (f\ i) \tag{4.1}$$
$$(with\text{-}int\ \mathcal{NE}[\![N]\!]\ f) = (f\ \mathcal{N}[\![N]\!]) \tag{4.2}$$
$$(with\text{-}int\ (Error \rightarrowtail Answer\ error)\ f) = (Error \rightarrowtail Answer\ error) \tag{4.3}$$

$\mathcal{P}[\![(\texttt{elmm (* (+ 1 2) (- 9 5)))}]\!]$

$= \mathcal{NE}[\![(\texttt{* (+ 1 2) (- 9 5))}]\!]$, by definition of $\mathcal{P}$

$= \textbf{match}\ \langle \mathcal{NE}[\![(\texttt{+ 1 2})]\!], \mathcal{NE}[\![(\texttt{- 9 5})]\!]\rangle$
    $\triangleright\ \langle(Int\rightarrowtail Answer\ i_1), (Int\rightarrowtail Answer\ i_2)\rangle\ [\![\ (\mathcal{A}[\![\texttt{*}]\!]\ i_1\ i_2)$
    $\triangleright\ \textbf{else}\ (Error\rightarrowtail Answer\ error)\ \textbf{end}$, by definition of $\mathcal{NE}$ on arithmetic operations

$= \textbf{match}\ \langle \textbf{match}\ \langle \mathcal{NE}[\![\texttt{1}]\!], \mathcal{NE}[\![\texttt{2}]\!]\rangle$
           $\triangleright\ \langle(Int\rightarrowtail Answer\ i_3), (Int\rightarrowtail Answer\ i_4)\rangle\ [\![\ (\mathcal{A}[\![\texttt{+}]\!]\ i_3\ i_4)$
           $\triangleright\ \textbf{else}\ (Error\rightarrowtail Answer\ error)\ \textbf{end}$,
          $\textbf{match}\ \langle \mathcal{NE}[\![\texttt{9}]\!], \mathcal{NE}[\![\texttt{5}]\!]\rangle$
           $\triangleright\ \langle(Int\rightarrowtail Answer\ i_5), (Int\rightarrowtail Answer\ i_6)\rangle\ [\![\ (\mathcal{A}[\![\texttt{-}]\!]\ i_5\ i_6)$
           $\triangleright\ \textbf{else}\ (Error\rightarrowtail Answer\ error)\ \textbf{end}\rangle$
    $\triangleright\ \langle(Int\rightarrowtail Answer\ i_1), (Int\rightarrowtail Answer\ i_2)\rangle\ [\![\ (\mathcal{A}[\![\texttt{*}]\!]\ i_1\ i_2)$
    $\triangleright\ \textbf{else}\ (Error\rightarrowtail Answer\ error)\ \textbf{end}$, by definition of $\mathcal{NE}$ on arithmetic operations

$= \textbf{match}\ \langle \textbf{match}\ \langle(Int\rightarrowtail Answer\ 1), (Int\rightarrowtail Answer\ 2)\rangle$
           $\triangleright\ \langle(Int\rightarrowtail Answer\ i_3), (Int\rightarrowtail Answer\ i_4)\rangle\ [\![\ (\mathcal{A}[\![\texttt{+}]\!]\ i_3\ i_4)$
           $\triangleright\ \textbf{else}\ (Error\rightarrowtail Answer\ error)\ \textbf{end}$,
          $\textbf{match}\ \langle(Int\rightarrowtail Answer\ 9), (Int\rightarrowtail Answer\ 5)\rangle$
           $\triangleright\ \langle(Int\rightarrowtail Answer\ i_5), (Int\rightarrowtail Answer\ i_6)\rangle\ [\![\ (\mathcal{A}[\![\texttt{-}]\!]\ i_5\ i_6)$
           $\triangleright\ \textbf{else}\ (Error\rightarrowtail Answer\ error)\ \textbf{end}\rangle$
    $\triangleright\ \langle(Int\rightarrowtail Answer\ i_1), (Int\rightarrowtail Answer\ i_2)\rangle\ [\![\ (\mathcal{A}[\![\texttt{*}]\!]\ i_1\ i_2)$
    $\triangleright\ \textbf{else}\ (Error\rightarrowtail Answer\ error)\ \textbf{end}$, by definition of $\mathcal{NE}$ on integer literals

$= \textbf{match}\ \langle(\mathcal{A}[\![\texttt{+}]\!]\ 1\ 2), (\mathcal{A}[\![\texttt{-}]\!]\ 9\ 5)\rangle$
    $\triangleright\ \langle(Int\rightarrowtail Answer\ i_1), (Int\rightarrowtail Answer\ i_2)\rangle\ [\![\ (\mathcal{A}[\![\texttt{*}]\!]\ i_1\ i_2)$
    $\triangleright\ \textbf{else}\ (Error\rightarrowtail Answer\ error)\ \textbf{end}$, by pattern matching of $\textbf{match}$

$= \textbf{match}\ \langle(Int\rightarrowtail Answer\ (1 +_{Int} 2)), (Int\rightarrowtail Answer\ (9 -_{Int} 5))\rangle$
    $\triangleright\ \langle(Int\rightarrowtail Answer\ i_1), (Int\rightarrowtail Answer\ i_2)\rangle\ [\![\ (\mathcal{A}[\![\texttt{*}]\!]\ i_1\ i_2)$
    $\triangleright\ \textbf{else}\ (Error\rightarrowtail Answer\ error)\ \textbf{end}$, by definition of $\mathcal{A}$

$= \textbf{match}\ \langle(Int\rightarrowtail Answer\ 3), (Int\rightarrowtail Answer\ 4)\rangle$
    $\triangleright\ \langle(Int\rightarrowtail Answer\ i_1), (Int\rightarrowtail Answer\ i_2)\rangle\ [\![\ (\mathcal{A}[\![\texttt{*}]\!]\ i_1\ i_2)$
    $\triangleright\ \textbf{else}\ (Error\rightarrowtail Answer\ error)\ \textbf{end}$, by definitions of $+_{Int}$ and $-_{Int}$

$= (\mathcal{A}[\![\texttt{*}]\!]\ 3\ 4)$, by pattern matching of $\textbf{match}$

$= (Int\rightarrowtail Answer\ (3 \times_{Int} 4))$, by definition of $\mathcal{A}$

$= (Int\rightarrowtail Answer\ 12)$, by definition of $\times_{Int}$

Figure 4.5   Meaning of a sample program in full ELMM.

Using *with-int*, the $\mathcal{NE}$ valuation clause for arithmetic expressions can be redefined as:

$\mathcal{NE}[\![(A\ NE_1\ NE_2)]\!]$
   $= \textit{with-int}\ \mathcal{NE}[\![NE_1]\!]\ (\lambda i_1 .\ (\textit{with-int}\ \mathcal{NE}[\![NE_2]\!]\ (\lambda i_2 .\ (\mathcal{A}[\![A]\!]\ i_1\ i_2))))$

With this modified definition and the above *with-int* equalities, details of error propagation can be hidden in equational proofs for ELMM meanings (see Figure 4.6).

One of the powers of lambda notation is that it supports the invention of new binding constructs like *with-int* via higher-order functions without requiring any new syntactic extensions to the metalanguage. We will make extensive use of this power to simplify our future denotational definitions. Later we will see how this idea appears in practical programming in monadic style (Section 8.3), continuation-passing style (Sections 9.2 and 17.9), and pattern matching (Section 10.5).

4.2.3   Step 3: ELM

The ELM language (Exercise 3.10 on page 67) is obtained from ELMM by adding indexed input via the expression (arg N_{index}), where N_{index} specifies the index (starting at 1) of a program argument. The form of a program is (elm $N_{numargs}$ NE_{body}), where $N_{numargs}$ indicates the number of integer arguments expected by the program when it is executed.

Intuitively, the meaning of ELM programs and numerical expressions must now be extended to include the program arguments. In Figure 4.7, this is expressed by modeling the meaning of programs and expressions as functions with signature $Int^* \rightarrow Answer$ that map the context domain Int^* (a sequence of integers representing the program arguments) to the answer domain $Answer$ (either an integer or an error). The program argument sequence i^* must be "passed down" the syntax tree to the body of a program and the operands of an arithmetic operation so that they can eventually be referenced in an arg expression at a leaf of the syntax tree. The valuation function for an ELM program must check that the number of supplied arguments matches the expected number of arguments $\mathcal{N}[\![N_{numargs}]\!]$, and the valuation function for an arg expression must check that the index $\mathcal{N}[\![N_{index}]\!]$ is between 1 and the number of arguments, inclusive.[2]

Figure 4.8 uses denotational definitions to find the result of applying the ELM program (elm 2 (+ (arg 2) (* (arg 1) 3))) to the argument sequence $[4, 5]$. The equational proof assumes the following equalities, which are easy to verify:

---

[2]In these valuation clauses, we take a few liberties involving the types of metalanguage expressions. (See Section A.3 for a discussion of types in the metalanguage.) Each occurrence of (*length* i^*) should really be $Nat \hookrightarrow Int$ (*length* i^*) since *length* returns a natural number, but this number is used in contexts where an integer is expected. Also, in the application (*nth* $\mathcal{N}[\![N_{index}]\!]$ i^*), the first argument of *nth* should have type *Pos*, but $\mathcal{N}[\![N_{index}]\!]$ has type *Int*. However, this application occurs in a context where $\mathcal{N}[\![N_{index}]\!]$ is guaranteed to be a positive integer, so $\mathcal{N}[\![N_{index}]\!]$ effectively denotes an element of *Pos* in this context. We will take similar liberties in other denotational definitions without comment.

$\mathcal{P}[\![\text{(elmm (* (+ 1 2) (- 9 5)))}]\!]$

$= \mathcal{NE}[\![\text{(* (+ 1 2) (- 9 5))}]\!]$, by definition of $\mathcal{P}$

$= \textit{with-int } \mathcal{NE}[\![\text{(+ 1 2)}]\!]$
  $(\lambda i_1 \text{ . } \textit{with-int } \mathcal{NE}[\![\text{(- 9 5)}]\!]$
    $(\lambda i_2 \text{ . } (\mathcal{A}[\![\text{*}]\!] \ i_1 \ i_2)))$, by new definition of $\mathcal{NE}$ on arithmetic operations

$= \textit{with-int } (\textit{with-int } \mathcal{NE}[\![1]\!]$
      $(\lambda i_3 \text{ . } \textit{with-int } \mathcal{NE}[\![2]\!]$
        $(\lambda i_4 \text{ . } (\mathcal{A}[\![\text{+}]\!] \ i_3 \ i_4))))$
  $(\lambda i_1 \text{ . } \textit{with-int } (\textit{with-int } \mathcal{NE}[\![9]\!]$
          $(\lambda i_5 \text{ . } \textit{with-int } \mathcal{NE}[\![5]\!]$
            $(\lambda i_6 \text{ . } (\mathcal{A}[\![\text{-}]\!] \ i_5 \ i_6))))$
    $(\lambda i_2 \text{ . } (\mathcal{A}[\![\text{*}]\!] \ i_1 \ i_2)))$, by new definition of $\mathcal{NE}$ on arithmetic operations

$= \textit{with-int } (\mathcal{A}[\![\text{+}]\!] \ 1 \ 2)$
  $(\lambda i_1 \text{ . } \textit{with-int } (\mathcal{A}[\![\text{-}]\!] \ 9 \ 5)$
    $(\lambda i_2 \text{ . } (\mathcal{A}[\![\text{*}]\!] \ i_1 \ i_2)))$, by (4.2)

$= \textit{with-int } (Int \rightarrowtail Answer \ (1 +_{Int} 2))$
  $(\lambda i_1 \text{ . } \textit{with-int } (Int \rightarrowtail Answer \ (9 -_{Int} 5))$
    $(\lambda i_2 \text{ . } (Int \rightarrowtail Answer \ (i_1 \times_{Int} i_2))))$, by definition of $\mathcal{A}$

$= (Int \rightarrowtail Answer \ ((1 +_{Int} 2) \times_{Int} (9 -_{Int} 5)))$, by (4.1)

$= (Int \rightarrowtail Answer \ (3 \times_{Int} 4))$, by definitions of $+_{Int}$ and $\times_{Int}$

$= (Int \rightarrowtail Answer \ 12)$, by definition of $\times_{Int}$

Figure 4.6 Example illustrating how *with-int* hides error propagation.

$$(\textit{with-int } (\mathcal{NE}[\![N]\!] \ i^*) \ f) = (f \ \mathcal{N}[\![N]\!]) \qquad (4.4)$$

$$(\textit{with-int } (\mathcal{NE}[\![\text{(arg } N)]\!] \ [i_1, \ldots, i_k, \ldots, i_n]) \ f) = (f \ i_k), \quad (4.5)$$
$$\text{where } \mathcal{N}[\![N]\!] = k$$

$$(\textit{with-int } (\mathcal{A}[\![A]\!] \ i_1 \ i_2) \ f) = (f \ i_{ans}), \qquad (4.6)$$
$$\text{where } (\mathcal{A}[\![A]\!] \ i_1 \ i_2) = (Int \rightarrowtail Answer \ i_{ans})$$

In Figure 4.8, if we replace the concrete argument integers 4 and 5 by abstract integers i_{arg1} and i_{arg2}, respectively, then the result would be

$$(Int \rightarrowtail Answer \ (i_{arg2} +_{Int} (i_{arg1} \times_{Int} 3)))$$

Based on this observation, we can give a meaning to the sample program itself (i.e., without applying it to particular arguments). Such a meaning must be abstracted over an arbitrary argument sequence:

Semantic Algebra

$i \in Int = \{\ldots, -2, -1, 0, 1, 2, \ldots\}$
    $Error = \{error\}$
$a \in Answer = Int + Error$

Operations on Int: $+_{Int}$, $-_{Int}$, $\times_{Int}$, $\div_{Int}$, $\%_{Int}$
Operation on $Answer$: $with\text{-}int$ (defined on page 122)

Valuation Functions

$\mathcal{P} : \text{Prog} \to Int^* \to Answer$

$\mathcal{P}[\![(\texttt{elm } N_{numargs} \ NE_{body})]\!]$
    $= \lambda i^*$. $\textbf{if } (length \ i^*) =_{Int} \mathcal{N}[\![N_{numargs}]\!]$
            $\textbf{then } \mathcal{NE}[\![NE]\!] \ i^*$
            $\textbf{else } (Error \rightarrowtail Answer \ error) \ \textbf{end}$

$\mathcal{NE} : \text{NumExp} \to Int^* \to Answer$

$\mathcal{NE}[\![N_{num}]\!] = \lambda i^*$. $(Int \rightarrowtail Answer \ \mathcal{N}[\![N_{num}]\!])$

$\mathcal{NE}[\![(\texttt{arg } N_{index})]\!] = \lambda i^*$. $\textbf{if } (1 \leq_{Int} \mathcal{N}[\![N_{index}]\!]) \wedge (\mathcal{N}[\![N_{index}]\!] \leq_{Int} (length \ i^*))$
                        $\textbf{then } (Int \rightarrowtail Answer \ (nth \ \mathcal{N}[\![N_{index}]\!] \ i^*))$
                        $\textbf{else } (Error \rightarrowtail Answer \ error) \ \textbf{end}$

$\mathcal{NE}[\![(A \ NE_1 \ NE_2)]\!]$
    $= \lambda i^*$. $with\text{-}int \ (\mathcal{NE}[\![NE_1]\!] \ i^*)$
              $(\lambda i_1 \ . \ with\text{-}int \ (\mathcal{NE}[\![NE_2]\!] \ i^*) \ (\lambda i_2 \ . \ (\mathcal{A}[\![A]\!] \ i_1 \ i_2)))$

$\mathcal{N} : \text{IntLit} \to Int$ and $\mathcal{A} : \text{ArithmeticOperator} \to (Int \to Int \to Answer)$
are unchanged from ELMM (Figure 4.4).

Figure 4.7   Denotational semantics for ELM.

$\mathcal{P}[\![(\texttt{elmm 2 (+ (arg 2) (* (arg 1) 3)))}]\!]$
    $= \lambda i^*$. $\textbf{match } i^*$
            $\triangleright [i_{arg1}, i_{arg2}] \ [\!] \ (Int \rightarrowtail Answer \ (i_{arg2} +_{Int} (i_{arg1} \times_{Int} 3)))$
            $\triangleright \textbf{else } (Error \rightarrowtail Answer \ error) \ \textbf{end}$

Here we have translated the **if** that appears in the $\mathcal{P}$ definition in Figure 4.7 into
an equivalent **match** construct that gives the names i_{arg1} and i_{arg2} to the two
integer arguments in the case where the argument sequence i^* has two elements.
We showed above that the result in this case is correct, and we know that an
error is returned for any other length.

$\mathcal{P}[\![\texttt{(elm 2 (+ (arg 2) (* (arg 1) 3)))}]\!]\ [4,5]$

$= \textbf{if}\ (length\ [4,5]) =_{Int} \mathcal{N}[\![2]\!]$
     $\textbf{then}\ \mathcal{NE}[\![\texttt{(+ (arg 2) (* (arg 1) 3))}]\!]\ [4,5]$
     $\textbf{else}\ (Error \rightarrowtail Answer\ error)\ \textbf{end}$, by the definition of $\mathcal{P}$

$= \mathcal{NE}[\![\texttt{(+ (arg 2) (* (arg 1) 3))}]\!]\ [4,5]$, by $length$, $=_{Int}$, and $\textbf{if}$

$= with\text{-}int\ (\mathcal{NE}[\![\texttt{(arg 2)}]\!]\ [4,5])$
     $(\lambda i_1 .\ with\text{-}int\ (\mathcal{NE}[\![\texttt{(* (arg 1) 3)}]\!]\ [4,5])$
         $(\lambda i_2 .\ (\mathcal{A}[\![\texttt{+}]\!]\ i_1\ i_2)))$, by the definition of $\mathcal{NE}$

$= with\text{-}int\ (\mathcal{NE}[\![\texttt{(* (arg 1) 3)}]\!]\ [4,5])$
     $(\lambda i_2 .\ (\mathcal{A}[\![\texttt{+}]\!]\ 5\ i_2))$, by (4.5)

$= with\text{-}int\ (with\text{-}int\ (\mathcal{NE}[\![\texttt{(arg 1)}]\!]\ [4,5])$
         $(\lambda i_3 .\ with\text{-}int\ (\mathcal{NE}[\![3]\!]\ [4,5])$
             $(\lambda i_4 .\ (\mathcal{A}[\![\texttt{*}]\!]\ i_3\ i_4)))$
     $(\lambda i_2 .\ (\mathcal{A}[\![\texttt{+}]\!]\ 5\ i_2))$, by the definition of $\mathcal{NE}$

$= with\text{-}int\ (with\text{-}int\ (\mathcal{NE}[\![3]\!]\ [4,5])$
         $(\lambda i_4 .\ (\mathcal{A}[\![\texttt{*}]\!]\ 4\ i_4))$
     $(\lambda i_2 .\ (\mathcal{A}[\![\texttt{+}]\!]\ 5\ i_2))$, by (4.5)

$= (with\text{-}int\ (\mathcal{A}[\![\texttt{*}]\!]\ 4\ 3)\ (\lambda i_2 .\ (\mathcal{A}[\![\texttt{+}]\!]\ 5\ i_2)))$, by (4.4)

$= (\mathcal{A}[\![\texttt{+}]\!]\ 5\ 12)$, by (4.6)

$= (Int \rightarrowtail Answer\ 17)$, by the definition of $\mathcal{A}$

Figure 4.8 Meaning of an ELM program applied to two arguments.

4.2.4 Step 4: EL

Full EL (Figure 2.4, page 25) is obtained from ELM by adding a numerical `if` expression and boolean expressions for controlling the `if` expressions. Boolean expressions BE include the boolean literals `true` and `false`, relational expressions like (< NE_1 NE_2), and logical expressions like (`and` BE_1 BE_2). Since boolean expressions can include numerical expressions as subexpressions and such subexpressions can denote errors, boolean expressions can also denote errors (e.g. (< 1 (/ 2 0))). In Figure 4.9, we model this by having the valuation function $\mathcal{BE}$ for boolean expressions return an element in the domain *BoolAnswer* of "boolean answers" that is distinct from the domain *Answer* of "integer answers." Since a numerical subexpression of a relational expression could be an `arg` expression, the meaning of a boolean expression is a function with signature $Int^* \to BoolAnswer$ that maps implicit program arguments to a boolean answer.

The error handling for relational and logical operations is performed by $\mathcal{BE}$, so the $\mathcal{R}$ and $\mathcal{L}$ valuation functions manipulate only nonerror values.

Note that the error-handling in $\mathcal{BE}[\![(R_{rator}\ NE_1\ NE_2)]\!]$ is performed by pattern matching. Could it instead be done via *with-int*? No. The final return value of *with-int* is in *Answer*, but the final return value of $\mathcal{BE}$ is in *BoolAnswer*. However, we could define and use a new auxiliary function that is like *with-int* but returns an element of *BoolAnswer* (see Exercise 4.3 on page 131).

Something that stands out in our study of the denotational semantics of the EL dialects is the importance of semantic domains and the signatures of valuation functions. Studying these yields insight into the fundamental nature of a language, even if the detailed valuation clause definitions are unavailable. For example, consider the signature of the numerical expression valuation function $\mathcal{NE}$ in the various dialects we studied. In ELMM without / and %, the signature

$$\mathcal{NE} : \text{NumExp} \rightarrow \textit{Int}$$

indicates that an expression simply stands for an integer. In full ELMM, the "unwound" signature

$$\mathcal{NE} : \text{NumExp} \rightarrow (\textit{Int} + \textit{Error})$$

indicates that errors may be encountered in the evaluation of some expressions. The ELM (and EL) signature

$$\mathcal{NE} : \text{NumExp} \rightarrow \textit{Int}^* \rightarrow (\textit{Int} + \textit{Error})$$

has a context domain $\textit{Int}^*$ representing program arguments that are passed down the abstract syntax tree. We will see many kinds of context domains in our study of other languages. Some, like ELM program arguments, flow down only to subexpressions. We shall see later that elements of other context domains can have more complex flows, and that these flows are reflected in the valuation function signatures.

4.2.5   A Denotational Semantics Is Not a Program

You may have noticed that the denotational definitions for the dialects of EL strongly resemble programs in certain programming languages. In fact, it is straightforward to write an executable EL interpreter that reflects the structure of its valuation clauses, especially in functional programming languages like ML, Haskell, and Scheme. Of course, an interpreter has to be explicit about many of the details suppressed in the denotational definition (parsing the concrete syntax, choosing appropriate data structures to represent domain elements, etc.). Furthermore, details of the implementation language may complicate matters.

Semantic Algebra

$i \in Int = \{\dots, -2, -1, 0, 1, 2, \dots\}$

$b \in Bool = \{\text{true}, \text{false}\}$

$Error = \{\text{error}\}$

$a \in Answer = Int + Error$

$ba \in BoolAnswer = Bool + Error$

Operations on $Bool$: $\wedge$ (conjunction), $\vee$ (disjunction)

Operations on Int: $+_{Int}$, $-_{Int}$, $\times_{Int}$, $\div_{Int}$, $\%_{Int}$, $<_{Int}$, $=_{Int}$, $>_{Int}$

Operation on $Answer$: with-int (defined on page 122)

Valuation Functions

$\mathcal{P} : \text{Prog} \rightarrow Int^* \rightarrow Answer$

$\mathcal{P}$ is unchanged from ELM (Figure 4.4, except the keyword `elm` becomes `el`).

$\mathcal{NE} : \text{NumExp} \rightarrow Int^* \rightarrow Answer$

$\mathcal{NE}[\![(\text{if } BE_{test} \ NE_{then} \ NE_{else})]\!]$
$\quad = \lambda i^* . \ \textbf{match} \ (\mathcal{BE}[\![BE_{test}]\!] \ i^*)$
$\qquad\qquad \triangleright (Bool \rightarrowtail BoolAnswer \ b) \ [\![$
$\qquad\qquad\quad \textbf{if } b \ \textbf{then } \mathcal{NE}[\![NE_{then}]\!] \ i^* \ \textbf{else } \mathcal{NE}[\![NE_{else}]\!] \ i^* \ \textbf{end}$
$\qquad\qquad \triangleright \textbf{else} \ (Error \rightarrowtail Answer \ \text{error}) \ \textbf{end}$

The other $\mathcal{NE}$ clauses are unchanged from ELM (Figure 4.7).

$\mathcal{BE} : \text{BoolExp} \rightarrow Int^* \rightarrow BoolAnswer$

$\mathcal{BE}[\![\text{true}]\!] = \lambda i^* . \ (Bool \rightarrowtail BoolAnswer \ \text{true})$

$\mathcal{BE}[\![\text{false}]\!] = \lambda i^* . \ (Bool \rightarrowtail BoolAnswer \ \text{false})$

$\mathcal{BE}[\![(R_{rator} \ NE_1 \ NE_2)]\!]$
$\quad = \lambda i^* . \ \textbf{match} \ \langle \mathcal{NE}[\![NE_1]\!] \ i^*, \mathcal{NE}[\![NE_2]\!] \ i^* \rangle$
$\qquad\qquad \triangleright \langle (Int \rightarrowtail Answer \ i_1), (Int \rightarrowtail Answer \ i_2) \rangle \ [\![$
$\qquad\qquad\quad (Bool \rightarrowtail BoolAnswer \ (\mathcal{R}[\![R]\!] \ i_1 \ i_2))$
$\qquad\qquad \triangleright \textbf{else} \ (Error \rightarrowtail BoolAnswer \ \text{error}) \ \textbf{end}$

$\mathcal{BE}[\![(L_{rator} \ BE_1 \ BE_2)]\!]$
$\quad = \lambda i^* . \ \textbf{match} \ \langle \mathcal{BE}[\![BE_1]\!] \ i^*, \mathcal{BE}[\![BE_2]\!] \ i^* \rangle$
$\qquad\qquad \triangleright \langle (Bool \rightarrowtail BoolAnswer \ b_1), (Bool \rightarrowtail BoolAnswer \ b_2) \rangle \ [\![$
$\qquad\qquad\quad (Bool \rightarrowtail BoolAnswer \ (\mathcal{L}[\![L]\!] \ b_1 \ b_2))$
$\qquad\qquad \triangleright \textbf{else} \ (Error \rightarrowtail BoolAnswer \ \text{error}) \ \textbf{end}$

$\mathcal{R} : \text{RelationalOperator} \rightarrow (Int \rightarrow Int \rightarrow Bool)$
$\mathcal{R}[\![\text{<}]\!] = <_{Int} \qquad \mathcal{R}[\![\text{=}]\!] = =_{Int} \qquad \mathcal{R}[\![\text{>}]\!] = >_{Int}$

$\mathcal{L} : \text{LogicalOperator} \rightarrow (Bool \rightarrow Bool \rightarrow Bool)$
$\mathcal{L}[\![\text{and}]\!] = \wedge \qquad \mathcal{L}[\![\text{or}]\!] = \vee$

$\mathcal{N} : \text{IntLit} \rightarrow Int$ and $\mathcal{A} : \text{ArithmeticOperator} \rightarrow (Int \rightarrow Int \rightarrow Answer)$
are unchanged from ELMM (Figure 4.4).

Figure 4.9 Denotational semantics for EL.

In particular, the correspondence will be much less direct if the implementation programming language does not support first-class procedures.

Although a denotational definition often suggests an approach for implementing an interpreter program, it can be misleading to think of the denotational definition itself as a program. Programming language procedures typically imply computation; denotational specifications do not. An interpreter specifies a process for evaluating program phrases, often one with particular operational properties. In contrast, there is no notion of process associated with a valuation function: it is simply a declarative description for a mathematical function (i.e., a triple of a source, a target, and a graph).

For example, consider the following metalanguage expression, which might arise in the context of reasoning about an ELMM program:

$$\lambda i_0 \,.\, \textit{with-int} \ (\mathcal{A}[\![/]\!] \ i_0 \ 2) \ (\lambda i_1 \,.\, (\textit{with-int} \ (\mathcal{A}[\![-]\!] \ 3 \ 3) \ (\lambda i_2 \,.\, (\mathcal{A}[\![*]\!] \ i_1 \ i_2))))$$

If we (incorrectly) view this as an expression in a programming language like ML or SCHEME, we might think that no evaluation can take place until an integer is supplied for i_0, and that after this happens, the division must be performed first, followed by the subtraction, and finally the multiplication. But there is no inherent notion of evaluation order associated with the metalanguage expression. We can perform any mathematical simplifications in any order on this expression. For example, observing that $(\mathcal{A}[\![-]\!] \ 3 \ 3)$ has the same meaning as $(\mathcal{N}\mathcal{E}[\![0]\!])$ allows us to rewrite the expression to

$$\lambda i_0 \,.\, \textit{with-int} \ (\mathcal{A}[\![/]\!] \ i_0 \ 2) \ (\lambda i_1 \,.\, (\textit{with-int} \ (\mathcal{N}\mathcal{E}[\![0]\!]) \ (\lambda i_2 \,.\, (\mathcal{A}[\![*]\!] \ i_1 \ i_2))))$$

This is equivalent to

$$\lambda i_0 \,.\, \textit{with-int} \ (\mathcal{A}[\![/]\!] \ i_0 \ 2) \ (\lambda i_1 \,.\, (\mathcal{A}[\![*]\!] \ i_1 \ 0))$$

which is in turn equivalent to

$$\lambda i_0 \,.\, \textit{with-int} \ (\mathcal{A}[\![/]\!] \ i_0 \ 2) \ (\lambda i_1 \,.\, (\textit{Int} \rightarrowtail \textit{Answer} \ 0))$$

since the product of 0 and any integer is 0. A division result cannot be an error when the second argument is nonzero, so this can be further simplified to

$$\lambda i_0 \,.\, (\textit{Int} \rightarrowtail \textit{Answer} \ 0)$$

The moral of this example is that many simplifications can be done with metalanguage expressions that would be difficult to justify with expressions in most programming languages.[3]

---

[3]Certain real-world programming languages, particularly the purely functional language HASKELL, were designed to support the kind of mathematical reasoning that can be done with metalanguage expressions.

Exercise 4.1 We have treated integer numerals atomically, but we could express them in terms of their component signs and digits via an s-expression grammar:

$SN \in$ SignedNumeral ::= (+ *UN*) | (- *UN*) | *UN*

$UN \in$ UnsignedNumeral ::= *D* | (@ *UN* *D*)

$D \in$ Digit ::= 0 | 1 | 2 | 3 | 4 | 5 | 6 | 7 | 8 | 9

For example, the numeral traditionally written as -273 would be written in s-expression form as (- (@ (@ 2 7) 3)). Give a denotational semantics for numerals by providing valuation functions for each of SignedNumeral, UnsignedNumeral, and Digit.

Exercise 4.2 Use the ELM semantics to determine the meaning of the following ELM program: (elm 2 (/ (arg 1) (- (arg 1) (arg 2)))).

Exercise 4.3 By analogy with the *with-int* auxiliary function in the ELM semantics, define functions with the following signatures and use them to "hide" error handling in the EL valuation clauses for conditional expressions, relational operations, and logical operations:

with-bool : *BoolAnswer* → (*Bool* → *Answer*) → *Answer*

with-int$_{BA}$: *Answer* → (*Int* → *BoolAnswer*) → *BoolAnswer*

with-bool$_{BA}$: *BoolAnswer* → (*Bool* → *BoolAnswer*) → *BoolAnswer*

4.3 A Denotational Semantics for PostFix

We are now ready to flesh out the details of the denotational description of POSTFIX that were sketched in Section 4.1. The abstract syntax for POSTFIX was provided in Figure 2.12 on page 40, so the syntactic algebra is already taken care of. We need to construct the semantic algebra and the meaning function.

4.3.1 A Semantic Algebra for PostFix

What kind of mathematical entities should we use to model POSTFIX programs? Suppose that we have some sort of entity representing stacks. Then it's natural to model both POSTFIX commands and command sequences as functions that transform one stack entity into another. For example, the swap command could be modeled by a function that takes a stack as an argument, and returns a stack in which the top two elements have been swapped.

We need to make some provision for the case where the stack contains an insufficient number of elements or the wrong type of elements. For this purpose we will assume that there is a distinguished stack, *errorStack*, that signifies an error. For example, applying the transform associated with the swap command to a stack with fewer than two elements should return *errorStack*. All transforms should return *errorStack* when given *errorStack* as an argument.

$$
\begin{aligned}
&t \in StackTransform \;=\; Stack \rightarrow Stack\\
&s \in Stack \;=\; Value^* + Error\\
&v \in Value \;=\; Int + StackTransform\\
&r \in Result \;=\; Value + Error\\
&a \in Answer \;=\; Int + Error\\
&\quad\; Error \;=\; \{error\}\\
&i \in Int \;=\; \{\ldots,\; -2,\; -1,\; 0,\; 1,\; 2,\; \ldots\}\\
&b \in Bool \;=\; \{true, false\}
\end{aligned}
$$

Figure 4.10   Semantic domains for the POSTFIX denotational semantics.

Figure 4.10 presents domain definitions that describe one implementation of this approach. The *StackTransform* domain consists of functions from stacks to stacks, where an element of the domain *Stack* is either a sequence of values or the distinguished error stack (here modeled by the single element of the unit domain *Error*). The domain *Value* of stackable values includes not only integers but also stack transforms, which model executable sequences that have been pushed onto the stack. The *Result* domain models intermediate results obtained from stack manipulations or arithmetic operations. It includes an error result to model situations like popping an empty stack and dividing by zero. The *Answer* domain models the final outcome of a POSTFIX program. Like *Result*, *Answer* includes an error answer, but its only nonerror answers are integers (because an executable sequence at the top of a final stack is treated as an error).

A somewhat unsettling property of the domain definitions in the figure is that they are recursive — transforms operate on stacks, which themselves may contain transforms. In Chapter 5 we will discuss how to understand a set of recursively defined domain equations. For now, we'll just assume that these equations have a sensible interpretation.[4]

We extend the semantic domains into a semantic algebra by defining a collection of constants and functions on the domains. For now we'll just specify the interfaces to these constants and functions. We'll defer the details of their definitions until we've studied the meaning function. This will allow us to move more quickly to the core of the denotational semantics — the meaning function — without getting sidetracked by details of the definitions of the semantic functions.

Figure 4.11 gives informal specifications for the constants and functions we will use to manipulate the semantic domains. We will study the implementa-

---

[4]It turns out that the domain definitions for *Stack* and *Answer* aren't quite right as stated, because they are missing a "bottom" element denoting nontermination. See the discussion in Section 4.4.3.

errorResult : *Result*
  An error in the domain *Result*.

errorAnswer : *Answer*
  An error in the domain *Answer*.

errorStack : *Stack*
  The distinguished error stack.

errorTransform : *StackTransform*
  A transform that maps all stacks to *errorStack*.

push : *Result* → *StackTransform*
  Given a result that is a value v, return a transform that pushes v onto a stack; otherwise return *errorTransform*.

pop : *StackTransform*
  For a nonempty stack s, return the stack resulting from popping the top value; otherwise return *errorStack*.

top : *Stack* → *Result*
  Given a nonempty stack s, return a result that is the top element of s; otherwise return *errorResult*.

intAt : *Int* → *Stack* → *Result*
  Given an integer i_{index} and a stack whose i_{index}th element (starting from 1) is the integer i_{result}, return i_{result}; otherwise return *errorResult*.

arithop : (*Int* → *Int* → *Result*) → *StackTransform*
  Let $f : Int \rightarrow Int \rightarrow Result$ be the functional argument to *arithop*. Return a transform with the following behavior: if the given stack has two integers i_1 and i_2 followed by s_{rest}, then return a stack whose top value v_{result} is followed by s_{rest}, where (*Value* ↣*Result* v_{result}) is the result of the application (f i_2 i_1). If the given stack is not of this form or if the result of applying f is *errorResult*, then return *errorStack*.

transform : *Result* → *StackTransform*
  Given a result that is a stack transform, return it; otherwise return *errorTransform*.

resToAns : *Result* → *Answer*
  Given a result that is an integer, return it as an answer; otherwise return *errorAnswer*.

Figure 4.11 Specifications for constants and functions on POSTFIX semantic domains.

tion of these later, in Section 4.3.3. *errorResult*, *errorAnswer*, *errorStack*, and *errorTransform* are just names for useful constants involving errors. *push*, *pop*, and *top* are the usual stack operations. Their specifications are complicated somewhat by the details of error handling. For example, *top* returns an element of *Result* rather than *Value* because it must return *errorResult* in the case where the given stack is empty. *push* takes its argument from *Result* rather than *Value* so that it can be composed with *top*. *intAt* is an auxiliary function that simplifies the specification of `nget`. *arithop* simplifies the specifications for arithmetic and relational commands; it serves to abstract over a common behavior (replacing the top two integers on the stack by some value that depends on them) while suppressing error-handling detail (returning an error stack if any error is encountered along the way). *transform* facilitates error handling when a result that is expected to be a transform turns out to be an integer or an error result instead. *resToAns* handles the conversion from results to answers.

The signatures of the stack functions *push*, *pop*, *arithop*, *transform*, and *errorTransform* may seem strange at first glance, because they don't explicitly refer to the *Stack* domain. But recall that *StackTransform* is defined to be *Stack* → *Stack*, so that the signature of *push*, for instance, is really

$$Result \rightarrow (Stack \rightarrow Stack)$$

From this perspective, *push* probably seems more familiar: it is a function that takes a result and stack (in curried form) and returns a stack. However, since stack transforms are the key abstraction of this semantics, we have written the signatures in a way that emphasizes this fact. Under this view, *push* is a function that takes a result and returns a stack transform. Of course, in either case *push* is exactly the same mathematical entity; the only difference is in how we think about it!

4.3.2   A Meaning Function for PostFix

Now we're ready to study the meaning function for PostFix. As in EL, we specify the meaning function by a collection of valuation functions, one for each syntactic domain defined by the abstract syntax for the language.

As we learned in studying the denotational semantics of EL, the signatures of valuation functions contain valuable information about the meaning of the language. It is always prudent to study the signatures before delving into the details of the definitions for the valuation functions.

The signatures for the PostFix valuation functions appear in Figure 4.12. In the case of PostFix, one of the things the signatures say is that a PostFix program is like an EL program in that it takes a sequence of integers as arguments

$$\mathcal{P} : \text{Prog} \rightarrow Int^* \rightarrow Answer$$
$$\mathcal{Q} : \text{CommandSeq} \rightarrow StackTransform$$
$$\mathcal{C} : \text{Command} \rightarrow StackTransform$$
$$\mathcal{A} : \text{ArithmeticOperator} \rightarrow (Int \rightarrow Int \rightarrow Result)$$
$$\mathcal{R} : \text{RelationalOperator} \rightarrow (Int \rightarrow Int \rightarrow Bool)$$
$$\mathcal{N} : \text{IntLit} \rightarrow Int$$

Figure 4.12   Signatures of the PostFix valuation functions.

and either returns an integer or signals an error: $\mathcal{P} : \text{Prog} \rightarrow Int^* \rightarrow Answer$. If the signature of $\mathcal{P}$ were instead $\mathcal{P} : \text{Prog} \rightarrow Int^* \rightarrow Result$, it would indicate that some PostFix programs could return a stack transform (corresponding to an executable sequence) instead of an integer. If the signature were one of $\mathcal{P} : \text{Prog} \rightarrow Int^* \rightarrow Int$ or $\mathcal{P} : \text{Prog} \rightarrow Int^* \rightarrow Value$, it would tell us that errors could not be signaled by a PostFix program.

The signatures also tell us that both commands and command sequences map to stack transforms. Since stack transforms are easily composable, this suggests that the meaning of a command sequence will be some sort of composition of the meanings of its component commands. This turns out to be the case. The return type of $\mathcal{A}$ matches the argument type of *arithop*, one of the auxiliary functions specified in Figure 4.11. This is more than coincidence: the auxiliary functions and valuation functions were designed to dovetail in a nice way.

Now we're ready to study the definitions of the PostFix valuation functions, which appear in Figure 4.13. The meaning of a program (postfix $N_{numargs}$ Q) is a function that transforms an initial stack consisting of the integers in the argument sequence i^* via the transform $\mathcal{Q}[\![Q]\!]$ and returns the top integer of the resulting stack. The definitions of *resToAns* and *top* guarantee that an error answer is returned when the stack is empty or does not have an integer as its top element. An error is also signaled when the number of arguments does not match the expected number $N_{numargs}$.

The meaning of a command sequence is the composition of the transforms of its component commands. The order of the composition

$$\mathcal{Q}[\![Q]\!] \circ \mathcal{C}[\![C]\!] = \lambda s \,.\, (\mathcal{Q}[\![Q]\!]\ (\mathcal{C}[\![C]\!]\ s))$$

is crucial, because it guarantees that the stack manipulations of the first command can be observed by the subsequent commands. Reversing the order of the composition would have the effect of executing commands in a right-to-left order instead. The stack transform associated with the empty command sequence is the identity function on stacks.

For valuation functions like $\mathcal{Q}$ that manipulate sequences of program phrases, we will often take notational liberties to avoid explicit sequences between the double brackets, $[\![\;]\!]$. For example, $\mathcal{Q}[\![\;]\!]$ is an abbreviation for $\mathcal{Q}[\![[\,]_{\text{Command}}]\!]$, and $\mathcal{Q}[\![3\ \mathtt{sub}\ \mathtt{swap}\ \mathtt{pop}]\!]$ is an abbreviation for $\mathcal{Q}[\![[3, \mathtt{sub}, \mathtt{swap}, \mathtt{pop}]_{\text{Command}}]\!]$.

Most of the clauses for the command valuation function $\mathcal{C}$ are straightforward. The integers and transforms corresponding to numerals and executable sequences are simply pushed onto the stack after appropriate injections into the *Value* and *Result* domains.[5] The transform associated with the $\mathtt{pop}$ command is simply the *pop* auxiliary function, while the transform associated with $\mathtt{swap}$ is expressed as a composition of *push*, *top*, and *pop*. If the top stack element is an integer i, the $\mathtt{nget}$ transform replaces it by the ith element from the rest of the stack if that element is an integer; in all other cases, $\mathtt{nget}$ returns an error stack. The $\mathtt{sel}$ transform selects one of the top two stack elements based on the numeric value of the third stack element; an error is signaled if the third element is not an integer. In the $\mathtt{exec}$ transform, the top stack element is expected to be a stack transform t representing an executable sequence. Applying t to the rest of the stack yields the stack resulting from executing the executable sequence. If the top stack element is not a stack transform, an error is signaled. The meaning of arithmetic and relational commands is determined by *arithop* in conjunction with $\mathcal{A}$ and $\mathcal{R}$, valuation functions that map operator symbols like $\mathtt{add}$ and $\mathtt{lt}$ to the expected functions and predicates. $\mathcal{A}$ treats $\mathtt{div}$ and $\mathtt{rem}$ specially so that division by 0 signals an error.

Before we move on, a few notes about reading the POSTFIX denotational definitions are in order. Valuation functions tend to be remarkably elegant and concise. But this does not mean that they are always easy to read! To the contrary, the density of information in a denotational definition often demands meticulous attention from the reader. The ability to read semantic functions and valuation functions is a skill that requires patient practice to acquire. At first, unraveling such a definition may seem like solving a puzzle or doing detective work. However, the time invested in reading definitions of this sort pays off handsomely in terms of deep insights into the meanings of programming languages.

The conciseness of a denotational definition is due in large part to the liberal use of higher-order functions, i.e., functions that take other functions as arguments or return them as results. *arithop* is an excellent example of such

---

[5]Whereas the operational semantics uses a stack with syntactic values — integer numerals and command sequences — the denotational semantics uses a stack of semantic values — integers and stack transforms. This is because the valuation functions $\mathcal{N}$ and $\mathcal{Q}$ are readily available for translating the syntactic elements to the semantic ones. Here and elsewhere, we will follow the convention of using explicit injections in denotational descriptions.

$\mathcal{P}[\![(\texttt{postfix}\ N_{numargs}\ Q)]\!]$
$\quad = \lambda i^*\ .\ \textbf{if}\ (length\ i^*) =_{Int} \mathcal{N}[\![N_{numargs}]\!]$
$\qquad\qquad \textbf{then}\ resToAns\ (top\ (\mathcal{Q}[\![Q]\!]\ (Value^* \rightarrowtail Stack\ (map\ Int \rightarrowtail Value\ i^*))))$
$\qquad\qquad \textbf{else}\ errorAnswer\ \textbf{end}$

$\mathcal{Q}[\![C\ .\ Q]\!]\ =\ \mathcal{Q}[\![Q]\!] \circ \mathcal{C}[\![C]\!]$

$\mathcal{Q}[\![]\!] = \lambda s\ .\ \ s$

$\mathcal{C}[\![N]\!]\ =\ push\ (Value \rightarrowtail Result\ (Int \rightarrowtail Value\ \mathcal{N}[\![N]\!]))$

$\mathcal{C}[\![(Q)]\!]\ =\ push\ (Value \rightarrowtail Result\ (StackTransform \rightarrowtail Value\ \mathcal{Q}[\![Q]\!]))$

$\mathcal{C}[\![\texttt{pop}]\!]\ =\ pop$

$\mathcal{C}[\![\texttt{swap}]\!]\ =\ \lambda s\ .\ (push\ (top\ (pop\ s))\ (push\ (top\ s)\ (pop\ (pop\ s))))$

$\mathcal{C}[\![\texttt{nget}]\!]\ =\ \lambda s\ .\ \textbf{match}\ top\ s$
$\qquad\qquad\qquad \triangleright (Value \rightarrowtail Result\ (Int \rightarrowtail Value\ i))\ [\![\ push\ (intAt\ i\ (pop\ s))\ (pop\ s)$
$\qquad\qquad\qquad \triangleright \textbf{else}\ errorStack\ \textbf{end}$

$\mathcal{C}[\![\texttt{sel}]\!]\ =\ \lambda s\ .\ \textbf{match}\ top\ (pop\ (pop\ s))$
$\qquad\qquad\qquad \triangleright (Value \rightarrowtail Result\ (Int \rightarrowtail Value\ i))\ [\![$
$\qquad\qquad\qquad push\ (\textbf{if}\ i =_{Int} 0\ \textbf{then}\ top\ s\ \textbf{else}\ top\ (pop\ s)\ \textbf{end})$
$\qquad\qquad\qquad\qquad (pop\ (pop\ (pop\ s)))$
$\qquad\qquad\qquad \triangleright \textbf{else}\ errorStack\ \textbf{end}$

$\mathcal{C}[\![\texttt{exec}]\!]\ =\ \lambda s\ .\ (transform\ (top\ s)\ (pop\ s))$

$\mathcal{C}[\![A]\!]\ =\ arithop\ \mathcal{A}[\![A]\!]$

$\mathcal{C}[\![R]\!]\ =\ arithop\ (\lambda i_1 i_2\ .\ (Value \rightarrowtail Result$
$\qquad\qquad\qquad\qquad\qquad (Int \rightarrowtail Value\ (\textbf{if}\ (\mathcal{R}[\![R]\!]\ i_1\ i_2)\ \textbf{then}\ 1\ \textbf{else}\ 0\ \textbf{end}))))$

$\mathcal{A}[\![\texttt{sub}]\!]\ =\ \lambda i_1 i_2\ .\ (Value \rightarrowtail Result\ (Int \rightarrowtail Value\ (i_1 -_{Int} i_2)))$
Similarly for add, mul

$\mathcal{A}[\![\texttt{div}]\!]\ =\ \lambda i_1 i_2\ .\ \textbf{if}\ i_2 =_{Int} 0$
$\qquad\qquad\qquad \textbf{then}\ errorResult$
$\qquad\qquad\qquad \textbf{else}\ (Value \rightarrowtail Result\ (Int \rightarrowtail Value\ (i_1 \div_{Int} i_2)))\ \textbf{end}$
Similarly for rem

$\mathcal{R}[\![\texttt{lt}]\!]\ =\ <_{Int}$
Similarly for eq and gt

$\mathcal{N}$ maps integer numerals to the integer numbers they denote.

Figure 4.13 Valuation functions for POSTFIX.

a function: it takes an argument in the function domain $Int \rightarrow Int \rightarrow Result$, and returns a stack transform, which itself is an element of the function domain $Stack \rightarrow Stack$.

Definitions involving higher-order functions can be rather daunting to read until you acquire a knack for them. A typical problem is to think that pieces are missing. For example, a common reaction to the valuation clause for numerals,

$$\mathcal{C}[\![N]\!] = (push \ (Value \rightarrowtail Result \ (Int \rightarrowtail Value \ (\mathcal{N}[\![N]\!]))))$$

is that a stack is somehow missing. After all, the value has to be pushed onto *something* — where is it? Carefully considering types, however, will show that nothing is missing. (Consult Sections A.3.2 and A.4 for more on types in the metalanguage.) Recall that the signature of *push* is $Result \rightarrow StackTransform$. Since ($Value \rightarrowtail Result \ (Int \rightarrowtail Value \ \mathcal{N}[\![N]\!])$) is clearly an element of *Result*, the result of the *push* application is a stack transform. Since $\mathcal{C}$ is supposed to map commands to stack transforms, the definition is well typed. It's possible to introduce an explicit stack in this valuation clause by wrapping the right-hand side in a λ of a stack argument:

$$\mathcal{C}[\![N]\!] = \lambda s \ . \ (push \ (Value \rightarrowtail Result \ (Int \rightarrowtail Value \ \mathcal{N}[\![N]\!])) \ s)$$

This form of the definition probably seems much more familiar, because it's more apparent that the meaning of the command is a function that takes a stack and returns a stack, and *push* is actually given a stack on which to push its value. But the two definitions are equivalent. In order to stress the power of higher-order functions, we will continue to use the more concise versions. We encourage you to type-check the definitions and expand them with extra λs to improve your skill at reading them.

Figure 4.14 illustrates using the POSTFIX denotational semantics to determine the result of executing the program (postfix 2 3 sub swap pop) on the argument integers [7, 8]. To make the figure more concise, we use the shorthand $\hat{n}$ to stand for ($Int \rightarrowtail Value \ n$). Each line of the equational proof is justified by simple mathematical reasoning. For example, the equality

$resToAns \ (top \ ((\mathcal{Q}[\![pop]\!] \ \circ \ \mathcal{C}[\![swap]\!]) \ (Value^* \rightarrowtail Stack \ [\hat{4}, \hat{8}])))$

$= resToAns \ (top \ (\mathcal{Q}[\![pop]\!] \ (\mathcal{C}[\![swap]\!] \ (Value^* \rightarrowtail Stack \ [\hat{4}, \hat{8}]))))$

is justified by the definition of function composition, while the equality

$$resToAns \ (top \ (\mathcal{Q}[\![\text{swap pop}]\!] \ (push \ (Value \rightarrowtail Result \ \widehat{7 -_{Int} 3})$$
$$(Value^* \rightarrowtail Stack \ [\hat{8}]))))$$
$$= \ resToAns \ \big(top \ \big(\mathcal{Q}[\![\text{swap pop}]\!] \ (Value^* \rightarrowtail Stack \ [\hat{4}, \hat{8}])\big)\big)$$

is justified by the definition of $-_{Int}$ and the specification for the *push* function. The proof shows that the result of the program execution is the integer 4.

Just as programs can be simplified by introducing procedural abstractions, equational proofs can often be simplified by structuring them more hierarchically. In the case of proofs, the analogue of a programming language procedure is a theorem. For example, it's not difficult to prove a theorem stating that for any numeral N, any command sequence Q, and any stack s, the following equality is valid:

$$(\mathcal{Q}[\![N \ . \ Q]\!] \ (Value^* \rightarrowtail Stack \ v^*))$$
$$= (\mathcal{Q}[\![Q]\!] \ (Value^* \rightarrowtail Stack \ ((Int \rightarrowtail Value \ \mathcal{N}[\![N]\!]) \ . \ v^*)))$$

This theorem is analogous to the operational rewrite rule for handling integer numeral commands. It can be used to justify equalities like

$$(\mathcal{Q}[\![\text{3 sub swap pop}]\!] \ (Value^* \rightarrowtail Stack \ [\hat{7}, \hat{8}]))$$
$$= (\mathcal{Q}[\![\text{sub swap pop}]\!] \ (Value^* \rightarrowtail Stack \ [\hat{3}, \hat{7}, \hat{8}]))$$

which took four steps in Figure 4.14. A few such theorems can greatly reduce the length of the sample proof. In fact, if we prove other theorems analogous to the operational rules, we can obtain a proof whose structure closely corresponds to the configuration sequence for an operational execution of the program (see Figure 4.15).

Figure 4.16 shows how the equational proof in Figure 4.15 can be generalized to handle two arbitrary integer arguments. Based on this result, we conclude that the meaning of the POSTFIX program (postfix 2 3 sub swap pop) is:

$$\mathcal{P}[\![(\text{postfix 2 3 sub swap pop})]\!]$$
$$= \lambda i^* . \ \mathbf{match} \ i^*$$
$$\rhd \ [i_1, i_2] \ [\!] \ (Int \rightarrowtail Answer \ (i_1 -_{Int} 3))$$
$$\rhd \mathbf{else} \ errorAnswer \ \mathbf{end}$$

Exercise 4.4 Use the POSTFIX denotational semantics to determine the values of the POSTFIX programs in Exercise 1.1 on page 13.

Note: $\hat{n}$ is a shorthand for $(Int \rightarrowtail Value \; n)$

$\mathcal{P}[\![(\texttt{postfix 2 3 sub swap pop})]\!] \; [7, 8]$

$= \mathbf{if} \; (length \; [7, 8]) =_{Int} \mathcal{N}[\![2]\!]$
    $\mathbf{then} \; resToAns \; \big(top \; (\mathcal{Q}[\![\texttt{3 sub swap pop}]\!] \; (Value^* \rightarrowtail Stack \; [\hat{7}, \hat{8}])))$
    $\mathbf{else} \; errorAnswer \; \mathbf{end}$

$= resToAns \; \big(top \; (\mathcal{Q}[\![\texttt{3 sub swap pop}]\!] \; (Value^* \rightarrowtail Stack \; [\hat{7}, \hat{8}])))$

$= resToAns \; \big(top \; ((\mathcal{Q}[\![\texttt{sub swap pop}]\!] \circ \mathcal{C}[\![\texttt{3}]\!]) \; (Value^* \rightarrowtail Stack \; [\hat{7}, \hat{8}])))$

$= resToAns \; \big(top \; (\mathcal{Q}[\![\texttt{sub swap pop}]\!] \; (\mathcal{C}[\![\texttt{3}]\!] \; (Value^* \rightarrowtail Stack \; [\hat{7}, \hat{8}]))))$

$= resToAns \; (top \; (\mathcal{Q}[\![\texttt{sub swap pop}]\!] \; (push \; (Value \rightarrowtail Result \; \hat{3})$
                                         $(Value^* \rightarrowtail Stack \; [\hat{7}, \hat{8}]))))$

$= resToAns \; \big(top \; (\mathcal{Q}[\![\texttt{sub swap pop}]\!] \; (Value^* \rightarrowtail Stack \; [\hat{3}, \hat{7}, \hat{8}])))$

$= resToAns \; \big(top \; ((\mathcal{Q}[\![\texttt{swap pop}]\!] \circ \mathcal{C}[\![\texttt{sub}]\!]) \; (Value^* \rightarrowtail Stack \; [\hat{3}, \hat{7}, \hat{8}])))$

$= resToAns \; \big(top \; (\mathcal{Q}[\![\texttt{swap pop}]\!] \; (\mathcal{C}[\![\texttt{sub}]\!] \; (Value^* \rightarrowtail Stack \; [\hat{3}, \hat{7}, \hat{8}]))))$

$= resToAns \; \big(top \; (\mathcal{Q}[\![\texttt{swap pop}]\!] \; (arithop \; \mathcal{A}[\![\texttt{sub}]\!] \; (Value^* \rightarrowtail Stack \; [\hat{3}, \hat{7}, \hat{8}]))))$

$= resToAns \; (top \; (\mathcal{Q}[\![\texttt{swap pop}]\!] \; (push \; (Value \rightarrowtail Result \; \widehat{7 -_{Int} 3})$
                                      $(Value^* \rightarrowtail Stack \; [\hat{8}]))))$

$= resToAns \; \big(top \; (\mathcal{Q}[\![\texttt{swap pop}]\!] \; (Value^* \rightarrowtail Stack \; [\hat{4}, \hat{8}])))$

$= resToAns \; \big(top \; ((\mathcal{Q}[\![\texttt{pop}]\!] \circ \mathcal{C}[\![\texttt{swap}]\!]) \; (Value^* \rightarrowtail Stack \; [\hat{4}, \hat{8}])))$

$= resToAns \; \big(top \; (\mathcal{Q}[\![\texttt{pop}]\!] \; (\mathcal{C}[\![\texttt{swap}]\!] \; (Value^* \rightarrowtail Stack \; [\hat{4}, \hat{8}]))))$

$= resToAns \; (top \; (\mathcal{Q}[\![\texttt{pop}]\!] \; (push \;\; (top \; (pop \; (Value^* \rightarrowtail Stack \; [\hat{4}, \hat{8}])))$
                                  $(push \;\; (top \; (Value^* \rightarrowtail Stack \; [\hat{4}, \hat{8}]))$
                                        $(pop \; (pop \; (Value^* \rightarrowtail Stack \; [\hat{4}, \hat{8}])))))))))$

$= resToAns \; (top \; (\mathcal{Q}[\![\texttt{pop}]\!] \; (push \; (top \; (Value^* \rightarrowtail Stack \; [\hat{8}]))$
                                  $(push \; (Value \rightarrowtail Result \; \hat{4})$
                                  $(Value^* \rightarrowtail Stack \; []))))))$

$= resToAns \; \big(top \; (\mathcal{Q}[\![\texttt{pop}]\!] \; (push \; (Value \rightarrowtail Result \; \hat{8}) \; (Value^* \rightarrowtail Stack \; [\hat{4}]))))$

$= resToAns \; \big(top \; (\mathcal{Q}[\![\texttt{pop}]\!] \; (Value^* \rightarrowtail Stack \; [\hat{8}, \hat{4}])))$

$= resToAns \; \big(top \; ((\mathcal{Q}[\![]\!] \circ \mathcal{C}[\![\texttt{pop}]\!]) \; (Value^* \rightarrowtail Stack \; [\hat{8}, \hat{4}])))$

$= resToAns \; \big(top \; (\mathcal{Q}[\![]\!] \; (\mathcal{C}[\![\texttt{pop}]\!] \; (Value^* \rightarrowtail Stack \; [\hat{8}, \hat{4}]))))$

$= resToAns \; \big(top \; (\mathcal{Q}[\![]\!] \; (Value^* \rightarrowtail Stack \; [\hat{4}])))$

$= resToAns \; \big(top \; ((\lambda s \, . \, s) \; (Value^* \rightarrowtail Stack \; [\hat{4}])))$

$= resToAns \; \big(top \; (Value^* \rightarrowtail Stack \; [\hat{4}]))$

$= resToAns \; (Value \rightarrowtail Result \; \hat{4})$

$= (Int \rightarrowtail Answer \; 4)$

Figure 4.14   Equational proof that executing the POSTFIX program (`postfix 2 3 sub swap pop`) on the arguments $[7, 8]$ yields the answer 4.

$$\mathcal{P}[\![(\texttt{postfix 2 3 sub swap pop})]\!] \ [7,8]$$
$$= \ resToAns \ \left(top \ \left(\mathcal{Q}[\![\texttt{3 sub swap pop}]\!] \ (Value^* \rightarrowtail Stack \ [\hat{7}, \hat{8}])\right)\right)$$
$$= \ resToAns \ \left(top \ \left(\mathcal{Q}[\![\texttt{sub swap pop}]\!] \ (Value^* \rightarrowtail Stack \ [\hat{3}, \hat{7}, \hat{8}])\right)\right)$$
$$= \ resToAns \ \left(top \ \left(\mathcal{Q}[\![\texttt{swap pop}]\!] \ (Value^* \rightarrowtail Stack \ [\hat{4}, \hat{8}])\right)\right)$$
$$= \ resToAns \ \left(top \ \left(\mathcal{Q}[\![\texttt{pop}]\!] \ (Value^* \rightarrowtail Stack \ [\hat{8}, \hat{4}])\right)\right)$$
$$= \ resToAns \ \left(top \ \left(\mathcal{Q}[\![]\!] \ (Value^* \rightarrowtail Stack \ [\hat{4}])\right)\right)$$
$$= \ resToAns \ \left(top \ (Value^* \rightarrowtail Stack \ [\hat{4}])\right)$$
$$= \ resToAns \ (Value \rightarrowtail Result \ \hat{4})$$
$$= \ (Int \rightarrowtail Answer \ 4)$$

Figure 4.15 Alternative equational proof with an operational flavor.

$$\mathcal{P}[\![(\texttt{postfix 2 3 sub swap pop})]\!] \ [i_1, i_2]$$
$$= \ resToAns \ \left(top \ \left(\mathcal{Q}[\![\texttt{3 sub swap pop}]\!] \ (Value^* \rightarrowtail Stack \ [\hat{i_1}, \hat{i_2}])\right)\right)$$
$$= \ resToAns \ \left(top \ \left(\mathcal{Q}[\![\texttt{sub swap pop}]\!] \ (Value^* \rightarrowtail Stack \ [\hat{3}, \hat{i_1}, \hat{i_2}])\right)\right)$$
$$= \ resToAns \ \left(top \ \left(\mathcal{Q}[\![\texttt{swap pop}]\!] \ (Value^* \rightarrowtail Stack \ [\widehat{i_1 -_{Int} 3}, \hat{i_2}])\right)\right)$$
$$= \ resToAns \ \left(top \ \left(\mathcal{Q}[\![\texttt{pop}]\!] \ (Value^* \rightarrowtail Stack \ [\hat{i_2}, \widehat{i_1 -_{Int} 3}])\right)\right)$$
$$= \ resToAns \ \left(top \ \left(\mathcal{Q}[\![]\!] \ (Value^* \rightarrowtail Stack \ [\widehat{i_1 -_{Int} 3}])\right)\right)$$
$$= \ resToAns \ \left(top \ (Value^* \rightarrowtail Stack \ [\widehat{i_1 -_{Int} 3}])\right)$$
$$= \ resToAns \ (Value \rightarrowtail Result \ \widehat{i_1 -_{Int} 3})$$
$$= \ (Int \rightarrowtail Answer \ (i_1 -_{Int} 3))$$

Figure 4.16 Version of equational proof for two arbitrary integer arguments.

Exercise 4.5 Modify the POSTFIX denotational semantics to handle POSTFIX2. Include valuation clauses for (: C_{com1} C_{com2}), (skip), and (exec).

Exercise 4.6 For each of the following, modify the POSTFIX denotational semantics to handle the specified extensions:

a. The pair, fst, and snd commands from Exercise 3.37 on page 102.

b. The for and repeat commands from Exercise 3.40 on page 103.

c. The I, def, and ref commands from Exercise 3.44 on page 106.

4.3.3   Semantic Functions for PostFix: the Details

Now that we've studied the core of the PostFix semantics, we'll flesh out the
details of the functions specified in Figure 4.11. Figure 4.17 presents one implementation of the specifications. As an exercise, you should make sure that these
definitions type-check, and that they satisfy the specifications in Figure 4.11.

Notice that several functions in Figure 4.17 describe similar manipulations.
push, *pop*, and *arithop* all check to see if their input stack is a suitable stack of
values. If so, they perform some manipulation on the sequence of values in the
stack; if not, they return *errorStack*. We can abstract over these similarities by
introducing three abstractions (Figure 4.18) similar to the *with-int* error-hiding
function defined in the EL denotational semantics:

- *with-stack-values* takes a function f from value sequences to stacks and returns
  a stack transform that (1) maps a nonerror stack to the result of applying f to
  the value sequence in the stack, and (2) maps an error stack to an error stack.

- *with-val&stack* takes a function f from a value to a stack transform and returns
  a stack transform that (1) maps any stack whose value sequence consists of the
  value v followed by v_{rest}^* to the result of applying f to v and the stack whose
  values are v_{rest}^*, and (2) maps any stack not of this form to the error stack.

- *with-int&stack* takes a function f from an integer to a stack transform and
  returns a stack transform that (1) maps any stack whose value sequence consists
  of an integer i followed by v_{rest}^* to the result of applying f to i and the stack
  whose values are v_{rest}^*, and (2) maps any stack not of this form to the error
  stack.

The purpose of these new functions is to hide the details of error handling in order
to highlight more important manipulations. As shown in Figure 4.18, rewriting
push in terms of *with-stack-values* removes an error check from the definition.
Using *with-val&stack* and *with-int&stack* greatly simplifies *pop* and *arithop*; the
updated versions concisely capture the essence of these functions without the
distraction of case analyses and error checks.

As with the valuation functions, these highly condensed semantic functions
can be challenging for the uninitiated to read. The fact that *push*, *pop*, and
arithop are ultimately manipulating a stack is even harder to see in the new
versions than it was in the original ones. As suggested before, reasoning about
types and inserting extra λs can help. For example, since the result of a call to
with-int&stack is a stack transform t, and t is equivalent to $\lambda s . (t\ s)$, the new
version of *arithop* can be rewritten as:

$errorResult : Result = (Error \rightarrowtail Result \ error)$
$errorAnswer : Answer = (Error \rightarrowtail Answer \ error)$
$errorStack : Stack = (Error \rightarrowtail Stack \ error)$
$errorTransform : StackTransform = \lambda s \ . \ errorStack$

$push : Result \rightarrow StackTransform$
$= \lambda r \ . \ (\lambda s \ . \ \textbf{match} \ \langle r, s \rangle$
$\qquad\qquad \triangleright \langle (Value \rightarrowtail Result \ v), (Value^* \rightarrowtail Stack \ v^*) \rangle \ [\![\ (v \ . \ v^*)$
$\qquad\qquad \triangleright \textbf{else} \ errorStack \ \textbf{end} \ )$

$pop : StackTransform$
$= \lambda s \ . \ \textbf{match} \ s$
$\qquad\qquad \triangleright (Value^* \rightarrowtail Stack \ (v_{head} \ . \ v^*_{tail})) \ [\![\ (Value^* \rightarrowtail Stack \ v^*_{tail})$
$\qquad\qquad \triangleright \textbf{else} \ errorStack \ \textbf{end}$

$top : Stack \rightarrow Result$
$= \lambda s \ . \ \textbf{match} \ s$
$\qquad\qquad \triangleright (Value^* \rightarrowtail Stack \ (v_{head} \ . \ v^*_{tail})) \ [\![\ (Value \rightarrowtail Result \ v_{head})$
$\qquad\qquad \triangleright \textbf{else} \ errorResult \ \textbf{end}$

$intAt : Int \rightarrow Stack \rightarrow Result$
$= \lambda is \ . \ \textbf{match} \ s$
$\qquad \triangleright (Value^* \rightarrowtail Stack \ v^*) \ [\![$
$\qquad\quad \textbf{if} \ 1 \leq_{Int} i \ \textbf{and} \ i \leq_{Int} (length \ v^*)$
$\qquad\quad \textbf{then match} \ (nth \ i \ v^*)$
$\qquad\qquad\qquad \triangleright (Int \rightarrowtail Value \ i_{result}) \ [\![\ (Value \rightarrowtail Result \ (Int \rightarrowtail Value \ i_{result}))$
$\qquad\qquad\qquad \triangleright \textbf{else} \ errorResult$
$\qquad\qquad \textbf{else} \ errorResult \ \textbf{end}$
$\qquad \triangleright \textbf{else} \ errorResult \ \textbf{end}$

$arithop : (Int \rightarrow Int \rightarrow Result) \rightarrow StackTransform$
$= \lambda f \ . \ (\lambda s \ . \ \textbf{match} \ s$
$\qquad\qquad \triangleright (Value^* \rightarrowtail Stack \ ((Int \rightarrowtail Value \ i_1) \ . \ (Int \rightarrowtail Value \ i_2) \ . \ v^*_{rest})) \ [\![$
$\qquad\qquad \ (push \ (f \ i_2 \ i_1) \ v^*_{rest})$
$\qquad\qquad \triangleright \textbf{else} \ errorStack \ \textbf{end} \ )$

$transform : Result \rightarrow StackTransform$
$= \lambda r \ . \ \textbf{match} \ r$
$\qquad\qquad \triangleright (Value \rightarrowtail Result \ (StackTransform \rightarrowtail Value \ t)) \ [\![\ t$
$\qquad\qquad \triangleright \textbf{else} \ errorTransform \ \textbf{end}$

$resToAns : Result \rightarrow Answer$
$= \lambda r \ . \ \textbf{match} \ r$
$\qquad\qquad \triangleright (Value \rightarrowtail Result \ (Int \rightarrowtail Value \ i)) \ [\![\ (Int \rightarrowtail Answer \ i)$
$\qquad\qquad \triangleright \textbf{else} \ errorAnswer \ \textbf{end}$

Figure 4.17   Functions manipulating the semantic domains for POSTFIX.

$with\text{-}stack\text{-}values : (Value^* \to Stack) \to StackTransform$
$= \lambda f . (\lambda s . \mathbf{match}\ s$
$\qquad\qquad \triangleright (Value^* \rightarrowtail Stack\ v^*) [\!] (f\ v^*)$
$\qquad\qquad \triangleright \mathbf{else}\ errorStack\ \mathbf{end}\ )$

$with\text{-}val\&stack : (Value \to StackTransform) \to StackTransform$
$= \lambda f . (with\text{-}stack\text{-}values$
$\qquad\quad (\lambda v^* . \mathbf{match}\ v^*$
$\qquad\qquad\quad \triangleright v_1 . v^*_{rest} [\!] (f\ v_1\ (Value^* \rightarrowtail Stack\ v^*_{rest}))$
$\qquad\qquad\quad \triangleright \mathbf{else}\ errorStack\ \mathbf{end}\ ))$

$with\text{-}int\&stack : (Int \to StackTransform) \to StackTransform$
$= \lambda f . (with\text{-}val\&stack$
$\qquad\quad (\lambda v . \mathbf{match}\ v$
$\qquad\qquad\quad \triangleright (Int \rightarrowtail Value\ i) [\!] (f\ i)$
$\qquad\qquad\quad \triangleright \mathbf{else}\ errorTransform\ \mathbf{end}\ ))$

$push : Result \to StackTransform$
$= \lambda r . \mathbf{match}\ r$
$\qquad \triangleright (Value \rightarrowtail Result\ v) [\!] (with\text{-}stack\text{-}values\ (\lambda v^* . (Value^* \rightarrowtail Stack\ (v . v^*))))$
$\qquad \triangleright \mathbf{else}\ errorTransform\ \mathbf{end}$

$pop : StackTransform = with\text{-}val\&stack\ (\lambda v_{head} . (\lambda s_{tail} . s_{tail}))$

$arithop : (Int \to Int \to Result) \to StackTransform$
$= \lambda f . (with\text{-}int\&stack\ (\lambda i_1 . (with\text{-}int\&stack\ (\lambda i_2 . (push\ (f\ i_2\ i_1))))))$

Figure 4.18 The functions *with-stack-values*, *with-val&stack*, and *with-integer&stack* simplify some of the semantic functions for POSTFIX. (Only the modified functions are shown.)

$\lambda f s_0 . ((with\text{-}int\&stack$
$\qquad\quad (\lambda i_1 s_1 . ((with\text{-}int\&stack$
$\qquad\qquad\qquad (\lambda i_2 s_2 . (push\ (f\ i_2\ i_1)\ s_2)))$
$\qquad\qquad\quad s_1)))$
$\qquad s_0)$

In this form, it's easier to see that there are stacks from which each occurrence of *with-int&stack* can extract an integer and substack.

From this expanded form we can understand *with-int&stack* as a construct that binds names to values. The pattern $((with\text{-}int\&stack\ (\lambda is_{rest} . E))\ s)$ can be read as:

Let i be the top value of s and s_{rest} be all but the top value of s in the expression E. Return the value of E, except when s is empty or its top value isn't an integer, in which cases the error stack should be returned instead.

Some of the POSTFIX valuation functions can be reexpressed using the error-hiding functions directly. For example, the valuation clause for `swap` can be written as:

$$\mathcal{C}[\![\texttt{swap}]\!] = \textit{with-val\&stack} \ (\lambda v_1 \ . \ (\textit{with-val\&stack} \ (\lambda v_2 \ . \ (\textit{push} \ v_2) \ \circ \ (\textit{push} \ v_1))))$$

You should convince yourself that this has the same meaning as the version written using *push*, *top*, and *pop*.

Exercise 4.7

a. By analogy with *with-int&stack*, define a function *with-trans&stack* whose signature is $(\textit{StackTransform} \rightarrow \textit{StackTransform}) \rightarrow \textit{StackTransform}$.

b. Using *with-val&stack*, *with-int&stack*, and *with-trans&stack*, rewrite the valuation clauses for `nget`, `sel`, and `exec` to eliminate all occurrences of *top*, *pop*, *transform*, and **match**.

4.4 Denotational Reasoning

The denotational definitions of EL and POSTFIX presented in the previous section are mathematically elegant, but how useful are they? We have already shown how they can be used to determine the meanings of particular programs. In this section we show how denotational semantics helps us to reason about program equality and safe program transformations. The compositional structure of the denotational semantics makes it more amenable to proving certain properties than the operational semantics. In Section 4.5 we study the relationship between operational semantics and denotational semantics.

4.4.1 Program Equality

In Section 4.3.2, we studied the program (postfix 2 3 sub swap pop), which takes two integer arguments and returns three less than the first argument:

$$\mathcal{P}[\![(\texttt{postfix 2 3 sub swap pop})]\!]$$
$$= \lambda i^* \ . \ \textbf{match} \ i^*$$
$$\vartriangleright \ [i_1, i_2] \ [\![\ (\textit{Int} \rightarrowtail \textit{Answer} \ (i_1 -_{\textit{Int}} 3))$$
$$\vartriangleright \textbf{else} \ \textit{errorAnswer} \ \textbf{end}$$

$$\mathcal{P}[\![(\texttt{postfix 2 3 sub})]\!] \; [i_1, i_2]$$

$$= \mathit{resToAns} \left(\mathit{top} \, \left(\mathcal{Q}[\![\texttt{3 sub}]\!] \; (\mathit{Value}^* \rightarrowtail \mathit{Stack} \; [\hat{i_1}, \hat{i_2}]) \right) \right)$$

$$= \mathit{resToAns} \left(\mathit{top} \, \left(\mathcal{Q}[\![\texttt{sub}]\!] \; (\mathit{Value}^* \rightarrowtail \mathit{Stack} \; [\hat{3}, \hat{i_1}, \hat{i_2}]) \right) \right)$$

$$= \mathit{resToAns} \left(\mathit{top} \, \left(\mathcal{Q}[\![\,]\!] \; (\mathit{Value}^* \rightarrowtail \mathit{Stack} \; [\widehat{i_1 -_{Int} 3}, \hat{i_2}]) \right) \right)$$

$$= \mathit{resToAns} \left(\mathit{top} \, (\mathit{Value}^* \rightarrowtail \mathit{Stack} \; [\widehat{i_1 -_{Int} 3}, \hat{i_2}]) \right)$$

$$= \mathit{resToAns} \, (\mathit{Value} \rightarrowtail \mathit{Result} \; \widehat{i_1 -_{Int} 3})$$

$$= (\mathit{Int} \rightarrowtail \mathit{Answer} \; (i_1 -_{Int} 3))$$

Figure 4.19   The meaning of (`postfix 2 3 sub`) on two integer arguments (compare Figure 4.16).

Intuitively, the purpose of the `swap pop` is to get rid of the second argument, which is ignored by the program. But in a POSTFIX program, only the integer at the top of the final stack can be observed and any other stack values are ignored. So we should be able to remove the `swap pop` from the program without changing its behavior.

We can formalize this reasoning using denotational semantics. Figure 4.19 shows a derivation of the meaning of the program (`postfix 2 3 sub`) when it is applied to two arguments. From this, we deduce that the meaning of (`postfix 2 3 sub`) is:

$$\mathcal{P}[\![(\texttt{postfix 2 3 sub})]\!]$$
$$= \lambda i^* . \; \textbf{match} \; i^*$$
$$\quad \triangleright \; [i_1, i_2] \; [\!] \; (\mathit{Int} \rightarrowtail \mathit{Answer} \; (i_1 -_{Int} 3))$$
$$\quad \triangleright \textbf{else} \; \mathit{errorAnswer} \; \textbf{end}$$

Since (`postfix 2 3 sub`) and (`postfix 2 3 sub swap pop`) have exactly the same meaning, they cannot be distinguished as programs.

Denotational semantics can also be used to show that programs from different languages have the same meaning. For example, it is not hard to show that the meaning of the EL program (`el 2 (- (arg 1) 3)`) is:

$$\mathcal{P}[\![(\texttt{el 2 (- (arg 1) 3)})]\!]$$
$$= \lambda i^* . \; \textbf{match} \; i^*$$
$$\quad \triangleright \; [i_1, i_2] \; [\!] \; (\mathit{Int} \rightarrowtail \mathit{Answer} \; (i_1 -_{Int} 3))$$
$$\quad \triangleright \textbf{else} \; \mathit{errorAnswer} \; \textbf{end}$$

If you review the semantic domains for EL and PostFix, you will see that the *Answer* domain is the same for both languages. So the above fact means that this EL program is interchangeable with the two PostFix programs whose meanings are given above.

4.4.2 Safe Transformations: A Denotational Approach

Because denotational semantics is compositional, it is a natural tool for proving that it is safe to replace one phrase by another. Recall the following three facts from the operational semantics of PostFix:

1. Two PostFix command sequences are observationally equivalent if they behave indistinguishably in all program contexts.

2. Two PostFix command sequences are transform equivalent if they map equivalent stacks to equivalent stacks.

3. Transform equivalence implies observational equivalence.

Since the PostFix denotational semantics models command sequences as stack transforms, the denotational equivalence of PostFix command sequences corresponds to transform equivalence in the observational framework. So we expect the following theorem:

Theorem 4.7 (PostFix Denotational Equivalence)
$\mathcal{Q}[\![Q_1]\!] = \mathcal{Q}[\![Q_2]\!]$ *implies* $Q_1 =_{obs} Q_2$.

This theorem is a consequence of a so-called **adequacy property** of PostFix, which we will study later in Section 4.5.2.

We can use this theorem to help us prove the behavioral equivalence of two command sequences. For instance, consider the pair of command sequences [1, add, 2, add] and [3, add]. Figure 4.20 shows that these are denotationally equivalent, so, by the above theorem, they must be observationally equivalent. The equational reasoning in Figure 4.20 uses the following three equalities, whose proofs are left as exercises (see Exercise 4.8):

$$(\mathcal{Q}[\![C_1 \ C_2 \ \ldots \ C_n]\!]) = (\mathcal{C}[\![C_n]\!]) \circ \ldots \circ (\mathcal{C}[\![C_2]\!]) \circ (\mathcal{C}[\![C_1]\!]) \tag{4.8}$$

$$(\textit{with-int\&stack } f) \circ (\textit{push } (\textit{Value} \rightarrowtail \textit{Result } (\textit{Int} \rightarrowtail \textit{Value } i))) = (f \ i) \tag{4.9}$$

$$t \circ (\textit{with-int\&stack } f) = (\textit{with-int\&stack } (\lambda i . (t \circ (f \ i)))) \tag{4.10}$$
$$\text{where } t \in \textit{StackTransform} \text{ maps } \textit{errorStack} \text{ to } \textit{errorStack}$$

$(\mathcal{Q}[\![\texttt{1 add 2 add}]\!])$

$= (\mathcal{C}[\![\texttt{add}]\!]) \circ (\mathcal{C}[\![\texttt{2}]\!]) \circ (\mathcal{C}[\![\texttt{add}]\!]) \circ (\mathcal{C}[\![\texttt{1}]\!])$, by (4.8)

$= (\textit{with-int\&stack}$
$\qquad (\lambda i_1' \,.\, (\textit{with-int\&stack}$
$\qquad\qquad (\lambda i_2' \,.\, \textit{push} \; (\textit{Value} \rightarrowtail \textit{Result} \; (\textit{Int} \rightarrowtail \textit{Value} \; (i_2' +_{\textit{Int}} i_1')))))))$
$\quad \circ \; \textit{push} \; (\textit{Value} \rightarrowtail \textit{Result} \; (\textit{Int} \rightarrowtail \textit{Value} \; \mathcal{N}[\![\texttt{2}]\!]))$
$\quad \circ \; (\textit{with-int\&stack}$
$\qquad (\lambda i_1 \,.\, (\textit{with-int\&stack}$
$\qquad\qquad (\lambda i_2 \,.\, \textit{push} \; (\textit{Value} \rightarrowtail \textit{Result} \; (\textit{Int} \rightarrowtail \textit{Value} \; (i_2 +_{\textit{Int}} i_1)))))))$
$\quad \circ \; \textit{push} \; (\textit{Value} \rightarrowtail \textit{Result} \; (\textit{Int} \rightarrowtail \textit{Value} \; \mathcal{N}[\![\texttt{1}]\!]))$, by definition of $\mathcal{C}$

$= (\textit{with-int\&stack}$
$\qquad (\lambda i_2' \,.\, \textit{push} \; (\textit{Value} \rightarrowtail \textit{Result} \; (\textit{Int} \rightarrowtail \textit{Value} \; (i_2' +_{\textit{Int}} 2)))))$
$\quad \circ \; (\textit{with-int\&stack}$
$\qquad (\lambda i_2 \,.\, \textit{push} \; (\textit{Value} \rightarrowtail \textit{Result} \; (\textit{Int} \rightarrowtail \textit{Value} \; (i_2 +_{\textit{Int}} 1)))))$, by (4.9)

$= (\textit{with-int\&stack}$
$\qquad (\lambda i_2 \,.\, (\textit{with-int\&stack}$
$\qquad\qquad (\lambda i_2' \,.\, (\textit{push} \; (\textit{Value} \rightarrowtail \textit{Result} \; (\textit{Int} \rightarrowtail \textit{Value} \; (i_2' +_{\textit{Int}} 2))))))$
$\qquad \circ \; (\textit{push} \; (\textit{Value} \rightarrowtail \textit{Result} \; (\textit{Int} \rightarrowtail \textit{Value} \; (i_2 +_{\textit{Int}} 1))))))$, by (4.10)

$= (\textit{with-int\&stack}$
$\qquad (\lambda i_2 \,.\, \textit{push} \; (\textit{Value} \rightarrowtail \textit{Result} \; (\textit{Int} \rightarrowtail \textit{Value} \; ((i_2 +_{\textit{Int}} 1) +_{\textit{Int}} 2)))))$, by (4.9)

$= (\textit{with-int\&stack}$
$\qquad (\lambda i_2 \,.\, \textit{push} \; (\textit{Value} \rightarrowtail \textit{Result} \; (\textit{Int} \rightarrowtail \textit{Value} \; (i_2 +_{\textit{Int}} 3)))))$, by definition of $+_{\textit{Int}}$

$= (\textit{with-int\&stack}$
$\qquad (\lambda i_1'' \,.\, (\textit{with-int\&stack}$
$\qquad\qquad (\lambda i_2 \,.\, \textit{push} \; (\textit{Value} \rightarrowtail \textit{Result} \; (\textit{Int} \rightarrowtail \textit{Value} \; (i_2 +_{\textit{Int}} i_1'')))))))$
$\quad \circ \; \textit{push} \; (\textit{Value} \rightarrowtail \textit{Result} \; (\textit{Int} \rightarrowtail \textit{Value} \; \mathcal{N}[\![\texttt{3}]\!]))$, by (4.9)

$= (\mathcal{C}[\![\texttt{add}]\!]) \circ (\mathcal{C}[\![\texttt{3}]\!])$, by definition of $\mathcal{C}$

$= (\mathcal{Q}[\![\texttt{3 add}]\!])$, by (4.8)

Figure 4.20 Proof that $[\texttt{1}, \texttt{add}, \texttt{2}, \texttt{add}]$ and $[\texttt{3}, \texttt{add}]$ are denotationally equivalent. This implies that the two sequences are observationally equivalent.

It is worth noting that the denotational proof that $[\texttt{1}, \texttt{add}, \texttt{2}, \texttt{add}] =_{obs} [\texttt{3}, \texttt{add}]$ has a very different flavor from the operational proof of this fact given in Section 3.7.2. The operational proof worked by case analysis on the initial stack. The denotational proof in Figure 4.20 works purely by equational reasoning — there is no hint of case analysis here. This is because all the case analyses are hidden within the carefully chosen abstractions *with-int&stack* and *push* (Fig-

$\mathcal{NE}[\![(+\ NE\ NE)]\!]$

$= \lambda i^* . \textit{with-int}\ (\mathcal{NE}[\![NE]\!]\ i^*)\ (\lambda i_1 . \textit{with-int}\ (\mathcal{NE}[\![NE]\!]\ i^*)\ (\lambda i_2 . (\mathcal{A}[\![+]\!]\ i_1\ i_2)))$

$= \lambda i^* . \textit{with-int}\ (\mathcal{NE}[\![NE]\!]\ i^*)\ (\lambda i_2 . (\textit{Int} \rightarrowtail \textit{Answer}\ (\mathcal{A}[\![+]\!]\ i_2\ i_2)))$

$= \lambda i^* . \textit{with-int}\ (\mathcal{NE}[\![NE]\!]\ i^*)\ (\lambda i_2 . (\textit{Int} \rightarrowtail \textit{Answer}\ (i_2 +_{\textit{Int}} i_2)))$

$= \lambda i^* . \textit{with-int}\ (\mathcal{NE}[\![NE]\!]\ i^*)\ (\lambda i_2 . (2 \times_{\textit{Int}} i_2))$

$= \lambda i^* . \textit{with-int}\ (\mathcal{NE}[\![NE]\!]\ i^*)\ (\lambda i_2 . (\mathcal{A}[\![*]\!]\ 2\ i_2))$

$= \lambda i^* . \textit{with-int}\ (\mathcal{NE}[\![2]\!]\ i^*)\ (\lambda i_1 . \textit{with-int}\ (\mathcal{NE}[\![NE]\!]\ i^*)\ (\lambda i_2 . (\mathcal{A}[\![*]\!]\ i_1\ i_2)))$

$= \mathcal{NE}[\![(*\ 2\ NE)]\!]$

Figure 4.21   Denotational proof that the EL expression (+ *NE NE*) may safely be replaced by (* 2 *NE*).

ure 4.18) and equalities (4.8)–(4.10). The case analyses would become apparent if these were expanded to show explicit **match** expressions.

Denotational justifications for the safety of transformations are not limited to POSTFIX. For example, Figure 4.21 shows that the EL numerical expressions (+ *NE NE*) and (* 2 *NE*) have the same meaning. So one can safely be substituted for the other in any EL program without changing the meaning of the program.

Exercise 4.8

a. Prove equalities (4.8)–(4.10).

b. Equality (4.10) requires that t map *errorStack* to *errorStack*. Show that the equality is not true if this requirement is violated.

Exercise 4.9

a. We have seen that (`postfix 2 3 sub swap pop`) and (`postfix 2 3 sub`) are equivalent programs. But in general it is *not* safe to replace the command sequence `3 sub swap pop` by `3 sub`. Give a context in which this replacement would change the meaning of a program.

b. Use denotational reasoning to show that it is safe to replace any of the following command sequences by `3 sub swap pop`:

   i.   `swap pop 3 sub`

   ii.   `(3 sub) swap pop exec`

   iii. `3 2 nget swap sub swap pop swap pop`

Exercise 4.10 Use the POSTFIX denotational semantics to either prove or disprove the purported observational equivalences in Exercise 3.28 on page 98.

Exercise 4.11 Use the EL denotational semantics to either prove or disprove the safety of the EL transformations in Exercise 3.33 on page 99.

4.4.3   Technical Difficulties

The denotational definition of POSTFIX depends crucially on some subtle details. As a hint of the subtlety, consider what happens to our denotational definition if we extend POSTFIX with our old friend **dup**. A valuation clause for **dup** seems straightforward:

$$\mathcal{C}[\![\text{dup}]\!] = \lambda s \,.\, (push \; (top \; s) \; s)$$

At the same time we know that adding **dup** to the language introduces the possibility that programs may not terminate. Yet, the signature for $\mathcal{P}$ declares that programs map to the *Answer* domain, and the *Answer* domain does not include any entity that represents nontermination. What's going on here?

   The source of the problem is the recursive structure of the semantic domains for POSTFIX. As the domain definitions show, the *StackTransform*, *Stack*, and *Value* domains are mutually recursive:

$$StackTransform = Stack \rightarrow Stack$$
$$Stack = Value^* + Error$$
$$Value = Int + StackTransform$$

It turns out that solving such recursive domain equations sometimes requires extending some domains with an element that models nontermination, written $\bot$ and pronounced "bottom." We will study this element in more detail in the next chapter, where it plays a prominent role. In the case of POSTFIX — whether or not we add **dup** — it turns out that both the *Stack* and *Answer* domains must include $\bot$, and this allows the domains to model the meaning of nonterminating command sequences.

4.5   Relating Operational and Denotational Semantics

We have presented the operational and denotational semantics of several simple languages, but have not studied the connection between them. What is the relationship between these two forms of semantics? How can we be sure that reasoning done with one form of semantics is valid in the other?

4.5.1 Soundness

Assume that an operational semantics has a deterministic behavior function of the form

$$beh_{det} : (\text{Prog} \times \text{Inputs}) \rightarrow \text{Outcome}$$

and that the related denotational semantics has a meaning function

$$meaning : (\text{Prog} \times Args) \rightarrow Answer$$

where *Args* is a domain of program arguments and *Answer* is the domain of final answers. Further suppose that there is a function *in* that maps between the syntactic and semantic input domains.

$$in : \text{Inputs} \rightarrow Args$$

Finally suppose that there is an **agreement relation** $\bowtie \subseteq Answer \times \text{Outcome}$ that relates denotational meanings with operational behaviors. We will pronounce $a \bowtie o$ as "the denotational answer a agrees with the operational outcome o." Then we define the following notion of soundness:

> **Definition 4.11 (Denotational Soundness)** *A denotational semantics* **is sound with respect to (wrt)** *an operational semantics iff for all programs P and inputs I, meaning $\langle P, (in\ I) \rangle \bowtie beh_{det} \langle P, I \rangle$.*

This definition says that the denotational semantics agrees with the operational semantics on the result of executing a program on any given inputs. Figure 4.22 shows how the parts of the soundness definition can be instantiated for EL and POSTFIX. Note that the Outcome domain does not include the nontermination domain LoopOut (see page 50) because both EL and POSTFIX are terminating languages.

We will now sketch a proof that the denotational semantics for POSTFIX is sound wrt the operational semantics for POSTFIX. The details of this proof, and a denotational soundness proof for EL, are left as Exercises 4.13 and 4.14. The essence of a denotational soundness proof for terminating languages like POSTFIX and EL is (1) defining the meaning of an operational configuration, (2) showing that each transition in the POSTFIX SOS preserves this meaning, and (3) showing that the meanings of final and stuck configurations agree with the outcomes of these configurations. Restricting attention to terminating languages simplifies the proof, because it is not necessary to consider the case of infinitely long transition paths (in which case $beh_{det} \langle P, I \rangle = \infty$). For languages containing

$I \in \text{Inputs} = \text{IntLit}^*$
$o \in \text{Outcome} = \text{IntLit} + \text{StuckOut}$
$\quad \text{StuckOut} = \{\text{stuckout}\}$
$ar \in Args = Int^*$
$a \in Answer = Int + Error$
$\quad Error = \{\text{error}\}$
$\text{stuck} : \text{Outcome} = (\text{StuckOut} \rightarrowtail \text{Outcome}\ \text{stuckout})$

$errorAnswer : Answer = (Error \rightarrowtail Answer\ error)$

$in : \text{Inputs} \rightarrow Args = \lambda N^* .\ (map\ \mathcal{N}\ N^*)$

$\ltimes\ \subseteq Answer \times \text{Outcome}$
$\ltimes\ = \{\langle(Int \rightarrowtail Answer\ (\mathcal{N}[\![N]\!])), (\text{IntLit} \rightarrowtail \text{Outcome}\ N)\rangle \mid N \in \text{IntLit}\}$
$\quad \cup\ \{\langle errorAnswer, \text{stuck}\rangle\}$

$beh_{det} : (\text{Prog} \times \text{Inputs}) \rightarrow \text{Outcome}$
$beh_{det\,EL}$ is the beh_{det} defined on page 51 in conjunction with the EL SOS.
$beh_{det\,PostFix}$ is the beh_{det} defined on page 51 in conjunction with the POSTFIX SOS.

$meaning : (\text{Prog} \times Args) \rightarrow Answer$
$meaning_{EL} = \lambda\langle P, ar\rangle .\ (\mathcal{P}_{EL}[\![P]\!]\ ar)$,
$\quad$ where $\mathcal{P}_{EL}$ is defined in Figure 4.9 on page 129.
$meaning_{PostFix} = \lambda\langle P, ar\rangle .\ (\mathcal{P}_{PostFix}[\![P]\!]\ ar)$,
$\quad$ where $\mathcal{P}_{PostFix}$ is defined in Figure 4.13 on page 137.

Figure 4.22   Instantiation of soundness components for EL and POSTFIX.

nonterminating programs, a denotational soundness proof must also explicitly handle this case, which can be challenging.

Recall that a configuration in the POSTFIX SOS has the form CommandSeq $\times$ Stack, where

$S \in \text{Stack} = \text{Value}^*$
$V \in \text{Value} = \text{IntLit} + \text{CommandSeq}$

Figure 4.23 defines a function $\mathcal{V}$ that maps an operational value to a denotational one, a function $\mathcal{S}$ that maps an operational stack to a denotational one, and a function $\mathcal{CF}$ that maps an operational configuration to an element of $Answer$.[6] Using these functions, we establish three lemmas that will lead to a proof of denotational soundness.

---

[6]When we talk about operational and denotational semantics together, note the distinction between syntactic or SOS domains, such as Value, and semantic domains, such as $Value$.

$$\mathcal{V} : \text{Value} \rightarrow \textit{Value}$$
$$\mathcal{V}[\![N]\!] = (Int \rightarrowtail Value\ \mathcal{N}[\![N]\!])$$
$$\mathcal{V}[\![(Q)]\!] = (StackTransform \rightarrowtail Value\ \mathcal{Q}[\![Q]\!])$$
$$\mathcal{S} : \text{Stack} \rightarrow \textit{Stack} = \lambda V^* . \ (Value^* \rightarrowtail Stack \ (\text{map}\ \mathcal{V}\ V^*))$$
$$\mathcal{CF} : \text{CommandSeq} \times \text{Stack} \rightarrow \textit{Answer} = \lambda\langle Q, S\rangle . \ resToAns \ (top \ (\mathcal{Q}[\![Q]\!]\ \mathcal{S}[\![S]\!]))$$

Figure 4.23 Meaning of a POSTFIX configuration.

Lemma 4.12 ($\mathcal{CF}$ Calculates the Meaning of PostFix Program) *For any* POSTFIX *program* $P = (\texttt{postfix}\ N_{numargs}\ Q)$ *and numerals* N^*,

$$(\mathcal{P}[\![P]\!]\ (in\ N^*)) = \mathcal{CF}[\![(IF\ \langle P, N^*\rangle)]\!]$$

where IF is the input function defined in Figure 3.3 on page 53 that maps a POSTFIX *program and inputs into an initial SOS configuration.*

Lemma 4.13 (PostFix Transitions Preserve Meaning) *For any transition* $cf \Rightarrow cf'$, $\mathcal{CF}[\![cf]\!] = \mathcal{CF}[\![cf']\!]$.

Lemma 4.14 (PostFix Stuck Configurations Denote Errors) *For any stuck configuration* cf, $\mathcal{CF}[\![cf]\!] = errorAnswer$.

We now give proofs of these three lemmas. In the proofs, we will use the following equalities, which are left as exercises (Exercise 4.12).

$$\mathcal{Q}[\![Q_1 @ Q_2]\!] = (\mathcal{Q}[\![Q_1]\!] \circ \mathcal{Q}[\![Q_2]\!]) \quad (4.15)$$
$$(\mathcal{Q}[\![Q]\!]\ errorStack) = errorStack \quad (4.16)$$

Proof of Lemma 4.12 ($\mathcal{CF}$ Calculates the Meaning of PostFix Program):
There are two cases:

1. When $\mathcal{N}[\![N_{numargs}]\!] = (length\ N^*)$, both the left- and right-hand sides of the equation denote

$$resToAns \ (top \ (\mathcal{Q}[\![Q]\!]\ (Value^* \rightarrowtail Stack \ (\text{map}\ (Int \rightarrowtail Value \circ \mathcal{N})\ N^*))))$$

2. When $\mathcal{N}[\![N_{numargs}]\!] \neq (length\ N^*)$, the left-hand side of the equation denotes *errorAnswer* and the right-hand side denotes

$$\mathcal{CF}[\![\langle \mathbf{exec} . Q_{rest}, (Q_{exec}) . S\rangle]\!]$$

$$= resToAns \ (top \ (\mathcal{Q}[\![\mathbf{exec} . Q_{rest}]\!] \ (Value^* {\rightarrowtail} Stack \ (\mathcal{V}[\![(Q_{exec})]\!] . v^*)))),$$
$$\text{where } v^* = (map \ \mathcal{V} \ S)$$

$$= resToAns$$
$$\quad (top \ (\mathcal{Q}[\![Q_{rest}]\!] \ (\mathcal{C}[\![\mathbf{exec}]\!] \ (Value^* {\rightarrowtail} Stack \ (\mathcal{V}[\![(Q_{exec})]\!] . v^*)))))$$

$$= resToAns$$
$$\quad (top \ (\mathcal{Q}[\![Q_{rest}]\!]$$
$$\qquad (transform \ (top \ (Value^* {\rightarrowtail} Stack \ (\mathcal{V}[\![(Q_{exec})]\!] . v^*)))$$
$$\qquad\qquad (pop \ (Value^* {\rightarrowtail} Stack \ (\mathcal{V}[\![(Q_{exec})]\!] . v^*))))))$$

$$= resToAns$$
$$\quad (top \ (\mathcal{Q}[\![Q_{rest}]\!]$$
$$\qquad (transform \ (Value {\rightarrowtail} Result \ (StackTransform {\rightarrowtail} Value \ \mathcal{Q}[\![Q_{exec}]\!]))$$
$$\qquad\qquad (Value^* {\rightarrowtail} Stack \ v^*))))$$

$$= resToAns \ (top \ (\mathcal{Q}[\![Q_{rest}]\!] \ (\mathcal{Q}[\![Q_{exec}]\!] \ (Value^* {\rightarrowtail} Stack \ v^*))))$$

$$= resToAns \ (top \ ((\mathcal{Q}[\![Q_{rest}]\!] \circ \mathcal{Q}[\![Q_{exec}]\!]) \ (Value^* {\rightarrowtail} Stack \ v^*)))$$

$$= resToAns \ (top \ (\mathcal{Q}[\![Q_{rest} @ Q_{exec}]\!] \ (Value^* {\rightarrowtail} Stack \ (map \ \mathcal{V} \ S)))) \ , \text{ by } (4.15)$$

$$= \mathcal{CF}[\![\langle Q_{exec} @ Q_{rest}, S\rangle]\!]$$

Figure 4.24 Proof that the [*execute*] transition preserves meaning.

$$\mathcal{CF}[\![(IF \ \langle P, N^*\rangle)]\!]$$
$$= \mathcal{CF}[\![\langle [\,]_{\text{Command}}, [\,]_{\text{Value}}\rangle]\!]$$
$$= resToAns \ (top \ (\mathcal{Q}[\![[\,]_{\text{Command}}]\!] \ (Value^* {\rightarrowtail} Stack \ [\,]_{\text{Value}})))$$
$$= resToAns \ (top \ (Value^* {\rightarrowtail} Stack \ [\,]_{\text{Value}}))$$
$$= errorAnswer \qquad\qquad\qquad\qquad\qquad\qquad\qquad\qquad\qquad \diamond$$

Proof of Lemma 4.13 (PostFix Transitions Preserve Meaning):   This can be shown by demonstrating this equality for each of the POSTFIX rewrite rules in Figure 3.4 on page 55. For example, one such rule is:

$$\langle \mathbf{exec} . Q_{rest}, (Q_{exec}) . S\rangle \Rightarrow \langle Q_{exec} @ Q_{rest}, S\rangle \qquad\qquad [execute]$$

An equational proof that this rule preserves meaning is presented in Figure 4.24. In this proof, we use the equality $\mathcal{Q}[\![Q_{rest} @ Q_{exec}]\!] = (\mathcal{Q}[\![Q_{rest}]\!] \circ \mathcal{Q}[\![Q_{exec}]\!])$. In Exercise 4.13, you are asked to prove this equality and also show that the other POSTFIX rewrite rules preserve meaning. $\diamond$

Proof of Lemma 4.14 (PostFix Stuck Configurations Denote Errors): This can be shown by enumerating the finite number of configuration patterns

$\boxed{\begin{aligned}
&\mathcal{CF}[\![\langle \texttt{swap}\,.\,Q,\,[V]\rangle]\!] \\
&= \mathit{resToAns}\ (\mathit{top}\ (\mathcal{Q}[\![\texttt{swap}\,.\,Q]\!]\ (\mathit{Value}^* \rightarrowtail \mathit{Stack}\ [\mathcal{V}[\![V]\!]]))) \\
&= \mathit{resToAns} \\
&\qquad (\mathit{top}\ (\mathcal{Q}[\![Q]\!]\ (\mathit{push}\ (\mathit{top}\ (\mathit{pop}\ (\mathit{Value}^* \rightarrowtail \mathit{Stack}\ [\mathcal{V}[\![V]\!]]))) \\
&\qquad\qquad\qquad\qquad\qquad (\mathit{push}\ (\mathit{top}\ (\mathit{Value}^* \rightarrowtail \mathit{Stack}\ [\mathcal{V}[\![V]\!]])) \\
&\qquad\qquad\qquad\qquad\qquad\qquad (\mathit{pop}\ (\mathit{pop}\ (\mathit{Value}^* \rightarrowtail \mathit{Stack}\ [\mathcal{V}[\![V]\!]])))))))) \\
&= \mathit{resToAns}\ (\mathit{top}\ (\mathcal{Q}[\![Q]\!]\ (\mathit{push}\ (\mathit{top}\ (\mathit{Value}^* \rightarrowtail \mathit{Stack}\ [\,]))) \\
&\qquad\qquad\qquad\qquad\qquad\qquad (\mathit{push}\ (\mathit{Value} \rightarrowtail \mathit{Result}\ \mathcal{V}[\![V]\!]) \\
&\qquad\qquad\qquad\qquad\qquad\qquad\qquad (\mathit{pop}\ (\mathit{Value}^* \rightarrowtail \mathit{Stack}\ [\,]))))))) \\
&= \mathit{resToAns}\ (\mathit{top}\ (\mathcal{Q}[\![Q]\!]\ (\mathit{push}\ \mathit{errorResult} \\
&\qquad\qquad\qquad\qquad\qquad\qquad (\mathit{push}\ (\mathit{Value} \rightarrowtail \mathit{Result}\ \mathcal{V}[\![V]\!])\ \mathit{errorStack})))) \\
&= \mathit{resToAns}\ (\mathit{top}\ (\mathcal{Q}[\![Q]\!]\ \mathit{errorStack})) \\
&= \mathit{resToAns}\ (\mathit{top}\ \mathit{errorStack}),\ \text{by}\ (4.16) \\
&= \mathit{errorAnswer}
\end{aligned}}$

Figure 4.25   Proof that the configuration $\langle \texttt{swap}\,.\,Q,\,[V]\rangle$ denotes the error answer.

that stand for configurations in $\mathit{Irreducible}_{PFSOS}$, and showing that each denotes the error answer. For example, one such pattern is $\langle \texttt{swap}\,.\,Q,\,[V]\rangle$. Figure 4.25 shows that this configuration pattern denotes the error answer. In this figure, we use the equality $(\mathcal{Q}[\![Q]\!]\ \mathit{errorStack}) = \mathit{errorStack}$ for any Q, which you are asked to prove in Exercise 4.13. $\diamond$

We're now ready to put the lemmas together to show denotational soundness for a POSTFIX program $(\texttt{postfix}\ N_{numargs}\ Q_{body})$ executed on inputs N^*_{inputs}. There are two cases:

1. $\mathcal{N}[\![N_{numargs}]\!] = \left(\mathit{length}\ N^*_{inputs}\right)$ and the initial program configuration has a transition path to a final configuration:

$$\langle Q_{body},\ N^*_{inputs}\rangle \xrightarrow{*} \langle [\,]_{\mathrm{Command}},\ N_{ans}\,.\,V^*_{rest}\rangle$$

In this case,

$\qquad$ meaning $\langle (\texttt{postfix}\ N_{numargs}\ Q_{body}),\left(\texttt{in}\ N^*_{inputs}\right)\rangle$

$\qquad = \mathcal{P}[\![(\texttt{postfix}\ N_{numargs}\ Q_{body})]\!]\ \left(\texttt{in}\ N^*_{inputs}\right)$

$\qquad = \mathcal{CF}[\![(\mathit{IF}\ \langle (\texttt{postfix}\ N_{numargs}\ Q_{body}),N^*_{inputs}\rangle)]\!]$, by Lemma 4.12.

$\qquad = \mathcal{CF}[\![\langle Q_{body},\ N^*_{inputs}\rangle]\!]$, where the IntLit $\rightarrowtail$ Value injections on the elements
$\qquad\qquad\qquad\qquad\qquad$ of N^*_{inputs} are omitted by the convention on page 56.

$= \mathcal{CF}[\![\langle[\,]_{\text{Command}}, N_{ans} \cdot V^*_{rest}\rangle]\!]$, by Lemma 4.13 on each $\Rightarrow$.

$= resToAns$
$\quad\quad (top\ (\mathcal{Q}[\![]\!]\ (Value^* \rightarrowtail Stack\ ((Int \rightarrowtail Value\ \mathcal{N}[\![N_{ans}]\!]) \cdot (map\ \mathcal{V}\ V^*_{rest}))))))$

$= resToAns\ (top\ (Value^* \rightarrowtail Stack\ ((Int \rightarrowtail Value\ \mathcal{N}[\![N_{ans}]\!]) \cdot (map\ \mathcal{V}\ V^*_{rest}))))$

$= (Int \rightarrowtail Answer\ \mathcal{N}[\![N_{ans}]\!])$

$\Bowtie (\text{IntLit} \rightarrowtail Outcome\ N_{ans})$

$= beh_{det\,PostFix}\ \langle(\texttt{postfix}\ N_{numargs}\ Q_{body}), N^*_{inputs}\rangle$

2. $\mathcal{N}[\![N_{numargs}]\!] \neq \left(length\ N^*_{inputs}\right)$ or the initial program configuration has a transition path to a stuck configuration. In these cases,

$$IF\ \langle(\texttt{postfix}\ N_{numargs}\ Q_{body}), N^*\rangle \overset{*}{\Rightarrow} cf_{stuck}$$

where cf_{stuck} is a stuck configuration. Then we have:

$meaning\ \langle(\texttt{postfix}\ N_{numargs}\ Q_{body}), \left(in\ N^*_{inputs}\right)\rangle$

$= \mathcal{P}[\![(\texttt{postfix}\ N_{numargs}\ Q_{body})]\!]\ \left(in\ N^*_{inputs}\right)$

$= \mathcal{CF}[\![\left(IF\ \langle(\texttt{postfix}\ N_{numargs}\ Q_{body}), N^*_{inputs}\rangle\right)]\!]$, by Lemma 4.12.

$= \mathcal{CF}[\![cf_{stuck}]\!]$, by Lemma 4.13 on each $\Rightarrow$.

$= errorAnswer$, by Lemma 4.14.

$\Bowtie \texttt{stuck}$

$= beh_{det\,PostFix}\ \langle(\texttt{postfix}\ N_{numargs}\ Q_{body}), N^*_{inputs}\rangle$

This completes the sketch of the proof that the denotational semantics for POSTFIX is sound with respect to the operational semantics for POSTFIX.

Exercise 4.12 Prove equalities (4.15) and (4.16).

Exercise 4.13 Complete the proof that the denotational semantics for POSTFIX is sound with respect to its operational semantics by fleshing out the following details:

a. Show that Lemma 4.13 holds for each transition rule in Figure 3.4 on page 55.

b. Make a list of all stuck configuration patterns in the POSTFIX SOS and show that Lemma 4.14 holds for each such pattern.

Exercise 4.14 Show that the denotational semantics for each of the following languages is sound with respect to its operational semantics: (1) a version of ELMM whose operators include only +, -, and *; (2) full ELMM; (3) ELM; and (4) EL.

4.5.2   Adequacy

The notion of soundness developed above works at the level of a whole program. But often we want to reason about smaller phrases within a program. In particular, we want to reason that we can substitute one phrase for another without changing the operational behavior of the program. The following adequacy property says that denotational equivalence implies the operational notion of observational equivalence:

> **Definition 4.17 (Adequacy)**   *Suppose that $\mathbb{P}$ ranges over program contexts, H ranges over the kinds of phrases that fill the holes in program contexts, and $\mathcal{H}$ is a denotational meaning function for phrases. A denotational semantics is* **adequate with respect to (wrt)** *an operational semantics if the following holds:*
>
> $$\mathcal{H}[\![H_1]\!] = \mathcal{H}[\![H_2]\!] \text{ implies } H_1 =_{obs} H_2$$

Recall from page 91 that $H_1 =_{obs} H_2$ means that for all program contexts $\mathbb{P}$ and all inputs I, $beh \ \langle \mathbb{P}\{H_1\}, I \rangle = beh \ \langle \mathbb{P}\{H_2\}, I \rangle$.

In the case of a deterministic behavior function, the following reasoning shows that adequacy is *almost* implied by denotational soundness:

$\mathcal{H}[\![H_1]\!] = \mathcal{H}[\![H_2]\!]$

implies $\mathcal{P}[\![\mathbb{P}\{H_1\}]\!] = \mathcal{P}[\![\mathbb{P}\{H_2\}]\!]$, by compositionality of denotational semantics

implies $meaning \ \langle \mathbb{P}\{H_1\}, (in \ I) \rangle = meaning \ \langle \mathbb{P}\{H_2\}, (in \ I) \rangle$ for any inputs I

implies $beh_{det} \ \langle \mathbb{P}\{H_1\}, I \rangle \bowtie a \ltimes beh_{det} \ \langle \mathbb{P}\{H_2\}, I \rangle$, by soundness,
     where $meaning \ \langle \mathbb{P}\{H_1\}, (in \ I) \rangle = a = meaning \ \langle \mathbb{P}\{H_2\}, (in \ I) \rangle$

(In the final step, the symbol $\bowtie$ stands for the relation in Outcome $\times$ *Answer* that is the inverse of the relation $\ltimes$ in *Answer* $\times$ Outcome.) But demonstrating the observational equivalence $H_1 =_{obs} H_2$ requires showing that

$$beh_{det} \ \langle \mathbb{P}\{H_1\}, I \rangle = beh_{det} \ \langle \mathbb{P}\{H_2\}, I \rangle$$

To conclude this from the above line of reasoning requires the following property for $\ltimes$:

> **Definition 4.18 (Observational Uniqueness)**   *The agreement relation $\ltimes \subseteq$ Answer $\times$ Outcome is* **observationally unique** *iff for every $a \in$ Answer and $o_1, o_2 \in$ Outcome, $a \ltimes o_1$ and $a \ltimes o_2$ implies $o_1 = o_2$.*

Observational uniqueness says that every denotational answer agrees with at most one operational outcome. In other words, ⋉ is a partial function from *Answer* to Outcome: an answer may not agree with any outcome, but if it does, it can agree with exactly one.

The agreement relation for EL and PostFix in Figure 4.22 has observational uniqueness. In each language, observable outcomes are either integer numerals or a `stuck` token. Assuming that only canonical integer numerals are used (e.g., 17 rather than 017 or +17) every integer answer agrees with only the unique numeral that represents it. And the error answer agrees with only the `stuck` token. Since the agreement relation has observational uniqueness, we can conclude that the denotational semantics for EL and PostFix are adequate.

Note that the agreement relation for PostFix would *not* have observational uniqueness if executable sequences at the top of a final stack could be returned as observable outcomes. For this extension to PostFix, we would need to extend the agreement relation so that a new semantic answer (a stack transform) would agree with any new observable syntactic outcome (an executable sequence) that denotes it. For example, the executable sequences (1 add 2 add) and (3 add) both denote the stack transform ($push$ ($Value \rightarrowtail Result$ ($Int \rightarrowtail Value$ 3))), so this stack transform would agree with both sequences. In such a framework, two outcomes that a given answer agrees with would not necessarily be syntactically identical, and the reasoning sketched above for adequacy would fail. However, as shown in Exercise 4.15, adequacy can be restored in this situation if the output function of the SOS maps all executable sequence outcomes to the token `executable`.

The above discussion allows us to conclude that any language with denotational soundness and an observationally unique agreement relation has the adequacy property. Since EL and PostFix satisfy both of these conditions, they have the adequacy property. In turn, this property justifies the use of denotational reasoning for proving the safety of program transformations. For example, the PostFix Denotational Equivalence Theorem on page 147 is a corollary of the adequacy of PostFix.

Exercise 4.15 Consider a variant of PostFix in which the SOS outcome of a PostFix program whose final configuration has an executable sequence at the top is the token `executable` (see Exercise 3.31 on page 99).

a. Modify the denotational semantics of PostFix (both domains and valuation functions) so that the transform at the top of the final stack can be the result of executing a PostFix program.

b. Show that your modified denotational semantics is denotationally sound with respect to the modified operational semantics by tweaking the denotational soundness proof for PostFix presented in Section 4.5.1.

c. Show that this POSTFIX variant has the adequacy property. This provides an alternative proof to the one in Exercise 3.31 that transform equivalence implies observational equivalence for this variant of POSTFIX.

4.5.3 Full Abstraction

Changing the unidirectional implication of adequacy to a bidirectional implication yields a stronger property called **full abstraction**:

> **Definition 4.19 (Full Abstraction)** *Suppose that $\mathbb{P}$ ranges over program contexts, H ranges over the kinds of phrases that fill the holes in program contexts, and $\mathcal{H}$ is a denotational meaning function for phrases. A denotational semantics is* **fully abstract with respect to (wrt)** *an operational semantics if the following holds:*
>
> $$\mathcal{H}[\![H_1]\!] = \mathcal{H}[\![H_2]\!] \quad iff \quad H_1 =_{obs} H_2$$

In addition to adequacy, full abstraction requires that observational equivalence imply denotational equivalence. That is, program fragments that behave the same in all contexts must have the same denotational meaning.

The denotational semantics of the various dialects of EL we have considered are all fully abstract. Consider the restricted version of ELMM in which the only operations are +, -, and *. In this language, every numerical expression denotes an integer. We already know that the denotational semantics for this language is adequate wrt the operational semantics; to prove full abstraction, we need to show that observational equivalence implies denotational equivalence. Suppose that $NE_1 =_{obs} NE_2$. Modeling nonexistent inputs by *unit*, this means that for all restricted ELMM program contexts $\mathbb{P}$, $beh_{det} \langle \mathbb{P}\{NE_1\}, unit \rangle = beh_{det} \langle \mathbb{P}\{NE_2\}, unit \rangle$. The program context $\mathbb{P} = (\texttt{elmm } \square)$ is particularly useful because the denotational soundness of restricted ELMM implies that $\mathcal{NE}[\![NE]\!] \ltimes beh_{det} \langle (\texttt{elmm } NE), unit \rangle$ for any numerical expression NE. Let $o = beh_{det} \langle (\texttt{elmm } NE_1), unit \rangle = beh_{det} \langle (\texttt{elmm } NE_2), unit \rangle$. Then the denotational soundness of restricted ELMM implies:

$$\mathcal{NE}[\![NE_1]\!] \ltimes o \rtimes \mathcal{NE}[\![NE_2]\!]$$

In restricted ELMM, the agreement relation is defined as:

$$\ltimes = \{\langle (Int \rightarrowtail Answer \; \mathcal{N}[\![N]\!]), (\text{IntLit} \rightarrowtail Outcome \; N) \rangle \mid N \in \text{IntLit}\}$$

Assuming that only canonical numerals are used, this relation defines a bijection between integer answers and integer numeral outcomes. So $\mathcal{NE}[\![NE_1]\!] \ltimes o \rtimes \mathcal{NE}[\![NE_2]\!]$ implies $\mathcal{NE}[\![NE_1]\!] = \mathcal{NE}[\![NE_2]\!]$. Via similar reasoning, we can show that all the dialects of EL we have studied have a fully abstract denotational semantics.

Surprisingly, the denotational semantics for POSTFIX is *not* fully abstract! As argued in Section 4.4.3, even though all POSTFIX programs terminate, the denotational domains for answers and stacks in POSTFIX must include an entity denoting nontermination, which we will write as $\bot$. This is the denotational analogue of the operational token ∞. Even though no POSTFIX command sequence can loop, the presence of $\bot$ in the semantics can distinguish the meanings of some observationally equivalent command sequences.

For example, consider the following two command sequences:

$$Q_1 = \texttt{1 0 div}$$
$$Q_2 = \texttt{exec 1 0 div}$$

Q_1 signals an error for any stack. Q_2 first executes the top value V_{top} on the stack and then executes `1 0 div`. We argue that Q_2 is observationally equivalent to Q_1, because it will also signal an error for any stack:

- if the stack is empty or if V_{top} is not an executable sequence, the attempt to perform `exec` will fail with an error;

- if V_{top} is an executable sequence, Q_2 will execute it. Since all POSTFIX command sequences terminate, the execution of V_{top} will either signal an error, or it will terminate without an error. In the latter case, the execution continues with `1 0 div`, which necessarily signals an error.

Even though $Q_1 =_{obs} Q_2$, they do not denote the same stack transform! To see this, consider a stack transform $t_{weird} = \lambda s . \bot$ and a stack s_{weird} whose top value is $(StackTransform \rightarrowtail Value \ t_{weird})$. Both t_{weird} and s_{weird} are "weird" in the sense that they can never arise during a POSTFIX computation, in which all stack transforms necessarily terminate. Nevertheless, t_{weird} is a legal element of the domain *StackTransform*, and it must be considered as a legal stack element in denotational reasoning. Observe that $(\mathcal{Q}[\![Q_1]\!] \ s_{weird}) = errorStack$, but $(\mathcal{Q}[\![Q_2]\!] \ s_{weird}) = \bot$ — i.e., the latter computation does not terminate. So Q_1 and Q_2 denote distinct stack transforms even though they are observationally equivalent.

Intuitively, full abstraction says that the semantic domains don't contain any extra "junk" that can't be expressed by phrases in the language. In the case of POSTFIX, the domains harbor $\bot$ even though it cannot be expressed in the language.

4.5.4 Operational versus Denotational: A Comparison

We have noted in this chapter that a denotational semantics expresses the meaning of a program in a much more direct way than an operational semantics. Furthermore, the compositional nature of a denotational semantics is a real boon for proving properties of programs and languages and for constructing interpreters and translators. Why would we ever want to choose an operational semantics over a denotational semantics?

For one thing, an operational semantics is usually a more natural medium for expressing the step-by-step nature of program execution. The notion of "step" is an important one: it is at the heart of a mechanistic view of computation; it provides a measure by which computations can be compared (e.g., which takes the fewest steps); and it provides a natural way to talk about nondeterminism (choice between steps) and concurrency (interleaving the steps of more than one process). What counts as a natural step for a program is explicit in the rewrite rules of an SOS. These notions cannot always be expressed straightforwardly in a denotational approach. Furthermore, in computer science, the bottom line is often what actually runs on a machine, and the operational approach is much closer to this bottom line.

From a mathematical perspective, the advantage of an operational semantics is that it's often much easier to construct than a denotational semantics. Since the objects manipulated by an SOS are simple syntactic entities, there are very few constraints on the form of an operational semantics. Any SOS with a deterministic set of rewrite rules specifies a well-defined behavior function from programs to answer expressions. Creating or extending a set of rewrite rules is fairly painless since it rarely requires any deep mathematical reasoning. Of course, the same emphasis on syntax that facilitates the construction of an operational semantics limits its usefulness for reasoning about programs. For example, it's difficult to see how some local change to the rewrite rules affects the global properties of a language.

Constructing a denotational semantics, on the other hand, is mathematically much more intensive. It is necessary to build consistent mathematical representations for each kind of meaning object. The difficulty of building such models in general is illustrated by the fact that there was no mathematically viable interpretation for recursive domain equations until Dana Scott invented one in the early 1970s. Since then, various tools and techniques have been developed that make it easier to construct a denotational semantics that maps programs into a restricted set of meanings. Extending this set of meanings requires potentially difficult proofs that the extensions are sound, so most semanticists are content to stick with the well-understood meanings. This class of meanings is large enough, however, to facilitate a wide range of formal reasoning about programs and programming languages.

Notes

Landin observed a correspondence between ALGOL 60 and the lambda calculus and suggested that this correspondence could be the basis for a formal description of the semantics of ALGOL 60 [Lan65a, Lan65b]. The notion of using the lambda calculus to define programming language semantics in a formal way is the essence of denotational semantics, which was developed by Strachey and Scott [Str00, SS71, MS76].

For a tutorial introduction to denotational semantics, we recommend the articles [Ten76] and [Mos90]. Coverage of both operational and denotational semantics, along with their use in reasoning about several simple programming languages, can be found in several semantics textbooks [Gun92, Win93, Mit96]. Full-length books devoted to denotational semantics include [Gor79, Sto85, Sch86].

Our notions of denotational soundness and adequacy are somewhat different from (but related to) those in the literature. For a discussion of the traditional approach to soundness, adequacy, and full abstraction, see [Gun92]. Seminal papers on full abstraction are [Mil77] and [Plo77].

5

Fixed Points

This is a quotation for the Fixed Points chapter.

— Turbak and Gifford with Sheldon
Design Concepts in Programming Languages, Chapter 5

Recursive definitions are a powerful and elegant tool for specifying complex structures and processes. While such definitions are second nature to experienced programmers, novices are often mystified by recursive definitions. Their confusion often centers on the question: "How can something be defined in terms of itself?" Sometimes there is a justifiable cause for confusion — not all recursive definitions make sense!

In this chapter, we carve out a class of recursive definitions that *do* make sense, and present a technique for assigning meaning to them. The technique involves finding a *fixed point* of a function derived from the recursive definition. The results and techniques of this chapter will find frequent application in later denotational descriptions of programming languages as we define recursive valuation functions and recursive domains.

5.1 The Fixed Point Game

There are fixed limits beyond which and short of which right cannot find a resting place.

— Horace, *Satires*

5.1.1 Recursive Definitions

For our purposes, a **recursive definition** is an equation of the form

$$x \;=\; \ldots \, x \, \ldots$$

where $\ldots x \ldots$ designates a mathematical expression that contains occurrences of the defined variable x. Mutually recursive definitions of the form

$$x_1 \;\; = \;\; \ldots \; x_1 \; \ldots \; x_n \; \ldots$$
$$\vdots$$
$$x_n \;\; = \;\; \ldots \; x_1 \; \ldots \; x_n \; \ldots$$

can always be rephrased as a single recursive definition

$$x \;\; = \;\; \langle \ldots (\mathit{Proj}\,1\;\, x) \, \ldots \, (\mathit{Proj}\,n\;\, x) \, \ldots \,,$$
$$\vdots$$
$$\ldots (\mathit{Proj}\,1\;\, x) \, \ldots \, (\mathit{Proj}\,n\;\, x) \, \ldots \rangle$$

where x stands for the n-tuple $\langle x_1, \ldots, x_n \rangle$ and $\mathit{Proj}\,i$ extracts the ith element of the tuple. For this reason, it is sufficient to focus on recursive definitions involving a single variable.

A **solution** to a recursive definition is a value that makes the equation true when substituted for all occurrences of the defined variable. A recursive definition may have zero, one, or more solutions. For example, suppose that x ranges over the integers. Then:

- $x = 1 + x$ has no solutions;

- $x = 4 - x$ has exactly one solution (2);

- $x = \frac{9}{x}$ has two solutions $(-3, 3)$;

- $x = x$ has an infinite number of solutions (each integer).

It is important to specify the domain of the defined variable in a recursive definition, since the set of solutions depends on this domain. For example, the recursive definition $x = \frac{1}{16x^3}$ has

- zero solutions over the integers (with division interpreted as a quotient function on integers);

- one solution over the positive rationals ($\frac{1}{2}$);

- two solutions over the rationals ($\frac{1}{2}, -\frac{1}{2}$);

- four solutions over the complex numbers ($\frac{1}{2}, -\frac{1}{2}, \frac{i}{2}, -\frac{i}{2}$).

In fact, many numerical domains were invented precisely to solve classes of equations that were insoluble with existing domains.

Although we are most familiar with equations that involve numeric variables, equations can involve variables from *any* domain, including product, sum, sequence, and function domains. For example, consider the following recursive definitions involving an element p of the product domain $Nat \times Nat$:

- $p = \langle (Proj\,2\ p), (Proj\,1\ p) \rangle$ has an infinite number of solutions of the form $\langle n, n \rangle$, where $n : Nat$.

- $p = \langle (Proj\,2\ p), (Proj\,1\ p) -_{Nat} 1 \rangle$ has the unique solution $\langle 0, 0 \rangle$. (As noted on page 1163, the natural number subtraction operation $n_1 -_{Nat} n_2$ is defined to be 0 when $n_1 \leq_{Nat} n_2$.)

- $p = \langle (Proj\,2\ p), (Proj\,1\ p) +1 \rangle$ has no solutions in $Nat \times Nat$. The first element n of a solution $p = \langle n, \ldots \rangle$ would have to satisfy the equation $n = n + 1$, and this equation has no solutions.

We can also have recursive definitions involving an element s of the sequence domain Nat^*:

- $s = (cons\ 3\ (tail\ s))$ has an infinite number of solutions: all nonempty sequences s whose first element is 3.

- $s = (cons\ 3\ s)$ has no solutions in Nat^*, which includes only finite sequences of natural numbers and so does not contain an infinite sequence of 3s. However, this equation *does* have a solution in a domain that includes infinite sequences of numbers in addition to the finite ones. We shall use the notation $\overline{Nat^*}$ to designate this domain.

- $s = (cons\ 3\ (tail\ (tail\ s)))$ has the unique solution [3]. This definition requires that (a) $(head\ s) = 3$ and (b) $(tail\ s) = (tail\ (tail\ s))$. In Nat^*, (b) is satisfied only if s is an empty sequence or a singleton sequence (recall that $(tail\ [\,])$ is defined to be $[\,]$). Since (a) requires s to be a nonempty sequence beginning with 3, (a) and (b) imply that s must be [3]. However, in $\overline{Nat^*}$, this equation has an infinite number of solutions, since for any natural number n, an infinite sequence of ns satisfies (b).

We will be especially interested in recursive definitions over function domains. Suppose that f is an element of the domain $Nat \rightarrow Nat$. Consider the following recursive function definition of f:

$$f = \lambda n \,.\, \textbf{if}\ (n = 0)\ \textbf{then}\ 0\ \textbf{else}\ (2 + (f\ (n-1)))\ \textbf{end}$$

Intuitively, this equation is solved when f is a doubling function, but how do we show this more formally? Recall that a function in $Nat \rightarrow Nat$ can be viewed as its graph, the set of argument/result pairs for the function. The graph associated with the lambda expression is

$$\{\langle 0, \textbf{if } (0 = 0) \textbf{ then } 0 \textbf{ else } (2 + (f\ 0))\rangle,$$
$$\langle 1, \textbf{if } (1 = 0) \textbf{ then } 0 \textbf{ else } (2 + (f\ 0))\rangle,$$
$$\langle 2, \textbf{if } (2 = 0) \textbf{ then } 0 \textbf{ else } (2 + (f\ 1))\rangle,$$
$$\langle 3, \textbf{if } (3 = 0) \textbf{ then } 0 \textbf{ else } (2 + (f\ 2))\rangle,$$
$$\ldots\}$$

After simplification, this becomes

$$\{\langle 0, 0\rangle, \langle 1, (2 + (f\ 0))\rangle,\ \langle 2, (2 + (f\ 1))\rangle,\ \langle 3, (2 + (f\ 2))\rangle,\ \ldots\ \}$$

If f is a doubling function, then the graph of the right-hand side can be further simplified to

$$\{\langle 0, 0\rangle,\ \langle 1, 2\rangle,\ \langle 2, 4\rangle,\ \langle 3, 6\rangle,\ \ldots\ \}$$

This is precisely the graph of the doubling function f on the left-hand side of the equation, so the equation holds true. It is not difficult to show that the doubling function is the *only* solution to the equation; we leave this as an exercise.

As with recursive definitions over other domains, recursive definitions of functions may have zero, one, or more solutions. Maintaining the assumption that $f : Nat \rightarrow Nat$, the definition

$$f \quad = \quad \lambda n\,.\,(1 + (f\ n))$$

has no solutions, because the result n_r for any given argument would have to satisfy $n_r = n_r + 1$. On the other hand, the definition

$$f \quad = \quad \lambda n\,.\,(f\ (1 + n))$$

has an infinite number of solutions: for any given constant n_c, a function with the graph $\{\langle n, n_c\rangle \mid n : Nat\}$ is a solution to the equation.

5.1.2   Fixed Points

If d ranges over domain D, then a recursive definition

$$d \quad = \quad (\ldots\ d\ \ldots)$$

can always be encoded as the $D \rightarrow D$ function

$$\lambda d\,.\,(\ \ldots\ d\ \ldots)$$

We will call this the **generating function** for the recursive definition. For example, if $r : Real$, the numeric equation $r = 1 - (r \times r)$ can be represented by the $Real \to Real$ generating function $\lambda r \,.\, (1 - (r \times r))$. Similarly, the recursive function definition

$$dbl : Nat \to Nat = \lambda n \,.\, \textbf{if } (n = 0) \textbf{ then } 0 \textbf{ else } (2 + (dbl \ (n-1))) \textbf{ end}$$

can be represented by the generating function

$$g_{dbl} : (Nat \to Nat) \to (Nat \to Nat)$$
$$= \lambda f \,.\, \lambda n \,.\, \textbf{if } (n = 0) \textbf{ then } 0 \textbf{ else } (2 + (f \ (n-1))) \textbf{ end}$$

where $f : Nat \to Nat$. A generating function is not recursive, so its meaning can be straightforwardly determined from its component parts.

A solution to a recursive definition is a fixed point of its associated generating function. A **fixed point** of a function $g : D \to D$ is an element $d : D$ such that $(g \ d) = d$. If a function in $D \to D$ is viewed as moving elements around the space D, elements satisfying the recursive definition are the only ones that remain stationary; hence the name "fixed point."

To build intuitions about fixed points, consider functions from the unit interval[1] $[0; 1]$ to itself. Such functions can be graphed in the unit square, with arguments along the horizontal axis and results along the vertical axis:

Every point where the function graph intersects the diagonal is a fixed point of the function. Figure 5.1 shows the graphs of functions with zero, one, two, and an infinite number of fixed points.

It is especially worthwhile to consider how a generating function like g_{dbl} moves elements around a domain of functions. Here are a few examples of how g_{dbl} maps various functions $f : Nat \to Nat$:

- If f is the identity function $\lambda n \,.\, n$, then $(g_{dbl} \ f)$ is the function that increments positive numbers and returns 0 for 0:

$$\lambda n \,.\, \textbf{if } (n = 0) \textbf{ then } 0 \textbf{ else } (n+1) \textbf{ end}$$

---

[1]The unit interval is the set of real numbers between 0 and 1, inclusive. We use the notation $[0; 1]$ rather than the more traditional notation $[0, 1]$ because in our domain notation the latter means a sequence of the two numbers 0 and 1.

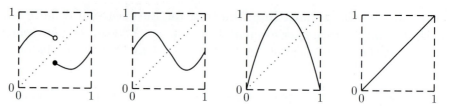

Figure 5.1   Functions on the unit interval with zero, one, two, and an infinite number of fixed points.

- If f is the function $\lambda n\,.\,\left((n+1)^2 - 2\right)$ then $(g_{dbl}\ f)$ is the function $\lambda n\,.\,n^2$

- If f is a doubling function, then $(g_{dbl}\ f)$ is also the doubling function, so the doubling function is a fixed point of g_{dbl}. Indeed, it is the only fixed point of g_{dbl}.

Since generating functions $D \to D$ correspond to recursive definitions, their fixed points have all the properties of solutions to recursive definitions. In particular, a generating function may have zero, one, or more fixed points, and the existence and character of fixed points depends on the details of the function and the nature of the domain D.

5.1.3   The Iterative Fixed Point Technique

Above, we saw that recursive definitions can make sense over any domain. However, the methods we used to find and/or verify solutions in the examples were rather ad hoc. In the case of numeric definitions, there are many familiar techniques for manipulating equations to find solutions. Are there any techniques that will help us solve recursive definitions over more general domains?

There is a class of recursive definitions for which an **iterative fixed point technique** will find a solution of the definition by finding a fixed point of the generating function encoding the recursive definition. The iterative fixed point technique is motivated by the observation that it is often possible to find a fixed point for a generating function by iterating the function starting with an appropriate initial value.

As a graphical example of the iteration technique, consider a transformation T on two-dimensional line drawings that is the sequential composition of the following three steps:

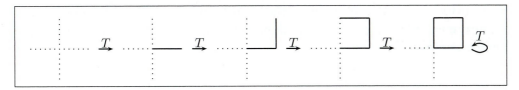

Figure 5.2 Iterating the transformation T starting with an empty line drawing leads to a fixed point in four steps.

1. Rotate the drawing 90 degrees counterclockwise about the origin.

2. Translate the drawing right by one unit.

3. Add a line from (0,0) to (0,1).

Figure 5.2 shows what happens when T is iterated starting with the empty drawing. Each of the first four applications of T adds a new line until the unit square is produced. Subsequent applications of T do not modify the square; it is a fixed point of T.

In the line drawing example, a fixed point is reached after four iterations of the transformation. Often, iterating a generating function does not yield a fixed point in a finite number of steps, but only approaches one in the limit. A classic numerical example is finding square roots. The square root of a nonnegative rational number n is a solution of the recursive definition

$$x = \frac{x + \frac{n}{x}}{2}$$

Iterating the generating function for this definition starting with n yields a sequence of approximations that converge to $\sqrt{n}$. For example, for $n = 3$ the generating function is

$$g_{sqrt3} : Rat \rightarrow Rat = \lambda q \cdot \frac{q + \frac{3}{q}}{2}$$

and the first few iteration steps are:

$$\left(g_{sqrt3}^{0} \; 3\right) \;=\; 3$$

$$\left(g_{sqrt3}^{1} \; 3\right) \;=\; 2$$

$$\left(g_{sqrt3}^{2} \; 3\right) \;=\; \tfrac{7}{4} \;=\; 1.75$$

$$\left(g_{sqrt3}^{3} \; 3\right) \;=\; \tfrac{97}{56} \;\approx\; 1.7321428571428572$$

$$\left(g_{sqrt3}^{4} \; 3\right) \;=\; \tfrac{18817}{10864} \;\approx\; 1.7320508100147276$$

$$\vdots$$

Since $\sqrt{3}$ is not a rational number, the fixed point clearly cannot be reached in a finite number of steps, but it is approached as the limit of the sequence of approximations.

Even in nonnumeric domains, generating functions can produce sequences of values approaching a limiting fixed point. For example, consider the following recursive definition of the even natural numbers:

$$evens = \{0\} \cup \{(n+2) \mid n \in evens\}$$

The associated generating function is

$$g_{evens} : \mathcal{P}(Nat) \to \mathcal{P}(Nat) = \lambda s \,.\, \{0\} \cup \{(n+2) \mid n \in s\}$$

where s ranges over the powerset of Nat. Iterating g_{evens} starting with the empty set yields a sequence of sets that approaches the set of even numbers in the limit:

$$
\begin{aligned}
\left(g_{evens}^{0} \ \{\}\right) &= \{\} \\
\left(g_{evens}^{1} \ \{\}\right) &= \{0\} \\
\left(g_{evens}^{2} \ \{\}\right) &= \{0,\ 2\} \\
\left(g_{evens}^{3} \ \{\}\right) &= \{0,\ 2,\ 4\} \\
\left(g_{evens}^{4} \ \{\}\right) &= \{0,\ 2,\ 4,\ 6\} \\
&\ \ \vdots
\end{aligned}
$$

The above examples of the iterative fixed point technique involve different domains but exhibit a common structure. In each case, the generating function maps an approximation of the fixed point to another approximation that is at least as good, where the notion of "at least as good" depends on the details of the function:

- In the line-drawing example, picture b is at least as good as picture a if b contains at least as many lines of the unit square as a.

- In the square-root example, number b is an approximation to $\sqrt{n}$ that is at least as good as number a if $|b^2 - n| \leq |a^2 - n|$.

- In the even-number example, set b is at least as good as set a if $a \subseteq b$.

Moreover, in each of the examples, the sequence of approximations produced by the generating function converges to a fixed point in the limit. This doesn't necessarily follow from the fact that each approximation is better than the previous one. For example, each element of the sequence $0, 0.9, 0.99, 0.999, \ldots$ is

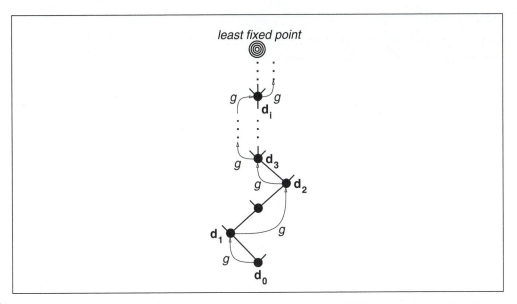

Figure 5.3 The "game board" for the iterative fixed point technique. Starting at element d_0, the generating function g calculates a sequence of domain elements, each of which is a better approximation to the fixed point of g. For an appropriate domain, generating function g, and starting element d_0, this process reaches the fixed point or approaches it as a limiting value.

closer to $\sqrt{2}$ than the previous element, but the sequence converges to 1, not to $\sqrt{2}$. The notion of approaching a limiting value is central to the iterative fixed point technique.

The basic structure of the iterative fixed point technique is depicted in Figure 5.3. The generating function $g : D \to D$ is defined over a domain D whose values are assumed to be ordered by their information content. A line connects two values when the lower value is an approximation to the higher value. That is, the higher value contains all the information of the lower value plus some extra information. What counts as "information" and "approximation" depends on the problem domain. When values are sets, for instance, a line from a up to b might indicate that $a \subseteq b$. In general, a lower value may approximate many higher values. In Figure 5.3, this is represented by multiple branches leading upward from a node. (To keep the diagram uncluttered, only the initial stubs of most branches are depicted.)

In the iterative fixed point technique, iteratively applying g from an appropriate starting value d_0 yields a sequence of values with increasing information content. Intuitively, iterative applications of g climb up through the ordered

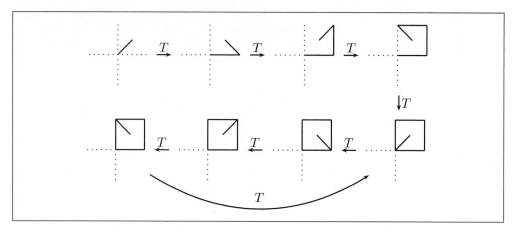

Figure 5.4   An example in which the iterative fixed point technique cannot find a fixed point of the picture transformation T for a nonempty initial picture.

values by refining the information of successive approximations. If this process reaches a value d_i such that $d_i = (g\ d_i)$, then the fixed point d_i has been found. If this process never actually reaches a fixed point, it should at least approach a fixed point as a limiting value.

The iterative fixed point technique does not work for every generating function $g : D \to D$. It depends on the details of the domain D, the function g, and the starting point d_0. The technique must certainly fail for generating functions that have no fixed points. Even when a generating function has a fixed point, the iterative technique won't necessarily find it. E.g., iterating the generating function for $n = \frac{3}{n}$ starting with any nonzero rational number q yields an alternating sequence q, $\frac{3}{q}$, q, $\frac{3}{q}$, ... that never gets any closer to the fixed point $\sqrt{3}$. Figure 5.4 shows an example in which the technique does not find a fixed point of T for an initial picture. Instead, it eventually cycles among four distinct pictures.

Moreover, there may be more than one fixed point, and which one you find may depend on where you start. As shown in Figure 5.5, if we start with an "X" in the upper right quadrant, the iterative fixed point technique applied to the picture transformation T yields a different fixed point than when we start with an empty picture.

In the next section, we will describe an important class of generating functions that are *guaranteed* to have a fixed point. A fixed point of these functions can be found by applying the iterative fixed point technique starting with a special informationless element called **bottom**. Such functions may have more than one

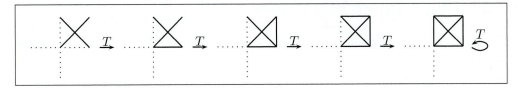

Figure 5.5   A different initial picture can lead to a different fixed point for the picture transformation T.

fixed point, but the one found by iterating from bottom has less information than all the others — it is the **least fixed point**. We will choose this distinguished fixed point as *the* solution of the associated recursive definition. This solution matches our operational intuitions about what solution the computer will find when the recursive definition is expressed as a program. We are guaranteed to be able to solve any recursive definition whose generating function is in this special class.

Exercise 5.1   Above, we showed two fixed points of the picture transformation T.

a. Draw a third line drawing that is a fixed point of T.

b. How many fixed points does T have?

c. Characterize all the fixed points of T. That is, what properties must a picture have in order to be a fixed point of T?

d. Figure 5.4 shows an initial picture for which the iterative technique finds a cycle of four distinct pictures related by T rather than a fixed point of T. Give an initial picture for which the iterative technique finds a cycle containing only two distinct pictures related by T. In the case of T, can the iterative technique find cycles of pictures with periods other than 1, 2, and 4?

Exercise 5.2 For each of the following classes of functions from the unit interval to itself, indicate the minimum and maximum number of fixed points of functions in the class:

a. constant functions (i.e., functions of the form $\lambda x \,.\, a$);

b. linear functions (i.e., functions of the form $\lambda x \,.\, ax + b$);

c. quadratic functions (i.e., functions of the form $\lambda x \,.\, ax^2 + bx + c$);

d. continuous functions (i.e., functions whose graph is an unbroken curve);

e. nondecreasing functions (i.e., functions f for which $a \leq b$ implies $(f\ a) \leq (f\ b)$;

f. nonincreasing functions (i.e., functions f for which $a \leq b$ implies $(f\ a) \geq (f\ b)$.

5.2   Fixed Point Machinery

In this section we present the mathematical machinery for defining a class of functions for which a distinguished fixed point always exists and illustrate the use of this machinery via several examples.

We begin in Section 5.2.1 by introducing the notion of a *partial order*, which will be used to model the information content of domain elements. We will see how the information ordering on the elements of a compound domain can be derived from the information ordering on its component domains. Some domains have a least element, called *bottom*, that can serve as the starting point for the iterative fixed point technique. It can also be viewed as the representation of a nonterminating computation.

We are most interested in partial orders for which the information-climbing process illustrated in Figure 5.3 approaches a limiting value. These are called *complete partial orders* or *CPOs*. We study these in Section 5.2.2. CPOs with a bottom element are said to be *pointed* (Section 5.2.3). Pointed CPOs are good domains for the iterative fixed point technique because their bottom element is the natural starting point for the technique.

In Section 5.2.4, we define two information-preserving properties of functions: *monotonicity* and *continuity*. Iterative application of a generating function g with these two properties starting at the bottom element of a pointed CPO yields a sequence of elements that approaches the least fixed point of g. This fundamental result, known as the *Least Fixed Point Theorem*, is shown in Section 5.2.5. Several examples of this theorem are illustrated in Section 5.2.6. Section 5.2.7 shows that a broad class of functions expressible in the metalanguage notation summarized in Section A.4 are monotonic and continuous.

5.2.1   Partial Orders

A **partial order** is a pair $\langle D, \sqsubseteq \rangle$ of a domain D and a binary ordering relation $\sqsubseteq$ on D that is reflexive, transitive, and antisymmetric. Recall that a relation is antisymmetric if $a \sqsubseteq b$ and $b \sqsubseteq a$ together imply $a =_D b$. The notation $a \sqsubseteq b$ is pronounced "a is weaker than b" or "b is stronger than a." Later, we shall be ordering elements by information content, so we will also pronounce $a \sqsubseteq b$ as "a approximates b." When the relation $\sqsubseteq$ is understood from context, it is common to refer to the partial order $\langle D, \sqsubseteq \rangle$ as D.

Partial orders are commonly depicted by **Hasse diagrams**, in which elements (represented by points) are connected by lines. In such a diagram, $a \sqsubseteq b$ if and only if there is a path from the point representing a to the point representing b

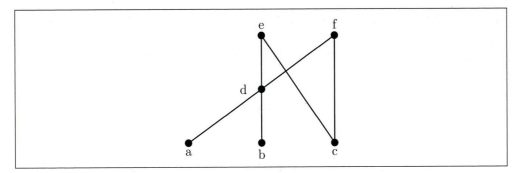

Figure 5.6 A Hasse diagram for the partial order PO.

such that each link of the path goes upward on the page. For example, Figure 5.6 shows the Hasse diagram for the partial order PO on six symbols whose relation is defined by the following graph:

$$\{\langle a, a\rangle,\ \langle a, d\rangle,\ \langle a, e\rangle,\ \langle a, f\rangle,\ \ \langle b, b\rangle,\ \langle b, d\rangle,\ \langle b, e\rangle,\ \langle b, f\rangle,$$
$$\langle c, c\rangle,\ \langle c, e\rangle,\ \langle c, f\rangle,\ \ \langle d, d\rangle,\ \langle d, e\rangle,\ \langle d, f\rangle,\ \ \langle e, e\rangle,\ \langle f, f\rangle\}$$

A partial order need not relate all the elements of its domain. Two elements of a partial order that are unrelated by $\sqsubseteq$ are said to be **incomparable**. For example, the pairs of incomparable elements in PO are $\{a, b\}$, $\{a, c\}$, $\{b, c\}$, $\{c, d\}$, and $\{e, f\}$.

A **total order** is a partial order in which every two elements are related (i.e., no two elements are incomparable). For example, the natural numbers under the traditional value-based ordering $\leq_{Nat}$ form a total order called ω (omega). The elements of a total order can be arranged in a vertical line in a Hasse diagram (see Figure 5.7).

Although $\leq_{Nat}$ may be the most familiar ordering on natural numbers, in the context of our discussion of fixed points we will consider some alternative orderings that are based on information content and may seem nonintuitive at first glance. For example, a **discrete** partial order is one in which every pair of elements is incomparable. Figure 5.8 depicts the discrete ordering $\sqsubseteq_{Nat}$ for *Nat*. In this partial order, numbers are not ordered by their value, but by their information content. Each number approximates only itself. The $\sqsubseteq_{Nat}$ relation is clearly very different from the familiar $\leq_{Nat}$ relation. From the perspective of information content, we will often consider primitive semantic domains to have the discrete ordering.

An **upper bound** of a subset $X \subseteq D$ of a partial order $\langle D, \sqsubseteq\rangle$ is an element $u \in D$ that is stronger than every element of X; i.e., for every x in X, $x \sqsubseteq u$.

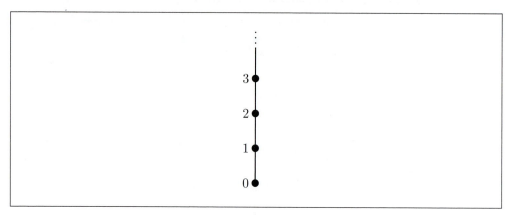

Figure 5.7 The total order ω of natural numbers under the traditional value-based ordering $\leq_{Nat}$.

In PO, the subset $\{\mathtt{a},\mathtt{b}\}$ has upper bounds $\mathtt{d}$, $\mathtt{e}$, and $\mathtt{f}$; the subset $\{\mathtt{a},\mathtt{b},\mathtt{c}\}$ has upper bounds $\mathtt{e}$ and $\mathtt{f}$; and the subset $\{\mathtt{e},\mathtt{f}\}$ has no upper bounds. The **least upper bound (lub[2])** of a subset X of D, written $\bigsqcup_D X$, is the upper bound of X that is weaker than every other upper bound of X; such an element may not exist. In PO, the lub of $\{\mathtt{a},\mathtt{b}\}$ is $\mathtt{d}$, but neither $\{\mathtt{a},\mathtt{b},\mathtt{c}\}$ nor $\{\mathtt{e},\mathtt{f}\}$ has a lub. There are symmetric notions of **lower bound** and **greatest lower bound (glb[3])**, but our fixed point machinery will mainly use upper bounds.

An element that is weaker than all other elements in a partial order D is called the **bottom** element and is denoted $\bot_D$. Symmetrically, an element that is stronger than all other elements in D is the **top** element (written $\top_D$). Partial orders need not have bottom and top elements. For example, PO and Nat (ordered by $\sqsubseteq_{Nat}$) have neither. The total order ω has a bottom element (0) but not a top element.

Any partial order D can be **lifted** to another partial order $D_\bot$ that has all the elements and orderings of D, but includes a new element $\bot_{D_\bot}$ that is weaker than all elements of D. If D already has a bottom element $\bot_D$, then $\bot_D$ and $\bot_{D_\bot}$ are distinct, with $\bot_{D_\bot}$ being the weaker of the two. Symmetrically, the notation $D^\top$ designates the result of extending D with a new top element.

A **flat** partial order D is a lifted discrete partial order. Figure 5.9 depicts the flat partial order $Nat_\bot$ of natural numbers. The element $\bot_{Nat_\bot}$ acts as an "unknown natural number" that approximates every natural number. It is often interpreted as representing the "result" of a nonterminating computational pro-

---

[2]The pronunciation of "lub" rhymes with "club."
[3]The abbreviation "glb" is pronounced "glub."

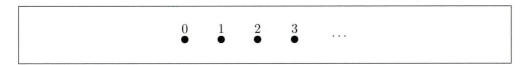

Figure 5.8 The semantic domain Nat with the discrete ordering $\sqsubseteq_{Nat}$.

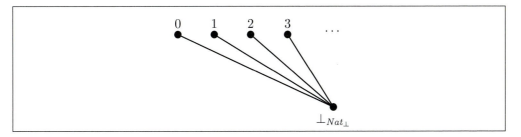

Figure 5.9 The flat partial order $Nat_\perp$.

cess. Flat partial orders will play an important role in understanding recursively defined functions that return elements of primitive semantic domains like the natural numbers (see Sections 5.2.4–5.2.7). In this context, we do not care about the usual numerical ordering of the numbers in Nat, but instead care about an information ordering that tells us whether the function diverges (i.e., returns the bottom element $\perp_{Nat_\perp}$ of $Nat_\perp$) or terminates (i.e., returns a nonbottom element of $Nat_\perp$).

A **chain** is a totally ordered, nonempty subset of a partial order. The chains of PO include $\{\mathtt{a},\mathtt{d},\mathtt{e}\}$, $\{\mathtt{c},\mathtt{f}\}$, $\{\mathtt{b},\mathtt{f}\}$, and $\{\mathtt{d}\}$. In $Nat_\perp$, the only chains are (1) singleton sets and (2) doubleton sets containing $\perp_{Nat_\perp}$ and a natural number.

Given partially ordered domains, we would like to define orderings on product, sum, sequence, and function domains such that the resulting domains are also partially ordered. That way, we will be able to view all our semantic domains as partial orders. In the following definitions, assume that D and E are arbitrary partial orders ordered by $\sqsubseteq_D$ and $\sqsubseteq_E$, respectively. We will illustrate the definitions with examples involving the two concrete partial orders G and H in Figure 5.10.

Product Domains

$D \times E$ is a partial order under the following ordering:

$$\langle d_1, e_1 \rangle \sqsubseteq_{D \times E} \langle d_2, e_2 \rangle \text{ iff } d_1 \sqsubseteq_D d_2 \text{ and } e_1 \sqsubseteq_E e_2$$

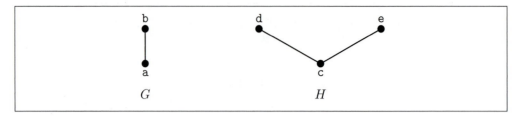

Figure 5.10   Two simple partial orders.

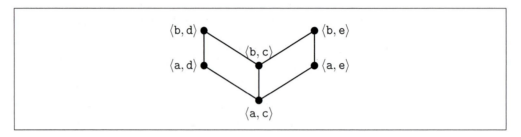

Figure 5.11   The product partial order $G \times H$.

The partial order $G \times H$ is depicted in Figure 5.11. Note how the Hasse diagram for $G \times H$ is visually the product of the Hasse diagrams for G and H. $G \times H$ results from making a copy of G at every point of H (or, symmetrically, making a copy of H at every point of G) and adding the extra lines specified by the ordering.

Sum Domains

$D + E$ is a partial order under the following ordering:

$$(D \rightarrowtail (D + E)\ d_1) \sqsubseteq_{D+E} (D \rightarrowtail (D + E)\ d_2)\ \text{ iff }\ d_1 \sqsubseteq_D d_2$$

$$(E \rightarrowtail (D + E)\ e_1) \sqsubseteq_{D+E} (E \rightarrowtail (D + E)\ e_2)\ \text{ iff }\ e_1 \sqsubseteq_E e_2$$

This ordering preserves the order between elements of the same summand domain, but treats elements from different summands as incomparable. The Hasse diagram for a sum partial order is simply the juxtaposition of the diagrams for the summands (see Figure 5.12).

Function Domains

$D \rightarrow E$ is a partial order under the following ordering:

$$f_1 \sqsubseteq_{D \rightarrow E} f_2 \text{ iff, for all } d \text{ in } D, (f_1\ d) \sqsubseteq_E (f_2\ d).$$

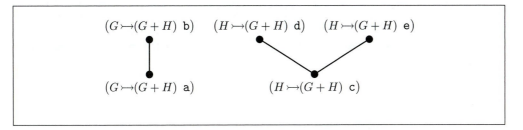

Figure 5.12   The sum partial order $G + H$.

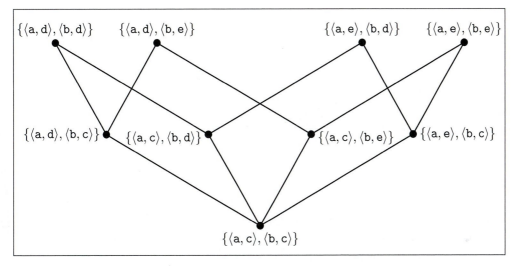

Figure 5.13   The function partial order $G \rightarrow H$. Each node is labeled with a function graph.

Consider using this ordering on the elements of $G \rightarrow H$. As usual, a total function from G to H can be represented by a graph of argument/result pairs. Figure 5.13 uses this notation to depict the partial order $G \rightarrow H$.

Sequence Domains

There are two common ways to order the elements of D^*. These differ in whether sequence elements of different lengths are comparable.

- Under the **prefix ordering**,

$$[d_1, \; d_2, \; \ldots, \; d_k] \sqsubseteq_{D^*} [d'_1, \; d'_2, \; \ldots, \; d'_l]$$
$$\text{iff } k \leq l \text{ and } d_i \sqsubseteq_D d'_i \text{ for all } 1 \leq i \leq k$$

If D is a discrete domain, this implies that a sequence s_1 is weaker than s_2 if and only if s_1 is a prefix of s_2 — i.e., $s_2 = s_1 @ s'$ for some sequence s'.

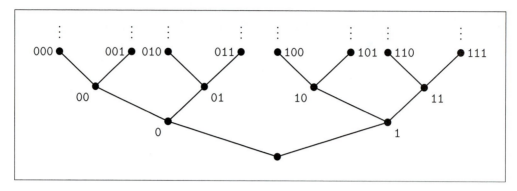

Figure 5.14   The sequence partial order Bit* under the prefix ordering.

As an example, suppose that Bit is the discrete partial order of the binary digits 0 and 1. Then Bit* under the prefix order is isomorphic to the partial order of binary numerals shown in Figure 5.14. (For example, the numeral 110 corresponds to the sequence $[1, 1, 0]_{\text{Bit}}$. The "empty numeral" consisting of no digits corresponds to the sequence $[\,]_{\text{Bit}}$ that is the bottom element of Bit*.) This partial order is an infinite binary tree rooted at the empty sequence. Each element of the tree can be viewed as an approximation to all of the elements of the subtree rooted at it. For example, 110 is an approximation to 1100, 1101, 11000, 11001, 11010, etc. In computational terms, this notion of approximation corresponds to the behavior of a computation process that produces its answer by printing out a string of 0s and 1s from left to right, one character at a time. At any time, the characters already printed are the current approximation to the final string that will be produced by the process.

Note that if D has a nontrivial ordering relation — i.e., D is not a discrete domain — the prefix ordering of D* is more complex than a simple tree.

- Under the **sum-of-products ordering**, D* is treated as isomorphic to the infinite sum of products $D^0 + D^1 + D^2 + D^3 + \cdots$.

  That is,

  $$[d_1,\ d_2,\ \ldots,\ d_k] \sqsubseteq_{D*} [d_1',\ d_2',\ \ldots,\ d_k']$$
  $$\text{iff } d_i \sqsubseteq_D d_i' \text{ for all } 1 \le i \le k$$

As in the prefix ordering, sequences are ordered component-wise by their elements, but the sum-of-products ordering treats sequences of different lengths as incomparable. For example, under the sum-of-products ordering, Bit$_\perp$* is isomorphic to the partial order depicted in Figure 5.15.

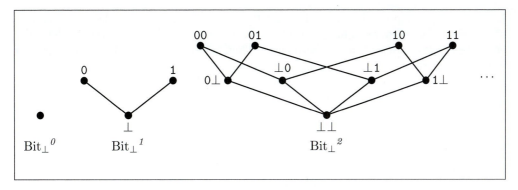

Figure 5.15   The sequence partial order $Bit_\perp{}^*$ under the sum-of-products ordering.

Discussion

Although we have stated that the above definitions are partial orders, we have not argued that each ordering is in fact reflexive, transitive, and antisymmetric. We encourage the reader to verify that these properties hold for each of the definitions (Exercise 5.6).

The orderings defined above are not the only ways to order compound domains, but they are relatively natural and are useful in many situations. Later, we will refine some of these orderings (particularly in the case of function domains). But, for the most part, these are the orderings that will prove useful for our study of semantic domains.

Exercise 5.3 Using the partial orders G and H in Figure 5.10, draw a Hasse diagram for each of the following nine compound partial orders:

a. $G \times G$

b. $H \times H$

c. $G \to G$

d. $H \to H$

e. $H \to G$

f. G^* under the prefix ordering (show the first four levels)

g. H^* under the prefix ordering (show the first four levels)

h. G^* under the sum-of-products ordering (show the first three summands)

i. H^* under the sum-of-products ordering (show the first three summands)

Exercise 5.4 Suppose that A and B are finite partial orders with the same number of elements, but they are not isomorphic. Partition the following partial orders into equivalence classes based on isomorphism. That is, each class should contain all the partial orders that are isomorphic to each other.

$$
\begin{array}{cccc}
A \times A, & A \times B, & B \times A, & B \times B, \\
A + A, & A + B, & B + A, & B + B, \\
A \to A, & A \to B, & B \to A, & B \to B
\end{array}
$$

Exercise 5.5 Given a discretely ordered domain D, the **powerdomain** $\mathcal{P}(D)$ is a partial order under the **subset ordering**:

$$
S \sqsubseteq_{\mathcal{P}(D)} S' \text{ if } S \subseteq S'
$$

Draw the Hasse diagram for the partial order $\mathcal{P}(\{a, b, c\})$ under the subset ordering.

If D is a partial order that is not discrete, it turns out that there are many "natural" ways to order the elements of the powerdomain $\mathcal{P}(D)$, each of which is useful for different purposes. See [Sch86] or [GS90] for details.

Exercise 5.6 For each ordering on a compound domain defined above, show that the ordering is indeed a partial order. I.e., show that the orderings defined for product, sum, function, and sequence domains are reflexive, transitive, and antisymmetric.

5.2.2   Complete Partial Orders (CPOs)

A partial order D is **complete** if every chain in D has a least upper bound in D. The term "complete partial order" is usually abbreviated **CPO**. Intuitively, completeness means that any sequence of elements visited on an upward path through a Hasse diagram must converge to a limit. Completeness is important because it guarantees that the iterative fixed point technique converges to a limiting value.

Here are some examples of CPOs:

- Any partial order with a finite number of elements is a CPO because every chain is finite and necessarily contains its lub. PO, G, and H from the previous section are all finite CPOs.

- Any flat partial order is a CPO because every chain has at most two elements, the stronger of which must be the lub. $Nat_\perp$ is a CPO with an infinite number of elements.

- $\mathcal{P}(Nat)$ is a CPO in which the elements (each of which is a subset of the naturals) are ordered by subset inclusion (see Exercise 5.5). It is complete because the lub of every chain C is the (possibly infinite) union of the elements of C. Unlike the previous examples of CPOs, this is one in which a chain may be infinite and not contain its own lub. Consider the chain C with elements c_i, where c_i is defined to be $\{n \mid n \leq i, n : Nat\}$ Then:

$$\bigsqcup_{\mathcal{P}(Nat)} C \ = \ \bigcup \{\{0\}, \{0, 1\}, \{0, 1, 2\}, \ldots\} \ = \ Nat$$

The lub of C is the entire set of natural numbers, but no individual c_i is equal to this set.

- The unit interval under the usual ordering of real numbers is a CPO. It is complete because the construction of the reals guarantees that it contains the least upper bound of every subset of the interval. The unit interval is another CPO in which chains do not necessarily contain their own lubs. For example, the set of all rational numbers less than $\sqrt{\frac{1}{2}}$ does not contain $\sqrt{\frac{1}{2}}$.

- The partial functions from Nat to Nat (denoted $Nat \rightharpoonup Nat$) form a CPO. Recall that a partial function can be represented by a graph of argument/result pairs. So the function that is undefined everywhere is represented by $\{\}$, the function that returns 23 given 17 and is elsewhere undefined is represented by $\{\langle 17, 23 \rangle\}$, and so on. The ordering of elements in this CPO is just subset inclusion on the graphs of the functions. It is complete for the same reason that $\mathcal{P}(Nat)$ is complete.

It is worthwhile to consider examples of partial orders that are *not* CPOs:

- The total order ω depicted in Figure 5.7 is not a CPO because the chain consisting of the entire set has no least upper bound (i.e., there is no largest natural number). This partial order can be turned into a CPO $\omega^\top$ by extending it with a top element $\top_{\omega^\top}$ that by definition is larger than every natural number (see Figure 5.16).

- The partial order of rational numbers (under the usual ordering) between 0 and 1, inclusive, is not complete because it does not contain irrational numbers like $\sqrt{\frac{1}{2}}$, and thus does not contain the lub of chains such as the set of all rational numbers less than $\sqrt{\frac{1}{2}}$. It can be made complete by extending it with the irrationals between 0 and 1; this results in the unit interval $[0; 1]$.

- The partial order of sequences Bit* under the prefix ordering is not a CPO. By definition, D^* is the set of *finite* sequences whose elements are taken from D. But the chain $\{[\,], [1], [1, 1], [1, 1, 1], \ldots\}$ has as its lub an infinite sequence of 1s, which is not an element of Bit*. To make this partial order complete, it is necessary to extend it with the set of infinite sequences over 0 and 1, written Bit$^\infty$. So the set of sequences Bit* $\cup$ Bit$^\infty$ under the prefix ordering is a CPO.

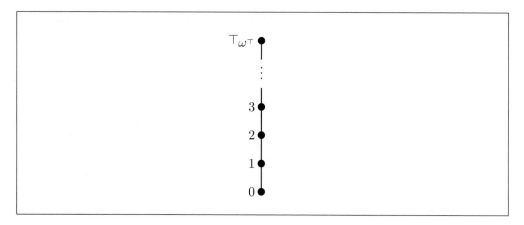

Figure 5.16 The partial order $\omega^\top$ is the partial order ω of natural numbers extended with a largest element $\top_{\omega\top}$.

Generalizing Bit$^\infty$, we introduce the notation D^∞ to denote the set of all infinite sequences whose elements are taken from the domain D. We also introduce the notation $\overline{D^*}$ to stand for $D^* \cup D^\infty$ under the prefix ordering. (The overbar notation is commonly used to designate the **completion** of a set, which adds to a set all of its limit points.)

As with partial orders, we are interested in combination properties of CPOs. As indicated by the following theorem, we can use $\bot$, $\times$, $+$, $\rightarrow$, and $*$ to build new CPOs out of existing CPOs.

Theorem 5.1 (CPO Construction) *Suppose that D and E are CPOs. Then:*

1.   *$D_\bot$ is a CPO;*

2.   *$D \times E$ is a CPO under the partial order for products;*

3.   *$D + E$ is a CPO under the partial order for sums;*

4.   *$D \rightarrow E$ is a CPO under the partial order for functions;*

5.   *D^* is a CPO under the sum-of-products ordering for sequences;*

6.   *$\overline{D^*}$ is a CPO under the prefix ordering for sequences.*

Exercise 5.7 Prove Theorem 5.1 by showing that each of the compound CPOs it mentions is indeed complete. That is, show that the completeness property of D and E implies that each chain of the compound domain has a lub in the compound domain.

5.2.3   Pointedness

Bottom! O most courageous day! O most happy hour!
                    — William Shakespeare, *A Midsummer Night's Dream*

A partial order is **pointed** if it has a bottom element. Pointedness is important because the bottom element of a CPO is the natural place for the iterative fixed point technique to start. Here are some of the pointed CPOs we have studied, listed with their bottom elements:

- G, bottom = a;

- H, bottom = c;

- $Nat_\perp$, bottom = $\perp_{Nat_\perp}$

- $\mathcal{P}(Nat)$, bottom = {};

- $[0; 1]$, bottom = 0;

- $Nat \rightharpoonup Nat$, bottom = the function whose graph is {};

- $\omega^\top$, bottom = 0;

- Bit*, bottom = [].

CPOs that we have studied that are *not* pointed include PO, $G + H$, and $Bit_\perp^*$ under the sum-of-products ordering.

In the iterative fixed point technique, the bottom element of a pointed CPO is treated as the element with the least information — the "worst" approximation to the desired value. For example, $\perp_{Nat_\perp}$ is the unknown natural number, [] is a (bad) approximation to any sequence of 0s and 1s, and {} is a (bad) approximation to the graph of any partial function from Nat to Nat.

In computational terms, the bottom element of a CPO can informally be viewed as representing a process that **diverges** (i.e., goes into an infinite loop). For example, a procedure that returns a boolean for even numbers but diverges on odd numbers can be modeled as an element of the domain $Int \rightarrow Bool_\perp$ that maps every odd number to $\perp_{Bool_\perp}$.

Pointed CPOs are commonly used to encode partial functions as total functions. Any partial function f in $D \rightharpoonup E$ can be represented as a total function f' in $D \rightarrow E_\perp$ by having f' map to $\perp_{E_\perp}$ every element $d : D$ on which f is undefined. For example, the partial function in $PO \rightharpoonup PO$ with graph

$$\{\langle \mathsf{a}, \mathsf{d}\rangle, \ \langle \mathsf{c}, \mathsf{b}\rangle, \ \langle \mathsf{f}, \mathsf{f}\rangle\}$$

can be represented as the total function in $PO \to PO_\perp$ with graph

$$\{\langle \mathsf{a}, \mathsf{d}\rangle, \ \langle \mathsf{b}, \perp_{PO_\perp}\rangle, \ \langle \mathsf{c}, \mathsf{b}\rangle, \ \langle \mathsf{d}, \perp_{PO_\perp}\rangle, \ \langle \mathsf{e}, \perp_{PO_\perp}\rangle, \ \langle \mathsf{f}, \mathsf{f}\rangle\}$$

Because of the isomorphism between $D \rightharpoonup E$ and $D \to E_\perp$, we casually perform implicit conversions between the two representations.

The following theorem summarizes some handy facts about the pointedness of partial orders constructed out of parts.

Theorem 5.2 (Pointedness of Compound Domains) *Suppose that D and E are arbitrary partial orders (not necessarily pointed). Then:*

1. $D_\perp$ *is pointed.*

2. $D \times E$ *is pointed iff D and E are pointed.*

3. $D + E$ *is never pointed.*

4. $D \to E$ *is pointed iff E is pointed.*

5. D^* *under the sum-of-products ordering is never pointed.*

6. $\overline{D^*}$ *and D^* under the prefix ordering are pointed.*

Note that unpointed compound domains like $D + E$ and D^* under the sum-of-products ordering can always be made pointed by lifting them with a new bottom element or by coalescing their bottom elements if they are pointed (see Exercise 5.9).

Exercise 5.8 Prove each of the facts about pointedness in Theorem 5.2.

Exercise 5.9 The **smash sum** (also known as **coalesced sum**) of two pointed partial orders D and E, written $D \oplus E$, consists of the elements

$$\{\perp_{D\oplus E}\} \cup \{(D' \rightarrowtail (D' + E') \ d) \mid d \in D'\} \cup \{(E' \rightarrowtail (D' + E') \ e) \mid e \in E'\}$$

where $D' = (D - \perp_D)$, $E' = (E - \perp_E)$, and $\perp_{D\oplus E}$ is a single new bottom element that combines the bottom elements $\perp_D$ and $\perp_E$. $D \oplus E$ is a partial order under the following ordering:

$\perp_{D\oplus E} \sqsubseteq_{D\oplus E} x$ for all $x \in D \oplus E$;

$(D' \rightarrowtail (D' + E') \ d_1) \sqsubseteq_{D\oplus E} (D' \rightarrowtail (D' + E') \ d_2)$ iff $d_1, d_2 \in D'$ and $d_1 \sqsubseteq_{D'} d_2$;

$(E' \rightarrowtail (D' + E') \ e_1) \sqsubseteq_{D\oplus E} (E' \rightarrowtail (D' + E') \ e_2)$ iff $e_1, e_2 \in E'$ and $e_1 \sqsubseteq_{E'} e_2$

a. Using the CPOs G and H from Figure 5.10, draw a Hasse diagram for the partial order $G \oplus H$.

b. If D and E are CPOs, show that $D \oplus E$ is a CPO.

c. What benefit does $D \oplus E$ have over $D + E$?

d. Suppose that D is a pointed CPO. Extend the notion of smash sum to a **smash sequence** $D^{\circledast}$ such that $D^{\circledast}$ is a pointed CPO under an ordering analogous to the sum-of-products ordering. What does $\text{Bit}_{\perp}{}^{\circledast}$ look like?

5.2.4 Monotonicity and Continuity

Suppose that $f : D \to E$, where D and E are CPOs (not necessarily pointed). Then

- f is **monotonic** iff $d_1 \sqsubseteq_D d_2$ implies $(f\ d_1) \sqsubseteq_E (f\ d_2)$.

- f is **continuous** iff, for all chains C in D, $(f\ (\bigsqcup_D C)) = \bigsqcup_E \{(f\ c) \mid c \in C\}$.

A monotonic function preserves order between CPOs, while a continuous function preserves limits. In the iterative fixed point technique, monotonicity is important because when $f : D \to D$ is monotonic, the set of values

$$\{\perp,\ (f\ \perp),\ (f\ (f\ \perp)),\ (f\ (f\ (f\ \perp))),\ \dots\}$$

is guaranteed to form a chain. The completeness of D guarantees that this chain approaches a limit in D, and it turns out that this limit is a fixed point of f. Continuity plays a key role in the proof of the Least Fixed Point Theorem (Section 5.2.5).

As an example of these properties, consider the CPO of functions $G \to H$ depicted in Figure 5.13. Any function whose graph is $\{\langle \mathsf{a}, x\rangle, \langle \mathsf{b}, y\rangle\}$ is monotonic if and only if $x \sqsubseteq y$. Although there are $3^2 = 9$ total functions from G to H, only five of these are monotonic:

$$\{\{\langle \mathsf{a}, \mathsf{c}\rangle, \langle \mathsf{b}, \mathsf{c}\rangle\},\ \{\langle \mathsf{a}, \mathsf{c}\rangle, \langle \mathsf{b}, \mathsf{d}\rangle\},\ \{\langle \mathsf{a}, \mathsf{d}\rangle, \langle \mathsf{b}, \mathsf{d}\rangle\},\ \{\langle \mathsf{a}, \mathsf{c}\rangle, \langle \mathsf{b}, \mathsf{e}\rangle\},\ \{\langle \mathsf{a}, \mathsf{e}\rangle, \langle \mathsf{b}, \mathsf{e}\rangle\}\}$$

The reason that there are fewer monotonic functions than total functions is that choosing the target element t for a particular source element s constrains all the source elements stronger than s to map to a target element stronger than t. For example, a monotonic function that maps a to e must necessarily map b to e. With larger domains, the reduction from total functions to monotonic functions can be more dramatic.

What functions from G to H are continuous? The only nonsingleton chain in G is $\{\mathsf{a}, \mathsf{b}\}$. By the definition of continuity, this means that a function $f : G \to H$ is continuous iff $(f\ (\bigsqcup_G \{\mathsf{a}, \mathsf{b}\})) = \bigsqcup_H \{(f\ \mathsf{a}), (f\ \mathsf{b})\}$. In this case, this condition simplifies to $(f\ \mathsf{a}) \sqsubseteq_H (f\ \mathsf{b})$, which is equivalent to saying that f is monotonic. Thus, the continuous functions from G to H are exactly the five monotonic functions listed above.

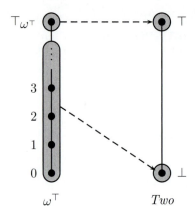

Figure 5.17   An example of a function that is monotonic but not continuous.

The relationship between monotonic and continuous functions in this example is more than coincidence. Monotonicity and continuity are closely related, as indicated by the following theorem:

Theorem 5.3 (Monotonicity/Continuity Relationship)

1.   *On finite CPOs (and even infinite CPOs with only finite chains), monotonicity implies continuity.*

2.   *On any CPO, continuity implies monotonicity.*

We leave the proof of this theorem as an exercise (see Exercise 5.12).

Although monotonicity and continuity coincide on finite-chain CPOs, monotonicity *does not* imply continuity in general. To see this, consider the following function from $\omega^\top$ to the two-point CPO $Two = \{\bot, \top\}$:

$$mon\text{-}not\text{-}con : \omega^\top \to Two = \lambda n \,.\, \textbf{if } (n = \top_{\omega^\top}) \textbf{ then } \top \textbf{ else } \bot \textbf{ end}$$

(See Figure 5.17 for a depiction of this function.) This function is clearly monotonic, but it is not continuous because on the subset ω of $\omega^\top$,

$$(f \, (\bigsqcup \omega)) = (f \, \top_{\omega^\top}) = \top \neq \bot = \bigsqcup{}_{Two}\{\bot\} = \bigsqcup{}_{Two}\{(f \; n) \mid n \in \omega\}$$

An important fact about continuous functions is that the set of continuous functions between CPOs D and E is itself a CPO under the usual ordering of functions. For example, Figure 5.18 depicts the CPO of the five continuous functions between G and H. If E is pointed, the function that maps all elements of D to $\bot_E$ is continuous and serves as the bottom element of the continuous-function CPO.

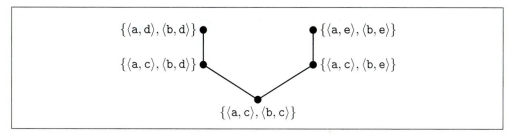

Figure 5.18 The CPO $G \xrightarrow{C} H$ of continuous functions between G and H.

Since the CPO of total functions between D and E and the CPO of continuous functions between D and E are usually distinct, it will be helpful to have a notation that distinguishes them. We will use $D \xrightarrow{T} E$ to designate the CPO of total functions from D to E and $D \xrightarrow{C} E$ to designate the CPO of continuous functions from D to E. As we shall see later in this chapter, the CPO of continuous functions plays an important role in constructing fixed points of recursive functions and solving recursive domain equations. For this reason, we adopt the convention that, throughout the rest of this text, any unannotated $\rightarrow$ should be interpreted as $\xrightarrow{C}$ whenever information ordering matters (i.e., when constructing fixed points of recursive functions or solving recursive domain equations). We shall use $\xrightarrow{T}$ whenever we wish to discuss total functions, and will explicitly use $\xrightarrow{C}$ only when we wish to emphasize the difference between $\xrightarrow{T}$ and $\xrightarrow{C}$.

Exercise 5.10 Using the CPOs G and H from Figure 5.10, draw Hasse diagrams for the following CPOs:

a. $G \xrightarrow{C} G$

b. $H \xrightarrow{C} H$

c. $H \xrightarrow{C} G$

Exercise 5.11 Consider the CPOs A and B pictured in Figure 5.19. For each of the following function domains, give the number of (1) total, (2) monotonic, and (3) continuous functions in the domain:

a. $A \xrightarrow{T} A$

b. $B \xrightarrow{T} B$

c. $A \xrightarrow{T} B$

d. $B \xrightarrow{T} A$

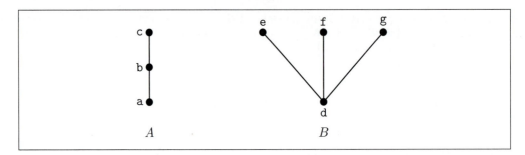

Figure 5.19   CPOs A and B.

Exercise 5.12

a. Show that a continuous function between CPOs is necessarily monotonic.

b. Show that a monotonic function must also be continuous if its source is a CPO all of whose chains are finite.

c. Show that if D is a CPO and E is a pointed CPO then $D \xrightarrow{C} E$ is a pointed CPO.

Exercise 5.13 This problem considers functions f from $[0; 1]$ to itself. We will say that f is *continuous in the CPO sense* if it is a member of $[0; 1] \xrightarrow{C} [0; 1]$, where $[0; 1]$ is assumed to have the traditional ordering. We will say that f is *continuous in the classical sense* if for all x and ϵ there exists a δ such that

$$(f \ [x - \delta; x + \delta]) \subseteq [(f \ x) - \epsilon; (f \ x) + \epsilon]$$

(Here we are abusing the function call notation to designate the image of all of the elements of the interval.)

a. Does classical continuity imply CPO continuity? If so, give a proof; if not, provide a counterexample of a function that is continuous in the classical sense but not in the CPO sense.

b. Does CPO continuity imply classical continuity? If so, give a proof; if not, provide a counterexample of a function that is continuous in the CPO sense but not in the classical sense.

5.2.5   The Least Fixed Point Theorem

Suppose D is a domain and $f : D \to D$. Then $d : D$ is a **fixed point** of f if $(f \ d) = d$. If $\langle D, \sqsubseteq \rangle$ is a partial order, then $d : D$ is the **least fixed point** of f if it is a fixed point of f and $d \sqsubseteq d'$ for every fixed point d' of f.

Everything is now in place to prove the following fixed point theorem:

Theorem 5.4 (Least Fixed Point Theorem) *If D is a pointed CPO, then a continuous function $f : D \to D$ has a least fixed point ($\mathbf{fix}_D\ f$) defined by $\bigsqcup_D \{(f^n\ \perp_D) \mid n \geq 0\}$.*

Proof:

First we show that the above definition of ($\mathbf{fix}_D\ f$) is a fixed point of f:

- Since $\perp_D$ is the least element in D, $\perp_D \sqsubseteq (f\ \perp_D)$.

- Since f is monotonic (continuity implies monotonicity by Theorem 5.3), $\perp_D \sqsubseteq (f\ \perp_D)$ implies $(f\ \perp_D) \sqsubseteq (f\ (f\ \perp_D))$. By induction, $(f^n\ \perp_D) \sqsubseteq (f^{n+1}\ \perp_D)$ for every $n \geq 0$, so $\{(f^n\ \perp_D) \mid n \geq 0\}$ is a chain in D.

- Now,

$$
\begin{aligned}
&(f\ (\mathbf{fix}_D\ f)) \\
&= (f\ \bigsqcup_D \{(f^n\ \perp_D) \mid n \geq 0\}) && \text{by definition of } \mathbf{fix}_D \\
&= \bigsqcup_D \{(f\ (f^n\ \perp_D)) \mid n \geq 0\} && \text{by continuity of } f \\
&= \bigsqcup_D \{(f^n\ \perp_D) \mid n \geq 1\} \\
&= \bigsqcup_D \{(f^n\ \perp_D) \mid n \geq 0\} && (f^0\ \perp_D) = \perp_D \text{ can't change lub} \\
&= (\mathbf{fix}_D\ f) && \text{by definition of } \mathbf{fix}_D.
\end{aligned}
$$

Thus, $(f\ (\mathbf{fix}_D\ f)) = (\mathbf{fix}_D\ f)$, showing that $(\mathbf{fix}_D\ f)$ is indeed a fixed point of f.

To see that this is the *least* fixed point of f, suppose there is some other fixed point d'. Then clearly $\perp_D \sqsubseteq d'$, and by the monotonicity of f, $(f^n\ \perp_D) \sqsubseteq (f^n\ d') = d'$. So d' is an upper bound of the set $S = \{(f^n\ \perp_D) \mid n \geq 0\}$. But then, by the definition of least upper bound, $(\mathbf{fix}_D\ f) = (\bigsqcup_D S) \sqsubseteq d'$. $\diamond$

We can treat $\mathbf{fix}_D$ as a function of type $(D \to D) \to D$. It turns out that $\mathbf{fix}_D$ is itself a continuous function, and satisfies some other properties that make it useful for many semantic purposes (see [GS90]).

The Least Fixed Point Theorem describes an important class of situations in which fixed points exist, and we shall use it to specify the meaning of various recursive definitions. However, there are many generating functions that have least fixed points but do not satisfy the conditions of the Least Fixed Point Theorem. In these cases, other means must be used to find the least fixed point.

5.2.6 Fixed Point Examples

Here we present several brief examples of the Least Fixed Point Theorem in action. We have discussed many of these examples informally already but will now show how the fixed point machinery formalizes the intuition underlying the iterative fixed point technique.

Sequence Examples

In order to model sequences of natural numbers, we will use the domain of finite and infinite sequences from $Nat_\perp$:

$$s \in Natseq = \overline{Nat_\perp}{}^*$$

We use the flat domain $Nat_\perp$ instead of Nat to model the elements of a sequence so that there is a distinguished bottom element to which $head$ can map the empty sequence. We will assume that $(tail \; []) = []$, though we could alternatively introduce a new bottom element for sequences if we wanted to distinguish $(tail \; [])$ from $[]$. We use $\overline{Nat_\perp}{}^*$ (with the prefix ordering) rather than $Nat_\perp{}^*$ because the former is a pointed CPO that contains all the limiting values that are missing from the latter.

The equation $s = (cons \; 3 \; (cons \; (1 + (head \; s)) \; []))$ has as its associated generating function the following:

$$g_{seq1} : Natseq \rightarrow Natseq = \lambda s \, . \, (cons \; 3 \; (cons \; (1 + (head \; s)) \; []))$$

$Natseq$ is a pointed CPO with bottom element $[]$, and it is not hard to show that g_{seq1} is continuous. Thus, the Least Fixed Point Theorem applies, and the least fixed point can be found by iterating g starting with $[]$:

$$
\begin{aligned}
&\left(\mathbf{fix}_{Natseq} \; g_{seq1}\right) \\
&\quad = \; \bigsqcup\nolimits_{Natseq} \{ (g_{seq1}^0 \; []), \; (g_{seq1}^1 \; []), \; (g_{seq1}^2 \; []), \; (g_{seq1}^3 \; []), \; \cdots \} \\
&\quad = \; \bigsqcup\nolimits_{Natseq} \{ [], \; [3, \perp_{Nat_\perp}], \; [3, 4] \} \\
&\quad = \; [3, 4]
\end{aligned}
$$

In this case, the unique fixed point [3,4] of g_{seq1} is reached after two iterations of g_{seq1}.

What happens when we apply this technique to an equation like

$$s = (cons \; (head \; s) \; (cons \; (1 + (head \; s)) \; []))$$

which has an infinite number of fixed points? The corresponding generating function is

$$g_{seq2} : Natseq \rightarrow Natseq = \lambda s \, . \, (cons \; (head \; s) \; (cons \; (1 + (head \; s)) \; []))$$

This function is continuous as long as $+$ returns $\perp_{Nat_\perp}$ when one of its arguments is $\perp_{Nat_\perp}$. The Least Fixed Point Theorem applies, and iterating g_{seq2} on $[]$ gives:

$$\left(\textbf{fix}_{Natseq}\ g_{seq2}\right)$$
$$=\ \bigsqcup\nolimits_{Natseq}\{(g_{seq2}^{0}\ []),\ (g_{seq2}^{1}\ []),\ (g_{seq2}^{2}\ []),\ (g_{seq2}^{3}\ []),\ \dots\ \}$$
$$=\ \bigsqcup\nolimits_{Natseq}\{[],\ [\bot_{Nat_\bot},\bot_{Nat_\bot}]\}$$
$$=\ [\bot_{Nat_\bot},\bot_{Nat_\bot}]$$

After one iteration, the iterative fixed point technique finds the fixed point $[\bot_{Nat_\bot},\bot_{Nat_\bot}]$, which is indeed less than all the other fixed points $[n,(n+1)]$. Intuitively, this result indicates that the solution is a sequence of two numbers, but that the value of those numbers cannot be determined without making an arbitrary decision. Note the crucial roles that the bottom elements $[]$ and $\bot_{Nat_\bot}$ play in this example. Each represents the value with the least information from a domain. Iterative application of the generating function may or may not refine these values by adding information.

A similar story holds for equations like

$$s\ =\ (cons_a\ (1+(head\ s))\ (cons\ (head\ s)\ []))$$

that have no solutions in Nat^*. The reader can verify that this equation *does* have the unique solution $[\bot_{Nat_\bot},\bot_{Nat_\bot}]$ in $Natseq$ and that this solution can be found by an application of the Least Fixed Point Theorem.

As a final sequence example, we consider the equation $s=(cons\ 1\ s)$, whose associated generating function is

$$g_{seq3}:Natseq\rightarrow Natseq=\lambda s\,.\,(cons\ 1\ s)$$

This function is continuous, and the Least Fixed Point Theorem can be invoked to find a solution to the original equation:

$$\left(\textbf{fix}_{Natseq}\ g_{seq3}\right)$$
$$=\ \bigsqcup\nolimits_{Natseq}\{(g_{seq3}^{0}\ []),\ (g_{seq3}^{1}\ []),\ (g_{seq3}^{2}\ []),\ (g_{seq3}^{3}\ []),\ \dots\ \}$$
$$=\ \bigsqcup\nolimits_{Natseq}\{[],\ [1],\ [1,\ 1],\ [1,\ 1,\ 1],\ \dots\ \}$$
$$=\ [1,\ 1,\ 1,\ \dots]$$

In this case, the unique fixed point of g_{seq3} is an infinite sequence of 1s. This fixed point is not reached in a finite number of iterations, but is the limit of the sequence of approximations whose nth element (starting at index $n=0$) is $(g_{seq3}^{n}\ [])$. This example underscores why it is necessary to extend $Nat_\bot{}^*$ with $Nat_\bot^\infty$ to make $Natseq$ a CPO. Without the infinite sequences in $Nat_\bot^\infty$, the iterative fixed point technique could not find a solution to some equations.

Function Examples

In the remainder of this book, we will typically apply the iterative fixed point technique to generating functions over function domains. Here we consider a few examples involving fixed points over the following domain of functions:

$$f \in \mathit{Natfun} = \mathit{Nat} \rightarrow \mathit{Nat}_\perp$$

Since we assume that $\rightarrow$ designates *continuous* functions, *Natfun* is a domain of the continuous functions between *Nat* and $\mathit{Nat}_\perp$. *Natfun* is a CPO because the set of continuous functions between CPOs is itself a CPO under the usual ordering of functions. Furthermore, *Natfun* is pointed because $\mathit{Nat}_\perp$ is pointed. Recall that $\mathit{Nat} \rightarrow \mathit{Nat}_\perp$ is isomorphic to $\mathit{Nat} \rightharpoonup \mathit{Nat}$, so elements of *Natfun* can be represented by a function graph in which pairs whose target element is $\perp_{\mathit{Nat}_\perp}$ are omitted.

Our first example is the definition of the doubling function studied earlier:

$$dbl = \lambda n \,.\, \textbf{if } (n = 0) \textbf{ then } 0 \textbf{ else } (2 + (dbl \ (n - 1))) \textbf{ end}$$

A solution to this definition is the fixed point of the generating function g_{dbl}:

$$g_{dbl} : \mathit{Natfun} \rightarrow \mathit{Natfun}$$
$$= \lambda f \,.\, \lambda n \,.\, \textbf{if } (n = 0) \textbf{ then } 0 \textbf{ else } (2 + (f \ (n - 1))) \textbf{ end}$$

Natfun is a pointed CPO, and *Natfun*'s bottom element is the function whose graph is $\{\}$. In this CPO, $\bigsqcup$ on a chain of functions in $\mathit{Nat} \rightarrow \mathit{Nat}$ is equivalent to $\bigsqcup$ on a chain of graphs of functions in $\mathit{Nat} \rightharpoonup \mathit{Nat}$. It can be shown that g_{dbl} is continuous, so the Least Fixed Point Theorem applies:

$$(\textbf{fix}_{\mathit{Natfun}} \ g_{dbl})$$
$$= \bigsqcup_{\mathit{Natfun}} \{(g_{dbl}^{0} \ \{\}),\ (g_{dbl}^{1} \ \{\}),\ (g_{dbl}^{2} \ \{\}),\ (g_{dbl}^{3} \ \{\}),\ \dots \}$$
$$= \bigsqcup_{\mathit{Natfun}} \{\{\},\ \{\langle 0,0 \rangle\},\ \{\langle 0,0 \rangle, \langle 1,2 \rangle\},\ \{\langle 0,0 \rangle, \langle 1,2 \rangle, \langle 2,4 \rangle\},\ \dots \}$$
$$= \{\langle n, 2n \rangle \mid n : \mathit{Nat}\}$$

Each $(g_{dbl}^{n} \ \{\})$ is a finite approximation of the doubling function that is defined only on the naturals in $[0..(n-1)]$. The least (and only) fixed point is the limit of these approximations: a doubling function defined on all naturals.

As an example of a function with an infinite number of fixed points, consider the following recursive definition of a function in *Natfun*:

$$\mathit{even0} : \mathit{Natfun} = \lambda n \,.\, \textbf{if } (n = 0) \textbf{ then } 0 \textbf{ else } (\mathit{even0} \ (n \ \% \ 2)) \textbf{ end}$$

Here $(a \% b)$ returns the remainder of dividing a by b. For each constant c in $Nat_\perp$, the function whose graph is

$$\bigcup n : Nat\{\langle 2n, 0 \rangle, \langle 2n+1, c \rangle\}$$

is a solution for $even0$. Each solution maps all even numbers to zero and maps every odd number to the same constant c, where c is a parameter that distinguishes one solution from another. Each of these solutions is a fixed point of the generating function g_{even0}:

$$g_{even0} : Natfun \rightarrow Natfun$$
$$= \lambda f . \lambda n . \textbf{if } (n = 0) \textbf{ then } 0 \textbf{ else } (f \ (n \% 2)) \textbf{ end}$$

It turns out that this function is continuous, so the Least Fixed Point Theorem gives:

$$(\textbf{fix}_{Natfun} \ g_{even0})$$
$$= \bigsqcup_{Natfun} \{(g^0_{even0} \ \{\}), \ (g^1_{even0} \ \{\}), \ (g^2_{even0} \ \{\}), \ (g^3_{even0} \ \{\}), \ \ldots \}$$
$$= \bigsqcup_{Natfun}\{\{\}, \ \{\langle 0,0 \rangle\}, \ \{\langle 2n,0 \rangle \mid n : Nat\}\}$$
$$= \{\langle 2n,0 \rangle \mid n : Nat\}$$

The least fixed point is a function that maps every even number to zero, but is undefined (i.e., yields $\perp_{Nat_\perp}$) on the odd numbers. Indeed, this is the least element of the class of fixed points described above; it uses the least arbitrary value for the constant c.

The solution for $even0$ matches our intuitions about the operational behavior of programming language procedures for computing $even0$. For example, the definition for $even0$ can be expressed in the SCHEME programming language via the following procedure:

```
(define (even0 n)
  (if (= n 0)
      0
      (even0 (mod n 2))))
```

We expect this procedure to return zero in at most two steps for an even natural number, but to diverge for an odd natural number. The fact that the function $even0$ maps odd numbers to $\perp_{Nat_\perp}$ can be interpreted as signifying that the procedure even0 diverges on odd inputs.

Exercise 5.14 For each of the following equations:

- Characterize the set of all solutions to the equation in the specified solution domain.

- Use the iterative fixed point technique to determine the least solution to the equation.

Assume that $s : Natseq$, $p : \mathcal{P}(Nat)$, $f : Natfun$, and $h : Int \rightarrow Int_\perp$.

a. $s = (cons\ 2\ (cons\ (head\ (tail\ s))\ s))$

b. $s = (cons\ (1 + (head\ (tail\ s)))\ (cons\ 3\ s))$

c. $s = (cons\ 5\ (mapinc\ s))$, where $mapinc$ is a function in $Natseq \rightarrow Natseq$ that maps every sequence $[n_1,\ n_2,\ \ldots]$ to the sequence $[(1 + n_1),\ (1 + n_2),\ \ldots]$

d. $p = \{1\} \cup \{x + 3 \mid x \in p\}$

e. $p = \{1\} \cup \{2x \mid x \in p\}$

f. $p = \{1\} \cup \{|2x - 4| \mid x \in p\}$

g. $f = \lambda n \,.\ (f\ n)$

h. $f = \lambda n \,.\ (f\ (1 + n))$

i. $f = \lambda n \,.\ (1 + (f\ n))$

j. $f = \lambda n \,.\ \mathbf{if}\ (n = 1)$
    $\qquad\qquad \mathbf{then}\ 0$
    $\qquad\qquad \mathbf{else\ if}\ (even?\ n)\ \mathbf{then}\ (1 + (f\ (n \div 2)))\ \mathbf{else}\ (f\ (n + 2))\ \mathbf{end}$
    $\qquad\qquad \mathbf{end}$

where $even?$ is a predicate determining if a number is even.

k. $h = \lambda i \,.\ \mathbf{if}\ (i = 0)\ \mathbf{then}\ 0\ \mathbf{else}\ (h\ (i - 2))\ \mathbf{end}$

Exercise 5.15 Section 5.1.3 sketches an example involving the solution of an equation on line drawings involving the transformation T. Formalize this example by completing the following steps:

a. Represent line drawings as an appropriate pointed CPO *Lines*.

b. Express the transformation T as a continuous function g_T in *Lines* $\rightarrow$ *Lines*.

c. Use the iterative fixed point technique to find the least fixed point of g_T.

Exercise 5.16 A binary relation R on a set A is a subset of $A \times A$. The **reflexive transitive closure** of R is the smallest subset R' of $A \times A$ satisfying the following properties:

- If $a \in A$, then $\langle a, a \rangle \in R'$;

- If $\langle a, b \rangle$ is in R' and $\langle b, c \rangle$ is in R, then $\langle a, c \rangle$ is in R'.

a. Describe how the reflexive transitive closure of a binary relation can be expressed as an instance of the Least Fixed Point Theorem. What is the pointed CPO? What is the bottom element? What is the generating function?

b. Use the iterative fixed point technique to determine the reflexive transitive closure of the following binary relation R on the set $\{a, b, c, d, e\}$:

$$R = \{\langle a, c\rangle,\ \langle c, e\rangle,\ \langle d, a\rangle,\ \langle d, b\rangle,\ \langle e, c\rangle\}$$

Exercise 5.17 Show that each of the generating functions g_{seq1}, g_{seq2}, g_{seq3}, g_{dbl}, g_{even0} from the examples in this section is continuous.

5.2.7 Continuity and Strictness

We have seen how compound CPOs can be constructed out of component CPOs using the domain operators $\perp$, $\times$, $+$, *, and $\to$. We have also seen how the pointedness of a compound CPO is in some cases dependent on the pointedness of its components.

But a pointed CPO D is not the only prerequisite of the Least Fixed Point Theorem. The other prerequisite is that the generating function $f : D \to D$ must be continuous. In the examples of the previous section, we waved our hands about the continuity of the generating functions, but did not actually prove continuity in any of the cases. The proofs are not difficult, but they are tedious. Below, we argue that all functions that can be expressed in the metalanguage summarized in Section A.4 are guaranteed to be continuous as long as we make certain assumptions about operations on primitive domains. The upshot is that we generally do not need to worry about the continuity of generating functions. We also introduce strictness, an important property for characterizing functions on pointed domains.

Recall that metalanguage expressions include:

- constants (both primitive values and primitive functions on such values);

- variables;

- construction and deconstruction operators for compound domains (e.g., $\langle \ldots \rangle$ and *Proj i* notation for products; *Inj i* and **cases** notation for sums; *cons*, *empty?*, *head*, and *tail* for sequences; λ abstraction and application for functions);

- syntactic sugar like **if**, **let**, and **match**.

It turns out that all of the construction and deconstruction operators for compound domains are continuous and that the composition of continuous functions is continuous (see [Sch86] for the details). This implies that any function expressed as a composition of construction and deconstruction operators is continuous. As long as primitive functions are continuous and the **if**, **let**, and **match** notations preserve continuity, all functions expressible in this metalanguage subset must be continuous. Below, we refine our interpretation of primitive functions and the sugar notations so that continuity is guaranteed.

Assume for now that all primitive domains are flat CPOs. What does it mean for a function between primitive domains to be continuous? Since all chains on a flat domain D can contain at most two elements ($\bot_D$ and a nonbottom element d), the continuity of a function $f : D \to E$ between flat domains D and E is equivalent to the following monotonicity condition:

$$(f \ \bot_D) \sqsubseteq_E (f \ d)$$

This condition is satisfied only in the following two cases:

- f maps $\bot_D$ to $\bot_E$, in which case d can map to any element of E;

- f maps *all* elements of D to the same nonbottom element of E.

In particular, f is *not* continuous if it maps $\bot_D$ and d to distinct nonbottom elements of E.

For example, a function *sqr* in $Nat_\bot \to Nat_\bot$ that maps $\bot_{Nat_\bot}$ to $\bot_{Nat_\bot}$ and every number to its square is continuous. So is the constant function *three* that maps every element of $Nat_\bot$ (including $\bot_{Nat_\bot}$) to 3. But a function *noncont* that maps every nonbottom number n to its square and maps $\bot_{Nat_\bot}$ to 3 is *not* continuous, because $(f \ n)$ is not a refinement of the approximation $(noncont \ \bot_{Nat_\bot}) = 3$ (because $(noncont \ n)$ and $(noncont \ \bot_{Nat_\bot})$ are incomparable).

Perhaps the most interesting example of a noncontinuous function is the celebrated **halting function**. For our purposes, the halting function has the signature

$$halts : (Nat \to Nat_\bot) \to Nat \to Bool$$

and the following behavior: if $f : Nat \to Nat_\bot$ and $n : Nat$, then $(halts \ f \ n)$ returns *true* iff $(f \ n)$ is a natural number (i.e., a nonbottom element of $Nat_\bot$) and returns *false* iff $(f \ n)$ is $\bot_{Nat_\bot}$. Intuitively, the *halts* function is noncontinuous for the same reason as *noncont*. It requires a mechanism for detecting whether a computation is caught in an infinite loop, and such a mechanism must map $\perp_{Nat_\perp}$ (representing a diverging computation) to one result (*false*) and all stronger elements in *Nat* to an incomparable result (*true*).

The halting function is the canonical example of an uncomputable function — a mathematical function whose results cannot be determined from its arguments by executing a computational process. In the study of programming languages, we expect that we should be able to model only computable functions, since these, by definition, are what procedures in a programming language can denote. It turns out that the continuous functions correspond exactly to the computable functions, which is why continuity is such an important property in the study of programming languages.

What we seek now is an easy way in our metalanguage to outlaw functions like *noncont* and *halts* while permitting functions like *sqr* and *three*. We do this based on a notion of strictness. If D and E are pointed domains, a function $f : D \to E$ is **strict** if $(f \perp_D) = \perp_E$. Otherwise, f is **nonstrict**. For example, the *sqr* function described above is strict, while the *three* function is nonstrict. Although strictness and continuity are orthogonal properties in general, strictness does imply continuity for functions between flat domains (see Exercise 5.18).

Strictness is important because it captures the operational notion that a computation will diverge if it depends on an input that diverges. For example, strictness models the parameter-passing strategies of most modern languages, in which a procedure call will diverge if the evaluation of any of its arguments diverges. Nonstrictness models the parameter-passing strategies of so-called lazy languages. See Sections 7.1, 8.4.3, and 10.1.3 for a discussion of these parameter-passing mechanisms.

When pointed CPOs are manipulated in our metalanguage, we shall assume the strictness of various operations:

- All the primitive functions on flat domains are strict. When such a function has multiple arguments, we will assume it is strict in each of its arguments. Thus, $+_{Nat_\perp}$ returns $\perp_{Nat_\perp}$ if either argument is $\perp_{Nat_\perp}$, and $=_{Nat_\perp}$ returns $\perp_{Bool_\perp}$ if either argument is $\perp_{Nat_\perp}$.

- An **if** expression is strict in its test value whenever it is an element of $Bool_\perp$ rather than *Bool*. Thus the expression

$$\textbf{if } x =_{Nat_\perp} y \textbf{ then } 3 \textbf{ else } 3 \textbf{ end}$$

is guaranteed to return $\perp_{Nat_\perp}$ (*not* 3) if either x or y is $\perp_{Nat_\perp}$. Together with the strictness of $=_{Nat_\perp}$, the strictness of **if** test values thwarts attempts to express uncomputable functions. For example, consider the following failed attempt to define the *noncont* function described above:

$$\lambda n \,.\, \textbf{if } n =_{Nat_\perp} \perp_{Nat_\perp} \textbf{ then } 3 \textbf{ else } n \times_{Nat_\perp} n \textbf{ end}$$

Because of the strictness of $=_{Nat_\perp}$, this function returns $\perp_{Nat_\perp}$ for *every* n in $Nat_\perp$, and so is continuous. Similarly, here is an attempt to define a variant of the *halts* function that returns *true* if applying the given function f to the argument n yields 0 and otherwise returns *false*:

$$\lambda fn \,.\, \textbf{if } (f\ n) =_{Nat_\perp} 0 \textbf{ then } \textit{true} \textbf{ else } \textit{false} \textbf{ end}$$

In the case where $(f\ n)$ is $\perp_{Nat_\perp}$, this function must return $\perp_{Bool_\perp}$, not *false*, and so it is continuous.

- A **match** expression is strict in its discriminant whenever it is an element of a pointed CPO. As with the strictness of **if** test values, this restriction matches computational intuitions and prevents the expression of uncomputable functions.

- If D is a pointed domain, we require the *head* operation on sequences to be strict on D^* under the prefix ordering. That is, $(head\ [\,])$ must equal $\perp_D$. If D is not pointed, or if D^* has the sum-of-products ordering, *head* is undefined for $[\,]$; i.e., it is only a partial function.

With the above provisions for strictness, it turns out that all functions expressible in the metalanguage are continuous.

We sometimes want to specify new strict functions, so it is helpful to have a convenient notation for expressing strictness. If f is any function between pointed domains D and E, then $(\textbf{strict}_{D,E}\ f)$ is a strict version of f. That is, $(\textbf{strict}_{D,E}\ f)$ maps $\perp_D$ to $\perp_E$ and maps every nonbottom element d of D to $(f\ d)$. As usual, we will omit the subscripts on **strict** when they are clear from context. For example, a strict function in $Nat_\perp \to Nat_\perp$ that returns 3 for all nonbottom arguments can be defined as:

$$\textit{strict-three} = (\textbf{strict } (\lambda n \,.\, 3))$$

We adopt the abbreviation $\underline{\lambda} \,.\, \ldots$ for $(\textbf{strict } (\lambda \,.\, \ldots))$, so $\underline{\lambda} n \,.\, 3$ is another way to write the above function.

Exercise 5.18

a. Show that strictness and continuity are orthogonal by exhibiting functions in $D \rightarrow D$ that have the properties listed below. You may choose different Ds for different parts.

    i.   Strict and continuous;

    ii.   Nonstrict and continuous;

    iii.   Strict and noncontinuous;

    iv.   Nonstrict and noncontinuous.

b. Which combinations of properties from the previous part cannot be achieved if D is required to be a flat domain? Justify your answer.

5.3 Reflexive Domains

Reflexive domains are domains that are defined by recursive domain equations. We have already seen reflexive domains in the context of PostFix:

$$StackTransform = Stack \rightarrow Stack$$
$$Stack = Value^* + Error$$
$$Value = Int + StackTransform$$

These equations imply that a stack may contain as one of its values a function that maps stacks to stacks. A simpler example of reflexive domains is provided by the lambda calculus (see Section 6.6), which is based on a single domain Fcn defined as follows:

$$Fcn = Fcn \rightarrow Fcn$$

We know from set theory that descriptions of sets that contain themselves (even indirectly) as members are not necessarily well defined. In fact, a simple counting argument shows that equations like the above are nonsensical if interpreted in the normal set-theoretic way. For example, if we (improperly) view $\rightarrow$ as the domain constructor for set-theoretic functions from Fcn to Fcn, by counting the size of each set we find:

$$|Fcn| = |Fcn|^{|Fcn|}$$

For any set Fcn with more than one element, $|Fcn|^{|Fcn|}$ is bigger than $|Fcn|$. Even if $|Fcn|$ is infinite, $|Fcn|^{|Fcn|}$ is a "bigger" infinity! In the usual theory of sets, the only solution to this equation is a trivial domain Fcn with one element. A computational world with a single value is certainly not very interesting, and is a far cry from the computationally complete world of the lambda calculus!

Dana Scott had the insight that the functions that can be implemented on a computer are limited to continuous functions. There are fewer continuous functions than set-theoretic functions on a given CPO, since the set-theoretic functions do not have to be monotonic (you can get more information out of them than you put in!). If we treat $\rightarrow$ as a constructor that describes computable (continuous) functions and we interpret "equality" in domain equations as isomorphisms, then we have a much more interesting world than with set-theoretic functions. In this world, we can show an isomorphism between Fcn and $Fcn \rightarrow Fcn$:

$$Fcn \approx Fcn \rightarrow Fcn$$

The breakthrough came when Scott provided a constructive technique (the so-called **inverse limit construction**) that showed how to build such a domain and prove the isomorphism. Models exist as well for all of the other domain constructors we have introduced (lifting, products, sums, sum-of-products, prefix ordering of sequences), and as long as we stick to well-defined domain constructors, we can be assured that there is a nontrivial solution to our reflexive domain equations.

The beauty of this mathematical approach is that there is a formal way of giving meaning to programming language constructs without any use of computation. We shall not describe the details of the inverse limit construction here. This construction was first presented in [Sco73]. For a high-level retrospective on this construction, see Scott's 1976 Turing Award Lecture [Sco77]. A readable account of the construction can be found in [Sch86, Chapter 11].

It is important to note that this construction requires that certain domains have bottom elements. For example, in order to solve the POSTFIX domain equations, we need to lift the *Stack* and *Answer* domains:

$$StackTransform = Stack \rightarrow Stack$$
$$Stack = (Value^* + Error)_\bot$$
$$Value = Int + StackTransform$$
$$Answer = (Int + Error)_\bot$$

This lifting explains how nontermination can "creep in" when POSTFIX is extended with dup. (Recall that we proved that programs in ordinary POSTFIX terminate regardless of lifting.)

The inverse limit construction is only one way to understand recursive domain equations. Many approaches to interpreting such equations have been proposed over the years. One approach is to interpret solution domains as subdomains of $\mathcal{P}(\omega)$, the powerset of natural numbers ordered by set inclusion [Sco76],[Sto85, Chapter 7]. Another popular approach is based on the notion of *information systems* [GS90, Gun92, Win93].

5.4 Summary

Here are the main ideas of this chapter:

- The meaning of a recursive definition over a domain D can be understood as the fixed point of a function $D \to D$.

- Complete partial orders (CPOs) model domain elements as approximations that are ordered by information. In a CPO, every sequence of information-consistent approximations has a well-defined limit.

- A CPO D is pointed if it has a least element (bottom, written $\perp_D$). The bottom element, which stands for "no information," is used as a starting point for the fixed point process. Bottom can be used to represent a partial function as a total function. It is often used to model computations that diverge (go into an infinite loop). A function between pointed CPOs is strict if it preserves bottom.

- Functions between CPOs are monotonic if they preserve the information ordering and continuous if they preserve the limits. Continuity implies monotonicity, but not vice versa.

- If D is a pointed CPO, every continuous function $f : D \to D$ has a least fixed point ($\mathbf{fix}_d\ f$) that is defined as the limit of iterating f starting at $\perp_D$.

- The domain constructors $_\perp$, $\times$, $+$, $\to$, and $\overline{}^*$ can be viewed as operators on CPOs. In particular, $D_1 \to D_2$ is interpreted as the CPO of *continuous* functions from D_1 to D_2. Only some of these constructors preserve pointedness. The new domain constructor $_\perp$ extends a domain with a new bottom element, guaranteeing that it is pointed.

- Functions that can be expressed in the metalanguage of Section A.4 are guaranteed to be continuous. Intuitively, such functions correspond to the computable functions.

- Recursive domain equations that are not solvable when domains are viewed as sets can become solvable when domains are viewed as CPOs. The key ideas (due to Scott) are to interpret equality as isomorphism and to focus only on continuous functions rather than all set-theoretic functions. There are restricted kinds of CPOs for which any domain equations over a rich set of operators are guaranteed to have a solution.

Notes

This chapter was inspired by Schmidt's presentation in [Sch86, Chapter 6]. The excellent overview article by Gunter and Scott [GS90] presents alternative approaches involving more restricted domains and touches upon many technical details omitted above. See Mosses's article on denotational semantics [Mos90] to see how these more restricted domains are used in practice. Gunter's book [Gun92] discusses many domain issues in detail.

For more information on domain theory and an introduction to the techniques of solving recursive domain equations, see [Sto85, Sch86, GS90, Gun92, Win93].

Part II

Dynamic Semantics

6

FL: A Functional Language

Things used as language are inexhaustibly attractive.

— Ralph Waldo Emerson, *The Philosopher*

FL (for *Functional Language*[1]) is a mini-language that exemplifies what is traditionally known as the **functional programming paradigm**. As we shall see, functional programming languages are characterized by a compositional style of expressing values and an emphasis on the manipulation of values that model mathematical functions. The name "functional language" is a little bit odd, since it suggests that languages not fitting this paradigm are somehow *dys*functional — a perception that many functional language aficionados actively promote! Perhaps **function-oriented languages** would be a more accurate term for this class of languages.

FL will form the basis of many languages in this book. It will provide us with the opportunity to use the semantic tools developed in the previous chapters to analyze a programming language that is much closer to a "real" programming language than POSTFIX or EL (see Section 6.4 and Section 6.5). But before we get there, we shall study a technique of **programming language decomposition** that enables the application of our analytical tools to practical languages. We shall also introduce two approaches for modeling names in a programming language: substitution and environments.

6.1 Decomposing Language Descriptions

The study of a programming language can often be simplified if it is decomposed into three parts:

1. A **kernel** language that forms the essential core of the language.

---

[1]Our FL language is not to be confused with any other similarly named language. In particular, our FL is *not* related to the FL functional programming language [BWW90, BWW+89] based on Backus's FP [Bac78].

2. **Syntactic sugar** that extends the kernel with convenient constructs. Such constructs can be automatically translated into kernel constructs via a process known as **desugaring**.

3. A **standard library** of procedures, constants, and operators supplied with the language.

We shall refer to the combination of a kernel, syntactic sugar, and a standard library as a **full language** to distinguish it from its components.

Decomposing a programming language definition into parts relieves a common tension in the design and analysis of programming languages. From the standpoint of reasoning about a language, it is desirable for a language to have only a few, simple parts. However, from the perspective of programming in a language, it is desirable to concisely and conveniently express common programming idioms. A language that is too pared down may be easy to reason about but horrendous to program in — try writing factorial in POSTFIX+{dup}. On the other hand, a language with many features may be convenient to program in but difficult to reason about — try proving some nontrivial properties about your next JAVA, C, ADA, or COMMON LISP program.

The technique of viewing a full language as mostly sugar-coating around a kernel lets us have our cake and eat it too. When we want to reason about the language, we consider only the small kernel upon which everything else is built. But when we want to program in the language, we make heavy use of the syntactic sugar and standard library to express what we want in a readable fashion. Indeed, we can even add new syntactic sugar and new primitives modularly without changing the properties of the kernel.

There are limitations to this approach. We'd like the kernel and full language to be close enough so that the desugaring is easy to understand. Otherwise we might have a situation where the kernel is a machine instruction set and the desugaring is a full-fledged compilation from high-level programs into object code. For this reason, we require that syntactic sugar be expressed via simple local transformations; no global program analysis is allowed.

6.2   The Structure of FL

FL is a typical functional programming language for computing with numeric, boolean, symbolic, procedural, and compound data values. The computational model of FL is based on the functional programming paradigm exemplified by

such languages as HASKELL, ML, SCHEME, and ERLANG. Syntactically, FL bears
a strong resemblance to SCHEME, but we shall see that semantically it is closer to
so-called **purely functional lazy languages** like HASKELL and MIRANDA. FL
programs are free of side effects and make heavy use of first-class functional values
(here called **procedures**). We shall consistently use the term **procedure** to refer
to entities in programming languages that denote mathematical functions, and
function to refer to the mathematical notion of function. In some languages,
these two terms are used to distinguish different kinds of programming language
entities. For example, in PASCAL, "function" refers to a subroutine that returns
a result whereas "procedure" refers to a subroutine that performs its work via
side effects and returns no result. Much of the functional programming literature
uses the term "function" to refer both to the programming language entity and
the mathematical entity it denotes, which we find confusing.

6.2.1 FLK: The Kernel of the FL Language

We begin by presenting the syntax and informal semantics of FLK, the FL kernel.

The Syntax of FLK

An FLK program is a member of the syntactic domain Prog defined by the s-
expression grammar in Figure 6.1. It has the form $(\texttt{flk}\ (I_{i=1}^{n})\ E_{body})$, where
$I_1, \ldots, I_n$ ($n \geq 0$) are the **formal parameters** of the program and E_{body} is
the **body expression** of the program. Intuitively, the formal parameters name
program inputs and the body expression specifies the result value computed by
the program for its inputs. When a program is applied to actual arguments, we
will say that the program **binds** the parameters to those values. (Section 6.3
spells out this notion of binding more formally.)

FLK expressions are s-expressions that represent ASTs whose leaves are either
literals or variable references. FLK **literals** include the unit literal, booleans,
integers, and symbols. We adopt the SCHEME convention of writing the boolean
literals as `#t` (true) and `#f` (false). The unit literal (`#u`) is used where the value
of an expression is irrelevant, such as in situations where C and JAVA use the
`void` return type. For symbolic (i.e., nonnumeric) processing, FLK supports the
LISP-like notion of a **symbol**. Symbols are similar to the character-string values
supported by many languages, except that: (1) they are atomic entities that
cannot be decomposed into their constituent characters; (2) they are written using
a different syntax (e.g. `(sym foobar)` rather than `"foobar"`); and (3) certain
sequences of characters are forbidden as symbols:

- any character sequence that is a valid representation of a number (e.g., 42 and -17);

- any character sequence beginning with # (e.g., #u, #t, and #f); and

- any character sequence that includes whitespace, grouping characters ({, }, (,), [,]), or quotation characters (", ', ').

Later we shall see how symbols make it easy for an FL program to manipulate s-expressions representing ASTs with symbolic leaves. Since s-expressions are a simple way to represent the abstract syntax trees of programs (see Section 2.3), symbols facilitate writing FL programs that manipulate programs, such as interpreters and translators.

A key difference between FLK and POSTFIX/EL is that FLK provides constructs (flk, lam, and rec) that introduce names for values. Syntactically, names are expressed via **identifiers**. The rules for what constitutes a well-formed identifier differ from language to language. In FLK we shall assume that any symbol can be an identifier except for (1) symbols starting with the character @[2] and (2) **reserved keywords** of the language (app, error, flk, if, pair, prim, lam, rec, sym). This means that expressions like x-y and 4/3*pi*r^2 are treated as atomic identifiers in FLK. In many other languages, these would be infix specifications of trees of binary operator applications.

For compound expressions, FLK supports procedural abstractions (lam) and applications (app), primitive applications (prim), conditionals (if), pair creation (pair), simple recursion (rec), and error signaling (error).

Although many of the syntactic conventions of FLK are borrowed from LISP-like languages, especially SCHEME, it's worth emphasizing that FLK differs from these languages in some important ways. For example, in SCHEME, abstractions may take any number of formal parameters, are introduced via the keyword lambda, and are invoked via an application syntax with no keyword. In contrast, FLK abstractions have exactly one formal parameter, are introduced via the keyword lam, and are applied via the keyword app.

An Informal Semantics for FLK

Because many readers may not be familiar with functional programming and FLK is the basis for most of the mini-languages presented in the rest of this book, we will begin with an informal explanation of the semantics of FLK via examples. Later, in Sections 6.4 and 6.5, will use our operational and denotational tools to specify the semantics of FLK formally.

---

[2]We disallow identifiers beginning with @ in order to support the syntactic sugar for prim explained in Section 6.2.2.

$P \in \mathrm{Prog} ::= (\mathtt{flk}\ (I_{formal}^{*})\ E_{body})\ \ [\text{Program}]$

$E \in \mathrm{Exp} ::= L$ [Literal]

$\quad\quad\quad\ \ |\ I$ [VariableReference]

$\quad\quad\quad\ \ |\ (\mathtt{error}\ Y_{message})$ [Errors]

$\quad\quad\quad\ \ |\ (\mathtt{if}\ E_{test}\ E_{then}\ E_{else})$ [Conditional]

$\quad\quad\quad\ \ |\ (\mathtt{prim}\ O_{primop}\ E_{arg}^{*})$ [PrimitiveApplication]

$\quad\quad\quad\ \ |\ (\mathtt{lam}\ I_{formal}\ E_{body})$ [Abstraction]

$\quad\quad\quad\ \ |\ (\mathtt{app}\ E_{rator}\ E_{rand})$ [Application]

$\quad\quad\quad\ \ |\ (\mathtt{pair}\ E_{fst}\ E_{snd})$ [Pairing]

$\quad\quad\quad\ \ |\ (\mathtt{rec}\ I_{name}\ E_{body})$ [Recursion]

$L \in \mathrm{Lit} ::= \mathtt{\#u}$ [UnitLiteral]

$\quad\quad\quad\ |\ B$ [BooleanLiteral]

$\quad\quad\quad\ |\ N$ [IntegerLiteral]

$\quad\quad\quad\ |\ (\mathtt{sym}\ Y)$ [SymbolicLiteral]

$B \in \mathrm{BoolLit} = \{\mathtt{\#t}, \mathtt{\#f}\}$

$N \in \mathrm{IntLit} = \{\ldots, \mathtt{-2}, \mathtt{-1}, \mathtt{0}, \mathtt{1}, \mathtt{2}, \ldots\}$

$Y \in \mathrm{SymLit} = \{\mathtt{x}, \mathtt{lst}, \mathtt{make\text{-}point}, \mathtt{map\_tree}, \mathtt{4/3*pi*r\char`^2}, \ldots\}$

$\quad\quad \mathrm{Keyword} = \{\mathtt{app}, \mathtt{error}, \mathtt{flk}, \mathtt{if}, \mathtt{pair}, \mathtt{prim}, \mathtt{lam}, \mathtt{rec}, \mathtt{sym}\}$

$\quad I \in \mathrm{Ident} = \mathrm{SymLit} - (\{Y \mid Y \text{ begins with } \mathtt{@}\} \cup \mathrm{Keyword})$

$O \in \mathrm{Primop} = \textit{Defined in Figure 6.2}$

Figure 6.1 An s-expression grammar for FLK.

Intuitively, every FLK expression denotes a value that is tagged with its type in addition to whatever information distinguishes it from other values of the same type. The primitive values supported by FLK include the unit value, boolean truth values, integers, and textual symbols. The unit value is the unique value of a distinguished type that has a single element. In addition, FLK supports pairs and procedures. A pair is a compound value that allows any two values (which may themselves be pairs) to be glued together to form a single value. A procedure is a value that represents a mathematical function by specifying how to map a single input value to a single output value. Procedures are applied using the application (app) construct. Primitive operators such as + are *not* procedure values and will be described below.

To help build intuitions about FLK, here we will informally illustrate the semantics of FLK constructs by considering some sample evaluations of FLK expressions. The notation $E \xrightarrow[FLK]{} o$ indicates that the expression E evaluates to the outcome o, where an outcome is a value, an error, or an infinite loop. Here are some examples that indicate our conventions for writing FLK outcomes:

unit	The unit value
false, true	The boolean values
17, −3	Integer values
*'abstraction', '4/3 * pi * r^2'*	Symbolic values
procedure	Procedural values
error:divide-by-zero, error:not-an-integer	Errors
∞	Nontermination
	(represents an infinite loop)
⟨*17, true*⟩,	Pair values
⟨*procedure*, ⟨*'abstraction', unit*⟩⟩,	
⟨*error:not-an-integer, ∞*⟩	
{*this is a comment*}	Comment about an outcome

For simplicity, our outcome notation does not distinguish procedural values that denote different mathematical functions. For instance, a squaring procedure and a doubling procedure are both written *procedure*. Our notation for errors does distinguish errors with different messages. Note that FLK pair values ⟨o_1, o_2⟩ can combine any two outcomes o_1 and o_2, which may include errors and infinite loops. Additionally, we will use the following abbreviation for representing lists of outcomes that are encoded as a unit-terminated sequence of pairs chained together via their second components:

$$\triangleleft o_1, o_2, \ldots, o_n \triangleright = \langle o_1, \langle o_2, \ldots \langle o_n, unit \rangle \ldots \rangle \rangle$$

For example, the notation $\triangleleft$*17, true, ⟨'foo', procedure⟩*$\triangleright$ is an abbreviation for the three-element list ⟨*17*, ⟨*true*, ⟨⟨*'foo', procedure*⟩, *unit*⟩⟩⟩.

The literal expressions designate constants in the language:

#u $\xrightarrow[FLK]{}$ *unit*
#t $\xrightarrow[FLK]{}$ *true*
23 $\xrightarrow[FLK]{}$ *23*
(sym captain) $\xrightarrow[FLK]{}$ *'captain'*

The primitive application (prim O E_1 ... E_n) denotes the result of applying the primitive operator named by O to the n values of the argument expressions E_i. Figure 6.2 presents the primitive operator names $O \in$ Primop in FL and their associated meanings.

(prim not #t) $\xrightarrow[FLK]{}$ *false*
(prim int? 1) $\xrightarrow[FLK]{}$ *true*
(prim int? #t) $\xrightarrow[FLK]{}$ *false*
(prim + 1 2) $\xrightarrow[FLK]{}$ *3*
(prim / 17 5) $\xrightarrow[FLK]{}$ *3* {*integer division*}
(prim % 17 5) $\xrightarrow[FLK]{}$ *2* {*integer remainder*}
(prim sym=? (sym captain) (sym captain)) $\xrightarrow[FLK]{}$ *true*
(prim sym=? (sym captain) (sym abstraction)) $\xrightarrow[FLK]{}$ *false*

Operator	Meaning
unit?	Unary type predicate for the unit value.
bool?	Unary type predicate for booleans.
int?	Unary type predicate for integers.
sym?	Unary type predicate for symbols.
proc?	Unary type predicate for procedures.
pair?	Unary type predicate for pairs.
not	Unary boolean negation.
and	Binary boolean conjunction (not short-circuit).
or	Binary boolean disjunction (not short-circuit).
bool=?	Binary boolean equality predicate.
+	Binary integer addition.
−	Binary integer subtraction.
*	Binary integer multiplication.
/	Binary integer division.
%	Binary integer remainder.
=	Binary integer equality predicate.
!=	Binary integer inequality predicate.
<	Binary integer less-than predicate.
<=	Binary integer less-than-or-equal-to predicate.
>	Binary integer greater-than predicate.
>=	Binary integer greater-than-or-equal-to predicate.
sym=?	Binary symbol equality.
fst	Unary selector of the first element of a given pair.
snd	Unary selector of the second element of a given pair.

Figure 6.2 The primitive operators $O \in$ Primop in FLK.

The value of a primitive application is not defined when a primitive operator is given the wrong number of arguments, when an argument has an unexpected type, or when integer division or remainder by 0 is performed. These situations are considered errors:

$$(\texttt{prim + 1}) \xrightarrow[FLK]{} \textit{error:wrong-number-of-args}$$
$$(\texttt{prim + 1 2 3}) \xrightarrow[FLK]{} \textit{error:wrong-number-of-args}$$
$$(\texttt{prim not 1}) \xrightarrow[FLK]{} \textit{error:not-a-boolean}$$
$$(\texttt{prim + \#t 1}) \xrightarrow[FLK]{} \textit{error:not-an-integer}$$
$$(\texttt{prim / 1 0}) \xrightarrow[FLK]{} \textit{error:divide-by-zero}$$

The error expression (**error** $Y_{message}$) signals an error with the symbolic message $Y_{message}$:

$$(\texttt{error index-out-of-range}) \xrightarrow[FLK]{} \textit{error:index-out-of-range}$$

The conditional expression (if E_{test} E_{then} E_{else}) requires the value of E_{test} to be a boolean, and evaluates one of E_{then} or E_{else} depending on whether the test is true or false:

```
(if (prim > 8 7) (prim + 2 3) (prim * 2 3))  FLK→ 5
(if (prim < 8 7) (prim + 2 3) (prim * 2 3))  FLK→ 6
(if (prim - 8 7) (prim + 2 3) (prim * 2 3))
      FLK→ error:nonbool-in-if-test
```

The abstraction (lam I E) specifies a procedural value that represents a mathematical function. I names the procedure's single **formal parameter**, and the expression E is the **procedure body**. The procedure application[3] (app E_1 E_2) stands for the result of applying the procedure denoted by the **operator** (or **rator**) expression E_1 to the value denoted by the **operand** (or **rand**) expression E_2. Intuitively, this result is determined by evaluating the procedure's body with all occurrences of its formal parameter replaced by the expression E_2, whose value is called the **actual parameter** or **argument** of the application. We say that the formal parameter is **bound to** the argument during the evaluation of the procedure body. In the application (app E_1 E_2), it is an error if E_1 doesn't denote a procedure.

```
(lam x (prim * x x))  FLK→ procedure {squaring procedure}
(app (lam x (prim * x x)) 5)  FLK→ 25
(app 3 5)  FLK→ error:nonprocedural-rator
(app not #t)  FLK→ error:unbound-variable
   {not is a primitive operator, not a variable naming a procedure}
```

Multiple-argument procedures can be simulated by currying (see Section A.2.5):

```
(app (app (lam n (lam x (prim - x n))) 5) 8)  FLK→ 3
```

A hallmark of functional programming is that procedures can be passed as arguments to other procedures and returned as results from other procedures, just like any other value:

```
(lam f (app f 5))  FLK→ procedure {apply-to-5 procedure}
(app (lam f (app f 5)) (lam x (prim * x x)))  FLK→ 25
(lam n (lam x (prim - x n)))
   FLK→ procedure {make-subtract-n procedure}
(app (lam n (lam x (prim - x n))) 1)
   FLK→ procedure {subtract-1 procedure}
(app (lam f (app f 5))
     (app (lam n (lam x (prim - x n))) 1))  FLK→ 4
```

---

[3]Common synonyms for procedure application are **procedure call** and **procedure invocation**, so we will also say that a procedure is "called" or "invoked" with an argument value.

```
(app (lam f (app f 5)) (lam n (lam x (prim - x n))))
  ⟶  procedure {subtract-5 procedure}
    FLK
(app (app (lam f (app f 5))
    (lam n (lam x (prim - x n)))) 8)  ⟶  3
                                        FLK
(app (lam x (app x x)) (lam x (app x x)))  ⟶  ∞
                                            FLK
  {similar to the POSTFIX command sequence (dup exec) dup exec}
```

Because they can be used in the same ways as values like integers and pairs, procedures in FLK are said to be **first class**. Procedures that take other procedures as arguments or return them as results are called **higher-order procedures**.

As in HASKELL, FLK's procedures are **nonstrict**. This means that a procedure application may return a value even if one of its arguments denotes an error or a nonterminating computation. Intuitively, nonstrictness means that an expression will never be evaluated if the rest of the computation does not require its value. For example:

```
(app (lam x 3) (prim / 1 0))  ⟶  3
                               FLK
(app (lam x (prim + x 3)) (prim / 1 0))  ⟶  error:divide-by-zero
                                          FLK
(app (lam x 3)
    (app (lam x (app x x)) (lam x (app x x))))  ⟶  3
                                                 FLK
(app (lam x (prim + x 3))
    (app (lam x (app x x)) (lam x (app x x))))  ⟶  ∞
                                                 FLK
```

Unlike FLK, most real-world languages (including C, JAVA, ML, PASCAL, and SCHEME) have **strict** procedures. In these languages, operands of procedure applications are always evaluated, even if they are never referenced by the procedure body. We shall explore strict versus nonstrict procedures in more detail in Sections 7.1 and 8.4.3.

The pairing expression (pair E_{fst} E_{snd}) glues two outcomes together into a single value of the pair type. The two components of a pair can be extracted with the primitive operators fst and snd.

```
(prim fst (pair (+ 1 2) (* 3 4)))  ⟶  3
                                    FLK
(prim snd (pair (+ 1 2) (* 3 4)))  ⟶  12
                                    FLK
```

A chain of pairs linked by their second components and terminated by the unit value is a standard way of encoding a list:

```
(pair 8 (pair 2 (pair 1 #u)))  ⟶  ⊲8, 2, 1⊳
                                FLK
(prim fst (pair 8 (pair 2 (pair 1 #u))))  ⟶  8
                                           FLK
(prim snd (pair 8 (pair 2 (pair 1 #u))))  ⟶  ⊲2, 1⊳
                                           FLK
(prim fst (prim snd (pair 8 (pair 2 (pair 1 #u)))))  ⟶  2
                                                     FLK
(prim snd (prim fst (pair 8 (pair 2 (pair 1 #u)))))
  ⟶  error:not-a-pair
    FLK
```

Like procedure applications, pairing in FLK is nonstrict. The result of a `pair` expression is always a well-defined pair even if one (or both) of its argument expressions does not denote an FLK value. The unspecified nature of a contained value can be detected only when it is extracted from the pair.

```
(pair (prim not #f) (prim / 1 0))  ⟶   ⟨true, error:divide-by-zero⟩
                                   FLK
(prim fst (pair (prim not #f) (prim / 1 0)))  ⟶   true
                                              FLK
(prim snd (pair (prim not #f) (prim / 1 0)))
     ⟶   error:divide-by-zero
    FLK
```

As we shall see in Section 10.1.3, nonstrict data structures are an important mechanism for supporting modularity in programs.

We choose to make `pair` a kernel construct rather than a primitive operator like `not` or `+` to emphasize the fact that pairing is nonstrict. If we made `pair` a primitive operator, we would still have to treat it specially when we describe the semantics of the `prim` construct because all the other primitives are strict. Treating `pair` as a separate syntactic construct provides a cleaner description of the semantics. This is a purely stylistic decision; it is also possible to treat `pair` as a binary primitive operator (see Exercise 6.27).

The recursion construct (`rec` I E) allows the expression of recursion equations over one variable. The value of the `rec` expression is the value of its body, where the value of I within E is the value of the entire `rec` expression; i.e., the value returned by a recursion is the solution to the equation $I = E$. `rec` is used to specify recursive procedures and data structures: it allows us to give a name to a value so that the value itself can be used in the expression that determines that value. For example:

```
(rec fact (lam n
            (if (prim = n 0)
                1
                (prim * n (app fact (prim - n 1))))))
    ⟶   procedure  {A factorial procedure.}
   FLK

(app (rec fact (lam n
                 (if (prim = n 0)
                     1
                     (prim * n (app fact (prim - n 1))))))
     5)  ⟶   120  {5! = 120.}
        FLK
(rec ones (pair 1 ones))  ⟶   ◁1, 1, 1, ...▷  {an infinite list of 1s}
                          FLK
(prim fst (rec ones (pair 1 ones)))  ⟶   1
                                     FLK
(prim fst (prim snd (rec ones (pair 1 ones))))  ⟶   1
                                                FLK
```

The **ones** example above illustrates a list that is conceptually infinite in length. Conceptually infinite data structures are an important programming idiom; see Section 10.1.3 for a discussion and examples.

FLK programs are parameterized. We use the notation $P \xrightarrow[FLK]{[V_1,\ldots,V_n]} o$ to indicate that running the FLK program P on argument values $V_1, \ldots, V_n$ yields outcome o. For example:

$$\text{(flk (x) (prim * x x))} \xrightarrow[FLK]{[5]} 25 \;\{\textit{squaring program}\}$$

$$\text{(flk (a b) (prim / (prim + a b) 2))} \xrightarrow[FLK]{[2,8]} 5 \;\{\textit{averaging program}\}$$

```
(flk (a b) (prim / (prim + a b) 2))
```
$$\xrightarrow[FLK]{[2,8,11]} \textit{error:wrong-number-of-args}$$

```
(flk (x ns)                        {x is a scaling factor; ns is a list of ints}
  (app (rec scale                  {A recursive procedure}
         (lam ys                   {to scale the ints in ys by x.}
           (if (prim unit? ys)          {Is ys the empty list?}
               ys                       {If so, return it;}
               (pair                    {otherwise, prepend the}
                 (prim * x (prim fst ys))  {scaled first int}
                 (app scale                {to the result of scaling}
                   (prim snd ys)))))))     {the rest of the ints.}
    ns))
```
$$\xrightarrow[FLK]{[3,\triangleleft 7,2,5 \triangleright]} \triangleleft 21, 6, 15 \triangleright$$

The penultimate example illustrates that it is an error if the number of arguments supplied to the program differs from the number of formal parameters declared. The final example illustrates that FLK program arguments may include values other than integers, such as lists of integers in this case.

In general, the values considered to be valid program arguments will be a proper subset of the values manipulated by a language. In languages such as C and JAVA, program arguments are passed as an array of strings, and these strings can be parsed into other kinds of values (such as integers, floating-point numbers, arrays of numbers, etc.) where necessary. Program arguments are typically limited to literal data with simple textual representations, which excludes procedural values as program arguments. In the case of FLK, we shall assume that program arguments may be any of the literal values (unit, booleans, integers, symbols) and "**pair** trees"[4] (i.e., binary trees with **pair** nodes) whose leaves are literals. Since s-expressions can be represented as such trees, this will allow us to write FLK programs that manipulate representations of programming language ASTs (e.g., see the ELM interpreter on page 241).

---

[4]sans partridge!

6.2.2   FL Syntactic Sugar

While FLK has considerably more expressive punch than PostFix or EL, expressing even simple programs with FLK is rather cumbersome. We will now show how to extend the kernel FLK language with syntactic sugar to yield another language, FL, that has the same semantic simplicity as FLK but is more practical for writing and reading nontrivial programs.

Syntactic Sugar Syntax

Figure 6.3 shows the new constructs that constitute FL's syntactic sugar. In the definition of E, the ellipsis (. . .) stands for all the expression productions in the FLK grammar. The new expressions in Figure 6.3 can be used anywhere the nonterminal E appears in the kernel FLK grammar as well as in the new syntactic constructs. Many of these syntactic abbreviations are inspired by constructs in Lisp dialects, but some of them have somewhat different meanings in FL than in Lisp.

Desugaring Expressions

FL expressions are desugared to FLK expressions via the desugaring function $\mathcal{DS}$ defined in Figure 6.4. This function traverses an FL expression AST, performing local transformations that replace the syntactic sugar constructs of FL by FLK constructs. The top clauses process the expressions of FL that are inherited from FLK, recursively applying $\mathcal{DS}$ to all subexpressions. This will expand any syntactic sugar constructs appearing in the subexpressions. $\mathcal{DS}$ acts as the identity function when applied to an FLK expression.

The FL sugar construct $(@O\ E_1\ \ldots\ E_n)$ is an abbreviation of the kernel construct $(\texttt{prim}\ O\ E_1\ \ldots\ E_n)$. With this sugar, the verbose FLK expression

```
(prim - (prim * b b) (prim * 4 (prim * a c)))
```

can be shortened to the concise expression

```
(@- (@* b b) (@* 4 (@* a c)))
```

We will take advantage of this conciseness below by leaving this abbreviation intact even after desugaring everything else in our examples, i.e., we will sometimes show only *partially* desugared expressions that still contain sugared primitive applications.

This abbreviation is the reason that FL identifiers can't begin with @. Otherwise, procedures like `(lam @+ (@+ 2 3))` would be ambiguous: should this procedure apply its argument to 2 and 3, or should it always add 2 and 3?

Modified Domains

Keyword = Keyword$_{FLK}$ $\cup$ {abs, cond, def, else, fl, let, letrec, list,
quote, scand, scor}

New Domains

$D \in$ Def

$SX \in$ SExp

New Productions

$P ::=$ (flk (I_{formal}^*) E_{body})   [UnsugaredProgram]

   $\mid$ (fl (I_{formal}^*) E_{body} D_{defn}^*) [SugaredProgram]

$D ::=$ (def I_{name} E_{defn})   [ValueDefinition]

   $\mid$ (def (I_{proc} I_{formal}^*) E_{body}) [FunctionDefinition]

$E ::= \ldots$ FLK *expressions* $\ldots$

   $\mid$ (@O_{primop} E_{rand}^*)   [AbbreviatedPrimitiveApplication]

   $\mid$ (abs (I_{formal}^*) E_{body})   [MultiAbstraction]

   $\mid$ (E_{rator} E_{rand}^*)   [MultiApplication]

   $\mid$ (list $E_{element}^*$)   [List]

   $\mid$ (quote SX_{quoted})   [S-Expression]

   $\mid$ (cond (E_{test} E_{then})* (else $E_{default}$)) [NWayConditional]

   $\mid$ (scand $E_{conjunct}^*$)   [ShortCircuitAnd]

   $\mid$ (scor $E_{disjunct}^*$)   [ShortCircuitOr]

   $\mid$ (let ((I_{name} E_{defn})*) E_{body})   [LocalBinding]

   $\mid$ (letrec ((I_{name} E_{defn})*) E_{body})   [RecursiveBinding]

   $\mid$ (recur I_{proc} ((I_{name} E_{init})*) E_{body}) [RecursiveFunctionCall]

$SX ::= Y$ [Symbol]

   $\mid$ #u   [UnitLiteral]

   $\mid$ B [BooleanLiteral]

   $\mid$ N [IntegerLiteral]

   $\mid$ ($SX_{element}^*$) [List]

Figure 6.3   Grammar for FL syntactic sugar.

FL's abs construct can bind any number (possibly zero) of identifiers within a procedure body. In the tagless multiapplication construct, a procedure can be applied to any number (possibly zero) of arguments. The rules for desugaring multiabstractions into lam and multiapplications into app are based on the same currying technique that we use extensively in the metalanguage. (See Exercise 6.21 for an alternative approach to desugaring these expressions.) For example, suppose that E_{abs3} is the three-parameter multiabstraction

```
(abs (a b c) (@* a (@+ b c)))
```

$\mathcal{DS} : \mathrm{Exp}_{FL} \rightarrow \mathrm{Exp}_{FLK}$

$\mathcal{DS}[\![L]\!] = L$
$\mathcal{DS}[\![I]\!] = I$
$\mathcal{DS}[\![(\texttt{error}\ Y)]\!] = (\texttt{error}\ Y)$
$\mathcal{DS}[\![(\texttt{if}\ E_{test}\ E_{then}\ E_{else})]\!] = (\texttt{if}\ \mathcal{DS}[\![E_{test}]\!]\ \mathcal{DS}[\![E_{then}]\!]\ \mathcal{DS}[\![E_{else}]\!])$
$\mathcal{DS}[\![(\texttt{prim}\ O\ E_{i=1}^{n})]\!] = (\texttt{prim}\ O\ \mathcal{DS}[\![E_i]\!]_{i=1}^{n})$
$\mathcal{DS}[\![(\texttt{lam}\ I_{formal}\ E_{body})]\!] = (\texttt{lam}\ I_{formal}\ \mathcal{DS}[\![E_{body}]\!])$
$\mathcal{DS}[\![(\texttt{app}\ E_{rator}\ E_{rand})]\!] = (\texttt{app}\ \mathcal{DS}[\![E_{rator}]\!]\ \mathcal{DS}[\![E_{rand}]\!])$
$\mathcal{DS}[\![(\texttt{pair}\ E_{fst}\ E_{snd})]\!] = (\texttt{pair}\ \mathcal{DS}[\![E_{fst}]\!]\ \mathcal{DS}[\![E_{snd}]\!])$
$\mathcal{DS}[\![(\texttt{rec}\ I_{name}\ E_{body})]\!] = (\texttt{rec}\ I_{name}\ \mathcal{DS}[\![E_{body}]\!])$

$\mathcal{DS}[\![(@O\ E_{i=1}^{n})]\!] = (\texttt{prim}\ O\ \mathcal{DS}[\![E_i]\!]_{i=1}^{n})$

$\mathcal{DS}[\![(\texttt{abs}\ ()\ E)]\!] = (\texttt{lam}\ I_{fresh}\ \mathcal{DS}[\![E]\!])$, where I_{fresh} is fresh
$\mathcal{DS}[\![(\texttt{abs}\ (I)\ E)]\!] = (\texttt{lam}\ I\ \mathcal{DS}[\![E]\!])$
$\mathcal{DS}[\![(\texttt{abs}\ (I_1\ I_{rest}^{+})\ E)]\!] = (\texttt{lam}\ I_1\ \mathcal{DS}[\![(\texttt{abs}\ (I_{rest}^{+})\ E)]\!])$

$\mathcal{DS}[\![(E)]\!] = (\texttt{app}\ \mathcal{DS}[\![E]\!]\ \texttt{\#u})$
$\mathcal{DS}[\![(E_1\ E_2)]\!] = (\texttt{app}\ \mathcal{DS}[\![E_1]\!]\ \mathcal{DS}[\![E_2]\!])$
$\mathcal{DS}[\![(E_1\ E_2\ E_{rest}^{+})]\!] = \mathcal{DS}[\![((\texttt{app}\ E_1\ E_2)\ E_{rest}^{+})]\!]$

$\mathcal{DS}[\![(\texttt{list})]\!] = \texttt{\#u}$
$\mathcal{DS}[\![(\texttt{list}\ E_1\ E_{rest}^{*})]\!] = (\texttt{pair}\ \mathcal{DS}[\![E_1]\!]\ \mathcal{DS}[\![(\texttt{list}\ E_{rest}^{*})]\!])$

$\mathcal{DS}[\![(\texttt{quote}\ \texttt{\#u})]\!] = \texttt{\#u}$
$\mathcal{DS}[\![(\texttt{quote}\ B)]\!] = B$
$\mathcal{DS}[\![(\texttt{quote}\ N)]\!] = N$
$\mathcal{DS}[\![(\texttt{quote}\ Y)]\!] = (\texttt{sym}\ Y)$
$\mathcal{DS}[\![(\texttt{quote}\ (SX_{i=1}^{n}))]\!] = \mathcal{DS}[\![(\texttt{list}\ (\texttt{quote}\ SX_i)_{i=1}^{n})]\!]$

$\mathcal{DS}[\![(\texttt{cond}\ (\texttt{else}\ E_{default}))]\!] = \mathcal{DS}[\![E_{default}]\!]$
$\mathcal{DS}[\![(\texttt{cond}\ (E_{test_1}\ E_{then_1})\ (E_{test_i}\ E_{then_i})_{i=2}^{n}\ (\texttt{else}\ E_{default}))]\!]$
$\quad = (\texttt{if}\ \mathcal{DS}[\![E_{test_1}]\!]\ \mathcal{DS}[\![E_{then_1}]\!]\ \mathcal{DS}[\![(\texttt{cond}\ (E_{test_i}\ E_{then_i})_{i=2}^{n}\ (\texttt{else}\ E_{default}))]\!])$

$\mathcal{DS}[\![(\texttt{scand}\ E_{conjunct}^{*})]\!] = \text{left as an exercise.}$
$\mathcal{DS}[\![(\texttt{scor}\ E_{disjunct}^{*})]\!] = \text{left as an exercise.}$

$\mathcal{DS}[\![(\texttt{let}\ ((I_i\ E_i)_{i=1}^{n})\ E_{body})]\!] = \mathcal{DS}[\![((\texttt{abs}\ (I_{i=1}^{n})\ E_{body})\ E_{i=1}^{n})]\!]$

$\mathcal{DS}[\![(\texttt{letrec}\ ((I_i\ E_i)_{i=1}^{n})\ E_{body})]\!]$
$\quad = \mathcal{DS}[\![(\texttt{app}\ (\texttt{rec}\ I_{ChurchTuple}$
$\qquad\qquad (\texttt{lam}\ I_{selector}\ (I_{selector}\ (I_{ChurchTuple}\ (\texttt{abs}\ (I_{j=1}^{n})\ E_i))_{i=1}^{n})))$
$\qquad\qquad (\texttt{abs}\ (I_{i=1}^{n})\ E_{body}))]\!]$, where $I_{ChurchTuple}$ and $I_{selector}$ are fresh.

$\mathcal{DS}[\![(\texttt{recur}\ I_{proc}\ ((I_i\ E_i)_{i=1}^{n})\ E_{body})]\!]$
$\quad = \mathcal{DS}[\![(\texttt{letrec}\ ((I_{proc}\ (\texttt{abs}\ (I_{i=1}^{n})\ E_{body})))\ (I_{proc}\ E_{i=1}^{n}))]\!]$

Figure 6.4 The $\mathcal{DS}$ function desugars FL expressions into FLK expressions.

Then (E_{abs3} 2 3 4) desugars into

```
(app (app (app (lam a
                (lam b
                  (lam c (prim * a (prim + b c)))))
              2)
            3)
      4)
```

So (E_{abs3} 2 3 4) evaluates to *14*, (E_{abs3} 2 3) evaluates to the same procedure as (abs (c) (@* 2 (@+ 3 c))), and (E_{abs3} 2) evaluates to the same procedure as (abs (b c) (@* 2 (@+ b c))).

Because multiapplications are the only tagless construct, the lack of an explicit tag is not ambiguous. Because applications tend to be the most common kind of compound expression, eliminating the explicit tag for this case makes expressions more concise. The multiabstraction and multiapplication syntax is inspired by LISP, but, unlike FLK, LISP does not support implicit currying.

The main desugaring clause for multiabstractions (those that have the form (abs (I_1 I_{rest}^+) E)) is defined in a recursive way that processes one parameter at a time. The argument abstraction to $\mathcal{DS}$ is made smaller by one parameter on each call until the base case of a single parameter is reached. A similar recursive strategy is used for desugaring multiapplications.

The nullary (zero-parameter) case for app is special because it is necessary to invent an arbitrary operand expression. We choose #u, but any expression would do. The nullary case for abs is special because it is necessary to invent a parameter name for the lam that results from the desugaring. As we shall see in Section 6.3.4, it is important to choose a name that does not conflict with other names that already appear in the program. In definitions of program transformations like desugaring, we will often declare that new names must be **fresh**. This is an informal way of specifying that the new name should be different from any name appearing elsewhere in the program. In Section 6.3.5, we will formalize a way of choosing new names that do not conflict with existing ones.

The list construct is a shorthand for creating lists by a sequence of nested pairings. (list E_1 ... E_n) constructs a unit-terminated chain of n pairs linked by their second components, where the value of E_i is the value of the first element of the ith pair in the chain. For example,

```
(list (@+ 1 2) (@= 3 4) (pair 4 5) (sym end))
```

is equivalent to

```
(pair (@+ 1 2)
      (pair (@= 3 4)
            (pair (pair 4 5)
                  (pair (sym end)
                        #u))))
```

The `quote` expression facilitates the construction of s-expressions in FL. These are recursively defined to be literals (unit, numeric, boolean, and symbolic) and lists of s-expressions. Quoted s-expressions are a very concise way to specify tree-structured data. The `quote` construct can be viewed as a means of constructing a tree from a printed representation of the tree. For example, the s-expression (`quote (1 (#t three) (four 5 six))`) desugars to

```
(list 1
      (list #t (sym three))
      (list (sym four) 5 (sym six)))
```

The concise `quote` notation for s-expressions facilitates writing program phrases from languages with s-expression syntax that are to be used as inputs for program-manipulating programs (like interpreters, translators, and analyzers). For example, the POSTFIX program (`postfix 1 (2 mul) exec`) can be represented as the FL s-expression (`quote (postfix 1 (2 mul) exec)`). This is *much* simpler for programmers to read and write than the corresponding kernel expression:

```
(pair (sym postfix)
      (pair 1
            (pair (pair 2 (pair (sym mul) #u))
                  (pair (sym exec)
                        #u))))
```

The `cond` construct is an *n*-way conditional that stands for a nested sequence of `if` expressions. For example,

```
(cond ((@>= grade 90) (sym A))
      ((@>= grade 80) (sym B))
      ((@>= grade 70) (sym C))
      ((@>= grade 60) (sym D))
      (else (sym F)))
```

desugars to

```
(if (@>= grade 90) (sym A)
    (if (@>= grade 80) (sym B)
        (if (@>= grade 70) (sym C)
            (if (@>= grade 60) (sym D) (sym F)))))
```

The `scand` and `scor` expressions provide for so-called **short-circuit** evaluation of logical conjunctions and disjunctions, respectively. If a false value is encountered in the left-to-right evaluation of the conjuncts of a **scand** expression, then its result is the false value, regardless of whether subsequent conjuncts contain errors or infinite loops. So (**scand** (@= 1 2) (@/ 3 0) (@< 4 5)) evaluates to *false* but (**scand** (@/ 3 0) (@= 1 2) (@< 4 5)) signals a divide-by-zero error. Similarly, if a true value is encountered in the left-to-right evaluation of the disjuncts of a **scor** expression, then the result is the true value, regardless of whether the subsequent disjuncts contain errors or infinite loops. Primitive applications involving the primitive operators **and** and **or** do *not* use short-circuit evaluation; they evaluate all operand expressions. So (@**and** (@= 1 2) (@/ 3 0)) and (@**or** (@< 1 2) (@/ 3 0)) both signal a divide-by-zero error. The desugaring definitions for **scand** and **scor** are left as Exercise 6.1.

The **let** expression is a convenient way to name intermediate results in a computation. The expression (**let** ((I_1 E_1) ... (I_n E_n)) E_{body}) evaluates the body expression E_{body} in a context where the names I_1, ..., I_n are bound to the values of the expressions E_1, ..., E_n. For example,

```
(let ((a (@* 4 5))
      (b (@+ 3 4)))
  (@/ (@+ a b) (@- a b)))
```

has the same value as (@/ (@+ 20 7) (@- 20 7)) or (@/ 27 13), namely *2*. The names I_1, ..., I_n introduced by the **let** can be referenced only in the body, not in the definition expressions E_1, ..., E_n:

```
(let ((a 1))
  (@* (let ((a 20)
            (b (@+ a 300)))  {refers to outer a, so b is 301}
        (@- b a))  {refers to inner a, so difference is 281}
      a))  {refers to outer a, so product is 281}
```

The **let** construct desugars into a multiapplication of a multiabstraction. That is, (**let** ((I_1 E_1) ... (I_n E_n)) E_{body}) desugars to

((**abs** (I_1 ... I_n) E_{body}) E_1 ... E_n)

Note that E_1, ..., E_n appear outside the **abs** and so cannot reference the parameters I_1, ..., I_n. The part of the program in which a declared name can be referenced is called its **scope**; we will study this notion in Section 6.3.1. That **let** can be expressed in terms of an abstraction underscores the fact that abstractions are a fundamental means of naming in FLK. Here is a (partial) desugaring of the two **let** examples from above:

((**abs** (a b) (@/ (@+ a b) (@- a b))) (@* 4 5) (@+ 3 4))

```
((abs (a)
   (@* ((abs (a b) (@- b a))
        20
        (@+ a 300))
       a))
 1)
```

The (letrec ((*I₁* *E₁*) ... (*Iₙ* *Eₙ*)) *E_body*) expression is similar to the let expression except that the names $I_1, \ldots, I_n$ *can* be referenced inside the definition expressions $E_1, \ldots, E_n$. The letrec expression is similar to the rec expression, except that it can be thought of as solving a group of mutually recursive equations. For example,

```
(letrec ((even? (abs (x) (if (@= x 0) #t (odd? (@- x 1)))))
         (odd? (abs (y) (if (@= y 0) #f (even? (@- y 1))))))
  (list (even? 0) (odd? 1) (odd? 2) (even? 3)))
```

evaluates to ◁*true, true, false, false*▷.

The letrec desugaring is inspired by the observation made in Section 5.1.1 that n mutually recursive definitions can always be rephrased as a single recursive definition of a tuple with n components. Because FLK's rec construct is able to "solve" a single recursive definition, we can use it to solve mutually recursive definitions as long as we can combine them into a tuple-like structure.

Since the letrec desugaring is tricky, we develop it in two passes. In the first pass, we combine the mutually recursive definitions into a list. As a concrete example, we can express the even?/odd? example using rec and list as follows:

```
(let ((outer (rec inner
               (let ((even? (nth 1 inner))
                     (odd? (nth 2 inner)))
                 (list (abs (x)
                         (if (@= x 0) #t (odd? (@- x 1))))
                       (abs (y)
                         (if (@= y 0) #f (even? (@- y 1)))))))))
  (let ((even? (nth 1 outer))
        (odd? (nth 2 outer)))
    (list (even? 0) (odd? 1) (odd? 2) (even? 3))))
```

Here we assume that nth is an identifier in the standard library bound to a procedure that takes an integer i and a list and returns the ith element of the list, where elements are indexed starting at 1. (See Figure 6.8 for a definition of nth.) In the expression (rec inner ...), inner denotes a list of the even? and odd? functions. The nth function is used to extract the two functions from this list, let is used to name these functions even? and odd?, and list glues together abstractions that define these functions. Because let and list are both nonstrict in FL, the solution to (rec inner ...) (as computed using the least fixed point technique from Chapter 5) is indeed a list of the two desired functions. This list is then named outer and is deconstructed into named components that become available for the evaluation of the body expression of the original letrec.

We can generalize this example into the following almost-correct desugaring for letrec:

$$\mathcal{DS}[\![(\texttt{letrec } ((I_i \ E_i)_{i=1}^n) \ E_{body})]\!]$$
$$= \mathcal{DS}[\![(\texttt{let } ((I_{outer} \ (\texttt{rec } I_{inner}$$
$$(\texttt{let } ((I_i \ (\texttt{nth } i \ I_{inner}))_{i=1}^n) \ (\texttt{list } E_{i=1}^n)))))$$
$$(\texttt{let } ((I_i \ (\texttt{nth } i \ I_{outer}))_{i=1}^n) \ E_{body}))]\!],$$
where I_{outer} and I_{inner} are fresh identifiers.

Note that both I_{inner} and I_{outer} must be fresh names. Whenever we choose more than one fresh name, we always assume that the fresh names are pairwise distinct, so I_{inner} is necessarily a different name from I_{outer}.[5]

The above desugaring is almost right but is problematic for two technical reasons. First, it assumes that the index arguments of nth can be *integers* when in fact they must be numerals denoting the corresponding integers. Second, employing the standard identifier nth is not only unaesthetic but also can lead to bugs as a result of name capture (see Section 6.3.4).

For these reasons, we present an alternative desugaring that circumvents both problems. This desugaring is based on the same idea but represents tuples as procedures. In this representation, which we shall call a **Church tuple**, an n-element list is represented as a unary procedure whose single argument is an n-argument selector procedure that is applied to the n elements of the list. If $I_{ChurchTuple}$ is bound to an n-element Church tuple, then the application

$(I_{ChurchTuple} \ (\texttt{abs } (I_1 \ \dots \ I_n) \ I_i))$

extracts the ith element of the list. More generally, the application

$(I_{ChurchTuple} \ (\texttt{abs } (I_1 \ \dots \ I_n) \ E))$

returns the value of E in a context where each I_i is bound to the ith element of the list. For example, suppose I_{CT} is bound to the Church tuple

$(\texttt{abs } (I_{selector}) \ (I_{selector} \ 2 \ 8 \ 1 \ 6))$

Then

$(I_{CT} \ (\texttt{abs } (\texttt{a b c d}) \ \texttt{a})) \ \xrightarrow[FL]{} \ 2$
$(I_{CT} \ (\texttt{abs } (\texttt{a b c d}) \ \texttt{c})) \ \xrightarrow[FL]{} \ 1$

---

[5]This fact is not important here since the desugaring has the same meaning if I_{inner} and I_{outer} are the same name.

$(I_{CT}$ (abs (a b c d) (@- (@* b d) d))) $\xrightarrow[FL]{}$ *42*
$(I_{CT}$ (abs (a b c d) (list d b a c))) $\xrightarrow[FL]{}$ *◁6, 8, 2, 1▷*

If we modify the even?/odd? example to use Church tuples in place of regular lists, we obtain the following:

```
(app (rec ct
        (lam s (s (ct (abs (even? odd?)
                      (abs (x)
                         (if (@= x 0) #t (odd? (@- x 1)))))
                   (ct (abs (even? odd?)
                      (abs (y)
                         (if (@= y 0) #f (even? (@- y 1)))))))))
     (abs (even? odd?)
       (list (even? 0) (odd? 1) (odd? 2) (even? 3))))
```

Here, ct names a Church tuple of the even? and odd? procedures. In the body of the rec, these two components are extracted by applying ct to selector procedures of the form (abs (even? odd?) ...). The Church tuple returned by the rec is also directly applied to such a selector to evaluate the body of the original letrec. Note how this approach avoids the use of nth and let to extract and name parts.

This example can be generalized to our official letrec desugaring:

$$\mathcal{DS}[\![\text{(letrec} \ ((I_1 \ E_1) \ \ldots \ (I_n \ E_n)) \ E_{body})]\!]$$
$$= \mathcal{DS}[\![\text{(app (rec} \ I_{ChurchTuple}$$
$$\text{(lam} \ I_{selector} \ (I_{selector} \ (I_{ChurchTuple} \ \text{(abs} \ (I_1 \ \ldots \ I_n) \ E_1))$$
$$\vdots$$
$$(I_{ChurchTuple} \ \text{(abs} \ (I_1 \ \ldots \ I_n) \ E_n)))))$$
$$\text{(abs} \ (I_1 \ \ldots \ I_n) \ E_{body}))]\!], \text{where } I_{ChurchTuple} \text{ and } I_{selector} \text{ are fresh.}$$

In this case, $I_{ChurchTuple}$ and $I_{selector}$ must not only be fresh, they must also be distinct.

A common idiom is to create a locally recursive procedure and then apply it immediately to initial values to start a computation. For example, an iterative factorial procedure can be expressed in FL as:

```
(abs (n)
  (letrec ((iter (abs (num ans)
                   (if (= num 0)
                       ans
                       (iter (- num 1) (* num ans)))))))
      (iter n 1)))
```

We can make this idiom easier to express by providing a new sugar construct

(recur I_{proc} ((I_1 E_{init_1}) ... (I_n E_{init_n})) E_{body})

that desugars to

(letrec ((I_{proc} (abs (I_1 ... I_n) E_{body})))
  (I_{proc} E_{init_1} ... E_{init_n}))

The recur expression is similar in structure to a let expression except that it has an additional identifier I_{proc}. Each of the n variables I_i is first bound to the value of the corresponding initialization expression E_{init_i} and then E_{body} is evaluated in a context where these bindings are in effect *and* the name I_{proc} refers to a procedure with parameters I_1, ..., I_n that computes E_{body}. Using recur, the iterative factorial procedure from above can be expressed more succinctly as

```
(abs (n)
  (recur iter ((num n) (ans 1))
    (if (= num 0)
        ans
        (iter (- num 1) (* num ans)))))
```

Exercise 6.1 Provide the missing desugarings for FL's scand and scor constructs (see Figure 6.4).

Exercise 6.2 It is often useful for the value of a let-bound variable to depend on the value of a previous let-bound variable. In FL, achieving this behavior requires nested let expressions. For example:

```
(abs (a b)
  (let ((r (@+ a b)))
    (let ((r-squared (@* r r)))
      (let ((r-cubed (@* r r-squared)))
        (@+ r (@+ r-squared r-cubed)))))))
```

Many LISP dialects support a let* construct that (other than the keyword let*) looks just like a let construct. However, the meaning of let* differs from let: its variables are guaranteed to be bound to the values of the associated definitions in the order in which they appear in the list of bindings. A definition expression in let* can refer to the result of a previous binding within the same let*. Using let*, the above example can be rendered:

```
(abs (a b)
  (let* ((r (@+ a b))
         (r-squared (@* r r))
         (r-cubed (@* r r-squared)))
    (@+ r (@+ r-squared r-cubed))))
```

Extend the desugaring function $\mathcal{DS}$ to desugar let* expressions.

Exercise 6.3 Ben Bitdiddle is upset by the desugaring for nullary (i.e., zero-parameter) abstractions and applications. He argues (correctly) that, according to the desugarings, the FL expression ((abs (x) x)) will return #u. He believes that evaluating this expression should give an error.

One way to fix this problem is to package up multiple arguments into some sort of data structure. See Exercise 6.21 for an example of this approach. Here we will consider other approaches for handling nullary abstractions and applications.

a. Bud Lojack suggests desugaring (abs () E) into E and (E) into E. Give examples of FL expressions that have a questionable behavior under this desugaring.

b. Abby Stracksen suggests a desugaring in which

$$\mathcal{DS}[\![(E)]\!] = \text{(app (app } \mathcal{DS}[\![E]\!] \text{ \#t) \#u)}$$
$$\mathcal{DS}[\![(E_1\ E_2)]\!] = \text{(app (app } \mathcal{DS}[\![E_1]\!] \text{ \#f) } \mathcal{DS}[\![E_2]\!])$$
$$\mathcal{DS}[\![(E_1\ E_2\ E_{rest}^+)]\!] = \text{((app (app } \mathcal{DS}[\![E_1]\!] \text{ \#f) } \mathcal{DS}[\![E_2]\!])$$
$$\mathcal{DS}[\![(E_{rest}^+)]\!])$$

   i. Give the corresponding desugarings for multiabstractions.

   ii. What value does ((abs (x) x)) have under this desugaring?

c. Ben reasons that the fundamental problem exhibited by the nullary desugarings is that there is no way to call a procedure without passing it an argument. He decides to extend FLK with the following kernel construct for parameterless procedures:

   (freeze E) returns a "frozen" value containing the unevaluated expression E.

   (thaw E) evaluates the expression within a frozen value. It gives an error if called on any value other than one created by freeze.

   Show how freeze and thaw can be used to fix Ben's problem.

d. Sam Antics doesn't like the fact that multiabstractions and multiapplications both have three desugaring clauses. Figuring that only two clauses should suffice in each case, he develops the following desugaring rules based on Ben's freeze and thaw commands:

$$\mathcal{DS}[\![\text{(abs () } E)]\!] = \mathcal{DS}[\![\text{(freeze } E)]\!]$$
$$\mathcal{DS}[\![\text{(abs } (I_1\ I_{rest}^*)\ E)]\!] = \text{(lam } I_1\ \mathcal{DS}[\![\text{(abs } (I_{rest}^*)\ E)]\!])$$
$$\mathcal{DS}[\![(E)]\!] = \mathcal{DS}[\![\text{(thaw } E)]\!]$$
$$\mathcal{DS}[\![(E_1\ E_{rest}^*)]\!] = \mathcal{DS}[\![\text{((app } E_1\ E_2)\ \mathcal{DS}[\![E_{rest}^*]\!])]\!]$$

   Discuss the strengths and weaknesses of Sam's desugaring.

Exercise 6.4 We will say that two constructs are **equipotent** (roughly, "of equal power") if each can be expressed as a desugaring into the other. For example, multiargument procedures and single-argument procedures are equipotent: multiargument abstractions and applications can be desugared into single-argument ones via currying;

and single-argument abstractions and applications are a special subcase of the multi-argument ones. On the other hand, lists and procedures are *not* equipotent; although Church tuples are a technique to represent lists as procedures, procedure abstractions and applications cannot be represented as pairs.

We have considered a version of FLK where `rec` is the kernel recursion construct and FL's `letrec` is desugared into `rec`. Show that `rec` and `letrec` are equipotent by providing a desugaring of `rec` into `letrec` (i.e., suppose that `letrec` is the kernel FLK construct and define `rec` as syntactic sugar).

Exercise 6.5 The `letrec` desugaring based on `nth` presented in the above discussion used three `let` expressions and two fresh identifiers. It is possible to simplify this desugaring to one that uses only one `let` expression and one fresh identifier. The simplified desugaring has the following form:

$$\mathcal{DS}[\![(\texttt{letrec } ((I_i \; E_i)_{i=1}^n) \; E_0)]\!]$$
$$= \mathcal{DS}[\![(\texttt{nth } index \; (\texttt{rec } I_{list} \; (\texttt{let } bindings \; body)))]\!], \text{ where } I_{list} \text{ is fresh}.$$

Complete the desugaring by fleshing out *index*, *bindings*, and *body*.

Exercise 6.6 The desugaring for `letrec` in Figure 6.4 requires a pair of fresh identifiers. There is another desugaring for `letrec` that requires no fresh identifiers whatsoever. This desugaring, known as the **Bekić expansion**, has a recursive structure not exhibited by the other versions. Below is a skeleton of the desugaring.

$$\mathcal{DS}[\![(\texttt{letrec } ((I_1 \; E_1) \; \ldots \; (I_n \; E_n)) \; E_0)]\!]$$
$$= \mathcal{DS}[\![(\texttt{let } ((I_1 \; (\texttt{rec } I_1 \; \square_1)) \; \ldots \; (I_n \; (\texttt{rec } I_n \; \square_n))) \; E_0)]\!]$$

where the boxes $\square_i$ are to be filled in appropriately.

a. Give the general form for expressions that fill the boxes $\square_i$ in such a way that the above skeleton defines a correct desugaring for `letrec`.

b. Using your approach, how many `rec`s will appear in a desugaring of a `letrec` with 5 bindings?

c. Give a closed-form solution for the number of `rec`s that will appear in a desugaring of a `letrec` with n bindings.

d. Comment on the practicality of this `letrec` desugaring.

Exercise 6.7 Prove that the expression-desugaring function $\mathcal{DS}$ specified in Figure 6.4 is well defined. That is, prove that if E is a valid FL expression, then $\mathcal{DS}[\![E]\!]$ is a valid FLK expression. Your proof should be by induction. However, it cannot be by structural induction, since in many clauses of the definition, $\mathcal{DS}$ is called on an expression that is *not* a subexpression of the original expression. The key challenge of this proof is developing a metric on FL expressions that decreases with every call to $\mathcal{DS}$.

Desugaring Definitions and Programs

The top-level program construct (fl $(I_1 \ldots I_n)$ $E_{pgmBody}$ $D_1 \ldots D_k$) evaluates the program body expression $E_{pgmBody}$ in a context where

- the formal program parameters $I_1, \ldots, I_n$ are bound to the program arguments;

- each name I_{name} in a definition D of the form (def I_{name} E_{defn}) is bound to the value of the definition expression E_{defn};

- each procedure name $I_{procName}$ in a definition of the form

$$\text{(def } (I_{procName} \; I'_1 \; \ldots \; I'_n) \; E_{procBody})$$

  is bound to a (curried) procedure with formal parameters $I'_1, \ldots, I'_n$ and body $E_{procBody}$; and

- each member of a set of **standard identifiers** (names in the standard library) is bound to the value specified by the library. We will assume that the standard library at the very least binds each primitive operator name to a procedure performing the corresponding operation. E.g., not is bound to (abs (a) (@not a)), + is bound to (abs (a b) (@+ a b)), etc. We will have more to say about the standard library in Section 6.2.3.

Definitions make it convenient to name top-level program values (typically procedures) that are used within the program body E_{body}. The value expressions of the definitions are evaluated in a mutually recursive context: the expression in one definition may refer to any name defined by any other definition. The program parameters and standard identifiers are visible within the definitions as well as within the program body.

Consider the following sample FL program:

```
(fl (a b) (pair (even? sum) (odd? prod))
  (def sum (+ a b))
  (def prod (* a b))
  (def (even? x) (if (= x 0) #t (odd? (- x 1))))
  (def (odd? y) (if (= y 0) #f (even? (- y 1)))))
```

The program body expression (pair (even? sum) (odd? prod)) refers to the values sum and prod and to the procedures even? and odd? introduced via def. Note that even? and odd? have mutually recursive definitions. The fact that standard identifiers are bound to appropriate procedures in the definitions and program body means that =, -, +, and * can all be used without the prim tag or @ sugar.

$$\mathcal{DS}_{pgm} : \text{Prog}_{FL} \rightarrow \text{Prog}_{FLK}$$

$$\mathcal{DS}_{pgm}[\![(\texttt{fl } (I^*_{pgmFormal})\ E_{pgmBody}\ (\texttt{def } I_{name_i}\ E_{defn_i})_{i=1}^{k-1}$$
$$\qquad (\texttt{def } (I_{procName}\ I^*_{procFormal})\ E_{procBody})\ D^n_{j=k+1})]\!]$$
$$= \mathcal{DS}_{pgm}[\![(\texttt{fl } (I^*_{pgmFormal})\ E_{pgmBody}\ (\texttt{def } I_{name_i}\ E_{defn_i})_{i=1}^{k-1}$$
$$\qquad\quad (\texttt{def } I_{procName}\ (\texttt{abs } (I^*_{procFormal})\ E_{procBody}))\ D^n_{j=k+1})]\!]$$

$$\mathcal{DS}_{pgm}\ [\![(\texttt{fl } (I^*_{pgmFormal})\ E_{pgmBody}\ (\texttt{def } I_{name_i}\ E_{defn_i})_{i=1}^{n})$$
$$= (\texttt{flk } (I^*_{pgmFormal})$$
$$\quad \mathcal{DS}[\![(\texttt{letrec } ((\texttt{not } (\texttt{abs } (\texttt{x})\ (\texttt{prim not x})))$$
$$\qquad\qquad\qquad (\texttt{+ } (\texttt{abs } (\texttt{x y})\ (\texttt{prim + x y})))$$
$$\qquad\qquad\qquad ;\ldots \textit{other standard library bindings}\ldots$$
$$\qquad\qquad\qquad)$$
$$\qquad\qquad\quad (\texttt{letrec } ((I_{name_i}\ E_{defn_i})_{i=1}^{n})$$
$$\qquad\qquad\quad E_{pgmBody}))]\!])$$

Figure 6.5 Desugaring FL programs into FLK programs.

The desugaring of an FL program into an FLK program is performed by the function $\mathcal{DS}_{pgm}$ defined in Figure 6.5. The first clause is responsible for desugaring each definition of the form $(\texttt{def } (I_{procName}\ I^*_{procFormal})\ E_{procBody})$ into one of the form $(\texttt{def } I_{procName}\ (\texttt{abs } (I^*_{procFormal})\ E_{procBody}))$. Once all the appropriate procedure definitions have been desugared in this way, the second clause transforms an FL program into an FLK program by wrapping the body expression in (1) a letrec that introduces standard bindings (which may be mutually recursive) and (2) a letrec that introduces the mutually recursive definitions. Because the letrec for definitions is defined inside the letrec for standard bindings, the definition expressions $E_{defn_1}, \ldots, E_{defn_n}$ can refer to the standard bindings.

Note that if a program parameter name is the same as a standard binding name or a name introduced by def, it will be impossible to refer to the parameter in the definition expressions or body because it will be "shadowed" by the other name. It is also possible for the names introduced by standard bindings to be shadowed within the definitions or body of a program. For instance, the expression (+ 2 3) does not necessarily denote 5 within the body or a definition of an FL program. Why? Because it might occur in a context like (let ((+ (abs (x y) (@* x y))) $\square$), in which case the name + stands for a multiplication procedure and (+ 2 3) denotes 6. In order to unambiguously specify addition in any context, it is necessary to use (prim + ...).

Desugaring Contexts

$\mathbb{DC} \in \text{DesugaringContext}$

$\mathbb{DC} ::= \Box \mid \text{(fl } (I_{formal}^*) \; E_{body} \; D_{i=1}^{k-1} \; \mathbb{DC} \; D_{j=k+1}^n) \mid \text{(flk } (I_{formal}^*) \; \mathbb{DC})$
$\qquad \mid \text{(if } \mathbb{DC} \; E_{then} \; E_{else}) \mid \text{(if } E_{test} \; \mathbb{DC} \; E_{else}) \mid \text{(if } E_{test} \; E_{then} \; \mathbb{DC})$
$\qquad \mid \text{(prim } O_{primop} \; E_{i=1}^{k-1} \; \mathbb{DC} \; E_{j=k+1}^n)$
$\qquad \mid \text{(lam } I_{formal} \; \mathbb{DC}) \mid \text{(app } \mathbb{DC} \; E_{rand}) \mid \text{(app } E_{rator} \; \mathbb{DC})$
$\qquad \mid \text{(pair } \mathbb{DC} \; E_{snd}) \mid \text{(pair } E_{fst} \; \mathbb{DC}) \mid \text{(rec } I_{name} \; \mathbb{DC})$

Figure 6.6   Rewriting approach to desugaring FL into FLK, Part 1.

Exercise 6.8 In FL, definitions are allowed only within the `fl` construct at "top level"; yet a local form of definition within `abs` and `let` expressions would often be useful. Generalize the idea of definitions by modifying FL to support local definitions. Design a syntax for your change, and show how to express it in terms of a desugaring.

Rewriting-based Approach to Desugaring

Intuitively, desugaring is a program transformation in which sugar constructs are rewritten to kernel constructs. The rewriting nature of desugaring is somewhat obscured in the definition of the desugaring function $\mathcal{DS}$ in Figures 6.4 and 6.5. Because of the recursive nature of the $\mathcal{DS}$ function, it rewrites an FL expression to an FLK expression "all at once" rather than "one step at a time."

Here we present an alternative specification of FL desugaring that describes the desugaring process as a sequence of discrete desugaring steps. In this approach, based on rewriting, the recursive nature of the desugaring process will be implicit rather than explicit. Since the rewriting-based approach to desugaring is easier to specify than desugaring functions, we will often use the rewriting-based approach in the remainder of this book.

Figure 6.7 presents one-step desugaring rules of the form $S \leadsto_{ds} S'$, where S and S' are viewed as generic s-expressions rather than FL or FLK expressions, definitions, or programs. These rules describe desugaring at the expression, definition, and program level. These desugaring rules cannot be applied just anywhere, but only in the desugaring contexts described by the productions for $\mathbb{DC}$ in Figure 6.6. These contexts allow the desugaring of FL program expressions, definitions within an FL program, and FL sugar constructs appearing within an FLK expression.

Restricting the context in which the desugaring rules can be applied is essential for prohibiting invalid desugarings. For example, without the restrictions, the parameter list $(I_1 \; I_2)$ in an `abs` expression could be misinterpreted as a

---

Desugaring Reduction Rules ($\leadsto_{ds}$)

$(@ O_{primop} \; E_{i=1}^n) \leadsto_{ds} (\texttt{prim} \; O_{primop} \; E_{i=1}^n)$

$(\texttt{abs} \; () \; E) \leadsto_{ds} (\texttt{lam} \; I_{fresh} \; E)$, where I_{fresh} is fresh
$(\texttt{abs} \; (I) \; E) \leadsto_{ds} (\texttt{lam} \; I \; E)$
$(\texttt{abs} \; (I_1 \; I_{rest}^+) \; E) \leadsto_{ds} (\texttt{lam} \; I_1 \; (\texttt{abs} \; (I_{rest}^+) \; E))$

$(E) \leadsto_{ds} (\texttt{app} \; E \; \texttt{\#u})$ \qquad $(E_1 \; E_2) \leadsto_{ds} (\texttt{app} \; E_1 \; E_2)$
$(E_1 \; E_2 \; E_{rest}^+) \leadsto_{ds} ((\texttt{app} \; E_1 \; E_2) \; E_{rest}^+)$

$(\texttt{list}) \leadsto_{ds} \texttt{\#u}$ \qquad $(\texttt{list} \; E_1 \; E_{rest}^*) \leadsto_{ds} (\texttt{pair} \; E_1 \; (\texttt{list} \; E_{rest}^*))$

$(\texttt{quote} \; \texttt{\#u}) \leadsto_{ds} \texttt{\#u}$ \qquad $(\texttt{quote} \; B) \leadsto_{ds} B$ \qquad $(\texttt{quote} \; N) \leadsto_{ds} N$
$(\texttt{quote} \; Y) \leadsto_{ds} (\texttt{sym} \; Y)$
$(\texttt{quote} \; (SX_{i=1}^n)) \leadsto_{ds} (\texttt{list} \; (\texttt{quote} \; SX_i)_{i=1}^n)$

$(\texttt{cond} \; (\texttt{else} \; E_{default})) \leadsto_{ds} E_{default}$
$(\texttt{cond} \; (E_{test_1} \; E_{then_1}) \; (E_{test_i} \; E_{then_i})_{i=2}^n \; (\texttt{else} \; E_{default}))$
$\quad \leadsto_{ds} (\texttt{if} \; E_{test_1} \; E_{then_1} \; (\texttt{cond} \; (E_{test_i} \; E_{then_i})_{i=2}^n \; (\texttt{else} \; E_{default})))$

$(\texttt{scand} \; E_{conjunct}^*) \leadsto_{ds}$ left as an exercise.
$(\texttt{scor} \; E_{conjunct}^*) \leadsto_{ds}$ left as an exercise.

$(\texttt{let} \; ((I_i \; E_i)_{i=1}^n) \; E_{body}) \leadsto_{ds} ((\texttt{abs} \; (I_{i=1}^n) \; E_{body}) \; E_{i=1}^n)$

$(\texttt{letrec} \; ((I_i \; E_i)_{i=1}^n) \; E_{body})$
$\quad \leadsto_{ds} (\texttt{app} \; (\texttt{rec} \; I_{ChurchTuple}$
$\qquad\qquad\qquad (\texttt{lam} \; I_{selector}$
$\qquad\qquad\qquad\quad (I_{selector} \; (I_{ChurchTuple} \; (\texttt{abs} \; (I_{j=1}^n) \; E_i))_{i=1}^n)))$
$\qquad\qquad (\texttt{abs} \; (I_{i=1}^n) \; E_{body}))$, where $I_{ChurchTuple}, I_{selector}$ are fresh.

$(\texttt{recur} \; I_{proc} \; ((I_i \; E_i)_{i=1}^n) \; E_{body})$
$\quad \leadsto_{ds} (\texttt{letrec} \; ((I_{proc} \; (\texttt{abs} \; (I_{i=1}^n) \; E_{body}))) \; (I_{proc} \; E_{i=1}^n))$

$(\texttt{def} \; (I_{procName} \; I_{procFormal}^*) \; E_{procBody})$
$\quad \leadsto_{ds} (\texttt{def} \; I_{procName} \; (\texttt{abs} \; (I_{procFormal}^*) \; E_{procBody}))$

$(\texttt{fl} \; (I_{pgmFormal}^*) \; E_{pgmBody} \; (\texttt{def} \; I_{name_i} \; E_{defn_i})_{i=1}^n)$
$\quad \leadsto_{ds} (\texttt{flk} \; (I_{pgmFormal}^*)$
$\qquad\quad (\texttt{letrec} \; (\dots \; standard \; library \; bindings \; \dots)$
$\qquad\qquad (\texttt{letrec} \; ((I_{name_i} \; E_{defn_i})_{i=1}^n)$
$\qquad\qquad\quad E_{pgmBody})))$

Desugaring Transition Relation ($\Rightarrow_{ds}$)
$\quad \mathbb{DC}\{\mathcal{S}\} \Rightarrow_{ds} \mathbb{DC}\{\mathcal{S}'\}$, where $\mathcal{S} \leadsto_{ds} \mathcal{S}'$

Figure 6.7 Rewriting approach to desugaring FL into FLK, Part 2.

procedure application and incorrectly be desugared to (app I_1 I_2). Similarly, a binding $(I\ E)$ within an let or letrec could be misinterpreted as a procedure application without the context restriction.

Desugaring contexts and desugaring rules combine to define desugaring transitions. If $S \leadsto_{ds} S'$ then $\mathbb{DC}\{S\} \Rightarrow_{ds} \mathbb{DC}\{S'\}$ for all desugaring contexts $\mathbb{DC}$ (including $\square$). For example:

```
  (abs (a b) (list (@+ a b) (@- a b)))
⇒ds (lam a (abs (b) (list (@+ a b) (@- a b))))
⇒ds (lam a (lam b (list (@+ a b) (@- a b))))
⇒ds (lam a (lam b (pair (@+ a b) (list (@- a b)))))
⇒ds (lam a (lam b (pair (prim + a b) (list (@- a b)))))
⇒ds (lam a (lam b (pair (prim + a b) (pair (@- a b) (list)))))
⇒ds (lam a (lam b (pair (prim + a b) (pair (@- a b) #u))))
⇒ds (lam a (lam b (pair (prim + a b) (pair (prim - a b) #u))))
```

Because desugaring contexts $\mathbb{DC}$ allow desugarings to take place in an arbitrary subexpression of a prim, app, if, or pair expression, the transition relation $\Rightarrow_{ds}$ is not deterministic. However, it is possible to show that $\Rightarrow_{ds}$ is confluent and terminating. So it is sensible to define desugaring functions as follows:

$$\mathcal{DS} : \mathrm{Exp}_{FL} \to \mathrm{Exp}_{FLK} = \lambda E\ .\ E',\ \text{where}\ E \overset{*}{\Rightarrow}_{ds} E' \not\Rightarrow_{ds}$$
$$\mathcal{DS}_{pgm} : \mathrm{Prog}_{FL} \to \mathrm{Prog}_{FLK} = \lambda P\ .\ P',\ \text{where}\ P \overset{*}{\Rightarrow}_{ds} P' \not\Rightarrow_{ds}$$

In fact, these are the same functions as those defined via the recursive function approach.

Exercise 6.9

a. Prove that $\Rightarrow_{ds}$ is confluent.

b. Prove that $\Rightarrow_{ds}$ is terminating. That is, if S is an s-expression, then there is no infinite transition path beginning with S.

c. Prove that if S is an s-expression for a valid FL expression and $S \Rightarrow_{ds} S' \not\Rightarrow_{ds}$, then S' is an s-expression for a valid FLK expression.

d. Prove that if S is an s-expression for a valid FL program and $S \Rightarrow_{ds} S' \not\Rightarrow_{ds}$, then S' is an s-expression for a valid FLK program.

e. Prove that the expression-desugaring function $\mathcal{DS}$ defined in terms of $\Rightarrow_{ds}$ is the same as the desugaring function $\mathcal{DS}$ defined in Figure 6.4 on page 220.

f. Prove that the program-desugaring function $\mathcal{DS}_{pgm}$ defined in terms of $\Rightarrow_{ds}$ is the same as the desugaring function $\mathcal{DS}_{pgm}$ defined in Figure 6.5 on page 231.

6.2.3   The FL Standard Library

A **standard library** is a collection of named values (frequently procedural values) that may be used within a program. The library often consists of two parts:

1. a collection of **built-in values** (such as FLK's #u, #t, #f, and $O \in$ Primop) that often must be used in the context of special syntax (such as prim in FLK);

2. a collection of **top-level values** that can be assumed to be defined in the outermost scope of a program.

Typically, built-in operators *cannot* (or at least cannot easily or efficiently) be defined by the programmer. These include operators for fundamental values like booleans, characters, and numbers (floating point as well as integer) as well as data structures like strings, arrays, and message-passing objects. In contrast, top-level values are values that *can* be defined by the programmer, but it is more convenient if the language provides these as "predefined" values.

The advantage of a standard library is that it allows many constants and procedures to be factored out of the syntax of the language. For example, we can easily extend FLK with such values as floating point numbers, characters, and strings by adding (1) new literal expression forms for each kind of value and (2) new primitive operators in Primop for manipulating these values. Such additions are modular in the sense that no new kernel expressions (except for the literal values) must be added to the language. It is even easier to extend FLK with data structures like matrices, stacks, queues, lists, trees, and graphs, since these can all be defined via top-level procedures that create and manipulate such data structures.

Of course, it is still necessary to specify the components of the library somewhere in a language description. Typically the library is specified by listing all elements in the library along with a description of the semantics of each one. We have already seen such a listing for FLK's primitive operators in Figure 6.2 on page 213. For real-world languages like JAVA and C++, such descriptions usually come in the form of an **Application Programming Interface (API)**, which specifies the number and types of arguments for each function/procedure/method along with an informal English description of its semantics.

We have seen in the FL program-desugaring function $\mathcal{DS}_{pgm}$ (defined in Figure 6.5 on page 231) that top-level standard library values can be specified via a sequence of bindings of the form $(I_{name}\ E_{value})$. So another way of specifying such top-level values is to list these bindings. Figures 6.8 and 6.9 show the top-

```
(not (lam x (@not x)))

    ⋮ Similar for other unary primitives.
(+ (abs (x y) (@+ x y)))

    ⋮ Similar for other binary primitives.
(true #t)

(false #f)

(cons (abs (x xs) (pair x xs)))

(car (lam xs (@fst xs)))

(cdr (lam xs (@snd xs)))

(nil #u)

(null (abs () #u))

(null? (lam xs (@unit? xs)))

(min (abs (x y) (if (@<= x y) x y)))

(max (abs (x y) (if (@>= x y) x y)))

(list? (abs (val) (scor (null? val)
                        (scand (@pair? val) (list? (snd val))))))

(length (abs (xs)
         (if (null? xs)
             0
             (@+ 1 (length (cdr xs)))))))

(nth (abs (i xs)
      (cond ((scor (null? xs) (@< i 1))
             (error nth-index-out-of-bounds))
            ((@= i 1) (car xs))
            (else (nth (@- i 1) (cdr xs)))))))
```

Figure 6.8   FL standard library bindings, Part 1.

level bindings that we will assume for FL. There are several kinds of bindings in the figure:

- There is one binding for each primitive operator in Primop, which binds the name of the primitive to a procedure performing the primitive operation. This allows writing (+ E_1 E_2) within the program instead of (@+ E_1 E_2) or (prim + E_1 E_2).

```
(reverse (abs (xs)
          ((rec loop
             (abs (old new)
                (if (null? old) new
                    (loop (cdr old) (cons (car old) new))))))
           xs nil)))
(append (abs (xs ys)
          (if (null? xs)
              ys
              (cons (car xs) (append (cdr xs) ys)))))
(equal? (abs (x y)
          (scor (scand (@unit? x) (@unit? y))
                (scand (@bool? x) (@bool? y) (@bool=? x y))
                (scand (@int? x) (@int? y) (@= x y))
                (scand (@sym? x) (@sym? y) (@sym=? x y))
                (scand (@pair? x) (@pair? y)
                       (equal? (@fst x) (@fst y))
                       (equal? (@snd x) (@snd y))))))
(member? (abs (elt lst)
          (scand (not (null? lst))
                 (scor (equal? elt (car lst))
                       (member? elt (cdr lst))))))
```
⋮ *higher-order list procedures from Figure 6.11.*

Figure 6.9   FL standard library bindings, Part 2.

- Synonyms are introduced for several constants and procedures. The names true and false are synonyms for #t and #f. The names min and max are given, respectively, to procedures that return the minimum or maximum of two integers. The LISP-inspired list-manipulation names cons, car, cdr, nil, null, and null? are introduced as synonyms for manipulations on unit-terminated chains of pairs. These functions highlight situations where pairs are being viewed as lists rather than raw pairs.

- list?, length, nth, reverse, append, equal?, and member? are recursive list procedures frequently used in list-manipulation programs. For examples involving these procedures, see Figure 6.10. There are many other recursive list procedures that could be included in the standard library for FLK. The fact that $\mathcal{DS}_{pgm}$ introduces standard bindings via letrec as opposed to let means that the standard bindings may be mutually recursive. So no explicit

```
(list? 17)   ⟶  false
        FL
(list? (list 7 2 5))   ⟶  true
                   FL
(list? (pair 3 (pair 4 5)))   ⟶  false
                          FL

(length (list))   ⟶  0
              FL
(length (list 7 2 5))   ⟶  3
                    FL
(length (list #u #t (sym foo) (pair 1 2) (list (sym a) (sym b))))   ⟶  5
                                                               FL

(nth 1 (list 7 #t (sym foo)))   ⟶  7
                            FL
(nth 3 (list 7 #t (sym foo)))   ⟶  'foo'
                            FL
(nth 0 (list 7 #t (sym foo)))   ⟶  error:nth-index-out-of-bounds
                            FL
(nth 4 (list 7 #t (sym foo)))   ⟶  error:nth-index-out-of-bounds
                            FL

(reverse (list 7 #t (sym foo)))   ⟶  ⊲'foo', true, 7⊳
                              FL
(reverse (list 7 (list 2 5)))   ⟶  ⊲⊲2, 5⊳, 7⊳
                            FL
(reverse (list))   ⟶  ⊲⊳
               FL

(append (list 7 #t (sym foo)) (list #f 4))   ⟶  ⊲7, true, 'foo', false, 4⊳
                                         FL
(append (list) (list #f 4))   ⟶  ⊲false, 4⊳
                          FL
(append (list 7 #t (sym foo)) (list))   ⟶  ⊲7, true, 'foo'⊳
                                    FL

(equal? 1 #f)   ⟶  false
            FL
(equal? 1 1)   ⟶  true
           FL
(equal? #f #f)   ⟶  true
             FL
(equal? (list 7 (pair #u (sym foo)) #f)
        (list 7 (pair #u (sym foo)) #t))   ⟶  false
                                       FL
(equal? (list 7 (pair #u (sym foo)) #f)
        (pair 7 (pair (pair #u (sym foo)) (pair #f #u))))   ⟶  true
                                                        FL

(member? 2 (list 7 2 5))   ⟶  true
                       FL
(member? 17 (list 7 2 5))   ⟶  false
                        FL
(member? (sym *) (quote (+ - * /)))   ⟶  true
                                  FL
```

Figure 6.10 Sample invocations of standard list procedures.

rec or letrec is necessary to define recursive procedures like length or nth, and each of these definitions may refer to other standard bindings (such as cons, car, cdr).

Desugaring a top-level program construct is only one way to include standard bindings within a program. Some programming language implementations support a notion of linking program modules together before executing a program (see Chapter 15). In such implementations, a program is linked with modules that implement the standard library. In some languages, programmers may declare extra libraries they wish to load in addition to the standard library.

The practical utility of a programming language depends in large part on the libraries it supplies. FORTRAN and C became popular languages for number crunching because of their extensive libraries for numerical methods. APL has impressive libraries for matrix manipulation. The standard libraries for functional languages (e.g., HASKELL, ML dialects, LISP dialects) include many procedures for processing lists and trees. Both JAVA and C++ have huge libraries of procedures and data structures for many purposes (numerical manipulation, graphics, network communication, cryptography, etc.).

6.2.4 Examples

Although FL is a toy language, it packs a fair bit of expressive punch. We have already seen several list-processing examples in the context of the standard library. Here we illustrate the expressive power of FL with a few more examples.

Higher-Order List Procedures

In functional languages it is common to abstract over list-processing idioms by supplying procedural arguments. Figure 6.11 presents some classic higher-order list procedures written as FL definitions. Since these functions are so useful, we will assume that they are included in the FL standard library. The `map` procedure returns the list that results from performing a given procedure on every element of a given list.

```
(map (abs (x) (* x x)) (list 7 2 5))  ⟶_FL  ⊲49, 4, 25⊳
(map not (list #t #f))  ⟶_FL  ⊲false, true⊳
(map (abs (y) (pair 3 y)) (list 7 #t (sym foo)))
     ⟶_FL  ⊲⟨3, 7⟩, ⟨3, true⟩, ⟨3, 'foo'⟩⊳
```

The `filter` procedure returns a list containing the elements of the given list that satisfy the given predicate.

```
(filter (abs (x) (= 1 (% x 2))) (list 7 2 5 3 4))  ⟶_FL  ⊲7, 5, 3⊳
(filter sym? (list 7 #t (sym foo) (pair #u (sym bar)) (sym baz))
     ⟶_FL  ⊲'foo', 'baz'⊳
```

The `forall?` procedure determines whether all the elements of a list satisfy a predicate. The `exists?` procedure determines whether at least one element of a list satisfies a predicate.

```
(forall? (abs (x) (= 1 (% x 2))) (list 7 3 5))  ⟶_FL  true
(forall? (abs (x) (= 1 (% x 2))) (list 7 3 2 5))  ⟶_FL  false
(exists? (abs (x) (= 1 (% x 2))) (list 7 3 2 5))  ⟶_FL  true
(exists? (abs (x) (= 1 (% x 2))) (list 6 2 8 4))  ⟶_FL  false
```

The `foldr` (short for "fold right") procedure accumulates a result value from a list by using `binop` to combine each element into the result starting with `nullval` as the initial result.

```
(foldr + 0 (list 7 2 3))  FL→  12
(foldr * 1 (list 7 2 3))  FL→  42
(foldr (abs (x bs) (cons (> x 2) bs))
       nil
       (list 7 2 3))  FL→  ⊲true, false, true⊳
```

Exercise 6.10 The `foldr` procedure abstracts over the general list-recursion idiom. Demonstrate the generality of `foldr` by defining each of `map`, `filter`, `forall?`, and `exists?` as nonrecursive procedures implemented in terms of `foldr`. E.g., the definition of `map` should have the form

```
(def (map f xs) (foldr Ebinop Enullval xs))
```

This can be simplified further to

```
(def (map f) (foldr Ebinop Enullval))
```

Merge Sort

Figure 6.12 presents a `merge-sort` procedure that uses the merge sort algorithm to sort a list of elements according to a less-than-or-equal-to predicate, `before?`. For example:

```
(merge-sort <= (list 7 2 4 1 5 4 3))  FL→  ⊲1, 2, 3, 4, 4, 5, 7⊳
(merge-sort >= (list 7 2 4 1 5 4 3))  FL→  ⊲7, 5, 4, 4, 3, 2, 1⊳
(merge-sort (abs (a b) (<= (% a 4) (% b 4)))
            (list 7 2 4 1 5 4 3))  FL→  ⊲4, 4, 1, 5, 2, 7, 3⊳
```

The procedure is implemented in terms of three auxiliary procedures: `merge`, `alts`, and `ms`. The `merge` procedure takes two lists `xs` and `ys` that are assumed to be sorted according to the `before?` predicate and returns the sorted list containing all the elements of both lists (including duplicates, if any). Note that because `merge` is defined as a local recursive procedure inside `merge-sort`, it can refer to the `before?` parameter of `merge-sort` without receiving it as an explicit argument. The `alts` procedure returns a pair of (1) all the odd-indexed[6] elements and (2) all the even-indexed elements of a given list, preserving the relative order of elements in each sublist.

```
(alts (list))  FL→  ⟨⊲⊳, ⊲⊳⟩
(alts (list 7))  FL→  ⟨⊲7⊳, ⊲⊳⟩
(alts (list 7 2))  FL→  ⟨⊲7⊳, ⊲2⊳⟩
(alts (list 7 2 4 5 1 4 3))  FL→  ⟨⊲7, 4, 1, 3⊳, ⊲2, 5, 4⊳⟩
```

---

[6]Assume that list elements are indexed starting with 1.

```
(def (map f xs)
  (if (null? xs) xs (cons (f (car xs)) (map f (cdr xs)))))
(def (filter pred xs)
  (cond ((null? xs) xs)
        ((pred (car xs)) (cons (car xs) (filter pred (cdr xs))))
        (else (filter pred (cdr xs)))))
(def (forall? pred xs)
  (scor (null? xs)
        (scand (pred (car xs)) (forall? pred (cdr xs)))))
(def (exists? pred xs)
  (scand (not (null? xs))
         (scor (pred (car xs)) (exists? pred (cdr xs)))))
(def (foldr binop nullval xs)
  (if (null? xs)
      nullval
      (binop (car xs) (foldr binop nullval (cdr xs)))))
```

Figure 6.11 Some higher-order list procedures written in FL and included in the standard library.

We could have written `alts` as a recursive procedure, but have instead chosen to implement it in terms of `foldr`. The `ms` procedure implements the divide-conquer-and-glue steps of the merge sort algorithm.

An ELM Interpreter

As a more interesting example of an FL program, in Figure 6.13 we use FL to write an interpreter for the ELM subset of the EL language (Exercise 3.10 on page 67). Recall that ELM is EL without conditional and boolean expressions. The `elm-eval` procedure evaluates an ELM expression relative to a list of numbers, `args`, which are the program inputs. ELM expressions are represented as FL s-expressions. `elm-eval` is written as a dispatch on the type of expression, which is determined by the syntax predicates `lit?`, `arg?`, and `arithop?`. The selectors `lit-num`, `arg-index`, `arithop-op`, `arithop-rand1`, `arithop-rand2` extract components of s-expressions. The `get-arg` procedure returns the `index`th element of the given list `nums` (where indices are assumed to start at 1). The `op->proc` procedure converts a symbol (such as `(sym +)`) to a binary FL procedure (such as the addition procedure `+`).

Both arguments to the ELM interpreter are expected to be s-expressions: `pgm` is an s-expression representing the structure of the ELM program and `args`

```
(def (merge-sort before? vs)
  (letrec
      ((merge (abs (xs ys)
                  (cond ((null? xs) ys)
                        ((null? ys) xs)
                        ((before? (car xs) (car ys))
                         (cons (car xs) (merge (cdr xs) ys)))
                        (else (cons (car ys) (merge xs (cdr ys)))))))
       (alts (abs (ws)
                (foldr (abs (w listpair)
                           (pair (snd listpair) (cons (w (fst listpair)))))
                       (pair nil nil)
                       ws)))
       (ms (abs (zs)
              (if (scor (null? zs) (null? (cdr zs)))
                  zs
                  (let ((split (alts zs)))
                    (merge (ms (fst split)) (ms (snd split))))))))
    (ms vs)))
```

Figure 6.12   A procedure that uses the merge sort algorithm to sort a list.

is an s-expression representing the program arguments, which must be a list of integers. Suppose that $P_{elm-eval}$ is the FL program in Figure 6.13. Then here are some sample executions of $P_{elm-eval}$:[7]

$$P_{elm-eval} \xrightarrow[FL]{[(quote\ (*\ (arg\ 1)\ (arg\ 1))),\ \triangleleft 5\triangleright]} 25$$

$$P_{elm-eval} \xrightarrow[FL]{[(quote\ (/\ (+\ (arg\ 1)\ (arg\ 2))\ 2)),\ \triangleleft 6,\ 8\triangleright]} 7$$

$$P_{elm-eval} \xrightarrow[FL]{[(quote\ (+\ (arg\ 1)\ (arg\ 2))),\ \triangleleft 3\triangleright]} error:arg\text{-}index\text{-}out\text{-}of\text{-}bounds$$

Exercise 6.11 Extend the ELM interpreter to handle full EL.

Exercise 6.12 Write a POSTFIX interpreter in FL.

Exercise 6.13 Write an FL interpreter in FL. An interpreter that happens to be written in the same programming language that is being interpreted is called a **metacircular interpreter**.

---

[7]We have taken the liberty of writing the program argument in FL s-expression notation. We assume that this stands for the desugared FL value s-expression constructed out of pairs and literals.

```
(fl (pgm args)
  (cond ((not (elm-program? pgm)) (error ill-formed-program))
        ((not (scand (list? args) (forall? int? args)))
         (error ill-formed-argument-list))
        ((not (= (elm-nargs pgm) (length args)))
         (error wrong-number-of-args))
        (else (elm-eval (elm-body pgm) args)))

  (def (elm-eval exp args)
    (cond ((lit? exp) (lit-num exp))
          ((arg? exp) (get-arg (arg-index exp) args))
          ((arithop? exp) ((op->proc (arithop-op exp))
                              (elm-eval (arithop-rand1 exp) args)
                              (elm-eval (arithop-rand2 exp) args)))
          (else (error illegal-expression))))

  (def (get-arg index nums)
    (cond ((scor (<= index 0) (null? nums))
            (error arg-index-out-of-bounds))
          ((= index 1) (car nums))
          (else (get-arg (- index 1) (cdr nums)))))

  (def (op->proc s)
    (cond ((sym=? s (sym +)) +) ((sym=? s (sym -)) -)
          ((sym=? s (sym *)) *) ((sym=? s (sym /)) /)
          ((sym=? s (sym %)) %)
          (else (error illegal-op))))

  {Abstract syntax}
  (def (elm-program? sexp)
    (scand (list? sexp) (= (length sexp) 3)
           (sym=? (car exp) (sym elm))))
  (def (elm-nargs sexp) (car (cdr sexp)))
  (def (elm-body sexp) (car (cdr (cdr sexp))))
  (def lit? int?)
  (def (lit-num lit) lit)
  (def (arg? sexp)
    (scand (list? sexp) (= (length sexp) 2)
           (sym=? (car sexp) (sym arg))))
  (def (arg-index sexp) (car (cdr sexp)))
  (def (arithop? sexp)
    (scand (list? sexp) (= (length sexp) 3)
           (member? (car exp) (quote (+ - * /)))))
  (def (arithop-op sexp) (car sexp))
  (def (arithop-rand1 sexp) (car (cdr sexp)))
  (def (arithop-rand2 sexp) (car (cdr (cdr exp)))))
```

Figure 6.13 An interpreter for ELM, a subset of EL.

6.3 Variables and Substitution

Intuitively, the meaning of an FLK abstraction (lam I E) shouldn't depend on the particular name chosen for I, which is known as its **formal parameter**. Just as we expect the meaning of an integral to be independent of the choice of the variable of integration (so that $\int_a^b f(x)dx = \int_a^b f(y)dy$), we expect the meaning of an FLK abstraction to be invariant under a change to the name of its variable. Thus, the identity abstraction (lam a a) should also be expressible as (lam x x) or (lam square square). Furthermore, the variable references named by a, x, and square are logically distinct from any variable references coincidentally sharing the same name in other expressions.

This section formalizes this intuition about names in FLK expressions.

6.3.1 Terminology

Notations for mathematics and computation contain many **binding constructs** that introduce syntactic placeholders ranging over some set of semantic entities. Examples of binding constructs include FLK's programs, abstractions, and recursion expressions; the summation ($\sum$) and integration ($\int$) notations in calculus; and universal ($\forall$) and existential ($\exists$) quantifiers in logic.

We reserve the word **variable** for the conceptual placeholder introduced by a binding construct and will use the word **identifier** to designate the name that stands for a given variable. The identity abstraction discussed above has a single variable, and the identifier that names it is arbitrary. In the expression (lam x (app x (lam x x))) there are two logically distinct variables introduced by the two abstractions, but they happen to be named by the same identifier.

An identifier naming a variable may be used in two different ways:

1. as a **variable declaration** that introduces the variable in a binding construct;

2. as a **variable reference** that refers to a previously declared variable.

For example, in the FLK expression (lam x (app x x)), the leftmost occurrence of x is a variable declaration and the other two occurrences are variable references. In general, declarations and references are distinguished in the format of expressions. For example, compare how variables are declared and referenced in notations for FLK, integration, summation, union, and logical quantification (in each case, the declaration of the variable x has been underlined):

$$(\text{lam } \underline{\text{x}} \text{ x}) \qquad \int_a^b x \, d\underline{x} \qquad \sum_{\underline{x}=1}^n x^2 \qquad \bigcup_{\underline{x} \in A} x \qquad \forall \underline{x}.f(x) = g(x)$$

The region of a program phrase in which a particular variable may be referenced is called the **scope** of that variable. For example:

- In (lam I E_{body}), the scope of the variable declared by I is E_{body}.

- In (let ((I_1 E_1) (I_2 E_2)) E_3), the scope of both I_1 and I_2 is E_3. The variables declared by I_1 and I_2 cannot be referenced in E_1 or E_2.

- In (letrec ((I_1 E_1) (I_2 E_2)) E_3), the scope of both I_1 and I_2 is all three expressions E_1, E_2 and E_3.

Notations in which variables are represented by identifiers share the following properties:

1. Ignoring certain restrictions (to be discussed shortly), it is possible to consistently rename a variable within its scope without changing the meaning of the entire expression. Thus, in each of the notations considered above, the x can be changed to y without changing the meaning:

$$(\text{lam y y}) \quad \int_a^b y \; dy \quad \sum_{y=1}^n y^2 \quad \bigcup_{y \in A} y \quad \forall y. f(y) = g(y)$$

2. Within the scope S of a variable named I, the declaration of a new variable with the same name I creates a new scope S' in which the outer variable cannot be referenced. The region S' is called a **hole in the scope** of the outer variable I. For example, any reference to x within the context $\square$ in the following examples refers to the variable declared by the inner x, not the outer x.

$$(\text{lam x (app x (lam x } \square))) \quad \int_a^b x \cdot \left(\int_c^x \square \; dx \right) dx \quad \prod_{x=1}^n \left(\sum_{x=1}^x \square \right)$$

$$\bigcup_{x \in A} \langle x, \bigcap_{x \in B} \square \rangle \quad \forall x. \left((f(x) = g(x)) \wedge \exists x. \square \right)$$

If a binding construct declares a variable named I, we shall say that the construct **binds** I and will sometimes use the term **binding occurrence** for the occurrence of I that is the variable declaration. An occurrence of an identifier I in an expression is **bound** if it is a binding occurrence or it is a variable reference in the scope of some binding construct that binds I; otherwise, that occurrence of the identifier is said to be **free**. For example, in (lam a (lam b (app a c))), the single occurrence of b and both occurrences of a are bound, while the single occurrence of c is free.

Whether an identifier is free or bound depends on the context in which the identifier is viewed. Thus, in the previous example, the second occurrence of a is free in (app a c) and in (lam b (app a c)) but not in the expression (lam a (lam b (app a c))). It is possible in one expression to have some occurrences of an identifier that are bound and other occurrences of the same identifier that are free. In (app (lam a a) a) the first and second occurrences of a are bound, while the third occurrence is free.

An identifier (as opposed to an *occurrence* of an identifier) is said to be a **free identifier** (likewise, **bound identifier**) in an expression if at least one of its occurrences is free (likewise, bound) in the expression. For instance, in the expression (app b (lam a (lam b (app a c)))), a and b are bound identifiers and b and c are free identifiers.

Similarly, we say that a **variable** is **free** (likewise, **bound**) in an expression if the identifier occurrences referring to it are free (likewise, bound). Using our terminology, an identifier may be both bound and free in an expression, but a variable can be only one or the other. In the literature, the terms *free variable* and *bound variable* are often used for what we call free and bound identifiers.

A phrase (expression, program, etc.) is **closed** if it contains no free identifiers (or, equivalently, no free variables). Otherwise, it is said to be **open**.

Expressions with free variables often arise when considering subexpressions of a given expression. For instance, in the subexpression (lam b (app b a)) of the closed expression (lam a (lam b (app b a))), the identifier a names a free variable.

Using definition by structural induction, it is straightforward to define functions *FrIds* and *BdIds* that map FLK expressions to sets of their free and bound identifiers, respectively. These functions are presented in Figure 6.14. Both functions have the signature $\text{Exp} \to \mathcal{P}(\text{Ident})$, where $\mathcal{P}(\text{Ident})$ is the powerset (set of all subsets) of Ident. For example,

$$FrIds[\![(\text{app b (lam a (lam b (app a c)))})]\!] = \{\text{b}, \text{c}\}$$
$$BdIds[\![(\text{app b (lam a (lam b (app a c)))})]\!] = \{\text{a}, \text{b}\}$$

There is one subtlety in these definitions: An *I* that appears within double brackets on the left-hand side of the definitions stands for a variable reference that is an element of the syntactic domain Exp. On the other hand, an unbracketed *I* on the right-hand side of the definitions stands for an element of the syntactic domain Ident.

$$FrIds : \mathrm{Exp} \rightarrow \mathcal{P}(\mathrm{Ident})$$
$$FrIds[\![L]\!] = \{\}$$
$$FrIds[\![I]\!] = \{I\}$$
$$FrIds[\![(\texttt{error } Y)]\!] = \{\}$$
$$FrIds[\![(\texttt{if } E_1 \ E_2 \ E_3)]\!] = \cup_{i=1}^{3} FrIds[\![E_i]\!]$$
$$FrIds[\![(\texttt{prim } O \ E_1 \ \dots \ E_n)]\!] = \cup_{i=1}^{n} FrIds[\![E_i]\!]$$
$$FrIds[\![(\texttt{lam } I_{formal} \ E_{body})]\!] = FrIds[\![E_{body}]\!] - \{I_{formal}\}$$
$$FrIds[\![(\texttt{app } E_{rator} \ E_{rand})]\!] = FrIds[\![E_{rator}]\!] \cup FrIds[\![E_{rand}]\!]$$
$$FrIds[\![(\texttt{pair } E_{fst} \ E_{snd})]\!] = FrIds[\![E_{fst}]\!] \cup FrIds[\![E_{snd}]\!]$$
$$FrIds[\![(\texttt{rec } I_{name} \ E_{body})]\!] = FrIds[\![E_{body}]\!] - \{I_{name}\}$$

$$FrIds_{pgm} : \mathrm{Prog} \rightarrow \mathcal{P}(\mathrm{Ident})$$
$$FrIds_{pgm}[\![(\texttt{flk } (I_1 \ \dots \ I_n) \ E_{body})]\!] = FrIds[\![E_{body}]\!] - \{I_1, \dots, I_n\}$$

$$BdIds : \mathrm{Exp} \rightarrow \mathcal{P}(\mathrm{Ident})$$
$$BdIds[\![L]\!] = \{\}$$
$$BdIds[\![I]\!] = \{\}$$
$$BdIds[\![(\texttt{error } Y)]\!] = \{\}$$
$$BdIds[\![(\texttt{if } E_1 \ E_2 \ E_3)]\!] = \cup_{i=1}^{3} BdIds[\![E_i]\!]$$
$$BdIds[\![(\texttt{prim } O \ E_1 \ \dots \ E_n)]\!] = \cup_{i=1}^{n} BdIds[\![E_i]\!]$$
$$BdIds[\![(\texttt{lam } I_{formal} \ E_{body})]\!] = BdIds[\![E_{body}]\!] \cup \{I_{formal}\}$$
$$BdIds[\![(\texttt{app } E_{rator} \ E_{rand})]\!] = BdIds[\![E_{rator}]\!] \cup BdIds[\![E_{rand}]\!]$$
$$BdIds[\![(\texttt{pair } E_{fst} \ E_{snd})]\!] = BdIds[\![E_{fst}]\!] \cup BdIds[\![E_{snd}]\!]$$
$$BdIds[\![(\texttt{rec } I_{name} \ E_{body})]\!] \ BdIds[\![E_{body}]\!] \cup \{I_{name}\}$$

$$BdIds_{pgm} : \mathrm{Prog} \rightarrow \mathcal{P}(\mathrm{Ident})$$
$$BdIds_{pgm}[\![(\texttt{flk } (I_1 \ \dots \ I_n) \ E_{body})]\!] = BdIds[\![E_{body}]\!] \cup \{I_1, \dots, I_n\}$$

Figure 6.14   Definition of free and bound identifiers for FLK.

The functions $FrIds_{pgm}$ and $BdIds_{pgm}$ define the free and bound identifiers of a program. It is reasonable to expect that each FLK program P we study will be closed: i.e., $FrIds_{pgm}[\![P]\!] = \{\}$. Otherwise, executing P might lead to an unbound variable error. Calculating the free variables of a program is a very simple example of a **static program analysis**, a terminating analysis that determines properties of a program that do not depend on its dynamic inputs. A static analysis can increase a programmer's confidence in the correctness of a program by providing guarantees that the program will not exhibit certain undesirable behaviors. For example, if P is closed, there is a guarantee that executing P cannot lead to an unbound variable error. Forms of static analysis that are more informative include type analysis and effect analysis. We will study these in Chapters 11–16.

Exercise 6.14 For each of the following four FLK expressions:

- Indicate for every occurrence of an identifier whether it is bound or free.

- Determine the free identifiers and bound identifiers of the expression.

a. `(lam x (app x y))`

b. `(app (lam z (lam x (app (app x y) z))) z)`

c. `(app z (lam y (app (lam z (app x y)) z)))`

d. `(lam x (app (app (lam y (app (lam z (app x r)) y)) y) z))`

6.3.2   Abstract Syntax DAGs and Stoy Diagrams

The chief structural feature of variables is that they permit sharing in an expression: the same variable introduced by a declaration can be used by many variable-reference occurrences. We have said before that syntactic expressions can be viewed as abstract syntax trees, but since trees allow no sharing of substructure, they are inadequate for illustrating the sharing nature of variables. We need the more general **directed acyclic graph (DAG)** to faithfully show the structure of an expression with variables.

As an example, consider the following FLK expression:[8]

`(app (lam a (app a a)) (lam a (lam b a)))`

In this expression, there are two distinct variables named a, and the variable named by b is declared without being referenced. Figure 6.15 shows an abstract syntax DAG corresponding to this expression. In the DAG, the three distinct variables in the expression are represented by distinct nodes labeled Variable.

Since sharing is explicit in the structure of the DAG, no identifiers are necessary in the DAG representation of the expression. The key reason variables are traditionally represented with identifiers is that they allow DAGs to be encoded with linear and tree-based notational frameworks (e.g., character strings and abstract syntax trees). Unfortunately, encodings of DAGs based on identifiers complicate reasoning about expressions because of incidental properties of the identifiers. For example, the notion of a "hole in the scope" introduced earlier is not inherent in the nature of variables, but results from the fact that, when variables are represented by identifiers, a nested pair of variables can accidentally share the same name. We'll see below that identifiers are the major sore spot when we need to do renaming and substitution on FLK expressions.

---

[8]In the following discussion, we shall focus only on FLK expressions, but the same techniques could be applied to any notation using variables.

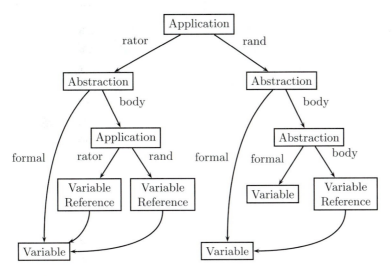

Figure 6.15 Abstract syntax DAG for `(app (lam a (app a a))`
`(lam a (lam b a)))`

Every closed expression can always be represented by a DAG with no identifiers. However, expressions containing free variables pose a problem because they contain references to a variable without also containing its declaration. Since expressions with free variables are common, we'd like to handle them within the DAG framework. The DAG representation must include the names of any free identifiers because the names of free identifiers actually matter. For example, the expression `(lam b (app b a))` does not have the same meaning as `(lam b (app b c))` in every context. Figure 6.16 shows the DAG representation of `(lam b (app b a))`. The free variable is declared by a special FreeVariable node annotated with the name of the variable.

Abstract syntax DAGs take up a lot of real estate on the printed page, so we shall use a more compact notation due to Joseph Stoy [Sto85]. Stoy's notation is a kind of wiring diagram for expressions in which the position corresponding to a variable reference is connected by a wire to the position corresponding to the variable declaration. For example, a **Stoy diagram** for the expression

`(app (lam a (app a a)) (lam a (lam b (lam c (app c a)))))`

is

`(app (lam  ●  (app  ●  ●)) (lam  ●  (lam  ●  (lam  ●  (app  ●  ●)))))`

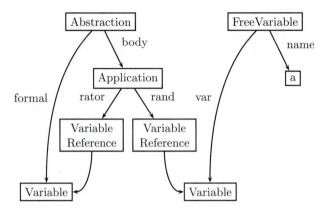

Figure 6.16   Abstract syntax DAG for (lam b (app b a)).

We extend Stoy's notation to handle free variables by simply leaving every free variable reference where it occurs in the expression. Thus, the modified Stoy diagram for (lam b (app a (app b a))) is:

$$\text{(lam} \quad \bullet \quad \text{(app a (app} \quad \bullet \quad \text{a)))}$$

All identifiers sharing the same name in a Stoy diagram must name the same free variable.

6.3.3   Alpha-Equivalence

Since we really care about the implied DAG structure of an expression and not the vagaries of particular choices of identifiers for variable names, it is natural to equate FLK expressions that share the same DAG representation. We shall use the notation $E_1 =_\alpha E_2$ (pronounced "E_1 is alpha-equivalent to E_2") to mean that E_1 and E_2 designate the same abstract syntax DAG. Thus,

$$\text{(lam a (lam b (app b a)))} =_\alpha \text{(lam b (lam a (app a b)))}$$
$$=_\alpha \text{(lam one (lam two (app two one)))}$$

and (lam b (app b a)) $=_\alpha$ (lam c (app c a)),

but (lam a (lam b (app b a))) $\neq_\alpha$ (lam a (lam a (app a a)))

and (lam b (app b a)) $\neq_\alpha$ (lam b (app b c)).

Since alpha-equivalence is an equivalence relation, it partitions FLK expressions into equivalence classes that share the same DAG. We shall generally assume throughout the rest of our discussion on FLK that each FLK expression serves as a representative of its equivalence class and that syntactic manipulations on expressions are functions on these equivalence classes rather than on individual expressions. For example, $FrIds$ is a well-defined function not only on FLK expressions but also on alpha-equivalence classes of FLK expressions because $E_1 =_\alpha E_2$ implies $FrIds[\![E_1]\!] = FrIds[\![E_2]\!]$. On the other hand, $BdIds$ is not a well-defined function on alpha-equivalence classes, because it depends on syntactic details of an expression that are not represented in its DAG structure. Thus (lam a a) $=_\alpha$ (lam b b), but

$$BdIds[\![(\texttt{lam a a})]\!] = \{\texttt{a}\} \neq_\alpha \{\texttt{b}\} = BdIds[\![(\texttt{lam b b})]\!]$$

6.3.4 Renaming and Variable Capture

Consistently renaming the variables of an expression in a way that preserves its alpha-equivalence class is called **alpha-renaming**. For example, the expression

```
(lam x (app (lam x x) (app (lam x x) x)))
```

can be alpha-renamed to any of the following:

```
(lam a (app (lam a a) (app (lam a a) a)))
(lam b (app (lam c c) (app (lam b b) b)))
(lam d (app (lam e e) (app (lam f f) d)))
```

Alpha-renaming is not required to choose distinct names for logically distinct variables, but it is often used for this purpose.

Although the notion of alpha-renaming may seem straightforward, specifying a procedure that performs it correctly is surprisingly tricky. We will begin by considering the subtleties of renaming a variable introduced by an abstraction. A correct variable renaming is one that preserves the alpha-equivalence class of the expression — i.e., does not alter its abstract syntax DAG or Stoy diagram. The naive approach of consistently renaming the variable's declaration and all its references is not always appropriate because of a situation known as **variable capture**. There are two kinds of variable capture, both of which will be illustrated in the following example.

Consider the expression (lam a (lam b (app a c))), whose Stoy diagram is shown below:

```
(lam • (lam • (app • c)))
```

Suppose we want to rename the variable named a in this expression. For almost all possible identifiers, a simple consistent renaming will do. For example, renaming a to x produces the expression (lam x (lam b (app x c))), which has the same Stoy diagram as the original.

Suppose, however, that we choose the identifier b as the new name for a. Then the naive renaming method yields (lam b (lam b (app b c))), whose Stoy diagram

$$\text{(lam} \bullet \text{(lam} \bullet \text{(app} \bullet \text{c)))}$$

is *not* the same as that for the original expression. The inner binding occurrence of b has created a hole in the scope of the outer binding occurrence of b. Because an inner abstraction just happens to bind the new name, all references to the new name within the body of the inner abstraction are accidentally captured by that abstraction. We call this **internal variable capture**.

A slightly different problem is encountered if we choose c as the new name for a. In that case, naive renaming yields (lam c (lam b (app c c))), whose Stoy diagram is

$$\text{(lam} \bullet \text{(lam} \bullet \text{(app} \bullet \bullet \text{)))}$$

Here a free identifier, c, in the body of a renamed binding construct has accidentally been captured by the declaration of the new name. We call this **external variable capture**, because the captured variable is declared somewhere external to the renamed abstraction.

Internal and external variable capture are not unique to FLK. They can occur in any naming system in which logically distinct variables can accidentally be merged together. As we shall see, in the programming language world, variable capture rears its ugly head in program transformations (including expression substitution) used in language implementation and in languages supporting dynamic scoping or macro expansion.

We would prefer that coincidental choices of identifiers not destroy the structural integrity of a renamed FLK expression. One way to ensure this is to guarantee that each new variable name introduced by a renaming appears nowhere else in the FLK expression, but this approach is more restrictive than necessary and gives little insight into the true nature of the problem. The following section defines a general syntactic renaming operator that avoids both forms of variable capture.

6.3.5 Substitution

Variable renaming is a special case of a more general syntactic operation called **substitution**. It is often desirable to substitute a particular expression for all free references of a variable named by a given identifier in another expression. For example, we might want to replace each free a in

```
(app a (lam b (app (lam a (app a b)) a)))
```

by the application (app c d) to yield

```
(app (app c d) (lam b (app (lam a (app a b)) (app c d))))
```

We use the notation $[E/I]$ to denote a function that maps a given expression into another expression in which E has been substituted for all free variable references named by I. Thus, $[E_1/I]E_2$ denotes the result of substituting E_1 for the free occurrences of I in E_2. Using this notation, the above example can be expressed as

```
[(app c d)/a](app a (lam b (app (lam a (app a b)) a)))
= (app (app c d) (lam b (app (lam a (app a b)) (app c d))))
```

A correct substitution is one that preserves the logical structure both of the expression being substituted (E_1) and the expression substituted into (E_2), except, of course, for the free variable being substituted for. Substitution may seem like a straightforward idea, but, like renaming, it is plagued with variable-capture subtleties.

As an example of a problematic situation, suppose that (app b d) rather than (app c d), were being substituted for a in the above example. Since the expression being substituted into has the Stoy diagram

```
(app a (lam • (app (lam • (app • •)) a)))
```

$[(app\ b\ d)/a](app\ a\ (lam\ b\ (app\ (lam\ a\ (app\ a\ b))\ a)))$ should have the Stoy diagram

```
(app (app b d) (lam • (app (lam • (app • •)) (app b d))))
```

However, a naive syntactic approach to substitution would yield the expression

```
(app (app b d) (lam b (app (lam a (app a b)) (app b d))))
```

whose Stoy diagram

```
(app (app b d) (lam • (app (lam • (app • •)) (app • d))))
```

shows the capture of the free occurrence of b in (app b d).

$subst : \mathrm{Exp} \to \mathrm{Ident} \to \mathrm{Exp} \to \mathrm{Exp}$

　The notation $[E_1/I]E_2$ abbreviates $(subst\ E_1\ I\ E_2)$.

　This notation associates to the right: $[E_2/I_2][E_1/I_1]E = [E_2/I_2]([E_1/I_1]E)$.

$[E/I]L = L$

$[E/I]I = E$

$[E/I]I' = I'$, where $I \neq I'$

$[E/I](\texttt{error}\ Y) = (\texttt{error}\ Y)$

$[E/I](\texttt{if}\ E_{test}\ E_{then}\ E_{else}) = (\texttt{if}\ [E/I]E_{test}\ [E/I]E_{then}\ [E/I]E_{else})$

$[E/I](\texttt{prim}\ O\ E_1\ ...\ E_n) = (\texttt{prim}\ O\ [E/I]E_1\ ...\ [E/I]E_n)$

$[E/I](\texttt{lam}\ I\ E_{body}) = (\texttt{lam}\ I\ E_{body})$

$[E/I](\texttt{lam}\ I'\ E_{body}) = (\texttt{lam}\ I_{fresh}\ [E/I][I_{fresh}/I']E_{body})$,
　　where $I \neq I'$ and $I_{fresh} \notin \{I\} \cup (FrIds[\![E]\!]) \cup (FrIds[\![E_{body}]\!])$

$[E/I](\texttt{app}\ E_{rator}\ E_{rand}) = (\texttt{app}\ [E/I]E_{rator}\ [E/I]E_{rand})$

$[E/I](\texttt{pair}\ E_{fst}\ E_{snd}) = (\texttt{pair}\ [E/I]E_{fst}\ [E/I]E_{snd})$

$[E/I](\texttt{rec}\ I\ E_{body}) = (\texttt{rec}\ I\ E_{body})$

$[E/I](\texttt{rec}\ I'\ E_{body}) = (\texttt{rec}\ I_{fresh}\ [E/I][I_{fresh}/I']E_{body})$,
　　where $I \neq I'$ and $I_{fresh} \notin \{I\} \cup (FrIds[\![E]\!]) \cup (FrIds[\![E_{body}]\!])$

Figure 6.17   The definition of substitution for FLK.

　　Figure 6.17 presents a method of substitution that avoids variable capture. Substitution is defined by structural induction on the expression substituted into. However, there is sometimes more than one clause per expression type because some expression types have subcases that depend on interactions between the variable I being replaced and variables within the expression substituted into. For example, $[E/I]I'$ is E if I and I' are syntactically identical, but is the original expression I' if I and I' are not the same. These different subcases are expressed in Figure 6.17 by implicit pattern matching or explicit restrictions.

　　As seen in Figure 6.17, most of the rules simply distribute the substitution over the subexpressions of an expression. The tricky case is substituting into a binding construct (`lam` or `rec` in FLK). For example, consider the case for `lam`:

$$[E/I](\texttt{lam}\ I'\ E_{body})$$

In the case where I and I' are the same, the declaration of I' creates a hole in the scope of the outer variable named by I. There can be no references to this outer variable within E_{body}, so no substitutions should be performed inside E_{body}.

When I and I' are distinct, the crucial case to handle is where I appears free in E_{body} (so a substitution will definitely take place) *and* E contains a free reference to I'. This reference will be captured by the bound variable I' of the abstraction unless we're careful. A simple example of this situation is:

$$[\text{b/a}](\text{lam b (app b a)})$$

Here, the substituted expression b contains (in fact, is) a free reference to a variable whose name happens to be the same as the name of the variable bound by the abstraction. A naive substitution would yield (lam b (app b b)), in which the outer variable named b has been accidentally captured by the inner binding of the same name. To prevent this internal variable capture, it is necessary to first consistently rename the bound variable of the abstraction with an identifier that is not the same as I and is free neither in E nor in E_{body}. After this renaming, substitution can be performed on E_{body} without threat of variable capture. In our example, the bound variable b can be renamed to c, say, yielding the alpha-equivalent abstraction (lam c (app c a)). Then substitution can be performed on the body to yield the correct expression

$$(\text{lam c } [\text{b/a}](\text{app c a})) = (\text{lam c (app c b)})$$

In the case where $I \neq I'$, it is always correct to perform the described renaming of the bound variable of the abstraction, but it is not always necessary. If I is not free in E_{body}, renaming is not required because no substitution will be performed inside the abstraction anyway. And if I' doesn't appear in E, no internal variable capture can arise, and it is safe to directly substitute into the body of the abstraction without a renaming step.

The notion of choosing an unused identifier often arises when manipulating syntactic expressions in which variables are represented by identifiers. Such an identifier is said to be **fresh**. When describing a syntactic manipulation formally, it is necessary to specify any constraints involved in choosing fresh identifiers (e.g., see the restrictions for lam and rec). However, informally we will often just say that a name is fresh without specifying any restrictions. In this case, we mean that the fresh name must be different from any identifier occurring anywhere else in the program under consideration. When we introduce more than one fresh name at once, we will also assume that the fresh names are pairwise distinct.

Keep in mind that all the complexity for renaming and substitution arises from the use of linear (in this case, textual) representations for declaration/reference relationships that are not linear or even tree-like. If FLK expressions were represented as DAGs or Stoy diagrams, renaming would be unnecessary and substitution (e.g., of a Stoy diagram into a Stoy diagram) would be straightforward.

The notion of **simultaneous substitution** is an extension to the substitution function we have seen. A simultaneous substitution of the expressions $E_1, \ldots,$ E_n for the identifiers $I_1, \ldots, I_n$, written

$$[E_1, \ldots, E_n/I_1, \ldots, I_n] \text{ or } [E_i/I_i]_{i=1}^n$$

is a function of a single expression that performs the substitutions $[E_1/I_1], \ldots,$ $[E_n/I_n]$ in parallel on that expression. It differs from a sequence of substitutions in that an I_i appearing in one of the E_j is never replaced. For example, simultaneous substitution of I_2 for I_1 and I_1 for I_2 in the expression (app I_1 I_2) swaps the two identifiers,

$$[I_2, I_1/I_1, I_2](\text{app } I_1 \ I_2) = (\text{app } I_2 \ I_1)$$

whereas neither ordering of two single substitutions has this behavior:

$$[I_2/I_1]([I_1/I_2](\text{app } I_1 \ I_2)) = (\text{app } I_2 \ I_2)$$
$$[I_1/I_2]([I_2/I_1](\text{app } I_1 \ I_2)) = (\text{app } I_1 \ I_1)$$

Exercise 6.15 Use the definition of substitution in Figure 6.17 to determine the results of the following substitutions. Assume that fresh identifiers are taken from the list v1, v2, v3, ..., and that the first identifier from the list that satisfies the given constraint is chosen as the fresh identifier.

a. [(app (app b c) d)/a](lam a (lam b (app (app c b) a)))

b. [(app (app b c) d)/b](lam a (lam b (app (app c b) a)))

c. [(app (app b c) d)/c](lam a (lam b (app (app c b) a)))

d. [(app (app b c) d)/d](lam a (lam b (app (app c b) a)))

e. [(app (app b c) d)/b](lam a (lam b (app c a)))

Exercise 6.16 Consider the case for substituting into abstractions,

$$[E/I](\text{lam } I' \ E_{body})$$

where $I \neq I'$. Here I' is consistently renamed to be a variable I_{fresh} that is not free in either E or E_{body} and is not equal to I.

a. Provide an example of an incorrect substitution that would be permitted if the restriction $I_{fresh} \notin FrIds[\![E]\!]$ were lifted.

b. Provide an example of an incorrect substitution that would be permitted if the restriction $I_{fresh} \notin FrIds[\![E_{body}]\!]$ were lifted.

c. Provide an example of an incorrect substitution that would be permitted if the restriction $I_{fresh} \neq I$ were lifted.

d. Would it be possible to consistently rename the free variables of E (within both E and E_{body}) instead of renaming I'? Explain your answer, using examples where appropriate.

Exercise 6.17 In the definition of the FL desugaring function $\mathcal{DS}$ in Figure 6.4 on page 220, fresh identifiers are introduced in the desugarings for nullary abstractions and `letrec`. For each identifier declared fresh in these cases, give an example of variable capture that could occur if the freshness condition were omitted.

Exercise 6.18 A `letrec` desugaring assuming a standard library function `nth` is presented on page 225. A purported problem with this desugaring is that it is susceptible to variable capture involving the name `nth`. Illustrate this by writing an FL expression $E_{capture}$ containing a `letrec` expression such that $E_{capture}$ does not desugar properly via this desugaring due to variable capture.

Exercise 6.19 Assuming that I_1 and I_2 are distinct, and that $I_2 \notin FrIds[\![E_1]\!]$, prove the following useful equivalence. (Hint: Use induction on the structure of E_3.)

$$[E_1/I_1]\,([E_2/I_2]E_3) = [([E_1/I_1]E_2)\,/I_2]\,([E_1/I_1]E_3)$$

Exercise 6.20 Write a formal definition of simultaneous substitution for FLK.

Exercise 6.21 Suppose that FL is extended with the following constructs for manipulating tuples of elements:

(tuple $E_{i=1}^n$): Returns a tuple whose n components are the outcomes of $E_{i=1}^n$.

(tuple-ref E N): Suppose N is the numeral for a positive integer i and E evaluates to a tuple t. Returns the ith element of t (assume 1-based indexing).

(tuple-length E): Returns the number of elements in the tuple denoted by E.

(tuple? E): Predicate determining if E is a tuple.

Tuples provide an alternative way to desugar multiabstractions and multiapplications. Multiapplications can package arguments into a tuple that is unpackaged by a multiabstraction.

a. Provide tuple-based desugarings for multiabstractions and multiapplications. Substitution is helpful for handling variable references in the body of a multiabstraction. Explain any design choices that you make.

b. Discuss the advantages and disadvantages of the tuple-based desugaring versus the desugaring based on currying.

Domains
Syntactic domains from FLK *grammar (Figure 6.1 on page 211).*
$V \in$ ValueExp ::= L | (lam I_{formal} E_{body}) | (pair E_{fst} E_{snd})
$IE \in$ InputExp ::= L | (pair IE_{fst} IE_{snd})
$A \in$ AnsExp ::= L | procans | pairans

SOS
The FLK SOS is defined by the tuple $\langle$Exp, $\Rightarrow$, ValueExp, IF, $OF\rangle$, where:

$\Rightarrow$ is the deterministic evaluation relation defined in Figure 6.19.

IF : (Prog $\times$ InputExp*) $\rightarrow$ Exp
IF $\langle$(flk $(I_1 \ldots I_n)$ E_{body}), $[IE_1, \ldots, IE_k]\rangle$
    = if $n \neq k$ then (error wrong-number-of-args) else $[IE_i / I_i]_{i=1}^n E_{body}$ end

OF : ValueExp $\rightarrow$ AnsExp
OF L = L
OF (lam I E) = procans
OF (pair E_1 E_2) = pairans

Behavior
beh_{det} : (Prog $\times$ InputExp*) $\rightarrow$ Outcome

beh_{det} $\langle P, IE^* \rangle$ = $\begin{cases} \text{(AnsExp} \rightarrowtail \text{Outcome } (OF\ E_{fin})) & \text{if } E_{init} \overset{*}{\Rightarrow} E_{fin} \in \text{ValueExp} \\ \text{stuck} & \text{if } E_{init} \overset{*}{\Rightarrow} E_{fin} \not\Rightarrow \\ & \quad \text{and } E_{fin} \notin \text{ValueExp} \\ \infty & \text{if } E_{init} \overset{\infty}{\Rightarrow} \end{cases}$
    where E_{init} = $(IF$ $\langle P, IE^* \rangle)$

Figure 6.18   An SOS for FLK.

6.4   An Operational Semantics for FLK

6.4.1   FLK Evaluation

Figures 6.18 and 6.19 present an SOS for FLK. In addition to the syntactic domains defined by the FLK s-expression grammar (Figure 6.1 on page 211), the SOS uses the following domains:

- The ValueExp domain contains expressions that model the values that are manipulated by FLK programs. The value expressions include all the literals, abstractions (representing procedural values), and pair expressions (representing pair values).

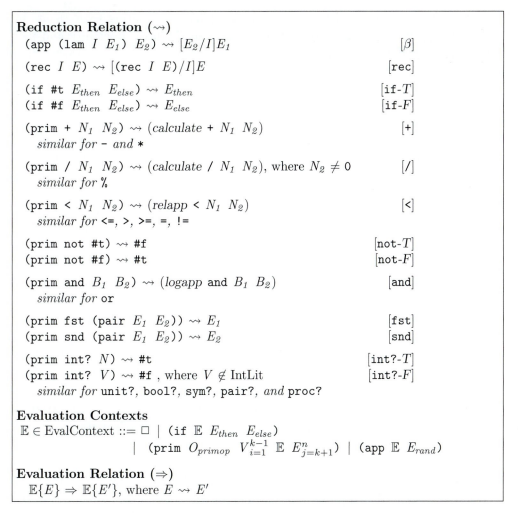

Reduction Relation ($\rightsquigarrow$)

$(\text{app } (\text{lam } I \ E_1) \ E_2) \rightsquigarrow [E_2/I]E_1$ $\qquad\qquad$ $[\beta]$

$(\text{rec } I \ E) \rightsquigarrow [(\text{rec } I \ E)/I]E$ $\qquad\qquad$ $[\text{rec}]$

$(\text{if \#t } E_{then} \ E_{else}) \rightsquigarrow E_{then}$ $\qquad\qquad$ $[\text{if-}T]$
$(\text{if \#f } E_{then} \ E_{else}) \rightsquigarrow E_{else}$ $\qquad\qquad$ $[\text{if-}F]$

$(\text{prim + } N_1 \ N_2) \rightsquigarrow (calculate \ \text{+} \ N_1 \ N_2)$ $\qquad\qquad$ $[\text{+}]$
$\quad$ *similar for* - *and* *

$(\text{prim / } N_1 \ N_2) \rightsquigarrow (calculate \ \text{/} \ N_1 \ N_2), \text{ where } N_2 \neq 0$ $\qquad$ $[\text{/}]$
$\quad$ *similar for* %

$(\text{prim < } N_1 \ N_2) \rightsquigarrow (relapp \ \text{<} \ N_1 \ N_2)$ $\qquad\qquad$ $[\text{<}]$
$\quad$ *similar for* <=, >, >=, =, !=

$(\text{prim not \#t}) \rightsquigarrow \text{\#f}$ $\qquad\qquad$ $[\text{not-}T]$
$(\text{prim not \#f}) \rightsquigarrow \text{\#t}$ $\qquad\qquad$ $[\text{not-}F]$

$(\text{prim and } B_1 \ B_2) \rightsquigarrow (logapp \ \text{and} \ B_1 \ B_2)$ $\qquad\qquad$ $[\text{and}]$
$\quad$ *similar for* or

$(\text{prim fst } (\text{pair } E_1 \ E_2)) \rightsquigarrow E_1$ $\qquad\qquad$ $[\text{fst}]$
$(\text{prim snd } (\text{pair } E_1 \ E_2)) \rightsquigarrow E_2$ $\qquad\qquad$ $[\text{snd}]$

$(\text{prim int? } N) \rightsquigarrow \text{\#t}$ $\qquad\qquad$ $[\text{int?-}T]$
$(\text{prim int? } V) \rightsquigarrow \text{\#f} \text{ , where } V \notin \text{IntLit}$ $\qquad\qquad$ $[\text{int?-}F]$
$\quad$ *similar for* unit?, bool?, sym?, pair?, *and* proc?

Evaluation Contexts

$\mathbb{E} \in \text{EvalContext} ::= \square \mid (\text{if } \mathbb{E} \ E_{then} \ E_{else})$
$\qquad\qquad\qquad \mid (\text{prim } O_{primop} \ V_{i=1}^{k-1} \ \mathbb{E} \ E_{j=k+1}^{n}) \mid (\text{app } \mathbb{E} \ E_{rand})$

Evaluation Relation ($\Rightarrow$)

$\mathbb{E}\{E\} \Rightarrow \mathbb{E}\{E'\}, \text{ where } E \rightsquigarrow E'$

Figure 6.19 A context-based description of the FLK evaluation relation.

- The InputExp domain models inputs to an FLK program. We restrict the inputs to those values that can be written as s-expressions *within* FL — i.e., values that can be written as (quote *SX*), where *SX* is defined in Figure 6.3. Such values are either literals or "pair trees" whose leaves are literals. So InputExp contains all values constructed out of literals and pairs but excludes any values mentioning procedures.

- The AnsExp domain models final answers in the execution of FLK programs. It is similar to ValueExp except that it replaces all abstraction expressions by

the procedure answer token `procans` and replaces all pairing expressions by
the pair answer token `pairans`. These tokens distinguish procedure and pair
answers from literal answers, but the component structure of these procedure
and pair answers is not observable.

Technically, the ValueExp and InputExp domains are disjoint and distinct from
the Exp domain. Informally, however, ValueExp can be viewed as a subset of
Exp and InputExp can be viewed as a subset of ValueExp. There are simple inclusion functions (which we do not define here) that can be used to formalize this
interpretation. To simplify our notation, we will not show such inclusion functions explicitly, but will assume that they are used implicitly when needed. For
example, in the simultaneous substitution notation $[IE_i/I_i]_{i=1}^n E_{body}$ used in the
definition of IF, we assume that each IE_i is first converted to the corresponding
element of Exp before the substitution is performed.

The configuration space for the FLK SOS consists of FLK expressions. The
input function IF maps an FLK program and a sequence of input values to
an initial configuration. If the number of inputs matches the number of formal
parameters in the program, the initial configuration is the result of substituting
the inputs for the formal parameters in the body of the program. Otherwise,
the initial configuration is an `error` expression indicating a mismatch. The final
configurations of the SOS are modeled by the ValueExp domain. The output
function OF erases the details of all procedure and pair values.

The SOS transition relation $\Rightarrow$ is defined by the context-based specification in
Figure 6.19. We shall call this relation the **evaluation relation** to distinguish
it from the simplification relation we will study in the next subsection. The
evaluation relation $\Rightarrow$ is defined by reductions ($\rightsquigarrow$) that take place in evaluation
contexts ($\mathbb{E}$). Most of the reduction rules deal with applications of primitives.
The *calculate* function used in the [+] rule serves the same purpose as it did in the
POSTFIX SOS. The *relapp* function returns the boolean literal encoding the result
of comparing two numerals with a given relational operator (`<`, `<=`, etc.). E.g.,
(*relapp* `<` 1 2) = `#t` and (*relapp* `>=` 1 2) = `#f`. The *logapp* function returns the
boolean literal that is the result of combining two boolean literals with `and` or `or`.
E.g., (*logapp* `and` `#f` `#t`) = `#f`, (*logapp* `and` `#t` `#t`) = `#t`, (*logapp* `or` `#f` `#t`)
= `#t`, and (*logapp* `or` `#f` `#f`) = `#f`.

Most `prim` reduction rules require their operand values to be of specific types.
For example, `+` and `<` require two integer operands; `and` requires two boolean
operands; and `fst` requires a pair operand.

Every primitive-application reduction rule requires operands that are value expressions. The evaluation context $(\texttt{prim}\ O_{primop}\ V_{i=1}^{k-1}\ \mathbb{E}\ E_{j=k+1}^{n})$ is responsible for evaluating the operands of a primitive application in left-to-right order. The $\mathbb{E}$ appearing after $V_{i=1}^{k-1}$ indicates that evaluation can take place in the kth operand position only when the first $k-1$ operands are already values. For example:

```
(prim / (prim * (prim + 4 7) (prim % 9 5)) (prim - 6 1))
⇒[+] (prim / (prim * 11 (prim % 9 5)) (prim - 6 1))
⇒[%] (prim / (prim * 11 4) (prim - 6 1))
⇒[*] (prim / 44 (prim - 6 1)) ⇒[-] (prim / 44 5) ⇒[/] 8
```

In the above evaluation sequence, we have annotated each evaluation arrow with the label of the reduction rule applied. Of course, each evaluation step also requires an evaluation context in which the reduction takes place.

The $(\texttt{if}\ \mathbb{E}\ E_{then}\ E_{else})$ evaluation context evaluates the test subexpression of a conditional. When this becomes a boolean literal, the [if-T] and [if-F] rules choose the appropriate branch. No evaluation takes place in the branch not chosen. For example,

```
(if (prim > (prim * 2 3) (prim + 4 5)) (prim * 6 7) (prim + 8 9))
⇒[*] (if (prim > 6 (prim + 4 5)) (prim * 6 7) (prim + 8 9))
⇒[+] (if (prim > 6 9) (prim * 6 7) (prim + 8 9))
⇒[>] (if #f (prim * 6 7) (prim + 8 9)) ⇒[if-F] (prim + 8 9) ⇒[+] 17
```

Procedure application is explained by the [β] rule, which substitutes the operand expression for the formal parameter in the procedure body. The left-hand side of this rule is called a **beta-redex** and the transformation is called **beta reduction**. Here is an example:

```
(app (app (lam x (lam y (prim * (prim - x y) (prim % x y)))) 20) 6)
⇒[β] (app (lam y (prim * (prim - 20 y) (prim % 20 y))) 6)
⇒[β] (prim * (prim - 20 6) (prim % 20 6))
⇒[-] (prim * 14 (prim % 20 6)) ⇒[%] (prim * 14 3) ⇒[*] 42
```

In FLK, the rator position can be an expression that is not an abstraction but may evaluate to an abstraction. The evaluation context $(\texttt{app}\ \mathbb{E}\ E_{rand})$ evaluates the rator position of an application. In the following evaluation, this evaluation context is needed to justify the evaluation steps labeled $\Rightarrow_{[>]}$ and $\Rightarrow_{[\texttt{if-}T]}$, which rewrite a conditional expression in the rator position to an abstraction:

```
(app (lam x (app (if (prim > x 0)
                     (lam y (prim + y 1))
                     (lam z (prim * z 2)))
                 (prim * x x)))
     4)
```
$\Rightarrow_{[\beta]}$ (app (if (prim > 4 0)
                       (lam y (prim + y 1))
                       (lam z (prim * z 2)))
                   (prim * 4 4))
$\Rightarrow_{[>]}$ (app (if #t (lam y (prim + y 1)) (lam z (prim * z 2)))
             (prim * 4 4))
$\Rightarrow_{[\text{if-}T]}$ (app (lam y (prim + y 1)) (prim * 4 4))
$\Rightarrow_{[\beta]}$ (prim + (prim * 4 4) 1) $\Rightarrow_{[*]}$ (prim + 16 1) $\Rightarrow_{[+]}$ 17

There is no evaluation context for evaluating the operand position of an application: the unevaluated operand expression is substituted for the formal parameter in the procedure body. This specifies that FLK procedures are nonstrict. (We will study a strict variant of FLK in Section 7.1.) If the substituted argument expression is never encountered in the evaluation of the body, it is never evaluated:

(app (lam x 1) (prim / 2 0)) $\Rightarrow_{[\beta]}$ 1

(app (lam x (if (prim < 1 2) 3 x)) (prim / 4 0))
$\Rightarrow_{[\beta]}$ (if (prim < 1 2) 3 (prim / 4 0))
$\Rightarrow_{[<]}$ (if #t 3 (prim / 4 0)) $\Rightarrow_{[\text{if-}T]}$ 3

If the formal parameter occurs more than once in the body, the operand expression may be evaluated multiple times. In the following example, the operand expression (prim + 2 3) is evaluated twice when substituted for x in the body of (lam x (prim * x x)):

(app (lam x (prim * x x)) (prim + 2 3))
$\Rightarrow_{[\beta]}$ (prim * (prim + 2 3) (prim + 2 3))
$\Rightarrow_{[+]}$ (prim * 5 (prim + 2 3)) $\Rightarrow_{[+]}$ (prim * 5 5) $\Rightarrow_{[*]}$ 25

The repeated evaluation of operand expressions is avoided in some alternative approaches to procedure application (see Sections 7.1 and 8.4.3).

Because abstractions are elements of the ValueExp domain, the $[\beta]$ rule is sufficient for explaining how FLK procedures can be passed as arguments to, and returned as results from, other procedures. We illustrate this in the following example, where

- (lam f (app f 5)) is a procedure that takes a procedural argument, f, and applies it to 5; and

- (lam n (lam x (prim - x n))) is a procedure that takes an integer argument, n, and returns a subtract-n procedure.

```
(app (app (lam f (app f 5))
          (lam n (lam x (prim - x n))))
     3)
⇒[β] (app (app (lam n (lam x (prim - x n))) 5)
     3)
⇒[β] (app (lam x (prim - x 5)) 3) ⇒[β] (prim - 3 5) ⇒[-] -2
```

The semantics of recursion (the [rec] rule) is especially simple in the SOS framework. It is obtained by unwinding the recursion equation one level at a time. Programmers often follow the same approach when trying to hand-simulate the behavior of recursive procedures. Figure 6.20 shows the evaluation of the following application of a recursive summation procedure that adds the numbers from 1 to its argument:

```
(app (rec sum (lam n (if (prim = n 0)
                         0
                         (prim + n (app sum (prim - n 1))))))
     3)
```

This example highlights the potential inefficiencies associated with nonstrict evaluation. For instance, the operand expression (prim - 3 1) ends up being evaluated five times!

It is easy to write a nonterminating expression with rec. For instance:

```
(app (rec loop (lam x (app loop x))) 0)
⇒[rec] (app (lam x (app (rec loop (lam x (app loop x))) x)) 0)
⇒[β]  (app (rec loop (lam x (app loop x))) 0)
⇒[rec] ···
```

Remarkably, it is possible to write nonterminating expressions without rec. Here is one example, which is similar in spirit to the POSTFIX command sequence (dup exec) dup exec :

```
(app (lam x (app x x)) (lam x (app x x)))
⇒[β] (app (lam x (app x x)) (lam x (app x x)))
⇒[β] ···
```

Although we have assumed that rec is a kernel construct of FLK, amazingly it turns out that it can be expressed as syntactic sugar in terms of abstractions and applications. We will study this on page 303.

As shown in Section 6.2.1, there are many kinds of errors in FLK. These include using the wrong number or types of values in various contexts or encountering an explicit `error` expression. Like the POSTFIX SOS, the FLK SOS models all errors with stuck states. There are no reduction rules that mention errors, so when an error situation is encountered in an evaluation context, the configuration is stuck. For example, not only is `(prim < 1 #t)` stuck, but all of the following expressions containing it are also stuck because no reduction can be performed on `(prim < 1 #t)` when it appears in an evaluation context:

```
(prim and (prim < 1 #t) (prim > 3 4))

(if (prim and (prim < 1 #t) (prim > 3 4))
    (lam x (prim + x 1))
    (lam y (prim * y 2)))

(app (if (prim and (prim < 1 #t) (prim > 3 4))
         (lam x (prim + x 1))
         (lam y (prim * y 2)))
     (prim / 6 2))
```

However, the left-hand sides of the following evaluation steps are *not* stuck, because each is an evaluation context filled with a reducible expression that allows progress to be made before `(prim < 1 #t)` is encountered:

$$(\text{prim and (prim > 3 4) (prim < 1 \#t))} \Rightarrow_{[>]} (\text{prim and \#f (prim < 1 \#t))}$$

$$(\text{app (lam b (if b 3 4)) (prim < 1 \#t))} \Rightarrow_{[\beta]} (\text{if (prim < 1 \#t) 3 4})$$

$$(\text{if (prim < 3 4) (prim < 1 \#t) \#f)} \Rightarrow_{[>]} (\text{if \#t (prim < 1 \#t) \#f)}$$

Instead of relying on stuck states to model errors, we could extend the FLK SOS to introduce and propagate explicit error values. This alternative approach to treating errors is explored in Exercise 6.28.

A notion of operational behavior for FLK can be obtained by instantiating the general notion of operational behavior introduced on page 51 with the FLK SOS. Because the FLK evaluation relation $\Rightarrow$ is deterministic (this is easy to see from inspection of the FLK evaluation relation), the result of this instantiation is the deterministic behavior function beh_{det} presented in Figure 6.18. For example, suppose P_{sum} is the following FLK program:

```
(flk (x)
  (app (rec sum (lam n (if (prim = n 0)
                           0
                           (prim + n (app sum (prim - n 1)))))))
       x))
```

Abbreviations

(@O E_1 ... E_n) abbreviates (prim O E_1 ... E_n) (usual FL sugar).

S = (rec sum (lam n (if (@= n 0) 0 (@+ n (app sum (@- n 1))))))

S' = (lam n (if (@= n 0) 0 (@+ n (app S (@- n 1)))))

Evaluation

(app S 3)

$\Rightarrow_{[\text{rec}]}$ (app S' 3)

$\Rightarrow_{[\beta]}$ (if (@= 3 0) 0 (@+ 3 (app S (@- 3 1))))

$\Rightarrow_{[=]}$ (if #f 0 (@+ 3 (app S (@- 3 1))))

$\Rightarrow_{[\text{if-}F]}$ (@+ 3 (app S (@- 3 1)))

$\Rightarrow_{[\text{rec}]}$ (@+ 3 (app S' (@- 3 1)))

$\Rightarrow_{[\beta]}$ (@+ 3 (if (@= (@- 3 1) 0) 0
                   (@+ (@- 3 1) (app S (@- (@- 3 1) 1)))))

$\Rightarrow_{[-]}$ (@+ 3 (if (@= 2 0) 0
                   (@+ (@- 3 1) (app S (@- (@- 3 1) 1)))))

$\Rightarrow_{[=]}$ (@+ 3 (if #f 0 (@+ (@- 3 1) (app S (@- (@- 3 1) 1)))))

$\Rightarrow_{[\text{if-}F]}$ (@+ 3 (@+ (@- 3 1) (app S (@- (@- 3 1) 1))))

$\Rightarrow_{[-]}$ (@+ 3 (@+ 2 (app S (@- (@- 3 1) 1))))

$\Rightarrow_{[\text{rec}]}$ (@+ 3 (@+ 2 (app S' (@- (@- 3 1) 1))))

$\Rightarrow_{[\beta]}$ (@+ 3 (@+ 2 (if (@= (@- (@- 3 1) 1) 0) 0
                       (@+ (@- (@- 3 1) 1) (app S (@- (@- (@- 3 1) 1) 1))))))

$\Rightarrow_{[-]}$ (@+ 3 (@+ 2 (if (@= (@- 2 1) 0) 0
                       (@+ (@- (@- 3 1) 1) (app S (@- (@- (@- 3 1) 1) 1))))))

$\Rightarrow_{[-]}$ (@+ 3 (@+ 2 (if (@= 1 0) 0
                       (@+ (@- (@- 3 1) 1) (app S (@- (@- (@- 3 1) 1) 1))))))

$\Rightarrow_{[=]}$ (@+ 3 (@+ 2 (if #f 0
                       (@+ (@- (@- 3 1) 1) (app S (@- (@- (@- 3 1) 1) 1))))))

$\Rightarrow_{[\text{if-}F]}$ (@+ 3 (@+ 2 (@+ (@- (@- 3 1) 1) (app S (@- (@- (@- 3 1) 1) 1)))))

$\Rightarrow_{[-]}$ (@+ 3 (@+ 2 (@+ (@- 2 1) (app S (@- (@- (@- 3 1) 1) 1)))))

$\Rightarrow_{[-]}$ (@+ 3 (@+ 2 (@+ 1 (app S (@- (@- (@- 3 1) 1) 1)))))

$\Rightarrow_{[\text{rec}]}$ (@+ 3 (@+ 2 (@+ 1 (app S' (@- (@- (@- 3 1) 1) 1)))))

$\Rightarrow_{[\beta]}$ (@+ 3 (@+ 2 (@+ 1 (if (@= (@- (@- (@- 3 1) 1) 1) 0) 0
                           (@+ (@- (@- (@- 3 1) 1) 1)
                               (app S (@- (@- (@- (@- 3 1) 1) 1) 1)))))))

$\Rightarrow_{[-]}$ (@+ 3 (@+ 2 (@+ 1 (if (@= (@- (@- 2 1) 1) 0) 0
                           (@+ (@- (@- (@- 3 1) 1) 1)
                               (app S (@- (@- (@- (@- 3 1) 1) 1) 1)))))))

$\Rightarrow_{[-]}$ (@+ 3 (@+ 2 (@+ 1 (if (@= (@- 1 1) 0) 0
                           (@+ (@- (@- (@- 3 1) 1) 1)
                               (app S (@- (@- (@- (@- 3 1) 1) 1) 1)))))))

$\Rightarrow_{[-]}$ (@+ 3 (@+ 2 (@+ 1 (if (@= 0 0) 0
                           (@+ (@- (@- (@- 3 1) 1) 1)
                               (app S (@- (@- (@- (@- 3 1) 1) 1) 1)))))))

$\Rightarrow_{[=]}$ (@+ 3 (@+ 2 (@+ 1 (if #t 0
                           (@+ (@- (@- (@- 3 1) 1) 1)
                               (app S (@- (@- (@- (@- 3 1) 1) 1) 1)))))))

$\Rightarrow_{[\text{if-}T]}$ (@+ 3 (@+ 2 (@+ 1 0)))

$\Rightarrow_{[+]}$ (@+ 3 (@+ 2 1)) $\Rightarrow_{[+]}$ (@+ 3 3) $\Rightarrow_{[+]}$ 6

Figure 6.20   FLK evaluation of an application of a recursive summation procedure.

Then beh_{det} $\langle P_{sum}, [IE_1 \ldots IE_k] \rangle$ is defined as follows:

$(\text{AnsExp} \rightarrowtail \text{Outcome } N_{ans})$ if $k = 1$, $IE_1 = N_{arg}$, $(compare >= N_{arg} \ 0)$,

and N_{ans} is the numeral for $\Sigma_{i=1}^{n} i$.

where n is the integer denoted by numeral N_{arg}.

∞ if $k = 1$, $IE_1 = N_{arg}$, and $(compare < N_{arg} \ 0)$

stuck   if $k \neq 1$ or $IE_1 \notin \text{IntLit}$.

The beh_{det} function departs in two ways from the informal notion of program execution introduced in Section 6.2.1:

- Because errors are modeled by stuck states, all programs encountering an error yield the outcome stuck rather than an error outcome with an associated message (e.g., *error:divide-by-zero*). The latter can be obtained by using an SOS that propagates errors (see Exercise 6.28).

- All programs returning a pair value result in the outcome

$$(\text{AnsExp} \rightarrowtail \text{Outcome } \texttt{pairans})$$

which does not show the components of the pair. Any attempt to flesh out the components of a nonstrict pair might encounter an error or an infinite loop. So we will interpret the informal outcome notation $\langle o_1, o_2 \rangle$ as:

the result of the program is a pair, and if the body of the program were wrapped in (prim fst □), then the outcome would be o_1, and if the body of the program were wrapped in (prim snd □), then the outcome would be o_2.

Exercise 6.22 Consider the following FLK abstractions:

E_{sub} = (lam x (lam y (prim - x y)))
E_{app5} = (lam f (app f 5))
E_{flip} = (lam g (lam a (lam b (app (app g b) a))))

Use the evaluation relation to show the evaluation of the following expressions:

a. (app E_{app5} (app E_{sub} 1))

b. (app (app E_{app5} E_{sub}) 2)

c. (app (app E_{app5} (app E_{flip} E_{sub})) 3)

d. (app (app (app E_{flip} E_{app5}) 4) E_{sub})

e. (app (app (app (app E_{flip} E_{flip}) 3) E_{sub}) 5)

Exercise 6.23 Use the FLK evaluation relation to show the evaluation of the following expressions:

a. (prim fst (pair 1 (prim not 3)))

b. (prim fst (prim snd (prim snd (rec p (pair 1 (pair 2 p))))))

The first expression illustrates the nonstrictness of `pair`, while the second illustrates the unwinding nature of `rec`.

Exercise 6.24 Consider the following FL expression E_0:

```
(letrec ((even? (abs (x) (if (@= x 0) #t (odd? (@- x 1)))))
         (odd? (abs (y) (@not (even? y)))))
  (list (even? 0) (odd? 1)))
```

a. What is the expression E_1 that is the result of desugaring E_0?

b. Use the FLK evaluation relation to show the evaluation of E_1. To simplify your task, introduce abbreviations for large unchanging expressions.

c. Bud Lojack thinks that the `letrec` desugaring in Figure 6.4 on page 220 can be simplified to:

$$\mathcal{DS}[\![(\texttt{letrec } ((I_i \; E_i)_{i=1}^n) \; E_{body})]\!]$$
$$=\mathcal{DS}[\![(\texttt{app } (\texttt{rec } I_{ChurchTuple}$$
$$(\texttt{lam } I_{selector} \; (I_{ChurchTuple} \; (\texttt{abs } (I_{i=1}^n) \; (I_{selector} \; E_{i=1}^n)))))$$
$$(\texttt{abs } (I_{i=1}^n) \; E_{body}))]\!], \text{ where } I_{ChurchTuple} \text{ and } I_{selector} \text{ are fresh}.$$

What is the expression E_2 that is the result of desugaring E_0 in Bud's modified approach?

d. Use the FLK rewrite rules to show the evaluation of E_2. What is the problem with Bud's desugaring?

Exercise 6.25 Since FLK is nonstrict, it is not necessary for `if` to be a distinguished construct. Instead, `if` could be a unary primitive operator that returns a (curried) binary function. That is, instead of being written (if E_1 E_2 E_3), conditionals could be expressed as

(app (app (primop if E_1) E_2) E_3)

Give the reduction rules for `if` as a unary primitive operator.

Exercise 6.26 Suppose we want to extend FL with a `least` construct. Given a numeric predicate, `least` returns the smallest nonnegative integer that satisfies the predicate:

```
(least (lam (x) (= x (* x x))))        ──→   0
                                    FL
(least (lam (a) (> (* a a) 10)))       ──→   4
                                    FL
(least (lam (x) (< x 0)))              ──→   ∞ {Looks, but no solution}
                                    FL
(least (lam (x) x))                    ──→   error:non-bool-in-if-test
                                    FL
```

a. Must the argument to `least` always be an abstraction (a `lam` expression)? If so, explain why; if not, give a counterexample.

b. One way to add `least` is to extend the syntax of FLK to include (`least` E) as a new kernel expression. Extend the operational semantics of FLK to handle the `least` expression. Keep in mind that an SOS has five parts; make the appropriate modifications to each of the parts. *Hint:* In addition to adding (`least` E) to the configuration space, it is also desirable to add a configuration of the form (`*least*` E N). Configurations like `*least*` that are not valid as expressions in the language are often useful for representing intermediate states of computations.

c. Alternatively, `least` can be written as a user-defined procedure that can be referenced in the definitions and body of an FL program. Show how to implement `least` with this approach.

Exercise 6.27 In FLK, `pair` is a kernel expression, but it can be handled in other ways.

a. One option is to treat `pair` as a primitive operator in Primop. Implement this change by modifying the grammar of FLK and the SOS for FLK. Show any changes you make to the domains and reduction rules. Do any of the evaluation contexts need to be modified?

b. Another option is to treat `pair` as a user-defined procedure. Here is such a definition:

```
(def pair (abs (x y) (abs (s) (s x y))))
```

Give corresponding definitions for unary selection procedures `fst` and `snd`. Can you define `pair?` in this approach?

Exercise 6.28 Like the POSTFIX SOS, the FLK SOS uses stuck states to model errors. Rather than using stuck states to model errors, we can explicitly represent and propagate errors by extending ValueExp to include `error` expressions as value expressions:

$V ::= \ldots \mid$ (`error` Y)

Then we need to modify the reduction rules to (1) convert stuck expressions to an appropriate `error` expression and (2) propagate `error` forms so that they eventually become final configurations (i.e., expressions in ValueExp). For example, we could have the rule

$$(\text{app } V \ E) \rightsquigarrow (\text{error non-procedural-rator}),$$
$$\text{where } V \text{ is not an abstraction} \qquad \qquad [\textit{rator-error}]$$

to express the fact that it is an error to use any value other than an abstraction in the rator position of an application.

a. Make all necessary modifications and additions to the FLK reduction relation in order to handle the explicit introduction and propagation of `error` expressions. Make sure that errors propagate appropriately; e.g., (`primop + 1 (primop / 1 0)`) should evaluate to an error because it has a subexpression that evaluates to an error.

b. Modify the AnsExp domain and the output function *OF* of the FLK SOS so that errors with messages can be outcomes of program execution.

Exercise 6.29 After carefully studying the SOS for FLK, Sam Antics proclaims that it is safe to use a naive substitution strategy (i.e., one that does not rename bound identifiers) in the [β] and [rec] rules as long as the original expression being evaluated does not contain any free identifiers.

a. Show that Sam is right. That is, show that the name capture problems addressed by the definition of substitution in Figure 6.17 cannot occur during the evaluation of an FLK expression that has no free identifiers.

b. Give an example of an FLK expression containing a free identifier that evaluates to the wrong answer if the naive substitution strategy is used.

c. Suppose that every FLK expression were alpha-renamed so that all variables had distinct identifiers and no bound variable used the same identifier as any free variable. Under these conditions, is it always safe to use the naive substitution strategy? If so, explain; if not, give a counterexample.

Exercise 6.30 Computation in the presence of nonstrictness can be viewed as a bureaucracy where envelopes (values containing a type and other information) are shuffled around by the interpreting agent that performs the computation.[9] In many steps of the computation, envelopes are simply moved around without being opened. In the formation of a nonstrict pair, for instance, two envelopes are simply stuffed into a larger envelope without ever having their contents examined. During other stages — a primitive addition, for instance — the contents (type and content information) of envelopes must definitely be examined.

With this perspective in mind, for each FLK expression describe when the contents of envelopes must be examined. In other words, which contexts demand the value of an expression?

Exercise 6.31 In your favorite programming language, implement an evaluator for FLK expressions based on the FLK SOS. Your evaluator should show the step-by-step evaluation of an FLK expression by displaying the result of each evaluation step. You will need an expression substitution procedure for implementing the [β] and [rec] rules.

Exercise 6.32

a. Write a big-step operational semantics (BOS) for FLK. (See Section 3.3 for an explanation of BOS.) As in Exercise 6.28, your rules should introduce and propagate errors. For example, Figure 6.21 shows the BOS rules for not.

b. In your favorite programming language, implement an evaluator for FLK expressions based on your FLK BOS. Your evaluator should show the result of evaluating an FLK expression. You will need an expression substitution procedure in order to handle procedure application and the unwinding of rec.

---

[9]Phil Agre introduced us to this point of view.

$$\frac{E \longrightarrow \texttt{\#t}}{(\texttt{prim not } E) \longrightarrow \texttt{\#f}} \qquad\qquad [\text{not-}T]$$

$$\frac{E \longrightarrow \texttt{\#f}}{(\texttt{prim not } E) \longrightarrow \texttt{\#t}} \qquad\qquad [\text{not-}F]$$

$$\frac{E \longrightarrow V}{(\texttt{prim not } E) \longrightarrow (\texttt{error not-a-bool})} \qquad\qquad [\text{not-}nonbool]$$
where V is not a boolean or an error.

$$(\texttt{prim not}) \longrightarrow (\texttt{error too-few-args}) \qquad\qquad [\text{not-}few]$$

$$\frac{\forall_{i=1}^{n} \, . \, E_i \longrightarrow V_i}{(\texttt{prim not } E_1 \, \ldots \, E_n) \longrightarrow (\texttt{error too-many-args})} \qquad\qquad [\text{not-}many]$$
where $n > 1$ and none of the V_i is an error.

$$\frac{\forall_{i=1}^{k-1} \, . \, E_i \longrightarrow V_i \quad ; \quad E_k \longrightarrow (\texttt{error } Y)}{(\texttt{prim } O \; E_1 \, \ldots \, E_n) \longrightarrow (\texttt{error } Y)} \qquad\qquad [\text{prim-error-prop}]$$
where $k \leq n$ and none of $V_{i=1}^{k-1}$ is an error.

Figure 6.21   Rewrite rules for `not` in a big-step operational semantics for FLK.

6.4.2   FLK Simplification

In our study of POSTFIX, we introduced the notion of safe transformations — changes to program phrases that are guaranteed to preserve program behavior. Here we revisit safe transformations in the context of behavior-preserving simplifications of FL expressions. The purpose of this exploration is twofold:

1. We want to explore safe transformations in the context of a language (FLK) that has many features not enjoyed by POSTFIX: e.g., names, recursion, and data structures (via `pair`). Such transformations are important for program optimization by both programmers and compiler writers.

2. The properties of simplification will be used to justify several important results later on. In particular, they will help us to show the relationship between parameter-passing mechanisms in Section 7.1, and will help us to show the strong normalization of a typed version of FLK in Section 11.7.

We will use the following FLK program P to motivate simplification:

```
(flk (n)
  (app (lam f (prim + (app f n) (app f 5)))
       (lam x (prim * (prim + 1 2) x))))
```

Reduction Relation ($\rightsquigarrow$)

  Same reduction rules as in Figure 6.19 on page 259

Simplification Contexts

$\mathbb{S} \in \mathrm{SimpContext}_{FL}$

$\mathbb{S} ::= \square \mid (\texttt{if } \mathbb{S} \ E_{then} \ E_{else}) \mid (\texttt{if } E_{test} \ \mathbb{S} \ E_{else}) \mid (\texttt{if } E_{test} \ E_{then} \ \mathbb{S})$
$\quad \mid (\texttt{prim } O_{primop} \ E_{i=1}^{k-1} \ \mathbb{S} \ E_{j=k+1}^{n})$
$\quad \mid (\texttt{lam } I_{formal} \ \mathbb{S}) \mid (\texttt{app } \mathbb{S} \ E_{rand}) \mid (\texttt{app } E_{rator} \ \mathbb{S})$
$\quad \mid (\texttt{pair } \mathbb{S} \ E_{snd}) \mid (\texttt{pair } E_{fst} \ \mathbb{S}) \mid (\texttt{rec } I_{name} \ \mathbb{S})$

Simplification Relation ($\rightarrow$)

  $\mathbb{S}\{E\} \rightarrow \mathbb{S}\{E'\}$, where $E \rightsquigarrow E'$

Nonevaluation Step ($\Longrightarrow\!\!\!\!\circ$)

  $\Longrightarrow\!\!\!\!\circ \ = (\rightarrow - \Rightarrow)$; *the set difference of the two relations*

Figure 6.22 A context-based description of the FLK simplification relation.

Executing this program on the argument 4 yields the following transition path:

```
     (app (lam f (prim + (app f 4) (app f 5)))
          (lam x (prim * (prim + 1 2) x))))
⇒[β] (prim + (app (lam x (prim * (prim + 1 2) x)) 4)
             (app (lam x (prim * (prim + 1 2) x)) 5))
⇒[β] (prim + (prim * (prim + 1 2) 4)
             (app (lam x (prim * (prim + 1 2) x)) 5))
⇒[+] (prim + (prim * 3 4)
             (app (lam x (prim * (prim + 1 2) x)) 5))
⇒[*] (prim + 12 (app (lam x (prim * (prim + 1 2) x)) 5))
⇒[β] (prim + 12 (prim * (prim + 1 2) 5))
⇒[+] (prim + 12 (prim * 3 5))
⇒[*] (prim + 12 15)
⇒[+] 27
```

The program contains several inefficiencies. Every time the program is executed, the abstraction (lam x (prim * (prim + 1 2) x)) is duplicated and applied to the arguments n and 5. This causes the primitive application (prim + 1 2), which always evaluates to 3, to be evaluated twice. We expect to be able to replace the abstraction by (lam x (prim * 3 x)). Moreover, applying this abstraction to 5 always yields 15 and applying it to n yields (prim * 3 n). So we should be able to simplify P to (flk (n) (+ (prim * 3 n) 15)), which we will call P'.

We can formalize these sorts of simplifications by defining a simplification relation $\rightarrow$ on expressions (Figure 6.22). This simplification relation supports the same basic reductions as the evaluation relation $\Rightarrow$ but allows them to be performed in arbitrary expression contexts (which we'll call **simplification con-**

texts) rather than restricting them to specialized evaluation contexts. We pronounce $E_1 \rightarrow E_2$ as "E_1 simplifies to E_2 in one step." For example, we can simplify the body of P to the body of P' via the following steps:

```
(app (lam f (prim + (app f n) (app f 5)))
     (lam x (prim * (prim + 1 2) x))))
  →[+] (app (lam f (prim + (app f n) (app f 5)))
          (lam x (prim * 3 x)))
  →[β] (prim + (app (lam x (prim * 3 x)) n)
              (app (lam x (prim * 3 x)) 5))
  →[β] (prim + (app (lam x (prim * 3 x)) n)
              (prim * 3 5))
  →[*] (prim + (app (lam x (prim * 3 x)) n) 15)
  →[β] (prim + (prim * 3 n) 15)
```

In this case, the final expression is a normal form with respect to $\rightarrow$; it is not possible to simplify it further.

Since evaluation and simplification are based on the same reductions and evaluation contexts are a subset of the simplification contexts, the evaluation relation $\Rightarrow$ is a subrelation of the simplification relation $\rightarrow$. So every evaluation step $E \Rightarrow E'$ can also be viewed as a simplification step $E \rightarrow E'$. We use the notation $E \Longrightarrow E'$ for any simplification step that is not an evaluation step, and call such a step a **nonevaluation step**. For example, here is a version of the above transition path annotated with evaluation and nonevaluation steps:

```
(app (lam f (prim + (app f n) (app f 5)))
     (lam x (prim * (prim + 1 2) x))))
  ⟜⇒[+] (app (lam f (prim + (app f n) (app f 5)))
           (lam x (prim * 3 x)))
  ⇒[β]  (prim + (app (lam x (prim * 3 x)) n)
               (app (lam x (prim * 3 x)) 5))
  ⟜⇒[β] (prim + (app (lam x (prim * 3 x)) n)
               (prim * 3 5))
  ⟜⇒[*] (prim + (app (lam x (prim * 3 x)) n) 15)
  ⇒[β]  (prim + (prim * 3 n) 15)
```

As illustrated by this example, evaluation and nonevaluation steps may be interleaved in a simplification sequence.

An FLK expression E belongs to one of three classes that describe its status relative to evaluation:

1. **reducible**: E can be reduced by an evaluation step. I.e., there is an E' such that $E \Rightarrow E'$.

2. **value**: E is an element of V.

3. **stuck**: E has no evaluation redex and is not an element of V.

The class of an expression is denoted (*classify E*). An important property of nonevaluation steps is that they preserve this classification:

Theorem 6.1 (Nonevaluation Steps Preserve Classification)

If $E_1 \overset{*}{\Rightarrow} E_2$, then (classify E_1) = (classify E_2).

This is easy to show by case analysis on the structure of E_1. In contrast, evaluation steps are not guaranteed to preserve classification: An evaluation step can change a reducible expression to a value or a stuck expression.

Whereas $\Rightarrow$ is deterministic, $\rightarrow$ is not because the general nature of simplification contexts often allows many different simplification steps to be performed in a given expression. However, $\rightarrow$ *is* confluent:

Theorem 6.2 (Confluence of FLK Simplification) *The* FLK *simplification relation is confluent. I.e., if $E_1 \overset{*}{\rightarrow} E_2$ and $E_1 \overset{*}{\rightarrow} E_3$ then there exists an E_4 such that $E_2 \overset{*}{\rightarrow} E_4$ and $E_3 \overset{*}{\rightarrow} E_4$.*

$$
\begin{array}{ccc}
E_1 & \overset{*}{\longrightarrow} & E_2 \\
\Big\downarrow{\scriptstyle *} & & \Big\downarrow{\scriptstyle *} \\
E_3 & \overset{*}{\dashrightarrow} & E_4
\end{array}
$$

As usual, in the diagram, the solid lines are the given relations and the dashed lines are the ones whose existence is implied by the theorem.

The proof of this and several other FLK simplification theorems can be found in the Web Supplement.

The confluence of simplification means that it is often possible to arrive at the same result via many different simplification paths. In particular, if $E_1 \overset{*}{\rightarrow} E_2$ and $E_1 \overset{*}{\rightarrow} E_3$ and both E_2 and E_3 are normal forms with respect to $\rightarrow$, then $E_2 = E_3$ (because both must be the E_4 implied by confluence). For example, here is a different simplification path for the body of P:

```
          (app (lam f (prim + (app f n) (app f 5)))
               (lam x (prim * (prim + 1 2) x))))
    ⇒[β]  (prim + (app (lam x (prim * (prim + 1 2) x)) n)
                  (app (lam x (prim * (prim + 1 2) x)) 5))
    ⇒[β]  (prim + (prim * (prim + 1 2) n)
                  (app (lam x (prim * (prim + 1 2) x)) 5))
    ⇒[+]  (prim + (prim * 3 n)
                  (app (lam x (prim * (prim + 1 2) x)) 5))
   ⟹[β]  (prim + (prim * 3 n) (prim * (prim + 1 2) 5))
   ⟹[+]  (prim + (prim * 3 n) (prim * 3 5))
   ⟹[*]  (prim + (prim * 3 n) 15)
```

In the alternative path, all evaluation steps are performed first until evaluation cannot proceed, and then nonevaluation steps are performed until a normal form is reached. The following theorem says that *any* FLK sequence of simplification steps can be replaced by a **standard path** consisting of a sequence of evaluation steps followed by a sequence of nonevaluation steps:

Theorem 6.3 (Standardization of FLK Simplification) *If $E_1 \xrightarrow{*} E_2$, then there exists an E' such that $E_1 \overset{*}{\Rightarrow} E'$ and $E' \overset{*}{\Longrightarrow} E_2$.*

Are simplification steps safe? Yes, it turns out that every simplification step is guaranteed to preserve the behavior of a program:

Theorem 6.4 (FLK Simplification Preserves Observational Equivalence) *If $E_1 \xrightarrow{*} E_2$ then $E_1 =_{obs} E_2$.*

This theorem can be proved using the confluence (Theorem 6.2) and standardization (Theorem 6.3) properties of FLK in conjunction with the fact that nonnormalization step preserve classification (Theorem 6.1). See the Web Supplement for details.

Theorem 6.4 gives FL programmers and compiler writers the confidence that they can simplify a program via $\rightarrow$ steps without changing its behavior. However, simplification steps cover only a small subset of safe transformations on FLK expressions. For example, they do not permit transforming (prim + 0 E) to E or (prim + E E) to (prim * 2 E). Nevertheless, simplification steps are still fundamental for reasoning about programs.

Note that the converse of Theorem 6.4 is not true. If E_1 and E_2 are observationally equivalent, it is not generally possible to show that one of these simplifies to the other. For example, we expect that (lam x (prim + x x)) and (lam x (prim * 2 x)) are observationally equivalent, but since both are normal forms with respect to $\rightarrow$, it is not possible to use $\rightarrow$ to simplify one to the other.

Exercise 6.33 Bud Lojack decides to implement an optimizer for FLK that performs all possible simplification steps on a program before running it on any inputs. Describe a fundamental problem with Bud's plan, using a concrete example to illustrate the problem.

6.5   A Denotational Semantics for FLK

Now we will develop a denotational semantics for FLK. As with EL and POST-FIX, the denotational semantics of FLK has a very different "feel" from the operational semantics. It gives us new ways to reason about FLK programs and suggests new techniques for implementing FLK. In particular, it employs a notion of **environment** that is an alternative to substitution for explaining the meaning of names in a program.

6.5.1   Semantic Algebra

As usual, we begin our study of the denotational semantics of FLK by carefully examining its semantic algebra: the semantic domains and the functions on these domains. The semantic domains of FLK are presented in Figure 6.23.

The values that can be expressed by an FLK expression are modeled by **expressible values** from the *Expressible* domain, which is a lifted sum of *Value* and *Error*. *Value* contains unit, boolean, integer, and symbol values, as well as pair and procedure values, which are recursively defined (indirectly via the *Comp* domain, explained below) in terms of *Expressible*. The fact that *Value* (and therefore *Expressible*) contains procedural values is an essential feature of a functional language: it indicates that procedural values may be used in all the same contexts where integers, booleans, and the like may be used. Errors, like symbols, are modeled as symbolic literals; in the case of errors, these represent the error messages. The bottom element of the *Expressible* domain represents a nonterminating computation in FLK.

We will see that the meaning of an FLK expression involves a notion of **computation**, which is an element of the domain *Comp*. In FLK, *Comp* is just a synonym for *Expressible*. So what is the *Comp* domain for? It is a commonly used domain that allows us to modularize our denotational semantics in support of various features. When we study variants of FL in later chapters, we will be able to tweak the definition of the *Comp* domain and leave the rest of the semantic algebra intact.

Similarly, the meaning of an FLK program involves an **answer** in the domain *Answer*. In FLK, *Answer* is another synonym for *Expressible*. We give it a separate name so that we can consider changing its definition later.

Whereas the SOS for FLK uses substitution to model naming, the denotational semantics uses **environments**, elements of the domain *Env*. An environment can be viewed as a virtual substitution that associates names (elements of the domain Ident) with so-called **nameable values** (elements of the domain

$c \in Comp\ =\ Expressible$; *Result of evaluating an expression*
$a \in Answer\ =\ Expressible$; *Result of running a program*
$x \in Expressible\ =\ (Value + Error)_\perp$; *Can be computed*
   $Error\ =\ \text{SymLit}$
$v \in Value\ =\ Unit\ +\ Bool\ +\ Int\ +\ Sym\ +\ Pair\ +\ Proc$
   $Unit\ =\ \{\text{unit}\}$
$b \in Bool\ =\ \{\text{true}, \text{false}\}$
$i \in Int\ =\ \{\ldots, \text{-}2, \text{-}1, 0, 1, 2, \ldots\}$
$y \in Sym\ =\ \text{SymLit}$
   $Pair\ =\ Comp \times Comp$
$p \in Proc\ =\ Nameable \to Comp$
$n \in Nameable\ =\ Comp$; *Can be named*
$\beta \in BindingVal\ =\ (Nameable + Unbound)_\perp$
$e \in Env\ =\ \text{Ident} \to BindingVal$; *Environment*
   $Unbound\ =\ \{\text{unbound}\}$

Ident and SymLit are the domains defined in Figure 6.1 on page 211.

Usual operations on *Bool*: $\neg$ (negation), $\wedge$ (conjunction), $\vee$ (disjunction), $=_{Bool}$
Usual operations on *Int*: $+_{Int}$, $-_{Int}$, $\times_{Int}$, $\div_{Int}$(quotient), $\%_{Int}$(remainder),
$$<_{Int},\ \leq_{Int},\ =_{Int},\ \neq_{Int},\ \geq_{Int},\ >_{Int}$$
Equality operation on *Sym*: $=_{Sym}$
Equality operation on Ident: $=_{\text{Ident}}$
Operations on *Env*: see Figure 6.24
Operations on *Comp*: see Figure 6.26

Figure 6.23   The semantic domains for FLK.

Nameable, which in FLK is a synonym for *Comp* and *Expressible*). An association between a name and a nameable value is called a **binding**. We say that the name is **bound to** the nameable value.

In the denotational semantics of FLK, expressions will be evaluated relative to an environment that specifies the values of the free variables in that expression. When a binding construct is encountered, the current environment will be extended by binding the bound name of the construct to an appropriate value. The extended environment will then be used to evaluate expressions within the scope of the bound name.

The *Env* domain consists of functions that map names to elements of the domain *BindingVal*, which is a lifted sum of nameable values and the trivial domain *Unbound*. The trivial element *unbound* acts as an "unbound marker" indicating that a name is not bound in an environment. The bottom element

---

Environment Operations

$empty\text{-}env : Env = \lambda I \, . \, (Unbound \rightarrowtail BindingVal \ \text{unbound})$

$lookup : \text{Ident} \to Env \to BindingVal = \lambda Ie \, . \, (e \ I)$

$extend : \text{Ident} \to Nameable \to Env \to Env$
$= \lambda Ine \, . \, \lambda I_2 \, . \ \textbf{if } I =_{\text{Ident}} I_2 \ \textbf{then } (Nameable \rightarrowtail BindingVal \ n)$
$\qquad\qquad\qquad \textbf{else } (lookup \ I_2 \ e) \ \textbf{end}$

$extend^* : \text{Ident}^* \to Nameable^* \to Env \to Env$
$= \lambda I^* n^* e \, . \ \textbf{match } \langle I^*, n^* \rangle$
$\qquad\qquad \triangleright \langle I_1 \, . \, I^*_{rest}, n_1 \, . \, n^*_{rest} \rangle \ [\![\ (extend \ I_1 \ n_1 \ (extend^* \ I^*_{rest} \ n^*_{rest} \ e))$
$\qquad\qquad \triangleright \textbf{else } e \ \textbf{end}$

$merge : Env \to Env \to Env$
$= \lambda e_1 e_2 \, . \ \lambda I \, . \ \textbf{match } (lookup \ I \ e_1)$
$\qquad\qquad \triangleright (Nameable \rightarrowtail BindingVal \ n) \ [\![\ (lookup \ I \ e_1)$
$\qquad\qquad \triangleright (Unbound \rightarrowtail BindingVal \ \text{unbound}) [\![\ (lookup \ I \ e_2)$
$\qquad\qquad \textbf{end}$

Notational Abbreviations

$[I \mapsto n]e$ abbreviates $(extend \ I \ n \ e)$.
This notation associates to the right: $[I_2 \mapsto n_2][I_1 \mapsto n_1]e = [I_2 \mapsto n_2]([I_1 \mapsto n_1]e)$.

$e_1 \uplus e_2$ abbreviates $(merge \ e_1 \ e_2)$.

$\{I_1 \mapsto n_1, \ldots, I_k \mapsto n_k\}$ abbreviates $[I_1 \mapsto n_1] \ldots [I_k \mapsto n_k]empty\text{-}env$,
 where $I_1, \ldots, I_k$ must be pairwise distinct.

Figure 6.24 Environment functions.

of $BindingVal$ is not strictly necessary for the semantics of FLK, but will be necessary for fixed-point calculations in variants of FLK that we will study later.

Environments are manipulated using the constants and functions in Figure 6.24. In the empty environment, $empty\text{-}env$, every name is unbound. The invocation $(lookup \ I \ e)$ returns the element of $BindingVal$ associated with the name I in environment e. The invocation $(extend \ I \ n \ e)$ (abbreviated $[I \mapsto n]e$) is similar, except it binds the name I to the nameable value n (overriding any existing binding). The invocation $(extend^* \ [I_1, \ldots, I_n] \ [n_1, \ldots, n_n] \ e)$ returns the environment that results from binding each I_i to n_i $(1 \le i \le n)$ in e. The invocation $(merge \ e_1 \ e_2)$ (abbreviated $e_1 \uplus e_2$) returns an environment that merges the bindings of e_1 and e_2; if a name is bound in both environments, the binding in e_1 takes precedence. The notation $\{I_1 \mapsto n_1, \ldots, I_n \mapsto n_n\}$ represents

Environment definition	Resulting environment
$e_0 = empty\text{-}env$	$\{\}$
$e_1 = [\mathsf{a} \mapsto \hat{1}]e_0$	$\{\mathsf{a} \mapsto \hat{1}\}$
$e_2 = [\mathsf{b} \mapsto \hat{2}]e_1$	$\{\mathsf{a} \mapsto \hat{1}, \mathsf{b} \mapsto \hat{2}\}$
$e_3 = [\mathsf{a} \mapsto \hat{3}]e_2$	$\{\mathsf{a} \mapsto \hat{3}, \mathsf{b} \mapsto \hat{2}\}$
$e_4 = \{\mathsf{b} \mapsto \hat{4}, \mathsf{c} \mapsto \hat{5}\}$	$\{\mathsf{b} \mapsto \hat{4}, \mathsf{c} \mapsto \hat{5}\}$
$e_5 = e_3 \uplus e_4$	$\{\mathsf{a} \mapsto \hat{3}, \mathsf{b} \mapsto \hat{2}, \mathsf{c} \mapsto \hat{5}\}$
$e_6 = e_4 \uplus e_3$	$\{\mathsf{a} \mapsto \hat{3}, \mathsf{b} \mapsto \hat{4}, \mathsf{c} \mapsto \hat{5}\}$
$e_7 = e_1 \uplus e_3$	$\{\mathsf{a} \mapsto \hat{1}, \mathsf{b} \mapsto \hat{2}\}$

Figure 6.25 Example environment manipulations. The notation $\hat{i}$ is an abbreviation for $(Value \rightarrowtail Comp\ (Int \rightarrowtail Value\ i))$.

an environment in which $I_1, \ldots, I_n$ (assumed to be pairwise distinct) are bound to nameable values $n_1, \ldots, n_n$, respectively, and all other identifiers are unbound. Figure 6.25 shows some sample uses of the environment functions.

The semantic domain *Nameable* of nameable values consists of those values that can be named in environments. The *Proc* domain's argument value must be nameable — otherwise the argument could not be named by a formal parameter. In FLK, *Nameable* and *Expressible* are the same domain, but there is no a priori reason why the entities that can be named in an environment have to be the same as those that can be the results of arbitrary expressions. In general, there are many other possible relationships between *Nameable* and *Expressible*:

- *Nameable* may be a superset of *Expressible* — some entities may be named but not written as expressions. For example, languages in which procedures are not first class typically have ways to name procedures (usually via a declaration) even though procedures cannot be values of expressions.

- *Nameable* may be a subset of *Expressible* — some entities that may be the results of expressions cannot be named. For example, in certain languages identifiers cannot name entities that represent errors and infinite loops. We shall study this example in detail when we discuss call-by-value semantics in Chapter 7.

- The relationship between *Nameable* and *Expressible* may be more complex. Consider a language in which procedures are nameable but not expressible, and errors are expressible but not nameable. (FORTRAN is in this category.)

Thus, the definitions of *Nameable* and *Expressible* in the denotational semantics of a given language contain some important information about high-level features of the language. The availability of this kind of information is the reason why, when reading a denotational semantics, it is advisable to first carefully study domain definitions and function signatures before delving into the details of the valuation functions.

Like *Value*, *Nameable*, and *Expressible*, the *Comp* domain is a "knob" that that can be tweaked as to specify different languages. The *Comp* domain provides a level of abstraction over the meaning of an expression relative to an environment. The valuation function $\mathcal{E}$ for expressions will always have the signature $\mathcal{E} : \mathrm{Exp} \rightarrow Env \rightarrow Comp$.

The purpose of the *Comp* domain is to highlight the essential meaning of expressions while factoring out cumbersome details like the propagation of errors and the management of context domains we will encounter in later chapters. In FLK, operations on the *Comp* domain serve mainly to simplify the description of error propagation. When we extend FL by adding state in Chapter 8 and continuations in Chapter 9, *Comp* and its associated operations will be become more complex, but the valuation functions for many expressions will remain unchanged. Elements of the state and control domains will be mentioned explicitly only in meanings of those expressions that use the state and control features of the language in an essential way.

The *Comp* domain is equipped with the functions shown in Figure 6.26. *val-to-comp* converts a value to a computation, *err-to-comp* converts an error to a computation, and *nam-to-comp* converts a nameable value to a computation. In FLK, *nam-to-comp* is the identity function because *Nameable* and *Comp* are the same. However, in other languages we study, *Nameable* and *Comp* will be different. Judiciously using *nam-to-comp* in some valuation clauses will allow us to keep the same valuation clause when we move from language to language; only the definition of *nam-to-comp* will change.

The purpose of the *with-value* function is to hide the explicit propagation of errors and infinite loops. The invocation (*with-value c f*) checks whether the computation c is a value. If so, it applies the function f (which returns another computation) to that value; otherwise it simply returns the original computation c. The invocation (*with-values c^* f*) is similar, except that it processes a sequence of computations c^*. If all computations in c^* are values, it applies f to these values (returning a computation); otherwise, the first non-value computation encountered in c^* is returned. The other functions whose names begin with *with-* are similar, except that (1) they may process elements other than computations and (2) they may generate new error computations rather than just passing along old ones. For example, the invocation (*with-boolean-val v f*) tests if v is a boolean value b. If so, the computation (f b) is returned. Otherwise, an error computation indicating that v is not a boolean is returned. The *with-boolean-comp* function is similar, except that it takes a computation rather than a value as its first argument. The *with-nameable* function processes the nameable value that results from looking up a name in an environment (or returns an `unbound-var` error computation if the name is unbound).

Some useful equalities involving the computation functions are presented in Figure 6.27. When we change the *Comp* domain in later chapters, we will change the definitions of its associated functions so that these equalities will still hold.

6.5.2   Valuation Functions

The valuation functions for FLK are presented in Figures 6.28 and 6.29. There are many valuation functions because there is one function for each syntactic domain that denotes a node in an abstract syntax tree, and there are many such syntactic domains (see Figure 6.18 on page 258).

The key valuation function is $\mathcal{E}$, whose signature is Exp $\rightarrow$ *Env* $\rightarrow$ *Comp*. This says that the meaning of an expression is a function from environments to computations.

- The function that is the meaning of an expression takes an environment because expressions may have free variables and an environment is necessary to resolve the meanings of these variables. The environment serves as a context domain that plays the role of substitution in the SOS. Indeed, an environment can be viewed as a virtual substitution that is passed down an expression AST and is performed in a "just-in-time" fashion when a variable reference is reached (in the clause $\mathcal{E}[\![I]\!]$).

- The function that is the meaning of an expression returns a computation. In FLK, the computation domain *Comp* is the same as *Expressible*, whose definition is $(Value + Error)_\bot$. So evaluating an expression relative to an environment can result in one of three kinds of answers: (1) a value (i.e., the unit value, a boolean, an integer, a symbol, a pair, or a procedure); (2) an error (one that carries an error message); or (3) an infinite loop.

The valuation clauses for $\mathcal{E}$ are written in a compact style, thanks in large part to the *Comp* abstraction and its associated helper functions. However, it takes time and effort to learn how to read clauses written in this style. It is helpful first to "type check" the clauses — that is, based on the declared signatures of the valuation functions and helper functions from the semantic domains, to reason that each clause has the type declared by the signature. It is also sometimes

$val\text{-}to\text{-}comp : Value \rightarrow Comp \ = \ Value \rightarrowtail Comp$
$err\text{-}to\text{-}comp : Error \rightarrow Comp \ = \ Error \rightarrowtail Comp$
$nam\text{-}to\text{-}comp : Nameable \rightarrow Comp \ = \ \lambda n \,.\, n$

$with\text{-}value : Comp \rightarrow (Value \rightarrow Comp) \rightarrow Comp$
$= \lambda cf \,.\, \textbf{match } c$
$\qquad \triangleright (Value \rightarrowtail Comp \ v) \ \| \ (f \ v)$
$\qquad \triangleright \textbf{else } c$
$\qquad \textbf{end}$

$with\text{-}values : Comp^* \rightarrow (Value^* \rightarrow Comp) \rightarrow Comp$
$= \lambda c^* f \,.\, \textbf{match } c^*$
$\qquad \triangleright [\,]_{Comp} \ \| \ (f \ [\,]_{Value})$
$\qquad \triangleright c_{fst} \cdot c^*_{rest} \ \| \ (with\text{-}value \ c_{fst}$
$\qquad\qquad\qquad (\lambda v_{fst} \,.\, (with\text{-}values \ c^*_{rest} \ (\lambda v^*_{rest} \,.\, (f \ (v_{fst} \cdot v^*_{rest})))))))$
$\qquad \textbf{end}$

$with\text{-}boolean\text{-}val : Value \rightarrow (Bool \rightarrow Comp) \rightarrow Comp$
$= \lambda vf \,.\, \textbf{match } v$
$\qquad \triangleright (Bool \rightarrowtail Value \ b) \ \| \ (f \ b)$
$\qquad \triangleright \textbf{else } (err\text{-}to\text{-}comp \ \texttt{not-a-boolean})$
$\qquad \textbf{end}$
similar for with-integer-val, with-pair-val, etc.

$with\text{-}boolean\text{-}comp : Comp \rightarrow (Bool \rightarrow Comp) \rightarrow Comp$
$= \lambda cf \,.\, (with\text{-}value \ c \ (\lambda v \,.\, (with\text{-}boolean\text{-}val \ v \ f)))$
similar for with-integer-comp, with-procedure-comp, etc.

$with\text{-}nameable : BindingVal \rightarrow (Nameable \rightarrow Comp) \rightarrow Comp$
$= \lambda \beta f \,.\, \textbf{match } \beta$
$\qquad \triangleright (Nameable \rightarrowtail BindingVal \ n) \ \| \ (f \ n)$
$\qquad \triangleright (Unbound \rightarrowtail BindingVal \ unbound) \ \| \ (err\text{-}to\text{-}comp \ \texttt{unbound-var})$
$\qquad \textbf{end}$

Figure 6.26   Computation functions.

helpful to expand some of the helper functions in a clause to understand it better. For example, here is an expanded version of the $\mathcal{E}$ clause for `if`:

$\mathcal{E}[\![(\texttt{if} \ E_1 \ E_2 \ E_3)]\!] =$
$\quad \lambda e \,.\, \textbf{match } (\mathcal{E}[\![E_1]\!] \ e)$
$\qquad \triangleright (Value \rightarrowtail Comp \ v) \ \| \ \textbf{match } v$
$\qquad\qquad\qquad \triangleright (Bool \rightarrowtail Value \ b) \ \|$
$\qquad\qquad\qquad\quad \textbf{if } b \ \textbf{then } (\mathcal{E}[\![E_2]\!] \ e) \ \textbf{else } (\mathcal{E}[\![E_3]\!] \ e) \ \textbf{end}$
$\qquad\qquad\qquad \triangleright \textbf{else } (err\text{-}to\text{-}comp \ \texttt{not-a-boolean}) \ \textbf{end}$
$\qquad \triangleright \textbf{else } (\mathcal{E}[\![E_1]\!] \ e) \ \textbf{end}$

$$(\text{with-value }(\text{val-to-comp } v)\ f) = (f\ v) \tag{6.5}$$

$$(\text{with-value } c\ (\lambda v\ .\ (\text{val-to-comp } v))) = c \tag{6.6}$$

$$(\text{with-value }(\text{with-value } c\ f)\ g)$$
$$= (\text{with-value } c\ (\lambda v\ .\ (\text{with-value }(f\ v)\ g))) \tag{6.7}$$

$$(\text{with-value }(\text{err-to-comp } Y_{msg})\ f) = (\text{err-to-comp } Y_{msg}) \tag{6.8}$$

$$(\text{with-boolean-val }(Bool \rightarrowtail Value\ b)\ f) = (f\ b) \tag{6.9}$$
similar for with-integer-val, *etc.*

$$(\text{with-boolean-comp }(\text{val-to-comp }(Bool \rightarrowtail Value\ b))\ f) = (f\ b) \tag{6.10}$$
similar for with-integer-comp, *etc.*

$$(\text{with-boolean-comp }(\text{err-to-comp } Y_{msg})\ f) = (\text{err-to-comp } Y_{msg}) \tag{6.11}$$
similar for with-integer-comp, *etc.*

$$(\text{with-nameable }(\text{lookup } I\ e)\ f) = (f\ n)\ ,\ \text{where } I \text{ is bound to } n \text{ in } e \tag{6.12}$$

$$(\text{with-nameable }(\text{lookup } I\ e)\ f) = (\text{err-to-comp unbound-var}),$$
$$\text{where } I \text{ is unbound in } e \tag{6.13}$$

Figure 6.27   Useful equalities on computations.

The expanded version makes explicit all the details of error checking that are hidden in the compact version. When the *Comp* domain is extended to handle state and control, even more details will be hidden by the compact versions of the clauses.

The meaning $\mathcal{E}[\![L]\!]$ of a literal L is a function that ignores its environment and simply injects the literal value into the *Comp* domain. It implicitly uses the $\mathcal{L}$, $\mathcal{B}$, and $\mathcal{N}$ functions, all of which are straightforward. The meaning of $\mathcal{E}[\![(\text{error } Y)]\!]$ is similar, except that it injects an error into the *Comp* domain.

The meaning $\mathcal{E}[\![I]\!]$ of an identifier is a function that looks up I in the environment e. If I is bound to the nameable value n (which is a computation) in e, then n is returned. Otherwise, I is unbound, and a computation specifying an unbound variable error is returned.

In the invocation $(\mathcal{E}[\![(\text{if } E_{test}\ E_{then}\ E_{else})]\!]\ e)$, if $(\mathcal{E}[\![E_{test}]\!]\ e)$ is a boolean value b, then b is used to choose between the computations $(\mathcal{E}[\![E_{then}]\!]\ e)$ and $(\mathcal{E}[\![E_{else}]\!]\ e)$. If $(\mathcal{E}[\![E_{test}]\!]\ e)$ is a value that is not a boolean, the resulting computation is an error. If $(\mathcal{E}[\![E_{test}]\!]\ e)$ is an error or infinite loop, these become the resulting computation of the if.

$(\mathcal{E}[\![(\text{pair } E_1\ E_2)]\!]\ e)$ simply returns a pair value whose components are the computations $(\mathcal{E}[\![E_1]\!]\ e)$ and $(\mathcal{E}[\![E_2]\!]\ e)$. As required for the nonstrictness of FLK's pairs, this always succeeds with a pair value, even when one or both of $(\mathcal{E}[\![E_1]\!]\ e)$ and $(\mathcal{E}[\![E_2]\!]\ e)$ is an error or an infinite loop.

$\mathcal{B} : \text{BoolLit} \to \textit{Bool}$

$\mathcal{N} : \text{IntLit} \to \textit{Int}$

$\mathcal{L} : \text{Lit} \to \textit{Value}$

$\mathcal{E} : \text{Exp} \to \textit{Env} \to \textit{Comp}$; $\textit{Comp} = \textit{Expressible in FLK}$

$\mathcal{E}^* : \text{Exp}^* \to \textit{Env} \to \textit{Comp}^*$

$\mathcal{O} : \text{Primop} \to \textit{Value}^* \to \textit{Comp}$

$\mathcal{IE} : \text{InputExp} \to \textit{Comp}$

$\mathcal{IE}^* : \text{InputExp}^* \to \textit{Comp}^*$

$\mathcal{P} : \text{Prog} \to \text{InputExp}^* \to \textit{Answer}$; $\textit{Answer} = \textit{Expressible in FLK}$

$\mathcal{B}[\![\texttt{\#t}]\!] = \textit{true}$

$\mathcal{B}[\![\texttt{\#f}]\!] = \textit{false}$

$\mathcal{N}$ maps integer numerals to the integer numbers they denote.

$\mathcal{L}[\![\texttt{\#u}]\!] = (\textit{Unit} \rightarrowtail \textit{Value } \textit{unit})$

$\mathcal{L}[\![B]\!] = (\textit{Bool} \rightarrowtail \textit{Value } \mathcal{B}[\![B]\!])$

$\mathcal{L}[\![N]\!] = (\textit{Int} \rightarrowtail \textit{Value } \mathcal{N}[\![N]\!])$

$\mathcal{L}[\![(\texttt{sym } Y)]\!] = (\textit{Sym} \rightarrowtail \textit{Value } Y)$

$\mathcal{E}[\![L]\!] = \lambda e \,.\, (\textit{val-to-comp } \mathcal{L}[\![L]\!])$

$\mathcal{E}[\![(\texttt{error } Y)]\!] = \lambda e \,.\, (\textit{err-to-comp } Y)$

$\mathcal{E}[\![I]\!] = \lambda e \,.\, (\textit{with-nameable } (\textit{lookup } I \; e) \; (\lambda n \,.\, (\textit{nam-to-comp } n)))$

$\mathcal{E}[\![(\texttt{if } E_1 \; E_2 \; E_3)]\!] = \lambda e \,.\, (\textit{with-boolean-comp } (\mathcal{E}[\![E_1]\!] \; e)$
$$(\lambda b \,.\, \textbf{if } b \textbf{ then } (\mathcal{E}[\![E_2]\!] \; e) \textbf{ else } (\mathcal{E}[\![E_3]\!] \; e) \,\textbf{end}))$$

$\mathcal{E}[\![(\texttt{pair } E_1 \; E_2)]\!] = \lambda e \,.\, (\textit{val-to-comp } (\textit{Pair} \rightarrowtail \textit{Value } \langle (\mathcal{E}[\![E_1]\!] \; e), (\mathcal{E}[\![E_2]\!] \; e) \rangle))$

$\mathcal{E}[\![(\texttt{prim } O \; E^*)]\!] = \lambda e \,.\, (\textit{with-values } (\mathcal{E}^*[\![E^*]\!] \; e) \; (\lambda v^* \,.\, (\mathcal{O}[\![O]\!] \; v^*)))$

$\mathcal{E}[\![(\texttt{lam } I \; E)]\!] = \lambda e \,.\, (\textit{val-to-comp } (\textit{Proc} \rightarrowtail \textit{Value } (\lambda n \,.\, (\mathcal{E}[\![E]\!] \; [I \mapsto n]e))))$

$\mathcal{E}[\![(\texttt{app } E_1 \; E_2)]\!] = \lambda e \,.\, (\textit{with-procedure-comp } (\mathcal{E}[\![E_1]\!] \; e) \; (\lambda p \,.\, (p \; (\mathcal{E}[\![E_2]\!] \; e))))$

$\mathcal{E}[\![(\texttt{rec } I \; E)]\!] = \lambda e \,.\, (\textbf{fix}_{\textit{Comp}} \; (\lambda c \,.\, (\mathcal{E}[\![E]\!] \; [I \mapsto c]e)))$

$\mathcal{E}^*[\![]\!] = \lambda e \,.\, [\,]_{\textit{Comp}}$

$\mathcal{E}^*[\![E_1 \,.\, E_{rest}^*]\!] = \lambda e \,.\, (\mathcal{E}[\![E_1]\!] \; e) \,.\, (\mathcal{E}^*[\![E_{rest}^*]\!] \; e)$

$\mathcal{IE}[\![L]\!] = (\textit{val-to-comp } \mathcal{L}[\![L]\!])$

$\mathcal{IE}[\![(\texttt{pair } IE_1 \; IE_2)]\!] = (\textit{val-to-comp } (\textit{Pair} \rightarrowtail \textit{Value } \langle \mathcal{IE}[\![IE_1]\!], \mathcal{IE}[\![IE_2]\!] \rangle))$

$\mathcal{IE}^*[\![]\!] = [\,]_{\textit{Comp}}$

$\mathcal{IE}^*[\![IE_1 \,.\, IE_{rest}^*]\!] = (\mathcal{IE}[\![IE_1]\!]) \,.\, (\mathcal{IE}^*[\![IE_{rest}^*]\!])$

$\mathcal{P}[\![(\texttt{flk } (I^*) \; E_{body})]\!]$
$= \lambda IE^* \,.\, \textbf{if } (\textit{length } I^*) =_{\textit{Int}} (\textit{length } IE^*)$
$\qquad \textbf{then } (\mathcal{E}[\![E_{body}]\!] \; (\textit{extend}^* \; I^* \; (\mathcal{IE}^*[\![IE^*]\!]) \; \textit{empty-env}))$
$\qquad \textbf{else } (\textit{err-to-comp } \texttt{wrong-number-of-args})$

Figure 6.28 Valuation functions for FLK (except primitive operators).

$(\mathcal{E}[\![(\text{prim } O \text{ } E^*)]\!] \text{ } e)$ uses the valuation function $\mathcal{E}^*$ to find the meanings of all expressions in E^* relative to the environment e. These are processed by *with-values*, which propagates errors and infinite loops appropriately. In the case where all of the expressions in E^* have values, these values v^* are processed by $\mathcal{O}[\![O]\!]$, the meaning of the primitive operator O. The $\mathcal{O}$ function is defined in Figure 6.29. Most of the work done by the $\mathcal{O}$ clauses is checking that the number and types of arguments are correct, removing injections to access the raw operand values, and injecting the result of the operation into the computation domain.

We can specialize the `prim` clause to the two-argument case as follows:

$$\mathcal{E}[\![(\text{prim } O \text{ } E_1 \text{ } E_2)]\!]$$
$$= \lambda e \text{ . } \text{with-values } (\mathcal{E}^*[\![[E_1, E_2]]\!] \text{ } e) \text{ } f_1 \text{ , where } f_1 \text{ } = \text{ } \lambda v^*_{seq1} \text{ . } (\mathcal{O}[\![O]\!] \text{ } v^*_{seq1})$$
$$= \lambda e \text{ . } \text{with-value } (\mathcal{E}[\![E_1]\!] \text{ } e)$$
$$\qquad (\lambda v_1 \text{ . } \text{with-values } (\mathcal{E}^*[\![[E_2]]\!] \text{ } e) \text{ } f_2),$$
$$\qquad\qquad \text{where } f_2 \text{ } = \text{ } \lambda v^*_{seq2} \text{ . } (f_1 \text{ } (v_1 \text{ . } v^*_{seq2}))$$
$$= \lambda e \text{ . } \text{with-value } (\mathcal{E}[\![E_1]\!] \text{ } e)$$
$$\qquad (\lambda v_1 \text{ . } \text{with-value } (\mathcal{E}[\![E_2]\!] \text{ } e) \text{ } (\lambda v_2 \text{ . } \text{with-values } (\mathcal{E}^*[\![]\!] \text{ } e) \text{ } f_3)),$$
$$\qquad\qquad \text{where } f_3 \text{ } = \text{ } \lambda v^*_{seq3} \text{ . } (f_2 \text{ } (v_2 \text{ . } v^*_{seq3}))$$
$$= \lambda e \text{ . } \text{with-value } (\mathcal{E}[\![E_1]\!] \text{ } e)$$
$$\qquad (\lambda v_1 \text{ . } \text{with-value } (\mathcal{E}[\![E_2]\!] \text{ } e) \text{ } (\lambda v_2 \text{ . } (f_3 \text{ } [])))$$
$$= \lambda e \text{ . } \text{with-value } (\mathcal{E}[\![E_1]\!] \text{ } e)$$
$$\qquad (\lambda v_1 \text{ . } \text{with-value } (\mathcal{E}[\![E_2]\!] \text{ } e) \text{ } (\lambda v_2 \text{ . } (f_2 \text{ } [v_2])))$$
$$= \lambda e \text{ . } \text{with-value } (\mathcal{E}[\![E_1]\!] \text{ } e)$$
$$\qquad (\lambda v_1 \text{ . } \text{with-value } (\mathcal{E}[\![E_2]\!] \text{ } e) \text{ } (\lambda v_2 \text{ . } (f_1 \text{ } [v_1, v_2])))$$
$$= \lambda e \text{ . } \text{with-value } (\mathcal{E}[\![E_1]\!] \text{ } e)$$
$$\qquad (\lambda v_1 \text{ . } \text{with-value } (\mathcal{E}[\![E_2]\!] \text{ } e) \text{ } (\lambda v_2 \text{ . } (\mathcal{O}[\![O]\!] \text{ } [v_1, v_2])))$$

We can further specialize this version of `prim` to `+`:

$$\mathcal{E}[\![(\text{prim } + \text{ } E_1 \text{ } E_2)]\!]$$
$$= \lambda e \text{ . } \text{with-value } (\mathcal{E}[\![E_1]\!] \text{ } e)$$
$$\qquad (\lambda v_1 \text{ . } \text{with-value } (\mathcal{E}[\![E_2]\!] \text{ } e)$$
$$\qquad\qquad (\lambda v_2 \text{ . } \text{with-integer-val } v_1$$
$$\qquad\qquad\qquad (\lambda i_1 \text{ . } (\text{with-integer-val } v_2$$
$$\qquad\qquad\qquad\qquad (\lambda i_2 \text{ . } (\text{val-to-comp}$$
$$\qquad\qquad\qquad\qquad\qquad (Int \rightarrowtail Value \text{ } (i_1 +_{Int} i_2)))))))))$$

Observe that $\mathcal{E}[\![(\text{prim } + \text{ } E_1 \text{ } E_2)]\!]$ is *not* equal to $\mathcal{E}[\![(\text{prim } + \text{ } E_2 \text{ } E_1)]\!]$. The operands of a primitive application are evaluated from left to right, and whether E_1 or E_2 is evaluated first can be detected using errors, possibly in conjunction with an infinite loop. For example, suppose $(\mathcal{E}[\![E_1]\!] \text{ } e)$ results in an error with message `err1` and $(\mathcal{E}[\![E_2]\!] \text{ } e)$ results in an error with message `err2`. Then $\mathcal{E}[\![(\text{prim } + \text{ } E_1 \text{ } E_2)]\!]e$ will yield $(Error \rightarrowtail Comp \text{ } \text{err1})$ and $\mathcal{E}[\![(\text{prim } + \text{ } E_2 \text{ } E_1)]\!]e$ will yield $(Error \rightarrowtail Comp \text{ } \text{err2})$. Similar reasoning applies if one of E_1 or E_2

$\mathcal{O}[\![\text{not}]\!] = \lambda v^* . \textbf{ match } v^*$
$\qquad\qquad \triangleright [v]_{Value} \;\|\; (\text{with-boolean-val } v$
$\qquad\qquad\qquad\qquad\qquad (\lambda b . \; (\text{val-to-comp } (Bool \rightarrowtail Value \; \neg b))))$
$\qquad\qquad \triangleright \textbf{else } (err\text{-}to\text{-}comp \; \texttt{not-wrong-number-of-args})$
$\qquad\qquad \textbf{end}$

$\mathcal{O}[\![\text{and}]\!] = \lambda v^* . \textbf{ match } v^*$
$\qquad\qquad \triangleright [v_1, v_2]_{Value} \;\|\; (\text{with-boolean-val } v_1$
$\qquad\qquad\qquad\qquad\qquad\qquad (\lambda b_1 . \; (\text{with-boolean-val } v_2$
$\qquad\qquad\qquad\qquad\qquad\qquad\qquad\qquad (\lambda b_2 . \; (\text{val-to-comp}$
$\qquad\qquad\qquad\qquad\qquad\qquad\qquad\qquad\qquad\qquad (Bool \rightarrowtail Value \; (b_1 \wedge b_2)))))))$
$\qquad\qquad \triangleright \textbf{else } (err\text{-}to\text{-}comp \; \texttt{and-wrong-number-of-args}) \textbf{ end}$
similar for `or`

$\mathcal{O}[\![\text{+}]\!] = \lambda v^* . \textbf{ match } v^*$
$\qquad\qquad \triangleright [v_1, v_2]_{Value} \;\|\; (\text{with-integer-val } v_1$
$\qquad\qquad\qquad\qquad\qquad\qquad (\lambda i_1 . \; (\text{with-integer-val } v_2$
$\qquad\qquad\qquad\qquad\qquad\qquad\qquad\qquad (\lambda i_2 . \; (\text{val-to-comp}$
$\qquad\qquad\qquad\qquad\qquad\qquad\qquad\qquad\qquad\qquad (Int \rightarrowtail Value \; (i_1 +_{Int} i_2)))))))$
$\qquad\qquad \triangleright \textbf{else } (err\text{-}to\text{-}comp \; \texttt{+-wrong-number-of-args}) \textbf{ end}$
similar for `-`, `*`, `/`, *and* `%`, *except that* `/` *and* `%` *return an error when* $i_2 = 0$

$\mathcal{O}[\![\text{<}]\!] = \lambda v^* . \textbf{ match } v^*$
$\qquad\qquad \triangleright [v_1, v_2]_{Value} \;\|\; (\text{with-integer-val } v_1$
$\qquad\qquad\qquad\qquad\qquad\qquad (\lambda i_1 . \; (\text{with-integer-val } v_2$
$\qquad\qquad\qquad\qquad\qquad\qquad\qquad\qquad (\lambda i_2 . \; (\text{val-to-comp}$
$\qquad\qquad\qquad\qquad\qquad\qquad\qquad\qquad\qquad\qquad (Bool \rightarrowtail Value \; (i_1 <_{Int} i_2)))))))$
$\qquad\qquad \triangleright \textbf{else } (err\text{-}to\text{-}comp \; \texttt{<-wrong-number-of-args}) \textbf{ end}$
similar for `<=`, `=`, `!=`, `>=`, *and* `>`; `bool=?` *and* `sym=?` *are also similar, except that they use with-boolean-val and with-symbol-val, respectively, in place of with-integer-val*

$\mathcal{O}[\![\text{fst}]\!] = \lambda v^* . \textbf{ match } v^*$
$\qquad\qquad \triangleright [v]_{Value} \;\|\; (\text{with-pair-val } v \; (\lambda \langle c_1, c_2 \rangle . \; c_1))$
$\qquad\qquad \triangleright \textbf{else } (err\text{-}to\text{-}comp \; \texttt{fst-wrong-number-of-args}) \textbf{ end}$
similar for `snd`

$\mathcal{O}[\![\text{int?}]\!] = \lambda v^* . \textbf{ match } v^*$
$\qquad\qquad \triangleright [v]_{Value} \;\|\; \textbf{match } v$
$\qquad\qquad\qquad\qquad \triangleright (Int \rightarrowtail Value \; i) \;\|\; (\text{val-to-comp } (Bool \rightarrowtail Value \; true))$
$\qquad\qquad\qquad\qquad \triangleright \textbf{else } (\text{val-to-comp } (Bool \rightarrowtail Value \; false))$
$\qquad\qquad\qquad\qquad \textbf{end}$
$\qquad\qquad \triangleright \textbf{else } (err\text{-}to\text{-}comp \; \texttt{int?-wrong-number-of-args}) \textbf{ end}$
similar for `unit?`, `bool?`, `sym?`, `pair?`, `proc?`

Figure 6.29 Valuation functions for FLK primitive operators.

generates an infinite loop. So in FLK, it is not safe to swap the operands of
+, since this may change the meaning of the program. However, swapping the
operands of + *would* be safe if we modified the semantics of FLK so that it represented all errors as $\perp_{Expressible}$, in which case divergence and all errors would
be indistinguishable (see the discussion on page 427).

The $\mathcal{E}$ clauses for lam and app describe the creation and application of procedural values. $\mathcal{E}[\![(\texttt{lam } I_{formal} \ E_{body})]\!]$ never yields an error or loop; it always
returns the following element of the *Proc* domain injected into a computation:
$\lambda n_{arg} \ . \ (\mathcal{E}[\![E_{body}]\!] \ [I_{formal} \mapsto n_{arg}]e)$. This abstraction "remembers" the environment e in force at the point of the lam. Whenever it is later applied, the body
expression E_{body} will be evaluated in an extension of e in which the formal parameter I_{formal} is bound to the actual argument value n_{arg}. This environment
extension serves the same purpose as the substitution $[n_{arg}/I_{formal}]E_{body}$ in the
SOS. Recall that *Nameable* = *Comp* in FLK, so n_{arg} may be an error or an
infinite loop.

$(\mathcal{E}[\![(\texttt{app } E_{rator} \ E_{rand})]\!] \ e)$ checks that $\mathcal{E}[\![E_{rator}]\!]e$ is a procedure value p. If
so, p is invoked on the operand computation $\mathcal{E}[\![E_{rand}]\!]e$. If the rator yields a
value that is not a procedure, the application results in a not-a-procedure
error. Otherwise, any error or infinite loop in the rator is propagated to become
the resulting computation.

The clauses for lam and app are illustrated in Figures 6.30–6.32, which show
the calculation of the meaning of the application

```
(app (lam f (app f 5))
     (lam n (lam x (prim - x n))))
```

(Figure 6.30 uses the specialization of prim derived on page 284. Many of the
equational steps in Figure 6.32 are justified by the equalities in Figure 6.27.) The
meaning of this application is the same meaning that would be calculated for
the FL abstraction (lam x (prim - x 5)), so this abstraction can be substituted for the original application expression without changing the meaning of a
program.

$(\mathcal{E}[\![(\texttt{rec } I \ E)]\!] \ e)$ uses $\textbf{fix}_{Comp}$ to find the "least" computation c satisfying
the equation $c = (\mathcal{E}[\![E]\!] \ [I \mapsto c]e)$. Because *Comp* is a pointed CPO (see Sections 5.2.2–5.2.3) the Least Fixed Point Theorem from Section 5.2.5 guarantees
that at least one fixed point exists and the iterative fixed point technique will
find the least of all the fixed points.

For example, consider the summation procedure (rec sum E_{abs}), where E_{abs}
is the abstraction

```
(lam n (if (prim = n 0)
           0
           (prim + n (app sum (prim - n 1)))))
```

It is possible to show that

$$\mathcal{E}[\![E_{abs}]\!]$$
$$= \mathcal{E}[\![\texttt{(lam n (if (prim = n 0) 0 (prim + n (app sum (prim - n 1)))))}]\!]$$
$$= \lambda e \,.\, (\textit{val-to-comp}$$
$$\qquad (\textit{Proc} \rightarrowtail \textit{Value}$$
$$\qquad\quad (\lambda n_n \,.\, (\textit{with-value } n_n$$
$$\qquad\qquad (\lambda v_n \,.\, (\textit{with-integer-val } v_n$$
$$\qquad\qquad\quad (\lambda i_n \,.\, \textbf{if } i_n =_{Int} 0$$
$$\qquad\qquad\qquad \textbf{then } \textit{val-to-comp } (\textit{Int} \rightarrowtail \textit{Value } 0)$$
$$\qquad\qquad\qquad \textbf{else } \textit{with-value } (\textit{with-procedure-comp } (\mathcal{E}[\![\texttt{sum}]\!] \ e)$$
$$\qquad\qquad\qquad\qquad (\lambda p \,.\, (p \ (\textit{val-to-comp}$$
$$\qquad\qquad\qquad\qquad\qquad (\textit{Int} \rightarrowtail \textit{Value } (i_n -_{Int} 1)))))$$
$$\qquad\qquad\qquad\quad (\lambda v_{sum} \,.\, (\textit{with-integer-val } v_{sum}$$
$$\qquad\qquad\qquad\qquad (\lambda i_{sum} \,.\, (\textit{val-to-comp}$$
$$\qquad\qquad\qquad\qquad\quad (\textit{Int} \rightarrowtail \textit{Value } (i_n +_{Int} i_{sum}))))))))))))))$$

Note how the meaning of E_{abs} depends on the meaning of the name $\texttt{sum}$ in the environment. The expression $\texttt{(rec sum } E_{abs}\texttt{)}$ "ties the knot" of recursion by binding the name $\texttt{sum}$ to the procedure-returning computation denoted by E_{abs} in the environment relative to which E_{abs} is evaluated. This knot-tying is achieved by a fixed point calculation in the meaning of $\texttt{(rec sum } E_{abs}\texttt{)}$:

$$\mathcal{E}[\![\texttt{(rec sum } E_{abs}\texttt{)}]\!]$$
$$= \lambda e \,.\, (\textbf{fix}_{Comp} \ (\lambda c \,.\, (\mathcal{E}[\![E_{abs}]\!] \ [\texttt{sum} \mapsto c]e)))$$
$$= \lambda e \,.\, c_{sum}$$
$$\quad \textbf{where} \ \ c_{sum} = (\textit{val-to-comp}$$
$$\qquad\qquad\qquad (\textit{Proc} \rightarrowtail \textit{Value}$$
$$\qquad\qquad\qquad\quad (\lambda n_n \,.\, (\textit{with-value } n_n$$
$$\qquad\qquad\qquad\qquad (\lambda v_n \,.\, (\textit{with-integer-val } v_n$$
$$\qquad\qquad\qquad\qquad\quad (\lambda i_n \,.\, \textbf{if } i_n <_{Int} 0 \ \textbf{then } \perp_{Comp}$$
$$\qquad\qquad\qquad\qquad\qquad \textbf{else } \textit{val-to-comp}$$
$$\qquad\qquad\qquad\qquad\qquad\quad (\textit{Int} \rightarrowtail \textit{Value}$$
$$\qquad\qquad\qquad\qquad\qquad\qquad ((i_n \times_{Int} (i_n +_{Int} 1)) \div_{Int} 2))$$
$$\qquad\qquad\qquad \textbf{end})))))$$

The generating function $\lambda c \,.\, (\mathcal{E}[\![E_{abs}]\!] \ [\texttt{sum} \mapsto c]e)$ applies the meaning of E_{abs} presented earlier to an environment in which the name $\texttt{sum}$ is bound to the argument c. You should convince yourself that the least fixed point of this function is the computation c_{sum} that returns a summation procedure that

$\mathcal{E}[\![(\text{lam n (lam x (prim - x n)))}]\!]$
$= \lambda e \, . \, (\textit{val-to-comp} \ (\textit{Proc} \rightarrowtail \textit{Value} \ p_n))$
$\quad \text{where} \quad p_n \ = \ \lambda n_n \, . \, (\mathcal{E}[\![(\text{lam x (prim - x n))}]\!] \ [\text{n} \mapsto n_n]e)$
$\qquad\qquad\qquad = \lambda n_n \, . \, (\textit{val-to-comp}$
$\qquad\qquad\qquad\qquad\quad (\textit{Proc} \rightarrowtail \textit{Value}$
$\qquad\qquad\qquad\qquad\qquad (\lambda n_x \, . \, (\mathcal{E}[\![(\text{prim - x n)}]\!] \ [\text{x} \mapsto n_x][\text{n} \mapsto n_n]e))))$
$\qquad\qquad\qquad = \lambda n_n \, . \, (\textit{val-to-comp}$
$\qquad\qquad\qquad\qquad\quad (\textit{Proc} \rightarrowtail \textit{Value}$
$\qquad\qquad\qquad\qquad\qquad (\lambda n_x \, . \, (\textit{with-value} \ (\mathcal{E}[\![\text{x}]\!] \ [\text{x} \mapsto n_x][\text{n} \mapsto n_n]e)$
$\qquad\qquad\qquad\qquad\qquad\quad (\lambda v_x \, . \, (\textit{with-value} \ (\mathcal{E}[\![\text{n}]\!] \ [\text{x} \mapsto n_x][\text{n} \mapsto n_n]e)$
$\qquad\qquad\qquad\qquad\qquad\quad\ (\lambda v_n \, . \, (\textit{with-integer-val} \ v_x$
$\qquad\qquad\qquad\qquad\qquad\qquad (\lambda i_x \, . \, (\textit{with-integer-val} \ v_n$
$\qquad\qquad\qquad\qquad\qquad\qquad\quad (\lambda i_n \, . \, (\textit{val-to-comp}$
$\qquad\qquad\qquad\qquad\qquad\qquad\qquad (\textit{Int} \rightarrowtail \textit{Value} \ (i_x -_{\textit{Int}} i_n))))))))))))))$
$\qquad\qquad\qquad = \lambda n_n \, . \, (\textit{val-to-comp}$
$\qquad\qquad\qquad\qquad\quad (\textit{Proc} \rightarrowtail \textit{Value}$
$\qquad\qquad\qquad\qquad\qquad (\lambda n_x \, . \, (\textit{with-value} \ n_x$
$\qquad\qquad\qquad\qquad\qquad\quad (\lambda v_x \, . \, (\textit{with-value} \ n_n$
$\qquad\qquad\qquad\qquad\qquad\quad\ (\lambda v_n \, . \, (\textit{with-integer-val} \ v_x$
$\qquad\qquad\qquad\qquad\qquad\qquad (\lambda i_x \, . \, (\textit{with-integer-val} \ v_n$
$\qquad\qquad\qquad\qquad\qquad\qquad\quad (\lambda i_n \, . \, (\textit{val-to-comp}$
$\qquad\qquad\qquad\qquad\qquad\qquad\qquad (\textit{Int} \rightarrowtail \textit{Value} \ (i_x -_{\textit{Int}} i_n))))))))))))))$

Figure 6.30   The meaning of (lam n (lam x (prim - x n))).

$\mathcal{E}[\![(\text{lam f (app f 5))}]\!]$
$= \lambda e \, . \, (\textit{val-to-comp} \ (\textit{Proc} \rightarrowtail \textit{Value} \ p_f))$
$\quad \text{where} \quad p_f \ = \ \lambda n_f \, . \, (\mathcal{E}[\![(\text{app f 5)}]\!] \ [\text{f} \mapsto n_f]e)$
$\qquad\qquad\qquad = \lambda n_f \, . \, (\textit{with-procedure-comp} \ (\mathcal{E}[\![\text{f}]\!] \ [\text{f} \mapsto n_f]e)$
$\qquad\qquad\qquad\qquad\qquad (\lambda p \, . \, (p \ (\mathcal{E}[\![5]\!] \ [\text{f} \mapsto n_f]e)))$
$\qquad\qquad\qquad = \lambda n_f \, . \, (\textit{with-procedure-comp} \ n_f$
$\qquad\qquad\qquad\qquad\qquad (\lambda p \, . \, (p \ (\textit{val-to-comp} \ (\textit{Int} \rightarrowtail \textit{Value} \ 5)))))$

Figure 6.31   The meaning of (lam f (app f 5)).

- returns $\sum_{k=1}^{i_n} k = \frac{i_n \cdot (i_n+1)}{2}$ if its argument is a nonnegative integer i_n;

- diverges (i.e., returns $\bot_{\textit{Comp}}$) if its argument is a negative integer;

- signals an error (i.e., returns an error computation) if its argument is not an integer.

$\mathcal{E}[\![\text{(app (lam f (app f 5)) (lam n (lam x (prim - x n))))}]\!]$
$= \lambda e \,.\; (\textit{with-procedure-comp} \; (\mathcal{E}[\![\text{(lam f (app f 5))}]\!] \; e)$
$\qquad\qquad (\lambda p \,.\; (p \; (\mathcal{E}[\![\text{(lam n (lam x (prim - x n)))}]\!] \; e))))$
$= \lambda e \,.\; (\textit{with-procedure-comp} \; (\textit{val-to-comp} \; (\textit{Proc} \rightarrowtail \textit{Value} \; p_f)) \; ; \; p_f \; \text{from Figure 6.31}$
$\qquad\qquad (\lambda p \,.\; (p \; (\textit{val-to-comp} \; (\textit{Proc} \rightarrowtail \textit{Value} \; p_n))))) \; ; \; p_n \; \text{from Figure 6.30}$
$= \lambda e \,.\; (p_f \; (\textit{val-to-comp} \; (\textit{Proc} \rightarrowtail \textit{Value} \; p_n)))$
$= \lambda e \,.\; (\textit{with-procedure-comp} \; (\textit{val-to-comp} \; (\textit{Proc} \rightarrowtail \textit{Value} \; p_n))$
$\qquad\qquad (\lambda p \,.\; (p \; (\textit{val-to-comp} \; (\textit{Int} \rightarrowtail \textit{Value} \; 5)))))$
$= \lambda e \,.\; (p_n \; (\textit{val-to-comp} \; (\textit{Int} \rightarrowtail \textit{Value} \; 5)))$
$= \lambda e \,.\; (\textit{val-to-comp}$
$\qquad\qquad (\textit{Proc} \rightarrowtail \textit{Value}$
$\qquad\qquad\quad (\lambda n_x \,.\; (\textit{with-value} \; n_x$
$\qquad\qquad\qquad (\lambda v_x \,.\; (\textit{with-value} \; (\textit{val-to-comp} \; (\textit{Int} \rightarrowtail \textit{Value} \; 5))$
$\qquad\qquad\qquad\quad (\lambda v_n \,.\; (\textit{with-integer-val} \; v_x$
$\qquad\qquad\qquad\qquad (\lambda i_x \,.\; (\textit{with-integer-val} \; v_n$
$\qquad\qquad\qquad\qquad\quad (\lambda i_n \,.\; (\textit{val-to-comp} \; (\textit{Int} \rightarrowtail \textit{Value} \; (i_x -_{Int} i_n)))))))))))))))))$
$= \lambda e \,.\; (\textit{val-to-comp}$
$\qquad\qquad (\textit{Proc} \rightarrowtail \textit{Value}$
$\qquad\qquad\quad (\lambda n_x \,.\; (\textit{with-value} \; n_x$
$\qquad\qquad\qquad (\lambda v_x \,.\; (\textit{with-integer-val} \; v_x$
$\qquad\qquad\qquad\quad (\lambda i_x \,.\; (\textit{with-integer-val} \; (\textit{Int} \rightarrowtail \textit{Value} \; 5)$
$\qquad\qquad\qquad\qquad (\lambda i_n \,.\; (\textit{val-to-comp} \; (\textit{Int} \rightarrowtail \textit{Value} \; (i_x -_{Int} i_n)))))))))))))$
$= \lambda e \,.\; (\textit{val-to-comp}$
$\qquad\qquad (\textit{Proc} \rightarrowtail \textit{Value}$
$\qquad\qquad\quad (\lambda n_x \,.\; (\textit{with-value} \; n_x$
$\qquad\qquad\qquad (\lambda v_x \,.\; (\textit{with-integer-val} \; v_x$
$\qquad\qquad\qquad\quad (\lambda i_x \,.\; (\textit{val-to-comp} \; (\textit{Int} \rightarrowtail \textit{Value} \; (i_x -_{Int} 5)))))))))))$

Figure 6.32 The meaning of (app (lam f (app f 5))
(lam n (lam x (prim - x n)))).

Note that replacing $\perp_{Comp}$ by any computation c_{neg} in the negative integer case yields a valid fixed point of the generating function, but the least fixed point is the case where $c_{neg} = \perp_{Comp}$.

The meaning of a program is determined by the $\mathcal{P}$ function. A program is a function that maps the input (assumed to be a sequence of value s-expressions in InputExp) to an answer (an expressible value in the case of FLK). The computation is determined by evaluating the body of the program in an environment that binds each formal parameter to the associated argument value. If there is a mismatch between the number of formal parameters and the number of actual arguments, the result is a wrong-number-of-args error computation.

Exercise 6.34 In FLK, `error` expressions take a symbol as the name of the error. There are other possible error strategies. One is to have only a single error value, which might simplify the semantics while making errors less helpful in practice. Another approach is to allow the argument of `error` to be a computed value. Suppose we alter the syntax of FLK to support the expression (`error` *E*).

a. Write the valuation clause for (`error` *E*).

b. What is the meaning of an `error` expression whose argument expression has an error?

Exercise 6.35 Construct an operational semantics for FLK that uses explicit environments rather than substitution. Is it easier to do this using an SOS or a BOS? *Hint:* Whether you choose an SOS or a BOS, it is a good idea to introduce a **closure value** that pairs a lambda expression with the environment it is evaluated in.

Exercise 6.36 Write a denotational semantics for FL that does not depend on its desugaring into FLK. That is, the valuation clauses should directly handle features such as `def`, `let`, `letrec`, and procedures with multiple arguments.

6.6   The Lambda Calculus

FLK is a relatively small kernel for a universal programming language. It is natural to wonder whether there is a smaller and more elegant kernel. Remarkably, a language with just three constructs — abstractions, applications, and variable references — is universal. This language is known as the **lambda calculus** (sometimes abbreviated LC). Because the lambda calculus is at the core of any programming language with function-like entities (such as procedures, methods, and subroutines) it has been intensively investigated by theoreticians. The lambda calculus plays such a pervasive role in the study of programming languages that some knowledge of the lambda calculus is required to understand much of the programming languages literature.

Many studies of programming language semantics and analysis start with the lambda calculus and then consider various extensions that result in more full-featured languages. In this book, we take a different approach. We started with a more full-featured kernel language (FLK) to help build intuitions about function-oriented programming. Now we present some of the key ideas and results from the lambda calculus, making comparisons with FLK along the way. We begin by specifying the syntax of the lambda calculus (Section 6.6.1) and describing its operational semantics (Section 6.6.2) and denotational semantics (Section 6.6.3). Then we show that, even though the syntax of the lambda calculus is extremely simple, it is powerful enough to express FLK features like numbers, booleans, conditionals, pairs, and recursion (Section 6.6.4).

Kernel Grammar

$E \in \text{Exp} ::= I$ [VariableReference]

          $|$ `(lam` I_{formal} E_{body}`)` [Abstraction]

          $|$ `(app` E_{rator} E_{rand}`)` [Application]

$I \in \text{Ident} = $ *any name except for* `lam`, `app`, *and* `abs`

Syntactic Sugar

`(abs () ` E`)` $\rightsquigarrow_{ds}$ `(lam` I_{fresh} E`)`, where I_{fresh} is fresh

`(abs (`I`) ` E`)` $\rightsquigarrow_{ds}$ `(lam` I E`)`

`(abs (`I_1 I_{rest}^+`) ` E`)` $\rightsquigarrow_{ds}$ `(lam` I_1 `(abs (`I_{rest}^+`) ` E`))`

`(`E`)` $\rightsquigarrow_{ds}$ `(app` E `(lam x x))`

`(`E_1 E_2`)` $\rightsquigarrow_{ds}$ `(app` E_1 E_2`)`

`(`E_1 E_2 E_{rest}^+`)` $\rightsquigarrow_{ds}$ `((app` E_1 E_2`) ` E_{rest}^+`)`

Figure 6.33 An s-expression grammar for the lambda calculus

6.6.1 Syntax of the Lambda Calculus

Syntactically, the lambda calculus is the subset of FLK consisting of only three kinds of expressions: abstractions, applications, and variable references. For consistency, we will use an s-expression syntax for the lambda calculus (Figure 6.33), but the traditional syntax for the lambda calculus is our more concise metalanguage notation (i.e., using $\lambda I . E$ for abstractions, juxtaposition for application, and parentheses for disambiguation). For convenience, we will use FL's syntactic sugar for multiparameter abstractions and multiargument applications. A lambda calculus expression is traditionally called a **term**, but we will continue to use the word expression for consistency with FLK.

The definitions of free identifiers and substitution for the lambda calculus are the ones for FLK (see Figures 6.14 and 6.17) specialized to the lambda calculus subset. A closed expression (i.e., one with no free variables) is called a **combinator**. For our purposes, a lambda calculus "program" will just be a combinator; we will not use any sort of special keyword to distinguish a program from an expression.

6.6.2 Operational Semantics of the Lambda Calculus

An operational semantics for the lambda calculus is presented in Figure 6.34. The simplification relation ($\rightarrow$) is just the FLK simplification relation restricted to its lambda calculus subset. In particular, the lambda calculus has only one kind of redex: a beta-redex that can be reduced via $[\beta]$.

Reduction Relation ($\leadsto$)

  (app (lam I E_1) E_2) $\leadsto$ $[E_2/I]E_1$ [β]

Simplification

Simplification Contexts

$\mathbb{S} \in$ SimpContext ::= $\square$ | (lam I $\mathbb{S}$) | (app $\mathbb{S}$ E_{rand}) | (app E_{rator} $\mathbb{S}$)

Simplification relation ($\rightarrow$)

    $\mathbb{S}\{E\} \rightarrow \mathbb{S}\{E'\}$, where $E \leadsto E'$

Normalization

Normal Forms

    $NF \in$ NormalForm ::= (lam I NF) | $NLNF$

$NLNF \in$ NonLambdaNormalForm ::= I | (app $NLNF$ NF)

Normalization Contexts

    $\mathbb{NC} \in$ NormContext ::= (lam I $\mathbb{NC}$) | $NLNC$

$\mathbb{NLNC} \in$ NonLambdaNormContext ::= $\square$ | (app $\mathbb{NLNC}$ E_{rand})
                                        | (app $NLNF_{rator}$ $\mathbb{NC}$)

Normalization relation ($\xrightarrow{n.o.}$)

    $\mathbb{NC}\{E\} \xrightarrow{n.o.} \mathbb{NC}\{E'\}$, where $E \leadsto E'$

Nonnormalization step ($\circ\xrightarrow{n.o.}$)

    $\circ\xrightarrow{n.o.} = \left(\rightarrow - \xrightarrow{n.o.}\right)$ *the set difference of the two relations*

Figure 6.34   Simplification and normalization in the lambda calculus.

As in FLK, simplification in the lambda calculus is confluent:

Theorem 6.14 (Confluence of Lambda Calculus Simplification)
The lambda calculus simplification relation is confluent. I.e., if $E_1 \xrightarrow{*} E_2$ and $E_1 \xrightarrow{*} E_3$ then there exists an E_4 such that $E_2 \xrightarrow{*} E_4$ and $E_3 \xrightarrow{*} E_4$.

Indeed, confluence of simplification in FLK can be shown by adapting traditional techniques for proving confluence in the lambda calculus [Bar84].

A lambda calculus expression that contains no beta-redexes is in **normal form**. An expression is said to **have a normal form** if it can be simplified to an expression in normal form. Confluence of simplification implies that if a lambda calculus expression has a normal form, it is unique (see page 82). Not every lambda calculus expression has a normal form. For example, just as in FLK, the expression

`(app (lam x (app x x)) (lam x (app x x)))`

simplifies only to itself and so can never be simplified to a normal form. The FLK expression

`(lam y (app (lam x (app x x)) (lam x (app x x))))`

is an evaluation normal form in FLK, but in the lambda calculus it is not a normal form and can never be simplified to one.

Not every simplification strategy is guaranteed to find the normal form of an expression that has one. For example, in the expression

`(app (lam y (lam z z)) (app (lam x (app x x)) (lam x (app x x))))`

reducing the outer beta-redex finds the normal form, `(lam z z)`, in one step. But reducing the inner beta-redex makes no progress toward the normal form.

If an expression has a normal form, it can be found by the **normal-order reduction strategy**, a deterministic approach to simplification that always reduces the **leftmost beta-redex** — i.e., the first beta-redex encountered in a left-to-right, depth-first walk of the abstract syntax tree of the expression. We shall call a simplification step taken by this strategy a **normalization step**, written $\xrightarrow[n.o.]{}$. Here is an example of normalization:

```
(app (lam f (app f (app (lam v (app v v))
                        (app (lam w w) (lam x x)))))
     (lam y (lam z y)))
```
$\xrightarrow[n.o.]{}$ `(app (lam y (lam z y))`
              `(app (lam v (app v v)) (app (lam w w) (lam x x))))`
$\xrightarrow[n.o.]{}$ `(lam z (app (lam v (app v v)) (app (lam w w) (lam x x))))`
$\xrightarrow[n.o.]{}$ `(lam z (app (app (lam w w) (lam x x)) (app (lam w w) (lam x x))))`
$\xrightarrow[n.o.]{}$ `(lam z (app (lam x x) (app (lam w w) (lam x x))))`
$\xrightarrow[n.o.]{}$ `(lam z (app (lam w w) (lam x x))))`
$\xrightarrow[n.o.]{}$ `(lam z (lam x x))`

Normalization is similar to FLK evaluation except that it can perform simplifications in the body of an abstraction. In FLK, evaluation of the above example would stop after two steps with

`(lam z (app (lam v (app v v)) (app (lam w w) (lam x x))))`

because the evaluation process does not attempt to simplify the body of an abstraction.

In the lambda calculus, the analogue of the nonevaluation relation $\Rightarrow$ from FLK is the nonnormalization relation $\circ\!\!\xrightarrow{n.o.}$. This is a simplification step that is not a normalization step. For example, here is an alternative reduction sequence for the example considered above that performs some nonnormalization steps:

```
(app (lam f (app f (app (lam v (app v v))
                        (app (lam w w) (lam x x)))))
     (lam y (lam z y)))
n.o.⟶ (app (lam f (app f (app (lam v (app v v))
                          (lam x x))))
     (lam y (lam z y)))
n.o.⟶ (app (lam f (app f (app (lam x x) (lam x x))))
     (lam y (lam z y)))
n.o.⟶ (app (lam f (app f (lam x x)))
     (lam y (lam z y)))
n.o.⟶ (app (lam y (lam z y)) (lam x x))
n.o.⟶ (lam z (lam x x))
```

The first three steps are nonnormalization steps because they simplify a beta-redex that is not the leftmost one. The final normal form is the same as before because normal forms are unique (up to alpha-equivalence). Note that the second sequence is one step shorter than the first sequence because the first nonnormalization step reduces the redex (app (lam w w) (lam x x)) to (lam x x) before this operand is duplicated by the abstraction (lam v (app v v)). In the first sequence, this redex is duplicated and must be reduced twice.

In any sequence of lambda calculus simplification steps that ends with a normal form, the last step must be a normalization step. Why? Because the last redex reduced is necessarily the leftmost one.

Why is the normal-order reduction strategy guaranteed to find the normal form of an expression (if it exists)? Intuitively, it reduces only those redexes that *must* be reduced in order to normalize the expression. In particular, it avoids reducing an inner redex in an expression that is currently (or might become) the rand of an outer redex. This is important, because the reduction of the outer redex can eliminate the entire rand expression if the rator's parameter does not appear in its body, in which case any effort expended simplifying the rand would have been wasted.

We now show that the leftmost redex E_{left} of an expression E cannot appear in a subexpression E_{rand} of E that is (or might become) the rand of an outer redex. To see this, suppose otherwise: i.e., assume E_{left} appears in E_{rand} and E_{rand} appears in $E_{app} = $ (app E_{rator} E_{rand}). If E_{rator} is an abstraction, then

E_{app} is a redex to the left of E_{left}, contradicting the leftmost status of E_{left}. If E_{rator} is not an abstraction, but can be simplified to one, it must contain at least one redex to the left of E_{left}, again contradicting the leftmost status of E_{left}. Since E_{left} must be reduced in the normalization of E, we choose to reduce it first.

More formally, the normalizing nature of $\xrightarrow[n.o.]{}$ is a consequence of the following theorem,[10] which is the lambda calculus analogue of standardization for FLK evaluation:

Theorem 6.15 (Standardization of Lambda Calculus Simplification) *If $E_1 \xrightarrow{*} E_2$, then there exists an E' such that $E_1 \xrightarrow[n.o.]{*} E'$ and $E' \circ\!\!\xrightarrow[n.o.]{*} E_2$.*

Using this theorem, we can show that if an expression has a normal form, the normal-order reduction strategy will find it. Suppose that $E \xrightarrow{*} E_{nf}$, where E_{nf} is a normal form. By standardization, there exists an E' such that $E \xrightarrow[n.o.]{*} E'$ $\circ\!\!\xrightarrow[n.o.]{*} E_{nf}$. As noted above, the last step in a simplification sequence ending in a normal form must be a normalization step. So the sequence $E' \circ\!\!\xrightarrow[n.o.]{*} E_{nf}$ must have zero steps, implying $E' = E_{nf}$.

Two other reduction rules besides $[\beta]$ are sometimes considered in the lambda calculus literature. The first rule is **alpha reduction**:

$$(\texttt{lam } I \ E) \rightsquigarrow (\texttt{lam } I' \ [I'/I]E), \text{ where } I' \notin \textit{FrIds}[\![E]\!] \quad [\alpha]$$

This rule says that the bound variable of an abstraction may be consistently renamed. Since we often think of lambda calculus expressions in terms of alpha-equivalence classes, there is little need to use the $[\alpha]$ rule explicitly.

The second rule is **eta reduction**:

$$(\texttt{lam } I \ (\texttt{app } E \ I)) \rightsquigarrow E, \text{ where } I \notin \textit{FrIds}[\![E]\!] \quad [\eta]$$

The intuition behind $[\eta]$ is that every lambda calculus value is a function, so wrapping E in an abstraction that applies E yields a function that behaves the same as E. We often use eta reduction (and its inverse, **eta expansion**) in our mathematical metalanguage, especially in denotational semantics of FL dialects involving the *Comp* abstraction.

---

[10]This is a somewhat different notion of standardization than the one traditionally presented in the lambda calculus literature. In the traditional approach, a "standard step" is defined as one that "freezes" all redexes to its left, allowing what we call a nonnormalization step to be a standard step in some situations. The traditional standardization theorem says than if E simplifies to E', then E simplifies to E' by a sequence of standard steps.

Exercise 6.37 Any closed lambda calculus expression can be written as applications involving only the following two combinators:

$$K = \texttt{(abs (x y) x)}$$
$$S = \texttt{(abs (x y z) ((x z) (y z)))}$$

a. Determine the normal forms of the following expressions:

   (S K K)

   (S (K S) K)

   (S (K (S K K)) (S (K K) (S K K)))

b. Express the following combinators using only applications of K and S:

   (abs (x y) y)

   (abs (x) (x x))

   (abs (x y) (x (y y)))

(For a general method of translating combinators to K and S, see [Hug82].)

6.6.3   Denotational Semantics of the Lambda Calculus

A denotational semantics for the lambda calculus is presented in Figure 6.35. The domain structure here is much simpler than in the denotational semantics for FLK. There is one main domain, *Fcn*, for modeling functions (the only kind of "value" in the lambda calculus), and one auxiliary domain, *Env*, for modeling bindings of names to elements of *Fcn*. Although the *Fcn* domain does not have an explicit bottom element, it turns out that solving the domain equation *Fcn* = $(Fcn \rightarrow Fcn)$ using the inverse limit construction mentioned in Section 5.3 introduces a bottom element $\perp_{Fcn}$. In addition to being viewed as a diverging computation in the *Fcn* domain, $\perp_{Fcn}$ is the least fixed point of $\lambda f' . (\lambda f . f')$ and so can also be viewed as the function that is the solution to the equation $f' = (\lambda f . f')$. So $\perp_{Fcn} = (\lambda f . \perp_{Fcn})$; applying $\perp_{Fcn}$ to any function yields $\perp_{Fcn}$.

As in FLK, the valuation function $\mathcal{E}$ determines the meaning of a lambda calculus expression relative to an environment that specifies the meanings of free variables in the expression. However, here the meaning is a function value in *Fcn*. The three valuation clauses for $\mathcal{E}$ are essentially the same as the corresponding clauses for FLK minus all the machinery for dealing with the distinctions between divergence, errors, and different kinds of values. In the lambda calculus, there is only one kind of value — a function — and particular functions are used to represent divergence and errors.

There is no need for any sort of error domain because every lambda calculus expression denotes *some* function. What about unbound variables (e.g., foo in

---

Domains

$f \in Fcn = Fcn \rightarrow Fcn$
$e \in Env = \text{Ident} \rightarrow Fcn$

Environments

$e_{top} : Env = \lambda I \,.\, \bot_{Fcn}$

$[I \mapsto f]e$ abbreviates $\lambda I' \,.\,$ **if** $I =_{\text{Ident}} I'$ **then** f **else** $(e \; I')$ **end**

Valuation Function

$\mathcal{E} : \text{Exp} \rightarrow Env \rightarrow Fcn$

$\mathcal{E}[\![I]\!] = \lambda e \,.\, (e \; I)$

$\mathcal{E}[\![(\texttt{lam } I \; E_{body})]\!] = \lambda e \,.\, (\lambda f \,.\, (\mathcal{E}[\![E_{body}]\!] \; [I \mapsto f]e))$

$\mathcal{E}[\![(\texttt{app } E_{rator} \; E_{rand})]\!] = \lambda e \,.\, ((\mathcal{E}[\![E_{rator}]\!] \; e) \; (\mathcal{E}[\![E_{rand}]\!] \; e))$

Figure 6.35 A denotational semantics for the lambda calculus.

(`lam x foo`))? The fact that the meaning of every expression is defined relative to an environment and the fact that environments are total functions that *must* specify *some* element of *Fcn* for every name (such as `foo` in the above example) mean that no variable reference can ever actually be unbound. We choose to use $\bot_{Fcn}$ to represent unbound variable errors as well as a divergence. We take the meaning of any expression relative to a top-level environment e_{top} that binds every name to $\bot_{Fcn}$, so that any free variable in an expression will denote $\bot_{Fcn}$.

Here are some examples illustrating the valuation function $\mathcal{E}$:

$\mathcal{E}[\![(\texttt{lam x x})]\!] \; e_{top} = \lambda f \,.\, (\mathcal{E}[\![\texttt{x}]\!] \; [\texttt{x} \mapsto f]e_{top}) = \lambda f \,.\, f$

$\mathcal{E}[\![(\texttt{lam x foo})]\!] \; e_{top} = \lambda f \,.\, (\mathcal{E}[\![\texttt{foo}]\!] \; [\texttt{x} \mapsto f]e_{top}) = (\lambda f \,.\, \bot_{Fcn}) = \bot_{Fcn}$

$\mathcal{E}[\![(\texttt{app (lam x x) (lam x x)})]\!] \; e_{top}$
$= ((\mathcal{E}[\![(\texttt{lam x x})]\!] \; e_{top}) \; (\mathcal{E}[\![(\texttt{lam x x})]\!] \; e_{top}))$
$= ((\lambda f \,.\, f) \; (\lambda f \,.\, f))$
$= \lambda f \,.\, f$

6.6.4 Representational Games

At first glance, the lambda calculus might seem impoverished because functions are the only kind of values manipulated in the language. However, it turns out that many of FLK's features — such as natural numbers, booleans, conditionals, pairs, and even recursion — can be expressed in the lambda calculus via clever encodings. Here we sketch some of these encodings.

Natural Numbers

The only "data structure" that lambda calculus expressions can represent is functions, so we must find a way to represent the natural numbers as functions. The classic approach is to encode each natural number as the n-fold composition function. When given a function f as its argument, the n-fold composition function returns f^n — i.e., f composed with itself n times. For example, applying the n-fold composition function to an incrementing function yields the add-n function.

For each natural number n, we can straightforwardly define a lambda calculus expression that represents the n-fold composition function:

$$
\begin{aligned}
\overline{0} &= \texttt{(abs (f v) v)} \\
\overline{1} &= \texttt{(abs (f v) (f v))} \\
\overline{2} &= \texttt{(abs (f v) (f (f v)))} \\
\overline{3} &= \texttt{(abs (f v) (f (f (f v))))} \\
&\vdots \\
\overline{n} &= \texttt{(abs (f v)} \overbrace{\texttt{(f (f ... (f v) ...)))}}^{n\ times}
\end{aligned}
$$

(Here and throughout the rest of this section we rely on syntactic sugar to make expressions more concise.) These lambda-based representation of numbers are called **Church numerals** after their inventor, Alonzo Church. We use the convention that $\overline{n}$ is a syntactic abbreviation for the Church numeral representing n.

A pictorial representation of n-fold compositions is useful for helping us reason about operations on Church numerals. We can associate with each $\overline{n}$ the following diagram:

Each box contains the mathematical function f that is the meaning of the lambda calculus variable f. The concatenation of n such boxes indicates the result of the application $(\overline{n}\ \texttt{f})$, which is the n-fold composition of f. The application $((\overline{n}\ \texttt{f})\ \texttt{v})$ represents the result of applying f^n to the value v denoted by v. It can also be viewed as an iterator or loop that applies f n times to an initial value of v.

This notation makes it easier to understand how to write functions that manipulate Church numerals. Since the number n is encoded in the number of times that the argument f is composed, we do manipulations on Church numerals by changing the number of times that f is composed. For example, to write the incrementing function INC that takes a Church numeral $\overline{n}$ and returns $\overline{n+1}$, we must add one extra application of f to the sequence of applications encoded in $\overline{n}$. We can draw a picture of this process and translate it into the appropriate lambda expression:

$$INC = \text{(abs (n) (abs (f v) (f ((n f) v))))}$$

From the above picture, though, it should be apparent that we could just as well add the extra f at the beginning of the sequence rather than at the end. This motivates the following alternative definition of INC:

$$INC' = \text{(abs (n) (abs (f v) ((n f) (f v))))}$$

It is possible to use similar pictures to derive the lambda calculus expression $PLUS$ for the two-argument (i.e., in curried form) function that returns the "sum" of its arguments.

$$PLUS = \text{(abs (m n) (abs (f v) ((n f) ((m f) v))))}$$

Of course, since the composition shown in the diagram is commutative, it is possible to swap the m and the n in the body ((n f) ((m f) v)) to yield a slightly different definition. But a very different definition for $PLUS$ can be constructed by realizing that the Church numeral $\overline{n}$ essentially describes a machine that iterates a given function n times on some initial input. Note that it is possible to describe the sum of m and n as the n-fold repetition of the incrementing function starting with the initial value m. Expressed in pictorial form:

This picture leads directly to the definition:

$$PLUS' = (\texttt{abs (m n) ((n } INC\texttt{) m))}$$

Again, it is possible to obtain a slightly different definition by interchanging the roles of m and n.

It is possible to define other arithmetic operations, such as decrementing (i.e., subtract one), multiplication, and exponentiation. These are left as exercises (Exercise 6.39 and Exercise 6.43).

Exercise 6.38 Show that the operations presented above behave appropriately by reducing each of the following expressions to normal form.

a. $(INC\ \overline{2})$

b. $(INC'\ \overline{2})$

c. $(PLUS\ \overline{2}\ \overline{3})$

d. $(PLUS'\ \overline{2}\ \overline{3})$

Exercise 6.39 Suppose that $\overline{m}$ and $\overline{n}$ are Church numerals. *Without using the Y operator introduced later*, define expressions *TIMES* and *EXPT* such that:

$$(TIMES\ \overline{m}\ \overline{n}) = \overline{m \times n}$$
$$(EXPT\ \overline{m}\ \overline{n}) = \overline{m^n}$$

Hint: As with *PLUS*, there are two very different ways to define each of *TIMES* and *EXPT*. Try to find both ways if you can.

Booleans and Conditionals

It is possible to represent boolean truth values in the lambda calculus as well. The only operation that depends on truth or falsity is a conditional that chooses between two alternatives. Consider an *IF* function that takes three arguments — a boolean test value, a then expression, and an else expression — and returns one of the then or else expressions depending on the value of the boolean. *IF* should observe the following functional behavior:

$$(IF\ TRUE\ E_{then}\ E_{else}) \xrightarrow[n.o.]{*} E_{then}$$
$$(IF\ FALSE\ E_{then}\ E_{else}) \xrightarrow[n.o.]{*} E_{else}$$

An implementation of this functionality is provided by the following definitions:

$$IF = (\text{abs (t x y) (t x y))}$$
$$TRUE = (\text{abs (a b) a})$$
$$FALSE = (\text{abs (a b) b})$$

Here *TRUE* and *FALSE* are represented as functions of two arguments that choose one of the two arguments. We shall call these **Church booleans** because they are functional representations of booleans. All *IF* does is apply the Church boolean to the then and else expressions.

Using Church booleans, it is possible to define a numeric predicate *ZERO?* that tests its numeric argument for equality to $\overline{0}$. Viewing numbers as iterators again, note that every number greater than $\overline{0}$ applies the function denoted by f at least once, but $\overline{0}$ never applies the function denoted by f at all. Since for any f, $f^0(v) = v$, $\overline{0}$ can be distinguished from other Church numerals in a context where the unary function that always returns *FALSE* is iterated n times starting with the initial value *TRUE*. If the function is applied zero times, the result is the initial value *TRUE*, but if it is applied one or more times, the result will be *FALSE*. Here's the definition of *ZERO?* based on this approach:

$$ZERO? = (\text{lam n ((n (lam x FALSE)) TRUE))}$$

Note that *FALSE* has the same (modulo alpha-renaming) definition as the Church numeral $\overline{0}$. This underscores the fact that lambda calculus expressions are not typed in any way. Thus, an expression that acts like 0 in a numeric context may act like falsity in a boolean context. This also means that there are no type errors in the lambda calculus. It is perfectly possible to provide *INC* with an argument that is not a Church numeral or provide a test to *IF* that is not a boolean. In these cases, the results will be valid expressions, but it will not be possible to interpret the results meaningfully as numbers or booleans. It is possible, however, to extend our representations to explicitly encode types for all objects and to model type errors.

Exercise 6.40 Assuming a normal-order reduction strategy, show that the definitions for *IF*, *TRUE*, and *FALSE* satisfy the desired behavior for conditionals.

Exercise 6.41 Define a lambda calculus expression *EVEN?* that denotes a function that returns a boolean indicating whether its single numeric argument is even. Do not use the *Y* operator introduced later.

Exercise 6.42 Suppose that $\widehat{p}$ and $\widehat{q}$ are Church booleans. Define lambda calculus expressions *AND*, *OR*, and *NOT* that, respectively, compute logical conjunction, disjunction, and negation.

Pairs

From a functional point of view, pairs are defined by the three operators *PAIR*, *FST*, and *SND*, such that for all expressions E_{fst} and E_{snd}:

$$(FST \ (PAIR \ E_{fst} \ E_{snd})) \xrightarrow[n.o.]{*} E_{fst}$$
$$(SND \ (PAIR \ E_{fst} \ E_{snd})) \xrightarrow[n.o.]{*} E_{snd}$$

A standard implementation of these three operators in the lambda calculus is:

$$
\begin{aligned}
PAIR \ &= \ \texttt{(abs (x y) (abs (s) (s x y)))} \\
FST \ &= \ \texttt{(abs (p) (p (abs (x y) x)))} \\
SND \ &= \ \texttt{(abs (p) (p (abs (x y) y)))}
\end{aligned}
$$

PAIR takes the two components of the pair and returns a pair, where the pair is represented as a function that takes a selector function s and applies s to the components of the pair. For example, (lam s (s $\overline{1}$ $\overline{2}$)) represents the pair $\langle \overline{1}, \overline{2} \rangle$. *FST* takes a pair and applies it to the selection function that extracts the first component, while *SND* uses a selection function that extracts the second component. Pairs encoded in this way are called **Church pairs**.

The notion of Church pairs can be generalized to tuples of any length. Indeed, we have already encountered Church tuples in the context of the letrec desugaring in Section 6.2.2. There are also ways to string Church pairs together to form linked lists.

Given Church pairs and iterators (i.e., Church numerals), it is possible to construct expressions for procedures like the iterative factorial procedure. The state of a factorial iteration can be captured by a pair of Church numerals $\langle \overline{n}, \overline{a} \rangle$, where one step of the iteration computes the next state $\langle \overline{n-1}, \overline{n*a} \rangle$. Starting with the initial state $\langle \overline{n}, \overline{1} \rangle$ and iterating the above process n times yields the pair $\langle \overline{0}, \overline{n!} \rangle$. Extracting the second element of this pair yields the factorial of $\overline{n}$. This leads to the definition of an iterative factorial in the lambda calculus:

$$
\begin{aligned}
ITER\text{-}FACT = \ &\texttt{(lam n} \ (SND \ \texttt{(n (lam p} \ (PAIR \ (DEC \ (FST \ \texttt{p})) \\
&\qquad\qquad\qquad\qquad\qquad (TIMES \ (FST \ \texttt{p}) \ (SND \ \texttt{p}))))) \\
&\qquad (PAIR \ \texttt{n} \ \overline{1}))))
\end{aligned}
$$

The above definition assumes that the decrementing function *DEC* and the multiplication function *TIMES* are defined. *TIMES* (Exercise 6.39) is not difficult to define, but *DEC* (Exercise 6.43) is quite a brain-teaser!

Exercise 6.43 Define a lambda calculus expression *DEC* that decrements a Church numeral by 1. Recall that for natural-number subtraction, $0 -_{Nat} 1 = 0$. *Hint:* Perform an iteration on pairs similar to the one performed by *ITER-FACT*.

Recursion

Amazingly, the raw lambda calculus is even powerful enough to express recursion. We will demonstrate this by showing that the FLK `rec` construct can be translated into the lambda calculus. Recall that this construct has the following reduction rule:

$$\texttt{(rec } I \texttt{ } E \texttt{)} \rightsquigarrow [\texttt{(rec } I \texttt{ } E \texttt{)}/I]E$$

Now suppose that E is an expression in the lambda calculus subset of FLK. We will translate the FLK expression $E_{FLK} = \texttt{(rec } I \texttt{ } E \texttt{)}$ into the following lambda calculus expression, E_{LC}, and then use normal-order reduction:

$$
\begin{aligned}
E_{LC} &= \texttt{(app (lam x (app (lam } I \texttt{ } E \texttt{) (app x x)))} \\
&\qquad \texttt{(lam x (app (lam } I \texttt{ } E \texttt{) (app x x))))} \\
&\xrightarrow[n.o.]{} \texttt{(app (lam } I \texttt{ } E \texttt{) (app (lam x (app (lam } I \texttt{ } E \texttt{) (app x x)))} \\
&\qquad\qquad\qquad\qquad\qquad \texttt{(lam x (app (lam } I \texttt{ } E \texttt{) (app x x)))))} \\
&= \texttt{(app (lam } I \texttt{ } E \texttt{) } E_{LC} \texttt{)} \\
&\xrightarrow[n.o.]{} [E_{LC}/I]E
\end{aligned}
$$

If we now translate $[E_{LC}/I]E$ back to E_{FLK}, we obtain $[\texttt{(rec } I \texttt{ } E \texttt{)}/I]E$. We have just shown that E_{LC} has exactly the same behavior as $\texttt{(rec } I \texttt{ } E \texttt{)}$. So there is no need for the latter construct since it can always be expressed by the former!

We will also reach the expression $[E_{LC}/I]E$ if we start with the expression $\texttt{(app } Y \texttt{ (lam } I \texttt{ } E \texttt{))}$, where Y is the following lambda calculus expression, which is known as the **Y operator**:

$$
\begin{aligned}
Y = \texttt{(lam f (app (lam x (app f (app x x)))} \\
\texttt{(lam x (app f (app x x)))))}
\end{aligned}
$$

Clearly, $\texttt{(app } Y \texttt{ (lam } I \texttt{ } E \texttt{))} \xrightarrow[n.o.]{} E_{LC} \xrightarrow[n.o.]{*} [E_{LC}/I]$. Here, $\texttt{(lam } I \texttt{ } E \texttt{)}$ acts like a generating function in the domain $Fcn \rightarrow Fcn$ in the iterative fixed point technique (Chapter 5) and Y acts like $\mathbf{fix}_{Fcn}$, which finds the least fixed point of this generating function. For this reason, Y is also called the **fixed-point combinator**.

As a concrete example, consider the following generating function:

$$
\begin{aligned}
\textit{FACT-GEN} = \texttt{(lam f (lam n (} \textit{IF} \texttt{ (} \textit{ZERO?} \texttt{ n)} \\
\overline{0} \\
\texttt{(} \textit{TIMES} \texttt{ n (f (} \textit{DEC} \texttt{ n))))))}
\end{aligned}
$$

The least fixed point of *FACT-GEN* is the factorial function. So we can write a "recursive" factorial function in the lambda calculus as (*Y FACT-GEN*). For

example, $((Y \; \textit{FACT-GEN}) \; \overline{5})$ normalizes to $\overline{120}$. We can also write an FLK
version of the factorial function without `rec` as follows:

$$(Y \; (\text{lam f } (\text{lam n } (\text{if } (= \text{n 0}) \; 0 \; (* \; \text{n } (\text{f } (- \; \text{n 1}))))))))$$

Exercise 6.44

a. What is the solution to the *numerical* equation $x = 2x$?

b. What is the solution to the *functional* equation $x = (\textit{TIMES} \; \overline{2} \; x)$ as found by
   reducing the lambda calculus expression $(Y \; (\text{lam x } (\textit{TIMES} \; \overline{2} \; \text{x})))$?

c. Explain any discrepancies between the solutions to the two parts above.

Exercise 6.45 Here we explore how to use Y to solve a set of simultaneous equations
in multiple variables. Our example will be based on a pair of functions that determines
whether a natural number is even or odd. It's easy to define the corresponding generating
functions for these:

$$
\begin{aligned}
\textit{EVEN?-GEN} \; = \; &(\text{abs (even? odd?}) \\
&\qquad (\text{lam n } (\textit{IF} \; (\textit{ZERO?} \; \text{n}) \\
&\qquad\qquad\quad \textit{TRUE} \\
&\qquad\qquad\quad (\text{odd? } (\textit{DEC} \; \text{n})))))
\end{aligned}
$$

$$
\begin{aligned}
\textit{ODD?-GEN} \; = \; &(\text{abs (even? odd?}) \\
&\qquad (\text{lam n } (\textit{IF} \; (\textit{ZERO?} \; \text{n}) \\
&\qquad\qquad\quad \textit{FALSE} \\
&\qquad\qquad\quad (\text{even? } (\textit{DEC} \; \text{n})))))
\end{aligned}
$$

However, neither $\textit{EVEN?-GEN}$ nor $\textit{ODD?-GEN}$ by itself is of the right form to represent
a pair of equations. Furthermore, Y can naturally only find the fixed point of a single
equation in a single variable.

We need some method of gluing together $\textit{EVEN?-GEN}$ and $\textit{ODD?-GEN}$ such that
they represent a single equation in a single variable. We can accomplish this with Church
pairs: a single pair can contain the solutions to both equations. And since Church pairs
are functions, Y can find fixed points that are Church pairs.

Based on this idea, use Y, $\textit{PAIR}$, $\textit{FST}$, $\textit{SND}$, $\textit{EVEN?-GEN}$, and $\textit{ODD?-GEN}$ to write
a lambda calculus expression that denotes the $\textit{EVEN?}$ function. Your expression should
solve the pair of equations and return the answer to the first one.

Notes

Despite some differences in syntax and semantics, FL is representative of real-
world function-oriented languages like HASKELL [HPW$^+$92], SML [MTHM97,
MT91b], and SCHEME [KCR$^+$98]. In coming chapters, we will gain a better un-

derstanding of the features of these languages as we explore language dimensions like naming, state, control, data, and types in the context of FL.

In his Turing award paper [Bac78], Backus argues that *applicative languages* — languages based on function composition — can be easier to reason about and more efficient to execute than *von Neumann languages* — those based on step-by-step manipulation of a state-based machine. He also demonstrates that applicative programs are amenable to algebraic reasoning, a key idea that underlies much of the research in functional programming. Indeed, functional languages provide a framework for deriving efficient programs from high-level specifications algebraically (e.g., see [Gib94, BdM96]).

Interestingly, Backus believes that the ability to define arbitrary anonymous functions is *too* powerful, and the language he proposes supports only a few built-in higher-order functions. In contrast, Hughes [Hug89] explains why arbitrary higher-order functions are essential for decomposing programs into modular parts. For numerous examples of the expressive power of higher-order functions in function-oriented programming, consult some of the many excellent programming texts that employ a function-oriented language, such as [ASS96, Bir98, Hen80, Hud00, Pau96, SF89, Tho99].

An excellent survey article by Hudak [Hud89] describes the history and concepts of functional programming. The collection [GdM03] showcases applications of functional programming to domains like hardware description, graphics, music, and finance. A list of functional programs applied to real-world tasks can be found in [Wadb].

Lambda notation was introduced by Church in [Chu32] as a means of abstracting over logical formulas. In [Chu36], he introduced what were later called alpha, beta, and eta reduction in the context of a study of the "effective calculability" of functions. He presented the full-fledged lambda calculus in [Chu41]. [Sto85] contains a good introduction to the lambda calculus and its semantics. [Bar84] provides comprehensive coverage of the lambda calculus, including proofs of confluence and standardization.

One approach to proving that simplification in the lambda calculus preserves observational equivalence can be found in a seminal paper by Plotkin [Plo75]. Our approach to this proof for FLK is based on the presentation sketched in [MT00] and refined in [Mac02].

In the programming languages literature, the lambda calculus and its extensions are frequent objects of study. Landin introduced an influential extension named ISWIM (If you See What I Mean) [Lan64, Lan65a, Lan65b, Lan66] that is effectively the core of modern call-by-value functional languages like SCHEME and ML. The full ISWIM language includes conditionals, local binding expressions, functions with call-by-value parameter passing, and recursive function definitions. These constructs can be desugared to a kernel language of so-called *applicative expressions* that is a call-by-value lambda calculus extended with a collection of primitives (e.g., numbers and arithmetic operators, a conditional operator, a fixed-point operator). Landin's description of ISWIM pioneered the modular description of programming languages in terms of a kernel language, syntactic sugar, and a library of primitives. Formal properties of the ISWIM kernel (such as confluence, standardization, observational equivalence) are presented in [FFF].

7

Naming

A good name is rather to be chosen than great riches.

— Proverbs 22:1

Naming is a central issue in programming language design. The fact that programming languages use names to refer to various objects and processes is at the heart of what makes them languages.

At the very least, a programming language must have a primitive set of names (literals and standard identifiers) and a means of combining the names into compound names (expressions). In a language without side effects (mutable data, input/output primitives, control jumps, etc.), every expression is a structured name for the value it computes relative to a given environment. In FL, for instance, 9, (+ 4 5), and ((abs (a) (* a a)) (+ 1 2)) are just three different names for the number nine in the standard environment. In languages with side effects, there are more complex relationships between names and values that we shall explore later.

Expressions built merely out of primitives and a means of combination quickly become complex and cumbersome. Any practical language must also provide a means of abstraction for abbreviating a long name with a shorter one. Programming languages typically use symbolic identifiers as abbreviations and have binding constructs that specify the association between the abbreviation and the entity for which it stands. FLK had two binding constructs, lam and rec, and FL offers several other binding constructs built on top of these: abs, let, letrec, and def. Using such constructs, it is possible to remove duplications to obtain more concise, readable, and efficient expressions. For example, naming allows us to transform the procedure

```
(abs (a b c)
  (list (+ (- 0 b)
           (sqrt (- (* b b)
                    (* 4 (* a c)))))
        (- (- 0 b)
           (sqrt (- (* b b)
                    (* 4 (* a c)))))))
```

into the equivalent procedure

```
(abs (a b c)
  (let ((sqrt-discriminant (sqrt (- (* b b)
                                    (* 4 (* a c)))))
        (-b (- 0 b)))
    (list (+ -b sqrt-discriminant)
          (- -b sqrt-discriminant)))))
```

Naming seems like such a simple idea that it's hard to imagine the subtleties hidden therein. A sampling of naming facilities in modern programming languages reveals a surprising number of ways to think about names. Some of the dimensions along which these facilities vary are:

- *Nameable values*: What entities in a language can be named by global variables? By local variables? By formal parameters of procedures? By field names of a record?

- *Parameter-passing mechanisms*: What is the relationship between the actual arguments provided to a procedure call and the values named by the formal parameters of the procedure?

- *Scoping*: How are new variables declared? Over what part of the program text and its associated computation does a declaration extend? How are references to a variable matched up with the associated declaration?

- *Name control*: What mechanisms exist for structuring names to minimize name clashes in large programs?

- *Multiple namespaces*: Can an identifier refer to more than one variable within a single expression?

- *Name capture*: Does the language exhibit any name capture problems like those that cropped up with naive substitution in FLK?

- *Side effects*: Can the value associated with a name change over time?

The goal of this chapter is to explore many of the above dimensions. We already introduced some of the basic concepts and terminology of naming in our discussion of FL: scope, free and bound variables, name capture, substitution, and environments. Here we give a fuller account of the issues involved in naming. Along the way, we shall pay particular attention to the effects that choices in naming design have on the expressive power of a language.

Certain naming issues (e.g., side effects, many parameter-passing mechanisms) are intertwined with state, control, data, and concurrency, which we will cover later. We defer these naming issues until the necessary concepts have been introduced.

7.1 Parameter Passing

Procedure application is the inverse operation to procedural abstraction. An abstraction packages formal parameters together with a body expression that refers to them, while application unpackages the body and evaluates it in a context where the formal parameters are associated with the actual arguments. There are numerous methods for associating the formal parameter names with the arguments. These methods are called **parameter-passing mechanisms**. Here we shall focus on two such mechanisms:

- In the **call-by-name (CBN)** mechanism, a formal parameter names the computation designated by an unevaluated argument expression. This corresponds to the nonstrict argument evaluation strategy exhibited by FL in the previous chapter. CBN is closely related to the normal-order reduction strategy for the lambda calculus, and variants of CBN have found their way into ALGOL 60 and various functional programming languages (such as HASKELL and MIRANDA).

- In the **call-by-value (CBV)** mechanism, a formal parameter names the value of an evaluated argument expression. This corresponds to the strict argument evaluation strategy used by most modern languages (C, JAVA, PASCAL, SCHEME, ML, SMALLTALK, POSTSCRIPT, etc.).

Numerous additional features may be layered on top of the above mechanisms to yield further variations in parameter passing for functional languages. For example, it is possible to pass parameters by keyword, to specify optional arguments, or to describe formal parameters that are pattern-matched against arguments that are compound data structures. While these are important ways of capturing common patterns of usage, they are orthogonal to and less fundamental than the CBN versus CBV distinction. The introduction of side effects, on the other hand, will lead to fundamental variations of the above mechanisms, such as call-by-need and call-by-reference (Section 8.4) and call-by-value-sharing and call-by-value-copy (Section 10.1.4). It is possible to include more than one parameter-passing mechanism within a single language. This possibility is explored in Exercise 7.12 on page 327.

Reduction Relation ($\rightsquigarrow$)

$\vdots$

(app (lam I_{formal} E_{body}) E_{rand}) $\rightsquigarrow$ $[E_{rand}/I_{formal}]E_{body}$ $[\beta]$

Evaluation Contexts ($\mathbb{E}^{CBN}$)

$\mathbb{E}^{CBN}$ ::= ... *non*-app *contexts* ... | (app $\mathbb{E}^{CBN}$ E_{rand})

Call-By-Name

Reduction Relation ($\rightsquigarrow$)

$\vdots$

(app (lam I_{formal} E_{body}) V_{rand}) $\rightsquigarrow$ $[V_{rand}/I_{formal}]E_{body}$ $[\beta\text{-}value]$

Evaluation Contexts ($\mathbb{E}^{CBV}$)

$\mathbb{E}^{CBV}$ ::= ... *non*-app *contexts* ... | (app $\mathbb{E}^{CBV}$ E_{rand}) | (app V_{rator} $\mathbb{E}^{CBV}$)

Call-By-Value

Figure 7.1 The essence of the operational semantics of CBN and CBV parameter passing in FLK. Under CBN, the unevaluated operand expression is substituted for the formal parameter. Under CBV, the operand expression is evaluated before being substituted for the formal parameter.

7.1.1   Call-by-Name vs. Call-by-Value: The Operational View

Figure 7.1 summarizes the difference between CBN and CBV in an operational framework. Both mechanisms share an evaluation context (app $\mathbb{E}$ E_{rand}), which allows the operator position of an application to be evaluated to an abstraction. When this occurs in CBN, the unevaluated operand expression E_{rand} is substituted for the formal parameter of the abstraction via the $[\beta]$ rule. But in CBV, the evaluation context (app V_{rator} $\mathbb{E}^{CBV}$) first forces evaluation of the operand expression E_{rand} to the operand value V_{rand}, an element of the syntactic domain ValueExp of value expressions. Only then will the $[\beta\text{-}value]$ rule substitute this value for the formal parameter within the body of the abstraction.

Figure 7.2 shows examples that highlight the differences between CBN and CBV. (We have labeled each reduction arrow with CBN or CBV to indicate which system is being used.) The number of times the operand expression is evaluated under CBN depends on how many times the formal parameter is used within the procedure body. If the formal is never used, the operand is never evaluated. In contrast, in CBV, the operand expression is evaluated exactly once, regardless of how many times the formal is referenced within the body. If operand evaluation

CBN	**CBV**

`(app (lam x (prim * x x))`
`     (prim + 2 3))`
$\xrightarrow[CBN]{[\beta]}$ `(prim * (prim + 2 3)`
`            (prim + 2 3))`
$\xrightarrow[CBN]{[+]}$ `(prim * 5 (prim + 2 3))`
$\xrightarrow[CBN]{[+]}$ `(prim * 5 5)`
$\xrightarrow[CBN]{[*]}$ `25`
	`(app (lam x (prim * x x))`
	`     (prim + 2 3))`
	$\xrightarrow[CBV]{[+]}$ `(app (lam x (prim * x x))`
	`          5)`
	$\xrightarrow[CBV]{[\beta\text{-}value]}$ `(prim * 5 5)`
	$\xrightarrow[CBV]{[*]}$ `25`

`(app (lam x 2) (prim / 1 0))` $\xrightarrow[CBN]{[\beta]}$ `2`	`(app (lam x 2) (prim / 1 0))` *{This stuck expression models an error}*

`(app (lam x 3)`
`     (app (lam a (app a a))`
`          (lam a (app a a))))`
$\xrightarrow[CBN]{[\beta]}$ `3`
	`(app (lam x 3)`
	`     (app (lam a (app a a))`
	`          (lam a (app a a))))`
	$\xrightarrow[CBV]{[\beta\text{-}value]}$
	`(app (lam x 3)`
	`     (app (lam a (app a a))`
	`          (lam a (app a a))))`
	$\xrightarrow[CBV]{[\beta\text{-}value]}$ `...` *{Infinite loop}*

Figure 7.2 Examples illustrating the difference between CBN and CBV.

encounters an error or diverges (goes into a loop), CBV won't return a value in some cases where CBN would — i.e., when the formal is never referenced during the evaluation of the body.

Despite these differences, CBN and CBV are closely related in FLK:

Theorem 7.1 (FLK CBN/CBV Relationship) *If E is an FLK expression and $E \xrightarrow[CBV]{*} V$, then $E \xrightarrow[CBN]{*} V'$, where $V' =_{obs} V$.*

This theorem says that if an FLK expression E evaluates to a value V using the CBV strategy, it evaluates to an observationally equivalent value V' using the CBN strategy. V and V' might not be syntactically identical, but they must behave the same in all FLK program contexts. For example, if V is `(lam x 3)` then V' might be `(lam x (prim + 1 2))`. The theorem also says that if E does not evaluate to a value under CBN (i.e., it diverges or gets stuck at an error), then it cannot evaluate to a value under CBV. Figure 7.2 shows that CBN can sometimes yield a value in cases where CBV doesn't. So the CBN strategy yields values in more cases than the CBV strategy; and when both strategies yield values for a given expression, the values must be observationally equivalent.

Proof of Theorem 7.1:   Suppose $E \xrightarrow[CBV]{*} V$. Observe that each CBV evaluation context is a valid FLK simplification context and each CBV reduction rule is a valid FLK simplification rule (see Section 6.4.2). So each CBV evaluation step is a valid FLK simplification step, implying $E \xrightarrow{*} V$. By standardization for FLK simplification (Theorem 6.3), there exists an expression E' such that $E \xrightarrow[CBN]{*} E' \overset{*}{\Longrightarrow} V$ — i.e., a sequence $\xrightarrow[CBN]{*}$ of FLK (CBN) evaluation steps followed by a sequence $\overset{*}{\Longrightarrow}$ of nonevaluation steps. Since each simplification step in $E' \overset{*}{\Longrightarrow} V$ is a nonevaluation step, and, by Theorem 6.1, nonevaluation steps preserve expression classification, E' must be a value expression; call it V'. By Theorem 6.4, $V' \overset{*}{\Longrightarrow} V$ implies $V' =_{obs} V$. $\diamond$

From the theoretical perspective, CBN seems superior to CBV because it can succeed with an answer in cases where CBV fails. Then why do so many languages use CBV and hardly any use CBN? As hinted above, one reason is that CBN implies certain implementation inefficiencies in practice. Perhaps an even more important reason is that CBN and side effects do not mix well. As we shall see in the next chapter, imperative programs using CBN are notoriously hard to reason about. But here we shall focus only on the issue of implementation efficiency.

As a nontrivial example, let's compare the CBN and CBV mechanisms on the following call to a recursive summation procedure written in FLK:

```
(app (rec sum (lam n (if (prim = n 0)
                         0
                         (prim + n (app sum (prim - n 1)))))))
     3)
```

The transition sequence for CBN evaluation of this expression was presented in Figure 6.20 on page 265. The CBV sequence is presented in Figure 7.3. Both sequences use the abbreviations S for the **rec** subexpression and S' for the result of unwinding S via the [rec] rule (Figure 6.19).

As indicated by the transition sequences, CBN can be much less efficient than CBV. There are two kinds of overhead:

1. CBN often requires more *time*[1] than CBV in the case where an argument is used more than once in the body of an abstraction, because then the same argument expression must be evaluated multiple times. For example, in Fig-

---

[1] Assume that the time taken by an evaluation is the length of its SOS transition sequence.

Abbreviations

(@O E_1 ... E_n) abbreviates (prim O E_1 ... E_n) (usual FL sugar).

S = (rec sum (lam n (if (@= n 0) 0 (@+ n (app sum (@- n 1)))))))

S'= (lam n (if (@= n 0) 0 (@+ n (app S (@- n 1)))))

Evaluation

(app S 3)

$\overrightarrow{CBV}_{[rec]}$ (app S' 3)

$\overrightarrow{CBV}_{[\beta\text{-value}]}$ (if (@= 3 0) 0 (@+ 3 (app S (@- 3 1))))

$\overrightarrow{CBV}_{[=]}$ (if #f 0 (@+ 3 (app S (@- 3 1))))

$\overrightarrow{CBV}_{[if\text{-}F]}$ (@+ 3 (app S (@- 3 1)))

$\overrightarrow{CBV}_{[rec]}$ (@+ 3 (app S' (@- 3 1)))

$\overrightarrow{CBV}_{[-]}$ (@+ 3 (app S' 2))

$\overrightarrow{CBV}_{[\beta\text{-value}]}$ (@+ 3 (if (@= 2 0) 0 (@+ 2 (app S (@- 2 1)))))

$\overrightarrow{CBV}_{[=]}$ (@+ 3 (if #f 0 (@+ 2 (app S (@- 2 1)))))

$\overrightarrow{CBV}_{[if\text{-}F]}$ (@+ 3 (@+ 2 (app S (@- 2 1))))

$\overrightarrow{CBV}_{[rec]}$ (@+ 3 (@+ 2 (app S' (@- 2 1))))

$\overrightarrow{CBV}_{[-]}$ (@+ 3 (@+ 2 (app S' 1)))

$\overrightarrow{CBV}_{[\beta\text{-value}]}$ (@+ 3 (@+ 2 (if (@= 1 0) 0 (@+ 1 (app S (@- 1 1))))))

$\overrightarrow{CBV}_{[=]}$ (@+ 3 (@+ 2 (if #f 0 (@+ 1 (app S (@- 1 1))))))

$\overrightarrow{CBV}_{[if\text{-}F]}$ (@+ 3 (@+ 2 (@+ 1 (app S (@- 1 1)))))

$\overrightarrow{CBV}_{[rec]}$ (@+ 3 (@+ 2 (@+ 1 (app S' (@- 1 1)))))

$\overrightarrow{CBV}_{[-]}$ (@+ 3 (@+ 2 (@+ 1 (app S' 0))))

$\overrightarrow{CBV}_{[\beta\text{-value}]}$ (@+ 3 (@+ 2 (@+ 1 (if (@= 0 0) 0 (@+ 0 (app S (@- 0 1)))))))

$\overrightarrow{CBV}_{[=]}$ (@+ 3 (@+ 2 (@+ 1 (if #t 0 (@+ 0 (app S (@- 0 1)))))))

$\overrightarrow{CBV}_{[if\text{-}T]}$ (@+ 3 (@+ 2 (@+ 1 0)))

$\overrightarrow{CBV}_{[+]}$ (@+ 3 (@+ 2 1))

$\overrightarrow{CBV}_{[+]}$ (@+ 3 3)

$\overrightarrow{CBV}_{[+]}$ 6

Figure 7.3 CBV evaluation involving a recursive summation procedure.

ure 6.20, the value of (prim - 3 1) is calculated five times, compared to only once in Figure 7.3. In general, evaluating (app S n) can take quadratic time (time proportional to n^2) using CBN but only linear time (time proportional to n) using CBV.

2. CBN often requires more *space*[2] than CBV because expressions whose values
   are not currently needed may grow as their evaluations are deferred until later.
   For example, unwinding S to S' creates a new application of S. The operand
   of this new application contains exactly one subtraction in CBV, but this
   operand grows by one subtraction with every recursive call in CBN.

In practice, there are techniques for ameliorating both of these sources of overhead. The time inefficiency is typically finessed by **memoization**,[3] a technique
that evaluates an operand and caches its value the first time it is referenced. Further references simply return the cached value rather than evaluating the operand
again. We shall investigate this more fully when we study **lazy evaluation** in
Section 8.4.3.

The space overhead is perhaps more insidious. It can be improved by using so-
called **graph reduction** to perform rewrites on shared graph structure [Pey87].
However, this technique does not prevent the space consumed by operands for
certain parameters from growing in size with every recursive call. There are cases
where CBN evaluation requires asymptotically more space than CBV evaluation
in FL programs, even in the presence of graph reduction (see Exercise 7.3). When
executing these programs on a machine with finite storage resources, a CBN
strategy is more likely to run out of space than a CBV strategy. A technique called
strictness analysis [Myc80, Pey87, KM89] can improve CBN by modifying it
to use CBV for operand evaluation when it is possible to prove that the value of
the operand will be required at least once.

These techniques for improving CBN make it much more palatable, but the
techniques themselves still involve overheads that some implementers find unacceptable. For example, memoization implies that a flag must be tested at every
variable reference. Since variable references are rather common, the extra check
is often considered prohibitive without special hardware support.

Parameter-passing mechanisms are used to describe not only procedure calls,
but also other constructs that bind names to values. For example, the FL
binding constructs `abs` and `let` have an implicit method for associating names
with values because they desugar into FLK's abstractions and applications. So
`(let ((a (/ 1 0))) 3)` evaluates to 3 in a CBN language, but signals an error in a CBV language. There are some thorny issues surrounding constructs
involving recursion (such as `rec`, `letrec`, and `def`) in CBV; we defer discussion
of these until Section 7.1.4.

---

[2]Assume that the space taken by an evaluation is the size (measured by number of AST
nodes) of the largest expression in its SOS transition sequence.

[3]That's memoizing — making a memo or note about something — not memorizing, although
this has a similar meaning.

Exercise 7.1 Is the following statement true? *If E diverges under CBN then it diverges under CBV.* If so, prove it; if not, give a counterexample.

Exercise 7.2 In a CBV language, it is often useful to delay the evaluation of an argument until a later time. This behavior can be specified with the pair of constructs (`wrap` E) and (`unwrap` E). Informally, (`wrap` E) wraps E up without evaluating it, while (`unwrap` E) unwraps E until it is no longer embedded in a `wrap`. On a non-`wrap` value, `unwrap` acts as an identity. For example, in CBV FLK:

```
(unwrap (prim + 1 2))  CBVFLK⟶  3

(unwrap (wrap (prim + 1 2)))  CBVFLK⟶  3

(unwrap (wrap (wrap (prim + 1 2))))  CBVFLK⟶  3

(app (app (lam a (lam b (unwrap a)))
          (wrap (prim + 1 2)))
     (wrap (prim / 1 0)))  CBVFLK⟶  3

(app (app (lam a (lam b (unwrap b)))
          (wrap (prim + 1 2)))
     (wrap (prim / 1 0)))  CBVFLK⟶  error:divide-by-zero
```

a. Extend the operational semantics of FLK to handle `wrap` and `unwrap`. Recall that an SOS has five parts; make whatever changes are necessary to each of the parts.

b. Can `wrap` and `unwrap` be implemented by syntactic sugar? If so, give the desugarings; if not, explain why.

c. Show how to translate CBN FLK into a CBV version of FLK that is equipped with `wrap` and `unwrap`.

Exercise 7.3 Consider the following two versions of an FLK factorial function:

```
F₁ = (rec fact-rec
        (lam n
          (if (prim = n 0) 1 (prim * n (app fact-rec (prim - n 1))))))
F₂ = (lam n (app (app LOOP n) 1))
     where LOOP = (rec fact-loop
                      (lam num
                        (lam ans
                          (if (prim = num 0)
                              ans
                              (app (app fact-loop (prim - num 1))
                                   (prim * num ans)))))))
```

Suppose that n is a nonnegative integer. For each F_i, calculate the time and space of the transition sequence starting with (`app` F_i n) as a function of n using (1) the CBN strategy and (2) the CBV strategy. Measure the time as the number of steps in the transition path. Measure the space as the maximum number of primitive applications in an expression in the transition path.

The space for F_1 can be reduced by using graph reduction techniques. But such techniques do not reduce the space required for the `ans` parameter in F_2. This problem, known as a **dragging tail**, causes what should intuitively be a constant-space iteration to take linear space.

7.1.2   Call-by-Name vs. Call-by-Value: The Denotational View

Figure 7.4 summarizes the difference between CBN and CBV in a denotational framework. For each mechanism, it shows the definition of the *Nameable* domain, the *nam-to-comp* function, and the valuation clause for app. The valuation clauses for variable references and lam are the same for both mechanisms and are shown in a separate box at the bottom of the figure. Since the *nam-to-comp* function differs in the two mechanisms and the valuation clause for variable references uses this function, the CBN and CBV versions of $\mathcal{E}[\![I]\!]$ actually differ slightly in terms of how entities from the environment are converted to computations. But the $\mathcal{E}[\![I]\!]$ clause is written in a way that abstracts over this difference.

The denotational framework clarifies the key difference between CBN and CBV for FLK: CBN allows errors and divergence to be named in environments whereas CBV does not. We can see this from the definitions of the *Nameable* domain for the two mechanisms. (Recall the *Nameable* is the domain that describes which values may be associated with names in environments.) In CBV FLK, *Nameable* = *Value*, which contains the "regular" values (unit, integers, booleans, symbols, pairs, and procedures). But in CBN FLK, *Nameable* = *Comp* = *Expressible* = $(Value + Error)_\perp$, which includes error and divergence in addition to the "regular" values.

In CBN, a procedure application can return an element of *Value* even when the operand denotes an error or divergence. In other words, CBN procedures are not strict. Here's an example (where e is an arbitrary environment and *diverr* is an abbreviation for $(Error \rightarrowtail Expressible\ \text{divide-by-zero})$):

$\mathcal{E}[\![(\text{app (lam x 3) (prim / 1 0))}]\!]\ e$

$= \textit{with-procedure-comp}\ (\mathcal{E}[\![(\text{lam x 3})]\!]\ e)\ (\lambda p\,.\,(p\ (\mathcal{E}[\![(\text{prim / 1 0})]\!]\ e)))$

$= \textit{with-procedure-comp}\ (\textit{val-to-comp}\ (Proc \rightarrowtail Value\ (\lambda n\,.\,(\mathcal{E}[\![3]\!]\ [\text{x} \mapsto n]e))))$
$\quad (\lambda p\,.\,(p\ \textit{diverr}))$

$= (\lambda n\,.\,(\mathcal{E}[\![3]\!]\ [\text{x} \mapsto n]e))\ \textit{diverr}$

$= \mathcal{E}[\![3]\!][\text{x} \mapsto \textit{diverr}]e$

$= \textit{val-to-comp}\ (Int \rightarrowtail Value\ 3)$

The CBV clause for app uses *with-value* to guarantee that only elements of the domain *Value* are passed to p. This accounts for the strict nature of CBV

$n \in \textit{Nameable} = \textit{Comp}$

$\textit{nam-to-comp} : \textit{Nameable} \rightarrow \textit{Comp} = \lambda n \,.\, n$

$\mathcal{E}[\![(\texttt{app } E_1 \ E_2)]\!] = \lambda e \,.\, (\textit{with-procedure-comp} \ (\mathcal{E}[\![E_1]\!] \ e) \ (\lambda p \,.\, (p \ (\mathcal{E}[\![E_2]\!] \ e))))$

Call-By-Name (CBN)

$n \in \textit{Nameable} = \textit{Value}$

$\textit{nam-to-comp} : \textit{Nameable} \rightarrow \textit{Comp} = \textit{val-to-comp}$

$\mathcal{E}[\![(\texttt{app } E_1 \ E_2)]\!] = \lambda e \,.\, (\textit{with-procedure-comp} \ (\mathcal{E}[\![E_1]\!] \ e)$
$\qquad\qquad\qquad\qquad\qquad (\lambda p \,.\, (\textit{with-value} \ (\mathcal{E}[\![E_2]\!] \ e) \ p)))$

Call-By-Value (CBV)

$\mathcal{E}[\![I]\!] = \lambda e \,.\, (\textit{with-nameable} \ (\textit{lookup } I \ e) \ (\lambda n \,.\, (\textit{nam-to-comp } n)))$

$\mathcal{E}[\![(\texttt{lam } I \ E)]\!] = \lambda e \,.\, (\textit{val-to-comp} \ (\textit{Proc} \rightarrowtail \textit{Value} \ (\lambda n \,.\, (\mathcal{E}[\![E]\!] \ [I \mapsto n]e))))$

Clauses shared by CBN and CBV

Figure 7.4 The essence of the denotational semantics of CBN and CBV parameter passing. For FLK, *Comp* = *Expressible*, but the CBN semantics will still be valid later when *Comp* is updated to reflect extensions to FLK. Likewise, the CBV semantics will still be valid when the *Value* domain is extended.

evaluation. As an illustration of CBV, let's evaluate the above example expression in CBV:

$\mathcal{E}[\![(\texttt{app (lam x 3) (prim / 1 0))}]\!] \ e$

$= \textit{with-procedure-comp} \ (\mathcal{E}[\![(\texttt{lam x 3})]\!] \ e)$
$\quad (\lambda p \,.\, (\textit{with-value} \ (\mathcal{E}[\![(\texttt{prim / 1 0})]\!] \ e) \ p))$

$= \textit{with-procedure-comp} \ (\mathcal{E}[\![(\texttt{lam x 3})]\!] \ e) \ (\lambda p \,.\, (\textit{with-value diverr } p))$

$= \textit{with-procedure-comp} \ (\mathcal{E}[\![(\texttt{lam x 3})]\!] \ e) \ (\lambda p \,.\, \textit{diverr})$

$= \textit{with-procedure-comp} \ (\textit{val-to-comp} \ (\textit{Proc} \rightarrowtail \textit{Value} \ (\lambda n \,.\, (\mathcal{E}[\![3]\!] \ [\texttt{x} \mapsto n]e))))$
$\quad (\lambda p \,.\, \textit{diverr})$

$= \textit{diverr}$

It is natural to wonder at this point how error or divergence in an argument can *ever* lead to error or divergence for an application in a CBN language. That is, if an argument is simply inserted into the environment upon call and retrieved upon lookup, when is the value denoted by the argument ever actually examined? There are several spots in the denotational definition where information about the values is required. For example, in the clause for $[\![(\text{app } E_1 \; E_2)]\!]$ the value of E_1 is required to be a procedure; the semantics must check the value to ensure that this is the case (such checks are hidden in the abstraction *with-procedure-comp*). Similarly, an `if` valuation clause must not only check that the test expression denotes a boolean, but also use the boolean value in order to determine which arm is denoted by the entire conditional construct. Handling primitive operators in FLK is perhaps the most common case where details of the values must be examined.

Exercise 7.4

a. In CBN FLK, show that for all environments e:

$$(\mathcal{E}[\![(\text{app } (\text{lam } I \; E_{body}) \; E_{rand})]\!] \; e) = (\mathcal{E}[\![E_{body}]\!] \; [I \mapsto (\mathcal{E}[\![E_{rand}]\!] \; e)]e)$$

b. In CBV FLK, show that for all environments e:

$$\begin{aligned}(\mathcal{E}[\![(\text{app } (\text{lam } I \; E_{body}) \; E_{rand})]\!] \; e) = {} & \textit{with-value } (\mathcal{E}[\![E_{rand}]\!] \; e) \\ & (\lambda v \, . \; (\mathcal{E}[\![E_{body}]\!] \; [I \mapsto v]e))\end{aligned}$$

7.1.3   Nonstrict versus Strict Pairs

In most programming languages, data constructors (such as `pair` in FLK) tend to have the same strictness properties as procedures. So they are typically nonstrict in a CBN language but strict in a CBV language. For example, consider the following expression $E_{pairTest}$:

```
(prim snd (pair (prim / 1 0) (prim + 2 3)))
```

We expect that $E_{pairTest}$ should evaluate to *5* in CBN FLK but should signal a divide-by-zero error in CBV FLK.

The key semantic differences between nonstrict and strict pairs are summarized in Figure 7.5. The figure omits the operational and denotational semantics of the `fst` and `snd` primitives, which do not differ between the nonstrict and strict versions and so are the same as those presented for FLK (see Figure 6.19 on page 259 for their operational semantics and Figure 6.29 on page 285 for their denotational semantics). In both operational and denotational perspectives, the difference boils down to whether the components of pair values must themselves be values (yes for CBV and no for CBN).

Strict data structures permit a more interesting output function to be defined for a language's operational semantics. If a program in a language with strict pairs terminates with a pair, the output function can produce a result based on

Operational:

$V \in \text{ValueExp} ::= \dots \text{ nonpair FLK } values \dots \mid (\texttt{pair } E_{fst} \ E_{snd})$

$\mathbb{E} \in \text{EvalContext} ::= \dots \text{ FLK } evaluation \ contexts \dots$

Nonstrict Pairs

$V \in \text{ValueExp} ::= \dots \text{ nonpair FLK } values \dots \mid (\texttt{pair } V_{fst} \ V_{snd})$

$\mathbb{E} \in \text{EvalContext} ::= \dots \text{ FLK } evaluation \ contexts \dots$
$\mid (\texttt{pair } \mathbb{E} \ E_{snd}) \mid (\texttt{pair } V_{fst} \ \mathbb{E})$

Strict Pairs

Denotational:

$Pair = Comp \times Comp$

$\mathcal{E}[\![(\texttt{pair } E_1 \ E_2)]\!] = \lambda e \, . \, (\textit{val-to-comp } (Pair \rightarrowtail Value \ \langle (\mathcal{E}[\![E_1]\!] \ e), (\mathcal{E}[\![E_2]\!] \ e) \rangle))$

Nonstrict Pairs

$Pair = Value \times Value$

$\mathcal{E}[\![(\texttt{pair } E_1 \ E_2)]\!] =$
$\quad \lambda e \, . \, (\textit{with-value } (\mathcal{E}[\![E_1]\!] \ e)$
$\quad\quad\quad (\lambda v_1 \, . \, (\textit{with-value } (\mathcal{E}[\![E_2]\!] \ e)$
$\quad\quad\quad\quad\quad (\lambda v_2 \, . \, (\textit{val-to-comp } (Pair \rightarrowtail Value \ \langle v_1, v_2 \rangle)))))))$

Strict Pairs

Figure 7.5 Operational and denotational views of nonstrict and strict pairs.

recursively computing output representations for the pair's components rather than yielding a generic output like `pairans` (see Section 6.4.1, page 266). The output function is well defined and guaranteed to terminate, because all the components are already values. In contrast, the output function for a language with nonstrict pairs cannot do this: the components of a pair may not be values and may contain errors or infinite computations.

Pairs are a special instance of a more general data structure called a **product**. We will study many design dimensions of products, including alternative approaches to nonstrictness, in Section 10.1.

We have assumed in our discussion up to this point that every entity that is nameable may be passed as an argument or bundled into a pair. While this tends to be true in functional languages (and is a major source of power in such languages), it is not true in general. For example, while procedures are almost universally nameable, there are many languages (e.g., FORTRAN, BASIC, PASCAL) in which procedures cannot be passed as arguments, or can be passed only in a limited way. Similarly, many languages do not permit data-structure components to be procedures. In order to give an accurate denotational description of such languages, it is necessary to distinguish the class of nameable entities from those which may be passed as arguments and those which can be components of data structures. To model such languages we would need to introduce new domains, *Passable* and *Component*, that describe these classes of values.

Exercise 7.5

a. Using the operational semantics of pairs presented in Figure 7.5, show the evaluation of $E_{pairTest}$ in both CBN and CBV versions of FLK.

b. Using the denotational semantics of pairs presented in Figure 7.5, show the evaluation of $E_{pairTest}$ in both CBN and CBV versions of FLK.

Exercise 7.6 One justification for giving data constructors the same strictness properties as procedures is that this is consistent with procedural encodings of data (such as the Church pair encoding in Section 6.6). For example, consider the following expressions for constructing and deconstructing pairs:

$$E_{pair} = \texttt{(lam x (lam y (lam f (app (app f x) y))))}$$

$$E_{fst} = \texttt{(lam pr (app pr (lam x (lam y x))))}$$

$$E_{snd} = \texttt{(lam pr (app pr (lam x (lam y y))))}$$

Using these expressions, we can "translate" the $E_{pairTest}$ example to the following expression:

$$E'_{pairTest} = \texttt{(app } E_{snd} \texttt{ (app (app } E_{pair} \texttt{ (prim / 1 0)) (prim + 2 3)))}$$

Show that $E'_{pairTest}$ behaves like $E_{pairTest}$ by doing Exercise 7.5 with $E_{pairTest}$ replaced by $E'_{pairTest}$. Use the results of Exercise 7.4 to simplify your reasoning for the denotational case.

7.1.4   Handling `rec` in a CBV Language

In an operational semantics, `rec` can be handled by the same rule regardless of whether the language is CBN or CBV:

$$\texttt{(rec } I \texttt{ } E) \rightsquigarrow [\texttt{(rec } I \texttt{ } E)/I]E \quad [\texttt{rec}]$$

(An alternative approach to handling `rec` under CBV is explored in Exercise 7.8.)

Unfortunately, things are not so simple in a denotational semantics. In CBN, where *Nameable = Comp*, the valuation clause for a CBN version of `rec` is very elegant:

$$\mathcal{E}[\![(\texttt{rec } I \; E)]\!] = \lambda e \, . \; (\mathbf{fix}_{Comp} \; (\lambda c \, . \, (\mathcal{E}[\![E]\!] \; [I \mapsto c]e)))$$

The fixed point defined by this clause is well defined as long as *Comp* is a pointed CPO. For this reason, we will always guarantee that *Comp* is a pointed domain.

However, developing a valuation clause for `rec` in a CBV language is rather tricky. In CBV, the corresponding version of the CBN clause is:

$$\mathcal{E}[\![(\texttt{rec } I \; E)]\!] = \lambda e \, . \; (\mathbf{fix}_{Value} \; (\lambda v \, . \, (\mathcal{E}[\![E]\!] \; [I \mapsto v]e)))$$

But since *Nameable = Value* is *not* a pointed domain, the fixed point is not well defined, and the clause is nonsensical.

There are several ways of circumventing this impasse. Here we present two approaches:

1. In (`rec` $I \; E$), we can limit E to be a subset of expressions that are syntactically guaranteed to be procedures. In CBV, *Proc = Nameable → Comp = Value → Comp* is a pointed CPO (because *Comp* is always pointed), so it is always possible to find a fixed point over *Proc*. That is, suppose we modify the syntax of FLK as follows:

$$E ::= \; \dots \; \textit{non-\texttt{rec} expressions } \dots \; | \; (\texttt{rec } I_{var} \; AB_{body})$$
$$AB \in \text{Abstraction} ::= (\texttt{lam } I_{formal} \; E_{body})$$

   If we suppose that $\mathcal{AB} : \text{Abstraction} \to Env \to Proc$ is the valuation function for abstractions, then `rec` is definable as:

$$\mathcal{E}[\![(\texttt{rec } I \; AB)]\!]$$
$$= \lambda e \, . \; (\textit{val-to-comp}$$
$$\quad (Proc \rightarrowtail Value \; (\mathbf{fix}_{Proc} \; (\lambda p \, . \, (\mathcal{AB}[\![AB]\!] \; [I \mapsto (Proc \rightarrowtail Value \; p)]e)))))$$

SML is an example of a CBV language that takes this approach. The SML grammar permits recursion only over explicit abstractions, not arbitrary expressions.

A drawback of restricting recursion to syntactic abstractions is that it reduces the expressive power of `rec`. For example, in FLK it would no longer be possible to specify recursions over pairs or over procedures denoted by an expression that is not an explicit `lam`. The following FL examples, though

$\mathcal{E}[\![(\text{rec } I \ E)]\!] = \lambda e \ . \ (\mathbf{fix}_{Comp} \ (\lambda c \ . \ (\mathcal{E}[\![E]\!] \ (bind \ I \ (extract\text{-}value \ c) \ e))))$

$bind : Ident \rightarrow BindingVal \rightarrow Env \rightarrow Env$
$= \lambda I\beta e \ . \ \lambda I_2 \ . \ \text{if } I =_{Ident} I_2 \ \text{then } \beta \ \text{else } (lookup \ I_2 \ e) \ \text{end}$

$extract\text{-}value : Expressible \rightarrow BindingVal$
$= \lambda c \ . \ \mathbf{match} \ c$
$\qquad \triangleright (Value \rightarrowtail Expressible \ v) \ [\!] \ (Nameable \rightarrowtail BindingVal \ v)$
$\qquad \triangleright (Error \rightarrowtail Expressible \ Y) \ [\!] \ \perp_{BindingVal}$
$\qquad \mathbf{end}$

Figure 7.6 A CBV version of `rec` that assumes $Comp = Expressible$.

contrived, are indicative of useful patterns that are disallowed by an approach
that requires the body of a `rec` to be an explicit abstraction in a CBV language:

```
(rec ones (pair 1 (abs () ones)))
(rec fact
  (let ((fact-of-0 1))
    (abs (n)
      (if (= n 0) fact-of-0 (* n (fact (- n 1)))))))
```

2. Recall that the *BindingVal* domain was defined as a lifted domain:

$\beta \in BindingVal = (Nameable + Unbound)_{\perp}$

An alternative strategy for CBV `rec` is to make use of $\perp_{BindingVal}$ to compute fixed points. Figure 7.6 presents a version of the `rec` valuation clause
that works in the case where $Comp = Expressible$. *bind* is an environment
extension function that is like *extend* except that it takes an element of *BindingVal* where *extend* takes an element of *Nameable*. *extract-value* coerces
a computation into a binding value that can be associated with a name in
the environment. The resulting binding value is either an injected element of
$Nameable = Value$ or it is $\perp_{BindingVal}$. (Recall from Section 5.2.7 that **match**
is strict in its discriminant, so that *extract-value* maps $\perp_{Comp}$ to $\perp_{BindingVal}$.)

By effectively naming a bottom element in the environment, this approach
provides a suitable starting point for the fixed point iteration technique. It
would also be possible to add a bottom element directly to the *Nameable*
domain, but that would not faithfully model the intuition that divergence is
not nameable in CBV. The $\perp_{BindingVal}$ element helps to clarify the difference
between using bottom to solve a recursion equation expressed by a `rec` and
allowing bottom to be passed as an argument to a procedure.

We emphasize that the *extract-value* function in Figure 7.6 works only for case where *Comp* = *Expressible* and needs to be tweaked if the *Comp* domain changes. For some definitions of *Comp*, it may not be possible to define a suitable *extract-value* function.

In the remainder of the text, we will assume that the second of these two approaches is taken whenever recursion is used in CBV FLK.

Exercise 7.7 Use both the operational and denotational `rec` semantics to compute the values of the following expressions in both CBN and CBV versions of FLK:

a. `(rec a 1)`

b. `(rec a (prim / 2 0))`

c. `(rec a a)`

d. `(rec a (if #t 3 a))`

e. `(rec a (lam x a))`

f. `(rec a (pair 4 a))`

g. `(rec a (pair 5 (lam x a)))`

Exercise 7.8 An alternative reduction rule for `rec` is:

$$(\text{rec } I \ V) \rightsquigarrow [(\text{rec } I \ V)/I]V \quad [\text{rec}']$$

This rule assumes that evaluation contexts have been extended as follows to allow evaluation of a `rec` body:

$$\mathbb{E} \in \text{EvalContext} ::= \ \dots \text{ FLK } evaluation \ contexts \ \dots \ | \ (\text{rec } I \ \mathbb{E})$$

a. Write an FLK expression involving `rec` that takes fewer steps to evaluate in CBV FLK when [`rec`'] is used in place of [`rec`].

b. For which expressions in Exercise 7.7 does [`rec`'] give rise to different behavior than [`rec`]?

c. Prove that if a CBV FLK expression evaluates to a value V' using the [`rec`'] rule, then it evaluates to a value V using the [`rec`] rule, where $V =_{obs} V'$.

Exercise 7.9 Bud Lojack has designed the following CBV `rec` clause, which finds fixed points over the *Env* domain rather than the *Comp* domain.

$$\mathcal{E}[\![(\text{rec } I \ E)]\!]$$
$$= \lambda e_{rec} . \ \mathcal{E}[\![E]\!] \ (\mathbf{fix}_{Env} \ (\lambda e_{fix} . \ \mathbf{match} \ (\mathcal{E}[\![E]\!] \ e_{fix})$$
$$\rhd (Value \!\rightarrowtail\! Expressible \ v) \ [\![\ [I \mapsto v] e_{rec}$$
$$\rhd \mathbf{else} \ e_{rec}$$
$$\mathbf{end} \ ))$$

a. As explained in Chapter 5, $\mathbf{fix}_D$ is sensible only when the domain D is a pointed CPO. Explain why Env is a pointed CPO.

b. Characterize the situations in which Bud's clause gives a different meaning from the standard CBV rec clause in Figure 7.6. You should consider the rec examples in Exercise 7.7 as well as design some rec examples of your own.

7.1.5   Thunking

Some important idioms used in CBN do not work in CBV. For example, consider the following FL unless procedure:

```
(def unless
  (abs (test default exception)
    (if test exception default)))
```

Because procedure arguments that are never referenced in the evaluation of the procedure body are not evaluated in CBN FL, at most one of the default and exception arguments will be evaluated. E.g., (unless #f (* 2 3) (/ 4 0)) returns 6 because (/ 4 0) is never evaluated in CBN. However, in CBV FL, the same invocation of unless signals a divide-by-zero error because all procedure arguments are evaluated before the procedure is applied.

As another example, in CBN it is possible to define infinite data structures, such as the following infinite list of the powers of two:[4]

```
(def twos
  (let ((gen-twos (abs (n) (pair n (gen-twos (* 2 n))))))
    (gen-twos 1)))
```

The elements of twos can be extracted using the nth procedure from FL's standard library (Figure 6.8 on page 236). E.g., (nth 11 twos) returns 1024. But in CBV FL, the application (gen-twos 1) diverges because no pair in the list can be returned until *all* the pairs in the list have been created (and this can't happen in finite time).

Can we somehow express these idioms in CBV FL? Yes! The key idea is to delay the evaluation of certain expressions. In CBV FL, a simple way to delay the evaluation of an expression $E_{wrapped}$ is to wrap it in a parameterless procedure, (abs () $E_{wrapped}$), which is known as a **thunk**.[5] If E_{thunk} denotes a thunk, its

---

[4]See Section 10.1.3 for a detailed discussion of conceptually infinite data structures.

[5]The earliest use we know of this term is in [Ing61], but its origins are not explained there. In computer-science folklore, two etymologies are given for this term. One is that it is called a "thunk" because all the thinking for it has already been done. The other is that "thunk" is the sound made when this entity is pushed onto the stack. The terms **delay**, **promise**, and

```
(app (app (app (lam test {lam begins unless desugaring}
                   (lam default-thunk
                     (lam exception-thunk
                       (if test
                           (app exception-thunk #u)
                           (app default-thunk #u))))) {end desugaring}
                #f)
            (lam ignore.1 (prim * 2 3))) {ignore.1 is fresh}
        (lam ignore.2 (prim / 4 0))) {ignore.2 is fresh}
```

$\xrightarrow[\text{[β-value]}]{*}_{CBV}$ (if #f
                                              (app (lam ignore.2 (prim / 4 0)) #u)
                                              (app (lam ignore.1 (prim * 2 3)) #u))

$\xrightarrow[\text{[if-F]}]{}_{CBV}$ (app (lam ignore.1 (prim * 2 3)) #u)

$\xrightarrow[\text{[β-value]}]{}_{CBV}$ (prim * 2 3)

$\xrightarrow[\text{[*]}]{}_{CBV}$ 6

Figure 7.7   CBV evaluation sequence for the sample `unless` application.

wrapped expression $E_{wrapped}$ can be evaluated via (E_{thunk}), which applies E_{thunk} to zero arguments. We will also use "thunk" as a verb: we "thunk" $E_{wrapped}$ via $E_{thunk} = (\texttt{abs ()}\ E_{wrapped})$ and "dethunk" E_{thunk} via (E_{thunk}).

To implement `unless` in CBV FL, we assume that its second and third arguments are thunked, as in

```
(unless #f (abs () (* 2 3)) (abs () (/ 4 0)))
```

The CBV `unless` procedure dethunks at most one of these thunks:

```
(def unless
  (abs (test default-thunk exception-thunk)
    (if test (exception-thunk) (default-thunk))))
```

Figure 7.7 presents the CBV evaluation sequence for the sample `unless` application after desugaring. The multiplication and division operations are delayed by thunking because CBV evaluation contexts do not permit evaluation to take place inside the body of an abstraction.

Thunks can also be used to represent conceptually infinite lists in CBV FL. Finiteness is achieved by making the second element of each pair a thunk that, when dethunked, returns the next pair in the list:

---

suspension are also used, though these terms sometimes imply thunks with memoization, as discussed in Section 10.1.3.

```
(def twos {CBV version}
  (let ((gen-twos (abs (n) (pair n (abs () (gen-twos (* 2 n)))))))
    (gen-twos 1)))
```

Of course, we also need a modified version of `nth` that performs the appropriate dethunking.

```
(def nth-inf {CBV version of nth for infinite lists}
  (abs (i xs)
    (cond ((scor (null? xs) (< i 1))
           (error nth-index-out-of-bounds))
          ((= i 1) (car xs))
          (else (nth-inf (- i 1) ((cdr xs)))))))  {dethunk the cdr}
```

Encoding CBN idioms in CBV via thunking and dethunking introduces time and space execution overheads and can be cumbersome for the programmer. Some of the overheads are fundamental, but memoization can ameliorate the execution time overhead; see the discussion in Section 10.1.3. Programming effort can be reduced by developing abstractions that hide the explicit thunking and dethunking. The transformation from CBN to CBV can also be automated by a translation process that inserts the appropriate thunk-manipulation code [Amt93, SW94].

From a denotational perspective, the essence of simulating CBN in CBV is finding a way to name errors and $\perp_{Comp}$ in CBV environments. It is not possible to name these directly, but it is always possible to name them indirectly, via procedures. For every computation c, we can construct a procedural value that returns c when called:

$$(val\text{-}to\text{-}comp \ (Proc \rightarrowtail Value \ (\lambda n \, . \, c)))$$

This means that we can effectively put any computation into an environment by transforming it into the above form before it is bound to a name and then perform the inverse transformation when the name is looked up. Since the parameter n is ignored, the transform and its inverse are equivalent to, respectively, thunking and dethunking.

Exercise 7.10

a. Can a CBN FL interpreter be written in CBV FL?

b. Can a CBV FL interpreter be written in CBN FL?

Justify your answers.

Exercise 7.11 The `letrec` to `rec` desugaring presented in Figure 6.4 (page 220) does not work in CBV FLK.

a. Develop a simple example demonstrating that the desugaring does not preserve the expected semantics of a CBV `letrec` construct.

b. Show how to fix the desugaring for CBV FLK using thunking and dethunking. You may use substitution in your desugaring.

c. Does the Bekić expansion desugaring for `letrec` introduced in Exercise 6.6 work in CBV? Explain.

Exercise 7.12 In this exercise we explore combining call-by-name and call-by-value in a single language. Imagine a language NAVAL (NAme/VAlue Language) that is just like CBN FLK except that (`lam` I E) has been replaced by the two constructs (`vlam` I E) and (`nlam` I E). Both of these constructs act like `lam` in that they create single-argument procedures. The only difference between them is that parameters of procedures created by `nlam` are passed using CBN, while those created by `vlam` use CBV. For example:

```
(app (nlam x 3) (prim / 1 0))  ⎯⎯⎯⎯→  3
                                NAVAL
(app (vlam x 3) (prim / 1 0))  ⎯⎯⎯⎯→  error:divide-by-zero
                                NAVAL
```

a. Give an operational semantics for NAVAL by modifying the FLK reduction rules in Figure 6.19 (page 259). Describe only your changes.

b. Give a denotational semantics for NAVAL by modifying the CBN FLK domain definitions in Figure 6.23 (page 276) and the valuation clauses in Figure 6.28 (page 283). Describe only your changes. *Hint:* In a simple approach to this problem, by-name and by-value procedures can both be elements of a single *Proc* domain. What should *Nameable* be?

c. Just as it was convenient to extend FLK with the notion of multiple-argument procedures, it would be nice to extend NAVAL with a similar notion. Some method must be chosen for specifying which parameters are by name and which are by value. For example, parameters might default to the by-value mechanism, but could be declared by-name with the token `name`, as illustrated below:

```
(def unless
  (abs (test (name default) (name exception))
    (if test exception default)))
```

Give the rules for desugaring such a multiple-argument `abs` construct into NAVAL's one-argument `nlam` and `vlam`.

d. We have seen how CBN can be simulated in a CBV language by using thunks. Formalize this transformation by defining a function that translates NAVAL into CBV FLK.

$n \in Nameable \ = \ Env \rightarrow Comp$

$\mathcal{E}[\![I]\!] \ = \ \lambda e \,.\, (\textit{with-nameable} \ (\textit{lookup} \ I \ e) \ (\lambda n \,.\, (n \ e)))$

$\mathcal{E}[\![(\texttt{app} \ E_1 \ E_2)]\!] \ = \ \lambda e \,.\, (\textit{with-procedure-comp} \ (\mathcal{E}[\![E_1]\!] \ e) \ (\lambda p \,.\, (p \ \mathcal{E}[\![E_2]\!])))$

Call-By-Denotation

Figure 7.8   Essence of the call-by-denotation semantics.

Exercise 7.13 In your favorite programming language, write a program that translates CBN FL into CBV FL. (Note that a very similar program could be used to translate CBN FL into SCHEME.)

7.1.6   Call-by-Denotation

Sometimes a denotational semantics suggests a feature that is an alternative point in a dimension of the programming-language design space. A case in point is **call-by-denotation (CBD)**, a parameter-passing mechanism that is obtained by tweaking CBN semantics in a straightforward way (see Figure 7.8). Whereas CBN determines the meaning of an operand expression relative to the environment available at the point of call, CBD instead determines the meaning of an operand expression relative to the environment where the formal parameter is referenced.

In CBD, the domain definition

$$n \in Nameable \ = \ Env \rightarrow Comp$$

indicates that the nameable entities in the language are functions that map environments to computations. Because the signature of $\mathcal{E}$ is $\mathrm{Exp} \rightarrow Env \rightarrow Comp$, applying $\mathcal{E}$ to an expression creates an element of $Nameable$. In the app clause, the expression $\mathcal{E}[\![E_2]\!]$ creates an operand-evaluation function of type $Nameable$ that is passed as an argument to the applied procedure. In the body of the applied procedure, the operand-evaluation function is invoked at every variable reference, where it is supplied with the environment in effect where the variable is referenced.

As a simple example of CBD, consider the meaning of the FL expression

```
((abs (y)
   (let ((x 3))
     y))
  x)
```

$\mathcal{E}[\![\text{y}]\!]\ e_1$
$= (\lambda e\,.\,(\textit{with-nameable}\ (\textit{lookup}\ \text{y}\ e)\ (\lambda n\,.\,(n\ e))))\ e_1$
$= (\textit{with-nameable}\ (\textit{lookup}\ \text{y}\ e_1)\ (\lambda n\,.\,(n\ e_1)))$
$= (\textit{with-nameable}\ (\textit{Nameable} {\rightarrowtail} \textit{BindingVal}$
$\qquad\qquad\qquad (\lambda e\,.\,(\textit{with-nameable}\ (\textit{lookup}\ \text{x}\ e)\ (\lambda n\,.\,(n\ e)))))$
$\qquad (\lambda n\,.\,(n\ e_1)))$
$= (\lambda e\,.\,(\textit{with-nameable}\ (\textit{lookup}\ \text{x}\ e)\ (\lambda n\,.\,(n\ e))))\ e_1$
$= (\textit{with-nameable}\ (\textit{lookup}\ \text{x}\ e_1)\ (\lambda n\,.\,(n\ e_1)))$
$= (\textit{with-nameable}\ (\textit{Nameable} {\rightarrowtail} \textit{BindingVal}$
$\qquad\qquad\qquad (\lambda e\,.\,(\textit{val-to-comp}\ (\textit{Int} {\rightarrowtail} \textit{Value}\ 3))))$
$\qquad (\lambda n\,.\,(n\ e_1)))$
$= (\lambda e\,.\,(\textit{val-to-comp}\ (\textit{Int} {\rightarrowtail} \textit{Value}\ 3)))\ e_1$
$= (\textit{val-to-comp}\ (\textit{Int} {\rightarrowtail} \textit{Value}\ 3))$

Figure 7.9 A calculation of the meaning of y in environment e_1.

in an environment e_0 in which the identifier x is unbound. This expression desugars to

```
(app (lam y
         (app (lam x y)
              3))
     x)
```

In both CBN and CBV, the meaning of this expression is an unbound-variable error, because the value of (the outer) x is required but nowhere defined. In CBD, however, the unevaluated outer x is effectively substituted for y to yield the application (app (lam x x) 3), whose value is 3. The outer x is no longer unbound because it is captured by the inner x.

Let's understand this example in more detail. The value of the given expression will end up being the value of the variable y evaluated in the following environment e_1:

$e_1 = \{\text{x} \mapsto (\textit{Nameable} {\rightarrowtail} \textit{BindingVal}\ (\lambda e\,.\,(\textit{val-to-comp}\ (\textit{Int} {\rightarrowtail} \textit{Value}\ 3)))),$
$\qquad\ \text{y} \mapsto (\textit{Nameable} {\rightarrowtail} \textit{BindingVal}\ (\lambda e\,.\,(\textit{with-nameable}\ (\textit{lookup}\ \text{x}\ e)\ (\lambda n\,.\,(n\ e)))))\}$

(We leave the details of how this point is reached as an exercise.) The meaning of y in e_1 at this point is presented in Figure 7.9, which shows that the expression indeed evaluates to 3.

The somewhat bizarre behavior of call-by-denotation in this example is due to a kind of name capture. The evaluation of the outer x yields not what we would normally think of as a value but an environment accessor that is eventually applied to an environment that has a binding for the inner x. Had the inner x been named something other than x or y, no capture would have occurred, and the expression would have denoted an unbound variable error, as in CBN and CBD. Interestingly, x is not the only outer name that causes trouble. If we replace the outer x by a reference to y, the expression diverges! (Check it and see.)

Because the semantics of call-by-denotation are so convoluted, it is hardly surprising that this mechanism is not used in any real programming language that we know of. What is our purpose in introducing so contrived a mechanism? First, we want to emphasize that in a denotational semantics, names can be bound to entities much more complex than simple values or expressible values. We shall see many examples of this later in the text. Second, call-by-denotation highlights variable capture problems that can be encountered in various programming language features that allow programmers to manipulate unevaluated expressions. Two such features are **user-definable macros** (such as C's #define mechanism), which allow programmers to define new syntactic sugar constructs in a language, and mechanisms in various Lisp dialects (such as MacLisp's FEXPR abstractions) that allow the definition of procedures whose arguments are passed as unevaluated s-expressions.

As a realistic example of the sort of name capture that can occur in CBD systems, consider the following desugaring rule, which a programmer might be able to specify via a macro definition:

$$(\texttt{ifpos } E_1 \; E_2) \rightsquigarrow_{ds} (\texttt{let } ((\texttt{n } E_1)) \; (\texttt{if } (\texttt{@> n 0) n } E_2))$$

The (ifpos E_1 E_2) construct evaluates and returns E_1 if its value is a positive number and otherwise returns the value of E_2. The desugaring gives the name n to E_1's value so that it needn't be evaluated again if it's positive. The problem with hardwiring a particular name like n into the desugaring is that it can capture a free n appearing in E_2. For example, consider the expression:

```
(let ((n 5)) (ifpos (@- 3 10) (@* n -6)))
```

From the specification of ifpos, we expect that this should evaluate to -30, but applying the ifpos desugaring rule yields

```
(let ((n 5)) (let ((n (@- 3 10))) (if (@> n 0) n (@* n -6))))
```

which evaluates to 42 as a result of capture of the variable n.

This example underscores the importance of choosing fresh variable names in desugarings. The simplest macro systems do not provide any means for avoiding hardwired names like n in the above example. In these systems, programmers

be aware of the entire namespace. For this reason, a global namespace is not scalable in a cognitive sense; large programs are much harder to comprehend than shorter ones.

- The reader has to infer structural groupings intended by the writer but not expressed because of the flatness of the namespace.

- Every time a new name is needed, the writer must find one that does not clash with any names already in use.

In order to reduce such unreasonable cognitive demands, programming languages typically provide mechanisms for reusing names and structuring the scope of names. Even when these are not supported by the naming system, programmers often develop naming conventions to simulate such mechanisms.

From an engineering point of view, more names can mean more complex interactions between program parts. One of the chief methods of controlling the complexity of large programs is to break them up into smaller units (such as procedures, methods, classes, abstract data types, modules) having well-defined **interfaces** that separate the use of a unit from its implementation. An interface specifies:

- the names defined external to the unit that are to be **imported** for use within the implementation of the unit; and

- the names defined internal to the unit that are to be **exported** for use outside of the unit.

It is desirable to make such interfaces narrow — i.e., importing and exporting few names — to limit dependencies among program parts. Wide interfaces give rise to spaghetti-like dependencies among program units that are difficult for a programmer to keep track of. And the complexities are exacerbated in the more common situation where a large program is developed in collaboration with others. In this case, wider interfaces imply increased communication and coordination between members of a programming team.

From this engineering perspective, a programming language should provide mechanisms that facilitate the construction of narrow interfaces. The simple approach of a single global namespace fails here because it allows every name to be used everywhere throughout a program. A crucial ingredient for narrow interfaces is some means of **name hiding**, whereby names purely local to the implementation of a unit are effectively hidden from the rest of a program.

In this section, we shall investigate techniques for **name control** that address the cognitive and engineering problems outlined above. Unlike our discussion of names up to this point, these issues are largely orthogonal to the choice of nameable values. Rather, they specify the relationship between patterns of name usage and the logical structure of variables in the program.

7.2.1   Hierarchical Scoping: Static and Dynamic

Recall the following terms from our study of variables in FLK:

- A **variable** is a placeholder for entities manipulated by a program.

- An **identifier** is a name for a variable. Distinct variables may be named by the same identifier.

- A **binding construct** is a construct that introduces a variable.

- A **variable declaration** is the part of the binding construct that specifies the identifier to be used for the variable.

- A **variable reference** is a phrase that stands for the entity denoted by the variable.

- The **scope** of a variable is the portion of the program text in which the variable may be referenced.

For example, in FL, the binding constructs are `lam`, `rec`, `abs`, `let`, and `letrec` expressions, `def` declarations, and the `fl` program construct. All variable references in FL are written as unadorned identifiers.

For a given language, it may or may not be possible to determine the scope of a given declaration without running the program. If the scope of a declaration can always be determined from the abstract syntax tree of a program, the scope of the declaration is said to be **static** or **lexical**. In this case, the variable declaration associated with any variable reference is apparent from the lexical structure of the program. If the scope of a declaration depends on details of the run-time execution of a program, the declaration is said to have **dynamic scope**. A language in which all declarations have static (respectively, dynamic) scope is said to be a **statically scoped** (respectively, **dynamically scoped**) language.

Figure 7.10 summarizes the difference between static and dynamic scoping in both CBN and CBV versions of FLK. We will refer to this figure as we explain these scoping mechanisms in more detail.

$p \in Proc \; = \; Nameable \to Comp$

$\mathcal{E}[\![(\text{lam } I \; E)]\!] \; = \; \lambda e_{lam} \,.\, (\textit{val-to-comp } (Proc \rightarrowtail Value \; (\lambda n \,.\, (\mathcal{E}[\![E]\!] \; [I \mapsto n]e_{lam}))))$

$\mathcal{E}[\![(\text{app } E_1 \; E_2)]\!] \; = \; \lambda e_{app} \,.\, (\textit{with-procedure-comp } (\mathcal{E}[\![E_1]\!] \; e_{app})$
$\qquad\qquad\qquad\qquad\qquad (\lambda p \,.\, (p \; (\mathcal{E}[\![E_2]\!] \; e_{app}))))$

Statically Scoped CBN Procedures

$p \in Proc \; = \; Nameable \to Env \to Comp$

$\mathcal{E}[\![(\text{lam } I \; E)]\!] \; = \; \lambda e_{lam} \,.\, (\textit{val-to-comp } (Proc \rightarrowtail Value \; (\lambda ne_{app} \,.\, (\mathcal{E}[\![E]\!] \; [I \mapsto n]e_{app}))))$

$\mathcal{E}[\![(\text{app } E_1 \; E_2)]\!] \; = \; \lambda e_{app} \,.\, (\textit{with-procedure-comp } (\mathcal{E}[\![E_1]\!] \; e_{app})$
$\qquad\qquad\qquad\qquad\qquad (\lambda p \,.\, (p \; (\mathcal{E}[\![E_2]\!] \; e_{app}) \; e_{app})))$

Dynamically Scoped CBN Procedures

$p \in Proc \; = \; Nameable \to Comp$

$\mathcal{E}[\![(\text{lam } I \; E)]\!] \; = \; \lambda e_{lam} \,.\, (\textit{val-to-comp } (Proc \rightarrowtail Value \; (\lambda n \,.\, (\mathcal{E}[\![E]\!] \; [I \mapsto n]e_{lam}))))$

$\mathcal{E}[\![(\text{app } E_1 \; E_2)]\!] \; = \; \lambda e_{app} \,.\, (\textit{with-procedure-comp } (\mathcal{E}[\![E_1]\!] \; e_{app})$
$\qquad\qquad\qquad\qquad\qquad (\lambda p \,.\, (\textit{with-value } (\mathcal{E}[\![E_2]\!] \; e_{app}) \; (\lambda v \,.\, (p \; v)))))$

Statically Scoped CBV Procedures

$p \in Proc \; = \; Nameable \to Env \to Comp$

$\mathcal{E}[\![(\text{lam } I \; E)]\!] \; = \; \lambda e_{lam} \,.\, (\textit{val-to-comp } (Proc \rightarrowtail Value \; (\lambda ne_{app} \,.\, (\mathcal{E}[\![E]\!] \; [I \mapsto n]e_{app}))))$

$\mathcal{E}[\![(\text{app } E_1 \; E_2)]\!] \; = \; \lambda e_{app} \,.\, (\textit{with-procedure-comp } (\mathcal{E}[\![E_1]\!] \; e_{app})$
$\qquad\qquad\qquad\qquad\qquad (\lambda p \,.\, (\textit{with-value } (\mathcal{E}[\![E_2]\!] \; e_{app}) \; (\lambda v \,.\, (p \; v \; e_{app})))))$

Dynamically Scoped CBV Procedures

Figure 7.10 The essence of the semantics of statically and dynamically scoped CBN and CBV procedures. In a statically (lexically) scoped procedure, free identifiers appearing in a `lam` body are resolved relative to e_{lam}, the environment determined by the program text lexically enclosing the `lam` expression. In a dynamically scoped procedure, free identifiers appearing in a `lam` body are resolved relative to e_{app}, the environment determined by the dynamic chain of procedure calls in which the procedure is being called.

Static Scope

All of the languages we have studied so far (other than call-by-denotation FL) have been statically scoped. In a statically scoped language, every variable reference refers to the variable introduced by the nearest lexically enclosing variable declaration of that identifier in the abstract syntax tree of the program. The nearest lexically enclosing declaration is found by starting at the identifier and tracing a path up the abstract syntax tree until a binding construct introducing the identifier is found that has the path in its scope.

As an example, consider the CBN FL expression

```
(let ((x 20))
  ((let ((inc-by-x (abs (y) (+ x y)))
         (double (abs (x) (* x 2)))))
     (letrec ((x (cons 1 x)))
       (abs (z)
         (cons (double (inc-by-x (double z)))
               x))))
   (- x 15)))
```

In this expression there are three distinct variables named x declared by three binding constructs:

1. (let ((x 20)) ...) declares x and binds it to the number 20.

2. The (abs (x) (* x 2)) expression named by **double** declares x but does not bind it; x will be bound on application of the procedural value of this abstraction. (The binding of x may be different for every distinct application of this procedure.)

3. (letrec ((x (cons 1 x))) ...) declares x and binds it to an infinite list of 1s.

There are also five variable references involving x:

1. In (+ x y), x is a reference to the **let**-bound variable named x, so its meaning in this context is 20. This means that **inc-by-x** is a procedure that always adds 20 to its argument, regardless of the binding for x in the environment in which it happens to be applied.

2. In (* x 2), x is a reference to the **abs**-bound variable named x, whose meaning will be determined at application time.

3. In `(cons 1 x)`, x is a reference to the `letrec`-bound variable named x, so its meaning is an infinite list of 1s.

4. In `(cons (double (inc-by-x (double z))) x)`, x refers to the variable introduced by the first lexically enclosing declaration of x, which in this case is the `letrec`-bound variable. So here x is an infinite list of 1s as well.

5. In `(- x 15)`, x is a reference to the variable introduced by the first lexically enclosing declaration of x, which in this case is the `let`-bound variable. So here x means the number 20.

Putting together all of the above information, the value of the example expression is an infinite list whose first element is 60, and the rest of whose elements are all 1.

In the above expression, some variables references (`+`, `-`, `*`, and `cons`) refer to variables in the standard library, which are implicitly declared by the top-level program in which the expression is embedded.

As we noted before for FLK, when the scope of a declaration contains another declaration of the same name, the inner declaration carves out a **hole in the scope** of the outer one. The Stoy diagrams we used to represent the structure of variables in FLK can easily be adapted to show declaration/reference relationships in any statically scoped language.

The essence of static scope is in the way environments are handled by abstractions. Figure 7.10 shows the domains and valuation functions that are crucial for static scope in CBN and CBV FLK. The clause for `lam` is exactly the same for CBN and CBV; it dictates that the body of the abstraction will be evaluated with respect to the environment in effect *when the procedure was created*. In particular, the environment in which the procedure is called can have no effect on the meaning of names within the abstraction body. This is clear from the domain definition for *Proc*, which simply maps nameable values to computations and ignores whatever the current environment might be. Though the details of nameable values and computations might differ, the handling of environments will have this form in any statically scoped language.

All of the FL variants we have studied support a particular discipline of static scoping known as **block structure**. In a block-structured language, any of the kinds of declarations that can be made at the top level of a program can be made inside of procedures. In particular, block-structured languages allow procedures to be declared inside of other procedures. Examples of block-structured languages include PASCAL, SCHEME, ML, and HASKELL. Popular languages that are not block-structured include C, C++, JAVA, and FORTRAN. For example, C does not allow defining a function inside another function, and JAVA does not permit defining a method inside another method.[6]

Dynamic Scope

SNOBOL4, APL, most early LISP dialects, and many macro languages are dynamically scoped. In each of these languages, a free variable in a procedure (or macro) body gets its meaning from the environment at the point where the procedure is called rather than the environment at the point where the procedure is created. Thus, in these languages, it is not possible to determine a unique declaration corresponding to a given free variable reference; the effective declaration depends on where the procedure is called. It is therefore generally impossible to determine the scope of a declaration simply by considering the abstract syntax tree of the program.

Instead, in a dynamically scoped language, the scope of a variable declaration is determined by the **execution tree** of a program. An execution tree describes the relationship between binding constructs encountered as the program is executed. Each node in an execution tree, which we shall call an **execution frame**, contains the bindings introduced by a binding construct. The subtrees of a node represent the execution of each subexpression evaluated during the evaluation of the binding construct before it is exited. In dynamic scope, free variables are evaluated relative to the dynamic chain of execution frames that starts at the current execution frame and goes to the top of the execution tree. This chain of execution frames corresponds to the stack of invocation frames in traditional stack-based implementations of procedure calls.

Figure 7.10 shows the essence of the semantics of dynamic scoping for CBN and CBV languages. In both case, the *Proc* domain has been modified to indicate that procedures take an extra argument: the dynamic environment (i.e., the call-time environment), which represents the dynamic chain of execution frames described above. In the valuation clause for `lam` (which is exactly the same for CBN and CBV), the body of the abstraction is evaluated in the dynamic environment rather than the lexical one. The CBN and CBV clauses for `app` have been modified to pass the current environment to the procedure being called.

---

[6]C supports nested blocks of local variable declarations, but since functions cannot be declared in these blocks, it does not satisfy our definition of block structure. JAVA's *inner class* feature allows a limited form of block structure in which a method-declaring class can be declared inside another method.

Example

As an example of static versus dynamic scoping, consider the following FL expression:

```
(let ((a 1))
  (let ((f (abs (x) (@+ x a))))
    (let ((a 20))
      (f 300))))
```

Informally, we can reason as follows. The procedure named f refers to a free variable a. Under static scoping, this variable is bound to the value of a where the procedure is defined (i.e., 1). Thus, the binding between a and 20 is irrelevant, and the result of the call (f 300) is 301. On the other hand, under dynamic scoping, the free variable gets its value from whatever binding of a is dynamically apparent. In the call (f 300), the binding between a and 20 shadows the binding between a and 1, so the value of the call is 320.

We can use the denotational definitions of scoping to analyze this example formally. The example FL expression above desugars into the following FLK expression:

```
(app (lam a {E_lam:a1}
        (app (lam f {E_lam:f}
                (app (lam a (app f 300)) {E_lam:a20}
                    20))
              (lam x (primop + x a)))) {E_lam:x}
    1)
```

The four lam expressions have been annotated with names that will be used to abbreviate them. Figures 7.11 and 7.12 highlight the key steps for using the denotational definitions to derive the value of the desugared expression under static scoping and dynamic scoping in CBV FLK. The calculations in the two figures begin similarly, because the following equality holds in both statically and dynamically scoped CBV FLK, as you should verify:

$$(\mathcal{E}[\![(\text{app } (\text{lam } I \ E_{body}) \ E_{rand})]\!] \ e) = \textit{with-value} \ (\mathcal{E}[\![E_{rand}]\!] \ e)$$
$$(\lambda v \ . \ (\mathcal{E}[\![E_{body}]\!] \ [I \mapsto v]e))$$

$\mathcal{E}[\![(\texttt{app } E_{lam:a1} \texttt{ 1})]\!] \ e_0$

$= (\textit{with-value } (\mathcal{E}[\![1]\!] \ e_0) \ (\lambda v . (\mathcal{E}[\![(\texttt{app } E_{lam:f} \ E_{lam:x})]\!] \ [\texttt{a} \mapsto v]e_0)))$

$= \mathcal{E}[\![(\texttt{app } E_{lam:f} \ E_{lam:x})]\!] \ e_1, \text{ where } e_1 \ = \ [\texttt{a} \mapsto (\textit{Int} \rightarrowtail \textit{Value } 1)]e_0$

$= (\textit{with-value } (\mathcal{E}[\![E_{lam:x}]\!] \ e_1) \ (\lambda v . (\mathcal{E}[\![(\texttt{app } E_{lam:a20} \texttt{ 20})]\!] \ [\texttt{f} \mapsto v]e_1)))$

$= \mathcal{E}[\![(\texttt{app } E_{lam:a20} \texttt{ 20})]\!] \ e_2, \text{ where } e_2 \ = \ [\texttt{f} \mapsto v_{lam:x}]e_1$
$\qquad \text{and } v_{lam:x} \ = \ (\textit{Proc} \rightarrowtail \textit{Value } (\lambda n . (\mathcal{E}[\![(\texttt{primop + x a})]\!] \ [\texttt{x} \mapsto n]e_1)))$

$= (\textit{with-value } (\mathcal{E}[\![20]\!] \ e_2) \ (\lambda v . (\mathcal{E}[\![(\texttt{app f 300})]\!] \ [\texttt{a} \mapsto v]e_2)))$

$= \mathcal{E}[\![(\texttt{app f 300})]\!] \ e_3, \text{ where } e_3 \ = \ [\texttt{a} \mapsto (\textit{Int} \rightarrowtail \textit{Value } 20)]e_2$

$= \textit{with-procedure-comp } (\mathcal{E}[\![\texttt{f}]\!] \ e_3) \ (\lambda p . (\textit{with-value } (\mathcal{E}[\![300]\!] \ e_3) \ p))$

$= \textit{with-procedure-comp } (\textit{val-to-comp } v_{lam:x}) \ (\lambda p . (p \ (\textit{Int} \rightarrowtail \textit{Value } 300)))$

$= (\lambda p . (p \ (\textit{Int} \rightarrowtail \textit{Value } 300))) \ (\lambda n . (\mathcal{E}[\![(\texttt{primop + x a})]\!] \ [\texttt{x} \mapsto n]e_1))$

$= (\lambda n . (\mathcal{E}[\![(\texttt{primop + x a})]\!] \ [\texttt{x} \mapsto n]e_1)) \ (\textit{Int} \rightarrowtail \textit{Value } 300)$

$= \mathcal{E}[\![(\texttt{primop + x a})]\!] \ [\texttt{x} \mapsto (\textit{Int} \rightarrowtail \textit{Value } 300)]e_1$

$= \mathcal{E}[\![(\texttt{primop + x a})]\!] \ [\texttt{x} \mapsto (\textit{Int} \rightarrowtail \textit{Value } 300)][\texttt{a} \mapsto (\textit{Int} \rightarrowtail \textit{Value } 1)]e_0$

$= (\textit{Int} \rightarrowtail \textit{Value } 301)$

Figure 7.11   Calculation of $\mathcal{E}[\![(\texttt{app } E_{lam:a1} \texttt{ 1})]\!] \ e_0$ in statically scoped CBV FLK.

The key differences between the two figures are:

1. The procedure value associated with $E_{lam:x}$ in static scope is

$$v_{lam:x} \ = \ (\textit{Proc} \rightarrowtail \textit{Value } \ (\lambda n . (\mathcal{E}[\![(\texttt{primop + x a})]\!] \ [\texttt{x} \mapsto n]e_1)))$$

whereas in dynamic scope it is

$$v'_{lam:x} \ = \ (\textit{Proc} \rightarrowtail \textit{Value } \ (\lambda n \ e' . (\mathcal{E}[\![(\texttt{primop + x a})]\!] \ [\texttt{x} \mapsto n]e')))$$

2. In static scope, $\mathcal{E}[\![(\texttt{app f 300})]\!] \ e_3$ is equal to

$$\textit{with-procedure-comp } (\textit{val-to-comp } v_{lam:x}) \ (\lambda p . (p \ (\textit{Int} \rightarrowtail \textit{Value } 300)))$$

whereas in dynamic scope it is equal to

$$\textit{with-procedure-comp } (\textit{val-to-comp } v'_{lam:x}) \ (\lambda p . (p \ (\textit{Int} \rightarrowtail \textit{Value } 300) \ e_3))$$

The upshot of these two differences is that the environment extended by the binding $[\texttt{x} \mapsto (\textit{Int} \rightarrowtail \textit{Value } 300)]$ is e_1 in static scope but e_3 in dynamic scope. Since $\texttt{a}$ has the value 1 in e_1 but 20 in e_3, the final results are different.

$\mathcal{E}[\![(\texttt{app}\ E_{lam:a1}\ \texttt{1})]\!]\ e_0$

$= (with\text{-}value\ (\mathcal{E}[\![\texttt{1}]\!]\ e_0)\ (\lambda v\ .\ (\mathcal{E}[\![(\texttt{app}\ E_{lam:f}\ E_{lam:x})]\!]\ [\texttt{a}\mapsto v]e_0)))$

$= \mathcal{E}[\![(\texttt{app}\ E_{lam:f}\ E_{lam:x})]\!]\ e_1,\ \text{where}\ e_1\ =\ [\texttt{a}\mapsto(Int\rightarrowtail Value\ 1)]e_0$

$= (with\text{-}value\ (\mathcal{E}[\![E_{lam:x}]\!]\ e_1)\ (\lambda v\ .\ (\mathcal{E}[\![(\texttt{app}\ E_{lam:a20}\ \texttt{20})]\!]\ [\texttt{f}\mapsto v]e_1)))$

$= \mathcal{E}[\![(\texttt{app}\ E_{lam:a20}\ \texttt{20})]\!]\ e_2,\ \text{where}\ e_2\ =\ [\texttt{f}\mapsto v'_{lam:x}]e_1$
$\quad\quad\text{and}\ v'_{lam:x}\ =\ (Proc\rightarrowtail Value\ (\lambda n\ e'\ .\ (\mathcal{E}[\![(\texttt{primop} + \texttt{x a})]\!]\ [\texttt{x}\mapsto n]e')))$

$= (with\text{-}value\ (\mathcal{E}[\![\texttt{20}]\!]\ e_2)\ (\lambda v\ .\ (\mathcal{E}[\![(\texttt{app f 300})]\!]\ [\texttt{a}\mapsto v]e_2)))$

$= \mathcal{E}[\![(\texttt{app f 300})]\!]\ e_3,\ \text{where}\ e_3\ =\ [\texttt{a}\mapsto(Int\rightarrowtail Value\ 20)]e_2$

$= with\text{-}procedure\text{-}comp\ (\mathcal{E}[\![\texttt{f}]\!]\ e_3)\ (\lambda p\ .\ (with\text{-}value\ (\mathcal{E}[\![\texttt{300}]\!]\ e_3)\ (\lambda v\ .\ (p\ v\ e_3))))$

$= with\text{-}procedure\text{-}comp\ (val\text{-}to\text{-}comp\ v'_{lam:x})\ (\lambda p\ .\ (p\ (Int\rightarrowtail Value\ 300)\ e_3))$

$= (\lambda p\ .\ (p\ (Int\rightarrowtail Value\ 300)\ e_3))\ (\lambda n\ e'\ .\ (\mathcal{E}[\![(\texttt{primop} + \texttt{x a})]\!]\ [\texttt{x}\mapsto n]e'))$

$= (\lambda n\ e'\ .\ (\mathcal{E}[\![(\texttt{primop} + \texttt{x a})]\!]\ [\texttt{x}\mapsto n]e'))\ (Int\rightarrowtail Value\ 300)\ e_3$

$= \mathcal{E}[\![(\texttt{primop} + \texttt{x a})]\!]\ [\texttt{x}\mapsto(Int\rightarrowtail Value\ 300)]e_3$

$= \mathcal{E}[\![(\texttt{primop} + \texttt{x a})]\!]\ [\texttt{x}\mapsto(Int\rightarrowtail Value\ 300)][\texttt{a}\mapsto(Int\rightarrowtail Value\ 20)]e_2$

$= (Int\rightarrowtail Value\ 320)$

Figure 7.12 Calculation of $\mathcal{E}[\![(\texttt{app}\ E_{lam:a1}\ \texttt{1})]\!]\ e_0$ in dynamically scoped CBV FLK.

A more graphical perspective of these derivations appears in Figure 7.13. Each derivation is summarized by an **environment diagram** that shows key expressions along with the environments they are evaluated in. An environment is represented by a chain of bindings that go up the page; this helps to clarify the relationship between the different environments. The static-scoping example is depicted in Figure 7.13(a). The arrow from within the procedural value to the environment starting with $[\texttt{a}\mapsto(Int\rightarrowtail Value\ 1)]$ emphasizes that a statically scoped procedure "remembers" the environment in which it was created. This **lexical environment** is determined by the text lexically surrounding the lam expression that gave rise to the procedure value.

The dynamic-scoping example is depicted in Figure 7.13(b). Here, there is no arrow emanating from the procedural value because the environment e' in which the body is evaluated will be the **dynamic environment** in effect when the procedure is called. The dynamic environment is determined by the bindings in the current branch of the tree of procedure calls made during the execution of the program. In this example, it is constructed by the procedure calls associated with the three nested lam expressions.

Although the environment chains happen to be the same for these two examples, lexically scoped languages tend to give rise to shallow, bushy environment diagrams, whereas dynamically scoped languages tend to give rise to deep thin ones (see Exercise 7.20).

Discussion

In practice, static scoping is often preferable to dynamic scoping. There are several reasons for this:

- Static scoping has better modularity properties than dynamic scoping. In a statically scoped language, the particular names chosen for variables in a procedure do not affect its behavior, so it is always safe to rename them in a consistent fashion. In contrast, in dynamically scoped systems, the particular names chosen for variables matter because a local variable name can interact with a free variable name of a procedure invoked in its scope. Procedure interfaces are more complex under dynamic scoping because they must mention the free variables of the procedure.

- Static scoping works nicely with block structure to create higher-order procedures that "remember" information from outer scopes. Many of the functional-programming idioms we have studied depend critically on this "memory" to work properly. As a simple example, consider the FLK definition

  ```
  (def add (lam x (lam y (prim + x y))))
  ```

  Under static scope, (app add 1) stands for an incrementing procedure because the returned procedure "remembers" that x is 1. But under dynamic scope, (app add 1) "forgets" that x is 1. The returned procedure is equivalent to (lam y (prim + x y)) and will use whatever value for x it finds (if there is one) in the context where it is called. Clearly, dynamic scope and higher-order procedures do not mix well!

- Statically scoped variables can be implemented more efficiently than dynamically scoped variables. In a compiler, references to statically scoped variables can be compiled to code that accesses the variable value efficiently using its **lexical address**, a description of its location that can be calculated from the program's abstract syntax tree (see Section 17.10). In contrast, looking up dynamically scoped variables implies an inefficient search through a chain of bindings for one that has the desired name.

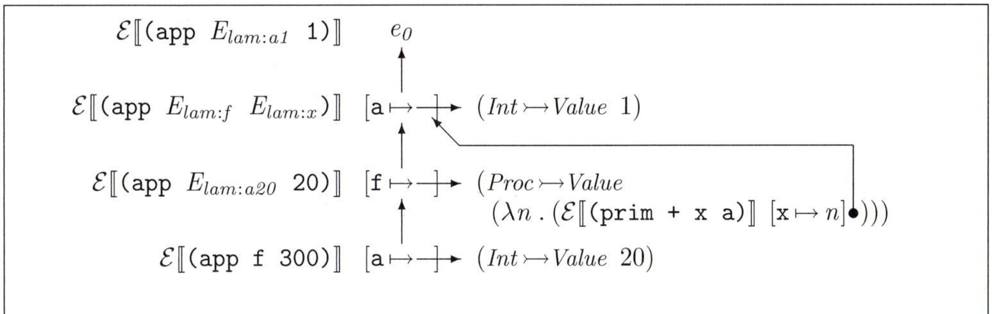

(a) Environment diagram for the sample expression under static scoping.

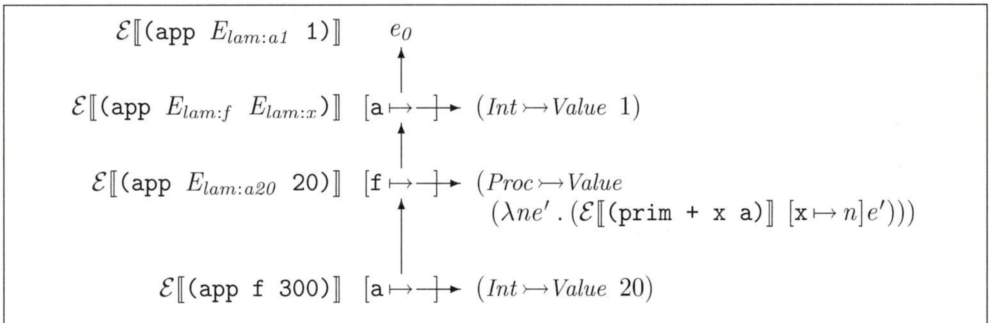

(b) Environment diagram for the sample expression under dynamic scoping.

Figure 7.13 Environment diagrams illustrating the difference between static and dynamic scoping for the example expression.

Is dynamic scoping ever useful? Yes! There are at least two situations in which dynamic scoping is important:

- *Exception Handling*: In the languages we have studied so far, computations cannot proceed after encountering an error. However, in Section 9.6, we will study ways to specify so-called **exception handlers** that describe how a computation can proceed from certain kinds of errors. Since exception handlers are typically in effect for certain subtrees of a program's execution tree, dynamic scope is the most natural scoping mechanism for the namespace of exception handlers.

- *Implicit Parameters*: Dynamic scope is also convenient for specifying the values of **implicit parameters** that are cumbersome to list explicitly as formal parameters to procedures. For example, consider the following `derivative` procedure in a version of FL with floating point operations (prefixed with `fp`):

```
(def derivative
  (abs (f x)
    (fp/ (fp- (f (fp+ x epsilon))
              (f x))
         epsilon)))
```

Note that `epsilon` appears as a free variable in `derivative`. With dynamic scoping, it is possible to dynamically specify the value of `epsilon` via any binding construct. For example, the expression

```
(let ((epsilon 0.001))
  (derivative (abs (x) (fp* x x)) 5.0))
```

environment where `epsilon` is bound to 0.001.

However, with lexical scoping, the variable `epsilon` must be defined at top level, and, without using mutation, there is no way to temporarily change the value of `epsilon` while the program is running. If we really want to abstract over `epsilon` with lexical scoping, we must pass it to `derivative` as an explicit argument:

```
(def derivative
  (abs (f x epsilon)
    (fp/ (fp- (f (fp+ x epsilon))
              (f x))
         epsilon)))
```

But then any procedure that uses `derivative` and wants to abstract over `epsilon` must also include `epsilon` as a formal parameter. In the case of `derivative`, this is only a small inconvenience. But in a system with a large number of tweakable parameters, the desire for fine-grained specification of variables like `epsilon` can lead to an explosion in the number of formal parameters throughout a program.

As an example along these lines, consider the huge parameter space of a typical graphics system (colors, fonts, stippling patterns, line thicknesses, etc.). It is untenable to specify each of these as a formal parameter to every graphics routine. At the very least, all these parameters can be bundled up into a data structure that represents the graphics state. But then we still want a means of executing window routines in a temporary graphics state in such a way that the old graphics state is restored when the routines are done. This behavior can be achieved with dynamic scoping; alternatively, it can be done with side effects (see Exercise 8.21).

Exercise 7.17 Consider a version of FL called FLAT in which a procedure (an `abs` or kernel `lam` expression) is not allowed to have free identifiers. Can the meaning of a FLAT expression differ under lexical and dynamic scope? If so, exhibit such an expression; if not, explain why.

Exercise 7.18 Write a single FL expression that exhibits a different behavior in each of the four following scenarios:

a. statically scoped CBN FL

b. statically scoped CBV FL

c. dynamically scoped CBN FL

d. dynamically scoped CBV FL

Exercise 7.19

a. Can a dynamically scoped FL interpreter be written in statically scoped FL?

b. Can a statically scoped FL interpreter be written in dynamically scoped FL?

Exercise 7.20 This problem considers a dynamically scoped variant of CBV FL called FLUID. The abstract syntax for FLUID is the same as that for FL except that the grammar for FLUID does not include any recursion constructs. That is, the FLUID kernel does not contain the `rec` construct, and the full FLUID language does not contain the `letrec` construct. The denotational semantics for the FLUID kernel is the same as that for CBV FLK except for the changes specified for dynamic scope in (a CBV version of) Figure 7.10.

a. For each of the expressions below, show the result of evaluating the expression both in FL and in FLUID. Refer to the denotational semantics as necessary to reason about the evaluation process, but don't get lost in a symbol-manipulation quagmire. You may find environment diagrams helpful for thinking about these problems.

```
i.    (let ((a 1))
        (let ((f (abs (a) (prim + a 20))))
          (f a)))
ii.   (let ((a 1))
        (let ((f (abs (a b) (@+ a b))))
          (f 20 300)))
iii.  (let ((a 1))
        (let ((a 20)
              (b 300))
          (@+ a b)))
iv.   (let ((a 1))
        (let ((f (abs (b) (@+ a b))))
          (f (let ((a (f 20)))
               (f 300)))))
```

   v.   `(let ((a 1))`
          `(let ((f (abs (b) (@+ a b))))`
           `(let ((g (abs (a) (f a))))`
            `(g (g a)))))`

b. In FLUID, the desugaring of multiple-argument abstractions into single-argument abstractions no longer behaves as expected. Explain what goes wrong with the usual desugaring. (You do *not* need to describe how to fix the problem.)

c. In FLK, the factorial procedure is written as the expression:

```
(rec fact (lam n
             (if (prim = n 0)
                 1
                 (prim * n (fact (prim - n 1)))))))
```

FLUID has no recursion constructs, but such constructs are not needed to write recursive definitions.

   i.   Briefly explain why FLUID doesn't need recursion constructs.

   ii.   Show the definition for the factorial procedure in FLUID.

   iii. Explain why your FLUID definition for factorial wouldn't work in FL.

d. Consider the factorial procedure from part **c**. When using the denotational semantics to determine the meaning of (`app fact 3`) in environment e_0, the meaning of (`prim = n 0`) is determined in four distinct environments. For both CBV FL and for FLUID, draw an environment diagram that shows the relationship among these four environments.

Exercise 7.21 The static scope expressed in Figure 7.10 is typical of block-structured languages. However, other kinds of static scope are imaginable. For example, suppose that e_{global} is the top-level FL environment — the one that defines the meanings of the standard library names (`+`, `bool?`, `cons`, etc.). Then **global scoping** is a static scoping mechanism in which free identifiers in a `lam` expression are resolved relative to e_{global} rather than the environment at the time of procedure creation or at the time of procedure call.

a. Write the valuation clauses for `lam` and `app` for a CBV variant of FL with global scoping.

b. Write a single FL expression whose value is one of the symbols `global`, `dynamic`, or `block-structure`, indicating the scoping mechanism under which it is evaluated.

Exercise 7.22 Develop an operational semantics for CBV FL that uses explicit environments instead of substitution.

Exercise 7.23 Develop an operational semantics for a dynamically scoped version of CBV FL.

Exercise 7.24 In response to customer demand, the Analog Equipment Corporation has hired Alyssa P. Hacker to develop a dynamically scoped version of FL. Alyssa is asked to do this over a weekend, but she does not panic. Instead, she realizes that with just a few new primitives, the entire job can be accomplished with a clever translation from the new dynamically scoped FLK to the existing statically scoped FLK.

Alyssa extends the regular FLK implementation with the following three new primitives for manipulating an explicit user-level enviroment data structure:

(prim new) creates a new, empty environment.

(prim extend *sym val env*) returns a new environment that extends the bindings of the environment *env* with a binding of the name *sym* (which should be a symbol) to the value *val*. Any previous binding for *sym* is shadowed by the new binding. It is an error if *sym* is not a symbol or *env* is not an environment.

(prim lookup *sym env*) returns the value bound to the name *sym* in the environment *env*. It is an error if *sym* is not a symbol, *env* is not an environment, or *sym* is not bound in *env*.

In Alyssa's translation, the *dynenv* variable is always assumed to be bound to the current dynamic environment. Here is Alyssa's translation rule for app:

$$\mathcal{T}[\![(\text{app } E_1 \ E_2)]\!] = (\text{app (app } \mathcal{T}[\![E_1]\!] \ \text{*dynenv*) } \mathcal{T}[\![E_2]\!])$$

a. What is the translation rule for I (variable reference)?

b. What is the translation rule for (lam I E)?

c. Do all identifiers have to be looked up in the dynamic environment? If not, state what optimizations of the translations for identifiers and abs are possible, and when and how they could be accomplished.

d. Desugar and then apply your translation to the following expression:

```
(let ((x 1))
  (let ((f (lam y (+ x y))))
    (let ((x 20))
      (f x))))
```

7.2.2 Multiple Namespaces

Sometimes a single environment is not sufficient to model the naming features of a programming language. Languages commonly support **multiple namespaces** — i.e., several different contexts in which names are associated with values of various sorts. For example, Figure 7.14 shows a piece of COMMON LISP code in which the name x is used to name five different entities at the same time: an exit point, a special (dynamic) variable, a lexical variable, a procedure, and a tagbody tag (which serves as a goto label).

```
(block x                    ; x₁, a exit point
  (let ((x 2))              ; x₂, declared to be a special (dynamic) variable
    (declare (special x))
    (let ((x 3))            ; x₃, a normal lexical variable
      (flet ((x (y) (+ x y))) ; x₄, a procedure referring to x₃ in its body
        (tagbody x          ; x₅, a tagbody tag (serves as a goto label)
          (if (> x 6)       ; this x = x₃ = 3
            (go x)          ; jump to label x₅
            (return-from x  ; return from exit point x₁ with following value
              (locally
                (declare (special x)) ; reference to 2nd x below is special
                (x x)       ; apply procedure x₄ to special variable x₂
                ))))))))    ; the value of this block expression is 3+2 = 5
```

Figure 7.14   COMMON LISP code that uses multiple namespaces

There are two typical situations in which multiple namespaces are useful:

1. The language provides multiple scoping mechanisms. In this case, different namespaces can be used for different scoping mechanisms. COMMON LISP, for example, supports both lexical and dynamic scoping of variables; variables are ordinarily scoped lexically, but those marked as `special` are dynamically scoped.

2. Different namespaces are used to name different kinds of entities. For example, exit points, `tagbody` tags, and procedures are in nonoverlapping namespaces in COMMON LISP. Namespaces used this way are especially useful for modeling values that are not first class.

Of course, any language with multiple namespaces must provide constructs for both declaring names and referencing names within each namespace. For example, consider the namespaces for exit points and tags in the COMMON LISP example above:

- `block` declares a name in the exit-point namespace, and `return-from` references names in this namespace;

- `tagbody` declares names in the tag namespace, and `go` references names in this namespace.

Multiple namespaces are modeled in denotational semantics by using multiple environments, one per namespace. For example, using two namespaces, we can develop variants of FL that support both lexical and dynamic scoping (see Exercise 7.25) or put second-class procedures in a separate namespace from other values (see Exercise 7.26).

Exercise 7.25 Understanding the virtues of both lexical and dynamic scoping, Dinah McScoop designs a language, DYNALEX, that supports both kinds of scoping mechanisms. The kernel of DYNALEX is statically scoped CBV FLK extended with the following extra constructs to support dynamic scoping:

(dyabs (I_{dyn}^*) E_{body}) is like abs, but binds the names I_{dyn}^* in a dynamic environment rather than a static one.

(dyref I) looks up I in the dynamic environment rather than the lexical one.

The full DYNALEX language includes the usual FL sugar as well as the following sugar for the dylet construct:

$$(\text{dylet } ((I_i \ E_i)_{i=1}^n) \ E_{body}) \rightsquigarrow_{ds} ((\text{dyabs } (I_{i=1}^n) \ E_{body}) \ E_{i=1}^n)$$

The following DYNALEX expression illustrates both dynamic and lexical scoping:

```
(let ((a 1) (b 20))
  (let ((f (abs () (+ a (dyref b)))))
    (dylet ((a 300) (b 4000))
      (f)))) ─DYNALEX→ 4001
```

a. Give a denotational semantics for DYNALEX that includes the signature of $\mathcal{E}$ and the valuation clauses for the following constructs: I, lam, app, dyref, and dyabs.

b. Explain why Dinah chose to make the multiparameter dyabs abstraction a kernel form rather than treating dyabs as sugar for a single-parameter abstraction for dynamic variables.

c. Write translation functions that translate DYNALEX kernel programs and kernel expressions into, respectively, FLK programs and expressions. The FLK program P' that results from translating a DYNALEX program P should have the same behavior as P on all inputs.

Exercise 7.26 All the variants of FL we have studied thus far treat procedures as first-class values. A first-class value is one that can be (1) named (denoted) by a variable; (2) passed to a procedure as an argument; (3) returned from a procedure as a result; (4) stored in a data structure (e.g., a pair); and (5) created in any context. In FL, all elements of *Value* (which includes all elements of *Proc*) satisfy all of these properties. Yet in numerous real-world programming languages, procedures are *not* first class; their use is restricted in various ways. Here we explore how to model the semantics of a language with second-class procedures.

We define a variant of FL named FL^{--} whose kernel syntax is as follows:

$$E \in \text{Exp} ::=\ L \mid I \mid (\texttt{error}\ Y) \mid (\texttt{prim}\ O\ E^*) \mid (\texttt{if}\ E\ E\ E) \mid (\texttt{pair}\ E\ E)$$
$$\mid\ (\texttt{app}\ I\ E) \mid (\texttt{vlet}\ I\ E\ E) \mid (\texttt{plet}\ I\ D\ E)$$

$$D \in \text{ProcDecl} ::=\ (\texttt{lam}\ I\ E) \mid (\texttt{rec}\ I\ (\texttt{lam}\ I\ E))$$

Other syntactic domains are unchanged from FLK.

The kernel syntax of FL^{--} is similar to that of FLK except that:

- The $\texttt{app}$ expression must have an identifier, rather than an arbitrary expression, as its operator.

- There are two new binding constructs: a local binding construct $\texttt{vlet}$ for values and a local binding construct $\texttt{plet}$ for procedures.

- FL^{--} has no stand-alone $\texttt{lam}$ or $\texttt{rec}$ expressions. Instead, these are procedure declarations that must always appear as the second subexpression of a $\texttt{plet}$. Also, the $\texttt{rec}$ declaration must have a $\texttt{lam}$ declaration rather than an arbitrary expression as its second subexpression.

FL^{--} has two statically scoped namespaces:

- The *value* namespace: variables are declared in this namespace with $\texttt{vlet}$ and $\texttt{lam}$ and are referenced via identifiers I not appearing in the $\texttt{app}$ operator position.

- The *procedure* namespace: variables are declared in this namespace with $\texttt{plet}$ and $\texttt{rec}$ and are referenced via identifiers I appearing in the $\texttt{app}$ operator position.

The semantics of FL^{--} is similar to that of CBN FLK except for the following:

- The $(\texttt{vlet}\ I_{val}\ E_{defn}\ E_{vbody})$ construct evaluates and returns the value of E_{vbody} relative to a value namespace extended by binding I_{val} to the value of E_{defn}. The scope of I_{val} is E_{vbody}.

- The $(\texttt{plet}\ I_{proc}\ D_{defn}\ E_{pbody})$ construct declares that D_{defn} is a procedure named I_{proc} that may be invoked within E_{pbody} and returns the value of E_{pbody}. The scope of I_{proc} is E_{pbody}. If D_{defn} is the declaration $(\texttt{rec}\ I_{rec}\ (\texttt{lam}\ I_{fml}\ E_{lbody}))$, then I_{rec} is bound to the procedure D_{defn} within E_{lbody}.

- The application $(\texttt{app}\ I_{proc}\ E_{rand})$ invokes the procedure named by I_{proc} in the current procedure namespace to the result of evaluating E_{rand} relative to both current namespaces.

- An identifier I that does not appear as the operator of an $\texttt{app}$ is evaluated relative to the current value namespace.

Figure 7.15 presents examples that illustrate key features of FL^{--}.

```
(plet sqr (lam x (prim * x x))
  (app sqr 5))  ───FL⁻⁻⟹  25
(vlet sqr 5
  (plet sqr (lam x (prim * x x))
    (app sqr sqr)))  ───FL⁻⁻⟹  25  {illustrates two distinct namespaces}
(vlet scale 7
  (plet scale (lam x (prim * x scale))
    (plet scale (lam y (prim + scale (app scale y)))
      (vlet scale 5
        (app scale scale)))))  ───FL⁻⁻⟹  42  {illustrates lexical scoping}
(plet fact (rec inner-fact
              (lam n
                (if (prim = n 0)
                    1
                    (prim * n (app inner-fact (prim - n 1))))))
  (app fact 5))  ───FL⁻⁻⟹  120  {illustrates recursion}
```

Figure 7.15 Some FL⁻⁻ examples.

a. Explain why procedures are second-class values in FL⁻⁻. As part of your explanation, give examples of FL programs that cannot be expressed straightforwardly in FL⁻⁻.

b. Give a denotational semantics for lexically scoped, CBN FL⁻⁻, modeling the two separate namespaces as two distinct environments. You should modify the FLK semantic domains as necessary and define three valuation functions: $\mathcal{E}$ (for expressions), $\mathcal{D}$ (for declarations), and $\mathcal{P}$ (for programs). Specify a signature for each of these valuation functions and define valuation clauses for each language construct except literals, errors, and primitive applications.

c. In FL, the vlet construct could be considered syntactic sugar for lam and app:

$$(\text{vlet } I_{val} \ E_{defn} \ E_{vbody}) \leadsto_{ds} (\text{app } (\text{lam } I_{val} \ E_{vbody}) \ E_{defn})$$

Consider an analogous desugaring for vlet in FL⁻⁻:

$$(\text{vlet } I_{val} \ E_{defn} \ E_{vbody}) \leadsto_{ds} (\text{plet } I_{proc} \ (\text{lam } I_{val} \ E_{vbody}) \ \{I_{proc} \ fresh\}$$
$$(\text{app } I_{proc} \ E_{defn}))$$

Is this a valid desugaring for vlet in FL⁻⁻? If so, explain why; if not, give an FL⁻⁻ expression whose meaning differs under this desugaring from the meaning in part **b**.

7.2.3   Nonhierarchical Scope

Philosophy

The binding constructs we have seen so far are all **hierarchical** in nature. Each construct establishes a parent/child relationship between an outer context in which the declaration is not visible and an inner (body) context in which the declaration is visible. In static scoping, the hierarchy is determined by the abstract syntax tree, while in dynamic scoping, the hierarchy is determined by the tree of procedure calls generated at run time. In both of these scoping mechanisms, there is no natural way to communicate a declaration *laterally* across the tree structure imposed by the hierarchy.

For small programs, this is not ordinarily a problem, but when a large program is broken into independent pieces, or **modules**, the constraint of hierarchy can be a problem. Modules communicate with each other via collections of bindings. A module provides services to other modules, called **clients**, by exporting a set of bindings, and makes use of other modules' services by importing bindings from those other modules. These services are specified by its interface. In a hierarchical language, the scope of a binding is a single subtree of a program's abstract syntax tree or procedure-invocation tree. The fact that all clients of a module must reside in the subtree where the module's bindings are in scope forces programs to be organized as trees whose nodes declare module bindings. This organization is not at all modular: the constraints involved in positioning each module carefully in a particular program tree discourage viewing it as an independent entity with a well-defined interface that can be reused in other programs. A strict hierarchy also prohibits having two modules that use each other's services.

A popular and somewhat better approach to organize communicating modules into a program is to use **global scoping**. In this approach, all exported bindings from all modules are defined in a single global namespace, and every module gets all of its imported bindings from this namespace. This technique is more modular than hierarchical approaches, but it has some major drawbacks:

- In order to avoid accidental name collisions, a programmer writing a module must be aware of all names exported by all other modules, even those that are completely irrelevant. This violates basic modularity principles.

- In practice, the dependencies among modules are often poorly documented, making intermodule dependencies difficult to track. A small change in one module can have widespread and unanticipated effects on other modules.

`(record (I E)*)`	Creates a record in which each field name I is bound to the value of the corresponding expression E.
`(select I E)`	Returns the value of the field named I in the record denoted by E. Signals an error if E doesn't denote a record or it denotes a record that does not contain a field named I.
`(override E₁ E₂)`	Returns a new record that combines the fields of the two records denoted by E_1 and E_2, giving precedence to fields in E_1. Signals an error if E_1 or E_2 doesn't denote a record.
`(conceal (I*) E)`	Returns a new record containing all the fields of the record denoted by E except for those with names in I^*. Signals an error if E doesn't denote a record.

Figure 7.16   Kernel record constructs.

A way for languages to overcome the limitations of hierarchical scoping and global scoping is to provide a value that contains a collection of bindings. Such a value can bundle up the bindings at one point in a program and communicate them to another point that is related neither lexically nor dynamically to the declarations of those bindings. We shall use the term **record** for a value that consists of name/value bindings, also known as **fields**. When their fields define procedures and constants that implement an interface, records serve as simple kinds of modules. For example, we can represent a matrix module via a record that defines matrix operations like transposing a matrix and multiplying two matrices. We use the term "record" rather than "module" for our collection-of-name/value-bindings value because we are reserving the latter term for more expressive values whose bindings can name types in addition to values (see Chapter 15). The records described here are similar to C structures, PERL hashes, and PASCAL records except that, unlike the latter two kinds of values, the values named in our record fields may be procedures.

Record Constructs

We will study records in the context of a version of FL that is extended with the kernel constructs in Figure 7.16.

The `record` construct builds a data structure of name/value bindings. For example, the definitions

```
(def r1 (record
         (a (@+ 2 3))
         (square (abs (x) (* x x)))))
(def r2 (record (a 7) (b 11)))
```

define two records: a record named `r1` whose `a` field is 5 and whose `square` field
is a squaring procedure; and a record named `r2` whose `a` field is 7 and whose `b`
field is 11.

Field values are extracted by field name using the `select` construct. E.g.:

(select a r1) $\xrightarrow[FL]{}$ *5*
((select square r1) (select a r1)) $\xrightarrow[FL]{}$ *25*
((select square r1) (select a r2)) $\xrightarrow[FL]{}$ *49*
(select b r1) $\xrightarrow[FL]{}$ *error:no-such-field*

Two records can be combined into a new record with the `override` construct.
When the two records share field names, precedence is given to the field in the
first record argument. E.g.:

(select a (override r1 r2)) $\xrightarrow[FL]{}$ *5*
(select a (override r2 r1)) $\xrightarrow[FL]{}$ *7*
(select b (override r1 r2)) $\xrightarrow[FL]{}$ *11*
(select b (override r2 r1)) $\xrightarrow[FL]{}$ *11*

The `conceal` construct returns a new record in which some bindings of the
original record have been removed. E.g.:

(select a (conceal (a) r2)) $\xrightarrow[FL]{}$ *error:no-such-field*
(select b (conceal (a) r2)) $\xrightarrow[FL]{}$ *11*
(select b (conceal (a b) r2)) $\xrightarrow[FL]{}$ *error:no-such-field*
(select a (override (conceal (a) r1) r2)) $\xrightarrow[FL]{}$ *7*

Notice that there is a design choice in the semantics of `conceal`: the English
description for this construct does not specify whether or not it is an error when
`conceal` attempts to hide a field that isn't present in the record.

The desugaring rules in Figure 7.17 define additional record constructs that
capture handy idioms that programmers would otherwise invent on their own.
The `recordrec` construct is like `record` except that it is a binding construct
in which each of the field names is a declaration whose scope is all the field
expressions. It is used to create records whose fields contain values that may be
mutually recursive. E.g.:

$$
\begin{array}{l}
\texttt{(recordrec } (I_i \ E_i)_{i=1}^n) \leadsto_{ds} \texttt{(letrec } ((I_i \ E_i)_{i=1}^n) \texttt{ (record } (I_i \ I_i)_{i=1}^n)) \\[4pt]
\texttt{(with-fields } (I_{i=1}^n) \ E_{rcd} \ E_{body}) \leadsto_{ds} \texttt{(let } ((I_{rcd} \ E_{rcd})) \quad ; I_{rcd} \text{ is fresh} \\
\hspace{7.5cm} \texttt{(let } ((I_i \ \texttt{(select } I_i \ I_{rcd}))_{i=1}^n) \\
\hspace{7.5cm} E_{body})) \\[4pt]
\texttt{(restrict } (I_{i=1}^n) \ E_{rcd}) \leadsto_{ds} \texttt{(with-fields } (I_{i=1}^n) \ E_{rcd} \texttt{ (record } (I_i \ I_i)_{i=1}^n)) \\[4pt]
\texttt{(rename } ((I_i \ I_i')_{i=1}^n) \ E_{rcd}) \\
\quad \leadsto_{ds} \texttt{(let } ((I_{rcd} \ E_{rcd})) \quad ; I_{rcd} \text{ is fresh} \\
\hspace{1.5cm} \texttt{(override } \texttt{(conceal } (I_{i=1}^n) \ I_{rcd}) \\
\hspace{3cm} \texttt{(record } (I_i' \ \texttt{(select } I_i \ I_{rcd}))_{i=1}^n)))
\end{array}
$$

Figure 7.17 Desugarings for the record syntactic sugar.

```
(def r3
  (recordrec (fact (abs (n) (if (@= n 0) 1 (@* n (fact (@- n 1))))))
             (even? (abs (n) (if (@= n 0) #t (odd? (@- n 1)))))
             (odd? (abs (n) (if (@= n 0) #f (even? (@- n 1)))))
             (zero-ones (cons 0 one-zeroes))
             (one-zeroes (cons 1 zero-ones))))
```

$(\texttt{with-fields } (I^*) \ E_{rcd} \ E_{body})$ evaluates E_{body} in the current environment extended with bindings for the specified names I^* from the record denoted by E_{rcd}. This spares the programmer the tiresome task of writing explicit selects everywhere or manually introducing lets that name the selects. E.g.:

```
(with-fields (fact even? zero-ones one-zeroes) r3
  (even? (+ (fact (car zero-ones)) (fact (car one-zeroes)))))
```

The explicit identifier list in with-fields is necessary for preserving static scope. Without this list, it would be impossible in general to match up a variable reference with its variable declaration. For instance, suppose the language permitted expressions of the form $(\texttt{with-fields } E_{rcd} \ E_{body})$. Then in the expression

```
(lam a (lam r (with-fields r a)))
```

we wouldn't be able to determine if the reference a is declared by lam or is introduced from the record r by with-fields. This would make it impossible to determine the free variables of a with-fields expression. We will see later in Chapters 11 and 14 that an explicit identifier list is unnecessary in a statically typed language because it can be automatically deduced from type information.

What if a name listed in $(\texttt{with-fields } (I^*) \ E_{rcd} \ E_{body})$ isn't in the record denoted by E_{rcd}? According to the desugaring rule for with-fields, this will be an error in a CBV language because the `select` on the nonexistent field will signal an error. However, in a CBN language, any error from the selection of a nonexistent field I will be delayed until I is referenced in E_{body} (if ever).

(`restrict` (I^*) E_{rcd}) returns a new record containing only the specified fields from the record denoted by E_{rcd}. It is a dual to `conceal` that is useful when exporting comparatively few names from a record. E.g., (`restrict` (`fact`) `r3`) is equivalent to:

```
(conceal (even? odd? zero-ones one-zeroes) r3)
```

The `rename` construct helps programmers to avoid name conflicts when using records that export the same name. For example,

```
(override (rename ((a a1)) r1) (rename ((a a2)) r2))
```

creates a record in which `a1` is bound to 5 and `a2` is bound to 7.

Record Semantics

Figure 7.18 presents a denotational semantics for the kernel record constructs in an extension to CBV FLK. Since both records and environments associate names and values, the denotational semantics models a record simply as an environment. The meanings of the `record` and `override` constructs are defined, respectively, in terms of the *extend** and *merge* functions from Figure 6.24 on page 277. To model records in a CBN language, the clause for the `record` construct would be modified as follows to bind the field names directly to computations of the field values:

$$
\begin{aligned}
&\mathcal{E}[\![(\texttt{record}\ ((I_1\ E_1)\ \dots\ (I_n\ E_n)))]\!] \\
&= \lambda e\ .\ (\textit{val-to-comp} \\
&\qquad\qquad (\textit{Record} \rightarrowtail \textit{Value}\ (\textit{extend}^*\ [I_1, \dots, I_n]\ [E_1, \dots, E_n]\ \textit{empty-env})))
\end{aligned}
$$

Record Examples

Figure 7.19 presents two arithmetic modules implemented as records of operations, one for integers and one for rational numbers. Both export the same names: $\{\texttt{zero}, \texttt{add}, \texttt{sub}, \texttt{mul}, \texttt{div}, \texttt{neg}, \texttt{recip}, \texttt{eq}, \texttt{lt}, \texttt{gt}\}$. In `rats`, the `rat` procedure creates a canonical numerator/denominator pair for a rational number in which common factors (as calculated by the `gcd` procedure) have been eliminated. The parts of such a pair can be extracted via `num` and `den`. Because `recordrec` (and not `record`) is used to create `rats`, the recursive `gcd` procedure can be defined in a field and it, along with the `rat`, `num`, and `den` procedures, is visible in the other field expressions.

Semantic Algebra

$v \in \mathit{Value} = \ldots \mathit{usual}$ FLK $\mathit{values} \ldots + \mathit{Record}$

$r \in \mathit{Record} = \mathit{Env}$

$\mathit{with\text{-}record\text{-}comp} : \mathit{Comp} \rightarrow (\mathit{Record} \rightarrow \mathit{Comp}) \rightarrow \mathit{Comp}$
$\mathit{defined\ like}\ \mathit{with\text{-}boolean\text{-}comp}\ \mathit{in\ Figure\ 6.26\ on\ page\ 281}$

Valuation Clauses

$\mathcal{E}[\![(\texttt{record}\ ((I_1\ E_1)\ \ldots\ (I_n\ E_n)))]\!]$
$= \lambda e\,.\ (\mathit{with\text{-}values}\ (\mathcal{E}^*[\![E_1\ \ldots\ E_n]\!]\ e)$
$\qquad\qquad (\lambda v^*\,.\ (\mathit{val\text{-}to\text{-}comp}$
$\qquad\qquad\qquad\qquad (\mathit{Record} \rightarrowtail \mathit{Value}\ (\mathit{extend}^*\ [I_1, \ldots, I_n]\ v^*\ \mathit{empty\text{-}env})))))$

$\mathcal{E}[\![(\texttt{select}\ I\ E)]\!]$
$= \lambda e\,.\ (\mathit{with\text{-}record\text{-}comp}\ (\mathcal{E}[\![E]\!]\ e)$
$\qquad\qquad (\lambda r\,.\ \mathbf{match}\ (\mathit{lookup}\ I\ r)$
$\qquad\qquad\qquad\qquad \triangleright (\mathit{Nameable} \rightarrowtail \mathit{BindingVal}\ n)\ [\![\ (\mathit{nam\text{-}to\text{-}comp}\ n)$
$\qquad\qquad\qquad\qquad \triangleright (\mathit{Unbound} \rightarrowtail \mathit{BindingVal}\ \mathit{unbound})\ [\![\ (\mathit{err\text{-}to\text{-}comp}\ \texttt{no-such-field})$
$\qquad\qquad\qquad \mathbf{end}\ ))$

$\mathcal{E}[\![(\texttt{override}\ E_1\ E_2)]\!]$
$= \lambda e\,.\ (\mathit{with\text{-}record\text{-}comp}\ (\mathcal{E}[\![E_1]\!]\ e)$
$\qquad\qquad (\lambda r_1\,.\ (\mathit{with\text{-}record\text{-}comp}\ (\mathcal{E}[\![E_2]\!]\ e)$
$\qquad\qquad\qquad (\lambda r_2\,.\ (\mathit{val\text{-}to\text{-}comp}\ (\mathit{Record} \rightarrowtail \mathit{Value}\ (\mathit{merge}\ r_1\ r_2)))))))$

$\mathcal{E}[\![(\texttt{conceal}\ (I_1\ \ldots\ I_n)\ E)]\!]$
$= \lambda e\,.\ (\mathit{with\text{-}record\text{-}comp}\ (\mathcal{E}[\![E]\!]\ e)$
$\qquad\qquad (\lambda r\,.\ (\mathit{val\text{-}to\text{-}comp}$
$\qquad\qquad\qquad (\mathit{Record} \rightarrowtail \mathit{Value}$
$\qquad\qquad\qquad\qquad (\lambda I\,.\ \mathbf{if}\ I \in \{I_1, \ldots, I_n\}$
$\qquad\qquad\qquad\qquad\qquad \mathbf{then}\ (\mathit{Unbound} \rightarrowtail \mathit{BindingVal}\ \mathit{unbound})$
$\qquad\qquad\qquad\qquad\qquad \mathbf{else}\ (\mathit{lookup}\ I\ r)\ \mathbf{end})))))$

Figure 7.18 Denotational semantics for CBV kernel record constructs.

The `gcd` procedure is intended only for use within the `rat` procedure and so is eliminated from the exported fields via `conceal`. However, the `rat`, `den`, and `num` procedures are exported along with the other operations so that clients can construct and deconstruct rational numbers without relying on their concrete implementations. Of course, since rational numbers are really just pairs, clients could manipulate them using pair operations instead. Manipulating elements of an abstract data type (in this case, rational numbers) via operations other than the ones provided by the interface to the abstraction (in this case, `rat`, `den`, and `num`) is called an **abstraction violation**. In Chapter 14, we will study ways to prevent such abstraction violations.

```
(def ints (record (zero 0) (add +) (sub -) (mul *) (div /)
                  (neg (abs (x) (- 0 x)))
                  (recip (abs (x) (/ 1 x)))
                  (eq =) (lt <) (gt >)))

(def rats
  (conceal (gcd)
    (recordrec
      (rat (abs (num den)
             (let ((common (gcd num den)))
               (pair (/ num common) (/ den common)))))
      (num fst)
      (den snd)
      (gcd (abs (a b) (if (= b 0) a (gcd b (% a b)))))
      (zero (rat 0 1))
      (add (abs (r1 r2)
             (rat (+ (* (num r1) (den r2)) (* (den r1) (num r2)))
                  (* (den r1) (den r2)))))
      (sub (abs (r1 r2) (add r1 (neg r2))))
      (mul (abs (r1 r2)
             (rat (* (num r1) (num r2))
                  (* (den r1) (den r2)))))
      (div (abs (r1 r2) (mul r1 (recip r2))))
      (neg (abs (r) (rat (- 0 (num r)) (den r))))
      (recip (abs (r) (rat (den r) (num r))))
      (eq (abs (r1 r2)
            (scand (= (num r1) (num r2))
                   (= (den r1) (den r2)))))
      (lt (abs (r1 r2) (< (* (num r1) (den r2))
                          (* (den r1) (num r2)))))
      (gt (abs (r1 r2) (lt r2 r1))))))
```

Figure 7.19   Two modules for arithmetic.

A benefit of defining records with common interfaces is that we can define
other operations that are generic for these interfaces. For example, the following
`sum-of-squares` procedure works for both integers and rationals:

```
(def sum-of-squares
  (abs (ops)
    (with-fields (add mul) ops
      (abs (a b)
        (add (mul a a) (mul b b))))))

((sum-of-squares ints) 3 4) $\xrightarrow{FL}$ 25
```

```
(with-fields (rat) rats
  ((sum-of-squares rats) (rat 1 3) (rat 1 4)))  FL⟶  ⟨25, 144⟩
```

For a meatier example of using these arithmetic modules, consider the matrix-module generator `make-matrix-ops` in Figure 7.20. We assume that $n{\times}n$ matrices are represented as length-n lists of rows, which are themselves represented as length-n lists of elements. `make-matrix-ops` takes a number n and an arithmetic module a and constructs a record representing a new module that implements $n{\times}n$ matrices whose components are manipulated by a. For example, if n is 3 and a is `rats`, then `make-matrix-ops` returns a record of operations for 3×3 matrices over the rational numbers. The input module a must supply a `zero` constant and binary `add` and `mul` procedures. The resulting module is a record that also exports these names as matrix operations. This means it is possible to use $n{\times}n$ matrices as elements in another matrix. Figure 7.21 shows matrix examples involving $2{\times}2$ matrices whose elements are (1) integers, (2) rationals, and (3) $2{\times}2$ matrices whose elements are integers.

The definition of `make-matrix-ops` uses `recordrec` to permit recursive definitions of the procedures in the `transpose`, `map2`, and `make-list` fields. Because `add`, `mul`, and `zero` are also fields defined by the `recordrec`, it is necessary to rename these fields from the `elt-ops` record in order to use them in the `recordrec` fields. The `map2` and `make-list` fields are eliminated from the returned record because they are intended for internal use only.

Exercise 7.27

a. Give an operational semantics for records in CBN FLK by doing the following:

- Extend the ValueExp domain in Figure 6.18 on page 258 to include record values.

- Extend the evaluation relation of CBN FLK in Figure 6.19 on page 259 to handle the kernel record constructs (`record`, `select`, `override`, and `conceal`). You should extend both the evaluation contexts and the reduction rules. You may assume the existence of the following auxiliary function:

  $deleteBindings :$ Ident* $\rightarrow$ (Ident $\times$ Exp) $*$ $\rightarrow$ (Ident $\times$ Exp)*
  ($deleteBindings$ $names$ $bindings$) returns a sequence of the bindings (i.e. name and expression pairs) in $bindings$ whose names do not appear in the sequence $names$.

  For example, the bindings in the record

  ```
  (record (a 3) (b (prim + x y)) (c (prim - x y)) (d (prim * x y)))
  ```

  are represented by the metalanguage binding sequence

  $$B = [\langle \mathsf{a}, 3\rangle, \langle \mathsf{b}, (\mathtt{prim + x\ y})\rangle, \langle \mathsf{c}, (\mathtt{prim - x\ y})\rangle, \langle \mathsf{d}, (\mathtt{prim * x\ y})\rangle]$$

  and ($deleteBindings$ $[\mathsf{b}, \mathsf{d}]$ B) $= [\langle \mathsf{a}, 3\rangle, \langle \mathsf{c}, (\mathtt{prim - x\ y})\rangle]$.

b. What changes need to be made to part **a** for a CBV version of FLK?

```
(def make-matrix-ops
  (abs (n elt-ops)
    (with-fields (elt-add elt-mul elt-zero)
      (rename ((add elt-add) (mul elt-mul) (zero elt-zero)) elt-ops)
      (conceal (map2 make-list)
        (recordrec
          (zero (make-list n (make-list n elt-zero)))
          (add (abs (m1 m2)
                 (map2 (abs (row1 row2) (map2 elt-add row1 row2))
                       m1
                       m2)))
          (mul (abs (m1 m2)
                 (map (abs (row1)
                        (map (abs (row2)
                               (foldr elt-add
                                      elt-zero
                                      (map2 elt-mul row1 row2)))
                             (transpose m2)))
                      m1)))
          (transpose (abs (m)
                       (if (null? (car m))
                           nil
                           (cons (map car m)
                                 (transpose (map cdr m))))))
          (map2 (abs (f lst1 lst2)
                  (if (or (null? lst1) (null? lst2))
                      nil
                      (cons (f (car lst1) (car lst2))
                            (map2 f (cdr lst1) (cdr lst2))))))
          (make-list (abs (n elt)
                       (if (= n 0)
                           nil
                           (cons elt (make-list (- n 1) elt)))))))))))
```

Figure 7.20 A generator for $n \times n$ matrix modules.

```
(def 2x2-int-matrices (make-matrix-ops 2 ints))
(def im1 (quote ((1 2) (3 4))))
(def im2 (quote ((2 3) (4 5))))
```

im1 $\xrightarrow[CBVFL]{}$ ⊲⊲$1, 2$⊳,⊲$3, 4$⊳⊳

im2 $\xrightarrow[CBVFL]{}$ ⊲⊲$2, 3$⊳,⊲$4, 5$⊳⊳

```
((select add 2x2-int-matrices) im1 im2)
```
$\xrightarrow[CBVFL]{}$ ⊲⊲$3, 5$⊳,⊲$7, 9$⊳⊳

```
((select mul 2x2-int-matrices) im1 im2)
```
$\xrightarrow[CBVFL]{}$ ⊲⊲$10, 13$⊳,⊲$22, 29$⊳⊳

```
(def 2x2-rat-matrices (make-matrix-ops 2 rats))
(def rm1 (with-fields (rat) rats
            (list (list (rat 1 4) (rat 2 4))
                  (list (rat 3 4) (rat 4 4)))))
```

rm1 $\xrightarrow[CBVFL]{}$ ⊲⊲$\langle 1, 4\rangle, \langle 1, 2\rangle$⊳,⊲$\langle 3, 4\rangle, \langle 1, 1\rangle$⊳⊳

```
(def rm2 (with-fields (rat) rats
            (list (list (rat 1 5) (rat 2 5))
                  (list (rat 3 5) (rat 4 5)))))
```

rm2 $\xrightarrow[CBVFL]{}$ ⊲⊲$\langle 1, 5\rangle, \langle 2, 5\rangle$⊳,⊲$\langle 3, 5\rangle, \langle 4, 5\rangle$⊳⊳

```
((select add 2x2-rat-matrices) rm1 rm2)
```
$\xrightarrow[CBVFL]{}$ ⊲⊲$\langle 9, 20\rangle, \langle 9, 10\rangle$⊳,⊲$\langle 27, 20\rangle, \langle 9, 5\rangle$⊳⊳

```
((select mul 2x2-rat-matrices) rm1 rm2)
```
$\xrightarrow[CBVFL]{}$ ⊲⊲$\langle 7, 20\rangle, \langle 1, 2\rangle$⊳,⊲$\langle 3, 4\rangle, \langle 11, 10\rangle$⊳⊳

```
(def 2x2-matrices-of-2x2-int-matrices
  (make-matrix-ops 2 2x2-int-matrices))
(def im3 (quote ((3 4) (5 6))))
(def im4 (quote ((5 6) (7 8))))
```

im3 $\xrightarrow[CBVFL]{}$ ⊲⊲$3, 4$⊳,⊲$5, 6$⊳⊳

im4 $\xrightarrow[CBVFL]{}$ ⊲⊲$5, 6$⊳,⊲$7, 8$⊳⊳

```
(def imm1 (list (list im1 im2) (list im3 im4)))
```
imm1 $\xrightarrow[CBVFL]{}$ ⊲⊲⊲$\langle 1, 2\rangle, \langle 3, 4\rangle$⊳,⊲$\langle 2, 3\rangle, \langle 4, 5\rangle$⊳⊳,
⊲⊲$\langle 3, 4\rangle, \langle 5, 6\rangle$⊳,⊲$\langle 5, 6\rangle, \langle 7, 8\rangle$⊳⊳⊳

```
(def imm2 (list (list im2 im3) (list im4 im1)))
```
imm2 $\xrightarrow[CBVFL]{}$ ⊲⊲⊲$\langle 2, 3\rangle, \langle 4, 5\rangle$⊳,⊲$\langle 3, 4\rangle, \langle 5, 6\rangle$⊳⊳,
⊲⊲$\langle 5, 6\rangle, \langle 7, 8\rangle$⊳,⊲$\langle 1, 2\rangle, \langle 3, 4\rangle$⊳⊳⊳

```
((select add 2x2-matrices-of-2x2-int-matrices) imm1 imm2)
```
$\xrightarrow[CBVFL]{}$ ⊲⊲⊲$\langle 3, 5\rangle, \langle 7, 9\rangle$⊳,⊲$\langle 5, 7\rangle, \langle 9, 11\rangle$⊳⊳,
⊲⊲$\langle 4, 5\rangle, \langle 6, 7\rangle$⊳,⊲$\langle 3, 4\rangle, \langle 5, 6\rangle$⊳⊳⊳

```
((select mul 2x2-matrices-of-2x2-int-matrices) imm1 imm2)
```
$\xrightarrow[CBVFL]{}$ ⊲⊲⊲$\langle 41, 49\rangle, \langle 77, 93\rangle$⊳,⊲$\langle 3, 4\rangle, \langle 3, 4\rangle$⊳⊳,
⊲⊲$\langle 89, 107\rangle, \langle 125, 151\rangle$⊳,⊲$\langle 26, 35\rangle, \langle 38, 51\rangle$⊳⊳⊳

Figure 7.21 Examples of 2×2 matrices.

7.3   Object-oriented Programming

Classification is the objectification of ness*ness.*
> — Daniel H. H. Ingalls, *Design Principles Behind Smalltalk*

Object-oriented programming (OOP) has emerged as an extremely popular programming paradigm. Definitions of what constitutes object-oriented programming vary, but they typically involve state-based entities called **objects** that communicate by sending **messages** to each other. The behavior of a related collection of objects is often defined by a **class**, which specifies the state variables of an object (its **instance variables**) and how an object responds to messages (its **instance methods**). Objects created from a class specification are called **instances** of the class. Classes are often organized into **inheritance hierarchies**, trees or DAGs of classes that specify how the instance variables and instance methods of one class in the hierarchy can be **inherited**, i.e., shared, by its descendants in the hierarchy. Classes themselves are sometimes treated as objects that can have variables (**class variables**) and methods (**class methods**).

SIMULA 67 is generally regarded as the first programming language to embody the object-oriented paradigm. The paradigm matured with the development of SMALLTALK and object-oriented packages for several dialects of LISP. Today, object-oriented features are embraced by a wide array of languages, including JAVA, C++, C#, COMMON LISP, OCAML, DYLAN, EIFFEL, and JAVASCRIPT.

Although we will not discuss issues of state until the next chapter, we introduce object-oriented programming here because most of the issues involved in this paradigm are issues of naming, not issues of state. We will introduce the key ideas of the object-oriented paradigm in the context of an object-oriented kernel called HOOK (Humble Object-Oriented Kernel) and its associated full language, HOOPLA (Humble Object-Oriented Programming Language), which is defined by extending HOOK with syntactic sugar. Both HOOK and HOOPLA were designed by Jonathan Rees. Rather than giving an operational or denotational semantics of HOOK, we will specify its semantics by showing how to translate it into FL. Defining the semantics of a language by its translation into an already understood language is an important technique.

7.3.1   HOOK: An Object-oriented Kernel

An s-expression grammar for HOOK is presented in Figure 7.22. The HOOK syntactic domains are similar to those for FL. One new domain HOOK has is Message, which is used for naming the messages sent between objects. The

$$P \in \text{Prog} ::= (\text{hook } (I^*_{formal}) \ E_{body} \ D^*_{defn}) \ [\text{Program}]$$

$$D \in \text{Def} ::= (\text{def } I_{name} \ E_{defn}) \ [\text{Definition}]$$

$$
\begin{aligned}
E \in \text{Exp} ::= \ & L && [\text{Literal}] \\
\mid \ & I && [\text{VariableReference}] \\
\mid \ & (\text{method } M_{message} \ (I_{receiver} \ I^*_{formal}) \ E_{body}) && [\text{SimpleObject}] \\
\mid \ & (\text{compose } E_{obj1} \ E_{obj2}) && [\text{ObjectComposition}] \\
\mid \ & (\text{null-object}) && [\text{NullObject}] \\
\mid \ & (\text{send } M_{message} \ E_{receiver} \ E^*_{arg}) && [\text{MessageSend}]
\end{aligned}
$$

$$
\begin{aligned}
L \in \text{Lit} ::= \ & B && [\text{BooleanLiteral}] \\
\mid \ & N && [\text{IntegerLiteral}] \\
\mid \ & (\text{sym } Y) \ [\text{SymbolicLiteral}]
\end{aligned}
$$

$$B \in \text{BoolLit} = \{\texttt{\#t}, \texttt{\#f}\}$$

$$N \in \text{IntLit} = \{\ldots, \texttt{-2}, \texttt{-1}, \texttt{0}, \texttt{1}, \texttt{2}, \ldots\}$$

$$Y \in \text{SymLit} = \{\texttt{x}, \texttt{lst}, \texttt{make-point}, \texttt{map\_tree}, \texttt{4/3*pi*r\^{}2}, \ldots\}$$

$I \in \text{Ident} = \textit{symbols } Y \textit{ that are not keywords and do not begin with } \texttt{\$}$

$M \in \text{Message} = \textit{symbols } Y \textit{ that do not begin with } \texttt{\$}$

Figure 7.22 An s-expression grammar for HOOK.

names in Ident and Message cannot begin with $ because names beginning with this prefix have a special meaning in the HOOK-to-FL translation.

The simplest object that can be constructed in HOOK is an object that responds to a single message. Such an object is created by the method construct:

$$(\text{method } M \ (I_{receiver} \ I^*_{formal}) \ E_{body})$$

Evaluating this construct returns an object that responds to the single message M by invoking the method. (Traditionally a method is defined in a class, but in our approach a method *is* a simple object.) The message should be accompanied by a number of arguments that matches the number of formal parameters in I^*_{formal}. Invoking the method on the message arguments evaluates E_{body} in an environment in which the **receiver parameter** $I_{receiver}$ is bound to the object that is the **receiver** of the message and the **formal parameters** I^*_{formal} are bound to the arguments of the message. The receiver parameter is a generalization of the special self variable in SMALLTALK and this variable in JAVA, which are used to refer to the receiver within a method body.

For example, FL procedures can be encoded in HOOK as objects that respond to the call message and ignore their receiver parameter:

```
(method call (_) 3) {A nullary procedure that returns three}
(method call (_ x) x) {The identity procedure}
(method call (_ y z) y) {A procedure returning the 1st of 2 args}
(method call (_ y z) z) {A procedure returning the 2nd of 2 args}
```

By convention, we will use the underscore identifier, _ , for a receiver parameter that is ignored.

We will often use HOOK's `def` construct to name objects.

```
(def three (method call (_) 3))
(def id (method call (_ x) x))
(def first (method call (_ y z) y))
(def second (method call (_ y z) z))
```

Technically, such definitions can appear only at the top level of a HOOK program, but for the purposes of exposition we will often interleave such definitions with HOOK expressions to simplify examples.

A message can be sent to an object via the **send** expression:

$$(\text{send } M_{message} \ E_{receiver} \ E^*_{arg})$$

This expression is pronounced "send the message $M_{message}$ to the object $E_{receiver}$ with the arguments E^*_{arg}." It is evaluated by first evaluating the expressions $E_{receiver}$ and E^*_{arg} to obtain, respectively, the receiver and arguments of the message M. The receiver is consulted to find a method for handling M. If such a method exists, it is invoked on the receiver and all of the arguments and its result is returned as the value of the **send** expression. An error is signaled if no method is found.

```
(send call three)    HOOK→  3     {This is the integer object 3}
(send call id #t)     HOOK→  #t     {This is the boolean truth object}
(send call first 17 #f)   HOOK→  17
(send call second 17 #f)  HOOK→  #f
(send foo id 17)     HOOK→  error:no-such-method
```

In HOOK, an integer like 3 is not just an integer value, but is a message-passing object that bundles up the usual integer value with methods for handling all the usual operations on integers (+, *, <, =, etc.):

```
(send + 2 3)   HOOK→  5
(send * 2 3)   HOOK→  6
(send < 2 3)   HOOK→  #t
(send = 2 3)   HOOK→  #f
```

Booleans and symbols are also message-passing objects:

```
(send not #f) ──────▸ #t
              HOOK
(send and #t #f) ──────▸ #f
                 HOOK
(send or #t #f) ──────▸ #t
                HOOK
(send = #f #f) ──────▸ #t
               HOOK
(send = #t #f) ──────▸ #f
               HOOK
(send = (sym a) (sym a)) ──────▸ #t
                         HOOK
(send = (sym a) (sym b)) ──────▸ #f
                         HOOK
(send = #t (sym c)) ──────▸ #f
                    HOOK
```

The last few examples show that the HOOK = message can be used to test the equality of booleans and symbols as well as integers and can even test equality of different kinds of objects. This differs from FL, where = is reserved for integer equality, `bool=?` tests boolean equality, and `sym=?` tests symbol equality. The ability of different objects to respond to the same message in different ways is a key feature of object-oriented programming.

In HOOK, booleans can be used for conditional evaluation because they also respond to the `if-true` message. The object `#t` handles the `if-true` message with two arguments, each of which should represent a nullary procedure (i.e., a thunk). It returns the result of invoking the first thunk by sending it a `call` message with no arguments. The `#f` object is similar except that it returns the result of invoking the second thunk.

```
(send if-true #t (method call (_) 2) (method call (_) 3) ──────▸ 2
                                                          HOOK
(send if-true #f (method call (_) 2) (method call (_) 3) ──────▸ 3
                                                          HOOK
```

Treating integers and booleans as full-fledged message-passing objects is in the spirit of SMALLTALK. In contrast, languages such as JAVA, C++, and C# treat integers and booleans as traditional non-object values like those in FL.

The expression (compose E_{obj1} E_{obj2}) builds complex objects out of simpler ones. This construct evaluates E_{obj1} and E_{obj2}, obtaining two objects. These are combined into a single object whose methods are the union of those of the two objects. If both objects have methods for handling some message M, the method belonging to the value of E_{obj1} takes precedence.

As a simple example of object composition, consider an object `square5` that represents the side length and area of a square with side length 5:

```
(def square5 (compose (method side (_) 5)
                      (method area (_) 25)))
(send + (send side square5) (send area square5)) ──────▸ 30
                                                  HOOK
```

We would like to be able to create many square objects with different side lengths. In many object-oriented languages, a description of related objects is called a **class** and each object generated from this description is called an **instance** of the class. A class typically specifies **instance variables** that characterize the state of an instance (e.g., side length in the square example) and **instance methods** specifying how each instance responds to messages (e.g., `side` and `area` in the square example).

In HOOK, we can represent a class as an object that responds to the `new` message by returning an instance of the class. For example, here is a class that creates square objects:

```
(def square-class
  (method new (_ s)
    (compose (method side (_) s)
             (method area (self) (send * (send side self)
                                          (send side self))))))
(def square3 (send new square-class 3))
(def square4 (send new square-class 4))
(send + (send side square3) (send side square4))  HOOK→ 7
(send + (send area square3) (send area square4))  HOOK→ 25
```

In `square-class`, the parameter `s` of the new method plays the role of an instance variable and the `side` and `area` methods serve as instance methods. Like FL, HOOK has static scoping of identifiers, so the `s` in the `side` method inside of `square-class` refers to the formal parameter `s` of the `new` method. The `new` method of `square-class` corresponds to what is called a **constructor method** in languages like JAVA and C++. For this reason, we will say that it **constructs an instance** of `square-class`.

The `area` instance method is the first method we have seen that refers to its receiver parameter (which we will typically call `self` or variations thereof). Its body determines the side length via the message send `(send side self)` rather than by directly referencing the instance variable `s`. As we shall see shortly, this level of indirection makes it easier to modify method behavior via inheritance. For this reason, it is a common idiom to send messages to the receiver parameter in instance method bodies.

A key feature of many object-oriented programming languages is that one class (a so-called **subclass**) can **inherit** instance variables and instance methods from one or more other classes (its so-called **superclasses**). This encourages a style of programming known as **programming by differences** in which a class specification implicitly shares the code of its superclasses and only explicitly defines the code that distinguishes it from its superclasses.

As an example of inheritance, consider the following class of scalable squares:

```
(def scalable-square-class
  (method new (_ s)
    (compose (send new square-class s)
             (method scale (unscaled-self factor)
               (compose (method side (scaled-self)
                          (send * (send unscaled-self side) factor))
                        unscaled-self)))))
```

Instances of `scalable-square-class` inherit behavior from `square-class` because they respond to the `side` and `area` messages using the methods from (an instance of) this class. But they also respond to a new message, `scale`, which returns a new object whose side length is the previous side length scaled by the parameter `factor`. The recipient of the `scale` message (which is named `unscaled-self` within the `scale` method) is expected to be an instance of `scalable-square-class`. The result of `scale` is a new object that has the same behavior as `unscaled-self` except that it responds to the `side` message with a scaled version of the side length of `unscaled-self`. Because the `area` method of square objects determines side length via `(send side self)`, the area of a scaled square will be calculated correctly. Moreover, a scaled square can itself be scaled:

```
(def ss1 (send new scalable-square-class 7))
(send side ss1)  HOOK-> -> 7
(send area ss1)  HOOK-> -> 49
(def ss2 (send scale ss1 2))
(send side ss2)  HOOK-> -> 14
(send area ss2)  HOOK-> -> 196
(def ss3 (send scale ss2 3))
(send side ss3)  HOOK-> -> 42
(send area ss3)  HOOK-> -> 1764
(send side ss2)  HOOK-> -> 14
(send side ss1)  HOOK-> -> 7
```

The last two evaluations illustrate that, because HOOK has no side effects, no existing objects are changed by sending the `scale` message.

By composing a new object with the recipient of the method, the `scale` method returns an object that has all the behavior of the recipient except for the behavior that is overridden or newly specified by the new object. This composition idiom elegantly supports **mixins**, which are combinations of orthogonal object behaviors. We illustrate mixins by an example. Consider the following class for objects that maintain a color attribute:

```
(def color-class
  (method new (_ col)
    (compose (method color (self) col)
             (method new-color (self new-col)
               (compose (send new color-class new-col)
                        self)))))
```

Not only can we make standalone instances of this class, but we can also use `compose` to give existing objects a color attribute. The fact that `new-color` returns a new instance of `color-class` composed with the recipient `self` means that all methods in `self` that are orthogonal to colors will be preserved when `new-color` is invoked. This is the sense in which the color attribute can be "mixed into" other objects. For example:

```
(def red (send new color-class (sym red)))
(def ss4 (compose red ss1))
(send side ss4)  ──HOOK→  7
(send color ss4)  ──HOOK→  (sym red) {This is a symbol object}
(def ss5 (send scale ss4 2))
(send side ss5)  ──HOOK→  14
(send color ss5)  ──HOOK→  (sym red) {scale preserves color}
(def ss6 (send new-color ss5 (sym blue)))
(send side ss6)  ──HOOK→  14 {new-color preserves side length}
(send color ss6)  ──HOOK→  (sym blue)
```

Much of the power and flexibility illustrated by the above examples is due to the fact that the receiver parameter of a method denotes the whole object of which the method may be only one component. When a message is sent to the result of combining objects via `compose`, the receiver parameter of the invoked method is bound to the result of the `compose`. So the behavior of a method body is dependent on how the method has been bundled up with other methods to form objects.

The one HOOK expression we haven't illustrated yet is `(null-object)`. This simply creates an object with no methods. It acts as the identity object for `compose`.

7.3.2   HOOPLA

The kinds of HOOK programming idioms seen above can be made more convenient by extending HOOK with the syntactic sugar defined in Figure 7.23. We give the name HOOPLA to the full language (HOOK + syntactic sugar).

The HOOPLA `object` expression builds an object by composing arbitrarily many other objects. The `class` expression creates an instance-creating object

$$(\texttt{hoopla}\ (I_{formal}^*)\ E_{body}\ D_{defn}^*)\ \leadsto_{ds}\ (\texttt{hook}\ (I_{formal}^*)\ E_{body}\ D_{defn}^*)$$

$$(\texttt{object})\ \leadsto_{ds}\ (\texttt{null-object})$$

$$(\texttt{object}\ E_1\ E_{rest}^*)\ \leadsto_{ds}\ (\texttt{compose}\ E_1\ (\texttt{object}\ E_{rest}^*))$$

$$(\texttt{class}\ (I_{init}^*)\ E_{object}^*)$$
$$\leadsto_{ds}\ (\texttt{method new}\ (I_{ignore}\ I_{init}^*)\ (\texttt{object}\ E_{object}^*))\ \{I_{ignore}\ \textit{is fresh}\}$$

$$(\texttt{abs}\ (I_{formal}^*)\ E_{body})$$
$$\leadsto_{ds}\ (\texttt{method call}\ (I_{ignore}\ I_{formal}^*)\ E_{body})\ \{I_{ignore}\ \textit{is fresh}\}$$

$$(E_{rator}\ E_{rand}^*)\ \leadsto_{ds}\ (\texttt{send call}\ E_{rator}\ E_{rand}^*)$$

$$(\texttt{let}\ ((I_{name}\ E_{defn})^*)\ E_{body})\ \leadsto_{ds}\ ((\texttt{abs}\ (I_{name}^*)\ E_{body})\ E_{defn}^*)$$

$$(\texttt{if}\ E_{test}\ E_{then}\ E_{else})$$
$$\leadsto_{ds}\ (\texttt{send if-true}\ E_{test}\ (\texttt{abs}\ ()\ E_{then})\ (\texttt{abs}\ ()\ E_{else}))$$

Figure 7.23 Desugaring rules for HOOPLA. The HOOPLA language is the HOOK language extended with syntactic sugar defined by these rules.

that responds to the single `new` message. Using these two sugar constructs, we can give more succinct definitions to the classes studied earlier. (By convention, we drop the suffix `-class` from the class names to make them shorter.)

```
(def square
  (class (s)
    (method side (self) s)
    (method area (self)
      (send * (send side self) (send side self)))))
(def scalable-square
  (class (s)
    (send new square s)
    (method scale (unscaled-self factor)
      (object (method side (scaled-self)
                (send * (send unscaled-self side) factor))
              unscaled-self)))) {Support mixins}
(def color
  (class (col)
    (method color (self) col)
    (method new-color (self new-col)
      (object (send new color new-col)
              self)))) {Support mixins}
```

Some additional HOOPLA classes are presented in Figure 7.24. They define colored "turtles": objects that have position, angle, and color. Below are some example turtle manipulations:

```
(def t1 (send new colored-turtle 0 0 0 (sym green)))
  {Define a turtle t1}
(send x t1)      HOOPLA→ 0
(send y t1)      HOOPLA→ 0
(send angle t1)  HOOPLA→ 0
(send color t1)  HOOPLA→ (sym green)

(def t2 (send move (send turn t1 45) 17 23))
  {t2 is a rotated and translated version of t1}
(send x t2)      HOOPLA→ 17
(send y t2)      HOOPLA→ 23
(send angle t2)  HOOPLA→ 45)
(send color t2)  HOOPLA→ (sym green)

(def t3 (send home t2)) {t3 is a version of t2 sent home}
(send x t3)      HOOPLA→ 0
(send y t3)      HOOPLA→ 0
(send angle t3)  HOOPLA→ 0
(send color t3)  HOOPLA→ (sym green)
```

Note that instances of `colored-turtle` are composed of `point`, `direction`, and `color` instances, so a turtle instance responds to any of the messages handled by these instances. Because HOOPLA does not support side effects, methods like `move` and `turn` create new objects rather than changing existing ones.

The HOOPLA syntactic sugar also supports familiar constructs from FL: `abs`, `let`, `if`, and procedure application. This makes it possible to write FL-like program fragments within HOOPLA.

7.3.3   Semantics of HOOK

Object composition in HOOK is reminiscent of record overriding in FL. In fact, the similarity is so great that we will define the semantics of HOOK programs by translating them into the version of the FL language extended with records that was presented in Section 7.2.3. The key to this translation is that objects are represented as records that bind message names to procedures that represent methods. A message send is then handled by simply looking up the method/procedure in the receiver record and applying it to the actual arguments.

We formally define the translation from HOOK code to FL code in Figure 7.25 in terms of the translation functions $\mathcal{T}_{pgm}$, $\mathcal{T}_{exp}$, and $\mathcal{T}_{lit}$, which translate, respectively, HOOK programs, expressions, and literals to FL. The core

```
(def point
  (class (init-x init-y)
    (method x (self) init-x)
    (method y (self) init-y)
    (method move (self dx dy)
      (object (send new point
                      (send + (send x self) dx)
                      (send + (send y self) dy))
              self)))) {Support mixins}

(def direction
  (class (init-angle)
    (method angle (self) init-angle)
    (method turn (self delta)
      (object (send new direction
                      (send + (send angle self) delta))
              self)))) {Support mixins}

(def turtle
  (class (x y angle)
    (method home (self)
      (object (send new turtle x y angle)
              self)) {Support mixins}
    (send new point x y)
    (send new direction angle)))

(def colored-turtle
  (class (x y angle col)
    (send new turtle x y angle)
    (send new color col)))
```

Figure 7.24   Sample HOOPLA classes.

of the translation is the handling of methods, objects, and message sends. A
HOOK method construct is translated to an FL record construct with a single
binding of the message name to a procedure that does the work of the method.
A HOOK compose construct is translated to an FL override construct; the
semantics of override are such that methods from E_{obj1} will take precedence
over methods from E_{obj2}. A HOOK send translates to a procedure application
in FL; the procedure is found by looking up the message name in the record that
represents the receiver.

$\mathcal{T}_{pgm} : \text{Prog}_{HOOK} \to \text{Prog}_{FL}$

$\mathcal{T}_{pgm}[\![(\text{hook } (I_{i=1}^{k}) \ E_{body} \ (\text{def } I_{def_j} \ E_j)_{j=1}^{n})]\!]$
$= (\text{fl } (I_{i=1}^{k}) \ (\text{let } ((I_i \ (\text{\$new-integer } I_i))_{i=1}^{k}) \ \mathcal{T}_{exp}[\![E_{body}]\!])$

```
    (def $new-integer
      (abs (n)
        (record
          ($val n)
          (+ (abs (self arg)
                (override ($new-integer (@+ n (select $val arg)))
                          self))) {Support mixins}
            ⋮ {similar for -, *, /, %}
          (= (abs (self arg)
                ($new-boolean (let ((v (select $val arg)))
                                (scand (@int? v) (@= v n)))))))
            ⋮ {similar for !=}
          (< (abs (self arg)
                ($new-boolean (@< n (select $val arg)))))
            ⋮ {similar for <=, >=, >}
        )))
    (def $new-boolean … left as an exercise … )
    (def $new-symbol … left as an exercise … )
    (def I_{def_j} 𝒯_{exp}[[E_j]])_{j=1}^{n}
    )
```

$\mathcal{T}_{exp} : \text{Exp}_{HOOK} \to \text{Exp}_{FL}$

$\mathcal{T}_{exp}[\![I]\!] = I$

$\mathcal{T}_{exp}[\![L]\!] = \mathcal{T}_{lit}[\![L]\!]$

$\mathcal{T}_{exp}[\![(\text{method } M_{message} \ (I_{self} \ I_{formal}^{*}) \ E_{body})]\!]$
$= (\text{record } (M_{message} \ (\text{abs } (I_{self} \ I_{formal}^{*}) \ \mathcal{T}_{exp}[\![E_{body}]\!])))$

$\mathcal{T}_{exp}[\![(\text{compose } E_{obj_1} \ E_{obj_2})]\!] = (\text{override } \mathcal{T}_{exp}[\![E_{obj_1}]\!] \ \mathcal{T}_{exp}[\![E_{obj_2}]\!])$

$\mathcal{T}_{exp}[\![(\text{null-object})]\!] = (\text{record})$

$\mathcal{T}_{exp}[\![(\text{send } M_{message} \ E_{receiver} \ E_{arg_1} \ \dots \ E_{arg_n})]\!]$
$= (\text{let } ((I_{receiver} \ \mathcal{T}_{exp}[\![E_{receiver}]\!])) \ ; I_{receiver} \text{ is fresh.}$
$\quad ((\text{select } M_{message} \ I_{receiver}) \ I_{receiver} \ \mathcal{T}_{exp}[\![E_{arg_1}]\!] \ \dots \ \mathcal{T}_{exp}[\![E_{arg_n}]\!]))$

$\mathcal{T}_{lit} : \text{Lit}_{HOOK} \to \text{Exp}_{FL}$

$\mathcal{T}_{lit}[\![N]\!] = (\text{\$new-integer } N)$

$\mathcal{T}_{lit}[\![B]\!] = (\text{\$new-boolean } B)$

$\mathcal{T}_{lit}[\![(\text{sym } Y)]\!] = (\text{\$new-symbol } (\text{sym } Y))$

Figure 7.25   The HOOK-to-FL translation function.

The handling of literals (via $\mathcal{T}_{lit}$) is perhaps the trickiest part of the translation. HOOK literals stand not for simple values but for full-fledged message-passing objects. A HOOK number object, for instance, must translate into an FL record that has methods for all the numeric operations. The translation uses the top-level FL procedure `$new-integer` to create such a record. The record must also be able to supply the unadorned version of the value it is holding onto; this is the purpose of the record binding with the special field named `$val`. Note that operations returning the same kind of object being defined (e.g., `+`, `*`) return an extended version of `self` rather than just a fresh instance of the object. This means that the returned object retains all the behavior of the receiver that is not explicitly specified by the definition; this is explored in Exercise 7.32. Note also that the definition of `=` uses `scand` and `int?` so as to allow the comparison of a number and a nonnumber to return false. The `$new-boolean` and `$new-symbol` procedures are analogous to `$new-integer` and are left as Exercise 7.35.

At the program level, HOOK top-level definitions translate to FL top-level definitions, which have recursive scope. For simplicity, we assume that all HOOK program arguments are integers. In the translation, the FL arguments will be regular FL integer values, so they are converted to objects via `$new-integer` for use in the translation of the program body expression E_{body}.

The fact that HOOK identifiers and message names cannot begin with `$` means that there cannot be any name capture issues in translated HOOK expressions involving the record field $val and top-level procedure names like $new-integer. We chose this naming convention to highlight the special nature of procedures and fields beginning with `$`, but an alternative solution to the problem would have been to choose fresh identifiers for these special names. Another naming issue not addressed in the translation is that FL identifiers cannot include the FL keywords, but certain of these (e.g., `letrec`) are permitted as identifiers in HOOPLA. This problem can be solved by alpha-renaming any problematic names in the HOOK program before performing the translation.

The HOOK-to-FL translation is elegant, but it doesn't handle certain error situations in a robust fashion. For example, the message send

```
(send foo (method bar (_) 17))
```

should give rise to a `no-such-method` error, but in the translation semantics it gives rise to a `no-such-field` error. As another example, the informal semantics for HOOK specifies that the number of arguments in a message send should match the number of formal parameters in the invoked method; presumably, an error indicating this fact should be reported when there is a mismatch. However, because of the details of the translation, such mismatches are not flagged in an appropriate way (see Exercise 7.34).

Exercise 7.28 What is the value of the following HOOPLA expression?

```
(let ((ob1 (object (method value (self) 1)))
      (ob2 (object (method value (self) 2)))
      (ob3 (object (method value (self) 3)
                   (method evaluate (self) (send value self)))))
  (send evaluate (object ob1 ob2 ob3)))
```

Exercise 7.29 Here we reconsider the `square` and `scalable-square` classes from Section 7.3.2.

```
(def square
  (class (s)
    (method side (self) s)
    (method area (self)
      (send * (send side self) (send side self)))))
(def scalable-square
  (class (s)
    (method scale (unscaled-self factor)
      (object (method side (scaled-self)
                (send * (send unscaled-self side) factor))
              unscaled-self)) {Support mixins}
    (send new square s)))
```

a. What is the value of the following HOOPLA expression using the above classes?

```
(let ((ss1 (send new scalable-square 10)))
  (let ((ss2 (send scale ss1 2)))
    (send + (send area ss1) (send area ss2))))
```

b. Redo part **a** after `square` and/or `scalable-square` are modified in each of the ways described below.

  i.   The `area` method of `square` is changed to

```
(method area (self) (send * s s))
```

  ii. The `scale` method of `scalable-square` is changed to:

```
(method scale (unscaled-self factor)
  (object unscaled-self
          (method side (scaled-self)
            (send * (send unscaled-self side) factor))))
```

  iii. The `scale` method of `scalable-square` is changed to:

```
(method scale (self factor)
  (object (method side (self)
            (send * (send self side) factor))
          self))
```

iv.   The `scalable-square` class is changed to:

```
(def scalable-square
  (class (s)
    (method scale (unscaled-self factor)
      (method side (scaled-self)
        (send * (send unscaled-self side) factor)))
    (send new square s)))
```

v.   The `scalable-square` class is changed to:

```
(def scalable-square
  (class (s)
    (method scale (self factor)
      (send new scalable-square (send * s factor)))
    (send new square s)))
```

Exercise 7.30 The HOOK-to-FL translation does not specify whether the target language is a CBN or CBV version of FL. Does it matter? Explain.

Exercise 7.31

a. Extend HOOPLA to handle FL's `pair` and `prim` constructs by extending the grammar and desugaring rules in Figure 7.23.

b. Assuming that the semantics of HOOK is defined by a translation into CBN FL, extend HOOPLA to handle FL's `rec` construct by extending the grammar and desugaring rules in Figure 7.23.

c. Can `rec` be defined as a desugaring if the semantics of HOOK is defined by a translation into CBV FL? Explain.

Exercise 7.32 Using the definition of the `color` class from Section 7.3.2, is the value of the following HOOPLA expression well defined?

```
(let ((n (send + (object 1 (send new color 10))
                 (object 2 (send new color 20)))))
  (send * n (send color n)))
```

Explain your answer. *Hint:* Study the definition of `$new-integer` in Figure 7.25.

Exercise 7.33 Does HOOPLA's `abs` construct support currying? Explain.

Exercise 7.34 This problem explores error reporting in HOOPLA. Consider the following object:

```
(def adder (method add (_ x y) (send + x y)))
```

Based on the HOOK-to-FL translation, what are the values of the following HOOPLA expressions?

a. (send mul adder 2 3)

b. (send add adder 2)

c. (send add adder 2 3 4)

d. (send add adder 2 #t)

Exercise 7.35 Following the example for integer literals, show how boolean and symbol literals in HOOK translate into FL by fleshing out the definitions of the `$new-boolean` and `$new-symbol` procedures in Figure 7.25.

Exercise 7.36 Anoop Hacker is confused about namespace issues in HOOPLA. For example, he observes that the `color` class presented in Section 7.3.2 has a method named `color` as well, and wonders if these names can interact in unexpected ways. In the syntax of the full language, there are several binding constructs: `class`, `abs`, `let`, and `method`. The first three constructs all bind formal parameters; the last one binds a message name and a name for the receiver (i.e., *self*) parameter in addition to the formal parameters of the method.

You have volunteered to help Anoop answer the following questions. Carefully study the definitions of HOOPLA to HOOK desugaring and HOOK to FL translation to justify your answers. Give examples where appropriate.

a. How many distinct namespaces are there in HOOPLA?

b. Is it possible for a method formal parameter named `x` to be shadowed by a message named `x`?

c. Is it possible for a message named `x` to be shadowed by a method formal parameter named `x`?

d. Do the answers to parts **b** and **c** change if the `record` in the translation for `method` becomes a `recordrec` instead? If so, how?

Exercise 7.37 Polly Morwicz doesn't like the fact that it's always necessary to explicitly name *self* within a HOOPLA method. She decides to implement a version of HOOPLA called SELFISH in which a reserved word `self` is implicitly bound within every method body. For example, in SELFISH the point class of Figure 7.24 would be written as follows:

```
(def point
  (class (init-x init-y)
    (method x () init-x)
    (method y () init-y)
    (method move (dx dy)
      (object (send new point
                    (send + (send x self) dx)
                    (send + (send y self) dy))
              self)))) {Support mixins}
```

In this example, the occurrences of `self` within the `move` method evaluate to the receiver of the `move` message. Because `self` is a reserved word in SELFISH, it is illegal to use it as a formal parameter to a method.

a. Describe what modifications would have to be made to the following in order to specify the semantics of SELFISH:

    i.   The HOOK grammar.

    ii.   The HOOPLA to HOOK desugarer.

    iii. The HOOK to FL translator.

b. Unfortunately, SELFISH doesn't always give the behavior Polly expects. For example, she makes a simple modification to the definition of the point class:

```
(def point
  (class (init-x init-y)
    (method x () init-x)
    (method y () init-y)
    (method move (dx dy)
      (let ((new-x (send + (send x self) dx))
            (new-y (send + (send y self) dy)))
        (object (method x () new-x)
                (method y () new-y)
                self)))))
```

After this change, turtle objects (which are implemented in terms of points) no longer work as expected. Explain what has gone wrong.

c. Show how to get Polly's new point definition to work as expected. You can add new code, but not remove any. You may perform alpha-renaming where necessary.

d. Which do you think is better: the explicit `self` approach of HOOPLA or the implicit `self` approach of SELFISH? Explain your answer.

Notes

The call-by-name and call-by-value parameter-passing mechanisms have their roots in evaluation strategies of the lambda calculus. In the lambda calculus, the *normal-order* strategy reduces the leftmost beta redex, so the operand is not normalized before it is substituted into the body of the operator. This is similar to CBN. In contrast, the *applicative-order* strategy resembles CBV, because it normalizes both the operator and operand before performing a beta reduction. Unlike the lambda calculus evaluation strategies, which perform beta reductions in the body of a lambda expression as part of normalizing it, FL (like most real-world programming languages) does *not* evaluate the body of a procedure until it is applied to an argument. This corresponds to the notion of *weak head normal form* in the lambda calculus.

The essence of CBN and CBV is distilled in a classic paper by Plotkin [Plo75]. Plotkin developed a CBV version of the lambda calculus corresponding to the CBV operational semantics of Landin's ISWIM language [Lan66]. He also defined a CBN variant of ISWIM and showed that it corresponded to the traditional lambda calculus. Finally, Plotkin showed how to simulate CBV in CBN and vice versa. More recently, Wadler has developed a framework that demonstrates a duality between CBN and CBV [Wad03, Wad05].

Although CBN has more pleasing theoretical properties than CBV, most real programming languages use CBV (or some variant) for reasons of efficiency.

The challenges we have seen in developing a CBV (as opposed to CBN) semantics of recursion are reflected in special mechanisms needed for implementing recursion in call-by-value languages (e.g., [BZ02, WSD02, HLW03]). Interestingly, all these mechanisms involve state and side effects.

In order to resolve the meaning of free variables in a procedure body correctly, static scoping conceptually involves procedural values that pair the procedure body with the environment in which the abstraction for the procedure was evaluated. This pairing was dubbed a *closure* by Landin [Lan64]. As we will see in Section 17.10, closures play a key role in the implementation of statically scoped languages with first-class procedures.

Moses [Mos70] observed that closures could address the *FUNARG problem* in early versions of LISP [McC60], in which dynamic scoping led to the incorrect resolution of free variables in the bodies of procedures passed as arguments or returned as results. The SCHEME language of Steele and Sussman solved the FUNARG problem by creating closures for all procedural values, yielding the first statically scoped dialect of LISP [SS75, Ste76, SS78]. They noted that static scoping led to more efficient variable access than dynamic scoping, and that the ALGOL 60-like block structure enabled by static scoping facilitated the construction of complex programs. They also observed that a closure consisting of a lambda abstraction and an environment was isomorphic to the script and acquaintance list of actors in actor languages [HBS73, GH75]. The environment/closure diagrams presented in [ASS96, Section 3.2] are helpful for reasoning about statically scoped procedures.

The history, applications, and theory of dynamic scoping are explained in [Mor98]. The two-namespace approach in Exercise 7.25 for supporting both lexical and dynamic scope was presented in [SS78], where it was observed that dynamic scope can be viewed as a kind of side effect. This view suggests that dynamic scope can be simulated in a statically scoped system using side effects, the approach taken with SCHEME's `fluid-let` construct (see Exercise 8.21). HASKELL's *implicit parameters* [LLMS00] provide some of the features of dynamic scope within a purely functional framework.

User-definable macros are a powerful feature allowing programmers to extend a programming language with new syntactic sugar. Because s-expressions are convenient for describing syntactic transformations, macro research has mostly been conducted in the context of LISP dialects (particularly SCHEME). Name-capture problems that naturally arise in these systems have been addressed by various notions of *hygiene* [KFFD86, BR88, CR91, RKDB92]. A high-level language for defining macros [KW87] has been incorporated into the SCHEME language definition [KCR+98].

Object-oriented programming has become a popular programming paradigm, but the term "object-oriented" is an overloaded one with a host of different meanings [Ree01]. The design landscape for object-oriented languages is rather muddy, but a tutorial paper by Wegner [Weg87] identifies six orthogonal dimensions of object-based language design: objects (modular state-based computing agents), delegation (a resource-sharing mechanism), abstraction (an interface specification mechanism), types (an expression classification mechanism), concurrency (a mechanism for multiple active threads of control), and persistence (a mechanism for data structures to outlive the lifetime of the process creating them). A later tutorial paper by Wegner [Weg90] expands on these ideas and explains other concepts of object-oriented programming.

In traditional object-oriented languages, the state and behavior of objects are specified by classes, and delegation is achieved by having subclasses inherit state and behavior from superclasses. The first language to include objects, classes, and inheritance was SIMULA 67 [DMN70, ND81], an extension of ALGOL 60 in which these features were designed to support discrete-event simulations. SMALLTALK [KG77, Ing81, GR83] was the first language to completely embrace the object-oriented paradigm. All SMALLTALK values (including numbers, booleans, and characters) are full-fledged message-passing objects that are instances of classes. The entire SMALLTALK system, including the operating system, a garbage collector, and a graphical user interface that was cutting edge for its time, is implemented in SMALLTALK itself. EIFFEL [Mey92, Mey97] is another example of a purely object-oriented language. But the two most popular exemplars of this style of object-oriented programming, C++ [Str86] and JAVA [GJS96], stray from the pure object-oriented paradigm. Both languages have numerous values (particularly "small values" like numbers, booleans, and characters) that are not objects, and C++ includes many additional non-object-oriented features of the C language it extends.

In the class-based object-oriented languages discussed above, the behavior of objects in a class is specified by methods (called virtual functions in C++) that are declared within the class and its superclasses. When a message is sent to a receiver object, the particular method invoked is determined by the class of the receiver. An alternative approach is to specify object behavior via *generic functions* that are not associated with any class. In this approach, numerous methods may be declared for a given generic function, each of which specifies the classes for some of its parameters. When a generic function is invoked on object arguments, the particular method invoked is determined by the classes of its object arguments. This approach was pioneered in the object systems for several dialects of LISP. In the FLAVORS object system of LISP MACHINE LISP [Moo86], a generic function dispatches to a method based on the class of a single argument, which corresponds to the receiver in traditional systems. In the COMMON LISP Object System (CLOS) [DG87] and in the DYLAN language [Sha96], the dispatch can depend on the classes of multiple arguments, in which case the methods are called *multimethods*. Another language supporting multimethods is CECIL [Cha92].

An alternative to using classes to specify objects is to create a new object by specifying any state/behavior that distinguishes it from one or more existing *prototype* objects. Any other state/behavior of the new object is delegated to (shared with) the prototypes [Lie86]. Early examples of this approach were various so-called *actor languages* [HBS73, GH75, Agh86], the SELF language [US87], and the object system of the T dialect of SCHEME [AR88]. More recent examples of prototype-based languages are CECIL and JAVASCRIPT (standardized under the name ECMASCRIPT [ECM99]).

Some object-oriented systems support *multiple inheritance*, in which the behavior of an object can be determined by multiple classes or prototypes. Examples include C++, EIFFEL, CLOS, and FLAVORS. Multiple inheritance supports the composition of orthogonal behaviors in mixins. Indeed, the FLAVORS system was inspired by the practice of some ice-cream parlors of creating specialized flavors for individual customers by mixing requested goodies into a base flavor of ice cream.[7]

The HOOPLA language presented in this chapter was designed in 1989 by Jonathan Rees, who was inspired by the object systems of SELF and T. HOOPLA is flexible and expressive. Although the underlying kernel language, HOOK, is prototype-based, the full language supports class-based programming by treating certain objects as instantiable classes. As illustrated by the

---

[7]The base class in FLAVORS is named `Vanilla`.

`color-class` example, it also supports mixins and multiple inheritance. Although the version of HOOPLA presented here does not support stateful instance variables, these are easy to add. The only sophisticated feature discussed above that is not supported in HOOPLA is multimethods; method dispatch is based on a single distinguished receiver object.

The dynamic semantics of objects and modules (including features like inheritance, mixins, and recursive bindings) are often described in terms of a lambda calculus extended with record-like structures, e.g [CM91, BL92, AZ02, Bru02]. An alternative approach for modeling objects is Abadi and Cardelli's sigma calculus [AC96], in which the fundamental entity is an object with named methods that can be invoked or updated. Extending these systems with static semantics (types) involves additional theoretical challenges, some of which are discussed in the notes at the end of Chapter 12 on page 767.

8

State

Man's yesterday may ne'er be like his morrow;
Nought may endure but Mutability

— Percy Bysshe Shelley, "Mutability," st. 4

What Is State?

I woke up one morning and looked around the room. Something wasn't
right. I realized that someone had broken in the night before and replaced
everything in my apartment with an exact replica. I couldn't believe it ...
I got my roommate and showed him. I said, "Look at this — everything's
been replaced with an exact replica!" He said, "Do I know you?"

— Steven Wright

We naturally view the world around us in terms of objects. Each object is characterized by a set of attributes that can vary with time. The **state** of an object is the set of particular attributes it has at a given time. For example, the state of a box of chocolates includes its size, shape, color, location, whether its lid is on or off, and the number, types, and positions of the chocolates inside.

Every object has a unique, time-independent attribute that distinguishes it from other objects: its **identity**. The notion of identity is at the very heart of objectness, for it formalizes the intuition that objects exist over extents of time rather than just at instants of time. Identity allows us to say that an object at one point in time is the "same" as that at another point, regardless of any changes of state that may have taken place in between. It also gives us a way of saying that two objects with otherwise indistinguishable states are "different."

Consider our box of chocolates again. If we open the lid, the state of the box has changed, but we still consider it to be the same box of chocolates. Even after we eat all the goodies inside, we think that the box has become empty, not that we have a different box of chocolates.

On the other hand, suppose we leave an unopened box of chocolates on the kitchen table one day and find an unopened box there the next day. We are likely to assume that it's the same box. However, a housemate might later confess to consuming the entire original box but then buying a replacement box after feeling pangs of guilt. In light of this confession, we concede that the box on the table is not the same as the one we bought, even though, from our perspective, its state is indistinguishable from that of the box we left there the day before.

How could we monitor similar situations in the future without the help of explicit confessions? Before placing an unopened box of chocolates on the table we could alter the box in some irreversible way. The next day we could check whether the box on the table had the same alteration. If the box on the table the next day does not exhibit the alteration, we are sure that the new box is not the same as the original. If it does have the alteration, we aren't 100% sure (our housemate might have diabolically copied our alteration, or a new box by chance might exhibit the same alteration), but there is reasonable evidence that the box is in fact the same one we left the previous day.

This example emphasizes that the notions of time, state, identity, and change are all inextricably intertwined.[1] The purpose of this chapter is to see how these notions are expressed in a computational framework. We shall see that state provides new ways to decompose problems but can greatly complicate reasoning about programs.

8.1 FL Is a Stateless Language

Computing with time-varying state-based entities is an extremely popular programming paradigm in traditional **imperative languages**, such as FORTRAN, COBOL, PASCAL, C, and ADA as well as in **object-oriented languages** like SMALLTALK, C++, C#, and JAVA. We call such languages **stateful**. One reason that stateful languages are so popular is that they resonate with our experience of interacting with objects that change over time in the world. At the opposite side of the spectrum are **stateless** languages like HASKELL and MIRANDA, which are sometimes called **purely functional** languages. **Mostly functional** languages are those, like ML, COMMON LISP, and SCHEME, that add stateful features on top of a stateless function-oriented core.

The FL language we have studied thus far is a stateless language — it provides no support for expressing computational objects with identity and state. In particular, neither variables nor data structures (pairs) may exhibit time-dependent behavior. To underscore this point, we will show the difficulties encountered in modeling a classic example of state — bank accounts — within FL. Our goal is to implement the following bank account procedures in FL:

---

[1]For a further discussion of this philosophical point in a computational framework, see Chapter 3 of [ASS96].

(make-account *amount*): Creates and returns an account with *amount* as its initial balance.

(balance *account*): Returns the balance in *account*.

(deposit! *amount account*): If *amount* is nonnegative, increases the balance of *account* by *amount* and returns the symbol succeeded. If *amount* is negative, leaves the balance unchanged and returns the symbol failed.

(withdraw! *amount account*): If *amount* is less than or equal to the balance of *account*, decreases the balance of *account* by *amount*, and returns the symbol succeeded. If *amount* is negative or is greater than the balance of *account*, leaves the balance unchanged and returns the symbol failed.

We adopt the convention that names of procedures that change the state of an object (such as deposit! and withdraw!) end in the "!" character (pronounced "bang").

Note that the specifications of deposit! and withdraw! indicate not only what **value** the procedures return (in both cases, one of the symbols succeeded or failed) but also what **effect** the procedure has on the state of the account (increasing or decreasing the balance). Even make-account can be viewed as having an effect on the state of the bank account system because it updates the system with a new account. Such changes in state are referred to as **side effects** or **mutations**. In programming languages supporting state, the specification of a procedure includes both its return value and its side effects.[2]

It turns out that it is impossible to write a set of FL procedures that satisfies the above specifications. We will show this by studying a nullary procedure test-deposit! that performs the following steps in order:

1. create an account *acct* with a balance of 100;

2. determine the balance *bal* of *acct*;

3. deposit 17 dollars into *acct*;

4. determine the new balance *bal′* of *acct*;

5. return the difference $bal′ - bal$.

---

[2]This is true for subroutines that can be invoked in value-accepting contexts, such as functions in ADA, FORTRAN, LISP, and PASCAL, non-void functions in C, and non-void methods in JAVA. Many languages have a distinct kind of subroutine that does not produce a value and is invoked only for its effect. Examples include ADA, FORTRAN, and PASCAL procedures, void functions in C, and void methods in JAVA.

Operational Semantics

Reduction Rules ($\rightsquigarrow$)

$\quad\vdots$ *non*-begin *reduction rules*
(begin V E) $\rightsquigarrow$ E [begin]

Evaluation Contexts ($\mathbb{E}$)

$\mathbb{E} ::= \ldots$ *non*-begin *contexts* $\ldots$ | (begin $\mathbb{E}$ E)

Denotational Semantics

$\quad \mathcal{E}[\![(\text{begin } E_1 \text{ } E_2)]\!] = \lambda e \,.\, (\textit{with-value} \; (\mathcal{E}[\![E_1]\!] \; e) \; (\lambda v \,.\, (\mathcal{E}[\![E_2]\!] \; e)))$

Figure 8.1   Operational and denotational semantics of begin in CBN and CBV.

In a stateful language, (test-deposit!) should return 17. We will demonstrate that FL is a stateless language by arguing that it must return 0 for (test-deposit!).

If we try to write test-deposit! in FL, we immediately run into a stumbling block. The specified actions are clearly ordered by time, but FL provides no explicit construct for specifying that expressions should be evaluated in any particular order. To circumvent this problem, we assume the existence of a construct (begin E_1 E_2) that evaluates E_1 before E_2. Since all FL expressions must return a value, we dictate that the value returned by a begin expression is the value of E_2. The formal semantics of begin are specified by the operational reduction rules and the denotational valuation clause in Figure 8.1.

Using begin, we can write test-deposit! in FL as follows:

```
(def test-deposit!
  (abs ()
    (let ((acct (make-account 100)))
      (let ((old (balance acct)))
        (begin (deposit! 17 acct)
               (- (balance acct) old))))))
```

The abstraction can be desugared into FLK as follows:

```
(lam ignore {E_lam:ignore}
  (app (lam acct {E_lam:acct}
         (app (lam old {E_lam:old}
                (begin
                  (app (app deposit! 17) acct) {E_seq1}
                  (prim - (app balance acct) old) {E_seq2}
                  ))
              (app balance acct)))
       (app make-account 100)))
```

```
(app E_{lam:ignore} #u)

 ==CBN=>_{[β]}  (app (lam acct
                       (app (lam old
                               (begin (app (app deposit! 17) acct)
                                         (prim - (app balance acct) old)))
                            (app balance acct)))
                    (app make-account 100))

 ==CBN=>_{[β]}  (app (lam old
                       (begin (app (app deposit! 17) (app make-account 100))
                                 (prim - (app balance (app make-account 100))
                                         old)))
                    (app balance (app make-account 100)))

 ==CBN=>_{[β]}  (begin (app (app deposit! 17) (app make-account 100))
                       (prim - (app balance (app make-account 100))
                               (app balance (app make-account 100))))

 ==CBN=>^{*}   (prim - (app balance (app make-account 100))
                       (app balance (app make-account 100)))

 ==CBN=>^{*}   (prim - 100 100)

 ==CBN=>_{[-]}  0
```

Figure 8.2 Operational evaluation sequence showing that (app test-deposit! #u) evaluates to 0.

We can now use our semantics frameworks to show that the FLK application (app test-deposit! #u) must evaluate to 0 regardless of how deposit! is defined. We will use a CBN version of FLK in the example. Since errors and divergence do not play a role here, the result will be the same for CBV.

An operational trace of the evaluation of (app test-deposit! #u) appears in Figure 8.2. In the second $[β]$ step, three copies of (app make-account 100) are made by the substitution process. In FL's operational semantics, an expression representing a data structure (an account in this case) for all intents and purposes *is* the data structure. Since the second operand of deposit! and the operand of the two applications of balance are syntactically distinct copies of (app make-account 100), any operation performed by deposit! on one copy can't possibly affect the copies in the operands of the balance calls. If we make the assumption that (app balance (app make-account 100)) $\xrightarrow[CBN]{*}$ 100 (this would seem to be required of any reasonable bank account implementation), then the trace shows that (test-deposit!) indeed evaluates to 0.

Denotational semantics offers another perspective on this example. Recall that CBN FL's valuation function $\mathcal{E}$ maps expressions and environments to com-

$\mathcal{E}[\![(\text{app } E_{lam:ignore} \text{ \#u})]\!] \; e_0$

$= \mathcal{E}[\![(\text{app } E_{lam:acct} \text{ (app make-account 100))}]\!] \; e_1,$
   where $e_1 = [\text{ignore} \mapsto (\mathcal{E}[\![\text{\#u}]\!] \; e_0)]e_0$

$= \mathcal{E}[\![(\text{app } E_{lam:old} \text{ (app balance acct))}]\!] \; e_2,$
   where $e_2 = [\text{acct} \mapsto (\mathcal{E}[\![(\text{app make-account 100})]\!] \; e_1)]e_1$

$= \mathcal{E}[\![(\text{begin } E_{seq1} \; E_{seq2})]\!] \; e_3,$
   where $e_3 = [\text{old} \mapsto (\mathcal{E}[\![(\text{app balance acct})]\!] \; e_2)]e_2$

$= (\textit{with-value} \; (\mathcal{E}[\![E_{seq1}]\!] \; e_3) \; (\lambda v \, . \, (\mathcal{E}[\![E_{seq2}]\!] \; e_3)))$

$= \mathcal{E}[\![(\text{prim - (app balance acct) old})]\!] \; e_3,$
   assuming $(\mathcal{E}[\![E_{seq1}]\!] \; e_3) = (\mathcal{E}[\![(\text{app (app deposit! 17) acct})]\!] \; e_3)$
                does not denote an error or divergence

$= \textit{with-value} \; (\mathcal{E}[\![(\text{app balance acct})]\!] \; e_3)$
   $(\lambda v_1 \, . \, \textit{with-value} \; (\mathcal{E}[\![\text{old}]\!] \; e_3) \; (\lambda v_2 \, . \, (\mathcal{O}[\![\text{-}]\!] \; [v_1, v_2]))),$
   using the specialization of prim to the two-argument case shown on page 284

$= \textit{with-value} \; (\mathcal{E}[\![(\text{app balance acct})]\!] \; e_3)$
   $(\lambda v_1 \, . \, \textit{with-value} \; (\mathcal{E}[\![(\text{app balance acct})]\!] \; e_2) \; (\lambda v_2 \, . \, (\mathcal{O}[\![\text{-}]\!] \; [v_1, v_2]))),$
   because $(\mathcal{E}[\![\text{old}]\!] \; e_3) = (\mathcal{E}[\![(\text{app balance acct})]\!] \; e_2)$

$= \textit{with-value} \; (\textit{val-to-comp} \; (Int \rightarrowtail Value \; i_{bal}))$
   $(\lambda v_1 \, . \, \textit{with-value} \; (\textit{val-to-comp} \; (Int \rightarrowtail Value \; i_{bal})) \; (\lambda v_2 \, . \, (\mathcal{O}[\![\text{-}]\!] \; [v_1, v_2]))),$
   where $(\mathcal{E}[\![(\text{app balance acct})]\!] \; e_3)$
        $= (\mathcal{E}[\![(\text{app balance acct})]\!] \; e_2)$
        $= (\textit{val-to-comp} \; (Int \rightarrowtail Value \; i_{bal}))$

$= (\mathcal{O}[\![\text{-}]\!] \; [(Int \rightarrowtail Value \; i_{bal}), (Int \rightarrowtail Value \; i_{bal})]))$

$= \textit{with-integer-val} \; (Int \rightarrowtail Value \; i_{bal})$
   $(\lambda i_1 \, . \, (\textit{with-integer-val} \; (Int \rightarrowtail Value \; i_{bal})$
        $(\lambda i_2 \, . \, (\textit{val-to-comp} \; (Int \rightarrowtail Value \; (i_1 -_{Int} i_2))))))$

$= (\textit{val-to-comp} \; (Int \rightarrowtail Value \; (i_{bal} -_{Int} i_{bal})))$

$= (\textit{val-to-comp} \; (Int \rightarrowtail Value \; 0))$

Figure 8.3   Denotational calculation showing that (app $E_{lam:ignore}$ #u) in the empty environment e_0 denotes the 0 computation.

putations that are expressible values. Figure 8.3 shows a calculation of the expressible value for the expression (app $E_{lam:ignore}$ #u) in the empty environment e_0. This calculation shows that the meaning of (app $E_{lam:ignore}$ #u) in e_0 is equivalent to the meaning of (prim - (app balance acct) old) in an environment e_3 in which old is bound to $(\mathcal{E}[\![(\text{app balance acct})]\!] \; e_2)$. The only difference between e_3 and e_2 is the binding for old, which isn't referenced in the expression (app balance acct), so $(\mathcal{E}[\![(\text{app balance acct})]\!] \; e_3)$ must be equal to $(\mathcal{E}[\![(\texttt{app balance acct})]\!]\ e_2)$. If we assume that these denote the integer computation $(val\text{-}to\text{-}comp\ (Int \rightarrowtail Value\ i_{bal}))$ for some integer i_{bal}, we conclude that the subtraction must yield the computation of the integer 0. In both the operational and denotational analyses, the fundamental insight is that (test-deposit!) returns the difference of the values of two occurrences of the expression (app balance acct), and these must necessarily be the same.

A language in which distinct occurrences of any expression always have the same meaning within a given naming context is said to be **referentially transparent**. Of course, the notion of "naming context" needs to be fully specified. Intuitively, two occurrences of an expression are in the same naming context if they share the same Stoy diagram — i.e., if every occurrence of a free identifier in the two expressions refers to a variable declared by the same variable declaration. Stateless languages, such as our mini-language FL and the real language HASKELL, are referentially transparent, while stateful languages are not.

Referential transparency is a property that we frequently use in mathematical reasoning in the form of "substituting equals for equals." But it is seriously at odds with the notions of state and time. State is predicated on the idea that observable properties of an object can change. But if we make the reasonable assumption that a property of an object can be accessed by applying a single-argument procedure to that object (as in (app balance acct) above), referential transparency dictates that all occurrences of such an expression within a given environment must denote the same value. Thus, the observable properties of an object cannot change. And if changes to the state of objects cannot be observed, how meaningful is it to talk about one action happening before or after another? We shall have more to say about referential transparency and state in Section 8.3.6.

Finally, suppose we actually try to write the definition of deposit! in FL. What kind of difficulties do we run into? Below is a skeleton for such a procedure:

```
(def deposit!
  (abs (amount account)
    (if (< amount 0)
        (sym failed)
        (begin E_increaseBalance
               (sym succeeded)))))
```

The body of deposit! returns the right value (one of the symbols failed or succeeded). But how do we write $E_{increaseBalance}$? By reasoning similar to that used above, no FL expression can possibly alter the state of the account. Obviously, we are missing something. Shortly, we will introduce constructs that allow us to fill in the blanks here, and we will explore how the semantics of FL needs to be changed to accommodate their introduction.

8.2   Simulating State in FL

FL is an extension to the lambda calculus, which is **computationally universal**
in the sense that any computation can be encoded in it. So FL must also be
computationally universal. Surely examples such as the bank account scenario
must be expressible within FL *somehow*, albeit not necessarily in a way that
corresponds to our intuitions about the physical world. We will now explore some
ways in which state can be simulated in FL. The purpose of this exploration is
to give us insight into the nature of state. Later, we will be able to apply what
we learn to the semantics for a stateful dialect of FL.

8.2.1   Iteration

The simulation of state in FL is exemplified by the handling of iteration. An
iteration is a computation that characterizes the state of a system in terms of
the values of a set of variables known as its **state variables**. The value of each
state variable in an iteration at time t is a function of the values of the state
variables at time $t - 1$.

As an example of an iteration, consider the problem of reversing the order of
cards in a deck of playing cards. A natural solution is to use two piles, called *old*
and *new*, where *old* is initially the original deck and *new* is an empty pile. Then,
one by one, cards can be moved from the old pile to the new pile until the old
pile is empty. At this point, the new pile contains the reversed deck of cards. In
this example the state variables are the (ordered) contents of the old and new
piles. These two variables completely characterize the state of the system. If a
person performing the reversal for some reason had to leave before completing
the task, someone else could take over as long as it was apparent which was the
old pile and which was the new.

It is straightforward to express iterations in FL. For example, the above
technique can be applied to list reversal as follows:

```
(def reverse
  (abs (elements) {E_abs:reverse}
    (letrec ((iterate
                (abs (old-pile new-pile) {E_abs:iterate}
                  (if (null? old-pile)
                      new-pile
                      (iterate (cdr old-pile)
                               (cons (car old-pile) new-pile)))))))
      (iterate elements (list)))))
```

In this case, the state variables are the parameters `old-pile` and `new-pile` of the local recursive procedure `iterate`. For example, here is the evaluation sequence of the reversal of a three-element list:

$$
\begin{aligned}
&(E_{abs:reverse}\ (\texttt{list 1 2 3})) \\
&\xRightarrow[CBV]{*} (E_{abs:iterate}\ (\texttt{list 1 2 3})\quad (\texttt{list}) \qquad\qquad) \\
&\xRightarrow[CBV]{*} (E_{abs:iterate}\ (\texttt{list 2 3})\quad\ (\texttt{list 1}) \qquad\ ) \\
&\xRightarrow[CBV]{*} (E_{abs:iterate}\ (\texttt{list 3})\quad\ \ (\texttt{list 2 1}) \quad\ ) \\
&\xRightarrow[CBV]{*} (E_{abs:iterate}\ (\texttt{list})\qquad (\texttt{list 3 2 1})) \\
&\xRightarrow[CBV]{*} (\texttt{list 3 2 1})
\end{aligned}
$$

We are using CBV instead of CBN here because we want to see the actual list values that are the arguments to $E_{abs:iterate}$ at each step, not the expressions that would produce those list values.

The above example suggests a general approach for expressing iterations in FL. State variables simply become the arguments to an iterating procedure, and updating the state variables is expressed by calling the iterating procedure on values computed from the previous values of the state variables.

Note carefully how an iteration manages to circumvent the constraints of referential transparency to represent state and time. The state at any point in time is represented by the values bound to formal parameters associated with a particular application of the iterating procedure. In the list-reversal example, the state variables correspond to the formal parameters `old-pile` and `new-pile`. The value of a particular variable named `old-pile` or `new-pile` never changes. However, each application of the `iterate` procedure effectively creates new variables that happen to be named by these same identifiers. So for each point in time t, there are distinct variables $\texttt{old-pile}_t$ and $\texttt{new-pile}_t$. State is encoded not as the changing value of a variable, but rather as the values of a sequence of immutable variables.

Events in time are ordered by the only means available for ordering in a stateless language: data dependency. If the value of E_1 is needed to compute E_2, then E_2 is said to have a **data dependency** on E_1. In the list reversal example, since $\texttt{old-pile}_t$ is bound to the value of (`cdr` $\texttt{old-pile}_{t-1}$), it has a data dependency on $\texttt{old-pile}_{t-1}$; $\texttt{new-pile}_t$ is dependent on both $\texttt{old-pile}_{t-1}$ and $\texttt{new-pile}_{t-1}$. Data dependencies can be interpreted as a kind of time: if E_2 depends on the result of E_1, it is natural to view the evaluation of E_1 as happening *before* the evaluation of E_2.

8.2.2   Single-Threaded Data Flow

Iteration is an instance of a general technique for simulating state in a stateless language. State can always be simulated by adding state variables both as arguments and return values to every procedure in a program whose body either accesses or changes the state variables. The state of the program upon entering a procedure is encoded in the values of the state-variable arguments, and the state of the program upon exiting a procedure is encoded in the values of the state variables returned as results. Because state is based on a notion of linearly ordered time, we must guarantee that the data dependencies among the state variables form a linear chain. State variables satisfying this constraint are said to be passed through the program in a **single-threaded** fashion.

From this perspective, the problem with the bank account procedures is that the state of the system is not appropriately threaded through calls to these procedures. Suppose the state of the banking system is modeled by an entity called a *bank state*. Then we can simulate state with the bank account procedures by extending each procedure to accept an additional bank state argument and to return a pair of its usual return value and a (potentially updated) bank state.

Suppose that every bank account bears a unique account number. Then we can represent a bank state as a list of pairs of an account number and the current balance of the account with that number. For example, the bank state ◁⟨*1729*, *200*⟩, ⟨*6821*, *17*⟩▷ indicates that account 1729 has a current balance of 200 dollars and account 6821 has a current balance of 17 dollars. We will allow the same account number to appear more than once in a bank state; in this case, the leftmost pair with a given account number indicates the current balance of that account. For example, in bank state ◁⟨*6821*, *52*⟩, ⟨*1729*, *200*⟩, ⟨*6821*, *17*⟩▷, account 6821 has 52 dollars.

In FL, we can define versions of the bank account procedures that single-thread the bank state through a computation. We shall prefix the names of these procedures with a *, pronounced "star," which stands for *single-threaded action routine*. Here is an implementation of the depositing procedure in this approach:

```
(def *deposit!
  (abs (amount account bank0)
    (if (< amount 0)
        (pair (sym failed) bank0)
        (let ((old&bank1 (*balance account bank0)))
          (let ((old (fst old&bank1))
                (bank1 (snd old&bank1)))
            (pair (sym succeeded)
                  (cons (pair account (+ old amount)) bank1))))))))
```

```
(def *test-deposit!
  (abs (bank0)
    (let ((acct&bank1 (*make-account 100 bank0)))
      (let ((acct (fst acct&bank1))
            (bank1 (snd acct&bank1)))
        (let ((old&bank2 (*balance acct bank1)))
          (let ((old (fst old&bank2))
                (bank2 (snd old&bank2)))
            (let ((status&bank3 (*deposit! 17 acct bank2)))
              (let ((status (fst status&bank3))
                    (bank3 (snd status&bank3)))
                (let ((new&bank4 (*balance acct bank3)))
                  (let ((new (fst new&bank4))
                        (bank4 (snd new&bank4)))
                    (pair (- new old) bank4)))))))))))
```

Figure 8.4 Definition of *test-deposit, a state-threading version of `test-deposit!`.

We assume that accounts are represented by their account numbers and that *balance is a state-threading version of the `balance` procedure. When it succeeds, *deposit! creates a new bank state by prepending a new account number/current balance pair to the old one, effectively overriding the old balance information. A bank state can be threaded through *make-account,[3] *balance, and *withdraw! in a similar fashion.

The `test-deposit!` procedure can be changed to a *test-deposit! procedure that takes a bank state and threads it through each of the bank account operations (Figure 8.4). Given any initial bank state, *test-deposit! will return a pair of 17 (the desired result) and an updated bank state. Using the single-threading idiom, we have been able to successfully model the bank account scenario in the stateless FL language.

Exercise 8.1 Provide definitions of *make-account, *balance, and *withdraw! in which a bank state is single-threaded through each procedure.

Exercise 8.2 It is only necessary to single-thread state information through procedures that may update the state. For procedures that only access the state without updating

---

[3] *make-account must also create a new, previously unused account number. Asking the caller to specify the number is an option, but it is better to include the next available account number as part of the bank state. If we don't care about wasting computational resources, we can compute a fresh account number from the current bank state representation by adding 1 to the largest account number in the bank state.

```
(def *test-deposit!
  (abs (bank0)
    (with-pair (*make-account 100 bank0)
      (abs (acct bank1)
        (with-pair (*balance acct bank1)
          (abs (old bank2)
            (with-pair (*deposit! 17 acct bank2)
              (abs (status bank3)
                (with-pair (*balance acct bank3)
                  (abs (new bank4)
                    (pair (- new old) bank4)))))))))))
```

Figure 8.5   Version of *test-deposit using with-pair.

it, it is sufficient to pass the state as an argument; such a procedure need not return the
state as its result. An example of such a procedure is *balance, which reads the balance
of a bank account but does not write it.

- Write a version of *balance that takes an account and a bank state and returns only
  the balance of the account.

- Modify the definitions of *deposit!, *withdraw!, and *test-deposit! to use the
  new version of *balance.

8.2.3   Monadic Style

State-threading details make the *test-deposit! code hard to read, but some
well-chosen abstractions can significantly increase readability. It helps to have a
with-pair procedure that decomposes a pair into its component parts and passes
these to a **receiver procedure**[4] that names them:

```
(def with-pair
  (abs (pair receiver)
    (receiver (fst pair) (snd pair))))
```

Using with-pair, *test-deposit! can be simplified as shown in Figure 8.5.

Readability can be increased even further by hiding the threading of the bank
state altogether. Suppose that we define an **action** as any procedure that takes
an initial state and returns a pair of a value and an updated state. In order to
perform an action, we apply the action to a state, which returns a value/state

---

[4]This use of the term "receiver" is different from the one used in object-oriented programming
in Section 7.3, where it referred to the object receiving a message.

```
(def after
  (abs (action1 val-to-action2)
    (abs (state0)
      (with-pair (action1 state0)
        (abs (val state1)
          ((val-to-action2 val) state1))))))

{Could simplify (abs (val state1) ((val-to-action2 val) state1))
 to (abs (val) (val-to-action2 val))
 or even to val-to-action2}

(def return
  (abs (val)
    (abs (state) (pair val state))))
```

Figure 8.6 The `after` and `return` procedures support a monadic style of threading state through a program.

pair. Such actions can be glued together by the `after` procedure in Figure 8.6, which takes two arguments — a first action and a procedure that maps the value from performing the first action to a second action — and returns a single action that performs the first action followed by the second. The figure also contains a `return` procedure that converts a value into an action. With these abstractions, the `*test-deposit!` procedure can be composed using four occurrences of `after` and one `return` (Figure 8.7). This version of `*test-deposit!` implicitly depends on the currying of FL procedures. For example, `*make-account` is a curried two-argument procedure that takes an initial balance and a bank state and returns a pair of an account and a new bank state. When supplied with only one argument, `*make-account` returns an action — i.e., a procedure that takes a bank state and returns a pair of an account and a new bank state.

The version of `*test-deposit!` using `after` and `return` illustrates a technique for threading state through a program that is known as **monadic style**. This style is based on gluing together state-threading components like the bank account actions in a way that hides the details of the "state plumbing." We have already seen monadic style in the denotational semantics of FL in Section 6.5. There, the *Comp* domain and functions like *with-value* are used to hide the messy details of propagating errors. In Section 8.3.4, we will extend the *Comp* domain to include a threaded "store." By changing the meanings of a few functions like *with-value*, it is possible to thread the state through the semantics without changing many of the existing valuation functions. This illustrates the power of the monadic style.

```
(def *test-deposit!
  (after (*make-account 100)
    (abs (acct)
      (after (*balance acct)
        (abs (old)
          (after (*deposit! 17 acct)
            (abs (status)
              (after (*balance acct)
                (abs (new)
                  (return (- new old)))))))))))
```

Figure 8.7   A version of `*test-deposit!` written in monadic style.

In stateless languages, monadic style is commonly used to express stateful computations. The awkwardness of using a combiner like `after` can be avoided by syntactic sugar. For example, HASKELL supports a `do` notation in which the bank account testing function can be written as:

```
testDeposit =
  do a <- makeAccount 100
     b1 <- balance a
     deposit 17 a
     b2 <- balance a
     return (b2 - b1)
```

As we shall see, this notation is not far from the way that stateful computations are expressed in stateful languages. A similar notation can be developed for FL (Exercise 8.3).

The name "monadic style" is derived from an algebraic structure, the **monad**, that captures the essence of manipulating information that is single-threaded through a computation. For more information on monads and how monadic style can be used to express stateful computations in stateless languages like HASKELL, see [PW93] and [Wad95].

Exercise 8.3 We can express HASKELL-like do notation in FL via desugaring. Define desugaring rules for a (do $((I\ E)^*)$ E) construct in FL that would permit the following definition of `*test-deposit!`:

```
(def *test-deposit!
  (do ((acct (*make-account 100))
       (old (*balance acct))
       (status (*deposit! 17 acct))
       (new (*balance acct)))
    (return (- new old))))
```

8.2.4 Imperative Programming

The bank account example demonstrates how it is possible to simulate state within a stateless language. However, even in monadic style, such simulations can be cumbersome. An alternative strategy is to develop a language paradigm that abstracts over the notion of state in such a way that the details of single-threading are automatically managed by the language. This is the essence of the **imperative programming paradigm**. In the imperative paradigm, all program state is conceptually bundled into a single entity called a **store** that is implicitly single-threaded through the program execution. Elements of the store are addressed by **locations**, unique identifiers that serve as unchanging names for time-dependent values. In the bank account example, bank states correspond to stores and account numbers correspond to locations.

The advantage of the imperative programming paradigm is that programs can be shorter and more modular when the details of single-threading are implicitly handled by the language. However, implicit single-threading has a downside: making explicit state variables implicit destroys referential transparency and thus makes programs harder to reason about.

The rest of this chapter explores how to model languages that exhibit state. We will see that the notions of store, location, and single-threading crop up in both operational and denotational descriptions of stateful languages.

8.3 Mutable Data: FLIC

8.3.1 Mutable Cells

> *A one-slot cons is called a cell,*
> *A two-slot cons makes pairs as well.*
> *But I would bet a coin of bronze*
> *There isn't any three-slot cons.*

> — Guy L. Steele Jr.

Data structures whose components can change over time are said to be **mutable**; otherwise they are said to be **immutable**. The simplest kind of mutable data is the **mutable cell**, a data structure characterized by a single time-dependent value called its **content**. A mutable cell corresponds to a mutable reference in ML, a one-slot mutable cons cell in LISP, or a pointer variable in languages like C and PASCAL. We will study mutable data in the context of FLIC, a version of **FL I**ncluding mutable **C**ells. We will use CBV as the default evaluation strategy for FLIC because, as we shall see later, CBV makes more sense than CBN in languages that support mutation.

$P \in \text{Prog} ::= (\texttt{flick}\ (I^*_{formal})\ E_{body})$ [Program]

$E \in \text{Exp} ::= \ldots$ FLK *expressions* $\ldots$

           | $(\texttt{cell}\ E_{initialContent})$ [CellCreation]

           | $(\texttt{begin}\ E_{sequent_1}\ E_{sequent_2})$ [SimpleSequencing]

$L \in \text{Lit} = \text{Lit}_{FLK}$

$O \in \text{Primop} = \text{Primop}_{FLK} \cup \{\texttt{\^{}}, \texttt{:=}, \texttt{cell=?}, \texttt{cell?}\}$

$I \in \text{Ident} = $ *FLK identifiers, but excluding all keywords*

Figure 8.8   An s-expression grammar for FLICK.

We begin by extending CBV FLK with features for supporting mutable cells. The modified kernel, which we shall call FLICK, has the syntax shown in Figure 8.8. We have already studied `begin` in Section 8.1. Here is an informal specification of the other extensions:

- (`cell` E) returns a new mutable cell whose initial content is the value of E. We shall write cells as *loc\$val*, where *loc* is a natural-number location that uniquely identifies the cell, and *val* is the content of the cell. In the following example, the expression allocates a cell with *loc* number 1729 and content 3:

  (cell (+ 1 2)) $\xrightarrow[\text{FLICK}]{}$ *1729\$3*

- (`prim` `^` E) fetches the content of the cell denoted by E. If the value of E is not a cell, this expression yields an error.

  (prim ^ (cell (+ 1 2))) $\xrightarrow[\text{FLICK}]{}$ *3*
  (prim ^ (+ 1 2)) $\xrightarrow[\text{FLICK}]{}$ *error:not-a-cell*

- (`prim` `:=` E_1 E_2) stores the value of E_2 in the cell denoted by E_1. If the value of E_1 is not a cell, this expression signals an error. Since every FLICK expression must have a value, we shall arbitrarily specify that the value returned by a cell assignment expression is the unit value.

  ```
  (let ((c (cell (+ 1 2))))
    (list (prim ^ c)
          (prim := c 4)
          (prim ^ c)))
  ```
  $\xrightarrow[\text{FLICK}]{}$ $\triangleleft 3, unit, 4 \triangleright$

Here and in other examples, we use standard FL sugar to enhance readability. Note that the answer depends critically on the fact that the subexpressions of `pair` (and therefore of `list`) are evaluated in left-to-right order.

- (prim cell=? E_1 E_2) returns *true* if E_1 and E_2 evaluate to the same cell (i.e., at the same location) and *false* otherwise. If at least one of E_1 or E_2 is not a cell, the expression signals an error.

  ```
  (let ((c1 (cell 1))
        (c2 (cell 1)))
    (let ((c3 c1))
      (list (prim cell=? c1 c1)
            (prim cell=? c1 c2)
            (prim cell=? c1 c3))))   FLICK→  ◁true, false, true▷
  ```

- (prim cell? E) returns *true* if E evaluates to a cell and *false* if it evaluates to some other value.

  ```
  (pair (prim cell? 0) (prim cell? (cell 0)))  FLICK→  ⟨false, true⟩
  ```

FLIC (Figure 8.9) is built on top of the kernel provided by FLICK by adding the syntactic sugar of FL as well as a few new constructs:

- Unlike the kernel `begin` construct, which has two sequents, the extended sequencing expression (begin E_1 ... E_n) can have an arbitrary number of sequents. This is the first time we've seen a sugar construct that has the same phrase tag as a kernel construct. This situation is common in practice. Of course, the desugaring for such a construct must guarantee that the general sugar form rewrites to the more restricted kernel form.

- Unlike the kernel `if` construct, which has both a then and an else expression, the sugar expression (if E_{test} E_{then}) omits the else expression when it is `#u`. This pattern is common in imperative programs — e.g., see the `while` desugaring.

- The looping construct (while E_{test} E_{body}) performs the body expression E_{body} expression every time the test expression E_{test} evaluates to *true* and returns *unit* the first time E_{body} evaluates to *false*. In languages like FLIC, traditional looping constructs like `while` loops can always be expressed via sugar involving local recursive procedures, but in languages without local recursive procedures, at least one looping construct must be a kernel construct.

- The `flic` construct permits top-level definitions and bindings for standard identifiers as in FL. The only difference from FL is that `^`, `:=`, `cell=?`, and `cell?` are new standard identifiers in FLIC.

8.3.2   Examples of Imperative Programming

The imperative programming paradigm is characterized by the use of side effects to perform computations. Because it is equipped with mutable cells, FLIC supports the imperative paradigm. In this section, we present a few FLIC programs that illustrate the imperative programming style.

Factorial

Here is an imperative version of an iterative factorial procedure written in FLIC:

```
(def (fact-imperative n)
  (let ((num (cell n))
        (ans (cell 1)))
    (begin (while (> (^ num) 0)
             (begin (:= ans (* (^ num) (^ ans)))
                    (:= num (- (^ num) 1))))
           (^ ans))))
```

The cells named `num` and `ans` serve as the state variables of the iteration. On each iteration of the `while` loop, the contents of these state variables are updated appropriately. The loop terminates when the content of `num` becomes zero, at which point the content of the `ans` cell is returned as the result of the `factorial` procedure.

It is instructive to compare the imperative version to a stateless version:

```
(def (fact-stateless n)
  (letrec ((loop (abs (num ans)
                   (if (= num 0)
                       ans
                       (loop (- num 1) (* num ans))))))
    (loop n 1)))
```

In the stateless version, every call to `loop` creates a new pair of variables named `num` and `ans`. In contrast, the imperative version shares one `num` and one `ans` variable across all the calls to the implicit looping procedure created by the `while` desugaring. The correctness of the imperative version depends crucially on the order of the assignment expressions `(:= ans ...)` and `(:= num ...)`. If these expressions are swapped, then the imperative version no longer computes the right answer. This bug is due purely to the time-based nature of the imperative paradigm; the stateless version does not exhibit the potential for this bug since

---

New Productions

$P \in \text{Prog} ::= $ `(flick` (I^*_{formal}) E_{body}`)`   [UnsugaredProgram]

        | `(flic` (I^*_{formal}) E_{body} $D^*_{definition}$`)` [SugaredProgram]

$D \in \text{Def} ::= \ldots \text{ as in FL} \ldots$

$E \in \text{Exp} ::= \ldots \text{ as in FL } and \text{ FLICK} \ldots$

        | `(begin` $E^*_{sequent}$`)`   [ExtendedSequencing]

        | `(if` E_{test} E_{then}`)`   [ElselessIf]

        | `(while` E_{test} E_{body}`)`   [WhileLoop]

$SX \in \text{SExp} ::= \ldots \text{ as in FL} \ldots$

Desugaring Rules

`(begin)` $\leadsto_{ds}$ `#u`

`(begin` E`)` $\leadsto_{ds}$ E

`(begin` E_1 E_2 E^*_{rest}`)` $\leadsto_{ds}$ `(begin` E_1 `(begin` E_2 E^*_{rest}`))`

`(if` E_{test} E_{then}`)` $\leadsto_{ds}$ `(if` E_{test} E_{then} `#u)`

`(while` E_{test} E_{body}`)` $\leadsto_{ds}$ `(letrec` $((I_{loop}$ $\{I_{loop}$ *is fresh*$\}$

                           `(abs ()`

                              `(if` E_{test} `(begin` E_{body} (I_{loop})`))))))`

                (I_{loop})`)`

The `flic` to `flick` desugaring is like the `fl` to `flk` desugaring except that the standard identifiers of FL are extended with `^`, `:=`, `cell=?`, and `cell?`.

The desugarings for constructs inherited from FL are as in FL.

Figure 8.9 FLIC grammar and sugar.

all expressions have time-independent values. This illustrates one of the dangers of imperative programming: since many dependencies are implicit rather than explicit, subtle bugs are more likely, and they are harder to locate.

Bank Accounts

Figure 8.10 shows how the bank account procedures introduced in Section 8.1 can be expressed in FLIC using mutable cells. Each account is represented by a distinct cell, and the bank account operations examine and change the content of this cell. Here are some sample bank account manipulations:

```
(def (make-account amount)
  (if (< amount 0)
      (sym failed)
      (cell amount)))
(def (balance account) (^ account))
(def (deposit! amount account)
  (if (< amount 0)
      (sym failed)
      (begin (:= account (+ amount (^ account)))
             (sym succeeded))))
(def (withdraw! amount account)
  (let ((bal (^ account)))
    (if (scor (< amount 0) (> amount bal))
        (sym failed)
        (begin (:= account (- bal amount))
               (sym succeeded)))))
```

Figure 8.10   Bank account procedures written in FLIC.

```
(def a (make-account 100))
(def b (make-account 100))
(pair (balance a) (balance b))   FLIC→  ⟨100, 100⟩

(deposit! 17 b)   FLIC→  'succeeded'

(pair (balance a) (balance b))   FLIC→  ⟨100, 117⟩

(list (deposit! 23 a) (deposit! -23 b)
      (withdraw! 120 a) (withdraw! 120 b))
  FLIC→  ⊲'succeeded', 'failed', 'succeeded', 'failed'⊳

(pair (balance a) (balance b))   FLIC→  ⟨3, 117⟩
```

While it is natural to represent accounts directly as cells, it is also insecure to do so. For example, every account should maintain the invariant that the balance never slips below zero. But if an account is just a cell, then it is possible to violate this invariant by using := directly to store a negative number into an account. It is also possible to use ^ and := to add and remove money from accounts without calling deposit! or withdraw!, thus violating the abstraction barrier provided by these procedures.

In general, it is wise to package up mutable data in a way that guarantees that important invariants cannot be violated (either accidentally or maliciously) by some other part of a software system. First-class procedures provide an elegant means of encapsulating state so that it can be manipulated only in constrained ways. Figure 8.11 presents an alternative implementation, inspired by

```
(def (make-account amount)
  (if (< amount 0)
      (sym failed)
      (let ((account (cell amount)))
        (abs (message)
          (cond ((sym=? message (sym balance))
                 (^ account))
                ((sym=? message (sym deposit!))
                 (abs (amount)
                   (if (< amount 0)
                       (sym failed)
                       (begin (:= account (+ amount (^ account)))
                              (sym succeeded)))))
                ((sym=? message (sym withdraw!))
                 (abs (amount)
                   (let ((bal (^ account)))
                     (if (scor (< amount 0) (> amount bal))
                         (sym failed)
                         (begin (:= account (- bal amount))
                                (sym succeeded)))))))))))
(def (balance account) (account (sym balance)))
(def (deposit! amount account) ((account (sym deposit!)) amount))
(def (withdraw! amount account) ((account (sym withdraw!)) amount))
```

Figure 8.11 A message-passing implementation of bank accounts.

the message-sending metaphor of object-oriented programming, in which a bank account is represented as a procedure that dispatches on a message. The advantage to this approach is that the message-passing account procedure provides a security wall for accessing and updating the account balance. In particular, this implementation guarantees that the balance can never fall below zero. In Chapter 14, we will study several other mechanisms for guaranteeing the safety of data abstractions.

Object-oriented programming languages are based on the ideas of message passing, inheritance of behavior, and encapsulation of behavior and state. We saw how to build a powerful object-oriented language without state in Section 7.3. However, the encapsulation of state is the basis for much of the appeal of object-oriented languages: it is hard to imagine good real-world simulations without it. Adding mutable cells (or the mutable variables of Section 8.4) to HOOK/HOOPLA is a very simple matter, and results in a simple and powerful object-oriented language.

Tree Decoration

As a final example of imperative programming, we present in Figure 8.12 a FLIC procedure `decorate` for "decorating" a "tree" with "ornaments." For the purposes of this procedure, a tree is recursively defined as either (1) a leaf, which we defined as any FLIC value that is not the unit value or a pair, or (2) a list of trees. The "ornaments" used for decorating a tree are any FLIC values collected together in a nonempty list. Given a tree and an ornament list, the tree decoration procedure returns a new tree that has the same shape as the original tree, but in which every original leaf has been replaced by an element of the ornament list. As each leaf is encountered in a left-to-right, depth-first traversal of the tree, the next ornament in the ornament list becomes the corresponding leaf of the new tree. If there are still more leaves to process when the end of the ornament list is reached, the decoration process should continue starting with the original ornament list. For example:

```
(def sample-tree (list 17
                       (list #t
                             (list (sym foo) (lam x x)))
                       (sym bar)))
```

sample-tree $\xrightarrow[\text{FLIC}]{}$ $\triangleleft 17, \triangleleft true, \triangleleft 'foo', procedure \triangleright \triangleright, 'bar' \triangleright$

(decorate sample-tree (list 1 2 3 4 5 6 7)) $\xrightarrow[\text{FLIC}]{}$ $\triangleleft 1, \triangleleft 2, \triangleleft 3, 4 \triangleright \triangleright, 5 \triangleright$

(decorate sample-tree (list 1 2 3)) $\xrightarrow[\text{FLIC}]{}$ $\triangleleft 1, \triangleleft 2, \triangleleft 3, 1 \triangleright \triangleright, 2 \triangleright$

(decorate sample-tree (list 1)) $\xrightarrow[\text{FLIC}]{}$ $\triangleleft 1, \triangleleft 1, \triangleleft 1, 1 \triangleright \triangleright, 1 \triangleright$

In an imperative setting, the `decorate` procedure is easy to implement. The as-yet-unprocessed ornaments are stored in a mutable cell `orns`, and the `next-ornament!` procedure is used to return the next ornament from this list, cycling back to the front of the list if necessary. The `walk` procedure copies the tree structure in a left-to-right, depth-first walk, invoking `next-ornament!` every time a leaf is encountered.

Of course, the `decorate` procedure can also be defined in a stateless language like FL by using the single-threading idiom studied (Exercise 8.4). However, threading the additional state information can make the procedure harder to read and write. Indeed, a key benefit of stateful languages is that they abstract over this single-threading idiom and hide its messy details from the programmer.

Exercise 8.4 Write a version of the `decorate` procedure in FL.

```
(def (decorate tree ornaments)
  (if (null? ornaments)
      (error no-ornaments)
      (let ((orns (cell ornaments)))
        (letrec
            ((leaf? (abs (t) (not (scor (unit? t) (pair? t)))))
             (next-ornament! (abs ()
                                  (let ((rest (if (null? (^ orns))
                                                  ornaments
                                                  (^ orns))))
                                    (begin (:= orns (cdr rest))
                                           (car rest)))))
             (walk (abs (tr)
                        (cond ((null? tr) tr)
                              ((leaf? tr) (next-ornament!))
                              (else (cons (walk (car tr))
                                          (walk (cdr tr))))))))
          (walk tree)))))
```

Figure 8.12 A FLIC procedure for decorating a "tree" with "ornaments."

8.3.3 An Operational Semantics for FLICK

In order to model the state exhibited by FLICK, we will use the notions of a **location** and a **store** introduced in Section 8.2.4. A location is a unique identifier for a mutable entity, and a store is a structure that associates each location with its value at a particular point in time. There are many ways to represent locations and stores. In our operational treatment, we will represent locations as natural-number literals in the domain Location and stores as elements of a sequence domain Store over assignments (elements of Assignment), which are pairs of locations and value expressions (see Figure 8.13).

The function $get :$ Location $\rightarrow$ Store $\rightharpoonup$ ValueExp finds the first value associated with a location in a store. It is a partial function that is undefined in the case where no assignment in the store mentions the given location. For example, given the store $S_0 = [\langle 1, (\mathtt{sym\ foo})\rangle, \langle 0, \mathtt{\#t}\rangle]$, here are some sample invocations of get:

$(get\ 0\ S_0) = \mathtt{\#t}$
$(get\ 1\ S_0) = (\mathtt{sym\ foo})$
$(get\ 2\ S_0) = undefined$
$(get\ 0\ (\langle 0, 17\rangle . S_0)) = 17$
$(get\ 2\ (\langle 2, (\mathtt{lam\ x\ x})\rangle . S_0)) = (\mathtt{lam\ x\ x})$

Domains

Syntactic domains from FLICK *grammar (Figure 8.8 on page 398) except for Exp,*
which is extended as follows:

$E \in \text{Exp}_{SOS} ::= \ \dots \ as \ in \ \text{FLICK} \ \dots \ | \ (\texttt{*cell*} \ LC)$

$IE \in \text{InputExp} ::= \ L \ | \ (\texttt{pair} \ IE_{fst} \ IE_{snd})$

$V \in \text{ValueExp} ::= \ L \ | \ (\texttt{lam} \ I_{formal} \ E_{body}) \ | \ (\texttt{pair} \ V_{fst} \ V_{snd}) \ | \ (\texttt{*cell*} \ LC)$

$A \in \text{AnsExp} ::= \ L \ | \ \texttt{procans} \ | \ \texttt{pairans} \ | \ \texttt{cellans}$

$NT \in \text{NatLit} \ = \ \{0, 1, 2, \dots\}$

$LC \in \text{Location} \ = \ \text{NatLit}$

$Z \in \text{Assignment} \ = \ \text{Location} \times \text{ValueExp}$

$S \in \text{Store} \ = \ \text{Assignment*}$

Auxiliary Function

$get : \text{Location} \to \text{Store} \rightharpoonup \text{ValueExp}$

$(get \ LC \ (\langle LC, V \rangle . S)) \ = \ V$

$(get \ LC_1 \ (\langle LC_2, V \rangle . S)) \ = \ (get \ LC_1 \ S), \text{ where } LC_1 \neq_{\text{Location}} LC_2$

SOS

The FLICK SOS is defined by the tuple $\langle CF, \Rightarrow, FC, IF, OF \rangle$, where:

$CF \ = \ \text{Exp}_{SOS} \times \text{Store}$

$\Rightarrow$ is the deterministic evaluation relation defined in Figure 8.14.

$FC \ = \ \text{ValueExp} \times \text{Store}$

$IF : (\text{Prog} \times \text{InputExp*}) \to CF$

$IF \ \langle (\texttt{flick} \ (I_1 \ \dots \ I_n) \ E_{body}), [IE_1, \dots, IE_k] \rangle$
$\ \ \ = \langle \textbf{if} \ n = k \ \textbf{then} \ ([IE_i/I_i]_{i=1}^{n}) E_{body}$
$\ \ \ \ \ \ \ \ \ \ \textbf{else} \ (\texttt{error wrong-number-of-args}) \ \textbf{end}, \ [\ ]_{\text{Assignment}} \rangle$

$OF : FC \to \text{AnsExp}$

$OF \ \langle (\texttt{lam} \ I \ E), \ S \rangle \ = \ \texttt{procans}$

$OF \ \langle (\texttt{pair} \ V_1 \ V_2), \ S \rangle \ = \ \texttt{pairans}$

$OF \ \langle (\texttt{*cell*} \ LC), \ S \rangle \ = \ \texttt{cellans}$

$OF \ \langle L, \ S \rangle \ = \ L$

Behavior

$beh_{det} : (\text{Prog} \times \text{InputExp*}) \to \text{Outcome}$

$beh_{det} \ \langle P, IE^* \rangle \ = \ \begin{cases} (\text{AnsExp} \rightharpoonup \text{Outcome} \ (OF \ cf_{fin})) & \text{if } cf_{init} \overset{*}{\Rightarrow} cf_{fin} \in FC \\ \texttt{stuck} & \text{if } cf_{init} \overset{*}{\Rightarrow} cf_{fin} \not\Rightarrow \\ & \quad \text{and } cf_{fin} \notin FC \\ \infty & \text{if } cf_{init} \overset{\infty}{\Rightarrow} \end{cases}$

$\ \ \ \ \ \ \text{where } cf_{init} = (IF \ \langle P, IE^* \rangle)$

Figure 8.13   An SOS for FLICK.

An SOS for FLICK is specified in Figure 8.13. It is similar to the SOS for CBV FL except for a few key differences:

- The expressions Exp_{SOS} that may arise during an operational execution of a FLICK program are defined by the expression grammar of FLICK extended with the new construct (*cell* LC). This represents the cell value associated with location LC. The *cell* construct may not appear in a user program, but can be introduced into a configuration during the execution of a program. The value expressions ValueExp are those of CBV FLK extended with these new cell values. The answer expressions AnsExp are those of FL extended with a new token, cellans, that represents an answer that is a cell value.

- Unlike FL, but like POSTFIX, the FLICK SOS has configurations that include both a code component (an expression in Exp_{SOS}) and a nontrivial context component (a store in Store) that represents the current state of the computation. The input function (IF) and output function (OF) are those from FLK SOS, suitably modified to handle the store component. A computation begins with an initial configuration consisting of the initial program body (into which program arguments have been substituted) and an empty store, $[]_{\text{Assignment}}$. A computation runs until the code component becomes a value expression or the configuration becomes stuck. At this point, an answer representing the final value is returned as the result of the FLICK program.

- The evaluation relation $\Rightarrow$ (defined in Figure 8.14 and discussed in more detail below) maps one stateful configuration to another. This allows evaluation rules to refer to the store component of a configuration as well as to the code component.

The definition of the evaluation relation in Figure 8.14 uses two distinct reduction relations to represent basic computational steps. One is the stateless reduction relation $\rightsquigarrow \in (\text{Exp}_{SOS} \times \text{Exp}_{SOS})$ with which we are already familiar. But for the three FLICK constructs — cell, ^, and := — that need to manipulate the store, a stateful reduction relation $\overset{s}{\rightsquigarrow} \in (CF \times CF)$ is needed. The [cell] stateful reduction rule allocates a new location, LC_{fresh}, which does not appear in the store, and extends the store with a new association between LC_{fresh} and the given value. The result of this operation is a *cell* value that maintains an index into the store. The [^] rule uses *get* to extract the value stored at the location specified by the *cell* value. The [:=] rule returns the unit value but also prepends a new location/value pair to the store to reflect the assignment.

The definition of the stateful reduction relation guarantees that the store is single-threaded through a program execution. Each stateful reduction step $\overset{s}{\leadsto}$ either adds a new assignment to the front of the store (in the [cell] and [:=] rules) or leaves the store unchanged (in all other rules). The evaluation relation inherits this property from the stateful reduction relation. So we can think of an executing program as having a single global store consisting of a sequence of assignments that only grows over time.

The single-threaded nature of the store is important for reasoning about properties of state-based programs. For example, even though *get* is only a partial function, an expression of the form (^ (*cell* LC)) can never be stuck. The location LC must have been allocated in the store earlier in the computation by a cell expression, and, because stores only grow over time, LC must still be a valid index into the store. The single-threaded nature of the store is also is essential for implementing stores in terms of physical computer memory devices that have addressable slots whose contents can change over time. Some interesting programming language constructs such as backtracking (Exercise 8.14 on page 422) and transactions (Exercise 8.15 on page 422) violate the single-threaded property of the store by allowing a computation to save a store and later reinstall it. Such constructs are very powerful, but can be challenging to implement efficiently.

We have chosen to represent stores as explicit sequences of assignments, but other representations are certainly possible (e.g., representing stores as functions that map locations to values). In our approach, the number of assignments in a store is equal to the number of cell and := operations performed by the program. An actual implementation based on such a strategy would be disastrously inefficient: the size of the store would grow throughout the computation, and cell references would take time linear in the size of the growing store. But our goal here is to give a simple semantics for stores, not to implement them efficiently. Any reasonable implementation of FLICK would represent stores in a way that takes advantage of the state-based nature of addressable memory in physical computers.

Since constructs other than cell, ^, and := do not access or update the store, any stateless reduction $E \leadsto E'$ can be viewed as a stateful reduction $\langle E,\ S \rangle \overset{s}{\leadsto} \langle E',\ S \rangle$ that leaves an arbitrary store S unchanged. An evaluation step is the result of performing a stateful reduction step in any evaluation context. That is, for any evaluation context $\mathbb{E}$ and any stateful reduction $\langle E,\ S \rangle \overset{s}{\leadsto} \langle E',\ S' \rangle$, we consider $\langle \mathbb{E}\{E\},\ S \rangle \Rightarrow \langle \mathbb{E}\{E'\},\ S' \rangle$ to be a valid evaluation step.

The evaluation contexts of FLICK are those of CBV FLK extended with new contexts for begin, cell, and rec. The stateless reduction rules for FLICK are those of CBV FLK extended with rules for begin, rec, and the primitive operators cell=? and cell?.

Stateless Reduction Relation ($\rightsquigarrow$)

  $\vdots$ *reduction rules for CBV FLK except* [rec]

(begin V E) $\rightsquigarrow$ E	[begin]
(rec I V) $\rightsquigarrow$ [(rec I V)/I]V	[CBV-rec]
(prim cell=? (*cell* LC) (*cell* LC)) $\rightsquigarrow$ #t	[cell=?-T]
(prim cell=? (*cell* LC_1) (*cell* LC_2)) $\rightsquigarrow$ #f,	[cell=?-F]
where $LC_1 \neq_{\text{Location}} LC_2$	
(prim cell? (*cell* LC)) $\rightsquigarrow$ #t	[cell?-T]
(prim cell? V) $\rightsquigarrow$ #f , where $V \neq$ (*cell* LC)	[cell?-F]

Stateful Reduction Relation ($\overset{s}{\rightsquigarrow}$)

$\langle$(cell V), $S\rangle \overset{s}{\rightsquigarrow} \langle$(*cell* LC_{fresh}), $\langle\langle LC_{fresh}, V\rangle . S\rangle\rangle$,	[cell]
where LC_{fresh} is a location that does not appear in S.	
$\langle$(prim ^ (*cell* LC)), $S\rangle \overset{s}{\rightsquigarrow} \langle V$, $S\rangle$, where $(get\ LC\ S) = V$	[^]
$\langle$(prim := (*cell* LC) V), $S\rangle \overset{s}{\rightsquigarrow} \langle$#u, $\langle LC, V\rangle . S\rangle$	[:=]
$\langle E$, $S\rangle \overset{s}{\rightsquigarrow} \langle E'$, $S\rangle$, where $E \rightsquigarrow E'$ via [*label*]	[*label*]

Evaluation Contexts

$\mathbb{E} \in \text{EvalContext} ::= \dots$ *as in CBV* FLK $\dots$
         | (rec I $\mathbb{E}$) | (cell $\mathbb{E}$) | (begin $\mathbb{E}$ E)

Evaluation Relation ($\Rightarrow$)

$\langle\mathbb{E}\{E\}$, $S\rangle \Rightarrow \langle\mathbb{E}\{E'\}$, $S'\rangle$, where $\langle E$, $S\rangle \overset{s}{\rightsquigarrow} \langle E'$, $S'\rangle$

Figure 8.14 The FLICK evaluation relation.

The reason for the new rec reduction rule and evaluation context is that handling recursion in a CBV language is a bit tricky in the presence of side effects. The basic problem is illustrated by the following FLIC example:

```
(let ((counter (cell 0)))
  (pair ((rec fact
              (begin (:= counter (+ (^ counter) 1))
                     (abs (n)
                       (if (= n 0)
                           1
                           (* n (fact (- n 1)))))))
         5)
        (^ counter)))
```

The value computed by the `rec` expression is a factorial procedure, so the value of the first component of the pair returned by the above expression should be 120. But for understanding CBV `rec` in the presence of state, we're more interested in the value of the second component of the pair. This value tells us how many times the `counter` cell is incremented during the evaluation of the `rec` expression. Presumably, this value should be 1, since intuitively the `begin` expression defining `fact` need be evaluated only once. However, if the CBN rule (`rec` I E) $\rightsquigarrow$ [(`rec` I E)/I]E were used, then the second component of the pair would be 6 because the `begin` expression that is the body of the `rec` would be copied in each unwinding and would be evaluated six times.

To avoid this behavior, the [CBV-`rec`] rule unwinds the `rec` only when the body is a value. The evaluation context (`rec` I $\mathbb{E}$) allows the `rec` body to be evaluated to a member of ValueExp so that the [CBV-`rec`] rule will be enabled. This means that any side effects encountered during the evaluation of the `rec` body are performed only once. In a CBV semantics, the rewriting of the `rec` body will terminate in a non-stuck state only when all uses of the formal parameter introduced by `rec` that appear in the body are "shielded" from immediate evaluation by a `lam`. For example, (`rec a a`) is stuck (because `a` is not a value expression), but (`rec a (lam x a)`) evaluates to a procedure that returns itself when called on any argument.

As a simple example of the FLICK SOS, consider the operational evaluation of the expression (`app` E_{lam} (`cell 3`)) where E_{lam} is:

```
(lam c (begin (prim := c (prim + 1 (prim ^ c)))
              (prim ^ c)))
```

Figure 8.15 shows the transition sequence associated with this expression. Note how the location 0 in the cell value (`*cell* 0`) serves as an unchanging index into the time-dependent store.

Exercise 8.5 The `begin` construct need not be primitive in FLICK. A desugaring of `begin` into other FLICK constructs must take advantage of the fact that the only notion of time in FL has to do with data dependency. That is, the only thing that forces an expression to be evaluated is that its value is used in the evaluation of another expression. This suggests the following desugaring for `begin` into other FLICK expressions.

(`begin` E_1 E_2) $\rightsquigarrow_{ds}$ (`app` (`lam` (I_{ignore}) E_2) E_1) {I_{ignore} *is fresh*}

a. The desugaring for `begin` given above uses constructs only from FLK, which does not support state. Is it possible to determine whether `begin` actually works as advertised (i.e., evaluates E_1 before E_2) in a stateless language like FL? Explain your answer, using examples where appropriate.

```
⟨(app E_lam (cell 3)), []⟩
⇒_[cell]    ⟨(app E_lam (*cell* 0)), [⟨0,3⟩]⟩
⇒_[β-value] ⟨(begin (prim := (*cell* 0) (prim + 1 (prim ^ (*cell* 0))))
                    (prim ^ (*cell* 0))),
             [⟨0,3⟩]⟩
⇒_[^]       ⟨(begin (prim := (*cell* 0) (prim + 1 3))
                    (prim ^ (*cell* 0))),
             [⟨0,3⟩]⟩
⇒_[+]       ⟨(begin (prim := (*cell* 0) 4)
                    (prim ^ (*cell* 0))),
             [⟨0,3⟩]⟩
⇒_[:=]      ⟨(begin #u (prim ^ (*cell* 0))), [⟨0,4⟩,⟨0,3⟩]⟩
⇒_[begin]   ⟨(prim ^ (*cell* 0)), [⟨0,4⟩,⟨0,3⟩]⟩
⇒_[^]       ⟨4, [⟨0,4⟩,⟨0,3⟩]⟩
```

Figure 8.15 Operational evaluation of a sample FLICK expression.

b. Explain why the above desugaring would not work for a CBN version of FLICK.

c. Write a desugaring for `begin` in CBV FLICK that does not require any condition involving the free variables of E_1 or E_2. (Hint: use thunks!)

d. Is it possible to write a desugaring for `begin` that works in both CBV and CBN FLICK ? If so, give the desugaring; if not, explain why not.

8.3.4   A Denotational Semantics for FLICK

Now we'll study the semantics of FLICK from the denotational perspective. As in the operational approach, notions of location and store will be used to model state. The notion of computation will be modified so that stores flow through a computation in a single-threaded fashion. The power of the computation abstraction will be illustrated by the fact that only those constructs that explicitly refer to the store need new valuation clauses; other constructs are described by their (unmodified) FLK valuation clauses.

Stores

The denotational treatment of stores and locations is summarized in Figure 8.16. Locations are represented as natural numbers and stores are represented as functions that map locations to elements of the *AssignedVal* domain. Stores do not map locations directly to values because it is necessary to encode the fact that not

$s \in Store = Location \rightarrow AssignedVal$

$l \in Location = Nat$

$\alpha \in AssignedVal = (Storable + Unassigned)_{\perp}$

$\sigma \in Storable = \text{language dependent} \qquad ; = Value \text{ in CBV}$

$\qquad Unassigned = \{\text{unassigned}\}$

$\text{next-location} : Location \rightarrow Location = \lambda l \,.\, (l +_{Nat} 1)$

$\text{empty-store} : Store = \lambda l \,.\, (Unassigned \rightarrowtail AssignedVal \text{ unassigned})$

$\text{fetch} : Location \rightarrow Store \rightarrow AssignedVal = \lambda ls \,.\, (s\ l)$

$\text{assign} : Location \rightarrow Storable \rightarrow Store \rightarrow Store$
$= \lambda l_1 \sigma s \,.\, \lambda l_2 \,.\, \textbf{if } l_1 =_{Location} l_2$
$\qquad\qquad\qquad \textbf{then } (Storable \rightarrowtail AssignedVal\ \sigma)$
$\qquad\qquad\qquad \textbf{else } (\text{fetch } l_2\ s)$
$\qquad\qquad\qquad \textbf{end}$

$\text{fresh-loc} : Store \rightarrow Location = \lambda s \,.\, (\text{first-fresh } s\ 0)$

$\text{first-fresh} : Store \rightarrow Location \rightarrow Location$
$= \lambda sl \,.\, \textbf{match } (\text{fetch } l\ s)$
$\qquad\quad \triangleright (Unassigned \rightarrowtail AssignedVal \text{ unassigned}) \ [\!] \ l$
$\qquad\quad \triangleright \textbf{else } (\text{first-fresh } s\ (\text{next-location } l))$
$\qquad\quad \textbf{end}$

Figure 8.16   Denotational treatment of locations and stores.

all locations have values assigned to them. The distinguished element *unassigned* in the lifted sum domain *AssignedVal* is used to indicate that a location is unassigned. *unassigned* serves the same purpose for stores that *unbound* serves for environments.

The domain *Storable* of storable entities varies from language to language. In FLICK, which is a CBV language, *Storable* = *Value*, but a CBN version of FLICK would have *Storable* = *Comp*. In both CBV and CBN FLICK, it happens that *Storable* = *Nameable*, but this need not be the case in general. For example, in PASCAL, procedures can be named and (with certain restrictions) passed as arguments, but they may not be assigned to variables or stored as the components of data structures.

There are several auxiliary functions for manipulating stores. *fetch* and *assign* are functions on stores that are reminiscent of *lookup* and *extend* on environments. The purpose of *fresh-loc* is to return an unassigned location from the given store. Since locations are natural numbers, one way of doing this is by scanning the store starting with location 0 and incrementing the location until an unassigned location is found. We assume an unbounded store, so that *fresh-loc* never fails to return a fresh location. To model a bounded store (which would be more realistic), *fresh-loc* could be modified to return an indication that the attempt to find a fresh location failed in some cases.

Exercise 8.6 Mima Rhee doesn't like the functional representation of the *Store* domain and decides to experiment with another representation. In Mima's representation, a store is a pair of (1) a natural number n that is the next free location and (2) a length-n sequence of storable values such that the value at location k is stored at index $(n - k)$ in the sequence. Recall that sequence elements are indexed starting at 1 and can be retrieved via the *nth* function defined on page 1183.

a. Give definitions of the *Store* domain, *empty-store*, *fetch*, *assign*, and *fresh-loc* for Mima's representation.

b. In what ways is Mima's representation closer than the functional representation to traditional efficient representations of stores as indexable arrays in physical computer memory? In what ways does it still fall short?

Computations

In all the stateless variants of FL we studied, a computation was just an expressible value. But in the presence of state, a computation needs to embody the single-threaded nature of stores. The following domain definition captures this idea:

$$c \in \mathit{Comp} \; = \; \mathit{Store} \rightarrow (\mathit{Expressible} \times \mathit{Store})$$

Here, a computation accepts an initial store and returns two entities:

• The expressible value computed by the computation.

• A final store that reflects all the allocations and assignments performed by the computation.

When composing two computations, single-threadedness can be achieved by supplying the final store of the first computation as the initial store of the second. This definition of stateful computations is very similar to the notion of a monadic action studied in Section 8.2.3.

It is not difficult to show that the new *Comp* domain is pointed (Exercise 8.7). This means that it is possible to find fixed points over computations, a fact that will be important when we discuss the semantics of `rec`.

Recall that numerous auxiliary functions are defined as part of the computation abstraction. Figure 8.17 shows the definitions of these functions for the

$c \in Comp = Store \rightarrow (Expressible \times Store)$
$x \in Expressible = (Value + Error)_\perp$
$\quad Error = \text{SymLit}$
$v \in Value = Unit + Bool + Int + Sym + Pair + Proc + Location$

$expr\text{-}to\text{-}comp : Expressible \rightarrow Comp = \lambda x \,.\, \lambda s \,.\, \langle x, s \rangle$

$val\text{-}to\text{-}comp : Value \rightarrow Comp = \lambda v \,.\, (expr\text{-}to\text{-}comp \; (Value \rightarrowtail Expressible \; v))$

$err\text{-}to\text{-}comp : Error \rightarrow Comp = \lambda Y \,.\, (expr\text{-}to\text{-}comp \; (Error \rightarrowtail Expressible \; Y))$

$with\text{-}value : Comp \rightarrow (Value \rightarrow Comp) \rightarrow Comp$
$= \lambda cf \,.\, \lambda s_1 \,.\, \textbf{match} \, (c \; s_1)$
$\qquad\qquad \triangleright \, \langle (Value \rightarrowtail Expressible \; v), s_2 \rangle \; [\![\; (f \; v \; s_2)$
$\qquad\qquad \triangleright \, \langle x_{err}, s_2 \rangle \; [\![\; \langle x_{err}, s_2 \rangle \; ; \; x_{err} \text{ must be } (Error \rightarrowtail Expressible \; Y)$
$\qquad\qquad \textbf{end}$

$with\text{-}location\text{-}val : Value \rightarrow (Location \rightarrow Comp) \rightarrow Comp$
$= \lambda vf \,.\, \textbf{match} \, v$
$\qquad\qquad \triangleright \, (Location \rightarrowtail Value \; l) \; [\![\; (f \; l)$
$\qquad\qquad \triangleright \, \textbf{else} \, (err\text{-}to\text{-}comp \; \texttt{not-a-location})$
$\qquad\qquad \textbf{end}$

with-values, *with-boolean-val*, *with-boolean-comp*, etc. are all written in terms of *with-value* and *err-to-comp*, so their definitions are unchanged from Figure 6.26 on page 281.

Figure 8.17   Store-based implementation of the computation abstraction.

store-based version of *Comp*. *val-to-comp* converts a value into a computation by threading an unchanged store around the result of injecting the value into an expressible value. *err-to-comp* converts an error message to a computation in a similar fashion. These functions are similar to the monadic **return** function studied in Section 8.2.3.

The main means of gluing computations together is *with-value*. It takes a computation c and a function f that maps a value to a computation c' and returns the computation that results from composing c and c'. Like the action-combining **after** procedure in Section 8.2.3, the main purpose of *with-value* is to support the monadic style of threading state by handling the "plumbing" between computations. The value argument to f is the (non-error) expressible value produced by c and the initial store of c' is the final store of c. In the case where c produces an error rather than a value, f is ignored and the resulting computation is equivalent to c. Unwinding the type of f

$$Value \rightarrow Comp = Value \rightarrow Store \rightarrow (Expressible \times Store)$$

$allocating : Storable \rightarrow (Location \rightarrow Comp) \rightarrow Comp$
$= \lambda \sigma f . \lambda s . (f (fresh\text{-}loc\ s) (assign (fresh\text{-}loc\ s)\ \sigma\ s))$

$fetching : Location \rightarrow (Storable \rightarrow Comp) \rightarrow Comp$
$= \lambda l f . \lambda s .$ **match** $(fetch\ l\ s)$
$\quad\quad\quad \triangleright (Storable \rightarrowtail AssignedVal\ \sigma) \parallel (f\ \sigma\ s)$
$\quad\quad\quad \triangleright$ **else** $(err\text{-}to\text{-}comp\ \texttt{unassigned-location}\ s)$
$\quad\quad\quad$ **end**

$update : Location \rightarrow Storable \rightarrow Comp$
$= \lambda l \sigma . \lambda s . (val\text{-}to\text{-}comp\ unit\ (assign\ l\ \sigma\ s))$

$sequence : Comp \rightarrow Comp \rightarrow Comp$
$= \lambda c_1 c_2 . (with\text{-}value\ c_1\ (\lambda v . c_2))$

Figure 8.18 Auxiliary functions for store-based computations.

makes it clear that f can be viewed as a function that maps two (curried) arguments (a value and a store) to two (paired) results (an expressible value and a store).

Other *with-* functions we have seen before (in Figure 6.26 on page 281) like *with-values*, *with-boolean-val*, *with-boolean-comp*, etc., were written in terms of *with-value* and *err-to-comp*, so their definitions for stateful computations are unchanged as long as we use the definitions of *with-value* and *err-to-comp* that are appropriate for stateful computations. This highlights the power of using these abstractions.

In FLICK, the *Value* domain includes *Location* to represent cell values. Figure 8.17 defines a *with-location-val* function we will later use for manipulating cells in the valuation clauses for FLICK. It is defined like *with-boolean-val*, *with-procedure-val*, etc.

In the presence of state, there are a few more auxiliary functions involving computations that are especially handy. These are defined in Figure 8.18. *allocating* allocates a location for a storable value and passes it (and the updated store) to a computation-producing function. *fetching* finds the storable value at a location and passes it (and the unchanged store) to a computation-producing function. *update* takes a location and storable value and returns a unit-producing computation whose final store includes an assignment between the location and value. *sequence* glues two computations together by supplying the final store of the first computation as the initial store of the second computation; the expressible value produced by the first computation is ignored.

$$(\textit{with-location-val} \ (\textit{Location} \rightarrowtail \textit{Value} \ l) \ f) = (f \ l) \qquad\qquad (8.1)$$

$$\begin{aligned}(\textit{with-value} \ &(\textit{allocating} \ \sigma \ f) \ g) \\ &= (\textit{allocating} \ \sigma \ (\lambda l \ . \ (\textit{with-value} \ (f \ l) \ g)))\end{aligned} \qquad (8.2)$$

$$\begin{aligned}(\textit{with-value} \ &(\textit{fetching} \ l \ f) \ g) \\ &= (\textit{fetching} \ l \ (\lambda \sigma \ . \ (\textit{with-value} \ (f \ \sigma) \ g)))\end{aligned} \qquad (8.3)$$

$$\begin{aligned}(\textit{with-value} \ &(\textit{update} \ l \ \sigma) \ f) \\ &= (\textit{sequence} \ (\textit{update} \ l \ \sigma) \ (f \ (\textit{Unit} \rightarrowtail \textit{Value} \ \textit{unit})))\end{aligned} \qquad (8.4)$$

$$\begin{aligned}(\textit{with-value} \ &(\textit{sequence} \ c1 \ c2) \ f) \\ &= (\textit{sequence} \ c1 \ (\textit{with-value} \ c2 \ f))\end{aligned} \qquad (8.5)$$

Figure 8.19 Useful equalities on store-based computations. It is assumed that new bound variables do not conflict with free identifiers elsewhere in the expressions.

Since reasoning about computations directly in terms of the auxiliary functions can be very tedious, we seek computational laws that simplify such reasoning. Remarkably, all of the computational laws presented in Figure 6.27 on page 282 still hold for stateful computations. Figure 8.19 presents some new laws involving auxiliary functions for stateful computations. We leave the proofs of these equalities as Exercise 8.8.

Exercise 8.7 Show that the store-based definition of *Comp* is pointed.

Exercise 8.8 Assume that *Comp* = *Store* → (*Expressible* × *Store*).

a. Prove that all of the equalities in Figure 6.27 on page 282 hold.

b. Prove that all of the equalities in Figure 8.19 hold.

Valuation Clauses

The denotational specification of FLICK is summarized in Figures 8.21 and 8.22. The *Value* domain has been extended with locations, which represent cell values. Since FLICK is a CBV language, both *Nameable* and *Storable* equal *Value*. As always, $\mathcal{E}$ has the signature Exp → *Env* → *Comp*. There are two valuation functions for primitives. $\mathcal{O}_{\mathrm{FLICK}}$ is the version for FLICK, while $\mathcal{O}_{\mathrm{FLK}}$ is the version inherited from FLK. The valuation function $\mathcal{P}$ for programs maps a program and its inputs to an answer, which is an expressible value in FLICK.

With the help of the auxiliary functions, the valuation clauses are surprisingly compact. In fact, only one clause (rec) explicitly mentions the store! begin sequences two computations. cell allocates a location for its content and returns

$$
\begin{aligned}
&check\text{-}unary : Value^* \to (Value \to Comp) \to Comp \\
&= \lambda v^* f \,.\; \textbf{match } v^* \\
&\qquad\qquad \rhd [v]_{Value} \parallel (f\ v) \\
&\qquad\qquad \rhd \textbf{else } (err\text{-}to\text{-}comp\ \texttt{wrong-number-of-args}) \\
&\qquad\qquad \textbf{end} \\[4pt]
&check\text{-}binary : Value^* \to (Value \to Value \to Comp) \to Comp \\
&= \lambda v^* f \,.\; \textbf{match } v^* \\
&\qquad\qquad \rhd [v_1, v_2]_{Value} \parallel (f\ v_1\ v_2) \\
&\qquad\qquad \rhd \textbf{else } (err\text{-}to\text{-}comp\ \texttt{wrong-number-of-args}) \\
&\qquad\qquad \textbf{end}
\end{aligned}
$$

Figure 8.20   Auxiliary functions for arity checking.

the location as its resulting value. `^` fetches the value of a location and returns it, while `:=` updates a location to contain a new value. `cell=?` compares the locations of two cells. `cell?` checks whether its argument is a location. (The cell operations make use of the auxiliary arity-checking functions defined in Figure 8.20.) Other primitives are handled by passing them off to $\mathcal{O}_{\text{FLK}}$ and converting the result into a computation. This works because none of the primitives inherited from FLK has any effect on the store. The meaning of a FLICK program is calculated like that of an FLK program except that the meaning of the body is determined relative to an empty store in addition to an initial environment that binds the formal parameters of the program to its inputs.

The only really tricky clause is the one for `rec`. The valuation clause presented here is a variant of the CBV version presented in Figure 7.6 on page 322. The only difference is that it is necessary to supply *extract-value* with the current store in order to coerce the computation into a binding value.

And that's it! By the magic of the monadic style, all the other valuation clauses are inherited unchanged from the denotational definition of CBV FLK. For example, the clause for `app` is still:

$$
\begin{aligned}
\mathcal{E}[\![(\texttt{app}\ E_1\ E_2)]\!] = \lambda e \,.\; &(with\text{-}procedure\text{-}comp\ (\mathcal{E}[\![E_1]\!]\ e) \\
&(\lambda p \,.\; (with\text{-}value\ (\mathcal{E}[\![E_2]\!]\ e)\ p)))
\end{aligned}
$$

The valuation clauses are very concise, but their level of abstraction can make them difficult to understand. To get a better feel for the valuation clauses, it can be helpful to strip away the abstractions by "inlining" the definitions of auxiliary functions. For example, here is a version of the `app` clause without any auxiliary functions:

$$c \in Comp = Store \rightarrow (Expressible \times Store)$$
$$x \in Expressible = (Value + Error)_\perp$$
$$\quad Error = \text{SymLit}$$
$$v \in Value = Unit + Bool + Int + Sym + Pair + Proc + Location$$
$$n \in Nameable = Value$$
$$\sigma \in Storable = Value$$
$$p \in Proc = Nameable \rightarrow Comp$$
$$\quad Pair = Value \times Value$$

$$\mathcal{E} : \text{Exp} \rightarrow Env \rightarrow Comp$$
$$\mathcal{O}_{\text{FLK}} : \text{Primop} \rightarrow Value^* \rightarrow Expressible$$
$$\mathcal{O}_{\text{FLICK}} : \text{Primop} \rightarrow Value^* \rightarrow Comp$$
$$\mathcal{P} : \text{Prog} \rightarrow \text{InputExp}^* \rightarrow Answer \quad ; Answer = Expressible \text{ in FLICK}$$

$$\mathcal{E}[\![(\texttt{begin } E_1 \ E_2)]\!] = \lambda e . \ (\text{sequence } (\mathcal{E}[\![E_1]\!] \ e) \ (\mathcal{E}[\![E_2]\!] \ e))$$

$$\mathcal{E}[\![(\texttt{cell } E)]\!] = \lambda e . \ (\text{with-value } (\mathcal{E}[\![E]\!] \ e)$$
$$\quad\quad\quad (\lambda v . \ \text{allocating } v$$
$$\quad\quad\quad\quad (\lambda l . \ (\text{val-to-comp } (Location \rightarrowtail Value \ l)))))$$

$$\mathcal{E}[\![(\texttt{rec } I \ E)]\!] = \lambda e . \ \mathbf{fix}_{Comp} \ (\lambda c . \lambda s . \ (\mathcal{E}[\![E]\!] \ (\text{bind } I \ (\text{extract-value } c \ s) \ e) \ s))$$

$$\text{extract-value} : Comp \rightarrow Store \rightarrow BindingVal$$
$$= \lambda cs . \ \mathbf{match} \ (c \ s)$$
$$\quad\quad \triangleright \langle (Value \rightarrowtail Expressible \ v), s' \rangle \ [\![\ (Nameable \rightarrowtail BindingVal \ v)$$
$$\quad\quad \triangleright \langle (Error \rightarrowtail Expressible \ Y), s' \rangle \ [\![\ \perp_{BindingVal}$$
$$\quad\quad \mathbf{end}$$

Figure 8.21 Fundamental valuation clauses for FLICK, Part 1. Clauses not shown here have the same definition as in CBV FLK.

$$\mathcal{E}[\![(\texttt{app } E_1 \ E_2)]\!] =$$
$$\lambda es_0 . \ \mathbf{match} \ (\mathcal{E}[\![E_1]\!] \ e \ s_0)$$
$$\quad \triangleright \langle (Value \rightarrowtail Expressible \ v), s_1 \rangle \ [\![$$
$$\quad\quad \mathbf{match} \ v$$
$$\quad\quad \triangleright (Proc \rightarrowtail Value \ p) \ [\![\ \mathbf{match} \ (\mathcal{E}[\![E_2]\!] \ e \ s_1)$$
$$\quad\quad\quad\quad \triangleright \langle (Value \rightarrowtail Expressible \ v), s_2 \rangle \ [\![\ (p \ v \ s_2)$$
$$\quad\quad\quad\quad \triangleright \langle x_{err}, s_2 \rangle \ [\![\ \langle x_{err}, s_2 \rangle$$
$$\quad\quad\quad\quad \mathbf{end}$$
$$\quad\quad \triangleright \mathbf{else} \ \langle (Error \rightarrowtail Expressible \ \texttt{not-a-procedure}), s_1 \rangle$$
$$\quad\quad \mathbf{end}$$
$$\quad \triangleright \langle x_{err}, s_1 \rangle \ [\![\ \langle x_{err}, s_1 \rangle$$
$$\quad \mathbf{end}$$

The single-threaded nature of the store that is implicit in the original clause is explicit in the expanded clause. Evaluating E_1 in an environment e and store s_0

$\mathcal{O}_{\text{FLICK}}\llbracket\texttt{^}\rrbracket$
$= \lambda v^* . (\textit{check-unary } v^* (\lambda v . (\textit{with-location-val } v (\lambda l . (\textit{fetching } l \textit{ val-to-comp})))))$

$\mathcal{O}_{\text{FLICK}}\llbracket\texttt{:=}\rrbracket$
$= \lambda v^* . (\textit{check-binary } v^* (\lambda v_1 v_2 . (\textit{with-location-val } v_1 (\lambda l . (\textit{update } l \ v_2)))))$

$\mathcal{O}_{\text{FLICK}}\llbracket\texttt{cell=?}\rrbracket$
$= \lambda v^* . (\textit{check-binary } v^*$
$\qquad (\lambda v_1 v_2 . (\textit{with-location-val } v_1$
$\qquad\qquad (\lambda l_1 . (\textit{with-location-val } v_2$
$\qquad\qquad\qquad (\lambda l_2 . (\textit{val-to-comp}$
$\qquad\qquad\qquad\qquad (Bool \rightarrowtail Value \ (l_1 =_{Location} l_2)))))))))$

$\mathcal{O}_{\text{FLICK}}\llbracket\texttt{cell?}\rrbracket$
$= \lambda v^* . (\textit{check-unary } v^*$
$\qquad (\lambda v . (\textit{val-to-comp } (Bool \rightarrowtail Value \ \textbf{match } v$
$\qquad\qquad\qquad\qquad\qquad \triangleright (Location \rightarrowtail Value \ l) \ \| \ true$
$\qquad\qquad\qquad\qquad\qquad \triangleright \textbf{else } false \ \textbf{end})))) $

$\mathcal{O}_{\text{FLICK}}\llbracket O \rrbracket = \lambda v^* . (\textit{expr-to-comp } (\mathcal{O}_{\text{FLK}}\llbracket O \rrbracket \ v^*)), \text{ where } O \in \text{Primop}_{FLK}$

$\mathcal{P}\llbracket(\texttt{flick } (I^*) \ E_{body})\rrbracket$
$= \lambda IE^* . \textbf{ if } (length \ I^*) =_{Int} (length \ IE^*)$
$\qquad \textbf{then let } \langle x, s \rangle \textbf{ be } \mathcal{E}\llbracket E_{body} \rrbracket \ (extend^* \ I^* \ (\mathcal{IE}^*\llbracket IE^* \rrbracket) \ \textit{empty-env})$
$\qquad\qquad\qquad\qquad\qquad\qquad\qquad \textit{empty-store}$
$\qquad\qquad \textbf{in } x$
$\qquad \textbf{else } (Error \rightarrowtail Expressible \ \texttt{wrong-number-of-args}) \ \textbf{end}$

Figure 8.22 Fundamental valuation clauses for FLICK, Part 2. Clauses not shown here have the same definition as in CBV FLK.

yields an expressible value (call it x_1) and a store s_1. If x_1 is a procedure value p, E_2 is evaluated in environment e and store s_1 to yield another expressible value (call it x_2) and another store, s_2. If x_2 is a value v, then p, whose signature is

$$Nameable \to Comp = Value \to Store \to (Expressible \times Store)$$

is applied to x_2 and s_2. In error situations (x_1 is not a procedure or x_2 is not a value), expressible error values are propagated along with the updated store.

It is worth commenting on the signature of procedures just mentioned. In CBV FLK, *Proc* maps values to expressible values. In FLICK, procedures take an extra argument, a store, and return a pair of an expressible value and a store. The input store represents the state of the computation when the procedure is called, and the output store represents the state of the computation when the procedure returns its result.

You may find it helpful to expand other valuation clauses. After you have done several, you may start to appreciate the purpose of the *Comp* abstraction and its associated auxiliary functions! As usual, it is also instructive to make sure that all of the valuation clauses type-check.

Exercise 8.9 Use the FLICK denotational semantics to calculate the meaning of the following expression studied in Section 8.3.3:

```
(app (lam c {E_lam}
        (begin (prim := c (prim + 1 (prim ^ c)))
               (prim ^ c)))
     (cell 3))
```

Use the laws in Figure 6.27 (page 282), Figure 8.19 (page 416), and Exercise 7.4 (page 318) to simplify your calculations.

Exercise 8.10 Instead of defining `while` as syntactic sugar in FLIC, we could make it a kernel construct in FLICK.

a. Extend the evaluation contexts and reduction rules of the FLICK SOS to specify the semantics of `while`. Do *not* rewrite `while` to expressions using `if` or `begin` in your reduction rules. *Hint:* Introduce one or more new intermediate expression constructs (like `*cell*`) into the language.

b. Write an $\mathcal{E}$ valuation clause that specifies the semantics of `while`.

Exercise 8.11 Inspired by the `repeat`/`until` construct of Pascal, Dewey Lupe suggests that FLICK be extended with the following looping construct:

(repeat E_{body} E_{test}) specifies a loop in which each iteration of the loop first evaluates E_{body} and then evaluates E_{test}. As long as E_{test} is false, the loop continues with the next iteration. If E_{test} is true, the loop terminates and the `repeat` expression returns *unit*. If E_{test} does not evaluate to a boolean, or if E_{body} or E_{test} signals an error, the `repeat` expression signals an error.

a. Suppose that `repeat` is a kernel construct. Extend the operational and denotational semantics of FLICK to handle `repeat` (compare to Exercise 8.10).

b. It is simpler to define `repeat` as syntactic sugar for other FLIC constructs. Give a desugaring rule for `repeat`.

Exercise 8.12

a. What is the value of (`rec a a`) under the call-by-value denotational semantics for FLK in the previous chapter?

b. What is the value of (`rec a a`) under the operational semantics for FLICK?

c. What is the value of (`rec a a`) under the denotational semantics for FLICK?

d. Explain any discrepancies in your answers to the first three parts of this exercise.

Exercise 8.13 FLICK's pair data structure is immutable. In this problem, we introduce a mutable pair, a simple kind of mutable structure similar to the mutable records found in many imperative languages. (See Section 10.1.4 for a discussion of mutable data structures.)

Suppose that FLICK is extended with the following five constructs for mutable pairs:

$$E ::= \ldots \text{ as in FLICK } \ldots$$
$$| \text{ (mpair } E_{fst} \text{ } E_{snd}) \text{ } | \text{ (mfst } E_{mp}) \text{ } | \text{ (msnd } E_{mp})$$
$$| \text{ (set-mfst! } E_{mp} \text{ } E_{new}) \text{ } | \text{ (set-msnd! } E_{mp} \text{ } E_{new})$$

The new constructs have the following informal semantics:

(mpair E_{fst} E_{snd}) creates a new mutable pair value with two fields called *mfst* and *msnd*. The values of E_{fst} and E_{snd} are stored in the *mfst* and *msnd* fields, respectively.

(mfst E_{mp}) returns the content of the *mfst* field of the mutable pair value of E_{mp}. Signals an error if mfst does not evaluate to a mutable pair. Similarly for msnd.

(set-mfst! E_{mp} E_{new}) mutates the mutable pair value of E_{mp} so that the *mfst* field contains the value of E_{new}. If E_{mp} does not evaluate to a mutable pair, or if evaluating E_{new} signals an error, then set-mfst! signals an error. Similarly for set-msnd!.

For example, here are some expressions involving mutable pairs in the full FLIC language:

```
(let ((foo (mpair 1 2)))
  (begin
    (set-mfst! foo 6)
    (+ (mfst foo) (msnd foo))))  FLIC↝ 8

(let ((bar (mpair 8 (mpair 4 3))))
  (begin
    (set-mfst! bar (msnd bar))
    (set-msnd! (msnd bar) (mfst (mfst bar)))
    (+ (mfst (msnd bar)) (msnd (mfst bar)))))  FLIC↝ 8
```

a. Extend the denotational semantics of FLICK to handle the five mutable pair constructs.

   i. Describe any additions or modifications you make to the semantic domains of FLICK.

   ii. Give valuation clauses for the five constructs. (You should not have to modify any of the existing valuation clauses.)

   iii. Define any auxiliary functions necessary for your valuation clauses.

b. Define the five mutable pair constructs as syntactic sugar using existing FLIC constructs.

Exercise 8.14 Clark Smarter of the Photocopy Research Center has developed a new backtracking construct for FLICK called `try`:

$$E ::= \ldots \mid (\text{try } E_1 \ E_2) \text{ [Backtracking]}$$

The informal semantics of (`try` E_1 E_2) is as follows: First E_1 is evaluated, and if E_1 evaluates to *true*, then `try` ignores E_2 and returns *true*. If E_1 evaluates to *false*, then the side effects of E_1 are discarded, and the value of `try` is the value of E_2. If the value of E_1 is neither *true* nor *false*, then the `try` expression yields an error. `try` is thus an elementary backtracking construct. It allows the exploration of one alternative, and, if that does not work, restores the initial state and tries a second alternative.

Here's an expression illustrating `try`:

```
(let ((balance (cell 200)))
  (let ((withdraw (abs (n)
                       (begin (:= balance (- (^ balance) n))
                              (>= (^ balance) 0)))))
    {First try to withdraw 250; if that fails, withdraw 10 from}
    {the original balance.}
    (begin (try (withdraw 250) (withdraw 10))
           (^ balance))))) ⎯FLIC⟶ 190
```

Clark knows the pitfalls of informal semantics. When writing up the documentation for `try`, he decides to give a formal operational and denotational description for his new construct.

a. First Clark works on an operational semantics for `try`:

   i. In attempting to give an operational semantics for `try`, Clark realizes that he must extend the configuration space *CF*, so he adds a new intermediate expression to *E*. Describe the new intermediate form and its purpose. *Hint:* you may want to think about the next part before answering this one.

   ii. Provide all of the new evaluation contexts and reduction rules that are necessary for handling the `try` construct.

b. Clark is having trouble extending the denotational semantics of FLICK to handle `try`. Help Clark by writing the $\mathcal{E}$ valuation clause that handles the `try` expression.

c. Clark shows his operational and denotational semantics definitions of `try` to language implementer Hardy Ware. Hardy says, "These semantic definitions are all well and good, but implementing `try` efficiently is going to be tough."

   i. Explain what Hardy means by describing what difficulties would be encountered in implementing `try` efficiently on physical computers where state-based memory devices implement the binding of locations to values.

   ii. Sketch a strategy for implementing `try` that does not require making a copy of the entire store.

Exercise 8.15 A common problem when working with state is data consistency. For example, consider a database application that manages bank accounts. Transferring an amount of money between two accounts implies subtracting the amount from the first account and adding it to the second one. If we transfer money only between accounts of the same bank, the total amount of money present in all the accounts should remain the same. However, if something bad occurs between the subtraction and the addition (e.g., a system crash), a certain amount might simply vanish!

This situation can be prevented in database programming by requiring all modifications to the database to occur within a *transaction*. Intuitively, a transaction is a series of modifications to a database that become permanent only when the transaction is successfully terminated (the technical term is *committed*). If the user decides to *abort* (i.e., cancel) the transaction, or the system crashes before the transaction is committed, all the modifications are "undone."

Abby Stracksen, president and CEO of Intrusive Databases, Inc., decides to add transactions to FLIC. In Abby's language, the store will act as the database: queries of the database are performed by ^, and modifications are performed by :=. It is an error to perform := when there is no active transaction.

Abby extends the grammar of FLICK by the following clauses:

$E ::= \ldots$ *as in* FLICK $\ldots$ | (begin-transaction!) | (commit!) | (abort!)

The informal semantics of transactions are:

(begin-transaction!) begins a transaction. The transaction continues until either a commit! or an abort! is encountered. It is an error if the program ends and a transaction has not been committed or aborted.

(commit!) successfully terminates the current transaction. It is an error if no transaction is in progress.

(abort!) ends the current transaction and undoes all of its modifications. It is an error if no transaction is in progress.

Like :=, the three transaction operations all return *unit*.

Transactions may be nested, in which case abort! and commit! end only the current (innermost) transaction. An abort! of a transaction undoes the modifications of the transaction including modifications made by nested transactions.

Here is how Abby writes a transfer between two bank accounts (represented as cells) using transactions:

```
(def transfer
  (abs (from to amount)
    (begin (begin-transaction!)
           (:= from (- (^ from) amount))
           (:= to   (+ (^ to)   amount))
           (if (< (^ from) 0)
               (begin (abort!) (sym failed))
               (begin (commit!) (sym succeeded))))))
```

Below are some more examples of the behavior of transactions. Assume that the expressions are evaluated in order:

```
(def c1 (cell 0))
(def c2 (cell 10))
(def (inc! a-cell) (:= a-cell (+ (^ a-cell) 1)))
(def (current-state) (list (^ c1) (^ c2)))

(current-state)  FLIC→ ⊲0, 10⊳

(begin (begin-transaction!)
       (inc! c1)
       (commit!)
       (current-state))  FLIC→ ⊲1, 10⊳

(begin (begin-transaction!)
       (inc! c2)
       (abort!)
       (current-state))  FLIC→ ⊲1, 10⊳

(begin (begin-transaction!)
       (inc! c1)
       (begin (begin-transaction!)
              (inc! c2)
              (abort!))
       (commit!)
       (current-state))  FLIC→ ⊲2, 10⊳

(begin (begin-transaction!)
       (inc! c1)
       (begin (begin-transaction!)
              (inc! c2)
              (commit!))  {End inner transaction,}
       (abort!)          {but abort! outer transaction.}
       (current-state))  FLIC→ ⊲2, 10⊳

(begin (begin-transaction!)
       (inc! c2)
       (commit!))  FLIC→ unit  {commit! returns #u}

(current-state)  FLIC→ ⊲2, 11⊳
```

Abby also points out some expressions that generate errors (assume that each interacts with the database in a completely independent session):

```
(begin-transaction!)  FLIC→ error:transaction-not-terminated

(commit!)  FLIC→ error:no-current-transaction

(let ((a-cell (cell 0)))
  (begin (:= a-cell 5)
         (^ a-cell)))  FLIC→ error:not-in-a-transaction
```

```
(let ((a-cell (cell 0)))
  (begin (begin-transaction!)
         (:= a-cell 5)
         (commit!)
         (:= a-cell 7) {commit! ends transaction,}
                       {so invalid modification}
         (^ a-cell)))   ‾FLIC‾→ error:not-in-a-transaction
```

a. Extend the SOS of FLICK to handle transactions:

   i. Define the configurations, the set of final configurations, the input function, and the output function.

   ii. Provide reduction rules for `begin-transaction!`, `commit!`, `abort!`, and `:=`.

b. Modify the denotational semantics of FLICK to handle transactions.

   i. Give the necessary additions or modifications to FLICK's semantic domains.

   ii. Some auxiliary functions used by the FLICK denotational semantics might need to be modified (e.g., as a result of the changes in the semantic domains). Give their new definitions.

   iii. Write the valuation clauses for `begin-transaction!`, `commit!`, `abort!`, and `:=`.

8.3.5 Call-by-Name versus Call-by-Value Revisited

The nonstrict nature of CBN does not interact well with mutable cells. To illustrate this, we reconsider the following expression studied earlier:

```
(app (lam c {E_lam}
         (begin (prim := c (prim + 1 (prim ^ c)))
                (prim ^ c)))
     (cell 3))
```

In Figure 8.15 on page 411, we saw how this expression evaluates to 4 in CBV FLICK. But we will see that in CBN FLICK this expression evaluates to 3!

To see why we get a different answer, we first need to develop the CBN semantics for FLICK. We can obtain an SOS for CBN FLICK by making the following modifications to the SOS for CBV FLICK:

- Use the CBN reduction rule and evaluation contexts for `app` in Figure 7.1 on page 310.

- Use the evaluation contexts for nonstrict pairs in Figure 7.5 on page 319.

- Use the CBN reduction rule for `rec` from Figure 6.19 on page 259.

$\langle$(app E_{lam} (cell 3)), []$\rangle$

$\xrightarrow[\text{CBN}]{}_{[\beta]}$ $\langle$(begin (prim := (cell 3) (prim + 1 (prim ^ (cell 3))))
                    (prim ^ (cell 3))),
               []$\rangle$

$\xrightarrow[\text{CBN}]{}_{[\text{cell}]}$ $\langle$(begin (prim := (*cell* 0) (prim + 1 (prim ^ (cell 3))))
                    (prim ^ (cell 3))),
               $[\langle 0, 3 \rangle]\rangle$

$\xrightarrow[\text{CBN}]{}_{[\text{cell}]}$ $\langle$(begin (prim := (*cell* 0) (prim + 1 (prim ^ (*cell* 1))))
                    (prim ^ (cell 3))),
               $[\langle 1, 3 \rangle, \langle 0, 3 \rangle]\rangle$

$\xrightarrow[\text{CBN}]{}_{[\text{^}]}$ $\langle$(begin (prim := (*cell* 0) (prim + 1 3))
                    (prim ^ (cell 3))),
               $[\langle 1, 3 \rangle, \langle 0, 3 \rangle]\rangle$

$\xrightarrow[\text{CBN}]{}_{[+]}$ $\langle$(begin (prim := (*cell* 0) 4)
                    (prim ^ (cell 3))),
               $[\langle 1, 3 \rangle, \langle 0, 3 \rangle]\rangle$

$\xrightarrow[\text{CBN}]{}_{[:=]}$ $\langle$(begin #u (prim ^ (cell 3))), $[\langle 0, 4 \rangle, \langle 1, 3 \rangle, \langle 0, 3 \rangle]\rangle$

$\xrightarrow[\text{CBN}]{}_{[\text{begin}]}$ $\langle$(prim ^ (cell 3)), $[\langle 0, 4 \rangle, \langle 1, 3 \rangle, \langle 0, 3 \rangle]\rangle$

$\xrightarrow[\text{CBN}]{}_{[\text{cell}]}$ $\langle$(prim ^ (*cell* 2)), $[\langle 2, 3 \rangle, \langle 0, 4 \rangle, \langle 1, 3 \rangle, \langle 0, 3 \rangle]\rangle$

$\xrightarrow[\text{CBN}]{}_{[\text{^}]}$ $\langle$3, $[\langle 2, 3 \rangle, \langle 0, 4 \rangle, \langle 1, 3 \rangle, \langle 0, 3 \rangle]\rangle$

Figure 8.23   Operational evaluation of a sample expression in CBN FLICK.

Figure 8.23 shows the evaluation of the example expression in CBN FLICK. The reason it evaluates to 3 rather than 4 is that in CBN each of the three references to the formal parameter c of E_{lam} is replaced by the operand expression (cell 3). Since each occurrence of cell creates a different cell, three distinct and unrelated cells are created, and the changes to one cell do not affect the others.

It should be clear from this example that mutable data cannot be used effectively in CBN FLIC because there is no way to reference the same cell twice. In Section 8.4.3, we will see a variant of FLIC in which CBN makes more sense, though it is still difficult to reason about. The example also demonstrates that side effects destroy the elegant relationship between CBN and CBV (as expressed in Theorem 7.1 on page 311) enjoyed by stateless languages.

Exercise 8.16 What changes need to be made to the CBV FLICK denotational semantics to obtain a denotational semantics for CBN FLICK?

8.3.6 Referential Transparency, Interference, and Purity

We noted earlier (page 389) that stateless languages like FL are referentially transparent. Referential transparency is an important property when reasoning about programs, especially when analyzing and transforming programs.

Consider the following two program transformations:

$$\text{T1: } (\texttt{prim + } E_a \ E_a) \xrightarrow{simp} (\texttt{prim * 2 } E_a)$$
$$\text{T2: } (\texttt{prim + } E_b \ E_c) \xrightarrow{simp} (\texttt{prim + } E_c \ E_b)$$

Under what conditions are such transformations **safe**, i.e., guaranteed to preserve the meaning of a program?

For the present discussion, imagine that we modify the definition of the behavior of FLK and FLICK programs so that programs terminating with stuck configurations map to the same outcome (∞) as diverging programs. Treating all errors and divergence as observationally equivalent significantly enlarges the set of safe transformations. For example, we do not care if a transformation changes the error signaled by a program or changes an error-signaling program to a diverging one (or vice versa).

In a referentially transparent language like FL, these two transformations are always safe. In T1, E_a always has the same value no matter how many times it is evaluated. In T2, reordering E_b and E_c cannot change their values because they are still in the same naming context as before.

However, in a stateful language like FLIC, neither of these transformations is always safe. For example, in T1, suppose that E_a increments a counter in addition to returning a value. Then (`prim + ` E_a E_a) will increment the counter twice, but (`prim * 2 ` E_a) will increment it only once. In T2, suppose that E_b increments a counter whose value is returned by E_c. Then swapping E_b and E_c changes the value returned by E_c. The problem in these cases is that expressions can depend on the implicit store threaded through their evaluation, so it is generally not safe to replace them by a value or change their relative positions. An expression can depend on the store by:

- allocating a location in the store (which includes initialization in our semantics),

- reading the value stored at a location, or

- writing a value into a location.

Nevertheless, there are still many situations in which the transformations are safe, even in a stateful language. Let us say that an expression E_1 **interferes** with E_2 when E_1 allocates or writes a store location that is read and/or written by E_2. Then T1 is safe as long as E_a does not interfere with itself or the rest of the program and T2 is safe as long as E_b or E_c do not interfere with each other. Classical compiler optimizations like code motion, common-subexpression elimination, and dead-code removal require reasoning about the interference between expressions (see Section 17.6.2).

A particularly simple form of noninterference involves expressions that do not depend on the store at all. An expression is **pure** when it does not allocate, read, or write any store locations. A pure expression does not interfere with any other expression, and so it can be treated as if it were in a referentially transparent language. For instance, it is safe to replace a pure expression by another pure expression having the same value or to move a pure expression to a different position in the same naming context.

Neither interference nor purity is a computable property. That is, it is impossible to write a program that decides whether an arbitrary expression is pure. However, we can define a simpler property, **syntactic purity**, that *is* computable. It is a conservative approximation to purity in that every syntactically pure expression is in fact pure; but not every pure expression is syntactically pure. For FLICK, we define syntactically pure expressions, called **syntactic values**, as follows:

- literals, variable references, and abstractions (`lam` expressions) do not depend on the store and so are syntactically pure;

- conditionals, `rec` expressions, `pair` expressions, and primitive applications (except those involving cell primitives) are syntactically pure if all their subexpressions are syntactically pure.

All other expressions, including applications of cell primitives and procedure applications, are assumed to be impure.

For FLIC, we would also want `let` and `letrec` expressions to be syntactically pure if all their subexpressions are syntactically pure. Because the desugarings for `let` and `letrec` include procedure applications, which are deemed impure by our syntactic purity test, it would be necessary to perform purity analysis on FLIC *before* desugaring.

We shall use this notion of syntactic values later, in our discussion of polymorphic types (Chapter 12), type reconstruction (Chapter 13), and abstract types (Chapter 14). Chapter 16 will present a more flexible mechanism for statically determining the side effects (and therefore interference properties) that an expression may have.

Exercise 8.17 Indicate whether each of the following nine expression transformations (1) is safe in CBV FL and (2) is safe in CBV FLIC. Initially assume that errors and divergence are observationally indistinguishable. Which answers change if errors and divergence are not observationally equivalent?

a. $(\texttt{prim + } I \text{ } I) \xrightarrow{simp} (\texttt{prim * 2 } I)$

b. $(\texttt{let ((x } E_1\texttt{)) (prim + x } E_2\texttt{))} \xrightarrow{simp} (\texttt{prim + } E_1 \text{ } E_2)$

c. $(\texttt{app (lam } I \text{ } E_1\texttt{) } E_2) \xrightarrow{simp} [E_2/I]E_1$

d. $(\texttt{lam } I_1 \texttt{ (app (lam } I_2 \text{ } E\texttt{) } I_1\texttt{))} \xrightarrow{simp} (\texttt{lam } I_2 \text{ } E)$, where $I_1 \notin \mathit{FrIds}[\![E]\!]$

e. $(\texttt{if \#t } E_1 \text{ } E_2) \xrightarrow{simp} E_1$

f. $(\texttt{if } E_1 \text{ } E_2 \text{ } E_2) \xrightarrow{simp} E_2$

g. $(\texttt{if } E_1 \texttt{ (if } E_1 \text{ } E_2 \text{ } E_3\texttt{) (if } E_1 \text{ } E_4 \text{ } E_5\texttt{))} \xrightarrow{simp} (\texttt{if } E_1 \text{ } E_2 \text{ } E_5)$

h. $(\texttt{if (if } E_1 \text{ } E_2 \text{ } E_3\texttt{) } E_4 \text{ } E_5)$
$\xrightarrow{simp} (\texttt{if } E_1 \texttt{ (if } E_2 \text{ } E_4 \text{ } E_5\texttt{) (if } E_3 \text{ } E_4 \text{ } E_5\texttt{))}$

i. $(\texttt{app } E_1 \texttt{ (if } E_2 \text{ } E_3 \text{ } E_4\texttt{))} \xrightarrow{simp} (\texttt{if } E_2 \texttt{ (app } E_1 \text{ } E_3\texttt{) (app } E_1 \text{ } E_4\texttt{))}$

8.4 Mutable Variables: FLAVAR

In FLICK, the only thing that can change over time is the content of a mutable cell. So-called "variables" are actually constants whose value cannot change during the execution of a program. Mutable cells are sufficient for implementing any state-based program, and they are the basis for stateful programming in real-world languages like ML. However, they are not always convenient to use. Here we explore a variant of FLIC called FLAVAR (**FL A**nd mutable **VAR**iables). in which every variable becomes a mutable entity. We will also revisit the issue of parameter passing in the context of state by examining four parameter-passing mechanisms for FLAVAR.

8.4.1 Mutable Variables

In FLIC, it can be difficult to modify a program to make a previously constant quantity mutable. For example, suppose a FLIC program binds the variable **addresses** to a list of names and addresses. Since both variables and pairs are immutable in FLIC, the meaning of **addresses** cannot change during the execution of the program. Suppose that we later decide to modify the program so that it dynamically updates the address list. Then it is necessary to rebind

addresses to a mutable cell whose content is a list. Furthermore, we must find all references to **addresses** in the existing program and replace them by (prim ^ addresses).[5]

Most programming languages offer a more convenient way of making such changes: **mutable variables**. A variable is mutable if the value it is bound to can change over time. The variables of FL and FLIC aren't *variable* at all, because their values can't vary over time; rather, they are names for constants. In contrast, variables in languages like SCHEME, C, PASCAL, and FORTRAN can have their values changed by assignment during the execution of the program. In these languages, modifying the address program would not require finding and updating all references to **addresses**, because all variables are assignable by default. On the other hand, programs in these languages can be tougher to reason about, because it can be hard to determine which variables change over time and which do not. This situation can be improved by providing so-called **constant declarations** for declaring that certain named entities are immutable.

We have two motivations for studying mutable variables:

1. Many real languages support mutable variables. We want to model this feature in our mini-languages.

2. Mutable variables shift the way we think about naming. In languages with mutable variables, names do not denote values, but instead denote locations in the store at which values are stored.

8.4.2   FLAVAR

We will study mutable variables in FLAVAR, a dialect of FLIC that supports assignments to variables. The syntax of FLAVAR (and its kernel, FLAVARK) is the same as that for FLIC (and its kernel, FLICK) except for the addition of a SCHEME-like set! construct:

$$E_{\text{FLAVARK}} ::= \ldots \text{FLICK } expressions \ldots \mid (\texttt{set! } I_{var} \ E_{val}) \text{ [Assignment]}$$

Informally, (set! I_{var} E_{val}) assigns the value of the expression E_{val} to the variable named by I_{var} and returns the unit value. For example:

$$(\texttt{let } ((\texttt{a 3})) \texttt{ (list a (set! a 4) a))} \xrightarrow[\text{FLAVAR}]{} \triangleleft 3, unit, 4 \triangleright$$

(Recall that list elements are evaluated from left to right.)

---

[5]We shall see in Section 17.5 that compilers often perform a program transformation like this called **assignment conversion**.

$n \in Nameable = Location$

$\sigma \in Storable = depends\ on\ parameter\text{-}passing\ mechanism$

$val\text{-}to\text{-}storable : Value \rightarrow Storable = depends\ on\ parameter\text{-}passing\ mechanism$

$\mathcal{E}[\![I]\!] = depends\ on\ parameter\text{-}passing\ mechanism$

$\mathcal{E}[\![(\texttt{app}\ E_1\ E_2)]\!] = depends\ on\ parameter\text{-}passing\ mechanism$

$\mathcal{E}[\![(\texttt{set!}\ I\ E)]\!] = \lambda e\,.\ (with\text{-}value\ (\mathcal{E}[\![E]\!]\ e)$
$\qquad\qquad\qquad (\lambda v\,.\ (with\text{-}nameable\ (lookup\ I\ e)$
$\qquad\qquad\qquad\qquad (\lambda l\,.\ (update\ l\ (val\text{-}to\text{-}storable\ v))))))$

Figure 8.24 Semantics of mutable variables. The definitions of *val-to-storable* and *Storable* and the valuation clauses for I and app depend on the parameter-passing mechanism (see Section 8.4.3).

Note the differences between the cell assignment operator, :=, and the variable assignment construct, set!. The former changes the value of a first-class data value (a cell), while the latter changes the value of a variable (which is not a first-class value). In (:= E_1 E_2), E_1 can be any expression that evaluates to a cell, while in (set! I E), I must be an identifier visible in the current scope. Mutable cells and mutable variables are orthogonal language features. FLAVAR contains both.

The denotational semantics of FLAVARK is based on that of FLICK as presented in Section 8.3.4. Figure 8.24 shows the key differences. The principal feature of FLAVARK is that variables, like mutable cells, are represented as locations in the store. This means that locations are the only entity in the language that can be named, i.e., *Nameable = Location*. The association between a name I and a value v that is represented by a single environment binding in FLIC is represented by *two* bindings in FLAVAR: an environment binding between a name I and a location l, and an assignment in the store between l and v. The indirection through l allows the value associated with the name to be changed. The details of how the locations are allocated, how they are looked up, and what values may legally be stored in them are determined by the parameter-passing mechanism of the language. We shall discuss several mechanisms shortly.

The other key aspect of the FLAVAR semantics is the valuation clause for set!. In (set! I E), E is evaluated and stored in the location named by I. The auxiliary function *val-to-storable*, which depends on the definition of *Storable*, is needed to inject the value into the *Storable* domain. Note that in the expression (set! a a), the left and right occurrences of a are treated differently. The left occurrence specifies a location, but the right occurrence specifies the value to

```
(letrec ((I₁ E₁) ... (Iₙ Eₙ)) E_body)
  ⤳_ds (let ((I₁ #u) ... (Iₙ #u))
          (begin (set! I₁ E₁)
                      ⋮
                  (set! Iₙ Eₙ)
                  E_body))
```

Figure 8.25   Desugaring for `letrec` in FLAVAR.

be stored at that location. For this reason, the location is called the **L-value** (left value) of the variable, and the value stored at that location is called the **R-value** (right value) of the variable. Determining the R-value associated with an L-value is called **dereferencing** the variable. The notions of L-value and R-value can be extended to expressions. Variables can be viewed as cells in which dereferencing corresponds to automatically performing the ^ operation at every variable reference, and (`set!` I E) performs := on the L-value of I and the R-value of E.

A somewhat unexpected benefit of mutable variables is that they considerably simplify the treatment of CBV recursion. Figure 8.25 shows how the `letrec` construct in FLAVAR can be desugared into other constructs that do not involve **rec**. Why does this work? Intuitively, the hard part of recursion, especially mutual recursion, is "tying the knot" between the declaration of a recursive variable and all of its references. In a language with mutable variables, the knots can be tied by initially declaring the variables to be bound to dummy values (`#u` in the desugaring) and then using `set!` to assign to each variable I_i the value of the corresponding definition expression E_i. Since each E_i is in the scope of all the $I_1, \ldots, I_n$, the `set!` changes the meaning of the references to these identifiers within E_i. Of course, in a CBV language, if such references are not "protected" by a `lam`, their evaluation will yield the (incorrect) dummy value rather than the (correct) recursive value.

8.4.3   Parameter-passing Mechanisms for FLAVAR

Parameter-passing mechanisms for languages with mutable variables are determined by the domain *Storable*, the function *val-to-storable*, and the valuation clauses for **app** and I. Figures 8.26 and 8.27 summarize four parameter-passing mechanisms for FLAVAR. These are explained below.

Call-by-value

The CBV mechanism for FLAVAR (shown in Figure 8.26) is similar to CBV
for FL and FLIC, except that a procedure call allocates a new location for the
argument value and passes this location (rather than the value) to the procedure.
Since the meaning of an identifier is a location and not a value, every variable
reference requires both a lookup in the environment (to find the location) and a
fetch from the store (to dereference the variable at that location). In CBV, only
elements of the domain *Value* are storable. For example:

```
(let ((a 0)
      (f (abs (x) (+ x x))))
  (f (begin (set! a (+ a 1)) a)))
```
$\xrightarrow[CBV\ FLAVAR]{}$ *2*

```
((abs (x) 3) (/ 1 0))
```
$\xrightarrow[CBV\ FLAVAR]{}$ *error:divide-by-zero*

Call-by-name

CBN in FLAVAR (shown in Figure 8.26) is similar to CBN in FL, except that
here it is *Storable* (not *Nameable*) that equals *Comp*. The app clause indicates
that the computation of the argument expression (not its value) is stored at a
newly allocated location. In FLAVAR, computations are functions that accept
a store, so the current store is supplied to a computation every time the variable
that names it is referenced. If the computation performs a side effect, this
side effect will be performed every time the variable is looked up. Consider the
following example:

```
(let ((a 0)
      (f (abs (x) (+ x x))))
  (f (begin (set! a (+ a 1)) a)))
```
$\xrightarrow[CBN\ FLAVAR]{}$ *3*

In the example, calling f binds x to a location that holds the computation
($\mathcal{E}[\![$(begin (set! a (+ a 1)) a)$]\!]$ e_1), where e_1 is an environment with bindings for a and f. Each variable reference to x within the procedure body (+ x x)
performs this computation with the current store. So the left reference to x increments a and returns 1, while the right reference to x increments a again and
returns 2. This example illustrates the perils of mixing state with CBN parameter
passing in a language with mutable variables.

As in FL, certain computations in FLAVAR correspond to errors or divergence. Because such computations are nameable in CBN (by an indirection
through the store), procedures can be nonstrict:

```
((abs (x) 3) (/ 1 0))
```
$\xrightarrow[CBN\ FLAVAR]{}$ *3*

$\sigma \in \textit{Storable} \; = \; \textit{Value}$

$\textit{val-to-storable} = \; \lambda v \cdot v$

$\mathcal{E}[\![(\texttt{app} \; E_1 \; E_2)]\!] \; = \; \lambda e \cdot (\textit{with-procedure-comp} \; (\mathcal{E}[\![E_1]\!] \; e)$
$\qquad\qquad\qquad\qquad\qquad (\lambda p \cdot (\textit{with-value} \; (\mathcal{E}[\![E_2]\!] \; e)$
$\qquad\qquad\qquad\qquad\qquad\qquad\qquad (\lambda v \cdot (\textit{allocating} \; v \; p)))))$

$\mathcal{E}[\![I]\!] \; = \; \lambda e \cdot (\textit{with-nameable} \; (\textit{lookup} \; I \; e) \; (\lambda l \cdot (\textit{fetching} \; l \; \textit{val-to-comp})))$

Call-by-Value

$\sigma \in \textit{Storable} \; = \; \textit{Comp}$

$\textit{val-to-storable} = \; \textit{val-to-comp}$

$\mathcal{E}[\![(\texttt{app} \; E_1 \; E_2)]\!] \; = \; \lambda e \cdot (\textit{with-procedure-comp} \; (\mathcal{E}[\![E_1]\!] \; e)$
$\qquad\qquad\qquad\qquad\qquad (\lambda p \cdot (\textit{allocating} \; (\mathcal{E}[\![E_2]\!] \; e) \; p)))$

$\mathcal{E}[\![I]\!] \; = \; \lambda e \cdot (\textit{with-nameable} \; (\textit{lookup} \; I \; e) \; (\lambda l \cdot (\textit{fetching} \; l \; (\lambda c \cdot c))))$

Call-by-Name

Figure 8.26   Parameter-passing mechanisms in FLAVAR, part I.

Call-by-need (Lazy Evaluation)

The presence of state in FLAVAR suggests a parameter-passing mechanism based on a technique called **memoization**. In this technique, the formal parameter name can be bound to a location that originally stores the computation of the argument expression. The first time the parameter is referenced, the computation is performed, but the resulting value is cached at the location and is used on every subsequent reference. Thus, the argument expression is evaluated at most once and is never evaluated at all if the parameter is never referenced. This mechanism is called **call-by-need** or **lazy evaluation**. Because the acronym CBN is already taken, we will call this mechanism **call-by-lazy** and abbreviate it CBL. (See Figure 8.27.)

Call-by-need can exhibit the desirable behavior of both CBV and CBN:

```
(let ((a 0)
      (f (abs (x) (+ x x))))
  (f (begin (set! a (+ a 1)) a)))
```
$\xrightarrow[\textit{CBL FLAVAR}]{} 2$

```
((abs (x) 3) (/ 1 0))
```
$\xrightarrow[\textit{CBL FLAVAR}]{} 3$

$\sigma \in Storable = Memo$

$mm \in Memo = Comp + Value$

$val\text{-}to\text{-}storable = \lambda v \,.\, (Value \rightarrowtail Memo\ v)$

$\mathcal{E}[\![(\text{app}\ E_1\ E_2)]\!] = \lambda e \,.\, (with\text{-}procedure\text{-}comp\ (\mathcal{E}[\![E_1]\!]\ e)$
$\qquad\qquad\qquad\qquad (\lambda p \,.\, (allocating\ (Comp \rightarrowtail Memo\ (\mathcal{E}[\![E_2]\!]\ e))\ p)))$

$\mathcal{E}[\![I]\!] = \lambda e \,.\, (with\text{-}nameable\ (lookup\ I\ e)$
$\qquad\qquad\quad (\lambda l \,.\, (fetching\ l$
$\qquad\qquad\qquad (\lambda mm \,.\, \textbf{match}\ mm$
$\qquad\qquad\qquad\qquad \rhd (Comp \rightarrowtail Memo\ c)$
$\qquad\qquad\qquad\qquad \| \ (with\text{-}value\ c$
$\qquad\qquad\qquad\qquad\qquad (\lambda v \,.\, (sequence\ (update\ l\ (Value \rightarrowtail Memo\ v))$
$\qquad\qquad\qquad\qquad\qquad\qquad\qquad (val\text{-}to\text{-}comp\ v))))$
$\qquad\qquad\qquad\qquad \rhd (Value \rightarrowtail Memo\ v)\ \| \ (val\text{-}to\text{-}comp\ v)$
$\qquad\qquad\qquad\qquad \textbf{end}\ ))))$

Call-by-Need (Lazy Evaluation)

$\sigma \in Storable = Value$

$\mathcal{E} : \text{Exp} \to Env \to Comp$

$\mathcal{LV} : \text{Exp} \to Env \to Comp$

$val\text{-}to\text{-}storable = \lambda v \,.\, v$

$\mathcal{E}[\![(\text{app}\ E_1\ E_2)]\!] = \lambda e \,.\, (with\text{-}procedure\text{-}comp\ (\mathcal{E}[\![E_1]\!]\ e)$
$\qquad\qquad\qquad\qquad (\lambda p \,.\, (with\text{-}location\ (\mathcal{LV}[\![E_2]\!]\ e)\ p)))$

$\mathcal{E}[\![I]\!] = \lambda e \,.\, (with\text{-}nameable\ (lookup\ I\ e)\ (\lambda l \,.\, (fetching\ l\ val\text{-}to\text{-}comp)))$

$\mathcal{LV}[\![I]\!] = \lambda e \,.\, (with\text{-}nameable\ (lookup\ I\ e)$
$\qquad\qquad\qquad (\lambda l \,.\, (val\text{-}to\text{-}comp\ (Location \rightarrowtail Value\ l))))$

$\mathcal{LV}[\![(\text{begin}\ E_1\ E_2)]\!] = \lambda e \,.\, (sequence\ (\mathcal{E}[\![E_1]\!]\ e)\ (\mathcal{LV}[\![E_2]\!]\ e))$

$\mathcal{LV}[\![E_{other}]\!]$; where E_{other} is not I or $(\text{begin}\ E_1\ E_2)$
$= \lambda e \,.\, (with\text{-}value\ (\mathcal{E}[\![E_{other}]\!]\ e)$
$\qquad\qquad (\lambda v \,.\, (allocating\ v\ (\lambda l \,.\, (val\text{-}to\text{-}comp\ (Location \rightarrowtail Value\ l))))))$

Call-by-Reference

Figure 8.27 Parameter-passing mechanisms in FLAVAR, part II.

However, because side effects in argument expressions are performed at the time
of lookup rather than at the time of call, CBL can exhibit different behavior from
CBV. For example, consider the following expression:

```
(let ((a 0))
  (let ((f (abs (x)
              (begin (set! a 17)
                     (+ x x)))))
    (f (begin (set! a (+ a 1)) a))))
```

Under CBV, the call to f first increments a and then binds x to a location
holding 1. The assignment of 17 to a does not affect x, so the result is 2. However,
under CBL, the call to f binds x to a location that holds the computation of
(begin (set! a (+ a 1)) a). This computation is not performed until the
first reference of x, which occurs *after* a has been set to 17. So this expression
returns 36 under CBL.

Call-by-reference

So far, all the parameter-passing mechanisms we have discussed allocate a new
location for every argument. But in the case where the argument expression is a
variable reference, there is already a location associated with the variable. This
suggests a mechanism that uses the existing location rather than allocating a new
one. Such a mechanism is termed **call-by-reference (CBR)**, and is described in
Figure 8.27. FORTRAN and PASCAL are examples of languages that support CBR.

In CBR, there is the question of what to do with an argument that is not an
explicit identifier. For example, in the application (test (+ 1 2)), the value of
(+ 1 2) has no associated location. Languages handle this situation in different
ways. In PASCAL, it is an error to supply anything but an identifier as a CBR
argument. In FORTRAN, however, a new location will be allocated for any argument that is not an identifier. The semantics in Figure 8.27 takes this latter
approach. In fact, this is the *only* mechanism for creating new mutable variables
in CBR FLAVAR. This is a somewhat unrealistic aspect of our language; real
CBR languages have special declarations for introducing new variables.

The denotational semantics for CBR models the special handling of variables
as arguments by providing two valuation functions for expressions: $\mathcal{E}$ and $\mathcal{LV}$.
$\mathcal{LV}$ finds the L-value of an expression, while $\mathcal{E}$ finds the R-value of an expression.
For an expression that is an identifier, $\mathcal{LV}$ returns the location associated with
that identifier. For a begin expression, the L-value of the second subexpression
is used, which can make begin expressions ending with a variable reference work
nicely. For any other expression, $\mathcal{LV}$ allocates a new location for the R-value of the

expression and returns this location. The key feature of the CBR semantics is that $\mathcal{LV}$ (rather than $\mathcal{E}$) is used to evaluate the operand of a procedure application.

In FLAVAR, procedure calls are expressions that return results, but in many imperative languages, procedure calls are commands that do not return results. In such languages, CBR is useful as a means of extracting a result from a procedure call. An argument to a procedure can be a variable that the procedure uses to communicate the result back to the caller. Here is an example of this idiom in CBR FLAVAR:

```
(let ((a 0)
      (double (abs (in out)
                (set! out (+ in in)))))
  (begin
  {a is 0 here}
  (double 17 a)
  {now a is 34}
  (+ a 1)))  CBR FLAVAR→ 35
```

The `double` procedure takes a numeric argument (`in`) and a variable (`out`) for returning the result of doubling `in`. In the example, the variable `a` is used to communicate the result of the doubling operation back to the point of call.

One characteristic of CBR (or any paradigm that allows mutable entities to be passed as arguments) is that two different names may refer to the same location. This situation is known as **aliasing**. Consider the following example:

```
(let ((x 1))
  (let ((test (abs (a)
                (begin
                  (set! x 20)
                  (+ a x)))))
    (test x)))  CBR FLAVAR→ 40
```

Within the call (`test x`), both `x` and `a` are aliases for the same location, so the assignment to `x` changes `a`. Aliasing is often considered undesirable because it complicates reasoning about programs.

CBR is similar to passing a mutable cell as an argument to a procedure. The difference is that variables are more restricted than cells. A mutable cell is a first-class value: it may be named, passed as an argument to a procedure, returned as a result from a procedure, and stored in any data structure, including another cell. On the other hand, while a variable may be named by an identifier and passed as an argument to a procedure, it cannot be returned as a result from a procedure, and it cannot be stored in a data structure (including another variable). Unlike cells, therefore, variables are not first-class values. Although this

restricts the expressive power of variables, it permits variables to be implemented
more efficiently than cells. A variable may be allocated on a run-time execution
stack, while cells generally must be allocated from a garbage-collected heap. We
will have much more to say about tradeoffs between expressiveness and efficiency
when we study pragmatic issues later on.

Exercise 8.18 Give the value of the following FLAVAR expression under each of the
following four parameter-passing mechanisms: call-by-value, call-by-name, call-by-need,
and call-by-reference.

```
(let ((a 1))
  (let ((inc! (abs () (begin (set! a (+ a 1)) a))))
    (let ((f (abs (y z)
                (begin (set! y (+ y 3))
                       (+ a (* z z))))))
      (f a (inc!)))))
```

Exercise 8.19 Suppose that you have been provided with a FLAVAR interpreter that
uses one of the four parameter-passing mechanisms described above, but you have not
been told which one. Write a single FLAVAR expression E_{param} that you can use to
determine the parameter-passing mechanism of the interpreter. Your expression should
evaluate to one of the following four symbols that names the mechanism used by the
interpreter: (sym value), (sym name), (sym need), or (sym reference). The only
values that you are allowed to use in E_{param} are symbols and procedures; you may not
use numbers, pairs, booleans, or cells. Of course, you may use mutable variables as well.

Exercise 8.20 Cy D. Fect thinks that set! should return the previous value of the
variable rather than the unit value. Cy gives the following example of his desired behavior
for set!:

$$\overline{(let\ ((a\ 20))\ (list\ (set!\ a\ (+\ a\ 1))\ (set!\ a\ (*\ a\ 2))\ a)}$$
$$\overline{\ CBV\ FLAVAR\ }^{\rightarrow}\ \triangleleft 20,\ 21,\ 42\triangleright$$

a. Change the denotational semantics for CBV FLAVARK to implement Cy's version
   of set!.

b. Use your denotational semantics to explain the meaning of the following idiom using
   Cy's version of set!: (set! I_1 (set! I_2 I_1)).

Exercise 8.21 Renowned naming expert Dinah McScoop has hired you to implement
in FLAVAR a new construct that she calls fluid-let. Here is Dinah's specification for
her construct:

(fluid-let ((I E_{def})) E_{body}) temporarily assigns to an existing bound variable I
    the value of E_{def} during the evaluation of E_{body} and then resets I to its original value.
    Returns the value of E_{body}. Signals an error if I is not already bound in the enclosing
    lexical scope.

Note that `fluid-let` is not a binding construct because it does not declare I as a new variable. Rather, it temporarily changes the value of an existing variable. Dinah has designed `fluid-let` to have a syntax similar to that of `let`, but for simplicity the construct only supports one binding.

a. Dinah claims that `fluid-let` gives much of the behavior associated with dynamic scoping within a statically scoped language like FLAVAR. What are the values of the following three FLAVAR expressions using `fluid-let`?

  i.
```
(let ((a 1))
  (let f (abs (x) (+ x a))
    (+ (fluid-let ((a 20)) (f 300))
       (f 4000))))
```

  ii.
```
(let ((a 1))
  (+ (fluid-let ((a 20))
       (begin (set! a (+ a 300)) a))
     a))
```

  iii.
```
(let ((a 1))
  (let ((p (fluid-let ((a 20))
             (let ((f (abs (x) (+ x a))))
               (pair (f a) f)))))
    ((snd p) (fst p))))
```

b. `fluid-let` can be implemented in FLAVAR via desugaring. Extend the desugaring rules of FLAVAR to implement `fluid-let`.

Exercise 8.22

a. Mutable variables provide no more expressive power than mutable cells. Show this by defining a translation from CBV FLAVARK programs to CBV FLICK programs. Because `rec` can be expressed as syntactic sugar in FLAVARK, you need not describe how to translate `rec` expressions. (Transforming mutable variables to mutable cells is known as **assignment conversion**; see Section 17.5 for a discussion of assignment conversion in the context of a transformation-based compiler.)

b. Modify your translation from part **a** to handle each of the following alternative parameter-passing mechanisms for FLAVARK: CBN, CBL, and CBR.

Exercise 8.23 The FLAVAR language was defined denotationally but not operationally.

a. Modify the SOS for CBV FLICK to yield an SOS for CBV FLAVARK.

b. Modify your SOS for CBV FLAVARK to implement CBN parameter passing.

c. Modify your SOS for CBV FLAVARK to implement CBL parameter passing.

d. Modify your SOS for CBV FLAVARK to implement CBR parameter passing.

Notes

What "state" means is far from obvious. For some interesting reflections on the notion of state, see [SS78, Part Two], [ASS96, Section 3.1], [Baw93, Chapter 6].

In our operational semantics for FLICK, we model state as a global store component separate from the program that is threaded through the execution of a program. An alternative approach is to represent the store as part of the program itself, as in [FH92]. Regardless of how the store is represented, such an operational semantics makes it possible to reason about the equivalence of expressions in a stateful language (e.g., [MT91a, FH92]).

Moggi observed that the *monad* notion from category theory is useful for describing the semantics of programming language features like side effects, exceptions, continuations, input/output, and nondeterminism [Mog89, Mog91]. Tutorial papers by Wadler [Wad92, Wad95] show how monads can be used to structure an interpreter to support these kinds of features. Many features/systems that at first glance might seem to require state can be expressed in a purely functional framework by using monads or monad-like techniques, including input/ouput and arrays with in-place update [PW93, LJ95], animations [EH97], and robotic controllers [HCNP03].

However, monadic approaches to state suffer from a major modularity problem: In order to add stateful behavior to a program, it is often necessary to restructure large chunks of it to use a monad. In contrast, traditional approaches to representing state are more modular for such changes — an observation made long before the advent of monadic programming [SS78, Part Two].

Alternatively, guided by denotational semantics, programs in stateful languages can be translated to programs in purely functional ones. For example, Morris claims that the EUCLID language [LHL+77], a restricted subset of PASCAL, is effectively a functional language, and backs up this claim by outlining a simple translation from EUCLID to a functional language [Mor82]. He notes that such a translation is also possible for PASCAL, but it would be much more complicated because of additional stateful features of PASCAL.

Hughes argues that lazy evaluation is an essential modularity mechanism in functional programming because it allows producers and consumers of information to work in a coroutining fashion [Hug89].

Lazy evaluation requires some way to share the results of subexpressions evaluated during a computation. Frameworks for modeling such sharing include *graph reduction* [Pey87], a big-step semantics for lazy evaluation [Lau93], the *call-by-need lambda calculus* [AMO+95], and the *cyclic lambda calculus* [AB97].

In this text, we have chosen to introduce state in the context of an existing functional language. An alternative approach is to study the semantics of state in the context of a very simple imperative language, such as one with mutable variables and `while` loops. Examples of this approach are [Sto85, Chapter 9] and [Win93, Chapters 2–6].

What about stateful objects? As noted earlier, stateful object-oriented programming can be achieved by extending the HOOK/HOOPLA languages from Section 7.3 with mutable cell objects or mutable variables. Another way to do object-oriented programming in a function-oriented language is to represent objects as message-passing closures where state is stored in the environment of the closure. See Exercise 14.1 on page 842 for an example of the message-passing idiom. This idiom was discussed in early Scheme papers [SS75, Ste76] and is used extensively for object-oriented programming in Scheme (e.g., [ASS96, AR88]). The power and flexibility of this idiom led Norman Adams to quip, "objects are a poor man's closures" [Dic92].

It has been suggested that the opposite ("closures are a poor man's objects") may also be true [vS]. After all, as illustrated in HOOPLA, a closure can be implemented as an object responding to a single message, `call`. But the ease with which objects can implement closures in HOOPLA depends critically on the fact that HOOK object declarations (via `method`) are statically scoped and can appear in arbitrary expressions. In many class-based object-oriented languages, objects can be declared only in top-level classes, not in arbitrary scopes, which severely impedes their ability to simulate closures. So-called *closure conversion* techniques (see Section 17.10) can be used to translate all closures into instances of top-level classes. Indeed, Java's *inner classes* are based on such a translation. But the translation is complex enough that it is challenging for object-oriented programmers to perform it by hand on a regular basis, which means that powerful function-oriented idioms like mapping, filtering, and folding remain out of their reach. In contrast, object-oriented techniques are more accessible to function-oriented programmers, especially in dynamically typed languages, where static typing problems associated with objects are not an issue.

Using operational or denotational semantics to prove properties of individual programs or program phrases in stateful languages can be tedious. An alternative approach, known as *axiomatic semantics*, is often used to describe the meaning of a program phrase by relating the states of a computation before and after the execution of the phrase. For an introduction to axiomatic semantics, see [Win93, Chapter 6], [Gri87].

9

Control

I shall be telling this with a sigh
Somewhere ages and ages hence:
Two roads diverged in a wood, and I —
I took the one less traveled by,
And that has made all the difference.

— Robert Frost, "The Road Not Taken"

9.1 Motivation: Control Contexts and Continuations

So far, we have studied two kinds of denotational context important in the evaluation of programming language expressions:

- A naming context that determines the meaning of free identifiers within an expression.

- A state context that specifies the time-dependent behavior of mutable entities.

By reifying both of these contexts as mathematical entities — environments for naming contexts and stores for state contexts — the denotational approach provides significant leverage for us to investigate the space of language features that depend on these contexts. In the case of naming, environments help us to understand issues like parameter passing, scoping, and inheritance. In the case of state, stores help us to understand issues involving mutable variables and mutable data structures.

There is a third major context that is still missing from our toolbox: a **control** context. Informally, control describes the path taken by a programmer's eyes and fingertips when hand-simulating the execution of code. For example, when simulating a `while` or `for` loop in an imperative language, it is often necessary to refocus attention to the beginning of the loop after the end of the loop code is reached. Conditional expressions and procedure calls are other simple examples of control constructs that we have seen.

What does it mean for expressions to have a control *context*? As an example, consider the following FLIC expression:

```
(let ((square (abs (x) (@* x x))))
  (@+ (square 5) (@* (@- 6 2) (square 5))))
```

There are two occurrences of the `(square 5)` expression. What is the difference between them? Both are evaluated in the same environment and the same store, so they are guaranteed to yield the same value. What distinguishes them is how their value is used by the rest of the program. Reading from left to right, the first `(square 5)` returns 25 to a process that is collecting the first of two arguments to the application of the `+` primitive. The second `(square 5)` yields its result to a process that is collecting the second of two arguments to an application of the `*` primitive (whose first argument is already known to be 4). This, in turn, is a subtask of the process that is collecting the second of two arguments to the application of the `+` primitive (whose first argument is known to be 25), which itself is a subtask of whatever process is waiting for the answer to the entire `let` expression. What distinguishes the occurrences of `(square 5)` is their control context: the part of the computation that remains to be done after the expression is evaluated.

In an operational framework, evaluation contexts are a way to specify control contexts. In the above squaring example, the control context of the first occurrence of `(square 5)` can be written as

```
(@+ □ (@* (@- 6 2) ((abs (x) (@* x x)) 5)))
```

and the control context of the second occurrence can be written as

```
(@+ 25 (@* 4 □))
```

Even though FLIC is a stateful language, note that the control context does not mention the state in any way.

The key topic we will study in this chapter is how to represent a control context in a denotational setting. The denotational descriptions we have employed so far have not explicitly represented the notion of an evaluation context or "the rest of the computation." A denotational semantics without an explicit control model is said to be a **direct semantics**. A direct semantics for a programming language cannot deal elegantly with interruptions of the normal flow of control of a program. As long as valuation clauses are defined by structural induction on the abstract syntax tree of a program, the flow of control in the clauses has no choice but to follow the structure of this abstract syntax tree.

A simple example of the limitation of direct semantics can be seen in its clumsy handling of error conditions in the languages that we have already encountered.

An error is detected in one part of the semantics, and every other part of the semantics must be able to cope with the possibility that some subexpression has produced an error instead of a normal result. This approach to error checking does not capture the intuition that a computation encountering an error immediately aborts without further processing. Abstractions like *with-value* help to hide this error checking, but they do not eliminate it. Indeed, interpreters based on the direct semantics of FL and its variants expend considerable effort performing such checks.

More generally, a direct denotational semantics cannot easily explain constructs that interrupt the "normal" flow of control:

- *early termination of procedures and loops* as provided by JAVA's and C's `return`, `break`, and `continue` constructs;

- *nonlocal exits* as provided by `setjmp`/`longjmp` in C and `throw`/`catch` in COMMON LISP;

- *unrestricted jumps* permitted in numerous languages via `goto`;

- sophisticated *exception handling* as seen in JAVA, ML, COMMON LISP, DYLAN, and CLU;

- *coroutines*, such as CLU's iterators, ICON's generators, and SATHER's iters, which permit control to pass back and forth between producer and consumer processes;

- *backtracking*, which is used to model nondeterministic choices to solve problems, e.g., to search a tree of possibilities. Backtracking is a common strategy in artificial intelligence programs and is an essential feature provided by PROLOG and other logic-oriented programming languages.

In each of these cases, a program phrase does not simply return some value and/or an updated store, but instead bypasses the control context in which it was executed and transfers control to some other place in the program.

Such control transfers can be modeled denotationally using mathematical entities called **continuations**, which are denotational analogues of the evaluation contexts from operational semantics. A continuation explicitly represents the "rest" of some computation. In implementation terms, it corresponds to a pair of (1) the current run-time stack of procedure-call invocation frames and (2) a return address that specifies what code to run when the currently executing procedure returns a value. The continuation corresponding to the textually subsequent code in a program is usually referred to as the **normal continuation**. Many control constructs achieve their effect by substituting some other continuation for the normal one.

This chapter shows how continuations simplify the descriptions of the languages we have studied so far and allow the modeling of advanced control features in these languages. Be forewarned that control constructs are notoriously hard to think about. Even though many of the formal descriptions of control constructs are surprisingly concise, this does not imply that they are easy to understand. The often convoluted nature of control can lead the reader into mental gymnastics that are likely to leave the brain a little bit sore at first. Fortunately, with sufficient practice, the concepts begin to seem natural, and it becomes clear that continuations are a remarkably powerful tool for understanding and designing complex control structures. Indeed, the area of control is the big payoff for our investment in denotational semantics. Many advanced control constructs that have succinct denotational descriptions are cumbersome to model in an operational framework.

To help build up some intuitions about continuations, we will first discuss how to achieve some sophisticated control behavior using only first-class procedures. Then we will be better prepared to understand the use of continuations in denotational semantics.

9.2   Using Procedures to Model Control

9.2.1   Representing Continuations as Procedures

In the dialects of FL we have studied, the continuation for an expression E is the rest of the computation "waiting for" the value of E. It is natural to think of this continuation as being a unary procedure that takes the value of E and performs the rest of the computation. For example, in the FL expression

```
(let ((square (abs (x) (@* x x))))
  (@+ (square 5) (@* (@- 6 2) (square 5))))
```

the continuation of the first (square 5) can be written as the procedure

```
(abs (v1) (@+ v1 (@* (@- 6 2) ((abs (x) (@* x x)) 5))))
```

and the continuation for the second (square 5) can be written as

```
(abs (v2) (@+ 25 (@* 4 v2)))
```

What we have done in both cases is represent an evaluation context as a procedure by abstracting over the content of its hole.

Even in languages that do not support side effects, continuations require a computation to be viewed in a purely sequential way: some expressions are evaluated "before" other expressions. For example, the above continuations highlight the fact that the operands of an FL primitive application are evaluated in left-to-right order. When the first call to `square` is being evaluated, the second operand to + is the unevaluated expression (@* (@- 6 2) (square 5)). But by the time the second call to `square` is evaluated, the first (square 5) has been evaluated to 25 and the (@- 6 2) operand to * has been evaluated to 4.

When continuations are represented explicitly, every computation can be viewed as an iteration in two state variables: (1) the expression currently being evaluated and (2) the continuation of the current expression. For example, the following table summarizes this iteration for a simple arithmetic calculation:

Expression	Continuation
(@/ (@+ (@* 6 5) (@- 7 3)) 2)	k_{top}
(@+ (@* 6 5) (@- 7 3))	k_1 = (abs (v1) (k_{top} (@/ v1 2)))
(@* 6 5)	k_2 = (abs (v2) (k_1 (@+ v2 (@- 7 3))))
30	k_2
(@- 7 3)	k_3 = (abs (v3) (k_1 (@+ 30 v3)))
4	k_3
(@+ 30 4)	k_1
34	k_1
(@/ 34 2)	k_{top}
17	k_{top}

By convention, we use the variable k to name continuations. We assume that an expression is initially evaluated relative to the top-level continuation k_{top}. In this case, k_{top} can be thought of as the identity procedure (abs (v) v), but sometimes it can be more complex. For example, in an interactive read-eval-print loop, k_{top} would be a unary procedure that prints its argument (the value of the last expression entered by the user) and then prompts the user to enter the next expression to evaluate.

As a more complex example of the iterative view of computation, consider the following factorial example written in FL:

```
((rec fact-rec {E_{fact-rec}}
   (abs (n)
     (if (@= n 0)
         1
         (@* n (fact-rec (@- n 1)))))))
 3)
```

This iteration table summarizes key steps in the evaluation of this expression:

Expression	Continuation
$(E_{fact-rec}$ 3)	k_{top}
$(E_{fact-rec}$ 2)	k_1 = (abs (v1) (k_{top} (@* 3 v1)))
$(E_{fact-rec}$ 1)	k_2 = (abs (v2) (k_1 (@* 2 v2)))
$(E_{fact-rec}$ 0)	k_3 = (abs (v3) (k_2 (@* 1 v3)))
(@* 1 1)	k_2
(@* 2 1)	k_1
(@* 3 2)	k_{top}
6	k_{top}

Note the stack-like nature of the continuations. When the base case of 0 is reached in the factorial computation, the continuation is k_3. This continuation references k_2, k_2 references k_1, and k_1 references k_{top}. Each of these continuations can be viewed as representing a procedure-call invocation frame in a traditional stack-based implementation of procedure calls. Calling a procedure creates a new continuation that corresponds to the frame that is pushed onto the top of the call stack. Invoking a continuation corresponds to popping the top frame off the call stack and returning control to code in the calling procedure, whose frame becomes the new top-of-stack frame.

It is worthwhile comparing the recursive factorial computation above to another way of computing factorial:

```
((abs (n) {E_fact-iter}
   ((rec fact-loop {E_fact-loop}
      (abs (num ans)
        (if (@= num 0)
            ans
            (fact-loop (@- num 1) (@* num ans)))))
    n 1))
 3)
```

In the iteration table summarizing the evaluation of this expression, note that the continuation for every application of $E_{fact-loop}$ is the same as the continuation for the top-level application $(E_{fact-iter}$ 3):

Expression	Continuation
$(E_{fact-iter}$ 3)	k_{top}
$(E_{fact-loop}$ 3 1)	k_{top}
$(E_{fact-loop}$ 2 3)	k_{top}
$(E_{fact-loop}$ 1 6)	k_{top}
$(E_{fact-loop}$ 0 6)	k_{top}
6	k_{top}

We will say that a recursive procedure like `fact-loop` is **iterative** because invoking it generates a computation like that expected for iteration constructs such as `while`, `for`, and `repeat/until` loops in many languages. The defining characteristic of such iteration constructs is that they repeat a computation using only constant **control space**. That is, the space required to control the iteration (the state variables themselves — e.g., `num` and `ans` in the `fact-loop` example — and any code pointers needed for the execution) is constant. The control space is distinguished from the **data space** required to represent any compound data stored in the state variables.

Because the `fact-loop` computation does not involve any new continuations, an implementation need not push a new invocation frame onto the procedure-call stack when the `fact-loop` procedure is called, so the stack size can remain constant during this factorial computation. In contrast, invocations of the `fact-rec` procedure do involve new continuations and their corresponding invocation frames, so `fact-rec` is not iterative. When we study compilation, we will see how a compiler can guarantee that an invocation of an iterative procedure like `fact-loop` does not create an invocation frame and so is executed like a looping construct (see the discussion of the *tail-call optimization* on page 1064).

9.2.2 Continuation-Passing Style (CPS)

We saw above that every procedure application is evaluated relative to an implicit continuation. It turns out that we can implement some sophisticated control behavior if we make this continuation explicit. We will say that a procedure that takes an explicit representation of its continuation is written in **continuation-passing style (CPS)**. For example, here is a CPS version of the recursive factorial procedure studied above:

```
(def fact-rec-cps
  (abs (n k)
    (if (@= n 0)
        (k 1)
        (fact-rec-cps (@- n 1)
          (abs (v) (k (@* n v)))))))
```

The body of a CPS procedure "returns" a value by invoking its continuation on that value. In the body of `fact-rec-cps`, there are two such invocations: `(k 1)` returns 1 in the base case and `(k (@* n v))` returns a product of `n` and the value `v` of the recursive call in the general case. A CPS procedure is invoked with a second argument that explicitly specifies what to do with the result of the invocation. For example, in the body of `fact-rec-cps`, the invocation

```
(fact-rec-cps (@- n 1)
  (abs (v) (k (@* n v))))
```

can be read as

> Call `fact-rec-cps` on the result of decrementing `n`. Name the result of
> this call `v`. Then return the result of multiplying `n` and `v`.

When `fact-rec-cps` is invoked from other parts of a program, a continuation
specifying how to process the result must be supplied. For example:

$$\text{(fact-rec-cps 3 (abs (v) v))} \xrightarrow[FL]{} 6$$

$$\text{(fact-rec-cps 3 (abs (v) (@* v 7)))} \xrightarrow[FL]{} 42$$

The fact that continuations can be explicitly represented as procedures is
intellectually interesting, but is it practically useful? Yes! We shall study two
key applications of this fact:

1. In the remainder of this section, we shall explore some sophisticated control behavior that can be realized when certain continuations are explicitly
   represented as first-class procedures. In particular, we will see how explicit
   continuations can be used to implement multiple-value-returning procedures,
   nonlocal exits, coroutines, error handling, and backtracking.

2. When we study compilation in Chapter 17, we will see that control aspects
   of a program can be made concrete by automatically converting all code into
   continuation-passing style (see Section 17.9). Remarkably, this CPS conversion
   stage of the compiler makes it unnecessary for the implementation to have
   explicit stacks of procedure-call invocation frames; all such invocation frames
   are implicit in the continuations.

9.2.3   Multiple-value Returns

It is often useful for a procedure to return more than one value. A classic example
of the utility of multiple-value returns concerns integer division and remainder.
Languages often provide two primitives for these operations even though the same
algorithm computes both. It would make more sense to have a single operation
that returns two values.

As another example, suppose that we want to write an FL program that,
given a binary tree with integer leaves, computes the product of (1) the height of
the tree and (2) the sum of the leaves in the tree. We will assume that such trees
are manipulated using the procedures in Figure 9.1. One approach is to apply

```
(def (node left right) (pair left right))
(def (left tree) (fst tree))
(def (right tree) (snd tree))
(def (leaf? tree) (not (pair? tree)))
```

Figure 9.1   Procedures for manipulating binary trees.

```
(def (height*sum₁ tree)
  (letrec ((height (abs (tr)
                   (if (leaf? tr)
                       0
                       (+ 1 (max (height (left tr))
                                 (height (right tr)))))))

          (sum (abs (tr)
                (if (leaf? tr)
                    tr
                    (+ (sum (left tr))
                       (sum (right tr)))))))
    (* (height tree) (sum tree))))
```

Figure 9.2   The first version of `height*sum` performs two tree traversals.

two different procedures to the tree and combine the results as in Figure 9.2.[1]
Notice that $height*sum_1$ requires two walks over the given tree.

A procedure that returns multiple values enables the computation to be performed in a single tree walk. A simple method of doing this is to return a pair at each node of the tree as in Figure 9.3. However, the bundling and unbundling of values makes this approach to multiple values messy and hard to read in FL. This approach is far more palatable in languages like ML and HASKELL that support the deconstruction of structured values via pattern-matching notation.

An alternative approach for returning multiple values is to use first-class procedures to represent continuations that accept multiple values. If procedure M is supposed to return multiple values, we can modify it to take an extra argument R, called the **receiver** (which, by convention, usually comes last). The

---

[1]Henceforth, we will not use @ with arithmetic operators in examples unless we are concerned about name capture or are focusing on formal properties of expressions in the context of operational rewriting steps or denotational calculations. Otherwise, it doesn't matter whether we use the primitive arithmetic operators or the corresponding arithmetic procedures from the standard library.

receiver is a procedure that expects the multiple values as its arguments and
combines them into some result. M returns its results by calling R on them.
We have already seen numerous examples of this strategy in metalanguage functions (Section A.2.5) and in the discussion of monadic style (Section 8.2.3). Figure 9.4 shows how to apply this idea to our current example. This style of
code can be difficult to read. The `receiver` argument to the `inner` procedure
acts as a continuation encoding what computation needs to be performed on the
two values that `inner` "returns." For example, suppose E_{inner} is the expression
`(rec inner (abs (tr receiver) ...))`. Then the call $(E_{inner}$ `tree *)` starts
off the process by applying the abstraction `(abs (tr receiver) ...)` (obtained
from unwinding the `rec` expression E_{inner}) to the tree `tree` with a receiver `*` that
will take the two results and return their product.

Even though the receiver is an argument, it is typical to ignore its argument
status and view it as a different entity when reading a call to a procedure like
`inner`. So `(inner` E_1 `(abs (`I_1 I_2`)` E_2`))` can be read as "Call `inner` on E_1
and apply the procedure `(abs (`I_1 I_2`)` E_2`)` to the results" or "Evaluate E_2 in
an environment where I_1 and I_2 are bound to the two results of applying `inner`
to E_1." Note that these readings treat `inner` as a procedure of one argument
that returns two results, not a procedure of two arguments. Viewing continuation
argument(s) as different entities from other arguments is important for getting a
better working understanding of them.

Unlike the other two approaches, using a receiver forces us to choose a particular order for examining the branches of the binary tree. The main advantage
of a receiver is that it allows the multiple returned values to be named using the
standard naming construct, `abs`; it is not necessary to invent a new syntax for
naming intermediate values.

As a concrete example, consider the following application of `height*sum`$_3$:

$$\text{(height*sum}_3 \text{ (pair 6 (pair 7 8)))}$$

(We use `pair` directly rather than `node` to simplify the discussion of the evaluation
of this expression.) Figure 9.5 presents a sequence of key evaluation steps for
this example in a CBV version of FL. In this and subsequent figures showing
evaluation sequences, we take two liberties to simplify the notation:

- The evaluation relation is defined only on kernel expressions, but we will use
  it on sugared expressions as well. In this case, $E_1 \overset{*}{\Rightarrow} E_2$ means that the kernel
  expression that results from desugaring E_1 rewrites to the kernel expression
  that results from desugaring E_2 in some number of evaluation steps.

```
(def (height*sum₂ tree)
  (letrec ((inner (abs (tr)
                    (if (leaf? tr)
                        (pair 0 tr)
                        (let ((height&sum1 (inner (left tr)))
                              (height&sum2 (inner (right tr))))
                          (pair (+ 1 (max (fst height&sum1)
                                          (fst height&sum2)))
                                (+ (snd height&sum1)
                                   (snd height&sum2)))))))))
    (let ((height&sum (inner tree)))
      (* (fst height&sum) (snd height&sum)))))
```

Figure 9.3 The second version of `height*sum` uses pairs to return multiple values.

```
(def (height*sum₃ tree)
  ((rec inner {Let E_inner be (rec inner ... )}
     (abs (tr receiver)
       (if (leaf? tr)
           (receiver 0 tr)
           (inner (left tr)
                  (abs (h1 s1)
                    (inner (right tr)
                           (abs (h2 s2)
                             (receiver (+ 1 (max h1 h2))
                                       (+ s1 s2)))))))))
   tree {First argument to local recursive procedure inner}
   *    {Second argument to local recursive procedure inner}
  ))
```

Figure 9.4 The third version of `height*sum` passes multiple values to procedural continuations.

• We will use the names of standard procedures (e.g., `+`) in contexts where abstractions wrapping the associated primitives (e.g., `(abs (x y) (@+ x y))`) would actually be substituted for the names.

In Figure 9.5, note how the continuation argument to `inner` acts like a stack that keeps track of the pending operations.

```
(height*sum₃ (pair 6 (pair 7 8)))
 *
CBV⟹ (E_inner (pair 6 (pair 7 8)) *)
 *
CBV⟹ (E_inner 6
        (abs (h1 s1)
          (E_inner (pair 7 8)
            (abs (h2 s2)
              (* (+ 1 (max h1 h2)) (+ s1 s2))))))
 *
CBV⟹ ((abs (h1 s1)
          (E_inner (pair 7 8)
            (abs (h2 s2)
              (* (+ 1 (max h1 h2)) (+ s1 s2)))))
       0 6)
 *
CBV⟹ (E_inner (pair 7 8)
        (abs (h2 s2)
          (* (+ 1 (max 0 h2)) (+ 6 s2))))
 *
CBV⟹ (E_inner 7
        (abs (h1 s1)
          (E_inner 8
            (abs (h2 s2)
              ((abs (h2 s2) (* (+ 1 (max 0 h2)) (+ 6 s2)))
               (+ 1 (max h1 h2)) (+ s1 s2))))))
 *
CBV⟹ ((abs (h1 s1)
          (E_inner 8
            (abs (h2 s2)
              ((abs (h2 s2) (* (+ 1 (max 0 h2)) (+ 6 s2)))
               (+ 1 (max h1 h2)) (+ s1 s2)))))
       0 7)
 *
CBV⟹ (E_inner 8
        (abs (h2 s2)
          ((abs (h2 s2) (* (+ 1 (max 0 h2)) (+ 6 s2)))
           (+ 1 (max 0 h2)) (+ 7 s2))))
 *
CBV⟹ ((abs (h2 s2)
          ((abs (h2 s2) (* (+ 1 (max 0 h2)) (+ 6 s2)))
           (+ 1 (max 0 h2)) (+ 7 s2)))
       0 8)
 *
CBV⟹ ((abs (h2 s2) (* (+ 1 (max 0 h2)) (+ 6 s2)))
       (+ 1 (max 0 0)) (+ 7 8))
 *
CBV⟹ ((abs (h2 s2) (* (+ 1 (max 0 h2)) (+ 6 s2))) 1 15)
 *
CBV⟹ (* (+ 1 (max 0 1)) (+ 6 15))
 *
CBV⟹ (* 2 21)
 *
CBV⟹ 42
```

Figure 9.5   Key steps in the evaluation of an invocation of height*sum₃.

Exercise 9.1 Using the continuation-based approach to multiple-value returns, give definitions of the following procedures:

(p1 *int-list*): Assume *int-list* is a list of positive integers. Returns a list with three elements: (1) the product of the elements of *int-list*; (2) the maximum of the elements of *int-list*; and (3) a list that has the same length as *int-list* in which each element has twice the value of the corresponding element of *int-list*.

(p2 *int-tree*): Assume *int-tree* is a binary tree whose leaves are positive integers. Returns a list with three elements: (1) the product of the leaves of *int-tree*; (2) the maximum of the leaves of *int-tree*; and (3) a tree that has the same shape as *int-tree* in which each leaf has twice the value of the corresponding leaf of *int-tree*.

Each of your procedures should traverse its argument list or tree exactly once.

9.2.4 Nonlocal Exits

A continuation represents all of the pending operations that are waiting to be done after the current operation. When continuations are implicit, the computation can terminate successfully only when all of the pending operations have been performed. Yet we sometimes want a computation buried deep in pending operations to terminate immediately with a result or at least circumvent some of the pending operations. We can achieve these so-called **nonlocal exits** by using procedures to represent explicit continuations. The key idea is this: When continuations are represented explicitly, we can choose which continuation to invoke or perhaps choose not to invoke any continuation at all.

As a simple example, consider the task of multiplying the leaves in a binary tree of integers. Figure 9.6 shows the natural recursive solution to this problem in FL. For example:

(tree-product$_1$ (node (node 2 3) (node 4 5))) $\xrightarrow[FL]{}$ 120

(tree-product$_1$ (node (node 2 0) (node 4 5))) $\xrightarrow[FL]{}$ 0

Figure 9.7 shows a CPS version of tree-product$_1$. Its behavior is exactly the same as tree-product$_1$'s; we have just made the continuations explicit.

Notice that tree-product$_1$ and tree-product$_2$ dutifully multiply all the leaves of the tree even if it contains the leaf 0. This is wasteful since the answer is known to be 0 as soon as a 0 is encountered. There is no need to look at any other leaves or to perform any more multiplications. tree-product$_3$ in Figure 9.8 performs this optimization. To accomplish a nonlocal exit, tree-product$_3$ distinguishes the continuation passed to the initial call (k-outer) from continuations (k-inner) generated by calls to the local recursive procedure prod. The local recursive procedure behaves like tree-product$_2$ except that it "returns" imme-

```
(def (tree-product₁ tree)
  (if (leaf? tree)
      tree
      (* (tree-product₁ (left tree))
         (tree-product₁ (right tree)))))
```

Figure 9.6 A recursive procedure for computing the product of the leaves of a binary tree of integers.

```
(def (tree-product₂ tree k)
  (if (leaf? tree)
      (k tree)
      (tree-product₂ (left tree)
        (abs (vl)
          (tree-product₂ (right tree)
            (abs (vr)
              (k (* vl vr))))))))
```

Figure 9.7 A CPS procedure for computing the product of the leaves of a binary tree of integers.

```
(def (tree-product₃ tree k-outer)
  ((rec prod
     (abs (tr k-inner)
       (if (leaf? tr)
           (if (= tr 0)
               (k-outer 0)    {"return" 0 immediately from outer procedure}
               (k-inner tr))  {"return" integer leaf from inner procedure}
           (prod (left tr)
             (abs (vl)
               (prod (right tr)
                 (abs (vr)
                   (k-inner (* vl vr)))))))))
   tree     {First argument to local recursive procedure}
   k-outer  {Second argument to local recursive procedure}
   ))
```

Figure 9.8 A CPS tree-product procedure that exits immediately with 0 if a 0 leaf is encountered.

```
(def (tree-product₄ tree)
  ((rec prod {Let E_prod be (rec prod ... )}
     (abs (tr k-inner)
       (if (leaf? tr)
           (if (= tr 0)
               0                    {return 0 immediately from tree-product₄}
               (k-inner tr)) {"return" integer leaf to inner continuation}
           (prod (left tr)
             (abs (vl)
               (prod (right tr)
                 (abs (vr)
                   (k-inner (* vl vr)))))))))
    tree          {First argument to local recursive procedure}
    (abs (v) v) {Second argument to local recursive procedure}
    ))
```

Figure 9.9 A non-CPS tree-product procedure that exits immediately with 0 if a 0
leaf is encountered.

diately to `k-outer` upon encountering a 0. This avoids processing the rest of the
tree and bypasses all pending multiplications represented by `k-inner`.

In this example, there was actually no need to convert the outer procedure
to CPS form. The only continuations needed are those used by the internal
recursive procedure. This observation leads to the definition of `tree-product₄`
in Figure 9.9. In this procedure, if a 0 leaf is encountered, a 0 is directly returned
as the result of `tree-product₄`. Explicit continuations are used to represent
pending computations in the local recursive `prod` procedure so that they can be
bypassed if a 0 is encountered. Figure 9.10 shows key steps in the evaluation
of `(tree-product₄ (pair (pair 2 0) (pair 4 5)))`. In particular, it shows
that the continuation in place when 0 is encountered is never invoked; instead, 0
is returned immediately as the result of the invocation of `tree-product₄`.

9.2.5 Coroutines

Coroutining is a situation in which control jumps back and forth between conceptually independent processes. The most common version is producer/consum-
er coroutines, where a consumer process transfers control to a producer process
when it wants the next value generated by the producer, and the producer returns
control to the consumer along with the value. A classic example of this kind of
coroutine is a compiler front end in which a parser requests tokens from a lexical
scanner that produces them on an as-needed basis.

```
(tree-product₄ (pair (pair 2 0) (pair 4 5)))
```

$\xLongrightarrow[CBV]{*}$ $(E_{prod}$ (pair (pair 2 0) (pair 4 5)) (abs (v) v))

$\xLongrightarrow[CBV]{*}$ $(E_{prod}$ (pair 2 0)
            (abs (vl)
              (E_{prod} (pair 4 5)
                (abs (vr)
                  ((abs (v) v) (* vl vr)))))))

$\xLongrightarrow[CBV]{*}$ $(E_{prod}$ 2
            (abs (vl)
              (E_{prod} 0
                (abs (vr)
                  ((abs (vl)
                      (E_{prod} (pair 4 5)
                        (abs (vr)
                          ((abs (v) v) (* vl vr)))))
                    (* vl vr)))))))

$\xLongrightarrow[CBV]{*}$ $(E_{prod}$ 0
            (abs (vr)
              ((abs (vl)
                  (E_{prod} (pair 4 5)
                    (abs (vr)
                      ((abs (v) v) (* vl vr)))))
                (* 2 vr))))

$\xLongrightarrow[CBV]{*}$ (if (= 0 0)
            0
            ((abs (vr)
                ((abs (vl)
                    (E_{prod} (pair 4 5)
                      (abs (vr)
                        ((abs (v) v) (* vl vr)))))
                  (* 2 vr)))
              0))

$\xLongrightarrow[CBV]{*}$ 0 $\{$(abs (vr) ...) *is never invoked!*$\}$

Figure 9.10   Key steps in the evaluation of an invocation of tree-product₄.

```
(def (count-from num)
  ((rec new-producer
     (abs (n) {E_{abs:producer}}
       (abs (consumer)
         (consumer n (new-producer (+ n 1))))))
   num))
(def (add-first length)
  ((rec new-consumer
     (abs (len sum) {E_{abs:consumer}}
       (abs (value next-producer)
         (if (= len 0)
             sum
             (next-producer (new-consumer (- len 1) (+ value sum)))))))
   length 0))
```

Figure 9.11   A simple producer/consumer example.

Here, we will show how simple producer/consumer coroutines can be implemented by using first-class procedures to represent control. An alternative technique for implementing such coroutines is to have the producer and consumer communicate via conceptually infinite data structures like **streams**, a notion we study in Section 10.1.3.

We represent a producer as a procedure that takes a consumer as its argument and hands that consumer the requested value along with the next producer. We represent a consumer as a procedure that takes a value and a producer as arguments, and either returns or calls the producer on the next consumer.

For example, suppose (count-from n) makes a producer that generates the (conceptually infinite) increasing sequence of integers beginning with n, and (add-first m) makes a consumer that adds up the first m elements of the producer to which it's attached. Then ((count-from 3) (add-first 5)) returns the sum of the integers from 3 to 7, inclusive. Figure 9.11 presents FL definitions of count-from and add-first and Figure 9.12 shows key steps in the evaluation of ((count-from 13) (add-first 3)). Note how this coroutining technique is able to effectively interleave two independently defined loops — the producer loop (new-producer) and the consumer loop (new-consumer) — by having control jump back and forth between the loops.

{*Add up the 3 consecutive integers starting at 13*}
```
((count-from 13) (add-first 3))
```
$\xrightarrow[CBV]{*}$ ((abs (consumer) (consumer 13 ($E_{abs:producer}$ (+ 13 1))))
     (abs (value next-producer)
       (if (= 3 0) 0
         (next-producer ($E_{abs:consumer}$ (- 3 1) (+ value 0))))))

$\xrightarrow[CBV]{*}$ ((abs (value next-producer)
      (if (= 3 0) 0
        (next-producer ($E_{abs:consumer}$ (- 3 1) (+ value 0)))))
    13 (abs (consumer) (consumer 14 ($E_{abs:producer}$ (+ 14 1)))))

$\xrightarrow[CBV]{*}$ ((abs (consumer) (consumer 14 ($E_{abs:producer}$ (+ 14 1))))
     (abs (value next-producer)
       (if (= 2 0) 13
         (next-producer ($E_{abs:consumer}$ (- 2 1) (+ value 13))))))

$\xrightarrow[CBV]{*}$ ((abs (value next-producer)
      (if (= 2 0) 13
        (next-producer ($E_{abs:consumer}$ (- 2 1) (+ value 13)))))
    14 (abs (consumer) (consumer 15 ($E_{abs:producer}$ (+ 15 1)))))

$\xrightarrow[CBV]{*}$ ((abs (consumer) (consumer 15 ($E_{abs:producer}$ (+ 15 1))))
     (abs (value next-producer)
       (if (= 1 0) 27
         (next-producer ($E_{abs:consumer}$ (- 1 1) (+ value 27))))))

$\xrightarrow[CBV]{*}$ ((abs (value next-producer)
      (if (= 1 0) 27
        (next-producer ($E_{abs:consumer}$ (- 1 1) (+ value 27)))))
    15 (abs (consumer) (consumer 16 ($E_{abs:producer}$ (+ 16 1)))))

$\xrightarrow[CBV]{*}$ ((abs (consumer) (consumer 16 ($E_{abs:producer}$ (+ 16 1))))
     (abs (value next-producer)
       (if (= 0 0) 42
         (next-producer ($E_{abs:consumer}$ (- 0 1) (+ value 42))))))

$\xrightarrow[CBV]{*}$ ((abs (value next-producer)
      (if (= 0 0) 42
        (next-producer ($E_{abs:consumer}$ (- 0 1) (+ value 42)))))
    16 (abs (consumer) (consumer 17 ($E_{abs:producer}$ (+ 17 1)))))

$\xrightarrow[CBV]{*}$ 42

Figure 9.12   Key steps in the evaluation of ((count-from 13) (add-first 3)).

Exercise 9.2 A problem with the definitions in Figure 9.11 in a CBV version of FLK is that the producer resulting from `count-from` can "run ahead" of the consumer resulting from `add-first`. For example, in the evaluation sequence in Figure 9.12, the producer has produced two numbers (16 and 17) beyond the last number that is actually needed (15). Not only is this inefficient, but in some producers it can cause problems in situations where attempting to produce the next element beyond the last one needed would lead to an error. Modify the definitions of `count-from` and `add-first` so that no number is generated by the producer unless it is actually needed by the consumer. *Hint:* use thunks!

9.2.6 Error Handling

The dialects of FL that we have studied all use the `error` construct to indicate that a computation has encountered an abnormal situation. Executing this construct effectively halts the computation. However, there are many times we want to handle the error in a way that allows the computation to proceed. Additionally, we want the flexibility to handle the error in different ways under different circumstances.

For example, consider the implementation of an environment data structure that binds names to values. Suppose that (`env-lookup` *name env*) is an operation that returns the value bound to the name *name* in the environment *env*. What should `env-lookup` do if *env* doesn't have any binding for *name*? Sometimes we simply want to terminate the computation with an unbound-variable error. But there are many situations in which we want the computation to continue. Perhaps `env-lookup` is being used to implement an operation that merges two environments, à la *merge* in the environments we have studied in denotational semantics (Figure 6.24 on page 277). In this case, if looking up a name in one environment fails, we want to look up the name in another environment. Or perhaps `env-lookup` is being used to look up variables in the implementation of an interpreter for the FL programming language. If we are testing the interpreter on a test suite of programs, some of which have unbound-variable errors, we want looking up an unbound variable to indicate that the current test case resulted in an unbound-variable error but also continue to run the remaining test cases. And if we embed the same interpreter in an interactive read-eval-print loop, we want to handle an unbound variable by indicating that an error has occurred when evaluating the current expression and then prompt the user for the next expression to evaluate.

One technique for handling errors is to use two continuations: a **success continuation** that is used for normal flow of control and a **failure continuation** that is used to handle abnormal situations. For example, Figure 9.13 presents

an implementation of environments as lists of name/value pairs in which the
env-lookup function takes a success (succ) and failure (fail) continuation in
addition to the name and environment arguments. If the name is bound in the
given environment, the success continuation is called on the associated value.
Otherwise, the failure continuation (which is a nullary procedure) is invoked.
Here is a sample use of env-lookup:

```
(def e1 (env-extend (sym a) 3
          (env-extend (sym b) 2
            (env-extend (sym a) 1
              (env-empty)))))
(def (env-test1 names env)
  (map (abs (name)
          (env-lookup name env
            (abs (v) v)
            (abs () (sym *unbound*))))
        names))
(env-test1 (list (sym a) (sym b) (sym c)) e1)
    ⟶FL  ◁3, 2, '*unbound*'▷
```

In env-test1, the success continuation for env-lookup returns the value that is
found and the failure continuation returns the symbol *unbound*.

A more interesting use of env-lookup's failure continuation is illustrated by
env-test2 in Figure 9.14. The env-test2 procedure takes a list of names and an
environment and returns a list of name/value binding pairs for all of the bound
names; the unbound names are ignored. For example:

```
(env-test2 (list (sym a) (sym c) (sym b) (sym d)) e1)
    ⟶FL  ◁⟨'a', 3⟩, ⟨'b', 2⟩▷
```

The env-test2 procedure is implemented in terms of a loop procedure that uses
an explicit continuation k to collect the binding list. When a name is in the
environment, env-lookup's success continuation invokes k to add a new binding to the list that results from processing the remaining names. But when a
name is unbound, env-lookup's failure continuation just continues processing
the remaining names.

In Figure 9.13, success and failure continuations are also used in the implementation of (env-extend name val env) to avoid unnecessary data allocation
(pair creation). When name is bound in env, a list of env's bindings in which a
new binding of name to val is in the same position as the old binding for name
is returned. In this case it is necessary to create only one new binding (pairing
name and val) and to copy the list nodes (the pairs that make up the list) up

```
{Returns an empty list of bindings.}
(def (env-empty) (list))

{If there is a name/value binding pair that binds name in the
 environment, call the success continuation on the associated value.
 Otherwise invoke the failure continuation.}
(def (env-lookup name env succ fail)
  (if (null? env)
      (fail)
      (let ((binding (car env)))
        (if (sym=? name (fst binding))
            (succ (snd binding))
            (env-lookup name (cdr env) succ fail)))))

{If there is a name/value binding pair that binds name in the environment,
 return a binding list in which the new binding for name appears instead
 of the old binding, in the same position in the list. Otherwise return a
 binding list that has a new binding for name to value at the front.}
(def (env-extend name value env)
  (let ((new-binding (pair name value)))
    (env-extend-loop name value env
      (abs (bindings) bindings)
      (abs () (cons new-binding env)))))

(def (env-extend-loop name value env succ fail)
  (if (null? env)
      (fail)
      (let ((binding (car env)))
        (if (sym=? name (fst binding))
            (succ (cons (pair name value) (cdr env)))
            (env-extend-loop name value (cdr env)
              (abs (bindings) (succ (cons binding bindings)))
              fail)))))

{Returns an environment with all the bindings of the two given environments.
 If a name is bound in both, precedence is given to the binding in env1.}
(def (env-merge env1 env2)
  (foldr (abs (binding env)
             (env-extend (fst binding) (snd binding) env))
         env2
         env1))
```

Figure 9.13 Implementation of environments as lists of pairs that uses success and failure continuations.

```
(def (env-test2 names env)
  (letrec ((loop (abs (ns k)
                   (if (null? ns)
                       (k nil)
                       (env-lookup (car ns) env
                         (abs (val)
                           (loop (cdr ns)
                             (abs (bindings)
                               (k (cons (pair (car ns) val)
                                        bindings)))))
                         (abs () (loop (cdr ns) k)))))))
    (loop names (abs (bindings) bindings))))
```

Figure 9.14 The `env-test2` procedure uses the failure continuations of `env-lookup` to ignore names that are unbound in the environment.

to and including this new binding. But if *name* is not bound in *env*, the new binding of *name* and *val* is prepended to the front of the binding list, requiring only one new binding and one new list node. This behavior could be achieved in two passes over the bindings by first determining if *name* is bound in *env* and then prepending or updating the binding. But this behavior can be achieved in a single pass over the bindings using success and failure continuations.

Figure 9.15 presents a more elegant implementation of environments as lookup procedures that take (1) a name to be looked up; (2) a unary success continuation to invoke on the value associated with the name if it is bound in the environment; and (3) a nullary failure continuation to invoke if the name is not bound in the environment. The empty environment returned by `env-empty` is a lookup procedure that simply invokes its failure continuation. `env-lookup` invokes its given environment as a lookup procedure on the name and two continuations. (`env-extend` *name val env*) returns a lookup procedure that succeeds with *val* when given *name* and looks up any other name in *env*. (`env-merge` *env1 env2*) returns a lookup procedure that first looks up a name in *env1*. If the name is bound in *env1*, the success continuation is invoked on the associated value; otherwise the name is looked up in *env2*. Note that the `env-test1` and `env-test2` procedures defined earlier will also work with this new implementation of environments.

Exercise 9.3 In Figure 9.13, `env-extend-loop` is defined outside of `env-extend`. Using `letrec`, it is possible to define `env-extend-loop` as a local recursive procedure inside the body of `env-extend`. Show that if this is done, the desirable data allocation behavior of `env-extend-loop` can be achieved by using only a success continuation; no failure continuation is needed.

```
(def (env-empty)
  (abs (name succ fail) (fail)))
(def (env-lookup name env succ fail)
  (env name succ fail))
(def (env-extend name value env)
  (abs (name2 succ fail)
    (if (sym=? name name2)
        (succ value)
        (env name2 succ fail))))
(def (env-merge env1 env2)
  (abs (name succ fail)
    (env1 name succ (abs () (env2 name succ fail)))))
```

Figure 9.15 Implementation of environments as procedures using success and failure continuations.

9.2.7 Backtracking

In many problem-solving scenarios, a choice must be made between several ways to solve a subproblem. Some subproblem solutions may lead to a solution to the whole problem while others may not. When a particular choice makes it impossible to solve the whole problem, it is necessary to **backtrack** to the point where the choice was made and try a different choice. For example, suppose you are trying to get out of a maze and you come to a spot where you can either turn right or turn left. If you turn right and find that all paths lead to dead ends, you need to backtrack to the same spot and instead turn left.

Backtracking can be programmed using success and failure continuations. The success continuation represents the normal flow of control through the program. Every time a choice point is encountered, the success continuation is invoked on one choice but a new failure continuation is created that represents trying the other choices. This failure continuation is a nullary procedure that is invoked if it becomes apparent that the problem cannot be solved with the choices that have been made already. Invoking the failure continuation backtracks to the last choice point and makes a different choice at that point.

A good example of backtracking is finding variable assignments that satisfy a boolean formula. We will represent boolean formulas as s-expressions defined by the following grammar:

$$BF \in \text{BooleanFormula} ::= \quad \texttt{\#t} \mid \texttt{\#f} \mid Y \mid (\texttt{not } BF)$$
$$\mid \; (\texttt{and } BF_1 \; BF_2) \mid (\texttt{or } BF_1 \; BF_2)$$

```
(def (not? form)
  (and (list? form)
       (= (length form) 2)
       (sym=? (car form) (sym not))))
(def (negand form) (nth 2 form))

(def (and? form)
  (and (list? form)
       (= (length form) 3)
       (sym=? (car form) (sym and))))
(def (conjunct1 form) (nth 2 form))
(def (conjunct2 form) (nth 3 form))

(def (or? form)
  (and (list? form)
       (= (length form) 3)
       (sym=? (car form) (sym or))))
(def (disjunct1 form) (nth 2 form))
(def (disjunct2 form) (nth 3 form))
```

Figure 9.16   Procedures for manipulating boolean formulas.

As usual, the literals **#t** and **#f** stand for boolean true and false values. The symbol Y represents a boolean variable named Y. (not BF) is the formula that negates BF. The logical conjunction of formulas BF_1 and BF_2 is written (and BF_1 BF_2) while their logical disjunction is written (or BF_1 BF_2). Such formulas can be written in FL dialects using the **quote** sugar for s-expressions. E.g.:

```
(def bf1 (quote (and (or a (or b c)) (and (not a) (not b)))))
```

Figure 9.16 presents some FL procedures for manipulating such formulas.

A boolean formula is **satisfiable** if there is an assignment of truth values to the boolean variables in the formula that makes the formula true. For example, **bf1** is satisfiable if **a** is assigned false, **b** is assigned false, and **c** is assigned true. On the other hand, the formula (and a (not a)) is not satisfiable since it denotes false no matter what value is assigned to **a**.

Figure 9.17 presents the FL definition of a **satisfy** procedure that determines whether a boolean formula is satisfiable. If so, **satisfy** returns an environment representing a set of variable assignments under which the formula is true. If not, **satisfy** returns the symbol **failed**. Assuming that the binding-list implementation of environments from Figure 9.13 is used, here are some sample invocations of **satisfy**:

```
(satisfy (quote (and a (and (not b) c))))
```
$\xrightarrow{FL} \lhd \langle 'c', \mathit{true} \rangle, \langle 'b', \mathit{false} \rangle, \langle 'a', \mathit{true} \rangle \rhd$

```
(satisfy (quote (and a (not a))))
```
$\xrightarrow{FL} \mathit{'failed'}$

```
(satisfy bf1)
```
$\xrightarrow{FL} \lhd \langle 'c', \mathit{true} \rangle, \langle 'b', \mathit{false} \rangle, \langle 'a', \mathit{false} \rangle \rhd$

```
(satisfy (quote (or a (or b c))))
```
$\xrightarrow{FL} \lhd \langle 'a', \mathit{true} \rangle \rhd$

The last example shows that variables whose values are irrelevant might not appear in the result. In this example, once a is assigned the value true, the formula is satisfiable and no more work is done to examine the subformula (or b c).

The satisfy procedure is implemented in terms of the auxiliary procedure sat, which takes four arguments:

1. the boolean formula form to be processed;

2. an environment asst representing the variable assignments so far;

3. a success continuation succ that takes (1) the boolean value of the formula, (2) the updated variable assignments from processing the formula, and (3) the updated failure continuation from processing the formula; and

4. a nullary failure continuation.

Observe how the variable assignments and failure continuation are threaded through the computation. The success continuation must take the variable assignments and failure continuation as arguments in order to thread them appropriately. Backtracking is implemented via the interplay between the variable-handling clause of sat and the invocation (fail) in satisfy. Whenever a variable is encountered, it is looked up in the current variable assignments. If it is already bound, the computation proceeds with that binding. But if it isn't yet bound, a guess must be made as to whether the variable should be true or false. Here sat always first guesses true by invoking succ on #t with the variable assignments updated to reflect this guess. But it also updates the failure continuation to make the false guess if the true guess doesn't work out. The top-level satisfy procedure invokes sat with a success continuation that checks whether the formula is true under the guessed assignments. If so, those assignments are returned. If not, the invocation (fail) will cause the computation to go back to the most recent choice point and make a different guess.

For example, consider how satisfy processes the formula bf1:

```
(and (or a (or b c)) (and (not a) (not b)))
```

sat will first guess true for a and ignore (or b c); but (and (not a) ...) will then be false, so bf1 will be false. The failure continuation created at the first

```
(def (satisfy formula)
  (sat formula
       (env-empty)
       (abs (b asst fail) (if b asst (fail)))
       (abs () (sym failed))))

(def (sat form asst succ fail)
  (cond ((bool? form) (succ form asst fail))
        ((sym? form)
         (env-lookup form asst
           (abs (b) (succ b asst fail))
           (abs ()
             (succ #t
               (env-extend form #t asst)
               (abs () (succ #f (env-extend form #f asst) fail))))))
        ((not? form)
         (sat (negand form) asst
           (abs (b asst1 fail1) (succ (not b) asst1 fail1))
           fail))
        ((and? form)
         (sat (conjunct1 form) asst
           (abs (b1 asst1 fail1)
             (if b1
                 (sat (conjunct2 form) asst1 succ fail1)
                 (succ #f asst1 fail1)))
           fail))
        ((or? form)
         (sat (disjunct1 form)
           (abs (b1 asst1 fail1)
             (if b1
                 (succ #t asst1 fail1)
                 (sat (disjunct2 form) asst1 succ fail1)))))
        (else (error illegal-form))
        ))
```

Figure 9.17 A backtracking version of a `satisfy` procedure written in FL. If the given formula is satisfiable, `satisfy` returns an environment representing the variable assignment that makes the formula true. Otherwise, `satisfy` returns the symbol `failed`.

reference to `a` will be invoked to guess false instead. This forces (`or b c`) to be processed, and `sat` will guess that `b` is true. But `bf1` will still be false, so the failure continuation created at the first reference to `b` will also be invoked. Under the assumption that `b` is false, `sat` will guess that `c` is true. With this assignment

```
(def (satisfy formula)
  (sat formula
       (abs (b fail asst) (if b asst (fail)))
       (abs () (sym failed))
       (env-empty)))
(def (sat form succ)
  (cond ((bool? form) (succ form))
        ((sym? form)
         (abs (fail asst) {Only place where fail and asst are explicit}
           (env-lookup form asst
             (abs (b) (succ b fail asst))
             (abs ()
               (succ #t
                 (abs () (succ #f fail (env-extend form #f asst)))
                 (env-extend form #t asst))))))
        ((not? form)
         (sat (negand form) (abs (b) (succ (not b)))))
        ((and? form)
         (sat (conjunct1 form)
           (abs (b1) (if b1 (sat (conjunct2 form) succ) (succ #f)))))
        ((or? form)
         (sat (disjunct1 form)
           (abs (b1) (succ #t) (sat (disjunct2 form) succ))))
        (else (error illegal-form))
        ))
```

Figure 9.18 A version of `satisfy` in which most of the state-threading details are hidden by currying. The arguments of `sat` and the success continuations have been reordered to put the assignment argument last.

(i.e., `a` and `b` are false but `c` is true), `bf1` is satisfied, and the environment representing this assignment is returned. The failure continuation created at the reference to `c` is never invoked.

Much of the code in `sat` deals with threading the variable assignments and failure continuation through the computation. It turns out that if a different parameter order is chosen for the arguments to `sat` and the success continuation, many of the threading details can be hidden by currying (see Figure 9.18). These details need be made explicit only in the one place (the variable-handling clause of `sat`) that must explicitly manipulate them. This is reminiscent of the way that a single-threaded store is hidden in monadic style except for the spots where the store must be explicitly manipulated. If `satisfy` is implemented in a stateful language like FLIC, then the single-threading of the failure continuation can be replaced by a cell that holds the current failure continuation. However, the single-threading of the assignment is trickier to avoid. These issues are explored in Exercise 9.4.

Exercise 9.4

a. Implement versions of `satisfy` and `sat` that do not explicitly single-thread the failure continuation through the computation, but instead store a stack of failure continuations in a top-level cell named `sat-fail`. The stack of failure continuations can be represented as a list ordered from the top (most recent) continuation down. Each time an unassigned variable is encountered, a new failure continuation is pushed onto the stack. The top continuation should be popped and invoked by `satisfy` whenever the formula is false. If the failure stack is empty, `satisfy` should return the symbol `failed`.

b. Show that the explicit stack in part **a** is unnecessary by changing the implementation so `sat-fail` is a cell containing exactly one failure continuation. The invocation of this failure continuation should be responsible for resetting the content of `sat-fail` appropriately, thus effectively popping an implicit stack.

c. Bud Lojack modifies the implementation from part **a** to eliminate the single-threading of the variable assignments through the satisfiability computation by using a top-level cell named `sat-asst` that holds a single environment representing the current assignments. His version of `sat` begins as follows:

```
(def (sat form succ)
  (cond ((bool? form) (succ form))
        ((sym? form)
         (env-lookup form (^ sat-asst)
           (abs (b) (succ b))
           (abs ()
             (begin
               (:= sat-fail
                 (cons (abs ()
                         (begin (:= sat-asst
                                   (env-extend form #f (^ sat-asst)))
                                (succ #f)))
                       (^ sat-fail)))
               (:= sat-asst (env-extend form #t (^ sat-asst)))
               (succ #t)))))
        ⋮
        ))
```

However, he finds that `satisfy` sometimes returns the symbol `failed` for a satisfiable formula. Given an example formula in which this occurs and explain why it happens.

d. Help Bud fix his program from part **c** by changing `sat-asst` so that it contains a *stack* of environments representing variable assignments.

e. In a version of FLIC supporting the `try` construct from Exercise 8.14, show how Bud can fix his program from part **c** assuming that `sat-asst` contains a single environment representing a set of variable assignments.

f. Without using `try`, modify the implementation from part **b** to use a cell `sat-asst` that contains only a single variable assignment. *Hint:* Invoking a failure continuation needs to reset both `sat-asst` and `sat-fail`.

9.3 Continuation-based Semantics of FLICK

Now that we've built up some intuitions about continuations, it's time to model continuations explicitly in our denotational definitions. To handle state in our semantics, we took the idiom of single-threading a store through a computation and made it part of the computational model. Similarly, we will handle control in our semantics by embedding in our computational model the idiom of passing explicit continuations through a computation. The strategy of capturing common programming idioms in a semantic framework — or any language — is a powerful idea that lies at the foundation of programming language design. Indeed, languages can be considered expressive to the extent that they relieve the programmer of managing the details of common programming idioms.

Together, environments, stores, and continuations are sufficiently powerful to model most programming language features. As noted earlier, a semantics that uses only environments and stores is called a **direct semantics**. A semantics that adds continuations to a direct semantics is called a **continuation-based semantics**. A continuation-based semantics with particular conventions about the signatures of valuation functions is called a **standard semantics**, since most denotational definitions are written in this style. One advantage of standard semantics is that following a set of conventions simplifies the comparison of different programming languages defined by standard semantics. We already saw this kind of advantage when we studied parameter passing and scoping. Comparing different approaches was facilitated by the fact that the styles of the denotational definitions being compared were similar.

The conventions used for standard semantics are different from the conventions we've been using that involve computations (the *Comp* domain). Since both conventions are important, we will present the continuation-based semantics for FLICK in both styles. Because it manipulates continuations more concretely, we will first present the standard semantics for FLICK. Then we will present a continuation-based semantics in the *Comp* framework, which is more abstract because it hides the manipulation of continuations. In both semantics, FLICK phrases have exactly the same meaning, but these are written down in different ways that expose or hide details involving continuations.

Moreover, in both semantics, FLICK *programs* have exactly the same meaning as they have using the direct denotational semantics from Section 8.3.4. What, then, is the advantage of a continuation-based semantics? Even though *programs* have the same meaning under all these different forms of semantics, other phrases — particularly expressions — have very different meanings in a direct semantics and in a continuation-based semantics. Just as explicit procedural continuations allowed us to model advanced control idioms in Section 9.2, in the following sections of this chapter we will use the explicit continuations in the semantics to capture these idioms in sophisticated programming language control constructs. A continuation-based semantics is a much more powerful tool for studying control features than a direct semantics.

9.3.1   A Standard Semantics of FLICK

Semantic Algebra

Figure 9.19 presents the semantic algebra for the standard semantics of FLICK. The semantic algebra introduces three continuation domains:

$$\gamma \in Cmdcont = Store \rightarrow Answer$$
$$k \in Expcont = Value \rightarrow Cmdcont$$
$$j \in Explistcont = Value^* \rightarrow Cmdcont$$

Cmdcont is the domain of **command continuations**. These represent the rest of the computation for **commands** (also called **statements**), phrases that may have side effects but do not return values. Many real-world programming languages have distinct syntactic categories for commands (which do not return values) and expressions (which do return values). For example, in ADA, FORTRAN, and PASCAL, variable assignments, array updates, and program output are performed via commands. C, C++, and JAVA are expression-based languages, but invocations of functions/methods with the `void` return type are effectively commands.

FLICK does not have a separate syntactic domain for commands, but some expressions effectively serve as commands. For example, `:=` expressions return the uninteresting value `#u` simply because they are required to return *something*, but the reason to execute an assignment is to modify the store. Sequencing using `begin` is a natural command context: it exists to enforce an order of state transformations. In (`begin` E_1 E_2), the value of E_1 is ignored, effectively treating it as a command.

Domains

$\gamma \in Cmdcont = Store \rightarrow Answer$

$k \in Expcont = Value \rightarrow Cmdcont$

$j \in Explistcont = Value^* \rightarrow Cmdcont$

$\quad Answer = Expressible$; *language-dependent in general*

$\quad Nameable = Value$; FLICK *is CBV*

$\quad Storable = Value$; FLICK *is CBV*

$p \in Proc = Nameable \rightarrow Expcont \rightarrow Cmdcont$

$x \in Expressible = (Value + Error)_{\perp}$; *as before*

$v \in Value = \ldots$ *as in* FLICK *direct semantics* $\ldots$; *language-dependent in general*

$\quad Error = \mathrm{SymLit}$

Constants and Operations

top-level-cont : $Expcont = \lambda v . \lambda s . (Value {\rightarrowtail} Expressible \; v)$

error-cont : $Error \rightarrow Cmdcont = \lambda Y . \lambda s . (Error {\rightarrowtail} Expressible \; Y)$

check-location : $Value \rightarrow (Location \rightarrow Cmdcont) \rightarrow Cmdcont$
$= \lambda vf .$ **match** v
$\qquad \triangleright (Location {\rightarrowtail} Value \; l) \; [\![\; (f \; l)$
$\qquad \triangleright$ **else** (*error-cont* `not-a-location`) **end**

similar for *check-integer* : $Value \rightarrow (Int \rightarrow Cmdcont) \rightarrow Cmdcont$, etc.

ensure-nameable : $BindingVal \rightarrow Expcont \rightarrow Cmdcont$
$= \lambda \beta k .$ **match** β
$\qquad \triangleright (Nameable {\rightarrowtail} BindingVal \; v) \; [\![\; (k \; v)$
$\qquad$; FLICK *is CBV; CBN definition would differ*
$\qquad \triangleright (Unbound {\rightarrowtail} BindingVal \; \mathbf{unbound}) \; [\![\; (error\text{-}cont \; \texttt{unbound-variable}) \;$ **end**

similar for *ensure-storable* : $AssignedVal \rightarrow Expcont \rightarrow Cmdcont$
$\qquad\qquad$ *ensure-value* : $Expressible \rightarrow Expcont \rightarrow Cmdcont$, etc.

boolean-cont : $(Bool \rightarrow Cmdcont) \rightarrow Expcont$
$= \lambda f . (\lambda v .$ **match** v
$\qquad\qquad \triangleright (Bool {\rightarrowtail} Value \; b) \; [\![\; (f \; b)$
$\qquad\qquad \triangleright$ **else** (*error-cont* `non-boolean`) **end**)

similar for *procedure-cont* : $(Proc \rightarrow Cmdcont) \rightarrow Expcont$, etc.

one-arg : $(Value \rightarrow Expcont \rightarrow Cmdcont) \rightarrow (Value^* \rightarrow Expcont \rightarrow Cmdcont)$
$= \lambda f . (\lambda v^* k .$ **match** v^*
$\qquad\qquad \triangleright [v_1] \; [\![\; (f \; v_1 \; k)$
$\qquad\qquad \triangleright$ **else** (*error-cont* `wrong-number-of-args`) **end**)

two-args : $(Value \rightarrow Value \rightarrow Expcont \rightarrow Cmdcont)$
$\qquad\qquad \rightarrow (Value^* \rightarrow Expcont \rightarrow Cmdcont)$
$= \lambda f . (\lambda v^* k .$ **match** v^*
$\qquad\qquad \triangleright [v_1, v_2] \; [\![\; (f \; v_1 \; v_2 \; k)$
$\qquad\qquad \triangleright$ **else** (*error-cont* `wrong-number-of-args`) **end**)

Figure 9.19 Semantic algebra for the standard semantics of FLICK.

In a standard semantics, a command continuation maps the store representing the state of the computation after the command has executed to the final answer of the program. What counts as the "final answer" of a program varies from language to language and is modeled by the *Answer* domain. In FLICK, *Answer = Expressible*. In interpreter-based languages, the initial continuation might be an interpreter's read-eval-print loop, which never returns. In this case, *Answer* could be viewed as a mapping from a sequence of input strings read by the interpreter to the sequence of output strings printed by the interpreter. In languages like C, JAVA, and PASCAL, for simple programs *Answer* can be viewed as a mapping from the initial state of the file system to the final state of the file system. But a much more complex *Answer* domain is needed to model the kinds of input and output systems used with modern programs, e.g., those involving graphical user interfaces, network communication, robotic sensors and actuators, and a host of other peripheral devices.

Expcont is the domain of **expression continuations**, which represent the rest of the computation for **expressions**, phrases that return a value in addition to possibly having side effects. Since expressions both return a value and potentially modify the store, the continuation for an expression expects both the value and the store produced by that expression. In contrast, a command continuation expects only a store. Note that because *Cmdcont = Store → Answer*, we can also view *Expcont* as:

$$Expcont \ = \ Value \rightarrow Store \rightarrow Answer$$

That is, we can think of an expression continuation as taking a value and returning a command continuation; or we can think of it as taking a value and a store and returning an answer. Which perspective is more fruitful depends on the situation. The argument order (value before store) is arbitrary, but this order is the convention in a standard semantics because it helps to hide the store in certain situations.

The first argument of an expression continuation is an element of *Value* regardless of whether the language being modeled is a CBV or a CBN language. Such a continuation can never be directly applied to an element of *Expressible*; it can only be applied to an element of *Value*.

The final continuation domain is *Explistcont*, which is used in contexts in which a sequence of values is collected. Such a continuation maps the value sequence and store to the final answer of the program.

Most of the other domains in Figure 9.19 are familiar from the direct semantics for FLICK. One domain that has been modified from before is the *Proc* domain, which now takes an expression continuation in addition to a nameable value:

$$Proc \ = \ Nameable \to Expcont \to Cmdcont$$

Intuitively, the new *Expcont* argument is the "return address" that a procedure returns to when it returns a value. We can also view this *Proc* domain as:

$$Proc \ = \ Nameable \to Expcont \to Store \to Answer$$

The order of these domains (nameable value before expression continuation before store) is standard. We will see that this particular ordering enables the continuation and store to be hidden when they are not explicitly needed. We will see the idiom *Expcont* $\to$ *Cmdcont* in many other spots in the semantics. Keep in mind that it can always be viewed as *Expcont* $\to$ *Store* $\to$ *Answer*.

The semantic algebra in Figure 9.19 includes many constants and operations that are helpful in the valuation functions. *top-level-cont* is the top-level expression continuation. Given the value and store at the end of a program, it ignores the store and converts the value into an expressible value that is the "final answer" of the program. *error-cont* is similar, except that it converts an error message into a "final answer." There are many functions whose purpose is to hide error-handling details. These are grouped according to their signatures:

- *check-location* serves a purpose similar to that of *with-location-val* from the direct semantics, but it has a different signature.

- The *ensure-nameable*, *ensure-storable*, and *ensure-value* functions will invoke a given expression continuation on the value that results from converting a binding value from the environment, an assigned value from the store, or an expressible value to a value. But if these are not convertible to a value (i.e., in the case of unbound identifiers, unassigned locations, or errors), an error continuation is returned.

- The *boolean-cont* and *procedure-cont* functions convert an expression continuation for a boolean or procedure value, respectively, into a general expression continuation.

- The *one-arg* and *two-args* functions perform number-of-arguments checking for primitive operations.

Figure 9.20 presents laws involving these functions that are useful for denotational calculations.

$$(\textit{check-location} \ (\textit{Location} \rightarrowtail \textit{Value} \ l) \ f) \ = \ (f \ l) \tag{9.1}$$

$$(\textit{check-location} \ v \ f) \ = \ (\textit{error-cont} \ \texttt{not-a-location}), \tag{9.2}$$
where v is not a location

$\textit{check-integer}$, etc. have laws similar to (9.1) and (9.2)

$$(\textit{ensure-nameable} \ (\textit{lookup} \ I \ e) \ k) \ = \ (k \ v), \tag{9.3}$$
where I is bound to v in e

$$(\textit{ensure-nameable} \ (\textit{lookup} \ I \ e) \ k) \ = \ (\textit{error-cont} \ \texttt{unbound-variable}) \tag{9.4}$$
where I is unbound in e

$\textit{ensure-storable}$, $\textit{ensure-value}$, etc. have laws similar to (9.3) and (9.4)

$$((\textit{boolean-cont} \ f) \ (\textit{Bool} \rightarrowtail \textit{Value} \ b)) \ = \ (f \ b) \tag{9.5}$$

$$((\textit{boolean-cont} \ f) \ v) \ = \ (\textit{error-cont} \ \texttt{not-a-boolean}), \tag{9.6}$$
where v is not a boolean

$\textit{procedure-cont}$, etc. have laws similar to (9.5) and (9.6)

$$((\textit{one-arg} \ f) \ [v] \ k) \ = \ (f \ v \ k) \tag{9.7}$$

$$((\textit{one-arg} \ f) \ v^* \ k) \ = \ (\textit{error-cont} \ \texttt{wrong-number-of-args}), \tag{9.8}$$
where $(\textit{length} \ v^*) \neq_{Int} 1$

$$((\textit{two-args} \ f) \ [v_1, v_2] \ k) \ = \ (f \ v_1 \ v_2 \ k) \tag{9.9}$$

$$((\textit{two-args} \ f) \ v^* \ k) \ = \ (\textit{error-cont} \ \texttt{wrong-number-of-args}), \tag{9.10}$$
where $(\textit{length} \ v^*) \neq_{Int} 2$

Figure 9.20   Laws for reasoning about standard semantics.

Valuation Functions

Figure 9.21 presents the complete valuation functions for the standard semantics
of FLICK except for `rec`, which will be discussed in Section 9.3.2. (CBV `rec`
is rather complex and we prefer to use the $\textit{Comp}$-based "recipe" that we have
already developed for defining its semantics.) The signatures of $\mathcal{P}$, $\mathcal{O}_{\text{FLK}}$, and $\mathcal{L}$
are the same as in the direct semantics of FLICK. But the signatures of $\mathcal{E}$, $\mathcal{E}^*$,
and $\mathcal{O}$ have been modified. The signature of $\mathcal{E}$ is:

$$\mathcal{E} : \text{Exp} \rightarrow \textit{Env} \rightarrow \textit{Expcont} \rightarrow \textit{Cmdcont}$$

Since $\textit{Cmdcont} = \textit{Store} \rightarrow \textit{Answer}$ we can also view the signature of $\mathcal{E}$ as:

$$\mathcal{E} : \text{Exp} \rightarrow \textit{Env} \rightarrow \textit{Expcont} \rightarrow \textit{Store} \rightarrow \textit{Answer}$$

That is, $\mathcal{E}$ takes a syntactic expression and representations of the naming ($\textit{Env}$),
control ($\textit{Expcont}$), and state ($\textit{Store}$) contexts, and finds the meaning of the expression (an answer in $\textit{Answer}$) with respect to these contexts.

$\mathcal{L} : \mathrm{Lit} \to \mathit{Value}$; as in FLK

$\mathcal{E} : \mathrm{Exp} \to \mathit{Env} \to \mathit{Expcont} \to \mathit{Cmdcont}$

$\mathcal{E}^* : \mathrm{Exp}^* \to \mathit{Env} \to \mathit{Explistcont} \to \mathit{Cmdcont}$

$\mathcal{O}_{\mathrm{FLK}} : \mathrm{Primop} \to \mathit{Value}^* \to \mathit{Expressible}$; as in FLK

$\mathcal{O} : \mathrm{Primop} \to \mathit{Value}^* \to \mathit{Expcont} \to \mathit{Cmdcont}$

$\mathcal{P} : \mathrm{Prog} \to \mathrm{InputExp}^* \to \mathit{Answer}$; $\mathit{Answer} = \mathit{Expressible}$ in FLICK

$\mathcal{E}[\![L]\!] = \lambda ek . (k \; \mathcal{L}[\![L]\!])$

$\mathcal{E}[\![(\texttt{error } Y)]\!] = \lambda ek . (error\text{-}cont \; Y)$

$\mathcal{E}[\![I]\!] = \lambda ek . (ensure\text{-}nameable \; (lookup \; I \; e) \; k)$; $Nameable = Value$ in CBV

$\mathcal{E}[\![(\texttt{lam } I \; E)]\!] = \lambda ek_{lam} . (k_{lam} \; (Proc \rightarrowtail Value \; (\lambda nk_{app} . (\mathcal{E}[\![E]\!] \; [I \mapsto n]e \; k_{app}))))$

$\mathcal{E}[\![(\texttt{app } E_1 \; E_2)]\!] = \lambda ek_{app} . (\mathcal{E}[\![E_1]\!] \; e \; (procedure\text{-}cont$
$\qquad\qquad\qquad\qquad\qquad (\lambda p . (\mathcal{E}[\![E_2]\!] \; e \; (\lambda v . (p \; v \; k_{app}))))))$

$\mathcal{E}[\![(\texttt{if } E_1 \; E_2 \; E_3)]\!]$
$= \lambda ek . (\mathcal{E}[\![E_1]\!] \; e \; (boolean\text{-}cont$
$\qquad\qquad\qquad\quad (\lambda b . \textbf{if } b \textbf{ then } (\mathcal{E}[\![E_2]\!] \; e \; k) \textbf{ else } (\mathcal{E}[\![E_3]\!] \; e \; k) \textbf{ end})))$

$\mathcal{E}[\![(\texttt{pair } E_1 \; E_2)]\!]$
$= \lambda ek . (\mathcal{E}[\![E_1]\!] \; e \; (\lambda v_1 . (\mathcal{E}[\![E_2]\!] \; e \; (\lambda v_2 . (k \; (Pair \rightarrowtail Value \; \langle v_1, v_2 \rangle))))))$

$\mathcal{E}[\![(\texttt{begin } E_1 \; E_2)]\!] = \lambda ek . (\mathcal{E}[\![E_1]\!] \; e \; (\lambda v_{ignore} . (\mathcal{E}[\![E_2]\!] \; e \; k)))$

$\mathcal{E}[\![(\texttt{cell } E)]\!] = \lambda ek . (\mathcal{E}[\![E]\!] \; e \; (\lambda vs . (k \; (Location \rightarrowtail Value \; (fresh\text{-}loc \; s))$
$\qquad\qquad\qquad\qquad\qquad\qquad\qquad (assign \; (fresh\text{-}loc \; s) \; v \; s))))$

$\mathcal{E}[\![(\texttt{prim } O \; E^*)]\!] = \lambda ek . (\mathcal{E}^*[\![E^*]\!] \; e \; (\lambda v^* . (\mathcal{O}[\![O]\!] \; v^* \; k)))$

$\mathcal{E}^*[\![]\!] = \lambda ej . (j \; []_{Value})$

$\mathcal{E}^*[\![E_{first} . E_{rest}^*]\!] = \lambda ej . (\mathcal{E}[\![E_{first}]\!] \; e \; (\lambda v . (\mathcal{E}^*[\![E_{rest}^*]\!] \; e \; (\lambda v^* . (j \; (v . v^*))))))$

$\mathcal{O}[\![\texttt{^}]\!] = one\text{-}arg \; (\lambda vk . (check\text{-}location \; v \; (\lambda ls . (ensure\text{-}storable \; (fetch \; l \; s) \; k \; s))))$

$\mathcal{O}[\![\texttt{:=}]\!] = two\text{-}args \; (\lambda v_1 v_2 k . (check\text{-}location \; v_1$
$\qquad\qquad\qquad\qquad\qquad (\lambda ls . (k \; (Unit \rightarrowtail Value \; unit) \; (assign \; l \; v_2 \; s)))))$

$\mathcal{O}[\![\texttt{cell=?}]\!]$
$= two\text{-}args \; (\lambda v_1 v_2 k . (check\text{-}location \; v_1$
$\qquad\qquad\qquad\qquad\qquad (\lambda l_1 . (check\text{-}location \; v_2$
$\qquad\qquad\qquad\qquad\qquad\qquad (\lambda l_2 . (k \; (Bool \rightarrowtail Value \; (l_1 =_{Location} l_2)))))))))$

$\mathcal{O}[\![\texttt{cell?}]\!] = one\text{-}arg \; (\lambda vk . (k \; (Bool \rightarrowtail Value \; \textbf{match } v$
$\qquad\qquad\qquad\qquad\qquad\qquad\quad \triangleright (Location \rightarrowtail Value \; l) \; \| \; true$
$\qquad\qquad\qquad\qquad\qquad\qquad\quad \triangleright \textbf{else } false \textbf{ end})))$

$\mathcal{O}[\![O]\!] = \lambda v^* k . (ensure\text{-}value \; (\mathcal{O}_{\mathrm{FLK}}[\![O]\!] \; v^*) \; k)$, where $O \in \mathrm{Primop}_{\mathrm{FLK}}$

$\mathcal{P}[\![(\texttt{flick } (I^*) \; E_{body})]\!]$
$= \lambda IE^* . \textbf{if } (length \; I^*) =_{Int} (length \; IE^*)$
$\qquad\quad \textbf{then } \mathcal{E}[\![E_{body}]\!] \; (extend^* \; I^* \; (\mathcal{IE}^*[\![IE^*]\!]) \; empty\text{-}env)$
$\qquad\qquad\qquad\qquad top\text{-}level\text{-}cont \; empty\text{-}store$
$\qquad\quad \textbf{else } (Error \rightarrowtail Expressible \; \texttt{wrong-number-of-args}) \textbf{ end}$

Figure 9.21 Valuation clauses for the standard semantics of FLICK except for `rec`.

An expression of the form $(\mathcal{E}[\![E]\!] \ e \ (\lambda v \ . \ \Box))$ can be read as "evaluate E in e and name the resulting value v in $\Box$." For example, the valuation clause for pair is:

$$\mathcal{E}[\![(\texttt{pair} \ E_1 \ E_2)]\!]$$
$$= \lambda ek \ . \ (\mathcal{E}[\![E_1]\!] \ e \ (\lambda v_1 \ . \ (\mathcal{E}[\![E_2]\!] \ e \ (\lambda v_2 \ . \ (k \ (Pair \rightarrowtail Value \ \langle v_1, v_2 \rangle))))))$$

This can be read as:

> To evaluate (pair E_1 E_2) relative to environment e and continuation k, first evaluate E_1, which should yield a value v_1. Then evaluate E_2, which should yield a value v_2. Finally, continue with the rest of the computation by invoking the continuation k on the pair value $(Pair \rightarrowtail Value \ \langle v_1, v_2 \rangle)$.

As discussed below, error situations are also implicitly handled by such clauses.

In many cases, the value argument of a continuation has been elided by eta reduction (see page 295). For example, in the if clause, $(\mathcal{E}[\![E_2]\!] \ e \ k)$ is a simplified form of $(\mathcal{E}[\![E_2]\!] \ e \ (\lambda v_2 \ . \ (k \ v_2)))$. For this reason, an expression of the form $(\mathcal{E}[\![E]\!] \ e \ k)$ is pronounced as "find the value of E in e and pass it to the continuation k."

Since evaluating an expression requires a store in FLICK, why doesn't a store explicitly appear in the above examples? The reason is that the order of arguments to $\mathcal{E}$ has been chosen to have the store last, rather than the continuation. This argument order is one of the conventions of a standard semantics; it is used because it hides the store when it is threaded through an expression untouched. In essence, *Cmdcont* fulfills the role that the *Comp* domain did when we introduced state into FL.

To specify that an expression transforms a store s_0 to a store s_1, we can write $(\mathcal{E}[\![E]\!] \ e \ (\lambda v s_1 \ . \ \Box) \ s_0)$. In the valuation clauses, our convention is to hide all stores except those that must be explicitly mentioned (i.e., in cell, ^, and :=). However, it is possible to expand any clause with implicit stores into one with explicit stores. For example, the app clause can be written with explicit stores:

$$\mathcal{E}[\![(\texttt{app} \ E_1 \ E_2)]\!]$$
$$= \lambda ek_{app}s_0 \ . \ \mathcal{E}[\![E_1]\!] \ e$$
$$(procedure\text{-}cont$$
$$(\lambda ps_1 \ . \ \mathcal{E}[\![E_2]\!] \ e$$
$$(\lambda v_{arg}s_2 \ . \ (p \ v_{arg}$$
$$(\lambda v_{result}s_3 \ . \ (k_{app} \ v_{result} \ s_3))$$
$$s_2))$$
$$s_1))$$
$$s_0$$

In this expanded clause, s_0 is the store before the app expression is evaluated, s_1 is the store after E_1 is evaluated, s_2 is the store after E_2 is evaluated, and s_3 is the store after the procedure p denoted by E_1 returns. The expanded form also makes explicit the result value v_{result} returned by the procedure p.

Figure 9.22 shows the calculation of the meaning of a sample FLICK expression in standard semantics. Many of the steps in the calculation are justified by the laws in Figure 9.20. Other steps are due to lemmas that we can prove. For example, if O_{arith} is one of the binary arithmetic primitive operators +, -, or *, then

$$
\begin{aligned}
&\mathcal{E}[\![(\text{prim } O_{arith} \ E_1 \ E_2)]\!] \ e \ k \\
&= \mathcal{E}[\![E_1]\!] \ e \\
&\qquad (\lambda v_1 \ . \ (\mathcal{E}[\![E_2]\!] \ e \\
&\qquad\qquad (\lambda v_2 \ . \ (\textit{check-integer } v_1 \\
&\qquad\qquad\qquad (\lambda i_1 \ . \ (\textit{check-integer } v_2 \\
&\qquad\qquad\qquad\qquad (\lambda i_2 \ . \ (k \ (Int \rightarrowtail Value \\
&\qquad\qquad\qquad\qquad\qquad (i_1 \ op_{Int} \ i_2))))))))))), \\
&\text{where } op_{Int} \text{ is the integer operator associated with } O_{arith} \qquad (9.11)
\end{aligned}
$$

We can see that the above metalanguage expression is equivalent to the Figure 9.21 definition

$$
\mathcal{E}^*[\![E^*]\!] \ e \ (\lambda v^* \ . \ (\textit{ensure-value } (\mathcal{O}_{\text{FLK}}[\![O_{arith}]\!] \ v^*) \ k))
$$

by an exhaustive case analysis on E_1 and E_2:

- if E_1 signals an error with message Y_1, both metalanguage expressions are equivalent to $(\textit{error-cont } Y_1)$;

- if E_1 does not signal an error but E_2 signals an error with message Y_2, both expressions are equivalent to $(\textit{error-cont } Y_2)$;

- if E_1 evaluates to a value v_1 and E_2 evaluates to a value v_2, then:
  - if v_1 is not an integer or v_2 is not an integer, then both expressions are equivalent to $(\textit{error-cont } \texttt{not-an-integer})$;
  - if v_1 is $(Int \rightarrowtail Value \ i_1)$ and v_2 is $(Int \rightarrowtail Value \ i_2)$, then both expressions are equivalent to $(k \ (Int \rightarrowtail Value \ (i_1 \ op_{Int} \ i_2)))$

In the particular case where O_{arith} is applied to two integer literals, the above metalanguage expression can be simplified to:

$$
\mathcal{E}[\![(\text{prim } O_{arith} \ N_1 \ N_2)]\!] \ e \ k = k \ (Int \rightarrowtail Value \ (\mathcal{N}[\![N_1]\!] \ op_{Int} \ \mathcal{N}[\![N_2]\!])) \qquad (9.12)
$$

Note that keeping stores implicit in Figure 9.22 makes the example much easier
to read, especially since stores are not required to perform any of the calculation
steps.

One way to think of the standard semantics clauses in Figure 9.21 is that
they are the result of transforming the direct semantics clauses from Figures 8.21
and 8.22 on pages 418 and 419 into continuation-passing style. Even though
FLICK does not have any advanced control features (we'll add many in the remainder of this chapter), there is a benefit to making the continuations explicit:
it simplifies the handling of errors. In the tree-product$_4$ example from Section 9.2.4, we saw how a computation could terminate immediately by directly
returning a value rather than invoking a continuation. In the standard semantics, valuation clauses behave similarly: they signal errors by ignoring the current
continuation and terminating with an error. For example, suppose in Figure 9.22
that the value bound to a in e_1 were the integer 1 rather than a boolean. Then
at the point where a is looked up in e_1 we would have:

$$ensure\text{-}nameable \ (lookup \ \texttt{a} \ e_1) \ k_2$$
$$= \ k_2 \ (Int \rightarrowtail Value \ 1), \text{ by } (9.3)$$
$$= \ (boolean\text{-}cont \ (\lambda b \ . \ \dots)) \ (Int \rightarrowtail Value \ 1)$$
$$= \ (error\text{-}cont \ \texttt{not-a-boolean}), \text{ by } (9.5)$$
$$= \ \lambda s \ . \ (Error \rightarrowtail Expressible \ \texttt{not-a-boolean})$$

Note that an error is signaled directly without applying the boolean continuation $(\lambda b \ . \ \dots)$. The same thing happens no matter how deeply the expression
(if a ...) is nested in a program. This captures the intuition that an error
immediately aborts the computation. It also stands in contrast to error handling in the direct semantics, where the valuation clause for each expression must
propagate any errors generated in its subexpressions.

Exercise 9.5 Use the FLICK standard semantics to calculate the meaning of the following expression studied in Section 8.3.3:

```
(app (lam c {E_lam}
         (begin (prim := c (prim + 1 (prim ^ c)))
                (prim ^ c)))
     (cell 3))
```

To simplify your calculations, use the laws in Figure 9.20 and develop any lemmas you
find useful.

Suppose $p_1 = \lambda n_1 k_1 \, . \; (\text{check-integer } n_1 \; (\lambda i_1 \, . \; (k_1 \; (Int \rightarrowtail Value \; (i_1 +_{Int} 1)))))$

$\qquad e_1 = \{\mathtt{a} \mapsto (Bool \rightarrowtail Value \; true), \mathtt{inc} \mapsto (Proc \rightarrowtail Value \; p_1)\}$

$\qquad k_{top} = top\text{-}level\text{-}cont$

$\mathcal{E}[\![(\texttt{app (if a (lam x (prim * x 6)) inc) (prim + 3 4))}]\!] \; e_1 \; k_{top}$

$= \mathcal{E}[\![(\texttt{if a (lam x (prim * x 6)) inc)}]\!] \; e_1 \; k_1,$

$\qquad$ where $k_1 = procedure\text{-}cont \; (\lambda p_2 \, . \; (\mathcal{E}[\![(\texttt{prim + 3 4)}]\!] \; e_1 \; (\lambda v_2 \, . \; (p_2 \; v_2 \; k_{top}))))$

$= \mathcal{E}[\![\texttt{a}]\!] \; e_1 \; k_2,$

$\qquad$ where $k_2 = boolean\text{-}cont \; (\lambda b \, . \; \textbf{if } b \textbf{ then } (\mathcal{E}[\![(\texttt{lam x (prim * x 6))}]\!] \; e_1 \; k_1)$
$\qquad\qquad\qquad\qquad\qquad\qquad\qquad\qquad \textbf{else } (\mathcal{E}[\![\texttt{inc}]\!] \; e_1 \; k_1) \textbf{ end})$

$= ensure\text{-}nameable \; (lookup \; \texttt{a} \; e_1) \; k_2$

$= k_2 \; (Bool \rightarrowtail Value \; true), \text{ by } (9.3)$

$= \textbf{if } true \textbf{ then } (\mathcal{E}[\![(\texttt{lam x (prim * x 6))}]\!] \; e_1 \; k_1) \textbf{ else } (\mathcal{E}[\![\texttt{inc}]\!] \; e_1 \; k_1) \textbf{ end},$
$\qquad$ by (9.5)

$= \mathcal{E}[\![(\texttt{lam x (prim * x 6))}]\!] \; e_1 \; k_1$

$= k_1 \; (Proc \rightarrowtail Value \; p_3), \text{ where } p_3 = \lambda n_3 k_3 \, . \; (\mathcal{E}[\![(\texttt{prim * x 6)}]\!] \; [\texttt{x} \mapsto n_3] e_1 \; k_3)$

$= \mathcal{E}[\![(\texttt{prim + 3 4)}]\!] \; e_1 \; (\lambda v_2 \, . \; (p_3 \; v_2 \; k_{top})), \text{ by } (9.5) \text{ for } procedure\text{-}cont$

$= (\lambda v_2 \, . \; (p_3 \; v_2 \; k_{top})) \; (Int \rightarrowtail Value \; 7), \text{ by } (9.12)$

$= p_3 \; (Int \rightarrowtail Value \; 7) \; k_{top}$

$= \mathcal{E}[\![(\texttt{prim * x 6)}]\!] \; e_2 \; k_{top}, \text{ where } e_2 = [\texttt{x} \mapsto (Int \rightarrowtail Value \; 7)] e_1$

$= \mathcal{E}[\![\texttt{x}]\!] \; e_2 \; k_4,$

$\qquad$ where $k_4 = \lambda v_4 \, . \; (\text{check-integer } v_4 \; (\lambda i_4 \, . \; (k_{top} \; (Int \rightarrowtail Value \; (i_4 \times_{Int} 6))))),$
$\qquad$ by (9.11)

$= ensure\text{-}nameable \; (lookup \; \texttt{x} \; e_2) \; k_4$

$= k_4 \; (Int \rightarrowtail Value \; 7), \text{ by } (9.3)$

$= \text{check-integer} \; (Int \rightarrowtail Value \; 7) \; (\lambda i_4 \, . \; (k_{top} \; (Int \rightarrowtail Value \; (i_4 \times_{Int} 6))))$

$= k_{top} \; (Int \rightarrowtail Value \; (7 \times_{Int} 6)), \text{ by } (9.1) \text{ for } \text{check-integer}$

$= k_{top} \; (Int \rightarrowtail Value \; 42)$

$= \lambda s \, . \; (Value \rightarrowtail Expressible \; (Int \rightarrowtail Value \; 42)), \text{ by the definition of } k_{top} = top\text{-}level\text{-}cont$

Figure 9.22 Calculation of the meaning of a sample FLICK expression in standard semantics.

9.3.2   A Computation-based Continuation Semantics of FLICK

The valuation functions for FLICK defined in Figure 9.21 do not employ the *Comp* abstraction that we have used in all of our other denotational descriptions of FL dialects. Instead, to help build intuitions about continuations, they are presented in a way that makes the manipulation of continuations explicit. However, we want to be able to compare the continuation-based semantics with other semantics we have studied. And we want to leverage the work done so far in defining notions like CBN versus CBV and lexical versus dynamic scope, which were defined in terms of the *Comp* domain. For these reasons, here we will recast the standard semantics of FLICK into the computation framework.

Let's begin by reviewing our use of the *Comp* domain thus far. Intuitively, an element of the *Comp* domain is the meaning of an expression relative to an environment. In the stateless FLK, *Comp* is defined as

$$Comp \ = \ Expressible \ = \ (\mathit{Value} + \mathit{Error})_\perp$$

because evaluating an expression in an environment in a stateless language yields either a value, an error, or divergence. In Figure 6.26 on page 281, we defined a collection of operations, including *val-to-comp*, *err-to-comp*, *with-value*, *with-values*, *with-boolean-comp*, *with-boolean-val*, and *with-nameable*, that manipulate elements of the *Comp* domain. In Figure 6.28 (page 283) and Figure 6.29 (page 285) we wrote the valuation functions for FLK using these computation operations.

When we added state to FLK to create FLICK, we changed the definition of *Comp* to be

$$Comp \ = \ Store \rightarrow (\mathit{Expressible} \times \mathit{Store})$$

This captures the intuitions that in a stateful language (1) the value of an expression may depend on the current state and (2) evaluating an expression may perform side effects that change the state. In Figure 8.17 on page 414, we gave modified definitions of *val-to-comp*, *err-to-comp*, and *with-value* in terms of the state-based definition of *Comp*. Since other computation operations, like *with-values*, *with-boolean-comp*, *with-boolean-val*, and *with-nameable*, were all defined in terms of *err-to-comp* and *with-value*, the definitions of these operations were simply inherited from Figure 6.26 on page 281. Remarkably, because they were written in terms of the *Comp* abstraction, the valuation clauses for all FLICK expressions inherited from FLK (except for `rec`) had exactly the same definitions in FLICK as in FLK. This is because the *Comp* domain and its associated operations hide the details of how state is single-threaded through the execution of a program.

As discussed in Section 7.1.4, the definition of `rec` in CBV languages is always somewhat problematic and depends on particular details of the *Comp* domain that cannot be abstracted away. So we expect that the valuation clause for `rec` will need tweaking whenever *Comp* is changed.

Of course, FLICK also introduced some new stateful constructs (`cell`, `^`, `:=`, and `begin`). For writing the valuation clauses of these constructs, some new stateful computation operations were introduced in Figure 8.18 on page 415: *allocating*, *fetching*, *update*, and *sequence*.

Our goal now is to define a continuation-based version of the *Comp* domain and to define versions of the associated operations such that the valuation clauses of FLICK in Figures 8.21 and 8.22 (for the stateful constructs of FLICK) and in Figures 6.28 and 6.29 (for the stateless constructs of FLICK inherited from FLK) are unchanged. We expect one exception — `rec` — because its clause depends on the details of *Comp*.

As noted above, an element of *Comp* is the meaning of an expression in an environment. In the standard semantics of FLICK in Figure 9.21, the meaning of an expression in an environment is a function with signature *Expcont* → *Cmdcont*, so we define the continuation-based version of *Comp* as

$$Comp \ = \ Expcont \rightarrow Cmdcont \ = \ Expcont \rightarrow Store \rightarrow Answer$$

As usual, for the case of FLICK, we will assume that *Answer* is synonymous with *Expressible*. Intuitively, the evaluation of each expression now takes a continuation k and a store s as implicit arguments. Under regular control assumptions, evaluation of the expression will yield a value v and a resulting store s' and these will be "returned" by invoking k on v and s'. But having an explicit continuation allows for control flows other than the regular ones.

Figure 9.23 presents new implementations of the computation operations that are consistent with this representation of the *Comp* abstraction. The application (*val-to-comp* v) yields a computation that "returns" v by invoking the expression continuation on it. (*err-to-comp* Y) yields a computation that terminates the computation with the error message Y by ignoring the expression continuation and signaling the error directly. The *with-value* function provides a standard way to "extract" the value v from a computation c and use it to create another computation $c' = (f \ v)$ via a function $f : Value \rightarrow Comp$. It does so by assuming that the expression continuation for c' will be k, and then using $\lambda v \,.\, (c' \ k) = \lambda v \,.\, (f \ v \ k)$ as the expression continuation for c. Unlike the previous definition of *with-value* in Figure 6.26 on page 281, the new definition of *with-value* does not need to perform a case analysis on the computation c in order to propagate errors. An error computation generated by *err-to-comp* will simply ignore the expression continuation $(\lambda v \, . \, (f \;\; v \;\; k))$ and signal the error. Figure 9.23 also reimplements the state-manipulating functions *allocating*, *fetching*, *update*, and *sequence* in a computation-based way.

With the definitions in Figure 9.23, all the computation laws in Figure 6.27 (page 282) and Figure 8.19 (page 416) still hold. Furthermore, all the valuation clauses in Figures 8.21 and 8.22 (for the stateful constructs of FLICK) and in Figures 6.28 and 6.29 (for the stateless constructs of FLICK inherited from FLK) except for `rec` still hold.

As an example of the computation-based continuation semantics, Figures 9.24 and 9.25 show the calculation of $\mathcal{E}[\![E_{test}]\!]\;e_1\;k_{top}$, where E_{test}, e_1, and k_{top} are the same expression, environment, and expression continuation from Figure 9.22. All but the final three reasoning steps in Figure 9.25 are justified using the valuation functions from Figures 6.28 and 6.29 and the computation laws from Figure 6.27. Remarkably, the very same steps could be used to calculate the meaning of $\mathcal{E}[\![E_{test}]\!]\;e_1$ in CBV FLK. This illustrates the power of the computation abstraction. Only the final three steps rely on details from the continuation-based definition of a computation.

The meaning calculated in Figures 9.24 and 9.25 is exactly the same as the one in Figure 9.22. Indeed, all FLICK expressions that do not use `rec` have exactly the same meaning under the standard semantics version of $\mathcal{E}$ (call this $\mathcal{E}_{std}$) and under the computation-based version of $\mathcal{E}$ (call this $\mathcal{E}_{comp}$). This can be formally proved by showing that for each FLICK expression construct E except `rec` that appears in the grammar of Exp, $\mathcal{E}_{comp}[\![E]\!] = \mathcal{E}_{std}[\![E]\!]$. In Exercise 9.7 we encourage you to show this for key constructs.

What about `rec`? To handle `rec` in the presence of a continuation-based *Comp* domain, we need to tweak the valuation clause for `rec` from Figure 8.21 as follows:

$$\mathcal{E}[\![(\texttt{rec}\;\; I \;\; E)]\!]$$
$$= \lambda e \, . \; \mathbf{fix}_{Comp} \, (\lambda c \, . \; \lambda ks \, . \; (\mathcal{E}[\![E]\!] \;\; (\textit{bind}\;\; I \;\; (\textit{extract-value}\;\; c \;\; s) \;\; e) \;\; k \;\; s))$$

$$\textit{extract-value} : Comp \rightarrow Store \rightarrow Binding\,Val$$
$$= \lambda cs \, . \; \mathbf{match}\;\; (c \;\; \textit{top-level-cont}\;\; s)$$
$$\quad\quad\quad\quad \vartriangleright (\textit{Value} \rightarrowtail \textit{Expressible}\;\; v) \;\| \; (\textit{Nameable} \rightarrowtail \textit{Binding\,Val}\;\; v)$$
$$\quad\quad\quad\quad \vartriangleright (\textit{Error} \rightarrowtail \textit{Expressible}\;\; Y) \;\| \; \bot_{Binding}$$
$$\quad\quad\quad \mathbf{end}$$

As in any CBV treatment of `rec`, the goal is to extract a value that can be named in the environment from an element of *Comp* that is defined as a fixed point of the `rec` expression. In Figure 8.21, a value was extracted from a computation by providing it with an initial store. This returned a pair of an ex-

---

Domains

$c \in Comp = Expcont \rightarrow Store \rightarrow Answer$; $Answer = Expressible$ in FLICK.
All other domains as in Figure 9.19.

Operations

$val\text{-}to\text{-}comp : Value \rightarrow Comp = \lambda v \,.\, \lambda ks \,.\, (k\ v\ s) = \lambda v \,.\, \lambda k \,.\, (k\ v)$

$err\text{-}to\text{-}comp : Error \rightarrow Comp = \lambda Y \,.\, \lambda ks \,.\, (Error \rightarrowtail Expressible\ Y)$

$with\text{-}value : Comp \rightarrow (Value \rightarrow Comp) \rightarrow Comp$
$= \lambda cf \,.\, \lambda k \,.\, (c\ (\lambda v \,.\, (f\ v\ k)))$

$with\text{-}values$, $with\text{-}boolean\text{-}val$, $with\text{-}boolean\text{-}comp$, etc. are all written in terms of
$with\text{-}value$ and $err\text{-}to\text{-}comp$, so their definitions are unchanged from Figure 6.26 on
page 281.

$allocating : Storable \rightarrow (Location \rightarrow Comp) \rightarrow Comp$
$= \lambda \sigma f \,.\, \lambda ks \,.\, (f\ (fresh\text{-}loc\ s)\ k\ (assign\ (fresh\text{-}loc\ s)\ \sigma\ s))$

$fetching : Location \rightarrow (Storable \rightarrow Comp) \rightarrow Comp$
$= \lambda lf \,.\, \lambda ks \,.\,$ **match** $(fetch\ l\ s)$
        $\triangleright (Storable \rightarrowtail AssignedVal\ \sigma) \,\|\, (f\ \sigma\ k\ s)$
        $\triangleright$ **else** $(err\text{-}to\text{-}comp\ \texttt{unassigned-location}\ k\ s)$
        end

$update : Location \rightarrow Storable \rightarrow Comp$
$= \lambda l\sigma \,.\, \lambda ks \,.\, (k\ (Unit \rightarrowtail Value\ \text{unit})\ (assign\ l\ \sigma\ s))$

$sequence : Comp \rightarrow Comp \rightarrow Comp$
$= \lambda c_1 c_2 \,.\, (with\text{-}value\ c_1\ (\lambda v_{ignore} \,.\, c_2))$; *unchanged from before*

Figure 9.23 Continuation-based computation abstraction.

pressible value and a store, and a value was extracted from the first component
of this pair. But here, extracting a value requires providing an initial continuation as well as an initial store. We use the initial continuation $top\text{-}level\text{-}cont =$
$(\lambda vs \,.\, (Value \rightarrowtail Expressible\ v))$ to get a computation to "cough up" an expressible
value, and then attempt to extract a value from this. The reason we handle $\texttt{rec}$
here but not in Section 9.3.1 is that CBV $\texttt{rec}$ is rather complex and we prefer
to use the $Comp$-based "recipe" that we have already developed for defining its
semantics.

The complexity in dealing with CBV $\texttt{rec}$ is due entirely to the fact that it
calculates a recursively defined value. In contrast, imperative looping constructs

Suppose $p_1 = \lambda v_1$. $\textit{with-integer-val}\ v_1\ (\lambda i_1\ .\ (\textit{val-to-comp}\ (Int \rightarrowtail Value\ (i_1 +_{Int} 1))))$
$\qquad e_1 = \{\mathsf{a} \mapsto (Bool \rightarrowtail Value\ true),\ \mathsf{inc} \mapsto (Proc \rightarrowtail Value\ p_1)\}$
$\qquad k_{top} = \textit{top-level-cont}$

$(\mathcal{E}[\![(\texttt{app (if a (lam x (prim * x 6)) inc) (prim + 3 4)})]\!]\ e_1)\ k_{top}$

$= (\textit{with-procedure-comp}\ c_1\ (\lambda p\ .\ (\textit{with-value}\ c_2\ p)))\ k_{top},$
$\quad$ where
$\qquad c_1 = \mathcal{E}[\![(\texttt{if a (lam x (prim * x 6)) inc})]\!]\ e_1$
$\qquad\quad = \textit{with-boolean-comp}\ (\mathcal{E}[\![\mathsf{a}]\!]\ e_1)\ f_1,$
$\qquad\qquad$ where $f_1 = \lambda b$. $\mathbf{if}\ b\ \mathbf{then}\ (\mathcal{E}[\![(\texttt{lam x (prim * x 6)})]\!]\ e_1)$
$\qquad\qquad\qquad\qquad\qquad\qquad \mathbf{else}\ (\mathcal{E}[\![\mathsf{inc}]\!]\ e_1)\ \mathbf{end}$
$\qquad\quad = \textit{with-boolean-comp}\ (\textit{with-nameable}\ (\textit{lookup}\ \mathsf{a}\ e_1)\ (\lambda v\ .\ (\textit{val-to-comp}\ v)))\ f_1$
$\qquad\quad = \textit{with-boolean-comp}\ (\textit{val-to-comp}\ (Bool \rightarrowtail Value\ true))\ f_1,\ \text{by (6.12)}$
$\qquad\quad = \mathbf{if}\ true\ \mathbf{then}\ (\mathcal{E}[\![(\texttt{lam x (prim * x 6)})]\!]\ e_1)\ \mathbf{else}\ (\mathcal{E}[\![\mathsf{inc}]\!]\ e_1)\ \mathbf{end},\ \text{by (6.10)}$
$\qquad\quad = \mathcal{E}[\![(\texttt{lam x (prim * x 6)})]\!]\ e_1$
$\qquad\quad = \textit{val-to-comp}\ (Proc \rightarrowtail Value\ p_2),$
$\qquad\qquad$ where
$\qquad\qquad p_2 = \lambda v_3$. $(\mathcal{E}[\![(\texttt{prim * x 6})]\!]\ [\mathsf{x} \mapsto v_3]e_1)$; CBV procedure
$\qquad\qquad\quad = \lambda v_3$. $\textit{with-value}\ (\mathcal{E}[\![\mathsf{x}]\!]\ [\mathsf{x} \mapsto v_3]e_1)$
$\qquad\qquad\qquad\qquad (\lambda v_1\ .\ (\textit{with-value}\ (\mathcal{E}[\![6]\!]\ [\mathsf{x} \mapsto v_3]e_1)\ f_2)),\ $; see page 284
$\qquad\qquad\qquad\quad$ where $f_2 = (\lambda v_2\ .\ \textit{with-integer-val}\ v_1$
$\qquad\qquad\qquad\qquad\qquad\qquad\qquad (\lambda i_1\ .\ \textit{with-integer-val}\ v_2$
$\qquad\qquad\qquad\qquad\qquad\qquad\qquad\qquad (\lambda i_2\ .\ (\textit{val-to-comp}$
$\qquad\qquad\qquad\qquad\qquad\qquad\qquad\qquad\qquad (Int \rightarrowtail Value\ (i_1 \times_{Int} i_2))))))$
$\qquad\qquad\quad = \lambda v_3$. $\textit{with-value}\ (\textit{with-nameable}\ (\textit{lookup}\ \mathsf{x}\ [\mathsf{x} \mapsto v_3]e_1)\ \textit{val-to-comp})$
$\qquad\qquad\qquad\qquad (\lambda v_1\ .\ (\textit{with-value}\ (\textit{val-to-comp}\ (Int \rightarrowtail Value\ 6))\ f_2))$
$\qquad\qquad\quad = \lambda v_3$. $\textit{with-value}\ (\textit{val-to-comp}\ v_3)$
$\qquad\qquad\qquad\qquad (\lambda v_1\ .\ (\textit{with-value}\ (\textit{val-to-comp}\ (Int \rightarrowtail Value\ 6))\ f_2)),\ \text{by (6.12)}$
$\qquad\qquad\quad = \lambda v_3$. $\textit{with-integer-val}\ v_3$
$\qquad\qquad\qquad\qquad (\lambda i_1\ .\ \textit{with-integer-val}\ (Int \rightarrowtail Value\ 6)$
$\qquad\qquad\qquad\qquad\qquad (\lambda i_2\ .\ (\textit{val-to-comp}$
$\qquad\qquad\qquad\qquad\qquad\qquad (Int \rightarrowtail Value\ (i_1 \times_{Int} i_2))))),\ \text{by (6.5)}$
$\qquad\qquad\quad = \lambda v_3$. $\textit{with-integer-val}\ v_3\ (\lambda i_1\ .\ (\textit{val-to-comp}\ (Int \rightarrowtail Value\ (i_1 \times_{Int} 6)))),$
$\qquad\qquad\qquad$ by (6.9) for $\textit{with-integer-val}$
$\qquad c_2 = \mathcal{E}[\![(\texttt{prim + 3 4})]\!]\ e_1$
$\qquad\quad = \textit{val-to-comp}\ (Int \rightarrowtail Value\ 7)$; similar to $\mathcal{E}[\![(\texttt{prim * x 6})]\!]\ [\mathsf{x} \mapsto v_3]e_1$

$= \ $ (continued in Figure 9.25)

Figure 9.24 Calculation of the meaning of a sample FLICK expression in a computation-based semantics (continued in Figure 9.25).

$(\text{with-procedure-comp } c_1 \ (\lambda p \ . \ (\text{with-value } c_2 \ p))) \ k_{top}$

$= (\text{with-procedure-comp } (\text{val-to-comp } (Proc \rightarrowtail Value \ p_2))$
$\qquad (\lambda p \ . \ (\text{with-value } (\text{val-to-comp } (Int \rightarrowtail Value \ 7)) \ p))) \ k_{top}$

$= (\text{with-value } (\text{val-to-comp } (Int \rightarrowtail Value \ 7)) \ p_2) \ k_{top},$
by (6.10) for $\text{with-procedure-comp}$

$= (p_2 \ (Int \rightarrowtail Value \ 7)) \ k_{top}, \text{ by (6.5)}$

$= (\text{with-integer-val } (Int \rightarrowtail Value \ 7) \ (\lambda i_1 \ . \ (\text{val-to-comp } (Int \rightarrowtail Value \ (i_1 \times_{Int} 6))))) \ k_{top}$

$= (\text{val-to-comp } (Int \rightarrowtail Value \ (7 \times_{Int} 6))) \ k_{top}, \text{ by (6.9) for } \text{with-integer-val}$

$= (\lambda v \ . \ \lambda k \ . \ (k \ v)) \ (Int \rightarrowtail Value \ 42) \ k_{top}, \text{ by the definition of } \text{val-to-comp} \text{ in Figure 9.23}$

$= k_{top} \ (Int \rightarrowtail Value \ 42)$

$= \lambda s \ . \ (Value \rightarrowtail Expressible \ (Int \rightarrowtail Value \ 42)), \text{ by the definition of } k_{top} = \text{top-level-cont}$

Figure 9.25 Continued from Figure 9.24.

that are executed for their side effects rather than their value are straightforward to model in a continuation-based semantics (see Exercises 9.8 and 9.10).

The power of continuation-based semantics is revealed in language features in which the normal expression continuation is replaced by some other continuation. We begin to explore such features in the following exercises and continue to explore them in the remaining sections of this chapter.

Exercise 9.6 Show that all the computation laws in Figure 6.27 (page 282) and Figure 8.19 (page 416) still hold when the $Comp$ domain and its associated operations have the definitions in Figure 9.23.

Exercise 9.7 For each of the following expression constructs E, use equational reasoning to show that $\mathcal{E}_{comp}[\![E]\!] = \mathcal{E}_{std}[\![E]\!]$: I, (lam I E_{body}), (app E_1 E_2), (cell E_{val}), (prim ^ E_{cell}), and (prim := E_1 E_2).

Exercise 9.8 Suppose that FLIC's (while E_{test} E_{body}) construct were a kernel construct rather than syntactic sugar. Recall that while is executed for side effects only and always returns the unit value.

a. Flesh out the following skeleton for the valuation clause for while written in the style of the standard semantics:

$$\mathcal{E}[\![(\text{while } E_{test} \ E_{body})]\!] = \lambda ek \ . \ (\textbf{fix}_{Cmdcont} \ (\lambda \gamma \ . \ \ldots))$$

b. Flesh out the following skeleton for the valuation clause for while written in the style of the computation-based semantics:

$$\mathcal{E}[\![(\text{while } E_{test} \ E_{body})]\!] = \lambda e \ . \ (\textbf{fix}_{Comp} \ (\lambda c \ . \ \ldots))$$

Exercise 9.9 Inspired by the capability of standard semantics for describing new control constructs, Ben Bitdiddle has extended FLICK with a new expression construct that allows a procedure to call itself without using `rec` or `letrec`.

$$E ::= \ \ldots \text{FLICK } expressions \ \ldots \mid (\texttt{self } E)$$

Informally, (`self` E) recursively calls the "current" procedure with an actual argument that is the result of evaluating E. For example:

```
(let ((fact (abs (n) (if (= n 0) 1 (* n (self (- n 1))))))
      (fib (abs (n) (if (< n 2) n (+ (self (- n 1)) (self (- n 2)))))))
     (pair (fact 4) (fib 6))  FLIC  ⟨24, 8⟩
```

When (`self` E) is used outside of any procedure, it causes the program to terminate immediately with a value that is the result of evaluating E.

Ben starts specifying the formal semantics of his extended language by modifying the signature of the meaning function $\mathcal{E}$ as follows:

$$
\begin{aligned}
\mathcal{E} : \mathrm{Exp} &\to Env \to Proc && ; \textit{the current procedure} \\
&\to Expcont && ; \textit{the normal expression continuation} \\
&\to Cmdcont && ; \textit{the normal command continuation}
\end{aligned}
$$

He has also modified $\mathcal{E}^*$ similarly.

In spite of his enthusiasm, Ben is still inexperienced with standard semantics and he has asked for your help in completing the standard semantics of his extension to FLICK.

a. Write the new $\mathcal{E}$ valuation clause for (`self` E) and the modified clauses for L, (`lam` I E), and (`app` E_1 E_2). Do the other $\mathcal{E}$ clauses need to be modified?

b. Write the modified definition of the $\mathcal{P}$ valuation function for programs.

c. Using the clauses from part **a** and part **b**:

    i.   Show that running the program (`flick () (self (self 1))`) on zero inputs yields the answer ($Value \rightarrowtail Expressible \ (Int \rightarrowtail Value \ 1)$).

    ii. Show that (`lam x (self 1)`) evaluates to a procedure that loops forever no matter what argument it is called with.

d. Ben has based the semantics for his FLICK extension on the standard semantics for FLICK in Figure 9.21, but he could have based it instead on the continuation-based computation abstraction in Figure 9.23. Show how to modify the *Comp* domain and the *val-to-comp*, *err-to-comp*, and *with-value* functions to describe Ben's language. With these changes, is it necessary to modify any of the $\mathcal{E}$ or $\mathcal{E}^*$ clauses for constructs inherited from FLICK? Explain.

Exercise 9.10 Unimpressed with FLIC's `while` loops, Dewey Lupe has designed a more general form of looping that uses the following new kernel constructs:

$$E ::= \ \ldots \text{FLICK } expressions \ \ldots \mid (\texttt{loop } E) \mid (\texttt{break } E) \mid (\texttt{continue})$$

Here is the informal semantics of Dewey's new constructs:

(loop E) evaluates E (the "looping expression") repeatedly forever.

(break E) terminates the innermost lexically enclosing loop, which then returns with the value of E.

(continue) restarts the evaluation of the looping expression for the innermost lexically enclosing loop.

It is an error to evaluate either a break or a continue expression outside of a loop expression.

Dewey writes the following procedure to illustrate his constructs:

```
(def (sum-list elts)
  (let ((sum (cell 0)) (es (cell elts)))
    (loop (if (null? (^ es))
              (break (^ sum))
              (let ((e (car es)))
                (begin (:= es (cdr (^ es)))
                       (:= sum (+ (^ sum) (if (int? e)
                                              e
                                              (continue))))
              ))))))
```

This procedure returns the sum of all integer elements in a given list; any noninteger elements are ignored.

a. Show how to desugar (while E_{test} E_{body}) in terms of Dewey's new constructs.

b. Show how to desugar a construct (repeat E_{body} E_{test}) from Exercise 8.11 in terms of Dewey's new constructs.

c. Consider a new looping construct (for I E_{lo} E_{hi} E_{body}) with the following informal semantics:

> First evaluate E_{lo} to an integer i_{lo} and E_{hi} to an integer i_{hi}. Then repeatedly evaluate E_{body} with I successively bound to each integer in the range $[i_{lo}..i_{hi}]$. If ($i_{lo} > i_{hi}$), E_{body} is not evaluated. After all evaluations of E_{body}, the for construct returns the unit value. The for construct signals an error if either E_{lo} or E_{hi} signals an error or does not denote an integer, or if E_{body} signals an error.

Show how to desugar the for construct in terms of Dewey's new constructs.

To better understand his new constructs, Dewey extends the standard denotational semantics of FLICK to handle them. He changes the signature of $\mathcal{E}$ to be

$$
\begin{aligned}
\mathcal{E} : \mathrm{Exp} \rightarrow Env \rightarrow{} & Expcont && \text{; the \textbf{break} continuation} \\
\rightarrow{} & Cmdcont && \text{; the \textbf{continue} continuation} \\
\rightarrow{} & Expcont && \text{; the normal expression continuation} \\
\rightarrow{} & Cmdcont && \text{; the normal command continuation}
\end{aligned}
$$

and changes $\mathcal{E}^*$ similarly. He also modifies the plumbing of $\mathcal{E}$ clauses for existing FLICK constructs to pass the additional continuations. For example:

$$\mathcal{E}[\![(\texttt{app } E_1 \ E_2)]\!]$$
$$= \lambda e \ k_{break} \ \gamma_{continue} \ k_{app} \ .$$
$$(\mathcal{E}[\![E_1]\!] \ e \ k_{break} \ \gamma_{continue}$$
$$(procedure\text{-}cont \ (\lambda p \ . \ (\mathcal{E}[\![E_2]\!] \ e \ k_{break} \ \gamma_{continue} \ (\lambda v \ . \ (p \ v \ k_{app})))))))$$

Assume that *procedure-cont* and similar functions have also been modified appropriately.

d. Write the $\mathcal{E}$ clauses for $(\texttt{loop } E)$, $(\texttt{break } E)$, and $(\texttt{continue})$.

e. Define the $\mathcal{P}$ valuation function for a program.

f. Procedures must be handled carefully in the formal semantics order for the extended language to have the informal semantics specified by Dewey.

   i.   What should the value of the following expression be?
$$E_{looptest} = (\texttt{loop } (\texttt{let } ((\texttt{f } (\texttt{lam x } (\texttt{break x}))))$$
$$(\texttt{break } (\texttt{+ 20 } (\texttt{loop } (\texttt{f 3}))))))$$

   ii. Assume that the *Proc* domain is not changed. Write the $\mathcal{E}$ clause for $(\texttt{lam } I \ E)$ so that occurrences of $\texttt{break}$ and $\texttt{continue}$ within a procedure body will refer to the *lexically* enclosing $\texttt{loop}$.

   iii. Describe all changes that need to be made to the semantics so that occurrences of $\texttt{break}$ and $\texttt{continue}$ within a procedure body will refer to the *dynamically* enclosing $\texttt{loop}$ rather than the lexically enclosing one. What is the value of $E_{looptest}$ after these changes?

g. Dewey has based the semantics for his FLICK extension on the standard semantics for FLICK in Figure 9.21, but he could have based it instead on the continuation-based computation abstraction in Figure 9.23. Show how to modify the *Comp* domain and the *val-to-comp*, *err-to-comp*, and *with-value* functions to describe Dewey's language. With these changes, is it necessary to modify any of the $\mathcal{E}$ or $\mathcal{E}^*$ clauses for constructs inherited from FLICK? Explain.

h. In JAVA, programmers may name a loop statement with a label and provide an optional label in the $\texttt{break}$ and $\texttt{continue}$ statements. When loops are nested, labels allows the programmer to specify *which* loop the $\texttt{break}$ or $\texttt{continue}$ statement refers to. Modify the syntax and semantics of Dewey's language to handle labeled loops.

Exercise 9.11 Abby Stracksen is aggressively using standard semantics to define the meaning of some rather nonstandard FLIC constructs. Most recently, she extended FLIC with some special constructs for Politically Oriented Programming (POP).

$$E ::= \dots \text{FLICK } expressions \ \dots \ | \ (\texttt{elect } E_{pres} \ E_{vp}) \ | \ (\texttt{impeach}) \ | \ (\texttt{reelect})$$

Here's the informal semantics of Abby's new constructs:

$(\texttt{elect } E_{pres} \ E_{vp})$: Evaluates to the value of E_{pres} unless $(\texttt{impeach})$ is evaluated in E_{pres}, in which case the $\texttt{elect}$ expression evaluates to the value of E_{vp}. It is possible to have nested `elect` constructs, in which case `(impeach)` affects the innermost lexically enclosing `elect` in whose E_{pres} it occurs.

`(impeach)`: When evaluated within the E_{pres} part of an `(elect` E_{pres} E_{vp}`)` expression, this causes the `elect` expression to evaluate and return E_{vp}. Otherwise, it signals an error.

`(reelect)`: When evaluated inside the E_{pres} part of an `(elect` E_{pres} E_{vp}`)` expression, this causes control to return to the beginning of the `elect` construct. Otherwise, it signals an error.

Abby provides some simple examples of her constructs in action:

```
(elect (- 1 2) (+ 3 4))  FLIC⟶  −1

(elect (- 1 (impeach)) (+ 3 4))  FLIC⟶  7

(elect (- 1 (impeach)) (+ 3 (impeach)))  FLIC⟶  error:no-elect-for-impeach

(elect (elect (- 1 (impeach)) (+ 3 (impeach))) (* 5 6))  FLIC⟶  30

(let ((scandals (cell 0)))
  (elect (if (< (^ scandals) 5)
             (begin (:= scandals (+ (^ scandals) 1))
                    (reelect))
             (impeach))
         (* (^ scandals) 2)))  FLIC⟶  10
```

In the last example, `(reelect)` is evaluated five times as the value in the `scandals` cell increases from 0 to 5. When `scandals` becomes 5, `(impeach)` is evaluated, and the result of `(* (^ scandals) 2)` is returned as the value of the `elect` expression.

You have been hired by Abby to modify the standard denotational semantics of FLICK in order to define the formal semantics of her new constructs. Abby has modified the signature of the meaning function $\mathcal{E}$ to be

$$
\begin{aligned}
\mathcal{E} : \mathrm{Exp} \rightarrow Env \rightarrow{} & Cmdcont &&; \text{the \texttt{impeach} continuation} \\
\rightarrow{} & Cmdcont &&; \text{the \texttt{reelect} continuation} \\
\rightarrow{} & Expcont &&; \text{the normal expression continuation} \\
\rightarrow{} & Cmdcont &&; \text{the normal command continuation}
\end{aligned}
$$

and has modified $\mathcal{E}^*$ similarly. She has also modified $\mathcal{E}$ clauses for existing FLICK constructs to appropriately pass along the two new command continuations.

a. Write the $\mathcal{E}$ valuation clauses for `(elect` E_{pres} E_{vp}`)`, `(impeach)`, and `(reelect)`.

b. Define the $\mathcal{P}$ valuation function for programs in Abby's language.

c. Use your meaning functions to compute the answer for running the nullary programs `(flick () (elect (+ 1 (impeach)) 2))` and `(flick () (elect (reelect) 3))` on zero arguments.

d. Abby shows the semantics for her extended language to Dewey Lupe, who is struck
   by the similarities between the semantics for Abby's `elect`, `impeach`, and `reelect`
   constructs and those for his own `loop`, `break`, and `continue` constructs (see Exercise 9.10). Dewey conjectures that it's possible to desugar Abby's constructs into
   his. Show that Dewey is right by writing a desugaring for (`elect` E_{pres} E_{vp}) into
   FLICK+{`loop`, `break`, `continue`}. Your desugaring should define local nullary procedures `impeach` and `reelect` that behave appropriately.

Exercise 9.12 As part of his new `.gov` platform for government customers, Sam Antics
has developed FLIC#, a version of FLIC that establishes user quotas for the store. An
important customer observed that government users tended to use the store carelessly,
resulting in expensive memory upgrades. To improve the situation, FLIC# tracks the
current user and maintains a per-user quota on the number of cells a user can create
during program execution.

In Sam's system, every user is identified by a distinct user ID (a nonnegative integer)
and at most one user can be logged in at any one time. The distinguished user ID 0 is
used to indicate that no one is currently logged in. Associated with each user ID is a
cell quota that is initially 100 cells. Whenever an attempt is made to create a cell, the
system checks that (1) a user is logged in (i.e., the user ID is not 0) and (2) the quota
for the current user is > 0. In this case, the current user's quota is decremented by 1;
otherwise, an error is signaled. Sam's system does not support garbage collection (see
Chapter 18), so there is no way to reclaim a cell that is no longer used.

The kernel FLICK# of FLIC# extends FLICK with the following constructs:

$E ::= \ldots$ FLICK *expressions* $\ldots$ | (`login!` N) | (`logout!`) | (`check-quota`)

Here is the informal semantics of these constructs:

(`login!` N) logs in the user whose ID is denoted by N and returns this ID. An error
   is signaled if another user is already logged in or if N denotes an integer ≤ 0. (Sam's
   system currently has no means of user authentication, so it simply "trusts" that N is
   an appropriate user ID.)

(`logout!`) logs the current user out and returns this user's ID. It signals an error if no
   user is currently logged in.

(`check-quota`) returns the number of cells remaining in the current user's quota. It
   signals an error if no user is currently logged in.

Sam has hired you, a top FLICK consultant, to assist in formalizing the semantics
of FLICK#. Sam has made the following modifications to the domains for the standard
semantics of FLICK:

$u \in UserID = Int$
$q \in QuotaEnv = UserID \rightarrow Int$
$\gamma \in Cmdcont = UserID \rightarrow QuotaEnv \rightarrow Store \rightarrow Answer$

UserID is just a synonym for the *Int* domain. *QuotaEnv* is an environment for user
quotas; it maps a user ID to the number of cells remaining in that user's quota. The

Cmdcont domain from the FLICK standard semantics has been redefined to take the user ID of the currently logged-in user and the current quota environment in addition to the store before yielding an answer. Sam redefines *Cmdcont* so that most of the semantic algebra definitions in Figure 9.19 and most of the valuation clauses in Figure 9.21 can remain unchanged. But Sam needs to redefine *top-level-cont* and *error-cont* by adding extra arguments:

$$top\text{-}level\text{-}cont : Expcont \; = \; \lambda v \,.\; \lambda uqs \,.\; (Value \rightarrowtail Expressible \; v)$$

$$error\text{-}cont : Error \rightarrow Cmdcont \; = \; \lambda Y \,.\; \lambda uqs \,.\; (Error \rightarrowtail Expressible \; Y)$$

Here is Sam's valuation clause for `check-quota`:

$$\mathcal{E}[\![(\texttt{check-quota})]\!] \; = \; \lambda ekuq \,.\; \textbf{if } u \; = \; 0$$
$$\textbf{then } (error\text{-}cont \; \texttt{no-user-logged-in} \; u \; q)$$
$$\textbf{else } (k \; (Int \rightarrowtail Value \; (q \; u)) \; u \; q) \; \textbf{end}$$

a. Help Sam finish his semantics by writing the $\mathcal{E}$ valuation clauses for (`login!` N), (`logout!`), and (`cell` E). and the $\mathcal{P}$ valuation function. Remember that a cell cannot be created unless a user is logged in.

b. Naturally, Sam Antics wants to embed some "trap doors" into the `.gov` platform to enable him to "learn more about his customers." One of these trap doors is the undocumented (`raise-quota!` N) command, which adds N cells to the quota of the current user and returns `#u`. Write the $\mathcal{E}$ valuation clause for (`raise-quota!` N).

9.4 Nonlocal Exits

A denotational semantics equipped with continuations is especially useful for modeling advanced control features of programming languages. One such feature is a **nonlocal exit**, a mechanism that aborts pending computation by forcing control to jump to a specified **control point** in the program. A control point is a new kind of invokable first-class value representing the rest of the computation that is waiting for the value of the expression currently being evaluated. When a control point is invoked with a value v, the computation it represents proceeds as if the currently evaluating expression evaluated to v. Thus, a control point is a first-class representation of an evaluation context in operational semantics and an expression continuation in denotational semantics. For this reason, control points are often called **first-class continuations**. However, to distinguish the first-class values manipulated in our mini-languages from the continuations in the denotational semantics, we will use the term "control point" for the former and "continuation" for the latter.

```
(@+ 1 (label exit (@* 2 (@- 3 (@+ 4 5)))))  ‾‾FLIC‾→  −11

(@+ 1 (label exit (@* 2 (@- 3 (@+ 4 (jump exit 5))))))  ‾‾FLIC‾→  6

(@+ 1 (label exit
         (@* 2 (@- 3 (@+ 4 (jump exit
                                   (@* 5 (jump exit 6)))))))))  ‾‾FLIC‾→  7

(@+ 1 (label exit1
         (@* 2 (label exit2
                  (@- 3 (@+ 4 (@* (jump exit2 5)
                                  (jump exit1 6)))))))))  ‾‾FLIC‾→  11
```

Figure 9.26   Some examples using `label` and `jump`.

9.4.1   `label` and `jump`

We study nonlocal exits by extending FLICK with two new constructs for capturing and manipulating control points:

$E ::= \ldots$ *usual* FLICK *expressions* $\ldots$
$\mid$ (`label` I_{ctrlPt} E_{body}) $\mid$ (`jump` E_{ctrlPt} E_{body})

The informal semantics of these constructs is as follows:

(`label` I_{ctrlPt} E_{body}) evaluates E_{body} in an environment that extends the current lexical environment with a binding of the name I_{ctrlPt} to a first-class control point value that represents the rest of the computation waiting for the value of the `label` expression. The `label` expression normally returns the value of E_{body}, but a different value can be returned by invoking the control point named I_{ctrlPt}.

(`jump` E_{ctrlPt} E_{val}) invokes the control point that is the value of E_{ctrlPt} with the value of E_{val}. If E_{ctrlPt} does not evaluate to a control point, `jump` signals an error.

Figure 9.26 shows some simple FLIC examples using `label` and `jump`. The first example illustrates that the value of (`label` I E) is the value of E if E performs no `jump`s. In the second example, (`jump exit 5`) aborts the pending (`@* 2 (@- 3 (@/ 4 □)`)) computation and returns 5 as the value of the `label` expression. The third example demonstrates that a pending `jump` can itself be aborted by a `jump` within one of its subexpressions. In the final example, the left-to-right evaluation of the operands of a primitive application causes 5 to be returned as the value of (`label exit2` ...). If the operands were evaluated in right-to-left order instead, the result of the final example would be 7.

In practice, nonlocal exits are a convenient means of communicating information between two points of a program separated by pending operations without performing any of the pending operations. For instance, here is a version of a recursive procedure for computing the product of integer leaves in a binary tree that uses `label` and `jump` to terminate the tree-walking process when a 0 leaf is encountered:

```
(def (tree-product tree)
  (label return
    (letrec ((prod (abs (tr)
                     (if (leaf? tr)
                         (if (= tr 0)
                             {return 0 immediately from tree-product}
                             (jump return 0)
                             tr)
                         (* (prod (left tr) (prod (right tr)))))))))
      (prod tree))))
```

Upon encountering a 0 leaf, the local recursive `prod` procedure uses `jump` to immediately return 0 as the result of a call to `tree-product`. Any pending multiplications generated by recursive calls to `prod` are aborted when the `jump` is performed. Compared to the versions of `tree-product` studied in Section 9.2.4, this one has the advantage that the `prod` procedure is written in the "natural" recursive way rather than in a continuation-passing style that explicitly manipulates procedural representations of continuations for calls to `prod`. This illustrates the key to the power of `label`/`jump`: programs never need mention continuations except in spots where they are actually needed.

Like all other values in FLIC, control point values are first class: they can be named, passed as arguments, returned as results, and stored in data structures (pairs, cells). An interesting consequence of this fact is that it is possible to return to the same control point more than once. Consider the following FLIC expression:

```
(let ((c (cell #u))) {#u is an arbitrary value that will be overwritten
                      by := before the first use of ^.}
  (let ((n (label bind-n (begin (:= c bind-n) 1))))
    (if (> n 17) n (jump (^ c) (* 2 n)))))  ═══⟶  32
                                             FLIC
```

Here, `bind-n` names the control point that is waiting for the value of the `label` expression. Invoking the control point on that value will bind `n` to that value and evaluate the `if` expression. This control point is stored in the cell `c` for later use, and then a 1 is returned as the value of the `label` expression, as part of the normal flow of control. Since this value for `n` is less than 17, the `jump` is performed, which returns the value of 2 to the same `bind-n` control point. This causes `n` to be rebound to 2 and the `if` expression to be evaluated a second time. Continuing in this manner, the expression behaves like a loop that successively binds `n` to the values 1, 2, 4, 8, 16, and 32. The final result is 32 because that is the first power of two that is greater than 17.

A similar technique can be used to phrase an imperative version of an iterative factorial procedure in terms of `label` and `jump`:

```
(def (fact n)
  (let ((ans (cell 1))
        (loop (cell #u)))  {#u is an arbitrary value that will be overwritten.}
    (let ((i (label top (begin (:= loop top) n))))
      (if (= i 0)
          (^ ans)
          (begin (:= ans (* i (^ ans)))
                 (jump (^ loop) (- i 1)))))))
```

This code is remarkable for using first-class control points to execute an iterative process without using any explicit looping or recursion constructs. It iterates from `n` down to 0, storing the product of the numbers processed so far in the cell `ans`. In each iteration, the name `i` is bound to the number currently being processed. In the first iteration, `i` is bound to the value of the expression (`label top (begin ... n)`), which is the value of `fact`'s argument `n`. But this `label` expression also stores into the cell named `loop` a control point that will perform an iteration of the loop starting with the integer on which it is invoked. The (`jump (^ loop) (- i 1)`) causes control to jump to the top of the loop with the next value of `i`. Note that jumping back to the top of the loop does *not* reset the value of the `ans` cell back to its initial value. The store continues to be single-threaded through the computation no matter how convoluted the control path might be.

It turns out that side effects are not necessary for exhibiting this sort of looping behavior in the presence of first-class control points. For example, a non-recursive factorial procedure can be written in a version of the stateless language FL extended with `label` and `jump` (see Exercise 9.15).

The above examples of first-class control points only scratch the surface of the strange and wonderful behaviors that they enable. As we shall see in Section 9.5 and the exercises, first-class control points provide a powerful mechanism by which programmers can implement advanced control features like coroutines,

---

Semantic Domains

$\quad ControlPoint = Expcont$

$v \in Value = \ldots \text{FLICK } values \ldots + ControlPoint$

Operations

$control\text{-}point\text{-}cont : (ControlPoint \rightarrow Cmdcont) \rightarrow Expcont$

$= \lambda f \, . \, (\lambda v \, . \, \mathbf{match} \; v$

$\qquad\qquad \triangleright (ControlPoint \rightarrowtail Value \; k) \, [\!|\!] \; (f \; k)$

$\qquad\qquad \triangleright \mathbf{else} \; (error\text{-}cont \; \texttt{non-control-point}) \; \mathbf{end} \,)$

New Valuation Clauses (Standard Version)

$\mathcal{E}[\![(\texttt{label} \; I_{ctrlPt} \; E_{body})]\!] = \lambda ek \, . \, (\mathcal{E}[\![E_{body}]\!] \; [I_{ctrlPt} \mapsto (ControlPoint \rightarrowtail Value \; k)]e \; k)$

$\mathcal{E}[\![(\texttt{jump} \; E_{ctrlPt} \; E_{val})]\!]$

$\quad = \lambda ek_{ignore} \, . \, (\mathcal{E}[\![E_{ctrlPt}]\!] \; e \; (control\text{-}point\text{-}cont \; (\lambda k_{ctrlPt} \, . \, (\mathcal{E}[\![E_{val}]\!] \; e \; k_{ctrlPt}))))$

Figure 9.27 The standard denotational semantics of `label` and `jump` in FLICK.

backtracking, and multithreading. But any control abstraction mechanism this powerful can easily lead to programs that are virtually impossible to understand and reason about. A key aspect of the so-called "structured programming" revolution of the 1970s was eliminating `goto`s (i.e., unrestricted jumps) from programs to avoid "spaghetti code" — programs in which tracking control flow was as difficult as following a strand of spaghetti through a bowlful of pasta. First-class control points turn the notion of `goto`-less programming on its head by promoting a `goto` label to a first-class value that can flow anywhere in a program, allowing jumps to that label from arbitrary other points in the program. Moreover, first-class control points can be challenging to implement efficiently, which is why so few real-world languages support them (SCHEME and various dialects of ML being the main exceptions). Clearly, great restraint should be exercised in the use of first-class control points. They should be used sparingly and judiciously — only in situations where their effect is not easily achievable in a more transparent fashion.

9.4.2   A Denotational Semantics for `label` and `jump`

A standard semantics for `label` and `jump` is presented in Figure 9.27. Control points are modeled as elements of the *ControlPoint* domain. These are just expression continuations that are treated as first-class values. Because *ControlPoint* = *Expcont*, we shall use the *Expcont* domain variable k to range over *Control-Point* as well. The valuation clause for `label` evaluates E_{body} in the environment

e extended with a binding between I_{ctrlPt} and the control point value that is the continuation of the label expression. jump ignores its default continuation and instead evaluates E_{val} with the continuation determined by E_{ctrlPt}.

Figure 9.28 shows the calculation of the meanings of the first two expressions in Figure 9.26 in the standard semantics. Since these two expressions are the same except for the innermost subexpression E_{hole}, Figure 9.28 begins by calculating the meaning of an expression in which E_{hole} is left abstract. When E_{hole} is instantiated to 5, the continuation k_4 of E_{hole} is applied to 5, which calculates $(1 +_{Int} (2 \times_{Int} (3 -_{Int} (4 +_{Int} 5)))) = -11$ and passes this result to the initial continuation k_0. But when E_{hole} is (jump exit 5), the continuation k_4 of E_{hole} is ignored. Instead, the exit continuation k_1 is applied to 5, which calculates $(1 +_{Int} 5) = 6$ and passes this result to the initial continuation k_0.

Figure 9.29 presents the denotational semantics of label and jump in the continuation-based computation style of Section 9.3.2. In addition to a function *with-control-point-comp* that is analogous to *with-boolean-comp*, there are two new operations on computations. *capturing-cont* duplicates the current continuation, passing it both as the control-point argument and the expression continuation to a given f. It is used in the valuation clause for label to capture the current continuation. (*install-cont* k_{new}) transforms a computation c into one that uses k_{new} instead of its regular continuation. It is used in the valuation clause for jump to replace the normal continuation of E_{val} by the control point denoted by E_{ctrlPt}.

Note that label refers to its continuation twice: it both binds it in the environment and uses it as the continuation of E_{body}. This is easier to see in the standard style than in the computation style, where the duplication is hidden inside *capturing-cont*. This means that a value can be returned from a label expression in two ways: (1) by normal evaluation of E_{body} (without any jumps) and (2) by using jump with a control point that is extracted from the environment. In contrast, jump does not refer to its normal continuation at all. This means that a jump expression can never return! So it is meaningless to ask what the value of a jump expression is. Similarly, expressions containing jump expressions may also have no value. This is the first time we have seen expressions without values in a dialect of FL.

Exercise 9.13

a. Use the standard denotational semantics for label and jump to calculate the meanings of the last two expressions in Figure 9.26.

b. Use the computation-based denotational semantics for label and jump to calculate the meanings of all four expressions in Figure 9.26.

$\mathcal{E}[\![(\texttt{@+ 1 (label exit (@* 2 (@- 3 (@+ 4 } E_{hole}\texttt{))))))}]\!]\ e_0\ k_0$

$= \mathcal{E}[\![(\texttt{label exit (@* 2 (@- 3 (@+ 4 } E_{hole}\texttt{)))))}]\!]\ e_0\ k_1,$
  where $k_1 = \lambda v_1\ .\ (\textit{check-integer}\ v_1\ (\lambda i_1\ .\ (k_0\ (\textit{Int} \rightarrowtail \textit{Value}\ (1 +_{Int} i_1)))))),$
  by (9.11)

$= \mathcal{E}[\![(\texttt{@* 2 (@- 3 (@+ 4 } E_{hole}\texttt{))))}]\!]\ e_1\ k_1,$
  where $e_1 = [\texttt{exit} \mapsto (\textit{ControlPoint} \rightarrowtail \textit{Value}\ k_1)]e_0$

$= \mathcal{E}[\![(\texttt{@- 3 (@+ 4 } E_{hole}\texttt{)))}]\!]\ e_1\ k_2,$
  where $k_2 = \lambda v_2\ .\ (\textit{check-integer}\ v_2\ (\lambda i_2\ .\ (k_1\ (\textit{Int} \rightarrowtail \textit{Value}\ (2 \times_{Int} i_2)))))),$
  by (9.11)

$= \mathcal{E}[\![(\texttt{@+ 4 } E_{hole}\texttt{))}]\!]\ e_1\ k_3,$
  where $k_3 = \lambda v_3\ .\ (\textit{check-integer}\ v_3\ (\lambda i_3\ .\ (k_2\ (\textit{Int} \rightarrowtail \textit{Value}\ (3 -_{Int} i_3)))))),$
  by (9.11)

$= \mathcal{E}[\![E_{hole}]\!]\ e_1\ k_4,$
  where $k_4 = \lambda v_4\ .\ (\textit{check-integer}\ v_4\ (\lambda i_4\ .\ (k_3\ (\textit{Int} \rightarrowtail \textit{Value}\ (4 +_{Int} i_4)))))),$
                by (9.11)
  $= \lambda v_4\ .\ (\textit{check-integer}\ v_4$
                $(\lambda i_4\ .\ (k_0\ (\textit{Int} \rightarrowtail \textit{Value}$
                              $(1 +_{Int} (2 \times_{Int} (3 -_{Int} (4 +_{Int} i_4)))))))))),$
        by simplifications involving (9.1) for $\textit{check-integer}$

Instantiating E_{hole} to 5:

$\mathcal{E}[\![(\texttt{@+ 1 (label exit (@* 2 (@- 3 (@+ 4 5)))))})]\!]\ e_0\ k_0$

$= \mathcal{E}[\![5]\!]\ e_1\ k_4,$ by the steps at the top of this figure

$= (k_4\ (\textit{Int} \rightarrowtail \textit{Value}\ 5))$

$= (k_0\ (1 +_{Int} (2 \times_{Int} (3 -_{Int} (4 +_{Int} 5))))),$
    by the definition of k_4 and (9.1) for $\textit{check-integer}$

$= (k_0\ -11)$

Instantiating E_{hole} to (jump exit 5):

$\mathcal{E}[\![(\texttt{@+ 1 (label exit (@* 2 (@- 3 (@+ 4 (jump exit 5)))))})]\!]\ e_0\ k_0$

$= \mathcal{E}[\![(\texttt{jump exit 5})]\!]\ e_1\ k_4,$ by the steps at the top of this figure

$= (\mathcal{E}[\![\texttt{exit}]\!]\ e_1\ (\textit{control-point-cont}\ (\lambda k_{ctrlPt}\ .\ (\mathcal{E}[\![5]\!]\ e\ k_{ctrlPt}))))$

$= (\textit{ensure-nameable}\ (\textit{lookup}\ \texttt{exit}\ e_1)$
                $(\textit{control-point-cont}\ (\lambda k_{ctrlPt}\ .\ (\mathcal{E}[\![5]\!]\ e\ k_{ctrlPt}))))$

$= (\textit{control-point-cont}\ (\lambda k_{ctrlPt}\ .\ (\mathcal{E}[\![5]\!]\ e\ k_{ctrlPt})))\ (\textit{ControlPoint} \rightarrowtail \textit{Value}\ k_1),$
    by (9.3)

$= \mathcal{E}[\![5]\!]\ e_1\ k_1,$ by (9.5) for $\textit{control-point-cont}$

$= (k_1\ (\textit{Int} \rightarrowtail \textit{Value}\ 5))$

$= (k_0\ (1 +_{Int} 5)),$ by the definition of k_1 and (9.1) for $\textit{check-integer}$

$= (k_0\ 6)$

Figure 9.28 Calculation of the meaning of some expressions with `label` and `jump` in standard semantics.

New Computation Operations for Control

$with\text{-}control\text{-}point\text{-}comp : Comp \to (ControlPoint \to Comp) \to Comp$
$= \lambda cf . (with\text{-}value \ c \ (\lambda v . \mathbf{match} \ v$
$\qquad\qquad\qquad \triangleright (ControlPoint \rightarrowtail Value \ k) \ [\![\ (f \ k)$
$\qquad\qquad\qquad \triangleright \mathbf{else} \ (err\text{-}to\text{-}comp \ \texttt{not-a-control-point})$
$\qquad\qquad\qquad \mathbf{end} \ ))$

$capturing\text{-}cont : (Expcont \to Comp) \to Comp \ = \ \lambda f . \lambda k . ((f \ k) \ k)$

$install\text{-}cont : Expcont \to Comp \to Comp \ = \ \lambda k_{new} c . \lambda k_{old} . (c \ k_{new})$

New Reasoning Laws

$(with\text{-}value \ (capturing\text{-}cont \ f) \ g)$ (9.13)
$\quad = (capturing\text{-}cont \ (\lambda k . (with\text{-}value \ (f \ (\lambda v . (g \ v \ k))) \ g))),$
$\qquad$ where k is not free in f or g

$(with\text{-}value \ (install\text{-}cont \ k \ c) \ f) = (install\text{-}cont \ k \ c)$ (9.14)

$(capturing\text{-}cont \ (\lambda k . (install\text{-}cont \ k \ c))) = c$, where k is not free in c (9.15)

New Valuation Clauses (Computation-based Version)

$\mathcal{E}[\![(\texttt{label} \ I_{ctrlPt} \ E_{body})]\!]$
$\quad = \lambda e . (capturing\text{-}cont \ (\lambda k . (\mathcal{E}[\![E_{body}]\!] \ [I_{ctrlPt} \mapsto (ControlPoint \rightarrowtail Value \ k)]e)))$
$\mathcal{E}[\![(\texttt{jump} \ E_{ctrlPt} \ E_{val})]\!]$
$\quad = \lambda e . (with\text{-}control\text{-}point\text{-}comp \ (\mathcal{E}[\![E_{ctrlPt}]\!] \ e)$
$\qquad\qquad (\lambda k_{ctrlPt} . (install\text{-}cont \ k_{ctrlPt} \ (\mathcal{E}[\![E_{val}]\!] \ e))))$

Figure 9.29 A computation-based denotational semantics of `label` and `jump` in FLICK.

Exercise 9.14 Suppose that `list-prod` is defined as follows:

```
(def (list-prod vals)
  (label return
    (recur prod ((vs vals))
      (cond ((null? vs) 1)
            ((= 0 (car vs)) (jump return 0))
            (else (* (car vs) (prod (cdr vs))))))))
```

What are the values of the following five expressions?

a. `(list-prod (list 2 3 4))`

b. `(list-prod (list 2 0 (sym yow!)))`

c. `(list-prod (list (sym yow!) 0 2))`

d. (let ((twice (abs (f x) (f (f x)))))
   (let ((f (label bind-f (abs (new-f) (jump bind-f new-f)))))
    ((f twice) (+ 1) 0)))

e. (jump (label a a) (label b b))

Exercise 9.15 It is possible to implement loops with `label` and `jump` without using mutation. As an example, here is a template for an iterative factorial procedure in FL + {`label`, `jump`} (recall that FL does not support mutation):

```
(def (fact n)
  (let ((triple E_triple))
    (let ((loop (nth 1 triple))
          (num  (nth 2 triple))
          (ans  (nth 3 triple)))
      (if (= num 0)
          ans
          (loop (list loop (- num 1) (* ans num)))))))
```

Using `label` and `jump`, write an expression E_{triple} such that `fact` is a procedure that calculates factorials.

Exercise 9.16 Sam Antics thinks that FLICK should be extended with a `(halt E)` expression that evaluates E to a value v and then terminates the current program with the answer v. For example, suppose

P = (flic (x)
   (+ (sq x) (sq (- x 5)))
   (def (sq n) (if (< n 0) (halt n) (* n n))))

Then here are some sample executions of P:

$$P \xrightarrow[FLIC]{[-3]} -3 \qquad P \xrightarrow[FLIC]{[4]} -1 \qquad P \xrightarrow[FLIC]{[7]} 53$$

Write the $\mathcal{E}$ valuation clause for `(halt E)`.

Exercise 9.17 In FLIC+{`label`, `jump`}, it is possible to express the `loop`, `break`, and `continue` constructs from Exercise 9.10 using syntactic sugar. Show this by writing a desugaring for `(loop E)`. Your desugaring should define local procedures named `break` and `continue` that behave like the `break` and `continue` constructs from Exercise 9.10.

Exercise 9.18 Chris Krenshall finds it hard to reason about FLIC+{`label`,`jump`} programs. He's never sure where the thread of control will end up! Chris would like more control over his control points. He wants to be able to declare *control regions* — areas of code such that a jump may be made to a control point within the same region but not to one in a different region.

Here are Chris's proposed kernel extensions:

$E ::=$ ... FLICK *expressions* ... | (**region** I E) | (**label** I E) | (**jump** E_1 E_2)

Informally, the `label` and `jump` constructs work as described above: `label` establishes first class control points and `jump` transfers control to them. However, there is one important difference, related to the `region` construct: It is only valid to jump to control points created in the current region, which is named by the identifier of the innermost lexically enclosing `region` declaration.

For example, consider the following procedure in Chris's language:

```
(def (p x)
  (region blue
    (label b
      (let ((f (abs (y) (if (> y 10) (jump I₁ y) (+ y 1))))
            (g (region red
                 (abs (z)
                   (label r
                     (* 2 (if (> z 5) (jump I₂ z) z)))))))
        (pair (f x) (g x)))))))
```

The label `b` is declared in the `blue` region, while the label `r` is declared in the `red` region. Since (`jump` I_1 `y`) occurs in the `blue` region, the jump is valid only if $I_1 = $ `b`. Similarly, since (`jump` I_2 `z`) occurs in the `red` region, it is valid only if $I_2 = $ `r`.

Assume that the validity of jumps is checked dynamically — i.e, when a `jump` expression is evaluated. (For static checking of control regions, see Section 16.3.1.) The following table shows the result of invoking `p` on various arguments for the given instantiations of I_1 and I_2:

Expression	$I_1 = $ b $I_2 = $ b	$I_1 = $ b $I_2 = $ r	$I_1 = $ r $I_2 = $ b	$I_1 = $ r $I_2 = $ r
(p 3) $\xrightarrow{\text{FLIC}}$	$\langle 4, 6 \rangle$	$\langle 4, 6 \rangle$	$\langle 4, 6 \rangle$	$\langle 4, 6 \rangle$
(p 7) $\xrightarrow{\text{FLIC}}$	error:invalid-jump	$\langle 8, 7 \rangle$	error:invalid-jump	$\langle 8, 7 \rangle$
(p 17) $\xrightarrow{\text{FLIC}}$	17	17	error:invalid-jump	error:invalid-jump

In this problem, you will modify the standard semantics for FLICK to specify the semantics of the `region`, `label`, and `jump` constructs. You may assume that all region names in a program are unique. (If this property does not hold, the regions can be renamed to make it hold.)

a. Suppose that the *ControlPoint* domain is modified as follows:

$k \in ControlPoint = Region \times Expcont$
$r \in Region = Ident$

Modify the signatures of $\mathcal{E}$ and $\mathcal{E}^*$ as necessary to support control regions.

b. Show the modified definitions of the $\mathcal{E}$ clauses for `lam` and `app`. (Assume that other clauses are changed in a similar fashion.)

c. Write the $\mathcal{E}$ valuation clauses for (`region` I E), (`label` I E), and (`jump` E_1 E_2).

d. Define a $\mathcal{P}$ valuation function for programs. Assume that the program body is evaluated in an implicit top-level region.

Expressions used in Configurations

$E \in \text{Exp}_{SOS} ::= \ldots \text{ as in FLICK } \ldots$
$\qquad\qquad | \text{ (label } I \text{ } E) \text{ } | \text{ (jump } E_1 \text{ } E_2) \text{ } | \text{ (*cp* } I \text{ } E)$

$V \in \text{ValueExp} ::= \ldots \text{ as in FLICK } \ldots | \text{ (*cp* } I \text{ } E)$

$A \in \text{AnsExp} ::= \ldots \text{ as in FLICK } \ldots | \text{ controlpointans}$

New Output Function Clause

$\quad OF \langle(\text{*cp* } I \text{ } E), \text{ } S\rangle = \text{controlpointans}$

Evaluation Contexts

$\mathbb{E} \in \text{EvalContext} ::= \ldots \text{ as in CBV FLICK } \ldots | \text{ (jump } \mathbb{E} \text{ } E) \text{ } | \text{ (jump } V \text{ } \mathbb{E})$

New Evaluation Rules (extending the FLICK evaluation relation)

$\quad\quad \langle\mathbb{E}\{(\text{label } I_{name} \text{ } E_{body})\}, \text{ } S\rangle$
$\quad\quad\quad \Rightarrow \langle\mathbb{E}\{[(\text{*cp* } I_{fresh} \text{ } \mathbb{E}\{I_{fresh}\})/I_{name}]E_{body}\}, \text{ } S\rangle, \quad \text{[label]}$
$\quad\quad\quad\quad \text{where } I_{fresh} \text{ is fresh}$

$\quad\quad \langle\mathbb{E}\{(\text{jump } (\text{*cp* } I \text{ } E) \text{ } V)\}, \text{ } S\rangle \Rightarrow \langle[V/I]E, \text{ } S\rangle \quad \text{[jump]}$

Figure 9.30 Changes to the FLICK SOS to handle `label` and `jump`.

9.4.3 An Operational Semantics for `label` and `jump`

Although many sophisticated control constructs are not straightforward to describe in operational semantics, `label` and `jump` are an exception. We will present an operational semantics for `label` and `jump` because it helps build operational intuitions for continuations. Figure 9.30 shows the changes that need to be made to the FLICK SOS from Figure 8.13 (page 406) and Figure 8.14 (page 409) in order to handle `label` and `jump`. The intermediate expressions Exp_{SOS} used in configurations are not only extended with the new constructs (`label` I E) and (`jump` E_1 E_2), but there is also a new expression (`*cp*` I E) that represents a first-class control point. This can be viewed like a procedure value (`lam` I E) except that it is applied to an argument value via `jump` rather than `app`. The ValueExp domain is extended to include control points as first-class values, and the output function OF is extended to map control points to the new AnsExp token `controlpointans`.

The key to the operational semantics is the [`label`] and [`jump`] evaluation rules, whose use is illustrated in Figure 9.31. The [`label`] rule captures the evaluation context $\mathbb{E}$ in which the `label` expression is being evaluated and wraps it up in a control-point value. The appearance of two copies of $\mathbb{E}$ in the right-hand side of this rule mirrors the duplication of the expression continuation in the denotational semantics. In the control-point value (`*cp*` I_{fresh} E), the fresh identifier I_{fresh} is used to represent the position of the hole in $\mathbb{E}$. This control-

---

; *Example where* exit *is not used as the target of a* jump.

`(@+ 1 (label exit (@* 2 (@- 3 (@+ 4 5)))))`

`= (@+ 1 □){(label exit (@* 2 (@- 3 (@+ 4 5)))))}`

$\overrightarrow{CBV}_{[label]}$ `(@+ 1 □){[(*cp* h (@+ 1 h))/exit](@* 2 (@- 3 (@+ 4 5)))}`

`= (@+ 1 □){(@* 2 (@- 3 (@+ 4 5)))}`

`= (@+ 1 (@* 2 (@- 3 (@+ 4 5))))`

$\overset{*}{\overrightarrow{CBV}}$ `-11`

; *Example where* exit *is used as the target of a* jump.

`(@+ 1 (label exit (@* 2 (@- 3 (@+ 4 (jump exit 5))))))`

`= (@+ 1 □){(label exit (@* 2 (@- 3 (@+ 4 (jump exit 5)))))}`

$\overrightarrow{CBV}_{[label]}$ `(@+ 1 □)`

`{[(*cp* h (@+ 1 h))/exit](@* 2 (@- 3 (@+ 4 (jump exit 5))))}`

`= (@+ 1 □){(@* 2 (@- 3 (@+ 4 (jump (*cp* h (@+ 1 h)) 5))))}`

`= (@+ 1 (@* 2 (@- 3 (@+ 4 (jump (*cp* h (@+ 1 h)) 5)))))`

`= (@+ 1 (@* 2 (@- 3 (@+ 4 □)))){(jump (*cp* h (@+ 1 h)) 5)}`

$\overrightarrow{CBV}_{[jump]}$ `[5/h](@+ 1 h)`

`= (@+ 1 5)`

$\overrightarrow{CBV}_{[+]}$ `6`

Figure 9.31 Examples illustrating the operational semantics of label and jump.

point value is substituted for the label name I_{name} in the body expression E_{body} of the label expression.

The [jump] rule is enabled when a control point is applied to an argument value. In this case, the evaluation context wrapping the jump expression is discarded (like the normal continuation in the denotational semantics) and the result of replacing the "hole" I in the "evaluation context" E by V becomes the next expression to be evaluated. The [jump] rule is similar to a beta-reduction step

$$\langle \mathbb{E}\{(\text{app }(\text{lam } I\ E)\ V)\},\ S \rangle \Rightarrow \langle \mathbb{E}\{[V/I]E\},\ S \rangle$$

except that beta reduction keeps the evaluation context discarded by [jump].

Figure 9.31 shows how the operational semantics explains the first two examples presented in Figure 9.26. Because none of these examples involves state, the store component is omitted from each of the configurations in the figure. This highlights that label and jump can be added to a stateless language like FL.

Exercise 9.19 Use the operational semantics for `label` and `jump` to show the evaluation of the last two expressions in Figure 9.26.

9.4.4 call-with-current-continuation (cwcc)

In the SCHEME programming language, first-class control points are made accessible by the standard procedure `call-with-current-continuation`, which we will abbreviate as `cwcc`.[2] In FLICK, this procedure can be written in terms of `label` and `jump` as follows:

```
(def (cwcc proc)
  (label here
    (proc (abs (val) (jump here val)))))
```

The `proc` argument is a unary procedure that is applied to an **escape procedure** that, when called, will return a result from the invocation of `cwcc`. For example, here is a version of `tree-product` written in terms of `cwcc`:

```
(def (tree-product tree)
  (cwcc (abs (return)
          (letrec ((prod (abs (tr)
                           (if (leaf? tr)
                               (if (= tr 0)
                                   (return 0) {the escape procedure
                                                return returns from cwcc}
                                   tr)
                               (* (prod (left tr) (right tr))))))))
            (prod tree)))))
```

Rather than defining `cwcc` as a procedure in terms of `label` and `jump`, we could instead make it a standard primitive operator. In this case, we would no longer need `label` and `jump` to be kernel constructs, because they could be expressed as syntactic sugar (see Exercise 9.20). The advantage of `cwcc` as an interface for capturing and invoking continuations is that it does not require extending a language with any new kernel constructs, just one new standard primitive. The binding performed by `label` is instead handled by the usual binding mechanism (`abs`), and a `jump` is encoded as a regular application of an escape procedure.

Some languages put restrictions on capturable continuations that make them easier to reason about and to implement. For example, the DYLAN language provides a (`bind-exit` (*I*) *E*) form that is similar to (`cwcc` (`abs` (*I*) *E*)) except that the lifetime of the escape procedure is limited by the lifetime of the

---

[2]Another common abbreviation is `call/cc`. Some dialects of ML provide a similar procedure; for example, STANDARD ML OF NEW JERSEY provides a `callcc` function for this purpose.

bind-exit construct. Similarly, the C programming language provides a setjmp construct for capturing an expression continuation whose lifetime is limited to the lifetime of the procedure call in which it is used; such a continuation is invoked via a longjmp construct. The catch and throw constructs of COMMON LISP are similar to label and jump except that throw jumps to a named control point declared by a dynamically enclosing catch. Dynamically declared control points are a good mechanism for exception handling, which is the topic of study in Section 9.6.

Exercise 9.20 We have shown that cwcc can be desugared into the kernel constructs label and jump. Here we suppose instead that cwcc is a kernel primitive operator $\in$ Primop in a language that does not have label and jump as kernel constructs.

a. Show how label and jump can be defined as syntactic sugar in a language that provides cwcc as a primitive operator.

b. Write a standard-style continuation-semantics valuation clause (e.g., $\mathcal{O}[\![\text{cwcc}]\!] = \ldots$) for the cwcc primitive operator.

c. Write a computation-style continuation-semantics valuation clause for the cwcc primitive operator. Use *capturing-cont* and *install-cont* in your clause.

9.5   Iterators: A Simple Coroutining Mechanism

An **iterator** is a simple kind of producer coroutine that yields a sequence of elements to a consumer coroutine. The iterator and the consumer can be viewed as separate computational processes. When a consumer process invokes an iterator to yield its next element, the consumer process is suspended and control transfers to the iterator process. The iterator process computes until it yields a value, at which point the iterator process is suspended and control is transferred back to the consumer process along with the yielded value. The consumer process is then resumed at the point of the iterator invocation with the iterated value returned as the value of the invocation. The next time the iterator is invoked, the iterator process is resumed at the point where it was last suspended. Control ping-pongs back and forth between the consumer process and the iterator process until either the consumer process requires no more elements or the iterator process has no more values to yield.

Iterators enhance program modularity because they allow the iterator and consumer processes to be written as two separate loops rather than as one complex loop. This makes it possible to mix and match different iterators with different consumers. Iterators were pioneered in the CLU programming language, but similar notions have been adopted in other languages. For example, in the ICON string-processing language, every procedure (known as a **generator**) is effectively an iterator that can return zero, one, or more results to its caller. SATHER is a dialect of EIFFEL supporting iterators (which it calls **iters**) in an object-oriented setting. C++ and JAVA also support object-oriented iterating abstractions called "iterators," but since they are not coroutines, they are less expressive than CLU-style iterators (see Exercise 9.23).

Here we will show how iterators can be added to FLIC using first-class control points to implement the suspension and resumption of the iterator process. We will begin by describing an `iterator` construct for creating iterators and will illustrate it with some examples. Then we will show how to implement `iterator` by desugaring it into FLIC using `label` and `jump`. Here is the informal specification of the `iterator` construct:

(iterator I_{yield} E_{body}) returns an **iterating procedure**, a regular FLIC nullary procedure that represents a sequence of iterated elements. Each time the iterating procedure is invoked, the next element of the sequence is returned. If there are no more elements, invoking the iterating procedure returns `#u`. The first time the iterating procedure is invoked, an iterating process is started that evaluates E_{body} in the lexical environment of `iterator` extended with a binding of I_{yield} to a **yielding procedure**. Calling the yielding procedure on a value suspends the iterating process and returns the yielded value to the invoker of the iterating procedure. The next time the iterating procedure is invoked, the iterating process is resumed by returning `#u` from the last invocation of I_{yield}. The iterating process continues to yield values until it terminates, at which point invoking the iterating procedure returns `#u`.

Figure 9.32 presents a few sample iterators. The application (between *lo hi*) returns an iterator that yields all the integers from *lo* through *hi*. Here is a summation consumer that adds up all the elements of an iterator that yields integers:

```
(def (sum next-int) {next-int is the name of an integer-yielding iterator}
  (recur loop ((total 0))
    (let ((int (next-int)))
      (if (unit? int)
          total
          (loop (+ total int))))))
```

For example, (sum (between 3 7)) $\xrightarrow[\text{FLIC}]{}$ *25*

Here is a listing consumer that lists all the elements produced by a finite iterator:

```
(def (to-list next-elt) {next-elt is the name of an iterator}
  (recur collect ((elt (next-elt)))
    (if (unit? elt)
        nil
        (cons elt (collect (next-elt)))))))
```

For example, (to-list (between 3 7)) $\xrightarrow[\text{FLIC}]{}$ ⊲*3, 4, 5, 6, 7*▷

Another example of an iterator from Figure 9.32 is (leaves *tree*), which returns an iterator that yields the leaves of a binary tree one by one, from left to right. Because of the modularity supported by iterators, we can use sum and to-list with leaves as well:

```
(sum (leaves (node 4 (node (node 1 3) 2))))    FLIC  10
(to-list (leaves (node 4 (node (node 1 3) 2)))) FLIC ⊲4, 1, 3, 2▷
```

Not all iterators are finite. The application (from *lo*) returns an iterator that yields all integers in the increasing sequence beginning with *lo*. Processing an infinite iterator requires a consumer that inspects only a finite number of the yielded values. The prefix iterator transformer is useful for this purpose. Given a nonnegative integer *n* and an iterator *iter*, the application (prefix *n iter*) returns an iterator yielding only the first *n* elements of *iter*. For example,

```
(to-list (prefix 4 (from 6)))    FLIC ⊲6, 7, 8, 9▷
(to-list (prefix 2 (leaves (node 4 (node 1 3)))))  FLIC ⊲4, 1▷
```

Now that we have seen iterators in action, we will study how they are implemented. Figure 9.33 shows how the iterator construct can be implemented via syntactic sugar in FLIC.

Every iterator has two local cells named with fresh identifiers. I_{resume} is a cell that holds a **resumption thunk** that, when dethunked, resumes the iteration process. I_{return} is a cell that holds the control point of the consumer that is waiting for the next value of the iterator. Both of these cells initially contain the arbitrary value #u, but in both cases this will be overwritten before the cell is dereferenced. The initial resumption thunk evaluates E_{body} in an environment where I_{yield} binds a unary yielding procedure. Invoking the yielding procedure suspends the iterating process (by setting I_{resume} to a resumption thunk that returns #u from the yielding procedure) and returns the yielded value to the consumer by jumping to the control point in I_{return}. The value of the iterator expression is a nullary iterating procedure that first remembers the control point of the consumer invoking the iterating procedure in the cell I_{return} and then re-

```
{Returns an iterator yielding all the integers from lo through hi.}
(def (between lo hi)
  (iterator yield
    (recur loop ((i lo))
      (if (<= i hi)
          (begin (yield i) (loop (+ i 1)))))))

{Returns an iterator yielding the leaves of a binary tree in a left-to-right traversal.}
(def (leaves tree)
  (iterator yield
    (recur walk ((tr tree))
      (if (leaf? tr)
          (yield tr)
          (begin (walk (left tr)) (walk (right tr)))))))

{Returns an iterator yielding all the integers from n up.}
(def (from n)
  (iterator yield
    (recur loop ((i n))
      (begin (yield i) (loop (+ i 1))))))

{Assume n is a nonnegative integer. Returns an iterator yielding the first n
 elements of the iterator next-elt. The returned iterator signals an error if
 an attempt is made to yield more elements than next-elt can yield.}
(def (prefix n next-elt)
  (iterator yield
    (recur loop ((i n))
      (if (> i 0)
          (let ((elt (next-elt)))
            (if (unit? elt)
                (error too-few-elements)
                (begin (yield elt) (loop (- i 1)))))
          {if i ≤ 0, iterator body terminates and iterator returns #u}
          ))))
```

Figure 9.32   Some examples of iterators.

sumes the execution of the iterator by dethunking the current resumption thunk. When the evaluation of E_{body} terminates, I_{resume} is set to a final resumption thunk that always returns #u to the consumer to indicate that no more values can be yielded.

```
(iterator I_yield E_body)
  ⤳_ds (let ((I_resume  (cell #u))   {I_resume is fresh}
             (I_return  (cell #u)))  {I_return is fresh}
         (let ((I_yield (abs (v)
                             (label resume {continuation of I_yield invocation}
                                    (begin (:= I_resume
                                                (abs () {return #u for I_yield invocation}
                                                     (jump resume #u)))
                                           {return v to consumer = caller of iterator}
                                           (jump (^ I_return) v)))))))
           (begin
             (:= I_resume
                 (abs () {initial resumption thunk}
                      (begin E_body {first evaluate body}
                             {then return #u thereafter}
                             (:= I_resume (abs () (jump (^ I_return) #u)))
                             ((^ I_resume)))))
             {return iterator = nullary iterating procedure}
             (abs ()
                  (label return {continuation of consumer = caller of iterator}
                         (begin (:= I_return return)
                                {resume iterator by dethunking resumption thunk}
                                ((^ I_resume)))))))))
```

Figure 9.33   Desugaring of the `iterator` construct.

For example, consider the steps in the evaluation of the expression

```
(let ((iter (iterator yield (begin (yield 4) (yield 2)))))
  (list (iter) (iter) (iter)))
```

- Initially, the I_{resume} cell for `iter` holds the resumption thunk

```
(abs () (begin (begin (yield 4) (yield 2))
               (:= I_resume (abs () (jump (^ I_return) #u)))
               ((^ I_resume))))
```

- The initial consumer expression is `(list (iter) (iter) (iter))`. When the leftmost `(iter)` call is made, the I_{return} cell is set to a continuation corresponding to the expression context `(list □ (iter) (iter))`, and the resumption thunk is dethunked. When `(yield 4)` is evaluated, the resumption thunk becomes a thunk that will supply `#u` to the hole in

```
(begin (begin □ (yield 2)) ... )
```

and 4 is supplied to the hole in (`list` □ `(iter) (iter)`), changing the consumer to (`list 4 (iter) (iter)`).

- Next the middle (`iter`) call is made. The I_{return} cell is set to a continuation corresponding to the expression context (`list 4` □ `(iter)`), and the resumption thunk is dethunked, which returns from (`yield 4`) by supplying `#u` for the hole in

  (`begin (begin` □ `(yield 2))` ...)

and then evaluates (`yield 2`). This sets the resumption thunk to a thunk that will supply `#u` to the hole in (`begin (begin #u` □ `)` ...) and supplies 2 to the hole in (`list 4` □ `(iter)`), changing the consumer to (`list 4 2 (iter)`).

- Finally, the rightmost (`iter`) call is made. The I_{return} cell is set to a continuation corresponding to the expression context (`list 4 2` □), and the resumption thunk is dethunked. This returns `#u` for (`yield 2`) and then evaluates

  (`begin (:=` I_{resume} `(abs () (jump (^` I_{return}`) #u)))`
          `((^` I_{resume}`)))`

This sets the resumption thunk to its final value

  (`abs () (jump (^` I_{return}`) #u)`)

and immediately dethunks it, which supplies `#u` to the hole in (`list 4 2` □) to give the final consumer value (`list 4 2 #u`). Note that any subsequent (`iter`) calls would also return `#u`.

The `iterator` construct is a good example of the sophisticated control constructs that can be implemented in a language that supports first-class control points. But first-class control points are not the only way to support interesting control relationships. In the case of iterators, a simpler way of achieving producer/consumer coroutines is to use so-called lazy data structures. We will study these in Section 10.1.3.

Exercise 9.21 Write a procedure (`trees` *elts*) that takes a list of elements *elts* and returns an iterator that yields all of the distinct binary trees whose leaves, from left to right, are *elts*. The order of the trees does not matter. For instance, the application (`trees (list 1 2 3 4)`) should return an iterator that yields the following trees in any order:

```
(node 1 (node 2 (node 3 4)))
(node 1 (node (node 2 3) 4))
(node (node 1 2) (node 3 4))
(node (node 1 (node 2 3)) 4)
(node (node (node 1 2) 3) 4)
```

Exercise 9.22

a. Write a procedure (`assignments` *vars*) that takes a list of variable names (i.e., symbols) and returns an iterator that yields all distinct assignments of the variables to *true* and *false*. As in Section 9.2.7, each set of variable assignments should be represented as an environment in which each of the variables is bound to either *true* or *false*. The order of the environments does not matter. For example, (`assignments` (`list` (`sym` a) (`sym` b) (`sym` c))) should return FLICK representations of the following environments in some order:

$$\{a \mapsto false, b \mapsto false, c \mapsto false\}, \quad \{a \mapsto false, b \mapsto false, c \mapsto true\},$$
$$\{a \mapsto false, b \mapsto true, c \mapsto false\}, \quad \{a \mapsto false, b \mapsto true, c \mapsto true\},$$
$$\{a \mapsto true, b \mapsto false, c \mapsto false\}, \quad \{a \mapsto true, b \mapsto false, c \mapsto true\},$$
$$\{a \mapsto true, b \mapsto true, c \mapsto false\}, \quad \{a \mapsto true, b \mapsto true, c \mapsto true\}$$

b. Problems that seem to require backtracking can sometimes be solved with a generate-and-test idiom in which an iterator generates possible solutions until a satisfactory one is found. For example, the iterator returned by (`assignments` *vars*) can be used to solve the satisfiability problem for boolean formulae discussed in Section 9.2.7. Implement an alternative version of the `satisfy` procedure defined there based on the following strategy:

- Determine the set of variable references in the given boolean formula;

- Use `assignments` to create an iterator yielding environments that represent all possible sets of variable assignment for the variables;

- Generate the environments one by one. For each environment, evaluate the boolean formula relative to the environment. If the value of the boolean formula is *true*, stop and return the environment. If the boolean formula is *false* for all environments, stop and return the symbol `failed`.

Exercise 9.23 In C++ and JAVA, iterators are stateful objects that respond to messages asking if there are any more values to be iterated and requesting the next value to be iterated. For example, a JAVA-style iterator for iterating the integers between `lo` and `hi` can be encoded in FLIC as the following message-passing procedure:

```
(def (between lo hi)
  (let ((i (cell lo)))
    (abs (msg)
      (cond ((sym=? msg (sym has-next?)) (<= (^ i) hi))
            ((sym=? msg (sym next))
             (let ((result (^ i)))
               (begin (:= i (+ result 1))
                      result)))
            (else (error unknown-message))))))
```

Here is a sample summation consumer that uses iterators written in this style:

```
(def (sum iter)
  (recur loop ((sum 0))
    (if (iter (sym has-next?))
        (loop (+ sum (iter (sym next))))
        sum)))
```

In simple cases like `between`, JAVA-style iterators are conceptually simpler than CLU-style iterators because they don't require the iterator process to be suspended and resumed. But JAVA-style iterators can be much more complex than CLU-style iterators because they effectively force the programmer to explicitly encode the state of a suspended process in an iterator. To see this, write versions of the following iterators studied above using JAVA-style message-passing procedures:

a. `(leaves` *tree*`)`

b. `(prefix` *n iterator*`)`

c. `(trees` *elts*`)` (Exercise 9.21)

d. `(assignments` *vars*`)` (Exercise 9.22)

Exercise 9.24 Abby Stracksen thinks it is inelegant that FLICK iterators use the unit value to indicate that they have no more values to yield. Instead, she thinks that an iterator should be a procedure that takes two arguments: (1) a *success continuation*, a unary procedure that is invoked on the yielded value, if there is one, and (2) a *failure continuation*, a nullary procedure that is invoked if there are no more values to yield. Here are versions of `between` and `sum` written using Abby's interface:

```
(def (between lo hi)
  (iterator yield fail {iterator now names the failure continuation}
    (recur loop ((i lo))
      (if (<= i hi)
          (begin (yield i) (loop (+ i 1)))
          (fail)))))
(def (sum next-int)
  (recur loop ((total 0))
    (next-int (abs (int) (loop (+ total int)))
              (abs () total))))
```

Modify the desugaring for `iterator` so that it implements Abby's interface.

9.6 Exception Handling

A common reason to alter the usual flow of control in a program is to respond to exceptional conditions. For example, upon encountering a divide-by-zero error, the caller of the division procedure may want the computation to proceed with a large number rather than terminate with an error. Dynamically responding to exceptional conditions is known as **exception handling**.

One strategy for exception handling is for every procedure to return values that are tagged with a **return code** that indicates whether the procedure is returning normally or in some exceptional way. The caller can then test for the return code and handle the situation accordingly. Although popular, the return code technique is unsatisfactory in many ways. It effectively requires every call to a procedure to explicitly test for all return codes the procedure could potentially generate. By treating normal and exceptional returns in the same fashion, return codes fail to capture the notion that exceptions are generally perceived as rare events compared to normal returns. In addition, return codes provide a very limited way in which to respond to exceptional conditions. All responsibility for dealing with the condition resides in the caller; in particular, the point at which the condition was generated has been lost.

Another strategy for handling exceptional conditions is to let a procedure **raise** (or **signal**) an **exception** as an alternative to returning a value. The immediate caller may then **handle** the exception, or it might decline to handle the exception and instead allow other callers in the current dynamic procedure-call chain to handle the exception. There are two basic strategies for handling the exception:

1. In **termination semantics**, the handler receives control from the signaler of the exception and keeps it. This is the approach taken by JAVA's `throw` and `try/catch`, COMMON LISP's `throw` and `catch`, SML's `raise` and `handle`, and CLU's `signal` and `except when`.

2. In **resumption semantics**, the handler receives control from the signaler of the exception but later passes control back to the computation that raised the exception. Operating system traps usually follow this model.

Some languages (such as CLU) require the caller to explicitly resignal exceptions in order to propagate them up the call chain. In other languages (including COMMON LISP and ML), unhandled exceptions propagate up the call chain until an appropriate handler is found. In these languages, programs are implicitly wrapped in a default handler that handles otherwise uncaught exceptions. JAVA uses a hybrid approach in which certain exceptions (instances of the `Error` or `RuntimeException` classes) are automatically propagated up the call chain, but others are resignaled by a method only if they are explicitly declared in the `throws` clause of the method definition.

An exception is usually an entity that glues a **tag** indicating the name or kind of the exception together with **information** summarizing the details of the exceptional situation. For example,

- dividing an integer i by 0 might raise an exception with tag `divide-by-zero` and information i;

- looking up an unbound symbol Y in an environment might raise an exception with tag `unbound-variable` and information Y;

- depositing a negative amount amt in a bank account $acct$ might raise an exception with tag `negative-deposit` and information that pairs amt and $acct$.

9.6.1 raise, handle, and trap

To study exception handling, we extend FLICK with the following constructs to accommodate both termination-style and resumption-style exception handling:

$$E ::= \ldots \text{FLICK } expressions \ldots \mid (\texttt{raise } I_{tag} \ E_{info})$$
$$\mid (\texttt{handle } I_{tag} \ E_{handler} \ E_{body}) \mid (\texttt{trap } I_{tag} \ E_{handler} \ E_{body})$$

The informal semantics of these constructs is as follows:

($\texttt{raise } I_{tag} \ E_{info}$) evaluates E_{info} to a value V_{info} and raises an exception with tag I_{tag} and information V_{info}.

($\texttt{handle } I_{tag} \ E_{handler} \ E_{body}$) is for termination-style exception handling. First $E_{handler}$ is evaluated to a unary **exception-handling procedure** $V_{handler}$. (It is an error if $E_{handler}$ does not denote a procedure.) Then E_{body} is evaluated. If no exception is raised in the evaluation of E_{body}, its value is the value of the `handle` expression. If an exception with tag I_{tag} and information V_{info} is raised and not handled within E_{body}, the value of the `handle` expression is the result of applying $V_{handler}$ to V_{info}. If an exception with a tag different from I_{tag} is raised and not handled within E_{body}, it should be handled by another exception handler that dynamically encloses the `handle` expression.

($\texttt{trap } I_{tag} \ E_{handler} \ E_{body}$) is for resumption-style exception handling. It is evaluated like a `handle` expression except that if an exception with tag I_{tag} and information V_{info} is raised and not handled within E_{body}, the value of the `raise` expression (rather than the `trap` expression) is the result of applying $V_{handler}$ to V_{info}.

Note that the expression (raise I_{tag} E_{info}) never returns a value if the handler for I_{tag} is defined by a handle expression: In this case, raise acts like a jump that returns from the handle expression. In contrast, when the handler for I_{tag} is defined by a trap expression, the raise expression *does* return a value (as long as E_{info} returns normally).

As a simple example of exceptions, consider a FLIC add procedure that normally returns the sum of its two arguments but raises a noninteger exception if one of its arguments is not an integer:

```
(def (add x y)
  (let ((check (abs (n) (if (@int? n) n (raise noninteger n)))))
    (@+ (check x) (check y))))
```

(In a language supporting exceptions, the underlying + primitive might raise a noninteger exception rather than signaling an error, but we are assuming the semantics of FLICK primitives here.) Now suppose we use add to find the sum of the elements in a list:

```
(def (list-sum elts) (foldr add 0 elts))
```

If the argument to list-sum is a list of integers, list-sum behaves as expected:

```
(list-sum (list 6 8 2 1)) FLIC→ 17
```

We can use exception handlers to specify what to do if the argument to list-sum is a list with noninteger elements, such as the following list elts1:

```
(def elts1 (list 3 #t 7 (sym foo) (list 4 5) 2))
```

For example we could find the sum of just the integers in the list by treating every noninteger as the number 0:

```
(trap noninteger (abs (_) 0) (list-sum elts1)) FLIC→ 12
```

(We often use the underscore identifier, _, for a procedure parameter that is ignored in the procedure body.) If we want to include the integers in embedded integer lists in the sum, we can express that, too:

```
(trap noninteger (abs (v) (if (list? v) (list-sum v) 0))
  (list-sum elts1)) FLIC→ 21
```

What happens if an embedded list itself contains nonintegers? For that detail we'll need to consult the formal semantics carefully later.

We can use handle in the case where we want to abort the list-summation computation. For example, to return 0 for the sum if there is a noninteger element in the list, we write:

```
(handle noninteger (abs (_) 0) (list-sum elts1)) FLIC→ 0
```

New and Modified Domains

$h \in HandlerEnv = \text{Ident} \to Proc$; as in Figure 9.35

$c \in Comp = HandlerEnv \to Expcont \to Cmdcont$

$p \in Proc = Nameable \to Comp$; as usual (Figure 6.23 on page 276)

Operations on the *HandlerEnv* Domain

default-handlers : $HandlerEnv = \lambda I \,.\, \lambda n \,.\, (\text{err-to-comp } I)$; Recall Ident $\subseteq$ SymLit

get-handler : Ident $\to HandlerEnv \to Proc = $ as defined in Figure 9.35

extend-handlers : Ident $\to Proc \to HandlerEnv \to HandlerEnv$
$= $ as defined in Figure 9.35

New Computation Operations Involving *HandlerEnv*

extending-handlers : Ident $\to Proc \to Comp \to Comp$
$= \lambda Ipc \,.\, \lambda h \,.\, (c \ (\text{extend-handlers } I \ p \ h))$

getting-handler : Ident $\to (Proc \to Comp) \to Comp$
$= \lambda If \,.\, \lambda h \,.\, (f \ (\text{get-handler } I \ h) \ h)$

Modified Computation Operations

val-to-comp : $Value \to Comp = \lambda v \,.\, \lambda hk \,.\, (k \ v)$

err-to-comp : $Error \to Comp = \lambda Y \,.\, \lambda hks \,.\, (Error \rightarrowtail Expressible \ Y)$

with-value : $Comp \to (Value \to Comp) \to Comp$
$= \lambda cf \,.\, \lambda hk \,.\, (c \ h \ (\lambda v \,.\, (f \ v \ h \ k)))$

with-values, with-boolean-val, with-boolean-comp, etc. are all written in terms of with-value and err-to-comp, so their definitions are unchanged from Figure 6.26 on page 281. The definitions of store-manipulating functions like *allocating* and *fetching* are unchanged from Figure 9.23 on page 485.

New Valuation Clauses (Computation Style)

$\mathcal{E} : \text{Exp} \to Env \to Comp$; as usual (Figure 6.28 on page 283)

$\mathcal{E}[\![(\text{trap } I_{tag} \ E_{handler} \ E_{body})]\!]$
  $= \lambda e \,.\, (\text{with-procedure-comp } (\mathcal{E}[\![E_{handler}]\!] \ e)$
      $(\lambda p \,.\, (\text{extending-handlers } I_{tag}$
          $(\lambda nh_{raise}k_{raise} \,.\, (p \ n \ h_{raise} \ k_{raise}))$
          ; can eta-reduce the above to p
          $(\mathcal{E}[\![E_{body}]\!] \ e))))$

$\mathcal{E}[\![(\text{handle } I_{tag} \ E_{handler} \ E_{body})]\!]$
  $= \lambda eh_{handle}k_{handle} \,.\,$
    $(\text{with-procedure-comp } (\mathcal{E}[\![E_{handler}]\!] \ e)$
      $(\lambda p \,.\, (\text{extending-handlers } I_{tag}$
          $(\lambda nh_{raise}k_{raise} \,.\, (p \ n \ h_{handle} \ k_{handle}))$
          $(\mathcal{E}[\![E_{body}]\!] \ e))))$
    $h_{handle} \ k_{handle}$; arguments to (with-procedure-comp ...) computation

$\mathcal{E}[\![(\text{raise } I_{tag} \ E_{info})]\!]$
  $= \lambda e \,.\, (\text{with-value } (\mathcal{E}[\![E_{info}]\!] \ e) \ (\lambda v_{info} \,.\, (\text{getting-handler } I_{tag} \ (\lambda p \,.\, (p \ v_{info})))))$

All other computation-style valuation clauses for FLICK are unchanged.

Figure 9.37 Computation-style continuation semantics of exception handling.

$\mathcal{E}[\![(\texttt{lam}\ I\ E_{body})]\!]$ in Figure 7.4

$=\ \lambda e\,.\,(\textit{val-to-comp}\ (Proc \rightarrowtail Value\ \ (\lambda n\,.\,(\mathcal{E}[\![E_{body}]\!]\ [I \mapsto n]e))))$

$=\ \lambda e\,.\,(\lambda hk\,.\,(k\ (Proc \rightarrowtail Value\ \ (\lambda n\,.\,(\mathcal{E}[\![E_{body}]\!]\ [I \mapsto n]e)))))$, by $\textit{val-to-comp}$ defn.

$=\ \lambda eh_{lam}k_{lam}\,.\,(k_{lam}\ (Proc \rightarrowtail Value\ \ (\lambda nh_{app}k_{app}\,.\,(\mathcal{E}[\![E_{body}]\!]\ [I \mapsto n]e\ h_{app}\ k_{app}))))$,
   by eta expansion of $(\lambda n\,.\,\ldots)$

$=\ \mathcal{E}[\![(\texttt{lam}\ I\ E_{body})]\!]$ in Figure 9.35

$\mathcal{E}[\![(\texttt{app}\ E_1\ E_2)]\!]$ in Figure 7.4

$=\ \lambda e\,.\,(\textit{with-procedure-comp}\ (\mathcal{E}[\![E_1]\!]\ e)\ (\lambda p\,.\,(\textit{with-value}\ (\mathcal{E}[\![E_2]\!]\ e)\ p)))$

$=\ \lambda e\,.\,(\textit{with-value}\ (\mathcal{E}[\![E_1]\!]\ e)$
   $\qquad\ (\lambda v\,.\,(\textit{with-procedure-val}\ v\ (\lambda p\,.\,(\textit{with-value}\ (\mathcal{E}[\![E_2]\!]\ e)\ p)))))$,
   by the definition of $\textit{with-procedure-comp}$ in Figure 6.26 on page 281

$=\ \lambda e\,.\,(\lambda hk\,.\,(\mathcal{E}[\![E_1]\!]\ e\ h$
   $\qquad\qquad\ (\lambda v\,.\,((\textit{with-procedure-val}\ v$
   $\qquad\qquad\qquad\ (\lambda p\,.\,(\lambda h'k'\,.\,(\mathcal{E}[\![E_2]\!]\ e\ h'\ (\lambda v'\,.\,(p\ v'\ h'\ k'))))))$
   $\qquad\qquad\ h\ k))))$,
   by the definition of $\textit{with-value}$ in Figure 9.37

$=\ \lambda e\,.\,(\lambda hk\,.\,(\mathcal{E}[\![E_1]\!]\ e\ h$
   $\qquad\qquad\ (\lambda v\,.\,(\textbf{match}\ v$
   $\qquad\qquad\qquad\ \triangleright (Proc \rightarrowtail Value\ p)$
   $\qquad\qquad\qquad\ [\![\ (\lambda h'k'\,.\,(\mathcal{E}[\![E_2]\!]\ e\ h'\ (\lambda v'\,.\,(p\ v'\ h'\ k'))))$
   $\qquad\qquad\qquad\ \triangleright \textbf{else}\ (\textit{err-to-comp}\ \texttt{not-a-procedure})$
   $\qquad\qquad\qquad\ \textbf{end}\ \ h\ k))))$,
   by the definition of $\textit{with-procedure-val}$ in Figure 6.26

$=\ \lambda e\,.\,(\lambda hk\,.\,(\mathcal{E}[\![E_1]\!]\ e\ h$
   $\qquad\qquad\ (\lambda v\,.\,\textbf{match}\ v$
   $\qquad\qquad\qquad\ \triangleright (Proc \rightarrowtail Value\ p)$
   $\qquad\qquad\qquad\ [\![\ (\mathcal{E}[\![E_2]\!]\ e\ h\ (\lambda v'\,.\,(p\ v'\ h\ k)))$
   $\qquad\qquad\qquad\ \triangleright \textbf{else}\ (\textit{error-cont}\ \texttt{not-a-procedure})$
   $\qquad\qquad\qquad\ \textbf{end}\ )))$,
   by distributing the operands h and k over the functions in the **match** clauses
   and by the definitions of $\textit{err-to-comp}$ (Figure 6.26) and $\textit{error-cont}$ (Figure 9.37)

$=\ \lambda eh_{app}k_{app}\,.\,(\mathcal{E}[\![E_1]\!]\ e\ h_{app}\ (\textit{procedure-cont}$
   $\qquad\qquad\qquad\qquad\ (\lambda p\,.\,(\mathcal{E}[\![E_2]\!]\ e\ h_{app}\ (\lambda v\,.\,(p\ v\ h_{app}\ k_{app})))))))$,
   by the definition of $\textit{procedure-cont}$ in Figure 9.19 on page 473

$=\ \mathcal{E}[\![(\texttt{app}\ E_1\ E_2)]\!]$ in Figure 9.35

Figure 9.38 Denotational equivalence of the $\mathcal{E}$ clauses for $\texttt{lam}$ and $\texttt{app}$ in the computation-style semantics and the standard semantics.

the handler environment of the application expression, which is essential for passing dynamic information from the caller to the called procedure.

2. In the computation-style valuation clause for $(\texttt{lam } I \; E_{body})$, the procedure body E_{body} is implicitly evaluated with respect to all of the arguments in the *Comp* domain in effect when the procedure is called, *not* the ones in effect when the abstraction expression is evaluated. This implements dynamic rather than static scoping.

3. *with-value* passes the same handler environment h to both the computation c and the *Value* $\rightarrow$ *Comp* function f. This means that h is treated like an environment (passed down from above to all subexpressions) rather than like a store (single-threaded through the computation).

It is possible to pass any information dynamically through a computation by treating it like handler environments in the computation-based semantics for exceptions.

The valuation clauses for **trap**, **handle**, and **raise** use the new computation operations *extending-handlers* and *getting-handler* to hide the explicit manipulation of handler environments. Given a tag I_{tag}, a handler $p_{handler}$, and a computation c, *extending-handlers* returns a new computation that will extend the dynamic handler environment with a binding of I_{tag} to $p_{handler}$ before proceeding with c. This is used to declare the handler in the **trap** and **handle** clauses. Given an exception tag I_{tag} and a function f mapping a handler procedure to a computation, *getting-handler* calls f on the handler associated with I_{tag} in the current handler environment. This is used in the **raise** clause to find the current handler. With these abstractions, all manipulations of the dynamic handler environment and expression continuation are hidden except in the **handle** clause, where the handler environment h_{handle} and continuation k_{handle} in effect at the handler declaration must be made explicit so that they can be used in the handler procedure to replace the dynamic handler environment h_{raise} and **raise** continuation k_{raise}.[3]

9.6.4 A Desugaring-based Implementation of Exceptions

Exception handling effectively combines dynamic scoping (for handler environments) with nonlocal exits (for exception handlers introduced by **handle**). This

---

[3]In the **trap** clause, we have eta-expanded the handler procedure p for the purpose of comparison with the handler procedure in the **handle** clause. But this could have been written simply as p, thereby hiding the handler environment and continuation.

is made clear by implementing exception handling via syntactic sugar in a language that supports (1) first-class control points and (2) a dynamically scoped namespace separate from the regular statically scoped one. Imagine a version of FLIC that is extended with `label` and `jump` from Section 9.4 and also supports a separate dynamically scoped namespace manipulated by the following constructs:

(`dylet` ((I_1 E_1) ... (I_n E_n)) E_{body}) is like `let`, but it binds the names I_1, ..., I_n to the values of E_1, ..., E_n, respectively, in the dynamic namespace rather than the static one.

(`dyref` I) looks up I in the dynamic namespace rather than the static one.

In this version of FLIC, `raise`, `trap`, and `handle` can be implemented via the desugarings in Figure 9.39. For comparison purposes, both nondismissal and dismissal versions of `handle` are presented. The desugarings for `trap` and `raise` highlight that these constructs are nothing more than ways to bind and look up procedures in a dynamic namespace. For comparison purposes, we can rewrite the desugaring for `trap` as:

```
; Nondismissal semantics for trap (the default trap semantics)
(trap I_tag E_handler E_body)
  ⇝_ds (let ((I_handler E_handler))
         (dylet ((I_tag (abs (vinfo) (I_handler vinfo))))
           E_body))
```

In this form, it is easy to see that the only difference between `trap` and the nondismissal version of `handle` is that a `handle` exception handler returns to the point of the `handle` (using (`jump` I_{return} ...)) rather than to the point of the `raise`. In the `handle` desugarings, there are two reasons to name the result of $E_{handler}$: (1) it forces $E_{handler}$ to be evaluated before E_{body} and (2) it guarantees that $E_{handler}$ is evaluated exactly once. Both of these are required by the semantics, but neither would be true if $I_{handler}$ were replaced by $E_{handler}$ within (`abs` (`vinfo`) ...).

In the first `handle` desugaring, whenever I_{tag} is raised in E_{body}, $I_{handler}$ will be invoked on the information value `vinfo` using the handler environment in place at the point of the `raise`, so this is a nondismissal semantics. For a dismissal semantics (the second desugaring) of `handle`, the application ($I_{handler}$ `vinfo`) is delayed in a thunk that is returned to a dethunking context at the point of the `handle`, where it will use the handler environment at that point when it is

```
(raise I_tag E_info) ⤳_ds ((dyref I_tag) E_info)

; Nondismissal semantics for trap (the default trap semantics)
(trap I_tag E_handler E_body) ⤳_ds (dylet ((I_tag E_handler)) E_body)

; The dismissal semantics for trap is Exercise 9.29.

; Nondismissal semantics for handle
(handle I_tag E_handler E_body)
  ⤳_ds (label I_return  {I_return is fresh}
          (let ((I_handler E_handler))  {I_handler is fresh. Evaluate E_handler before}
                                         {E_body and name it so only evaluated once}
             (dylet ((I_tag (abs (vinfo)
                               {Return vinfo from handle rather than raise}
                               (jump I_return (I_handler vinfo))))
                    E_body)))

; Dismissal semantics for handle (the default handle semantics)
(handle I_tag E_handler E_body)
  ⤳_ds (({This left paren begins the application dethunking
            the thunk returned by label}
          (label I_return  {I_return is fresh}
            (abs ()  {The "normal" thunk returned from the label}
              (let ((I_handler E_handler))  {I_handler is fresh}
                (dylet ((I_tag (abs (vinfo)
                               {Return a handler thunk from label}
                               (jump I_return (abs () (I_handler vinfo)))))
                      E_body)))))
```

Figure 9.39 Desugaring of exceptions in a language that supports first-class control points and a dynamically scoped namespace.

dethunked. Since label is assumed to return a thunk for the exception case, it must also return a thunk for the normal case. It is possible to give a desugaring for a dismissal version of trap and a thunkless desugaring for the dismissal version of handle (see Exercise 9.29).

The desugarings in Figure 9.39 assume that the exception-handling constructs have exclusive access to the dynamic environment. If programs could use dylet and dyref to explicitly access the dynamic environment, some method for preventing name clashes of exception tags with other names bound in the dynamic environment would have to be employed.

9.6.5   Examples Revisited

With the formal semantics in hand, we can now definitively answer questions about the evaluation of expressions that use exceptions in complex ways. For example, reconsider the expression

$$E_{handlerTest} = (handler_1 \text{ a (abs (x) (@+ 4000 x))}$$
$$(handler_2 \text{ b (abs (y) (@+ 300 (raise a (@+ y 4))))}$$
$$(handler_3 \text{ a (abs (z) (@+ 20 z))}$$
$$\text{(@+ 1 (raise b 2))))))}$$

in which each $handler_i$ is either `trap` or `handle`. First consider the case in which every $handler_i$ is `trap`. Because $handler_2$ is `trap`, `(@+ 1 (raise b 2))` is equivalent to

```
(@+ 1 ((abs (y) (@+ 300 (raise a (@+ y 4)))) 2))
```

evaluated in a dynamic environment that binds all three handlers. This is equivalent to $E_{raise} = $ `(@+ 1 (@+ 300 (raise a 6)))`. Under the default nondismissal semantics of `trap`, the handler found for a is the *inner* one (i.e., the one introduced by $handler_3$), yielding `(@+ 1 (@+ 300 ((abs (z) (@+ 20 z)) 6)))`, which evaluates to 327. If dismissal semantics were used instead, E_{raise} would be evaluated in an exception environment containing the binding for the *outer* a, and the result would be 4307.

For the case in which each $handler_i$ is `handle`, the result of each `raise` is returned directly to the point of the `handle`, so the `(@+ 1 ... )` and `(@+ 300 ... )` pending operations are bypassed. In the default dismissal semantics for `handle`, this leads to the result 4006, but the result would be 26 in a nondismissal semantics. There are many other possibilities for instantiating the $handler_i$ in this example, which you are asked to consider in Exercise 9.27.

What is the value of the following expression?

```
(trap noninteger (abs (v) (if (list? v) (list-sum v) 0))
  (list-sum (list 3 #t 7 (list #f 6) (sym foo) 2)))
```

Since `trap` uses nondismissal semantics, the `noninteger` handler introduced by the `trap` is still in effect when `list-sum` is applied in the handler to the element `(list #f 6)`. So this inner application of `list-sum` returns *6* and the outer application of `list-sum` (as well as the `trap` expression) returns *18*. But if `trap` used a dismissal semantics, the inner application of `list-sum` would raise an unhandled `noninteger` exception that would be converted to a `noninteger` error by the default exception handler.

Exercise 9.25 The following procedures are variants of the `add` and `list-sum` procedures discussed in the text.

```
(def (mul x y)
  (let ((check (abs (n)
                 (if (@int? n)
                     (if (@= n 0) (raise zero #u) {trivial info} n)
                     (raise noninteger n)))))
    (@* (check x) (check y))))

(def (list-prod elts) (foldr mul 1 elts))
```

Here are some lists whose definitions are used below:

```
(def elts1 (list 3 #t 7 (sym foo) (list 4 5) 2))
(def elts2 (list 3 #t 7 (sym foo) (list #f 5) 2))
(def elts3 (list 3 #t 0 (sym foo) (list 4 5) 2))
```

a. Evaluate each of the following expressions (1) when *handler* is `handle` and (2) when *handler* is `trap`.

  i.   (*handler* noninteger (abs (_) 1) (list-prod elts1))

  ii.   (*handler* noninteger (abs (_) 0) (list-prod elts1))

  iii.   (*handler* noninteger (abs (v) v) (list-prod elts1))

  iv.   (*handler* noninteger (abs (v) (if (list? v) (list-prod v) 1))
          (list-prod elts1))

  v.   (*handler* noninteger (abs (v) (if (list? v) (list-prod v) 1))
          (list-prod elts2))

  vi.   (*handler* zero (abs (_) 0) (list-prod elts3))

  vii.   (*handler* zero (abs (_) 0)
          (trap {*Fix this handler as* trap} noninteger (abs (v) 0)
            (list-prod elts3)))
       (How many multiplications are performed in this case?)

b. Here are two versions of `list-prod` that attempt to avoid unnecessary multiplications when a 0 is encountered. Compare the benefits and drawbacks of the two versions.

```
(def (list-prod2 elts)
  (handle zero (abs (_) 0)
    (foldr mul 1 elts)))

(def (list-prod3 elts)
  (label return
    (recur prod ((es elts))
      (if (@null? elts)
          1
          (let ((n (@car  elts)))
            (if (@= n 0)
                (jump return 0)
                (* n (prod (@cdr elts)))))))))
```

Exercise 9.26 Evaluate the following expression (1) when *handler* is `handle` and (2) when *handler* is `trap`:
```
(handler exn (abs (x) x)
  (handler exn (abs (y) (if (@= y 0) 1 (@* y (raise exn (@- y 1)))))
    (raise exn 5)))
```

Exercise 9.27 In the test expression $E_{handleTest}$ presented in the text, there are eight possible ways to instantiate *handler₁*, *handler₂*, *handler₃* from the set $\{\texttt{trap}, \texttt{handle}\}$. Two combinations have already been analyzed in the text.

a. Write the result of evaluating $E_{handleTest}$ for the other six combinations, assuming the default semantics for `trap` and `handle`.

b. Let V be the set of all result values from part **a**. If you instead assume dismissal semantics for `trap` and/or nondismissal semantics for `handle`, for which combinations does $E_{handleTest}$ have a different result value than any of the values in V?

Exercise 9.28 The implementation of `env-merge` in Figure 9.34 uses `handle` to catch an unbound variable exception from looking up the variable in `env1`. Could `trap` be used instead? Explain, using concrete examples where appropriate.

Exercise 9.29 Figure 9.39 presents desugarings for some versions of `trap` and `handle`.

a. The desugaring for `trap` in Figure 9.39 is for the default nondismissal version. Give a desugaring for a dismissal version of `trap`.

b. In Figure 9.39, the dismissal semantics for `handle` is achieved via thunks. Give a thunkless desugaring for the dismissal semantics of `handle` by fleshing out the $\square$ in the following skeleton:

$$(\texttt{handle}\ I_{tag}\ E_{handler}\ E_{body})$$
$$\leadsto_{ds} (\texttt{label}\ I_{normal}\ \{I_{normal}\ \textit{is fresh}\}$$
$$(E_{handler}\ (\texttt{label}\ I_{raise}\ \{I_{raise}\ \textit{is fresh}\}\ \square)))$$

Exercise 9.30 Inspired by JAVA features for exception handling, Abby Stracksen is experimenting with adding two kernel constructs to FLIC+$\{\texttt{handle}, \texttt{raise}\}$:

$$E ::= \ \dots \ \text{FLICK}+\{\texttt{raise}, \texttt{handle}\}\ \textit{expressions} \ \dots$$
$$\mid\ (\texttt{raises}\ (I^*_{tag})\ E_{body})\ \mid\ (\texttt{finally}\ E_{body}\ E_{finally})$$

Since JAVA uses termination semantics for exceptions, Abby does not include `trap` in her language.

Here is the informal semantics of Abby's constructs:

$(\texttt{raises}\ (I^*_{tag})\ E_{body})$ evaluates and returns the value of E_{body}. However, E_{body} is only allowed to raise exceptions whose tags are listed in I^*_{tag}. If E_{body} dynamically raises an exception that is not in I^*_{tag}, the program halts with an `illegal-exception` error. (A different approach would be to statically determine which exceptions E_{body} might raise; see Section 16.3.3.)

(finally E_{body} $E_{finally}$) first evaluates E_{body} to the value v_{body}, then evaluates $E_{finally}$ (whose value is discarded), and then returns v_{body}. If an exception is raised by E_{body}, $E_{finally}$ is still evaluated before the exception is handled. So $E_{finally}$ is evaluated regardless of whether E_{body} evaluates normally or raises an exception.

The **raises** construct is useful for documenting which exceptions an expression or procedure can raise. For example,

```
(def p (abs (x y) (raises (negative zero) E_pbody)))
```

declares that the procedure p might raise the **negative** or **zero** exceptions. So it's a good idea to wrap calls to p in **handle** expressions that handle these two exceptions. If p is invoked with arguments that cause E_{pbody} to raise an exception that is not **negative** or **zero**, the program will halt with an **illegal-exception** error.

The (**finally** E_{body} $E_{finally}$) construct is useful for guaranteeing that the cleanup operations in $E_{finally}$ are performed regardless of how E_{body} is exited. For example, consider the following procedure:

```
(def (with-cell-set-to c temp-value thunk)
  (let ((old-value (^ c)))
    (finally (begin (:= c temp-value) (thunk))
             (:= c old-value))))
```

This dethunks **thunk** in a context where the cell c is temporarily set to **temp-value** and then resets c to its original value. The cell c is reset to its original value even if dethunking **thunk** raises an exception. Here's an example illustrating **with-cell-set-to**:

```
(let ((a (cell 10)))
  (let ((f (abs (x) (@* (^ a) (if (@< x 0) (raise negative x) x))))))
    (list (f 2)
          (with-cell-set-to a 3 (abs () (f 4)))
          (handle negative (abs (v) (@- 0 v))
            (with-cell-set-to a 5 (abs () (f -6))))
          (f 7)))) ⟶_FLIC ◁20, 12, 6, 70▷
```

Note that cell a holds the value 10 before and after the evaluation of each of the four subexpressions in (**list** ...).

a. Write the $\mathcal{E}$ valuation clause for **raises**.

b. Write the $\mathcal{E}$ valuation clause for **finally**.

c. The informal semantics for **finally** does not specify what happens when an exception is raised within $E_{finally}$. According to your semantics for **finally**, what is the value of the following expression?

```
(let ((b (cell 10)))
  (handle exn1 (abs (x) (@* x (^ b)))
    (handle exn2 (abs (y) (@+ y (^ b)))
      (finally (begin (:= b 200)
                      (handle exn2 (abs (y) (:= b (@/ (^ b) y))))
                        (@* 3 (raise exn1 4))))
              (begin (@- 6 (raise exn2 5))
                     (:= b 10))))))
```

Exercise 9.31 Sam Antics thinks that exception handlers should be able to dynamically choose between termination and resumption semantics. Sam likes the termination semantics of `handle` but occasionally he would prefer the resumption semantics of `trap`. He decides to extend FLIC+{raise, handle} with a new expression construct (resume E) that helps to simulate some of the behavior of `trap`.

Informally, (resume E) causes a handler to resume at the point of the `raise` rather than terminating at the point of the `handle`. `resume` first evaluates E using the current dynamic handler environment and then returns control to the point of the most recent `raise` with the value of E. Any program that does not use `resume` should behave just as it would in FLIC+{raise, handle}. Figure 9.40 shows some examples that Sam has developed to illustrate his (resume E) construct.

a. Unfortunately, Sam has fallen ill, and you must flesh out his design. You should extend the standard semantics for FLIC+{raise, handle} as follows.

   i.   Modify the signatures of $\mathcal{E}$ and $\mathcal{E}^*$ and the definition of the semantic domain *Proc* to support the `resume` construct.

   ii. Give the valuation clauses for `lam`, `app`, `raise`, `handle`, and `resume`. (Assume that the clauses for other FLICK constructs are modified appropriately.)

   iii. Give the $\mathcal{P}$ valuation clause for a program.

b. It is possible to define a translation function $\mathcal{T}$ from FLIC+{trap, handle, raise} to FLIC+{handle, raise, resume} that preserves the meaning of expressions. This is a *translation* between two different languages and *not* a desugaring from a language to itself. The translation of most expressions is purely structural — i.e., translating the expression merely glues together the translation of its subexpressions. For example,

$$\mathcal{T}[\![(\text{app } E_1 \ E_2)]\!] = (\text{app } \mathcal{T}[\![E_1]\!] \ \mathcal{T}[\![E_2]\!])$$

Define the translation clauses for `trap`, `handle`, and `raise`. Recall that the `trap` construct presented in the text combines resumption semantics with nondismissal semantics. The resumption semantics can be achieved via `resume`; the tricky part is simulating the nondismissal semantics of `trap` using `handle` (which uses dismissal semantics).

Exercise 9.32 Sam Antics has developed SWITCHEROO, a version of FLIC extended with a kernel `switch` expression that allows a program to both generate and handle exceptions:

   $E ::= \dots$ FLICK *expressions* $\dots$ | (switch E)

In SWITCHEROO, every expression is implicitly provided with *two* expression continuations, which Sam calls the A and B continuations:

```
{handle behaves as normal}
(handle exn (abs (x) (@+ x 2))
  (@+ 20 (raise exn 1)))  ──FLIC→  3

{handle using resume is similar to trap}
(handle exn (abs (x) (resume (@+ x 2)))
  (@+ 20 (raise exn 1)))  ──FLIC→  23

{It is an error to use resume outside an exception handler}
(resume 7)  ──FLIC→  error:no-raise

{resume need not be syntactically inside the handler expression to work}
(let ((f (abs (x) (resume (@+ x 4)))))
  (handle exn (abs (y) (f (@+ y 300)))
    (@+ 20 (raise exn 1))))  ──FLIC→  324

{When resume is invoked, any pending computation in the}
{handler is discarded, including any other resumes}
(handle exn (abs (x) (resume (@+ 300 (resume (@+ x 2)))))
  (@+ 20 (raise exn 1)))  ──FLIC→  23

(handle exn1 (abs (x) (@+ 50000 (resume (@+ x 4))))
  (@+ 4000
      (handle exn2 (abs (x) (@+ 300 (raise exn1 (@+ x 2))))
        (@+ 20 (raise exn2 1)))))  ──FLIC→  4307

{handle with resume differs from trap: handle uses dismissal while trap does not.}
(handle exn1 (abs (x) (@+ 50000 (resume (@+ x 4))))
  (@+ 4000
      (handle exn2 (abs (x) (resume (@+ 300 (raise exn1 (@+ x 2)))))
        (handle exn1 (abs (x) (@+ 600000 x))
          (@+ 20 (raise exn2 1))))))  ──FLIC→  4327

{With resume, handlers can choose between termination and resumption}
(let ((f (abs (x)
           (handle exn (abs (y)
                         (if (@< y 3)
                             (@+ y 300)
                             (@+ 50000 (resume (@+ y 4000)))))
             (@+ 20 (raise exn x))))))
  (pair (f 2) (f 4)))  ──FLIC→  ⟨302, 4024⟩
```

Figure 9.40 Sam's examples illustrating his resume construct (Exercise 9.31).

$\mathcal{E} : \mathrm{Exp} \to Env \to Expcont$; the A continuation
$\qquad\qquad\qquad \to Expcont$; the B continuation
$\qquad\qquad\qquad \to Cmdcont$; the normal command continuation

$\mathcal{E}^* : \mathrm{Exp}^* \to Explistcont \to Explistcont \to Cmdcont$; takes both A and B continuations

$Proc = Nameable \to Expcont \to Expcont \to Cmdcont$; takes both A and B continuations

Sam has modified the $\mathcal{E}$ and $\mathcal{E}^*$ valuation clauses so that expressions and expression sequences inherited from FLICK provide their return value to the A continuation but pass the B continuation along as an extra argument. For example:

$\mathcal{E}[\![L]\!] = \lambda e k_a k_b \,.\, (k_a \ \mathcal{L}[\![L]\!])$

$\mathcal{E}[\![(\texttt{lam } I \ E)]\!]$
$= \lambda e k_{alam} k_{blam} \,.\, (k_{alam} \ (Proc \rightarrowtail Value \ (\lambda n k_{aapp} k_{bapp} \,.\, (\mathcal{E}[\![E]\!] \ [I \mapsto n] e \ k_{aapp} \ k_{bapp}))))$

$\mathcal{E}[\![(\texttt{app } E_1 \ E_2)]\!] = \lambda e k_{app} k_{bapp} \,.\, (\mathcal{E}[\![E_1]\!] \ e \ (procedure\text{-}cont$
$\qquad\qquad\qquad\qquad\qquad\qquad (\lambda p \,.\, (\mathcal{E}[\![E_2]\!] \ e \ (\lambda v \,.\, (p \ v \ k_{app} \ k_{bapp}))))$
$\qquad\qquad\qquad\qquad\qquad\qquad k_{bapp})$

The key feature of SWITCHEROO is that the (switch E) construct swaps the A and B continuations for the evaluation of the component expression E:

$\mathcal{E}[\![(\texttt{switch } E)]\!] = \lambda e k_a k_b \,.\, (\mathcal{E}[\![E]\!] \ e \ k_b \ k_a)$

Whereas the A continuation usually corresponds to a normal return, the B continuation usually corresponds to an exceptional return. Sam calls values that are passed to A continuations "A values" and values that are passed to B continuations "B values."

Sam gives the following example of using switch to generate and handle exceptions:

```
(let ((inc (lam x
             (if (@= x 0)
                 (switch (sym zero))
                 (if (@< x 0)
                     (switch (sym negative)
                     (@+ x 1)))))))
  (let ((f (lam y
             (switch (let ((exn (switch (inc (@* y 10)))))
                       (switch (if (sym=? exn (sym negative))
                                   -1
                                   0)))))))
    (list (f 5) (f 0) (f -5))))  FLIC  ⊲51, 0, −1⊳
```

The inc procedure increments a positive integer, but switch is used to raise exceptions (i.e., return B values) if the argument is zero or negative. In the f procedure, if the invocation of inc returns an A value v_{norm} (a normal value), then the switch around (inc ...) is canceled by the switch around (let ((exn ...)) ...), and f returns v_{norm} as well. But if the invocation of inc returns a B value v_{exn} (an exception value), this value is named exn, and f returns −1 for a negative exception and 0 for any other exception (i.e., zero). The switch around (if ...) is necessary for returning the −1 or 0 from f as a normal value rather than as an exception value.

a. Suppose that p_{inc} is the meaning of the `inc` procedure in Sam's example. Use Sam's semantics to find the meaning p_f of the `f` procedure and verify that it behaves like Sam claims on the arguments 5, 0, and -5.

b. Use Sam's semantics to show that `(switch (switch E))` has the same meaning as E.

c. Write the valuation function $\mathcal{P}$ for SWITCHEROO. If the body of a program returns a B value, the program should signal an `unhandled-exception` error.

d. Sam observes that, in SWITCHEROO, `raise` and `handle` can be defined as syntactic sugar. Here is Sam's desugaring for `raise`:

$$\texttt{(raise } I_{tag} \ E_{info}\texttt{)} \leadsto_{ds} \texttt{(switch (pair (sym } I_{tag}\texttt{) } E_{info}\texttt{))} \ ; \textit{Recall Ident} \subseteq \textit{SymLit}$$

Write a corresponding desugaring for `(handle `I_{tag}` `$E_{handler}$` `E_{body}`)`. Explain why your solution implements the termination semantics and dismissal semantics of the `handle` construct.

e. Basing the SWITCHEROO semantics on the standard semantics of FLICK requires making many minor changes to domain signatures and valuation clauses. Far fewer changes need to be made if the SWITCHEROO semantics is based on the computation-style semantics FLICK. Give the modified definition of the *Comp* domain and the *val-to-comp*, *err-to-comp*, and *with-value* functions for SWITCHEROO. With these definitions, explain why the computation-based $\mathcal{E}$ and $\mathcal{E}^*$ valuation clauses from FLICK can be used without modification in SWITCHEROO.

Notes

John Reynolds's history of continuations [Rey93] credits Adriaan van Wijngaarden with the discovery of the notion of continuation, but notes that many others — including F. Lockwood Morris, Chris Wadsworth, James Morris, and Michael Fischer — rediscovered the idea or contributed to its early development. It appears that the term "continuation" was coined by Wadsworth. Continuations played an important role in the development of actor languages [Hew77] and of SCHEME [SS75, Ste76, SS76, Ste78].

Strachey and Wadsworth used continuations to model control-point-capturing constructs in the denotational semantics framework [SW74]. For more coverage of the use of continuations in denotational semantics see [Ten76, Sto85, Sch86]. For treatments of control constructs in operational semantics, see [SF89, FH92, FFF].

Early examples of programming language constructs for capturing control points include Landin's J operator [Lan65a, Lan65b, Lan98], Reynolds's `escape` construct [Rey72], and the `catch` construct in the initial version of SCHEME [SS75]. Later versions of Scheme provide the power of these earlier constructs via a procedure in the standard library named `call-with-current-continuation` (often abbreviated `call/cc`) [AA+85]. Continuations have been used to implement a wide range of sophisticated control features, including backtracking [FHK84], coroutines [HFW86], multitasking with process threads [Wan80], timed preemption [HF87], and Web applications [Que04]. Many applications of continuations are surveyed in [SF89, Que93, FD01].

Continuations support *nondeterministic programming*, a paradigm in which expressions can have multiple values and there is a means of specifying when a suitable one has been found. This model is based on a pair of constructs: one, often called `amb`, `choice`, or `choose`, conceptually makes a nondeterministic choice between a set of alternatives; the other, typically called `fail`, indicates that the current alternative is unacceptable [McC67, ZMC87]. Such nondeterminism can be implemented by backtracking-based search techniques using success and failure continuations [ASS96, Section 4.3]. Combining unification (see Section 13.3.2) with nondeterministic choice is the basis for a style of programming known as *logic programming* (e.g., [RW89], [ASS96, Section 4.4]), whose goal is to separate the logic of an algorithm from its step-by-step realization in an executing program [Kow79]. The chief exemplar of the style is the PROLOG programming language [WPP77]. The relationship between nondeterministic programming and logic programming is discussed in [RH04, Chapter 9].

For more on continuation-passing style (CPS), see [DF92, SF93],[FWH01, Chapter 8]. CPS plays an important role in the transformation-based compiler we present in Chapter 17. Stoy argues that embedding continuations in the semantics is better for expressing the meaning of programs than transforming programs into CPS and then using direct semantics [Sto85].

The modularity benefits of coroutines were elucidated in [Con63] in the context of structuring a compiler. Coroutining-based forms of iteration were included in CLU[L+79], ICON [GG00], and SATHER [MOSS96]. The enumerations and iterators supported in C++ and JAVA provide the modularity benefits of these forms of iteration, but do so using hand-crafted state-based traversals of collections in place of coroutines.

10

Data

Conjunction Junction, what's their function?
I got "and"... and "or,"
They'll get you pretty far.

"And": That's an additive, like "this and that." ...
And then there's "or":
O-R, when you have a choice like "this or that".
"And"... and "or,"
Get you pretty far.

— Bob Dorough, "Conjunction Junction (Schoolhouse Rock)"

Well-designed data structures can make programs efficient, understandable, extensible, secure, and easy to debug. For this reason, programmers focus much of their energy on designing and using data structures. How successful they are depends in part on the tools provided by their programming language for declaring and manipulating data.

This chapter explores key data dimensions in programming languages, beginning with *products* (this *and* that) in Section 10.1 and then moving on to *sums* (this *or* that) in Section 10.2. Typical data structures are naturally expressed using a combination of these, yielding *sum-of-products* data introduced in Section 10.3. Sum-of-products data are more convenient to use if they can be manipulated with constructor and deconstructor procedures created by the data declarations presented in Section 10.4. Deconstructor procedures are somewhat awkward to use directly, but the pattern matching facility of Section 10.5 provides a simple and powerful interface for deconstructing sum-of-products data.

10.1 Products

Products are compound values that result from gluing other values together. They are data structures that correspond to the product domains we have been using in our mathematical metalanguage (see Section A.3.3) to represent structured mathematical values with components. Standard examples of products are two-dimensional points (consisting of x and y components), employee records (consisting of name, sex, age, identification number, hiring date, etc.), and the sequences of points in polygons.

There is a wide variety of product data structures in programming languages that differ along a surprising number of dimensions:

- How are product values created and later decomposed into parts?

- Are the components of the product indexed by position or by name?

- When accessing a component, can its index be calculated or must an index be an explicit constant?

- Are the components values (as in call-by-value) or computations (as in call-by-name/call-by-need)?

- Are the components of the product immutable or mutable?

- Is the length of the product fixed or variable?

- Are all components of the product required to have the "same type"? I.e., are products *homogeneous*?

- Can components of a product be products? If so, are the component products all required to have the same size and/or "shape"?

- How are products passed as arguments, returned as results, and stored via assignments?

- Can a product created within a procedure invocation outlive that invocation?

In this section, we will explore many of these dimensions, using our operational and denotational tools where appropriate to explain interesting points in the design space of products.

Products are known by a confusing variety of names — such as *array*, *vector*, *sequence*, *tuple*, *string*, *list*, *structure*, *record*, *environment*, *table*, *module*, and *association list* — that are used inconsistently between languages. We shall be using some of these names in our study of products, but it is important to keep in mind that our use of a name may denote a different kind of product than what you might be familiar with from your programming experience.

10.1.1 Positional Products

Simple Positional Products

The simplest kind of product is a pair, which glues two values together. In Section 7.1.3, we studied the semantics of strict and nonstrict pairs in FL.

Pairs are an example of a **positional product**, in which component values are indexed by their position in the product value. We can extend pairs into more general positional products by adding the following two kernel expressions to CBV FLIC:[1]

$$E ::= \ldots$$
$$| \; (\texttt{prod} \; E^*_{component}) \quad [\text{ProductCreation}]$$
$$| \; (\texttt{get} \; N_{index} \; E_{prod}) \quad [\text{ProductProjection}]$$

The expression ($\texttt{prod} \; E_1 \; \ldots \; E_n$) constructs an immutable positional product value whose n components are the values of the subexpressions E_1 through E_n. Such a value is traditionally known as a **tuple**. ($\texttt{get} \; N_{index} \; E_{prod}$) extracts the component of the tuple denoted by E_{prod} that is at the index denoted by the integer literal N_{index}, where the components of an n-component product are indexed from 1 to n. An attempt to extract a component outside this index range is an error. In the terminology of general products, the $\texttt{get}$ operation is often called a **projection**.

Because there is no mechanism to change a component of a tuple, tuples are an example of an immutable product. In our initial exploration of products, we will focus on immutable products because mutability introduces extra complexity into the semantics. We will study mutable products in Section 10.1.4.

The operational and denotational semantics of immutable positional products in CBV FLICK are presented in Figure 10.1. In the operational semantics, a $\texttt{prod}$ expression with value-expression components is considered a new kind of value expression. The new evaluation context ($\texttt{prod} \; V^{k-1}_{i=1} \; \mathbb{E} \; E^n_{j=k+1}$) dictates that the subexpressions of a $\texttt{prod}$ expression are evaluated from left to right. For example,

```
(let ((c (cell 3)))
  (prod c (:= c (* 2 (^ c))) c (:= c (+ 1 (^ c))) c))
```

evaluates to the value expression

```
(prod 3 #u 6 #u 7)
```

The new evaluation context ($\texttt{get} \; N_{index} \; \mathbb{E}$) evaluates the tuple argument to $\texttt{get}$. The [$\texttt{get}$] reduction rule extracts the value component denoted by index N_{index}.

---

[1]We use a stateful language to facilitate discussion of product design issues involving state.

Using these contexts and rule, it is straightforward to show that the following
FL expression evaluates to *9*:

```
(let ((p (prod (= 0 1) (* 2 3) (+ 4 5))))
  (if (get 1 p) (get 2 p) (get 3 p)))
```

In the corresponding denotational semantics, the *Value* domain is extended
with a new summand, *Prod*, whose elements — sequences of values — represent
product values. The evaluation of the subexpressions of a `prod` expression is
handled by *with-values*, and *nth* is used to extract the component at a given index
in a `get` expression. The *with-prod-and-checked-index* function ensures that (1)
the given computation produces a product value and (2) the given integer is in
the range of valid indices for the product value.

Both the operational and denotational treatments of `get` perform what is
known as a **bounds check** to ensure that the specified index is in the valid
range. If the bounds check fails, the `get` expression is an error. This is modeled
by a stuck expression in the operational semantics and an error computation
in the denotational semantics. In many programming languages, the size of a
product is known by the compiler or interpreter, and a bounds check for every
projection can be performed either at compile time or at run time. Important
exceptions are C and C++, in which arrays carry no size information and bounds
checks are not performed when array components are accessed. Programmers in
these languages must pass array size information separately from the array itself
and are expected to perform their own bounds checks. The lack of automatic
bounds checks in C/C++ is the root cause of a high percentage of security
flaws in modern software applications, many of which are due to so-called **buffer
overflow** exploits that take advantage of C's permissiveness to fill memory with
malicious code that can then be executed by a privileged process [KBO⁺05].

A product value with n components is often drawn as a box with n slots,
sometimes with explicit indices. For example, the three-component product value
`(prod #f 6 7)` would be drawn as

false	*6*	*7*
1	2	3

Such a diagram suggests a low-level implementation in which the n components
of a product are stored as the contents of n successive addresses in the memory
of the computer, something we shall explore in more detail in Section 18.2.3.

We emphasize that tuples in FLIC are immutable: there is no way to change
the value stored in a slot. We will study mutable products in Section 10.1.4. But
first we discuss many possible variants of the simple products presented above.

Values

$V \in \text{ValueExp} ::= \ldots \mid (\texttt{prod } V_1 \ldots V_n)$

The AnsExp domain and output function OF would also have to be extended to handle $\texttt{prod}$ values.

Evaluation Contexts

$\mathbb{E} \in \text{EvalContext} ::= \ldots \mid (\texttt{prod } V_{i=1}^{k-1} \ \mathbb{E} \ E_{j=k+1}^{n}) \mid (\texttt{get } N_{index} \ \mathbb{E})$

New Stateless Reduction Rule

$(\texttt{get } N_{index} \ (\texttt{prod } V_1 \ldots V_n)) \rightsquigarrow V_i, \quad [\text{get}]$
   where $i = \mathcal{N}[\![N_{index}]\!]$ and $1 \leq i \leq n$

Operational semantics for CBV products

New and Modified Semantic Domains

$\quad Prod = Value^*$

$v \in Value = \ldots + Prod$

New Computation Operation

$with\text{-}product\text{-}comp : Comp \rightarrow (Prod \rightarrow Comp) \rightarrow Comp$

The definition is similar to that of $with\text{-}boolean\text{-}comp$ in Figure 6.26 on page 281.

$with\text{-}prod\text{-}and\text{-}checked\text{-}index : Comp \rightarrow Int \rightarrow (Prod \rightarrow Int \rightarrow Comp) \rightarrow Comp$
$= \lambda cif . \ with\text{-}product\text{-}comp \ c$
$\qquad\qquad (\lambda v^* . \ \textbf{if} \ (1 \leq i) \ \wedge \ (i \leq (length \ v^*))$
$\qquad\qquad\qquad \textbf{then} \ (f \ v^* \ i)$
$\qquad\qquad\qquad \textbf{else} \ (err\text{-}to\text{-}comp \ \texttt{out-of-bounds-product-index})$
$\qquad\qquad\qquad \textbf{end})$

New Valuation Clauses

$\mathcal{E}[\![(\texttt{prod } E^*)]\!] = \lambda e . \ (with\text{-}values \ (\mathcal{E}^*[\![E^*]\!] \ e) \ (\lambda v^* . (Prod \rightarrowtail Value \ v^*)))$

$\mathcal{E}[\![(\texttt{get } N_{index} \ E_{prod})]\!]$
$= \lambda e . \ with\text{-}prod\text{-}and\text{-}checked\text{-}index \ (\mathcal{E}[\![E_{prod}]\!] \ e) \ \mathcal{N}[\![N_{index}]\!]$
$\qquad (\lambda v^* i . (val\text{-}to\text{-}comp \ (nth \ i \ v^*)))$

Denotational semantics for CBV products

Figure 10.1 Operational and denotational semantics of immutable positional products in CBV FLICK.

Sequences

In the projection expression considered above, the index is an integer literal, not
an integer expression. This means that the projection index cannot be calculated.
As we discuss later (page 548), literal indices facilitate reasoning about programs
written in statically typed languages.

The positional products studied above do not include any way to dynamically determine the size of the product, i.e., the number of components. It is
assumed that the programmer knows the size of every tuple when writing the
program. However, there are many situations where it is necessary or convenient
to determine the size of a product and to extract a product component at an
index calculated from an expression. For instance, given an arbitrary product
containing numbers, determining the average of these numbers requires knowing
the number of components and looping through all indices of the product to find
the sum of the components. Such capabilities are normally associated with products called **arrays**. But since arrays are usually mutable, we will instead use
the name **sequence** for immutable products with calculated indices and dynamically determinable sizes. This terminology is consistent with our use of the term
"sequence" in our mathematical metalanguage.

We can extend FLIC with immutable sequences by adding the following constructs to the language:

$$E ::= \ldots$$
$$| \ (\texttt{seq} \ E^*_{component}) \qquad \text{[SequenceCreation]}$$
$$| \ (\texttt{seq-get} \ E_{index} \ E_{seq}) \ \text{[SequenceProjection]}$$
$$| \ (\texttt{seq-size} \ E_{seq}) \qquad \text{[SequenceSize]}$$

The expression (seq E_1 ... E_n) creates and returns a size-n sequence whose
components are the values of the expressions E_1 through E_n. The expression
(seq-get E_{index} E_{seq}) returns the ith component of the sequence denoted by
E_{seq}, where i is the integer denoted by the arbitrary expression E_{index} (which must
be checked against the bounds of the sequence). The expression (seq-size E_{seq})
returns the number of components in the sequence. The formal semantics of
sequences is left as Exercise 10.1.

As an example of sequence manipulation, here is a procedure that finds the
average of a sequence of numbers:

```
(def (average s)
  (let ((n (seq-size s)))
    (recur loop ((i n) (sum 0))
      (if (= i 0)
          (/ sum n)
          (loop (- i 1) (+ sum (seq-get i s)))))))
```

Exercise 10.1

a. Give an operational semantics for sequences in CBV FLICK.

b. Give a denotational semantics for sequences in CBV FLICK.

c. Explicitly enumerating the elements of a sequence in a `seq` expression can be inconvenient. For example, a sequence of the squares of the integers from 1 to 5 would be written:

```
(seq (* 1 1) (* 2 2) (* 3 3) (* 4 4) (* 5 5))
```

An alternative means of specifying such sequences is via a new construct

$$(\text{tabulate } E_{size} \ E_{proc})$$

where E_{size} denotes the size of the sequence and E_{proc} denotes a unary procedure f that maps the index i to the value $(f \ i)$. For instance, using `tabulate`, the above five-element sequence could be written

```
(tabulate 5 (abs (i) (* i i)))
```

Give an operational and denotational semantics for `tabulate` in CBV FLICK.

Updatable Sequences

Even with immutable products, it is still useful to provide a facility for updating elements in, inserting elements into, and removing elements from a product. Since the product is immutable, these operations don't actually change a given product value: Instead they return a new product value that shares most of its components with the given product value. We shall call sequences that support one or more of these operations **updatable sequences**, though this is by no means a standard term. HASKELL's arrays, SML's vectors,[2] and CLU's sequences are examples of updatable sequences in real languages.

Consider the following constructs for one form of updatable sequence:

$$E ::= \ldots$$
$$| \ (\text{useq } E^*_{component}) \qquad\qquad\qquad [\text{UpdatableSequenceCreation}]$$
$$| \ (\text{useq-get } E_{index} \ E_{useq}) \qquad\qquad [\text{UpdatableSequenceProjection}]$$
$$| \ (\text{useq-size } E_{useq}) \qquad\qquad\qquad [\text{UpdatableSequenceSize}]$$
$$| \ (\text{useq-update } E_{index} \ E_{val} \ E_{useq}) \ [\text{UpdatableSequenceUpdate}]$$
$$| \ (\text{useq-insert } E_{index} \ E_{val} \ E_{useq}) \ [\text{UpdatableSequenceInsertion}]$$
$$| \ (\text{useq-delete } E_{index} \ E_{useq}) \qquad\quad [\text{UpdatableSequenceDeletion}]$$

The `useq`, `useq-get`, and `useq-size` constructs are the updatable sequence versions of the corresponding (non-updatable) sequence constructs. For the other constructs, suppose that E_{index} denotes an integer i, E_{val} denotes a value v_{new},

---

[2]Vectors are not part of the SML standard but are supported by many dialects.

and E_{useq} denotes a size-n updatable sequence v_{useq}. If v is an updatable sequence, let $\#v$ denote the size of v and $v \downarrow j$ denote the jth component value of v, where $1 \leq j \leq \#v$. Finally, for the following examples, suppose that u denotes the sequence with integer values $[7, 5, 8]$. Then:

- if $1 \leq i \leq n$, (useq-update E_{index} E_{val} E_{useq}) returns a size-n updatable sequence v_{useq2} such that

  $v_{useq2} \downarrow i = v_{new}$; and

  $v_{useq2} \downarrow j = v_{useq} \downarrow j$ for all $1 \leq j \leq n$ where $j \neq i$.

  For example, (useq-update 2 6 u) returns the updatable sequence $[7, 6, 8]$.

- if $1 \leq i \leq n + 1$, (useq-insert E_{index} E_{val} E_{useq}) returns a size-$(n + 1)$ updatable sequence v_{useq2} such that

  $v_{useq2} \downarrow j = v_{useq} \downarrow j$ for all $1 \leq j < i$;

  $v_{useq2} \downarrow i = v_{new}$; and

  $v_{useq2} \downarrow k = v_{useq} \downarrow (k - 1)$ for all $i < k \leq (n + 1)$;

  For example, (useq-insert 2 6 u) returns the updatable sequence $[7, 6, 5, 8]$.

- if $1 \leq i \leq n$, (useq-delete E_{index} E_{useq}) returns a size-$(n - 1)$ updatable sequence v_{useq2} such that

  $v_{useq2} \downarrow j = v_{useq} \downarrow j$ for all $1 \leq j < i$; and

  $v_{useq2} \downarrow k = v_{useq} \downarrow (k + 1)$ for all $i \leq k \leq (n - 1)$;

  For example, (useq-delete 2 u) returns the updatable sequence $[7, 8]$.

All of the above constructs signal an error when E_{useq} does not denote an updatable sequence or when E_{index} is not an integer or is out of bounds.

Exercise 10.2 Define a procedure (sort *less-than* *elts*) that takes a less-than predicate *less-than* and an updatable sequence *elts* and returns an updatable sequence with the same elements as *elts* sorted from low to high by *less-than*.

Exercise 10.3

a. Give an operational semantics for updatable sequences in call-by-value FLICK.

b. Give a denotational semantics for updatable sequences in call-by-value FLICK.

c. Show that useq-update is not strictly necessary in a language with updatable sequences by showing how to desugar it into other constructs.

d. Consider a language with updatable sequences that also has a (`useq-empty`) construct
that returns an empty updatable sequence. Show that `useq` is not strictly necessary
in such a language by showing how to desugar it into other constructs. What are the
benefits and drawbacks of such a desugaring?

Product indexing

The positional products discussed above use **1-based indexing**, in which the
components of an n-component tuple are accessed via the indices $1 \ldots n$. Many
languages instead have **0-based indexing**, in which the slots are accessed via
the indices $0 \ldots n - 1$. For example:

false	*6*	*7*
0	1	2

Why use the index 0 to access the first slot of a product? One reason is
that it can simplify some addressing calculations in the compiled code, which
results in the execution of fewer low-level instructions when projecting components from products. Another reason is that 0-based indexing simplifies certain
addressing calculations for the programmer. For example, compare the following
expressions for accessing the slot in row i and column j of a conceptually two-
dimensional matrix m with width w and height h that is actually represented as
a one-dimensional sequence with $w \times h$ components stored in row-major order:[3]

```
{0-based indexing of matrices and sequences}
(nth (+ (* w i) j) m)
```

```
{1-based indexing of matrices and sequences}
(nth (+ (* w (- i 1)) j) m)
```

The 0-based approach is simpler because it does not require the subtraction of 1
seen in the 1-based approach.

Using 0 or 1 as the index for the first component is not the only choice when
it comes to indexing. Some languages allow using any integer range for product
indices. PASCAL even allows using as index ranges any range of values that is
isomorphic to an integer range. For instance, a PASCAL array can be indexed by
the alphabetic characters from 'p' to 'u' or the days of the week from `monday`
through `friday` (where an enumeration of days has been declared elsewhere).

---

[3]**Row-major** order means the elements of each row are stored in consecutive locations in
the sequence. This makes accessing elements along a row very inexpensive. Likewise, **column-
major** order means elements of each column are stored in consecutive sequence locations.

Types

FL is a **dynamically typed language**, in which each value is conceptually tagged with its type, and type errors are not detected until the program is run. In contrast, many modern languages are **statically typed languages**, in which the type of every expression is known when the program is compiled. The goal of static typing affects the design of positional products in these languages. In particular, it must be possible for the type checker to determine the type of every value projected from a product value.

For instance, SML and HASKELL support so-called **heterogeneous tuples**, in which each tuple component may have a different type. In order to determine the type of a projection, both tuple indices and tuple sizes must be statically determinable (i.e., they cannot be determined at run time as the value of an arbitrary expression). In contrast, products whose projection indices or size can be dynamically computed must be **homogeneous** — i.e., all components are required to have the same type. Examples of homogeneous products are the mutable arrays of ADA, C, JAVA, and PASCAL and the immutable updatable sequences of HASKELL and CLU. Many languages treat homogeneous sequences of characters, known as **strings**, as a special kind of positional product. Immutable strings appear in languages such as JAVA, SML, HASKELL and CLU, while C and SCHEME provide mutable strings.

Product indices are usually restricted to the integer type, but, as mentioned above, some languages allow index types that are isomorphic to the integers or some finite range of the integers. For example, the HASKELL language allows arrays to be indexed by any type that provides the operations of an "indexable" type. In PASCAL, arrays can be indexed by any range type that is isomorphic to a finite integer range. Oddly, the index range (not merely the index type) is part of the array type in PASCAL, which means that the size of every PASCAL array is statically known, and it is not possible to write procedures that are parameterized over arrays of different lengths.

We will have much more to say about product types when we study types in more detail (see Section 11.8.1).

Specialized syntax

Many languages provide specialized syntax for product manipulation. For instance, SML tuples are constructed by comma-separated expressions delimited by parentheses, and the ith tuple component is extracted via the syntax #i. Here is an SML version of the example we expressed earlier in s-expression syntax:

```
let val p = (0=1, 2*3, 4+5)
 in if #1(p) then #2(p) else #3(p)
end
```

For immutable sequences (as well as for mutable arrays) a subscripting notation using square brackets is a standard way to project components, and := might be used for an update operation.

Exercise 10.4

a. What changes would need to be made in Exercise 10.1 (page 545) to specify 0-based indexing rather than 1-based indexing?

b. What changes would need to be made to the syntax for sequences and in Exercise 10.1 to specify an indexing scheme that starts at an arbitrary dynamically determinable value *low* rather than 0 or 1?

10.1.2 Named Products

In a **named product**, components are indexed by names rather than by positions. In Section 7.2.3, we introduced the **record**, a classic form of named product, and studied its semantics. We saw that records were effectively reified environments. Here we discuss some of the design issues for named products.

The simplest form of named product is a named version of positional products with a product creator (**record**) and a product projector (**select**):

$$E ::= \dots$$
$$| \; (\texttt{record} \; (I_{fieldName} \; E_{fieldDefn})^*) \quad [\text{RecordCreation}]$$
$$| \; (\texttt{select} \; I_{fieldName} \; E_{rcd}) \qquad\quad [\text{RecordProjection}]$$

As above, we assume that such constructs are embedded in a call-by-value language and denote immutable products.

As a simple example of records, consider the following expression, which evaluates to *9*:

```
(let ((r (record (test (= 0 1)) (yes (* 2 3)) (no (+ 4 5)))))
  (if (select test r) (select yes r) (select no r)))
```

The order of bindings in the record constructor is irrelevant, so the value of the above expression would not change if the **record** subexpression were changed to

```
(record ((no (+ 4 5)) (test (= 0 1)) (yes (* 2 3))))
```

Many languages with named products have special syntax for record creation and projection. For instance, here is our example expressed in SML record syntax:

```
let val r = {test=(0=1), yes=2*3, no=4+5}
 in if #test(r) then #yes(r) else #no(r)
end
```

A more common syntax for record selection is the "dot notation" used with C structures, PASCAL records, and JAVA objects, as in:

```
if r.test then r.yes else r.no fi
```

In a language like SML that permits numeric record labels, positional products can be viewed as syntactic sugar for named products. E.g., the SML tuple (true, 17) is syntactic sugar for {1=true, 2=17}.

Simple records can be augmented with operations that parallel many of the extensions for positional products:

(record-size E_{rcd}): Returns the number of components in a record.

(record-insert I E_{val} E_{rcd}): Let v_{rcd} be the record denoted by E_{rcd}. Then the record-insert expression returns a new record that has a binding of I to the value of E_{val} in addition to all the bindings of v_{rcd}. If v_{rcd} already has a binding for I, the new binding overrides it. With named products, record-insert corresponds to both useq-insert and useq-update for positional products.

(record-delete I E_{rcd}): Let v_{rcd} be the record denoted by E_{rcd}. Then the record-delete expression returns a new record that has all the bindings of v_{rcd} except for any with the name I.

The override construct of Section 7.2.3 is a generalization of record-insert that combines two environments, while the conceal construct presented there is a generalization of record-delete. Other forms of record combination and name manipulation are also possible. For instance, it is possible to take the "intersection" or "difference" of two records, or to specify the names that should be kept in a record rather than those that should be concealed.

It is even possible, but rare, to have a named index that can be calculated. In FL, such a construct might have the form (select-sym E_{sym} E_{rcd}), where E_{sym} is an expression denoting a symbol value v_{sym} and select-sym selects from the record denoted by E_{rcd} the value associated with v_{sym}. It would be hard to imagine such a construct in a statically typed language. However, this idiom is often used in dynamically typed languages (especially LISP dialects) in the form of **association lists**, which are lists of bindings between explicit symbols and values.

10.1.3 Nonstrict Products

Our discussion so far has focused on **strict products**, in which the expressions specifying the product components are fully evaluated into values that are stored within the resulting product value. Another option is to have **nonstrict products**, in which the component computations themselves are stored within the product value and are performed only when their values are "demanded." Such products are the default in nonstrict languages like HASKELL, but we will see that there are considerable benefits to integrating nonstrict products into a call-by-value language, which is the focus of this section.

Call-by-Name (CBN) Products

A simple approach to nonstrict products is to adapt the call-by-name parameter-passing mechanism to product formation. We will call the resulting data **call-by-name (CBN) products** in contrast to the **call-by-value (CBV) products** we have studied so far. An operational and denotational semantics for immutable positional CBN products in a call-by-value version of FLIC is presented in Figure 10.2. We use the names `nprod/nget` instead of `prod/get` to syntactically distinguish CBN products from CBV products. This allows us to support both kinds of products in the CBV FLIC language.

In the operational semantics, the delayed computation of CBN product components is modeled by *not* having any evaluation contexts for evaluating the component expressions of an `nprod` expression (but an evaluation context is still needed to evaluate the nonstrict-tuple argument to `nget`). In the denotational semantics, a product value is represented as a sequence of computations rather than as a sequence of values. Intuitively, these computations are "forced" into values only upon projection from the CBN product by the occurrences of *with-value* that are sprinkled throughout the rest of the denotational semantics for CBV FLICK.

As a simple example of how CBN products differ from CBV products, consider the following expression:

```
(let ((c (cell 5)))
  (let ((p (nprod (begin (:= c (+ (^ c) 1)) (^ c))
                  (begin (:= c (* (^ c) 2)) (^ c)))))
    (list (nget 2 p) (nget 1 p) (nget 1 p) (nget 2 p))))
```

The value of this expression is $\triangleleft 10, 11, 12, 24 \triangleright$, indicating that the increments and doublings of the argument expressions are performed at every projection rather than when the CBN product is formed. If we had instead used CBV products, the above expression would yield $\triangleleft 12, 6, 6, 12 \triangleright$, indicating that the

Values

$V \in \mathrm{ValueExp} ::= \ \dots \ | \ (\texttt{nprod} \ E_1 \ \dots \ E_n)$

The AnsExp domain and output function OF would also have to be extended to handle $\texttt{nprod}$ values.

Evaluation Contexts

$\mathbb{E} \in \mathrm{EvalContext} ::= \ \dots \ | \ (\texttt{nget} \ N_{index} \ \mathbb{E})$

New Stateless Reduction Rule

$(\texttt{nget} \ N_{index} \ (\texttt{nprod} \ E_1 \ \dots \ E_n)) \rightsquigarrow E_i, \quad [\text{nget}]$
$\quad$ where $i = \mathcal{N}[\![N_{index}]\!]$ and $1 \leq i \leq n$

Operational semantics for CBN products

New and Modified Semantic Domains

$\quad NProd \ = \ Comp^*$

$v \in Value \ = \ \dots + NProd$

New Computation Operation

$with\text{-}nprod\text{-}and\text{-}checked\text{-}index : Comp \to Int \to (NProd \to Int \to Comp) \to Comp$
The definition is similar to that of $with\text{-}prod\text{-}and\text{-}checked\text{-}index$ in Figure 10.1 on page 543.

New Valuation Clauses

$\mathcal{E}[\![(\texttt{nprod} \ E^*)]\!] \ = \ \lambda e \, . \, (NProd \rightarrowtail Value \ (\mathcal{E}^*[\![E^*]\!] \ e))$

$\mathcal{E}[\![(\texttt{nget} \ N_{index} \ E_{prod})]\!]$
$= \ \lambda e \, . \ with\text{-}nprod\text{-}and\text{-}checked\text{-}index \ (\mathcal{E}[\![E_{prod}]\!] \ e) \ \mathcal{N}[\![N_{index}]\!]$
$\qquad (\lambda c^* i \, . \, (nth \ i \ c^*))$

Denotational semantics for CBN products

Figure 10.2 Operational and denotational semantics for CBN positional products in call-by-value FLICK.

side effects of the argument expressions are performed exactly once, when the product is created.

Lazy (CBL) Products

In CBN products, the component computation is reevaluated at every projection. Another option, inspired by the call-by-need (a.k.a. call-by-lazy) parameter-passing mechanism, is to evaluate the component computation at the very first projection and memoize the resulting value for later projections. We shall call

---

Modified Domains

$LC \in \text{Location} = \text{NatLit}$ *; as usual*

$S \in \text{Store} = \text{Assignment}^*$ *; as usual*

$Z \in \text{Assignment} = \text{Location} \times \text{Exp}$; *use Exp rather than ValueExp*

                                         ; in Figure 8.13 on page 406

$V \in \text{ValueExp} ::= \ \ldots \ | \ (\texttt{*lprod*} \ LC_1 \ \ldots \ LC_n)$

The AnsExp domain and output function *OF* would also have to be extended to handle `*lprod*` values.

Modified Store Operations

$get : \text{Location} \to \text{Store} \rightharpoonup \text{Exp}$; *uses Exp rather than ValueExp*

The definition is similar to that of *get* in Figure 8.13 on page 406.

Evaluation Contexts

$\mathbb{E} \in \text{EvalContext} ::= \ \ldots \ | \ (\texttt{lget} \ N_{index} \ \mathbb{E})$

New Stateful Reduction Rules

$\langle (\texttt{lprod} \ E_1 \ \ldots \ E_n), \ S \rangle$
$\overset{s}{\leadsto} \langle (\texttt{*lprod*} \ LC_1 \ \ldots \ LC_n), \ [\langle LC_1, E_1 \rangle \ldots \langle LC_n, E_n \rangle] \, @ \, S \rangle$ [`lprod`]
    where $LC_1 \ \ldots \ LC_n$ are locations that do not appear in S.

$\langle (\texttt{lget} \ N \ (\texttt{*lprod*} \ LC_1 \ \ldots \ LC_n)), \ S \rangle \overset{s}{\leadsto} \langle V, \ S \rangle,$ [`lget`]
    where $i = \mathcal{N}[\![N]\!], \ 1 \leq i \leq n$, and $(get \ LC_i \ S) = V$

New Evaluation Progress Rule

$$\frac{\langle E, \ S \rangle \Rightarrow \langle E', \ S' \rangle}{\begin{array}{l} \langle \mathbb{E}\{(\texttt{lget} \ N \ (\texttt{*lprod*} \ LC_1 \ \ldots \ LC_n))\}, \ S \rangle \\ \Rightarrow \langle \mathbb{E}\{(\texttt{lget} \ N \ (\texttt{*lprod*} \ LC_1 \ \ldots \ LC_n))\}, \ (\langle LC_i, E' \rangle . S') \rangle \end{array}} \quad [\texttt{lget-}progress]$$
         where $i = \mathcal{N}[\![N]\!], \ 1 \leq i \leq n$, and $(get \ LC_i \ S) = E$

Figure 10.3 Operational semantics for lazy (CBL) products in call-by-value FLICK.

this form of nonstrict product a **lazy (CBL) product**. Using a lazy product in the above example would yield the list $\triangleleft 10, 11, 11, 10 \triangleright$, which indicates that the side effects are performed on the first projection of each component but not on subsequent projections.

The operational semantics of lazy products is presented in Figure 10.3. We use the names `lprod` and `lget` to distinguish lazy products from CBV and CBN products. A lazy product value (introduced by the keyword `*lprod*`) is a sequence of locations in a store that has been extended to map locations to arbitrary expressions, not just value expressions. Only lazy products will make use of this generality; cells will continue to store only values at locations. The new stateful reduction rule [`lprod`] allocates a location to hold each unevaluated

$\langle$(app (lam lp (prim * (lget 1 lp) (lget 1 lp)))
    (lprod (prim + 1 2) (prim - 9 5))), [ ]$\rangle$

$\overrightarrow{CBV}_{[\text{lprod}]}$ $\langle$(app (lam lp (prim * (lget 1 lp) (lget 1 lp)))
    (*lprod* 0 1)),
    $[\langle 0, (\text{prim + 1 2})\rangle, \langle 1, (\text{prim - 9 5})\rangle]\rangle$

$\overrightarrow{CBV}_{[\beta\text{-value}]}$ $\langle$(prim * (lget 1 (*lprod* 0 1)) (lget 1 (*lprod* 0 1))),
    $[\langle 0, (\text{prim + 1 2})\rangle, \langle 1, (\text{prim - 9 5})\rangle]\rangle$

$\overrightarrow{CBV}$ $\langle$(prim * (lget 1 (*lprod* 0 1)) (lget 1 (*lprod* 0 1))),
    $[\langle 0, 3\rangle, \langle 0, (\text{prim + 1 2})\rangle, \langle 1, (\text{prim - 9 5})\rangle]\rangle$

; *This step is justified by both [*lget-progress*] and [+]*

$\overrightarrow{CBV}_{[\text{lget}]}$ $\langle$(prim * 3 (lget 1 (*lprod* 0 1))),
    $[\langle 0, 3\rangle, \langle 0, (\text{prim + 1 2})\rangle, \langle 1, (\text{prim - 9 5})\rangle]\rangle$

$\overrightarrow{CBV}_{[\text{lget}]}$ $\langle$(prim * 3 3), $[\langle 0, 3\rangle, \langle 0, (\text{prim + 1 2})\rangle, \langle 1, (\text{prim - 9 5})\rangle]\rangle$

$\overrightarrow{CBV}_{[*]}$ $\langle 9, [\langle 0, 3\rangle, \langle 0, (\text{prim + 1 2})\rangle, \langle 1, (\text{prim - 9 5})\rangle]\rangle$

Figure 10.4   Evaluation steps in a lazy product example.

component expression. The [lget-*progress*] evaluation progress rule permits the evaluation process to "reach into" the store and perform an evaluation step on a stored expression E, but only when the value of that expression is demanded in an evaluation context as a projection of the ith component of a lazy product. Whatever progress is made in evaluating the configuration $\langle E, S\rangle$ to $\langle E', S'\rangle$ is "remembered" in the store by prepending the assignment $\langle LC_i, E'\rangle$ to S', where LC_i is the location of the ith component of the lazy product. A progress rule (rather than some sort of extended evaluation context) seems to be required here to handle cases in which projecting a lazy product component requires projecting other lazy product components. If the lazy-product projection process eventually massages the stored expression into a value, that value will be memoized at the component location and will be returned directly by every future lget of that component without further evaluation.

For example, Figure 10.4 shows the evaluation steps in a simple example involving a lazy product. Note that the expression (prim + 1 2), which is referenced twice as the first component of the lazy product lp, is evaluated only once. The second component of lp, the expression (prim - 9 5), is never referenced and so is never evaluated. The third step in the evaluation sequence is justified by *two* evaluation rules. First,

$$\langle(\text{prim + 1 2}), S\rangle \overrightarrow{CBV}_{[+]} \langle 3, S\rangle$$

for any store S, including $S_0 = [\langle 0, (\texttt{prim + 1 2})\rangle, \langle 1, (\texttt{prim - 9 5})\rangle]$. Since

```
(prim * (lget 1 (*lprod* 0 1)) (lget 1 (*lprod* 0 1)))
  = (prim * □ (lget 1 (*lprod* 0 1))){(lget 1 (*lprod* 0 1))}
```

the following evaluation step can be justified via the [lget-*progress*] rule in conjunction with the [+] evaluation step:

$\langle$(prim * □ (lget 1 (*lprod* 0 1))){(lget 1 (*lprod* 0 1))}, $S_0\rangle$

$\xRightarrow[\mathit{CBV}]{}$ $\langle$(prim * □ (lget 1 (*lprod* 0 1))){(lget 1 (*lprod* 0 1))},

$(\langle 0, 3\rangle \, . \, S_0)\rangle$

In the denotational semantics for lazy products (Figure 10.5), the memoizing behavior of lazy products is modeled by extending *Storable* to be *Memo*,[4] which includes both values and computations. For a CBV language, we modify the *allocating* function to inject the initial value to be stored in a location into *Memo*, and introduce *allocatingComp* and *allocatingComps* for storing computations in freshly allocated locations. We modify *fetching* so that whenever the content of a location is fetched, any computation stored at that location is evaluated to a value that is memoized at that location. A lazy product itself is modeled as a sequence of locations holding elements of *Memo*.

Nonstrict products may be also added to stateless languages like FL, something we have already seen in our study of CBN pairs in FL (Section 7.1.3). Here we have chosen to focus on the stateful language FLIC for two reasons:

1. It is easier to demonstrate the differences between the three forms of products (prod, nprod, lprod) in a language with state. In stateless FL, CBN and CBL products are observationally indistinguishable, and only termination and errors can be used to distinguish strict and nonstrict products.

2. Explaining the memoization of CBL products requires some form of state, so for presentational purposes it is easier to add these to a language like FLIC that already has state.

Streams

The main benefit of nonstrict products is that they enable the creation of conceptually infinite data structures that improve program modularity. For instance,

---

[4]This domain implies that computations could be stored at any location (such as cell locations), but in fact they can be stored only in lazy-product locations. A practical implementation of lazy products would localize the overhead of memoization to lazy-product component locations so that the efficiency of manipulating cell locations would not be affected.

we can introduce potentially infinite lists, sometimes called **streams**, into a CBV language with the following sugar for `scons` (stream `cons`):

$$(\texttt{scons } E_1 \; E_2) \rightsquigarrow_{ds} (\texttt{lprod } E_1 \; E_2)$$

along with the following definitions:

```
(def (scar s) (lget 1 s))
(def (scdr s) (lget 2 s))
(def snil #u)
(def (snull? s) (unit? s))
```

For example, the stream of all natural numbers can be created via `(from 0)`, where the `from` procedure is defined as

```
(def (from n) (scons n (from (+ n 1))))
```

The fact that the evaluation of the component expression `(from (+ n 1))` is delayed until it is accessed prevents what would otherwise be an infinite recursion if `cons` were used instead of `scons`.

To view a prefix of a stream as a regular list, we can use the following two procedures:

```
(def (prefix n str)
  (cond ((= n 0) snil)
        ((snull? str) (error empty-stream))
        (else (scons (scar str) (prefix (- n 1) (scdr str))))))

(def (to-list str)
  (if (snull? str)
      nil
      (cons (scar str) (to-list (scdr str)))))
```

For example:

```
(to-list (prefix 5 (from 3)))
```
$\xrightarrow[\text{FLIC}]{}$ ⊲3, 4, 5, 6, 7⊳

As illustrated by these examples, streams are a simpler way to represent the sequences of numbers generated by the coroutining iterators presented in Section 9.5. With streams, there is no need for complex manipulation of first-class control points to suspend an iterator process. Instead, the nonstrictness of lazy evaluation automatically effectively suspends the sequence-generating process. Moreover, the fact that streams are a data structure with memoized elements makes them more convenient to use in many situations than a nullary element-generation procedure that returns the next element each time it is called.

Modified Semantics Domains

$mm \in Memo = Comp + Value$

$\quad \sigma \in Storable = Memo$; *like call-by-need semantics in Figure 8.27 on page 435*

$\quad\quad LProd = Location^*$

$\quad v \in Value = \ldots + LProd$

New and Modified Computation Operations

with-lprod-and-checked-index : $Comp \rightarrow Int \rightarrow (LProd \rightarrow Int \rightarrow Comp) \rightarrow Comp$

The definition is similar to that of *with-prod-and-checked-index* in Figure 10.1 on page 543.

allocating : $Value \rightarrow (Location \rightarrow Comp) \rightarrow Comp$
$= \lambda vf . \lambda s . (f \ (\text{fresh-loc } s) \ (\text{assign} \ (\text{fresh-loc } s) \ (Value \rightarrowtail Memo \ v) \ s))$

allocatingComp : $Comp \rightarrow (Location \rightarrow Comp) \rightarrow Comp$
$= \lambda cf . \lambda s . (f \ (\text{fresh-loc } s) \ (\text{assign} \ (\text{fresh-loc } s) \ (Comp \rightarrowtail Memo \ c) \ s))$

allocatingComps : $Comp^* \rightarrow (Location^* \rightarrow Comp) \rightarrow Comp$
$= \lambda c^* f . (\textbf{match } c^*$
$\quad\quad\quad \triangleright [\,]_{Comp} \ [\!] \ (f \ [\,]_{Location})$
$\quad\quad\quad \triangleright (c . c^*) \ [\!] \ allocatingComp \ c \ (\lambda l . (allocatingComps \ c^* \ (\lambda l^* . (f \ (l . l^*)))))$
$\quad\quad\quad \textbf{end })$

fetching : $Location \rightarrow (Value \rightarrow Comp) \rightarrow Comp$
$= \lambda lf . \lambda s . \ \textbf{match} \ (\text{fetch } l \ s)$
$\quad\quad\quad\quad \triangleright (Storable \rightarrowtail AssignedVal \ mm) \ [\!]$
$\quad\quad\quad\quad \textbf{match } mm$
$\quad\quad\quad\quad \triangleright (Value \rightarrowtail Memo \ v) \ [\!] \ (f \ v \ s)$
$\quad\quad\quad\quad \triangleright (Comp \rightarrowtail Memo \ c) \ [\!]$
$\quad\quad\quad\quad\quad with\text{-}value \ c \ (\lambda vs' . (f \ v \ (\text{assign } l \ (Value \rightarrowtail Memo \ v) \ s')))$
$\quad\quad\quad\quad \textbf{end}$
$\quad\quad\quad\quad \triangleright \textbf{else} \ (err\text{-}to\text{-}comp \ \texttt{unassigned-location} \ s)$
$\quad\quad\quad\quad \textbf{end}$

New Valuation Clauses

$\mathcal{E}[\![(\texttt{lprod } E^*)]\!] = \lambda e . (allocatingComps \ (\mathcal{E}^*[\![E^*]\!] \ e) \ (\lambda l^* . (LProd \rightarrowtail Value \ l^*)))$

$\mathcal{E}[\![(\texttt{lget } N_{index} \ E_{prod})]\!]$
$= \lambda e . \ with\text{-}lprod\text{-}and\text{-}checked\text{-}index \ (\mathcal{E}[\![E_{prod}]\!] \ e) \ \mathcal{N}[\![N_{index}]\!]$
$\quad\quad\quad (\lambda l^* i . (fetching \ (nth \ i \ l^*) \ val\text{-}to\text{-}comp))$

Figure 10.5 Denotational semantics for CBL products in CBV FLICK.

```
{A stream of all natural numbers}
(def nats (scons 0 (smap (+ 1) nats)))  {(+ 1) is a curried incrementing proc.}
(to-list (prefix 5 nats)) ────▷ ◁0, 1, 2, 3, 4▷
                           FLIC

{A stream of all even natural numbers}
(def evens (sfilter (abs (x) (= (% x 2) 0)) nats))
(to-list (prefix 5 evens)) ────▷ ◁0, 2, 4, 6, 8▷
                            FLIC

{A stream of all powers of two}
(def twos (scons 1 (smap (* 2) twos)))  {(* 2) is a curried doubling proc.}
(to-list (prefix 5 twos)) ────▷ ◁1, 2, 4, 8, 16▷
                           FLIC

{A stream of all Fibonacci numbers}
(def fibs (scons 0 (scons 1 (smap2 + fibs (scdr fibs)))))
(to-list (prefix 10 fibs)) ────▷ ◁0, 1, 1, 2, 3, 5, 8, 13, 21, 34▷
                            FLIC

{A stream of all prime numbers (created via the sieve of Eratosthenes)}
(def primes
  (recur sieve ((str (from 2)))
    (scons (scar str)
           (sieve (sfilter (abs (x) (not (= (% x (scar str)) 0)))
                           (scdr str))))))
(prefix 10 primes) ────▷ ◁2, 3, 5, 7, 11, 13, 17, 19, 23▷
                    FLIC
```

Figure 10.6   Some sample streams of numbers.

Some of the power of streams is suggested by the examples in Figure 10.6, which use the stream mapping and filtering procedures in Figure 10.7. Note how laziness enables the streams `nats`, `twos`, and `fibs` to all be defined directly in terms of themselves, without the need for an explicit recursive generating function like `from`. The stream of prime numbers, `primes`, is calculated using the sieve of Eratosthenes method, which begins at 2 and keeps as primes only those following integers that are not multiples of previous primes. It is worth emphasizing that all of these examples could be implemented using regular lists (manipulated via `cons`, `car`, and `cdr`) in a call-by-name language or a call-by-need language; special lazy products are necessary only in a call-by-value language.

To appreciate the modularity benefits of the conceptually infinite data structures enabled by nonstrict products, consider the following `first-bigger-than` procedure, which returns the first value in an infinite numeric stream that is strictly bigger than a given threshold `n`.

```
{Returns the stream that results from the elementwise application
 of a unary procedure f to the stream str}
(def (smap f str)
  (if (snull? str)
      snil
      (scons (f (scar str)) (smap f (scdr str)))))

{Returns the stream that results from the elementwise application
 of a binary procedure g to the streams str1 and str2}
(def (smap2 g str1 str2)
  (if (scor (snull? str1) (snull? str2))
      snil
      (scons (g (scar str1) (scar str2))
             (smap2 g (scdr str1) (scdr str2)))))

{Returns a stream with only those elements of str satisfying the predicate pred}
(def (sfilter pred str)
  (cond ((snull? str) snil)
        ((pred (scar str))
         (scons (scar str) (sfilter pred (scdr str))))
        (else (sfilter pred (scdr str)))))
```

Figure 10.7   Mapping and filtering procedures for streams.

```
(def (first-bigger-than n str)
  {no base case since str is assumed to be infinite}
  (if (> (scar str) n)
      (scar str)
      (first-bigger-than n (scdr str))))
(first-bigger-than 1000 nats)   --FLIC-> 1001
(first-bigger-than 1000 evens)  --FLIC-> 1002
(first-bigger-than 1000 twos)   --FLIC-> 1024
(first-bigger-than 1000 fibs)   --FLIC-> 1597
(first-bigger-than 1000 primes) --FLIC-> 1009
```

Infinite lists allow a list-processing termination condition to be specified in the consumer of a list rather than in its producer. With strict lists, all lists must be finite, so the termination condition must be specified when the list is produced. To get the behavior of first-bigger-than with strict lists, it would be necessary to intertwine the details of generating the next element with checking it against the threshold — a strategy that would compromise the modularity of having a separate first-bigger-than procedure.

Exercise 10.5 Write stream versions of the following iterators from Section 9.5:

a. (between *lo hi*) (Figure 9.32)

b. (prefix *n iterator*) (Figure 9.32)

c. (trees *elts*) (Exercise 9.21)

d. (assignments *vars*) (Exercise 9.22)

Exercise 10.6 The **Hamming numbers** are all positive integers whose nontrivial factors are 2, 3, and 5 exclusively.

a. Define a stream of the Hamming numbers. *Hint:* Write auxiliary procedures to scale a stream of integers and to merge sorted streams of integers. What is the first Hamming number strictly larger than 1000?

b. Define an iterator that yields the Hamming numbers one by one.

c. Compare the stream approach to the iterator approach for generating the sequence of Hamming numbers. Which is easier?

Exercise 10.7 Even one-element lazy products are useful simply for delaying and memoizing a computation in the context of an abstraction variously known as a **suspension**, a **promise**, or a **delayed value**. They are often manipulated via the following delay and force constructs:

> (delay E) $\leadsto_{ds}$ (lprod E)
>
> (def (force suspension) (lget 1 suspension))

For example:

```
(let ((c (cell 0)))
  (let ((inc! (abs () (begin (:= c (+ 1 (^ c))) (^ c)))))
    (let ((susp (delay (inc!))))
        {susp is a suspension that will compute (inc!) later}
      (begin (:= c 17)
            (list (force susp) (force susp))))))  FLIC⟶ ⟨18, 18⟩
```

Here, the incrementing of the cell c is delayed (via delay) in the suspension susp and is performed (via force) only after c is set to 17. Once a suspension has been performed, its value is memoized, and subsequent forces return the same value as the first force.

a. In a stateful language like FLICK, lazy products are not necessary to implement delay and force. Give an alternative implementation of these (using desugaring and/or procedure definitions) in the kernel FLICK language without any extensions.

b. Using delay and force from part **a**, show how lprod and lget can be defined as nonkernel constructs in FLICK + {prod, get} (using desugaring and/or procedure definitions).

Exercise 10.8 Many SCHEME implementations support a form of stream created out of pairs where the second component is lazy but the first is not:

```
(cons-stream E₁ E₂) ⤳ds (pair E₁ (lprod E₂))
(def (head str) (fst str))
(def (tail str) (lget 1 (snd str)))
```

a. Show that it is possible to define all lazy lists illustrated in this section as SCHEME streams.

b. Design a stream in which laziness in the first component is essential — that is, a stream that can be defined via `scons`, `scar`, `scdr` but not via `cons-stream`, `head`, `tail`.

Exercise 10.9

a. Use `lprod`/`lget` to define procedures for creating and decomposing potentially infinite binary trees in which each node holds a value in addition to its left and right subtrees.

b. Use your procedures to define an infinite binary tree whose left-to-right breadth-first traversal yields the positive integers in order of magnitude.

c. Define a `breadth-first-elts` procedure that returns a stream of the elements of an infinite binary tree as they would be encountered in a left-to-right breadth-first traversal.

10.1.4 Mutable Products

Thus far we have discussed only immutable products — those whose components do not change over time. But in popular imperative languages, the vast majority of built-in data structures are mutable products. Here we explore some design dimensions of mutable products and some examples of mutable products in real languages.

All of the dimensions we explored above for immutable products are relevant to mutable products. For example, mutable product components are either named or positional. Examples of mutable products with named components include C's structures and PASCAL's records. An example of a fixed-size mutable product with positional components is SCHEME's pairs, whose two components may be altered via `set-car!` and `set-cdr!`. Mutable sequences are typically called arrays (as in C/C++, PASCAL, FORTRAN, and CLU) or vectors (as in SCHEME); JAVA supports both fixed-length mutable sequences (arrays) and dynamically sized mutable sequences (vectors). All of these support the ability to update the component at any index, often via a special subscripting notation, such as the array notation `a[i] = 2*a[i]` in C/C++/JAVA. Only some of these — CLU's arrays and Java's vectors (but not Java's arrays) — support the ability to expand or contract the size of the mutable sequence by inserting or removing elements. All of these examples of mutable products have 0-based indexing except for Fortran (which has 1-based arrays), CLU (whose arrays can have any lower bound but are 1-based by default), and Pascal (whose arrays support arbitrary enumerations as indices). In all of these array and vector examples, all components are required to be of the same type, except for Scheme's vectors (where any slot may contain any value) and Java's vectors (where any slot may contain any object).

Although the mutable products mentioned above seem similar on the surface, their semantics differ in fundamental ways. Below we explore some of the dimensions along which mutable products can differ. For simplicity, we consider only mutable fixed-length positional products of heterogeneous values, which we shall call **mutable tuples**. It is easy to generalize these to other kinds of mutable products. We will study the addition of mutable tuples to FLIC. We assume a CBV parameter-passing mechanism unless otherwise stated.

Here are the constructs we will consider:

$$
\begin{array}{lll}
E ::= & \ldots & \\
& \mid \text{(mprod } E^*_{component}) & \text{[MutableTupleCreation]} \\
& \mid \text{(mget } N_{index} \ E_{mprod}) & \text{[MutableTupleProjection]} \\
& \mid \text{(mset! } N_{index} \ E_{mprod} \ E_{new}) & \text{[MutableTupleAssignment]}
\end{array}
$$

Informally, these constructs have the following semantics:

(mprod E_1 ... E_n): Creates a new mutable tuple with n mutable slots, indexed from 1 to n, where slot i is initially filled with the value of E_i.

(mget N_{index} E_{mprod}): Let $i = \mathcal{N}[\![N_{index}]\!]$ and assume that E_{mprod} evaluates to a mutable tuple v_{mprod} with n slots, where $1 \leq i \leq n$. Then mget returns the value in the ith slot of v_{mprod}. Otherwise, mget signals an error.

(mset! N_{index} E_{mprod} E_{new}): Let $i = \mathcal{N}[\![N_{index}]\!]$ and assume that E_{mprod} evaluates to a mutable tuple v_{mprod} with n slots, where $1 \leq i \leq n$, and E_{new} evaluates to v. Then mset! changes the value in the ith slot of v_{mprod} to be v. Otherwise, mset! signals an error.

For example, here is an expression involving a mutable tuple:

```
(let ((m (mprod 3 4)))
  (begin
    (mset! 1 m (+ (mget 1 m) (mget 2 m)))  {1st slot is now 7}
    (mset! 2 m (+ (mget 1 m) (mget 2 m)))  {2nd slot is now 11}
    (* (mget 1 m) (mget 2 m))))  FLIC→ 77
```

A very simple way to include mutable products in a language is to have a single kind of mutable entity — such as a mutable cell — and allow this entity to be a component of otherwise immutable structures. This is the approach taken in SML, where immutable tuples, vectors, and user-defined data types may have mutable cells as components. We can model this approach in FLIC with the following desugarings for `mprod`, `mget`, and `mset!`:

$(\text{mprod } E_1 \dots E_n) \rightsquigarrow_{ds} (\text{prod } (\text{cell } E_1) \dots (\text{cell } E_n))$

$(\text{mget } N_{index} \; E_{mprod}) \rightsquigarrow_{ds} (\hat{} \; (\text{get } N_{index} \; E_{mprod}))$

$(\text{mset! } N_{index} \; E_{mprod} \; E_{new}) \rightsquigarrow_{ds} (:= (\text{get } N_{index} \; E_{mprod}) \; E_{new})$

In typical imperative languages, a more common design is to directly support various kinds of mutable products, perhaps along with some immutable ones. The CLU language, for example, supports a variety of different built-in data types, each of which comes in both mutable and immutable flavors.

In most imperative languages, mutable products would be modeled as a sequence of locations, as shown in the denotational semantics presented in Figure 10.8, which is a straightforward generalization of the semantics of mutable cells. Mutable tuple values are represented as sequences of locations. This is similar to the representation of lazy products, except that in `mprod`, the computed values of the subexpressions (rather than the computations for these subexpressions) are stored at the locations.

A key issue in the semantics of mutable products is how they are passed as parameters. When mutable products are added as values to the CBV version of FLIC we have studied, we shall say that they are passed via a **call-by-value-sharing (CBVS)** mechanism, because both the caller and the callee share access to the same locations in the mutable product. For example, in the following expression, `t` and `m` in the body of the procedure `f` refer to the same mutable product, so that changes to the components of one are visible in the other:

```
(let ((t (mprod 5 6)))
  (let ((f (abs (m)
              (begin
                (mset! 1 t (* 10 (mget 1 t)))
                (mset! 2 m (* 100 (mget 2 m)))
                (mget 1 m)))))
    (+ (f t) (mget 2 t))))   CBVS FLIC→ 650
```

This is the behavior exhibited for mutable products in languages such as JAVA and SCHEME. Conceptually, when a mutable product is assigned to a variable, passed as a parameter, returned as a result, or stored in a data structure, no new product locations are created; the existing product locations are simply shared in all parts of the program to which the given product value has "flowed."

Modified Semantic Domains

$MProd = Location^*$

$v \in Value = \ldots + MProd$

New Computation Operations

$allocatingVals : Value^* \to (Location^* \to Comp) \to Comp$

$= \lambda v^* f \,.\, \textbf{match } v^*$

$\qquad \triangleright [\,]_{Value} \,\|\, (f\,[\,]_{Location})$

$\qquad \triangleright (v \,.\, v^*) \,\|\, (allocating \; v \; (\lambda l \,.\, (allocatingVals \; v^* \; (\lambda l^* \,.\, (f \; (l \,.\, l^*))))))$

$\qquad \textbf{end}$

Use the following definitions from Figure 8.18 on page 415, where $Storable = Value$ (because FLICK is CBV):

$allocating : Storable \to (Location \to Comp) \to Comp$

$fetching : Location \to (Storable \to Comp) \to Comp$

$update : Location \to Storable \to Comp$

$with\text{-}mprod\text{-}and\text{-}checked\text{-}index : Comp \to Int \to (LProd \to Int \to Comp) \to Comp$

The definition is similar to that of $with\text{-}prod\text{-}and\text{-}checked\text{-}index$ in Figure 10.1 on page 543.

New Valuation Clauses

$\mathcal{E}[\![(\texttt{mprod } E^*)]\!]$

$= \lambda e \,.\, (with\text{-}values \; (\mathcal{E}^*[\![E^*]\!] \; e)$

$\qquad\qquad (\lambda v^* \,.\, (allocatingVals \; v^* \; (\lambda l^* \,.\, (MProd \rightarrowtail Value \; l^*)))))$

$\mathcal{E}[\![(\texttt{mget } N_{index} \; E_{mprod})]\!]$

$= \lambda e \,.\, with\text{-}mprod\text{-}and\text{-}checked\text{-}index \; (\mathcal{E}[\![E_{mprod}]\!] \; e) \; \mathcal{N}[\![N_{index}]\!]$

$\qquad\qquad (\lambda l^* i \,.\, (fetching \; (nth \; i \; l^*) \; val\text{-}to\text{-}comp))$

$\mathcal{E}[\![(\texttt{mset! } N_{index} \; E_{mprod} \; E_{new})]\!]$

$= \lambda e \,.\, with\text{-}mprod\text{-}and\text{-}checked\text{-}index \; (\mathcal{E}[\![E_{mprod}]\!] \; e) \; \mathcal{N}[\![N_{index}]\!]$

$\qquad\qquad (\lambda l^* i \,.\, (with\text{-}value \; (\mathcal{E}[\![E_{new}]\!] \; e) \; (\lambda v_{new} \,.\, (update \; (nth \; i \; l^*) \; v_{new}))))$

Figure 10.8   Denotational semantics of mutable tuples with CBVS parameter passing.

An alternative strategy for passing mutable products in a CBV language is to create a new product with new locations whenever a product is passed from one part of a program to another. This approach, which we shall term **call-by-value-copy (CBVC)** is explained by the denotational semantics in Figure 10.9. Before a value v is passed as an argument to a procedure p, it is "copied" by the *deepCopying* function. Primitive values, pairs, procedures, and locations (i.e., cells) are passed along unchanged, but a mutable tuple with n slots is copied by allocating n new locations and filling these with copies of the contents of the existing locations. In the *allocatingCopies* function, the g argument specifies how

---

New Computation Operations

$allocatingCopies: Location^* \rightarrow (Value \rightarrow (Value \rightarrow Comp) \rightarrow Comp)$
$$\rightarrow (Location^* \rightarrow Comp) \rightarrow Comp$$
$= \lambda l^* gf \;.\; \textbf{match } l^*$
$\qquad \rhd []_{Location} [\![(f \; []_{Location})$
$\qquad \rhd (l_{old} \cdot l^*_{old}) [\![\; fetching \; l_{old}$
$\qquad\qquad\qquad (\lambda v \;.\; g \; v \; (\lambda v' \;.\; allocating \; v'$
$\qquad\qquad\qquad\qquad\qquad (\lambda l_{new} \;.\; allocatingCopies \; l^*_{old}$
$\qquad\qquad\qquad\qquad\qquad\qquad (\lambda l^*_{new} \;.\; (f \; (l_{new} \cdot l^*_{new}))))))$

$deepCopying: Value \rightarrow (Value \rightarrow Comp) \rightarrow Comp$
$= \lambda vf \;.\; \textbf{match } v$
$\qquad \rhd (MProd \rightarrowtail Value \; l^*_{old})$
$\qquad\quad [\![\; (allocatingCopies \; l^*_{old} \; deepCopying \; (\lambda l^*_{new} \;.\; (f \; (MProd \rightarrowtail Value \; l^*_{new}))))$
$\qquad \rhd \textbf{else } f \; v$
$\qquad \textbf{end}$

Modified Valuation Clause

(compare to the CBVS **app** clause in Figure 7.4 on page 317)

$\mathcal{E}[\![(\text{app } E_1 \; E_2)]\!] = \lambda e \;.\; with\text{-}procedure\text{-}comp \; (\mathcal{E}[\![E_1]\!] \; e)$
$\qquad\qquad\qquad\qquad (\lambda p \;.\; with\text{-}value \; (\mathcal{E}[\![E_2]\!] \; e)$
$\qquad\qquad\qquad\qquad\qquad (\lambda v \;.\; (deepCopying \; v \; p)))$

Figure 10.9 Call-by-value-copy (CBVC) semantics for passing mutable tuples.

the components of a mutable tuple should be copied. The kind of data copying performed in Figure 10.9 is known as a **deep copy** because *deepCopying* is supplied as the *g* argument, recursively applying the copying process at all levels of the data. An alternative strategy, known as a **shallow copy**, is to copy only the first level of a data structure and share the contents of the other levels. Although it would be possible to use shallow copying in the CBVC strategy, we do not know of a real programming language that uses this strategy.

In a CBVC interpretation of the example expression considered above for CBVS, the names t and m refer to two distinct mutable tuples, so that changes to the components of one are not visible in the other:

```
(let ((t (mprod 5 6)))
  (let ((f (abs (m)
              (begin
                (mset! 1 t (* 10 (mget 1 t)))
                (mset! 2 m (* 100 (mget 2 m)))
                (mget 1 m)))))
    (+ (f t) (mget 2 t))))   CBVC FLIC  11
```

New Valuation Clause for $\mathcal{LV}$

(this extends $\mathcal{LV}$ for the CBR FLAVAR semantics in Figure 8.27 on page 435)

$\mathcal{LV}[\![(\text{mget } N_{index} \ E_{mprod})]\!]$
$= \lambda e \,.\, \text{with-mprod-and-checked-index} \ (\mathcal{E}[\![E_{mprod}]\!] \ e) \ \mathcal{N}[\![N_{index}]\!]$
$\quad\quad\quad (\lambda l^* i \,.\, (\text{val-to-comp} \ (Location \rightarrowtail Value \ (nth \ i \ l^*))))$

Figure 10.10   Extension to the CBR FLAVAR semantics to handle mutable tuples.

The CBVC strategy for passing mutable products is used for passing arrays and records by value in PASCAL and for passing structures by value in C. On the other hand, arrays in C are passed via CBVS. Passing arrays in C via CBVC can be achieved by embedding an array in a one-component structure! The inconsistency between the mechanisms for passing named versus positional products in C is perplexing from the viewpoint of semantics.

In languages supporting the call-by-reference (CBR) mechanism presented in Section 8.4.3, mutable products introduce new ways to alias locations between the caller and callee. When an `mget` construct is used in a parameter position, its L-value (the location of the product slot, as determined by $\mathcal{LV}$ in Figure 10.10) is passed rather than its R-value (the content of the L-value). In the following CBR example, the L-values of (`mget 2 u`) and `r` denote the same location:

```
(let ((u (mprod 7 8)))
  (let ((g (abs (p r)
              (begin
                (set! r (+ 20 r))
                (mset! 2 p (+ 100 (mget 2 p)))))))
    (begin (g u (mget 2 u))
           (mget 2 u))))  ───────────→  128
                            CBR FLAVAR
```

In contrast, under a CBV interpretation, changes to `r` would not affect `u` and `p`. The above expression would evaluate to 108 under CBVS and 8 under CBVC.

Exercise 10.10   Write a single FLIC expression that returns the symbol `sharing` under CBVS, `deep` under CBVC with deep copying, and `shallow` under CBVC with shallow copying. Your expression should use only symbols, mutable tuples, and procedures.

Exercise 10.11

a. Modify the CBVC denotational semantics in Figure 10.9 to use shallow rather than deep copying.

b. Write three versions of an operational semantics for FLIC with mutable tuples that differ in their parameter-passing mechanism: (1) CBVS (2) CBVC with deep copying (3) CBVC with shallow copying.

10.2   Sums

Here's hoping we meet now and then
It was great fun
But it was just one of those things.

— Cole Porter, "Jubilee"

A **sum** is a data structure that can hold one of several different kinds of values.
Sums are used in situations where programmers use the terms "either" or "one
of" to informally describe a data structure. For example:

- A linked list is either a list node (with head and tail components) or the empty
  list.

- A graphics system might support shapes that are either circles, rectangles, or
  triangles.

- In a banking system, a transaction might be one of deposit, withdrawal, transfer, or balance query.

Intuitively, a sum value pairs an underlying value, which we call its **payload**,
with a **tag** that indicates which kind of value the payload is. Processing a sum
value usually involves performing a case analysis on its tag and manipulating its
payload accordingly. For example, consider a system for manipulating geometric
figures that can either be circles of a given radius or squares of a given side length.
To determine the perimeter of a figure, we need to check its tag, because we can't
determine from the payload alone (a floating point number, say) what kind of
figure it is.

It may seem counterintuitive to view a sum as a pair — after all, isn't a
pair a product? While sums may be *implemented* as pairs, they are not treated
as full-fledged pairs, because the tag and payload are strongly linked and must
not be manipulated separately in an uncoordinated way. For example, a list
node payload should not be tagged with an empty-list tag. Many dynamically
typed languages like LISP do not provide built-in sum types, and programmers use
tag/payload pairs and certain programming idioms to keep the tag and payload in
sync.[5] It can still be valuable to provide support for these idioms in a dynamically
typed language, as we shall see in the extended-number arithmetic example below.

---

[5]Statically typed languages must provide linguistic types to avoid type loopholes that arise
from the ability to set tags and payloads separately. C's `union` and PASCAL's variant record
facility expose the pair representation of sums, and thus suffer from this type loophole.

Sums are data structures that correspond to the sum domains that we have been using in our mathematical metalanguage (see Section A.3.4) to represent mathematical values that can come from several different component domains. In programming languages, sums are known by such names as *tagged sums, unions, tagged unions, discriminated unions, oneofs*, and *variants*. Although sums are a very simple kind of data structure, they are rarely found in their pure form in real-world programming languages. Instead, as we shall see in the next section, sums are typically joined with products to form so-called sum-of-products data structures. Notable exceptions are CLU, which provides both immutable and mutable sum values, and HASKELL, which provides a two-summand positional sum called an `Either`. (Exercise 10.12 explores extending FLIC with a similar feature.) The `union` construct of C creates an *untagged* sum that the programmer must explicitly tag using C's `struct` construct. We will see an example of this in the next section (Figure 10.17 on page 582).

Example: Extended-Number Arithmetic

Consider the problem of defining arithmetic on **extended numbers**, where such a number can be (1) an integer, (2) positive infinity (`+inf`), (3) negative infinity (`-inf`), or (4) undefined (`undef`). Suppose (`int` i) converts an integer i to an extended number and *EN* stands for any extended number. We expect the following rules to hold for the `add` operator on extended numbers:

$$
\begin{aligned}
\text{(add (int } i_1\text{) (int } i_2\text{))} &= \quad \text{(int } (i_1 + i_2)\text{))}\\
\text{(add (int } i\text{) +inf)} = \text{(add +inf (int } i\text{))} &= \text{(add +inf +inf)} = \text{+inf}\\
\text{(add (int } i\text{) -inf)} = \text{(add -inf (int } i\text{))} &= \text{(add -inf -inf)} = \text{-inf}\\
\text{(add +inf -inf)} = \quad \text{(add -inf +inf)} &= \text{undef}\\
\text{(add } EN \text{ undef)} = \quad \text{(add undef } EN\text{)} &= \text{undef}
\end{aligned}
$$

Suppose we use the following conventions for representing extended numbers as sum values:

- All tags are represented as symbols.

- An integer is represented using the `integer` tag and an integer payload.

- The two infinities are represented by the `infinity` tag and a boolean payload (`#t` for `+inf` and `#f` for `-inf`).

- The undefined value `undef` is represented by the `undefined` tag and a `#u` payload.

```
(def (make-sum tag payload) (pair tag payload))
(def (tag oneof) (fst oneof))
(def (payload oneof) (snd oneof))

(def (int num) (make-sum (sym integer) num))
(def +inf (make-sum (sym infinity) #t))
(def -inf (make-sum (sym infinity) #f))
(def undef (make-sum (sym undefined) #u))

(def (add num1 num2)
  (cond ((sym=? (tag num1) (sym integer))
         (if (sym=? (tag num2) (sym integer))
             (int (+ (payload num1) (payload num2)))
             num2))
        ((sym=? (tag num1) (sym infinity))
         (cond ((sym=? (tag num2) (sym integer)) num1)
               ((sym=? (tag num2) (sym infinity))
                (if (bool=? (payload num1) (payload num2))
                    num1
                    undef))
               ((sym=? (tag num2) (sym undefined)) undef)
               ))
        ((sym=? (tag num1) (sym undefined)) undef)
        ))
```

Figure 10.11 Extended-number addition in FL using explicit tags.

Addition on extended numbers with these representations is a good example for illustrating sums because it involves several different kinds of payloads and a nontrivial case analysis. Figure 10.11 shows how extended-number addition can be expressed in FL using tag/payload pairs to represent sum values. The `make-sum` procedure creates such a pair, and the `tag` and `payload` procedures extract its components. The `int` procedure converts an integer to an extended number, and `+inf`, `-inf`, and `undef` are defined as particular sum values. The `add` procedure performs a case analysis on the tags of its arguments to determine the result. When adding two extended integers or two infinities, it is necessary to examine their payloads; in all other cases, the result can be determined from their tags.

Rather than rely on programming conventions, we can support sums directly by adding two new kernel constructs for manipulating sum values:

$E ::= \dots$
   $\mid$ (one I_{tag} $E_{payload}$)   [NamedInjection]
   $\mid$ (tagcase E_{disc} $I_{payload}$ (I_{tag} E_{body})* (else E_{else})$^?$) [NamedCaseAnalysis]

The expression (one I_{tag} $E_{payload}$) creates a sum value, which we shall call a **oneof**, that conceptually pairs the tag name I_{tag} with the payload value denoted by $E_{payload}$. We say that **one injects** the value of $E_{payload}$ into a sum value. We can imagine that **one** is defined by the following desugaring:

(one I_{tag} $E_{payload}$) $\leadsto_{ds}$ (pair (sym I_{tag}) $E_{payload}$)

Oneofs are decomposed with (tagcase E_{disc} $I_{payload}$ (I_{tag} E_{body})*), which evaluates the **discriminant** E_{disc} to what should be a oneof value v_{disc}, and dispatches to the **body clause** (I_i E_i) whose tag I_i matches the tag of v_{disc}. The value of the tagcase expression is the result of evaluating the **body expression** E_i of the matching body clause in a scope where $I_{payload}$ is bound to the payload of v_{disc}. A tagcase expression may have an optional[6] **else** clause whose body E_{else} is used when no body-clause tag matches the discriminant tag. $I_{payload}$ is unbound in the **else** clause. It is an error if E_{disc} does not evaluate to a oneof or if there is no clause in an **else**-less tagcase whose tag matches the discriminant tag. We can imagine that **tagcase** is defined by the following desugaring:

(tagcase E_{disc} $I_{payload}$ (I_i E_i)$_{i=1}^n$ (else E_{else})$^?$)
  $\leadsto_{ds}$ (let ((I_{disc} E_{disc})) $\{I_{disc}$ *fresh*$\}$
       (let ((I_{tag} (fst I_{disc}))) $\{I_{tag}$ *fresh*$\}$
          (cond
             ((sym=? I_{tag} (sym I_i)) (let (($I_{payload}$ (snd I_{disc}))) E_i))$_{i=1}^n$
             (else E_{else})$^?$)))

Figure 10.12 presents a definition of extended-number addition using **one** and **tagcase**. In the **add** procedure, **tagcase** clarifies the case analyses performed on the arguments **num1** and **num2** and highlights the cases where the payload values (**v1** and **v2**) are used instead of the oneofs that carry them.

Using **one** and **tagcase** to abstract over the creation and case analysis of tagged values has several advantages over using explicit pairs. As illustrated by the extended-number addition example, it makes programs that use tagged values easier to read, write, and debug. In Section 11.8.4, we shall see that the ability to associate different types with the payloads of different tags (e.g., the payload for the **integer** tag is an integer whereas the payload for the **infinity** tag is a boolean) allows oneofs to be type-checked. Finally, these abstractions give an implementer the freedom to use more efficient implementations. For instance, if

---

[6]Recall from page 32 that a postfix $^?$ indicates an optional syntactic element.

```
(def (int num) (one integer num))
(def +inf (one infinity #t))
(def -inf (one infinity #f))
(def undef (one undefined #u))

(def (add num1 num2)
  (tagcase num1 v1
    (integer (tagcase num2 v2
               (integer (int (+ v1 v2)))
               (else num2)))
    (infinity (tagcase num2 v2
                (integer num1)
                (infinity (if (bool=? v1 v2) num1 undef))
                (undefined undef)))
    (undefined undef)))
```

Figure 10.12   Extended-number addition in FL using oneofs.

tags are represented as small integers rather than symbols, in `tagcase` they can be used as indices that enable jumping into a dispatch table for `tagcase` clauses rather than linearly checking through all possible tags. In the extended-number example, the `integer`, `infinity`, and `undefined` tags could be represented as 0, 1, and 2, respectively.[7]

Design Dimensions of Sums

In category theory, sum domains are the mathematical dual of product domains: For any theorem about products, there is a dual theorem about sums. This duality carries over to the programming language notions of sums and products. A named product datum (i.e., record) can be viewed as an entity that is created by combining multiple named component values and is decomposed via a projection operator that supplies one named component value of the datum to a single continuation. Dually, a named sum datum (i.e., oneof) can be viewed as an entity

---

[7]Both type checking and the improved tagging scheme require some way of knowing which tags are used together — e.g., extended numbers use one of the three tags `integer`, `infinity`, and `undefined`. This information is not readily apparent in the setting considered here, but can be determined in other settings. For example, it can be explicitly declared by users in the form of data declarations that group related tags (e.g., see Section 10.4 and Section 13.5.4) or in the form of explicit type annotations on the `one` construct (see Section 11.8.4). Tag relationships can also be automatically deduced by a type-reconstruction process; see the discussion of row types in Section 13.5.3.

Values
$V \in \text{ValueExp} ::= \ \ldots \ | \ (\texttt{one} \ I_{tag} \ V_{payload})$

The AnsExp domain and output function OF would also have to be extended to handle $\texttt{one}$ values.

Evaluation Contexts
$\mathbb{E} \in \text{EvalContext} ::= \ \ldots \ | \ (\texttt{one} \ I_{tag} \ \mathbb{E})$
$\qquad\qquad\qquad | \ (\texttt{tagcase} \ \mathbb{E} \ I_{payload} \ (I_{tag} \ E_{body})^* \ (\texttt{else} \ E_{else})^?)$

New Stateless Reduction Rules
$(\texttt{tagcase} \ (\texttt{one} \ I_{tag} \ V_{payload}) \ I_{payload} \ (I_i \ E_i)_{i=1}^n \ (\texttt{else} \ E_{else})^?)$
$\quad \rightsquigarrow [V_{payload}/I_{payload}]E_j, \text{ where } 1 \le j \le n \text{ and } I_{tag} = I_j$ $\qquad$ [tagcase]

$(\texttt{tagcase} \ (\texttt{one} \ I_{tag} \ V_{payload}) \ I_{payload} \ (I_i \ E_i)_{i=1}^n \ (\texttt{else} \ E_{else}))$
$\quad \rightsquigarrow E_{else}, \text{ where } I_{tag} \notin \{I_1, \ldots, I_n\}$ $\qquad\qquad\qquad$ [tagcase-*else*]

Figure 10.13 CBV operational semantics for named sums (oneofs).

that is created by applying an injection operator to one named component value (i.e., a tagged payload) and is decomposed by supplying the datum to multiple named continuations (i.e., the clauses of $\texttt{tagcase}$). Because of this duality, sums vary along the same dimensions as products: e.g., positional versus named, immutable versus mutable, call-by-value versus call-by-name, and dynamically typed versus statically typed. Here, we focus on immutable, dynamically typed call-by-value sums with named components, but other variations (e.g., positional components) are considered in the exercises.

Operational Semantics of Oneofs

We have already given an informal semantics for call-by-value oneofs based on desugaring. A formal operational semantics for call-by-value oneofs is presented in Figure 10.13. The new evaluation contexts evaluate the payload of a $\texttt{one}$ expression and the discriminant of a $\texttt{tagcase}$ expression. The [tagcase] rule is enabled when the discriminant of a $\texttt{tagcase}$ is a value ($\texttt{one} \ I_{tag} \ V_{payload}$), in which case $V_{payload}$ is substituted for $I_{payload}$ in the matching body expression. The [tagcase-*else*] rule is for the case where the oneof tag does not match any of the tagged body clauses, in which case E_{else} is used as the body expression (and $I_{payload}$ is *not* substituted away). Stuck states arise when any of the subexpressions get stuck, when the discriminant does not evaluate to a oneof value, or when the discriminant's tag does not have a matching body in an $\texttt{else}$-less $\texttt{tagcase}$. Call-by-name sums would be treated similarly, except that no attempt would be made to evaluate the expression being injected by $\texttt{one}$.

Denotational Semantics of Oneofs

Figure 10.14 presents the denotational semantics for call-by-value oneofs. It might seem odd that the domain *Oneof* of sum values is modeled by a product domain that pairs an identifier tag and the injected value. But such a product domain is isomorphic to a domain that is an infinite sum, each of whose summands (one for each identifier) is the *Value* domain. That is, for each identifier $I \in$ Ident, imagine we define a domain D_I that is a synonym for *Value*. Then *Oneof* is isomorphic to the sum domain $\Sigma_{I \in \text{Ident}} D_I$.

The valuation clause for (one I_{tag} E) simply creates a oneof value that pairs I_{tag} with the value of E. The two clauses for `tagcase` use elements of the *TagEnv* domain to express how a `tagcase` body expression matching the tag of the discriminant value is found and evaluated. In (`tagcase` E_{disc} $I_{payload}$ $(I_i$ $E_i)_{i=1}^n$), each body expression E_i effectively stands for a "body abstraction" of the form (`abs` $(I_{payload})$ E_i) that will be applied to the payload of the discriminant value if its tag is I_i. If the `tagcase` expression is evaluated in an environment e, then the meaning of this body abstraction is a "body procedure": the element of *Proc* = *Nameable* $\rightarrow$ *Comp* that is $p_i = \lambda n . (\mathcal{E}[\![E_i]\!] \ [I_{payload} \mapsto n]e)$.

Elements of *TagEnv* are **tag environments** that simply bind tag names to body procedures. (*extend-tenv* I_{tag} E_i e $I_{payload}$ t_0) extends an initial tag environment t_0 with a binding of I_{tag} to the body procedure p_i described above. *extend-tenv** is similar, but works for a list of tags and their associated bodies. *empty-tenv* is the tag environment that for any tag I_{tag} returns a body procedure that, when called, gives an error indicating that I_{tag} is unmatched in the `tagcase`.

The valuation clause for an `else`-less `tagcase` looks up the tag I_{tag} of the discriminant oneof value in the tag environment corresponding to the `tagcase`'s body clauses and applies the resulting body procedure to the payload $v_{payload}$ of the oneof. The initial environment for *extend-tenv** in this case is *empty-tenv*, which will lead to an unmatched-tag error if there is no body expression tagged with I_{tag}. Handling a `tagcase` with an `else` clause is similar, except that the initial tag environment for *extend-tenv**, which is used for any tag not mentioned in a body clause, is a tag environment t_{else} that returns a body procedure for E_{else} that does not provide a binding for $I_{payload}$.

The use of tag environments in the denotational semantics of oneofs highlights their duality with records. Records use an environment to glue together named values, one of which is later chosen at each `select` site. Dually, `one` creates a oneof value that is later processed in the context of a `tagcase` that uses a tag environment to glue together named body procedures for processing the payload. In a continuation-based semantics, the tag environments used in the semantics of `tagcase` would map names to continuations for processing the payload.

Exercise 10.12 The simplest kind of positional product is a pair, which glues together two component values. Dually, the simplest kind of positional sum chooses between two component values. Such a sum value is called an **either**. It has two possible tags: *left* or *right*.

Here we consider an extension to FLICK that supports eithers:

$$E ::= \ldots$$
$$| \; (\text{inleft } E_{payload}) \qquad\qquad\qquad \text{[LeftInjection]}$$
$$| \; (\text{inright } E_{payload}) \qquad\qquad\qquad \text{[RightInjection]}$$
$$| \; (\text{ecase } E_{disc} \; I_{payload} \; E_{left} \; E_{right}) \; \text{[EitherAnalysis]}$$

$(\text{inleft } E_{payload})$ creates an either whose tag is *left* and whose payload is the value of $E_{payload}$.

$(\text{inright } E_{payload})$ creates an either whose tag is *right* and whose payload is the value of $E_{payload}$.

$(\text{ecase } E_{disc} \; I_{payload} \; E_{left} \; E_{right})$ examines the discriminant value represented by E_{disc}, binds its payload to the identifier $I_{payload}$, and then evaluates E_{left}, if the tag of the discriminant value is *left*, or E_{right}, if the tag is *right*. It is an error if E_{disc} is not an either.

For example, we can use eithers in a version of FLICK that also has floating point numbers to encode whether a geometric shape is a square (in which case the payload is the length of a side) or a circle (in which case the payload is the radius). We can then write a procedure for computing the area of a shape:

```
(def (square side) (inleft side))
(def (circle radius) (inright radius))
(def pi 3.14159)
(def (area shape)
  (ecase shape v
    (f* v v)  {square case (assume f* multiplies floating point numbers)}
    (f* pi (f* v v)) {circle case}
    ))
```

$$(\text{area (square 10.0))} \; \xrightarrow[\text{FLIC}]{} \; 100.0$$
$$(\text{area (circle 10.0))} \; \xrightarrow[\text{FLIC}]{} \; 314.159$$

a. Write an operational semantics for CBV eithers. What causes stuck states in your semantics?

b. Write a denotational semantics for CBV eithers. You may find it convenient to have a new domain for eithers as well as new *Left* and *Right* domains.

c. In CBN eithers, the expressions $(\text{inleft } E_{payload})$ and $(\text{inright } E_{payload})$ do not tag the *value* denoted by $E_{payload}$ but rather the *computation* denoted by $E_{payload}$. Make any necessary modifications to your semantics for both part **a** and part **b** to support CBN rather than CBV eithers.

New Semantic Domains

$Oneof = \text{Ident} \times Value$

$v \in Value = \ldots + Oneof$

$t \in TagEnv = \text{Ident} \to Proc$

$p \in Proc = Nameable \to Comp \text{ ; as usual}$

New Computation Operation

$\textit{with-oneof-comp} : Comp \to (Oneof \to Comp) \to Comp$

The definition is similar to that of *with-boolean-comp* in Figure 6.26 on page 281.

Operations on the *TagEnv* Domain

$\textit{empty-tenv} : TagEnv = \lambda I\, n\,.\, (\textit{err-to-comp}\ \texttt{unmatched-tagcase-tag})$

$\textit{extend-tenv} : \text{Ident} \to \text{Exp} \to Env \to \text{Ident} \to TagEnv \to TagEnv$
$= \lambda I\, E\, e\, I_{payload}\, t\,.\, (\lambda I'\, n\,.\, \textbf{if}\ I' = I\ \textbf{then}\ (\mathcal{E}[\![E]\!]\ [I_{payload} \mapsto n]e)\ \textbf{else}\ (t\ I'))$

$\textit{extend-tenv}^* : \text{Ident}^* \to \text{Exp}^* \to Env \to \text{Ident} \to TagEnv \to TagEnv$
$= \lambda I^*\, E^*\, e\, I_{payload}\, t\,.\, \textbf{match}\ \langle I^*, E^* \rangle$
$\qquad\qquad\qquad \rhd\ \langle [\,]_{\text{Ident}}, [\,]_{\text{Exp}} \rangle \parallel t$
$\qquad\qquad\qquad \rhd\ \langle I_{fst} \cdot I^*_{rest}, E_{fst} \cdot E^*_{rest} \rangle$
$\qquad\qquad\qquad\quad \parallel\ (\textit{extend-tenv}^*\ I^*_{rest}\ E^*_{rest}\ e\ I_{payload}$
$\qquad\qquad\qquad\qquad\qquad\qquad (\textit{extend-tenv}\ I_{fst}\ E_{fst}\ e\ I_{payload}\ t))$
$\qquad\qquad\qquad \rhd\ \textbf{else}\ \textit{empty-tenv}$
$\qquad\qquad\qquad \textbf{end}$

New Valuation Clauses

$\mathcal{E}[\![(\texttt{one}\ I_{tag}\ E_{payload})]\!]$
$= \lambda e\,.\, \textit{with-value}\ (\mathcal{E}[\![E_{payload}]\!]\ e)$
$\qquad\qquad (\lambda v_{payload}\,.\, (\textit{val-to-comp}\ (Oneof \rightarrowtail Value\ \langle I_{tag},\ v_{payload} \rangle)))$

$\mathcal{E}[\![(\texttt{tagcase}\ E_{disc}\ I_{payload}\ (I_1\ E_1)\ \ldots\ (I_n\ E_n))]\!]$
$= \lambda e\,.\, (\textit{with-oneof-comp}\ (\mathcal{E}[\![E_{disc}]\!]\ e)$
$\qquad\qquad (\lambda \langle I_{tag}, v_{payload} \rangle\,.$
$\qquad\qquad\qquad ((\textit{extend-tenv}^*\ [I_1 \ldots I_n]\ [E_1 \ldots E_n]\ e\ I_{payload}\ \textit{empty-tenv})$
$\qquad\qquad\qquad I_{tag}\ v_{payload})))$

$\mathcal{E}[\![(\texttt{tagcase}\ E_{disc}\ I_{payload}\ (I_1\ E_1)\ \ldots\ (I_n\ E_n)\ (\texttt{else}\ E_{else}))]\!]$
$= \lambda e\,.\, (\textit{with-oneof-comp}\ (\mathcal{E}[\![E_{disc}]\!]\ e)$
$\qquad\qquad (\lambda \langle I_{tag}, v_{payload} \rangle\,.$
$\qquad\qquad\qquad \textbf{let}\ t_{else}\ \textbf{be}\ (\lambda I\, n\,.\, (\mathcal{E}[\![E_{else}]\!]\ e))$
$\qquad\qquad\qquad \textbf{in}\ ((\textit{extend-tenv}^*\ [I_1 \ldots I_n]\ [E_1 \ldots E_n]\ e\ I_{payload}\ t_{else})$
$\qquad\qquad\qquad\qquad I_{tag}\ v_{payload})))$

Figure 10.14 CBV denotational semantics of named sums (oneofs).

Exercise 10.13 The two-summand positional sums considered in Exercise 10.12 can be generalized to positional sums with any number of summands. Just as positional product data structures use integer indices to distinguish product components, positional sums use integer tags to distinguish summands. To add positional sums to FLICK, we extend the kernel expression syntax as follows:

$$E ::= \ldots$$
$$\mid \text{(inj } N \; E_{payload}) \qquad\qquad \text{[PositionalInjection]}$$
$$\mid \text{(sumcase } E_{disc} \; I_{payload} \; E^*_{body}) \; \text{[PositionalCaseAnalysis]}$$

(inj N $E_{payload}$) creates a positional sum value whose tag is N, where N is an integer literal for a positive integer and not a computed value. Positional sum values are taken apart with the expression (sumcase E_{disc} $I_{payload}$ E_1 ... E_n), which evaluates the **discriminant** E_{disc} to what should be a positional sum value, examines the numeric tag N of this positional sum value (which should denote an integer i in the range $[1..n]$), and evaluates E_i with $I_{payload}$ bound to the payload. It is an error if E_{disc} is not a positional sum value or if i is not in the range $[1..n]$.

a. Express the addition of extended numbers in Figure 10.12 using positional sums rather than named sums. Which is better? Why?

b. Write an operational semantics for CBV positional sums. What causes stuck states in your semantics?

c. Write a denotational semantics for CBV positional sums.

d. In CBN positional sums, the expression (inj N $E_{payload}$) does not tag the *value* denoted by $E_{payload}$ but rather tags the *computation* denoted by $E_{payload}$. Modify the operational and denotational semantics for positional sums in part **b** and part **c** to be CBN rather than CBV.

Exercise 10.14

a. Modify the operational semantics for named sums in Figure 10.13 to be call-by-name rather than call-by-value.

b. Modify the denotational semantics for named sums in Figure 10.14 to be call-by-name rather than call-by-value.

c. Write a continuation-based denotational semantics for call-by-name and call-by-value named sums.

10.3   Sum of Products

I think that I shall never see
A matrix lovely as a tree.
. . .
But any fool can plainly see
Inherent flexibility
In data structured as a tree.
. . .
Arrays are used by clods like me,
But only LISP can make a tree.

— Guy L. Steele Jr.

In practice, sum and product data are often used together in idiomatic ways. Many common data structures can be viewed as a tree constructed from different kinds of nodes, each of which has multiple components. Here are some examples:

- A shape in a simple geometry system is either:
  - a circle with a radius;
  - a rectangle with a width and a height;
  - a triangle with three side lengths.

- A list of integers is either:
  - an empty list;
  - a list node with an integer head and an integer-list tail.

- An ELM expression is either:
  - an integer literal;
  - an argument expression with an index;
  - an arithmetic operation with an operator symbol, a left operand expression, and a right operand expression.

In each of the above examples, the variety of possible nodes for a data structure can be modeled as a sum, and each individual kind of node can be modeled as a product. For this reason, such data structures are known as **sum-of-products** structures.

As a simple example, consider the following list of geometric shapes:

```
(list (one rectangle (record (width 3) (height 4)))
      (one triangle (record (side1 5) (side2 6) (side3 7)))
      (one square (record (side 2))))
```

In this encoding, oneof tags are used to distinguish squares, rectangles, and triangles. The two sides of a rectangle (`width` and `height`) and three sides of a triangle (`side1`, `side2`, and `side3`) are named as fields in a record. Even though a square has only a single side length (`side`), it too is encapsulated in a record for uniformity. Of course, we could have used positional rather than named products, in which case the meaning of each position would need to be specified.

Manipulating a sum-of-products datum typically involves performing a case analysis on its tag and extracting the components of the associated record. For example, here is a procedure that calculates the perimeter of a shape:

```
(def (perim shape)
  (tagcase shape r
    (square (* 4 (select side r)))
    (rectangle (* 2 (+ (select width r) (select height r))))
    (triangle (+ (select side1 r)
                 (+ (select side2 r) (select side3 r))))))
```

As another example, consider the sum-of-products encoding of the ELM temperature conversion expression (/ (* 5 (- (arg 1) 32)) 9) shown in Figure 10.15. In this encoding, oneof tags distinguish integer literals (`lit`), arithmetic operations (`arithop`), and argument references (`arg`). The three components of an arithmetic operation — the operation symbol (`op`) and two operands (`rand1` and `rand2`) are represented as a record. As with square shapes, the single number component of a literal expression and the index component of an argument expression are boxed up into records for uniformity.

To handle this representation for ELM expressions, the `elm-eval` procedure from Figure 6.13 on page 243 would be rewritten:

```
(def (elm-eval exp args)
  (tagcase exp r
    (lit (select num r))
    (arg (get-arg (select index r) args))
    (arithop  ((primop->proc (select op r))
               (elm-eval (select rand1 r) args)
               (elm-eval (select rand2 r) args)))))
```

The rigidity of the above sum-of-products encodings is sometimes relaxed in practice. For instance, the case where a product has a single component can be optimized by replacing the product by the component value. If a product has no

```
(one arithop
  (record
    (op (sym /))
    (rand1 (one arithop
             (record
               (op (sym *))
               (rand1 (one lit (record (num 5))))
               (rand2 (one arithop
                        (record
                          (op (sym -))
                          (rand1 (one arg (record (index 1))))
                          (rand2 (one lit (record (num 32)))))))))))
    (rand2 (one lit (record (num 9)))))))
```

Figure 10.15 A sum-of-products encoding of the ELM temperature-conversion expression (/ (* 5 (- (arg 1) 32)) 9).

components, it can be replaced by the unit value. In several popular data structures (including linked lists and binary trees), there are only two summands, one of which has no components. This situation is often handled by representing the nontrivial summand (e.g., list or tree node) directly as a product and representing the no-component summand (e.g., empty list or tree leaf) as a distinguished **null pointer** value. Conceptually, there is still a sum in this case: a value is *either* a null pointer or a node. But pragmatically, it is not necessary to associate a tag with a node because it is assumed that there is a cheap test that determines whether a node is the null pointer. For example, many implementations represent a null pointer as zero to take advantage of (1) efficient machine instructions for testing for zero and (2) the fact that the zero memory address is protected in many architectures (so an attempt to dereference the null pointer causes a segmentation violation).

Programming languages differ widely in terms of their support for sum-of-products data. For example:

- The ML and HASKELL programming languages have powerful facilities for declaring and manipulating sum-of-products data. We shall see similar facilities in Sections 10.4 and 10.5.

- In object-oriented languages, such as JAVA, C++, and SMALLTALK, the dynamic dispatch performed when invoking a method on an object effectively performs a case analysis on the class (effectively a tag) of the object, whose instance variables can be viewed as a record.

- In LISP dialects, it is common to represent a sum-of-products datum as a list s-expression whose first element is a symbolic tag indicating the summand and whose remaining elements are the components of the product. For instance, the Fahrenheit-to-Celsius conversion expression given on page 578 can be represented as the following LISP s-expression:

```
(arithop /
        (arithop *
                (lit 5)
                (arithop - (arg 1) (lit 32)))
        (lit 9))
```

This, in turn, can be optimized without ambiguity into an s-expression identical to the ELM concrete s-expression syntax:

```
(/ (* 5 (- (arg 1) 32)) 9)
```

Indeed, syntax trees are without a doubt the most important sum-of-products data structure used in the study of programming languages. The ease with which they can be represented as s-expressions is the reason we have adopted s-expression grammars for the mini-languages in this book.

- In document-description languages like HTML and XML, summand tags appear in begin/end markups and product components are encoded in the association lists of markups as well as in components nested within the begin/end markups. For instance, Figure 10.16 shows how the Fahrenheit-to-Celsius expression might be encoded in XML. The reader is left to ponder why XML, which essentially is a verbose encoding of s-expressions, is a far more popular standard for expressing structured data than s-expressions. In fact, the WA-TER language [Plu02] goes even further, using XML as a representation for s-expressions in a language with SCHEME-like semantics.

- In the C programming language, programmers must "roll their own" sum-of-products data structures using the **union** and **struct** constructs. For instance, Figure 10.17 shows how the geometric shape example from above can be expressed in C. In C, **union** is used to declare storage that can contain one of several different kinds of values. However, there is no built-in support for tagging such values. Instead, an explicit **struct** is typically used to associate a tag (**shapetag** in the example) with the value (**sum** in the example). Values with multiple components (e.g., **rect** and **tri**) are themselves encoded via additional **struct** declarations.

As is apparent from the example in Figure 10.17, encoding sum-of-products data in C is awkward. Nesting **struct** declarations to provide explicit tags is

```
<arithop>
  <op name="/"/>
  <rand1>
    <arithop>
      <op name="*"/>
      <rand1>
        <lit num="5"/>
      </rand1>
      <rand2>
        <arithop>
          <op name="-"/>
          <rand1>
            <arg index="1"/>
          </rand1>
          <rand2>
            <lit num="32"/>
          </rand2>
        </arithop>
      </rand2>
    </arithop>
  </rand1>
  <rand2>
    <lit num="9"/>
  </rand2>
</arithop>
```

Figure 10.16   The ELM Fahrenheit-to-Celsius expression in XML notation.

cumbersome and leads to unwieldy name paths like `s.sum.rect.width`. But much worse is the fact that the language enforces no connection between the tag and the sum. For instance, consider the following sequence of C statements:

```
shape s4;
s4.tag = square;
s4.sum.rect.width = 8;
s4.sum.rect.height = 9;
printf("The perimeter of s4 is %d\n", perim(s4));
```

Although conceptually it makes no sense to manipulate a rectangle's components in a square, in many C implementations, the above code compiles and runs without error, yielding 32 as the perimeter of s4. Why? Because the storage set aside for a `union` type is that required for the largest summand (in this case, the three integers of a triangle) and `s4.sum.side`, `s4.sum.rect.width`, and `s4.sum.tri.side1` are just synonyms referencing the first slot of this storage.

```
typedef enum {square, rectangle, triangle} shapetag;

typedef struct {
  shapetag tag;
  union {
    int side;
    struct {int width; int height;} rect;
    struct {int side1; int side2; int side3;} tri;
  } sum;
} shape;

int perim (shape s) {
  switch (s.tag) {
  case square:
    return 4*(s.sum.side);
  case rectangle:
    return 2*(s.sum.rect.width + s.sum.rect.height);
  case triangle:
    return (s.sum.tri.side1 + s.sum.tri.side2 + s.sum.tri.side3);
  }
}

int main () {
  shape s1, s2, s3;
  s1.tag = square;
  s1.sum.side = 2;
  s2.tag = rectangle;
  s2.sum.rect.width = 3;
  s2.sum.rect.height = 4;
  s3.tag = triangle;
  s3.sum.tri.side1 = 5;
  s3.sum.tri.side2 = 6;
  s3.sum.tri.side3 = 7;
  printf("The perimeter of s1 is %d\n", perim(s1));
  printf("The perimeter of s2 is %d\n", perim(s2));
  printf("The perimeter of s3 is %d\n", perim(s3));
}
```

Figure 10.17   The shape example encoded using `struct` and `union` in C.

This is a classic example of a **type loophole** in C. PASCAL's variant records, which encode sum-of-products data types in a way reminiscent of C, exhibit a similar type loophole. The same sort of undesirable behavior can be exhibited with the LISP s-expression (`square 8 9`), for which a perimeter procedure would return 32 if the means of extracting the side of a square was returning the second element of an s-expression list. But the difference between LISP and C/PASCAL on this score is that C and PASCAL, unlike LISP, sport a static type system that might be expected to catch such type-related bugs at compile time. We will have much more to say about static typing in Chapter 11.

10.4 Data Declarations

Programming with "raw" sums and products is cumbersome and error-prone. Here we study a high-level facility for data declaration that simplifies the creation and manipulation of sum-of-products data. We extend our FL family of languages with a `def-data` declaration that specifies a new kind of sum-of-products data. We introduce this construct via a declaration for geometric shapes:

```
(def-data shape
  (square side)
  (rectangle width height)
  (triangle side1 side2 side3))
```

This declaration specifies that a shape is either a square with one component, a rectangle with two components, or a triangle with three components. Each of the names `square`, `rectangle`, and `triangle` is a **value constructor procedure** (or just **constructor** for short) that takes the specified number of components and returns a sum-of-products datum with those components. For example, the list of shapes

```
(list (square 2) (rectangle 3 4) (triangle 7 8 9))
```

is equivalent to the list

```
(list (one square (prod 2))
      (one rectangle (prod 3 4))
      (one triangle (prod 5 6 7)))
```

In contrast with Section 10.3, the sum-of-products data created by `def-data` constructors uses positional rather than named products.

In the example, the data name `shape` and the component names `side`, `width`, `height`, etc., are just comments. Only the *number* of components specified for

a constructor is relevant. For instance, we could emphasize that all components
are integers by writing

```
(def-data shape
  (square int)
  (rectangle int int)
  (triangle int int int))
```

or we could use nonsense words to specify an equivalent declaration, as in

```
(def-data frob
  (square foo)
  (rectangle bar baz)
  (triangle quux quuux quuuux))
```

The reason for requiring such comments is that the comment positions will assume
a nontrivial meaning when we study a typed version of def-data in Section 13.5.4.

For every constructor procedure C that takes n arguments, def-data also
declares an associated **deconstructor procedure** that takes three arguments:

1. the value v to be deconstructed;

2. a **success continuation**, an n-argument procedure that is applied to the n
   components of v in the case where v was constructed by C;

3. a **failure continuation**, a nullary procedure that is invoked in the case where
   v was not constructed by C.

We assume a convention in which the deconstructor has a name that is the
name of the constructor followed by the tilde character, ~, which is pronounced
"twiddle." For instance, the square~, rectangle~, and triangle~ deconstructors introduced by the shape declaration can be used to calculate the perimeter
of a shape:

```
(def (perim shape)
  (square~ shape (abs (s) (* 4 s))
    (abs ()
      (rectangle~ shape (abs (w h) (* 2 (+ w h)))
        (abs ()
          (triangle~ shape (abs (s1 s2 s3) (+ s1 (+ s2 s3)))
            (abs ()
              (error not-a-shape)))))))))
```

Deconstructors are somewhat awkward to use directly. In the next section we
will study a pattern-matching facility based on deconstructors that significantly
simplifies the deconstruction of sum-of-products data.

```
(def-data elm-exp
  (lit num)
  (arg index)
  (arithop op rand1 rand2))
(def f2c (arithop (sym /)
                  (arithop (sym *)
                           (lit 5)
                           (arithop (sym -)
                                    (arg 1)
                                    (lit 32)))
                  (lit 9)))
(def (elm-eval exp args)
  (lit~ exp (abs (n) n)
    (abs ()
      (arg~ exp (abs (i) (get-arg i args))
        (abs ()
          (arithop~ exp
            (abs (op r1 r2)
              ((primop->proc op) (elm-eval r1 args) (elm-eval r2 args)))
            (abs () (error not-an-elm-exp)))))))))
```

Figure 10.18   ELM examples.

As another example of constructors and deconstructors, consider the `elm-exp`
declaration in Figure 10.18. The `lit`, `arg`, and `arithop` constructors introduced
by this declaration are illustrated in the Fahrenheit-to-Celsius expression `f2c`,
and the deconstructors `lit~`, `arg~`, and `arithop~` are used to define `elm-eval`.

We can even use `def-data` to define list constructors and deconstructors
(Figure 10.19), replacing the list procedures in the FL standard library defined
in Figure 6.8 (page 236). The standard procedures for pairs can be defined in a
similar fashion (Figure 10.20).

A formal definition of `def-data` is presented in Figure 10.21. The syntax
of FLIC programs is extended to include `def-data` declarations along with the
usual definitions. The meaning of a `def-data` declaration can be explained by
desugaring the declaration into a sequence of procedure definitions via an explicit
desugaring function $\mathcal{DS}_{def}$, which has signature Def → Def*. We assume that
the resulting sequence of definitions is spliced into the `flic` program construct,
and that all program definitions are further desugared by the program desugaring
specified in Figure 6.5 on page 231. Each summand clause $(I_{tag}\ I_1\ \dots\ I_k)$ is
desugared by $\mathcal{DS}_{cl}$ into a sequence of two procedure definitions:

```
(def-data list-data
  (null)
  (cons car cdr))
(def (null? xs)
  (null~ xs (abs () #t) (abs () #f)))
(def nil (null))
(def (car xs)
  (cons~ xs (abs (hd tl) hd)
    (abs () (error car-of-nonlist-or-empty-list))))
(def (cdr xs)
  (cons~ xs (abs (hd tl) tl)
    (abs () (error cdr-of-nonlist-or-empty-list))))
```

Figure 10.19   Defining lists via def-data.

```
(def-data pair-data
  (pair x y))
(def (fst p)
  (pair~ p (abs (x y) x) (abs () (error fst-of-nonpair))))
(def (snd p)
  (pair~ p (abs (x y) y) (abs () (error snd-of-nonpair))))
```

Figure 10.20   Defining pairs via def-data.

1. A k-parameter constructor procedure named I_{tag} that constructs a oneof with tag I_{tag} of a product whose components are its k argument values. The notation $I \bowtie n$ stands for the identifier that results from concatenating the characters of the name I with the digit characters of the numeral for the natural number n. For example, $x \bowtie 3$ denotes the identifier x3. The parameters of the constructor procedure are constructed in this fashion to guarantee that they are distinct — something that may not be true for $I_1, \ldots, I_k$.

2. A three-argument deconstructor procedure that expects a oneof value as its first argument (val). If this oneof has the tag I_{tag}, the deconstructor applies its second argument (a k-argument success continuation, succ) to the k components of the product that is the oneof's payload. Otherwise, it invokes the nullary failure continuation, fail, that is its third argument. The name of this deconstructor procedure is created from the name I_{tag} by adding the character ~ as a suffix. The notation $I_1 \bowtie I_2$ stands for the identifier that results

Modified Syntax

$P ::= (\texttt{flic} \ (I^*_{formal}) \ E_{body} \ D^*_{defn})$ [Program]

$D ::= (\texttt{def} \ I_{name} \ E_{defn})$ [ValueDefinition]

     $| \ (\texttt{def} \ (I_{procName} \ I^*_{formal}) \ E_{body})$ [ProcedureDefinition]

     $| \ (\texttt{def-data} \ I_{data} \ (I_{tag} \ I^*)^*)$ [DataDeclaration]

New Desugaring

$\mathcal{DS}_{def} : \text{Def} \to \text{Def}^*$

$\mathcal{DS}_{def}[\![(\texttt{def-data} \ I_{data} \ (I_{tag_1} \ I_{1,1} \ \ldots \ I_{1,k_1}) \ \ldots \ (I_{tag_n} \ I_{n,1} \ \ldots \ I_{n,k_n}))]\!]$
    $= \mathcal{DS}_{cl}[\![(I_{tag_1} \ I_{1,1} \ \ldots \ I_{1,k_1})]\!] @ \cdots @ \mathcal{DS}_{cl}[\![(I_{tag_n} \ I_{n,1} \ \ldots \ I_{n,k_n})]\!]$
       where $\mathcal{DS}_{cl}[\![(I_{tag} \ I_1 \ \ldots \ I_k)]\!]$

            $= [(\texttt{def} \ (I_{tag} \ \texttt{x}\bowtie\texttt{1} \ \ldots \ \texttt{x}\bowtie k) \ ; \ constructor \ procedure$
                $(\texttt{one} \ I_{tag} \ (\texttt{prod} \ \texttt{x}\bowtie\texttt{1} \ \ldots \ \texttt{x}\bowtie k))),$
             $(\texttt{def} \ (I_{tag}\bowtie\texttt{\~{}} \ \texttt{val succ fail}) \ ; \ deconstructor \ procedure$
                $(\texttt{tagcase val payload}$
                   $(I_{tag} \ (\texttt{succ} \ (\texttt{get 1 payload}) \ \ldots \ (\texttt{get} \ \overline{k} \ \texttt{payload})))$
                       $; \ For \ i \in Int, \ the \ notation \ \overline{i} \ stands \ for$
                       $; \ the \ IntLit \ N \ such \ that \ \mathcal{N}[\![N]\!] = i$
                  $(\texttt{else (fail)})))$
            $]$

Figure 10.21 Syntax and desugaring of `def-data`.

from concatenating the characters of two identifiers. For example, `square`$\bowtie$`~` denotes the identifier `square~`.

For example, Figure 10.22 shows the constructors and deconstructors introduced by the `shape` declaration.

Exercise 10.15 Extend the declaration of `elm-exp` and the definition of `elm-eval` to handle the full EL language presented in Figure 2.4 on page 25.

Exercise 10.16 It is possible to tweak the desugaring of `def-data` to use more efficient representations than those given in Figure 10.21.

a. Modify the `def-data` desugaring to avoid creating products for constructors that take fewer than two arguments.

b. Modify the `def-data` desugaring to represent a sum-of-products datum with tag I_{tag} and components $v_1 \ \ldots \ v_n$ as the heterogeneous sequence

     $(\texttt{seq} \ (\texttt{sym} \ I_{tag}) \ v_1 \ \ldots \ v_n)$

(This desugaring makes sense for a dynamically typed language but not a statically typed one.)

The **shape** declaration

```
(def-data shape
  (square int)
  (rectangle int int)
  (triangle int int int))
```

desugars into the following constructors and deconstructors:

```
(def (square x1)
  (one square (prod x1)))

(def (square~ val succ fail)
  (tagcase val payload
    (square (succ (get 1 payload)))
    (else (fail))))

(def (rectangle x1 x2)
  (one rectangle (prod x1 x2)))

(def (rectangle~ val succ fail)
  (tagcase val payload
    (rectangle (succ (get 1 payload) (get 2 payload)))
    (else (fail))))

(def (triangle x1 x2 x3)
  (one triangle (prod x1 x2 x3)))

(def (triangle~ val succ fail)
  (tagcase val payload
    (triangle (succ (get 1 payload) (get 2 payload) (get 3 payload)))
    (else (fail))))
```

Figure 10.22   Value constructors and deconstructors introduced by the **shape** declaration.

Exercise 10.17 SML and HASKELL support user-defined data-type declarations. Below are the geometric shape declarations expressed in SML and HASKELL:

SML	HASKELL
datatype Shape =	data Shape =
Square of int	Square Int
| Rectangle of int * int	| Rectangle Int Int
| Triangle of int * int * int	| Triangle Int Int Int

In SML, passing multiple arguments to a data constructor is modeled by collecting the arguments into a tuple, as in `Triangle(5,6,7)`, where the tuple `(5,6,7)` has type `int * int * int`. It is a type error to supply the constructor with the wrong number of arguments, as in `Triangle(5,6)`.

In contrast, HASKELL data declarations allow curried constructors that can take multiple arguments one at a time. For instance, the invocation `Triangle 5 6` denotes a unary function that "expects" the third side of the triangle.

Is FL extended with `def-data` more like ML or HASKELL in this respect? For example, does (`triangle 5 6`) denote an error or a unary function? How would you change the desugaring of `def-data` to model the other language?

Exercise 10.18 The desugaring for `def-data` in Figure 10.21 introduces two procedures for each summand clause (I_{tag} I_1 ... I_k) — a constructor I_{tag} and a deconstructor $I_{tag}\bowtie\tilde{}$. An alternative approach is to introduce $k + 2$ procedures:

- A k-argument constructor procedure named I_{tag}.

- A unary predicate named $I_{tag}\bowtie$? that returns true for a oneof value with tag I_{tag} and false for any other oneof value. It is an error to apply this predicate to a value that is not a oneof value.

- k unary selector procedures named I_1 ... I_k, where I_i extracts the ith component of a product tagged with I_{tag}. It is an error to apply a selector procedure to a value that is not a oneof value or a oneof value with a tag that is not I_{tag}.

In this approach, the component names matter, since they are names of selectors, not just comments. For example, here is the `perim` procedure in this approach:

```
(def (perim s)
  (cond ((square? s) (* 4 (side s)))
        ((rectangle? s) (* 2 (+ (width s) (height s))))
        ((triangle? s) (+ (side1 s) (+ (side2 s) (side3 s))))
  ))
```

a. Give a desugaring for `def-data` that implements the new approach.

b. In your new desugaring, compare the evaluation of the conditional clause

```
        ((triangle? s) (+ (side1 s) (+ (side2 s) (side3 s))))
```

with the following deconstructor application in the original desugaring

```
        (triangle~ s (abs (s1 s2 s3) (+ s1 (+ s2 s3)))
          (abs () (error not-a-shape)))
```

Which evaluation is more efficient?

c. One drawback of having `def-data` desugar into so many procedures is that it increases the possibility of name conflicts. For instance, the `shape` declaration introduces procedures with names like `square`, `rectangle?`, and `width` that very well might be useful in other contexts. One way to address this problem is for programmers to use more specific names within data declarations, as in:

```
        (def-data shape
          (shape-square shape-side)
          (shape-rectangle shape-width shape-height)
          (shape-triangle shape-side1 shape-side2 shape-side3))
```

Another approach is to modify the desugaring for `def-data` to automatically concatenate the data name with the name of every constructor, predicate, and selector procedure. For instance, something like this is done in COMMON LISP's `defstruct` facility. Discuss the benefits and drawbacks of these two ways to address potential name conflicts in a program with data declarations.

d. Yet another way to address name conflicts is to treat constructor, predicate, and selector applications as kernel constructs that refer to a different namespace than the usual value namespace. Design an extension to FL that handles data declarations based on this idea. Do you think it is a good way to handle name conflicts?

10.5   Pattern Matching

10.5.1   Introduction to Pattern Matching

Deconstructors are a sufficient mechanism for dispatching on and extracting the components of sum-of-products data, but they are awkward to use in practice. It is more convenient to manipulate sum-of-products data using a **pattern matching** facility that simultaneously tests for a summand and names the components of the associated product when the test succeeds. We have made extensive use of a form of pattern matching (via the **match** construct) in the mathematical metalanguage of this book. Pattern matching is also an important feature of some real-world programming languages, such as PROLOG, ML, and HASKELL.

We will study pattern matching in the context of an extension to FL that includes `def-data` from the previous section along with a new `match` construct. First we will give an informal introduction to `match` via a series of examples. Then we will describe the semantics of `match` in detail by desugaring it into deconstructor applications.

The `match` construct has the form (`match` E_{disc} (PT_{pat} E_{body})*), where E_{disc} is the **discriminant** and each **match clause** of the form (PT_{pat} E_{body}) has a **pattern** PT_{pat} and a **body** E_{body}. A pattern PT consists of either an FL literal value, an identifier, a wild card[8] (_), or a constructor application pattern:

$$PT \in \text{Pattern} ::= L \qquad\qquad\qquad\ \text{[Literal]}$$
$$\mid I \qquad\qquad\qquad\ \ \text{[PatternVariable]}$$
$$\mid \_ \qquad\qquad\qquad\ \ \text{[WildCard]}$$
$$\mid (I_{constr}\ PT^*) \ \ \text{[ConstructorApplication]}$$

A `match` expression is evaluated by first evaluating E_{disc} into a value v_{disc}, then finding the first clause whose pattern PT_i matches v_{disc}, and finally evaluating

---

[8]We assume that the definition of Ident is modified so that it no longer contains _ as an identifier.

the associated body E_i of this clause relative to any bindings introduced by the successful match of v_{disc} to PT_i. If no clause has a pattern that matches v_{disc}, the match expression signals an error.

A literal pattern matches only the same literal value and does not introduce any bindings. An identifier pattern I matches any value v and binds I to v in the clause body. A wildcard pattern _ also matches any value v but does not introduce any bindings. Intuitively, a constructor application pattern $(I_{constr}\ PT_1\ ...\ PT_n)$ matches a value that could be the result of a constructor application $(I_{constr}\ v_1\ ...\ v_n)$. In this case, the patterns $PT_1\ ...\ PT_n$ are recursively matched against the values $v_1\ ...\ v_n$, and all bindings introduced by a successful matching process are available in the clause body.

We begin with a few examples of match involving patterns that are just literals, identifiers, or wild cards. Here is a procedure that converts a boolean to an integer (and signals an error for a nonboolean input).

```
(def (bool->int b)
  (match b
    (#f 0)
    (#t 1)))
```

The negate procedure below returns a symbol that negates the sense of a yes or no input but returns unknown for any other input. The underscore pattern is a wildcard pattern that matches any discriminant.

```
(def (negate s)
  (match s
    ((sym yes) (sym no))
    ((sym no) (sym yes))
    (_ (sym unknown))))
```

The following procedure returns one more than the square of a given number, except at the inputs −1 and 1, where it returns 0:

```
(def (squarish n)
  (match (* n n)
    (1 0)
    (x (+ 1 x))))
```

A pattern variable like x successfully matches any discriminant value, and the name may be used to denote this value in the associated body expression.

To introduce constructor application patterns, we consider pattern matching involving lists of integers. Consider the following two procedures, in which cons and null are constructors from the list-data declaration in Figure 10.19 on page 586:

```
(def (match-ints-1 ints)
  (match ints
    ((cons x (null)) (* x x))
    (_ 17)
    ))

(def (match-ints-2 ints)
  (match ints
    ((cons x (null)) (* x x))
    ((cons 3 (cons y ns)) (+ y (length ns)))
    (_ 17)
    ))
```

- The pattern (cons x (null)) matches a list that contains exactly one element, and names that element x in the scope of the body. So both procedures return the square of the first (only) element of the list when given a singleton list.

- The pattern (cons 3 (cons y ns)) matches a list that has at least two elements, the first of which is the integer 3. In the case of a match, the body is evaluated in a scope where the second element is named y and the list of all but the first two elements is named ns. So when this pattern matches, the second procedure returns the sum of the second element and the length of the rest of the list.

- The final wildcard pattern in both procedures matches any value not matched by the first two patterns, in which case a 17 is returned.

The following table shows the results returned by these two procedures when supplied with various integer lists as an argument:

	(list)	(list 3)	(list 3 4)	(list 6 8)	(list 3 6 8)
match-ints-1	17	9	17	17	17
match-ints-2	17	9	4	17	7

One restriction on patterns not reflected in the Pattern grammar is that the same variable name may not be used twice in the same pattern. For example, the pattern (cons x (cons x ns)) is illegal. To match lists whose first two elements are the same, the pattern (cons x (cons y ns)) can be used along with a body beginning with the test (if (equal? x y) ...).

The most important use of match is to perform pattern matching on user-defined sum-of-products data. For instance, here is a succinct version of the perimeter procedure of Section 10.4 based on pattern matching:

```
(def (perim shape)
  (match shape
    ((square s) (* 4 s))
    ((rectangle w h) (* 2 (+ w h)))
    ((triangle s1 s2 s3) (+ s1 (+ s2 s3))))))
```

The pattern (square s) matches a sum-of-products value constructed by the
constructor application (square v_{side}), in which case s names v_{side} in the body
of the match clause. Similarly, the pattern (rectangle w h) matches a value
constructed by (rectangle v_{width} v_{height}), where w names v_{width} and h names
v_{height}. The triangle pattern is handled similarly.

Examples involving the ELM language nicely illustrate the elegant conciseness of pattern matching. Figure 10.23 presents a complete ELM expression
evaluator based on pattern matching. The twelve lines of code are easy to understand and analyze. A compelling use of nested patterns is in the crude algebraic
simplifier for ELM expressions in Figure 10.24. The second match clause in
the simp procedure expresses the fact that literals and argument references are
self-evaluating (i.e., they simplify to themselves). The first clause simplifies an
arithop by simplifying the arguments and then attempting to further simplify
the resulting arithop. simp-arithop handles six special cases. The first four
clauses express the facts that zero is an identity for addition and one is an identity
for multiplication. The next two clauses capture the fact that multiplication by
zero yields zero.[9] In order to appreciate the succinctness of pattern matching,
the reader is encouraged to express the simp procedure in a version of FL that
does not support pattern matching.

All the examples so far are "well typed" in the sense that the discriminant of
the match is "expected" to be a particular type (e.g., a list of integers, a shape,
an ELM expression) and the results of all the clause bodies in a given match
have the same type as each other. But in a dynamically typed language, match
is not required to have this behavior, as indicated by the following example:

```
(def (dynamic x)
  (match x
    ((0 #f)
    (#t (sym zero))
    ((sym one) 17))))
```

In Chapter 11, we will study a statically typed version of FL in which dynamic
will not be a legal procedure. However, all the other match examples above will
still be legal.

---

[9]This is not a safe transformation when the other subexpression signals an error!

```
(def (elm-eval exp args)
  (match exp
    ((lit n) n)
    ((arg i) (get-arg i args))
    ((arithop op r1 r2)
     ((primop->proc op) (elm-eval r1 args) (elm-eval r2 args)))))

(def (get-arg index nums)
  (match (pair index nums)
    ((pair 1 (cons n _)) n)
    ((pair i (cons _ ns)) (get-arg (- i 1) ns))))

(def (primop->proc name)
  (match name
    ((sym +) +) ((sym -) -) ((sym *) *) ((sym /) /) ((sym %) %)))
```

Figure 10.23 A complete ELM evaluator based on pattern matching. This assumes the `def-data` declaration for ELM expressions in Figure 10.18 on page 585 and the declarations for list and pair data in Figures 10.19 and 10.20.

10.5.2   A Desugaring-based Semantics of `match`

In order to motivate the structure of the desugaring of `match`, which is rather complex, we will incrementally develop the desugaring in the context of some concrete `match` examples rather than simply present the final desugaring. We begin with the `bool->int` procedure from the previous subsection:

```
(def (bool->int b)
  (match b
    (#f 0)
    (#t 1)))
```

It would be natural to desugar the `match` in `bool->int` into a series of `if` expressions:

```
(def (bool->int b)
  (if (equal? b #f)
      0
      (if (equal? b #t)
          1
          (error no-match))))
```

The case where `b` is not a boolean is handled by an explicit `error` expression indicating that the value of the discriminant did not match the pattern of any `match` clause.

```
(def (simp exp)
  (match exp
    ((arithop p r1 r2) (simp-arithop (arithop p (simp r1) (simp r2))))
    (x x)))

(def (simp-arithop exp)
  (match exp
    ((arithop (sym +) (lit 0) x) x)
    ((arithop (sym +) x (lit 0)) x)
    ((arithop (sym *) (lit 1) x) x)
    ((arithop (sym *) x (lit 1)) x)
    ((arithop (sym *) (lit 0) _) (lit 0))
    ((arithop (sym *) _ (lit 0)) (lit 0))
    (_ exp)))
```

Figure 10.24 An algebraic simplifier for ELM expressions.

In general, the discriminant of a `match` will be an arbitrary expression whose value should be calculated only once. To avoid recalculation of the discriminant, our `match` desugaring first names the discriminant (using `let`) and then performs a case analysis on the name. As shown in Exercise 10.23, this name can be eliminated when it is not necessary. For example, in `bool->int`, the discriminant is already bound to the variable `b`. Here is a revised desugaring for `bool->int` that names the discriminant:[10]

```
(def (bool->int b)
  (let ((disc b))
    (if (equal? disc #f)
        0
        (if (equal? disc #t)
            1
            (error no-match)))))
```

Whenever a mismatch between a pattern and a discriminant value is discovered, the matching process should stop processing the pattern in the current `match` clause and begin processing the pattern in the next `match` clause. When we study the desugaring of constructor application patterns later, we will see that such a mismatch may be discovered at many different points in the processing of a given pattern. To avoid replicating the code that begins processing the pattern in the next `match` clause, our desugaring will wrap this code into a **failure thunk** that may potentially be invoked from several different points in the desugared

---

[10]In the examples, all new identifiers introduced by the desugaring are assumed to be fresh so they do not clash with any program variables.

code. Here is a version of the desugaring for `bool->int` that includes failure
thunks named `fail1` and `fail2`:

```
(def (bool->int b)
  (let ((disc b))
    (let ((fail1 (abs ()
                   (let ((fail2 (abs () (error no-match))))
                     (if (equal? disc #t)
                         1
                         (fail2))))))
      (if (equal? disc #f)
          0
          (fail1)))))
```

In the simple `match` within `bool->int`, each failure thunk is invoked exactly once.
But soon we will see examples in which the failure thunk is invoked multiple times.
In the case where the failure thunk is invoked zero or one times, it is possible for
the desugarer to avoid introducing a named failure thunk. We leave this as an
exercise (see Exercise 10.23).

The discussion so far leads to a first cut for the `match` desugaring, shown in
Figure 10.25. The desugaring of `match` is performed by $\mathcal{DS}_{match}$. For simplicity,
we assume that all `match` constructs are first eliminated by $\mathcal{DS}_{match}$ in a separate
pass over the program before other FL desugarings are performed. It is possible
to merge all desugarings into a single pass, but that would make the description
of the `match` desugaring more complex.

$\mathcal{DS}_{match}$ first introduces the fresh name I_{disc} for the value of the discriminant expression E_{disc} and then processes the `match` clauses with $\mathcal{DS}_{clauses}$. The
$\mathcal{DS}_{clauses}$ function takes three arguments: (1) a list of clause patterns, (2) a list
of clause body expressions, and (3) the identifier naming the discriminant. The
third argument allows the desugarer to refer to the discriminant by its identi-
fier when processing the clauses. The $\mathcal{DS}_{clauses}$ function uses $\mathcal{DS}_{pat}$ to process
the first pattern and body expression in a context where the fresh identifier I_{fail}
names the failure thunk that processes the rest of the clauses. When no clauses
remain, the desugarer yields an `error` expression that will be reached only when
the desugared code for processing the clauses finds no pattern that matches the
discriminant.

The core of the `match` desugaring is the $\mathcal{DS}_{pat}$ function. This takes four
arguments: (1) the pattern being matched, (2) the identifier naming the discriminant, (3) the **success expression** that is evaluated when the pattern matches
the discriminant, and (4) the name of the failure thunk that is invoked when the
pattern does not match the discriminant. A literal pattern is an easy case. The
desugared code first compares the literal and the discriminant via the equality
operator $equal_L$. In a dynamically typed language, $equal_L$ is just the generic

$\mathcal{DS}_{match} : \mathrm{Exp} \to \mathrm{Exp}$

$\mathcal{DS}_{match}[\![(\texttt{match}\ E_{disc}\ (PT_1\ E_1)\ \ldots\ (PT_n\ E_n))]\!] =$
  $(\texttt{let}\ ((I_{disc}\ E_{disc}))\ ;\ I_{disc}\ \text{is fresh}$
    $(\mathcal{DS}_{clauses}\ [PT_1, \ldots, PT_n]\ [E_1, \ldots, E_n]\ I_{disc}))$

$\mathcal{DS}_{clauses} : \mathrm{Pattern}^* \to \mathrm{Exp}^* \to \mathrm{Ident} \to \mathrm{Exp}$

$\mathcal{DS}_{clauses}\ []\ []\ I_{disc}\ =\ (\texttt{error no-match})$

$\mathcal{DS}_{clauses}\ (PT_1 . PT^*_{rest})\ (E_1 . E^*_{rest})\ I_{disc}\ =$
  $(\texttt{let}\ ((I_{fail}\ ;\ I_{fail}\ \text{is fresh}$
          $(\texttt{abs}\ ()\ ;\ \textit{Failure thunk: if } PT_1 \textit{ doesn't match, try the other clauses}$
             $(\mathcal{DS}_{clauses}\ PT^*_{rest}\ E^*_{rest}\ I_{disc}))))$
    $(\mathcal{DS}_{pat}[\![PT_1]\!]\ I_{disc}\ E_1\ I_{fail}))$

$\mathcal{DS}_{pat} : \mathrm{Pattern} \to \mathrm{Ident} \to \mathrm{Exp} \to \mathrm{Ident} \to \mathrm{Exp}$

$\mathcal{DS}_{pat}[\![L]\!]\ I_{disc}\ E_{succ}\ I_{fail}\ =\ (\texttt{if}\ (\texttt{equal}_L\ I_{disc}\ L)\ E_{succ}\ (I_{fail}))$

$\mathcal{DS}_{pat}[\![\_]\!]\ I_{disc}\ E_{succ}\ I_{fail}\ =\ \ldots\ \textit{to be added} \ldots$

$\mathcal{DS}_{pat}[\![I]\!]\ I_{disc}\ E_{succ}\ I_{fail}\ =\ \ldots\ \textit{to be added} \ldots$

$\mathcal{DS}_{pat}[\![(I_{constr}\ PT_1\ \ldots\ PT_n)]\!]\ I_{disc}\ E_{succ}\ I_{fail}\ =\ \ldots\ \textit{to be added} \ldots$

Figure 10.25 A first cut of the `match` desugaring.

equality-testing procedure `equal?`, but when desugaring `match` in a statically typed language (as in Section 13.5.4 or in Section 15.4.6), the equality operator $\texttt{equal}_L$ depends on the domain of the literal L. If the literal and discriminant are the same, the success expression is evaluated; otherwise, the failure thunk is invoked, which will either process the next `match` clause (if there is one) or signal a `no-match` error (if there is no next clause).

The literal case is the only $\mathcal{DS}_{pat}$ case that is needed to explain the `bool->int` desugaring. The desugarings for the other three types of patterns (wild cards, identifiers, and constructor applications) are not shown in Figure 10.25 but will be fleshed out in the following discussion.

We first consider the wildcard pattern, as used in the `negate` procedure:

```
(def (negate s)
  (match s
    ((sym yes) (sym no))
    ((sym no) (sym yes))
    (_ (sym unknown))))
```

The wildcard pattern always matches the discriminant, so the desugarer can simply emit the success expression for this case:

$$\mathcal{DS}_{pat}[\![\_]\!]\ I_{disc}\ E_{succ}\ I_{fail}\ =\ E_{succ}$$

The result of desugaring the `match` expression within the `negate` procedure is

```
(def (negate s)
  (let ((disc s))
    (let ((fail1
            (abs ()
              (let ((fail2
                      (abs ()
                        (let ((fail3 (abs ()
                                       (error no-match))))
                          (sym unknown))))
                (if (equal? disc (sym no)) (sym yes) (fail2))))))
      (if (equal? disc (sym yes)) (sym no) (fail1)))))
```

It turns out that `fail3` can never be referenced, so the subexpression

```
(let ((fail3 (abs () (error no-match))))
  (sym unknown))
```

could simply be replaced by `(sym unknown)`. This optimization could be performed by the desugarer itself or by a post-desugaring optimization pass (see Exercise 10.23).

The case of patterns that are identifiers is similar to the wildcard case, except that the success expression must be evaluated in an environment where the identifier is bound to the value of the discriminant:

$$\mathcal{DS}_{pat}[\![I]\!] \; I_{disc} \; E_{succ} \; I_{fail} = (\texttt{let} \; ((I \; I_{disc})) \; E_{succ})$$

As an example, consider the `squarish` procedure introduced above:

```
(def (squarish n)
  (match (* n n)
    (1 0)
    (x (+ 1 x))))
```

After the `match` expression within `squarish` is desugared, the procedure becomes:

```
(def (squarish n)
  (let ((disc (* n n)))
    (let ((fail1
            (abs ()
              (let ((fail2 (abs () (error no-match))))
                (let ((x disc))
                  (+ x 1))))))
      (if (equal? disc 1)
          0
          (fail1)))))
```

As in the `negate` example, the creation of the innermost failure thunk can be
eliminated by an optimization (see Exercise 10.23). Note that the binding of the
discriminant (`* n n`) to an identifier (`disc`) is significant here: (`* n n`) would
otherwise be evaluated twice. If the discriminant expression performed any side
effects, this would be a semantic issue as well as an efficiency concern.

The last case for $\mathcal{DS}_{pat}$ is a constructor application pattern of the form
(I_{constr} PT_1 ... PT_n). Recall that I_{constr} in this case is some sort of constructor procedure, such as `cons` or `triangle` in the earlier pattern-matching
examples. Handling this case is tricky because it requires decomposing a constructed discriminant value into parts and recursively matching the subpatterns
PT_1 ... PT_n against these parts. A deconstructor procedure is just the right
tool for decomposing the discriminant and matching the subpatterns:

$$\mathcal{DS}_{pat}[\![(I_{constr} \ PT_1 \ \ldots \ PT_n)]\!] \ I_{disc} \ E_{succ} \ I_{fail} =$$
$$(I_{constr} \bowtie^{\sim} I_{disc}$$
$$\quad (\texttt{abs} \ (I_1 \ \ldots \ I_n) \ \ ; \textit{Fresh identifiers for components}$$
$$\quad \quad ; \textit{Body (call it } E_{pats}\textit{) matches the component parts of the constructed value}$$
$$\quad \quad (\mathcal{DS}_{pats} \ [PT_1, \ldots , PT_n] \ [I_1, \ldots , I_n] \ E_{succ} \ I_{fail}))$$
$$\quad I_{fail})$$

$$\mathcal{DS}_{pats} \ [\,] \ [\,] \ E_{succ} \ I_{fail} = E_{succ}$$
$$\mathcal{DS}_{pats} \ (PT_1 \ . \ PT^*_{rest}) \ (I_1 \ . \ I^*_{rest}) \ E_{succ} \ I_{fail} =$$
$$\quad \mathcal{DS}_{pat}[\![PT_1]\!] \ I_1 \ (\mathcal{DS}_{pats} \ PT^*_{rest} \ I^*_{rest} \ E_{succ} \ I_{fail}) \ I_{fail}$$

The $\mathcal{DS}_{pat}$ function processes a constructor application pattern (I_{constr} PT_1 ...
PT_n) by emitting code that invokes the deconstructor associated with I_{constr}
on the discriminant value denoted by I_{disc}, a success continuation whose body
(call it E_{pats}) is constructed by $\mathcal{DS}_{pats}$, and the current failure thunk, denoted
by I_{fail}. The E_{pats} expression is constructed by recursively matching the patterns
PT_1 ... PT_n against the components of I_{disc} denoted by the success continuation
parameters I_1 ... I_n relative to the initial success expression E_{succ} and the failure
thunk I_{fail}. Observe that I_{fail} is the same for all invocations of $\mathcal{DS}_{pat}$ and $\mathcal{DS}_{pats}$ in
the processing of a single `match` clause, and that this I_{fail} denotes the failure thunk
that processes the rest of the `match` clauses. This means that should there be
any mismatch between the patterns and the component values of the discriminant
when E_{pats} is evaluated, I_{fail} will be invoked, terminating the attempt to match
the current `match` clause against the discriminant and starting to match the next
`match` clause against the discriminant. On the other hand, if no mismatch is
found when E_{pats} is evaluated, then the initial success expression E_{succ} will be
evaluated in a context where all pattern variables are bound to the appropriate
discriminant-component values.

As concrete examples of desugaring constructor application patterns, we will study the desugarings of `match` within the `match-ints-1` and `match-ints-2` procedures presented earlier. Recall that `match-ints-1` was defined as follows:

```
(def (match-ints-1 ints)
  (match ints
    ((cons x (null)) (* x x))
    (_ 17)
    ))
```

Here is a version of `match-ints-1` in which the `match` expression has been desugared:

```
(def (match-ints-1 ints)
  (let ((disc ints))
    (let ((fail1 (abs ()
                   (let ((fail2 (abs ()
                                  (error no-match))))
                     17))))
      (cons~ disc
        (abs (v1 v2)
          (let ((x v1))
            (null~ v2
              (abs () (* x x))
              fail1)))
        fail1)))))
```

If the value denoted by `ints` and `disc` is a singleton list, then the `cons~` and `null~` deconstructors will both succeed, and `(* x x)` will be evaluated in an environment where `x` is bound to the single element (denoted by `x` and `v1`). If the discriminant is not a singleton list, then one of `cons~` or `null~` will invoke the failure continuation `fail1`, which returns the 17 specified in the second clause.

The code generated by the desugarer for `match-ints-1` is inefficient in many respects. By making the desugarer cleverer and/or transforming the result of the desugarer by a simple optimizer, it is possible to generate the following more compact and efficient code:

```
(def (match-ints-1 ints)
  (let ((fail1 (abs () 17)))
    (cons~ ints
      (abs (v1 v2)
        (null~ v2
          (abs () (* v1 v1))
          fail1))
      fail1)))
```

As a second example of desugaring constructor application patterns, reconsider `match-ints-2`:

```
(def (match-ints-2 ints)
  (match ints
    ((cons x (null)) (* x x))
    ((cons 3 (cons y ns)) (+ y (length ns)))
    (_ 17)
    ))
```

The `match` desugaring functions yield the desugared definition in Figure 10.26. Everything is the same as the desugaring for `match-ints-1` except that the failure thunk `fail1` now corresponds to matching the second and third clauses of the `match` within `match-ints-2` and the failure thunk `fail2` now corresponds to matching the third clause. Note how the desugaring guarantees that the expression (+ y (length ns)) is evaluated in an environment that contains correct bindings for the names y and ns. Also observe that the second clause pattern (cons 3 (cons y ns)) can fail to match the discriminant for three distinct reasons, all of which cause the invocation of the failure thunk `fail2`:

1. the discriminant `disc` is not a pair;

2. the discriminant `disc` is a pair whose first element `v3` is not 3;

3. the discriminant `disc` is a pair whose first element `v3` is 3 but whose second element `v4` is not a pair.

In general, a failure thunk is invoked in only two situations: (1) a literal is not equal to the value it is matched against or (2) a deconstructor invokes the failure thunk as its failure continuation when the discriminant does not match the associated constructor.

With the handling of constructor application patterns, we have completed the presentation of the desugaring of `match`. Whew! The complete desugaring rules for `match` are presented in Figure 10.27. Recall that we assume that the usual FL desugaring is performed on the expression resulting from the `match` desugaring.

We have presented an approach to pattern matching based on desugaring and deconstructors. But this is by no means the only way to specify or implement pattern matching. For instance, the dynamic semantics for the core language of SML [MTHM97] treats pattern matching as a fundamental language feature that is explained via operational semantics rules. Whereas the deconstructor-based desugaring requires linearly testing the `match` clauses, one by one, in order, the SML definition does not imply a particular implementation. Indeed, there are clever implementations of SML pattern matching that can greatly reduce the number of tests that need to be performed [BM85].

```
(def (match-ints-2 ints)
  (let ((disc ints))
    (let ((fail1
            (abs ()
              (let ((fail2
                       (abs ()
                         (let ((fail3 (abs ()
                                        (error no-match))))
                           17))))
                (cons~ disc
                  (abs (v3 v4)
                    (if (equal? v3 3)
                        (cons~ v4
                          (abs (v5 v6)
                            (let ((y v5))
                              (let ((ns v6))
                                (+ y (length ns))))))
                        fail2)
                    (fail2)))
                fail2)))))
      (cons~ disc
        (abs (v1 v2)
          (let ((x v1))
            (null~ v2
              (abs () (* x x))
              fail1)))
        fail1))))
```

Figure 10.26   The result of desugaring `match` in `match-ints-2`.

Exercise 10.19 If `match` were a kernel expression rather than syntactic sugar, it would be necessary to define the free identifiers of `match`. Extend *FrIds* to handle `match` expressions.

Exercise 10.20 Extend the `match` desugaring to handle record and oneof patterns:

$$PT ::= \ldots \mid (\text{one } I_{tag}\ PT_{payload}) \mid (\text{record } (I_{field}\ PT_{field})^*)$$

As an example of such patterns, consider the following alternative definition of the perimeter procedure.

$\mathcal{DS}_{match}$: Exp $\to$ Exp

$\mathcal{DS}_{match}[\![$(match E_{disc} $(PT_1$ $E_1)$ $\ldots$ $(PT_n$ $E_n))]\!]$ =
  (let $((I_{disc}$ $E_{disc}))$; I_{disc} is fresh
    $(\mathcal{DS}_{clauses}$ $[PT_1 \ldots PT_n]$ $[E_1, \ldots, E_n]$ $I_{disc}))$

$\mathcal{DS}_{clauses}$: Pattern* $\to$ Exp* $\to$ Ident $\to$ Exp

$\mathcal{DS}_{clauses}$ $[]$ $[]$ I_{disc} = (error no-match)

$\mathcal{DS}_{clauses}$ $(PT_1 \,.\, PT^*_{rest})$ $(E_1 \,.\, E^*_{rest})$ I_{disc} =
  (let $((I_{fail}$; I_{fail} is fresh
        (abs () ; Failure thunk: if PT_1 doesn't match, try the other clauses
          $(\mathcal{DS}_{clauses}$ PT^*_{rest} E^*_{rest} $I_{disc}))))$
  $(\mathcal{DS}_{pat}[\![PT_1]\!]$ I_{disc} E_1 $I_{fail}))$

$\mathcal{DS}_{pat}$: Pattern $\to$ Ident $\to$ Exp $\to$ Ident $\to$ Exp

$\mathcal{DS}_{pat}[\![L]\!]$ I_{disc} E_{succ} I_{fail} = (if (equal$_L$ I_{disc} L) E_{succ} $(I_{fail}))$

$\mathcal{DS}_{pat}[\![\_]\!]$ I_{disc} E_{succ} I_{fail} = E_{succ}

$\mathcal{DS}_{pat}[\![I]\!]$ I_{disc} E_{succ} I_{fail} = (let $((I$ $I_{disc}))$ $E_{succ})$

$\mathcal{DS}_{pat}[\![(I_{constr}$ PT_1 $\ldots$ $PT_n)]\!]$ I_{disc} E_{succ} I_{fail} =
  $(I_{constr}\bowtie^{\sim}$ I_{disc}
    (abs $(I_1$ $\ldots$ $I_n)$; Fresh identifiers for components
      ; Body (call it E_{pats}) matches the component parts of the constructed value
      $(\mathcal{DS}_{pats}$ $[PT_1, \ldots, PT_n]$ $[I_1, \ldots, I_n]$ E_{succ} $I_{fail}))$
    $I_{fail})$

$\mathcal{DS}_{pats}$: Pattern* $\to$ Ident* $\to$ Exp $\to$ Ident $\to$ Exp

$\mathcal{DS}_{pats}$ $[]$ $[]$ E_{succ} I_{fail} = E_{succ}

$\mathcal{DS}_{pats}$ $(PT_1 \,.\, PT^*_{rest})$ $(I_1 \,.\, I^*_{rest})$ E_{succ} I_{fail} =
  $\mathcal{DS}_{pat}[\![PT_1]\!]$ I_1 $(\mathcal{DS}_{pats}$ PT^*_{rest} I^*_{rest} E_{succ} $I_{fail})$ I_{fail}

Figure 10.27 The final version of the `match` desugaring.

```
(def (perim shape)
  (match shape
    ((one square (record (side s)))
     (* 4 s))
    ((one rectangle (record (width w) (height h)))
     (* 2 (+ w h)))
    ((one triangle (record (side1 s1) (side2 s2) (side3 s3)))
     (+ s1 (+ s2 s3)))
    ))
```

Exercise 10.21 The definition of lists in Figure 10.19 on page 586 allows `cons` and `null` to be used in patterns. But it would be nice to handle `list` patterns as well:

$$PT ::= \ldots \mid (\text{list } PT^*_{elt})$$

For example:

```
(def (match-list ints)
  (match ints
    ((list x) (+ x 1))
    ((list _ y) (* 2 y))
    ((list x y 3) (* x y))
    (_ 0)
    ))
```

```
(match-list (list))    ⟶ 0
             FL
(match-list (list 4))    ⟶ 5
             FL
(match-list (list 7 8))    ⟶ 16
             FL
(match-list (list 5 4 3))    ⟶ 20
             FL
(match-list (list 3 4 5))    ⟶ 0
             FL
(match-list (list 1 2 3 4))    ⟶ 0
             FL
```

Extend the `match` desugaring to handle `list` patterns.

Exercise 10.22 Consider the following procedure for removing duplicates from a sorted list of integers:

```
(def (remove-dups sorted-list)
  (match sorted-list
    ((cons x (cons y zs))
     (if (= x y)
         (remove-dups (cons y zs))
         (cons x (remove-dups (cons y zs)))))
    (_ sorted-list)
    ))
```

Matching with nested constructor application patterns helps to extract the first two elements (`x` and `y`) of a list with at least two elements. But it is inelegant to name the remainder of such a list (`zs`) and to rebuild the tail of `sorted-list` via (`cons y zs`).

One way to avoid these problems is to use nested `match` constructs:

```
(def (remove-dups-2 sorted-list)
  (match sorted-list
    ((cons x ys)
     (match ys
       ((cons y _)
        (if (= x y)
            (remove-dups ys)
            (cons x (remove-dups ys))))
       (_ sorted-list)))
    (_ sorted-list)
    ))
```

But this is verbose and requires duplication of the last `match` clause, (_ `sorted-list`).

A more elegant approach is to introduce patterns of the form (`<->` *I PT*). When such a pattern is matched against a value *v*:

- if *PT* matches *v*, then (`<->` *I PT*) also matches *v*, and the environment is extended with a binding between *I* and *v* as well as with any bindings implied by the match of *PT* against *v*;

- if *PT* does not match *v*, then (`<->` *I PT*) does not match *v*.

For example, with named patterns, `remove-dups` can be elegantly expressed as:

```
(def (remove-dups-3 sorted-list)
  (match sorted-list
    ((cons x (<-> ys (cons y _)))
     (if (= x y)
         (remove-dups ys)
         (cons x (remove-dups ys))))
    (_ sorted-list)
    ))
```

Extend the `match` desugaring to handle `<->` patterns and show the result of your extended `match` desugaring for `remove-dups-3`.

Exercise 10.23 Modify the `match` desugaring functions and/or define a post-desugaring optimizer to make the desugared code more compact and efficient. You should handle at least the following optimizations:

- Optimize unnecessary renamings of the form (`let` ((I_1 I_2)) ...). E.g., the expression (`let` ((x v1)) (* x x)) should be replaced by (* v1 v1).

- Eliminate the creation of failure thunks that are never used. E.g., the expression (`let` ((fail (`abs` () E_1))) E_2) should be replaced by E_2 if `fail` is not free within E_2.

- Eliminate the naming of failure thunks that are referenced only once. The single reference should be replaced by the thunk itself. E.g., the expression

  (`let` ((fail E_1)) (`cons`~ E_2 E_3 fail))

  should be replaced by (`cons`~ E_2 E_3 E_1).

- Optimize the application of an explicit thunk. E.g., ((`abs` () E)) should be replaced by E.

10.5.3 Views

While the deconstructor-based desugaring of pattern matching may be inherently inefficient compared to other approaches, it provides an important advantage in expressiveness for the programmer. In languages like ML and HASKELL, sum-

of-products data types can be deconstructed only by referencing the constructor
in a pattern context. But using `match`, programmers can define arbitrary deconstructors from scratch and use them in patterns.

As an example, consider the `snoc`[11] procedure, which postpends an element
to the back of a list:

```
(def (snoc xs x)
  (if (null? xs)
      (list x)
      (cons (car xs) (snoc (cdr xs) x))))
```

It is often handy to have a deconstructor corresponding to `snoc` that decomposes
a nonempty list L into two values: the list of all elements in L excluding the last,
and the last element L. This can be expressed with the following deconstructor:[12]

```
(def (snoc˜ xs succ fail)
  (if (null? xs)
      (fail)
      (if (null? (cdr xs))
          (succ nil (car xs))
          (snoc˜ (cdr xs)
                 (abs (but-last last)
                   (succ (cons (car xs) but-last) last))
                 (abs () (error cant-fail))))))
```

For example:

```
(snoc˜ (list 1 2 3)
  (abs (ns n) (cons n ns))
  (abs () nil)) ⎯FL→ ◁3, 1, 2▷
```

Because of the way the `match` desugaring is defined, it is possible to invoke
`snoc˜` by referencing `snoc` in a pattern context, even though `snoc` was not defined
as a constructor in a `def-data`. For example, here is a compact definition of a
quadratic-time list-reversal procedure using `snoc˜` via pattern matching:

```
(def (reverse xs)
  (match xs
    ((null) xs)
    ((cons _ (null)) xs)
    ((snoc ys y) (cons y (reverse ys)))))
```

---

[11]So called because it is a "backward `cons`."

[12]An alternative approach to defining `snoc˜` would be to express it in terms of two auxiliary
procedures, one of which returns all but the last element of a nonempty list and the other of
which returns the last element of a nonempty list. In such a definition, `snoc˜` would walk over
the given list twice. The definition given above effectively uses the success continuation to return
multiple values and walks over the given list only once.

The ability to choose from multiple deconstructors when decomposing a data structure characterizes what is known as a **views facility**, so called because it allows a compound data value to be viewed from different perspectives depending on the context [Wad87]. For example, among the many possible views of a nonempty length-n list are

- the `cons` view: the list is the first element prepended to a list containing elements 2 through n.

- the `snoc` view: the list is the nth element postpended to the sublist containing elements 1 through $(n - 1)$.

- the `split` view: a list is the result of appending a left sublist (elements 1 through $\lceil n/2 \rceil$) and a right sublist (elements $\lceil n/2 \rceil + 1$ through n).

- the `interleave` view: a list is the result of interleaving a list containing all the odd-indexed elements with a list containing all the even-indexed elements.

- the `join` view: the list is the result of sandwiching element $\lceil n/2 \rceil$ between a left sublist (elements 1 through $\lceil n/2 \rceil - 1$) and a right sublist (elements $\lceil n/2 \rceil + 1$ through n).

These views show up in many standard list algorithms. For instance, the `interleave` (or `split`) view is at the heart of a merge sort algorithm for sorting lists:

```
(def (merge-sort nums)
  (match nums
    ((null) nums)
    ((cons _ (null)) nums)
    ((interleave ms ns) {Could decompose with split as well}
     (merge (merge-sort ms) {merge left as an exercise}
            (merge-sort ns)))))
```

In addition to allowing compound data to be decomposed via pattern matching in different ways in different contexts, the views facility provided by user-defined deconstructor procedures helps to overcome a key drawback of ML- and HASKELL-style pattern matching: the lack of abstraction in patterns. While such patterns are wonderful for concisely specifying algorithms that manipulate sum-of-products data, the fact that they expose concrete implementation details hinders program development by making it difficult to change the implementation of data abstractions.

As an example of the sort of flexibility lost with ML-style patterns, consider a simple implementation of binary trees with integers stored in the leaves:

```
(def (node left right) (prod left right))
(def (leaf n) n)
(def (leaf? t) (integer? t))
(def (left t) (get 1 t))
(def (right t) (get 2 t))
```

Given these basic tree-manipulation primitives, we can define many other tree procedures. For example:

```
(def (sum t)
  (if (leaf? t)
      t
      (+ (sum (left t))
         (sum (right t)))))

(def (height t)
  (if (leaf? t)
      0
      (+ 1 (max (height (left t))
                (height (right t)))))))
```

Suppose we wish to modify this implementation so that each node additionally keeps track of its height. This can be accomplished with only minor changes:

```
(def (node left right)
  (prod left right
        (+ 1 (max (height left)
                  (height right)))))

(def (height t) (get 3 t))
```

No other changes need to be made. In particular, procedures like sum that do not use the height remain unchanged.

Now instead suppose that we used sum-of-products data and pattern matching to implement the initial version of trees, where nodes did not maintain their height (Figure 10.28).

Let's now modify the nodes so that they maintain a height component. If we want node to remain a two-argument procedure, in an ML-style system, we must give a different name (say, hnode) to the constructor that takes a third argument, the height. In every pattern that uses node, we must change the constructor name to hnode and add an extra pattern to each hnode match clause to account for the height component (Figure 10.29).

```
(def-data int-tree
  (leaf int)
  (node left right))

(def (sum t)
  (match t
    ((leaf n) n)
    ((node l r) (+ (sum l) (sum r)))))

(def (height t)
  (match t
    ((leaf _) 0)
    ((node l r)
     (+ 1 (max (height l) (height r))))))
```

Figure 10.28 Integer binary trees expressed via def-data and match.

```
(def-data int-tree
  (leaf int)
  (hnode left right height))

(def (node l r)
  (hnode l r (+ 1 (max (height l) (height r)))))

(def (sum t)
  (match t
    ((leaf n) n)
    ((hnode l r _) (+ (sum l) (sum r)))))

(def (height t)
  (match t
    ((leaf _) 0)
    ((hnode l r h) h)))
```

Figure 10.29 Adding a height component requires changing all node patterns.

It might seem easy to make these changes. But suppose we have hundreds of tree procedures in our program that needed to be changed in this manner. It would be tedious and error-prone to make the change everywhere — so much so that we might avoid making such representation changes. The concrete nature of ML-style patterns thus stands in the way of a software engineering principle that dictates that programming languages should be designed in such a way as to facilitate changing representations.

A view mechanism like explicit deconstructors addresses this issue. When we introduce **hnode**, in addition to defining a new **node** procedure that has the same meaning as the old **node** constructor, we can define a new **node~** deconstructor:

```
(def (node~ val succ fail)
  (match val
    ((leaf _) (fail))
    ((hnode l r h) (succ l r))))
```

With this deconstructor, the original definition of **sum** that used **node** in its **match** clause need not be modified even though the representation of nodes has changed. In this way, user-defined deconstructors (and view facilities in general) facilitate representation changes to programs.

Exercise 10.24 Define the list deconstructors **split~**, **interleave~**, and **join~** described in the discussion on views. Give examples of algorithms where such views are helpful.

Exercise 10.25 Define a **partition~** deconstructor for a nonempty list of integers L that decomposes it into three parts:

a. the first element of L (known as the **pivot**);

b. a list of all elements in the tail of L less than or equal to the pivot (with the same relative order as in L);

c. a list of all elements in the tail of L that are strictly greater than the pivot (with the same relative order as in L).

Using your **partition~**, it should be possible to define the quicksort algorithm for sorting lists:

```
(def (quicksort nums)
  (match nums
    ((null) nums)
    ((cons _ (null)) nums)
    ((partition pivot lesses greaters)
     (append (quicksort lesses)
             (cons pivot (quicksort greaters)))))))
```

Exercise 10.26 The convention of naming deconstructors by extending the constructor name with the suffix ~ is really just a crude but simple way of associating a deconstructor with a constructor. Here we consider an alternative way to specify this association.

Suppose that FL is extended with a declaration construct, `def-constructor`, that associates a constructor name with *two* procedures: a constructor and its associated deconstructor. Using this construct, new list constructors `kons` and `knull` could be specified as follows:

```
(def-constructor kons
  (abs (elt lst) (pair elt lst))   {Constructor}
  (abs (val succ fail)             {Deconstructor}
    (if (pair? val)
        (succ (left pair) (right pair))
        (fail)))
)

(def-constructor knull
  (abs () #u)           {Constructor}
  (abs (val succ fail)  {Deconstructor}
    (if (unit? val) (succ) (fail)))
)
```

The intention is that the name declared by `def-constructor` can be used within expressions to denote the constructor procedure and within patterns to denote the deconstructor procedure. Sometimes it is necessary to access the deconstructor procedure within an expression; for this case, FL is also extended with a new expression (`decon` I) that accesses the "deconstructor part" of I. For example:

```
(kons 1 (kons 2 (knull)))  ──→  ◁1, 2▷
                           FL
```

```
(match (kons 1 (kons 2 (knull)))
  ((kons x (kons y (knull))) (+ x y)))  ──→  3
                                        FL
```

```
((decon kons) (kons 1 (kons 2 (knull)))
   (abs (hd tl) (kons hd (kons hd tl)))
   (abs () (kons 5 (knull))))  ──→  ◁1, 1, 2▷
                                FL
```

```
((decon kons) (knull)
   (abs (hd tl) (kons hd (kons hd tl)))
   (abs () (kons 5 (knull))))  ──→  ◁5▷
                                FL
```

The `match` desugaring for this extended version of FL is the same as before except that within $\mathcal{DS}_{pat}$, the occurrence of $I\bowtie$~ is replaced by (`decon` I).

a. One way to model the semantics of (`def-constructor` I E_1 E_2) is to say that it binds the name I to the *pair* of values that result from evaluating E_1 and E_2. Extend the denotational semantics of FL to reflect this model, and explain (1) the meaning of `def-constructor`, (2) the application of constructors, and (3) the semantics of `decon`.

b. Another way to model the semantics of (`def-constructor` I E_1 E_2) is to say that the extended version of FL has *two* namespaces: one for "normal" values (including constructors) and one for deconstructors. Extend the denotational semantics of FL to reflect this model, and explain (1) the meaning of `def-constructor`, (2) the application of constructors, and (3) the semantics of `decon`.

c. What are the benefits and drawbacks of using `def-constructor` and `decon` versus the convention of naming deconstructors with a ~?

Notes

Although algorithms have traditionally been described in terms of mutable data structures, algorithms using immutable data structures can be very elegant and surprisingly efficient [Oka98].

As emphasized by Hughes in [Hug89], lazy data structures (and laziness in general) enhance modularity between producers and consumers of data by allowing termination conditions to be chosen by the consumer rather than the producer. Lazy data structures effectively establish a coroutine between producers and consumers and constitute a much simpler mechanism for doing so than the iterator mechanism presented in Section 9.5. Compelling examples of streams and other lazy data structures can be found in [Hug89, Bir98, Tho99], [ASS96, Sections 3.5 and 4.4].

Not only can streams express coroutines, they can also represent a sequence of choices made in a backtracking system. This is nicely illustrated in [ASS96, Section 4.4], where streams are used to implement backtracking in a logic programming language. A formal correspondence between streams and the success/failure continuation approach to backtracking (see Section 9.2.7) has been shown in [WV04].

Numerous examples of sum-of-products data types with pattern matching can be found in textbooks for ML (e.g., [Pau96, Ull97, CM98, Hic08]) and HASKELL (e.g., [Bir98, Tho99, Hud00]).

An early description of a compiler for ML-style pattern-matching is in [Aug85]. An efficient pattern-matching compiler is presented in [Wada]. [Ses96] derives an efficient pattern-matching compiler from an inefficient one. The use of decision trees to improve ML pattern matching is described in [BM85]. This techinque is applicable only in strict dialects of ML like SML and OCAML, where match clauses can be examined in any order. In lazy dialects, pattern matching is sensitive to clause ordering.

The data-type facility and associated desugaring-based pattern matcher described in this chapter were developed by Jonathan Rees in 1989. The SCHEME+

language described in the Web Supplement includes similar facilities. Another data-declaration and pattern-matching facility for SCHEME is described in [WD94].

Sum and product data types have elegant descriptions in category theory (in which the notions of sum and product are dual) [Pie91]. Such descriptions have inspired generalizations of list operations like `map` and `foldr` on general recursive sum-of-products data types (e.g., see [MFP91]).

The kinds of data structures supported by a language can influence the way programmers solve problems. In [Bac78], Backus argues that applicative languages manipulating compound structures like sequences, arrays, and matrices free programmers from one-word-at-time programming and allows them to focus on the big picture. This style of programming, in which programs can be expressed in terms of higher-order operators that generate, map, filter, and accumulate compound data, was pioneered by LISP (using lists) and APL (using arrays). This style is also an elegant and effective way to describe algorithms for massively parallel processing systems (e.g., see [HS86a, Sab88, Ble90]). The MapReduce model [DG08] for the parallel processing of enormous data sets extracted from the Web is a shining example of the practical utility of this style.

Part III

Static Semantics

11

Simple Types

Type of the wise who soar, but never roam,
True to the kindred points of heaven and home
— William Wordsworth, "To a Skylark"

11.1 Static Semantics

Our emphasis until this point has been the **dynamic semantics** of programming languages, which covers the meaning of programming language constructs and the run-time behavior of programs. We will now shift our focus to **static semantics**, in which we describe properties of programs that can be determined without executing them.

Programs have both dynamic and static properties:

- A **dynamic property** is one that can be determined in general only by executing the program. Such a property is determined at **run time** — i.e., when the program is executed.

- A **static property** is one that can be determined without executing the program. Unlike a dynamic property, a static property must be independent of the particular argument values on which a parameterized program is invoked. A static property can be determined at **analysis time** — i.e., when the program is analyzed before execution. In many implementations, program analysis is performed by the compiler, in which case it happens at **compile time**. However, a program may be analyzed without compiling it (i.e., translating it to another, usually lower-level, language), so we distinguish these two times in general. When a program is compiled, we will generally assume that analysis time precedes compile time, though certain kinds of analysis may be performed during or even after compilation.

For instance, consider the following FL program:

```
(fl (n)
  (let ((sq (abs (x) (* x x))))
    (if (int? n)
        (+ (sq (- n 1)) (sq (+ n 1)))
        0)))
```

We assume that the program input n can be any input expression in InputExp. The result of the program is a dynamic property, because it cannot be known until run time what input will be entered by the user. However, there are numerous static properties of this program that can be determined at analysis time:

- the free identifiers of the program body are int?, +, -, and *;

- the result of the program is a nonnegative even integer;

- the program is guaranteed to terminate.

In general, we're interested in static properties that aid in the verification, optimization, and documentation of programs. For instance, we'd like to ask the following kinds of questions about a given program:

- Is this program consistent with a given specification?

- Can this program possibly encounter a certain error situation?

- When the program executes, is a certain variable guaranteed to contain a value consistent with its declared type?

- Can this program be optimized in a particular way without changing its meaning?

Of course, there are certain questions that simply cannot be answered in general. "Does this program halt?" is the most famous example of an undecidable question. Yet undecidability does not necessarily spell defeat for the goal of determining static properties of programs. There are two ways that undecidability is finessed in practice:

1. Make a conservative approximation to the desired property. E.g., for **termination analysis** (determining whether a program halts), allow three answers:

    (a)   yes, it definitely halts;

    (b)   it might not halt (but I'm not sure);

    (c)   no, it definitely doesn't halt.

A termination analysis is sound if it answers (a) or (b) for a program that halts and (b) or (c) for a program that doesn't halt. Of course, a trivial sound analysis answers (b) for all programs. In practice, we're interested in sound analyses that answer (a) or (c) in as many cases as possible.

2. Restrict the language to the point where it is possible to determine the property unequivocally. Such restrictions allow precise static information to be calculated at analysis time, but reduce expressiveness by forbidding many programs that would otherwise be valid.

For instance, languages with **static type systems** (see Section 11.3.1) prohibit writing many expressions whose evaluation would not signal dynamic type errors. Consider the following FL expression, in which the procedure f returns the square of a negative number but a scaling procedure for a nonnegative number:

```
(let ((f (abs (x)
           (if (< x 0) (* x x) (abs (y) (* x y)))))))
   (+ ((f 4) (f -3)) ((f 6) (f -1))))
```

This expression evaluates to 42 without encountering a type error at run time. But such an expression is illegal in most languages with static type systems, because the type system is too weak to specify that the type of the value returned by f depends on the value of f's argument.

Sometimes writing an expression in a different way permits it to be analyzed more precisely or transforms it from an illegal expression to a legal one. For example, many languages with static type systems can express a version of the above example in which f is split into a squaring procedure and a curried scaling procedure:

```
(let ((f1 (abs (x) (* x x)))
      (f2 (abs (x) (abs (y) (* x y)))))
  (+ ((f2 4) (f1 -3)) ((f2 6) (f1 -1))))
```

In our study of static semantics, we shall take the second approach to ensuring that the properties of interest are decidable. Starting with a general language about which we can determine very few properties, we shall remove features or add restrictions until the desired properties can be determined statically. Unfortunately, the increase in our ability to reason about the programs is offset by a decrease in the expressive power of the programming language. This is a fundamental tension in the design of programming languages: the more we can say *about* programs, the less we can say *with* them.

Static semantics adds new dimensions to the programming language design space. As we shall see, points in the design space can often be characterized by different tradeoffs among the expressive power of the language, the expressiveness of the static properties, and the complexity of the analyses that determine the static properties.

In this chapter, we introduce key concepts in static semantics in the context of a simple type system. In the following five chapters, we explore more sophisticated systems for static analysis.

11.2   What Is a Type?

When reading or writing code, it is common to describe expressions in terms of the kinds of values they manipulate. This is especially true when talking about procedures. For example, we typically describe > as a procedure that takes two integers and returns a boolean. At a more detailed level, > certainly performs an operation much more specific than indicated by this fuzzy description, but in many situations the fuzzy description is all we need.

For example, suppose we want to know whether > would make sense as the content of the hole in the following FL expression context:

```
(if (□ 1 2) (sym three) (sym four))
```

We can reason as follows about the content of the hole: because the hole appears as the leftmost subexpression of an application, it must be a procedure; because it is supplied with 1 and 2 as arguments, it must take two integer arguments; and because the result of the application is used as the test in an if expression, the procedure in the hole must return a boolean. Thus, > *would* make sense as the content of the hole. But more important, *any* value satisfying the description "a procedure that maps two integer arguments to a boolean result" would be valid as the content of the hole.

This example illustrates that it is not necessary to know precise values in order to reason about a program. The reasoning used above was based on abstract descriptions of values rather than on concrete values. Abstract descriptions of values are known as **types**. Types are often distinguished by the legal usage contexts for the values they describe. For example, in FL, integers may be used as the arguments to arithmetic and relational operators, but they cannot be applied to arguments or used to select a conditional branch. Types help programmers reason about a program, e.g., by enabling them to determine the number, order, and suitability of the actual arguments that should be passed to a given procedure. Types also guide programming language implementations by indicating the size and layout of values in computer memory.

There are many ways to think about types. One way to think of a type is as a value with only partial information. For example, the type "boolean" describes a value that may be used to control a conditional but doesn't indicate whether the value is true or false. From another perspective, a type is an approximation to a value. For example, the type "integer" is an approximation to the integers 1 and 2, while the type "procedures from two integers to a boolean" is an approximation to > and =. From yet another point of view, types are arbitrary sets. Some examples of such sets include the integers, the natural numbers less than 5, the prime numbers, and procedures that halt on the input 3.

The last example (procedures that halt on the input 3) shows that types we might like to describe may not even be computable. In other cases (e.g., the prime numbers), types might be exceedingly difficult to reason about in an automated way. It is often necessary to restrict these very general notions of type to ones that are less general, but simpler to reason about. A language incorporating such types must be carefully crafted to facilitate reasoning about them.

Types naturally arise from the fact that certain values can be meaningfully used only in certain contexts. For this reason, almost all programming languages support some notion of type and a **type system** for reasoning about types. The chief purpose of a type system is to detect **type errors** — attempts to perform an inappropriate operation on a value. Examples of type errors are adding an integer and a string, calling a procedure with the incorrect number and/or types of arguments, calling an integer as a procedure, and interpreting the bits of a floating point number as an integer, a memory address, or a machine instruction. Some type systems detect type errors when the program is executed, while others detect them when the program is analyzed before it is executed (see Section 11.3.1). We say that a programming language is **type-safe** if its type system prevents attempts to perform inappropriate operations. It might do this by aborting program execution when a type error is detected at run time, or by aborting program compilation when a type error is detected at compile time.

A type system has a **type loophole** if it allows a value of one type to masquerade as a value of another type. The C language is rife with type loopholes. An example of a type loophole involving C union types is presented on page 581; Pascal's variant records exhibit a similar loophole. As another C example, suppose a is declared as a local array of integers with two elements (accessed via a[0] and a[1]). C permits out-of-bounds array accesses (such as a[-1] and a[2]) that return the contents (interpreted as integers) of the memory slots directly before and after the slots where the elements of `a` are stored. A programmer who understands how the C compiler allocates local variables can store values of other types (e.g., floating-point numbers) in these slots and then use `a[-1]` and `a[2]` to interpret the bits of these values as integers. A programming language with type loopholes is obviously not type-safe.

Some languages have subsets that are type-safe, but the full language includes features that destroy type safety. For example, the ADA language provides certain safety guarantees as long as operations whose names begin with `UNCHECKED_` are not used. Even languages generally considered to be type-safe, such as ML, HASKELL, and COMMON LISP, have implementations supporting unsafe features like unchecked array accesses; such implementations are not type-safe if these unsafe features are used.

Not all programming languages have type systems. In order for a language to be truly **typeless**, it must be the case that every value can be used in every context. The untyped lambda calculus, in which every value is a function, is one example of a typeless language. Another example of a typeless language is a machine language in which all instructions, memory addresses, and data words have the same size and any bit pattern of this size can be interpreted as a legal instruction, address, or datum. However, if certain bit patterns are considered illegal as instructions, addresses, or data in certain contexts, then the distinctions between legal and illegal patterns are the basis of a type system. Moreover, even if all bit patterns can safely be used in all contexts, the fact that bit patterns have particular meanings to the programmer at certain points in the program (e.g., as instructions, addresses, or data) is the foundation for a type system.

11.3   Dimensions of Types

Types do not constitute a monolithic feature that is either present or absent in a language. Rather, there is a rich diversity of ways that types may appear in a programming language. In this section, we discuss three dimensions along which type systems vary:

1. dynamic versus static types;

2. explicit versus implicit types;

3. simple versus expressive types.

11.3.1 Dynamic versus Static Types

Languages in which all values conceptually carry type annotations that can be inspected at run time are said to be **dynamically typed** or **latently typed**. All the mini-languages we have studied so far are dynamically typed. FL, for instance, partitions nonerror values into six types: unit, integers, booleans, symbols, procedures, and pairs. The language includes primitive operators (`unit?`, `int?`, etc.) allowing the programmer to test if a value has one of these six types. The operational and denotational semantics for FL use the type information in values to determine the meanings of programs. For example, the value of the expression (`prim` + E_1 E_2) is an integer if both E_1 and E_2 have integer values, but is an error if one of E_1 or E_2 has a noninteger value. The process of inspecting type information at run time is called **dynamic type checking**. In implementations of dynamically typed languages, dynamic type checking incurs both space and time costs at run time: Space is necessary to encode the type of a value at the bit level, and inspecting these types when performing certain primitive operations takes time.

An alternative to processing types at run time is to statically analyze a program before executing it to determine whether type information is consistent. The process of analyzing the types of phrases is called **static type checking**, and languages using this approach are said to be **statically typed**. In static type checking, types are associated with phrases in the language rather than with run-time values. If types can be consistently assigned to all of its phrases, a program is said to be **well typed**. Typically, well-typed programs are guaranteed not to encounter type errors at run time, because all such errors should have been discovered during static type checking.

Examples of real-world statically typed languages include ADA, C, C++, FORTRAN, HASKELL, ML, and PASCAL. In most statically typed languages, static type information plays an important role in the process of translating programs to executable code. For example, the number of bits that need to be allocated in computer memory for a variable is typically determined by the static type of the variable.

Examples of real-world dynamically typed languages include APL, COMMON LISP, ERLANG, JAVASCRIPT, LOGO, PERL, PYTHON, SCHEME, SMALLTALK, and many scripting languages (such as those for LINUX shells). Many dynamically typed languages are **interpreted languages**, in which abstract syntax trees for whole programs and even program phrases can be directly executed without first being analyzed or translated into some execution language. Dynamic type checking is a natural choice for interpreted languages, because there is not necessarily any analysis phase during which static types can be determined. However, many dynamically typed languages are amenable to forms of type analysis and translation that can eliminate some of the overhead of dynamic type checking (e.g., see the discussion of **soft typing** on page 837).

Not all languages can be easily classified as statically or dynamically typed. For example, JAVA employs type checking at many different phases of program implementation. At compile time, static type checking is performed on a JAVA class with the available type information. But when a JAVA class is loaded for execution, it can load other classes that were not known at compile time. Some type checking must be performed at load time to ensure that the loaded classes are type-compatible with the given class. Various other features of JAVA (reflection, safe down-casts, safe array subtyping) require that JAVA objects carry dynamic type information and that certain type checks be delayed until run time.

The choice between dynamic and static typing has been a source of a great debate in the programming language community. Adherents of static typing offer the following arguments in favor of static types:

- *Safety:* Static type checking eliminates certain kinds of errors that can occur at run time. It is often extremely desirable to catch as many errors as possible before the program is run, especially in software that is safety critical (e.g., control software for airplanes, nuclear power plants, communication grids, and medical instruments) or financially important (e.g., software for banking, e-commerce sites, and satellites).

- *Efficiency:* Statically typed programs can execute more efficiently than dynamically typed ones, because no run-time storage is required for type information and static type checks eliminate the need to check types at run time.[1]

- *Documentation:* Static types provide documentation about the program that can facilitate reasoning about the program, both by humans and by other programs (e.g., analyzers and translators). Such information is especially valuable in large programs. For example, programmers can often deduce how to use the operations of a data-structure library based on the names of the operations along with their argument types and return types.

---

[1]Even in statically typed languages, there are still run-time space and time overheads for representing and checking the tags of sum values (see Section 10.2). Indeed, many dynamically typed languages can be viewed as having a single sum data type that describes all values.

- *Program Development:* Static types help programmers catch errors in their programs before running them and help programmers make representation changes. For example, suppose a programmer decides to change the interface of a procedure in a large program. The type checker helps the programmer by finding all the places in the program where there is a mismatch between the old and new interfaces.

Proponents of dynamic typing counter with the following claims:

- The restrictions placed on a language in order to make it statically type-checkable force the programmer into a straitjacket of reduced expressive power.

- In most statically typed languages, types serve mainly to make the language easier to implement, not easier for writing programs.

- Finding type errors at analysis time is overrated. The hard-to-find errors that occur in practice are logical errors, not type errors. Finding logical errors requires testing programs with extensive test suites that would uncover type errors anyway. Eliminating the time-consuming static type-checking phase allows programmers to test for logical errors sooner in the program development process.

- Using programmer time more efficiently is more important than using computer resources more efficiently. Dynamically typed languages allow programmers to be more productive. They can build prototype systems more quickly because they don't waste time wrestling with type annotations and static type checkers.

The relative benefits of static versus dynamic type checking are often debated in electronic forums. Some spirited discussions can be found at [LTU].

11.3.2   Explicit versus Implicit Types

Another dimension on which type systems vary is the extent to which they force a programmer to declare explicit types. Although some dynamically typed languages have simple type markers,[2] dynamically typed languages typically have no explicit type annotations. The converse is true in statically typed languages, where explicit type annotations are the norm. Most languages descended from ALGOL 68, such as ADA, C/C++, JAVA, and PASCAL, require that types be explicitly declared for all variables, all data-structure components, and all func-

---

[2]E.g., PERL variable names begin with a character that indicates the type of value: $ for scalar values, @ for array values, and % for hash values (key/value pairs).

tion/procedure/method parameters and return values. However, some languages (e.g., ML, HASKELL, FX, MIRANDA) achieve static typing without explicit type declarations via a technique called **type reconstruction** or **type inference**. We shall study type reconstruction in Chapter 13.

For example, here is a JAVA method that determines whether a string s contains a character c:

```java
public static boolean contains (String s, char c) {
  int len = s.length();
  for (int i = 0; i < len; i++) {
    if (s.charAt(i) == c) {
      return true;
    }
  }
  return false;
}
```

In JAVA, it is necessary to explicitly declare the types of the method parameters s (`String`) and c (`char`), the return type (`boolean`) of the method, and the types of the local variables `len` (`int`) and i (`int`). In contrast, the following declaration of the corresponding function in the SML dialect of ML has no explicit type annotations:

```
fun contains (s,c) =
  let val len = String.size s
  in let fun loop i =
         if i = len then false
         else if String.sub(s, i) = c then true
         else loop (i+1)
     in loop 0
     end
  end
```

SML is a statically typed language in which type information is deduced based on how variables are used within the program.

One argument for explicit types is that the types serve as important documentation in a program and therefore make programs easier to read and write. Often, however, explicit types make programs easier for compilers to read, not easier for humans to read. And explicit types are generally cumbersome for the program writer as well. In languages with sophisticated type systems, explicit type annotations can even be larger (in some case, *much* larger) than the underlying program being annotated. In such languages, programmers may spend more time writing the types to satisfy the type checker than writing the part of their program that expresses the desired computation.

Implicitly typed programming languages thus have clear advantages in terms of readability and writability. Unfortunately, certain restrictions must be placed on a language in order to make type reconstruction possible. This means that some programs that can be written with explicit types cannot be written with implicit ones. A compromise between the two approaches, adopted by ML, HASKELL, and FX, is to make most types implicit by default, but to allow (or require) explicit declarations in situations where types cannot be reconstructed.

11.3.3 Simple versus Expressive Types

A third dimension along which typed languages can vary is the expressiveness of their type systems. Languages with simple type systems facilitate type checking and type reconstruction, but generally severely restrict the kinds of programs that can be written. Advanced type features make it possible to express a broader range of programs at the cost of making the type system more complex.

For example, in PASCAL (at least in pre-ANSI PASCAL) the length of an array is a part of its type; this makes it impossible to write a sorting procedure that can accept an array of any length. The JAVA type system prohibits defining a single array reversal method that reverses the elements in both an array of integers and an array of strings.[3] In contrast, languages supporting **universal polymorphism** (such as HASKELL and ML) permit procedure declarations that are parameterized over the types of their inputs.[4] We will study polymorphism in Chapter 12.

We shall study several other sophisticated type features. **Subtyping** (Section 12.1) allows certain types to be used in contexts where a related type is expected. **Existential types** (Section 14.3) model aspects of abstract data types. Systems with **dependent types** allow the type of a phrase to depend on the value of an expression. We will study a simple form of dependent types in Section 14.5. **Module types** (Chapter 15) are a convenient way to package types (including abstract data types) together with procedures and values whose specifications use these types. **Effect systems** (Chapter 16) extend type systems to track descriptions of the side effects performed by a program phrase in addition to an approximation of the value of the phrase.

Each of these features extends the range of expressible programs and/or the kinds of reasoning that can be performed about programs. However, each feature

---

[3]In JAVA, it is possible to define a single array-reversal method that works for any array whose elements are objects. But arrays whose elements have a primitive type like `int` or `double` require different methods.

[4]The generics feature of JAVA 5.0 allows classes and static methods to be parameterized over types, but these types cannot be instantiated to primitive types. So the generics mechanism is not truly universal. See Section 12.2.5.

$P \in \text{Prog} ::= (\texttt{flexk} \ ((I_{formal} \ T_{formalType})^*) \ E_{body}) \ [\text{Program}]$

$E \in \text{Exp} ::= L \mid I \mid (\texttt{error} \ Y_{message} \ T_{errorType})$
$\qquad \mid (\texttt{if} \ E_{test} \ E_{then} \ E_{else}) \mid (\texttt{prim} \ O_{primop} \ E_{arg}^*)$
$\qquad \mid (\texttt{abs} \ ((I_{formal} \ T_{formalType})^*) \ E_{body}) \mid (E_{rator} \ E_{rand}^*)$
$\qquad \mid (\texttt{let} \ ((I_{name} \ E_{defn})^*) \ E_{body})$
$\qquad \mid (\texttt{letrec} \ ((I_{name} \ T_{defnType} \ E_{defn})^*) \ E_{body})$
$\qquad \mid (\texttt{the} \ T_{bodyType} \ E_{body}) \ [\text{TypeAscription}]$

$L \in \text{Lit} ::= \texttt{\#u} \mid B \mid N \mid (\texttt{sym} \ Y) \ ; \ \text{as in FL.}$

$B \in \text{BoolLit} = \{\texttt{\#t}, \texttt{\#f}\} \ \text{as in FL.}$

$N \in \text{IntLit} = \text{as in FL.}$

$Y \in \text{SymLit} = \text{as in FL.}$

$O \in \text{Primop} = \text{usual FL primitives except no type predicates or pair operators}$
$\qquad \text{Keyword} = \{\texttt{abs}, \texttt{error}, \texttt{flexk}, \texttt{if}, \texttt{let}, \texttt{letrec}, \texttt{prim}, \texttt{sym}, \texttt{the}\}$
$\qquad \text{SugarKeyword} = \text{defined in Figure 11.2}$

$I \in \text{Ident} = \text{SymLit} - (\{Y \mid Y \ \text{begins with} \ \texttt{@}\} \cup \text{Keyword} \cup \text{SugarKeyword})$

$T \in \text{Type} ::= BT \qquad\qquad\qquad [\text{BaseType}]$
$\qquad \mid \tau \qquad\qquad\qquad\qquad [\text{TypeIdentifier}]$
$\qquad \mid (\texttt{->} \ (T_{arg}^*) \ T_{result}) \ [\text{ArrowType}]$

$BT \in \text{BaseType} = \{\texttt{unit}, \texttt{int}, \texttt{bool}, \texttt{symb}\}$

$\tau \in \text{TypeId} = \text{SymLit} - (\text{BaseType} \cup \{\texttt{->}\})$

$PT \in \text{ProgType} ::= (\texttt{=>} \ (T_{arg}^*) \ T_{result}) \ [\text{ProgamType}]$

Figure 11.1 Kernel grammar for μFLEX, a monomorphic, explicitly typed language. This grammar will be extended with additional expressions and types to yield the full FLEX language in Figure 11.31 on page 697.

makes the type system more complex. Furthermore, many of these features do not interact well with type reconstruction, so programmers must often write complex type annotations in order to use these features.

In the remainder of this chapter, we will study an explicitly typed language whose type system has only the most basic features. We call such a system a **simple type system** because it does not support any of the advanced features mentioned above.

11.4 μFLEX: A Language with Explicit Types

Our study of types begins with the study of FLEX, a statically typed dialect of FL with **explicit types**. We use the name FLEX because the language combines

FL with **EX**plicit types and because it serves as a flexible base for exploring many aspects of type systems. Because it contains numerous features, the full-fledged FLEX language is daunting to cover all at once. So we will introduce the basic notions of types and type checking in the context of a small subset of FLEX named μFLEX (micro-FLEX). Once these notions are understood, it will be easier to explain the remaining features of FLEX.

FLEX has a **monomorphic** type system, which means that each valid expression in the language is described by exactly one type. In a monomorphic type system, procedures cannot be parameterized over the types of their arguments. For example, a procedure that reverses lists of integers cannot be used to reverse lists of strings, even though the reversal procedure never needs to examine the components of the list. Despite this lack of expressiveness, a monomorphic type system is worth studying because (1) it simplifies the discussion of many type issues and (2) a number of popular languages (e.g., C, FORTRAN, and PASCAL) have monomorphic type systems.[5] As evidenced by the success of these languages, monomorphic type systems can still be very useful in practice. As we shall see, such languages can even support features like higher-order procedures and recursive types.

The kernel grammar for μFLEX is presented in Figure 11.1. It is similar to the FL grammar, but there are some important differences. Most prominently, several expressions include explicit type annotations (using the domain variable T from the domain Type) and some expressions that were syntactic sugar in FL are kernel expressions in μFLEX. We discuss the features of μFLEX in detail in the remainder of this section.

11.4.1 Types

The μFLEX grammar has a new syntactic domain Type that is used to specify the types of μFLEX expressions. A μFLEX type has one of three forms:

1. a **base type**, which specifies one of the built-in types of primitive data:

   - `unit`, the type of the one-element set $\{$`#u`$\}$;
   - `bool`, the type of the two-element set $\{$`#t`, `#f`$\}$;
   - `int`, the type of integers; and
   - `symb`, the type of symbols.

---

[5]Some of these languages provide ad hoc overloading and type-casting mechanisms that make it possible to go beyond monomorphism in limited ways. However, because they provide no principled mechanisms for polymorphism, we consider them to be monomorphic.

2. an **arrow type** of the form (-> (T_{arg_1} ... T_{arg_n}) T_{result}), which specifies
the type of an n-argument procedure that takes arguments of type T_{arg_1}
through T_{arg_n} and returns a result of type T_{result}. Because it specifies the
type of a procedure, an arrow type is also called a **procedure type**. For example, an incrementing procedure on integers has type (-> (int) int), an
addition procedure on integers has type (-> (int int) int), and a less-than
procedure on integers has type (-> (int int) bool).

Arrow types can be nested, in which case they describe higher-order procedures. For example:

- a procedure that returns either an incrementing or decrementing procedure
based on a boolean argument has type (-> (bool) (-> (int) int));

- a procedure that takes an integer predicate and determines if it is true for
any numbers in the range [1..10] has type (-> ((-> (int) bool)) bool);
and

- a procedure that returns an approximation to the derivative of an integer
function has type (-> ((-> (int) int)) (-> (int) int)).

Because -> is used to combine simpler types into more complex types, it is
known as a **type constructor**. It is the first of several type constructors that
we will encounter in FLEX. We will meet several others in Section 11.8.

3. a **type identifier**, which is a name from the domain TypeId, a domain containing all symbols except for the names of base types and type constructors.[6]
Type identifiers can be associated with types via the let-type, let-type*,
and def-type syntactic sugar constructs (Section 11.4.3).

The prefix form of μFLEX arrow types may seem unusual to those accus-
tomed to the infix type notation that is standard in the types literature and in
languages like ML and HASKELL. The following table shows examples of the two
notations side by side:

μ**FLEX types**	**ML types**
(-> (bool) (-> (int) int))	bool -> (int -> int)
(-> ((-> (int) bool)) bool)	(int -> bool) -> bool
(-> ((-> (int) int)) (-> (int) int))	(int -> int) -> (int -> int)
(-> ((-> (int int) bool)) (-> (int int) int))	(int * int -> bool) -> int * int -> int

Because a program maps arguments to a result, the form of a program type,
(=> (T_{arg}^*) T_{result}), is similar to a procedure type, except that it uses the key-

---

[6]In μFLEX, the only type constructor is ->, but in Section 11.8 we will see that the full
FLEX language has more type constructors.

word => rather than ->. For example, the program type (=> (int bool) int)
describes a program that takes two arguments, an integer and a boolean, and
returns an integer. It is necessary to distinguish program and procedure types
because programs and procedures are invoked by different mechanisms and so are
not interoperable.

11.4.2 Expressions

Some μFLEX expressions — literals, variable references, conditionals, primitive
and nonprimitive applications, and let — are unchanged from FL. But other
expressions have been extended with type annotations that are used to determine
the types of the expressions:

- In abstractions, parameters are specified by a sequence of name/type associations $(I\ T)$ that specify both the name and the type of each formal parameter.[7] For example, an averaging abstraction is written

      (abs ((a int) (b int)) (/ (+ a b) 2))

  and an abstraction that chooses an incrementing or decrementing procedure
  based on a boolean argument is written

```
(abs ((b bool))
  (if b
      (abs ((x int)) (+ x 1))
      (abs ((x int)) (- x 1))))
```

- Unlike let expression bindings, which have the form $(I\ E)$, each letrec binding $(I\ T\ E)$ has a type T in addition to the name I and definition expression
  E. For example, the following letrec expression introduces a summer procedure that sums all the integer values in the range lo to hi satisfying a unary
  predicate pred. The letrec syntax requires that the type of summer be written
  down explicitly:

```
(letrec ((summer (-> ((-> (int) bool) int int) int)
         (abs ((pred (-> (int) bool)) (lo int) (hi int))
           (if (> lo hi)
               0
               (+ (if (pred lo) lo 0)
                  (summer pred (+ lo 1) hi))))))
   {Sum the multiples of 3 between 1 and 100}
   (summer (abs ((x int)) (= (% x 3) 0)) 1 100))
```

---

[7]Although not specified in the μFLEX grammar, the same name may not appear more than
once in a flexk or abs formal parameter list or in a let or letrec binding list.

- μFLEX requires the programmer to specify the type of an `error` construct explicitly. For example, consider the following higher-order procedure:

```
(abs ((n int))
  (if (< n 0)
      (error negative (-> (int) bool))
      (abs ((d int))
        (if (= d 0)
            (error zero bool)
            (= (% n d) 0)))))
```

Although `error` expressions never return a value, the type annotations specify that the first `error` expression should be treated as if it returns a procedure with type `(-> (int) bool)` and the second `error` expression should be treated as if it returns a boolean value. These type declarations specify that the `error` expressions have the same type as the other branches of their corresponding `if` expressions.

Unlike FL, μFLEX treats multiparameter abstractions (`abs`), multiargument applications, `let`, and `letrec` as kernel forms rather than as syntactic sugar. The reason for this is that such desugarings would not preserve expression types. In μFLEX, a two-argument procedure with type `(-> (int int) int)` is not equivalent to the curried procedure with type `(-> (int) (-> (int) int))`. A μFLEX `let` construct cannot desugar into an application of a multiargument abstraction because the parameter types necessary for the abstraction are not apparent. For instance, `(let ((x 2)) (* x 3))` cannot be desugared to the expression `((abs ((x` $T_?$`)) (* x 3)) 2)` because it is not apparent to the desugaring process what the type $T_?$ should be.

You may wonder why μFLEX has type annotations for some expressions but not others. For instance:

- Why are types required in `letrec` bindings but not `let` bindings?

- Why do abstractions require specifying the types of the parameters but not the type of the returned value? After all, procedure and method declarations in languages like C, JAVA, and PASCAL require explicit return types.

- Why are types required in `error` expressions?

The answer is that type annotations in μFLEX expressions were chosen to be the minimal annotations that allow the type of any expression in a program to be determined without "guessing" the types of any expressions. We will formalize this notion when we study the type checking of FLEX expressions in Section 11.5.

There are several other differences between μFLEX and FL:

- Unlike FL, which has pairs and lists, μFLEX has no data structures. However, full FLEX supports several forms of typed data. We will study these in Section 11.8.

- μFLEX supports fewer primitive operations than FL. In particular, because the type of every μFLEX expression is known at type-checking time, there is no need for type predicates like `bool?`, `int?`, `proc?`. Because μFLEX does not support pairs, the associated pair operations are not included.

- μFLEX has a new type-ascription construct (the T E) that asserts that expression E has type T. In other languages, type ascription is often written with a notation like $E : T$. The expression (the T E) returns the value of E, so it can be used wherever E is used. E.g., it can be used to explicitly declare that the return type of the following procedure is `int`:

    ```
    (abs ((b bool) (x int))
      (the int (if b (+ x 1) (- x 2))))
    ```

    The `the` construct is not strictly necessary, but it is handy for documenting the types of expressions. Assertions made with `the` are automatically verified by a type checker. For example:

    ```
    (+ 1 (the int (* 2 3)))  {well-typed}
    (+ 1 (the bool (* 2 3)))  {ill-typed: (* 2 3) is an int}
    ```

Type ascriptions in μFLEX are safe in the sense that inserting `the` can never change a fundamentally ill-typed expression into a well-typed one that can be executed. But in some languages, such a construct can indicate a **type conversion** that may be an unsafe type loophole. For example, consider the array subscripting expression `i[3]` in C. If the variable `i` is declared to be an integer, then this expression causes a compile-time type error, because `i` is an integer, not an array. However, the explicit type cast `((int*) i)` can be used to force the compiler to treat `i` as if it were a pointer to an integer (i.e., the address of a memory location storing an integer). Since pointers to integers and arrays of integers are indistinguishable in C, the expression `((int*) i)[3]` compiles without error, even though it may lead to a run-time error.

$SugarKeyword = \{$cond, def, def-type, else, flex,
$\qquad\qquad\qquad$ let-type, let-type*, scand, scor$\}$

$@O$, cond, scand, and scor are desugared as in FL.

(let-type $((\tau_i\ T_i)_{i=1}^n)\ E_{body}) \leadsto_{ds} [T_i/\tau_i]_{i=1}^n E_{body}$

(let-type* () $E_{body}) \leadsto_{ds} E_{body}$
(let-type* $((\tau_1\ T_1)\ (\tau_i\ T_i)_{i=2}^n)\ E_{body})$
$\quad \leadsto_{ds}$ (let-type $((\tau_1\ T_1))$ (let-type* $((\tau_i\ T_i)_{i=2}^n)\ E_{body}))$

(def $(I_{procName}\ T_{return}\ (I_i\ T_i)_{i=1}^n)\ E_{procBody})$
$\quad \leadsto_{ds}$ (def $I_{procName}$ (-> $(T_{i=1}^n)\ T_{return}$) (abs $((I_i\ T_i)_{i=1}^n)\ E_{procBody}))$

(flex $((I_{fml_i}\ T_{fml_i})_{i=1}^h)\ E_{body}$ (def-type $\tau_{dt_j}\ T_{dt_j})_{j=1}^m$ (def $I_{d_k}\ T_{d_k}\ E_{d_k})_{k=1}^n)$
$\quad$ {*Assume procedure defs already desugared to* (def $I\ T\ E$) *by previous rule.*}
$\leadsto_{ds}$ (flexk $((I_{fml_i}\ T_{fml_i})_{i=1}^h)$
$\qquad\qquad$ (let {*Standard library bindings*}
$\qquad\qquad\qquad$ ((not (abs ((x bool)) (prim not x)))
$\qquad\qquad\qquad$ (and (abs ((x bool) (y bool)) (prim and x y)))
$\qquad\qquad\qquad\qquad \vdots$ {*Similar for* or *and* bool=?}
$\qquad\qquad\qquad$ (+ (abs ((x int) (y int)) (prim + x y)))
$\qquad\qquad\qquad\qquad \vdots$ {*Similar for* -, *, /, %, <, <=, =, !=, >=, >}
$\qquad\qquad\qquad$ (sym=? (abs ((x symb) (y symb)) (prim sym=? x y)))
$\qquad\qquad\qquad$ (true #t) (false #f))
$\qquad\qquad$ (let-type* $((\tau_{dt_j}\ T_{dt_j})_{j=1}^m)$ {*Type definitions from program*}
$\qquad\qquad\qquad$ (letrec $((I_{d_k}\ T_{d_k}\ E_{d_k})_{k=1}^n)$ {*Value definitions from program*}
$\qquad\qquad\qquad\quad E_{body}))))$

Figure 11.2   Desugaring rules that define the syntactic sugar of μFLEX.

11.4.3   Programs and Syntactic Sugar

A kernel μFLEX program is like an FLK program except that (1) each program parameter is annotated with a type and (2) the program keyword is flexk rather than flk.

μFLEX also supports the syntactic sugar defined in Figure 11.2. The $@O$, cond, scand, and scor constructs are desugared exactly as in FL. The new expression construct (let-type $((\tau_i\ T_i)_{i=1}^n)\ E_{body})$ is sugar for the result of simultaneously substituting the types $T_{i=1}^n$ for the type identifiers $\tau_{i=1}^n$ in the expression E_{body}. (This notion of substitution is formalized in Section 11.4.4.) let-type* is like let-type but performs the substitutions sequentially rather than in parallel. The `let-type` and `let-type*` constructs improve the readability and writability of large and cumbersome types by allowing them to be locally abbreviated by type identifiers. For example,

```
(let-type* ((intfun (-> (int) int))
            (transform (-> (intfun) intfun)))
  (the (-> (transform transform) transform)
    (abs ((t1 transform) (t2 transform))
      (abs ((f intfun)) (t1 (t2 f))))))
```

is an alternative way of writing

```
(the (-> ((-> ((-> (int) int)) (-> (int) int))
          (-> ((-> (int) int)) (-> (int) int)))
         (-> ((-> (int) int)) (-> (int) int)))
  (abs ((t1 (-> ((-> (int) int)) (-> (int) int)))
        (t2 (-> ((-> (int) int)) (-> (int) int))))
    (abs ((f (-> (int) int))) (t1 (t2 f)))))
```

As suggested by this example, the `let-type` and `let-type*` constructs can make explicitly typed programs smaller (as measured by number of AST nodes) and easier to understand.

As we will see in Section 11.4.4, value identifiers (I) — which we have called just identifiers up to this point — and type identifiers (τ) are in separate namespaces, so they do not interact in any way. For example,

```
(let-type ((x bool)) (abs ((x int)) (abs ((y x)) x)))
```

and

```
(abs ((x int)) (let-type ((x bool)) (abs ((y x)) x)))
```

both are equivalent to `(abs ((x int)) (abs ((y bool)) x))`. Note that the domain TypeId of type identifiers excludes the base type names (`unit`, `bool`, `int`, and `symb`) and the arrow symbol (`->`), so these cannot be bound by `let-type` or `let-type*`. For example, `(let-type ((bool int)) (the bool 3))` is syntactically malformed.

The `flex` program sugar defines global procedures for each primitive operator and defines the standard library values `true` and `false`. It also permits top-level value definitions with `def` and type definitions with `def-type` in addition to a body expression. The μFLEX version of `def` has the form (`def` I T E), where T is the explicit type of E that is used when desugaring a `def` into a `letrec` binding. The procedure-defining sugar construct (`def` ($I_{procName}$ T_{return} (I_i T_i)$_{i=1}^{n}$) E_{body}) is also supported; the procedure return type T_{return} must be explicitly declared because it is needed for the definition of recursive procedures. The new declarations (def-type τ T) are sugar for global nested type definitions that surround the recursive value definitions. This desugaring allows a type identifier defined by one def-type to be used in subsequent def-types, and any type identifier defined by a def-type to be used in any def as well as in the body expression E_{body}.

Because μFLEX does not support lists, the flex desugaring does not include bindings for list procedures in the standard library. However, we will assume that these are included in the full FLEX language. One FL standard library function that is not included even in full FLEX is the generic equality-testing procedure equal?. In FL, this procedure tests the equality of two values having any (perhaps even different) types. But in FLEX, it is possible to test the equality only of two values with the *same* type via =, bool=?, and sym=?.

Here is an example program that determines whether the integer input i is positive or even, depending on the boolean input b:

```
(flex ((b bool) (i int)) (if b (pos? i) (even? i))
  (def-type intfun (-> (int) int))
  (def-type intpred (-> (int) bool))
  (def dec intfun (abs ((x int)) (- x 1)))
  (def pos? intpred (abs ((y int)) (> y 0)))
  (def even? intpred
    (abs ((x int)) (if (= x 0) #t (odd? (dec x)))))
  (def odd? intpred
    (abs ((y int)) (if (= y 0) #f (even? (dec y))))))
```

Note that the def desugaring rule in Figure 11.2 also permits the even? definition to be expressed as:

```
(def (even? bool (x int)) (if (= x 0) #t (odd? (dec x))))
```

The program type of the above program is (=> (bool int) bool).

11.4.4   Free Identifiers and Substitution

Notions of free identifiers and substitution are necessary for describing the dynamic and static semantics of μFLEX. A consequence of having two different namespaces, one for value identifiers and one for type identifiers, is that the notions of free identifiers and substitution are more complex in μFLEX than they were in FL. As shown in Figure 11.3, there are now three notions of free identifier:

1. *The free value identifiers in an expression (FrIds):* The interesting cases for *FrIds* are value identifiers (for which it returns a singleton set) and the value-identifier binding constructs abs, let, and letrec (for which it removes the

newly bound identifiers from the free identifiers of the subexpressions that are in the scope of the new identifiers). Otherwise *FrIds* simply calculates the union of the free value identifiers in the subexpressions of an expression. Note that *FrIds* never explores any types within an expression, because types cannot harbor value identifiers.[8]

2. *The free type identifiers in a type (FrTyIds$_{ty}$):* The definition of *FrTyIds$_{ty}$* is particularly simple because the Type domain contains no binding constructs.

3. *The free type identifiers in an expression (FrTyIds$_{exp}$):* The *FrTyIds$_{exp}$* definition is the most interesting of the three. *FrTyIds$_{exp}$* explores all the subexpressions of a given expression, but returns an empty set for both kinds of leaf expressions (literals and value identifiers). It does its work by using *FrTyIds$_{ty}$* to collect the free type identifiers residing in the types in all the expressions it visits.

As examples of free-identifier calculations, suppose that

$$E_{abs1} = \text{(abs ((f (-> (b intpred) i)))}$$
$$\text{(f y (abs ((x i)) (not (g x y))))))}$$

where `b` is a type identifier that is an abstracted form of `bool`, `i` is an abstracted form of `int`, and `intpred` is an abstracted form of `(-> (int) bool)`. Then:

$FrTyIds_{ty}[\![\text{(-> (int) bool)}]\!] = \{\}$

$FrTyIds_{ty}[\![\text{(-> (i) b)}]\!] = \{\text{b}, \text{i}\}$

$FrTyIds_{ty}[\![\text{(-> (b intpred) i)}]\!] = \{\text{b}, \text{i}, \text{intpred}\}$

$FrTyIds_{exp}[\![\text{(f y (abs ((x i)) (not (g x y))))}]\!] = \{\text{i}\}$

$FrIds[\![\text{(f y (abs ((x i)) (not (g x y))))}]\!] = \{\text{f}, \text{g}, \text{not}, \text{y}\}$

$FrTyIds_{exp}[\![E_{abs1}]\!] = \{\text{b}, \text{i}, \text{intpred}\}$

$FrIds[\![E_{abs1}]\!] = \{\text{g}, \text{not}, \text{y}\}$

Because there are now three notions of free identifiers, there are now three notions of substitution (Figures 11.4 and 11.5):

1. substituting expressions for free value identifiers in an expression ($[E_1/I]E_2$);

2. substituting types for free type identifiers in a type ($[T_1/\tau]T_2$); and

3. substituting types for free type identifiers in an expression ($[T/\tau]E$).

---

[8]That is, not until dependent types are introduced in Section 14.5.

$FrIds : \text{Exp} \to \mathcal{P}(\text{Ident})$

$FrIds[\![L]\!] = \{\}$

$FrIds[\![I]\!] = \{I\}$

$FrIds[\![(\texttt{prim } O \ E_{i=1}^n)]\!] = \cup_{i=1}^n FrIds[\![E_i]\!]$

$FrIds[\![(\texttt{if } E_1 \ E_2 \ E_3)]\!] = \cup_{i=1}^3 FrIds[\![E_i]\!]$

$FrIds[\![(\texttt{abs } ((I_i \ T_i)_{i=1}^n) \ E)]\!] = FrIds[\![E]\!] - \cup_{i=1}^n \{I_i\}$

$FrIds[\![(E_0 \ E_{i=1}^n)]\!] = \cup_{i=0}^n FrIds[\![E_i]\!]$

$FrIds[\![(\texttt{let } ((I_i \ E_i)_{i=1}^n) \ E_0)]\!] = (\cup_{i=1}^n FrIds[\![E_i]\!]) \cup (FrIds[\![E_0]\!] - \cup_{i=1}^n \{I_i\})$

$FrIds[\![(\texttt{letrec } ((I_i \ T_i \ E_i)_{i=1}^n) \ E_0)]\!] = (\cup_{i=0}^n FrIds[\![E_i]\!]) - \cup_{i=1}^n \{I_i\}$

$FrIds[\![(\texttt{error } Y \ T)]\!] = \{\}$

$FrIds[\![(\texttt{the } T \ E)]\!] = FrIds[\![E]\!]$

$FrTyIds_{ty} : \text{Type} \to \mathcal{P}(\text{TypeId})$

$FrTyIds_{ty}[\![BT]\!] = \{\}$

$FrTyIds_{ty}[\![\tau]\!] = \{\tau\}$

$FrTyIds_{ty}[\![(\texttt{->} \ (T_{i=1}^n) \ T_0)]\!] = \cup_{i=0}^n FrTyIds_{ty}[\![T_i]\!]$

$FrTyIds_{exp} : \text{Exp} \to \mathcal{P}(\text{TypeId})$

$FrTyIds_{exp}[\![L]\!] = \{\}$

$FrTyIds_{exp}[\![I]\!] = \{\}$

$FrTyIds_{exp}[\![(\texttt{prim } O \ E_{i=1}^n)]\!] = \cup_{i=1}^n FrTyIds_{exp}[\![E_i]\!]$

$FrTyIds_{exp}[\![(\texttt{if } E_1 \ E_2 \ E_3)]\!] = \cup_{i=1}^3 FrTyIds_{exp}[\![E_i]\!]$

$FrTyIds_{exp}[\![(\texttt{abs } ((I_i \ T_i)_{i=1}^n) \ E)]\!] = \left(\cup_{i=1}^n FrTyIds_{ty}[\![T_i]\!]\right) \cup FrTyIds_{exp}[\![E]\!]$

$FrTyIds_{exp}[\![(E_0 \ E_{i=1}^n)]\!] = \cup_{i=0}^n FrTyIds_{exp}[\![E_i]\!]$

$FrTyIds_{exp}[\![(\texttt{let } ((I_i \ E_i)_{i=1}^n) \ E_0)]\!] = \cup_{i=0}^n FrTyIds_{exp}[\![E_i]\!]$

$FrTyIds_{exp}[\![(\texttt{letrec } ((I_i \ T_i \ E_i)_{i=1}^n) \ E_0)]\!]$
$\quad = \left(\cup_{i=1}^n FrTyIds_{ty}[\![T_i]\!]\right) \cup \left(\cup_{i=0}^n FrTyIds_{exp}[\![E_i]\!]\right)$

$FrTyIds_{exp}[\![(\texttt{error } Y \ T)]\!] = FrTyIds_{ty}[\![T]\!]$

$FrTyIds_{exp}[\![(\texttt{the } T \ E)]\!] = FrTyIds_{ty}[\![T]\!] \cup FrTyIds_{exp}[\![E]\!]$

Figure 11.3 Definitions of free value and type identifiers for μFLEX.

The abbreviated notation $[A/B]C$ is used for all three substitution functions; we rely on the domains of the syntactic values A, B, and C for disambiguation. All three notions of substitution can be straightforwardly extended to the simultaneous substitution of multiple entities for multiple names.

$subst : \text{Exp} \to \text{Ident} \to \text{Exp} \to \text{Exp}$
    The notation $[E_1/I]E_2$ abbreviates $(subst\ E_1\ I\ E_2)$.

$[E/I]L = L$

$[E/I]I = E \qquad [E/I]I' = I'$, where $I \neq I'$

$[E/I](\text{prim}\ O\ E_{i=1}^n) = (\text{prim}\ O\ ([E/I]E_i)_{i=1}^n)$

$[E/I](\text{if}\ E_{test}\ E_{then}\ E_{else}) = (\text{if}\ [E/I]E_{test}\ [E/I]E_{then}\ [E/I]E_{else})$

$[E/I](\text{abs}\ ((I_i\ T_i)_{i=1}^n)\ E_{body}) = (\text{abs}\ ((I_i\ T_i)_{i=1}^n)\ E_{body})$, where $I \in \cup_{i=1}^n\{I_i\}$.

$[E/I](\text{abs}\ ((I_i\ T_i)_{i=1}^n)\ E_{body}) = (\text{abs}\ ((I_i'\ T_i)_{i=1}^n)\ [E/I]([I_j'/I_j]_{j=1}^n E_{body}))$,
    where $I \notin \cup_{i=1}^n\{I_i\}$ and $I_1',\ \ldots,\ I_n'$ are fresh.

$[E/I](E_{rator}\ E_{i=1}^n) = ([E/I]E_{rator}\ ([E/I]E_i)_{i=1}^n)$

$[E/I](\text{let}\ ((I_i\ E_i)_{i=1}^n)\ E_{body}) = (\text{let}\ ((I_i\ [E/I]E_i)_{i=1}^n)\ E_{body})$,
    where $I \in \cup_{i=1}^n\{I_i\}$.

$[E/I](\text{let}\ ((I_i\ E_i)_{i=1}^n)\ E_{body}) = (\text{let}\ ((I_i'\ [E/I]E_i)_{i=1}^n)\ [E/I]([I_j'/I_j]_{j=1}^n E_{body}))$,
    where $I \notin \cup_{i=1}^n\{I_i\}$ and $I_1',\ \ldots,\ I_n'$ are fresh.

$[E/I](\text{letrec}\ ((I_i\ T_i\ E_i)_{i=1}^n)\ E_{body}) = (\text{letrec}\ ((I_i\ T_i\ E_i)_{i=1}^n)\ E_{body})$,
    where $I \in \cup_{i=1}^n\{I_i\}$.

$[E/I](\text{letrec}\ ((I_i\ T_i\ E_i)_{i=1}^n)\ E_{body})$
    $= (\text{letrec}\ ((I_i'\ T_i\ [E/I]([I_j'/I_j]_{j=1}^n E_i))_{i=1}^n)\ [E/I]([I_j'/I_j]_{j=1}^n E_{body}))$,
    where $I \notin \cup_{i=1}^n\{I_i\}$ and $I_1',\ \ldots,\ I_n'$ are fresh.

$[E/I](\text{error}\ Y\ T) = (\text{error}\ Y\ T)$

$[E/I](\text{the}\ T\ E) = (\text{the}\ T\ [E/I]E)$

Figure 11.4 Expression substitution for μFLEX.

The substitution definitions have a structure similar to the free-identifier definitions in terms of how they process subphrases and handle binding constructs, but they return an expression or type instead of a set of identifiers. Here are some example substitutions:

```
[b/i](-> (b intpred) i) = (-> (b intpred) b)
[b/i]E_abs1 = (abs ((f (-> (b intpred) b)))
              (f y (abs ((x b)) (not (g x y)))))
[(> z 0)/y]E_abs1 = (abs ((f (-> (b intpred) i)))
                    (f (> z 0) (abs ((x i)) (not (g x (> z 0))))))
[(f x y)/g]E_abs1 = (abs ((f1 (-> (b intpred) i)))
                    (f1 y (abs ((x1 i)) (not ((f x y) x1 y)))))
```

Exercise 11.1 Handling type abbreviations via substitution-based desugarings (as with `let-type`, `let-type*`, and `def-type`) is simple, but can lead to kernel expressions containing large types, many of which are duplicated. E.g., the desugaring of the `let-type*` expression on page 635 contains many instances of the types `(-> (int) int)` and `(-> ((-> (int) int)) (-> (int) int))`.

One way to stem this blowup in the size of types in kernel expressions is to define type abbreviations via kernel constructs rather than desugarings. In this exercise, we explore this notion by extending μFLEX with a new kernel expression for local type abbreviations:

$$E ::= \ldots \mid (\texttt{tbind } ((\tau \ T))^* \ E_{body})$$

Like $(\texttt{let-type } ((\tau_i \ T_i)_{i=1}^n) \ E_{body})$, $(\texttt{tbind } ((\tau_i \ T_i)_{i=1}^n) \ E_{body})$ locally defines the type identifiers $\tau_{i=1}^n$ as abbreviations for the types $T_{i=1}^n$ within the scope of E_{body}. However, unlike `let-type`, `tbind` is a kernel binding construct for type identifiers, so the definitions of free identifiers and substitution must be extended to handle this new kernel form.

a. Extend *FrIds* and *FrTyIds*$_{exp}$ in Figure 11.3 on page 638 with clauses for `tbind`.

b. Here is an incorrect clause for substituting an expression E into a `tbind` expression:

$$[E/I](\texttt{tbind } ((\tau_i \ T_i)_{i=1}^n) \ E_{body}) = (\texttt{tbind } ((\tau_i \ T_i)_{i=1}^n) \ ([E/I]E_{body}))$$

Give a simple example exhibiting variable capture if this incorrect clause is used.

c. Extend *subst* and *substTy*$_{exp}$ in Figures 11.4 and 11.5 (pages 639 and 641) with correct clauses for `tbind`.

d. Consider the following μFLEX expression E_{test}:

```
(abs ((g t))
  (f (tbind ((t (-> (s) t)))
       (abs ((y s) (z t))
         (g y z f)))))
```

Using your substitution definitions from part **c**, give the results of the following substitutions:

i. $[\texttt{t/s}]E_{test}$ (assume $\texttt{s}, \texttt{t} \in \text{TypeId}$)

ii. $[(\texttt{abs } ((\texttt{h } (\texttt{-> } (\texttt{s}) \ \texttt{t}))) \ (\texttt{h } \texttt{g } \texttt{y}))/\texttt{f}]E_{test}$

11.5   Type Checking in μFLEX

11.5.1   Introduction to Type Checking

In a statically typed language, a program phrase is said to be **well typed** if it is possible to assign a type to the phrase based on a process known as **type checking**. This process is typically expressed using a collection of formal rules

$substTy_{ty}$: Type $\rightarrow$ TypeId $\rightarrow$ Type $\rightarrow$ Type
  The notation $[T_1/\tau]T_2$ abbreviates $(substTy_{ty}\ T_1\ \tau\ T_2)$.
$[T/\tau]BT = BT$
$[T/\tau]\tau = T \qquad [T/\tau]\tau' = \tau'$, where $\tau \neq \tau'$
$[T/\tau](\texttt{->}\ (T_{i=1}^n)\ T_{result}) = (\texttt{->}\ (([T/\tau]T_i)_{i=1}^n)\ [T/\tau]T_{result})$

$substTy_{exp}$: Type $\rightarrow$ TypeId $\rightarrow$ Exp $\rightarrow$ Exp
  The notation $[T/\tau]E$ abbreviates $(substTy_{exp}\ T\ \tau\ E)$.
$[T/\tau]L = L$
$[T/\tau]I = I$
$[T/\tau](\texttt{prim}\ O\ E_{i=1}^n) = (\texttt{prim}\ O\ ([T/\tau]E_i)_{i=1}^n)$
$[T/\tau](\texttt{if}\ E_{test}\ E_{then}\ E_{else}) = (\texttt{if}\ [T/\tau]E_{test}\ [T/\tau]E_{then}\ [T/\tau]E_{else})$
$[T/\tau](\texttt{abs}\ ((I_i\ T_i)_{i=1}^n)\ E_{body}) = (\texttt{abs}\ ((I_i\ [T/\tau]T_i)_{i=1}^n)\ [T/\tau]E_{body})$
$[T/\tau](E_{rator}\ E_{i=1}^n) = ([T/\tau]E_{rator}\ ([T/\tau]E_i)_{i=1}^n)$
$[T/\tau](\texttt{let}\ ((I_i\ E_i)_{i=1}^n)\ E_{body}) = (\texttt{let}\ ((I_i\ [T/\tau]E_i)_{i=1}^n)\ [T/\tau]E_{body})$
$[T/\tau](\texttt{letrec}\ ((I_i\ T_i\ E_i)_{i=1}^n)\ E_{body})$
  $= (\texttt{letrec}\ ((I_i\ [T/\tau]T_i\ [T/\tau]E_i)_{i=1}^n)\ [T/\tau]E_{body})$
$[T/\tau](\texttt{error}\ Y\ T) = (\texttt{error}\ Y\ [T/\tau]T)$
$[T/\tau](\texttt{the}\ T\ E) = (\texttt{the}\ [T/\tau]T\ [T/\tau]E)$

Figure 11.5 Type substitution for μFLEX.

and a reasoning system that uses these rules. A phrase is said to be **ill typed** if it is not possible to assign it a type. Only well-typed phrases are considered legal phrases of the language. Only well-typed programs can be executed.

Type checking is similar to evaluation, except that rather than manipulating the run-time values associated with expressions, it manipulates the static types associated with the expressions. Recall that it is possible to view types as approximations to values. From this perspective, a type checker evaluates the program with approximations rather than actual values.

As an example of the kind of reasoning used in type checking, consider the type analysis of the following μFLEX abstraction:

E_{abs2} = (abs ((b bool) (x int) (f (-> (int int) int)))
            (prim > (if b x (f x 2)) 0))

The type annotations on the parameters indicate that b is assumed to be a boolean, x is assumed to be an integer, and f is assumed to be a procedure that maps two integer arguments to an integer result. Based on the assumptions for x and f, the type of (f x 2) is int, because applying a procedure of type

(-> (int int) int) to two integers yields an integer. Based on this conclusion and the assumptions for b and x, the body expression (if b x (f x 2)) is well typed, because the test subexpression has type bool, and the two branches both have the same type, int. The type of the if expression is int, because that is the type of the value returned by the expression for any values of b, x, and f satisfying the type assumptions. The type of the (prim > ...) expression is bool, because both the if expression and 0 denote integers, and comparing two integers via > yields a boolean. Since the abstraction takes three parameters, a bool, an int, and a procedure of type (-> (int int) int), and it returns a bool, E_{abs2} has the arrow type (-> (bool int (-> (int int) int)) bool). Since we can assign a type to E_{abs2}, E_{abs2} is well typed.

If we changed the if expression in the example to (if x x (f x 2)), the if expression would not be well typed because the test subexpression does not have type bool. Similarly, the if expression would not be well typed if it were (if b b (f x 2)), because then the two conditional branches would have incompatible types: bool and int.[9] The expression (if #t b (f x 2)) is not considered to be well typed in our system, even though it is guaranteed to return a boolean value when executed. Why? Our type checker, like most type checkers, manipulates only approximations to values. It does not "know" that the test expression is the constant true value. All it "knows" is that the test expression is a boolean, and so it cannot determine which branch is taken.[10]

From the above examples, it is clear that just as the value of an expression is determined from the values of its subexpressions, so too is the type of the expression determined from the type of its subexpressions. However, the actual rules for determining the type of the whole from the types of the parts may be very different from the rules for determining the value of the whole from the values of the parts. For instance:

- An evaluator evaluates only *one* branch of a conditional, but a type checker checks *both* branches of a conditional.

- An evaluator does not evaluate the body of an abstraction until it is applied to arguments, but a type checker checks the body of an abstraction regardless of whether or not it is applied.

---

[9]There are sophisticated type systems in which (if b b (f x 2)) would be considered well typed with a so-called **union type** that is *either* bool *or* int. In order to guarantee type soundness (see Section 11.6), such systems must constrain the ways in which a value with union type may be manipulated. In this presentation, we focus on simpler type systems that do not allow union types.

[10]In some sophisticated type systems, (if #t b (f x 2)) would be considered well typed with type bool.

TE_{prim} = {not : (-> (bool) bool),   and : (-> (bool bool) bool),
        or : (-> (bool bool) bool),   bool=? : (-> (bool bool) bool),
        < : (-> (int int) bool),   <= : (-> (int int) bool),
        = : (-> (int int) bool),   != : (-> (int int) bool),
       >= : (-> (int int) bool),   > : (-> (int int) bool),
        + : (-> (int int) int),   - : (-> (int int) int),
        * : (-> (int int) int),   / : (-> (int int) int),
        % : (-> (int int) int),   sym=? : (-> (symb symb) bool) }

Figure 11.6 Primitive type environment TE_{prim} for μFLEX.

- An evaluator associates the actual arguments with the formal parameters when applying a procedure to arguments, but a type checker simply checks that the types of the actual arguments are compatible with the argument types expected by the procedure.

11.5.2 Type Environments

Just as expressions are evaluated with respect to a dynamic **value environment** that associates free value identifiers with their run-time values, they are type-checked with respect to a static **type environment** that associates free value identifiers with their types. Type environments are partial functions from value identifiers to types:

$$TE \in \text{TypeEnvironment} = \text{Ident} \rightharpoonup \text{Type}$$

If TE is a type environment and $I \in dom(TE)$, then the notation $TE(I)$ designates the type assigned to I in TE.

The association of a type T with a value identifier I is known as a **type assignment**, which is written $I : T$ and pronounced "I has type T." We will write a type environment as a set of type assignments whose names are distinct. For instance, {} is the empty type environment, and the type environment used to check the body of the abstraction E_{abs2} in the discussion on page 641 is

$$TE_1 = \{\texttt{b} : \texttt{bool}, \texttt{x} : \texttt{int}, \texttt{f} : \texttt{(-> (int int) int)}\}$$

So $dom(TE_1) = \{\texttt{b}, \texttt{f}, \texttt{x}\}$ and $TE_1(\texttt{b}) = \texttt{bool}$, $TE_1(\texttt{f}) = \texttt{(-> (int int) int)}$, and $TE_1(\texttt{x}) = \texttt{int}$. Figure 11.6 shows a type environment TE_{prim} that assigns an appropriate arrow type to each μFLEX primitive operator name. For example, $TE_{prim}(\texttt{<}) = \texttt{(-> (int int) bool)}$.

$$TE \vdash \texttt{\#u} : \texttt{unit} \quad [unit] \qquad TE \vdash N : \texttt{int} \quad [int] \qquad TE \vdash B : \texttt{bool} \quad [bool]$$

$$TE \vdash (\texttt{sym } Y) : \texttt{symb} \quad [symb] \qquad TE \vdash (\texttt{error } Y \; T) : T \; [error]$$

$$TE \vdash I : TE(I) \quad \text{where } I \in dom(TE) \qquad\qquad [var]$$

$$\frac{TE \vdash E_{test} : \texttt{bool} \quad TE \vdash E_{then} : T \quad TE \vdash E_{else} : T}{TE \vdash (\texttt{if } E_{test} \; E_{then} \; E_{else}) : T} \qquad [if]$$

$$\frac{TE[I_i : T_i]_{i=1}^n \vdash E_{body} : T_{body}}{TE \vdash (\texttt{abs } ((I_i \; T_i)_{i=1}^n) \; E_{body}) : (\texttt{->} \; (T_{i=1}^n) \; T_{body})} \qquad [\rightarrow\text{-}intro]$$

$$\frac{TE \vdash E_{rator} : (\texttt{->} \; (T_{i=1}^n) \; T_{result}) \quad \forall_{i=1}^n . \; TE \vdash E_i : T_i}{TE \vdash (E_{rator} \; E_{i=1}^n) : T_{result}} \qquad [\rightarrow\text{-}elim]$$

$$\frac{\forall_{i=1}^n . \; TE \vdash E_i : T_i \quad TE[I_i : T_i]_{i=1}^n \vdash E_0 : T_0}{TE \vdash (\texttt{let } ((I_i \; E_i)_{i=1}^n) \; E_0) : T_0} \qquad [let]$$

$$\frac{\forall_{i=0}^n . \; TE[I_j : T_j]_{j=1}^n \vdash E_i : T_i}{TE \vdash (\texttt{letrec } ((I_i \; T_i \; E_i)_{i=1}^n) \; E_0) : T_0} \qquad [letrec]$$

$$\frac{TE_{prim} \vdash O_{op} : (\texttt{->} \; (T_{i=1}^n) \; T_{result}) \quad \forall_{i=1}^n . \; TE \vdash E_i : T_i}{TE \vdash (\texttt{prim } O_{op} \; E_{i=1}^n) : T_{result}} \qquad [prim]$$

$$\frac{TE \vdash E : T}{TE \vdash (\texttt{the } T \; E) : T} \qquad [the]$$

$$\frac{\{I_i : T_i\}_{i=1}^n \vdash E_{body} : T_{body}}{\vdash_{prog} (\texttt{flexk } ((I_i \; T_i)_{i=1}^n) \; E_{body}) : (\texttt{=>} \; (T_{i=1}^n) \; T_{body})} \qquad [prog]$$

Figure 11.7   Type rules for μFLEX.

As with value environments, it is often necessary to extend a type environment with additional bindings. We use the notation

$$TE[I_1 : T_1, \dots, I_n : T_n]$$

(often abbreviated $TE[I_i : T_i]_{i=1}^n$) to indicate the type environment that results from extending TE with the given type assignments. The identifiers $I_1, \dots, I_n$ must be distinct, and the extensions override any assignments that TE may already have for them. E.g., suppose that $TE_2 = TE_1[\texttt{b} : \texttt{symb}, \texttt{t} : \texttt{bool}]$. Then $dom(TE_2) = \{\texttt{b}, \texttt{f}, \texttt{x}, \texttt{t}\}$ and $TE_2(\texttt{b}) = \texttt{symb}$, $TE_2(\texttt{f}) = (\texttt{->} \; (\texttt{int int}) \; \texttt{int})$, $TE_2(\texttt{x}) = \texttt{int}$, and $TE_2(\texttt{t}) = \texttt{bool}$.

11.5.3 Type Rules for μFLEX

We now describe a formal process for determining the types of μFLEX expressions and programs. The assertion that an expression E has type T with respect to type environment TE is known as a **type judgment** and is written

$$TE \vdash E : T$$

This is pronounced "expression E has type T in type environment TE" or, more loosely, "TE proves that E has type T." When such an assertion is true, we say that the type judgment is **valid**. If $TE \vdash E : T$ is valid for some T, we say that E is **well typed with respect to** TE. Otherwise, E is **ill typed with respect to** TE. If the type environment is understood from context, we just say that E is **well typed** or **ill typed**.

There are also type judgments for μFLEX programs. These have the form

$$\vdash_{prog} P : (\texttt{=>} \ (T_1 \ \ldots \ T_n) \ T_{result})$$

where $T_1 \ \ldots \ T_n$ are the types of the program arguments and T_{result} is the type of the value computed by the program. Program judgments use a different turnstile symbol, $\vdash_{prog}$, than the one used in expression judgments. Also, they do not have a type environment, because well-typed programs are required to have no free value identifiers. However, well-typed programs may mention free type identifiers (see Exercise 11.3 on page 652).

Valid type judgments can be determined via **type rules** that have a form similar to the rewrite rules we introduced for operational semantics in Section 3.2.3. Each type rule has the form

$$\frac{premise_1 \ \ldots \ premise_n}{conclusion} \qquad \textit{[rule-name]}$$

where *conclusion* and each *premise$_i$* are type judgments. A rule without any premises is an **axiom**, and is written without a horizontal line. We will call a type rule with a nonempty set of premises an **inference rule**. If all of the premises of a rule are valid, then the type judgment in the conclusion of the rule is valid.

The type rules for μFLEX are presented in Figure 11.7. The [*unit*], [*bool*], [*int*], [*symb*], and [*error*] rules are axioms that hold for any type environment TE. As in the operational semantics rules, type rules are really rule schemas in which every domain variable can be instantiated by any element of its domain. So [*int*] represents the infinite number of rules that can be obtained by instantiating TE with any type environment and N with any integer literal.

The [*if*] rule requires that the test expression denote a boolean and the two branches have the same type T. If these requirements are met, the type of the `if` expression is the type T of the branches. The constraint that the two branch types and return type must all be the same is specified by using the same domain variable, T, for all three types.

Many of the ways to instantiate the [*if*] rule schema may not make sense at first glance. For example, here is one instantiation of the `if` rule:

$$\frac{\{\} \vdash \texttt{1} : \texttt{bool} \quad \{\} \vdash \texttt{2} : \texttt{symb} \quad \{\} \vdash \texttt{3} : \texttt{symb}}{\{\} \vdash \texttt{(if 1 2 3)} : \texttt{symb}}$$

Certainly we should not be able to prove that (`if 1 2 3`) has type `symb`! But the rule doesn't say that (`if 1 2 3`) has type `symb`. Rather, it says that (`if 1 2 3`) *would* have type `symb` *if* the integer 1 had type `bool` and the integers 2 and 3 had type `symb`. But it is impossible to prove these false premises, and so the false conclusion will never be declared to be a valid judgment by the type system.

The [→-*intro*] and [→-*elim*] rules are the rules for abstractions and applications, respectively. The rule names emphasize that abstractions are the source expressions that produce values of arrow type and that applications are the sink expressions that use values of arrow type. In our study of typed data in Section 11.8, we shall see many other examples of introduction and elimination rules. In the [→-*intro*] rule, the type of an abstraction is an arrow type that maps the explicitly declared parameter types to the type of the body, where the body type is determined relative to an extended environment that includes type assignments for the parameters. The [→-*elim*] rule requires that the operator of an application be an arrow type whose number of parameters is the same as the number of supplied operands and whose parameter types are the same as the corresponding operand types. In this case, the type of the application is the result type of the operator type. When we reason that applying a procedure of type (`-> (int bool) symb`) to an `int` expression and a `bool` expression yields a value of type `symb`, we are using the [→-*elim*] rule.

The [*let*] and [*letrec*] rules are similar to the [→-*elim*] rule. Both type-check a body expression E_0 with respect to the given type environment TE extended with type assignments for the named definition expressions $E_1, \ldots, E_n$ in the bindings. The difference is that `let` definitions are not in the scope of the bindings, and so can be type-checked relative to TE. However, `letrec` definitions *are* in the scope of the bindings, and so must be type-checked relative to an environment TE' that extends TE with type assignments for the bindings. Since the definition types in a `let` can be determined from the supplied type environment TE, there is no need for the types of the definitions to be explicitly declared. But in the `letrec` case, determining the extended type environment TE' in general would require finding a fixed point over type environments. μFLEX requires the programmer to explicitly declare the types of `letrec` definitions so that the type checker need not compute fixed points.

The [*prim*] rule treats primitive operators as if they have arrow types determined by the primitive type environment TE_{prim}. This allows the type checker to handle primitive applications via what is essentially a specialized version of [$\rightarrow$-*elim*].

For the type ascription expression (`the` T E), the [*the*] rule simply checks that E has the specified type T.

The [*prog*] rule type-checks a program. It is similar to the [$\rightarrow$-*intro*] rule, except that: (1) because a program has no type environment, its body is checked only with respect to the type bindings for its formal parameters; and (2) a program type uses `=>` rather than `->`.

In the μFLEX type system, the standard library bindings in a program introduced by the `flex` keyword are handled by the `flex` desugaring rule presented in Figure 11.2. An alternative strategy is to handle `flex` programs directly via the following type rule (where, for simplicity, it is assumed that there are no `def-type`s):

$$\frac{\forall_{j=1}^{k} \;.\; TE_{body} \vdash E_{d_j} : T_{d_j} \qquad TE_{body} \vdash E_{body} : T_{body}}{\vdash_{prog} (\texttt{flex} \; ((I_{fml_h} \; T_{fml_h})_{h=1}^{m}) \; E_{body} \; (\texttt{def} \; I_{d_j} \; T_{d_j} \; E_{d_j})_{j=1}^{k})} \quad [prog']$$
$$: (\texttt{=>} \; (T_{fml_1} \; \ldots \; T_{fml_m}) \; T_{body})$$
$$\text{where} \quad TE_{body} = TE_{prim}[I_{fml_h} : T_{fml_h}]_{h=1}^{m}[I_{d_j} : T_{d_j}]_{j=i}^{k}$$

This reflects the way that top-level programs are usually type-checked in practice: The types of standard bindings are summarized in a standard type environment (such as TE_{prim}) rather than being type-checked anew for every program.

All the type rules are **purely structural** in the sense that the premise judgments involve subexpressions of the expression that appears in the conclusion judgment. Just as purely structural rewrite rules guarantee meaningful transitions in an SOS (see Section 3.2.5), purely structural type rules guarantee that the type checking process will terminate. The initial expression being type-checked has a finite AST. In any rule each premise subexpression necessarily has a strictly smaller AST than the conclusion expression. By structural induction, the type-checking process must eventually bottom out at the axioms.

Another important property of the μFLEX type system is that each μFLEX expression construct appears in the conclusion of exactly one type rule. A type system with this property is said to be **syntax directed**. It is straightforward to turn syntax-directed type rules into an efficient type-checking algorithm because the type-checking process is completely deterministic. For example, the type rules in Figure 11.7 can be encoded in a type-checking function TC that takes a type environment TE and an expression E and either returns the type T (in the case where $TE \vdash E : T$) or indicates that the expression is ill typed. The body of this function would be a dispatch on the kind of expression. If E is a primitive expression, TC would succeed or fail immediately as specified by the associated axiom. For compound expressions, TC would be called recursively on the subexpressions of E as specified by the premises of the single inference rule whose conclusion matches E. The syntax-directed nature of the type rules means that it is never necessary to guess which type rule should be used for a given expression, so the type-checking process can be performed without backtracking.

11.5.4   Type Derivations

The proof that a type judgment is valid is called a **type derivation**, also known as a **typing**. A type derivation is a tree in which each node is a type judgment. Each type judgment must be the conclusion of an instantiated type rule whose premises are its children in the tree. The root judgment of the tree is the desired type judgment and the leaf judgments are instantiated type-checking axioms.

Consider the following μFLEX expression E_{let}:

```
(let ((app5 (abs ((f (-> (int) bool))) (f 5)))
      (pos (abs ((x int)) (prim > x 0))))
  (app5 pos))
```

A type derivation TD_{let} proving that E_{let} has type `bool` in the empty type environment is shown in Figure 11.8. The figure employs several abbreviations for expressions, types, type environments, and three subderivations. Without these abbreviations, the derivation would be too wide to display on the page.

To reduce the width of type derivations, we will present them in a **vertical style**. In this style, horizontal-style type-rule instantiations of the form

$$\frac{premise_1 \ \dots \ premise_n}{conclusion} \qquad [\textit{rule-name}]$$

are presented vertically as

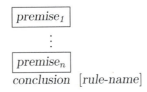

Abbreviations

T_{ib} = (-> (int) bool)

T_{iib} = (-> (int int) bool)

TE_f = {f : T_{ib}}

TE_x = {x : int}

TE_{body} = {app5 : (-> (T_{ib}) bool), pos : T_{ib}}

E_{app5} = (abs ((f T_{ib})) (f 5))

E_{pos} = (abs ((x int)) (prim > x 0))

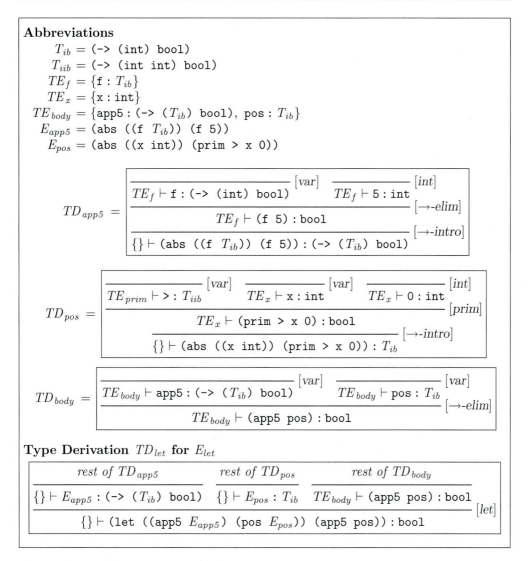

Type Derivation TD_{let} for E_{let}

Figure 11.8 Type derivation for E_{let}.

All premises of a conclusion are individually boxed and aligned vertically such that the leftmost sides of the boxes are directly above the leftmost side of the conclusion. For example, the horizontal-style derivation

$$\frac{\overline{TE_{prim} \vdash \mathtt{>} : (\mathtt{->}\ (\mathtt{int}\ \mathtt{int})\ \mathtt{bool})}\ [var] \quad \overline{TE_x \vdash \mathtt{x} : \mathtt{int}}\ [var] \quad \overline{TE_x \vdash \mathtt{0} : \mathtt{int}}\ [int]}{TE_x \vdash (\mathtt{prim}\ \mathtt{>}\ \mathtt{x}\ \mathtt{0}) : \mathtt{bool}}\ [prim]$$

is presented in the vertical style as

$$\boxed{\begin{array}{l}\boxed{TE_{prim} \vdash \mathtt{>} : (\mathtt{->}\ (\mathtt{int}\ \mathtt{int})\ \mathtt{bool})\ [var]} \\[4pt] \boxed{TE_x \vdash \mathtt{x} : \mathtt{int}\ [var]} \\[4pt] \boxed{TE_x \vdash \mathtt{0} : \mathtt{int}\ [int]} \\[2pt] TE_x \vdash (\mathtt{prim}\ \mathtt{>}\ \mathtt{x}\ \mathtt{0}) : \mathtt{bool}\ [prim]\end{array}}$$

The vertical style makes more efficient use of the real estate on the page. E.g., Figure 11.9 shows a vertical-style presentation for the type derivation TD_{let}. Note that a boxed premise may itself be a conclusion of other boxed premises, naturally leading to the nesting of boxes.

Figure 11.10 presents a program P_{pow} that exercises many features of μFLEX. Figure 11.12 shows the type derivation for P_{pow} that illustrates all of the μFLEX type rules except for [unit], [bool], [symb], and [error] in a single example.

The reason that we emphasize the structure of and notation for type derivations is that such derivations are essential for understanding typed programming languages. Every valid type judgment $TE \vdash E : T$ must be justified by a type derivation, so type derivations (rather than individual type judgments) are often the key entity manipulated when reasoning formally about type systems. For example, in Section 11.6 we will see that proving the soundness of a type system involves showing that when expression E rewrites to E', the type derivation for E can be transformed to an appropriate type derivation for E'. In Chapter 13 and Chapter 16, we will see that type and effect reconstruction can be understood using derivations that are remarkably similar to the ones presented here.

Additionally, visual representations of type derivations serve as compact execution traces for a type-checking algorithm. For example, when the type-checking function TC sketched on page 648 is executed on P_{pow}:

- each type judgment $TE \vdash E : T$ in Figure 11.12 represents a call to TC that takes two arguments (a type environment TE and an expression E) and returns a type T;

- each box appearing at the same indentation level above a judgment for E represents a recursive call to TC on a subexpression of E that is made as part of determining the type for E.

Abbreviations

$$T_{ib} = \texttt{(-> (int) bool)}$$
$$TE_f = \{\texttt{f} : T_{ib}\}$$
$$TE_x = \{\texttt{x} : \texttt{int}\}$$
$$TE_{body} = \{\texttt{app5} : \texttt{(-> (}T_{ib}\texttt{) bool)}, \texttt{pos} : T_{ib}\}$$
$$E_{app5} = \texttt{(abs ((f } T_{ib}\texttt{)) (f 5))}$$
$$E_{pos} = \texttt{(abs ((x int)) (prim > x 0))}$$

Type Derivation TD_{let} **for** E_{let}

$$TE_f \vdash \texttt{f} : \texttt{(-> (int) bool)} \quad [var]$$
$$TE_f \vdash \texttt{5} : \texttt{int} \quad [int]$$
$$TE_f \vdash \texttt{(f 5)} : \texttt{bool} \quad [\rightarrow\text{-}elim]$$
$$\{\} \vdash \texttt{(abs ((f } T_{ib}\texttt{)) (f 5))} : \texttt{(-> (}T_{ib}\texttt{) bool)} \quad [\rightarrow\text{-}intro]$$

$$TE_{prim} \vdash \texttt{>} : \texttt{(-> (int int) bool)} \quad [var]$$
$$TE_x \vdash \texttt{x} : \texttt{int} \quad [var]$$
$$TE_x \vdash \texttt{0} : \texttt{int} \quad [int]$$
$$TE_x \vdash \texttt{(prim > x 0)} : \texttt{bool} \quad [prim]$$
$$\{\} \vdash \texttt{(abs ((x int)) (prim > x 0))} : \texttt{(-> (int) bool)} \quad [\rightarrow\text{-}intro]$$

$$TE_{body} \vdash \texttt{app5} : \texttt{(-> (}T_{ib}\texttt{) bool)} \quad [var]$$
$$TE_{body} \vdash \texttt{pos} : T_{ib} \quad [var]$$
$$TE_{body} \vdash \texttt{(app5 pos)} : \texttt{bool} \quad [\rightarrow\text{-}elim]$$
$$\{\} \vdash \texttt{(let ((app5 } E_{app5}\texttt{) (pos } E_{pos}\texttt{)) (app5 pos))} : \texttt{bool} \quad [let]$$

Figure 11.9 Vertical-style type derivation for E_{let}.

Exercise 11.2 Consider the following closed FL expressions:

```
E₁ = (((abs (a b) (abs (f) (f b a)))
       1 #t)
      (abs (x y) (if x y 2)))
E₂ = (let ((add (abs (x y) (prim + x y))))
       (letrec ((sum (abs (i done? next)
                       (if (done? i)
                           0
                           (add i (sum (add i 1)))))))
         sum))
```

```
P_pow = (flexk ((n int))
            (let ((dbl (the (-> (int) int) (abs ((x int)) (prim * x 2)))))
                (letrec ((loop (-> (int) int)
                            (abs ((i int))
                                (if (prim >= i n)
                                    i
                                    (loop (dbl i))))))
                    (loop 1)))))
```

Figure 11.10   A sample μFLEX program, P_{pow}.

$$T_{ii} = (\text{->} \ (\text{int}) \ \text{int})$$
$$TE_{loop} = \{n : \text{int}, \ dbl : T_{ii}, \ loop : T_{ii}\}$$
$$P_{pow} = (\text{flexk} \ ((n \ \text{int})) \ E_{letdbl}))$$
$$E_{letdbl} = (\text{let} \ ((dbl \ (\text{the} \ T_{ii} \ E_{dblabs}))) \ E_{recloop})$$
$$E_{dblabs} = (\text{abs} \ ((x \ \text{int})) \ (\text{prim} \ * \ x \ 2))$$
$$E_{recloop} = (\text{letrec} \ ((loop \ T_{ii} \ E_{loopabs})) \ (loop \ 1))$$
$$E_{loopabs} = (\text{abs} \ ((i \ \text{int})) \ E_{if})$$
$$E_{if} = (\text{if} \ (\text{prim} \ \text{>=} \ i \ n) \ i \ (loop \ (dbl \ i)))$$

Figure 11.11   Abbreviations for Figure 11.12.

a. Translate each expression into a well-typed μFLEX expression by adding appropriate type annotations.

b. For each of your translations, give a type derivation that shows that it is well typed in the empty type environment.

Exercise 11.3

a. Give a type derivation showing that for any type T, the following μFLEX program has type (=> (int) T):

```
(flexk ((n int))
    (if (< n 0)
        (error negative T)
        (letrec ((loop (-> () T) (abs () (loop))))
            (loop))))
```

b. The type T used in part **a** could be any type, including one that contains type identifiers that are free in the program. Does this indicate that μFLEX has a type loophole? That is, might there be an expression whose static type does not match the dynamic type of the run-time value of that expression? Explain.

Type Derivation TD_{pow} **for** P_{pow}
See abbreviations in Figure 11.11.

$$
\boxed{
\begin{array}{l}
\boxed{
\begin{array}{l}
\boxed{\begin{array}{l}
\boxed{TE_{prim} \vdash * : (\text{-> (int int) int)} \;\; [var]} \\
\boxed{\{\texttt{n : int, x : int}\} \vdash \texttt{x : int} \;\; [var]} \\
\boxed{\{\texttt{n : int, x : int}\} \vdash \texttt{2 : int} \;\; [int]} \\
\{\texttt{n : int, x : int}\} \vdash \texttt{(prim * x 2) : int} \;\; [prim]
\end{array}} \\
\{\texttt{n : int}\} \vdash \texttt{(abs ((x int)) (prim * x 2)) :} T_{ii} \;\; [\text{->-intro}]
\end{array}} \\
\{\texttt{n : int}\} \vdash \texttt{(the } T_{ii} \texttt{ (abs ((x int)) (prim * x 2)))} : T_{ii} \;\; [the] \\
\\
\boxed{
\begin{array}{l}
\boxed{
\begin{array}{l}
\boxed{\begin{array}{l}
\boxed{TE_{prim} \vdash \texttt{>= : (-> (int int) bool)} \;\; [var]} \\
\boxed{TE_{loop}[\texttt{i : int}] \vdash \texttt{i : int} \;\; [var]} \\
\boxed{TE_{loop}[\texttt{i : int}] \vdash \texttt{n : int} \;\; [var]} \\
TE_{loop}[\texttt{i : int}] \vdash \texttt{(prim >= i n) : bool} \;\; [prim]
\end{array}} \\
\boxed{TE_{loop}[\texttt{i : int}] \vdash \texttt{i : int} \;\; [var]} \\
\boxed{\begin{array}{l}
\boxed{TE_{loop}[\texttt{i : int}] \vdash \texttt{loop : (-> (int) int)} \;\; [var]} \\
\boxed{\begin{array}{l}
\boxed{TE_{loop}[\texttt{i : int}] \vdash \texttt{dbl : (-> (int) int)} \;\; [var]} \\
\boxed{TE_{loop}[\texttt{i : int}] \vdash \texttt{i : int} \;\; [var]} \\
TE_{loop}[\texttt{i : int}] \vdash \texttt{(dbl i) : int} \;\; [\text{->-elim}]
\end{array}} \\
TE_{loop}[\texttt{i : int}] \vdash \texttt{(loop (dbl i)) : int} \;\; [\text{->-elim}]
\end{array}} \\
TE_{loop}[\texttt{i : int}] \vdash \texttt{(if (prim >= i n) i (loop (dbl i))) : int} \;\; [if]
\end{array}} \\
TE_{loop} \vdash \texttt{(abs ((i int))} E_{if}) : \texttt{(-> (int) int)} \;\; [\text{->-intro}]
\end{array}} \\
\boxed{
\begin{array}{l}
\boxed{TE_{loop} \vdash \texttt{loop : (-> (int) int)} \;\; [var]} \\
\boxed{TE_{loop} \vdash \texttt{1 : int} \;\; [int]} \\
TE_{loop} \vdash \texttt{(loop 1) : int} \;\; [\text{->-elim}]
\end{array}} \\
\{\texttt{n : int, dbl :} T_{ii}\} \vdash \texttt{(letrec ((loop } T_{ii} \; E_{loopabs}\texttt{)) (loop 1)) : int} \;\; [letrec]
\end{array}} \\
\{\texttt{n : int}\} \vdash \texttt{(let ((dbl (the } T_{ii} \; E_{dblabs}\texttt{)))} \; E_{recloop}\texttt{) : int} \;\; [let] \\
\vdash_{prog} \texttt{(flexk ((n int))} \; E_{letdbl}\texttt{) : (=> (int) int)} \;\; [prog]
\end{array}}
$$

Figure 11.12 Vertical-style type derivation for P_{pow}.

Exercise 11.4 Abby Stracksen likes the power of the POSTFIX+{dup} language from Section 3.8, but doesn't want to rely on dynamic typing. So she develops a type system for POSTFIX+{dup}. First, she defines the type grammar:

$$T ::= \texttt{int} \qquad\qquad\qquad \text{[IntType]}$$
$$| \ \texttt{(-> } (T^*) \ (T^*)\texttt{)} \ \text{[TransformType]}$$

A type is either an integer type `int` or a transform type of the form `(-> ` (T_{in}^*) ` ` (T_{out}^*)`)`. A transform type models the type of a stack transform that consumes some number of values from the top of the stack (by popping them off the input stack) and produces some (other) number of values for the top of the stack (by pushing them onto the output stack). In the transform type `(-> ` (T_{in}^*) ` ` (T_{out}^*)`)`, T_{in}^* are the types of the values, in order, that are consumed by the transform and T_{out}^* are the types of the values that are produced by the transform. In both sequences, the leftmost type represents the item on the top of the stack.

Next, Abby writes type rules of the form $\vdash_C C : T$ to describe the transform type T of a command C. Here are some of her rules:

$$\vdash_C N : \texttt{(-> () (int))} \qquad\qquad\qquad\qquad [int]$$

$$\vdash_C \texttt{pop} : \texttt{(-> } (T) \texttt{ ())} \qquad\qquad\qquad\qquad [pop]$$

$$\vdash_C \texttt{dup} : \texttt{(-> } (T) \ (T \ T)\texttt{)} \qquad\qquad\qquad\qquad [dup]$$

$$\vdash_C A_{op} : \texttt{(-> (int int) (int))} \qquad\qquad\qquad\qquad [arithop]$$

$$\vdash_C R_{op} : \texttt{(-> (int int) (int))} \qquad\qquad\qquad\qquad [relop]$$

The [arithop] rule works for all arithmetic commands A_{op} (`add`, `sub`, `mul`, `div`, and `rem`) and the [relop] rule works for all relational commands R_{op} (`lt`, `eq`, and `gt`).

a. Give type rules for the `swap` and `sel` commands.

b. The above type rules define the types of individual POSTFIX+{dup} commands, but Abby still needs the "glue" to paste together the transform types of individual commands to result in the transform type of a command sequence. For this purpose, Abby develops command-sequence type rules of the form $\vdash_Q Q : T$ to describe the transform type T of the command sequence Q. Complete the following type rules by filling in the holes with appropriate transform types:

$$\vdash_Q [\,] : \square \qquad\qquad\qquad\qquad\qquad [seq\text{-}empty]$$

$$\frac{\vdash_C C : \texttt{(-> } (T_1 \ \ldots \ T_i) \ (T_1' \ \ldots \ T_j')\texttt{)} \quad \vdash_Q Q : \texttt{(-> } (T_1' \ \ldots \ T_m') \ (T_1'' \ \ldots \ T_n'')\texttt{)}}{\vdash_Q C \,.\, Q : \square} \ \text{where } j < m \qquad [seq\text{-}<]$$

$$\frac{\vdash_C C : \texttt{(-> } (T_1 \ \ldots \ T_i) \ (T_1' \ \ldots \ T_j')\texttt{)} \quad \vdash_Q Q : \texttt{(-> } (T_1' \ \ldots \ T_m') \ (T_1'' \ \ldots \ T_n'')\texttt{)}}{\vdash_Q C \,.\, Q : \square} \ \text{where } j = m \qquad [seq\text{-}=]$$

$$\frac{\vdash_C C : (\text{->} (T_1 \ \dots \ T_i) \ (T'_1 \ \dots \ T'_j))}{\vdash_Q C \cdot Q : \Box} \quad \text{where } j > m \qquad [seq\text{-}>]$$

Rules like this naturally arise in other languages that manipulate a stack, including typed assembly languages (e.g., [MCG+99]).

c. Use the type rules for commands and command sequences developed so far to derive the transform type of the following command sequence:

> (pop swap 2 mul add dup)

d. One POSTFIX command not considered so far is nget.

    i. Explain why the nget command is problematic in a typed version of POSTFIX.

    ii. Suppose that nget is replaced by a command of the form (get N_{index}), where N_{index} specifies the index of the (not necessarily integer) stack value to be copied to the top of the stack. Write a type rule for (get N_{index}).

e. To handle command-sequence values within her typed version of POSTFIX+{dup}, Abby modifies the exec command. Instead of a single exec command she introduces a family of commands of the form exec-m-n, where m and n are nonnegative integers. exec-m-n works like exec, except that it expects the top of the stack to be a command sequence that consumes m stack values and produces n stack values. Give the type rules for the commands exec-m-n and (Q).

f. Translate the following POSTFIX command sequence into Abby's typed language and use the above type rules for commands and command sequences to derive the transform type of your translation:

> ((pop add) (exec) sel exec)

g. Abby uses the notation $\vdash_P$ (postfix N Q) to indicate that a program in her typed version of POSTFIX+{dup} is well typed. Write a type rule that defines $\vdash_P$.

11.5.5 Monomorphism

The μFLEX type system is **monomorphic**, meaning that each μFLEX expression can be assigned at most one type in a given type environment. This is formalized by the following theorem:

> **Theorem 11.1 (μFLEX Type Uniqueness)** *If a μFLEX expression E is well typed with respect to a type environment TE, then there is a unique type T such that $TE \vdash E : T$.*

This theorem formalizes the claim that a μFLEX type checker never has to guess types or perform any backtracking. Another consequence of this theorem is that there is a partial function *typeof* that maps pairs of expressions and type environments to their types:

$$typeof : (\text{Exp} \times \text{TypeEnvironment}) \rightharpoonup \text{Type}$$
$$typeof \; \langle E, TE \rangle \; = \; \begin{cases} T, \text{ if } TE \vdash E : T \\ undefined, \text{ otherwise} \end{cases}$$

In other words, it makes sense to talk about *the* type of a well-typed expression relative to a given environment.

It is worthwhile to prove this theorem both to understand why it is true and to see an example of how proofs involving types are structured.

Proof of Theorem 11.1:   Since E is well typed with respect to TE, there must be a judgment $TE \vdash E : T$ (call it TJ) that is the root of a type derivation TD. We will not only show that T is unique; we will prove the stronger claim that TD is unique. This implies that any type-checking process based on the type rules is deterministic.

The proof is by induction on the height of TD. The base cases of the induction are the type derivations for literals, variable references, and **error** expressions. In each of these cases, a type judgment matches exactly one type axiom, and the type derivation is uniquely determined by TE and E. Note that (1) TE only matters in the [*var*] case and (2) the explicit type T in (**error** Y T) is critical for making the theorem hold in the [*error*] case.

The uniqueness of the remaining cases can be shown by case analysis. Each remaining kind of type judgment TJ matches the conclusion of exactly one inference rule, which is determined by the structure of the expression E in TJ. For each such rule, we can argue that all the premise judgments are uniquely determined by the conclusion judgment. These premises must be the roots of the subderivations of TD. By induction, all these subderivations are unique, so TD is also unique.

The easy cases are the [*if*], [$\rightarrow$-*intro*], [*letrec*], and [*the*] rules, in which all syntactic entities mentioned in the rule premises are either constants (e.g., the type identifier **bool**, the type environment TE_{prim}) or domain variables that appear in the conclusion. So in every instantiation of these inference rules, the instantiations of the rule premises are uniquely determined by the instantiation of the conclusion.

In the other cases (the [$\rightarrow$-*elim*], [*let*], and [*prim*] rules), the argument is more delicate because the premises mention some domain variables that do *not* appear in the conclusion but *do* appear in other premises. We spell out the details for [$\rightarrow$-*elim*]; the other two rules are similar. Suppose TD is rooted at

$TE \vdash (E_{rator}\ E_{i=1}^n) : T_{result}$. By $[\rightarrow\text{-}elim]$, TD has subderivations TD_1, ..., TD_n rooted at judgments of the form $TE \vdash E_i : T_i$. By induction, these are unique, so the T_i are unique. The remaining judgment mentions these types in addition to TE, E_{rator}, and T_{result} from the conclusion, so it is completely determined and is also unique. $\diamond$

From the $[prog]$ rule, it is easy to see that the uniqueness of types and type derivations carries over from μFLEX expressions to μFLEX programs.

Minor modifications to the μFLEX syntax and type rules can invalidate the uniqueness of types. For example, consider a variant of μFLEX in which the error construct has the form (error Y) — i.e., it does not include an explicit type. Then a type rule for such a construct might be:

$$TE \vdash (\texttt{error}\ Y) : T \qquad\qquad [error']$$

In this rule, T is unconstrained, so an error expression may be assigned *any* type. Clearly its type would no longer be unique! Omitting the explicit type declarations for parameters in abs would also cause types to be unconstrained. For example, the expression (abs (x) x) could be assigned an infinite number of types, such as (-> (int) int) and (-> (bool) bool). Exercise 11.7 shows that changes to the letrec syntax and type rules can similarly lead to situations where the type checker must "guess" a type. Such changes aren't necessarily bad — indeed, we will institute such changes when we consider type reconstruction in Chapter 13. However, such changes can alter the character of a type system. For instance, the *typeof* function is not well defined after such changes.

A monomorphic type system is very simple to understand and to implement, but it can create headaches for the programmer. As a simple example, suppose we want to translate the following FL expression into μFLEX:

```
(let ((id (abs (x) x)))
  (if (id #t) 1 ((id id) 2)))
```

Intuitively, the identity function id takes a value of any type and returns the same value. But the monomorphism of μFLEX forbids us from specifying "any type"; we must write particular types. We can often circumvent this restriction by defining multiple copies of an expression that differ only in their type annotations. In this case, we need to define three versions of the identity function to achieve a well-typed μFLEX translation:

```
(let ((id_bool (abs ((x bool)) x))
      (id_int (abs ((x int)) x))
      (id_intfun (abs ((x (-> (int) int))) x)))
  (if (id_bool #t) 1 ((id_intfun id_int) 2)))
```

Although this example is contrived, it represents a real problem faced by programmers in languages like C, JAVA,[11] and PASCAL. In the next chapter, we will see how polymorphic type systems address this problem.

Exercise 11.5 Translate each of the following FL expressions into a well-typed μFLEX expression by (1) adding explicit type annotations and (2) duplicating expressions when necessary.

a. `(abs (a b c)`
```
   (let ((appc (abs (f) (f c)))
         (make-sub (abs (n) (abs (x) (prim - x n))))
         (make-geq (abs (k) (abs (y) (prim >= y k)))))
      (scand (appc (make-geq (appc (make-sub a))))
             ((appc make-geq) ((appc make-sub) b)))))
```

b. `(let ((inc (abs ((x int)) (prim + x 1)))`
```
       (compose (abs (f g) (abs (x) (f (g x)))))
       (thrice (abs (f) (abs (x) (f (f (f x)))))))
   (let ((nat (abs (g) ((g inc) 0))))
     (+ (nat (abs (h) (compose (thrice h) (thrice h))))
       (+ (nat (compose thrice thrice))
          (nat (thrice thrice))))))
```

Exercise 11.6 Suppose that the following two constructs were added to the μFLEX kernel (rather than being defined as syntactic sugar):

a. `(cond ($E_{test}$ $E_{then}$)* (else $E_{default}$))`

b. `(scand $E_{conjunct}^*$)` (The type rule for scor is similar.)

Give a type rule for each of these two constructs.

Exercise 11.7 Suppose that μFLEX's letrec were changed so that (1) letrec bindings had the form $(I\ E)$ rather than $(I\ T\ E)$ and (2) the type rule for letrec became:

$$\frac{\forall_{i=0}^{n}\ .\ TE[I_j : T_j]_{j=1}^{n} \vdash E_i : T_i}{TE \vdash (\mathtt{letrec}\ ((I_i\ E_i)_{i=1}^{n})\ E_0) : T_0} \qquad [letrec']$$

These modifications invalidate the unique type property of μFLEX (Theorem 11.1). Demonstrate this by constructing a type derivation showing that the following looping expression can be assigned any type T:

```
(letrec ((loop (abs () (loop)))) (loop))
```

Exercise 11.8 Thai Ping wants to extend μFLEX with label and jump from Section 9.4. Recall the informal semantics of these constructs:

---

[11]The generics feature of Java version 5.0 goes a long way toward addressing this problem, but does not eliminate it. See the discussion in Section 12.2.5.

(label I E) evaluates E in an environment where I is bound to the *control point* receiving the value of the label expression.

(jump E_1 E_2) first evaluates E_1 to a control point value, then evaluates E_2 to a value, and then "returns" the value of E_2 to the control point value.

Below are some simple examples of label and jump in a version of FL extended with these constructs. Assume that the names +, *, and < are bound to the usual standard procedures.

$$E_1 = \text{(+ 1 (label exit (* 2 3)))} \xrightarrow[FL]{} 7$$

$$E_2 = \text{(+ 1 (label exit (* 2 (jump exit (+ 3 (jump exit 4))))))} \xrightarrow[FL]{} 5$$

$$E_3 = \text{(* 2 (label out (if (label test (< 3 (if (jump test \#f)}$$
$$\text{(jump test \#t)}$$
$$\text{(jump out 4))))}$$
$$5$$
$$\text{((jump out 6) 7)))) } \xrightarrow[FL]{} 12$$

Thai modifies the grammar of μFLEX as follows:

$E ::= \ldots \mid \text{(label } T\ I\ E\text{)} \mid \text{(jump } T\ E_1\ E_2\text{)}$

$T ::= \ldots \mid \text{(controlpointof } T\text{)}$

The label and jump constructs have been annotated with explicit types that specify the types of these expressions. These annotations are similar to the explicit types in letrec and error expressions, respectively, which allow a type checker to determine the type of these expressions without "guessing" any types. The domain of types has been extended with a new type of the form (controlpointof T). This type describes control points that expect a value of type T. For example, in the μFLEX expression

    (+ 1 (label int return (if (jump bool return 2) 3 4)))

- the label expression is given the explicit type int because it appears in a context that expects an integer;

- the control point named return has type (controlpointof int), because the label expression returns an integer;

- the jump expression is given the explicit type bool because it appears in a context where a boolean is expected;

- the value passed to return by jump must be an integer because return has type (controlpointof int).

a. Using Thai's framework, give type rules for label and jump.

b. Translate E_1, E_2, and E_3 into Thai's extended version of μFLEX, and show that each translation is well typed by constructing a type derivation for it.

c. Is it possible to remove the explicit type annotation T from the label or jump construct without invalidating the type uniqueness property of μFLEX (Theorem 11.1)? Explain.

Exercise 11.9 Mona Morwicz is upset that expressions like let cannot be defined as syntactic sugar in μFLEX. To address this problem, she designs the following new μFLEX expression:

(bindtypeof τ E_1 E_2): In the dynamic semantics, this expression evaluates and returns E_2; it never evaluates E_1, whose only purpose is for type checking. In the static semantics, this expression is type-checked by finding the type T_1 of E_1 and substituting T_1 for τ in E_2 before type-checking it. The unique type derivation property of μFLEX guarantees that T_1 is unique.

The power of bindtypeof is illustrated by the following desugaring:

(test E_{test} E_{then}) $\leadsto_{ds}$ (if E_{test} E_{then} (bindtypeof t E_{then} (error fail t)))

This desugaring uses bindtypeof to automatically determine the type of the error expression. Without bindtypeof, the test construct would need to include an explicit type for E_{then}.

a. Write a type rule for bindtypeof.

b. Argue that adding bindtypeof to μFLEX preserves unique type derivations.

c. With Mona's new construct, show that let can be defined as syntactic sugar rather than being a kernel form.

d. Bud Lojack thinks that Mona's bindtypeof expression is too complex. He prefers to extend the type syntax of μFLEX with a typeof construct:

   $T ::= \ldots \mid$ (typeof E)

Bud explains that (typeof E) simply denotes the type of E. Using typeof, Bud gives a simpler desugaring for test:

   (test E_{test} E_{then}) $\leadsto_{ds}$ (if E_{test} E_{then} (error fail (typeof E_{then})))

Is Bud's construct a good idea? Discuss any difficulties that would be encountered in extending μFLEX with typeof.

Exercise 11.10 Based on the type-checking rules presented in Section 11.5.3, write a type checker for μFLEX programs in your favorite programming language. The core of the type checker can be structured as an interpreter that takes an expression and a type environment. If the expression is well typed, it returns the type of the expression; if the expression is ill typed, it should somehow indicate this fact.

Exercise 11.11 Just because μFLEX has explicit types doesn't necessarily imply that it must be type-checked at compile time. It is possible to imagine a version of μFLEX in which all type checking is done at run time. Demonstrate this by writing an interpreter for μFLEX that performs all type checking dynamically. For example, when a procedure is called, the types of the arguments should be checked before the body of the procedure is evaluated.

11.6   Type Soundness

11.6.1   What Is Type Soundness?

We expect that any language with a static type system should come with a guarantee that the execution of well-typed programs will not encounter **dynamic type errors**. The notion of what constitutes a dynamic type error depends on the language. In μFLEX, dynamic type errors include:

- a reference to an unbound variable (i.e., one that is free in the program);

- a primitive application with the wrong number of operands, such as the expressions (prim not #t #f), (prim + 1), and (prim < 1 2 3);

- a primitive application with an operand of the wrong type, such as the expressions (prim not 17) and (prim + 1 #t);

- a conditional expression with a nonboolean test, such as (if 1 2 3);

- an application of a nonprocedural value, such as (1 2 3);

- a procedure application with the wrong number of operands, such as the expressions ((abs ((x T_x)) E) 1 2) and ((abs ((y T_y) (z T_z)) E) 3).

There are also **dynamic nontype errors** that program execution may encounter. In μFLEX, these include division/remainder by zero and user-specified error conditions (using error). In languages with data structures, common dynamic nontype errors include out-of-bounds indexing of positional products and performing an operation on the wrong element of a sum type (e.g., taking the head of an empty list). Some sophisticated type systems are able to detect some of these errors at analysis time. But catching all such errors statically is usually undecidable, so no type system could possibly detect all of them.

A type system is said to be **sound** if a well-typed program cannot encounter a dynamic type error. This property is often summarized by the slogan "well-typed programs do not go wrong" [Mil78]. This slogan is somewhat misleading, since it seems to imply that well-typed programs cannot encounter any dynamic error. There are some very simple languages (such as the simply typed lambda calculus and some of its rudimentary extensions) in which all dynamic errors are indeed type errors. But, as illustrated above, more full-featured languages may encounter many kinds of nontype errors at run time. So a more accurate slogan is "well-typed programs do not encounter dynamic type errors (but may encounter other dynamic errors)."

Type soundness relates the dynamic semantics (usually an operational semantics) of a language to the static semantics (type system). A proof of type soundness is generally decomposed into two parts:

1. A **preservation** (also called **subject reduction**) theorem stating that if a configuration cf has type T and $cf \Rightarrow cf'$, then cf' has type T.

2. A **progress** theorem stating that if cf is well typed, then either it is reducible, a final configuration, or stuck at a nontype error. In other words, a well-typed configuration cannot be stuck at a type error.

With these two theorems, it is easy to prove two aspects of type soundness: (1) an initially well-typed configuration cf_0 can never lead to a dynamic type error and (2) if a final configuration is reached, it has the same type as the initial configuration. Suppose cf_0 has type T and $cf_0 \stackrel{n}{\Rightarrow} cf_n$, where cf_n is irreducible. By preservation, each configuration in the transition path from cf_0 to cf_n has type T. Since cf_n is well typed, by progress, it cannot be stuck at a type error, proving (1). If cf_n is a final configuration, it has the same type T as the initial configuration, proving (2).

In the remainder of this section, we follow this recipe to prove the type soundness of μFLEX. Since the proof strategy requires an operational semantics, we must first develop an operational semantics for μFLEX (Section 11.6.2). Then we will demonstrate the type soundness of μFLEX by developing appropriate preservation and progress theorems (Section 11.6.3).

11.6.2   An Operational Semantics for μFLEX

We begin by presenting an operational semantics for a CBN version of μFLEX. (The type soundness argument can be adapted to CBV, but the CBN version is simpler to describe because it involves checking fewer cases.) The SOS in Figures 11.13 and 11.14 is similar to the SOS for FL in Figure 6.18 (page 258) and Figure 6.19 (page 259) except that:

- Unlike FL, μFLEX does not support pairs, so the InputExp and ValueExp domains do not include pair expressions, and the AnsExp domain does not contain the `pairans` token. (All these domains must be extended appropriately when μFLEX is extended to full FLEX.)

- μFLEX's $[\beta]$ rule is a generalization of FL's $[\beta]$ rule to the case of applying a multiparameter abstraction to multiple arguments.

- μFLEX has rules for the `let`, `letrec`, and `the` constructs, which are new kernel constructs in μFLEX. The `let` rule substitutes the definition expressions for the associated names in the body. The `letrec` rule is similar to the `let` rule except that the definition expressions are wrapped in a `letrec` before substitution to implement the semantics of recursion. This is a generalization of FL's [rec] rule. The rule for `the` simply returns the underlying expression.

- In addition to checking the number of inputs, the input function *IF* checks the types of inputs (using the function $type_{inp}$) to verify that they match the declared types of the formal parameters of the program. Any mismatch results in an initial configuration that is an **error** expression. Such dynamic type checking of program inputs is performed in most real-world languages in some guise, either by the programmer or by the implementation. Program inputs are typically extracted from a command-line string, an input stream, one or more files, and/or input specifications entered via a graphical user interface. Such inputs must often be checked dynamically for well-formedness. For example, if a program expects a command-line argument string to represent an integer, the programmer must write code checking that the string is a sequence of characters representing a valid integer and indicate some sort of error if this check fails.

Note that in μFLEX it is possible to have well-typed programs that cannot be executed nontrivially on any inputs. For example, consider the following programs:

P_1 = (flexk ((x t)) x)
P_2 = (flexk ((f (-> (int) bool))) (f 5))

Both of these programs are well typed. But all μFLEX program inputs must be literals, and no literal has a type identifier (such as `t`) or an arrow type (such as `(-> (int) bool)`) as its type. So the execution of these programs on any input will immediately get stuck at a **bad-arg-type** error. This awkward situation could be avoided by modifying the μFLEX type system to restrict declared program parameter types to be the types of valid inputs (i.e., base types), in which case P_1 and P_2 would no longer be valid programs.

In order to prove the soundness of the μFLEX type system, we need to define type and nontype errors in μFLEX. This is the purpose of the following two lemmas, which can be proven via easy case analyses on the grammars for $\mathbb{E}$ and E.

Domains

Syntactic domains are from the μFLEX grammar (Figure 11.1 on page 628)

$V \in \text{ValueExp} ::= L \mid (\texttt{abs} \; ((I_{formal} \; T_{formalType})^*) \; E_{body})$

$IE \in \text{InputExp} ::= L$

$A \in \text{AnsExp} ::= L \mid \texttt{procans}$

Reduction Relation ($\rightsquigarrow$)

$((\texttt{abs} \; ((I_i \; T_i)_{i=1}^n) \; E_{body}) \; E_{i=1}^n) \rightsquigarrow [E_i/I_i]_{i=1}^n E_{body}$ $\qquad [\beta]$

$(\texttt{let} \; ((I_i \; E_i)_{i=1}^n) \; E_{body}) \rightsquigarrow [E_i/I_i]_{i=1}^n E_{body}$ $\qquad [let]$

$(\texttt{letrec} \; ((I_i \; T_i \; E_i)_{i=1}^n) \; E_{body})$

$\quad \rightsquigarrow [(\texttt{letrec} \; ((I_k \; T_k \; E_k)_{k=1}^n) \; E_i)/I_i]_{i=1}^n E_{body}$ $\qquad [letrec]$

$(\texttt{the} \; T \; E) \rightsquigarrow E$ $\qquad\qquad\qquad\qquad\qquad\qquad\qquad [the]$

The μFLEX reduction rules also include [if-T], [if-F], and application rules for μFLEX primitives from the FL reduction relation shown in Figure 6.19 (page 259).

Evaluation Contexts

$\mathbb{E} \in \text{EvalContext} ::= \square \mid (\texttt{if} \; \mathbb{E} \; E_{then} \; E_{else})$

$\qquad\qquad\qquad\qquad \mid (\texttt{prim} \; O_{primop} \; V_{i=1}^{k-1} \; \mathbb{E} \; E_{j=k+1}^n) \mid (\mathbb{E} \; E_{i=1}^n)$

Evaluation Relation ($\Rightarrow$)

$\mathbb{E}\{E\} \Rightarrow \mathbb{E}\{E'\}$, where $E \rightsquigarrow E'$

Figure 11.13 A context-based SOS for μFLEX, Part 1.

Lemma 11.2 (Decomposition of μFLEX Expressions) *If E is not a value expression V, then E can be uniquely decomposed into an evaluation context $\mathbb{E}$ and expression E' having one of the forms*

1. I

2. $(\texttt{if} \; V_{test} \; E_{then} \; E_{else})$

3. $(V_{rator} \; E_{i=1}^n)$

4. $(\texttt{let} \; ((I_i \; E_i)_{i=1}^n) \; E_{body})$

5. $(\texttt{letrec} \; ((I_i \; T_i \; E_i)_{i=1}^n) \; E_{body})$

6. $(\texttt{prim} \; O \; V_{i=1}^n)$

7. $(\texttt{error} \; Y \; T)$

8. $(\texttt{the} \; T \; E)$

such that $E = \mathbb{E}\{E'\}$.

SOS

The μFLEX SOS is defined by the tuple $\langle \text{Exp}, \Rightarrow, \text{ValueExp}, IF, OF \rangle$, where:

$IF : (\text{Prog} \times \text{InputExp}^*) \to \text{Exp}$
$IF \; \langle(\texttt{flexk} \; ((I_1 \; T_1) \; \ldots \; (I_n \; T_n)) \; E_{body}), \; [IE_1, \ldots, IE_k] \rangle$
$\quad = \textbf{if} \; n \neq k \; \textbf{then} \; (\texttt{error wrong-number-of-args int})$
$\qquad \textbf{else if} \; \forall i \in [1..n] \; . \; \big(type_{inp}[\![IE_i]\!] = T_i\big)$
$\qquad\qquad \textbf{then} \; [IE_i/I_i]_{i=1}^n E_{body}$
$\qquad\qquad \textbf{else} \; (\texttt{error bad-arg-type int}) \; \textbf{end}$
$\qquad \textbf{end}$

$type_{inp} : \text{InputExp} \to \text{Type}$
$type_{inp}[\![\texttt{\#u}]\!] = \texttt{unit}$
$type_{inp}[\![B]\!] = \texttt{bool}$
$type_{inp}[\![N]\!] = \texttt{int}$
$type_{inp}[\![(\texttt{sym} \; Y)]\!] = \texttt{symb}$

$OF : \text{ValueExp} \to \text{AnsExp}$
$OF \; L = L$
$OF \; (\texttt{abs} \; ((I \; T)^*) \; E) = \texttt{procans}$

Behavior

$beh_{det} : (\text{Prog} \times \text{InputExp}^*) \to \text{Outcome}$

$beh_{det} \; \langle P, IE^* \rangle = \begin{cases} (\text{AnsExp} \rightarrowtail \text{Outcome} \; (OF \; E_{fin})) & \text{if } E_{init} \stackrel{*}{\Rightarrow} E_{fin} \in \text{ValueExp} \\ \texttt{stuck} & \text{if } E_{init} \stackrel{*}{\Rightarrow} E_{fin} \not\Rightarrow \\ & \quad \text{and } E_{fin} \notin \text{ValueExp} \\ \infty & \text{if } E_{init} \stackrel{\infty}{\Rightarrow} \end{cases}$

$\qquad\qquad \text{where } E_{init} = (IF \; \langle P, IE^* \rangle)$

Figure 11.14 A context-based SOS for μFLEX, Part 2.

That is, $E = \mathbb{E}\{E'\}$ for a unique E' that cannot itself be expressed as a non-trivial (non-$\square$) evaluation context filled with something. E' is the next redex to be reduced in the evaluation of E; it cannot have one of the more general forms $(\texttt{if} \; E_{test} \; E_{then} \; E_{else})$, $(E_{rator} \; E_{i=1}^n)$, or $(\texttt{prim} \; O \; E_{i=1}^n)$, because the definition of evaluation contexts allows descending into a nonvalue E_{test} in an $\texttt{if}$, a nonvalue E_{rator} in an application, and a nonvalue operand E_i in a $\texttt{prim}$.

With the Decomposition Lemma, we can precisely characterize the μFLEX configurations (i.e., expressions) that are stuck: the cases where $E = \mathbb{E}\{E'\}$ and E' does not match the left-hand side of a reduction rule ($\rightsquigarrow$):

Lemma 11.3 (Characterization of μFLEX Stuck Expressions) *If E is a stuck expression in the μFLEX SOS, then it can be decomposed into $\mathbb{E}\{E'\}$ where E' has one of the following forms:*

1.   *I*

2.   *(if V E_{then} E_{else}), where V is not #t or #f*

3.   *(V $E_{i=1}^{n}$), where V is not an abstraction*

4.   *((abs ((I_i T_i)$_{i=1}^{m}$) E_{body}) $E_{j=1}^{n}$), where $m \neq n$*

5.   *(prim O $V_{i=1}^{n}$), where the number or type of arguments is incorrect for O*

6.   *(prim O N 0), where O is / or %*

7.   *(error Y T)*

*We will classify forms 1–5 as dynamic type errors and forms 6–7 as dynamic nontype errors.[12] Depending on the form of E', we will say that $\mathbb{E}\{E'\}$ is **stuck at a type error** or **stuck at a nontype error**.*

Note that although a stuck expression E may be a let, letrec, or the expression, the "place" E' where it is stuck cannot be one of these kinds of expressions.

The next section will show the soundness of the μFLEX type system by showing that a well-typed program cannot encounter a dynamic type error — that is, that the type rules prevent the dynamic type errors detailed above. In fact, the type rules prevent even more errors than those we have classified as dynamic type errors.

Because the μFLEX SOS does not keep track of the types of arbitrary expressions, there are certain ill-typed expressions that we might wish would produce dynamic type errors but will not become stuck in our SOS and thus are not covered by Lemma 11.3:

- A procedure application with an operand of the wrong type, such as the application ((abs ((x int)) E_{body}) (= 1 2)). In this case, the SOS will substitute (= 1 2) for x in E_{body} even though x is supposed to have type int but (= 1 2) has type bool.

- A letrec with a binding of the wrong type, such as

    (letrec ((f (-> (int) bool) (abs ((x int)) x))) (f 3))

---

[12]In case 1, I is an unbound variable. Since no binding has provided a type for I, we can consider the error to be a type error.

Here the SOS will eventually substitute (abs ((x int)) x) for f in (f 3) even though it has the type (-> (int) int) and not (-> (int) bool).

- A type ascription whose declared type does not match the value type, such as (the bool (+ 1 2)). The SOS will rewrite this to (+ 1 2) even though it has type int, not bool.

It is possible to modify the reduction rules to handle these cases using the *typeof* function from Section 11.5.5. This is left as an exercise. The type soundness proof can be extended to handle the resulting new cases of dynamic type errors.

Exercise 11.12 Using the *typeof* function, modify the reduction rules for the μFLEX SOS so that the uncaught dynamic type errors discussed above lead to stuck configurations. Think carefully about the type environment you should use for *typeof*.

11.6.3 Type Soundness of μFLEX

In this section, we present a proof of the type soundness for the μFLEX type system. This proof will be our main example of formal reasoning involving types. To avoid getting bogged down, we focus on a relatively high-level sketch of the proof and offload numerous details to the exercises and the Web Supplement.

To state the type soundness theorem for μFLEX, we need to relate SOS answers to types:

Definition 11.4 (μFLEX Answer Compatibility) *An answer A in AnsExp is* **compatible with a type** *T iff (1) A is a literal L and $\{\} \vdash L : T$ or (2) A is the token* procans *and T is an arrow type.*

Using this notion, we now formalize what we mean by type soundness in μFLEX:

Theorem 11.5 (Type Soundness of μFLEX) *Suppose that μFLEX program P is well typed with type ($=>$ ($T_{i=1}^n$) T_{ans}). Executing P on inputs $IE_{i=1}^n$ having corresponding types $T_{i=1}^n$ will either:*

1. *return an answer compatible with T_{ans};*

2. *get stuck at a nontype error;*

3. *loop infinitely.*

In particular, the execution of P will never get stuck at a type error.

In the first outcome, the program result type T_{ans} must accurately describe the answer computed by the program. This type is irrelevant in the other two outcomes, where no answer is returned. The theorem implies that the execution of a μFLEX program on appropriate inputs cannot get stuck at a type error, since this possibility is not allowed by any of the three outcomes.

In order to prove Theorem 11.5, we will first specialize the type soundness recipe discussed on page 662 to μFLEX by proving the following two theorems:

Theorem 11.6 (Preservation for μFLEX) *If $\{\} \vdash E : T$ and $E \Rightarrow E'$ then $\{\} \vdash E' : T$.*

Theorem 11.7 (Progress for μFLEX) *If $\{\} \vdash E : T$ then E is not stuck at a type error.*

The reason why both theorems use an empty type environment rather than an arbitrary one is that the expressions in the theorems represent SOS configurations, which in μFLEX must be closed expressions. Before we prove *these* two theorems, we will establish three technical lemmas that simplify the presentation of the proofs. After stating the three lemmas and sketching their justifications, we will then prove the Preservation and Progress Theorems, and conclude by proving the μFLEX Type Soundness Theorem.

The first lemma says that within a well-typed expression E, any free identifier I_i with type T_i can be replaced by an expression E_i with type T_i without changing the well-typedness of E:

Lemma 11.8 (Substitution) *Suppose that $TE[I_i : T_i]_{i=1}^{n} \vdash E : T$ and that $\forall_{i=1}^{n} . TE \vdash E_i : T_i$. Then $TE \vdash [E_i/I_i]_{i=1}^{n} E : T$.*

Intuitively, this is true because a type derivation for $TE \vdash [E_i/I_i]_{i=1}^{n} E : T$ can be constructed by starting with the type derivation for $TE[I_i : T_i]_{i=1}^{n} \vdash E : T$ and replacing each leaf judgment of the form $TE_{before} \vdash I_i : T_i$ by a derivation tree rooted at the judgment $TE_{after} \vdash E_i : T_i$. The tricky aspect of formalizing this intuition is choosing a TE_{after} for each TE_{before} that makes the new derivation valid. A proof of the Substitution Lemma can be found in the Web Supplement.

The second lemma says that each SOS reduction $E \rightsquigarrow E'$ preserves types:

Lemma 11.9 (Type Preservation of Reduction) *If $TE \vdash E : T$ and $E \rightsquigarrow E'$ then $TE \vdash E' : T$.*

Proof: This lemma is proved by showing that it holds for each reduction rule $E \rightsquigarrow E'$ in Figure 11.13. Here we show that it holds for the $[\beta]$ rule and leave the other cases as an exercise (Exercise 11.13).

Suppose that TJ is the type judgment

$$TE \vdash ((\texttt{abs } ((I_i \ T_i)_{i=1}^n) \ E_{body}) \ E_{i=1}^n) : T$$

Since $((\texttt{abs } ((I_i \ T_i)_{i=1}^n) \ E_{body}) \ E_{j=1}^n) \rightsquigarrow [E_i/I_i]_{i=1}^n E_{body}$, we need to show that $TE \vdash [E_i/I_i]_{i=1}^n E_{body} : T$. The type derivation for TJ must have the following form:

$$\frac{\boxed{\dfrac{\boxed{TE[I_i : T_i]_{i=1}^n \vdash E_{body} : T}}{TE \vdash (\texttt{abs } ((I_i \ T_i)_{i=1}^n) \ E_{body}) : (\text{-> } (T_{i=1}^n) \ T)} \ [\rightarrow\text{-}intro]} \quad \boxed{\forall_{i=1}^n \ . \ TE \vdash E_i : T_i}}{TE \vdash ((\texttt{abs } ((I_i \ T_i)_{i=1}^n) \ E_{body}) \ E_{i=1}^n) : T} \ [\rightarrow\text{-}elim]$$

Thus, we deduce that $TE[I_i : T_i]_{i=1}^n \vdash E_{body} : T$ and $\forall_{i=1}^n \ . \ TE \vdash E_i : T_i$. The Substitution Lemma (Lemma 11.8) implies that $TE \vdash [E_i/I_i]_{i=1}^n E_{body} : T$, which is what we need to show for this case. $\diamond$

The third lemma is useful for reasoning about μFLEX configurations:

Lemma 11.10 (Context Filling) *Suppose $\{\} \vdash \mathbb{E}\{E_1\} : T$. Then:*

1. *there exists a type T_1 such that $\{\} \vdash E_1 : T_1$;*

2. *if $\{\} \vdash E_1' : T_1$, then $\{\} \vdash \mathbb{E}\{E_1'\} : T$.*

The lemma uses empty type environments because configurations are guaranteed to be closed expressions. Why? A well-typed program cannot have any free variables, so the initial configuration (which is the result of substituting literal values for program parameters in the program body) is also closed. All subsequent configurations are closed because each SOS reduction step preserves the closed property of the configuration.

The first part of the lemma is based on the fact that holes in evaluation contexts do not appear in the scope of any identifiers (that is, holes do not appear inside the body of a let, letrec, or abs expression). Since the configuration is well typed in the empty environment (and therefore closed), this means that the expression filling the hole must also be well typed in the empty environment (and therefore closed). The second part of the lemma says that replacing the closed expression filling the hole of a context with another closed expression of the same type does not change the type of the filled context. Both parts are easy to prove by induction on the structure of the evaluation context $\mathbb{E}$ (Exercise 11.14).

Armed with Lemmas 11.8–11.10, we are now ready to prove the Preservation Theorem, Progress Theorem, and Type Soundness Theorem for μFLEX.

Theorem 11.6 (Preservation for μFLEX) *If $\{\} \vdash E : T$ and $E \Rightarrow E'$ then $\{\} \vdash E' : T$.*

Proof: Suppose $\{\} \vdash E : T$ and $E \Rightarrow E'$. We need to show $\{\} \vdash E' : T$. By the definition of $\Rightarrow$, it must be that $E = \mathbb{E}\{E_{redex}\}$, $E' = \mathbb{E}\{E'_{redex}\}$, and $E_{redex} \rightsquigarrow E'_{redex}$. So we are given $\{\} \vdash \mathbb{E}\{E_{redex}\} : T$ and we need to show $\{\} \vdash \mathbb{E}\{E'_{redex}\} : T$.

By part 1 of the Context Filling Lemma (Lemma 11.10), there is a type T_{redex} such that $\{\} \vdash E_{redex} : T_{redex}$. By Type Preservation of Reduction (Lemma 11.9), $\{\} \vdash E_{redex} : T_{redex}$ and $E_{redex} \rightsquigarrow E'_{redex}$ imply that $\{\} \vdash E'_{redex} : T_{redex}$. Finally, by part 2 of the Context Filling Lemma, $\{\} \vdash \mathbb{E}\{E'_{redex}\} : T$. $\diamond$

Theorem 11.7 (Progress for μFLEX) *If $\{\} \vdash E : T$ then E is not stuck at a type error.*

Proof: Suppose that $\{\} \vdash E : T$ — that is, E is well typed. Like any expression, E is either reducible, a value expression, or stuck. We wish to show that E cannot be stuck at a type error. By the Characterization of μFLEX Stuck Expressions (Lemma 11.3), if E is stuck, it must have the form $\mathbb{E}\{E'\}$, where E' has one of seven forms. By part 1 of the Context Filling Lemma, there is some type T' such that $\{\} \vdash E' : T'$. A case analysis of the type-error forms (cases 1–5) shows that none of them can be well typed:

1. $E' = I$: In an empty type environment, any identifier I is unbound, and so it cannot be the case that $\{\} \vdash I : T'$.

2. $E' = (\texttt{if}\ V\ E_{then}\ E_{else})$, where V is not #t or #f: The $[if]$ type rule requires $\{\} \vdash V : \texttt{bool}$, but #t or #f are the only value expressions with type $\texttt{bool}$.

3. $E' = (V\ E_{i=1}^{n})$, where V is not an abstraction: The $[\rightarrow\text{-}elim]$ rule requires $\{\} \vdash V : T_V$, where T_V is an arrow type, but abstractions are the only value expressions with an arrow type.

4. $E' = ((\texttt{abs}\ ((I_i\ T_i)_{i=1}^{m})\ E_{body})\ E_{j=1}^{n})$, where $m \neq n$: If the abstraction is well typed in the empty environment, the $[\rightarrow\text{-}intro]$ rule implies that its type must have the form $(\texttt{->}\ (T_{i=1}^{m})\ T_{result})$. But for the application of this abstraction to be well typed, the $[\rightarrow\text{-}elim]$ rule requires that $m = n$.[13]

---

[13] The $[\rightarrow\text{-}elim]$ rule also requires that the parameter and argument types match, but a mismatch would not result in a stuck expression in our SOS.

5. $E' = (\text{prim } O \ V_{i=1}^n)$, where the number or type of arguments is incorrect for O: The $[prim]$ rule requires that the number and type of arguments must be correct.

However, the nontype error forms can be well typed:

6. $E' = (\text{prim } O \ N \ 0)$, where O is / or %: E' is well typed in the empty environment by the $[prim]$ rule and has type int because $\{\} \vdash N : \text{int}$, $\{\} \vdash 0 : \text{int}$, and $TE_{prim} \vdash O : (\text{-> (int int) int})$.

7. $E' = (\text{error } Y \ T)$: By the $[error]$ rule, $\{\} \vdash (\text{error } Y \ T) : T$.

Since only the nontype errors can be well typed, E cannot be stuck at a type error. $\diamond$

Theorem 11.5 (Type Soundness of μFLEX) *Suppose that μFLEX program P is well typed with type $(\text{=> } (T_{i=1}^n) \ T_{ans})$. Executing P on inputs $IE_{i=1}^n$ having corresponding types $T_{i=1}^n$ will either:*

1. *return an answer compatible with T_{ans};*

2. *get stuck at a nontype error;*

3. *loop infinitely.*

In particular, the execution of P will never get stuck at a type error.

Proof: Suppose that μFLEX program P has program type $(\text{=> } (T_{i=1}^n) \ T_{ans})$. The $[prog]$ type rule implies that P has the form $(\text{flexk } ((I_i \ T_i)_{i=1}^n) \ E_{body})$ and $\{I_1 : T_1, \dots, I_n : T_n\} \vdash E_{body} : T_{ans}$. By the assumption that we have the correct number of program inputs $IE_{i=1}^n$ with the types specified by the program parameters, we know that $\forall_{i=1}^n \ . \ \{\} \vdash IE_i : T_i$. By the Substitution Lemma (Lemma 11.8), the initial configuration $E_0 = [IE_i/I_i]_{i=1}^n E_{body}$ is well typed via the judgment $\{\} \vdash E_0 : T_{ans}$.

The evaluation path starting at E_0 will either be an infinite path (outcome 3 in Theorem 11.5) or a finite path $E_0 \overset{n}{\Longrightarrow} E_n$, where E_n is irreducible. By preservation (Theorem 11.6), each E_i in the finite path will be well typed with the judgment $\{\} \vdash E_i : T_{ans}$. By progress (Theorem 11.7), E_n is not stuck at a type error, so it must either be stuck at a nontype error (outcome 2 in Theorem 11.5) or be a final configuration (i.e., a value expression). If E_n is a value expression V_n, then V_n has type T_{ans}, and it is easy to see that the answer $(OF \ V_n)$ is compatible with T_{ans} (outcome 1 in Theorem 11.5). $\diamond$

In Section 11.8, we will extend μFLEX to full FLEX by adding numerous constructs. This affects the details of the SOS (e.g., there are new input expressions, value expressions, answer expressions, reduction rules, and evaluation contexts) and the type soundness proof (e.g., type preservation must be shown for each new reduction rule). However, the basic structure of the type soundness proof for FLEX remains unchanged from μFLEX.

Exercise 11.13 For each of the following reduction rules in the μFLEX SOS (Figure 11.13), show that the Type Preservation of Reduction Lemma (Lemma 11.9) holds:

a. [+] (other primitive operators are similar)

b. [if-T] ([if-F] is similar)

c. [the]

d. [let]

e. [$letrec$]

Exercise 11.14 Prove both parts of the Context Filling Lemma (Lemma 11.10) by structural induction on evaluation contexts.

Exercise 11.15

a. Modify the evaluation contexts and reduction rules for the μFLEX SOS in Figure 11.13 to express CBV semantics rather than CBN semantics for application, `let`, and `letrec`.

b. Modify the Characterization of μFLEX Stuck Expressions (Lemma 11.3) to be consistent with a CBV version of μFLEX.

c. Describe any modifications that need to be made to the μFLEX type soundness proof to show type soundness for the CBV version of μFLEX.

Exercise 11.16 The FL language supports currying: the application of a procedure to too few arguments returns another procedure that takes the remaining arguments. For example, consider the following FL abstraction:

E_{linear} = (abs (a b x) (prim + (prim * a x) b))

- (E_{linear} 2 3 4) evaluates to 11;

- (E_{linear} 2 3) evaluates to a procedural value that is described by the abstraction (abs (x) (prim + (prim * 2 x) 3));

- (E_{linear} 2) evaluates to a procedural value that is described by the abstraction (abs (b x) (prim + (prim * 2 x) b)).

As described, μFLEX does not support currying. The μFLEX analogue of the E_{linear} abstraction is:

$$E'_{linear} = \texttt{(abs ((a int) (b int) (x int)) (prim + (prim * a x) b))}$$

In μFLEX (E'_{linear} 2 3 4) is well typed and evaluates to 11, but neither (E'_{linear} 2 3) nor (E'_{linear} 2) is well typed.

In this exercise, you will modify μFLEX to support currying. In the curried version of μFLEX, both (E'_{linear} 2 3) and (E'_{linear} 2) are well typed, but (E'_{linear} 2 #t) and (E'_{linear} #u) are not well typed.

a. Modify the μFLEX type rules in Figure 11.7 to describe a version of μFLEX that supports currying:

b. Using the modified type rules, (1) give type derivations showing that (E'_{linear} 2 3) and (E'_{linear} 2) are well typed and (2) argue that (E'_{linear} 2 #t) and (E'_{linear} #u) are not well typed.

c. Modify the dynamic semantics of μFLEX in Figure 11.13 to describe a version of μFLEX that supports currying.

d. Modify the Characterization of μFLEX Stuck Expressions (Lemma 11.3) to be consistent with a version of μFLEX that supports currying.

e. Describe the modifications that need to be made to the μFLEX type soundness proof to show type soundness for the curried version of μFLEX.

11.7 Types and Strong Normalization

In general, the evaluation of μFLEX expressions may not terminate. Here is a simple nonterminating expression:

```
(letrec ((loop (-> () unit) (abs () (loop))))
  (loop))
```

It is unsurprising that a language with a recursion construct like `letrec` can express infinite loops. But the following fact might come as a surprise: any well-typed μFLEX program that does not use `letrec` *is* guaranteed to terminate! That is, μFLEX$-\{\texttt{letrec}\}$ is strongly normalizing.

The reason that this may come as a surprise is that the same fact does not hold for FL$-\{\texttt{rec}\}$. Recall from page 263 that we can express an infinite loop in FL using just abstractions, applications, and variables:

$$E_{loop} = \texttt{((abs (x) (x x)) (abs (x) (x x)))}$$

The fact that μFLEX$-\{\texttt{letrec}\}$ is strongly normalizing implies that it is impossible to annotate E_{loop} with explicit types so that it is a well-typed μFLEX expression.

Why is μFLEX$-\{$letrec$\}$ strongly normalizing? Intuitively, μFLEX procedure types significantly constrain the way in which procedures can be used. It turns out that procedure types can be used to define an energy function on μFLEX$-\{$letrec$\}$ expressions that strictly decreases when certain beta reductions are performed, and this energy function can be used to show that evaluation in μFLEX$-\{$letrec$\}$ must terminate (see the Web Supplement for details). In particular, for $n > 1$, it is impossible to have a typed version E'_{loop} of E_{loop} such that $E'_{loop} \stackrel{n}{\Longrightarrow} E'_{loop}$ because the energy of E'_{loop} would not have decreased even though beta reductions were performed.

Does μFLEX$-\{$letrec$\}$ remain strongly normalizing if we extend it to support FLK-like simplification steps (see Section 6.4.2) — i.e., reductions in any context as opposed to reductions only in evaluation contexts? Unlike evaluation, which is deterministic in μFLEX$-\{$letrec$\}$, simplification is not deterministic — in general, there may be many different simplification steps that can be performed on a given expression. Strong normalization of evaluation in μFLEX$-\{$letrec$\}$ means that the unique evaluation path is finite. In contrast, strong normalization of simplification would mean that *all* simplification paths are finite.

Remarkably, even simplification in μFLEX$-\{$letrec$\}$ is strongly normalizing! This can be shown by adapting to μFLEX$-\{$letrec$\}$ techniques from the literature for proving the strong normalization of beta reduction in what is known as the **simply typed lambda calculus**, the subset of μFLEX including only single-parameter abstractions, single-operand applications, and variable references. Adding the additional features of μFLEX (except letrec) does not change this result. So any simplification strategy in μFLEX$-\{$letrec$\}$ is guaranteed to terminate, regardless of the order in which the simplifications are performed.

How important are these strong normalization results? Most realistic programs are likely to use looping/recursion constructs like letrec, so the results are unlikely to be of much use to the typical programmer. However, compiler writers care about these results because they guarantee that certain rewriting processes will terminate when performed on parts of a program that don't use looping/recursion constructs. The results are also important for the designers and implementers of statically typed languages. As we shall see in Section 12.3.2, powerful type systems include features at the type level (e.g., abstractions and applications) that are similar to the features μFLEX has at the expression level. Strong normalization at the type level means that types mentioning user-defined type abstractions can be normalized and guarantees that type checkers for these languages will terminate.

Syntax

$E ::= \ldots \mid (\texttt{pair}\ E_{fst}\ E_{snd}) \mid (\texttt{fst}\ E_{pair}) \mid (\texttt{snd}\ E_{pair})$

$T ::= \ldots \mid (\texttt{pairof}\ T_{fst}\ T_{snd})$

Type Rules

$$\frac{TE \vdash E_{fst} : T_{fst} \qquad TE \vdash E_{snd} : T_{snd}}{TE \vdash (\texttt{pair}\ E_{fst}\ E_{snd}) : (\texttt{pairof}\ T_{fst}\ T_{snd})} \qquad [\textit{pairof-intro}]$$

$$\frac{TE \vdash E_{pair} : (\texttt{pairof}\ T_{fst}\ T_{snd})}{TE \vdash (\texttt{fst}\ E_{pair}) : T_{fst}} \qquad [\textit{pairof-elim-fst}]$$

$$\frac{TE \vdash E_{pair} : (\texttt{pairof}\ T_{fst}\ T_{snd})}{TE \vdash (\texttt{snd}\ E_{pair}) : T_{snd}} \qquad [\textit{pairof-elim-snd}]$$

Figure 11.15 Static semantics of pairs in FLEX.

11.8 Full FLEX: Typed Data and Recursive Types

We now extend μFLEX to full FLEX by adding typed versions of the forms of data studied in Chapter 10, the mutable cells and mutable variables studied in Chapter 8, and recursive types. We will see that the goal of maintaining static type checking constrains the ways in which we create and manipulate some data structures.

Since we have already studied the dynamic semantics (i.e., evaluation rules) of all the constructs covered in this section, we will not describe how to extend the μFLEX SOS to handle each construct. Instead, we will focus on the static semantics (i.e., type rules). It is possible to extend the type soundness proof for μFLEX to full FLEX, but we will not present the details of this proof. Each new construct preserves the fundamental monomorphic nature of μFLEX (as embodied in Theorem 11.1), so every well-typed FLEX expression in a given type environment has a unique type (modulo the notion of type equivalence discussed in Section 11.8.2).

11.8.1 Typed Products

Pairs

Figure 11.15 shows the syntax and type rules needed to extend FLEX with pairs, the simplest kind of product. Types formed by the `pairof` type constructor keep track of the types of the first and second components of a pair. This type is introduced by the `pair` construct and eliminated by either `fst` or `snd`. For

---

Syntax

$E ::= \dots \mid (\texttt{prod}\ E^*_{component}) \mid (\texttt{get}\ N_{index}\ E_{prod})$

$T ::= \dots \mid (\texttt{prodof}\ T^*_{component})$

Type Rules

$$\frac{\forall_{i=1}^{n}\ .\ TE \vdash E_i : T_i}{TE \vdash (\texttt{prod}\ E_{i=1}^{n}) : (\texttt{prodof}\ T_{i=1}^{n})} \qquad \textit{[prodof-intro]}$$

$$\frac{TE \vdash E_{prod} : (\texttt{prodof}\ T_{j=1}^{n})}{TE \vdash (\texttt{get}\ N_{index}\ E_{prod}) : T_i} \qquad \textit{[prodof-elim]}$$

$$\text{where}\quad i = \mathcal{N}[\![N_{index}]\!]\ \text{and}\ 1 \le i \le n$$

Figure 11.16 Static semantics of immutable positional products (tuples) in FLEX.

example, the expression `(pair (+ 1 2) (pair (= 3 4) (sym yes)))` has the type `(pairof int (pairof bool symb))`.

Although `fst` and `snd` are primitive operators in FL, they cannot be primitive operators in FLEX because of the monomorphic nature of the language. For example, the *[pairof-elim-fst]* rule says that `fst` returns a value whose type is the first type component of the type `(pairof` T_{fst} T_{snd}`)`. Without some form of polymorphism (see Section 12.2) it is not possible to describe this behavior via a single type assignment for `fst` in the primitive type environment.

The type rules for pairs (and the other products we study) are the same regardless of whether they are strict or nonstrict.[14] A product component expression that does not terminate or signals an error must be given the same type in either case.

Tuples

Pairs can be generalized to tuples (positional products with an arbitrary number of components), whose syntax and type rules are presented in Figure 11.16. The `prodof` type tracks the number of components and type of each component in a product value. For example, the type of

    (prod (+ 1 2) (= 3 4) (abs (x) (> x 5)))

is

    (prodof int bool (-> (int) bool))

---

[14]Using the naming conventions of Section 10.1.3, we would have to replace `prod` by `nprod`/`lprod` and `get` by `nget`/`lget` in the type rules.

Syntax

$E ::= \ldots \mid$ (seq $E^{*}_{component}$) $\mid$ (seq-get E_{index} E_{seq}) $\mid$ (seq-size E_{seq})

$T ::= \ldots \mid$ (seqof $T_{component}$)

Type Rules

$$\frac{\forall^{n}_{i=1} \, . \, TE \vdash E_i : T}{TE \vdash (\texttt{seq} \; E^{n}_{i=1}) : (\texttt{seqof} \; T)} \qquad [seqof\text{-}intro]$$

$$\frac{TE \vdash E_{index} : \texttt{int} \qquad TE \vdash E_{seq} : (\texttt{seqof} \; T)}{TE \vdash (\texttt{seq-get} \; E_{index} \; E_{seq}) : T} \qquad [seqof\text{-}elim]$$

$$\frac{TE \vdash E_{seq} : (\texttt{seqof} \; T)}{TE \vdash (\texttt{seq-size} \; E_{seq}) : \texttt{int}} \qquad [seqof\text{-}size]$$

Figure 11.17 Static semantics of sequences in FLEX.

The [*prodof-elim*] rule clarifies why the index in a get form must be an explicit integer literal rather than the result of evaluating an arbitrary expression. Otherwise, the type checker would not "know" which component was being extracted and different types could not be allowed at different indices.

Sequences

Recall from Section 10.1.1 that sequences differ from tuples in that the index used to project a tuple component must be an integer literal while the index used to project a sequence component can be the result of evaluating an arbitrary expression that denotes an integer. The simplest way to handle sequences in a typed setting (Figure 11.17) is to require all sequence components to have the same type T, in which case the type of a sequence can be written (seqof T). We can then reason that performing seq-get on a sequence of type (seqof T) yields a component of type T regardless of which index is specified. Thus, computable indices (at least in simple type systems) imply homogeneous products, but explicit integer indices permit heterogeneous products.

Records

Handling named products in a typed language requires additional complexity. As shown in Figure 11.18, the recordof type associates record field names with types. Although the [*recordof-elim*] rule is concise, the ellipses in the premise type (recordof ... (I T) ...) obscure the fact that the type checker must somehow find the binding associated with the selected field name in the list of name/type associations. Moreover, the fact that the name/type associations may be in any

Syntax

$E ::= \ldots \mid (\texttt{record} \ (I_{name} \ E_{defn})^*) \mid (\texttt{select} \ I_{name} \ E_{rcd}) \mid (\texttt{with} \ E_{rcd} \ E_{body})$

$T ::= \ldots \mid (\texttt{recordof} \ (I_{name} \ T_{defn})^*)$

Type Rules

$$\frac{\forall_{i=1}^{n} . \ TE \vdash E_i : T_i}{TE \vdash (\texttt{record} \ (I_i \ E_i)_{i=1}^{n}) : (\texttt{recordof} \ (I_i \ T_i)_{i=1}^{n})} \qquad [\textit{recordof-intro}]$$

$$\frac{TE \vdash E : (\texttt{recordof} \ \ldots \ (I \ T) \ \ldots)}{TE \vdash (\texttt{select} \ I \ E) : T} \qquad [\textit{recordof-elim}]$$

$$\frac{TE \vdash E_{rcd} : (\texttt{recordof} \ (I_i \ T_i)_{i=1}^{n}) \quad TE[I_i : T_i]_{i=1}^{n} \vdash E_{body} : T_{body}}{TE \vdash (\texttt{with} \ E_{rcd} \ E_{body}) : T_{body}} \quad [\textit{recordof-with}]$$

Figure 11.18 Static semantics of records in FLEX.

order complicates the notion of type equivalence — an issue that we discuss next in Section 11.8.2.

The record operations in Figure 11.18 include (`with` E_{rcd} E_{body}), a statically typed analog of the (`with-fields` (I^*) E_{rcd} E_{body}) construct introduced on page 355 for the dynamically typed FL language. This construct evaluates E_{body} in an environment that extends the current environment with the bindings from the record value of E_{rcd}. In a dynamically typed language, the explicit identifier list I^* in `with-fields` is necessary to declare the names that will be extracted from the record value; otherwise the free identifiers of `with-fields` cannot be determined. But in the statically typed `with` construct, an explicit identifier list is not necessary because it can be determined from the type of the record value.[15] Other record constructs are considered in Exercise 11.18.

Exercise 11.17 Consider extending FLEX with a construct (`pair=?` E_{pair_1} E_{pair_2}) that returns *true* if the respective components of the pair values of E_{pair_1} and E_{pair_2} are equal, and returns *false* otherwise.

a. Give a type rule for `pair=?`.

b. In dynamically typed FL, write `pair=?` as a user-defined procedure (using the generic `equal?` procedure to compare components).

c. In FLEX, is it possible to write `pair=?` as a user-defined procedure? Explain.

---

[15]Because of this, the *FrIds* function in full FLEX must take an additional type environment argument in order to determine the type of the record expression in the `with` construct. However, we will typically omit this argument in discussions of FLEX and its extensions.

Exercise 11.18 Give a type rule for each of the following record constructs presented in the earlier discussion of records (pages 353–356):

a. (conceal (I^*_{name}) E_{rcd})

b. (override E_{rcd_1} E_{rcd_2})

c. (recordrec (I_{name} E_{defn})*)

d. (restrict (I^*_{name}) E_{rcd})

e. (rename ($I_{oldName}$ $I'_{newName}$)* E_{rcd})

11.8.2 Type Equivalence

Before the introduction of recordof types, it was reasonable to assume that two types were equivalent if and only if they were syntactically identical. This assumption is no longer valid in the presence of recordof types, because two recordof types with different binding orders can be considered equal. For example, (recordof (a int) (b bool)) and (recordof (b bool) (a int)) are equivalent types.

One way to handle record-type equivalence is to require that all recordof types be put into a canonical form — e.g., with name/type associations alphabetically ordered by name. However, not all forms of type equivalence we will discuss are easily addressed by canonical forms. So here we will instead develop a collection of rules that formalize when types T_1 and T_2 are equivalent, written $T_1 \approx T_2$. In this approach, two types are equivalent if and only if a proof of equivalence can be derived from the rules.

Figure 11.19 presents a collection of type-equivalence rules for the FLEX types studied thus far. The [*reflexive-≈*], [*symmetric-≈*], and [*transitive-≈*] rules guarantee that ≈ is an equivalence relation. The [$\rightarrow$-≈], [*pairof-≈*], [*prodof-≈*], and [*seqof-≈*] rules ensure that ≈ is a congruence over the ->, pairof, prodof, and seqof type constructors — that is, that the constructed types are equivalent if their component types are equivalent.[16] The [*recordof-≈*] rule allows the field-name/type associations of a recordof type to appear in permuted order as long as the types associated with each field name are equivalent.

How do we use type equivalence in proofs of well-typedness? The approach we adopt in Figure 11.20 is to introduce a new type rule, [*type-≈*], that allows a judgment $TE \vdash E : T'$ to be transformed to the judgment $TE \vdash E : T$ when $T' \approx T$.

---

[16]Suppose D is a recursive domain with a constructor $C : D^n \rightarrow D$. Then an equivalence relation $=_R$ on D is a **congruence** over C iff applications of C are equivalent when their operands are equivalent: $(\forall^n_{i=1} . d_i =_R d'_i)$ implies $(C\ d_1\ \ldots\ d_n) =_R (C\ d'_1\ \ldots\ d'_n)$.

$$T \approx T \qquad\qquad [\textit{reflexive-}\approx]$$

$$\frac{T_1 \approx T_2}{T_2 \approx T_1} \qquad\qquad [\textit{symmetric-}\approx]$$

$$\frac{T_1 \approx T_2 \quad T_2 \approx T_3}{T_1 \approx T_3} \qquad\qquad [\textit{transitive-}\approx]$$

$$\frac{\forall_{i=1}^{n} . \, (T'_i \approx T_i) \quad T'_{body} \approx T_{body}}{(\text{->} \ (T'^{n}_{i=1}) \ T'_{body}) \approx (\text{->} \ (T^{n}_{i=1}) \ T_{body})} \qquad\qquad [\rightarrow\text{-}\approx]$$

$$\frac{\forall_{i=1}^{2} . \, (T'_i \approx T_i)}{(\texttt{pairof} \ T'_1 \ T'_2) \approx (\texttt{pairof} \ T_1 \ T_2)} \qquad\qquad [\textit{pairof-}\approx]$$

$$\frac{\forall_{i=1}^{n} . \, (T'_i \approx T_i)}{(\texttt{prodof} \ T'^{n}_{i=1}) \approx (\texttt{prodof} \ T^{n}_{i=1})} \qquad\qquad [\textit{prodof-}\approx]$$

$$\frac{T' \approx T}{(\texttt{seqof} \ T') \approx (\texttt{seqof} \ T)} \qquad\qquad [\textit{seqof-}\approx]$$

$$\frac{\forall_{i=1}^{n} . \, \exists j \in [1..n] . \, \big((I'_j = I_i) \wedge (T'_j \approx T_i) \big)}{(\texttt{recordof} \ (I'_j \ T'_j)^{n}_{j=1}) \approx (\texttt{recordof} \ (I_i \ T_i)^{n}_{i=1})} \qquad\qquad [\textit{recordof-}\approx]$$

Figure 11.19   Type-equivalence rules for FLEX.

$$\frac{TE \vdash E : T' \quad T' \approx T}{TE \vdash E : T} \qquad\qquad [\textit{type-}\approx]$$

Figure 11.20   Type rule for using type-equivalence information in type derivations.

Rather than having a separate [*type-*≈] rule, an alternative approach would be to embed type-equivalence conditions into the other type rules. For example, we could modify the [*if*] rule to include explicit type-equivalence premises as follows:

$$\frac{\begin{array}{ccc} TE \vdash E_{test} : T_{test} & TE \vdash E_{then} : T_{then} & TE \vdash E_{else} : T_{else} \\ T_{test} \approx \texttt{bool} & T_{then} \approx T_{else} & T_{then} \approx T_{result} \end{array}}{TE \vdash (\texttt{if} \ E_{test} \ E_{then} \ E_{else}) : T_{result}} \qquad [\textit{if}']$$

With the introduction of type equivalence, the μFLEX type uniqueness theorem needs to be tweaked in order to hold for FLEX. In particular, the types of well-typed FLEX expressions are unique only *modulo type equivalence.*

Syntax

$E ::= \ldots \mid$ (begin E_1 E_2) $\mid$ (set! I_{var} E_{val})
$\mid$ (cell $E_{content}$) $\mid$ (^ E_{cell}) $\mid$ (:= E_{cell} E_{val}) $\mid$ (cell=? E_1 E_2)

$T ::= \ldots \mid$ (cellof $T_{content}$)

Syntactic Sugar

(begin) $\leadsto_{ds}$ #u

(begin E) $\leadsto_{ds}$ E

(begin E_1 E_2 E_{rest}^*) $\leadsto_{ds}$ (begin E_1 (begin E_2 E_{rest}^*))

Type Rules

$$\frac{\forall_{i=1}^2 \, . \, TE \vdash E_i : T_i}{TE \vdash (\text{begin } E_1 \, E_2) : T_2} \qquad [\textit{begin}]$$

$$\frac{TE \vdash I_{var} : T \qquad TE \vdash E_{val} : T}{TE \vdash (\text{set! } I_{var} \, E_{val}) : \texttt{unit}} \qquad [\textit{assign}]$$

$$\frac{TE \vdash E_{content} : T_{content}}{TE \vdash (\text{cell } E_{content}) : (\text{cellof } T_{content})} \qquad [\textit{cellof-intro}]$$

$$\frac{TE \vdash E_{cell} : (\text{cellof } T)}{TE \vdash (\text{^ } E_{cell}) : T} \qquad [\textit{cellof-elim}]$$

$$\frac{TE \vdash E_{cell} : (\text{cellof } T_{val}) \qquad TE \vdash E_{val} : T_{val}}{TE \vdash (\text{:= } E_{cell} \, E_{val}) : \texttt{unit}} \qquad [\textit{cell-set}]$$

$$\frac{\forall_{i=1}^2 \, . \, TE \vdash E_i : (\text{cellof } T)}{TE \vdash (\text{cell=? } E_1 \, E_2) : \texttt{bool}} \qquad [\textit{cell-eq}]$$

Type Equivalence

$$\frac{T_1 \approx T_2}{(\text{cellof } T_1) \approx (\text{cellof } T_2)} \qquad [\textit{cellof-}\approx]$$

Figure 11.21 Static semantics of mutable cells and mutable variables in FLEX.

11.8.3 Typed Mutable Data

Mutable variables and mutable data (such as mutable cells, tuples, records, and arrays) are straightforward to handle in an explicitly typed framework. The type rules for mutable variables and mutable cells are presented in Figure 11.21. Both subexpressions of a begin construct are required to be well typed, but only the type of the second expression appears in the result type. In the [*assign*] rule, the

682 Chapter 11 Simple Types

new value for the mutable variable I_{var} is constrained to have the same type as the value already in the variable. The `unit` result type of the `set!` construct indicates that it is performed for its side effect, not for its value.

The `cellof` type constructor tracks the type of the content of a cell. The content type is determined in the [*cellof-intro*] rule. It is used in the [*cellof-elim*] rule to determine the type of a cell reference, in the [*cell-set*] rule to constrain the new value to have the same type as the value already in the cell, and in the [*cell-eq*] rule to constrain the contents of the two argument cells to have the same type. Like `set!`, `:=` is performed for its side effect, not for its value. As with the pair operators `fst` and `snd`, FLEX's lack of polymorphism prevents treating the cell operators `^`, `:=`, and `cell=?` as primitive operators.

The type rules in Figure 11.21 are sound regardless of which parameter-passing mechanism is employed by μFLEX. When using the imperative features of FLEX in examples, we will generally assume CBV semantics, but we could just as well use CBN, CBL, or CBR semantics.

Note that Figure 11.21 includes a type-equivalence rule for `cellof` types. From now on, we must specify type-equivalence rules for each new type constructor in order to test for equivalence on the types it constructs.

11.8.4 Typed Sums

Recall from Section 10.2 that sums (such as oneof values) are used to express that a datum can be one of several different kinds of values. Conceptually, a oneof value pairs a tag indicating the "kind of value" with a payload value of the appropriate kind. In practice, sums are commonly used in conjunction with products to create sum-of-products data.

Oneofs can be incorporated into FLEX with the following expressions and types:

$$E ::= \ldots \mid (\texttt{one } T_{oneof} \; I_{tag} \; E_{payload})$$
$$\mid (\texttt{tagcase } E_{disc} \; I_{payload} \; (I_{tag} \; E_{body})^* \; (\texttt{else } E_{else})^?)$$
$$T ::= \ldots \mid (\texttt{oneof } (I_{tag} \; T_{payload})^*)$$

A `oneof` type lists all possible tags of a oneof value along with the types of their associated payloads. For example, the following `shape` type is an abbreviation for a `oneof` type with three tags:

```
(def-type shape
  (oneof (square int)                    {payload = side length}
         (rectangle (pairof int int))    {payload = width and height}
         (triangle (prodof int int int)) {payload = three side lengths}
  ))
```

Such abbreviations enhance code readability; any shape-manipulation procedures would be more verbose without the abbreviation. We could have consistently used `prodof` or `recordof` types for all of the oneof components, but have chosen to use different type constructors for different components just to show that this is possible.

Before we study the type rules for `one` and `tagcase`, we will consider a few motivating examples. The following `perim` procedure calculates the perimeter of a shape:

```
(def perim (-> (shape) int)
  (abs ((sh shape))
    (tagcase sh v
      (square (* 4 v))
      (rectangle (* 2 (+ (fst v) (snd v))))
      (triangle (+ (get 1 v) (+ (get 2 v) (get 3 v)))))))
```

The `tagcase` construct performs a case analysis on the three possible tags of the discriminant shape `sh`. Each `tagcase` clause uses the identifier `v` to name the payload of the discriminant in the body of the clause. Since the payloads have different types for different tags, `v` must assume a different type in different clauses: `v` has type `int` in the `square` clause, type `(pairof int int)` in the `rectangle` clause, and type `(prodof int int int)` in the `triangle` clause.

The following `scale` procedure, which scales a shape `sh` by a scaling factor `n`, illustrates the oneof introduction construct (`one` T_{oneof} I_{tag} $E_{payload}$):

```
(def scale (-> (shape int) shape)
  (abs ((sh shape) (n int))
    (tagcase sh v
      (square (one shape square (* n v)))
      (rectangle (one shape rectangle
                  (pair (* n (fst v)) (* n (snd v)))))
      (triangle (one shape triangle
                  (prod (* n (get 1 v))
                        (* n (get 2 v))
                        (* n (get 3 v))))))))
```

Note that the `one` construct explicitly specifies the type T_{oneof} of the resulting oneof value. This is necessary to preserve the monomorphism property of FLEX — i.e., the type of any FLEX expression in a given type environment is unique (up to type equivalence) and can be determined without any guessing.

The type rules for `one` and `tagcase` are presented in Figure 11.22. The [*oneof-intro*] rule simply assigns a `one` expression the specified `oneof` type T_{oneof} after verifying that the type of the payload expression $E_{payload}$ is the payload type

Syntax

$E ::= \ldots \mid$ (one T_{oneof} I_{tag} $E_{payload}$)

$\quad \mid$ (tagcase E_{disc} $I_{payload}$ (I_{tag} E_{body})* (else E_{else})$^?$)

$T ::= \ldots \mid$ (oneof (I_{tag} $T_{payload}$)*)

Type Rules

$$\frac{TE \vdash E_{payload} : T_{payload}}{TE \vdash (\text{one } T_{oneof}\ I_{tag}\ E_{payload}) : T_{oneof}} \qquad [\textit{oneof-intro}]$$

$$\text{where} \quad T_{oneof} = (\text{oneof} \ldots (I_{tag}\ T_{payload})\ \ldots)$$

$$\frac{TE \vdash E_{disc} : (\text{oneof } (I_i\ T_i)_{i=1}^n) \qquad \forall_{i=1}^n . \ TE[I_{payload} : T_i] \vdash E_i : T_{result}}{TE \vdash (\text{tagcase } E_{disc}\ I_{payload}\ (I_i\ E_i)_{i=1}^n) : T_{result}} \qquad [\textit{oneof-elim1}]$$

$$\text{where} \quad 1 \leq n$$

$$\frac{TE \vdash E_{disc} : (\text{oneof } (I_i\ T_i)_{i=1}^n) \qquad \forall_{i=1}^k . \ TE[I_{payload} : T_i] \vdash E_i : T_{result} \qquad TE \vdash E_{else} : T_{result}}{TE \vdash (\text{tagcase } E_{disc}\ I_{payload}\ (I_i\ E_i)_{i=1}^k\ (\text{else } E_{else})) : T_{result}} \qquad [\textit{oneof-elim2}]$$

$$\text{where} \quad k \leq n$$

Type Equivalence

$$\frac{\forall_{j=1}^n . \ \exists i \in [1..n] . \ \left(\left(I_j' = I_i \right) \wedge \left(T_j' \approx T_i \right) \right)}{(\text{oneof } (I_j'\ T_j')_{j=1}^n) \approx (\text{oneof } (I_i\ T_i)_{i=1}^n)} \qquad [\textit{oneof-}\approx]$$

Figure 11.22   Static semantics of oneofs in FLEX.

$T_{payload}$ in T_{oneof}. Note that the order of tagged types in a oneof type is irrelevant because they can be rearranged according to the [oneof-$\approx$] type equivalence rule.

There are two type rules for tagcase: [oneof-elim1] handles the case with no else clause and [oneof-elim2] handles the case with an else. In each tagcase clause (I_i E_i), the body E_i is type-checked in a type environment extended with a binding of the name $I_{payload}$ to the type T_i associated with the tag I_i in the oneof type of the discriminant. All clause bodies (including any else clause body E_{else}) must have the same type (T_{result}), which is the type of the whole tagcase expression. Note that a well-typed else-less tagcase expression must have at least one clause of the form (I_i E_i) in order to preserve the monomorphism property of FLEX (because the result type of a clauseless body would be unconstrained).

For simplicity, the [oneof-elim1] rule requires that the order of tags in the tagged types in the oneof type be the same as the order of tags in the tagged clauses in the tagcase construct. In the [oneof-elim2] rule, the ordered tags in a

```
(flavar (n) (test (make-cell))
  (def (make-cell)
    (let ((val #u))
      (record
        (get (abs () (if (int? val) val (error uninitialized))))
        (init (abs (v) (set! val v)))
        (set (abs (v)
                (if (int? val)
                    (let ((old val)) (begin (set! val v) old))
                    (error uninitialized)))))))
  (def (test c)
    (begin ((select init c) 2)
           (* ((select set c) n)
              ((select get c)))))))
```

Figure 11.23 A sample CBV FLAVAR program for Exercise 11.20.

`tagcase` expression with an `else` clause may be a prefix of the ordered tags in the `oneof` type. If the order were different, it would be necessary to use the [*type-≈*] type rule in conjunction with the [*oneof-≈*] type equivalence rule to reorder the tagged types appropriately within the `oneof` type.

In the [*oneof-elim2*] rule, note that the name $I_{payload}$ cannot be referenced within the `else` expression E_{else}. The type of the payload of the discriminant value is unknown in this case. To maintain type soundness, the type system forbids references to $I_{payload}$ within E_{else}. This is consistent with the dynamic semantics for `tagcase` studied in Section 10.2.

Exercise 11.19 Construct type derivations showing that the abstractions in the `perim` and `scale` definitions are well typed.

Exercise 11.20 Using `recordof` and `oneof` types, translate the CBV FLAVAR program in Figure 11.23 to a well-typed FLEX program that exhibits similar structure. We assume here that FLAVAR supports records.

11.8.5 Typed Lists

The shape examples from the previous section show that simple sum-of-products data types can be expressed in FLEX by composing sums and products. However, as it stands, FLEX does not have the power to express recursively structured sum-of-products data types like lists and trees. Here we extend FLEX with a built-in list data type. In Section 11.8.6, we extend FLEX with a recursive type mechanism that allows lists and trees to be constructed by programmers.

Syntax

$E ::= \ldots \mid$ (cons E_{head} E_{tail}) $\mid$ (car E_{list}) $\mid$ (cdr E_{list})
$\qquad \mid$ (null T_{elt}) $\mid$ (null? E_{list})

$T ::= \ldots \mid$ (listof T_{elt})

Syntactic Sugar

(list T) $\leadsto_{ds}$ (null T)

(list T E_1 E^*_{rest}) $\leadsto_{ds}$ (cons E_1 (list T E^*_{rest}))

Type Rules

$$\frac{TE \vdash E_{head} : T \quad TE \vdash E_{tail} : \text{(listof } T)}{TE \vdash \text{(cons } E_{head} \ E_{tail}) : \text{(listof } T)} \qquad [cons]$$

$$\frac{TE \vdash E_{list} : \text{(listof } T)}{TE \vdash \text{(car } E_{list}) : T} \qquad [car]$$

$$\frac{TE \vdash E_{list} : \text{(listof } T)}{TE \vdash \text{(cdr } E_{list}) : \text{(listof } T)} \qquad [cdr]$$

$$TE \vdash \text{(null } T) : \text{(listof } T) \qquad [null]$$

$$\frac{TE \vdash E_{list} : \text{(listof } T)}{TE \vdash \text{(null? } E_{list}) : \text{bool}} \qquad [null?]$$

Type Equivalence

$$\frac{T_1 \approx T_2}{\text{(listof } T_1) \approx \text{(listof } T_2)} \qquad [\text{listof-}\approx]$$

Figure 11.24   Static semantics of lists in FLEX.

Figure 11.24 presents the essence of typed lists in FLEX. Unlike in FL, where lists are just sugar for idiomatic uses of pairs, FLEX supplies kernel constructs for creating empty lists (null), creating nonempty lists (cons), decomposing nonempty lists (car and cdr), and testing for empty lists (null?). All of these manipulate values of types created with the listof type constructor. The type (listof T) describes lists whose elements all have the same type T. FLEX lists are said to be **homogeneous**, in contrast to the **heterogeneous** lists of FL. To model heterogeneous lists within FLEX, such as a list of integers and booleans, it is necessary to inject the different types into an explicit sum type.

To preserve the monomorphism property of FLEX, the null construct includes the element type of the empty list, which cannot otherwise be determined except by guessing. So (null int) is an empty integer list, (null bool) is an empty boolean list, and (null (listof int)) is an empty list of integer lists.

Because each empty list has an explicit type, the `list` syntactic sugar construct must also be modified to have an explicit element type, as in (`list int 5 2 3`).

In a monomorphic language like FLEX, it is not possible for the programmer to define generic list-processing procedures like `map`, `filter`, and `foldr` that work for any list, but it is possible to define specialized versions that work on lists with particular types. For example, here is a mapping procedure that maps a list of shapes to a list of integers:

```
(def map-shape-int (-> ((-> (shape) int) (listof shape))
                       (listof int))
  (abs ((f (-> (shape) int)) (ss (listof shape)))
    (if (null? ss)
        (null int)
        (cons (f (car ss))
              (map-shape-int f (cdr ss))))))

(map-shape-int perim
  (list shape
        (one shape rectangle (pair 4 5))
        (one shape triangle (product 7 8 9))
        (one shape square 3)))  FLEX→ ◁18, 24, 12▷
```

Exercise 11.21 Translate each of the following FL expressions into a well-typed FLEX expression by (1) adding explicit type annotations, (2) introducing oneofs when necessary, and (3) duplicating expressions when necessary.

a.
```
(letrec ((map (abs (f xs)
                (if (null? xs)
                    (null)
                    (cons (f (car xs)) (map f (cdr xs)))))))
  (map (abs (x) (if (bool? x) (if x 1 0) (= 0 (% x 2))))
       (list 2 3 #t #f 6)))
```

b.
```
(abs (b)
  (letrec ((gen (abs (seed next done?)
                  (if (done? seed)
                      (null)
                      (cons seed (gen (next seed) next done?)))))
           (foldr (abs (binop init xs)
                    (if (null? xs)
                        init
                        (binop (car xs)
                               (foldr binop init (cdr xs)))))))
    (let ((ns (gen b (abs (x) (- x 1)) (abs (y) (= y 0)))))
      (if (foldr (abs (x y) (or (> x 3) y)) #f ns)
          (foldr (abs (x y) (cons (= 0 (% x 2)) y)) (null) ns)
          (gen #t (abs (x) (not x)) (abs (y) y))))))
```

11.8.6   Recursive Types

Recursive procedures often manipulate recursively structured data that cannot be described in terms of compound types alone. `trec` and `tletrec` (Figure 11.25) are used to specify the types of such data.

`trec` allows the specification of a single recursive type in the same manner that the FL `rec` construct specifies a single recursive value. For example, here `trec` is used to specify the type of a binary tree with integer leaves:

```
(trec int-tree
  (oneof (leaf int)
         (node (recordof (left int-tree)
                         (right int-tree)))))
```

In the literature, recursive types are often expressed using μ notation. For example, the FLEX type (`trec t (pairof int (pairof bool t))`) is traditionally written $\mu t.\text{int} \times (\text{bool} \times t)$.

`tletrec` is the type-domain analogue to `letrec`. It permits a mutually recursive set of named types to be used in a body type. For example, here is a use of `tletrec` to specify a binary tree that has integers at odd-numbered levels and booleans at even-numbered levels:

```
(tletrec ((int-level (oneof (leaf int)
                            (node (recordof (left bool-level)
                                            (right bool-level)))))
          (bool-level (oneof (leaf bool)
                             (node (recordof (left int-level)
                                             (right int-level))))))
    int-level)
```

Just as `letrec` can be expressed as sugar for `rec` in FL, it is possible to express `tletrec` as sugar for `trec`. But since this is cumbersome, `tletrec` is provided as a kernel type construct.

Both `trec` and `tletrec` are binding constructs for type identifiers, so it is necessary to extend the $FrTyIds_{ty}$ function appropriately to handle them.

Introducing recursive types into a programming language can change its termination properties. In particular, although μFLEX$-\{$`letrec`$\}$ is strongly normalizing, FLEX$-\{$`letrec`$\}$ is *not* strong normalizing. For example, as explored in Exercise 11.24, recursive types make it is possible to annotate the looping FL expression (`(abs (x) (x x)) (abs (x) (x x))`) with types to yield a well-typed FLEX expression.

What does it mean for two recursive types to be equivalent? For example, consider the four types in Figure 11.26. All of the types describe infinite lists of

$$T ::= \ldots \mid (\texttt{trec}\ \tau_{name}\ T_{body}) \mid (\texttt{tletrec}\ ((\tau_{name}\ T_{defn})^*)\ T_{body})$$

Figure 11.25 Syntax for recursive types in FLEX.

```
T_ib1 = (trec iblist (pairof int (pairof bool iblist)))
T_ib2 = (trec int-bool-list (pairof int (pairof bool int-bool-list)))
T_ib3 = (pairof int
              (pairof bool
                      (trec iblist (pairof int (pairof bool iblist)))))
T_ib4 = (pairof int (trec bilist (pairof bool (pairof int bilist))))
```

Figure 11.26 Four types describing infinite lists with alternating integer and boolean values.

$$(\texttt{trec}\ \tau\ T) \approx (\texttt{trec}\ \tau_{new}\ [\tau_{new}/\tau]T) \quad \text{where } \tau_{new} \notin FrTyIds_{ty}[\![T]\!] \qquad [\textit{trec-}\alpha]$$

$$(\texttt{trec}\ \tau\ T) \approx [(\texttt{trec}\ \tau\ T)/\tau]T \qquad\qquad\qquad\qquad [\textit{trec-}\beta]$$

Figure 11.27 Isorecursive type-equivalence rules for `trec` types.

alternating integer and boolean values. T_{ib2} is a copy of T_{ib1} in which the `trec`-bound type identifier has been consistently renamed. T_{ib3} is a copy of T_{ib1} in which the definition of `iblist` has been unwound one level. In T_{ib4}, the recursive type `bilist` describes an infinite list of alternating boolean and integer values. Which pairs of these four types are equivalent?

We shall study two common approaches for determining the type equivalence of recursive types expressed via `trec`. (These can be extended to handle `tletrec` as well.) The so-called **isorecursive** approach to formalizing type equivalence is based on the two type-equivalence rules shown in Figure 11.27. The [*trec-*α] rule says that the name of the bound variable in a `trec` doesn't matter. So $T_{ib1} \approx T_{ib2}$ via [*trec-*α]. The [*trec-*β] rule says that a `trec` type is equivalent to the result of substituting the entire `trec` type expression for its bound identifier in the body of the `trec`. So $T_{ib1} \approx T_{ib3}$ via [*trec-*β], and $T_{ib2} \approx T_{ib3}$ by the symmetry and transitivity of type equivalence.

Can T_{ib4} be shown to be equivalent to T_{ib1}, T_{ib2}, or T_{ib3} using [*trec-*α] and [*trec-*β]? No! We can prove this via the following observation. In each of T_{ib1}, T_{ib2}, and T_{ib3}, the number of occurrences of the type `int` is equal to the number of occurrences of the type `bool`. In T_{ib4}, the number of occurrences of `int` is one more than the number of occurrences of `bool`. Since each application of [*trec-*α]

and [*trec-β*] preserves the difference between the number of occurrences of `int` and of `bool`, T_{ib4} can never be shown to be equivalent to the other types via these rules.

There is another approach to recursive type equivalence in which T_{ib4} *is* equivalent to the other types. In this so-called **equirecursive** approach, two recursive types are considered to be equivalent if their complete (potentially infinite) unwindings are equal. Under this criterion, all four of the types in Figure 11.26 are equivalent, because all of them unwind to an infinite type describing a list of alternating integers and booleans:

```
(pairof int (pairof bool (pairof int (pairof bool ...))))
```

In our subsequent discussion of types, equirecursive type equivalence will be assumed unless explicitly stated otherwise.

There are two ways to formalize equirecursive type equivalence: canonical forms for recursive types and type-equivalence rules with assumptions.

Canonical Forms for Recursive Types

The complete unwinding of a type can be viewed as a (potentially infinite) abstract syntax tree whose leaves are base types and type identifiers and whose nodes are type constructors (`->`, `pairof`, `cellof`, etc.). Even though it may be infinite, any tree generated in this fashion has the property that it contains only a finite number of distinct subtrees — the defining property of a **regular tree**. Such a tree is called "regular" because it can be described by a finite-state automaton accepting a language that describes all paths down the tree beginning at its root. For instance, here is a depiction of a finite-state automaton describing the types T_{ib1} through T_{ib4} (assume **PairState1** is the start state and all states are final states):

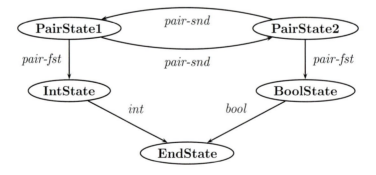

There is a straightforward correspondence between FLEX type expressions and such automata. Since finite-state automata can be minimized, FLEX type expressions can also be "minimized" to a canonical form. So FLEX type equivalence can be determined by finding the canonical forms of two type expressions and checking if they are the same.

Type-Equivalence Rules with Assumptions

Another approach to checking equirecursive type equivalence is a recursive "two-finger" process that simultaneously explores the tree structures denoted by two type expressions, T_1 and T_2. If a difference is detected between the two trees, the types are not equivalent. But if both trees are completely explored without detecting a difference, they must be equivalent.

The process compares the types pointed to by two "fingers," initially T_1 and T_2. If both fingers point to the same base type or the same childless type constructor (e.g., the empty product type (prodof)), the comparison of the types currently pointed at by the fingers succeeds. If both fingers point to a type with the same type constructor and the same number of children, the process checks the equivalence of the corresponding children in turn. If either finger points to a trec (or tletrec) type, that type is unwound and the comparison is performed again. In any other case, a difference is detected between the two types. The comparison process continues until a difference is detected (in which case T_1 and T_2 are not equivalent) or there are no more comparisons to perform (in which case T_1 and T_2 are equivalent).

As described, this comparison process has a problem: it may not terminate for types that denote infinite trees. This can be fixed by adopting a strategy similar to that of a person exploring a maze with cyclic paths: dropping breadcrumbs along the path already taken makes it possible to avoid taking any path more than once. In the realm of type equivalence, the analogue of breadcrumbs is the set of type pairs that have already been visited by the two fingers. We will call each such pair $\langle T, T' \rangle$ an **assumption** because the types are assumed to be equivalent. If the process encounters a comparison of two types in an assumption, the comparison succeeds because no evidence contradicting the assumed equivalence has been discovered since the last time the two types were encountered. Because T_1 and T_2 are finite expressions, there can be only a finite number of assumptions involving their parts. Since the set of assumptions grows whenever a new comparison is encountered and the set of assumptions is bounded, the comparison process must terminate. It is not necessary to store all type pairs encountered in the

---

New Domain

$AN \in \text{Assumption} = \text{Type} \times \text{Type}$

$AS \in \text{AssumptionSet} = \mathcal{P}(\text{Assumption})$

Type-Equivalence Rules

$$\frac{T_1 \approx_{\{\}} T_2}{T_1 \approx T_2} \qquad\qquad\qquad [\textit{simple-}\approx_{AS}]$$

$$T_1 \approx_{AS} T_2 \quad \text{where} \quad \langle T_1, T_2 \rangle \in AS \qquad\qquad [\textit{assumed-}\approx_{AS}]$$

$$\frac{[(\texttt{trec}\ \tau_1\ T_1)/\tau_1]T_1 \approx_{\{\langle(\texttt{trec}\ \tau_1\ T_1),T_2\rangle\}\cup AS} T_2}{(\texttt{trec}\ \tau_1\ T_1) \approx_{AS} T_2} \qquad [\textit{trec-}\approx_{AS}]$$

For each type-equivalence rule presented in Sections 11.8.2–11.8.5, there should be a similar rule here in which every occurrence of $\approx$ is replaced by $\approx_{AS}$. For example:

$$\frac{\forall_{i=1}^{2} \cdot (T_i' \approx_{AS} T_i)}{(\texttt{pairof}\ T_1'\ T_2') \approx_{AS} (\texttt{pairof}\ T_1\ T_2)} \qquad [\textit{pairof-}\approx_{AS}]$$

Figure 11.28   Rules for equirecursive type equivalence.

comparison process as assumptions; it is sufficient to store only those pairs in which at least one type is a `trec` (or `tletrec`) type.

Based on the idea of using assumptions, Figure 11.28 presents a set of type rules for equirecursive type equivalence. The notation $T_1 \approx_{AS} T_2$ indicates that T_1 and T_2 are equivalent relative to the assumptions in the set AS. The [$\textit{simple-}\approx_{AS}$] rule says that two types are equivalent if they are equivalent relative to the empty set of assumptions. The [$\textit{assumed-}\approx_{AS}$] rule says that T_1 and T_2 are equivalent relative to AS if the assumption $\langle T_1, T_2 \rangle$ is in AS. The [$\textit{trec-}\approx_{AS}$] rule says that a recursive type ($\texttt{trec}\ \tau_1\ T_1$) is equivalent to a type T_2 relative to the assumptions AS if the unwound type $[(\texttt{trec}\ \tau_1\ T_1)/\tau_1]T_1$ is equivalent to T_2 in AS extended with the new assumption $\langle(\texttt{trec}\ \tau_1\ T_1), T_2\rangle$. All other rules are versions of the type-equivalence rules presented in Sections 11.8.2–11.8.5 with $\approx$ replaced by $\approx_{AS}$. Note that a rule handling `trec` as the left component of $\approx_{AS}$ is sufficient because any `trec` in the right component can be handled by using the [$\textit{symmetric-}\approx_{AS}$] rule.

Figure 11.29 illustrates the equirecursive type-equivalence rules by showing that T_{ib1} and T_{ib4} from Figure 11.26 are equivalent in the equirecursive approach. Recall that these two types are *not* equivalent in the isorecursive approach.

Abbreviations

T'_{ib1} = (pairof int (pairof bool iblist))

T_{ib1} = (trec iblist T'_{ib1})

$\quad$ = (trec iblist (pairof int (pairof bool iblist)))

T''_{ib1} = (pairof bool T_{ib1}) = (pairof bool (trec iblist T'_{ib1}))

T''_{ib4} = (pairof bool (pairof int bilist))

T'_{ib4} = (trec bilist T''_{ib4})

$\quad$ = (trec bilist (pairof bool (pairof int bilist)))

T_{ib4} = (pairof int T'_{ib4})

$\quad$ = (pairof int (trec bilist T''_{ib4}))

$\quad$ = (pairof int (trec bilist (pairof bool (pairof int bilist))))

Derivation of Equirecursive Type Equivalence of T_{ib1} and T_{ib4}

$$\text{int} \approx_{\{\langle T_{ib1}, T_{ib4}\rangle\}} \text{int} \; [\textit{reflexive-}\approx_{AS}]$$

$$\text{bool} \approx_{\{\langle T'_{ib4}, T''_{ib1}\rangle, \langle T_{ib1}, T_{ib4}\rangle\}} \text{bool} \; [\textit{reflexive-}\approx_{AS}]$$

$$T_{ib1} \approx_{\{\langle T'_{ib4}, T''_{ib1}\rangle, \langle T_{ib1}, T_{ib4}\rangle\}} T_{ib4} \; [\textit{assumed-}\approx_{AS}]$$

$$T_{ib4} \approx_{\{\langle T'_{ib4}, T''_{ib1}\rangle, \langle T_{ib1}, T_{ib4}\rangle\}} T_{ib1} \; [\textit{symmetric-}\approx_{AS}]$$

(pairof bool T_{ib4})

$$\approx_{\{\langle T'_{ib4}, T''_{ib1}\rangle, \langle T_{ib1}, T_{ib4}\rangle\}} (\text{pairof bool } T_{ib1}) \; [\textit{pairof-}\approx_{AS}]$$

$$(\text{trec bilist } T''_{ib4}) \approx_{\{\langle T_{ib1}, T_{ib4}\rangle\}} (\text{pairof bool } T_{ib1}) \; [\textit{trec-}\approx_{AS}]$$

$$(\text{pairof bool } T_{ib1}) \approx_{\{\langle T_{ib1}, T_{ib4}\rangle\}} (\text{trec bilist } T''_{ib4}) \; [\textit{symmetric-}\approx_{AS}]$$

(pairof int (pairof bool T_{ib1}))

$$\approx_{\{\langle T_{ib1}, T_{ib4}\rangle\}} (\text{pairof int (trec bilist } T''_{ib4})) \; [\textit{pairof-}\approx_{AS}]$$

$$(\text{trec iblist } T'_{ib1}) \approx_{\{\}} (\text{pairof int (trec bilist } T''_{ib4})) \; [\textit{trec-}\approx_{AS}]$$

$$(\text{trec iblist } T'_{ib1}) \approx (\text{pairof int (trec bilist } T''_{ib4})) \; [\textit{simple-}\approx_{AS}]$$

Figure 11.29 A derivation of equirecursive type equivalence for two types, T_{ib1} and T_{ib4}, that are not isorecursive type-equivalent.

```
T₁ = (trec it
        (oneof (leaf int)
          (node (recordof (left it)
                          (right it)))))
T₂ = (trec int-tree
        (oneof (leaf int)
          (node (recordof (left int-tree)
                          (right int-tree)))))
T₃ = (trec it
        (oneof (leaf int)
          (node (recordof
                  (left (trec it2
                          (oneof (leaf int)
                            (node (recordof (left it2)
                                            (right it2))))))
                  (right it)))))
T₄ = (trec it
        (oneof (leaf int)
          (node (recordof
                  (left it)
                  (right (trec it2
                          (oneof (leaf int)
                            (node (recordof (left it2)
                                            (right it2)))))))))))
T₅ = (oneof (leaf int)
        (node (recordof
                (left (trec it
                        (oneof (leaf int)
                          (node (recordof (left it)
                                          (right it))))))
                (right (trec it
                        (oneof (leaf int)
                          (node (recordof (left it)
                                          (right it)))))))))
```

Figure 11.30   Five types for integer-leaved binary trees, for Exercise 11.22.

Exercise 11.22 Figure 11.30 presents five types. Which of these types are considered equivalent (a) under the isorecursive approach and (b) under the equirecursive approach?

Exercise 11.23 Give isorecursive and equirecursive type-equivalence rules for `tletrec`.

Exercise 11.24

a. Show that the following FLEX expression is well typed for any type T:

$$E_{self} = \text{(abs ((x (trec s (-> (s) } T\text{)))) (x x))}$$

b. Show that $(E_{self}\ E_{self})$ is well typed. Since evaluation of this expression does not terminate, this demonstrates that FLEX$-\{$letrec$\}$ is not strongly normalizing.

c. Here is a definition of a factorial procedure in CBN FL that does not use any explicit expression-level recursion constructs:

```
E_fact = ((abs (f)
             ((abs (x) (f (x x)))
              (abs (x) (f (x x)))))
           (abs (g)
            (abs (n)
             (if (= n 0) 1 (* n (g (- n 1)))))))
```

Using recursive types, annotate E_{fact} with types so that it is a well-typed expression denoting a factorial procedure in CBN FLEX.

d. Modify the expression in part **c** to yield a factorial procedure in CBV FLEX defined without letrec.

Exercise 11.25

a. Figure 6.13 on page 243 presents an interpreter for the ELM language written in FL. Here we consider an interpreter for ELM written in FLEX. Suppose that ELM expressions and programs are described in FLEX by the following types:

$$
\begin{aligned}
T_{elmExp} = &\text{ (trec numexp}\\
&\quad\text{(oneof (intval int)}\\
&\qquad\qquad\text{(input int)}\\
&\qquad\qquad\text{(arithop (prodof symb numexp numexp))))}\\
T_{elmPgm} = &\text{ (recordof (nargs int) (body } T_{elmExp}\text{))}
\end{aligned}
$$

Define a FLEX procedure with type $\text{(-> (}T_{elmPgm}\text{ (listof int)) int)}$ that runs an ELM program on a list of integer arguments. In your definition, use letrec to define any auxiliary procedures that you need (such as elm-eval and get-arg from Figure 6.13).

b. Define a procedure that runs a full EL program on a list of integer arguments. A grammar for EL is defined in Figure 2.4 on page 25. In your definition, use tletrec to define the mutually recursive types for numerical and boolean expressions.

Exercise 11.26 Define a FLEX procedure that executes a POSTFIX program on a list of integers. As part of your definition, you will need to write types that describe POSTFIX programs, commands, and command sequences.

Exercise 11.27 In your favorite programming language, write a program that determines equirecursive type equivalence for FLEX types using either the assumption-based approach or the canonicalization approach.

11.8.7   Full FLEX Summary

Thus far, we have presented the constructs of FLEX in bits and pieces. Figure 11.31 presents the entire kernel grammar of FLEX in one place. The syntactic sugar for FLEX (not shown) is that of μFLEX extended with the `begin` sugar from Figure 11.21 on page 681 and the `list` sugar from Figure 11.24 on page 686.

In order to specify the dynamic semantics of FLEX (which is necessary to prove type soundness), we could extend the dynamic semantics of μFLEX from Section 11.6.2 to handle the additional constructs of FLEX. Since the dynamic semantics of each of these constructs has been studied previously, we do not flesh out the details of the FLEX SOS. Note that the ValueExp and AnsExp domains of the SOS must be extended to handle product, sum, list, and cell values. The presence of mutable variables and cells means that configurations in the FLEX SOS must have a store component and that both variables and cells must be associated with locations in the store. As usual, we will assume a CBV semantics for procedure application and data components in the presence of imperative features.

The type soundness argument for μFLEX from Section 11.6 can be extended to full FLEX. In order to handle mutable variables and cells, each location in the store can be assigned a type, and only values of this type can be stored at the location [Pie02, Chapter 13].

Full FLEX is monomorphic in the sense that every well-typed expression has a unique type up to type equivalence.

As seen in Exercise 11.24 (page 694), the full FLEX language without `letrec` is not strongly normalizing. Recursive types make it possible to write nonterminating expressions in FLEX even without `letrec`.

Sum-of-products data types can be expressed in FLEX using typed sums, typed products, and recursive types, but this is rather cumbersome. It would be helpful to have a more convenient means for specifying such data types, such as a typed analogue of FL's `def-data`/`match` facility. However, as we shall see in Section 12.2.3, FLEX's monomorphism stands in the way of specifying the deconstructor procedures used by this facility. Nevertheless, as explored in Exercise 11.28, it is still helpful to extend FLEX with an s-expression data type for describing generic tree-structured data, and to extend the domain of program inputs in a similar fashion.

$P \in \text{Prog} ::= (\texttt{flexk} \ ((I_{formal} \ T_{formalType})^*) \ E_{body})$

$E \in \text{Exp} ::= L \mid I \mid (\texttt{error} \ Y_{message} \ T_{errorType})$
$\mid (\texttt{if} \ E_{test} \ E_{then} \ E_{else}) \mid (\texttt{prim} \ O_{primop} \ E_{arg}^*)$
$\mid (\texttt{abs} \ ((I_{formal} \ T_{formalType})^*) \ E_{body}) \mid (E_{rator} \ E_{rand}^*)$
$\mid (\texttt{let} \ ((I_{name} \ E_{defn})^*) \ E_{body})$
$\mid (\texttt{letrec} \ ((I_{name} \ T_{defnType} \ E_{defn})^*) \ E_{body})$
$\mid (\texttt{the} \ T_{bodyType} \ E_{body})$
$\mid (\texttt{begin} \ E_1 \ E_2) \mid (\texttt{set!} \ I_{var} \ E_{val})$
$\mid (\texttt{cell} \ E_{content}) \mid (\texttt{\^{}} \ E_{cell}) \mid (\texttt{:=} \ E_{cell} \ E_{val}) \mid (\texttt{cell=?} \ E_1 \ E_2)$
$\mid (\texttt{pair} \ E_{fst} \ E_{snd}) \mid (\texttt{fst} \ E_{pair}) \mid (\texttt{snd} \ E_{pair})$
$\mid (\texttt{prod} \ E_{component}^*) \mid (\texttt{get} \ N_{index} \ E_{prod})$
$\mid (\texttt{seq} \ E_{component}^*) \mid (\texttt{seq-get} \ E_{index} \ E_{seq}) \mid (\texttt{seq-size} \ E_{seq})$
$\mid (\texttt{cons} \ E_{head} \ E_{tail}) \mid (\texttt{car} \ E_{list}) \mid (\texttt{cdr} \ E_{list})$
$\mid (\texttt{null} \ T_{elt}) \mid (\texttt{null?} \ E_{list})$
$\mid (\texttt{record} \ (I_{name} \ E_{defn})^*) \mid (\texttt{select} \ I_{name} \ E_{rcd})$
$\mid (\texttt{with} \ E_{rcd} \ E_{body})$
$\mid (\texttt{one} \ T_{oneof} \ I_{tag} \ E_{payload})$
$\mid (\texttt{tagcase} \ E_{disc} \ I_{payload} \ (I_{tag} \ E_{body})^* \ (\texttt{else} \ E_{else})^?)$

$L \in \text{Lit} ::= \texttt{\#u} \mid B \mid N \mid (\texttt{sym} \ Y) \ ; \textit{as in} \ \text{FL}.$

$B \in \text{BoolLit} = \{\texttt{\#t}, \texttt{\#f}\} \text{ as in FL}.$

$N \in \text{IntLit} = \text{ as in FL}.$

$Y \in \text{SymLit} = \text{ as in FL}.$

$O \in \text{Primop} = \text{usual FL primitives except no type predicates or pair operators}$

$\quad \text{Keyword} = \text{the set of all FLEX kernel-expression and program keywords}$

$\quad \text{SugarKeyword} = \text{the set of all FLEX syntactic sugar keywords}$

$I \in \text{Ident} = \text{SymLit} - (\{Y \mid Y \text{ begins with } \texttt{@}\} \cup \text{Keyword} \cup \text{SugarKeyword})$

$T \in \text{Type} ::= BT \mid \tau \mid (\texttt{->} \ (T_{arg}^*) \ T_{result}) \mid (\texttt{cellof} \ T_{content})$
$\mid (\texttt{pairof} \ T_{fst} \ T_{snd}) \mid (\texttt{prodof} \ T_{component}^*)$
$\mid (\texttt{seqof} \ T_{component}) \mid (\texttt{listof} \ T_{elt})$
$\mid (\texttt{recordof} \ (I_{name} \ T_{defn})^*) \mid (\texttt{oneof} \ (I_{tag} \ T_{payload})^*)$
$\mid (\texttt{trec} \ \tau_{name} \ T_{body}) \mid (\texttt{tletrec} \ ((\tau_{name} \ T_{defn})^*) \ T_{body})$

$BT \in \text{BaseType} = \{\texttt{unit}, \texttt{int}, \texttt{bool}, \texttt{symb}\}$

$\quad \text{TypeKeyword} = \text{BaseType} \cup \{\texttt{->}, \texttt{cellof}, \texttt{listof}, \texttt{oneof}, \texttt{pairof}, \texttt{prodof},$
$\quad\quad\quad\quad\quad\quad\quad\quad\quad\quad \texttt{recordof}, \texttt{seqof}, \texttt{tletrec}, \texttt{trec}\}$

$\tau \in \text{TypeId} = \text{SymLit} - \text{TypeKeyword}$

$PT \in \text{ProgType} ::= (\texttt{=>} \ (T_{arg}^*) \ T_{result})$

Figure 11.31 Kernel grammar for full FLEX. The syntactic sugar for FLEX is that of μFLEX extended with the `begin` sugar from Figure 11.21 on page 681 and the `list` sugar from Figure 11.24 on page 686.

Exercise 11.28 This exercise considers extending FLEX with s-expressions having the following recursive type:

$$T_{sexp} = \text{(trec sexp}$$
$$\qquad \text{(oneof (unit->sexp unit)}$$
$$\qquad\qquad\qquad \text{(int->sexp int)}$$
$$\qquad\qquad\qquad \text{(bool->sexp bool)}$$
$$\qquad\qquad\qquad \text{(symb->sexp symb)}$$
$$\qquad\qquad\qquad \text{(list->sexp (listof sexp))))}$$

Assume that every free occurrence of the type identifier `sexp` appearing in a FLEX program (including in the types of its formal parameters) is replaced by T_{sexp}.

a. Write the s-expression `(1 #t ((a #u) #f))` as a FLEX expression with type T_{sexp}.

b. Extend FLEX with desugaring rules for an FL-like `quote` construct for conveniently writing s-expressions (see Figure 6.7 on page 233), so that the s-expression from part **a** can be written directly in FLEX as `(quote (1 #t ((a #u) #f)))`.

c. S-expressions representing phrases defined by an s-expression grammar can be parsed into FLEX sum-of-products values representing abstract syntax trees, such as the ELM expression type T_{elmExp} from part **a** of Exercise 11.25. Define a procedure `sexp->elm` with type `(-> (sexp)` T_{elmExp}`)` that parses s-expressions into ELM expressions. An `invalid-elm-exp` error should be generated for any input s-expression that does not correspond to a valid ELM expression.

d. A limitation of FLEX is that program inputs must be literals. It would be nice to allow inputs with type `sexp` in order to handle programs (list/tree manipulation programs, interpreters, compilers, etc.) with tree-structured inputs. This can be accomplished by modifying the InputExp domain in the SOS so that all inputs are s-expressions:

$$IE \in \text{InputExp} ::= \texttt{\#u} \mid N \mid B \mid Y \mid (IE^*)$$

For example, this allows the s-expression from part **a** to be used as a program input.

Give a modified definition of the input function *IF* that works with this new domain. Note that InputExp no longer describes a subset of Exp, so inputs must be converted to expressions before being substituted for program parameters. Your definition of *IF* should allow any integer literal input N to be used for an `int` parameter or an `sexp` parameter; unit, boolean, and symbol literals should be handled similarly.

Notes

A good introduction to various dimensions of type design is a survey article written by Cardelli and Wegner [CW85]. For more in-depth coverage on many facets of type systems and typed programming languages, we recommend [Pie02, Pie05, Mit96, Sch94].

Many dimensions of types have been fruitfully studied in the context of the lambda calculus. Church described an explicitly typed version of the lambda calculus in [Chu40], and Curry and his colleagues formulated implicitly typed versions of the lambda calculus in [CF58, CHS72]. These are two variants of what is known as the *simply typed lambda calculus*. Consult [HS86b, Hin97] for coverage of the simply typed lambda calculus. For a discussion of how to extend the simply typed lambda calculus with additional typing features, see [Bar92].

Another standard language in which types are studied is PCF, which stands for Programming Computable Functions [Plo77], [Mit96, Chapter 2]. PCF is an explicitly typed, monomorphic language that extends the simply typed lambda calculus with integers, booleans, conditionals, and a fixed-point operator. FLEX can be viewed as an extension to PCF with even more features: positional and named products, named sums, lists, mutable variables and cells, and recursive types. Extensions to PCF with these kinds of features are often considered in the literature.

The vertical-style type derivations in this text were inspired by the vertically oriented type derivations in [AC96]. The vertical style enables far more complex type derivations to fit on a standard page than does the traditional horizontal style.

The preservation/progress recipe for proving type soundness was championed by Wright and Felleisen in [WF94]. More detailed coverage of type soundness issues can be found in [Pie02].

In the literature, strong normalization of typed functional languages is usually studied in typed variants of the lambda calculus. A standard proof that simplification in the simply typed lambda calculus is strongly normalizing can be found in [HS86b, Appendix 2]; it uses a proof method known as *logical relations* pioneered in [Tai67], but does not call attention to this general technique. [Pie02, Chapter 12] presents a proof emphasizing the general logical relations technique and gives pointers to the history and uses of this technique. A different proof technique for strong normalization is presented in [KW95].

In [Pie02, Chapter 21], Pierce presents the theory underlying the equivalence and subtyping of equirecursive types. He explains how the assumption-based approach to equirecursive type equivalence calculates a *greatest* fixed point of a relation between types, and presents an alternative approach to equirecursive type equivalence that is more efficient than the one in Figure 11.28.

Type checking exemplifies a form of static analysis in which a program is "executed" in a way that is guaranteed to terminate by using a finite set of value approximations in place of an infinite set of values. This style of program analysis, known as *abstract interpretation* [CC77, JN95], [NNH98, Chapter 4], is used for many kinds of program analysis, such as termination analysis, strictness analysis, and flow analysis.

Throughout this book, we adopt the view that types are descriptions of values. But this is not the only interpretation. A very different perspective is that types are logical propositions, and an expression with a given type is a proof of the corresponding proposition. This *types-as-formulas* perspective is the foundation of what is known as the *Curry-Howard Isomorphism*. See [SU06] for detailed coverage of this notion.

12

Polymorphism and Higher-order Types

He will put some things behind, will pass an invisible boundary; new, universal, and more liberal laws will begin to establish themselves around and within him; or the old laws be expanded, and interpreted in his favor in a more liberal sense, and he will live with the license of a higher order of beings. ... If you have built castles in the air, your work need not be lost; that is where they should be. Now put the foundations under them.

— Henry David Thoreau, *Walden*

Types can be thought of as describing the size and shape of values manipulated by a program. Strictly monomorphic languages, like FLEX, impose two onerous requirements:

- Whenever two types must be compatible, they must be exactly the same (e.g., the two arms of a conditional or the formal-parameter and actual-argument types of a procedure).

- Every program expression has exactly one type.

Polymorphism allows program expressions that would previously have required data of a single size and shape to work with values of different sizes and shapes. It relaxes the above constraints and adds considerable expressive power to our language and its type system. **Subtyping** provides relief from the first restriction above; and **polymorphic types** provide relief from the second.

12.1 Subtyping

To understand why we want to develop a notion of compatible types looser than exact type equivalence, consider a `get-age` procedure that extracts the contents of the `age` field of a record:

```
(def get-age (-> ((recordof (age int))) int)
  (abs ((r (recordof (age int))))
    (select age r)))
```

In the FLEX type system, the following use of `get-age` does not type-check:

```
(get-age (record (name (symb Polly_Morwicz)) (age 35) (student? #f)))
```

The problem is that the given record has three fields, but the type of `get-age` dictates that the argument record must have exactly one field. Yet the presence of the extra fields does not compromise the type safety of the expression — i.e., evaluating the expression will not perform an illegal operation. We can reliably extract an integer from the `age` field of *any* record that binds `age` to an integer value. No constraints on the number or nature of other fields are implied by the extraction of the `age` field.

Situations like `get-age` can be addressed by the notion of **subtyping** (also called **type inclusion**). We say that T' is a **subtype** of T (written $T' \sqsubseteq T$) if all expressions of type T' can be used (in a type-safe manner) in every situation where an expression of type T is used. Viewing types as sets, $T' \sqsubseteq T$ means that $T' \subseteq T$. If T' is a subtype of T, we can also say that T is a **supertype** of T'.

12.1.1   FLEX/S: FLEX with Subtyping

FLEX/S is a variant of FLEX that supports subtyping. The type rules of FLEX/S are the same as those for FLEX except for the addition of the [*inclusion*] rule of Figure 12.1. This rule formalizes the notion that a subtype element can be used in any situation where a supertype element is expected. It says that E can be treated as having type T if it is known to have type T' and T' is a subtype of T.

Subtyping of Nonrecursive Types

The subtype relation for nonrecursive types in FLEX/S is defined by the subtype rules in Figure 12.2. The [*equiv-$\sqsubseteq$*] rule is a generalized reflexivity rule stating that any two type-equivalent types are in the subtype relation. It is possible to show that the subtype relation is antisymmetric: $T \sqsubseteq T'$ and $T' \sqsubseteq T$ imply $T \approx T'$. Because it is also reflexive and transitive, the subtype relation is a partial order on types.

The [*pairof-$\sqsubseteq$*] rule says that one `pairof` type is a subtype of another if its corresponding components are subtypes in the same direction. When two corresponding type components are related via subtyping in the same direction as their enclosing compound types, the subtyping relation on these component

$$\frac{TE \vdash E : T' \qquad T' \sqsubseteq T}{TE \vdash E : T} \qquad [inclusion]$$

Figure 12.1 The type rules of FLEX/S are those of FLEX extended with this single rule.

$$\frac{T' \approx T}{T' \sqsubseteq T} \qquad [equiv\text{-}\sqsubseteq]$$

$$\frac{T_1 \sqsubseteq T_2 \qquad T_2 \sqsubseteq T_3}{T_1 \sqsubseteq T_3} \qquad [transitive\text{-}\sqsubseteq]$$

$$\frac{\forall_{i=1}^{2} \cdot T_i' \sqsubseteq T_i}{(\texttt{pairof } T_1' \ T_2') \sqsubseteq (\texttt{pairof } T_1 \ T_2)} \qquad [pairof\text{-}\sqsubseteq]$$

$$\frac{\forall_{i=1}^{n} \cdot T_i' \sqsubseteq T_i}{(\texttt{prodof } T'^{n}_{i=1}) \sqsubseteq (\texttt{prodof } T^{n}_{i=1})} \qquad [prodof\text{-}\sqsubseteq]$$

$$\frac{T' \sqsubseteq T}{(\texttt{seqof } T') \sqsubseteq (\texttt{seqof } T)} \qquad [seqof\text{-}\sqsubseteq]$$

$$\frac{T' \sqsubseteq T}{(\texttt{listof } T') \sqsubseteq (\texttt{listof } T)} \qquad [listof\text{-}\sqsubseteq]$$

$$\frac{\forall_{i=1}^{n} \cdot \exists j \in [1..m] \cdot \left(\left(I_j' = I_i \right) \wedge \left(T_j' \sqsubseteq T_i \right) \right)}{(\texttt{recordof } (I_j' \ T_j')_{j=1}^{m}) \sqsubseteq (\texttt{recordof } (I_i \ T_i)_{i=1}^{n})} \qquad [recordof\text{-}\sqsubseteq]$$

$$\frac{\forall_{j=1}^{m} \cdot \exists i \in [1..n] \cdot \left(\left(I_j' = I_i \right) \wedge \left(T_j' \sqsubseteq T_i \right) \right)}{(\texttt{oneof } (I_j' \ T_j')_{j=1}^{m}) \sqsubseteq (\texttt{oneof } (I_i \ T_i)_{i=1}^{n})} \qquad [oneof\text{-}\sqsubseteq]$$

$$\frac{\left(\forall_{i=1}^{n} \cdot (T_i \sqsubseteq T_i') \right) \qquad T_{body}' \sqsubseteq T_{body}}{(\texttt{-> } (T'^{n}_{i=1}) \ T_{body}') \sqsubseteq (\texttt{-> } (T^{n}_{i=1}) \ T_{body})} \qquad [\rightarrow\text{-}\sqsubseteq]$$

Figure 12.2 Subtype rules for nonrecursive types in FLEX/S.

types is said to be **covariant**. Both component types of a `pairof` type have covariant subtyping. All components of `prodof`, `seqof`, and `listof` types also have covariant subtyping.

The [*recordof*-$\sqsubseteq$] rule says that a record type $T' = (\texttt{recordof } (I_j' \ T_j')_{j=1}^{m})$ is a subtype of a record type $T = (\texttt{recordof } (I_i \ T_i)_{i=1}^{n})$ if (1) T' has at least the fields of T and (2) for each of the common fields, the type of the field in T' is a subtype of the type of the field in T (i.e., the common fields have covariant

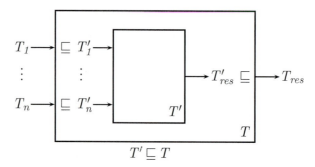

$$T' \sqsubseteq T$$

Figure 12.3 A depiction of $(\text{->}\ (T''^n_{i=1})\ T'_{res}) = T' \sqsubseteq T = (\text{->}\ (T^n_{i=1})\ T_{res})$ that suggests why procedure subtyping is covariant in result types but contravariant in argument types.

subtyping). It is safe for T' to have extra fields because those fields are ignored by any code that uses only the fields mentioned in T. For example:

```
(recordof (a int) (b (recordof (c bool) (d symb))))
⊑ (recordof (a int) (b (recordof (c bool))))
⊑ (recordof (b (recordof (c bool))))
```

The $[\textit{oneof-}\sqsubseteq]$ rule is a dual of the $[\textit{recordof-}\sqsubseteq]$ rule: a oneof type $T' = (\text{oneof}\ (I'_j\ T'_j)^m_{j=1})$ is a subtype of a oneof type $T = (\text{oneof}\ (I_i\ T_i)^n_{i=1})$ if it has *fewer* tags. This makes sense because if a program is prepared to handle all the cases of the supertype, T, then it is prepared for the fewer cases of the subtype, T'. Additionally, the types associated with the shared tags have covariant subtyping. For example:

```
(oneof (b (oneof (c bool))))
⊑ (oneof (a int) (b (oneof (c bool))))
⊑ (oneof (a int) (b (oneof (c bool) (d symb))))
```

In the $[\rightarrow\text{-}\sqsubseteq]$ rule for procedure subtyping, the subtyping of result types is covariant, but the subtyping of argument types is **contravariant** — that is, arrow types as a whole are related via subtyping in a direction that is opposite to the subtyping of argument types. The reason for this is suggested by Figure 12.3, which depicts a procedure with type $T' = (\text{->}\ (T''^n_{i=1})\ T'_{res})$ filling a context where a procedure of type $T = (\text{->}\ (T^n_{i=1})\ T_{res})$ is expected. The result type T'_{res} of T' is used where a type T_{res} is expected, so it is safe to use only a procedure that returns a "smaller" result type in place of one that returns a "larger" result type. In contrast, the argument type T_i is used in a context where T'_i is expected, so it is safe to use only a procedure that takes a "larger" argument type in place of one that takes a "smaller" argument type.

Subtyping for Mutable Structures

Note that there is no subtype rule for `cellof` types. This is not an oversight. Two `cellof` types are in a subtyping relation if and only if they are equivalent (as implied by the [*equiv-⊑*] rule), and two `cellof` types are equivalent if and only if their component types are equivalent (as specified by the [*cellof-≈*] rule). In other words, it is as if the `cellof` subtype rule were:

$$\frac{T' \approx T}{(\texttt{cellof}\ T') \sqsubseteq (\texttt{cellof}\ T)} \qquad [\textit{cellof-}\sqsubseteq]$$

This rule may be somewhat surprising. The following covariant subtype rule for `cellof` seems natural, but it is actually *unsound*:

$$\frac{T' \sqsubseteq T}{(\texttt{cellof}\ T') \sqsubseteq (\texttt{cellof}\ T)} \qquad [\textit{unsound-cellof-}\sqsubseteq]$$

To see why this second rule is incorrect, consider the following example:

```
(let ((stuffit (abs ((r (cellof (recordof (a int)))))
                  (:= r (record (a 2)))))
      (c (cell (record (a 1) (b #t)))))
  (begin (stuffit c)
         (select b (^ c))))
```

The type of `stuffit` is `(-> ((cellof (recordof (a int)))) unit)` and the type of the cell c is $T_c = $ `(cellof (record (a int) (b bool)))`. Using the [*unsound-cellof-⊑*] subtype rule in conjunction with the [*recordof-⊑*] rule, we can deduce that $T_c \sqsubseteq$ `(cellof (record (a int)))`. This together with the [*inclusion*] rule allows us to prove that the application (`stuffit c`) is well typed, and then it is easy to show that the whole expression is well typed.

However, evaluating this expression leads to a dynamic type error! The cell c initially contains a record with both a and b fields, but the application (`stuffit c`) changes c so that it contains a record with only an a field. So the attempt to select b from the record in c after `stuffit` is called is a dynamic type error. A type system is sound only if well-typed programs are guaranteed not to encounter any type errors at run time. Clearly the type system with the [*unsound-cellof-⊑*] type rule is unsound.

Requiring the `cellof` component types to be equivalent, as in the [*cellof-⊑*] subtype rule, maintains the soundness of the type system. In the above example, this subtype rule makes the call (`stuffit c`) ill typed. The intuition behind this rule is that cells are equivalent to a pair of a "getter" procedure with subtyping covariant in the component type and a "setter" procedure with subtyping contravariant in the component type. The only way to satisfy both constraints is to require that subtyping be **invariant** in the component type — that is, the component types must be equivalent regardless of the direction of subtyping of the compound types. This perspective is explored more fully in Exercise 12.2.

The invariance of component subtyping for `cellof` generalizes to any mutable data structure. For example, if we were to extend FLEX/S with mutable arrays with types of the form (`arrayof` T), then (`arrayof` T') would be a subtype of (`arrayof` T) if and only if $T' \approx T$. However, if the `arrayof` type described *immutable* arrays, then the subtyping of components would be covariant: (`arrayof` T') would be a subtype of (`arrayof` T) if and only if $T' \sqsubseteq T$. Some languages, like CLU, have both mutable and immutable product types. In such a language, the immutable product can support more flexible subtyping.

Subtyping of Recursive Types

The FLEX/S subtype rules in Figure 12.2 do not include any subtype rules involving `trec` or `tletrec`. Without any additional rules, a recursive type would be in a subtyping relation with another type if and only if it is equivalent to that type.

However, it is desirable to have a more permissive notion of subtyping involving recursive types. Suppose that T_a = (`recordof` (a int)) and T_{ab} = (`recordof` (a int) (b bool)), so that $T_{ab} \sqsubseteq T_a$. Now consider the following recursive types:

$$T_{rs} = (\texttt{trec s (pairof } T_{ab} \texttt{ s)})$$
$$T_{rt} = (\texttt{trec t (pairof } T_a \texttt{ t)})$$
$$T_{ru} = (\texttt{trec u (pairof } T_{ab} \texttt{ (-> (} T_a \texttt{) u)))}$$
$$T_{rv} = (\texttt{trec v (pairof } T_a \texttt{ (-> (} T_{ab} \texttt{) v)))}$$

Intuitively, we expect that T_{rs} is a subtype of T_{rt} because these specify infinite lists whose element types are in a covariant subtyping relation. We also expect that T_{ru} is a subtype of T_{rv} because (1) the first components of the pairs are related covariantly; (2) the argument types of the procedures in the second components of the pairs are related contravariantly; and (3) by assumption, the result types of the procedures in the second components of the pairs are related covariantly.

In order to express these sorts of nontrivial subtypings involving recursive types, we can modify the assumption-based approach to equirecursive type equivalence presented in Figure 11.28 on page 692 to handle subtyping instead. Figure 12.4 shows the new subtyping rules. The rules maintain a set of subtyping assumptions represented as a sequence of type pairs. If $\langle T_1, T_2 \rangle$ is in the set of assumptions AS, then T_1 is a subtype of T_2 by the [assumed-$\sqsubseteq_{AS}$] rule. When-

---

New Domain

$AN \in \text{Assumption} = \text{Type} \times \text{Type}$

$AS \in \text{AssumptionSet} = \mathcal{P}(\text{Assumption})$

Subtype Rules

$$\frac{T_1 \sqsubseteq_{\{\}} T_2}{T_1 \sqsubseteq T_2} \qquad\qquad\qquad\qquad [simple\text{-}\sqsubseteq_{AS}]$$

$$T_1 \sqsubseteq_{AS} T_2 \quad \text{where} \quad \langle T_1, T_2 \rangle \in AS \qquad\qquad [assumed\text{-}\sqsubseteq_{AS}]$$

$$\frac{[(\texttt{trec } \tau_1 \ T_1)/\tau_1]T_1 \sqsubseteq_{(\{\langle(\texttt{trec } \tau_1 \ T_1), T_2\rangle\}\cup AS)} T_2}{(\texttt{trec } \tau_1 \ T_1) \sqsubseteq_{AS} T_2} \qquad [trec\text{-}left\text{-}\sqsubseteq_{AS}]$$

$$\frac{T_1 \sqsubseteq_{(\{\langle T_1, (\texttt{trec } \tau_2 \ T_2)\rangle\}\cup AS)} [(\texttt{trec } \tau_2 \ T_2)/\tau_2]T_2}{T_1 \sqsubseteq_{AS} (\texttt{trec } \tau_2 \ T_2)} \qquad [trec\text{-}right\text{-}\sqsubseteq_{AS}]$$

For each subtype rule presented in Figure 12.2, there should be a similar rule here in which every occurrence of $\sqsubseteq$ is replaced by $\sqsubseteq_{AS}$. For example:

$$\frac{\forall_{i=1}^{2} \cdot (T_i' \sqsubseteq_{AS} T_i)}{(\texttt{pairof } T_1' \ T_2') \sqsubseteq_{AS} (\texttt{pairof } T_1 \ T_2)} \qquad [pairof\text{-}\sqsubseteq_{AS}]$$

Figure 12.4 Rules for equirecursive subtyping.

ever a recursive type is encountered, the set of type assumptions is extended with an assumption involving this type, and the subtype-checking process continues with the result of unwinding the recursive type. Because subtyping is an asymmetric relation, it is necessary to have two rules for handling recursive types: one where the recursive type appears to the left of $\sqsubseteq_{AS}$, and one where it appears to the right. It is also necessary to have assumption-based versions of each of the subtype rules in Figure 12.2. The $[simple\text{-}\sqsubseteq_{AS}]$ rule says that two types are related by $\sqsubseteq$ if they are related by the extended subtype relation with an empty set of assumptions.

With these new rules, it is possible to show that $T_{rs} \sqsubseteq T_{rt}$ and $T_{ru} \sqsubseteq T_{rv}$ (see Exercise 12.4).

Recall that assumption-based rules were only one approach for showing the equivalence of recursive types in Section 11.8.6. Another approach was based on viewing recursive types as finite-state automata. So it is natural to wonder whether it is possible to check the subtyping of recursive types using the automata approach. The answer is yes: an automata-based subtyping algorithm for recursive types is described in [KPS93].

Subtyping and Type Equivalence

In the subtype rules of Figure 12.2, the [*equiv-$\sqsubseteq$*] rule mediates between the type-equivalence relation $\approx$ and the subtype relation $\sqsubseteq$. This rule treats subtyping as a secondary relation defined in terms of a primary type-equivalence relation. An alternative approach is to make subtyping the primary relation and define two types to be type-equivalent if they are mutually inclusive according to the subtype relation. This can be formalized by replacing the [*equiv-$\sqsubseteq$*] subtype rule and all type-equivalence rules by the following two rules:

$$T \sqsubseteq T \qquad\qquad\qquad [\textit{reflexive-}\sqsubseteq]$$

$$\frac{T \sqsubseteq T' \quad T' \sqsubseteq T}{T \approx T'} \qquad\qquad [\textit{type-}\approx]$$

The Soundness of Subtyping

Any change in a language's type rules or dynamic semantics immediately raises the issue of type soundness. It is easy to extend the soundness argument for FLEX to show the soundness of FLEX/S, because the two languages have the same dynamic semantics, and the only difference in the type system is the introduction of the [*inclusion*] rule. The FLEX soundness proof (Section 11.6) consisted of two parts: *preservation*, which says that $\{\} \vdash E : T$ and $E \Rightarrow E'$ implies $\{\} \vdash E' : T$; and *progress*, which says that E is not stuck at a type error if $\{\} \vdash E : T$.

Preservation for FLEX/S is the more straightforward part. As before, this is proved by showing that reduction preserves types (if $TE \vdash E : T$ and $E \rightsquigarrow E'$ then $TE \vdash E' : T$) and that the well-typedness of a filled context $\mathbb{E}\{E\}$ is preserved if E is replaced by E', where both E and E' have the same type in the empty type environment. The only change is that the well-typedness of contexts in which reductions are performed may depend on the [*inclusion*] rule.

In the progress argument for FLEX/S, the analysis of each kind of stuck expression must account for possible use of the [*inclusion*] rule. Consider record-selection expressions as an example (other cases are similar). The expression $E_{select} = (\texttt{select } I \texttt{ (record } (I_i \; E_i)_{i=1}^n)$ is stuck (at a type error) only if $I \notin \cup_{i=1}^n \{I_i\}$. We need to argue that E_{select} cannot be stuck if it is well typed — i.e., we need to prove that if E_{select} is well typed, then I *must* be in $\cup_{i=1}^n \{I_i\}$.

The type derivation for E_{select} must use the [*recordof-elim*] rule to show that the $\texttt{record}$ expression has a type $(\texttt{recordof } (I_i' \; T_i)_{i=1}^n)$ such that $I \in \cup_{i=1}^n \{I_i'\}$. In FLEX, which does not have the [*inclusion*] rule, this $\texttt{record}$ expression has a type, determined by the [*recordof-intro*] rule, of the form $T_{record} =$

(recordof $(I_i\ T_i)_{i=1}^n$), so $I \in \cup_{i=1}^n\{I_i\}$, and we are done. But in FLEX/S, one or more instantiations of the [*inclusion*] rule can assign to (record $(I_i\ E_i)_{i=1}^n$) any supertype T'_{record} of T_{record}, where the fields $\cup_{i=1}^n\{I'_i\}$ in T'_{record} may be a subset of the fields $\cup_{i=1}^n\{I_i\}$ in T_{record}. In order for E_{select} to be well typed (via the [*recordof-elim*] rule), however, T'_{record} must still contain the I field, so $I \in \cup_{i=1}^n\{I'_i\} \subseteq \cup_{i=1}^n\{I_i\}$, as desired. In essence, subtyping can eliminate any fields except I, so the expression cannot be stuck.

This proof provides extra insight into what goes wrong if we choose an incorrect subtyping rule. Consider a proposal to define record subtyping so that the subtype has a subset of the fields and the supertype has *more* fields. Then the [*inclusion*] rule could be used to introduce I as a record field name in T'_{record} even though it didn't appear in the record expression, effectively promising the availability of a field the dynamic semantics cannot deliver. This record subtyping relation would be unsound because a well-typed expression could become stuck at a dynamic type error.

In practice, additional static or dynamic checks are sometimes used to ensure the soundness of type systems with subtyping rules that would otherwise be unsound. For example, the original definition of the EIFFEL object-oriented language included several features that made subtyping unsound [Coo89], including procedure-argument subtyping that was covariant rather than contravariant. By requiring additional static restrictions, it is possible to make EIFFEL type-safe even in the presence of procedure-argument covariance [Mey97, Chapter 17].

JAVA supports covariant subtyping on mutable arrays, which is unsound by itself, but preserves type safety by requiring a dynamic check for array subtyping [GJS96]. For example, the JAVA program in Figure 12.5 is an adaptation of the stuffit example from the earlier cellof subtyping discussion that compiles without error. The main program calls the stuffit method on an array bs whose single slot contains an instance of class B even though stuffit expects an array of instances of class A. JAVA accepts this because it treats B as a subtype of A (because of the subclass relationship between the B and A classes — see Section 12.1.3 below) and B[] as a subtype of A[].

If the program were allowed to run without intervention, there would be a dynamic type error: stuffit modifies the first slot of its array argument to contain an instance of A, and after the method invocation stuffit(bs) returns, bs[0] contains an instance of A rather than an instance of B. This is problematic, because the subsequent attempt to extract the b field of bs[0] will fail because instances of A do not have a b field.

To preserve type safety, the JAVA run-time system performs a dynamic check that prevents the assignment of an instance of class C to a slot of an array whose element type is a subclass of C. This check signals an `ArrayStoreException` error at run time for the array slot assignment in `stuffit` when it is called on `bs`. This is one reason that JAVA objects must carry dynamic type information.

Why doesn't JAVA simply disallow covariant subtyping on arrays? Because there are many situations where such subtyping is dynamically safe and useful for programming. In this case, the JAVA designers chose to make the language more expressive by replacing a static type check by a dynamic one.

Exercise 12.1 Bud Lojack thinks that the $[\rightarrow\text{-}\sqsubseteq]$ rule should be changed to specify covariant subtyping for procedure arguments rather than contravariant subtyping.

a. Define a procedure-subtyping rule $[\rightarrow\text{-}\sqsubseteq']$ based on Bud's idea. In the rest of this problem, assume that FLEX/S is modified by replacing $[\rightarrow\text{-}\sqsubseteq]$ by $[\rightarrow\text{-}\sqsubseteq']$.

b. Show that $[\rightarrow\text{-}\sqsubseteq']$ is unsound by defining a FLEX/S expression $E_{unsound}$ that is well typed in the modified version of FLEX/S but encounters a dynamic type error when it is evaluated. For simplicity, $E_{unsound}$ should use only values that are integers, records, and procedures.

c. Give a type derivation showing that $E_{unsound}$ is well typed in the modified version of FLEX/S.

d. Show that the evaluation of $E_{unsound}$ encounters a dynamic type error according to the SOS for FLEX (the SOS for μFLEX extended to handle the semantics of FLEX's data structures).

Exercise 12.2 In a language like FLEX/S that supports mutable variables, it is possible to represent cells as pairs of getter and setter procedures via the following desugarings:

```
(cell E) ⇝ds (let ((v E))
                (pair (abs () v) {getter procedure}
                      (abs (new) (set! v new))))) {setter procedure}
(^ Ecell) ⇝ds ((fst Ecell)) {extract and call nullary getter procedure}
(:= Ecell Enew) ⇝ds ((snd Ecell) Enew) {extract and call unary setter procedure}
```

a. What is the desugaring of the type (`cellof` T) that is consistent with the above expression desugarings?

b. Based on your answer from part **a**, use the $[pairof\text{-}\sqsubseteq]$ and $[\rightarrow\text{-}\sqsubseteq]$ subtype rules to explain why `cellof` subtyping needs to be invariant in the component type.

Exercise 12.3 Ben Bitdiddle wants to allow FLEX/S expressions (especially procedure applications) to return multiple values instead of just one. He extends the grammar of FLEX/S as follows:

$$E ::= \ldots \mid (\texttt{result } E^+) \mid (\texttt{result-bind } E_{result} \ (I^+) \ E_{body})$$

```
class A {
  public int a;
  public A (int initial_a) {a = initial_a;}
}

class B extends A {
  public boolean b;
  public B (int initial_a, boolean initial_b) {
    super(initial_a); b = initial_b;
  }
}

public class CovariantArrayTest {
  public static void stuffit (A[] as) {
    as[0] = new A(3);
  }

  public static void main (String [] args) {
    B[] bs = new B[1];
    bs[0] = new B(2, true);
    System.out.println("Before: " + bs[0].b);
    stuffit(bs);
    System.out.println("After: " + bs[0].b);
  }
}
```

Figure 12.5 JAVA program that compiles without error but signals a run-time type error involving an ill-typed array assignment.

The expression (result $E_{i=1}^n$) returns the values of the expressions $E_{i=1}^n$, where $n \geq 1$. The expression (result-bind E_{result} ($I_{i=1}^m$) E_{body}) denotes the value of E_{body} in an environment where the identifiers $I_{i=1}^m$ name the values $V_{i=1}^n$ returned by E_{result}; it is an error if $m \neq n$. For example:

```
(result-bind (result (* 2 3) (+ 4 5)) (x y)
  (- y x))  FLEX/S→ 3 {x names 6 and y names 9}

(let ((f (abs ((x int)) (result (* x x) (< x 10)))))
  (result-bind (f 4) (i b)
    (if b (+ i 1) 2)))  FLEX/S→ 17 {i names 16 and b names #t}
```

Like prod, result glues together an arbitrary number of values, but unlike prod, result does not create a first-class value: the entity denoted by result cannot be passed as an argument to a procedure, named by a let, or stored in a data structure. It is meaningful to use result only in a context where result-bind is waiting to deconstruct it. Although procedures may use result to return multiple values, they can still return a single value without using `result`, as in FLEX/S. Furthermore, (`result` E) and E are *not* equivalent — the former *must* be deconstructed by `result-bind` while the latter *cannot* be.

a. Extend the dynamic semantics of CBV FLEX/S (which is inherited from CBV FLEX) to handle the `result` and `result-bind` constructs. Because `result` does not create a first-class value, expressions like the following should become stuck in your semantics:

    ```
    (result-bind (let ((x (result 4 5))) x) (y z) (* y z))
    (result-bind (fst (pair (result 1 2) 3)) (x y) (+ x y))
    ```

b. Ben's intern Bud Lojack suggests that the Type domain include a new `resultof` type constructor to model the type of expressions returning multiple values:

    $T \in \text{Type} ::= \ \dots \ | \ (\texttt{resultof}\ T^+)$

    What is wrong with Bud's plan? *Hint:* Consider the following expressions:

    ```
    (fst (pair (result 1 2) 3))
    (let ((x (result 4 5))) x)
    (abs ((x (resultof int bool))) x)
    ```

c. Ben convinces Bud that there should be a new domain for specifying the type of expressions that might denote multiple values:

    $MMT \in \text{MaybeMultiType} ::= T \ | \ (\texttt{resultof}\ T^+)$

    "Of course," notes Ben, "type judgments may now have the form $TE \vdash E : MMT$."

    i.   The grammar of FLEX/S is the same as that of FLEX in Figure 11.31 on page 697. Which occurrences of the metavariable T should be replaced by MMT in expressions, types, programs, and program types?

    ii. Which FLEX/S type rules inherited from FLEX must be modified to replace occurrences of T by MMT?

    iii. Give the type rules for the `result` and `result-bind` constructs.

    iv. The binary subtyping relation on the Type domain can be extended to the MaybeMultiType domain. What is the subtype rule for `resultof`?

d. Except for the first subexpression position of `result-bind`, all FLEX/S evaluation contexts expect a single value. Ben's design treats `result` in any other evaluation context as an error. An alternative approach is that a `result` in a non-`result-bind` context should automatically be converted to its first value. For example, with this approach, the following expression evaluates without error.

    ```
    (let ((f (abs ((x int)) (result (* x x) (< x 10)))))
      (let ((p (pair (f 1) (f (f 2)))))  {p is a pair of 1 and 16}
        (+ (fst p) (snd p))))  FLEX/S   17
    ```

    Modify the dynamic and static semantics of FLEX/S to handle this alternative interpretation of multiple values.

Exercise 12.4 Using the type definitions on page 706 give derivations of the following subtypings:

a. $T_{rs} \sqsubseteq T_{rt}$

b. $T_{ru} \sqsubseteq T_{rv}$

Exercise 12.5 Bud Lojack suggests the following subtype rule for `trec`:

$$\frac{[\tau_{fresh}/\tau_1]\,T_1 \sqsubseteq [\tau_{fresh}/\tau_2]\,T_2}{(\text{trec } \tau_1 \ T_1) \sqsubseteq (\text{trec } \tau_2 \ T_2)} \quad \text{where } \tau_{fresh} \text{ is fresh} \qquad [\textit{unsound-trec-}\sqsubseteq]$$

Show that this rule is unsound. That is, write an expression that is well typed if this rule is used but encounters a dynamic type error when it is evaluated.

12.1.2 Dimensions of Subtyping

Having studied one approach to subtyping in FLEX/S, we now explore some dimensions of subtyping in the context of variations of FLEX/S as well as some real languages.

Implicit versus Explicit Subtyping

Type rules are often written to specify type properties of a language to humans. An expression is well typed if there is a way to use the rules to derive a type for that expression. In order to make rules compact or to leave room for future extensions, a set of type rules may not specify a deterministic way to derive a type for all typable expressions. A case in point is the [*inclusion*] rule of FLEX/S, a single type-inclusion rule that allows **implicit subtyping** to occur for any expression in a type derivation. Although the [*inclusion*] rule is very flexible and simple to specify, we shall see that it can create complex problems for a language implementer.

In FLEX, every expression has exactly one type, modulo type equivalence, because of the syntax-directed nature of the type rules. The [*inclusion*] rule destroys the syntax-directed nature of the type rules. Since the [*inclusion*] rule can be used for any kind of expression, the kind of expression no longer uniquely determines the type rule used for that expression. For instance, in FLEX/S, it is possible to prove that the expression

```
(record (a 3) (b #t))
```

has each of the following types:

```
(recordof (a int) (b bool))
(recordof (a int))
(recordof (b bool))
(recordof)
```

The lack of unique types is not itself a problem, but it can complicate other analyses. In the case of FLEX/S, the lack of unique types makes it difficult to write a type checker. The problem is that a straightforward type checker needs to choose one of many possible types before enough information is known to make a correct decision.

For example, consider the following expression:

```
(let ((c (cell (record (a 3) (b #t)))))
  (begin (:= c (record (a 4)))
         (select a (^ c))))
```

This expression is well typed according to the type rules of FLEX/S. The type derivation must use the [*inclusion*] rule to hide the b field of the first record so that c has the type (cellof (recordof (a int))). A straightforward type checker needs to assign a type to c before it examines the rest of the program. But when it encounters the definition of c, the type checker does not "know" which fields of the record stored in c will be accessed later and how c will be mutated. In fact, such details are undecidable in general. Without such knowledge, the type checker may make an inappropriate choice. For instance, upon encountering the cell expression, it seems prudent to assume that c has the type

```
(cellof (recordof (a int) (b bool)))
```

Unfortunately, the program is not well typed under this assumption. In this case, the correct type for c is

```
(cellof (recordof (a int)))
```

but this is OK only because it so happens that the program does not later extract the b field. Without backtracking or some sophisticated mechanism for managing constraints, simple expressions like the one above will not be type-checked properly.

It is possible to restore unique types and make type checking easier by using syntax-directed type rules that restrict the contexts in which subtyping is allowed. The simplest way to do this is to require that all type inclusions be specified by the programmer using declarations for **explicit subtyping**. For example, Figure 12.6 presents a [*the-inclusion*] type rule in which the is no longer merely a type declaration, but a means of **upward type conversion** — that is, a means of making a value appear to have as its type a supertype of its actual type. Replacing the [*inclusion*] and [*the*] type rules by [*the-inclusion*] in FLEX/S would make all subtyping explicit rather than implicit.

In this modified version of FLEX/S, reconsider the above example:

$$\frac{TE \vdash E : T' \qquad T' \sqsubseteq T}{TE \vdash (\texttt{the } T \ E) : T} \qquad \textit{[the-inclusion]}$$

Figure 12.6 A type rule for explicit subtyping specified by the `the` construct. Replacing the [*inclusion*] and [*the*] type rules by [*the-inclusion*] would make FLEX/S subtyping explicit rather than implicit.

```
(let ((c (cell (record (a 3) (b #t)))))
  (begin (:= c (record (a 4)))
         (select a (^ c))))
```

Under the alternative type rules, this expression is not well typed. The variable `c` is found to have the type `(cellof (recordof (a int) (b bool)))`. Because the [*cell-set*] type rule requires the new value to have the same type as that stored in the cell, type checking fails at the `:=` expression. However, well-typedness can be restored by using an explicit type conversion, as in the following well-typed variant of the example:

```
(let ((c (cell (the (recordof (a int)) (record (a 3) (b #t))))))
  (begin (:= c (record (a 4)))
         (select a (^ c))))
```

Here, `(the (recordof (a int)) ... )` effectively hides the `b` field of the record so that the variable `c` has type `(cellof (recordof (a int)))`.

Explicit subtyping declarations greatly simplify type checking by indicating exactly where type inclusions occur in a type derivation, thus eliminating any need for guessing/backtracking. But this design choice has a price: Programmers are burdened with declaring all type inclusions, many of which seem obvious. For example, suppose that `get-age` is a procedure with type `(-> ((recordof (age int))) int)` that extracts the `age` field of a record and E_{polly} is the record

```
(record (name (symb Polly_Morwicz)) (age 35) (student? #f))
```

In a version of FLEX/S with explicit subtyping, invoking `get-age` on E_{polly} requires a type inclusion declaration:

```
(get-age (the (recordof (age int)) E_polly))
```

This situation can be improved by allowing implicit subtyping in certain contexts that do not affect the deterministic type checking and only requiring programmers to use explicit subtyping elsewhere. Figure 12.7 illustrates how this strategy could be instituted in the FLEX/S type system. The [*inclusion*], [*the*], and [→-*elim*] type rules have been merged to form two type rules:

$$TE \vdash E_{rator} : (\text{->} \ (T^n_{i=1}) \ T_{result})$$
$$\frac{\forall^n_{i=1} \ . \ ((TE \vdash E_i : T'_i) \wedge (T'_i \sqsubseteq T_i))}{TE \vdash (E_{rator} \ E^n_{i=1}) : T_{result}} \qquad [\rightarrow\text{-}elim\text{-}inclusion]$$

$$\frac{TE \vdash E : T' \qquad T' \sqsubseteq T}{TE \vdash (\texttt{the} \ T \ E) : T} \qquad [the\text{-}inclusion]$$

Figure 12.7 Type rules for supporting a combination of implicit and explicit subtyping in FLEX/S. The $[\rightarrow\text{-}elim\text{-}inclusion]$ rule supports implicit subtyping for arguments to a procedure call, but all other contexts must use explicit subtyping via the $[the\text{-}inclusion]$ rule.

- The $[\rightarrow\text{-}elim\text{-}inclusion]$ rule permits actual arguments to be subtypes of the formal parameters of the called procedure, thus pinpointing procedure-call boundaries as the most useful places to support implicit subtyping. For example, this rule can be used to show that $(\texttt{get-age} \ E_{polly})$ is well typed without resorting to an explicit subtype declaration. This rule avoids any guessing by effectively using the explicitly declared parameter types of procedures as the type-inclusion supertype.

- The $[the\text{-}inclusion]$ rule allows programmers to explicitly specify type-inclusion supertypes in other contexts using **the**.

In practice, languages typically support some combination of implicit and explicit type conversions. Virtually all languages with subtyping permit implicit subtyping in procedure calls via a type rule like $[\rightarrow\text{-}elim\text{-}inclusion]$. For example, JAVA allows methods to accept arguments whose class is a subclass of the expected class. It is also common to allow a value to be assigned to a variable of any supertype of the value's type. The formal specifications for languages like ADA, C, C++, JAVA, and PASCAL include a complicated set of rules precisely describing all the contexts in which implicit type conversions may take place. They also provide ways for programmers to specify type conversions explicitly.

For example, in C/C++/JAVA, there are numerous rules governing the situations in which values of the integer type `int` are automatically converted to values of the floating-point number type `float`. Consider the expression x/y, which denotes an integer resulting from integer division if both x and y have type `int` but denotes a floating-point number if at least one of x and y has type `float`. In the latter case, if one of x and y has type `float` and the other has type `int`, the integer is first implicitly converted to a floating-point number before the division takes place. If both x and y are integers and a floating-point result is desired, one or both of the operands can be converted to a floating-point number via an explicit **type cast** expression. For example, the type cast expression (`float`) x denotes the result of converting the contents of x to a floating-point value.

Exercise 12.6 The type rules in Figure 12.7 can be extended to handle limited subtyping for certain data operations while still maintaining the unique-type property. For example, if `recs` is defined as

```
(def recs (listof (recordof (a int)))
  (cons (record (a 3)) (null (recordof (a int)))))
```

then it seems reasonable that

```
(cons (record (a 7) (b #t)) recs)
```

should be well typed with (`listof` (`recordof` (a int))) as its type.

Extend the rules of Figure 12.7 to permit implicit type inclusion in the type rules for the data operations for which this makes sense. Argue that your rules (1) are sound and (2) preserve the unique-type property of expressions.

Exercise 12.7 The $\sqsubseteq$ relation defines a partial order on types. Can we define a bottom element $(\perp_T)$ for this partial order, and might this be useful? Yes! We can extend the FLEX/S type system with a new base type, `void`, that serves as a bottom type — i.e., it is a subtype of every type:

$$\texttt{void} \sqsubseteq T \qquad \qquad [void]$$

Viewing types as sets, the only meaningful interpretation of `void` is the empty set, i.e., `void` is a type that contains *no* values.

The `void` type can simplify a type system by giving a type to expressions that do not return a value, such as `error` expressions, infinite loops, and jumps to nonlocal exits. For example, in a version of FLEX/S extended with `void`, the explicit type T appearing in an empty list expression (`null` T) or in an error expression (`error` Y T) can be eliminated and the associated type rules can be changed to:

$$TE \vdash (\texttt{null}) : (\texttt{listof void}) \qquad \qquad [null']$$

$$TE \vdash (\texttt{error}\ Y) : \texttt{void} \qquad \qquad [error']$$

a. Write a simple FLEX/S expression E_{loop} that loops infinitely and show it can be assigned the `void` type.

b. Argue that your E_{loop} expression from part **a** can be assigned *any* type.

c. Show how a `void` type can simplify the syntax and type rule for a `jump` construct (see Exercise 11.8) in a version of FLEX/S extended with nonlocal exits.

d. Give the syntax and type rule for a kernel version of the `cwcc` construct from Section 9.4.4 in a dialect of FLEX/S with `void`.

   Can you write the type rule without using `void`? Explain.

Subset Semantics versus Coercion Semantics of Subtyping

Thus far, we have assumed what is known as the **subset semantics** of subtyping, in which a value of a subtype may directly be used as a value of the supertype without performing any computation at run time. But many applications of subtyping use a **coercion semantics**, in which some sort of run-time computation (typically involving a change in representation) must be performed to convert a value of a subtype to a value of a supertype. For example, in C/C++/JAVA, integers and floating-point numbers have different, incompatible bit-level representations, so converting an `int` to a `float` requires a change in representation at run time. Henceforth, we will use the term **type coercion** to refer to any form of type conversion that implies a **representation conversion** — i.e., a change in representation at run time.

A subset semantics may be easy to express in an SOS, but it can imply implementation inefficiencies that are better addressed with a coercion semantics. Record implementations illustrate the tradeoffs between these two approaches. Suppose that a record value V_1 with type

$$T_1 = \texttt{(recordof (age int) (name symb) (salary int))}$$

is used in a context that selects the `salary` field from a value whose type is

$$T_2 = \texttt{(recordof (salary int))}$$

- In a subset semantics, no computation is done in order to view V_1 as having type T_2; the extra fields are just ignored. However, because the number and order of the fields in a record is unknown, (1) the run-time representation of a record must include the field names along with the field values, and (2) selecting a field from a record implies a search process that must examine field names at run time.

- In a coercion semantics, each value of record type (`recordof` $(I_i \ T_i)_{i=1}^{n}$) may be assumed to have *exactly* the fields $I_1, \ldots, I_n$, which are known at type-checking time and so do not need to be included in the run-time representation of a record. A record value can be implemented as a positional product whose components are the field values (stored in some canonical order), and field selection can be efficiently performed using an index for the field that is statically determined from the record type. For example, the `salary` component would be at index 3 in a record value with type T_1 but at index 1 in a record value with type T_2. But now converting V_1 from type T_1 to T_2 requires a run-time representation conversion that creates a new record value V_2 containing only the `salary` field of V_1.

A language designer can fiddle with subtype rules in order to reduce or eliminate the work of the run-time representation conversion in a coercion semantics. For example, if record subtyping is modified so that only field permutations are allowed (i.e., subtypes cannot add new fields), then an implementation can represent records using a canonical form (fields in alphabetical order, for example). This eliminates any need for representation conversion, but cannot handle more compelling examples of record subtyping, such as the `get-age` example on page 701. See Exercise 12.8 for yet another take on record subtyping.

The soundness argument for FLEX/S discussed on page 708 uses a subset semantics of subtyping, because it assumes that the SOS for FLEX/S is the same as the SOS for FLEX. Alternatively, we can give a coercion semantics to FLEX/S by translating any well-typed FLEX/S expression to a well-typed FLEX expression by performing an explicit representation conversion in FLEX from values of type T to values of type T' whenever the FLEX/S type derivation uses an [*inclusion*] rule to mediate between T and T'. For example, suppose that $(E_{proc}\ E_{rcd})$ is a FLEX/S expression well typed in the empty type environment via the following type derivation:

$$
\begin{array}{l}
\vdots \\
\{\} \vdash E_{proc} : \texttt{(-> ((recordof (age int) (salary int))) int)} \\[1ex]
\quad
\begin{array}{l}
\vdots \\
\{\} \vdash E_{rcd} : \texttt{(recordof (age int) (name symb) (salary int))} \\
\hline
\{\} \vdash E_{rcd} : \texttt{(recordof (age int) (salary int))} \ \ [\textit{inclusion}]
\end{array} \\
\hline
\{\} \vdash (E_{proc}\ E_{rcd}) : \texttt{int} \ \ [\rightarrow\text{-}elim]
\end{array}
$$

Since the type of E_{rcd} is `(recordof (age int) (name symb) (salary int))` but the argument type of E_{proc} is `(recordof (age int) (salary int))`, the [*inclusion*] type rule is needed to mediate between the record types. If E'_{proc} and E'_{rcd} are the FLEX expressions that result from translating E_{proc} and E_{rcd}, respectively, then here is a FLEX expression that explicitly performs a representation conversion (by constructing a new two-component record) in place of letting type inclusion take place, as happened in the example derivation:

```
(let ((I_rcd E'_rcd)) {I_rcd is fresh}
  (E'_proc (record (age (select age I_rcd))
                   (salary (select salary I_rcd)))))
```

The translation-based approach to defining the coercion semantics of subtyping for FLEX/S is further explored in Exercise 12.9.

Exercise 12.8 Why would a rational language designer propose to replace $[recordof\text{-}\sqsubseteq]$ by the following subtype rule for records?

$$\frac{\forall_{i=1}^{n} \cdot ((I_i' = I_i) \wedge (T_i' \sqsubseteq T_i))}{(\texttt{recordof} \ (I_j' \ T_j')_{j=1}^{m}) \sqsubseteq (\texttt{recordof} \ (I_i \ T_i)_{i=1}^{n})} \quad \text{where } m \geq n. \qquad [recordof\text{-}\sqsubseteq\,']$$

Discuss the implications of the new rule for run-time record representations and representation conversions.

Exercise 12.9 Thai Ping sets out to formally define the coercion semantics of subtyping for FLEX/S based on a translation function with the following specification:

$coerce : \text{Type} \rightarrow \text{Type} \rightarrow \text{Exp}_{\text{FLEX/S}} \rightharpoonup \text{Exp}_{\text{FLEX}}$

> Suppose E is a FLEX/S expression such that $TE \vdash_{\text{FLEX/S}} E : T$ for some type environment TE and type T, where $T \sqsubseteq T'$. Then $(coerce \ T \ T' \ E)$ denotes a FLEX expression E' such that $TE \vdash_{\text{FLEX}} E' : T'$.

To avoid certain technical difficulties, Thai assumes that the types T and T' mentioned in the specification of the $coerce$ function do not mention any `seqof` types or recursive types. Subject to this assumption, the $coerce$ function can be used to translate any expression that is well typed in FLEX/S to a corresponding expression that is well typed in FLEX by performing an explicit representation conversion in FLEX from values of type T to values of type T' whenever the FLEX/S type derivation uses an [*inclusion*] rule to mediate between T and T'.

The $coerce$ function is an example of a **type-directed translation** — a translation between languages that is guided by type information.

Here are two clauses from Thai's definition of $coerce$:

$(coerce \ T \ T \ E) = E$

$(coerce \ (\texttt{pairof} \ T_1 \ T_2) \ (\texttt{pairof} \ T_1' \ T_2') \ E)$
$= (\texttt{let} \ ((I_{pair} \ E)) \ \{I_{pair} \ fresh\}$
$\quad (\texttt{pair} \ (coerce \ T_1 \ T_1' \ (\texttt{fst} \ I_{pair})) \ (coerce \ T_2 \ T_2' \ (\texttt{snd} \ I_{pair}))))$

a. Give definitions for the following five clauses of $coerce$:

   i. $(coerce \ (\texttt{prodof} \ T_{i=1}^{n}) \ (\texttt{prodof} \ T_{i=1}'^{n}) \ E)$

   ii. $(coerce \ (\texttt{->} \ (T_{i=1}^{n}) \ T_{res}) \ (\texttt{->} \ (T_{i=1}'^{n}) \ T_{res}') \ E)$

   iii. $(coerce \ (\texttt{recordof} \ (I_j \ T_j)_{j=1}^{m}) \ (\texttt{recordof} \ (I_i' \ T_i')_{i=1}^{n}) \ E)$, where there is a function $f : [1..n] \rightarrow [1..m]$ such that $\forall_{i=1}^{n} \cdot ((I_{(f \ i)} = I_i') \wedge (T_{(f \ i)} \sqsubseteq T_i'))$.

   iv. $(coerce \ (\texttt{oneof} \ (I_j \ T_j)_{j=1}^{m}) \ (\texttt{oneof} \ (I_i' \ T_i')_{i=1}^{n}) \ E)$, where there is a function $f : [1..m] \rightarrow [1..n]$ such that $\forall_{j=1}^{m} \cdot ((I_j = I_{(f \ j)}') \wedge (T_j \sqsubseteq T_{(f \ j)}'))$.

   v. $(coerce \ (\texttt{listof} \ T) \ (\texttt{listof} \ T') \ E)$

b. Explain why Thai's $coerce$ function cannot handle `seqof` types. What if updatable sequences (see Section 10.1.1) were used instead?

c. For simplicity, Thai assumed that his *coerce* function did not have to handle recursive types. "However," observes Thai, "*coerce could* handle recursive types if it were modified to take an additional argument corresponding to the subtyping assumptions in Figure 12.4 on page 707." Based on Thai's comment, show how a modified *coerce* function can handle conversions involving recursive types. Comment on any efficiency issues in your solution.

Downward Type Conversions

In a version of FLEX/S with the [*the-inclusion*] type rule, `the` can convert a value of type T only to a value of a supertype of T, which is always type safe.[1] This sort of explicit upward type conversion is sometimes called an **upcast**.

Sometimes it is helpful to perform an explicit downward type conversion, or **downcast**. For example, consider the following abstraction written in FLEX/S (with mutable cells and immutable records):

$$E_{incAge} = \texttt{(abs ((r (recordof (age (cellof int)))))}$$
$$\texttt{(let ((age (select age r)))}$$
$$\texttt{(begin (:= age (+ (\^{} age) 1))}$$
$$\texttt{r))))}$$

This abstraction has the type

$$T_{incAge} = \texttt{(-> ((recordof (age (cellof int))))}$$
$$\texttt{(recordof (age (cellof int))))}$$

Using the [*inclusion*] type rule, E_{incAge} can be assigned any type that is a supertype of T_{incAge} — i.e., any type of the form $\texttt{(-> ((}T_{arg}\texttt{))} \; T_{res}\texttt{)}$, where

$$T_{arg} \sqsubseteq \texttt{(recordof (age (cellof int)))} \sqsubseteq T_{res}$$

The subtype relation on the argument type T_{arg} says that E_{incAge} can be used to increment the age of any record containing *at least* an updatable integer `age` field: student records, employee records, etc. But the subtype relation on the result type T_{res} says that E_{incAge} returns a record that the type system treats as having *at most* an updatable integer field. E.g., if E_{incAge} is applied to a record E_{rcd} of type `(recordof (age (cellof int)) (name symb))`, the type system necessarily "forgets" the `name` field in the result type, `(recordof (age (cellof int)))`. So `(select name (`E_{incAge} E_{rcd}`))` is ill typed, even though, according to a subset semantics of subtyping, the `name` field is still present in the record value returned by E_{incAge} and no dynamic type error would occur. The FLEX/S type system

---

[1]In fact, `the` as an upward conversion operator does not actually provide any new power to a language with implicit subtyping on procedure calls: Any upward conversion can be written as an appropriately typed identity procedure.

New Type Rule

$$\frac{TE \vdash E : T' \qquad T \sqsubseteq T'}{TE \vdash (\texttt{downcast}\ T\ E) : T} \qquad\qquad [\textit{downcast}]$$

New Evaluation Context

$\mathbb{E} \in \text{EvalContext} ::= \dots \mid (\texttt{downcast}\ T\ \mathbb{E})$

New Reduction Rules

$(\texttt{downcast}\ T\ V) \rightsquigarrow V$, where $\textit{typeof}\ \langle V, \{\}\rangle \sqsubseteq T$ $\qquad [\textit{downcast-succeed}]$

$(\texttt{downcast}\ T\ V) \rightsquigarrow (\texttt{error downcast-failure}\ T),$ $\qquad [\textit{downcast-fail}]$
$\qquad\qquad$ where $\textit{typeof}\ \langle V, \{\}\rangle \not\sqsubseteq T$

Figure 12.8   Static and dynamic semantics of downcasting in FLEX/S.

is simply too weak to express the idea that the return type of E_{incAge} is the same as the argument type for any subtype of (`recordof (age (cellof int))`).

One way to address this problem is to strengthen the type system so that it can express the relationship between the argument type and result type of E_{incAge}. This approach, which involves combining notions of subtyping and polymorphism, is explored in Section 12.2.4.

In practice, a simpler but less satisfying approach is often used: Allow the programmer to declare explicitly where a downward type conversion should take place. For example, we can extend FLEX/S with a downcasting expression (`downcast` T E) that asserts that E has a type T that is a subtype of E's type (Figure 12.8). We can then use `downcast` to create a well-typed expression that extracts the `name` field from the result of invoking E_{incAge} on E_{rcd}:

```
(select name (downcast (recordof (age (cellof int)) (name symb))
             (E_incAge  E_rcd)))
```

Unlike upcasting, which is always type-safe, downcasting is potentially dangerous. In (`downcast` T E), the type system simply accepts the programmer's assertion that the run-time value of E will actually have type T. But what if the programmer is wrong? For instance, in the above example, if the value of E_{rcd} does not have a `name` field at run time, then a dynamic type error will occur when the `name` field is selected.

As shown in Figure 12.8, we can fix this type-safety problem by modifying the SOS to force the evaluation of E to the value V, and dynamically check that V's type is compatible with T. This dynamic check preserves type safety by preventing illegal operations (e.g., attempting to select the `name` field from a record that does not have this field). Dynamic type checks are performed for all downcasts in Java, where downcasting is a common idiom. However, this approach is rather unsatisfying for a statically typed language, because it implies that values must carry dynamic type information that is checked at run time.

In some languages, such as C, the programmer's downcast assertions are simply trusted by the compiler without performing any run-time type check, giving rise to type loopholes that destroy type safety. For example, suppose that the C variable p has type int* — i.e., it is either a pointer to an integer or an array of integers. The declaration statement

```
void *q = (void *)p;
```

defines q as a copy of p whose type, void* (which means "a pointer to some unknown type"), effectively hides the representation of the value p points to. The expression (void *)p is an upcast — any pointer type can safely be cast to void*. But dereferencing the integer pointed at by q requires a downcast, as in *((int *)q). Although this is safe, C permits arbitrary casts on pointer types. For example, *((float *)q) treats the bits in the value pointed at by q as a floating point number rather than an integer, which is clearly not type-safe. A cast can even be used to treat an arbitrary memory address as a pointer to any type (e.g., (int *)3221202052), even though a compiler can't possibly know in general what kind of value will be in that address at run time.

Proponents of weak type systems often claim that they are necessary to support flexibility in systems programming. However, recent research (e.g. [JMG⁺02, NMW02]) suggests that many low-level programming tasks can be performed in a type-safe way.

12.1.3 Subtyping and Inheritance

There is a great deal of confusion about the relationship between inheritance in object-oriented languages and subtyping. A class is not really a type, and inheritance is not the same as subtyping. In particular, types are *specifications* of functionality whereas classes are *implementations* of some functionality.

Subtyping specifies an abstract relationship between values computed by program expressions: Any expression whose value is described by the subtype can be used anywhere the supertype is needed. In contrast, the purpose of class inheritance is to support sharing/reuse of implementation code. Java and many other object-oriented languages confuse the distinction between types and classes by creating a type corresponding to every class and treating a subclass as a subtype of its superclass in addition to having the subclass inherit code from its superclass. Though the languages and literature make these distinctions hard to notice, they are worth keeping in mind.

Classes are often motivated by a desire to model objects with state (sometimes even real-life objects). Good programmers design class hierarchies so that they represent some useful ontology, provide clean abstraction boundaries (with nicely related specifications), *and* maximize code reuse. But there are times when these goals are at odds.

A complication that arises when inheritance is used as a proxy for subtyping involves cases where specification should be inherited with only partial (or perhaps no) common implementation code. For example, JAVA provides two different mechanisms for this:

- An **interface** declares type specifications for instance methods without any associated code. A class can implement one or more interfaces by defining instance methods satisfying all the type specifications in the interface(s).

- An **abstract class**[2] declares type specifications (but no code) for so-called abstract instance methods, but can also include code for other components, which we will call concrete. It is not possible to make instances of an abstract class. A subclass inherits the concrete code components of an abstract class and also the unimplemented specifications of any abstract methods. The subclass can provide implementations for any of the abstract methods. If it implements all the abstract methods of its superclass, the subclass is no longer abstract and it is possible to make instances of the subclass.

For example, JAVA defines a `Graphics` abstract class for objects that support drawing on a display device. It has abstract specifications for methods like `drawLine` and `drawOval`. The class does not actually provide any implementation of these methods, because the implementation would depend on the particular device. One cannot, therefore, create a `Graphics` object directly: one must define a subclass of `Graphics` that provides implementations of all the abstract methods, and then create an object of the subclass. However, `Graphics` does define some concrete methods, such as `drawRect`, which draws the outline of a rectangle, presumably by drawing four lines with `drawLine`. A subclass of `Graphics` inherits the code for `drawRect`, something that would not be possible if `Graphics` were an interface.

It would seem that an interface is simply an abstract class with no concrete components. Then why does JAVA provide two mechanisms? Because JAVA's classes may implement any number of interfaces, but can inherit from only a

---

[2] EIFFEL uses the term **deferred classes** for this.

single superclass. Thus, interfaces and abstract classes fill gaps in an ontology and enforce a relationship on the specifications of several classes when there is no shared implementation code for some specifications (i.e., the functionality is not actually inherited, but the specification is).

A more vexing problem arises when there is code to inherit, but the specification should not be inherited. Consider a system for manipulating geometric shapes[3] in which there is a `Shape` class with abstract methods for drawing shapes, determining if a shape contains a given point, etc. Typically, there will be a variety of subclasses of `Shape` to support different sorts of shapes: `Circle`, `Rectangle`, and `Polygon`, for example. Suppose that instances of the `Polygon` class are constructed by creating an empty polygon and then adding vertices using an `add-vertex` method. Should the `Rectangle` class be a subclass of `Polygon`? From the code-reuse perspective, the answer should be yes, since `Rectangle` instances can then inherit code for drawing, point containment, etc., from the `Polygon` class. And mathematically, a rectangle is a polygon, so this subclass relation seems natural in the classes-are-types interpretation. But this interpretation also implies that we can safely pass a `Rectangle` instance to any code that manipulates `Polygon` instances. This isn't true for `Polygon` code that uses the `add-vertex` method, which should not be permitted for `Rectangle` instances!

In this case, there is an ontological relationship, and there is useful code to be appropriated, but there is not a subtype relationship. One solution to this problem is for the `Rectangle` class to override `add-vertex` with a method that generates a dynamic `method-not-implemented` error, but this undermines the goal of statically detecting all such errors. A better solution is to define the `Rectangle` class as a subclass of `Shape` (but not of `Polygon`) and store a hidden instance of a `Polygon` in each `Rectangle` instance. Then code reuse can still be achieved by delegating relevant messages to the `Polygon` instance.

12.2 Polymorphic Types

12.2.1 Monomorphic Types Are Not Expressive

Monomorphic type systems are easy to reason about, but they hinder the development of reusable code. In particular, monomorphic languages prevent the programmer from expressing **polymorphic** values — values (typically procedures) that can have different types in different contexts. In this section, we develop a type system that allows the expression of polymorphic values.

---

[3][Ros92] has a very good discussion of this and related issues. This is where we first saw this example, which originated in a debate on the `comp.lang.eiffel` bulletin board.

As an example of a polymorphic value, consider the FL `map` procedure:

```
(def map (abs (f xs)
              (if (null? xs)
                  (null)
                  (cons (f (car xs)) (map f (cdr xs))))))
```

We have seen that aggregate data operators like `map` are a powerful means of composing programs out of reusable, mix-and-match parts. In large part, this power is due to the fact that the same operator works over many types of operands. The `map` procedure, for instance, can be viewed as having an infinite number of possible types, including:

```
(-> ((-> (int) int) (listof int)) (listof int))
(-> ((-> (int) bool) (listof int)) (listof bool))
(-> ((-> ((listof int)) int) (listof (listof int))) (listof int))
(-> ((-> (int) (-> (bool) int)) (listof int))
    (listof (-> (bool) int)))
```

The type of `map` for any particular call depends on the types of its arguments. So, in the call

```
(map (abs (x) (* x x)) (list 1 2 3)) ,
```

`map` effectively has type

```
(-> ((-> (int) int) (listof int)) (listof int)) ,
```

whereas in the call

```
(map (abs (x) (< x 17)) (list 23 13 29)) ,
```

it has type

```
(-> ((-> (int) bool) (listof int)) (listof bool)) .
```

Other common examples of useful polymorphic procedures include the identity procedure, the procedure-composing procedure, searching and sorting procedures, and numerous list utilities like `length`, `reverse`, `filter`, and `foldr`.

Unfortunately, the type system of FLEX requires the types of values like `map` to be specified where they are defined, not where they are used. A programmer wishing to use `map` on different types of arguments must write a different version of `map` for every different set of argument types. For example, here are two FLEX versions of `map` that correspond to the two calls mentioned above:

```
(def map (-> ((-> (int) int) (listof int)) (listof int))
  (abs ((f (-> (int) int)) (xs (listof int)))
    (if (null? xs)
        (null int)
        (cons (f (car xs)) (map f (cdr xs))))))
(def map (-> ((-> (int) bool) (listof int)) (listof bool))
  (abs ((f (-> (int) bool)) (xs (listof int)))
    (if (null? xs)
        (null bool)
        (cons (f (car xs)) (map f (cdr xs))))))
```

Except for type information, the two definitions are exactly the same.

Any language like FLEX that forces the programmer to reimplement functionality in order to satisfy the type system thwarts the goal of writing reusable software components. There is a broad class of general-purpose procedures and data structures that are inexpressible in such languages because of the shackles of the type system. This lack of expressiveness is indicative of the price that programmers may have to pay for types. Indeed, fundamental limitations of languages such as PASCAL and C stem from their monomorphic type systems.

12.2.2   Universal Polymorphism: FLEX/SP

Polymorphism can be introduced into a language by generalizing the types of values where they are created and then specializing these types where the values are used. Reconsider the types of map listed above. All of them are instances of a common pattern:

```
(-> ((-> (T) T') (listof T)) (listof T'))
```

We would like to be able to declare that map has this general type, but then specialize this type (by specifying T and T') wherever map is applied. This approach to polymorphism is called **universal polymorphism** or **parametric polymorphism** because the types T and T' are parameters that may be independently instantiated to *any* types.

Constructs for Universal Polymorphism

A polymorphic language needs to specify polymorphic types and create and use polymorphic values. FLEX/SP (the **P** stands for **P**olymorphism) extends FLEX/S with three new constructs:[4]

---

[4]Since universal polymorphism does not depend on subtyping, we could also add universal polymorphism to a language without subtyping. We will use the name FLEX/P for FLEX extended with universal polymorphism. FLEX/P is FLEX/SP without the [*inclusion*] type rule.

(pabs (τ^*) E) creates a first-class **polymorphic value** that is parameterized over the type identifiers τ^*.

(pcall E T^*) **projects** the polymorphic value denoted by E onto the types T by instantiating the type identifiers of E.

(forall (τ^*) T) is a **polymorphic type** — a type in which the type T is parameterized over the type variables τ^*. Polymorphic values have polymorphic types.

We use forall to express the type of polymorphic values like map:

```
map : (forall (s t) (-> ((-> (s) t) (listof s)) (listof t)))
```

This says that map is a polymorphic value that, when projected onto any types s and t, yields a procedure that takes a procedure from s to t and a list of s and returns a list of t. Similarly, the type of the polymorphic identity procedure is (forall (t) (-> (t) t)), and the type of a polymorphic procedure returning the length of a list is (forall (t) (-> ((listof t)) int)).

The type identifiers τ^* in (forall (τ^*) T) are formal type parameters that stand in the place of actual types that will be supplied later. They serve the same role as the formal parameters of an abs, the only difference being that abs-bound names stand for values whereas forall-bound names stand for types. forall types can be nested, and their type identifiers obey standard scoping conventions. For instance, in the type

```
(forall (s t) (-> (s) (forall (u) (-> (u) t))))
```

the u introduced by the inner forall can be renamed to s without changing the meaning of the type, but it cannot be renamed to t because of variable capture.

In the literature, polymorphic types are often written using $\forall$ notation and are referred to as "universally quantified." In this notation, the type of map is

$$\forall\, s\, t\, .\, ((s \rightarrow t) \times (\mathit{list}\ s)) \rightarrow (\mathit{list}\ t)$$

Polymorphism allows general operations on data structures like pairs, sequences, lists, and cells to be built-in procedures in the standard library rather than kernel constructs. For example, here are types for the standard list procedures, which no longer require special syntactic support:

```
  cons : (forall (t) (-> (t (listof t)) (listof t)))
   car : (forall (t) (-> ((listof t)) t))
   cdr : (forall (t) (-> ((listof t)) (listof t)))
 null? : (forall (t) (-> ((listof t)) bool))
  null : (forall (t) (-> () (listof t)))
```

Without polymorphism, these must be kernel constructs, because there is no way to write their types. In FLEX, their polymorphic behavior is achieved by having a special type rule for each operation, but in FLEX/SP their types can be described using universal polymorphism. In FLEX/SP, it is even possible to have a polymorphic empty list `nil` with type `(forall (t) (listof t))`. This underscores the fact that polymorphism can be used with all values, not only procedures.

Assuming that we have some way to create polymorphic values (which we'll see below), we need some way to supply actual types for the formal type parameters in the `forall` type of a polymorphic value. This is accomplished by the **polymorphic projection** construct (pcall E_{poly} $T_{i=1}^n$). Here, E_{poly} must denote a polymorphic value with type $T_{poly} = $ (forall ($\tau_{i=1}^n$) T_{body}). The `pcall` construct specializes the type T_{poly} by substituting the actual type parameters $T_{i=1}^n$ for the formal type parameters $\tau_{i=1}^n$ in T_{body}. A `forall` type is somewhat like a procedure waiting for type arguments, where `pcall` is the "call" that supplies these "arguments." For example:

```
(pcall cons int) : (-> (int (listof int)) (listof int))
(pcall cons bool) : (-> (bool (listof bool)) (listof bool))
(pcall map int int) : (-> ((-> (int) int) (listof int)) (listof int))
(pcall map int bool) : (-> ((-> (int) bool) (listof int)) (listof bool))
```

The process of instantiating the type identifiers found in the universal type of a polymorphic value with particular types via `pcall` is called **projection**. For instance, (pcall map int bool) can be pronounced "the result of projecting the polymorphic `map` value onto `int` and `bool`."

Projecting a polymorphic procedure allows it to be used with different types of arguments in different calls. If `il` is an integer list and `bl` is a list of booleans, then ((pcall null? int) il) and ((pcall null? bool) bl) test each list for emptiness. The following expression makes a one-element integer list whose only element is 1:

```
((pcall cons int) 1 ((pcall null int)))
```

And here are two examples of different uses of `map`:

```
((pcall map int int) (abs ((x int)) (* x x)) (list int 1 2 3))
((pcall map int bool) (abs ((x int)) (< x 17)) (list int 23 13 29))
```

Finally, we need a way to create polymorphic values. This is the purpose of the construct (pabs (τ^*) E), which denotes a polymorphic value that abstracts over the type identifiers τ^* within E. For example, the polymorphic identity procedure is written (pabs (t) (abs ((x t)) x)). Here is a polymorphic version of map written in FLEX/SP, in which we assume that list procedures are polymorphic, as discussed above:

```
(def map (forall (s t)
            (-> ((-> (s) t) (listof s)) (listof t)))
  (pabs (s t)
    (abs ((f (-> (s) t)) (xs (listof s)))
      (if ((pcall null? s) xs)
          ((pcall null t))
          ((pcall cons t) (f ((pcall car s) xs))
                          ((pcall map s t)
                            f ((pcall cdr s) xs)))))))
```

The (pabs (s t) ...) creates a polymorphic value (in this case, a procedure) whose type is abstracted over the type identifiers s and t.

pabs and pcall have a similar contract to abs and procedure application. But whereas abs and procedure call imply computation at run time, pabs and pcall imply computation during type checking. That is, pabs builds abstractions over types during static analysis; these abstractions are also unwound by pcall during static analysis. Every polymorphic value must have its types instantiated (via pcall) before it can be used.

In the literature, abstraction over types is often written using Λ, and projection onto types is often written using brackets, juxtaposition, or subscripts. For example, the definition of map above might begin

$$\Lambda\, s\, t\, .\ \lambda\, f : (s \to t)\ \ xs : (list\ s)\, .\ \dots$$

and the projection (pcall map int bool) might be written $map\ [int]\ [bool]$.

FLEX/SP requires the explicit projection of polymorphic values via pcall. But some polymorphic languages support **implicit projection**, in which the type arguments of projection are automatically deduced from context. Implicit projection makes polymorphic programming more palatable by removing some of the overhead of writing explicit types. We shall study an example of implicit projection in Section 15.4.5.

Static Semantics of Universal Polymorphism

Figure 12.9 shows the changes to the FLEX/S type system to support universal polymorphism. The [∀-*intro*] rule gives a forall type to a pabs, while the [∀-*elim*] rule specifies a beta reduction in the type domain. To illustrate these two new type rules, we revisit the FL example from page 657:

Syntax

$E \in \mathrm{Exp} ::= \dots \mid \texttt{(pabs (τ^*) } E\texttt{)} \mid \texttt{(pcall } E \ T^*\texttt{)}$

$T \in \mathrm{Type} ::= \dots \mid \texttt{(forall (τ^*) } T\texttt{)}$

Free Identifiers

$FrIds[\![\texttt{(pabs ($\tau_{i=1}^n$) } E\texttt{)}]\!] = FrIds[\![E]\!]$

$FrIds[\![\texttt{(pcall } E \ T_{i=1}^n\texttt{)}]\!] = FrIds[\![E]\!]$

$FrTyIds_{ty}[\![\texttt{(forall ($\tau_{i=1}^n$) } T\texttt{)}]\!] = FrTyIds_{ty}[\![T]\!] - \cup_{i=1}^n\{\tau_i\}$

$FrTyIds_{exp}[\![\texttt{(pabs ($\tau_{i=1}^n$) } E\texttt{)}]\!] = FrTyIds_{exp}[\![E]\!] - \cup_{i=1}^n\{\tau_i\}$

$FrTyIds_{exp}[\![\texttt{(pcall } E \ T_{i=1}^n\texttt{)}]\!] = FrTyIds_{exp}[\![E]\!] \cup \left(\cup_{i=1}^n FrTyIds_{ty}[\![T_i]\!]\right)$

New Type Rules

$$\frac{TE \vdash E : T}{TE \vdash \texttt{(pabs ($\tau_{i=1}^n$) } E\texttt{)} : \texttt{(forall ($\tau_{i=1}^n$) } T\texttt{)}} \qquad [\forall\text{-}intro]$$

where $\quad \forall_{i=1}^n \ . \ \tau_i \notin \cup_{I \in FrIds[\![E]\!]} \left(FrTyIds_{ty}[\![TE(I)]\!]\right) \quad$ *[import restriction]*

$\qquad\qquad E$ is pure $\qquad\qquad\qquad\qquad\qquad\qquad\qquad\qquad$ *[purity restriction]*

$$\frac{TE \vdash E : \texttt{(forall ($\tau_{i=1}^n$) } T\texttt{)}}{TE \vdash \texttt{(pcall } E \ T_{i=1}^n\texttt{)} : ([T_i/\tau_i]_{i=1}^n)T} \qquad [\forall\text{-}elim]$$

New Type-Equivalence Rule

$$\frac{([\tau_i/\tau_i']_{i=1}^n)T' \approx T}{\texttt{(forall ($\tau_{i=1}'^n$) } T'\texttt{)} \approx \texttt{(forall ($\tau_{i=1}^n$) } T\texttt{)}} \qquad [\forall\text{-}\approx]$$

$$\text{where} \quad \forall_{i=1}^n \ . \ \left(\tau_i \notin FrTyIds_{ty}[\![T']\!]\right)$$

New Subtype Rule

$$\frac{([\tau_i/\tau_i']_{i=1}^n)T' \sqsubseteq T}{\texttt{(forall ($\tau_{i=1}'^n$) } T'\texttt{)} \sqsubseteq \texttt{(forall ($\tau_{i=1}^n$) } T\texttt{)}} \qquad [\forall\text{-}\sqsubseteq]$$

$$\text{where} \quad \forall_{i=1}^n \ . \ \left(\tau_i \notin FrTyIds_{ty}[\![T']\!]\right)$$

New Value

$V \in \mathrm{ValueExp} ::= \dots \mid \texttt{(pabs (τ^*) } E_{body}\texttt{)}$

New Evaluation Context

$\mathbb{E} \in \mathrm{EvalContext} ::= \dots \mid \texttt{(pcall } \mathbb{E} \ T^*\texttt{)}$

New Reduction Rule

$\texttt{(pcall (pabs ($\tau_{i=1}^n$) } E_{body}\texttt{) } T_{i=1}^n\texttt{)} \rightsquigarrow ([T_i/\tau_i]_{i=1}^n)E_{body}$ *[polymorphic projection]*

Figure 12.9 Changes to FLEX/S to handle universal polymorphism in FLEX/SP.

$$E_{id} = \texttt{(let ((id (abs (x) x)))}\;\{\text{FL }expression\}$$
$$\texttt{(if (id \#t) 1 ((id id) 2)))}$$

Translating this expression into FLEX required making three copies of the **id** procedure that differed only in type annotations. But translating this expression into FLEX/SP requires only a single polymorphic version of **id**:

$$E_{polyId} = \texttt{(let ((id (pabs (t) (abs ((x t)) x))))}\;\{\text{FLEX/SP }expression\}$$
$$\texttt{(if ((pcall id bool) \#t)}$$
$$\texttt{1}$$
$$\texttt{(((pcall id (-> (int) int)) (pcall id int)) 2)))}$$

Figure 12.10 presents a type derivation showing that this expression is well typed in the FLEX/SP type system.

The [∀-*intro*] rule includes a restriction that **pabs**-bound type identifiers cannot be elements of the set $FrTyIds_{ty}[\![TE(I)]\!]$ for any $I \in FrIds[\![E]\!]$ — i.e., they cannot appear in the free type identifiers of the types of free identifiers in the expression E. We call this the **import restriction** because it involves type identifiers that are "imported" as types of the free identifiers in E.

The import restriction prohibits a subtle form of variable capture. Consider the following example:

```
(def polytest
  (pabs (t)
    (abs ((x t))
      (pabs (t) x))))
```

What is the type of **polytest**? To say that it is

```
(forall (t) (-> (t) (forall (t) t)))
```

is incorrect, because the **t** introduced by the outer **pabs** and used as the type of **x** has been captured by the inner **pabs**. If this capture were allowed to happen, and **polytest** had the type above, then

```
(pcall ((pcall polytest int) 3) bool)
```

would have the type **bool**, thus misinterpreting an integer value as a boolean!

In the [∀-*intro*] rule, we simply outlaw such situations.[5] An implementation could insist that programmers enforce the rule, or it could alpha-rename type identifiers to guarantee that no capture is possible no matter what names the programmer used. E.g., in the **polytest** example, the two **pabs**-bound identifiers **t** would have different names, and the type of **x** would be the one bound by the outer **pabs**.

---

[5]Another way to outlaw such situations without the import restriction is to have the [∀-*intro*] rule extend the type environment with **forall**-bound variables and prohibit duplication of these variables in the type environment. This is the approach taken in [Pie02, Chapter 23].

Abbreviations

$TE_{letbody} = \{\texttt{id} : \texttt{(forall (t) (-> (t) t))}\}$

$E_{polyId} = \texttt{(let ((id } E_{pabs}\texttt{)) (if (}E_{boolId} \texttt{ \#t) 1 ((}E_{intProcId} \texttt{ } E_{intId}\texttt{) 2)))}$

$E_{pabs} = \texttt{(pabs (t) (abs ((x t)) x))}$

$E_{boolId} = \texttt{(pcall id bool)}$

$E_{intId} = \texttt{(pcall id int)}$

$E_{intProcId} = \texttt{(pcall id (-> (int) int))}$

Type Derivation for E_{polyId}

$\{\texttt{x} : \texttt{t}\} \vdash \texttt{x} : \texttt{t}$ $[var]$

$\{\} \vdash \texttt{(abs ((x t)) x)} : \texttt{(-> (t) t)}$ $[\rightarrow\text{-}intro]$

$\{\} \vdash \texttt{(pabs (t) (abs ((x t)) x))} : \texttt{(forall (t) (-> (t) t))}$ $[\forall\text{-}intro]$

$TE_{letbody} \vdash \texttt{id} : \texttt{(forall (t) (-> (t) t))}$ $[var]$

$TE_{letbody} \vdash \texttt{(pcall id bool)} : \texttt{(-> (bool) bool)}$ $[\forall\text{-}elim]$

$TE_{letbody} \vdash \texttt{\#t} : \texttt{bool}$ $[bool]$

$TE_{letbody} \vdash \texttt{(}E_{boolId} \texttt{ \#t)} : \texttt{bool}$ $[\rightarrow\text{-}elim]$

$TE_{letbody} \vdash \texttt{1} : \texttt{int}$ $[int]$

$TE_{letbody} \vdash \texttt{id} : \texttt{(forall (t) (-> (t) t))}$ $[var]$

$TE_{letbody} \vdash \texttt{(pcall id (-> (int) int))}$
$\qquad\qquad : \texttt{(-> ((-> (int) int)) (-> (int) int))}$ $[\forall\text{-}elim]$

$TE_{letbody} \vdash \texttt{id} : \texttt{(forall (t) (-> (t) t))}$ $[var]$

$TE_{letbody} \vdash \texttt{(pcall id int)} : \texttt{(-> (int) int)}$ $[\forall\text{-}elim]$

$TE_{letbody} \vdash \texttt{(}E_{intProcId} \texttt{ } E_{intId}\texttt{)} : \texttt{(-> (int) int)}$ $[\rightarrow\text{-}elim]$

$TE_{letbody} \vdash \texttt{2} : \texttt{int}$ $[int]$

$TE_{letbody} \vdash \texttt{((}E_{intProcId} \texttt{ } E_{intId}\texttt{) 2)} : \texttt{int}$ $[\rightarrow\text{-}elim]$

$TE_{letbody} \vdash \texttt{(if (}E_{boolId} \texttt{ \#t) 1 ((}E_{intProcId} \texttt{ } E_{intId}\texttt{) 2))} : \texttt{int}$ $[if]$

$\{\} \vdash \texttt{(let ((id } E_{pabs}\texttt{)) (if (}E_{boolId} \texttt{ \#t) 1 ((}E_{intProcId} \texttt{ } E_{intId}\texttt{) 2)))} : \texttt{int}$ $[let]$

Figure 12.10 Derivation showing the well-typedness of E_{polyId} in FLEX/SP.

The [∀-*intro*] rule also contains a **purity restriction** that insists that a polymorphic expression be referentially transparent. (Section 8.3.6 discusses referential transparency.) Chapter 16 will introduce a more precise way to enforce this restriction, but we shall require here that an expression be a syntactic value in the sense of Section 8.3.6, page 428. That is, the expression must be

- a variable reference (if there are no mutable variables) or an abstraction (`abs` expression), or

- a conditional, `let` expression, primitive application (except those dealing with cells), or an immutable data-structure constructor (e.g., `pair`) whose subexpressions are all syntactic values.

All other expressions — including procedure applications and invocations of cell primitives — are potentially impure and are not syntactic values.

The purity restriction in the [∀-*intro*] rule has both practical and theoretical motivations. The practical motivation is that we'd like to be able to define a dynamic semantics for FLEX/SP expressions that ignores all type information — an idea we formalize in Section 13.2.1 using a notion called **type erasure**. From this perspective, constructs like `pabs` and `pcall` are compile-time fictions that can be erased from a program after the type-checking phase because they don't affect the run-time behavior of a program. For instance, the FLEX/SP polymorphic procedure

```
(pabs (s t)
  (abs (p (pairof s t))
    ((pcall pair t s) ((pcall snd t) p) ((pcall fst s) p))))
```

can simply be implemented as if it were the FL procedure

```
(abs (p) (pair (snd p) (fst p)))
```

after type checking is performed.

Unfortunately, this implementation strategy no longer works if polymorphic values with impure bodies are allowed. For example, suppose that (`inc!`) increments a global cell holding an integer. Then the FLEX/SP expression

```
(let ((id (pabs (t) (begin (inc!) (abs ((x t)) x)))))
  ((pcall pair int bool) ((pcall id int) 1)
                         ((pcall id bool) #t)))
```

presumably should increment the cell twice, but the type-erased expression,

```
(let ((id (begin (inc!) (abs (x) x))))
  (pair (id 1) (id #t)))
```

increments the cell only once (assuming a CBV evaluation strategy). Requiring every pabs body E_{body} to be pure means that the number of times E_{body} is evaluated cannot affect program behavior and so erasing pabs and pcall remains a viable implementation strategy.

The theoretical motivation for the purity restriction in the [∀-*intro*] rule is that the FLEX/SP type system is unsound if pabs is allowed to abstract over the types in arbitrary impure expressions. To see why, we start with the following CBV FL expression:

$$E_{polyCell} = \texttt{(let ((c (cell (null))))}$$
$$\texttt{(begin (:= c (cons 1 (null)))}$$
$$\texttt{(not (car (^ c)))))}$$

This expression encounters a dynamic type error because it attempts to use the first element of an integer list in cell c as a boolean. We can translate $E_{polyCell}$ into the following FLEX/SP expression:

$$E'_{polyCell} =$$
```
(let ((c (pabs (t) ((pcall cell (listof t)) ((pcall null t))))))
  (begin ((pcall := (listof int))
          (pcall c int)
          ((pcall cons int) 1 ((pcall null int))))
         (not ((pcall car bool)
               ((pcall ^ (listof bool)) (pcall c bool))))))
```

If we removed the purity restriction from the [∀-*intro*] rule, then c could be given the type (forall (t) (cellof (listof t))) and $E'_{polyCell}$ would be well typed (verify this for yourself). But this well-typed expression would encounter a dynamic type error (at least according to the type-erasure semantics discussed above), so the type system would be unsound without the purity restriction.

Note that the rules for type equivalence and type inclusion allow alpha-renaming of the forall-bound type identifiers. E.g.,

$$\texttt{(forall (s) (-> (s) s))} \approx \texttt{(forall (t) (-> (t) t))}$$

The type (forall $(\tau_{i=1}^{n})$ T) is said to be a **universal type** because the type parameters $\tau_{i=1}^{n}$ range over the universe of types. Does the universe of types over which type parameters range include universal types themselves? If the answer is "yes" (as in the FLEX/SP type system), the type system is said to be **impredicative**, while if the answer is "no," the type system is said to be **predicative**. In a predicative type system, there is a hierarchy of types: there is a universe U_1 of "regular" types that does not include forall types, a universe U_2 that includes forall types quantified over the regular types in U_1, a universe U_3 that includes forall types quantified over the types in U_2, and so on. Although the FLEX/SP type system is impredicative, we shall see (in Section 13.4.2) that type reconstruction for universal types uses a predicative type system instead. For more on impredicative versus predicative polymorphism, see [Mit96, Chapter 9].

Dynamic Semantics of Universal Polymorphism

The dynamic semantics of universal polymorphism is expressed by extending the FLEX SOS in Figure 12.9. The new evaluation context (pcall $\mathbb{E}$ T^*) permits the evaluation of the expression E_{poly} in (pcall E_{poly} T^*) to a polymorphic value (pabs (τ^*) E_{body}), and the new [*polymorphic projection*] reduction rule substitutes the actual type arguments of the pcall for the formal type parameters of the pabs. The modified SOS can be used to show the type soundness of FLEX/SP by extending the preservation/progress recipe to handle the new constructs of FLEX/SP (Exercise 12.15).

Figure 12.9 does not describe the changes in the type rules or the SOS of FLEX/S that are needed to replace the kernel constructs for operations on lists, pairs, cells, and sequences by primitive operators or built-in procedures. The usual primitive-application construct (prim O E^*) is not sufficient for polymorphic primitives like cons and pair, which need to be projected onto type arguments. We could address this by modifying prim to specify the projection types for polymorphic primitives, as in (prim pair (int bool) 3 #t).

Exercise 12.10 As illustrated in Exercise 11.5 on page 658 and Exercise 11.21 on page 687, translating FL expressions into the monomorphic FLEX language often requires making duplicate copies of procedure definitions differing only in type annotations. FLEX/SP's universal polymorphism makes such duplication unnecessary. Show this by translating the expressions from these two exercises into FLEX/SP without duplicating any procedure definitions.

Exercise 12.11 Polly Morwicz wants to simplify FLEX/SP by introducing into the standard library a built-in polymorphic err procedure that replaces the kernel error construct.

a. Specify the type of Polly's err procedure.

b. Illustrate the use of Polly's err procedure by filling in the hole in the following example to produce a well-typed FLEX/SP expression:

```
(abs ((x int) (y int)) (if (= x 0) □ (/ y x)))
```

Exercise 12.12 Bud Lojack is having trouble implementing letrec in a call-by-name version of FLEX/SP. He decides that recursion should instead be specified by a polymorphic fix procedure in the standard library that computes the fixed point of a generating procedure. For example, here is Bud's correct definition of a factorial procedure:

```
(let ((fact-gen
        (abs ((fact (-> (int) int)))
          (abs ((n int))
            (if (= n 0) 1 (* n (fact (- n 1)))))))))
  ((pcall fix (-> (int) int)) fact-gen))
```

a. What is the type of `fact-gen`?

b. What is the type of `fix`?

c. What is the type of `((pcall fix (-> (int) int)) fact-gen)`?

d. Bud asks his friend Thai Ping to define a version of `fix` that works in call-by-name FLEX/SP, and Thai quickly produces the following:

```
(def fix T₀
  (pabs (t)
    (abs ((f  T₁))
      ((abs ((x  T₂)) (f (x x)))
       (abs ((x  T₂)) (f (x x)))))))
```

What are T_0, T_1, and T_2? *Hint:* Compare to Exercise 11.24 on page 694.

e. Is it possible to define a version of `fix` for call-by-value FLEX/SP?

f. Rather than making `fix` a standard library procedure, Bud could have made it a kernel construct of the form (`fix` E), in which case his factorial procedure would be written (`fix fact-gen`). What is the type rule for the kernel `fix` construct?

Exercise 12.13 Translate the following FL procedures for manipulating Church pairs into FLEX/SP:

```
(def church-pair (abs (x y) (abs (f) (f x y))))
(def church-fst (abs (p) (p (abs (x y) x))))
(def church-snd (abs (p) (p (abs (x y) y))))
```

Exercise 12.14 Consider a version of FLEX/SP that includes (`cwcc` E) from Section 9.4.4 as a kernel construct.

a. Give a type rule for (`cwcc` E).

b. Translate the following FL abstraction that uses `cwcc` to a FLEX/SP abstraction that is well typed assuming your type rule from part **a**.

```
(abs (x y)
  (cwcc (abs (return)
          (if (or (< x y) (and (< y (* 2 x)) (return x)))
              (return y)
              (+ x y)))))
```

c. Can (`cwcc` E) be added as a kernel construct to FLEX? Explain.

(See part **d** of Exercise 12.7 on page 717 for another approach to typing `cwcc`.)

Exercise 12.15

a. Sketch a proof for the following lemma:

$$\text{If } TE \vdash E : T, \text{ then } (([T_i/\tau_i]_{i=1}^n)\, TE) \vdash ([T_i/\tau_i]_{i=1}^n)E : ([T_i/\tau_i]_{i=1}^n)\, T$$

b. Using the lemma from part **a**, show that the [*polymorphic projection*] reduction rule preserves types in the empty type environment. This extends Lemma 11.9 on page 668, which is the key step in showing that the Preservation Theorem for μFLEX (Theorem 11.6 on page 668) holds for FLEX/SP.

c. Extend the proof of the Progress Theorem for μFLEX (Theorem 11.7 on page 668) to show that FLEX/SP expressions that are well typed in the empty environment cannot be stuck at a dynamic type error. You need only consider the new kinds of stuck expressions that are possible in the presence of `pabs` and `pcall`.

12.2.3   Deconstructible Data Types

Universal polymorphism makes it possible to express simple forms of the deconstructible sum-of-products data types from Section 10.4 in a statically typed language. Data-type deconstructors must be polymorphic because they need to return different types in different contexts. Such deconstructors cannot be defined as regular procedures in a monomorphic language.

An Example: Integer Lists

Consider the following data-type declaration for lists of integers:

```
(def-datatype intlist
  (inull)
  (icons int intlist))
```

As shown in Figure 12.11, this declaration can be viewed as introducing a recursive sum-of-products type, $T_{intlist}$, along with procedures for constructing (`inull`, `icons`) and deconstructing (`inull˜`, `icons˜`) values of this type.

The `intlist` deconstructors are polymorphic procedures that are parameterized over a type `t` specifying the type of the value returned when the deconstructor is invoked. For example, Figure 12.12 presents three recursive procedures in which these deconstructors are projected onto three different types:

1. the `sum` procedure (in which `t = int`) adds the elements of an integer list;

2. the `all-positive?` procedure (in which `t = bool`) determines whether all the elements of an integer list are positive; and

3. the `map-squares` procedure (in which `t = intlist`) returns an integer list containing the squares of the corresponding integers in a given list.

Data-Type Declaration
```
(def-datatype intlist
  (inull)
  (icons int intlist))
```

Sum-of-products Data Type

$T_{intlist}$ = (trec intlist
    (oneof (inull (prodof))
       (icons (prodof int intlist)))))

Constructors

(def inull (-> () $T_{intlist}$)
 (abs () (one $T_{intlist}$ inull (prod))))

(def icons (-> (int $T_{intlist}$) $T_{intlist}$)
 (abs ((x1 int) (x2 $T_{intlist}$))
  (one $T_{intlist}$ icons (prod x1 x2))))

Deconstructors

(def inull˜ (forall (t) (-> ($T_{intlist}$ (-> () t) (-> () t)) t))
 (pabs (t)
  (abs ((disc $T_{intlist}$)   {*discriminant*}
    (succ (-> () t)) {*success continuation*}
    (fail (-> () t))) {*failure continuation*}
   (tagcase disc payload
    (inull (succ))
    (else (fail))))))

(def icons˜
 (pabs (t) (forall (t) (-> ($T_{intlist}$ (-> (int $T_{intlist}$) t) (-> () t)) t))
  (abs ((disc $T_{intlist}$)   {*discriminant*}
    (succ (-> (int $T_{intlist}$) t)) {*success continuation*}
    (fail (-> () t)))   {*failure continuation*}
   (tagcase disc payload
    (icons (succ (get 1 payload) (get 2 payload)))
    (else (fail))))))
```

**Figure 12.11** The type, constructor procedures, and deconstructor procedures introduced by an `intlist` data-type declaration.

## The General Case

A formal definition of the desugaring for `def-datatype` is presented in Figure 12.13. This is similar to the desugaring of the `def-data` declaration (see Figure 10.21 on page 587) in a dynamically typed language except for the following differences:
```

```
(def sum (-> (T_intlist) int)
  (abs ((ns T_intlist))
    ((pcall inull~ int) ns
        (abs () 0)
        (abs ()
          ((pcall icons~ int) ns
              (abs ((n int) (ms T_intlist))
                (+ n (sum ms)))
              (abs () (error shouldnt-happen int)))))))
(def all-positive? (-> (T_intlist) bool)
  (abs ((ns T_intlist))
    ((pcall inull~ bool) ns
        (abs () #t)
        (abs ()
          ((pcall icons~ bool) ns
              (abs ((n int) (ms T_intlist))
                (scand (> n 0) (all-positive? ms)))
              (abs () (error shouldnt-happen bool)))))))
(def map-square (-> (T_intlist) T_intlist)
  (abs ((ns T_intlist))
    ((pcall inull~ T_intlist) ns
        (abs () (inull))
        (abs ()
          ((pcall icons~ T_intlist) ns
              (abs ((n int) (ms T_intlist))
                (cons (* n n) (map-square ms)))
              (abs () (error shouldnt-happen T_intlist)))))))
```

Figure 12.12   Three recursive procedures illustrating use of `intlist` deconstructors.

- In each `def-datatype` clause $(I_{tag_i}\ T_{i,1}\ \ldots\ T_{i,k_i})$, the entities $T_{i,1}\ \ldots\ T_{i,k_i}$ are not mere placeholders for product components but are bona fide types describing the product components.

- In addition to defining constructor and deconstructor procedures for each clause, the (`def-datatype` τ_{data} ...) declaration defines a recursive sum-of-products type named τ_{data}. The scope of the type identifier τ_{data} includes the clauses of the current `def-datatype` declaration, any following declarations, and the program body.[6]

---

[6]This scope is based on the assumption that all `def-type` declarations that result from the desugaring of `def-datatype` are moved in front of all `def` declarations, preserving their relative order, before the program desugaring in Figure 11.2 on page 634 is performed. The program desugaring replaces all occurrences of τ_{data} by the corresponding sum-of-products type.

Modified Syntax

$P ::= (\texttt{flex/SP} \; ((I_{formal} \; T_{formalType})^*) \; E_{body} \; D_{defn}^*) \;$ [Program]

$D ::= (\texttt{def} \; I_{name} \; T_{defnType} \; E_{defn}) \hspace{2.5cm}$ [ValueDefinition]

$\hspace{0.8cm} | \; (\texttt{def} \; (I_{proc} \; T_{return} \; (I_{formal} \; T_{formalType})^*) \; E_{body}) \;$ [ProcedureDefinition]

$\hspace{0.8cm} | \; (\texttt{def-datatype} \; \tau_{data} \; (I_{tag} \; T^*)^*) \hspace{1.6cm}$ [DataTypeDeclaration]

New Desugaring

; *This desugaring rule interleaves* `def-type` *and* `def` *declarations. We assume*
; *that all* `def-type` *declarations are moved in front of the* `def` *declarations*
; *before the program desugaring defined in Figure 11.2 on page 634 is performed.*

$\mathcal{DS}_{def} : \text{Def} \to \text{Def}^*$

$\mathcal{DS}_{def}[\![(\texttt{def-datatype} \; \tau_{data} \; (I_{tag_i} \; T_{i,1} \; \ldots \; T_{i,k_i})_{i=1}^n)]\!]$

$\quad = (\texttt{def-type} \; \tau_{data} \; T_{data}) \, . \, (@_{i=1}^n \mathcal{DS}_{cl}[\![(I_{tag_i} \; T_{i,1} \; \ldots \; T_{i,k_i})]\!])$

$\qquad \text{where } T_{data} = (\texttt{trec} \; \tau_{data} \; (\texttt{oneof} \; (I_{tag_i} \; (\texttt{prodof} \; T_{i,1} \; \ldots \; T_{i,k_i}))_{i=1}^n))$

$\qquad \text{and} \quad \mathcal{DS}_{cl}[\![(I_{tag} \; T_{i=1}^k)]\!]$

$\qquad\qquad = [; \textit{constructor procedure}$

$\qquad\qquad\quad (\texttt{def} \; I_{tag} \; (\texttt{->} \; (T_{i=1}^k) \; \tau_{data})$

$\qquad\qquad\qquad (\texttt{abs} \; ((\texttt{x}\bowtie\texttt{1} \; T_1) \; \ldots \; (\texttt{x}\bowtie k \; T_k))$

$\qquad\qquad\qquad\quad (\texttt{one} \; \tau_{data} \; I_{tag} \; (\texttt{prod} \; \texttt{x}\bowtie\texttt{1} \; \ldots \; \texttt{x}\bowtie k)))),$

$\qquad\qquad\quad ; \textit{polymorphic deconstructor procedure}$

$\qquad\qquad\quad (\texttt{def} \; I_{tag}\bowtie\texttt{\textasciitilde}$

$\qquad\qquad\qquad (\texttt{forall} \; (\tau_{ret}) \; ; \, \tau_{ret} \textit{ is the deconstructor return type}$

$\qquad\qquad\qquad\quad (\texttt{->} \; (\tau_{data} \hspace{2.3cm} ; \textit{ discriminant type}$

$\qquad\qquad\qquad\qquad (\texttt{->} \; (T_{i=1}^k) \; \tau_{ret}) \; ; \textit{ success continuation type}$

$\qquad\qquad\qquad\qquad (\texttt{->} \; () \; \tau_{ret})) \hspace{1cm} ; \textit{ failure continuation type}$

$\qquad\qquad\qquad\quad \tau_{ret}))$

$\qquad\qquad\qquad (\texttt{pabs} \; (\tau_{ret}) \; ; \, \tau_{ret} \textit{ is a fresh return type}$

$\qquad\qquad\qquad\quad (\texttt{abs} \; ((\texttt{val} \; \tau_{data}) \hspace{2.2cm} ; \textit{ discriminant}$

$\qquad\qquad\qquad\qquad (\texttt{succ} \; (\texttt{->} \; (T_{i=1}^k) \; \tau_{ret})) \; ; \textit{ success continuation}$

$\qquad\qquad\qquad\qquad (\texttt{fail} \; (\texttt{->} \; () \; \tau_{ret}))) \hspace{0.8cm} ; \textit{ failure continuation}$

$\qquad\qquad\qquad\quad (\texttt{tagcase} \; \texttt{val} \; \texttt{payload}$

$\qquad\qquad\qquad\qquad (I_{tag} \; (\texttt{succ} \; (\texttt{get} \; \bar{i} \; \texttt{payload})_{i=1}^k))$

$\qquad\qquad\qquad\qquad\quad ; \textit{ For } i \in \textit{Int, the notation } \bar{i} \textit{ stands for}$

$\qquad\qquad\qquad\qquad\quad ; \textit{ the IntLit N such that } \mathcal{N}[\![N]\!] = i$

$\qquad\qquad\qquad\qquad (\texttt{else} \; (\texttt{fail})))))))$

$\qquad\qquad]$

Figure 12.13 Syntax and desugaring of `def-datatype` in FLEX/SP.

- Each constructor procedure abstraction specifies explicit types for the formal parameters and the sum-of-products injection.

- Each deconstructor is a polymorphic procedure parameterized over the return type τ_{ret} used in the explicit types for the success and failure continuations.

Pattern Matching for Deconstructing Data Types

Since explicit deconstructor applications are cumbersome to read and write, it would be nice to have a more convenient way to write them, such as the `match` construct from Section 10.5. For example, we'd like to define the `all-positive?` procedure as

```
(def all-positive? (-> (T_intlist) bool)
  (abs ((ns T_intlist))
    (match ns
      ((inull) #t)
      ((icons n ms) (scand (> n 0) (all-positive? ms))))))
```

and have it automatically transformed into the definition in Figure 12.12. Unfortunately, the `match` desugaring for the dynamically typed FL language presented in Figure 10.27 on page 603 does not work in FLEX/SP because it doesn't handle the fact that FLEX/SP deconstructors are polymorphic procedures that need to be projected onto the return type of the `match` expression. Here are two ways to address this problem, which are explored further in Exercise 12.20.

1. We can extend the `match` construct with an explicit return type that can be used in a suitably modified desugaring. For example, in the `all-positive?` procedure, we could replace (`match ns ...`) by (`match ns bool ...`) to explicitly declare that this `match` returns a boolean value. Adding explicit type information is consistent with other FLEX/SP constructs (such as `error` and `null`), but is a hassle for the programmer. Intuitively, it is also unnecessary, because the type system must be able to determine the return type of the `match` expression when there is at least one clause. Explicit types become even more cumbersome when parameterized data types such as (`listof t`) and (`pairof s t`) are considered (see Exercise 12.25 on page 766).

2. A more flexible approach is to treat the `match` construct as a kernel construct for the purposes of type checking and to delay the transformation of `match` into deconstructor applications until after type checking is complete. Then the type of the `match` expression determined during type checking can be used as the projection type when `match` is transformed to deconstructor applications.

We will see in Section 13.5.4 that many of the complications involving pattern matching in an explicitly typed language disappear in the presence of type reconstruction.

Exercise 12.16 Suppose that the `shape` data type in Figure 10.22 on page 588 is defined in FLEX/SP using `def-datatype`.

a. Define a FLEX/SP procedure `perim` that calculates the perimeter of a shape.

b. Define a FLEX/SP procedure `scale` that, given a shape and an integer scaling factor, returns an appropriately scaled shape.

Exercise 12.17 Exercise 11.25 (page 695) considers an ELM interpreter written in FLEX based on explicit types T_{elmExp} and T_{elmPgm}.

a. Define T_{elmExp} and T_{elmPgm} using `def-datatype`.

b. Write an ELM interpreter in FLEX/SP in which all data-type deconstruction is performed via deconstruction procedures.

c. Using `def-datatype`, define an s-expression data type `sexp` (see Exercise 11.28 on page 698) and define a procedure `sexp->elm` that parses s-expressions into ELM expressions.

Exercise 12.18 Deconstructors for individual constructors are helpful when we want to define pattern-matching approaches to data-type deconstruction in FLEX/SP (e.g., see Exercise 12.20). However, they are clumsy in the common case where there is one deconstruction clause for each constructor. Later clauses end up being embedded in the failure continuations for earlier clauses, and the final failure continuation is an error expression (such as (`error shouldnt-happen int`) in Figure 12.12) that will never be executed because all cases have already been covered.

For this common case, it is helpful to define a single deconstructor that has one success continuation for each constructor tag, as suggested by the following example:

```
(def sum (-> (T_intlist) int)
  (abs ((ns T_intlist))
    ((pcall intlist~ int) ns
      (record (inull {success continuation for inull}
                (abs () 0))
              (icons {success continuation for icons}
                (abs ((n int) (ms T_intlist)) (+ n (sum ms))))))))
```

For a data type named τ_{data}, the new deconstructor is named $\tau_{data}\bowtie\tilde{}$. Its first argument is a value of type τ_{data} to be deconstructed and its second argument is a record of success continuations, one for each constructor tag in the data-type declaration.

Extend the desugaring of `def-datatype` to provide this new kind of deconstructor.

Exercise 12.19 Data types sometimes need to be mutually recursive. For example, mutually recursive data types would be needed to express the definitions of numerical expressions and boolean expressions in the EL language in Figure 2.4 on page 25:

```
(def-datatype numexp
  (intval int)
  (input int)
  (arithapp arithop numexp numexp)
  (conditional boolexp numexp numexp))

(def-datatype boolexp
  (boolval bool)
  (relapp relop numexp numexp)
  (logapp logop boolexp boolexp))

(def-datatype arithop (+) (-) (*) (/) (%))
(def-datatype relop (<) (=) (>))
(def-datatype logop (and) (or))
```

However, the desugaring for `def-datatype` defined in Figure 12.13 (in conjunction with the program desugaring defined in Figure 11.2 on page 634) does not support mutually recursive datatypes.

Modify the handling of `def-datatype` declarations within a FLEX/SP program to allow mutually recursive datatypes like `numexp` and `boolexp`.

Exercise 12.20

a. Suppose FLEX/SP is extended with the following `match` sugar expression for decomposing sum-of-products data types:

$$E \in \text{Exp} ::= \ldots \mid (\texttt{match } E_{disc} \ T_{match} \ (PT \ E)^*)$$
$$PT \in \text{Pattern} ::= L \mid I \mid \_ \mid (I_{constr} \ PT^*)$$

The programmer-supplied type T_{match} in the `match` construct describes the value of the `match` expression.

Modify the `match` desugaring in Figure 10.27 on page 603 to desugar the FLEX/SP `match` construct. You may assume that there is a type environment $TE_{datatypes}$ containing the types of constructor and deconstructor procedures for all programmer-declared data types in the program.

b. Now consider a FLEX/SP `match` construct (1) that does not have the explicit return type T_{match}; (2) that has at least one clause; and (3) in which patterns are restricted to constructor application patterns of the form $(I_{constr} \ I^*)$:

$$E \in \text{Exp} ::= \ldots \mid (\texttt{match } E_{disc} \ (PT \ E)^+)$$
$$PT \in \text{Pattern} ::= (I_{constr} \ I^*)$$

   i. Suppose that the type checker treats this `match` expression as a kernel construct. Give the type rule for `match`.

ii. Define the following translation function, $\mathcal{T}$, which transforms `match` expressions into appropriate deconstructor applications:

$\mathcal{T} : \mathrm{Exp}_{\mathrm{FLEX/SP+\{match\}}} \rightarrow \mathrm{TypeEnvironment} \rightarrow \mathrm{Exp}_{\mathrm{FLEX/SP}}$

If E is a FLEX/SP+{match} expression that is well typed in TE, then $\mathcal{T}[\![E]\!]\ TE$ should be a FLEX/SP expression that is well typed in TE and has the same meaning as E.

iii. Generalize parts **i** and **ii** to handle more expressive patterns defined by the following grammar:

$PT \in \mathrm{Pattern} ::= L \mid I \mid \_ \mid (I_{constr}\ PT^*)$

12.2.4 Bounded Quantification

A problem with the notion of subtyping studied in Section 12.1.1 is that there is no way to express dependencies between the argument types and result type of a procedure. For example, as explored on page 721, the procedure

```
E_incAge = (abs ((r (recordof (age (cellof int)))))
              (let ((age (select age r)))
                (begin (:= age (+ (^ age) 1))
                       r))))
```

can be given any supertype of the procedure type

```
T_incAge = (-> ((recordof (age (cellof int))))
               (recordof (age (cellof int))))
```

But any such type necessarily "forgets" any fields other than the `age` field. For example, if E_{rcd} is a record with type

```
T_rcd = (recordof (age (cellof int)) (name symb))
```

then (`select name` $(E_{incAge}\ E_{rcd})$) is ill typed. Even though $(E_{incAge}\ E_{rcd})$ has a `name` field at run time, the best the FLEX/S type system can do is assign to $(E_{incAge}\ E_{rcd})$ the type (`recordof (age (cellof int))`).

Bounded quantification combines subtyping with universal polymorphism to allow us to express the idea that the return type of E_{incAge} is the same as the argument type for any subtype of (`recordof (age (cellof int))`). Each `pabs` parameter specification (τ `<=` T) now includes an upper type bound T in addition to the type identifier τ. When a `pabs` is projected, each actual type parameter must be a subtype of the upper type bound in the corresponding formal parameter specification.

For example, we can now write our procedure that increments any record's updatable integer `age` field and returns the updated record as:

$$E'_{incAge} = \texttt{(pabs ((t <= (recordof (age (cellof int))))))}$$
$$\texttt{(abs ((r t))}$$
$$\texttt{(let ((age (select age r)))}$$
$$\texttt{(begin (:= age (+ (\^{} age) 1))}$$
$$\texttt{r))))}$$

This polymorphic procedure has the type:

$$T'_{incAge} = \texttt{(forall ((t <= (recordof (age (cellof int))))))}$$
$$\texttt{(-> (t) t))}$$

The `(-> (t) t)` in the polymorphic type specifies that the return type of E_{incAge} is the same as the argument type, and the bound in the parameter specification `(t <= (recordof (age (cellof int))))` says that this argument/result type can be any subtype of `(recordof (age (cellof int)))`.

This polymorphic procedure can be projected onto any record type containing an updatable integer age field; but it doesn't forget the other fields of the record type it is projected onto. For example, we can now safely extract the `name` field from the result of using E'_{incAge} to increment the `age` field of an expression E_{rcd} with a type T_{rcd} containing both an `age` and `name` field:

   `(select name ((pcall ` E'_{incAge} ` ` T_{rcd}`) ` E_{rcd}`))`

This is well typed because `(pcall ` E'_{incAge} ` ` T_{rcd}`)` has the type `(-> (` T_{rcd}`) ` T_{rcd}`)` that results from projecting the polymorphic type T'_{incAge} onto T_{rcd}. This projection is sensible because T_{rcd} is a subtype of the bound specified for `t` in E'_{incAge}: `(recordof (age (cellof int)))`.

Figure 12.14 shows the changes necessary to add bounded quantification to FLEX/SP. Of course, we still want the unrestricted polymorphism of FLEX/SP. Rather than have separate type abstraction and projection facilities for the two cases, we introduce the new type `top` as the top of the type lattice. Every type is a subtype of `top`, and every binding occurrence τ that appears in a FLEX/SP `pabs` expression or `forall` type without an upper bound is replaced by the bounded specification `(` τ ` <= top)`.

Exercise 12.21 Write the type-equivalence rule and subtype rule for `forall` types in a system with bounded quantification.

Syntax

$E \in \text{Exp} ::= \ \ldots \ all \ \text{FLEX/SP} \ expressions \ except \ \text{pabs} \ \ldots$
$\hspace{2.5em} | \ (\text{pabs} \ ((\tau \ \text{<=} \ T)^*) \ E)$

$T \in \text{Type} ::= \ \ldots \ all \ \text{FLEX/SP} \ types \ except \ \text{forall} \ \ldots$
$\hspace{3em} | \ (\text{forall} \ ((\tau \ \text{<=} \ T)^*) \ T) \ | \ \text{top}$

Syntactic Sugar

$(\text{forall} \ (\ldots \ \tau_i \ \ldots) \ E) \leadsto_{ds} (\text{forall} \ (\ldots \ (\tau_i \ \text{<=} \ \text{top}) \ \ldots) \ E)$

$(\text{pabs} \ (\ldots \ \tau_i \ \ldots) \ E) \leadsto_{ds} (\text{pabs} \ (\ldots \ (\tau_i \ \text{<=} \ \text{top}) \ \ldots) \ E)$

Free Identifiers

$FrIds[\![(\text{pabs} \ ((\tau_i \ \text{<=} \ T_i)_{i=1}^{n}) \ E)]\!] = FrIds[\![E]\!]$

$FrTyIds_{ty}[\![(\text{forall} \ ((\tau_i \ \text{<=} \ T_i)_{i=1}^{n}) \ T)]\!]$
$\hspace{1em} = \left(FrTyIds_{ty}[\![T]\!] - \cup_{i=1}^{n} \{\tau_i\}\right) \cup \left(\cup_{i=1}^{n} FrTyIds_{ty}[\![T_i]\!]\right)$

$FrTyIds_{exp}[\![(\text{pabs} \ ((\tau_i \ \text{<=} \ T_i)_{i=1}^{n}) \ E)]\!]$
$\hspace{1em} = \left(FrTyIds_{exp}[\![E]\!] - \cup_{i=1}^{n} \{\tau_i\}\right) \cup \left(\cup_{i=1}^{n} FrTyIds_{ty}[\![T_i]\!]\right)$

New Type Rules

$$\frac{TE \vdash E : T}{TE \vdash (\text{pabs} \ ((\tau_i \ \text{<=} \ T_i)_{i=1}^{n}) \ E) : (\text{forall} \ ((\tau_i \ \text{<=} \ T_i)_{i=1}^{n}) \ T)} \quad [\forall\text{-}intro_{BQ}]$$

$\hspace{2em} \text{where} \quad \forall_{i=1}^{n} . \ \tau_i \notin \cup_{I \in FrIds[\![E]\!]} \left(FrTyIds_{ty}[\![TE(I)]\!]\right) \quad \textit{[import restriction]}$
$\hspace{5em} E \ \text{is pure} \hspace{7em} \textit{[purity restriction]}$

$$\frac{TE \vdash E : (\text{forall} \ ((\tau_i \ \text{<=} \ T_i)_{i=1}^{n}) \ T) \quad \forall_{i=1}^{n} . \ T_i' \sqsubseteq T_i}{TE \vdash (\text{pcall} \ E \ T_i'^{n}_{i=1}) : ([T_i'/\tau_i]_{i=1}^{n}) T} \quad [\forall\text{-}elim_{BQ}]$$

New Type-Equivalence Rule

$\hspace{6em} \textit{Left as Exercise 12.21.} \hspace{6em} [\forall\text{-}\approx_{BQ}]$

New Subtype Rules

$\hspace{7em} T \sqsubseteq \text{top} \hspace{8em} [top\text{-}\sqsubseteq_{BQ}]$

$\hspace{5em} \textit{Left as Exercise 12.21.} \hspace{5em} [forall\text{-}\sqsubseteq_{BQ}]$

New Value

$V \in \text{ValueExp} ::= \ldots \ | \ (\text{pabs} \ ((\tau \ \text{<=} \ T)^*) \ E_{body})$

New Reduction Rule

$(\text{pcall} \ (\text{pabs} \ ((\tau_i \ \text{<=} \ T_i)_{i=1}^{n}) \ E_{body}) \ T_i'^{n}_{i=1}) \leadsto ([T_i'/\tau_i]_{i=1}^{n}) E_{body},$
$\hspace{1em} \text{where} \ \forall_{i=1}^{n} . \ T_i' \sqsubseteq T_i \hspace{9em} [polymorphic \ projection_{BQ}]$

Figure 12.14 Adding bounded quantification to FLEX/SP.

12.2.5   Ad Hoc Polymorphism

There is another way in which program code can have more than one type.
Consider the JAVA + operator, which can mean integer addition, floating point
addition, or string concatenation. So the type of + can be any of the following:

$(int \times int) \rightarrow int$
$(float \times float) \rightarrow float$
$(double \times double) \rightarrow double$
$(string \times string) \rightarrow string$

This is unlike universal polymorphism, because the program code that implements the + operator is different for each of these types. The different operators
just happen to share the same name.

When a procedure or operator has a different meaning depending on the
number and/or types of its arguments, this is called **ad hoc polymorphism** or
overloading. Overloading arises in three ways:

- As noted above, built-in operators like + can have multiple meanings. This
  feature is present in most common programming languages. Some languages
  allow the programmer to further overload built-in operators. For example, in
  C++ one can define a meaning for infix + (or any of a large number of built-in
  operators) when applied to objects of a user-defined class.

- Languages like JAVA, C++, and DYLAN generalize overloaded operators by
  supporting multiple methods/functions defined with the same name as long
  as they are distinguished by the number and/or types of their arguments. A
  particular method/function will be chosen by the compiler or run-time system
  based on the invocation context.

- In many object-oriented languages, dynamic method dispatch and the ability of
  a subclass to override a superclass's methods imply that the code implementing
  a method is chosen at run time depending on the actual class of an object.

This last form of ad hoc polymorphism is at the very heart of object-oriented
programming. When one hears people refer to object-oriented languages as polymorphic, this is typically the sort of polymorphism they have in mind.

There are other forms of ad hoc polymorphism that are closer in spirit to
universal polymorphism. C++ provides **templates** that allow class and function
declarations to be parameterized over types. For example, templates can be used
to define a stack whose elements have type T or a sorting function that sorts
arrays with elements of type T using a < operator. When these templates are

instantiated with a particular argument type, the compiler effectively makes a copy of the template code in which the argument type is substituted for the type parameter `T`. Although similar to universal polymorphism, this approach is still ad hoc because different instantiations use different code. For example, elements in an `int` stack have a different size than elements in a `double` stack, and `<` stands for a different less-than operator when used to compare two `int` values than when used to compare two `double` values.

In JAVA prior to version 5.0, programmers compensated for the lack of universal polymorphism by adopting a programming idiom that takes advantage of subtyping, the JAVA class hierarchy, and casts (with dynamic type checking). Because the `Object` class is at the top of the inheritance hierarchy in JAVA, it functions as the top of the type partial order for object types. Thus, code that one would like to work for any object type is written to use the `Object` type. For example, a stack class can be defined as a collection of values of type `Object`. Because any object has a type that is a subtype of `Object`, we can push elements of any object type, say `String`, onto a stack. However, when popping a `String` element from a stack, the type system only "knows" that the returned element is an `Object`; the programmer has to supply a downcast to declare that the result is really a `String`.

There are two main problems with this JAVA idiom. First, the use of explicit downcasts is inelegant and error-prone. Second, the idiom can only be used with object types and does not work for primitive types like `int` and `boolean`. Values of these primitive types must be packaged into instances of so-called wrapper classes (like the `Integer` class for holding `int` values) before they can be used in this idiom. For example, we can use our stack class to make a stack of `Integer` instances but not a stack of `int` values.

Version 5.0 of JAVA introduces several features for alleviating these problems. The most important of these is its **generics** facility, which allows classes, interfaces, and static methods to be parameterized over types and then instantiated with particular types. Unlike in C++ templates, all instantiations of a JAVA generic type use the same code, which is closer in spirit to universal polymorphism. For compatibility with earlier versions of JAVA, the semantics of generics is defined by erasing the generic type parameters and effectively translating generic code to the `Object`/downcast idiom described above. But from the programmer's perspective, generics provide most of the benefits of universal programming and bounded quantification. For example, it is possible to define a stack with elements of type `T` such that popping a stack of `String` elements returns a `String` object without an explicit downcast.

```
(def-type int-tree (trec tr (oneof (leaf int) (node (prodof tr tr)))))

(def make-int-node (-> (int-tree int-tree) int-tree)
  (abs ((l int-tree) (r int-tree))
    (one int-tree node (prod l r))))
```

Figure 12.15 Defining the `int-tree` type simplifies the definition of `make-int-node`.

Primitive types are still a sore point, but the autoboxing/autounboxing features of JAVA 5.0 will automatically wrap primitive values into and unwrap them from wrapper classes in many situations. For example, pushing an `int` onto a stack will implicitly wrap the `int` into an `Integer` instance before pushing it.

However, for many problems involving collections of elements, it is still not possible to define a single generic method that works for any type of element, including primitive types. E.g., reversing the elements of an array of `int` values requires a different method from one that reverses the elements of an array of objects.

12.3   Higher-order Types: Descriptions and Kinds

12.3.1   Descriptions: FLEX/SPD

Chapter 11 showed how type synonyms (introduced by `let-type`, `let-type*`, and `def-type`) can make explicitly typed programs more compact and readable, just as `let` allows us to give readable names to values. The remainder of this chapter explores the symmetry between programming with types and programming with values. In particular, we will motivate the need for functions on types and the need for checking the "types" (called the kinds) of such functions.

The desire to modularize a program into reusable components motivates procedural abstraction: procedures (constructed using FLEX's `abs`) allow us to write code that can be reused in different contexts with different arguments. Universal polymorphism extends this idea into the world of typed programs by allowing us to abstract an expression over type identifiers (using `pabs`) so it can be reused in various situations. The very same principle of abstraction can be used again to support modularity and reuse of type expressions.

To motivate abstractions at the type level, consider the `make-int-node` procedure (Figure 12.15), which glues two `int-trees` (binary trees with integer leaves) into a single `int-tree`. Using `def-type` to introduce the name `int-tree` as a synonym for a recursive sum-of-products type is essential for keeping the example succinct. Without this synonym, each of the six occurrences of `int-tree` in the

```
(def make-node
    (forall (t)
      (-> ((trec tr (oneof (leaf t) (node (prodof tr tr))))
           (trec tr (oneof (leaf t) (node (prodof tr tr)))))
          (trec tr (oneof (leaf t) (node (prodof tr tr))))))
  (pabs (t)
    (let-type ((t-tree (trec tr (oneof (leaf t)
                                (node (prodof tr tr)))))))
      (abs ((l t-tree) (r t-tree))
        (one t-tree node (prod l r))))))
```

Figure 12.16 make-node, a version of make-int-node parameterized over the leaf type.

definition of make-int-node would need to be a copy of the trec type specifying the type of integer trees.

The importance of type abstraction is highlighted when make-int-node is generalized to a make-node procedure that abstracts over the type t of the tree leaves (Figure 12.16). The definition of make-node contains four copies of the type (trec tr ...), which describes a binary tree with leaves of type t. In the body of the procedure, let-type is used to give this type the name t-tree. But let-type cannot be used to abstract over the three occurrences of the tree type within the forall type, because the body of let-type must be an expression, not a type. Nor can we use def-type to define t-tree globally, because it refers to the type t, which is declared locally by forall and pabs within make-node.

FLEX/SPD addresses this problem by generalizing types to more expressive phrases called **descriptions**. FLEX/SPD's description-naming construct, dlet, is similar to FLEX's let and let-type (renamed here to plet[7]) except that it names a description within another description.

Let Keyword	Binding Definitions	Body
let	expressions	expression
plet	descriptions	expression
dlet	descriptions	description

Using dlet, we can simplify the type of make-node to:

```
(forall (t)
  (dlet ((t-tree (drec tr {drec is FLEX/SPD's generalization of trec}
                  (oneof (leaf t) (node (prodof tr tr)))))))
    (-> (t-tree t-tree) t-tree)))
```

---

[7]In FLEX/SPD, let-type is renamed plet to emphasize the correspondences between let/abs, plet/pabs, and dlet/dabs.

```
(def-desc treeof {def-desc is FLEX/SPD's generalization of def-type}
  (dabs (leaf-type)
    (drec tr {drec is FLEX/SPD's generalization of trec}
      (oneof (leaf leaf-type) (node (prodof tr tr))))))

(def make-node (forall (t) (-> ((treeof t) (treeof t)) (treeof t)))
  (pabs (t)
    (abs ((l (treeof t)) (r (treeof t)))
      (one (treeof t) node (prod l r)))))
```

Figure 12.17   Version of `make-node` written in FLEX/SPD, which permits the definition of a `treeof` type constructor.

FLEX/SPD has a description abstraction construct, `dabs`, analogous to `abs` and `pabs`.

Abstraction Keyword	Operands	Body
abs	expressions	expression
pabs	descriptions	expression
dabs	descriptions	description

Using `dabs` it is possible to simplify the definition of `make-node` even more (Figure 12.17) by defining a global `treeof` type abstraction that maps a given leaf type `leaf-type` to a type of binary trees whose leaves have this type. An abstraction like `treeof` that maps types to types is called a **type constructor** or a **type operator**. `abs` and `pabs` are not adequate for defining type constructors: `abs` creates procedures that map values to values, and `pabs` creates polymorphic abstractions that map types to values, but a type constructor maps types to types.

The key syntactic changes needed to extend FLEX/SP to FLEX/SPD are summarized in Figure 12.18. FLEX/SPD replaces the notion of type with a more general notion of description. FLEX/SPD descriptions include[8]

- types, such as base types (`unit`, `int`, `bool`, and `symb`), arrow types (`->`), `recordof` types, `prodof` types, `oneof` types, and `forall` types;

- base type constructors (`cellof` and `seqof`);[9]

---

[8]Descriptions can be extended to include other information as well, such as **effects**, which describe the allocation, reading, or writing of mutable data structures (see Chapter 16).

[9]Types of the form (`cellof` T) and (`seqof` T) can now be expressed as description applications using a base type constructor. Intuitively, `->`, `oneof`, `recordof`, and `prodof` can also be viewed as base type constructors. However, although `prodof` types can be expressed using

---

New Kernel Syntax

$P \in \text{Prog} ::= (\texttt{flexk/SPD} \; ((I_{formal} \; D_{formalDesc})^*) \; E_{body})$

$E \in \text{Exp} ::= \; \dots \; \text{FLEX/SP } expressions \text{ with } T \text{ replaced by } D \; \dots$

$D \in \text{Desc} ::= \; \dots \; \text{FLEX/SP } types \; (excluding \; \texttt{cellof}, \texttt{listof}, \texttt{pairof},$
$\qquad\qquad\qquad \texttt{seqof}, \texttt{trec}, and \; \texttt{tletrec}) \; with \; \tau \; replaced \; by \; \delta$
$\qquad\qquad\qquad and \; T \; replaced \; by \; D \; \dots$
$\qquad\qquad | \; BTCR \; | \; (\texttt{dabs} \; (\delta^*_{formal}) \; D_{body})$
$\qquad\qquad | \; (D_{rator} \; D^*_{rand}) \; | \; (\texttt{dletrec} \; ((\delta_{name} \; D_{defn})^*) \; D_{body})$

$PD \in \text{ProgDesc} ::= (\texttt{=>} \; (D^*_{arg}) \; D_{result})$

$BTCR \in \text{BaseTypeConstructor} = \{\texttt{cellof}, \texttt{seqof}\}$

$DK \in \text{DescKeyword} = \text{BaseType} \cup \text{BaseTypeConstructor}$
$\qquad\qquad\qquad\qquad\qquad \cup \; \{\texttt{->}, \texttt{dabs}, \texttt{dletrec}, \texttt{forall}$
$\qquad\qquad\qquad\qquad\qquad\quad \texttt{oneof}, \texttt{prodof}, \texttt{recordof}\}; \; kernel \; keywords$
$\qquad\qquad\qquad\qquad\qquad \cup \; \{\texttt{dlet}, \texttt{drec}, \texttt{plet}, \texttt{pletrec}\} \; ; \; sugar \; keywords$

$\delta \in \text{DescId} = \text{SymLit} - \text{DescKeyword}$

New Syntactic Sugar

$(\texttt{dlet} \; ((\delta_i \; D_i)_{i=1}^{n}) \; D_{body}) \rightsquigarrow_{ds} [D_i/\delta_i]_{i=1}^{n} D_{body}$

$(\texttt{drec} \; \delta_{name} \; D_{body}) \rightsquigarrow_{ds} (\texttt{dletrec} \; ((\delta_{name} \; D_{body})) \; \delta_{name})$

$(\texttt{plet} \; ((\delta_i \; D_i)_{i=1}^{n}) \; E_{body}) \rightsquigarrow_{ds} [D_i/\delta_i]_{i=1}^{n} E_{body}$

$(\texttt{pletrec} \; ((\delta_i \; D_i)_{i=1}^{n}) \; E_{body}) \rightsquigarrow_{ds} [(\texttt{dletrec} \; ((\delta_j \; D_j)_{j=1}^{n}) \; \delta_i)/\delta_i]_{i=1}^{n} E_{body}$

Figure 12.18 Syntactic changes for adding descriptions to FLEX/SP to yield
FLEX/SPD.

- description abstractions (`dabs` (δ^*) D) that specify type constructors and other description operators that take descriptions as arguments and return descriptions as results;

- description applications (D_{rator} D^*_{rand}), used for applying type constructors and other description operators, as in (`(dabs (t) (prodof t t)) int`) and (`seqof int`);

- a description recursion construct, (`dletrec` $((\delta \; D)^*)$ D_{body}), and its associated sugar form (`drec` δ D), which are the description analogues of `tletrec` and `trec` types;

---

description applications, `->`, `oneof`, and `recordof` types cannot because of their special syntax. Moreover, even if we modified the syntax, we would not be able to assign kinds to `->`, `oneof`, `recordof`, and `prodof` in the kind system presented in Section 12.3.2, so we choose to treat them specially in FLEX/SPD.

```
(flex/SPD ((I_fml_i  D_fml_i)^h_{i=1}) E_body
   (def-desc δ_dd_j  D_dd_j)^m_{j=1} (def I_d_k  D_d_k  E_d_k)^n_{k=1})
     {Assume procedure defs are desugared to (def I D E)}
⤳_ds
   (flexk/SPD ((I_fml_i  D_fml_i)^h_{i=1})
     (pletrec ((pairof (dabs (s t) (prodof s t)))
               (listof (dabs (t)
                          (drec listof-t
                            (oneof (null unit)
                               (cons (prodof t listof-t)))))))
        (let {Standard library bindings for values}
           ((null (pabs (t) (abs () (one (listof t) null #u))))
            (cons (pabs (t) (abs ((x t) (xs (listof t)))
                               (one (listof t) cons (prod x xs)))))
            (null? (pabs (t) (abs ((xs (listof t)))
                                 (tagcase xs _ (null #t) (cons #f)))))
            (car (pabs (t) (abs ((xs (listof t)))
                               (tagcase xs p (null (error car-of-nil t))
                                  (cons (get 1 p)))))))
           ⋮ {cdr, pair operations, and other standard bindings go here}
        )
        (pletrec ((δ_dd_j  D_dd_j)^m_{j=1}) {Description definitions from program}
           (letrec (((I_d_k  D_d_k  E_d_k)^n_{k=1}) {Value definitions from program}
              E_body)))))
```

Figure 12.19 Desugaring rule for FLEX/SPD programs.

- a description-binding sugar construct (dlet ((δ D)*) D_{body}) that allows the naming of descriptions within other descriptions;

- description identifiers (δ ∈ Desc), the generalization of type identifiers, which are introduced via pabs, plet, pletrec, forall, dabs, dlet, dletrec, and drec.

Since descriptions include types, the description domain variable D is used everywhere in the FLEX/SPD grammar that the type domain variable T is used in the FLEX grammar.

The FLEX/SPD plet expression supersedes FLEX's let-type expression and the pletrec expression supports the definition of locally recursive descriptions. These are similar to dlet and dletrec except that they return values rather than descriptions, allowing the naming of descriptions within expressions. For example,

```
{dlet returns a description}
(dlet ((pairof (dabs (s t) (prodof s t))))
  (pairof int (pairof bool symb)))

{plet returns a value}
(plet ((pairof (dabs (s t) (prodof s t))))
  (the (pairof int (pairof bool symb))
       (prod 3 (prod #f (sym Abby)))))
```

The scope of `plet/dlet`-bound identifiers is only the body of the `plet/dlet`,
while the scope of `pletrec/dletrec`-bound identifiers includes all definitions as
well as the body.

Pair and list types and operations are not included in the kernel grammar of
FLEX/SPD because they can be defined in the standard library specified in the
desugaring of programs (Figure 12.19). This desugaring allows the definition of
top-level descriptions (via `def-desc`) and values (via `def`). `def-desc` can name
any description, including types, as in `(def-desc intlist (listof int))`, and
type constructors, as in `(def-desc twiceof (dabs (t) (prodof t t)))`.

Because the arguments and results of description operators may include arbitrary descriptions, it is possible to have higher-order description operators. As
an example where this power can be put to use, suppose we are defining mapping
procedures for several different homogeneous aggregate data structures, such as
lists and sequences. The types of the procedures `list-map` and `seq-map` would be:

```
list-map : (forall (in-type out-type)
              (-> ((-> (in-type) out-type) (listof in-type))
                  (listof out-type)))

 seq-map : (forall (in-type out-type)
              (-> ((-> (in-type) out-type) (seqof in-type))
                  (seqof out-type)))
```

Clearly there is a common pattern in the types of the two mapping procedures.
We can capture this pattern by creating a higher-order description operator
`mapperof`:

```
(def-desc mapperof
  (dabs (type-constructor)
    (forall (in-type out-type)
      (-> ((-> (in-type) out-type) (type-constructor in-type))
          (type-constructor out-type)))))
```

Then the types of `list-map` and `seq-map` can be written more succinctly as

```
list-map : (mapperof listof)
 seq-map : (mapperof seqof)
```

Type Rules

For each type rule in FLEX/SP, FLEX/SPD has a corresponding type rule that replaces all occurrences of T by D and replaces the notion of type equivalence by description equivalence.

Description-Equivalence Rules

$$\frac{([\delta_i'/\delta_i]_{i=1}^n)D \approx D'}{(\text{dabs } (\delta_{i=1}^n) \ D) \approx (\text{dabs } (\delta_{i=1}'^n) \ D')} \qquad [\textit{dabs-}\alpha\textit{-}\approx]$$
$$\text{where} \quad \forall_{i=1}^n . (\delta_i' \notin \textit{FrDescIds}_{desc}[\![D]\!])$$

$$((\text{dabs } (\delta_{i=1}^n) \ D_{body}) \ D_{i=1}^n) \approx ([D_i/\delta_i]_{i=1}^n)D_{body} \qquad [\textit{dabs-}\beta\textit{-}\approx]$$

$$(\text{dabs } (\delta_{i=1}^n) \ (D \ \delta_{i=1}^n)) \approx D \ , \text{where} \ \forall_{i=1}^n . (\delta_i \notin \textit{FrDescIds}_{desc}[\![D]\!]) \quad [\textit{dabs-}\eta\textit{-}\approx]$$

$$\frac{\forall_{i=0}^n . (D_i \approx D_i')}{(D_0 \ D_{i=1}^n) \approx (D_0' \ D'^n_{i=1})} \qquad [\textit{dapply-}\approx]$$

For each type-equivalence rule in FLEX/SP, FLEX/SPD has a corresponding description-equivalence rule that replaces all occurrences of T by D.

Figure 12.20   Static semantics of FLEX/SPD.

Intuitively, constructs in the description domain (`dabs`, description-operator application, `dlet`, and `dletrec`) have a close correspondence with value-domain constructs (`abs`, procedure application, `let`, and `letrec`). But how do we formally describe the meanings of the new descriptions that we have introduced?

Modulo replacing T by D, the type rules for FLEX/SPD are the same as those for FLEX/SP. What distinguishes FLEX/SPD from FLEX/SP is a notion of **description equivalence** that generalizes the notion of type equivalence and defines when two descriptions are considered to be the same. FLEX/SPD inherits all the type-equivalence rules of FLEX/SP (with T replaced by D) but also includes the new description-equivalence rules in Figure 12.20. Some of these rules use the function $\textit{FrDescIds}_{desc}$ to determine the free description identifiers in a description. $\textit{FrDescIds}_{desc}$ is a straightforward generalization of the $\textit{FrTyIds}_{ty}$ function defined in Figure 11.3 on page 638, so we leave its definition as an exercise (Exercise 12.22).

The $[\textit{dabs-}\alpha\textit{-}\approx]$, $[\textit{dabs-}\beta\textit{-}\approx]$, and $[\textit{dabs-}\eta\textit{-}\approx]$ rules correspond to the alpha, beta, and eta reduction rules of the lambda calculus, respectively. For example:

$$(\text{dabs (t) t}) \approx (\text{dabs (s) s}) \qquad \qquad (\text{via } [\textit{dabs-}\alpha\textit{-}\approx])$$

$$((\text{dabs (s t) (prodof s t)) int bool}) \approx (\text{prodof int bool}) \quad (\text{via } [\textit{dabs-}\beta\textit{-}\approx])$$

$$(\text{dabs (s t) (pairof s t)}) \approx \text{pairof} \qquad \qquad (\text{via } [\textit{dabs-}\eta\textit{-}\approx])$$

[*dapply-≈*] is a structural rule that permits description equivalence on the operator and operand positions of a description application.

We assume that equivalence of recursive descriptions involving `dletrec` is defined in an equirecursive fashion using a generalization of the rules for `trec` in Figure 11.28 on page 692.

There is an interesting design choice in the definitions of `dlet` and `plet`. These constructs are defined by desugarings that substitute away the bound description identifiers. But just as `let` can be desugared into an application of an abstraction, we might have defined `plet` by the desugaring

$$(\texttt{plet } ((\delta_i \ D_i)_{i=1}^{n}) \ E_{body}) \rightsquigarrow_{ds} ((\texttt{pabs } (\delta_{i=1}^{n}) \ E_{body}) \ D_{i=1}^{n})$$

and used a similar desugaring for `dlet`. In this alternative desugaring, the type bindings for `plet`/`dlet`-bound names are **opaque**, i.e., the names are *not* equivalent to their definitions. In particular, two description identifiers that have the same definition are not considered equivalent. In contrast, the substitution-based desugarings used in FLEX/SPD give rise to **transparent** type bindings in which description names *are* equivalent to their definitions. The difference between these approaches is illustrated by the expression

```
(plet ((s int) (t int))
  (abs ((b bool) (x s) (y t))
    (if b x y)))
```

which is well typed with transparent bindings (because both `if` branches have the type `int`) but ill typed with opaque bindings (because the types `s` and `t` of the `if` branches are not equivalent). Although we do not choose to use opaque types here, we do use them in Chapter 15 to implement abstract types in a module system.

Our system of descriptions, while adding considerable power to FLEX/SPD, has two big problems:

- It is possible to write meaningless descriptions in programs. Not all descriptions actually represent types of values. There is no value of type `cellof` or `(dabs (t) t)`, for instance. Yet there is nothing to prevent one from writing

  ```
  (abs ((x cellof) (y (dabs (t) t))) (prod x y))
  ```

One can also write description applications that have no meaning, such as `(int bool)`. In fact, the type rules for FLEX/SPD are problematic because an assignment $I : D$ in a type environment makes sense only if D is a type. Since one can never construct or use values of these meaningless types, it is "safe" nonsense, but it is disturbing nonetheless.

- Description equivalence is not decidable. We have embedded a general, untyped notion of abstraction and application (the untyped lambda calculus, a universal programming language) in the description domain. Since equality in a universal programming language is necessarily undecidable, there is no effective procedure to decide description equivalence using the rules in Figure 12.20. The fact that we can write pathological descriptions such as the looping description ((dabs (d) (d d)) (dabs (d) (d d))) or the Y operator underscores this problem and suggests that type checking may not terminate.

We will address these issues in the next section.

Exercise 12.22 Define the following functions for FLEX/SPD. The first three functions are generalizations of the free-identifier functions defined in Figure 11.3 on page 638. The last three functions are generalizations of the substitution functions defined in Figures 11.4 and 11.5 on pages 639 and 641.

a. $FrIds : \text{Exp} \rightarrow \mathcal{P}(\text{Ident})$
   $FrIds[\![E]\!]$ returns the set of free value identifiers in E.

b. $FrDescIds_{desc} : \text{Desc} \rightarrow \mathcal{P}(\text{DescId})$
   $FrDescIds_{desc}[\![D]\!]$ returns the set of free description identifiers in D.

c. $FrDescIds_{exp} : \text{Exp} \rightarrow \mathcal{P}(\text{DescId})$
   $FrDescIds_{exp}[\![E]\!]$ returns the set of free description identifiers in E.

d. $subst : \text{Exp} \rightarrow \text{Ident} \rightarrow \text{Exp} \rightarrow \text{Exp}$
   $(subst\ E_1\ I\ E_2)$, abbreviated $[E_1/I]E_2$, returns the expression that results from substituting E_1 for every free occurrence of I in E_2.

e. $substDesc_{desc} : \text{Desc} \rightarrow \text{DescId} \rightarrow \text{Desc} \rightarrow \text{Desc}$
   $(substDesc_{desc}\ D_1\ \delta\ D_2)$, abbreviated $[D_1/\delta]D_2$, returns the description that results from substituting D_1 for every free occurrence of δ in D_2.

f. $substDesc_{exp} : \text{Desc} \rightarrow \text{DescId} \rightarrow \text{Exp} \rightarrow \text{Exp}$
   $(substDesc_{desc}\ D\ \delta\ E)$, abbreviated $[D/\delta]E$, returns the expression that results from substituting D for every free occurrence of δ in E.

12.3.2   Kinds and Kind Checking: FLEX/SPDK

We would like to ensure that descriptions make sense, both intrinsically and in context (e.g., that one cannot apply int to bool, and that descriptions associated with actual program values must be types). Moreover, we want to guarantee that type checking in the presence of descriptions is still static — i.e., is guaranteed to terminate and can be performed before the program is executed.

$K \in \text{Kind} ::= \texttt{type} \mid (\texttt{->>}\ (K^*_{arg})\ K_{result})$

$E \in \text{Exp} ::= \ldots \textit{all FLEX/SPD expressions except }\texttt{pabs}\ \ldots$
$\phantom{E \in \text{Exp} ::=}\mid (\texttt{pabs}\ ((\delta\ K)^*)\ E)$

$D \in \text{Desc} ::= \ldots \textit{all FLEX/SPD descriptions except }\texttt{forall}\textit{ and }\texttt{dabs}\ \ldots$
$\phantom{D \in \text{Desc} ::=}\mid (\texttt{forall}\ ((\delta\ K)^*)\ D) \mid (\texttt{dabs}\ ((\delta\ K)^*)\ D)$

Figure 12.21 Grammar modifications to extend FLEX/SPD to FLEX/SPDK.

The first problem is a lot like the one we already solved for expressions by using types. Showing that (`int bool`) is not a meaningful description is similar to showing that (`1 2`) is not a meaningful expression. We'd like to have something akin to types for descriptions. These are called **kinds**; kinds are the types of descriptions.

The second problem is that the structure of descriptions is so general that they are powerful enough to express any computation. This means that they cannot always be normalized and there is no effective procedure for deciding the equivalence of descriptions. However, just as a simple type system is able to carve out a strongly normalizing subset of FL (see Section 11.7), a kind system can be used to carve out a restricted subset of descriptions on which equivalence is decidable.

We incorporate the notion of kinds into an extension of FLEX/SPD named FLEX/SPDK. Figure 12.21 shows the necessary changes to the grammar. The domain variable K ranges over kind expressions, which are now required to annotate all description identifiers declared in `pabs`, `forall`, and `dabs`.[10] The simplest kind is the base kind `type`. Intuitively, all well-formed FLEX types (suitably modified to be legal FLEX/SPDK descriptions) have kind `type`. For example, the following descriptions all have kind `type`:

```
int
(-> (int) bool)
(recordof (name symb) (age int))
(drec intlist (oneof (inull unit)
                     (icons (prodof int intlist)))))
```

A description operator has an **arrow kind** (`->>` $(K_{arg_1}\ \ldots\ K_{arg_n})\ K_{result}$) that reflects the kinds of the operator's arguments (K_{arg_1}, ..., K_{arg_n}) and the kind of the operator's result (K_{result}). We use the double arrow `->>` in the kind of a description operator to distinguish it from the arrow `->` used in the type

---

[10] `dletrec` doesn't need kind annotations because, as we'll see below, its declared identifiers are required to be of kind `type`.

Base Kind Environment

$KE_{base} = \{$unit::type, int::type, bool::type, symb::type,

cellof::(->> (type) type), seqof::(->> (type) type)$\}$

Kind Rules

$$KE \vdash BT :: KE_{base}(BT) \qquad\qquad [\textit{base-type}]$$

$$KE \vdash BTCR :: KE_{base}(BTCR) \qquad\qquad [\textit{base-tycon}]$$

$$KE \vdash \delta :: KE(\delta) \quad \text{where } \delta \in dom(KE) \qquad\qquad [\textit{var}]$$

$$\frac{\forall_{i=0}^{n} \, . \, (KE \vdash D_i :: \texttt{type})}{KE \vdash (\texttt{->} \; (D_{i=1}^{n}) \; D_0) :: \texttt{type}} \qquad\qquad [\rightarrow]$$

The kind-checking rules for prodof, recordof, and oneof are similar to $[\rightarrow]$.

$$\frac{KE[\delta_i :: K_i]_{i=1}^{n} \vdash D_{body} :: \texttt{type}}{KE \vdash (\texttt{forall} \; ((\delta_i \; K_i)_{i=1}^{n}) \; D_{body}) :: \texttt{type}} \qquad\qquad [\textit{forall}]$$

$$\frac{KE[\delta_i :: K_i]_{i=1}^{n} \vdash D_{body} :: K_{body}}{KE \vdash (\texttt{dabs} \; ((\delta_i \; K_i)_{i=1}^{n}) \; D_{body}) :: (\texttt{->>} \; (K_{i=1}^{n}) \; K_{body})} \qquad\qquad [\texttt{->>}\textit{-intro}]$$

$$\frac{KE \vdash D_{rator} :: (\texttt{->>} \; (K_{i=1}^{n}) \; K_{result}) \quad \forall_{i=1}^{n} \, . \, (KE \vdash D_i :: K_i)}{KE \vdash (D_{rator} \; D_{i=1}^{n}) :: K_{result}} \qquad\qquad [\texttt{->>}\textit{-elim}]$$

$$\frac{\forall_{i=1}^{n} \, . \, (KE' \vdash D_i :: \texttt{type}) \quad KE' \vdash D_{body} :: K_{body}}{KE \vdash (\texttt{dletrec} \; ((\delta_i \; D_i)_{i=1}^{n}) \; D_{body}) :: K_{body}} \qquad\qquad [\textit{dletrec}]$$

$$\text{where } KE' \; = \; KE[\delta_i::\texttt{type}]_{i=1}^{n}$$

Figure 12.22   Kind-checking rules for FLEX/SPDK.

of a procedure. This notational difference is not strictly necessary but serves to emphasize the distinction between the two levels. For example, the cellof, seqof, and listof type constructors all have kind (->> (type) type), because they take a single type and return a type. The pairof type constructor has kind (->> (type type) type), because it takes two types and returns a type. The mapperof operator on page 755 has kind (->> ((->> (type) type)) type) because it takes a unary type constructor and returns a forall type.

In the literature, the kind type is often written $\bullet$ or $*$ and our prefix kind arrow ->> is often written as an infix $\Rightarrow$. In this notation, the mapperof kind is $(\bullet \Rightarrow \bullet) \Rightarrow \bullet$.

A description is **well kinded** if it can be assigned a kind according to the kind-checking rules in Figure 12.22. Kind checking is analogous to type checking. The **kind judgment** $KE \vdash D :: K$ means that the description D has kind K relative to a **kind environment** KE, which is a partial function from kind names to kinds:

$KN \in$ KindName $=$ DescId $\cup$ BaseType $\cup$ BaseTypeConstructor

$KE \in$ KindEnvironment $=$ KindName $\rightharpoonup$ Kind

In addition to description identifiers, kind names include base types and base type constructors so that the meanings of these can be modeled by the **base kind environment**, KE_{base}. The **kind assignment** notation $KN{::}K$, pronounced "KN has kind K," represents the association of a kind K with a kind name KN. As with type environments, we write kind environments as sets of kind assignments and use the notation $KE[\delta_1{::}K_1, \ldots, \delta_n{::}K_n]$, abbreviated $KE[\delta_i{::}K_i]_{i=1}^n$, to indicate the kind environment that results from extending KE with the given kind assignments. Since base types and base type constructors appear as kind names only in the base kind environment, each kind name in the kind-environment extension notation is guaranteed to be a description identifier δ.

The kind-checking rules in Figure 12.22 prohibit nonsensical descriptions like (int bool) and guarantee that descriptions like cellof, (dabs (t type) t), and mapperof are always used as description operators and never as types. Furthermore, the rules are carefully formulated to ensure that description equivalence is decidable. The subset of the description language excluding dletrec is analogous to the simply typed lambda calculus and the simply typed μFLEX language without letrec (Section 11.7) — languages in which evaluation and simplification are strongly normalizing. All descriptions in this subset have a normal form that can be computed by the kind checker before equivalence is tested. The kind-checking rules prohibit using dabs and description application to write a description-level Y operator or looping descriptions like

$$((\text{dabs } ((\text{d } K)) \ (\text{d d})) \ (\text{dabs } ((\text{d } K)) \ (\text{d d}))).$$

To write these descriptions in an explicitly kinded system, we would need recursion at the kind level (see Exercise 12.24).

Recursive descriptions (expressed using dletrec) do not undermine the decidability of description equivalence. To see this, note that all descriptions named in a dletrec are required to have kind type. This prevents using them to define a recursive description operator like a looping operator or the Y operator. Once all descriptions in the strongly normalizing subset of the description language have been reduced to normal form, dletrec descriptions denote regular trees similar to those described in Section 11.8.6. Equivalence of regular trees is decidable for both isorecursive and equirecursive interpretations of recursive types.

The kind restrictions in dletrec constrain the way in which it can be used to define type constructors and other higher-order descriptions. For example, the listof type constructor *cannot* be defined as

```
(dletrec ((listof (dabs (t type)
                  (oneof (null unit)
                         (cons (prodof t (listof t)))))))
   listof)
```

because the `dletrec`-bound identifier `listof` has kind `(->> (type) type)` and not the required kind `type`. However, in this case, the `dletrec` and `dabs` constructs can be reordered to yield a well-kinded description:

$$D_{listof} = \texttt{(dabs (t type)}$$
```
             (dletrec ((listof-t (oneof (null unit)
                                        (cons (prodof t listof-t)))))
          listof-t))
```

The effect of kind restrictions on general parameterized sum-of-products datatype definitions is explored in Exercise 12.25.

How do kinds and kind checking interact with types and type checking? First, all programmer-supplied descriptions in an expression must be well kinded. Second, in some contexts, descriptions are required to be of a particular kind, typically **type**. For example, the descriptions annotating the formal parameters of an **abs** expression must be of kind **type**. We express these relationships in the type-checking rules for FLEX/SPDK (Figure 12.23) by including constraints on kinds in rule premises. The **type/kind judgment** $TE, KE \vdash E : D$ means that E has type D (that is, E has a description D whose kind is **type**) relative to the type environment TE and the kind environment KE. The rules in Figure 12.23 suggest that the type-checking and kind-checking processes can be interleaved into a single process that uses both a type environment and a kind environment. It is also possible to perform kind checking as a separate phase that precedes type checking.

The [$\rightarrow$-*intro*] and [*letrec*] rules in Figure 12.23 also extend the type environment with some bindings. Kind checking is used in these situations to guarantee that the extensions bind identifiers to types and not to arbitrary descriptions. That is, the notation $TE[I_i : D_i]_{i=1}^n$ makes sense only when all of the D_i have kind **type**.

In the FLEX/SPDK type-checking rules, if all descriptions in the image of TE have kind **type** with respect to KE, then $TE, KE \vdash E : D$ implies that $KE \vdash D :: \texttt{type}$. This property is easy to show by induction on the structure of a type derivation (see Exercise 12.23). It explains why the first four type rules do not need to kind-check D_{body}, D_0, or D, although the [*error*] and [*oneof-intro*] type rules need an explicit premise requiring the resulting description in the conclusion to be of kind **type**. It also explains why the [*desc-inclusion*] rule kind-checks D but does not need to kind-check D'.

$$\frac{\forall_{i=1}^{n} . (KE \vdash D_i :: \texttt{type}) \quad TE[I_i : D_i]_{i=1}^{n}, KE \vdash E_{body} : D_{body}}{TE, KE \vdash (\texttt{abs } ((I_i \ D_i)_{i=1}^{n}) \ E_{body}) : (\texttt{-> } (D_{i=1}^{n}) \ D_{body})} \quad [\rightarrow\text{-intro}]$$

$$\frac{\forall_{i=1}^{n} . (KE \vdash D_i :: \texttt{type}) \quad \forall_{i=0}^{n} . (TE[I_i : D_i]_{i=1}^{n}, KE \vdash E_i : D_i)}{TE, KE \vdash (\texttt{letrec } ((I_i \ D_i \ E_i)_{i=1}^{n}) \ E_0) : D_0} \quad [letrec]$$

$$\frac{TE, KE[\delta_i :: K_i]_{i=1}^{n} \vdash E : D}{TE, KE \vdash (\texttt{pabs } ((\delta_i \ K_i)_{i=1}^{n}) \ E) : (\texttt{forall } ((\delta_i \ K_i)_{i=1}^{n}) \ D)} \quad [\forall\text{-intro}]$$

where $\forall_{i=1}^{n} . \ \delta_i \notin \cup_{I \in FrIds[\![E]\!]} (FrDescIds_{desc}[\![TE(I)]\!])$ *[import restriction]*
  E is pure   *[purity restriction]*

$$\frac{TE, KE \vdash E : (\texttt{forall } ((\delta_i \ K_i)_{i=1}^{n}) \ D_{body}) \quad \forall_{i=1}^{n} . (KE \vdash D_i :: K_i)}{TE, KE \vdash (\texttt{pcall } E \ D_{i=1}^{n}) : ([D_i/\delta_i]_{i=1}^{n}) \ D_{body}} \quad [\forall\text{-elim}]$$

$$\frac{KE \vdash D_{oneof} :: \texttt{type} \quad TE, KE \vdash E_{payload} : D_{payload}}{TE \vdash (\texttt{one } D_{oneof} \ I_{tag} \ E_{payload}) : D_{oneof}} \quad [oneof\text{-intro}]$$

where $D_{oneof} = (\texttt{oneof } \ldots (I_{tag} \ D_{payload}) \ldots)$

$$\frac{KE \vdash D :: \texttt{type}}{TE, KE \vdash (\texttt{error } Y_{msg} \ D) : D} \quad [error]$$

$$\frac{TE, KE \vdash E : D' \quad KE \vdash D :: \texttt{type} \quad D' \sqsubseteq D}{TE, KE \vdash E : D} \quad [desc\text{-inclusion}]$$

All other type rules are inherited from FLEX, replacing each judgment of the form $TE \vdash E : T$ by one of the form $TE, KE \vdash E : D$.

Figure 12.23 Type rules for FLEX/SPDK.

The *[desc-inclusion]* rule uses the notation $D' \sqsubseteq D$, which we have not defined yet. Since both D' and D must have kind type, the notation $D' \sqsubseteq D$ can denote the subtyping relation for FLEX/SP (as defined in Figure 12.2 on page 703, Figure 12.4 on page 707, and Figure 12.9 on page 731) modulo the following changes:

- In the *[equiv-⊑]* rule from Figure 12.2 on page 703, $\approx$ denotes description equivalence as defined in Figure 12.20 on page 756 (where the dabs rules and the inherited *[∀-≈]* rule need to include kind annotations on bound description identifiers and check that corresponding kinds are the same);

- The *[∀-⊑]* rule from Figure 12.9 on page 731 must be extended to include kind annotations on bound description identifiers and check that corresponding kinds are the same;

- The rules for equirecursive subtyping in Figure 12.4 on page 707 must be generalized to handle dletrec.

Type System	Typed Calculus	Our Typed Language
System F_1	simply typed lambda calculus	FLEX (no explicit kinds, but all kinds implicitly in the domain $K^1 \in \mathrm{Kind}_1 ::= \texttt{type}$)
System F_2 (a.k.a. System F)	polymorphic (second-order) lambda calculus	FLEX/SP (no explicit kinds, but all kinds implicitly in the domain $K^2 \in \mathrm{Kind}_2 ::= \texttt{type}$)
System F_3	third-order lambda calculus	FLEX/SPDK with kinds in the domain $K^3 \in \mathrm{Kind}_3 ::= K^2 \mid (\texttt{->>}\ (K^{2*})\ K^3)$
$\vdots$	$\vdots$	$\vdots$
System F_i	ith-order lambda calculus	FLEX/SPDK with kinds in the domain $K^i \in \mathrm{Kind}_i ::= K^{i-1} \mid (\texttt{->>}\ (K^{i-1*})\ K^i)$
$\vdots$	$\vdots$	$\vdots$
System F_ω	higher-order polymorphic lambda calculus	FLEX/SPDK

Figure 12.24   Some typed lambda calculi and their relationship to languages we have studied.

12.3.3   Discussion

In the literature, typed versions of the lambda calculus are classified according to the structure of their kind system. Figure 12.24 presents a table of the traditional names for these languages and their correspondence to the languages we have studied. In each row of the table, the language we studied provides more features than the typed lambda calculus (e.g., recursion, side effects, data structures, recursive types, subtyping), but the typed lambda calculus is a proper subset of the language we studied. The **simply typed lambda calculus** is the lambda-calculus subset of FLEX, in which abstraction parameters are annotated with types. The **polymorphic lambda calculus** (also known as the second-order lambda calculus, System F, and System F_2) is the subset of FLEX/SP that extends the simply typed lambda calculus with polymorphic values (i.e., type abstraction over expressions), type projection, and polymorphic ($\forall$) types. There are no explicit kinds in this language; all kinds are implicitly in the trivial domain $K^2 \in \mathrm{Kind}_2 ::= \texttt{type}$. For $i \geq 3$, System F_i is the subset of FLEX/SPDK that extends the polymorphic lambda calculus with explicit kind annotations from the restricted kind domain $K^i \in \mathrm{Kind}_i$ (in which the arguments in arrow kinds must have kinds from System F_{i-1}). The **higher-order polymorphic**

lambda calculus (also known as **System** F_ω) is the lambda calculus subset of FLEX/SPDK without any kind restrictions.

If you're wondering whether it's possible for kinds themselves to have something similar to types or kinds, the answer is yes. We will use the term **sort** to refer to the "type" of a kind. All kind expressions we have examined have the base sort `kind`. But it is possible to consider operators on kinds that would have more interesting sorts. Similarly, we could construct a "typing" system for sorts that distinguishes base sorts from operators on sorts. This process can be repeated ad infinitum (and ad nauseam!), giving rise to an infinite "tower" of typing systems. However, only the lowest levels of the tower — types and kinds — are useful in most practical situations.

Earlier, we observed that FLEX/SPD has three kinds of abstractions: `abs` maps values to values, `pabs` maps descriptions to values, and `dabs` maps description to descriptions. There is a fourth kind of abstraction missing: one that takes values as arguments and returns descriptions. Such constructs are **dependent descriptions** — descriptions that contain value expressions.[11] The array-type constructor in PASCAL is a simple example of a dependent description; every array type has an integer that indicates the length of the array. Of course, in order to ensure static type checking, the argument values to such an abstraction would have to be statically determinable. We will investigate dependent descriptions in more detail in Section 14.5.

Some find four different constructs that are so similar disturbing. The need for the differing constructs arises from the fact that we have maintained a rigid distinction between descriptions and values. In the interest of notational (and perhaps conceptual) economy, some languages, such as PEBBLE, blur the distinction between descriptions and values; a single abstraction construct can do the job of `abs`, `pabs`, and `dabs` (and even the fourth kind of abstraction). Since types can be treated as values in these languages, type checking generally cannot be performed statically. Instead, it may have to be interleaved with the execution of the program; in such cases, type checking is effectively dynamic. In fact, in some languages with first-class types, type checking might never even terminate!

Exercise 12.23

a. Prove the following theorem by structural induction on the derivation of the type/kind judgment $TE, KE \vdash E : D$.

> **FLEX/SPDK Type/Kind Judgment Theorem**
> *If* $TE, KE \vdash E : D$ *and* $\forall (D' \in img(TE)) \,.\, (KE \vdash D' :: \texttt{type})$ *then*
> $KE \vdash D :: \texttt{type}$.

---

[11]**Dependent type** is the more common term in the literature.

b. The FLEX/SPDK type rule for **the** is:

$$\frac{TE, KE \vdash E : D}{TE, KE \vdash (\texttt{the } D \; E) : D} \qquad [the]$$

Based on part **a**, explain why it is not necesesary to kind-check D in the premise of the $[the]$ rule, even though D is an arbitrary user-supplied description.

c. Explain why the explicit kind checks are necessary in the premises of the $[oneof\text{-}intro]$ and $[desc\text{-}inclusion]$ type rules. What could go wrong if these checks were omitted?

Exercise 12.24

a. Show that there is no kind K in FLEX/SPDK that will make the following description well kinded:

```
((dabs ((d K)) (d d)) (dabs ((d K)) (d d)))
```

b. Suppose that the kind grammar for FLEX/SPDK is extended as follows:

$\kappa \in \mathrm{KindId} = \mathrm{SymLit} - \{\texttt{kind}\}$

$K \in \mathrm{Kind} ::= \ldots \; as \; in \; \mathrm{FLEX/SPDK} \; \ldots \mid \kappa \mid (\texttt{krec } \kappa \; K)$

Assume that **krec** is a kind-level recursion construct analogous to **rec** for expressions and **drec** for descriptions. Using the new kind constructs, write a kind K such that the description in part **a** is well kinded. Explicitly state any assumptions you need to make concerning (1) kind equivalence and (2) changes to the kind-checking rules.

Exercise 12.25

a. Extend FLEX/SPDK to have parameterized data-type declarations with the form

$$(\texttt{def-datatype } (\delta_{data} \; \delta_{j=1}^{h}) \; (I_{tag_i} \; D_{i,1} \; \ldots \; D_{i,k_i})_{i=1}^{n})$$

(Compare to **def-datatype** in Section 12.2.3.) This should introduce a type constructor named δ_{data} that takes h arguments of kind **type** and returns a recursive sum-of-products data type. For each tag I_{tag_i}, it should also introduce a polymorphic constructor procedure named I_{tag_i} with type

$$(\texttt{forall } (\delta_{j=1}^{h}) \; (\texttt{-> } (D_{i,1} \; \ldots \; D_{i,k_i}) \; (\delta_{data} \; \delta_{j=1}^{h})))$$

and a polymorphic deconstructor procedure named $I_{tag_i}\bowtie^{\sim}$ with type

$$
\begin{aligned}
&(\texttt{forall } (\delta_{return} \; \delta_{j=1}^{h}) \quad \{\delta_{return} \text{ is a fresh name for the return type.}\} \\
&\quad (\texttt{-> } ((\delta_{data} \; \delta_{j=1}^{h}) \qquad\qquad \{discriminant\ type\} \\
&\qquad\quad (\texttt{-> } (D_{i,1} \; \ldots \; D_{i,k_i}) \; \delta_{return}) \quad \{success\ continuation\ type\} \\
&\qquad\quad (\texttt{-> } () \; \delta_{return})) \qquad\qquad\quad \{failure\ continuation\ type\} \\
&\quad \delta_{return})
\end{aligned}
$$

For example, the **pairof** and **listof** type constructors can now be defined by the programmer as:

```
(def-datatype (pairof s t)
  (pair s t))

(def-datatype (listof t)
  (null)
  (cons t (listof t)))
```

The `listof` type constructor introduced by this definition should be the description D_{listof} on page 762.

As illustrated by D_{listof}, care must be taken to ensure that the type constructor δ_{data} is well kinded. In particular, `dletrec` cannot be used *outside* `dabs` to define a recursive type constructor; it must be used *inside* `dabs` to define a recursive sum-of-products type. To support this, we make the simplifying assumption that in the definition of δ_{data}, all uses of the type constructor δ_{data} within the clauses $(I_{tag_i}\ D_{i,1}\ \ldots\ D_{i,k_i})_{i=1}^{n}$ are description applications of the form $(\delta_{data}\ \delta_{j=1}^{h})$. E.g., in a data-type declaration `(def-datatype (mydataof s t) ...)`, all uses of `mydataof` in the declaration must have the form `(mydataof s t)`; uses like `(mydataof int t)`, `(mydataof t s)`, or `(mydataof s (mydataof s t))` are not permitted.

b. Parameterized data types like `pairof` and `listof` are more useful if data-type deconstruction can be performed via pattern matching. Exercise 12.20 on page 744 explores how this can be done for parameterless data types in FLEX/SP using two approaches. Generalize these two approaches to handle parameterized data types in FLEX/SPDK:

  i.   As in part **a** of Exercise 12.20: Extend the `match` construct with explicit type information that can be used for polymorphic projection in the desugaring of `match` into deconstructor applications.

  ii. As in part **b** of Exercise 12.20: For the purposes of type checking, treat `match` as a kernel construct with its own type rule, and then use the type information in the type derivation of `match` to guide a post-type-checking translation of `match` into deconstructor applications.

Notes

An early paper on the subtyping of recursive types, which uses an automata-based approach, is [KPS93]. For a tutorial on the theory and practice of subtyping on recursive types, see [GLP00] or [Pie02, Chapter 21]; these also present a more efficient subtyping algorithm for recursive types than the one presented here.

A nice example of balancing theory and practice in types is the design of HASKELL's extensible records [JP99].

The importance of separating inheritance from subtyping in object-oriented languages is argued in [CHC90, Ame91, Por92, Coo92]. The notion that inheritance compromises the benefits of data abstraction is presented in [Sny86].

The polymorphic lambda calculus (also known as System F) was invented by Girard ([Gir71]) and later independently reinvented by Reynolds [Rey74]. See [Hue90] for some papers on the polymorphic lambda calculus, including retrospectives by Reynolds [Rey90] and Girard [Gir90].

Cardelli [Car88b] recognized that record subtyping could model aspects of typed object-oriented languages. In [CW85], Cardelli and Wegner married subtyping with universal polymorphism to yield bounded quantification, which gave an even more powerful way to specify types in object-oriented languages. Their paper also serves as a good introduction to subtyping and universal and existential quantification in type systems. The standard type system with bounded quantification, known as system $F_{<:}$ (pronounced "F sub"), is described in [CMMS94]. An extension to bounded quantification known as *F-bounded polymorphism* was introduced in [CCH⁺89] to properly handle subtyping on the recursive types that are typically used to model objects.

The generics feature introduced in version 5.0 of JAVA is an example of bounded quantification in a real-world programming language [NW06]. This feature arose out of work in the language GJ [BOSW98], a key goal of which was to add a form of universal polymorphism to JAVA in a way that was backward-compatible with existing programs. Because JAVA is such a large, complex language, its semantics is often studied in the context of pared-down subsets. One such subset is FEATHERWEIGHT JAVA (FJ) [IPW01].

For more information about typing, subtyping, and polymorphism in object-oriented languages, we recommend starting with the following textbooks and collections: [GM94], [AC96], [Bru02], [Pie02], [Mit03, Chapters 10, 11, 12].

See [McC79] for an early description of a kinded type system. This idea was used as the basis for the language used in [Luc87] and [LG88]. These ideas were further developed into a system of types, kinds, and descriptions for FX87 [GJLS87] and FX91 [GJSO92], both of which supported implicit projection of polymorphic values.

Languages that eschew a kind system and instead allow `type` to have type `type` (i.e., in which `type : type`) include PEBBLE [BL84]. See [Car86] for an investigation into the meaning and utility of programs that rely on `type : type`.

Many people associate polymorphism with implicitly typed languages such as ML. Such languages do not have the full power of the polymorphic lambda calculus, but they relieve the programmer of the task of writing most or all types. We shall explore such languages in considerable detail in Chapter 13.

ML [MTHM97] introduced typed pattern matching and data definitions, which have been incorporated into its various implementations and successors as well as into other languages, such as HASKELL [HPW⁺92].

13

Type Reconstruction

The faculty of deduction is certainly contagious ...

— Sherlock Holmes in *The Problem of Thor Bridge*
by Sir Arthur Conan Doyle

13.1   Introduction

In the variants of FLEX that we've studied so far, it is necessary to specify
explicit type information in certain situations. All parameter names introduced
by an `abs` must be explicitly typed, for instance. Not all type information needs
to be explicitly specified, however. For example, the return type of a procedure
need not be declared.

The placement of explicit type annotations in FLEX is determined by the
top-down, evaluator-like structure of the type checker. Explicit types are used in
FLEX to avoid any guessing/backtracking in the type-checking process. Consider
the type checking of an `abs` expression. When entering an `abs` expression, the
type checker has no information about the types of the formal parameters, so
these must be provided explicitly. However, once the types of the formals are
known, it is easy for the type checker to determine the type of the body, so this
information need not be declared.

Could a more sophisticated type checker do its job with even less explicit
information? Certainly, programmers can reason proficiently about type information in many programs where there are no explicit types at all. Such reasoning
is important because understanding the type of an expression, especially one that
denotes a procedure, is often a major step in figuring out what purpose the expression serves in the program. As an example of this kind of type reasoning,
consider the following FL abstraction:

```
(abs (f g x y)
  (if (f x y) (prim + x 1) (g (f x (sym static)))))
```

By studying the various ways in which `f`, `g`, `x`, and `y` are used in the body of this
abstraction, we can piece together complete information about the types of these

names. For example, we know that the application (f x y) returns a boolean, because it is used as the predicate in an if expression. Thus, f is a procedure of two arguments that returns a boolean. The subexpression (prim + x 1), tells us that x is an integer. From the two calls (f x y) and (f x (sym static)), we know that the type of the first argument to f is an integer and the types of y and the second argument to f are symbols. So f must be a procedure that takes an integer and a symbol and returns a boolean. Since g is applied to the result of f, it must be a procedure that takes a single boolean argument. The fact that (prim + x 1) and (g (f x (sym static))) are branches of the same if implies that their return types must be the same. We deduce that the result type of g, the type of the if expression, and the return type of the abs expression must all be the same: an integer.

There is no reason that a program cannot carry out the same kinds of reasoning exhibited above. Automatically computing the type of an expression that does not contain type information is known as **type reconstruction** or **type inference**. Type reconstruction is more complicated than type checking because type reconstruction must operate properly without (or with only partial) programmer-supplied type information.

Type reconstruction formalizes the kind of reasoning seen in the example above. A type reconstruction algorithm is an automatic way of determining the type of an expression (and of all of its subexpressions). We can think of the various subexpressions in the above example as specifying constraints on the types of the expressions. It is possible to view these constraints as a set of simultaneous type equations that restrict the type of an expression. If these equations can be solved, then the expression is well typed; otherwise, it is ill typed.

Consider the abs expression discussed above. Let's introduce some type identifiers to stand for types that arise as we try to reconstruct types for the expression. We use a ? prefix on these identifiers to emphasize that they are the unknown variables in the type constraints. Assume:

- ?abs is the type of the abs expression;

- ?if is the type of the if expression;

- ?f is the type of f;

- ?g is the type of g;

- ?x is the type of x;

- ?y is the type of y;

- ?+res is the type of (prim + x 1);

- ?fres1 is the result type of the first call to f;

- ?fres2 is the result type of the second call to f; and

- ?gres is the result type of the call to g.

Then the type constraints (written using the notation $T_1 \doteq T_2$) that are implied by the expression are:

?f $\doteq$ (-> (?x ?y) ?fres1)	*Procedure type implied by first call to f*
?f $\doteq$ (-> (?x symb) ?fres2)	*Procedure type implied by second call to f*
?g $\doteq$ (-> (?fres2) ?gres)	*Procedure type implied by call to g*
?fres1 $\doteq$ bool	*Type of if test must be boolean*
?x $\doteq$ int	*Operand of addition must be an integer*
?+res $\doteq$ int	*Result of addition is an integer*
?+res $\doteq$?gres	*Branches of if must have the same type*
?if $\doteq$?+res	*Type of if is type of its first branch*
?abs $\doteq$ (-> (?f ?g ?x ?y) ?if)	*Procedure type is from arg types to body type*

A solution to the above type constraints yields the following bindings for the type identifiers:

$$
\begin{aligned}
?x &\mapsto \texttt{int} \\
?y &\mapsto \texttt{symb} \\
?fres1 &\mapsto \texttt{bool} \\
?f &\mapsto \texttt{(-> (int symb) bool)} \\
?fres2 &\mapsto \texttt{bool} \\
?+res &\mapsto \texttt{int} \\
?gres &\mapsto \texttt{int} \\
?g &\mapsto \texttt{(-> (bool) int)} \\
?if &\mapsto \texttt{int} \\
?abs &\mapsto \texttt{(-> ((-> (int symb) bool) (-> (bool) int) int symb) int)}
\end{aligned}
$$

A system of type equations need not always have such a neat solution, however. For example, the system associated with

```
(abs (f x)
  (if (f x) (f 3) (f (sym static)))))
```

has no solution since it is overconstrained: x (and the argument of f) must have type int and type symb, which is impossible. On the other hand, a system may be underconstrained, as in the following example:

```
(abs (h x y)
  (if (h x y) (h 3 y) (h x y)))
```

In this case, the type of y is unknown, and the type deduced for the expression will be something like

```
(-> ((-> (int ?y) bool) int ?y) bool)
```

The appearance of an unknown type identifier in a type suggests polymorphism; If we assume that h is polymorphic, then ?y can be instantiated to any type. In other notations we have seen, this type might be expressed as:

```
(forall (t) (-> ((-> (int t) bool) int t) bool))
```

or

$$\forall t \,.\, (((\texttt{int} \times t) \rightarrow \texttt{bool}) \times \texttt{int} \times t) \rightarrow \texttt{bool}$$

In Section 13.4, we will study an approach to type reconstruction that capitalizes on the polymorphism implied by underconstrained type identifiers.

13.2 μFLARE: A Language with Implicit Types

We will explore type reconstruction in the context of the language FLARE, so named because it combines FL **a**nd type **re**construction. We will first study a simple subset of FLARE named μFLARE, and then extend it to the full-featured FLARE language in Section 13.5.

13.2.1 μFLARE Syntax and Type Erasure

The syntax of μFLARE (Figure 13.1) is similar to that for FL, but its multiple-parameter abstractions, multiple-argument applications, and multiple-binding lets and letrecs are treated as kernel forms rather than as syntactic sugar. μFLARE can be viewed as a version of μFLEX in which all explicit type annotations have been erased. This view is formalized in Figure 13.2 by defining a **type erasure** transformation on μFLEX expressions (written $\lceil E \rceil$) and programs (written $\lceil P \rceil_{pgm}$) that yields μFLARE expressions and programs, respectively.

For example, reconsider the μFLEX program P_{pow} from page 652:

```
P_pow = (flexk ((n int))
          (let ((dbl (the (-> (int) int)
                          (abs ((x int)) (prim * x 2)))))
            (letrec ((loop (-> (int) int)
                        (abs ((i int))
                          (if (prim >= i n)
                              i
                              (loop (dbl i))))))
              (loop 1))))
```

Kernel Grammar

$P \in \text{Prog} ::= (\texttt{flarek} \ (I^*_{formal}) \ E_{body})$

$E \in \text{Exp} ::= L \mid I \mid (\texttt{error} \ Y_{message}) \mid (\texttt{if} \ E_{test} \ E_{then} \ E_{else})$
$\quad \mid (\texttt{prim} \ O_{primop} \ E^*_{arg}) \mid (\texttt{abs} \ (I^*_{formal}) \ E_{body}) \mid (E_{rator} \ E^*_{rand})$
$\quad \mid (\texttt{let} \ ((I_{name} \ E_{defn})^*) \ E_{body}) \mid (\texttt{letrec} \ ((I_{name} \ E_{defn})^*) \ E_{body})$

$L \in \text{Lit} ::= \texttt{\#u} \mid B \mid N \mid (\texttt{sym} \ Y) \ ; \ \textit{as in } \text{FL}.$

$B \in \text{BoolLit} = \{\texttt{\#t}, \texttt{\#f}\} \text{ as in } \text{FL}.$

$N \in \text{IntLit} = \text{as in } \text{FL}.$

$Y \in \text{SymLit} = \text{as in } \text{FL}.$

$O \in \text{Primop} = \text{as in } \mu\text{FLEX} \ — \ \text{i.e., usual FL primitives except}$
$\quad\quad\quad \text{no type predicates or pair operators}$

$\quad \text{Keyword} = \{\texttt{abs}, \texttt{error}, \texttt{flarek}, \texttt{if}, \texttt{let}, \texttt{letrec}, \texttt{prim}, \texttt{sym}\}$

$\quad \text{SugarKeyword} = \{\texttt{cond}, \texttt{def}, \texttt{flare}, \texttt{recur}, \texttt{scand}, \texttt{scor}\}$

$I \in \text{Ident} = \text{SymLit} - (\{Y \mid Y \text{ begins with } \texttt{@}\} \cup \text{Keyword} \cup \text{SugarKeyword})$

Syntactic Sugar

$\texttt{@}O$, $\texttt{cond}$, $\texttt{scand}$, $\texttt{scor}$, $\texttt{recur}$, and $\texttt{def}$ as in FL (page 233).

$(\texttt{flare} \ (I^*_{pgmFormal}) \ E_{pgmBody} \ (\texttt{def} \ I_{name_i} \ E_{defn_i})^n_{i=1})$
$\quad \{\textit{Assume procedure defs already desugared to} \ (\texttt{def} \ I \ E)$
$\quad \ \textit{by the} \ \texttt{def} \ \textit{desugaring rule inherited from} \ \text{FL}.\}$
$\leadsto_{ds} (\texttt{flarek} \ (I^*_{pgmFormal})$
$\quad\quad\quad (\texttt{letrec} \ \{\textit{Standard library bindings}\}$
$\quad\quad\quad\quad\quad\quad \{\textit{None of these bindings are recursive, but new ones might be.}\}$
$\quad\quad\quad\quad\quad\quad ((\texttt{not} \ (\texttt{abs} \ (\texttt{x}) \ (\texttt{prim} \ \texttt{not} \ \texttt{x})))$
$\quad\quad\quad\quad\quad\quad \ (\texttt{+} \ (\texttt{abs} \ (\texttt{x} \ \texttt{y}) \ (\texttt{prim} \ \texttt{+} \ \texttt{x} \ \texttt{y})))$
$\quad\quad\quad\quad\quad\quad\quad\quad \vdots \ \{\textit{Similar for other primitive operators.}\}$
$\quad\quad\quad\quad\quad\quad\quad (\texttt{true} \ \texttt{\#t}) \ (\texttt{false} \ \texttt{\#f}) \ \{\textit{Synonyms for literals.}\}$
$\quad\quad\quad\quad\quad\quad)$
$\quad\quad\quad\quad (\texttt{letrec} \ ((I_{name_i} \ E_{defn_i})^n_{i=1})$
$\quad\quad\quad\quad\quad E_{pgmBody})))$

Figure 13.1 Grammar and syntactic sugar for μFLARE.

The type erasure of P_{pow} is the following μFLARE program:

$$P'_{pow} = \lceil P_{pow} \rceil = (\texttt{flarek} \ (\texttt{n})$$

```
              (let ((dbl (abs (x) (prim * x 2))))
                  (letrec ((loop (abs (i)
                                     (if (prim >= i n)
                                         i
                                         (loop (dbl i)))))))
                      (loop 1))))
```

$typeErase_{pgm} : \text{Prog}_{\mu FLEX} \rightarrow \text{Prog}_{\mu FLARE}$

The notation $\lceil P \rceil_{pgm}$ abbreviates $(typeErase_{pgm}\ P)$.

$\lceil (\texttt{flexk}\ ((I_i\ T_i)_{i=1}^{n})\ E_{body}) \rceil_{pgm} = (\texttt{flarek}\ (I_{i=1}^{n})\ \lceil E_{body} \rceil)$

$typeErase_{exp} : \text{Exp}_{\mu FLEX} \rightarrow \text{Exp}_{\mu FLARE}$

The notation $\lceil E \rceil$ abbreviates $(typeErase_{exp}\ E)$.

$\lceil L \rceil = L \qquad \lceil I \rceil = I \qquad \lceil (\texttt{error}\ Y_{msg}\ T) \rceil = (\texttt{error}\ Y_{msg})$

$\lceil (\texttt{if}\ E_{test}\ E_{then}\ E_{else}) \rceil = (\texttt{if}\ \lceil E_{test} \rceil\ \lceil E_{then} \rceil\ \lceil E_{else} \rceil)$

$\lceil (\texttt{prim}\ O_{op}\ E_{i=1}^{n}) \rceil = (\texttt{prim}\ O_{op}\ \lceil E_i \rceil_{i=1}^{n})$

$\lceil (\texttt{abs}\ ((I_i\ T_i)_{i=1}^{n})\ E_{body}) \rceil = (\texttt{abs}\ (I_{i=1}^{n})\ \lceil E_{body} \rceil)$

$\lceil (E_{rator}\ E_{i=1}^{n}) \rceil = (\lceil E_{rator} \rceil\ \lceil E_i \rceil_{i=1}^{n})$

$\lceil (\texttt{let}\ ((I_i\ E_i)_{i=1}^{n})\ E_{body}) \rceil = (\texttt{let}\ ((I_i\ \lceil E_i \rceil)_{i=1}^{n})\ \lceil E_{body} \rceil)$

$\lceil (\texttt{letrec}\ ((I_i\ T_i\ E_i)_{i=1}^{n})\ E_{body}) \rceil = (\texttt{letrec}\ ((I_i\ \lceil E_i \rceil)_{i=1}^{n})\ \lceil E_{body} \rceil)$

$\lceil (\texttt{the}\ T\ E) \rceil = \lceil E \rceil$

Figure 13.2   Type-erasure function transforming μFLEX to μFLARE.

In addition, μFLARE supports many of the syntactic sugar constructs of FL. These are especially useful in the compiler source language we will study in Section 17.2.2 that is an extension to μFLARE.

13.2.2   Static Semantics of μFLARE

μFLARE is said to be an **implicitly typed language** because it has a type system even though the programmer does not have to write down any types explicitly. The type system for μFLARE is presented in Figure 13.3. Types and type environments are the same as in μFLEX. The μFLARE type rules are the same as the corresponding ones for μFLEX except that in the [error], [$\rightarrow$-intro], [letrec], and [prog] rules, the type system "guesses" certain types and checks that these guesses are correct. The type rules do not specify how to make such guesses. In Section 13.3, we will see how the type reconstruction algorithm generates a fresh type identifier whenever it needs to make a guess, and then determines the types designated by such identifiers by collecting and solving a collection of type constraints.

Observe that each of the type rules in Figure 13.3 can be obtained from the corresponding type rule for μFLEX (Figure 11.7 on page 644) by applying type erasure to each expression mentioned in the μFLEX rules. So we can naturally

Type Domains (as in μFLEX)

$T \in \text{Type} ::= BT \mid \tau \mid \text{(-> }(T^*)\ T_{result})$

$BT \in \text{BaseType} = \{\text{unit}, \text{int}, \text{bool}, \text{symb}\}$

$\tau \in \text{TypeId} = \text{SymLit} - (\text{BaseType} \cup \{\text{->}\})$

$PT \in \text{ProgType} ::= \text{(=> }(T_{arg}^*)\ T_{result})$

$TE \in \text{TypeEnvironment} = \text{Ident} \rightharpoonup \text{Type}$

Type Rules

$$TE \vdash \text{\#u} : \text{unit}\quad [\textit{unit}] \qquad TE \vdash N : \text{int}\quad [\textit{int}] \qquad TE \vdash B : \text{bool}\quad [\textit{bool}]$$

$$TE \vdash \text{(sym }Y) : \text{symb}\quad [\textit{symb}] \qquad TE \vdash \text{(error }Y) : T\quad [\textit{error}]$$

$$TE \vdash I : TE(I) \quad \text{where } I \in \text{dom}(TE) \hspace{3cm} [\textit{var}]$$

$$\frac{TE \vdash E_{test} : \text{bool} \quad TE \vdash E_{then} : T \quad TE \vdash E_{else} : T}{TE \vdash \text{(if }E_{test}\ E_{then}\ E_{else}) : T} \qquad [\textit{if}]$$

$$\frac{TE[I_i : T_i]_{i=1}^n \vdash E_{body} : T_{body}}{TE \vdash \text{(abs }(I_{i=1}^n)\ E_{body}) : \text{(-> }(T_{i=1}^n)\ T_{body})} \qquad [\rightarrow\text{-intro}]$$

$$\frac{TE \vdash E_{rator} : \text{(-> }(T_{i=1}^n)\ T_{result}) \quad \forall_{i=1}^n\ .\ TE \vdash E_i : T_i}{TE \vdash (E_{rator}\ E_{i=1}^n) : T_{result}} \qquad [\rightarrow\text{-elim}]$$

$$\frac{\forall_{i=1}^n\ .\ TE \vdash E_i : T_i \quad TE[I_i : T_i]_{i=1}^n \vdash E_0 : T_0}{TE \vdash \text{(let }((I_i\ E_i)_{i=1}^n)\ E_0) : T_0} \qquad [\textit{let}]$$

$$\frac{\forall_{i=0}^n\ .\ TE[I_j : T_j]_{j=1}^n \vdash E_i : T_i}{TE \vdash \text{(letrec }((I_i\ E_i)_{i=1}^n)\ E_0) : T_0} \qquad [\textit{letrec}]$$

$$\frac{TE_{prim} \vdash O_{op} : \text{(-> }(T_{i=1}^n)\ T_{result}) \quad \forall_{i=1}^n\ .\ TE \vdash E_i : T_i}{TE \vdash \text{(prim }O_{op}\ E_{i=1}^n) : T_{result}} \qquad [\textit{prim}]$$

$$\frac{\{I_i : T_i\}_{i=1}^n \vdash E_{body} : T_{body}}{\vdash_{prog} \text{(flarek }(I_{i=1}^n)\ E_{body}) : \text{(=> }(T_{i=1}^n)\ T_{body})} \qquad [\textit{prog}]$$

Figure 13.3   Types and type rules for μFLARE, an implicitly typed language.

extend the notion of type erasure to type judgments and type derivations, as shown in Figure 13.4. Type erasure for a judgment erases all types in the expression of the judgment. Type erasure for derivations removes derivation tree nodes for **the** and type-erases the judgment in every other tree node. For example, Figure 13.5 shows the type derivation $TD'_{pow} = \lceil TD_{pow} \rceil_{TD}$, where TD_{pow} (defined in Figure 11.12 on page 653) is the type derivation for the μFLEX program P_{pow}.

$typeErase_{TJ} : TypeJudgment_{\mu FLEX} \rightarrow TypeJudgment_{\mu FLARE}$

The notation $\lceil TJ \rceil_{TJ}$ abbreviates $(typeErase_{TJ}\ TJ)$.

$\lceil \vdash_{prog,\mu FLEX} P : PT \rceil_{TJ} = \vdash_{prog,\mu FLARE} \lceil P \rceil_{pgm} : PT$

$\lceil TE \vdash_{\mu FLEX} E : T \rceil_{TJ} = TE \vdash_{\mu FLARE} \lceil E \rceil : T$

$typeErase_{TD} : TypeDerivation_{\mu FLEX} \rightarrow TypeDerivation_{\mu FLARE}$

The notation $\lceil TD \rceil_{TD}$ abbreviates $(typeErase_{TD}\ TD)$.

$$\left\lceil \frac{TD}{TE \vdash_{\mu FLEX} (\text{the } T\ E) : T} \right\rceil_{TD} = \lceil TD \rceil_{TD}$$

$$\left\lceil \frac{TD_1 \ldots TD_n}{TJ} \right\rceil_{TD} = \frac{\lceil TD_1 \rceil_{TD} \ldots \lceil TD_n \rceil_{TD}}{\lceil TJ \rceil_{TJ}}, \text{ for all other type derivations.}$$

Figure 13.4   Type erasure for type judgments and type derivations.

Note that TD'_{pow} is also a type derivation of $P'_{pow} = \lceil P_{pow} \rceil$. This illustrates the following theorem relating μFLEX and μFLARE type judgments and type derivations.

Theorem 13.1 (μFLEX/μFLARE Static Correspondence)

1.   *If the μFLEX type judgment TJ_X is justified by the type derivation TD_X, then the μFLARE type judgment $\lceil TJ_X \rceil_{TJ}$ is justified by the type derivation $\lceil TD_X \rceil_{TD}$.*

2.   *If the μFLARE type judgment TJ_R is justified by the type derivation TD_R, then there exists a μFLEX type judgment TJ_X justified by TD_X such that $\lceil TJ_X \rceil_{TJ} = TJ_R$ and $\lceil TD_X \rceil_{TD} = TD_R$.*

Part 1 is easily shown by induction on the structure of TD_X. For part 2, an induction on the structure of TD_R leads to the construction of explicitly typed versions of the expressions (and possibly program) mentioned in TD_R. The explicit types need not be guessed because all relevant type information is already present in TD_R. (Any guessing of types already took place in the construction of TD_R.)

Unlike μFLEX, μFLARE does not have a unique-type property. Some μFLARE expressions can be assigned infinitely many types in a given type environment. For example, in μFLARE, (error Y) can be assigned any type and (abs (x) x) can be assigned the type (-> (T) T) for any type T. Nev-

Abbreviations

$T_{ii} = $ `(-> (int) int)`

$TE_{loop} = \{$`n`$:$`int`$,$ `dbl`$: T_{ii},$ `loop`$: T_{ii}\}$

$P'_{pow} = $ `(flarek (n) (let ((dbl` E'_{dblabs}`))` $E'_{recloop}$`))`

$E'_{dblabs} = $ `(abs (x) (prim * x 2))`

$E'_{recloop} = $ `(letrec ((loop` $E'_{loopabs}$`)) (loop 1))`

$E'_{loopabs} = $ `(abs (i)` E_{if}`)`

$E_{if} = $ `(if (prim >= i n) i (loop (dbl i)))`

Type Derivation TD'_{pow} **for** P'_{pow}

$TE_{prim} \vdash$ `*` $: $ `(-> (int int) int)` $[var]$

$\{$`n`$:$`int`$,$ `x`$:$`int`$\} \vdash$ `x` $:$ `int` $[var]$

$\{$`n`$:$`int`$,$ `x`$:$`int`$\} \vdash$ `2` $:$ `int` $[int]$

$\{$`n`$:$`int`$,$ `x`$:$`int`$\} \vdash$ `(prim * x 2)` $:$ `int` $[prim]$

$\{$`n`$:$`int`$\} \vdash$ `(abs (x) (prim * x 2))` $:$ `(-> (int) int)` $[\rightarrow\text{-}intro]$

$TE_{prim} \vdash$ `>=` $:$ `(-> (int int) bool)` $[var]$

$TE_{loop}[$`i`$:$`int`$] \vdash$ `i` $:$ `int` $[var]$

$TE_{loop}[$`i`$:$`int`$] \vdash$ `n` $:$ `int` $[var]$

$TE_{loop}[$`i`$:$`int`$] \vdash$ `(prim >= i n)` $:$ `bool` $[prim]$

$TE_{loop}[$`i`$:$`int`$] \vdash$ `i` $:$ `int` $[var]$

$TE_{loop}[$`i`$:$`int`$] \vdash$ `loop` $:$ `(-> (int) int)` $[var]$

$TE_{loop}[$`i`$:$`int`$] \vdash$ `dbl` $:$ `(-> (int) int)` $[var]$

$TE_{loop}[$`i`$:$`int`$] \vdash$ `i` $:$ `int` $[var]$

$TE_{loop}[$`i`$:$`int`$] \vdash$ `(dbl i)` $:$ `int` $[\rightarrow\text{-}elim]$

$TE_{loop}[$`i`$:$`int`$] \vdash$ `(loop (dbl i))` $:$ `int` $[\rightarrow\text{-}elim]$

$TE_{loop}[$`i`$:$`int`$] \vdash$ `(if (prim >= i n) i (loop (dbl i)))` $:$ `int` $[if]$

$TE_{loop} \vdash$ `(abs (i)` E_{if}`)` $:$ `(-> (int) int)` $[\rightarrow\text{-}intro]$

$TE_{loop} \vdash$ `loop` $:$ `(-> (int) int)` $[var]$

$TE_{loop} \vdash$ `1` $:$ `int` $[int]$

$TE_{loop} \vdash$ `(loop 1)` $:$ `int` $[\rightarrow\text{-}elim]$

$\{$`n`$:$`int`$,$ `dbl`$: T_{ii}\} \vdash$ `(letrec ((loop` $E'_{loopabs}$`)) (loop 1))` $:$ `int` $[letrec]$

$\{$`n`$:$`int`$\} \vdash$ `(let ((dbl` E'_{dblabs}`))` $E'_{recloop}$`)` $:$ `int` $[let]$

$\vdash_{prog}$ `(flarek (n) (let ((dbl` E'_{dblabs}`))` $E'_{recloop}$`))` $:$ `(=> (int) int)` $[prog]$

Figure 13.5 Vertical-style type derivation for P'_{pow}.

Domains
Syntactic domains are from the μFLEX grammar (Figure 11.1 on page 628)

$V \in \text{ValueExp} ::= L \mid (\text{abs } (I^*_{formal}) \ E_{body})$

$IE \in \text{InputExp} ::= L$

$A \in \text{AnsExp} ::= L \mid \text{procans}$

Reduction Relation ($\leadsto$)

$((\text{abs } (I^n_{i=1}) \ E_{body}) \ E^n_{i=1}) \leadsto ([E_i/I_i]^n_{i=1})E_{body}$ $[\beta]$

$(\text{let } ((I_i \ E_i)^n_{i=1}) \ E_{body}) \leadsto ([E_i/I_i]^n_{i=1})E_{body}$ $[let]$

$(\text{letrec } ((I_i \ E_i)^n_{i=1}) \ E_{body})$

$\qquad \leadsto ([(\text{letrec } ((I_k \ E_k)^n_{k=1}) \ E_i)/I_i]^n_{i=1})E_{body}$ $[letrec]$

The μFLARE reduction rules also include [if-T], [if-F], and application rules for μFLARE primitives from the FL reduction relation shown in Figure 6.19 on page 259.

Evaluation Contexts

$\mathbb{E} \in \text{EvalContext} ::= \square \mid (\text{if } \mathbb{E} \ E_{then} \ E_{else})$

$\qquad\qquad\qquad \mid (\text{prim } O_{primop} \ V^{k-1}_{i=1} \ \mathbb{E} \ E^n_{j=k+1}) \mid (\mathbb{E} \ E^n_{i=1})$

Evaluation Relation ($\Rightarrow$)

$\qquad \mathbb{E}\{E\} \Rightarrow \mathbb{E}\{E'\}, \text{ where } E \leadsto E'$

Figure 13.6   A context-based SOS for μFLARE, Part 1.

ertheless, μFLARE still has a monomorphic flavor because it does not have an effective form of polymorphism. For example, in μFLARE the expression

$$E_{id} = (\text{let } ((\text{id } (\text{abs } (x) \ x)))$$
$$\qquad\qquad (\text{if } (\text{id } \#t) \ 1 \ ((\text{id id}) \ 2)))$$

is not well typed because id has the type $(\text{-> } (T_x) \ T_x)$ for exactly one type T_x and each of the three references to id requires a different T_x. In Section 13.4 we will see how a small modification to the type rules and reconstruction algorithm can empower μFLARE with an effective form of polymorphism.

13.2.3   Dynamic Semantics and Type Soundness of μFLARE

In order to show the soundness of the μFLARE type system, we need a dynamic semantics for μFLARE. Figures 13.6 and 13.7 present a context-based SOS for μFLARE, which is essentially the result of erasing types in the μFLEX SOS in Figures 11.13 and 11.14 on pages 664 and 665.   In particular, (1) all type

---

SOS

The μFLARE SOS is defined by the tuple $\langle \text{Exp}, \Rightarrow, \text{ValueExp}, \textit{IF}, \textit{OF} \rangle$, where:

$\textit{IF} : (\text{Prog} \times \text{InputExp}^*) \to \text{Exp}$

$\textit{IF} \; \langle (\texttt{flarek} \; (I_{i=1}^{n}) \; E_{body}), \; [\textit{IE}_1, \dots, \textit{IE}_k] \rangle$
$\quad = \textbf{if} \; n \neq k \; \textbf{then} \; (\texttt{error wrong-number-of-args})$
$\qquad \textbf{else if} \; \exists T \; . \; ((\vdash_{prog} (\texttt{flarek} \; (I_{i=1}^{n}) \; E_{body}) : T)$
$\qquad\qquad\qquad \wedge (T = (\texttt{=>} \; (T_{i=1}^{n}) \; T_{body}))$
$\qquad\qquad\qquad \wedge (\forall i \in [1..n] \; . \; (type_{inp}[\![\textit{IE}_i]\!] = T_i)))$
$\qquad\qquad \textbf{then} \; [\textit{IE}_i/I_i]_{i=1}^{n} E_{body}$
$\qquad\qquad \textbf{else} \; (\texttt{error bad-arg-type}) \; \textbf{end}$
$\quad \textbf{end}$

$type_{inp} : \text{InputExp} \to \text{Type}$
$type_{inp}[\![\texttt{\#u}]\!] = \texttt{unit}$
$type_{inp}[\![B]\!] = \texttt{bool}$
$type_{inp}[\![N]\!] = \texttt{int}$
$type_{inp}[\![(\texttt{sym} \; Y)]\!] = \texttt{symb}$

$\textit{OF} : \text{ValueExp} \to \text{AnsExp}$
$\textit{OF} \; L = L$
$\textit{OF} \; (\texttt{abs} \; (I^* \; E)) = \texttt{procans}$

Behavior

$beh_{det} : (\text{Prog} \times \text{InputExp}^*) \to \text{Outcome}$

$$beh_{det} \; \langle P, \textit{IE}^* \rangle = \begin{cases} (\text{AnsExp} \rightarrowtail \text{Outcome} \; (\textit{OF} \; E_{fin})) & \text{if } E_{init} \overset{*}{\Rightarrow} E_{fin} \in \text{ValueExp} \\ \text{stuck} & \text{if } E_{init} \overset{*}{\Rightarrow} E_{fin} \not\Rightarrow \\ & \quad \text{and } E_{fin} \notin \text{ValueExp} \\ \infty & \text{if } E_{init} \overset{\infty}{\Rightarrow} \end{cases}$$
$\qquad\qquad \text{where } E_{init} = (\textit{IF} \; \langle P, \textit{IE}^* \rangle)$

Figure 13.7 A context-based SOS for μFLARE, Part 2.

---

annotations have been erased from $\texttt{abs}$ and $\texttt{letrec}$ expressions and the program form ($\texttt{flarek}$) and (2) there is no reduction rule for $\texttt{the}$, which is not a μFLARE expression. As in μFLEX, the input function $\textit{IF}$ must dynamically check that the types of the program inputs match those of the program parameters. But since the program parameter types are not explicitly declared, they must be determined by the type rules.

The following are the μFLARE versions of the corresponding lemmas and theorems for μFLEX. The proofs are all analogous to those for μFLEX.

Lemma 13.2 (Characterization of μFLARE Stuck Expressions) *If E is a stuck expression in the μFLARE SOS, then it can be decomposed into $\mathbb{E}\{E'\}$ where E' has one of the following forms:*

1. I

2. $(\texttt{if}\ V\ E_{then}\ E_{else})$, *where V is not* $\texttt{\#t}$ *or* $\texttt{\#f}$

3. $(V\ E_{i=1}^{n})$, *where V is not an abstraction*

4. $((\texttt{abs}\ (I_{i=1}^{m})\ E_0)\ E_{j=1}^{n})$, *where $m \neq n$*

5. $(\texttt{prim}\ O\ V_{i=1}^{n})$, *where the number or type of arguments is incorrect for O*

6. $(\texttt{prim}\ O\ N\ \texttt{0})$, *where O is* $\texttt{/}$ *or* $\texttt{\%}$

7. $(\texttt{error}\ Y)$

We classify the forms 1–5 as dynamic type errors and forms 6–7 as dynamic nontype errors. Depending on the form of E', we will say that $\mathbb{E}\{E'\}$ is stuck at a type error or stuck at a nontype error.

Theorem 13.3 (Preservation for μFLARE) *If $\{\} \vdash_{\mu FLARE} E : T$ and $E \Rightarrow_{\mu FLARE} E'$ then $\{\} \vdash_{\mu FLARE} E' : T$.*

Theorem 13.4 (Progress for μFLARE) *If $\{\} \vdash_{\mu FLARE} E : T$ then E is not stuck at a type error.*

Theorem 13.5 (Type Soundness of μFLARE) *If μFLARE program P is well typed with type $(\texttt{=>}\ (T_{i=1}^{n})\ T_{ans})$, then executing P on inputs $IE_{i=1}^{n}$ having corresponding types $T_{i=1}^{n}$ will either:*

1.   *return an answer compatible with T_{ans};*

2.   *get stuck at a nontype error; or*

3.   *loop infinitely.*

In particular, the execution of P will never get stuck at a type error.

An important consequence of the above results is that they allow us to dispense with the dynamic semantics for μFLEX — all we need is the dynamic semantics for μFLARE! Intuitively, types specify a static property of a μFLEX expression, not a dynamic one. So we should be able to express the dynamic semantics of μFLEX in terms of a language (μFLARE) with no explicit type information. We do this simply by applying type erasure to a given μFLEX expression/program and then using the μFLARE SOS on the result. When it comes to properties like preservation and progress for a μFLEX expression E, we can just use the preservation and progress results of μFLARE for $\lceil E \rceil$, relying on the fact that the Static Correspondence Theorem guarantees that if E is well typed with type T in μFLEX, then $\lceil E \rceil$ is well typed with type T in μFLARE.

Henceforth, whenever we extend FLEX with a new explicitly typed construct, we will define its dynamic semantics by type erasure to FLARE rather than by extending the FLEX SOS.

Exercise 13.1 Consider the following theorem:

Theorem 13.6 (μFLEX/μFLARE Dynamic Correspondence)
If $E_X \overset{n}{\Longrightarrow}_{\mu FLEX} E'_X$, then $\lceil E_X \rceil \overset{k}{\Longrightarrow}_{\mu FLARE} \lceil E'_X \rceil$, where $k \leq n$. Moreover, if E_X has type T in the empty type environment, then E'_X, $\lceil E_X \rceil$, and $\lceil E'_X \rceil$ all have type T in the empty type environment.

a. Give a concrete example where the length k in the μFLARE transition path is strictly less than the length n in the original μFLEX transition path.

b. Prove the theorem.

Exercise 13.2 Imagine that we had never defined an SOS for μFLEX. Using type erasure in conjunction with the SOS for μFLARE, state and prove (1) a Preservation Theorem for μFLEX and (2) a Progress Theorem for μFLEX. Use the Preservation and Progress Theorems for μFLARE and the Static Correspondence Theorem in your proofs.

13.3 Type Reconstruction for μFLARE

We are now ready to develop the technical machinery for performing type reconstruction in μFLARE. We start by presenting the notion of a **type substitution**, which we will use to represent the solution to a set of type constraints. Next, we present **unification**, a method for solving type constraints. Then we develop an interface for operations that collect and solve type-constraint sets and show that this interface has multiple implementations. Finally, we present an algorithm that uses the type-constraint set operations to reconstruct (where possible) the types for μFLARE expressions and programs.

13.3.1 Type Substitutions

We represent the solution to a set of type constraints using an entity called a **type substitution** or just plain **substitution**. A type substitution is a partial function from type identifiers to types:

$$\sigma \in \text{TypeSubst} = \text{TypeId} \rightharpoonup \text{Type}$$

A type substitution with a finite domain of definition can be written as a set of bindings between type identifiers and types. Here is a sample type substitution:

$$\sigma_1 = \{?a \mapsto \texttt{int}, ?b \mapsto ?d, ?c \mapsto \texttt{(-> (?e bool) ?d)}\}$$

Because type substitutions are partial functions, the type identifiers on the left-hand sides of the bindings must be distinct. Note that type identifiers may also appear in the right-hand side of a binding, either by themselves or as components of other types. Although the definition of type substitution allows bindings for any type identifiers, in the type substitutions we use in type reconstruction, the type identifiers are all generated by the type reconstruction process and by convention begin with the symbol ?.

Technically, type substitutions are partial functions on type identifiers, but it is natural to "lift" them to be total functions on types and type environments. Applying a type substitution σ to a type T yields a copy of T in which all occurrences of any $\tau \in dom(\sigma)$ have been replaced by $(\sigma\ \tau)$. We will abuse notation and write $(\sigma\ T)$ for the result of applying σ to T. For example, suppose that T_1 is

$$T_1 = \texttt{(-> (?a ?c) (-> (?d ?f) ?b))}$$

Then $(\sigma_1\ T_1)$ is

$$\texttt{(-> (int (-> (?e bool) ?d)) (-> (?d ?f) ?d))}$$

We can similarly lift application of a type substitution to type environments: $(\sigma\ TE)$ is a type environment such that $((\sigma\ TE)\ I) = (\sigma\ (TE\ I))$. E.g.:

$$(\sigma_1\ \{\texttt{x}:\texttt{(-> (?a) ?b)}, \texttt{y}:\texttt{(-> (?c) ?d)}, \texttt{z}:\texttt{(-> (?d) ?e)}\})$$
$$= \{\texttt{x}:\texttt{(-> (int) ?d)}, \texttt{y}:\texttt{(-> ((-> (?e bool) ?d)) ?d)}, \texttt{z}:\texttt{(-> (?d) ?e)}\}$$

When viewed as a total function from Type to Type, σ acts as the identity on any type that does not contain any type identifiers in $dom(\sigma)$. In particular, if $\tau \notin dom(\sigma)$, then $(\sigma\ \tau) = \tau$ if τ is interpreted as an element of Type. This definition is subtle, because if τ is interpreted as an element of TypeId, then $(\sigma\ \tau) = undefined$, because in this case σ is a partial function from TypeId to Type. The **identity substitution**, written σ_{id}, is the type substitution that, as an element of TypeId $\rightharpoonup$ Type, is undefined on every type identifier — i.e., it has an empty set of bindings. However, when interpreted as an element of Type $\rightarrow$ Type, σ_{id} is indeed the identity function.

When type substitutions are viewed as elements of Type $\rightarrow$ Type (not as elements of TypeId $\rightharpoonup$ Type), they can be composed. For example, if

$$\sigma_2 = \{?d \mapsto \texttt{(-> (?f) ?g)}, ?e \mapsto \texttt{symb}\}$$

then

$$\sigma_2 \circ \sigma_1 = \{\text{?a} \mapsto \text{int}, \text{?b} \mapsto \text{(-> (?f) ?g)}, \text{?c} \mapsto \text{(-> (symb bool) (-> (?f) ?g))},$$
$$\text{?d} \mapsto \text{(-> (?f) ?g)}, \text{?e} \mapsto \text{symb}\}$$

As with general functions, composition of type substitutions is not typically commutative. For instance,

$$\sigma_1 \circ \sigma_2 = \{\text{?a} \mapsto \text{int}, \text{?b} \mapsto \text{?d}, \text{?c} \mapsto \text{(-> (?e bool) ?d)},$$
$$\text{?d} \mapsto \text{(-> (?f) ?g)}, \text{?e} \mapsto \text{symb}\}$$

The identity substitution σ_{id} is the identity element of the composition operator.

If a type T' is the result $(\sigma\ T)$ of applying a type substitution σ to another type T, we say that T' is a **substitution instance** of T and that T can be **instantiated** to T'. For example, the following types are all substitution instances of (-> (?s ?t) ?s):

(-> (int bool) int)

(-> ((-> (int) bool) ?t) (-> (int) bool))

(-> (?s symb) ?s)

(-> (?a ?b) ?a)

(-> (?t ?s) ?t)

(-> ((-> (?a ?b) ?c) (-> (?a) ?b)) (-> (?a ?b) ?c))

13.3.2   Unification

Suppose that we are given a type constraint that equates two types, each of which may contain type identifiers. For example, we might be given $T_a \doteq T_b$, where

$$T_a = \text{(-> (?a (-> (?b) ?b)) int)}$$
$$T_b = \text{(-> (bool ?c) ?b)}$$

We would like to be able to "solve" such a type constraint. In algebra, solving an equation with variables means finding a substitution for the variables that makes both sides of the equation the same value or expression. The same is true for type constraints: a solution to a type constraint $T_1 \doteq T_2$ is a type substitution σ such that $(\sigma\ T_1) \approx (\sigma\ T_2)$. In the above example, a solution to $T_a \doteq T_b$ is the following substitution:

$$\sigma = \{\text{?a} \mapsto \text{bool}, \text{?b} \mapsto \text{int}, \text{?c} \mapsto \text{(-> (int) int)}\}$$

We can verify that $(\sigma\ T_a) = (\sigma\ T_b) = $ (-> (bool (-> (int) int)) int).

Domains

$\sigma \in \text{TypeSubst} = \text{TypeId} \rightharpoonup \text{Type}$

$TC \in \text{TypeConstraint} = \text{Type} \times \text{Type}$

      ; $T_1 \doteq T_2$ *stands for an element* $\langle T_1, T_2 \rangle$ *of TypeConstraint*

$us \in \text{UnifySoln} = \text{TypeSubst} + \text{Failure}$

      $\text{Failure} = \{\texttt{fail}\}$

Unification Algorithm

failsoln : UnifySoln $= (\text{Failure} \rightarrowtail \text{UnifySoln } \texttt{fail})$

unify : TypeConstraint* $\rightarrow$ UnifySoln $= \lambda TC^*$. *unifyLoop* $TC^* \ \sigma_{id}$

unifyLoop : TypeConstraint* $\rightarrow$ TypeSubst $\rightarrow$ UnifySoln
$= \lambda TC^* \ \sigma$.

    match TC^*
    $\triangleright [\,] \ \| \ (\text{TypeSubst} \rightarrowtail \text{UnifySoln } \sigma)$
    $\triangleright (T' \doteq T) . \ TC^*_{rest}$
      $\| \ $ **if** $T' \approx T$
       then *unifyLoop* $TC^*_{rest} \ \sigma$
       else match $T' \doteq T$
         $\triangleright (\texttt{->} \ (T'^n_{i=1}) \ T'_0) \doteq (\texttt{->} \ (T^n_{i=1}) \ T_0)$
         $\| \ $ *unifyLoop* $([T'_i \doteq T_i]^n_{i=0} \ @ \ TC^*_{rest}) \ \sigma$
         $\triangleright \tau \doteq T \ \| \ $ **if** $\tau \notin FrTyIds_{ty}[\![T]\!]$; *occurs check*
              then let σ_τ **be** $\{\tau \mapsto T\}$
                  in *unifyLoop* $(\sigma_\tau \ TC^*_{rest}) \ (\sigma_\tau \circ \sigma)$
              else *failsoln* **end**
         $\triangleright T \doteq \tau \ \| \ $; *handled just like the* $\tau \doteq T$ *case*
         $\triangleright$ **else** *failsoln*
       end
      end
    end

Figure 13.8   A unification algorithm that solves a sequence of type constraints.

A type substitution that makes the two types in a type constraint equivalent
is called a **unifier** for the two types. If a unifier exists, we say that the two types
can be **unified** and that the unifier is the result of the **unification** of the two
types. Not every pair of types can be unified; in the case where no unifier exists,
we say that unification **fails**. For instance, the type constraint $\texttt{int} \doteq \texttt{bool}$ is
clearly unsolvable, as is $(\texttt{-> (?t) int}) \doteq (\texttt{-> (bool) ?t})$, so unification fails
in both of these cases. A trickier case is $\texttt{?t} \doteq (\texttt{-> (int) ?t})$. Because μFLARE
types do not include recursive types, there is no finite type T such that $\{\texttt{?t} \mapsto T\}$

is a unifier, so the constraint is unsolvable.[1] By the same reasoning, any type constraint of the form $\tau \doteq T$ where $T \neq \tau$ and $\tau \in FrTyIds_{ty}[\![T]\!]$ is unsolvable. In this case, unification is said to fail because of the test $\tau \in FrTyIds_{ty}[\![T]\!]$, which is called an **occurs check**.

In some cases there may be many solutions to a type constraint. For instance, consider the following type constraint:

$$\text{(-> (?a) ?b)} \doteq \text{(-> (?b) ?c)}$$

This constraint can be solved by any unifier that binds ?a, ?b, and ?c to the same type. Examples of such unifiers are:

$$\sigma_1 = \{?\text{a} \mapsto \text{int}, ?\text{b} \mapsto \text{int}, ?\text{c} \mapsto \text{int}\}$$
$$\sigma_2 = \{?\text{a} \mapsto \text{bool}, ?\text{b} \mapsto \text{bool}, ?\text{c} \mapsto \text{bool}\}$$
$$\sigma_3 = \{?\text{a} \mapsto ?\text{c}, ?\text{b} \mapsto ?\text{c}\}$$
$$\sigma_4 = \{?\text{a} \mapsto ?\text{b}, ?\text{c} \mapsto ?\text{b}\}$$
$$\sigma_5 = \{?\text{a} \mapsto ?\text{d}, ?\text{b} \mapsto ?\text{d}, ?\text{c} \mapsto ?\text{d}\}$$

Intuitively, the substitutions σ_3, σ_4, and σ_5 are more general than σ_1 and σ_2, because the latter can be obtained from the former by instantiating more type identifiers. For instance, σ_1 can be obtained from σ_5 by instantiating ?d to int. We shall say that σ' is **at least as general as** σ (written $\sigma' \succeq \sigma$) if there exists an instantiation substitution σ_{inst} such that $\sigma_{inst} \circ \sigma' = \sigma$. It turns out that if μFLARE types T_1 and T_2 have a unifier, then they have a **most general unifier** σ_{mgu} such that $\sigma_{mgu} \succeq \sigma$ for every unifier σ of T_1 and T_2. In the above example, any unifier σ_T must map ?a, ?b, and ?c to the same type T. σ_5 is a most general unifier because it maps ?a, ?b, and ?c to ?d, and σ_5 can be instantiated to σ_T by mapping ?d to T. By the same reasoning, σ_3 and σ_4 are most general unifiers as well.

Figure 13.8 presents a unification algorithm *unify* that solves a sequence of type constraints $[T_i' \doteq T_i]_{i=1}^n$. If the constraints are solvable, *unify* returns $(\text{TypeSubst} \rightarrowtail \text{UnifySoln } \sigma_{soln})$, where σ_{soln} is a most general unifier for all the type constraints. I.e., $\forall_{i=1}^n . (\sigma_{soln} \; T_i') \doteq (\sigma_{soln} \; T_i)$, and for all σ' such that $\forall_{i=1}^n . (\sigma' \; T_i') \doteq (\sigma' \; T_i)$, $\sigma_{soln} \succeq \sigma'$. If the constraints are not solvable, *unify* returns *failsoln* = $(\text{Failure} \rightarrowtail \text{UnifySoln fail})$.

The unification algorithm works by using a helper function *unifyLoop* to build a solution substitution starting with the identity substitution σ_{id}. It processes the sequence of type constraints one by one, updating the current solution substi-

---

[1]If μFLARE had recursive types, the type $T = \text{(trec s (-> (int) s))}$ would be a solution. If infinite types were allowed, then the infinitely nested arrow type $T = \text{(-> (int) (-> (int) (-> (int) ...)))}$ would be a solution.

tution so that it is a most general unifier of all type constraints processed so far. If it processes all the type constraints without encountering a problem, it returns the result of injecting the final solution substitution into UnifySoln. However, it returns *failsoln* if it encounters an unsolvable constraint — i.e., a constraint involving types with the following forms:

1. two base types that are not equal, such as $\texttt{int} \doteq \texttt{bool}$;

2. a base type and an arrow type, such as $\texttt{symb} \doteq \texttt{(-> (?a) ?b)}$;

3. two arrow types with different numbers of argument types, such as the constraint $\texttt{(-> (?a) ?b)} \doteq \texttt{(-> (?c ?d) ?e)}$;

4. a type identifier τ and a type $T \neq \tau$ in which τ is a free type identifier, such as $\texttt{?x} \doteq \texttt{(-> (int) ?x)}$ (this case is the occurs check).

For a nonempty sequence of type constraints, *unifyLoop* processes the first constraint $T' \doteq T$ by case analysis:

- If the two types are equivalent, *unifyLoop* simply processes the remaining constraints with the current solution substitution. In μFLARE, two types are equivalent if and only if they are syntactically identical, but we phrase this case in terms of type equivalence ($\approx$) so that it will work if μFLARE is extended with more complicated types.

- If the constraint involves two arrow types with the same number of argument types, then new type constraints involving the corresponding argument types and result types are added to the sequence of unprocessed constraints that *unifyLoop* must process.

- The most interesting case is when the constraint has the form $\tau \doteq T$ or $T \doteq \tau$, and τ is not mentioned in T. (Note that constraints of the form $\tau \doteq \tau$ have already been handled by the $T' \approx T$ case.) In this case, the substitution $\sigma_\tau = \tau \mapsto T$ is used (1) to "remember" the solution of τ by updating the current substitution σ to $\sigma_\tau \circ \sigma$ and (2) to remove occurrences of τ in the unprocessed constraints by applying σ_τ to them. For the second purpose, we assume that the application of type substitutions is lifted to sequences of type constraints as follows: $\left(\sigma \; [T_i' \doteq T_i]_{i=1}^n\right) = [(\sigma \; T_i') \doteq (\sigma \; T_i)]_{i=1}^n$.

- In all other cases, the first type constraint is an unsolvable type constraint having one of the forms enumerated earlier, and unification fails.

$$
\begin{aligned}
&\textit{unify}\ [(\text{->}\ (?a)\ (\text{->}\ (?b)\ ?c))\ \doteq\ (\text{->}\ (?d)\ ?e),\\
&\qquad (\text{->}\ (?a\ ?e)\ \text{symb})\ \doteq\ (\text{->}\ (?a\ (\text{->}\ (?f)\ \text{int}))\ ?a)]\\[4pt]
&=\ \textit{unifyLoop}\ [(\text{->}\ (?a)\ (\text{->}\ (?b)\ ?c))\ \doteq\ (\text{->}\ (?d)\ ?e),\\
&\qquad\qquad\quad (\text{->}\ (?a\ ?e)\ \text{symb})\ \doteq\ (\text{->}\ (?a\ (\text{->}\ (?f)\ \text{int}))\ ?a)]\\
&\qquad\qquad\quad \sigma_{id}\\[4pt]
&=\ \textit{unifyLoop}\ [?a\ \doteq\ ?d,\ (\text{->}\ (?b)\ ?c)\ \doteq\ ?e,\\
&\qquad\qquad\quad (\text{->}\ (?a\ ?e)\ \text{symb})\ \doteq\ (\text{->}\ (?a\ (\text{->}\ (?f)\ \text{int}))\ ?a)]\\
&\qquad\qquad\quad \sigma_{id}\\[4pt]
&=\ \textit{unifyLoop}\ [(\text{->}\ (?b)\ ?c)\ \doteq\ ?e,\\
&\qquad\qquad\quad (\text{->}\ (?d\ ?e)\ \text{symb})\ \doteq\ (\text{->}\ (?d\ (\text{->}\ (?f)\ \text{int}))\ ?d)]\\
&\qquad\qquad\quad \{?a \mapsto ?d\}\\[4pt]
&=\ \textit{unifyLoop}\ [(\text{->}\ (?d\ (\text{->}\ (?b)\ ?c))\ \text{symb})\ \doteq\ (\text{->}\ (?d\ (\text{->}\ (?f)\ \text{int}))\ ?d)]\\
&\qquad\qquad\quad \{?a \mapsto ?d,\ ?e \mapsto (\text{->}\ (?b)\ ?c)\}\\[4pt]
&=\ \textit{unifyLoop}\ [?d\ \doteq\ ?d,\ (\text{->}\ (?b)\ ?c)\ \doteq\ (\text{->}\ (?f)\ \text{int}),\ \text{symb}\ \doteq\ ?d]\\
&\qquad\qquad\quad \{?a \mapsto ?d,\ ?e \mapsto (\text{->}\ (?b)\ ?c)\}\\[4pt]
&=\ \textit{unifyLoop}\ [(\text{->}\ (?b)\ ?c)\ \doteq\ (\text{->}\ (?f)\ \text{int}),\ \text{symb}\ \doteq\ ?d]\\
&\qquad\qquad\quad \{?a \mapsto ?d,\ ?e \mapsto (\text{->}\ (?b)\ ?c)\}\\[4pt]
&=\ \textit{unifyLoop}\ [?b\ \doteq\ ?f,\ ?c\ \doteq\ \text{int},\ \text{symb}\ \doteq\ ?d]\\
&\qquad\qquad\quad \{?a \mapsto ?d,\ ?e \mapsto (\text{->}\ (?b)\ ?c)\}\\[4pt]
&=\ \textit{unifyLoop}\ [?c\ \doteq\ \text{int},\ \text{symb}\ \doteq\ ?d]\\
&\qquad\qquad\quad \{?a \mapsto ?d,\ ?e \mapsto (\text{->}\ (?f)\ ?c),\ ?b \mapsto ?f\}\\[4pt]
&=\ \textit{unifyLoop}\ [\text{symb}\ \doteq\ ?d]\\
&\qquad\qquad\quad \{?a \mapsto ?d,\ ?e \mapsto (\text{->}\ (?f)\ \text{int}),\ ?b \mapsto ?f,\ ?c \mapsto \text{int}\}\\[4pt]
&=\ \textit{unifyLoop}\ [\,]\ \sigma_{soln},\ \text{where}\ \sigma_{soln}\ =\ \{?a \mapsto \text{symb},\ ?e \mapsto (\text{->}\ (?f)\ \text{int}),\\
&\qquad\qquad\qquad\qquad\qquad\qquad\qquad\qquad\ ?b \mapsto ?f,\ ?c \mapsto \text{int},\ ?d \mapsto \text{symb}\}\\[4pt]
&=\ (\text{TypeSubst} \rightarrowtail \text{UnifySoln}\ \sigma_{soln})
\end{aligned}
$$

Figure 13.9   A unification example.

Figure 13.9 presents an example of the unification algorithm on an initial sequence containing two type constraints. You should verify that the final type substitution is in fact a solution of the type constraints — i.e., $(\sigma_{soln}\ T_i')$ = $(\sigma_{soln}\ T_i)$ for both type constraints $T_i' \doteq T_i$ in the initial sequence.

13.3.3   The Type-Constraint-Set Abstraction

The core of the type reconstruction algorithm is collecting and solving a set of type constraints. The details of how the constraints are collected and when they

---

Abstract Domain

$TCS \in$ TypeConstraintSet

An element of TypeConstraintSet represents a finite set whose elements are type constraints from TypeConstraint. Different implementations of this abstraction will use different definitions for TypeConstraintSet.

Operations

$empty_{TCS}$: TypeConstraintSet

The empty type-constraint set, abbreviated $\{\}_{TCS}$.

$fail_{TCS}$: TypeConstraintSet

An unsolvable type-constraint set.

$make_{TCS}$: TypeConstraint* $\rightarrow$ TypeConstraintSet

$make_{TCS}[TC_1, \ldots, TC_n]$, abbreviated $\{TC_1, \ldots, TC_n\}_{TCS}$, returns a type-constraint set whose elements are the type constraints $TC_1, \ldots, TC_n$.

$union_{TCS}$: TypeConstraintSet $\rightarrow$ TypeConstraintSet $\rightarrow$ TypeConstraintSet

$(union_{TCS}\ TCS_1\ TCS_2)$, abbreviated $TCS_1 \uplus TCS_2$, returns a type-constraint set containing the union of the type constraints in TCS_1 and TCS_2.

$solve_{TCS}$: TypeConstraintSet $\rightarrow$ UnifySoln

If the type constraints of TCS are solvable, $(solve_{TCS}\ TCS)$ returns (TypeSubst$\rightarrowtail$UnifySoln σ_{mgu}), where σ_{mgu} is a most general unifier for these type constraints. If the type constraints of TCS are not solvable, $(solve_{TCS}\ TCS)$ returns $failsoln$ = (Failure$\rightarrowtail$UnifySoln `fail`).

Figure 13.10   An abstract domain TypeConstraintSet and its associated operations.

are solved affect our understanding of the algorithm and the efficiency of its implementation.

In order to abstract over these details, we present in Figure 13.10 an interface to an abstract TypeConstraintSet set domain and its associated operations. We will phrase the type reconstruction algorithm in terms of these abstract type-constraint sets. Like a data abstraction in programming, this abstraction allows us to separate how type-constraints sets are used from how they are implemented and allows us to experiment with different implementations without changing the description of the type reconstruction algorithm that uses them.

Each element of the TypeConstraintSet domain represents a finite set of type constraints from the TypeConstraint domain. $empty_{TCS}$ (abbreviated $\{\}_{TCS}$) is the empty set of type constraints. $fail_{TCS}$ is an unsolvable set of type constraints. $make_{TCS}$ converts a concrete sequence of type constraints to an abstract set of these constraints. $union_{TCS}$ takes the union of two type-constraint sets. $solve_{TCS}$ solves all the type constraints in a type-constraint set.

Domain

$TCS \in$ TypeConstraintSet $=$ TypeConstraint*

Operations

$empty_{TCS}$: TypeConstraintSet $= [\,]_{\text{TypeConstraint}}$

$fail_{TCS}$: TypeConstraintSet $= [\texttt{int} \doteq \texttt{bool}]_{\text{TypeConstraint}}$

$make_{TCS}$: TypeConstraint* $\to$ TypeConstraintSet $= \lambda TC^* . \; TC^*$

$union_{TCS}$: TypeConstraintSet $\to$ TypeConstraintSet $\to$ TypeConstraintSet
$= \lambda TC_1^* \; TC_2^* . \; TC_1^* @ TC_2^*$

$solve_{TCS}$: TypeConstraintSet $\to$ UnifySoln $= \lambda TC^* . \; unify \; TC^*$

Figure 13.11 A lazy implementation of type-constraint sets.

There are many concrete implementations of the TypeConstraintSet abstraction that might be used in practice. A particularly simple implementation (Figure 13.11) represents an element of TypeConstraintSet as a sequence of type constraints that might contain duplicate elements. In this representation,

- the empty type-constraint set is the empty sequence;

- the failure type-constraint set is a sequence with a single unsolvable constraint, $\texttt{int} \doteq \texttt{bool}$;

- converting a sequence of type constraints to a type-constraint set is the identity operation;

- forming the union of two type-constraint sets is accomplished by appending two sequences; and

- a type-constraint set is solved simply by calling the *unify* function from Figure 13.8.

We call this a "lazy" implementation because solving the constraints is delayed until the $solve_{TCS}$ function is called explicitly. There are many variants on this implementation that differ in minor ways (e.g., by removing duplicate constraints or organizing the constraints in a tree rather than a linear sequence), but this suffices for our purposes.

In contrast, Figure 13.12 presents a very different implementation strategy. In this approach, a solvable type-constraint set is represented as the type sub-

---

Domain

$TCS \in \text{TypeConstraintSet} = \text{UnifySoln}$

Operations

$empty_{TCS} : \text{TypeConstraintSet} = (\text{TypeSubst} \rightarrowtail \text{UnifySoln } \sigma_{id})$

$fail_{TCS} : \text{TypeConstraintSet} = failsoln$

$make_{TCS} : \text{TypeConstraint}^* \rightarrow \text{TypeConstraintSet} = \lambda TC^* . \; unify \; TC^*$

$union_{TCS} : \text{TypeConstraintSet} \rightarrow \text{TypeConstraintSet} \rightarrow \text{TypeConstraintSet}$
$= \lambda us_1 \; us_2 . \; \textbf{match} \; \langle us_1, us_2 \rangle$
$\qquad\qquad \triangleright \langle (\text{TypeSubst} \rightarrowtail \text{UnifySoln } \sigma_1), (\text{TypeSubst} \rightarrowtail \text{UnifySoln } \sigma_2) \rangle$
$\qquad\qquad \parallel \; unify \; ((substToTCSeq \; \sigma_1) \; @ \; (substToTCSeq \; \sigma_2))$
$\qquad\qquad \triangleright \textbf{else } failsoln \; \textbf{end}$

$substToTCSeq : \text{TypeSubst} \rightarrow \text{TypeConstraint}^* = \lambda \sigma . \; [\tau \doteq (\sigma \; \tau)]_{\tau \in dom(\sigma)}$

$solve_{TCS} : \text{TypeConstraintSet} \rightarrow \text{UnifySoln} = \lambda us . \; us$

Figure 13.12   An eager implementation of type-constraint sets.

stitution that results from solving the constraints in the set. In order to handle unsolvable type-constraint sets, each type-constraint set is an element of the UnifySoln domain, which is either a substitution (for solvable type-constraint sets) or the `fail` token (for unsolvable type-constraint sets). We call this an "eager" implementation because constraints are solved as soon as they are encountered. For example, $\{TC_1, \ldots , TC_n\}_{TCS}$ uses unification to solve the type constraints $TC_1, \ldots, TC_n$ and $TCS_1 \uplus TCS_2$ uses unification to solve the type constraints in the result of combining the two constraint sequences derived from the type substitutions σ_1 (from TCS_1) and σ_2 (from TCS_2). The helper function $substToTCSeq$ converts a type substitution to a sequence of type constraints. The notation $[\tau \doteq (\sigma \; \tau)]_{\tau \in dom(\sigma)}$ stands for a sequence of type constraints of the form $\tau \doteq (\sigma \; \tau)$ for each τ in $dom(\sigma)$.

13.3.4   A Reconstruction Algorithm for μFLARE

Now that we have developed operations on type-constraint sets, we present a type reconstruction algorithm for μFLARE in Figure 13.14. This algorithm is expressed in terms of two reconstruction functions:

1. The expression reconstruction function, R, has the signature:

$$R : \text{Exp} \rightarrow \text{TypeEnvironment} \rightarrow (\text{Type} \times \text{TypeConstraintSet})$$

It performs type reconstruction on an expression E relative to a type environment TE. It returns two results: (1) a type T_E and (2) a set TCS_E of type constraints that were collected in the process of determining T_E. If the type-constraint set TCS_E has a solution σ_E, then we say that Algorithm R **reconstructs the type** $(\sigma_E\ T_E)$ for E in TE, indicating that E is well typed in TE. If the type-constraint set TCS_E has no solution, then we say that Algorithm R **fails to reconstruct a type** for E in TE, indicating that E is ill typed in TE.

2. The program reconstruction function, R_{pgm}, has the signature:

$$R_{pgm} : \text{Prog} \rightarrow \text{ReconAns}$$

where ReconAns is a sum domain that is used to distinguish between the success and failure cases of the algorithm:

$RA \in \text{ReconAns} = \text{ProgType} + \text{Failure}$
    $\text{Failure} = \{\texttt{fail}\}$

If type reconstruction on the program succeeds, R_{pgm} returns an answer of the form $(\text{ProgType} \rightarrowtail \text{ReconAns}\ PT)$, where PT is the type of the program. If no type can be reconstructed for the program, R_{pgm} returns the answer $(\text{Failure} \rightarrowtail \text{ReconAns}\ \texttt{fail})$, indicating that the type reconstruction process has failed to find a type for the program.

The basic strategy of the algorithm is to process the nodes in the abstract syntax tree of a program in a recursive fashion. At each node of the abstract syntax tree, the algorithm takes as inputs (1) the node and (2) a type environment passed down from above that describes the types of all identifiers bound at that node. The algorithm produces as outputs two pieces of information for each node: (1) the type of the node and (2) the set of type constraints collected for the subtree rooted at the node.

Given the compositional, tree-recursive structure of R, we choose to define it in Figure 13.14 as a deduction system with rules involving judgments of the form $R[\![E]\!]\ TE = \langle T, TCS \rangle$. Such a judgment is pronounced "reconstructing the type of expression E in type environment TE yields the type T and type-constraint set TCS." The rule for each leaf node of the abstract syntax tree is an axiom in the deduction system. The rule for each non-leaf node is an inference rule whose conclusion is a judgment for the node and whose premises are judgments for the subnodes of the node. As expected in a compositional system, the type and type-constraint set of a conclusion judgment for E are determined from the types and type-constraint sets of premise judgments for the subexpressions of E.

Domains

$RA \in \text{ReconAns} = \text{ProgType} + \text{Failure}$

$\quad \text{Failure} = \{\texttt{fail}\}$

Type Reconstruction Function Signatures

$R_{pgm} : \text{Prog} \rightarrow \text{ReconAns}$

$R : \text{Exp} \rightarrow \text{TypeEnvironment} \rightarrow (\text{Type} \times \text{TypeConstraintSet})$

Figure 13.13   Domains and function signatures for Figure 13.14

The rules for the reconstruction algorithm are structured very much like the type rules for μFLARE presented in Figure 13.3. One key difference is that the reconstruction rules "return" a type-constraint set at each node in addition to "returning" a type. The other key difference is that the algorithm uses a fresh type identifier for any type that is unknown and needs to be guessed. The $[prog_R]$, $[\rightarrow\text{-}intro_R]$, and $[letrec_R]$ rules all introduce fresh type identifiers to represent the unknown types associated with the variables that they declare. These types are communicated from the variable declaration to the variable references by storing them in the type environment that is passed down the abstract syntax tree by the downward phase of the recursive algorithm. The $[error_R]$ rule introduces a fresh type identifier that represents the type guessed for the **error** expression. The $[\rightarrow\text{-}elim_R]$ introduces a fresh type identifier τ_{res} that represents the type guessed for the result of the application. This type identifier is used as the result type of an arrow type whose argument types are the rand types, and this arrow type is unified with the rator type via a type constraint. The $[prim_R]$ rule is similar to the $[\rightarrow\text{-}elim_R]$ rule except that the operator type is found in the primitive type environment TE_{prim}.

The type constraints at every node are the result of taking the union of the type constraints of its subnodes and adding any node-specific constraints. In a well-typed expression, all leaf nodes have empty type-constraint sets; constraints are added only at non-leaf nodes. In particular:

- The $[if_R]$ rule constrains the type of the test expression to be **bool** and the types of the then and else expressions to be equal.

- The $[\rightarrow\text{-}elim_R]$ and $[prim_R]$ rules constrain the rator/operator type to be an arrow type mapping the rand types to a (freshly generated) result type.

- The $[letrec_R]$ rule constrains the types of the **letrec**-bound names to be the same as their reconstructed types, thus "tying the recursive knot."

Domains and Function Signatures
See Figure 13.13.

Type Reconstruction Rules

$R[\![\texttt{\#u}]\!]\ TE\ =\ \langle \texttt{unit}, \{\}_{TCS}\rangle\ [unit_R]$ $R[\![N]\!]\ TE\ =\ \langle \texttt{int}, \{\}_{TCS}\rangle$ $[int_R]$

$R[\![B]\!]\ TE\ =\ \langle \texttt{bool}, \{\}_{TCS}\rangle\ [bool_R]$ $R[\![(\texttt{sym }Y)]\!]\ TE\ =\ \langle \texttt{symb}, \{\}_{TCS}\rangle\ [symb_R]$

$$R[\![(\texttt{error }Y)]\!]\ TE\ =\ \langle \tau, \{\}_{TCS}\rangle\ \text{where }\tau \text{ is fresh.} \qquad [error_R]$$

$$R[\![I]\!]\ TE\ =\ \langle TE(I), \{\}_{TCS}\rangle\ \text{where }I \in dom(TE) \qquad [var_R]$$

$$R[\![I]\!]\ TE\ =\ \langle \texttt{unit}, fail_{TCS}\rangle\ \text{where }I \notin dom(TE) \qquad [var\text{-}fail_R]$$

$$\frac{\forall_{i=1}^{3} \cdot (R[\![E_i]\!]\ TE\ =\ \langle T_i, TCS_i\rangle)}{R[\![(\texttt{if }E_1\ E_2\ E_3)]\!]\ TE\ =\ \langle T_2, \left(\biguplus_{i=1}^{3} TCS_i\right) \uplus \{T_1 \doteq \texttt{bool}, T_2 \doteq T_3\}_{TCS}\rangle}\ [if_R]$$

$$\frac{R[\![E_{body}]\!]\ TE[I_i : \tau_i]_{i=1}^{n}\ =\ \langle T_{body}, TCS_{body}\rangle}{R[\![(\texttt{abs }(I_{i=1}^{n})\ E_{body})]\!]\ TE\ =\ \langle (\texttt{-> }(\tau_{i=1}^{n})\ T_{body}), TCS_{body}\rangle}\ [\rightarrow\text{-}intro_R]$$
$$\text{where }\tau_{i=1}^{n}\text{ are fresh.}$$

$$\frac{\forall_{i=0}^{n} \cdot (R[\![E_i]\!]\ TE\ =\ \langle T_i, TCS_i\rangle)}{R[\![(E_0\ E_{i=1}^{n})]\!]\ TE = \langle \tau_{res}, (\biguplus_{i=0}^{n} TCS_i) \uplus \{T_0 \doteq (\texttt{-> }(T_{i=1}^{n})\ \tau_{res})\}_{TCS}\rangle}\ [\rightarrow\text{-}elim_R]$$
$$\text{where }\tau_{res}\text{ is fresh.}$$

$$\frac{\forall_{i=1}^{n} \cdot (R[\![E_i]\!]\ TE\ =\ \langle T_i, TCS_i\rangle) \quad R[\![E_0]\!]\ TE[I_i : T_i]_{i=1}^{n}\ =\ \langle T_0, TCS_0\rangle}{R[\![(\texttt{let }((I_i\ E_i)_{i=1}^{n})\ E_0)]\!]\ TE\ =\ \langle T_0, \biguplus_{i=0}^{n} TCS_i\rangle}\ [let_R]$$

$$\frac{\forall_{i=0}^{n} \cdot \left(R[\![E_i]\!]\ TE[I_j : \tau_j]_{j=1}^{n}\ =\ \langle T_i, TCS_i\rangle\right)}{\begin{array}{c} R[\![(\texttt{letrec }((I_i\ E_i)_{i=1}^{n})\ E_0)]\!]\ TE \\ =\ \langle T_0, (\biguplus_{i=0}^{n} TCS_i) \uplus (\biguplus_{i=1}^{n} \{\tau_i \doteq T_i\}_{TCS})\rangle \end{array}}\ [letrec_R]$$
$$\text{where }\tau_{i=1}^{n}\text{ are fresh.}$$

$$\frac{R[\![O_{op}]\!]\ TE_{prim}\ =\ \langle T_{op}, TCS_0\rangle \quad \forall_{i=1}^{n} \cdot (R[\![E_i]\!]\ TE\ =\ \langle T_i, TCS_i\rangle)}{\begin{array}{c} R[\![(\texttt{prim }O_{op}\ E_{i=1}^{n})]\!]\ TE \\ =\ \langle \tau_{res}, (\biguplus_{i=0}^{n} TCS_i) \uplus \{T_{op} \doteq (\texttt{-> }(T_{i=1}^{n})\ \tau_{res})\}_{TCS}\rangle \end{array}}\ [prim_R]$$
$$\text{where }\tau_{res}\text{ is fresh.}$$

$$\frac{R[\![E_{body}]\!]\ \{I_i : \tau_i\}_{i=1}^{n}\ =\ \langle T_{body}, TCS_{body}\rangle}{R_{pgm}[\![(\texttt{flarek }(I_{i=1}^{n})\ E_{body})]\!]\ =\ RA_{pgm}}\ [prog_R]$$
$$\text{where }\tau_{i=1}^{n}\text{ are fresh}$$

$$\text{and }RA_{pgm}\ =\ \begin{cases} (\text{ProgType}\rightarrowtail\text{ReconAns }(\sigma_{body}\ (\texttt{=> }(\tau_{i=1}^{n})\ T_{body}))), \\ \quad \text{if } solve_{TCS}\ TCS_{body}\ =\ (\text{TypeSubst}\rightarrowtail\text{UnifySoln }\sigma_{body}) \\ (\text{Failure}\rightarrowtail\text{ReconAns }\texttt{fail}), \text{ otherwise} \end{cases}$$

Figure 13.14 μFLARE type reconstruction algorithm expressed via deduction rules.

It is important to understand how the fresh type identifiers introduced by
the type reconstruction algorithm "flow" through the nodes of an abstract syntax tree. As already noted, the fresh type identifiers for program parameters,
abstraction parameters, and `letrec`-bound names are passed down the abstract
syntax tree via type environments. Type environments also pass down any fresh
type identifiers generated in the definition expressions associated with `let`-bound
names. The one place where fresh type identifiers flow from the type-environment
input to the type output is the $[var_R]$ rule. The $[error_R]$, $[\rightarrow\text{-}elim_R]$, and $[prim_R]$
rules introduce fresh type identifiers in the type output of a node. Fresh identi-
fiers in a type output may flow elsewhere in the program via the type environment
in the $[let_R]$ rule, or they may flow into the type and/or type-constraint set of a
parent node. Once fresh type identifiers appear in a type or type-constraint set,
they are effectively propagated up the abstract syntax tree in the upward phase
of the recursive algorithm.

When the type and constraint information percolates to the top of the program, the algorithm has determined a type T_{body} and type-constraint set TCS_{body}
for the body expression E_{body} of the program. At this point, the $[prog_R]$ rule,
which defines the R_{pgm} function, is applied. It attempts to solve all of the type
constraints TCS_{body} collected in the program body. If there is a solution substitution σ_{body} for these constraints, the program is well typed with a program
type that is the result of applying σ_{body} to (=> $(\tau_{i=1}^{n})$ $T_{body})$, where $\tau_{i=1}^{n}$ are
the type identifiers guessed for the program parameters. If there is no solution
substitution, the algorithm indicates that reconstruction has failed.

It is convenient to express R and R_{pgm} in the deduction style, but it is not
necessary. Alternatively, we can define the R function via a set of clauses written
in the same metalanguage notation that we have used extensively to define most
functions on expression trees that we have studied. For example, in this style the
`if` clause for R would be written:

$$R[\![(\texttt{if}\ E_{test}\ E_{then}\ E_{else})]\!]\ TE\ =$$
$$\textbf{let}\ \langle T_{test}, TCS_{test}\rangle\ \textbf{be}\ R[\![E_{test}]\!]\ TE\ \textbf{and}$$
$$\langle T_{then}, TCS_{then}\rangle\ \textbf{be}\ R[\![E_{then}]\!]\ TE\ \textbf{and}$$
$$\langle T_{else}, TCS_{else}\rangle\ \textbf{be}\ R[\![E_{else}]\!]\ TE$$
$$\textbf{in}\ \langle T_{then}, TCS_{test} \uplus TCS_{then} \uplus TCS_{else} \uplus \{T_{test} \doteq \texttt{bool}, T_{then} \doteq T_{else}\}_{TCS}\rangle$$

In the literature, type reconstruction algorithms are often presented in a more
imperative style in which type-constraint sets (or the substitutions that solve
them) are single-threaded through invocations of the reconstruction function. In
this style, the reconstruction function (we'll call it R') takes a third argument:
a type-constraint set that includes all type constraints collected by the recon-

struction process so far. $(R'[\![E]\!] \; TE \; TCS)$ returns a pair of E's type and a type-constraint set TCS' that augments TCS with any type constraints encountered in the reconstruction of E. Here is the `if` clause in this style:

$$R'[\![(\texttt{if} \; E_{test} \; E_{then} \; E_{else})]\!] \; TE \; TCS_0 =$$
$$\textbf{let} \; \langle T_{test}, TCS_1 \rangle \; \textbf{be} \; R'[\![E_{test}]\!] \; TE \; TCS_0$$
$$\textbf{in let} \; \langle T_{then}, TCS_2 \rangle \; \textbf{be} \; R'[\![E_{then}]\!] \; TE \; TCS_1$$
$$\textbf{in let} \; \langle T_{else}, TCS_3 \rangle \; \textbf{be} \; R'[\![E_{else}]\!] \; TE \; TCS_2$$
$$\textbf{in} \; \langle T_{then}, TCS_3 \uplus \{ T_{test} \doteq \texttt{bool}, T_{then} \doteq T_{else} \}_{TCS} \rangle$$

We choose to express the type reconstruction algorithm as a deduction system because it has two advantages over these other approaches:

1. The similarity in structure between the μFLARE type rules and the μFLARE type reconstruction algorithm highlights the relationship between these two formal systems and facilitates proving properties of the type reconstruction algorithm.

2. Deduction-style rules make it possible to present examples of the type reconstruction algorithm in a style that resembles type derivations.

As an example of the second benefit, Figure 13.16 is a vertical-style presentation of the type reconstruction algorithm for the μFLARE program P'_{pow} introduced on page 773. The constraints collected by the algorithm for the program body E'_{let} are:

$$(\texttt{->} \; (\texttt{int int}) \; \texttt{int}) \doteq (\texttt{->} \; (\texttt{?x int}) \; \texttt{?*res})$$
$$(\texttt{->} \; (\texttt{int int}) \; \texttt{bool}) \doteq (\texttt{->} \; (\texttt{?i ?n}) \; \texttt{?>=res})$$
$$(\texttt{->} \; (\texttt{?x}) \; \texttt{?*res}) \doteq (\texttt{->} \; (\texttt{?i}) \; \texttt{?dblres})$$
$$\texttt{?>=res} \doteq \texttt{bool}$$
$$\texttt{?i} \doteq \texttt{?loopres1}$$
$$\texttt{?loop} \doteq (\texttt{->} \; (\texttt{?dblres}) \; \texttt{?loopres1})$$
$$\texttt{?loop} \doteq (\texttt{->} \; (\texttt{int}) \; \texttt{?loopres2})$$
$$\texttt{?loop} \doteq (\texttt{->} \; (\texttt{?i}) \; \texttt{?i})$$

The solution to these constraints is a substitution with the following bindings:

$\texttt{?n} \mapsto \texttt{int}$	$\texttt{?*res} \mapsto \texttt{int}$	$\texttt{?loopres1} \mapsto \texttt{int}$
$\texttt{?x} \mapsto \texttt{int}$	$\texttt{?>=res} \mapsto \texttt{bool}$	$\texttt{?loopres2} \mapsto \texttt{int}$
$\texttt{?i} \mapsto \texttt{int}$	$\texttt{?dblres} \mapsto \texttt{int}$	$\texttt{?loop} \mapsto (\texttt{->} \; (\texttt{int}) \; \texttt{int})$

Applying this substitution to the program type $(\texttt{=>} \; (\texttt{?n}) \; \texttt{?loopres2})$ obtained from the algorithm yields the program type $(\texttt{=>} \; (\texttt{int}) \; \texttt{int})$. Note that the nested box structure in the μFLARE type reconstruction derivation depicted

---

Abbreviations

$TE_{loop} = \{\texttt{n} : \texttt{?n}, \texttt{dbl} : \texttt{(-> (?x) ?*res)}, \texttt{loop} : \texttt{?loop}\}$

$P'_{pow} = \texttt{(flarek (n) } E'_{let}\texttt{)}$

$E'_{let} = \texttt{(let ((dbl } E'_{dblabs}\texttt{)) } E'_{recloop}\texttt{)}$

$E'_{dblabs} = \texttt{(abs (x) (prim * x 2))}$

$E'_{recloop} = \texttt{(letrec ((loop } E'_{loopabs}\texttt{)) (loop 1))}$

$E'_{loopabs} = \texttt{(abs (i) } E_{if}\texttt{)}$

$E_{if} = \texttt{(if (prim >= i n) i (loop (dbl i)))}$

$TCS_* = \{\texttt{(-> (int int) int)} \doteq \texttt{(-> (?x int) ?*res)}\}_{TCS}$

$TCS_{>=} = \{\texttt{(-> (int int) bool)} \doteq \texttt{(-> (?i ?n) ?>=res)}\}_{TCS}$

$TCS_{dbl} = \{\texttt{(-> (?x) ?*res)} \doteq \texttt{(-> (?i) ?dblres)}\}_{TCS}$

$TCS_{loop1} = TCS_{dbl} \uplus \{\texttt{?loop} \doteq \texttt{(-> (?dblres) ?loopres1)}\}_{TCS}$

$TCS_{if} = TCS_{>=} \uplus TCS_{loop1} \uplus \{\texttt{?>=res} \doteq \texttt{bool}, \texttt{?i} \doteq \texttt{?loopres1}\}_{TCS}$

$TCS_{loop2} = \{\texttt{?loop} \doteq \texttt{(-> (int) ?loopres2)}\}_{TCS}$

$TCS_{recloop} = TCS_{loop2} \uplus TCS_{if} \uplus \{\texttt{?loop} \doteq \texttt{(-> (?i) ?i)}\}_{TCS}$

Figure 13.15   Abbreviations for Figure 13.16.

in Figure 13.16 is exactly the same as that of the μFLARE type derivation for the same program in Figure 13.5. This highlights the connection between type derivations and the type reconstruction process in the μFLARE type system.

For any given expression E and type environment TE, Algorithm R always returns a pair of a type T and a type-constraint set TCS. So in this sense it always "succeeds." But we say that Algorithm R reconstructs a type for E only if TCS is solvable. For example, consider

$$R[\![\texttt{(if x 1 x)}]\!]\ \{\} = \langle \texttt{int}, TCS_{if} \rangle$$

where $TCS_{if} = \{\texttt{?x} \doteq \texttt{bool}, \texttt{?x} \doteq \texttt{int}\}_{TCS}$. Since $(solve_{TCS}\ TCS_{if}) = failsoln$, we say that Algorithm R fails to reconstruct a type for E even though the type component of the result is $\texttt{int}$.

Algorithm R finds a **principal type** — i.e., a most general type — of an expression in a type environment. If $R[\![E]\!]\ TE = \langle T, TCS \rangle$, TCS is solvable, and σ_{mgu} is a most general unifier of TCS, then the type $T_E = (\sigma_{mgu}\ T)$ is a principal type in the sense that any type T' that can be assigned to E in $(\sigma_{mgu}\ TE)$ according to the type system in Figure 13.3 is a substitution instance of T_E. For example, consider reconstructing the type of the abstraction

$$E_{revapp}\ =\ \texttt{(abs (x) (abs (f) (f x)))}$$

in the empty type environment (Figure 13.17). $R[\![E_{revapp}]\!]\ \{\} = \langle T, TCS \rangle$, where $T = \texttt{(-> (?x) (-> (?f) ?r))}$ and $TCS = \{\texttt{?f} \doteq \texttt{(-> (?x) ?r)}\}_{TCS}$. Define

Type Reconstruction for P'_{pow}

See abbreviations in Figure 13.15

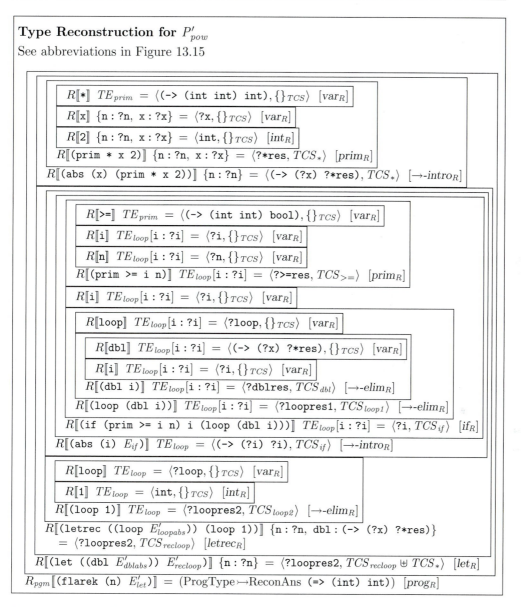

$R_{pgm}[\![(\text{flarek (n) } E'_{let})]\!] = (\text{ProgType} \rightarrowtail \text{ReconAns } (\Rightarrow (\text{int}) \text{ int})) \; [prog_R]$

Figure 13.16 Type reconstruction for P'_{pow}.

Abbreviations

E_{revapp} = (abs (x) (abs (f) (f x)))

TCS = {?f $\doteq$ (-> (?x) ?r)}$_{TCS}$

Type Reconstruction for E_{revapp}

$$R[\![\texttt{f}]\!] \ \{\texttt{x}:\texttt{?x}, \ \texttt{f}:\texttt{?f}\} \ = \ \langle\texttt{?f}, \{\}_{TCS}\rangle \ \ [var_R]$$

$$R[\![\texttt{x}]\!] \ \{\texttt{x}:\texttt{?x}, \ \texttt{f}:\texttt{?f}\} \ = \ \langle\texttt{?x}, \{\}_{TCS}\rangle \ \ [var_R]$$

$$R[\![(\texttt{f x})]\!] \ \{\texttt{x}:\texttt{?x}, \ \texttt{f}:\texttt{?f}\} \ = \ \langle\texttt{?r}, TCS\rangle \ \ [\rightarrow\text{-}elim_R]$$

$$R[\![(\texttt{abs (f) (f x)})]\!] \ \{\texttt{x}:\texttt{?x}\} \ = \ \langle(\texttt{-> (?f) ?r}), TCS\rangle \ \ [\rightarrow\text{-}intro_R]$$

$$R[\![(\texttt{abs (x) (abs (f) (f x))})]\!] \ \{\} = \langle(\texttt{-> (?x) (-> (?f) ?r)}), TCS\rangle \ \ [\rightarrow\text{-}intro_R]$$

Figure 13.17   Type reconstruction for E_{revapp}.

σ = ($solve_{TCS}$ TCS) = {?f $\mapsto$ (-> (?x) ?r)}. Then the principal type of E_{revapp} determined by R is

$$T_{revapp} = (\sigma \ T)$$
$$= (\{\texttt{?f} \mapsto (\texttt{-> (?x) ?r})\} \ (\texttt{-> (?x) (-> (?f) ?r)}))$$
$$= (\texttt{-> (?x) (-> ((-> (?x) ?r)) ?r))}$$

Any type that can be assigned to E_{revapp} is a substitution instance of T_{revapp}. For example, E_{revapp} can be assigned the type

```
(-> (int) (-> ((-> (int) bool)) bool))
```

which is the result of applying the type substitution {?x $\mapsto$ int, ?r $\mapsto$ bool} to T_{revapp}, and it can be assigned the type

```
(-> ((-> (?y) ?z))
    (-> ((-> ((-> (?y) ?z)) (-> (?w) symb)))
        (-> (?w) symb)))
```

which is the result of applying {?x $\mapsto$ (-> (?y) ?z), ?r $\mapsto$ (-> (?w) symb)} to T_{revapp}.

The following theorems (which are proved in the Web Supplement) formalize the correctness of Algorithm R. The soundness theorem says that if Algorithm R reconstructs a type for an expression relative to a type environment, then the expression is well typed in (an instantiation of) that environment.[2]   The

---

[2]In Theorem 13.7, applying the substitution σ to the type environment TE is necessary because TE might contain type identifiers that are resolved by the type reconstruction process. E.g., suppose TE = {b : bool, x : ?t} and E = (if b x 0). In this case, σ = {?t $\mapsto$ int} and the judgment (σ TE) $\vdash$ E : (σ ?t) holds but the judgment $TE \vdash E$: (σ ?t) does not hold.

completeness theorem says that if an expression has type T in a type environment, Algorithm R can reconstruct the type T for it.

> **Theorem 13.7 (Soundness of Algorithm R)** *Suppose $R[\![E]\!]$ TE $=$ $\langle T, TCS \rangle$. If σ is any solution of TCS, then $(\sigma\ TE) \vdash E : (\sigma\ T)$.*

> **Theorem 13.8 (Completeness of Algorithm R)** *If $TE \vdash E : T$ then $R[\![E]\!]$ TE $=$ $\langle T', TCS \rangle$ where there is a solution σ of TCS such that $(\sigma\ T')$ $= T$.*

The fact that Algorithm R finds a principal type follows from soundness and completeness:

> **Theorem 13.9 (Principal Types for Algorithm R)** *Suppose that $R[\![E]\!]$ TE $=$ $\langle T', TCS \rangle$ and TCS is a solvable type-constraint set with a most general unifier σ_{mgu}. Then T_{PT} $=$ $(\sigma_{mgu}\ T')$ is a **principal type** of E: That is, if $(\sigma_{mgu}\ TE) \vdash E : T$, then $T = (\sigma_{inst}\ T_{PT})$ for some instantiation substitution σ_{inst}.*

Proof: By the soundness of Algorithm R, $(\sigma_{mgu}\ TE) \vdash E : (\sigma_{mgu}\ T') = T_{PT}$. By the completeness of Algorithm R, $(\sigma_{mgu}\ TE) \vdash E : T$ implies there is a solution σ of TCS such that $T = (\sigma\ T')$. Since σ_{mgu} is a most general unifier of TCS, $\sigma = \sigma_{inst} \circ \sigma_{mgu}$ for some substitution σ_{inst}. So $T = (\sigma\ T') = ((\sigma_{inst} \circ \sigma_{mgu})\ T') = (\sigma_{inst}\ (\sigma_{mgu}\ T')) = (\sigma_{inst}\ T_{PT})$. $\diamond$

Because the type reconstruction algorithm uses the abstract operations for type-constraint sets from Section 13.3.3, it abstracts over the details of when the constraints are solved. In a lazy implementation of type-constraint sets (Figure 13.11), the algorithm first collects constraints from the entire program and then solves them all at once at the very end of the reconstruction process. Since the lazy implementation will not "notice" if unsolvable constraints like $int \doteq bool$ are encountered during the constraint collection process, it may do much more work than it has to in cases where the reconstruction process fails.

In an eager implementation of type-constraint sets (Figure 13.12), the algorithm solves constraints whenever a new type-constraint set is created and whenever two type-constraint sets are unioned. An eager implementation can be designed to fail immediately if an unsolvable constraint is encountered. Because all constraints encountered in the reconstruction process are eventually collected into one big type-constraint set, a variant of the eager implementation that is popular in practice is to represent the substitution solving all the type constraints collected so far as a global mutable data structure that is updated every time a new constraint is encountered. For example, this substitution can be represented as a mutable table mapping the fresh type identifiers generated by the algorithm to their current types in the global substitution.

Exercise 13.3

a. Construct a vertical-style μFLARE type reconstruction for the following program:

```
(flarek (i)
  (let ((make-gt (abs (n) (abs (x) (prim > x n))))
        (app5 (abs (f) (f 5)))
        (flip (abs (g) (abs (a) (abs (b) ((g b) a))))))
    (((flip app5) i) make-gt)))
```

As part of your answer, show the type substitution that is the solution of all the constraints collected by the reconstruction algorithm.

b. Write a well-typed program in the explicitly typed μFLEX language whose type erasure is the μFLARE program in part **a**.

Exercise 13.4 Thai Ping is excited when he realizes that the `label` and `jump` constructs he added to μFLEX (see Exercise 11.8 on page 658) can be handled in μFLARE without the need for any explicit type annotations. The expression and type grammars of μFLARE can be extended as follows:

$$E ::= \ldots \mid (\texttt{label}\ I\ E) \mid (\texttt{jump}\ E_1\ E_2)$$
$$T ::= \ldots \mid (\texttt{controlpointof}\ T)$$

a. Write μFLARE type rules for `label` and `jump`.

b. Using your type rules from part **a**, construct a type derivation for the expressions E_1, E_2, and E_3 from Exercise 11.8, showing that they are well typed.

c. Write μFLARE type-reconstruction rules for `label` and `jump`.

Exercise 13.5 Type reconstruction can be extended to construct explicitly typed versions of implicitly typed expressions and programs.

a. Modify R so that it returns a third result: an explicitly typed μFLEX expression $E_{\mu FLEX}$ whose type erasure is the μFLARE expression $E_{\mu FLARE}$ on which R was called. If the type constraints collected by R are solvable, then $E_{\mu FLEX}$ should be a well-typed expression. You may assume that applying a type substitution σ to a μFLEX expression $E_{\mu FLEX}$ yields a μFLEX expression $E'_{\mu FLEX}$ in which every occurrence of a type identifier τ in $dom(\sigma)$ has been replaced by $(\sigma\ \tau)$.

b. Modify R_{pgm} so that in the case where it succeeds with a type it returns a second result: an explicitly typed μFLEX program $P_{\mu FLEX}$ such that $P_{\mu FLEX}$ is well typed and the type erasure of $P_{\mu FLEX}$ is the μFLARE program $P_{\mu FLARE}$ on which R_{pgm} was called.

13.4   Let Polymorphism

13.4.1   Motivation

The type system of μFLARE and the associated type reconstruction algorithm
are a big improvement over the explicit type system of μFLEX. All types in
μFLARE are implicit and can be automatically inferred, so programmers never
need to write any explicit types in their programs.

However, the μFLARE type system is still not as expressive as we would like
it to be. There are many μFLARE expressions that are intuitively well typed but
are treated as ill typed by the μFLARE type system. For example, reconsider
the following expression discussed on page 778:

$$E_{id} = \texttt{(let ((id (abs (x) x)))}$$
$$\texttt{(if (id \#t) 1 ((id id) 2)))}$$

We might reasonably expect that type reconstruction should succeed on E_{id}, but
the μFLARE type reconstruction algorithm presented in Figure 13.14 fails on
this expression. It discovers that $\texttt{id}$ has the type $\texttt{(-> (?x) ?x)}$, which suggests
that $\texttt{id}$ should have type $\texttt{(-> } (T) \; T \texttt{)}$ for *any* type T. But it permits $\texttt{?x}$ to
be instantiated only once in the entire expression. Since $\texttt{?x}$ needs to be $\texttt{bool}$,
$\texttt{(-> (int) int)}$, and $\texttt{int}$, respectively, for the three different references to $\texttt{id}$,
the constraints collected by the type reconstruction algorithm for this expression
are unsolvable.

The problem is that the μFLARE type system and its associated reconstruction algorithm are essentially monomorphic. A $\texttt{let}$ definition expression like
$\texttt{(abs (x) x)}$ is typed exactly once even though it may be used in different ways
in different contexts. We would prefer a way to derive a different type for a $\texttt{let}$
definition expression for each of its uses in the $\texttt{let}$ body. That is, we would like
to get the effect of typing or reconstructing an expression in which each $\texttt{let}$ definition is substituted for its corresponding name in the $\texttt{let}$ body. For example,
the μFLARE expression

$$E'_{id} = \texttt{(let ((id (abs (x) x)))}$$
$$\texttt{(if ((abs (x) x) \#t) 1 (((abs (x) x) (abs (x) x)) 2)))}$$

is well typed because a different type can be chosen for $\texttt{x}$ in each of the three
copies of the abstraction $\texttt{(abs (x) x)}$.

In the polymorphic language FLEX/SP from Section 12.2, this effect is
achieved without copying $\texttt{let}$ definitions by giving them universal types that

can be instantiated differently at each use. For example, here is a FLEX/SP version of the identity example:

$$E_{idSP} = \text{(let ((id (pabs (t) (abs ((x t)) x))))}$$
$$\text{(if ((pcall id bool) \#t)}$$
$$\text{1}$$
$$\text{((pcall id (-> (int) int)) (pcall id int)) 2)))}$$

The polymorphism of FLEX/SP increases the expressive power of the typed language, but it forces the programmer to explicitly declare and instantiate universal types. The burning question is: Can this polymorphic approach be adapted to the implicitly typed μFLARE language? The answer is a qualified "yes": Some, but not all, of the power of universal polymorphism can be captured in an implicitly typed language. The key idea is to associate each **let**-bound and **letrec**-bound name with a **type schema** of the form (generic ($\tau_{i=1}^{n}$) T). This can be viewed as a weak form of the universal type (forall ($\tau_{i=1}^{n}$) T). Each time such a name is used, the **generic**-bound type identifiers $\tau_1, \ldots, \tau_n$ can be instantiated with different types. This allows a **let** or **letrec** definition to have a different type for each use of its associated name within the **let** or **letrec** body, just as if the definition were substituted for each occurrence of the name in the body. Since polymorphism in this approach is restricted to definition expressions in a **let** or **letrec** expression, it is called **let polymorphism**.

As an example of **let** polymorphism, Figure 13.18 presents a vertical-style type derivation showing that the identity example expression E_{id} is well typed in the empty type environment. The derivation uses some new rules (subscripted with LP, for *Let Polymorphism*) that will be presented in Section 13.4.2. In deriving the type for the identity abstraction (abs (x) x), the μFLEX type system allows any type to be used for x; we choose the type identifier ?x as the type of x. Because the identity abstraction is a **let** definition, the μFLARE$_{LP}$ type system with **let** polymorphism generalizes its type to the type schema (generic (?x) (-> (?x) ?x)) and extends the type environment with a binding of the name id to this type schema for type-checking the body of the **let** expression. Each reference to id in the **let** body instantiates the type identifier ?x in a different way. In (id \#t), ?x is instantiated to bool, so that id has the type (-> (bool) bool). In ((id id) 2), the ?x for the first occurrence of id is instantiated to (-> (int) int), giving the first id the type (-> ((-> (int) int)) (-> (int) int)), and the ?x for the second occurrence of id is instantiated to int, giving the second id the type (-> (int) int). Because **let** polymorphism allows each of the three references to id to have a different type, E_{id} is well typed with type int.

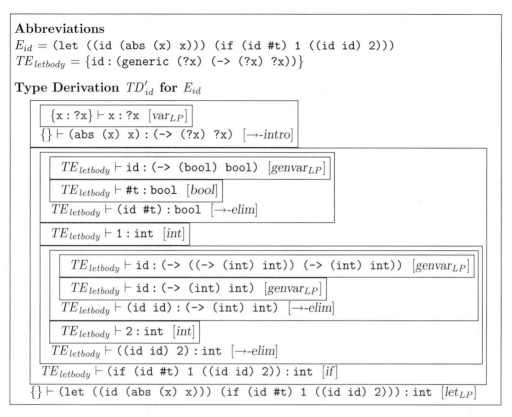

Figure 13.18 Type derivation for E_{id} in μFLARE with let polymorphism.

13.4.2 A μFLARE Type System with Let Polymorphism

Extending the μFLARE type system with let polymorphism requires only a few modifications, which are presented in Figure 13.19. We use the name μFLARE$_{LP}$ to refer to μFLARE with let polymorphism to distinguish it from μFLARE with the monomorphic type system. The new domain TypeSchema is the domain of type schemas, which are possibly instantiatable types. These include generic schemas of the form (generic $(\tau_{i=1}^n)$ T) introduced above. They also include plain types of the form T, which can be viewed as an abbreviated way of writing the trivial generic schema (generic () T).

Although type schemas include plain types, the Type domain is unchanged. In particular, the generic construct cannot appear in a type. This is the key way in which generic differs from the universal type constructor forall, which *can* appear in types.[3] As we shall discuss later, this difference makes `generic` less powerful than `forall` but makes type reconstruction possible.

To support `let` polymorphism, type environments are changed to bind value identifiers to type schemas rather than to types. The $[genvar_{LP}]$ type rule allows each reference to an identifier I bound to (`generic` ($\tau_{i=1}^{n}$) T) to be given a type that is a substitution instance of T in which each type identifier τ_i is replaced by an arbitrary type T_i. The substitution $([T_i/\tau_i]_{i=1}^{n}) T_{body}$ is effectively an implicit projection that serves the same purpose as the explicit projection (`pcall` I $T_{i=1}^{n}$) in an explicitly typed system (where I would be assumed to have the type (`forall` ($\tau_{i=1}^{n}$) T_{body})). The fact that each type T_i may be chosen differently for each reference to I is the sole source of polymorphism in a type system with `let` polymorphism.

The $[var_{LP}]$ type rule says that if I is bound to a plain type T, then there is no polymorphism and each reference to I has the same type T. This is consistent with the view that T is just an abbreviation of (`generic` () T).

The only other modification for `let` polymorphism is changing the type rules for `let` and `letrec` to introduce generic type schemas for the type T_i of each definition expression E_i. In an explicitly typed system, this would correspond to wrapping the definition expressions with `pabs` so that the bound identifiers would have `forall` types. The key decision to make is which type identifiers appearing in T_i can be parameterized when wrapping T_i in a `generic`. In the type derivation of E_{id}, the type (`->` (`?x`) `?x`) is abstracted into the type schema (`generic` (`?x`) (`->` (`?x`) `?x`)). But in general it is *not* sound to simply parameterize over all type identifiers that appear in T_i. To see why, consider the following variant of E_{id}:

E_{const} = (abs (c)
                (let ((const (abs (x) c)))
                  (if (const #t) 1 ((const const) 2))))

In E_{const}, the identity abstraction `id` has been replaced by the constant abstraction `const` that always returns the `abs`-bound value `c`. The most general type of (`abs` (`x`) `c`) is (`->` (`?x`) `?c`). If this is generalized to the type schema (`generic` (`?x` `?c`) (`->` (`?x`) `?c`)) and the type environment binds `const` to this schema, there is a problem: `?c` can be instantiated to a different type for each reference to `const`, and the expression is determined to be well typed. But E_{const} should *not* be well typed. The same value `c` is returned for both (`const` `#t`) and (`const` `const`). In the first application, `c` must be a boolean, since it is

---

[3]Using the terminology from page 735, the μFLARE type system is predicative, in contrast to the impredicative type system of FLEX/SP.

New and Modified Domains

$TS \in \text{TypeSchema} ::= T \mid (\texttt{generic} \ (\tau^*) \ T)$

$TE \in \text{TypeEnvironment} = \text{Ident} \rightharpoonup \text{TypeSchema}$

New Type Functions

$FrTyIds_{TS} : \text{TypeSchema} \rightarrow \mathcal{P}(\text{TypeId})$

$FrTyIds_{TS}[\![T]\!] = FrTyIds_{ty}[\![T]\!]$

$FrTyIds_{TS}[\![(\texttt{generic} \ (\tau_{i=1}^n) \ T_{body})]\!] = FrTyIds_{ty}[\![T_{body}]\!] - (\cup_{i=1}^n \{\tau_i\})$

$FrTyIds_{TE} : \text{TypeEnvironment} \rightarrow \mathcal{P}(\text{TypeId})$

$(FrTyIds_{TE} \ TE) = \cup_{I \in dom(TE)} FrTyIds_{TS}[\![TE(I)]\!]$

$gen : \text{Type} \rightarrow \text{TypeEnvironment} \rightarrow \text{TypeSchema}$

$(gen \ T \ TE) = (\texttt{generic} \ (\tau_{i=1}^n) \ T),$

$\quad$ where $\{\tau_1, \ldots, \tau_n\} = FrTyIds_{ty}[\![T]\!] - (FrTyIds_{TE} \ TE)$

Modified Type Rules

$$TE \vdash I : T \ \text{ where } TE(I) = T \qquad\qquad [\text{var}_{LP}]$$

$$TE \vdash I : ([T_i/\tau_i]_{i=1}^n) T_{body} \ \text{ where } TE(I) = (\texttt{generic} \ (\tau_{i=1}^n) \ T_{body}) \quad [\text{genvar}_{LP}]$$

$$\frac{\forall_{i=1}^n \ . \ TE \vdash E_i : T_i \qquad TE[I_i : (gen \ T_i \ TE)]_{i=1}^n \vdash E_0 : T_0}{TE \vdash (\texttt{let} \ ((I_i \ E_i)_{i=1}^n) \ E_0) : T_0} \qquad [\text{let}_{LP}]$$

$$\frac{\forall_{i=1}^n \ . \ TE[I_j : T_j]_{j=1}^n \vdash E_i : T_i \qquad TE[I_i : (gen \ T_i \ TE)]_{i=1}^n \vdash E_0 : T_0}{TE \vdash (\texttt{letrec} \ ((I_i \ E_i)_{i=1}^n) \ E_0) : T_0} \qquad [\text{letrec}_{LP}]$$

Figure 13.19 Modified domains and type rules for $\mu\text{FLARE}_{LP} = \mu\text{FLARE}$ with `let` polymorphism.

used in the test position of an `if` expression. In the second expression, `c` must be a procedure that maps an integer to an integer, since it is applied to `2` and must return an integer (to match the `1` returned in the other branch of the `if` expression). Clearly, no value `c` can be both a boolean and a procedure.

The correct generalization of `(-> (?x) ?c)` in this example is the type schema `(generic (?x) (-> (?x) ?c))`. It *is* safe to generalize the type identifier `?x` for each occurrence of **const** but is *not* safe to generalize the type identifier `?c`. With this generalization, E_{const} is ill typed, as it should be.

In general, how can we determine which type identifiers in a type T can be generalized? The key is to disallow generalization for any free type identifier in T that is mentioned in the type environment. It turns out that any free

type identifier in the type environment is a type associated with an **abs**-bound
identifier. Since the value associated with an **abs**-bound identifier is generally
unknown to the type checker, each such free type identifier must be assumed to
represent the same type everywhere it is used, and so such type identifiers cannot
be generalized.

The *gen* function in Figure 13.19 generalizes a type relative to a type environment. (*gen T TE*) calculates which type identifiers in T can be generalized
relative to TE and returns a type schema parameterized over these type identifiers. The function *FrTyIds*$_{TE}$ determines the free type identifiers in a type
environment by unioning the free type identifiers for each type schema in the
environment. The function *FrTyIds*$_{TS}$ determines the free type identifiers in a
type schema by subtracting any **generic**-bound type identifiers from the free
type identifiers of the generalized type. For example:

$(gen$ `(-> (?x) ?c)` `{})` $=$ `(generic (?x ?c) (-> (?x) ?c))`

$(gen$ `(-> (?x) ?c)` `{c : ?c})` $=$ `(generic (?x) (-> (?x) ?c))`

$(gen$ `(-> (?x) ?c)` `{f : (-> (?c) ?x)})` $=$ `(generic () (-> (?x) ?c))`

$(gen$ `(-> (?x) ?c)` `{g : (generic (?c) (-> (?c) ?x))})`
   $=$ `(generic (?c) (-> (?x) ?c))`

The [*let*$_{LP}$] and [*letrec*$_{LP}$] rules in Figure 13.19 are modified versions of the
[*let*] and [*letrec*] rules from Figure 13.3 that use *gen* to determine the type schema
for each **let** and **letrec** definition. Note that the [*letrec*$_{LP}$] rule generalizes the
type of a definition expression only in the body of the **letrec**; the type of a
letrec-bound name is treated monomorphically within the **letrec** definition
expressions. This restriction is motivated by the fact that the typability of expressions involving general polymorphic recursion is known to be undecidable
[KTU93]. With this treatment of **letrec**, the expression

```
(letrec ((id (abs (x) x))
         (inc (abs (y) (+ 1 (id y)))))
  (if (id #t) (id 1) (inc 2)))
```

is ill typed even in the presence of **let** polymorphism. The application `(id y)`
forces the type of **id** to be `(-> (int) int)` rather than `(-> (?x) ?x)`. Since
`(-> (int) int)` cannot be generalized to a nontrivial type schema, the application `(id #t)` is necessarily ill typed.

The polymorphic type system of μFLARE$_{LP}$ allows types to be derived for
many μFLARE programs that are ill typed in the basic monomorphic type system of μFLARE. Nevertheless, it is still not powerful enough to derive types for

the type erasures of all programs that are well typed using the universal types of
FLEX/SP. As a simple example, consider the following FLEX/SP abstraction:

$$E_{absSP} = \text{(abs ((f (forall (t) (-> (t) t))))}$$
$$\text{(if ((pcall f bool) \#t)}$$
$$1$$
$$\text{(((pcall f (-> (int) int)) (pcall f int)) 2)))}$$

E_{absSP} is well typed in FLEX/SP, where it can be applied to arguments like the
following, all of which have type (forall (t) (-> (t) t)):

```
(pabs (t) (abs ((x t)) t))

(pabs (t) (abs ((x t)) (error wrong t)))

(pabs (t)
  (abs ((x t))
    (letrec ((loop (-> (t) t) (abs ((y t)) (loop y))))
      (loop x))))
```

However, the type erasure of E_{absSP},[4]

$$E_{absR} = \lceil E_{absSP} \rceil = \text{(abs (f) (if (f \#t) 1 ((f f) 2)))}$$

is *not* well typed in μFLARE$_{LP}$. The reason is that f is an **abs**-bound identifier
and, as such, is assumed to have a plain (i.e., nongeneralizable) type. Clearly f
has an arrow type, but there is no μFLARE$_{LP}$ arrow type that is compatible
with an argument type **bool** and an argument type that is another arrow type.
So E_{absR} is ill typed. Indeed, any FLEX/SP expression that requires abstraction
parameters to be first-class polymorphic values — i.e., values with **forall** types
— has a type erasure that will be ill-typed in μFLARE for the same reason.

Sometimes an ill-typed μFLARE$_{LP}$ expression can be rewritten to make it
well typed. E.g., (E_{absR} (abs (x) x)), which is ill typed in μFLARE$_{LP}$, can
be rewritten as E_{id} from page 778, which is well typed in μFLARE$_{LP}$. The
reason that this rewriting makes the expression well typed is that it provides the
type checker with more information. When type-checking E_{absR}, the type checker
has no information about f and must treat it monomorphically. But when type
checking E_{id}, the type checker knows that the definition of f is (abs (x) x),
which it can treat polymorphically because it is a **let** definition.

Expressions like E_{absR} are ill typed in μFLARE$_{LP}$ because polymorphism is
provided only by type schemas, (generic $(\tau_{i=1}^{n})$ T), which can appear in type
environments but cannot appear in types. Why not simply make the μFLARE$_{LP}$

---

[4]For type erasure on FLEX/SP expressions, we assume that $\lceil$(pcall E $T_{i=1}^{n}$)$\rceil = \lceil E \rceil$ and
$\lceil$(pabs $(\tau_{i=1}^{n})$ E)$\rceil = \lceil E \rceil$.

type system more powerful by extending it with full-fledged universal types, (forall $(\tau_{i=1}^n)$ T)? The reason is that typability in an implicitly typed system with universal types is known to be undecidable [Wel99]. So type reconstruction is not possible for such a system.

Developing a type system that supports both reconstruction and some form of polymorphism requires weakening universal polymorphism in some way. The type-schema strategy discussed here is a standard approach that limits universal types by effectively allowing `pabs` only around `let`/`letrec` definition expressions and allowing `pcall` only at references to `let`-bound and `letrec`-bound names in the bodies of `let` and `letrec` expressions. Exploring other implicit type systems that support reconstruction along with other features (e.g., more powerful polymorphism, subtyping, bounded quantification, existential types) is an area of active research.

13.4.3 μFLARE Type Reconstruction with Let Polymorphism

Figure 13.20 shows the modifications to the μFLARE type reconstruction algorithm (Figure 13.14 on page 793) that are needed to handle `let` polymorphism. As in the μFLARE$_{LP}$ type system, type environments are modified to map identifiers to type schemas. Nontrivial schemas are introduced in the reconstruction of `let` and `letrec` expressions and are generalized at each variable reference by replacing `generic`-bound type identifiers by fresh type identifiers. The *rgen* function is the type reconstruction analogue of the *gen* function from the μFLARE$_{LP}$ type system. It differs from *gen* in two ways:

1. In addition to taking a type T and a type environment TE, *rgen* takes an additional argument: a type-constraint set TCS of the constraints collected in reconstructing the type T. These constraints must be solved and applied to both T and TE before the calculation of generalizable type identifiers can be performed.

2. Unlike *gen*, which is a total function, *rgen* is a partial function. It is undefined in the case where the type-constraint set TCS is unsolvable. Although this is not explicit in the algorithm, we assume that type reconstruction fails in the case where *rgen* is undefined.

The reason that type constraints must be solved before calculating which identifiers can be generalized is that these constraints may relate fresh type identifiers to each other and to free type identifiers in the type environment. For example, consider the case in which `(abs (f x) (f (if b c x)))` is a `let` defini-

---

Domains

TypeSchema and TypeEnvironment are defined as in Figure 13.19.

New Type Function

$rgen :$ Type $\rightarrow$ TypeEnvironment $\rightarrow$ TypeConstraintSet $\rightharpoonup$ TypeSchema

$$(rgen \ T \ TE \ TCS) = \begin{cases} (\text{generic } (\tau_1 \ \ldots \ \tau_n) \ (\sigma \ T)), \\ \quad \text{if } solve_{TCS} \ TCS \ = \ (\text{TypeSubst} \rightarrowtail \text{UnifySoln } \sigma) \\ \quad \text{and } \{\tau_1, \ldots, \tau_n\} = FrTyIds_{ty}[\![(\sigma \ T)]\!] \\ \qquad\qquad\qquad - (FrTyIds_{TE} \ (\sigma \ TE)) \\ \text{undefined, otherwise} \end{cases}$$

Modified Type Reconstruction Rules

$$R[\![I]\!] \ TE = \langle T, \{\}_{TCS}\rangle \text{ where } TE(I) = T \qquad\qquad [\text{var}_{LPR}]$$

$$R[\![I]\!] \ TE = \langle ([\tau_i'/\tau_i]_{i=1}^n) \, T_{body}, \{\}_{TCS}\rangle \qquad\qquad [\text{genvar}_{LPR}]$$
where $TE(I) = (\text{generic } (\tau_{i=1}^n) \ T_{body})$ and $\tau_1', \ldots, \tau_n'$ are fresh.

$$R[\![I]\!] \ TE = \langle \text{unit}, fail_{TCS}\rangle \text{ where } I \notin dom(TE) \qquad [\text{var-fail}_{LPR}]$$

$$\frac{\forall_{i=1}^n \, . \, (R[\![E_i]\!] \ TE = \langle T_i, TCS_i\rangle)}{R[\![E_0]\!] \ TE[I_i : (rgen \ T_i \ TE \ TCS_i)]_{i=1}^n = \langle T_0, TCS_0\rangle} \qquad\qquad [\text{let}_{LPR}]$$
$$\overline{R[\![(\text{let } ((I_i \ E_i)_{i=1}^n) \ E_0)]\!] \ TE = \langle T_0, TCS_0 \uplus TCS_{defns}\rangle}$$
$$\text{where } TCS_{defns} = \biguplus_{i=1}^n TCS_i$$

$$\frac{\forall_{i=1}^n \, . \, \left(R[\![E_i]\!] \ TE[I_j : \tau_j]_{j=1}^n = \langle T_i, TCS_i\rangle\right)}{R[\![E_0]\!] \ TE[I_i : (rgen \ T_i \ TE \ TCS_{defns})]_{i=1}^n = \langle T_0, TCS_0\rangle} \quad [\text{letrec}_{LPR}]$$
$$\overline{R[\![(\text{letrec } ((I_i \ E_i)_{i=1}^n) \ E_0)]\!] \ TE = \langle T_0, TCS_0 \uplus TCS_{defns}\rangle}$$
$$\text{where } \tau_{i=1}^n \text{ are fresh and } TCS_{defns} = \left(\biguplus_{i=1}^n TCS_i\right) \uplus \left(\biguplus_{i=1}^n \{\tau_i \doteq T_i\}_{TCS}\right)$$

Figure 13.20 Modified type reconstruction rules for μFLARE$_{LP}$.

tion whose type is being reconstructed relative to a type environment $TE_{abs} = \{\texttt{b}:\texttt{bool}, \texttt{c}:\texttt{?c}\}$. Type reconstruction (see Figure 13.21) yields the type $T_{abs} = (\texttt{->} \ (\texttt{?f} \ \texttt{?x}) \ \texttt{?fres})$, where $\texttt{?f}$ and $\texttt{?x}$ are the fresh type identifiers generated for the parameters $\texttt{f}$ and $\texttt{x}$ and $\texttt{?fres}$ is the fresh type identifier generated for the result of the application $(\texttt{f} \ (\texttt{if} \ \texttt{b} \ \texttt{x} \ \texttt{c}))$. Type reconstruction also yields the type-constraint set

$$TCS_{app} = \{\texttt{bool} \doteq \texttt{bool}, \texttt{?c} \doteq \texttt{?x}, \texttt{?f} \doteq (\texttt{->} \ (\texttt{?c}) \ \texttt{?fres})\}_{TCS}$$

which has the solution

$$\sigma_{abs} = \{\texttt{?f} \mapsto (\texttt{->} \ (\texttt{?x}) \ \texttt{?fres}), \texttt{?c} \mapsto \texttt{?x}\}$$

Abbreviations

T_{abs} = (-> (?f ?x) ?fres)

TCS_{if} = $\{\text{bool} \doteq \text{bool}, ?c \doteq ?x\}_{TCS}$

TCS_{app} = $TCS_{if} \uplus \{?f \doteq (\text{-> (?c) ?fres)}\}_{TCS}$

Type Reconstruction

$R[\![$f$]\!]$ {b : bool, c : ?c, f : ?f, x : ?x} = $\langle$?f, $\{\}_{TCS}\rangle$ $[var_{LPR}]$

$R[\![$b$]\!]$ {b : bool, c : ?c, f : ?f, x : ?x} = $\langle$bool, $\{\}_{TCS}\rangle$ $[var_{LPR}]$

$R[\![$c$]\!]$ {b : bool, c : ?c, f : ?f, x : ?x} = $\langle$?c, $\{\}_{TCS}\rangle$ $[var_{LPR}]$

$R[\![$x$]\!]$ {b : bool, c : ?c, f : ?f, x : ?x} = $\langle$?x, $\{\}_{TCS}\rangle$ $[var_{LPR}]$

$R[\![$(if b c x)$]\!]$ {b : bool, c : ?c, f : ?f, x : ?x} = $\langle$?c, $TCS_{if}\rangle$ $[if_R]$

$R[\![$(f (if b c x))$]\!]$ {b : bool, c : ?c, f : ?f, x : ?x}
= $\langle$?fres, $TCS_{app}\rangle$ $[\text{->-}elim_R]$

$R[\![$(abs (f x) (f (if b c x)))$]\!]$ {b : bool, c : ?c} = $\langle T_{abs}, TCS_{app}\rangle$ $[\text{->-}intro_R]$

Figure 13.21 Type reconstruction for (abs (f x) (f (if b c x))) relative to the type environment {b : bool, c : ?c}.

If σ_{abs} were not applied to T_{abs} and TE_{abs}, then $rgen$ would determine that ?f, ?x, and ?fres were the free type identifiers in T_{abs} not mentioned in TE_{abs} and would return the type schema

    (generic (?f ?x ?fres) (-> (?f ?x) ?fres))

This type fails to take into account that ?f is not an independently choosable type identifier but really depends on both the fresh type identifier ?fres and the type identifier ?c from the type environment. But when $(\sigma_{abs} \; T_{abs})$ = (-> ((-> (?x) ?fres) ?x) ?fres) and $(\sigma_{abs} \; TE_{abs})$ = {b : bool, c : ?x} are used, $rgen$ determines that ?fres is the only free type identifier in $(\sigma_{abs} \; T_{abs})$ that is not mentioned in TE_{abs}, and it returns the correct type schema,

    (generic (?fres) (-> ((-> (?x) ?fres) ?x) ?fres))

Note how σ_{abs} has replaced the free type identifier ?c in TE_{abs} by ?x.

Figure 13.22 presents the type reconstruction of our running example E_{id}. The let$_{LPR}$ rule generalizes the type (-> (?x) ?x) of (abs (x) x) to the type schema (generic (?x) (-> (?x) ?x)), and this type schema is instantiated with three fresh type identifiers (?x1, ?x2, and ?x3) at the three variable references to id. The type-constraint set TCS_{if} collected for E_{id} is

Abbreviations

E_{id} = (let ((id (abs (x) x))) (if (id #t) 1 ((id id) 2)))

$TE_{letbody}$ = {id : (generic (?x) (-> (?x) ?x))}

$TCS_{(id\ \#t)}$ = {(-> (?x1) ?x1) $\doteq$ (-> (bool) ?res1)}$_{TCS}$

$TCS_{(id\ id)}$ = {(-> (?x2) ?x2) $\doteq$ (-> ((-> (?x3) ?x3)) ?res2)}$_{TCS}$

$TCS_{((id\ id)\ 2)}$ = $TCS_{(id\ id)}$ $\uplus$ {?res2 $\doteq$ (-> (int) ?res3)}$_{TCS}$

TCS_{if} = $TCS_{(id\ \#t)}$ $\uplus$ $TCS_{((id\ id)\ 2)}$ $\uplus$ {?res1 $\doteq$ bool, int $\doteq$?res3}$_{TCS}$

Type Reconstruction for E_{id}

$R[\![x]\!]$ {x : ?x} = $\langle$?x, {}$_{TCS}\rangle$ [var$_{LPR}$]

$R[\![$(abs (x) x)$]\!]$ {} = $\langle$(-> (?x) ?x), {}$_{TCS}\rangle$ [$\rightarrow$-intro$_R$]

$R[\![id]\!]$ $TE_{letbody}$ = $\langle$(-> (?x1) ?x1), {}$_{TCS}\rangle$ [genvar$_{LPR}$]

$R[\![\#t]\!]$ $TE_{letbody}$ = $\langle$bool, {}$_{TCS}\rangle$ [bool$_R$]

$R[\![$(id #t)$]\!]$ $TE_{letbody}$ = $\langle$?res1, $TCS_{(id\ \#t)}\rangle$ [$\rightarrow$-elim$_R$]

$R[\![1]\!]$ $TE_{letbody}$ = $\langle$int, {}$_{TCS}\rangle$ [int$_R$]

$R[\![id]\!]$ $TE_{letbody}$ = $\langle$(-> (?x2) ?x2), {}$_{TCS}\rangle$ [genvar$_{LPR}$]

$R[\![id]\!]$ $TE_{letbody}$ = $\langle$(-> (?x3) ?x3), {}$_{TCS}\rangle$ [genvar$_{LPR}$]

$R[\![$(id id)$]\!]$ $TE_{letbody}$ = $\langle$?res2, $TCS_{(id\ id)}\rangle$ [$\rightarrow$-elim$_R$]

$R[\![2]\!]$ $TE_{letbody}$ = $\langle$int, {}$_{TCS}\rangle$ [int$_R$]

$R[\![$((id id) 2)$]\!]$ $TE_{letbody}$ = $\langle$?res3, $TCS_{((id\ id)\ 2)}\rangle$ [$\rightarrow$-elim$_R$]

$R[\![$(if (id #t) 1 ((id id) 2))$]\!]$ $TE_{letbody}$ = $\langle$int, $TCS_{if}\rangle$ [if$_R$]

$R[\![$(let ((id (abs (x) x))) (if (id #t) 1 ((id id) 2)))$]\!]$ {}
= $\langle$int, $TCS_{if}\rangle$ [let$_{LPR}$]

Figure 13.22 Type reconstruction for E_{id} in μFLARE$_{LP}$.

$$TCS_{if} = \{(\text{-> (?x1) ?x1}) \doteq (\text{-> (bool) ?res1}),$$
$$(\text{-> (?x2) ?x2}) \doteq (\text{-> ((-> (?x3) ?x3)) ?res2}),$$
$$?res2 \doteq (\text{-> (int) ?res3}), ?res1 \doteq bool, int \doteq ?res3\}_{CS},$$

and the solution to this type-constraint set is (TypeSubst $\rightarrowtail$ UnifySoln σ_{if}), where

$$\sigma_{if} = \{?x1 \mapsto bool, ?x2 \mapsto (\text{-> (int) int}), ?x3 \mapsto int$$
$$?res1 \mapsto bool, ?res2 \mapsto (\text{-> (int) int}), ?res3 \mapsto int\}$$

Transforming each judgment $R[\![E]\!]$ TE = $\langle T, TCS\rangle$ in Figure 13.22 to $(\sigma_{if}\ TE) \vdash$ $E : (\sigma_{if}\ T)$ yields the type derivation for E_{id} presented earlier (Figure 13.18 on page 803).

The approach to type reconstruction based on `let` polymorphism is sometimes called **Hindley-Damas-Milner (HDM) type reconstruction**, after its inventors. This approach is widely recognized as a "sweet spot" in the design space of type reconstruction systems and is used in many practical type reconstruction systems, most notably those of ML and HASKELL. Because it was first implemented in ML, this approach is also known as **ML-style type reconstruction**.

Exercise 13.6 For each of the following μFLARE expressions,

- if the expression is well typed, construct a vertical-style type derivation showing that the expression is well typed in the μFLARE$_{LP}$ type system;

- if the expression is ill typed, explain why, and show how to rewrite the expression so that it has the same meaning but is well typed in the μFLARE$_{LP}$ type system.

a. `(abs (a b)`
   `   (let ((revapp (abs (x) (abs (f) (f x)))))`
   `     (let ((appa (revapp a))`
   `           (appb (revapp b)))`
   `       (if (and (appa (abs (w) (prim > w 0)))`
   `                (appb (abs (x) (prim not x))))`
   `           (appa (abs (y) (prim + y 1)))`
   `           (appb (abs (z) (if z 1 0)))))))`

b. `(abs (b y z)`
   `   ((abs (f) (f z))`
   `    (if b (abs (w) w) (abs (x) y))))`

c. `(abs (b)`
   `   ((abs (f) (f f))`
   `    (if b (abs (w) w) (abs (x) (abs (y) x)))))`

d. `(abs (i)`
   `   (letrec ((id (abs (x) x))`
   `            (compose (abs (f g) (abs (x) (f (g x)))))`
   `            (repeated (abs (n h)`
   `                        (if (prim <= n 0)`
   `                            id`
   `                            (compose h (repeated (prim - n 1) h)))))`
   `            (incdbl (compose (abs (y) (prim + 1 y))`
   `                             (abs (z) (prim * 2 z)))))`
   `     (if ((repeated i not) #t) i ((repeated i incdbl) i))))`

e. `(let ((compose (abs (f g) (abs (x) (f (g x)))))`
   `      (thrice (abs (f) (abs (x) (f (f (f x)))))))`
   `   (let ((nat (abs (g) ((g (abs (x) (prim + x 1))) 0))))`
   `     (prim + (nat (abs (h) (compose (thrice h) (thrice h))))`
   `             (prim + (nat (compose thrice thrice))`
   `                     (nat (thrice thrice))))))`

Exercise 13.7 Consider the following definitions of Church pair operations in the FL language:

```
(def church-pair (abs (a b) (abs (f) (f a b))))
(def church-fst (abs (p) (p (abs (x y) x))))
(def church-snd (abs (p) (p (abs (x y) y))))
```

Can these definitions be used in μFLARE_{LP}? Explain. *Hint:* Compare to Exercise 12.13 on page 737.

13.5 Extensions

13.5.1 The Full FLARE Language

The full FLARE language extends μFLARE_{LP} with immutable pairs, homogeneous immutable lists, and mutable cells (Figure 13.23). We will assume that full FLARE is a CBV language. This allows us to treat `begin` as syntactic sugar and `cell` and `pair` as primitive operators. In a CBN version of FLARE, we would need to make `begin`, `pair`, and `cell` kernel constructs. Reducing the number of kernel constructs makes the language easier to analyze. For example, fewer type rules and type-reconstruction rules need to be specified when there are fewer kernel constructs. Furthermore, FLARE is the foundation for the source language for the transformation-based compiler we study in Chapter 17, and having fewer kernel constructs simplifies the compiler by reducing the number of cases that need to be handled by each transformation.

Since FLARE supports lists, it includes the `list` sugar from FL. Unlike in FLEX, no explicit type is needed in the `list` sugar construct because it can be inferred.

The dynamic semantics of FLARE can be obtained by modifying the CBN μFLARE semantics in Figures 13.6 and 13.7 to be CBV and extending it to handle state with cells (as in the SOS for FLICK defined in Figures 8.13 and 8.14) as well as pairs and lists.

The static semantics of FLARE is summarized in Figure 13.24. FLARE needs new type constructors to handle pairs (`pairof`), lists (`listof`), and cells (`cellof`). Most type rules are inherited from μFLARE_{LP}. There are no special type rules for pair, list, and cell operations; we assume that the primitive type environment TE_{prim} has been appropriately extended with generic type schemas for these primitives. For example:

```
pair : (generic (?a ?b) (-> (?a ?b) (pairof ?a ?b)))
 fst : (generic (?a ?b) (-> ((pairof ?a ?b)) ?a))
 snd : (generic (?a ?b) (-> ((pairof ?a ?b)) ?b))
```

Kernel Grammar

(as in μFLARE except where noted)

$P \in \text{Prog} ::= (\text{flarek } (I^*_{formal}) \ E_{body})$

$E \in \text{Exp} ::= L \mid I \mid (\text{error } Y_{message}) \mid (\text{if } E_{test} \ E_{then} \ E_{else})$
$\qquad \mid (\text{prim } O_{primop} \ E^*_{arg}) \mid (\text{abs } (I^*_{formal}) \ E_{body}) \mid (E_{rator} \ E^*_{rand})$
$\qquad \mid (\text{let } ((I_{name} \ E_{defn})^*) \ E_{body}) \mid (\text{letrec } ((I_{name} \ E_{defn})^*) \ E_{body})$

$L \in \text{Lit} ::= \texttt{\#u} \mid B \mid N \mid (\text{sym } Y)$

$B \in \text{BoolLit} = \{\texttt{\#t}, \texttt{\#f}\}$ as in FL and μFLARE.

$N \in \text{IntLit} = $ as in FL and μFLARE.

$Y \in \text{SymLit} = $ as in FL and μFLARE.

$O \in \text{Primop} ::= \ldots \mu$FLARE *primitive operators* $\ldots$
$\qquad\qquad\quad \mid \texttt{pair} \mid \texttt{fst} \mid \texttt{snd} \qquad\qquad\quad ; \textit{ pair ops}$
$\qquad\qquad\quad \mid \texttt{cons} \mid \texttt{car} \mid \texttt{cdr} \mid \texttt{null} \mid \texttt{null?} \ ; \textit{ list ops}$
$\qquad\qquad\quad \mid \texttt{cell} \mid \texttt{\textasciicircum} \mid \texttt{:=} \mid \texttt{cell=?} \qquad\quad ; \textit{ mutable cell ops}$

$\qquad$ Keyword $=$ as in μFLARE.

$\qquad$ SugarKeyword $=$ SugarKeyword$_{\mu\text{FLARE}} \cup \{\texttt{begin}, \texttt{list}\}$

$I \in \text{Ident} = \text{SymLit} - (\{Y \mid Y \text{ begins with } \texttt{@}\} \cup \text{Keyword} \cup \text{SugarKeyword})$

Syntactic Sugar

$\texttt{@}O$, cond, scand, scor, recur, and def as in FL (page 233).

$(\texttt{begin}) \rightsquigarrow_{ds} \texttt{\#u}$
$(\texttt{begin } E) \rightsquigarrow_{ds} E$
$(\texttt{begin } E_1 \ E^*_{rest}) \rightsquigarrow_{ds} (\texttt{let } ((\_ \ E_1)) \ (\texttt{begin } E^*_{rest})),$
$\qquad$ where $\_$ is a special identifier that can never be referenced

$(\texttt{list}) \rightsquigarrow_{ds} (\texttt{prim null})$
$(\texttt{list } E_1 \ E^*_{rest}) \rightsquigarrow_{ds} (\texttt{prim cons } E_1 \ (\texttt{list } E^*_{rest}))$

$(\texttt{flare } (I^*_{pgmFormal}) \ E_{pgmBody} \ (\texttt{def } I_{name_i} \ E_{defn_i})^n_{i=1})$
$\qquad \{\textit{Assume procedure defs already desugared to } (\texttt{def } I \ E)$
$\qquad\quad \textit{by the } \texttt{def} \ \textit{desugaring rule inherited from } FL.\}$
$\rightsquigarrow_{ds} (\texttt{flarek } (I^*_{pgmFormal})$
$\qquad\quad (\texttt{letrec } \{\textit{Standard library bindings}\}$
$\qquad\qquad\qquad \{\textit{None of these bindings are recursive, but new ones might be.}\}$
$\qquad\qquad\qquad ((\texttt{car } (\texttt{abs } (\texttt{x}) \ (\texttt{prim car x})))$
$\qquad\qquad\qquad\ (\texttt{cons } (\texttt{abs } (\texttt{x y}) \ (\texttt{prim cons x y})))$
$\qquad\qquad\qquad\quad \vdots \ \{\textit{Similar for other primitive operators.}\}$
$\qquad\qquad\qquad\ (\texttt{true \#t}) \ (\texttt{false \#f}) \ \{\textit{Synonyms for literals.}\}$
$\qquad\qquad\qquad)$
$\qquad\qquad (\texttt{letrec } ((I_{name_i} \ E_{defn_i})^n_{i=1})$
$\qquad\qquad\quad E_{pgmBody})))$

Figure 13.23   Grammar and syntactic sugar for the full FLARE language.

Domains

$T \in \text{Type} ::= BT \mid \tau \mid (\texttt{->} \ (T^*) \ T_{result}) \ ; \textit{as in } \mu\text{FLARE}$
$\qquad\qquad \mid (\texttt{pairof} \ T_{fst} \ T_{snd}) \mid (\texttt{listof} \ T) \mid (\texttt{cellof} \ T) \ ; \textit{as in FLEX}$

$BT \in \text{BaseType} = \{\texttt{unit}, \texttt{int}, \texttt{bool}, \texttt{symb}\} \ ; \textit{as in } \mu\text{FLARE}$

$\tau \in \text{TypeId} = \text{SymLit} - (\text{BaseType} \cup \{\texttt{->}, \texttt{pairof}, \texttt{listof}, \texttt{cellof}, \texttt{generic}\})$

$PT \in \text{ProgType} ::= (\texttt{=>} \ (T^*_{arg}) \ T_{result}) \ ; \textit{as in } \mu\text{FLARE}$

$TS \in \text{TypeSchema} ::= T \mid (\texttt{generic} \ (\tau^*) \ T) \ ; \textit{as in } \mu\text{FLARE}_{LP}$

$TE \in \text{TypeEnvironment} = \text{Ident} \rightharpoonup \text{TypeSchema} \ ; \textit{as in } \mu\text{FLARE}_{LP}$

New Type Functions

gen is defined as in μFLARE_{LP} (Figure 13.19 on page 805).

$genPure : \text{Type} \to \text{TypeEnvironment} \to \text{Exp} \to \text{TypeSchema}$

$$(genPure \ T_{defn} \ TE \ E_{defn}) = \begin{cases} (gen \ T_{defn} \ TE) & \text{if } E_{defn} \text{ is pure.} \\ T_{defn} & \text{otherwise} \end{cases}$$

Type Rules

$$\frac{\forall_{i=1}^n \ . \ TE \vdash E_i : T_i \qquad TE[I_i : (genPure \ T_i \ TE \ E_i)]_{i=1}^n \vdash E_0 : T_0}{TE \vdash (\texttt{let} \ ((I_i \ E_i)_{i=1}^n) \ E_0) : T_0} \qquad [let'_{LP}]$$

$$\frac{\forall_{i=1}^n \ . \ TE[I_j : T_j]_{j=1}^n \vdash E_i : T_i \qquad TE[I_i : (genPure \ T_i \ TE \ E_i)]_{i=1}^n \vdash E_0 : T_0}{TE \vdash (\texttt{letrec} \ ((I_i \ E_i)_{i=1}^n) \ E_0) : T_0} \qquad [letrec'_{LP}]$$

All other type rules are the same as in μFLARE_{LP}.

Figure 13.24 Type system for the full FLARE language with `let` polymorphism.

Interestingly, the fact that FLARE has imperative features (mutable cells) makes it necessary to modify the $[let_{LP}]$ and $[letrec_{LP}]$ rules from μFLARE_{LP}. In particular, it is safe to generalize the type of a `let` or `letrec` definition expression only if it is **pure** — i.e., evaluating it does not touch the store (see the discussion of purity on page 428).

To see what can go wrong with impure definition expressions, we revisit the $E_{polyCell}$ example from page 735 (which we now view as a FLARE expression rather than an FL expression):

```
E_polyCell = (let ((c (cell (null))))
               (begin (:= c (cons 1 (null)))
                      (not (car (^ c)))))
```

$$\vdash_{pure} L \qquad [\textit{lit-pure}] \qquad\qquad \vdash_{pure} I \qquad [\textit{var-pure}]$$

$$\vdash_{pure} (\texttt{abs}\ (I_{i=1}^n)\ E_{body})\ [\textit{abs-pure}] \qquad\qquad \vdash_{pure} (\texttt{error}\ Y) \qquad [\textit{error-pure}]$$

$$\frac{\forall_{i=1}^3 \cdot (\vdash_{pure} E_i)}{\vdash_{pure} (\texttt{if}\ E_1\ E_2\ E_3)}\ [\textit{if-pure}] \qquad \frac{\forall_{i=0}^n \cdot (\vdash_{pure} E_i)}{\vdash_{pure} (\texttt{let}\ ((I_i\ E_i)_{i=1}^n)\ E_0)}\ [\textit{let-pure}]$$

$$\frac{\forall_{i=0}^n \cdot (\vdash_{pure} E_i)}{\vdash_{pure} (\texttt{letrec}\ ((I_i\ E_i)_{i=1}^n)\ E_0)} \qquad\qquad [\textit{letrec-pure}]$$

$$\frac{\forall_{i=1}^n \cdot (\vdash_{pure} E_i)}{\vdash_{pure} (\texttt{prim}\ O\ E_{i=1}^n)}\ , \text{where}\ O \notin \{\texttt{cell}, \texttt{\textasciicircum}, \texttt{:=}\} \qquad [\textit{prim-pure}]$$

Figure 13.25 Deduction system to conservatively approximate the purity of FLARE expressions.

With the $[\textit{let}_{LP}]$ rule from μFLARE, the cell type $(\texttt{cellof}\ (\texttt{listof}\ \texttt{?t}))$ of $(\texttt{cell}\ (\texttt{null}))$ can be generalized to $(\texttt{generic}\ (\texttt{?t})\ (\texttt{cellof}\ (\texttt{listof}\ \texttt{?t})))$, which can be instantiated to $(\texttt{cellof}\ (\texttt{listof}\ \texttt{int}))$ for the reference of c in the := expression and instantiated to $(\texttt{cellof}\ (\texttt{listof}\ \texttt{bool}))$ for the reference of c in the ^ expression. So the expression is well typed. But at run time, a dynamic type error will be encountered when an attempt is made to apply **not** to the integer 1!

The problem here is that the type system effectively copies the definition expression $(\texttt{cell}\ (\texttt{null}))$ to the two variable references of c, and the expression is safe if these refer to different cells but not if they refer to the same cell. It is safe to copy the definition expression, and therefore safe to generalize the type of the definition expression, only when it is guaranteed that the expression will not perform any side effects. The new $[\textit{let}'_{LP}]$ and $[\textit{letrec}'_{LP}]$ rules use the new *genPure* function to restrict generalization to the cases where the definition expression is pure — i.e., evaluating it does not "touch" the store (look up information in or modify the store in an observable way). *genPure* is like *gen*, but takes an additional argument (the definition expression) in order to determine when generalization can take place. With the purity restriction, the above **cell** example is ill typed, because both references to c must have the same content type, which cannot be both **int** and **bool**.

Purity is an undecidable property in general, but it can be conservatively approximated. The deduction system in Figure 13.25 is a simple conservative approximation of purity that formalizes the notion of syntactic value introduced on page 428. If the judgment $\vdash_{pure} E$ can be proven via the rules in Figure 13.25, then we can argue that E does not touch the store. Literals, variable references, and error expressions clearly do not touch the store. An abstraction is always pure regardless of the purity of its body; although *invoking* a procedure can touch the store, *creating* a procedure does not touch it. An `if` expression is pure if all of its subexpressions are pure. The same is true for `let` and `letrec` expressions. Primitive applications are pure as long as the operand expressions are pure and the primitive operation is not a cell operation that touches the store (i.e., one of `cell`, `^`, or `:=`). It is important to understand why certain expressions are excluded from the deductive definition of purity:

- Primitive applications involving `cell`, `:=`, and `^` touch the store and so are clearly impure.

- Procedure applications are considered impure because evaluating the body of an invoked procedure might touch the store.

There are many ways in which this approximation of purity can be improved. For example, if the body of a procedure is pure, then an application of the procedure is also pure. In Chapter 16, we will see how some additional procedure applications can be considered pure by using an **effect system** that tracks the potential side effects of procedures.

The type reconstruction rules for FLARE are those of μFLARE_{LP} with modifications analogous to those made in changing the μFLARE_{LP} type system to the FLARE type system. These modifications are presented in Figure 13.26. In the modified reconstruction rules for `let` and `letrec`, the *rgen* function is replaced by *rgenPure*, which takes one additional argument: a definition expression to test for purity. Limiting `let` polymorphism to syntactic values is common in ML dialects, where it is known as the **value restriction** [Wri95].

It would be straightforward to extend FLARE with certain additional features, like immutable or mutable strings, immutable sequences, and mutable arrays. To keep FLARE compact, we do not include these in the standard version of the language, though we will sometimes consider variants of the language with these features.

Other features — such as mutable variables, tuples, records, oneofs, and general recursive sum-of-products data types — are more challenging to add to a language that supports type reconstruction. We discuss these features in more detail in the remainder of this chapter.

New Type Functions

rgen is defined as in Figure 13.20.

rgenPure : Type $\rightarrow$ TypeEnvironment $\rightarrow$ TypeConstraintSet $\rightarrow$ Exp $\rightarrow$ TypeSchema

$$(\textit{rgenPure } T_{defn} \; TE \; TCS \; E_{defn}) = \begin{cases} (\textit{rgen } T_{defn} \; TE \; TCS) & \text{if } E_{defn} \text{ is pure} \\ T_{defn} & \text{otherwise} \end{cases}$$

Modified Type Reconstruction Rules

$$\frac{\forall_{i=1}^{n} \, . \, (R[\![E_i]\!] \; TE = \langle T_i, TCS_i \rangle) \quad R[\![E_0]\!] \; TE[I_i : (\textit{rgenPure } T_i \; TE \; TCS_i \; E_i)]_{i=1}^{n} = \langle T_0, TCS_0 \rangle}{R[\![(\texttt{let } ((I_i \; E_i)_{i=1}^{n}) \; E_0)]\!] \; TE = \langle T_0, TCS_0 \uplus TCS_{defns} \rangle} \quad [\textit{let}'_{LPR}]$$
$$\text{where } TCS_{defns} = \biguplus_{i=1}^{n} TCS_i$$

$$\frac{\forall_{i=1}^{n} \, . \, \left(R[\![E_i]\!] \; TE[I_j : \tau_j]_{j=1}^{n} = \langle T_i, TCS_i \rangle \right) \quad R[\![E_0]\!] \; TE[I_i : (\textit{rgenPure } T_i \; TE \; TCS_{defns} \; E_i)]_{i=1}^{n} = \langle T_0, TCS_0 \rangle}{R[\![(\texttt{letrec } ((I_i \; E_i)_{i=1}^{n}) \; E_0)]\!] \; TE = \langle T_0, TCS_0 \uplus TCS_{defns} \rangle} \quad [\textit{letrec}'_{LPR}]$$
$$\text{where } \tau_{i=1}^{n} \text{ are fresh and } TCS_{defns} = \left(\biguplus_{i=1}^{n} TCS_i \right) \uplus \left(\biguplus_{i=1}^{n} \{\tau_i \doteq T_i\}_{TCS} \right)$$

Figure 13.26   Type reconstruction rules for FLARE.

Exercise 13.8 For each of the following FLARE abstractions,

- if the abstraction is well typed, give the principal type that the type reconstruction algorithm finds for the abstraction;

- if the abstraction is ill typed, explain why type reconstruction fails.

a. `(abs (x f g) (pair (f x) (g x)))`

b. `(abs (x f g) (pair (f x) (g (f x))))`

c. `(abs (x f g) (pair (g (f x)) (f (g x))))`

d. `(abs (x f g) (pair (f x) (g x (f x))))`

e. `(abs (x f g) (pair (f x) (g (f x) (f (g x)))))`

f. `(abs (x f g) (pair (f x) (g x (f (g x)))))`

Exercise 13.9 Assume that all of the definitions in Figure 13.27 are made in the same FLARE program. Give the type schema reconstructed for each definition.

Exercise 13.10 FLARE can be extended with updatable sequences, which were discussed on page 545. Assume that the Type domain is extended with types of the form

```
(def (swap-pair p)
  (pair (snd p) (fst p)))

(def (swap-cells! c1 c2)
  (let ((v (^ c1)))
    (begin (:= c1 (^ c2))
           (:= c2 v))))

(def (foldr binop nullval xs)
  (if (null? xs)
      nullval
      (binop (car xs) (foldr binop nullval (cdr xs)))))

(def (map f xs)
  (if (null? xs) xs (cons (f (car xs)) (map f (cdr xs)))))

(def (map-as-foldr f xs)
  (foldr (abs (x ans) (cons (f x) ans)) (null) xs))

(def (map! f xs)
  (if (null? xs)
      #u
      (begin (:= (car xs) (f (^ (car xs))))
             (map! f (cdr xs)))))

(def (filter pred xs)
  (cond ((null? xs) xs)
        ((pred (car xs)) (cons (car xs) (filter pred (cdr xs))))
        (else (filter pred (cdr xs)))))

(def (forall? pred xs)
  (scor (null? xs)
        (scand (pred (car xs)) (forall? pred (cdr xs)))))
```

Figure 13.27 Some sample FLARE definitions.

(useqof T) that model the type of an updatable sequence. Give a FLARE type rule and a FLARE type reconstruction rule for each of the following constructs:

```
(useq E*)
(useq-get Eindex Euseq)
(useq-size Euseq)
(useq-update Eindex Eval Euseq)
(useq-insert Eindex Eval Euseq)
(useq-delete Eindex Euseq)
```

13.5.2 Mutable Variables

FLARE can be extended with mutable variables that are changed via an assignment construct, such as the `set!` construct in the FLAVAR language presented in Section 8.4. This has two consequences:

1. Just as it is unsound to generalize the type of a `let` or `letrec` definition expression that touches the store via mutable cell operations, it is unsound to generalize the type of the expression when its associated name is assigned via `set!` in its scope. In a version of FLARE with `set!`, it is necessary to modify the *genPure* and *rgenPure* functions to prohibit such unsound generalizations.

2. In the presence of mutable variables, variable references are no longer necessarily pure since they read information from a mutable store. The simplest way to handle this is to change the definition of $\vdash_{pure}$ so that a variable reference I is no longer considered pure. A less crude approximation can be obtained by tracking which variables are assigned and considering I to be pure if it is never assigned.

These issues are explored in Exercise 13.11. To avoid these complications, we do not include mutable variables in FLARE. There is no loss of expressiveness, because FLARE+{`set!`} can be automatically transformed to FLARE by converting all variables that are mutated by `set!` into explicit cells. This transformation, which is known as **assignment conversion**, is a stage (Section 17.5) in the transformation-based compiler that we will study in Chapter 17.

Exercise 13.11 This exercise explores the consequences of extending FLARE with mutable variables (via the `set!` construct).

a. Extend the type rules in Figure 13.24 and the type reconstruction rules in Figure 13.26 to handle the `set!` construct.

b. Consider the following FLARE+{`set!`} expression:

```
(let ((f (abs (x) x)))
  (begin (set! f (abs (y) (prim + y 1)))
         (if (f #t) 1 (f 2))))
```

Using this expression, show that the $[let'_{LP}]$ type rule from Figure 13.24 is unsound for FLARE+{`set!`}. That is, show that the expression is well typed even though it encounters a dynamic type error.

c. Modify the $[let'_{LP}]$ and $[letrec'_{LP}]$ type rules from Figure 13.24 so that they are sound for FLARE+{`set!`}. Your rules should prevent generalizing the type of any variable that is assigned via `set!`. You should modify the definition of *genPure* appropriately. (*Hint:* add extra arguments). Assume that the definition of $\vdash_{pure}$ is changed so that a variable reference I is no longer considered pure. You may find the *MutIds* function in Figure 17.10 on page 1020 helpful for determining which variables are assigned.

d. Show that the expression in part **b** is ill typed using your modified $[let'_{LP}]$ rule from part **c**.

e. Modify the $[let'_{LPR}]$ and $[letrec'_{LPR}]$ type reconstruction rules from Figure 13.26 so that they are sound for FLARE+{`set!`}. You should modify the definition of *rgenPure* appropriately.

f. Explain why the following expression is ill typed in FLARE+{`set!`}:

```
(let ((first (abs (xs) (prim car xs)))
      (second (abs (ys) (prim car (prim cdr ys)))))
  (abs (b)
    (let ((g (if b first second)))
      (pair (g (list 1 2)) (g (list #t #f))))))
```

g. Argue that the expression in part **f** is safe to evaluate even though it is ill typed.

h. It is possible to change the definition of purity to be more accurate so that the expression in part **f** is well typed. In particular, a reference to a variable should be considered pure if that variable is never assigned via `set!`. To track which variables are never assigned, purity judgments can be changed to have the form $IS \vdash_{pure} E$ where $IS \in \mathcal{P}(\text{Ident})$ is a set of identifiers known not to be assigned in a program.

  i. Modify the purity rules in Figure 13.25 so they use the extended purity judgments.

  ii. Modify your definition of *genPure* and the `let` and `letrec` type rules from part **c** so that they explicitly use the extended purity judgments to allow more expressions to be well typed.

  iii. Show that the expression in part **f** is well typed using your modified type system.

13.5.3 Products and Sums

Homogeneous products like strings and arrays are easy to include in a language supporting type reconstruction because all components have the same type. But heterogeneous products (records and tuples) are problematic because the component-projection constructs provide only partial information about the product type. Similarly, injection constructs for sums (e.g., the oneof-creation construct `one`) provide only partial information about the sum type.

For example, the record-selection expression (`select` I_{field} E_{rcd}) implies that E_{rcd} denotes a record that has at least a field named I. The type of this field is constrained by the context of the `select` expression. But it doesn't say anything about the rest of the record. Consider the abstraction

```
(abs (r) (pair (+ 1 (select a r)) (not (select b r))))
```

(`select a r`) tells us that `r`'s type has the form (`recordof ... (a int) ...`), and (`select b r`) tells us that it has the form (`recordof ... (b bool) ...`). We could perhaps combine these pieces of information, but we are still left with only a partial record type (`recordof ... (a int) (b bool) ...`).

There are several ways to address the problem of partial type information. The most direct is to require each `select` expression to contain an explicit type, e.g., to be of the form (`select` I_{field} E_{rcd} T_{rcd}), where T_{rcd} is the type of the value of E_{rcd}. In this approach, the record example from above might become:

```
(abs (r)
    (pair (+ 1 (select a r (recordof (a int) (b bool) (c symb))))
          (not (select b r (recordof (a int) (b bool) (c symb))))))
```

Although explicit types are not in the spirit of type reconstruction, they are sometimes used to simplify the type reconstruction process.

Another way to address the problem of partial type information is to require the user to declare a unique association between field names and record types. In such a system, the type declaration

```
(def-type myrecord (recordof (a int) (b bool) (c symb)))
```

would not only define `myrecord` as a synonym for the specified record type, but would also restrict the field names `a`, `b`, and `c` to be used only in records of type `myrecord`. It would be an error to use these field names in any other record, which can be a frustrating restriction. But then we would know that the E in (`select a` E) must have type `myrecord`.[5]

The most general approach for reconstructing record types is to collect, and eventually solve, constraints on record field types. The basic idea is simple: we represent the constraints on a record type by a sequence of name/type bindings (known as a **row type**) that may terminate in a unification variable (known as a **row variable**). Here we give an example-based description of this approach that glosses over many technical details. For a formal presentation of row types, see the Web Supplement.

Consider the row type $RT_1 = [(b\ int), (d\ bool), \$x]$. This consists of the bindings (`b int`) and (`d bool`) as well as the row variable `$x`,[6] which provides a kind of hook onto which future bindings can be hung. Unlike the unification vari-

---

[5]This is precisely the mechanism used in OCAML for reconstructing record types.
[6]Our convention is that row variable names start with the symbol $.

ables we have seen so far, which stand for a single type, a row variable stands for a sequence of name/type bindings. A row type ending in a row variable is said to be **incomplete**, while one that does not is said to be **complete**. E.g., RT_1 above is incomplete, while $RT_2 = [\text{(a symb)},\text{(b int)},\text{(c unit)},\text{(d bool)},\text{(e int)}]$ is a complete row type.

The unification algorithm from Figure 13.8 on page 784 can be modified to unify row types. For example, unifying RT_1 with RT_2 yields a substitution in which x is the complete row type $[\text{(a symb)},\text{(c unit)},\text{(e int)}]$. And unifying RT_1 with the incomplete row type $RT_3 = [\text{(a symb)},\text{(d bool)},\$\text{y}]$ yields a substitution in which x is the incomplete row type $[\text{(a symb)},\$\text{z}]$ and y is the incomplete row type $[\text{(b int)},\$\text{z}]$. The fact that both new row types end in the same row variable z constrains RT_1 and RT_3 to be the same if further unifications involving x, y, and z are performed.

Using row types, it is easy to reconstruct the `record` and `select` constructs in FLARE. For the expression $(\text{record } (I_i \; E_i)_{i=1}^n)$, the type rule

$$\frac{\forall_{i=1}^n . \; \mathcal{R}[\![E_i]\!] \; TE \; = \; \langle T_i, TCS_i \rangle}{\begin{array}{l} \mathcal{R}[\![(\text{record } (I_i \; E_i)_{i=1}^n)]\!] \; TE \\ = \; \langle (\text{recordof } (I_i \; T_i)_{i=1}^n), \biguplus_{i=1}^n TCS_i \rangle \end{array}} \qquad [\textit{recordof-intro}_R]$$

reconstructs a `recordof` type with the complete row type $[(I_i \; T_i)_{i=1}^n]$, where each T_i is the type reconstructed for the corresponding record-field definition E_i. For the expression $(\text{select } I \; E_{rcd})$, the type rule

$$\frac{\mathcal{R}[\![E_{rcd}]\!] \; TE \; = \; \langle T_{rcd}, TCS_{rcd} \rangle}{\begin{array}{l} \mathcal{R}[\![(\text{select } I \; E_{rcd})]\!] \; TE \\ = \; \langle \tau, TCS_{rcd} \uplus \{T_{rcd} \doteq (\text{recordof } (I \; \tau) \; \rho)\}_{TCS} \rangle \end{array}} \qquad [\textit{recordof-elim}_R]$$
$$\text{where } \tau \text{ is a fresh type identifier and } \rho \text{ is a fresh row variable.}$$

constrains the type T_{rcd} reconstructed for the record expression E_{rcd} to have a `recordof` type with the incomplete row type $[(I \; \tau), \rho]$, where τ is a fresh type identifier that stands for the type of the record field named I (and also the result type of the `select` expression), and ρ is a fresh row variable that stands for all the other record fields.

For example, consider the reconstruction of the FLARE expression

```
(let ((f (abs (r) (pair (* 2 (select c r)) (select d r)))))
  (pair (f (record (c 1) (d #t)))
        (f (record (b 3) (d #u) (c 4) (e (sym foo)))))))
```

Processing (select c r) introduces the type constraint

$$?r \doteq (\text{recordof } (c \; ?c) \; \$x)$$

and processing `(select d r)` introduces the type constraint

$$\texttt{?r} \doteq \texttt{(recordof (d ?d) \$y)}$$

where `?r` is the type of the abstraction parameter `r`. The `(* 2 ...)` expression constrains `?c` to have type `int`, but `?d` remains unconstrained. The unification process sketched above will determine that `?r` is the type

$$\texttt{(recordof (c int) (d ?d) \$z)}$$

so the abstraction in the example has type

```
(-> ((recordof (c int) (d ?d) $z))
    (pairof int ?d))
```

Both the type identifier `?d` and the row variable `$z` can be generalized,[7] so `f` is bound to the type schema

```
(generic (?d $z)
  (-> ((recordof (c int) (d ?d) $z))
      (pairof int ?d)))
```

This schema can be instantiated to match the type of the record argument in the first call to `f`, `(recordof (c int) (d bool))`, by instantiating the type variable `?d` to `bool` and the row variable `$z` to the empty row type, `[]`. The schema can also be instantiated to match the type of the record argument in the second call to `f`, `(recordof (b int) (d unit) (c int) (e symb))`, by instantiating `?d` to `unit` and `$z` to `[(b int),(e symb)]`. This example not only illustrates how row types allow partial record-type information to be manipulated but also shows how row types support a form of record polymorphism that resembles record subtyping (see Section 12.1).

Row types can also be used to reconstruct tuple types. These can be reconstructed by treating them as records with the distinguished labels `#1`, `#2`, `#3`, etc. For example:

Tuple Type/Expression	Corresponding Record Type/Expression
`(prodof int bool symb)`	`(recordof (#1 int) (#2 bool) (#3 symb))`
`(prod 17 #t (sym cat))`	`(record (#1 17) (#2 #t) (#3 (sym cat)))`
`(get 2 p)`	`(select #2 p)`

Row types can also be used to reconstruct sum types. Exercise 13.13 explores how to reconstruct oneof types in FLARE.

---

[7]To yield this result, the FLARE generalization function *rgen* from Figure 13.20 on page 809 must be modified to handle free row variables in addition to free type variables.

Exercise 13.12 Sam Antics wants to extend FLARE with heterogeneous positional products like those manipulated via prod and get in Section 10.1.1. He thinks that row types are too complicated for this purpose, but he bristles at the thought of supplying a complete explicit product type in the get construct simply to aid type reconstruction. Sam chooses a design between these two extreme design points based on the following constructs for manipulating products:

$$E ::= \ldots \mid (\texttt{prod } E^*) \mid (\texttt{get } N_{index} \; E_{prod} \; N_{size})$$

As usual, $(\texttt{prod } E_1 \; \ldots \; E_n)$ creates a product value, or tuple, with n components that are the values of the expressions $E_1, \ldots, E_n$, all of which may have different types. The expression $(\texttt{get } N_{index} \; E_{prod} \; N_{size})$ extracts the element at index N_{index} (1-based) from the value of E_{prod}, which should be a tuple with N_{size} components. The get expression signals an error if E_{prod} does not denote a tuple, if $\mathcal{N}[\![N_{size}]\!] \leq 0$, or if $\mathcal{N}[\![N_{index}]\!]$ is not in the range $[1..\mathcal{N}[\![N_{size}]\!]]$.

The inclusion of N_{size} in the get expression is Sam's one concession for type reconstruction. He claims that this provides enough information for the type reconstruction process to succeed on tuple-manipulation programs that are intuitively well typed without requiring the complex machinery of row types.

Sam also extends the type system with a prodof type constructor to describe the types of tuples:

$$T ::= \ldots \mid (\texttt{prodof } T^*)$$

a. Give the FLARE type rules for prod and get in Sam's system.

b. Give the FLARE type reconstruction rules for prod and get in Sam's system.

c. Louis Reasoner studies Sam's system and thinks he can improve it: "I don't see why the N_{index} has to be an integer literal. Why not change the form of get to $(\texttt{get } E_{index} \; E_{prod} \; N_{size})$? Then the index could be computed!" Why is this a bad idea?

d. After studying Sam's design, Abby Stracksen suggests that he replace get by the following construct:

$(\texttt{match-prod } ((I_1 \; \ldots \; I_n) \; E_{prod}) \; E_{body})$ evaluates E_{prod} to a value, which should be a tuple with n components, and then returns the value of E_{body} evaluated in the current environment extended with bindings of the names $I_1, \ldots, I_n$ to the n component values of the tuple.[8]

i. Give the type rule for match-prod.

ii. Give the type reconstruction rule for match-prod.

iii. Which do you prefer: Sam's get or Abby's match-prod? Explain.

---

[8]This approach — extracting tuple components using a pattern for the whole tuple — is used in OCAML for reconstructing tuple types.

e. Thai Ping studies Sam's design and observes that a version of FLARE with products can use the simpler construct (get N_{index} E_{prod}) (i.e., with no size specification) without requiring the full machinery of row types. "In addition to the complete product types (prodof $T_{i=1}^n$)," notes Thai, "all you need is an incomplete product type of the form (prodof $T_{i=1}^n$ TSV), where TSV is a type-sequence variable that stands for a sequence of types." Flesh out Thai's idea by (1) giving a type reconstruction rule for the simpler get construct that uses incomplete product types and (2) describing how to change the unification algorithm to handle both complete and incomplete product types.

Exercise 13.13 Suppose that FLARE with records and row types is further extended to include oneofs (see Section 10.2):

$$E \in \text{Exp} ::= \ldots$$
$$\mid (\text{one } I_{tag} \; E_{payload})$$
$$\mid (\text{tagcase } E_{disc} \; I_{payload} \; (I_{tag} \; E_{body})^* \; (\text{else } E_{else})^?)$$

$$T \in \text{Type} ::= \ldots$$
$$\mid (\text{oneof } (I_{tag} \; T_{payload})^*) \quad [\text{CompleteOneofType}]$$
$$\mid (\text{oneof } (I_{tag} \; T_{payload})^* \; \rho) \quad [\text{IncompleteOneofType}]$$

$$\rho \in \text{RowId} = \{ Y \in \text{SymLit} \mid Y \text{ begins with } \$ \}$$

Assume that the unification algorithm is modified to unify the row types of two oneof types.

a. Write type reconstruction rules for: (1) the one expression; (2) a tagcase expression without an else clause; and (3) a tagcase expression with an else clause.

b. Consider the following expression:

```
(let ((g (abs (bval h) (list (h (one i 17)) (h (one b bval))))))
  (pair (g #t (abs (v) (tagcase v p (i p)
                                   (b (if p 1 0)))))
        (g (sym cat) (abs (w) (tagcase w q (i (prim = q 0))
                                          (x #f)
                                          (else #t)))))))
```

Using your type reconstruction rules, what type schema is bound to the variable g? How is this schema instantiated for each of the two calls to g?

13.5.4   Sum-of-products Data Types

Sum-of-products data with pattern matching (see Sections 10.3–10.5) are a powerful way to describe and manipulate tree-structured data like lists, binary trees, and abstract syntax trees. In the explicitly typed framework of FLEX, sum-of-products data types can be cumbersome to use, because they generally involve recursive types (Section 11.8.6), universal types (Section 12.2.2), and kinds (Section 12.3.2). These features make it challenging to adapt approaches for desug-

```
 null : (generic (?t) {?t is element type}
           (-> () (listof ?t)))
 null~ : (generic (?r ?t)    {?r is return type; ?t is element type}
             (-> ((listof ?t) {type of datum to deconstruct}
                (-> () ?r)   {type of success continuation}
                (-> () ?r))  {type of failure continuation}
              ?r))           {return type of deconstructor}
 cons : (generic (?t) {?t is element type}
           (-> (?t (listof ?t) (listof ?t))))
 cons~ : (generic (?r ?t)                        {?r is return type; ?t is element type}
             (-> ((listof ?t)                     {type of datum to deconstruct}
                (-> (?t (listof ?t)) ?r)          {type of success continuation}
                (-> () ?r))                        {type of failure continuation}
              ?r))                                 {return type of deconstructor}
```

Figure 13.28 The type schemas of the constructor and deconstructor procedures introduced by the listof data-type definition.

aring data-type declarations in an explicitly typed language (see Section 12.2.3 and Exercises 12.20 and 12.25) to an implicitly typed one (see Exercise 13.16). In this section, we will see how to hide these complexities in FLARE, thus making sum-of-products data types and pattern matching convenient to use in an implicitly typed framework.

We will define the dynamic semantics for sum-of-products data types in a similar manner as before, by desugaring a data-type definition to define constructor and deconstructor procedures. If that were all we did, however, the static semantics — the type reconstruction needed for type checking — would be very complex. We will avoid the complexity of reconstructing the constructor and deconstructor types by putting their type information, which can be automatically derived from the data-type definition, into the type environment. Then at type-checking time, the types needn't be reconstructed because they are found in the extended type environment.

Consider a parameterized data-type declaration for lists:

```
(def-datatype (listof t)
  (null)
  (cons t (listof t)))
```

In our approach, the listof data-type definition introduces the constructor and deconstructor type schemas in Figure 13.28 into the type environment. The type schemas of the constructors null and cons are parameterized over the element type `?t` of the list being constructed. The type schemas of the deconstructors `null˜` and `cons˜` are parameterized over two types: the return type `?r` of the deconstructor and the element type `?t` of the list being deconstructed.

Handling the static semantics of data-type definitions by extending the type environment with type schemas has numerous advantages over approaches (like the one presented in Section 12.2.3) that explicitly specify or implicitly reconstruct the types of the constructor and deconstructor procedures introduced by desugaring data-type definitions.

- *No universal types:* Using `generic` types rather than `forall` types allows parameterized types while avoiding the machinery (`pabs` and `pcall`) for universal types.

- *No kinds, sum types, product types, or recursive types:* Because the type schemas implicitly treat `listof` as a new one-argument type constructor, there is no need to provide an explicit definition of `listof`. This not only avoids the description and kind machinery, but it also allows recursive sum-of-products types to be defined without recursive types, sum types, or product types! Sum types are handled implicitly by having multiple constructor/deconstructor pairs for a data type (e.g., `null/null˜` and `cons/cons˜`) that conceptually create data-type instances with different tags. Product types are handled implicitly by having constructors (like `cons`) that create a data-type instance from multiple argument values and having deconstructors (like `cons˜`) that extract these values from the data-type instance. Recursive types are handled implicitly by having constructors/deconstructors (like `cons/cons˜`) that create a data-type instance from and decompose a data-type instance into values that include other instances of the same data type.

- *No complex machinery for type reconstruction:* The constructor/deconstructor type schemas can be derived automatically from data-type definitions (see below), so they need not be reconstructed from definitions of the constructor and deconstructor procedures. Indeed, for the purposes of the static semantics (type checking), the definitions of the constructor and deconstructor procedures aren't necessary, because the type schemas tell us all that we need to know about them. For the dynamic semantics, we can simply use the desugaring-based definitions of these procedures defined in Figure 10.21 on page 587 (where we treat `def-datatype` like `def-data`).

- *Simple pattern matching:* Avoiding the explicit manipulation of types simplifies pattern matching on data-type instances. Although deconstructors may be used explicitly in programs, they are usually used implicitly via the `match` construct introduced in Section 10.5. For example, the definition

```
(def (sum xs)
  (match xs
    ((null) 0)
    ((cons y ys) (+ y (sum ys)))))
```

desugars to[9]

```
(def sum
  (abs (xs)
    (null~ xs
            (abs () 0)
            (abs ()
              (cons~ xs
                     (abs (y ys) (+ y (sum ys)))
                     (abs () (error no-match)))))))
```

Indeed, a version of FLARE supporting data-type definitions and the `match` construct can be desugared exactly as in Figure 10.27 on page 603, except that in the clause

$$\mathcal{DS}_{pat}[\![L]\!] \ I_{disc} \ E_{succ} \ I_{fail} = (\texttt{if} \ (\texttt{equal?} \ I_{disc} \ L) \ E_{succ} \ (I_{fail}))$$

the generic equality procedure `equal?` must be replaced by an equality procedure `equal`$_L$ that is appropriate for the type of the literal L. For instance, `equal`$_{17}$ is =, `equal`$_{true}$ is `bool=?`, and `equal`$_{'foo'}$ is `sym=?`. In contrast, desugaring `match` in a language with explicit universal types is more complex (see Section 12.2.3 and Exercises 12.20 and 12.25).

The reason why sum-of-products data-type definitions are a good idea in languages with type reconstruction is that they allow the user to declare key type information that is otherwise difficult to reconstruct. The ease with which sum-of-products data-type definitions and pattern matching can be integrated into languages with type reconstruction explains why they are supported in many such languages, including ML and HASKELL, where they are popular programming features. They also are an easy way to support sums and products without complicated machinery, such as row types, for reconstructing the types of raw oneofs and records.

---

[9]This is a simplified version of the result yielded by the `match` desugaring in Figure 10.27 on page 603. Note that in a statically typed language, it is possible to prove that the `(error no-match)` expression in this example will never be executed, because any list value `xs` will cause the success continuation of either the `null~` or `cons~` call to be invoked.

Figure 13.29 summarizes the essential changes that need to be made to FLARE to support data-type definitions and pattern matching. The syntax of FLARE is modified to include top-level data-type definitions in kernel programs. Each data-type definition DD has the form

$$(\texttt{def-datatype}\ (\theta_{tycon}\ \tau_1\ \ldots\ \tau_m)$$
$$(I_{constructor_1}\ T_{1,1}\ \ldots\ T_{1,n_1})$$
$$\vdots$$
$$(I_{constructor_k}\ T_{k,1}\ \ldots\ T_{k,n_k}))$$

This definition declares θ_{tycon} as a new m-argument type constructor parameterized over the type identifiers $\tau_1,\ \ldots,\ \tau_m$. The name θ_{tycon} is a type constructor identifier that must not be one of the standard type constructor names (`->` and `cellof` in FLARE and `prodof`, `recordof`, and `oneof` in extensions to FLARE). The data-type definition also declares k constructor procedures $I_{constructor_1},\ \ldots,\ I_{constructor_k}$, the ith of which constructs an instance of the data type $(\theta_{tycon}\ \tau_1\ \ldots\ \tau_m)$ out of n_i components whose types are $T_{i,1},\ \ldots,\ T_{i,n_i}$. The component types may refer to the type parameter names $\tau_1,\ \ldots,\ \tau_m$ of the type constructor.

We have already studied the data-type definition for lists. Here are data-type definitions for pairs and binary trees:

```
(def-datatype (pairof s t)
  (pair s t))

(def-datatype (treeof t)
  (leaf)
  (node (treeof t) t (treeof t)))
```

The `pairof` definition illustrates that a type constructor may have more than one type parameter and may have only a single constructor. Data-type definitions may even be mutually recursive; see Exercise 13.14.

The FLARE type domain is extended to include type-constructor applications of the form $(\theta_{tycon}\ T^*_{arg})$. E.g., `(pairof (listof bool) (treeof bool))` is a nested type-constructor application. Pair and list types and operations are excluded from the kernel language in this extension to FLARE, because they can be defined by the programmer.

The only FLARE type reconstruction rule that needs to be modified to handle data-type definitions is the $[prog_R]$ rule. This rule uses the $\oplus$ operator to extend the program-parameter type environment $\{I_1 : \tau_1, \ldots, I_n : \tau_n\}$ with bindings for constructor and deconstructor type schemas defined by the data-type definitions.

Modified Syntax

$P \in \text{Prog} ::= (\texttt{flarek} \ (I^*_{formal}) \ DD^* \ E_{body})$

$DD \in \text{DatatypeDefinition} ::= (\texttt{def-datatype} \ (\theta_{tycon} \ \tau^*_{param})$
$\qquad\qquad\qquad\qquad\qquad (I_{constructor} \ T^*_{component})^*)$

$O \in \text{Primop} ::= \ldots \text{ FLARE } \textit{primitives except for pair and list operations } \ldots$

$T \in \text{Type} ::= \ldots \text{ FLARE } \textit{types except for } \texttt{pairof} \textit{ and } \texttt{listof} \textit{ types } \ldots$
$\qquad\qquad | \ (\theta_{tycon} \ T^*_{arg}) \ [\text{TypeConstructorApp}]$

$\theta \in \text{TyConId} = \text{SymLit} - \{\texttt{->}, \texttt{cellof}\}$
$\qquad ; \textit{ subtract off other type constructors (e.g., } \texttt{prodof}, \texttt{recordof}, \texttt{oneof})$
$\qquad ; \textit{ in extensions to FLARE}$

New Syntactic Sugar

$(\texttt{match} \ E_{disc} \ (PT \ E)^*) \leadsto_{ds} \mathcal{DS}_{match}[\![(\texttt{match} \ E_{disc} \ (PT \ E)^*)]\!]$
$\quad \text{where } PT \in \text{Pattern} ::= L \ | \ I \ | \ \_ \ | \ (I \ PT^*)$
$\quad \text{and } \mathcal{DS}_{match} \text{ is the pattern matching desugarer from Figure 10.27 on page 603}$
$\quad \text{with the modification to } \texttt{equal?} \text{ described in the text.}$

Extending Type Environments with Data-Type Declarations

$TE \in \text{TypeEnvironment} = \text{Ident} \rightharpoonup \text{TypeSchema}$

The notation $TE \oplus DD$ denotes a type environment such that

$$(TE \oplus DD)(I) = \begin{cases} (\texttt{generic} \ (\tau^m_{j=1}) \ (\texttt{->} \ (T^n_{h=1}) \ (\theta_{tycon} \ \tau^m_{j=1}))), \\ \quad \text{if } I =_{\text{Ident}} I_{con} \text{ and } DD = (\texttt{def-datatype} \ (\theta_{tycon} \ \tau^m_{j=1}) \\ \qquad\qquad\qquad\qquad\qquad\qquad \ldots (I_{con} \ T^n_{h=1}) \ldots) \\ (\texttt{generic} \ (\tau_{ret} \ \tau^m_{j=1}) \qquad \{\tau_{ret} \text{ is a fresh return type}\} \\ \quad (\texttt{->} \ ((\theta_{tycon} \ \tau^m_{j=1}) \quad \{\textit{type of datum to deconstruct}\} \\ \qquad (\texttt{->} \ (T^n_{h=1}) \ \tau_{ret}) \ \{\textit{type of success continuation}\} \\ \qquad (\texttt{->} \ () \ \tau_{ret})) \qquad \{\textit{type of failure continuation}\} \\ \quad \tau_{ret})) \qquad\qquad\quad \{\textit{return type of deconstructor}\}, \\ \quad \text{if } I =_{\text{Ident}} I_{con} \bowtie^{\sim} \\ \qquad \text{and } DD = (\texttt{def-datatype} \ (\theta_{tycon} \ \tau^m_{j=1}) \\ \qquad\qquad\qquad\qquad\qquad \ldots (I_{con} \ T^n_{h=1}) \ldots) \\ TE(I), \text{ otherwise} \end{cases}$$

$TE \oplus [DD_1, \ldots, DD_n]$ is an abbreviation for $((TE \oplus DD_1) \oplus \ldots) \oplus DD_n$.

New Type Reconstruction Rule for Programs

$$\frac{R[\![E_{body}]\!] \ \{I_i : \tau_i\}^n_{i=1} \oplus [DD_1, \ldots, DD_k] = \langle T_{body}, TCS_{body} \rangle}{R_{pgm}[\![(\texttt{flarek} \ (I^n_{i=1}) \ DD^k_{j=1} \ E_{body})]\!] = RA_{pgm}} \quad [\text{prog}_R]$$
$$\text{where } \tau^n_{i=1} \text{ are fresh}$$

$$\text{and } RA_{pgm} = \begin{cases} (\text{ProgType} \rightarrowtail \text{ReconAns} \ (\sigma_{body} \ (\texttt{=>} \ (\tau^n_{i=1}) \ T_{body}))), \\ \quad \text{if } solve_{TCS} \ TCS_{body} = (\text{TypeSubst} \rightarrowtail \text{UnifySoln} \ \sigma_{body}) \\ (\text{Failure} \rightarrowtail \text{ReconAns} \ \texttt{fail}), \text{ otherwise} \end{cases}$$

Figure 13.29 The essence of data-type definitions and pattern matching in FLARE.

```
 pair : (generic (?s ?t) (-> (?s ?t) (pairof ?s ?t)))
pair~ : (generic (?r ?s ?t)
            (-> ((pairof ?s ?t) (-> (?s ?t) ?r) (-> () ?r)) ?r))
 leaf : (generic (?t) (-> () (treeof ?t)))
leaf~ : (generic (?r ?t)
            (-> ((treeof ?t) (-> () ?r) (-> () ?r)) ?r))
 node : (generic (?t) (-> ((treeof ?t) ?t (treeof ?t)) (treeof ?t)))
node~ : (generic (?r ?t)
            (-> ((treeof ?t)
                  (-> ((treeof ?t) ?t (treeof ?t)) ?r)
                  (-> () ?r))
                ?r))
```

Figure 13.30   The type schemas of the constructor and deconstructor procedures introduced by the `pairof` and `treeof` data-type definitions.

The notation $TE \oplus [DD_1, \ldots, DD_n]$ is an abbreviation for $((TE \oplus DD_1) \oplus \ldots)$ $\oplus\, DD_n$, where the notation $TE \oplus DD$ denotes a type environment that extends TE with type schemas for the constructors and deconstructors declared by DD. For each constructor declaration $(I_{con}\ T_{i=1}^n)$ in the definition of the data type $(\theta_{tycon}\ \tau_{i=1}^m)$, $\oplus$ adds two type schemas to the type environment:

1. A constructor type schema named I_{con} having the form

    (generic $(\tau_{j=1}^m)$ (-> $(T_{h=1}^n)$ $(\theta_{tycon}\ \tau_{j=1}^m)))$)

    which is parameterized over the m type identifiers of the declared data type $(\theta_{tycon}\ \tau_{i=1}^m)$.

2. A deconstructor type schema named $I_{con}\bowtie^{\sim}$ having the form

    (generic $(\tau_{ret}\ \tau_{j=1}^m)$
        (-> $((\theta_{tycon}\ \tau_{j=1}^m)$ {type of datum to deconstruct}
            (-> $(T_{h=1}^n)$ $\tau_{ret})$ {type of success continuation}
            (-> () $\tau_{ret}))$ {type of failure continuation}
            $\tau_{ret}))$ {return type of deconstructor}

    which is parameterized over the return type τ_{ret} of the deconstructor as well as the m type identifiers of the data type $(\theta_{tycon}\ \tau_{i=1}^m)$.

We have already seen examples of these type schemas for the `listof` data type. Figure 13.30 shows the type schemas introduced by $\oplus$ for the `pairof` and `treeof` data-type definitions.

For simplicity, unparameterized data types are required to be written as applications of nullary type constructors. For instance, an integer list type can be declared as

```
(def-datatype (intlist)
  (inull)
  (icons int intlist))
```

in which case the integer list type would be `(intlist)` (the application of a nullary type constructor) and not `intlist` (which is a nullary type constructor, not a type). Exercise 13.15 explores how to support the declarations of new types in addition to new type constructors.

Exercise 13.14 Data-type definitions may be mutually recursive. For example, here is a pair of mutually recursive data types defining a so-called **rose tree** — a tree with element-bearing leaves whose nodes may have any number of children:

$$DD_{rosetree} = \texttt{(def-datatype (rtreeof t)}$$
$$\texttt{(rleaf t)}$$
$$\texttt{(rnode (rlistof t)))}$$
$$DD_{roselist} = \texttt{(def-datatype (rlistof t)}$$
$$\texttt{(rnull)}$$
$$\texttt{(rcons (rtreeof t) (rlistof t)))}$$

a. What are the bindings of the type environment $\{\} \oplus [DD_{rosetree}, DD_{roselist}]$?

b. Show that the following expression is well typed:

```
(rnode (rcons (rleaf 1)
              (rcons (rnode (rcons (rleaf 2) (rnull)))
                     (rnull))))
```

c. Define a procedure `rleaves` that takes a rose tree as its single argument and returns a list (a `listof`, not an `rlistof`) of all the leaves in the rose tree.

Exercise 13.15 Suppose that the syntax of data types is extended to allow the definition of new types in addition to new type constructors:

$$DD \in \text{DatatypeDefinition} ::= \ldots \textit{form for defining } (\theta_{tycon}\ \tau^*_{param}) \ldots$$
$$\mid \texttt{(def-datatype } \tau_{new}\ (I_{constructor}\ T^*_{component})^*\texttt{)}$$

For example, an integer list type could now be declared as

```
(def-datatype intlist
  (inull)
  (icons int intlist))
```

which defines a new type (not type constructor) `intlist`. Describe how to modify the $\oplus$ operator to handle this new form of data-type declaration.

Exercise 13.16 In this section, we have seen that FLARE can be extended with data-type declarations by extending the type environment with appropriate type bindings for their constructor and deconstructor procedures. In this exercise, we explore an alternative strategy: desugaring each data-type declaration into a recursive type and constructor and deconstructor procedures that manipulate this type.

For example, a data-type declaration of the form

```
(def-datatype intlist
  (inull)
  (icons int intlist))
```

can introduce a recursive integer-list type,[10]

$$T_{intlist} = \texttt{(trec intlist}$$
$$\texttt{(oneof (inull (prodof))}$$
$$\texttt{(icons (prodof int intlist))))}$$

and also introduce the following constructor and deconstructor definitions:

```
(def (inull) (one inull (prod) Tintlist))

(def (inull~ val succ fail)
  (tagcase val untagged (inull (succ)) (else (fail))))

(def (icons x1 x2) (one icons (prod x1 x2) Tintlist))

(def (icons~ val succ fail)
  (tagcase val untagged
    (icons (succ (get 1 untagged (prodof int Tintlist))
                 (get 2 untagged (prodof int Tintlist))))
    (else (fail))))
```

In this desugaring, we assume that the oneof-creation construct **one** and the product-selection construct **get** include explicit types to aid the type reconstruction process. Since these explicit types are automatically introduced by the desugaring and not written by the programmer, they do not make programming more cumbersome. We cannot omit these explicit types and use row types (Section 13.5.3) instead for reconstructing the sum and product types because the reconstruction algorithm we have presented is incapable of reconstructing recursive types like $T_{intlist}$ (see Exercise 13.17).

a. Write a transformation that desugars simple (unparameterized) data-type declarations like **intlist** into FLARE constructor and deconstructor procedures.

b. Although unparameterized user-defined data types can be handled in FLARE via desugaring, parameterized data types like (listof T),

```
(def-datatype (listof t)
  (null)
  (cons t (listof t)))
```

---

[10]To do this, we would need to augment the FLARE type domain with recursive types.

are much more challenging to handle in a desugaring-based approach. What changes would need to be made to the FLARE type system in order to adapt the desugaring-based approach to data-type declarations from the explicitly typed FLEX/SPDK language (see Exercise 12.25 on page 766) to the implicitly typed FLARE language?

Exercise 13.17 This exercise explores the problem of reconstructing recursive sum-of-products types. Imagine a version of FLARE that uses row types to reconstruct oneof types (see Exercise 13.13 on page 826). (This exercise also involves tuple types, but since it uses only the prod operation and not the get operation, there is no need to use row types for tuple-type reconstruction.) In this version of FLARE, consider the following expression:

```
(let ((inull (abs () (one inull (prod))))
      (icons (abs (i is) (one icons (prod i is)))))
  (letrec ((down (abs (n)
                   (if (= n 0)
                       (inull)
                       (icons n (down (prim - n 1)))))))
    (down 5)))
```

a. Assume that the type of the letrec expression is reconstructed with respect to a type environment TE. What are the type schemas for inull and icons in TE?

b. Assume that the type of down in TE is (-> (?n) ?res) and that the type environment $TE_{if} = TE[\mathtt{n} : \mathtt{?n}]$ is used to reconstruct the if expression E_{if} that is the body of (abs (n) ...). Then $R[\![E_{if}]\!]\ TE_{if} = \langle T_{if}, TCS_{if}\rangle$. Suppose $solve_{TCS}\ TCS_{if} = $ (TypeSubst $\rightarrowtail$ UnifySoln σ_{if}). What is $T'_{if} = (\sigma_{if}\ T_{if})$?

c. Reconstructing the type of the letrec expression introduces a type constraint that equates the type of down and the type of (abs (n) ...):

$$(\texttt{->}\ (\texttt{?n})\ \texttt{?res}) \doteq (\texttt{->}\ (\texttt{?n})\ T'_{if})$$

This constraint requires unifying ?res and T'_{if}, but this unification fails. Why?

d. Describe a modification to the unification algorithm that would allow the unification of ?res and T'_{if} to succeed. What is the result of unifying these two types in your modified algorithm?

Notes

The notion of reconstructing types for an implicitly typed language is due to Curry and Hindley. See [Hin97] for a summary of the history of this notion and an elegant formulation of type reconstruction in the context of the lambda calculus. In the late 1970s, Milner rediscovered this notion [Mil78], refined it with Damas [DM82], and made it a cornerstone of SML, a practical programming language

[MTHM97, MT91b]. A nice presentation of the concepts and implementation of HDM type reconstruction is [Car87]. Examples of other programming languages with HDM type reconstruction include MIRANDA [Tur85], HASKELL [HPW$^+$92], and FX [GJSO92]. For an overview of type reconstruction systems, see [Tiu90].

Unification is due to Robinson [Rob65]. For a survey on algorithms for and uses of unification, see [Kni89].

The occurs check in our unification algorithm is standard in many type reconstruction systems, but it is not mandatory. Indeed, removing the occurs check gives rise to a form of cyclic unification capable of constructing recursive types [CC91]. An example of a system using cyclic unification is described in [OJ97].

Using row variables to reconstruct record types was introduced by Wand [Wan91]. An alternative approach to type inference for extensible records is presented in [Rém94]. Type inference of records using row variables can be used to support object-oriented programming in a language with HDM type reconstruction, as demonstrated by OCAML's object system [RV98].

Type reconstruction algorithms, such as Milner's "bottom-up" Algorithm $\mathcal{W}$ [Mil78, DM82] or its "top-down" variant, Algorithm $\mathcal{M}$ [LY98], are often expressed in terms of constructing appropriate type substitutions during a tree walk of a program. The single-threaded nature of the substitutions in these algorithms enables implementing them as global mappings from type variables to types that are updated during the type reconstruction process [Car87].

Our Algorithm R separates the collection of type constraints from their solution as a type substitution. An extended treatment of the constraint-based approach to ML type reconstruction can be found in [PR05], which also includes a discussion of row variables for the type reconstruction of records. We have chosen to specify Algorithm R via deduction rules in order to highlight the relationship between the algorithm and the underlying type system. Another presentation of type reconstruction via deduction rules can be found in [Pie02].

An implicitly typed language has the *principal type* property if the typability of an expression E in a type environment TE implies that there is a most general type T for E that can be instantiated to any type of E in TE. HDM has this property [DM82]. A stronger notion is the *principal typing* property: the typabilty of an expression E in some type environment implies that there is a most general typing (i.e., type derivation) concluding with $TE \vdash E : T$ that can be instantiated to any typing of E. Principal typing is desirable for compositional approaches to type reconstruction, but many implicitly typed systems with principal types (such as HDM) do not have principal typings [Jim96, Wel02].

When HDM type reconstruction is used in the presence of imperative features, care must be taken to ensure that type soundness is maintained. One approach, adopted in an early version of SML [MTH90], is to distinguish *imperative type variables* for values that may be stored in cells from regular type variables, and to limit the generalization of imperative type variables. The *value restriction* approach, adopted in a later version of SML [MTHM97], restricts polymorphism to syntactic values [Wri95]. This is a simple way to guarantee type soundness, but prohibits certain imperative programming idioms that are well typed in other approaches. It is possible to relax the value restriction without affecting type soundness [Gar04].

The undecidability of type reconstruction in System F is a result due to Wells [Wel99]. Numerous decidable reconstruction systems have been developed for variants of System F in which programmers are required to supply explicit type annotations for certain polymorphic types, e.g. [OG89, OL96, GR99, BR03, Rém05, JVWS07].

Type reconstruction has been applied to dynamically typed languages in the context of so-called *soft typing* systems [CF91, AWL94, CF98]. Such systems can verify some (but not necessarily all) assertions about program phrases, such as assertions that the operand values of a primitive operation have the correct type at run time. When such assertions can be proven, the corresponding dynamic checks can be eliminated to improve the efficiency of the program. For example, experiments with a flow-based analysis system for eliminating run-time type checks found that between 5 and 40 percent of program execution time was spent performing checks that could be eliminated by the system [WJ98].

One drawback of many type-reconstruction systems is that when type mismatches arise during the constraint-solving process, it is often difficult for programmers to reason about which parts of their program are responsible for the unsolvable constraints. For an overview of work in this area and a *type-error slicing* technique for addressing the problem, see [HW04].

14

Abstract Types

Come, Abstraction,
by Will out of Demonic Ambition,
carry me lightly into the regions of the immortal.

— Louise Glück, "The Winged Horse"

14.1 Data Abstraction

A cornerstone of modern programming methodology is the principle of **data abstraction**, which states that programmers should be able to use data structures without understanding the details of how they are implemented. Data abstraction is based on establishing a **contract**, also known as an **Application Programming Interface (API)**, or just **interface**, that specifies the abstract behavior of all operations that manipulate a data structure without describing the representation of the data structure or the algorithms used in the operations.

The contract serves as an **abstraction barrier** that separates the concerns of the two parties that participate in a data abstraction. On one side of the barrier is the **implementer**, who is responsible for implementing the operations so that they satisfy the contract. On the other side of the barrier is the **client**, who is blissfully unaware of the hidden implementation details and uses the operations based purely on their advertised specifications in the contract. This arrangement gives the implementer the flexibility to change the implementation at any time as long as the contract is still satisfied. Such changes should not require the client to modify any code.[1] This separation of concerns is especially useful when large programs are being developed by multiple programmers, many of whom may never communicate except via contracts. But it is even helpful in programs written by a single person who plays the roles of implementer and client at different times in the programming process.

---

[1] However, the client may need to recompile existing code in order to use a modified implementation.

14.1.1   A Point Abstraction

As an extremely simple example of data abstraction, consider an abstraction for points on a two-dimensional grid. The point abstraction is defined by the following contract, which specifies an operation for creating a point from its two coordinates and operations for extracting each coordinate:

(make-pt *x y*) creates a point whose x coordinate is the integer *x* and whose y coordinate is the integer *y*.

(pt-x *p*) returns the x coordinate of the given point *p*.

(pt-y *p*) returns the y coordinate of the given point *p*.

An implementation of the point abstraction should satisfy the following axioms:

1. For any integers n_1 and n_2, (pt-x (make-pt n_1 n_2)) evaluates to n_1.

2. For any integers n_1 and n_2, (pt-y (make-pt n_1 n_2)) evaluates to n_2.

Even for this simple abstraction, there are a surprising number of possible implementations. For concreteness, below we give two point implementations in a version of the dynamically typed FL language that supports records. Our convention will be to package up the operations of a data abstraction into a record, but that is not essential.

```
(def pair-point-impl
  (record (make-pt (abs (x y) (pair x y)))
          (pt-x (abs (p) (fst p)))
          (pt-y (abs (p) (snd p)))))

(def proc-point-impl
  (record (make-pt (abs (x y) (abs (b) (if b x y))))
          (pt-x (abs (p) (p #t)))
          (pt-y (abs (p) (p #f)))))
```

In pair-point-impl, the two coordinates are stored in a pair. Alternatively, we could have stored them in the opposite order or glued them together in a different kind of product (record, sequence, list, etc.). In proc-point-impl, a point is represented as a first-class procedure that "remembers" the coordinates in its environment and uses a boolean argument to determine which coordinate to return when called. Alternatively, some other key (such as a symbol) could be used to select the coordinate.

As a sample client of the point abstraction, consider the following procedure, which, for a given point implementation, defines a coordinate-swapping `transpose` procedure and a `point->pair` procedure that converts a point to a concrete pair (regardless of its underlying representation) and uses these on the abstract point (1, 2):

```
(def test-point-impl
  (abs (point-impl)
    (with-fields (make-pt pt-x pt-y) point-impl
      (let ((transpose (abs (p) (make-pt (pt-y p) (pt-x p))))
            (point->pair (abs (p) (pair (pt-x p) (pt-y p)))))
        (point->pair (transpose (make-pt 1 2)))))))
```

The result of invoking `test-point-impl` on a valid point implementation should be the concrete pair value ⟨2, 1⟩.

In this example, there is little reason to prefer one of the implementations over the other. The pair implementation might be viewed as being more straightforward, requiring less memory space, or being more efficient because it requires fewer procedure calls. However, judgments about efficiency are often tricky and require a deep understanding of low-level implementation details. In more realistic examples, such as abstractions for data structures like stacks, queues, priority queues, sets, tables, databases, etc., one implementation might be preferred over another because of asymptotically better running times or memory usage for certain operations.

14.1.2 Procedural Abstraction Is Not Enough

Any language with procedural abstraction — i.e., the ability to capture common patterns in expressions and statements with parameterized procedures — can be used to implement data abstraction in the way illustrated in the point example. However, in order for the full benefits of data abstraction to be realized, this approach requires that the client never commit **abstraction violations** by using knowledge of the representation of an abstract value to manipulate abstract values concretely.

For instance, if points are represented as pairs, then the client might write `(fst p)` rather than `(pt-x p)` to extract the x coordinate of a point p, or might create a point "forgery" using `(pair 1 2)` in place of `(make-pt 1 2)`. Although these concrete manipulations will not cause errors, such abuses of the exposed representation are dangerous because they are not guaranteed to work if the implementation is changed. For example, `(fst p)` would lead to a run-time type error if the implementation were changed to use a procedural representation for points, and would give the incorrect value if the implementation were changed to put the y coordinate before the x coordinate in a pair.

Furthermore, many representations involve **representation invariants** that are maintained by the abstract operations but which concrete manipulations could violate. A representation invariant is a set of conceptual or actual predicates that a representation satisfies and the implementation may depend on. For instance, a string-collection implementation might store the strings in a sorted array. Thus a `sorted?` predicate would be true for this representation. If the client creates a forgery with an unsorted array, all bets are off concerning the behavior of the abstract operations on this forgery.

Without an enforcement of the relationship between abstract values and their operations, it is even possible to interchange values of different abstractions that happen to have the same concrete representation. For instance, if an implementation of a rational-number abstraction represents a rational number as a pair of two integers, then a rational number could be dissected with `pt-x` and `pt-y`, assuming that points are also represented as pairs of integers.

Although our examples have been for a dynamically typed language, the same problems occur in statically typed languages in which type equivalence is structural — i.e., two compound types are considered equivalent if their corresponding components are equivalent, as in FLEX's $\approx$ relation. Clearly, attempting to achieve data abstraction using procedural abstraction alone is fraught with peril. There must additionally be some sort of mechanism to guarantee that abstract data is secure. We will call a language **secure** when barriers associated with a data abstraction cannot be violated. Such a security mechanism must effectively hide the representation of abstract data by making it impossible to create or operate on abstract values with anything other than the appropriate abstract operations.

In the remainder of this chapter, we explore techniques for making data abstractions secure. In Section 14.2, we study how secure data abstractions can be achieved dynamically using a lock and key mechanism. Then we explore various ways to achieve such security statically using types: existential types (Section 14.3), nonce types (Section 14.4), and static dependent types (Section 14.5).

Exercise 14.1 In languages with first-class procedures, one approach to hiding the representations of data structures is to encapsulate them in message-passing objects. For example, the two point-making procedures in Figure 14.1 encapsulate the pair representation and procedural representation, respectively. How secure is this approach to hiding data abstraction representations? What kinds of abstraction violations are prevented by this technique? What kinds of abstraction violations can still occur?

```
(def (make-pair-point x y)
  (let ((point (pair x y)))
    (abs (msg) {return a message dispatcher}
      (cond ((sym=? msg (sym pt-x)) (fst point))
            ((sym=? msg (sym pt-y)) (snd point))
            (else (error unrecognized-message))))))
(def (make-proc-point x y)
  (let ((point (abs (b) (if b x y))))
    (abs (msg) {return a message dispatcher}
      (cond ((sym=? msg (sym pt-x)) (point #t))
            ((sym=? msg (sym pt-y)) (point #f))
            (else (error unrecognized-message))))))
```

Figure 14.1 Message-passing point implementations.

14.2 Dynamic Locks and Keys

The human heart has hidden treasures,
In secret kept, in silence sealed.

— Charlotte Brontë, "Evening Solace"

One approach for securely encapsulating a data-abstraction representation is to make it inaccessible by "locking" abstract values with a "key" in such a way that only the very same key can unlock a locked value to access the representation. We explore a dynamic lock and key mechanism by extending FLIC with the following primitive operators, which, as usual, are also assumed to be available as standard library procedures:

(new-key) generates a unique, unforgeable key value.

(lock *key value*) creates a new kind of "locked value" that pairs *key* with *value* in such a way that *key* cannot be extracted and *value* can be extracted only by supplying *key*.

(unlock *key locked*) returns the value stored in *locked* if *key* matches the key used to create *locked*. Otherwise, it signals an error.

We extend FLIC rather than FL because cells and a single-threaded store simplify specifying the semantics of these constructs. Indeed, new-key, lock, and unlock can all be implemented as user-defined procedures in FLIC (Fig-

```
(def (new-key) (cell 0))

(def (lock key val)
  (abs (key1)
    (if (cell=? key key1)
        val
        (error wrong-key))))

(def (unlock key locked)
  (locked key))
```

Figure 14.2   Implementation of a dynamic lock and key mechanism in FLIC.

```
(def pt-impl1
  (let ((key (new-key)))
    (let ((up (abs (x) (lock key x)))
          (down (abs (x) (unlock key x))))
      (record (make-pt (abs (x y) (up (pair x y))))
              (pt-x (abs (p) (fst (down p))))
              (pt-y (abs (p) (snd (down p))))))))

(def pt-impl2
  (let ((key (new-key)))
    (let ((up (abs (x) (lock key x)))
          (down (abs (x) (unlock key x))))
      (record (make-pt (abs (x y) (up (pair y x))))
              (pt-x (abs (p) (snd (down p))))
              (pt-y (abs (p) (fst (down p))))))))
```

Figure 14.3   Using the lock and key mechanism to hide point representations.

ure 14.2). The new-key procedure creates a new cell whose location *is* a unique and unforgeable key; the value in the cell is arbitrary and can be ignored. The lock procedure represents a locked value as a procedure that "remembers" the given key and value and returns the value only if it is invoked on the original key (as done in unlock). The procedural representation of locked values prevents direct access to the key, and the value can be extracted only by supplying the key, as desired.

Figure 14.3 shows how the lock and key mechanism can be used to securely encapsulate two representations of points as pairs that differ only in the order of the coordinates. The procedures up and down[2] use lock and unlock to mediate

---

[2]The name up is intended to suggest raising a value from a low (concrete) level to a high (abstract) level, while down suggests lowering the value between these levels.

between the concrete pair values and the abstract point values. Because all operators for a single implementation use the same key, the operators for `pt-impl1` work together, as do those for `pt-impl2`. For example:

```
((select pt-x pt-impl1) ((select make-pt pt-impl1) 1 2))  ⟶FLIC 1
((select pt-y pt-impl2) ((select make-pt pt-impl2) 1 2))  ⟶FLIC 2
```

However, because different implementations use different keys, point values created by one of the implementations cannot be dissected by operations of the other. Furthermore, because the operators create and use locked values, neither point implementation can be used with concrete pair operations. For example, all of the following four expressions generate dynamic errors when evaluated:

```
((select pt-x pt-impl1) ((select make-pt pt-impl2) 1 2))
((select pt-y pt-impl2) ((select make-pt pt-impl1) 1 2))
(fst ((select make-pt pt-impl1) 1 2))
((select pt-y pt-impl2) (pair 1 2))
```

Some syntactic sugar can facilitate the definition of implementation records. We introduce a `cluster` construct that abstracts over the pattern used in the point implementations:

$$(\text{cluster } (I\ E)^*) \rightsquigarrow_{ds} (\text{let } ((I_{key}\ (\text{new-key}))) \quad \{I_{key}\ \textit{fresh}\}$$
$$(\text{let } ((\text{up } (\text{abs } (x)\ (\text{lock } I_{key}\ x)))$$
$$(\text{down } (\text{abs } (x)\ (\text{unlock } I_{key}\ x))))$$
$$(\text{recordrec } (I\ E)^*)))$$

The `up` and `down` procedures implicitly introduced by the desugaring may be used in any of the cluster bindings. Using `recordrec` in place of `record` allows for mutually recursive operations. Here is the definition of `pt-impl1` expressed using the `cluster` notation:

```
(def pt-impl1
  (cluster (make-pt (abs (x y) (up (pair x y))))
           (pt-x (abs (p) (fst (down p))))
           (pt-y (abs (p) (snd (down p))))))
```

Note that `cluster` creates a new data abstraction every time it is evaluated. For instance, consider:

```
(def make-wrapper
  (abs ()
    (cluster (wrap (abs (x) (up x)))
             (unwrap (abs (x) (down x))))))

(def wrapper1 (make-wrapper))

(def wrapper2 (make-wrapper))
```

Evaluating ((select unwrap wrapper2) ((select wrap wrapper1) 17)) signals a dynamic error because the wrap procedure from wrapper1 and the unwrap
procedure from wrapper2 use different keys.

Exercise 14.2 Consider an integer-set abstraction that supports these operations:

(empty) creates an empty set of integers.

(insert *int intset*) returns the set that results from inserting *int* into the integer set
   intset.

(member? *int intset*) returns *true* if *int* is a member of the integer set *intset* and *false*
   otherwise.

a. Define a cluster list-intset-impl that represents an integer set as a list of integers
   without duplicates, sorted from low to high.

b. Define a cluster pred-intset-impl that represents an integer set as a predicate — a
   procedure that takes an integer and returns *true* if that integer is in the set represented
   by the predicate and false otherwise.

c. Extend both list-intset-impl and pred-intset-impl to handle union, intersection, and difference operations on two integer sets.

d. Some representations have advantages over others for implementing particular operations. Show that (size *intset*) (which returns the number of elements in *intset*) is
   easy to implement in the list-intset-impl cluster but impossible to implement in
   the pred-intset-impl cluster (without changing the representation). Similarly, show
   that (complement *intset*) (which returns the set of all integers not in *intset*) is easy to
   implement in pred-intset-impl but impossible to implement in list-intset-impl.

Exercise 14.3

a. Extend the SOS for FLICK in Figures 8.13 and 8.14 to directly handle the primitives
   new-key, lock, and unlock, without using cells. Assume that the syntactic domains
   Exp$_{SOS}$ and ValueExp are extended with expressions of the form (*key* *LC*) to
   represent keys and (*locked* *LC* *V*) to represent locked values.

b. It is helpful to have the following additional primitives:

   (key? *thing*) determines whether *thing* is a key value.

   (key=? *key1 key2*) determines whether *key1* is the same key value as *key2*. Signals
      an error if either *key1* or *key2* is not a key value.

   (locked? *thing*) determines whether *thing* is a locked value.

   Extend your SOS to handle these primitives.

c. Can you extend the implementation in Figure 14.2 to handle the additional primitives?
   Explain.

Exercise 14.4 It is not always desirable to export every binding of a cluster in the resulting record. For example, in the following implementation of a rational-number cluster, the `gcd` procedure (which calculates the greatest common divisor of two numbers) is intended to be an unexported local recursive procedure used by `make-rat`.

```
(def rat-impl
  (cluster (make-rat (abs (x y)
                      (let ((g (gcd x y)))
                        (up (pair (/ x g) (/ y g))))))
           (numer (abs (r) (fst (down r))))
           (denom (abs (r) (snd (down r))))
           (gcd (abs (a b) (if (= b 0) a (gcd b (% a b))))))))
```

In this case, we could make the definition of `gcd` local to `make-rat`, but this strategy does not work if the local value is used in more than one binding in the cluster. Alternatively, we can extend the `cluster` syntax to be (cluster (I^*_{exp}) $(I\ E)^*$), where (I^*_{exp}) is an explicit list of **exports** — those bindings we wish to be included in the resulting record. For instance, if we use (`make-rat numer denom`) as the export list in `rat-impl`, then `gcd` would not appear in the resulting record. Modify the desugaring of `cluster` to support explicit export lists.

Exercise 14.5 A dynamic lock and key mechanism can be added to statically typed languages like the explicitly typed FLEX language and the implicitly typed FLARE language.

a. Extend the type syntax and type rules of FLEX to handle `new-key`, `lock`, and `unlock`.

b. We can add a `cluster` construct to FLEX using the syntax

$$(\text{cluster}\ T_{rep}\ (I_i\ T_i\ E_i)_{i=1}^n)$$

where T_{rep} is the concrete representation type of the data abstraction and T_i is the type of E_i. Give a type rule for this explicitly typed `cluster` construct.

c. Why is it necessary to include T_{rep} and the T_i in the explicitly typed `cluster` construct? Would these be necessary in a `cluster` construct for FLARE?

14.3 Existential Types

The dynamic lock and key mechanism enforces data abstraction by signaling a run-time error whenever an abstraction violation is encountered. The main drawback of this approach is its dynamic nature. It would be desirable to have a static mechanism that reports abstraction violations when the program is type-checked. As usual, the constraints of computability prevent a static system from detecting exactly those violations that would be caught by a dynamic lock and key

mechanism. Nevertheless, by relinquishing some expressive power, it is possible
to design type systems that prevent abstraction violations via a static lock and
key mechanism known as an **abstract type**. In the next three sections, we shall
study three designs for abstract types.

Our first abstract type system is based on extending the explicitly typed
language FLEX/P[3] with **existential types**. To motivate existential types, consider the types of the `pair-point-impl` and `proc-point-impl` implementations
introduced in Section 14.1:

```
(def-type pair-point-impl-type
  (recordof (make-pt (-> (int int) (pairof int int)))
            (pt-x (-> ((pairof int int)) int))
            (pt-y (-> ((pairof int int)) int)))))

(def-type proc-point-impl-type
  (recordof (make-pt (-> (int int) (-> (bool) int)))
            (pt-x (-> ((-> (bool) int)) int))
            (pt-y (-> ((-> (bool) int)) int)))))
```

These two types are the same except for the concrete type used to represent an
abstract point value: `(pairof int int)` in the first case and `(-> (bool) int)`
in the second. We would like to be able to say that both implementations have the
same abstract type. Intuitively, we can do this by abstracting over the concrete
point type in the two implementation types.

Let's call a value that implements an abstract type a **package**. To represent
the type of a package, we introduce a type construct $(\text{packof}_{exist}\ \tau_{abs}\ T_{impl})$ in
which the type identifier τ_{abs} is used to abstract over references to the concrete
representation type within the implementation type T_{impl}. For instance, here
is a packof_{exist} type for the point example, in which the abstract type name
`point` stands for the concrete type used to represent a point in a particular
implementation.

```
(def-type pt-eface
  (packof_exist point
    (recordof (make-pt (-> (int int) point))
              (pt-x (-> (point) int))
              (pt-y (-> (point) int))))))
```

We informally read the above $(\text{packof}_{exist}\ \ldots)$ type as "there exists a concrete
point representation type (call it `point`) such that there are `make-pt`, `pt-x`, and
`pt-y` procedures with the specified arrow types that manipulate values with this

---

[3]Recall that FLEX/P is FLEX/SP without subtyping. We use FLEX/P here because
subtyping is not relevant to the discussion.

representation type." Such a type is called an **existential type** because it posits the existence of a type and indicates how it is used without saying anything about its concrete representation.[4] In the following discussion, we will often refer to this particular existential type, so we have given it the name pt-eface, where eface is short for **existential interface**.

A summary of existential types is presented in Figure 14.4. In the existential type $(\texttt{packof}_{exist}\ \tau_{abs}\ T_{impl})$, the abstract type name τ_{abs} is a binding occurrence of a type identifier whose scope is the implementation type T_{impl}, which is typically a recordof type describing the operations associated with the abstract type. The particular name of the abstract type variable is irrelevant; as is indicated by the [epackof-≈] type-equivalence rule, it can be consistently renamed without changing the essence of the type. So the type

```
(packof_exist q
  (recordof (make-pt (-> (int int) q))
            (pt-x (-> (q) int))
            (pt-y (-> (q) int))))
```

is equivalent to the existential type using **point** above.

Values of existential type, which we shall call **existential packages**, are created by the construct $(\texttt{pack}_{exist}\ \tau_{abs}\ T_{rep}\ E_{impl})$. The type identifier τ_{abs} is a type name that is used to hide the concrete representation type T_{rep} within the implementation expression E_{impl}. For example, Figure 14.5 shows two existential packages that implement the type contract specified by pt-eface. In the first package, the abstract name **point** stands for the type of pair of integers, while in the second package, it stands for the type of a procedure that maps a boolean to an integer.

Like the dynamic **cluster** construct shown in Section 14.2, the $\texttt{pack}_{exist}$ construct implicitly introduces **up** and **down** procedures. However, here these procedures have no interesting dynamic semantics; they behave like identity procedures. Instead, they are used by the type system to explicitly convert between concrete and abstract types. This is formalized by the [epack] type rule in Figure 14.4, which specifies how different implementations can have the same existential type. The implementation expression E_{impl} is checked in a type environment where **up** converts from the concrete representation type T_{rep} to the abstract type name τ_{abs} and **down** converts from τ_{abs} to T_{rep}.[5] If type checking of a $\texttt{pack}_{exist}$

---

[4]In the literature, such types are often written with ∃ or exists just as ∀ and forall are used for universal polymorphism. For example, a more standard syntax for the pt-eface type is: ∃ point . {make-pt : int*int → point, pt-x : point → int, pt-y : point → int}.

[5]up and down are just one way to distinguish concrete and abstract types in an existential type. Some alternative approaches are explored in Exercise 14.9.

Syntax

$E ::= \ldots \mid (\text{pack}_{exist}\ \tau_{abs}\ T_{rep}\ E_{impl}) \mid (\text{unpack}_{exist}\ E_{pkg}\ \tau_{ty}\ I_{impl}\ E_{body})$

$T ::= \ldots \mid (\text{packof}_{exist}\ \tau_{abs}\ T_{impl})$

Free Identifiers

$FrIds[\![(\text{pack}_{exist}\ \tau_{abs}\ T_{rep}\ E_{impl})]\!] = FrIds[\![E_{impl}]\!]$

$FrIds[\![(\text{unpack}_{exist}\ E_{pkg}\ \tau_{ty}\ I_{impl}\ E_{body})]\!] = FrIds[\![E_{pkg}]\!] \cup (FrIds[\![E_{body}]\!] - \{I_{impl}\})$

$FrTyIds_{ty}[\![(\text{packof}_{exist}\ \tau_{abs}\ T_{impl})]\!] = FrTyIds_{ty}[\![T_{impl}]\!] - \{\tau_{abs}\}$

$FrTyIds_{exp}[\![(\text{pack}_{exist}\ \tau_{abs}\ T_{rep}\ E_{impl})]\!]$
$\quad = FrTyIds_{ty}[\![T_{rep}]\!] \cup \big(FrTyIds_{exp}[\![E_{impl}]\!] - \{\tau_{abs}\}\big)$

$FrTyIds_{exp}[\![(\text{unpack}_{exist}\ E_{pkg}\ \tau_{ty}\ I_{impl}\ E_{body})]\!]$
$\quad = FrTyIds_{exp}[\![E_{pkg}]\!] \cup \big(FrTyIds_{exp}[\![E_{body}]\!] - \{\tau_{ty}\}\big)$

Dynamic Semantics (via Type Erasure)

$\lceil(\text{pack}_{exist}\ \tau_{abs}\ T_{rep}\ E_{impl})\rceil$
$\quad = (\texttt{let ((up (abs (x) x)) (down (abs (x) x)))}\ \lceil E_{impl}\rceil))$

$\lceil(\text{unpack}_{exist}\ E_{pkg}\ \tau_{ty}\ I_{impl}\ E_{body})\rceil = (\texttt{let ((}I_{impl}\ \lceil E_{pkg}\rceil))\ \lceil E_{body}\rceil)$

Type Equivalence

$$\frac{[\tau'/\tau]\,T \approx T'}{(\text{packof}_{exist}\ \tau\ T) \approx (\text{packof}_{exist}\ \tau'\ T')} \qquad \text{[epackof-}\approx\text{]}$$

Type Rules

$$\frac{TE[\texttt{up}: (\texttt{->}\ (T_{rep})\ \tau_{abs}),\ \texttt{down}: (\texttt{->}\ (\tau_{abs})\ T_{rep})] \vdash E_{impl} : T_{impl}}{TE \vdash (\text{pack}_{exist}\ \tau_{abs}\ T_{rep}\ E_{impl}) : (\text{packof}_{exist}\ \tau_{abs}\ T_{impl})} \qquad \text{[epack]}$$

$\quad$ where $\ \tau_{abs} \notin \cup_{I \in FrIds[\![E_{impl}]\!]} \big(FrTyIds_{ty}[\![TE(I)]\!]\big)$ $\quad$ *[import restriction]*

$$\frac{TE \vdash E_{pkg} : (\text{packof}_{exist}\ \tau_{abs}\ T_{impl})}{TE[I_{impl} : [\tau_{ty}/\tau_{abs}]\,T_{impl}] \vdash E_{body} : T_{body}}{TE \vdash (\text{unpack}_{exist}\ E_{pkg}\ \tau_{ty}\ I_{impl}\ E_{body}) : T_{body}} \qquad \text{[eunpack]}$$

$\quad$ where $\ \tau_{ty} \notin \cup_{I \in FrIds[\![E_{body}]\!]} \big(FrTyIds_{ty}[\![TE(I)]\!]\big)$ $\quad$ *[import restriction]*
$\qquad\qquad \tau_{ty} \notin FrTyIds_{ty}[\![T_{body}]\!]$ $\qquad\qquad\qquad$ *[export restriction]*

Figure 14.4 The essence of existential types in FLEX/P.

expression succeeds, we have a proof that there is at least one representation for τ_{abs} (namely T_{rep}) and one implementation using this representation (namely E_{impl}) that has the implementation type T_{impl}. This knowledge is recorded with the type $(\text{packof}_{exist}\ \tau_{abs}\ T_{impl})$, in which any implementation details related to T_{rep} and E_{impl} have been purposely omitted.

```
(def pair-point-epkg pt-eface
  (pack_exist point (pairof int int)
    (record (make-pt (abs ((x int) (y int)) (up (pair x y))))
            (pt-x (abs ((p point)) (fst (down p))))
            (pt-y (abs ((p point)) (snd (down p)))))))
(def proc-point-epkg pt-eface
  (pack_exist point (-> (bool) int)
    (record (make-pt (abs ((x int) (y int))
                          (up (abs ((b bool)) (if b x y)))))
            (pt-x (abs ((p point)) ((down p) #t)))
            (pt-y (abs ((p point)) ((down p) #f)))))))
```

Figure 14.5 Two existential packages that implement pt-eface.

For example, in the pair-point-epkg example in Figure 14.5, the up procedure has type (-> ((pairof int int)) point) and the down procedure has type (-> (point) (pairof int int)). We can use these types to show that

$$\begin{array}{l}\texttt{(abs ((x int) (y int)) (up (pair x y))):(-> (int int) point)}\\ \qquad\texttt{(abs ((p point)) (fst (down p))):(-> (point) int)}\\ \qquad\texttt{(abs ((p point)) (snd (down p))):(-> (point) int)}\end{array}$$

and then use the [epack] rule to conclude that the pack_exist expression in the pair-point-epkg definition has the existential type pt-eface. The same conclusion can be drawn in the proc-point-epkg example, where the up procedure has type (-> ((-> (bool) int)) point) and the down procedure has type (-> (point) (-> (bool) int)).

As indicated by the type erasure for pack_exist in Figure 14.4, the dynamic meaning of a pack_exist expression is just the implementation expression in a context where up and down are identity operations. So pack_exist does nothing interesting in terms of its dynamic semantics. Its sole purpose is to package up an implementation in such a way that the details of its representation type cannot be seen outside the implementation in the static semantics.

The only way to use the underlying implementation of an existential package E_{pkg} (such as the record of point operations in a point package) is to use the existential elimination construct, (unpack_exist E_{pkg} τ_{ty} I_{impl} E_{body}). The type erasure of this expression — (let ((I_{impl} $\lceil E_{pkg} \rceil$)) $\lceil E_{body} \rceil$) — indicates that the dynamic meaning of this expression is simply to give the name I_{impl} to the implementation in the scope of the body expression E_{body}. The type name τ_{ty}

serves as a local name for the abstract type of the existential package that can
be used within E_{body}.

As an example of unpack_{exist}, consider the following procedure, which is a
typed version of the `test-point-impl` procedure presented on page 841.

```
(def test-point-epkg (-> (pt-eface) (pairof int int))
  (abs ((point-epkg pt-eface))
    (unpackexist point-epkg pt point-ops
      (with point-ops
        (let ((transpose (abs ((p pt))
                           (make-pt (pt-y p) (pt-x p))))
              (point->pair (abs ((p pt))
                             (pair (pt-x p) (pt-y p)))))
          (point->pair (transpose (make-pt 1 2)))))))))
```

The `point-epkg` argument to `test-point-epkg` is any existential package with
type `pt-eface`. The unpack_{exist} gives the local name `pt` to the abstract point
type and the local name `point-ops` to the implementation record containing the
`make-pt`, `pt-x`, and `pt-y` procedures. So the type of `point-ops` is:

```
(recordof (make-pt (-> (int int) pt))
          (pt-x (-> (pt) int))
          (pt-y (-> (pt) int)))
```

In the context of local bindings for these procedures (made available by `with`),
the local `transpose` and `point->pair` procedures are created. Each of these
takes a point as an argument and so must refer to the local abstract type name
`pt` for the abstract point type. Finally, `test-point-epkg` returns a pair of the
swapped coordinates for the abstract point (1,2).

In the [*eunpack*] type rule, it is assumed that the package expression E_{pkg} has
type (packof_{exist} τ_{abs} T_{impl}). The body expression E_{body} is type-checked under
the assumption that I_{impl} has as its type a version of T_{impl} in which the bound
name τ_{abs} has been replaced by the local abstract type name τ_{ty}. For instance,
in the above unpack_{exist} example, where `pt` is the local abstract type name, the
`make-pt` procedure has type (-> (int int) pt). The fact that the result type
is `pt` rather than `point` is essential for matching up the return type of `transpose`
and the declared argument type of `point->pair`.

Why is it necessary for unpack_{exist} to introduce a new name τ_{ty} (`pt` in our
example) for the abstract type name τ_{abs} (`point` in our example) in the existential type (packof_{exist} τ_{abs} T_{impl}) of E_{pkg}? Why not just use τ_{abs} itself? The
reason is that τ_{abs} is the binding occurrence of a name whose scope is only T_{impl},

and so it has no meaning outside this scope. In particular, τ_{abs} is subject to renaming within the $\texttt{packof}_{exist}$ type, so the notion of "*the* abstract type name of a $\texttt{packof}_{exist}$ type" is ill defined.

Existential types support data abstractions whose security is enforced by the type checker. In $\texttt{pack}_{exist}$, the type checker verifies that the concrete representation type is used internally within the implementation in a consistent way. However, once the concrete representation type of an implementation is hidden via $\texttt{pack}_{exist}$, there is no way for the type system to extract the concrete type from a package. It forever remains hidden to clients of the package. In particular, $\texttt{unpack}_{exist}$ provides no access to the concrete type of a package — it only allows renaming the abstract type. Because clients can manipulate only the abstract type and never the concrete type, they cannot violate the abstraction barrier established by $\texttt{pack}_{exist}$.

In the [*epack*] rule, there is an **import restriction** on the abstract type name τ_{abs} that prevents it from accidentally capturing a type identifier mentioned in the type of a free variable in E_{impl}. Here is an expression that would unsoundly be declared well typed without this restriction:

$$E_{unsound} = \texttt{(pabs (t)}$$
$$\texttt{(abs ((z t))}$$
$$\texttt{(pack}_{exist} \texttt{ t int (+ 1 (down z)))))}$$

The application $\texttt{(down z)}$ applies the $\texttt{down}$ procedure to a value $\texttt{z}$ of arbitrary type $\texttt{t}$. But since $\texttt{down}$ has type $\texttt{(-> (t) int)}$, where $\texttt{t}$ abstracts over the concrete type $\texttt{int}$, this application (as well as $E_{unsound}$ itself) would unsoundly be declared well typed without the import restriction. For example, $\texttt{((pcall } E_{unsound} \texttt{ bool) \#t)}$ would be considered well typed even though it attempts to add the integer 1 to the boolean $\texttt{\#t}$. A similar import restriction is also needed in the [*eunpack*] rule. The import restriction is not a serious issue for programmers because it can be satisfied by automatically alpha-renaming a program to give distinct names to logically distinct type identifiers.

In contrast, the **export restriction** $\tau_{ty} \notin FrTyIds_{ty}[\![T_{body}]\!]$ in the [*eunpack*] rule can be a serious impediment. This restriction says that the local abstract type name τ_{ty} is not allowed to escape the scope of the $\texttt{unpack}_{exist}$ expression by appearing in the type T_{body} of the body expression E_{body}. A consequence is that no value of the abstract type can escape from $\texttt{unpack}_{exist}$ in any way.

Without the export restriction, the [*eunpack*] rule would be unsound, as illustrated by the following example:

$$E_{incompat} = \text{(let ((p (unpack}_{exist} \text{ proc-point-epkg t point-ops1}$$
$$\text{(with point-ops1 (make-pt 1 2)))))}$$
$$\text{(f (unpack}_{exist} \text{ pair-point-epkg t point-ops2}$$
$$\text{(with point-ops2 pt-x)))))}$$
$$\text{(f p))}$$

The first **unpack**$_{exist}$ makes a procedural point whose type within the **unpack**$_{exist}$ is the local abstract type t. This point escapes from the **unpack**$_{exist}$ and is let-bound to the name p. The type of the point at this time is still t, which is an unbound type identifier in this context. The second **unpack**$_{exist}$ unpackages a pair point implementation and returns its pt-x operation, which is renamed f. Since t is also used as the local abstract type in the second **unpack**$_{exist}$, the type of f is (-> (t) int), where t again is actually an unbound type variable. Since f has type (-> (t) int) and p has type t, the application (f p) would be well typed. But dynamically an attempt is being made to take the first component of a procedural point, which should be a type error! This example makes clear that although it is powerful to be able to locally name the abstract type within **unpack**$_{exist}$, the local type name has no meaning outside the scope of the **unpack**$_{exist}$ and so cannot be allowed to escape.

The export restriction fundamentally limits the usefulness of existential types in practice. Although the data and operations from *different* implementations of an abstract type are clearly incompatible (as in $E_{incompat}$), there are many situations where we would like the data and operations from two unpackings of the *same* implementation to work together. For example, we would like the following variant of $E_{incompat}$ to be well typed, since it cannot encounter any dynamic type error:

$$E_{compat} = \text{(let ((p (unpack}_{exist} \text{ pair-point-epkg t point-ops1}$$
$$\text{(with point-ops1 (make-pt 1 2)))))}$$
$$\text{(f (unpack}_{exist} \text{ pair-point-epkg t point-ops2}$$
$$\text{(with point-ops2 pt-x)))))}$$
$$\text{(f p))}$$

However, the overly conservative export restriction has no way to determine that both ts refer to the same abstract type in this case, so E_{compat} is ill typed.

The export restriction also prohibits defining a make-transpose procedure that takes a point package and returns a transpose procedure appropriate for that package. The type of make-transpose would presumably be something like (-> (pt-eface) (-> (τ_{abs}) τ_{abs})), where τ_{abs} is the name of the abstract type used by the given point package. But there is no way to refer to that type except within **unpack**$_{exist}$ expressions inside the body of make-transpose, and that type cannot escape any such expressions to occur in the result type of `make-transpose`.

In practice, there are a few ways to finesse the export type restriction. One approach is to organize programs in such a way that large regions of the program are within the body of unpack_{exist} expressions that open up commonly used data abstractions. Within these large regions, it is possible to freely manipulate values of the abstract type. The problem with this approach is that it can make it more difficult to take advantage of one of the key benefits of existential types: the ability to abstract code over different implementations of the same abstract type and choose implementations at run time based on dynamic conditions.

In cases where we really want to pass values that mention the abstract type outside the scope of an unpack_{exist}, we can program around the restriction by packaging up such values together with their abstract type into a new existential type. For example, Figure 14.6 shows how to define an `extend-point-epkg` procedure that can take any package with type `pt-eface` and return a new package that has new operations and values in addition to the old ones. While this technique addresses the problem, it can be cumbersome, especially since all values mentioning the same abstract type must always be put together into the same package (or else later they could not be used with each other). Furthermore, the components of the original package need to be repackaged to get the right abstract type (and satisfy the import restriction).[6]

One paradigm in which the packaging overhead is not too onerous is a simple form of object-oriented programming. Figure 14.7 shows how the pair and procedural point representations can be encapsulated as existential packages whose implementations combine the state and methods of an object. As shown in the figure, in this paradigm, it is possible to express a generic top-level `transpose` method that operates on any value with type `point-object`. For example, the following expression is well typed:

```
(let ((points (list point-object {explicit type of list elements}
                    (make-pair-point 1 2)
                    (make-proc-point 3 4))))
  ((pcall append point-object) {append two lists into one}
   points
   ((pcall map point-object point-object) {map a function over a list}
    transpose points)))
```

---

[6]This is an artifact of using `up`/`down` to convert between abstract and concrete types. Such repackaging is not necessary in some other approaches; see Exercise 14.9.

```
(def-type new-pt-eface
  (packof_exist point
    (recordof (make-pt (-> (int int) point))
              (pt-x (-> (point) int))
              (pt-y (-> (point) int))
              (transpose (-> (point) point))
              (point->pair (-> (point) (pairof int int)))
              (origin point)))))

(def extend-point-epkg (-> (pt-eface) new-pt-eface)
  (abs ((point-epkg pt-eface))
    (unpack_exist point-epkg pt point-ops
      (with point-ops
        (pack_exist newpt pt
          (record (make-pt (abs ((x int) (y int)) (up (make-pt x y))))
                  (pt-x (abs ((p newpt)) (pt-x (down p))))
                  (pt-y (abs ((p newpt)) (pt-y (down p))))
                  (transpose (abs ((p newpt))
                                  (up (make-pt (pt-y (down p))
                                               (pt-x (down p))))))
                  (point->pair (abs ((p newpt))
                                    (pair (pt-x (down p))
                                          (pt-y (down p)))))
                  (origin (up (make-pt 0 0)))))))))))
```

Figure 14.6   The `extend-point-epkg` procedure shows how values mentioning an abstract type can be passed outside unpack_{exist} as long as they are first packaged together with their abstract type.

For simplicity, the existential type system considered here does not permit parameterized abstract types, but it can be extended to do so. For instance, here is an interface type for immutable stacks that is parameterized over the stack component type `t`:

```
(def-type stack-eface
  (forall (t)
    (packof_exist (stackof t)
      (recordof (empty (-> () (stackof t)))
                (empty? (-> ((stackof t)) bool))
                (push (-> (t (stackof t)) (stackof t)))
                (pop (-> ((stackof t)) (stackof t)))
                (top (-> ((stackof t)) t))))))
```

Parameterized existential types are explored in Exercise 14.8.

```
(def-type point-object
  (packof_exist point
    (recordof
      (state point)
      (methods (recordof
                 (make-pt (-> (int int) point))
                 (pt-x (-> (point) int))
                 (pt-y (-> (point) int)))))))
(def make-pair-point (-> (int int) point-object)
  (abs ((x int) (y int))
    (pack_exist point (pairof int int)
      (let ((make-pt (abs ((x int) (y int)) (up (pair x y)))))
        (record
          (state (make-pt x y))
          (methods (record
                     (make-pt make-pt)
                     (pt-x (abs ((p point)) (fst (down p))))
                     (pt-y (abs ((p point)) (snd (down p)))))))))))
(def make-proc-point (-> (int int) point-object)
  (abs ((x int) (y int))
    (pack_exist point (-> (bool) int)
      (let ((make-pt (abs ((x int) (y int))
                          (up (abs ((b bool)) (if b x y))))))
        (record
          (state (make-pt x y))
          (methods (record
                     (make-pt make-pt)
                     (pt-x (abs ((p point)) ((down p) #t)))
                     (pt-y (abs ((p point)) ((down p) #f))))))))))
(def transpose (-> (point-object) point-object)
  (abs ((pobj point-object))
    (unpack_exist pobj pt impl
      (with impl
        (with methods
          (pack_exist newpt pt
            (record
              (state (up (make-pt (pt-y state) (pt-x state))))
              (methods
                (record
                  (make-pt (abs ((x int) (y int)) (up (make-pt x y))))
                  (pt-x (abs ((p newpt)) (pt-x (down p))))
                  (pt-y (abs ((p newpt)) (pt-y (down p))))))))))))))
```

Figure 14.7 Encoding two pair-object representations using existential types.

Exercise 14.6 This exercise revisits the integer-set abstraction introduced in Exercise 14.2 (Section 14.2).

a. Define an interface type `intset-eface` for integer sets supporting the operations `empty`, `insert`, and `member?`.

b. Define an existential package `list-intset-epkg` implementing `intset-eface` that represents integer sets as sorted integer lists without duplicates.

c. Define an existential package `pred-intset-epkg` implementing `intset-eface` that represents integer sets as predicates.

d. Define a testing procedure `test-intset` that takes any implementation satisfying the type `intset-eface`, creates a set `s` containing the integers 1 and 3, and returns a three-element boolean list whose ith element (1-indexed) indicates whether `s` contains the integer i.

Exercise 14.7

a. Illustrate the necessity of the import restriction for the [*eunpack*] rule by giving an expression that would unsoundly be well typed without the restriction.

b. Alf Aaron Ames claims that the import restriction in the [*epack*] rule and the import and export restrictions in the [*eunpack*] rule are all unnecessary if before type checking the program is alpha-renamed to make all logically distinct type identifiers unique. Is Alf correct? Use suitably modified versions of the unsoundness examples in this section to support your answer.

Exercise 14.8

a. Extend the syntax and type rules of FLEX/P to handle parameterized existential types like (`stackof t`), which appears in the `stack-eface` example above.

b. Define an implementation `stack-list-epkg` of immutable stacks that has the type `stack-eface` and represents a stack as a list of elements ordered from the top down.

c. Define a procedure `int-stack-test` that tests a stack package by (1) defining a `swap` procedure that swaps the top two elements of an integer stack; (2) defining a `stack->list` procedure that converts an integer stack to an integer list; and (3) returning the result of invoking `stack->list` on the result of calling `swap` on a stack that contains the elements 1 and 2.

d. Design an interface `mstack-eface` for *mutable* stacks and repeat parts **b** and **c** for mutable stacks.

Exercise 14.9 The pack$_{exist}$ construct uses `up` and `down` procedures to explicitly convert between a concrete representation type and an abstract type name. Here we explore alternative ways to specify abstract versus concrete types in pack$_{exist}$. These alternatives also work for the other variants of `pack` that we shall study in Sections 14.4 and 14.5.

a. One alternative to using up and down is to extend pack_{exist} to have the form

$$(\text{pack}_{exist} \; \tau_{abs} \; T_{rep} \; T_{impl} \; E_{impl})$$

in which the implementation type T_{impl} is explicitly supplied. For example, here is one way to express a pair implementation of points using this modified form of pack_{exist}:

```
(packexist point (pairof int int)
    (recordof (make-pt (-> (int int) point))
              (pt-x (-> (point) int))
              (pt-y (-> (point) int)))
    (record (make-pt (abs ((x int) (y int)) (pair x y)))
            (pt-x (abs ((p point)) (fst p)))
            (pt-y (abs ((p (pairof int int))) (snd p)))))))
```

Within E_{impl}, the abstract type point and the concrete type (pairof int int) are interconvertible.

Give a type rule for this form of pack_{exist}. Your rule should not introduce up and down procedures. Use examples to justify the design of your rule.

b. An alternative to specifying T_{impl} in pack_{exist} is to require the programmer to use explicit type ascriptions (via FLEX/P's (the T E) construct) to convert concrete to abstract types or vice versa. Explain, using examples.

c. Yet another way to convert between concrete and abstract types is to interpret the def-datatype construct presented in Section 12.2.3 in a creative way. (The module system in Chapter 15 follows this approach.) Each constructor can be viewed as performing a conversion up to an abstract type and each deconstructor can be viewed as performing a conversion down from this type. For example, here is a point-as-pair existential package declared via an alternative syntax for pack_{exist} that replaces τ_{abs} and T_{rep} by a def-datatype declaration:

```
(packexist (def-datatype point (pt (pairof int int)))
    (record (make-pt (abs ((x int) (y int)) (pt (pair x y))))
            (pt-x (abs ((p point)) (match p ((pt (pair x _)) x))))
            (pt-y (abs ((p point)) (match p ((pt (pair _ y)) y)))))))
```

Give a type rule for this modified form of pack_{exist}.

d. Express the examples in Figure 14.6 and Figure 14.7 using the alternative approaches to existential types introduced above.

14.4 Nonce Types

We have seen that existential types provide secure data abstractions in a typed language, but the export restriction makes them impractical in many situations. The export restriction is a consequence of the fact that the abstract type name in an existential type and the local abstract type names introduced by $\mathbf{unpack}_{exist}$ are not connected to each other or to the concrete type in any way. One way to address this problem is by replacing the abstract type names by globally unique type symbols that we call **nonce types**. We shall see that package types based on nonce types are in many ways a more flexible approach to abstract types than existential types, but suffer from problems of their own.

As an example, the type of one implementation of a point abstraction might be the nonce package type

$$T_{point\text{-}npkg} = (\mathtt{packof}_{nonce}\ \mathtt{\#1729}$$
$$(\mathtt{recordof}\ (\mathtt{make\text{-}pt}\ (\mathtt{->}\ (\mathtt{int}\ \mathtt{int})\ \mathtt{\#1729}))$$
$$(\mathtt{pt\text{-}x}\ (\mathtt{->}\ (\mathtt{\#1729})\ \mathtt{int}))$$
$$(\mathtt{pt\text{-}y}\ (\mathtt{->}\ (\mathtt{\#1729})\ \mathtt{int}))))$$

where $\mathtt{\#1729}^{7}$ is the notation for the globally unique nonce type for this particular implementation. Another point-abstraction implementation would have the same $\mathtt{packof}_{nonce}$ type, except that a different unique nonce type (say $\mathtt{\#6821}$) for that implementation would be substituted for each occurrence of $\mathtt{\#1729}$. Nonce types $\nu \in \mathrm{NonceType}$ are introduced automatically by the type checker and cannot be written down directly by the programmer.

Whereas $(\mathtt{packof}_{exist}\ \tau_{abs}\ T_{impl})$ is a binding construct declaring that the type name τ_{abs} may be used in the scope of T_{impl}, $(\mathtt{packof}_{nonce}\ \nu_{abs}\ T_{impl})$ is not a binding construct. Rather, it effectively pairs the nonce type ν_{abs} with an implementation type T_{impl} in such a way that the two components can be unbundled by the elimination construct ($\mathtt{unpack}_{nonce}$). Like τ_{abs}, ν_{abs} serves to hide a concrete representation type. But unlike τ_{abs}, which has no meaning outside the scope of the $\mathtt{packof}_{exist}$, ν_{abs} names a particular concrete representation throughout the entire program. It serves as a globally unique tag for guaranteeing that the operations of a data abstraction are performed only on the appropriate abstract values, regardless of how the operations and values are packaged and unpackaged. For example, a value of type $\mathtt{\#1729}$ is necessarily created by the $\mathtt{make\text{-}pt}$ operation with type $(\mathtt{->}\ (\mathtt{int}\ \mathtt{int})\ \mathtt{\#1729})$, and it is safe to operate on this value with $\mathtt{pt\text{-}x}$ and $\mathtt{pt\text{-}y}$ operations having type $(\mathtt{pt\text{-}x}\ (\mathtt{->}\ (\mathtt{\#1729})\ \mathtt{int}))$. In contrast, these operations are incompatible with abstract values having nonce type $\mathtt{\#6821}$.

The essence of the nonce-type approach to abstract data types in FLEX/P is presented in Figure 14.8. The syntax for creating and eliminating nonce packages (using $\mathtt{pack}_{nonce}$ and $\mathtt{unpack}_{nonce}$) is the same as that for existential packages (us-

---

[7]Nonce types are a new kind of primitive type distinct from type identifiers. We write nonce types by prepending $\mathtt{\#}$ to a sequence of digits.

Syntax

$E ::= \ldots \mid (\text{pack}_{nonce}\ \tau_{abs}\ T_{rep}\ E_{impl}) \mid (\text{unpack}_{nonce}\ E_{pkg}\ \tau_{ty}\ I_{impl}\ E_{body})$

$NT \in \text{NatLit} = \{0, 1, 2, \ldots\}$

$\nu \in \text{NonceType} = \{\#\bowtie NT \mid NT \in \text{NatLit}\}$

$\tau \in \text{TypeId} = \text{TypeId}_{\text{FLEX/P}} - (\text{NonceType} \cup \{\text{packof}_{nonce}\})$

$T ::= \ldots \mid \nu \mid (\text{packof}_{nonce}\ \nu\ T_{impl})$

Free Identifiers

$FrTyIds_{ty}[\![(\text{packof}_{nonce}\ \nu\ T_{impl})]\!] = FrTyIds_{ty}[\![T_{impl}]\!]$

All clauses for *FrIds* and *FrTyIds*$_{exp}$ are analogous to those for existential types in Figure 14.4 on page 850.

Dynamic Semantics (via Type Erasure)

Same as for $\text{pack}_{exist}/\text{unpack}_{exist}$ in Figure 14.4 on page 850.

Type Equivalence

$$\frac{T \approx T'}{(\text{packof}_{nonce}\ \nu\ T) \approx (\text{packof}_{nonce}\ \nu\ T')} \qquad [\textit{npackof-}\approx]$$

Type Rules

$$\frac{TE[\text{up} : (\text{->}\ (T_{rep})\ \nu),\ \text{down} : (\text{->}\ (\nu)\ T_{rep})] \vdash [\nu/\tau_{abs}]E_{impl} : T_{impl}}{TE \vdash (\text{pack}_{nonce}\ \tau_{abs}\ T_{rep}\ E_{impl}) : (\text{packof}_{nonce}\ \nu\ T_{impl})} \qquad [\textit{npack}]$$

where ν is a fresh nonce type $\qquad\qquad$ *[freshness condition]*

$\qquad\qquad T_{rep}$ does not contain any **pabs**-bound identifiers $\qquad$ *[rep restriction]*

$$\frac{TE \vdash E_{pkg} : (\text{packof}_{nonce}\ \nu\ T_{impl}) \qquad TE[I_{impl} : T_{impl}] \vdash [\nu/\tau_{ty}]E_{body} : T_{body}}{TE \vdash (\text{unpack}_{nonce}\ E_{pkg}\ \tau_{ty}\ I_{impl}\ E_{body}) : T_{body}} \qquad [\textit{nunpack}]$$

Figure 14.8 The essence of nonce types in FLEX/P.

ing pack_{exist} and unpack_{exist}). For example, here is an expression that describes a pair implementation of a point abstraction as a nonce package:

```
E_pair-point-npkg =
   (pack_nonce point (pairof int int)
      (record (make-pt (abs ((x int) (y int)) (up (pair x y))))
              (pt-x (abs ((p point)) (fst (down p))))
              (pt-y (abs ((p point)) (snd (down p)))))))
```

The same expression described an existential package implementing points as pairs (see Figure 14.5 on page 851); the difference is in the static semantics, not the syntax or dynamic semantics.

According to the [*npack*] type rule, $E_{pair\text{-}point\text{-}npkg}$ could have the $\texttt{packof}_{nonce}$ type $T_{point\text{-}npkg}$ given earlier. Each application of the [*npack*] rule introduces a fresh nonce type ν (in this case, #1729) that is not used in any other application of the [*npack*] rule. This nonce type replaces all occurrences of the programmer-specified abstract type name τ_{abs} (in this case, $\texttt{point}$) in E_{impl}. As in existential types, $\texttt{up}$ and $\texttt{down}$ procedures are used to mediate between the concrete and abstract types (but this can be accomplished in other ways; see Exercise 14.9 on page 858). Note that the Type domain must be extended to include nonce types $\nu \in \text{NonceType}$, which are distinct from type identifiers. They are instead type constants that are freshly generated, similar to Skolem constants used in logic.

The following expression is a use of the example package that is possible with nonce packages but not with existential packages (because of the export restriction, which prevents the transposed point from being returned):

```
E_pair-point-test  =
  (let ((pair-point-npkg E_pair-point-npkg))
    (let ((transpose (unpack_nonce pair-point-npkg t pair-point-ops
                       (with pair-point-ops
                         (abs ((p t))
                           (make-pt (pt-y p) (pt-x p))))))
          (pt (unpack_nonce pair-point-npkg t pair-point-ops
                (with pair-point-ops
                  (make-pt 1 2)))))
      (transpose pt)))
```

To see that $E_{pair\text{-}point\text{-}test}$ is well typed, note that the same nonce type, #1729, is used within both occurrences of $\texttt{unpack}_{nonce}$. By [*nunpack*], $\texttt{transpose}$ has type $\texttt{(-> (#1729) #1729)}$ and $\texttt{pt}$ has type #1729, so $\texttt{(transpose pt)}$ (as well as $E_{pair\text{-}point\text{-}test}$) has type #1729. As shown by [*nunpack*], the type identifier τ_{ty} in $\texttt{unpack}_{nonce}$ allows the programmer to locally name the nonce type of E_{pkg}, which cannot be written down directly. There are no import or export restrictions in [*nunpack*]. The substitution $[\nu/\tau_{ty}]E_{body}$ converts all local type identifiers into nonce types that may safely enter and escape from $\texttt{unpack}_{nonce}$ because they are globally unique type symbols that denote the same implementation in all contexts.

Although [*nunpack*] has no restrictions, there are two restrictions in [*npack*]. The freshness condition requires that a different nonce type be used for each occurrence of $\texttt{pack}_{nonce}$ encountered in the type-checking process.[8] The "rep

---

[8]The restriction requires careful attention in practice. One way to formalize it in the type rules would be to modify the type rules to pass a nonce-type counter through the type-checking process in a single-threaded fashion and increment the counter whenever [*npack*] is used. In

restriction" prohibits the concrete representation type T_{rep} from containing any pabs-bound type identifiers. In the simple form of nonce packages that we are studying, this restriction prevents a single nonce type from being implicitly parameterized over any types that are not known when type checking is performed on the pack_{nonce} expression. For example, consider the following expression, which would unsoundly be well typed without the restriction:

```
(let ((make-wrapper
        (pabs (t)
          (pack_nonce absty t
            (record (wrap (abs ((x t)) (up x)))
                    (unwrap (abs ((y absty)) (down y)))))))))
      (let ((wrap-int (unpack_nonce (pcall make-wrapper int) ity ircd
                        (select wrap ircd)))
            (unwrap-bool (unpack_nonce (pcall make-wrapper bool) bty brcd
                            (select unwrap brcd))))
        (unwrap-bool (wrap-int 3))))
```

If #6821 is used as the nonce type in the pack_{nonce} expression, then wrap-int has type (-> (int) #6821), unwrap-bool has type (-> (#6821) bool), and (unwrap-bool (wrap-int 3)) has type bool even though it dynamically evaluates to the integer 3! The problem is that #6821 should not be a single nonce type but some sort of nonce-type constructor that is parameterized over t.

The key advantage of nonce packages for expressing abstract types is that, unlike existential packages, they have no export restriction. As illustrated by $E_{pair\text{-}point\text{-}test}$, values of and operations on the abstract type may escape from unpack_{nonce} expressions. Programmers do not have to rearrange their programs or adopt an awkward programming style to prevent this from happening.

However, this advantage is offset by three major drawbacks that nonce packages suffer from as a mechanism for abstract types:

1. *Difficulties with writing nonce types.* The fact that nonce types cannot conveniently be written down directly by the programmer is problematic, especially in an explicitly typed language. For example, in FLEX/P, the programmer cannot write a top-level definition of the form

   (def pair-point-npkg T $E_{pair\text{-}point\text{-}npkg}$)

   because there is no way to write down the concrete nonce type needed in T. This is not just an issue of type syntax; the programmer does not know which

---

languages that allow separate analysis and compilation of modular units, nonce types could include a unique identifier of the computer on which type checking was performed along with a timestamp of the time when type checking took place.

nonce type the type checker will generate when checking $E_{pair\text{-}point\text{-}npkg}$. By contrast, with existential types this is easy to express, as shown in Figure 14.5 on page 851.

One way to address this problem is to embed nonce packages in a language with implicit types, where type reconstruction can infer nonce package types that the programmer cannot express (see Exercise 14.14). This is the approach taken in SML, where the nonce-based `abstype` mechanism allows the local declaration of abstract data types (independent of SML's module system). But in reconstructible languages, it is still sometimes necessary to write down explicit types, and the inability to express nonce package types reduces expressivity in these cases.

Another alternative is to require that the abstract type name τ_{abs} appearing in ($\texttt{pack}_{nonce}\ \tau_{abs}\ T_{rep}\ E_{impl}$) be a globally unique name that serves as a concrete nonce type (see Exercise 14.12). This lets the programmer rather than the type checker choose the abstract type name. In this case, the programmer *can* write down the abstract type name and there is no need for the local abstract type name in $\texttt{unpack}_{nonce}$. There are serious modularity problems with this approach, but it makes sense in restricted systems where all nonce packages are created at top level (see Exercise 14.15). This is the approach to abstract types taken in languages like ADA, PASCAL, and JAVA, in which type equivalence is determined by the declared name of a type (**name equivalence**) rather than the structure of the type (**structural equivalence**). For example, consider the following type declarations in PASCAL:

```
type point = array [1..2] of integer;
     rational = array [1..2] of integer;
```

The two types are structurally identical, but a value of type `point` cannot be used where a `rational` is expected because the type names are different.

2. *Difficulties abstracting over different implementations.* As demonstrated by the `test-point-epkg` example on page 852, it is possible to define procedures that abstract over existential packages. However, even if there were a way for programmers to write nonce types directly, the fact that nonce package types mention particular nonce types makes it difficult to abstract over nonce packages. For instance, what type T_{npkg} can be given to the nonce package argument in the following abstraction, which creates a transpose procedure from any point implementation?

$$E_{make\text{-}transpose} = \text{(abs ((npkg } T_{npkg}\text{))}$$
$$\text{(unpack}_{nonce}\text{ npkg t impl}$$
$$\text{(with impl}$$
$$\text{(abs ((p t))}$$
$$\text{(make-pt (pt-y p) (pt-x p))))))}$$

Presumably, T_{npkg} has the form

```
(packof_nonce ν
  (recordof (make-pt (-> (int int) ν))
            (pt-x (-> (ν) int))
            (pt-y (-> (ν) int))))
```

but then it will match at most one point implementation. What we really want is to abstract over the nonce type so that (a suitably modified version of) $E_{make\text{-}transpose}$ has a type that is something like:

```
(forall (point)
  (-> ((packof_nonce point
          (recordof (make-pt (-> (int int) point))
                    (pt-x (-> (point) int))
                    (pt-y (-> (point) int)))))
      (-> (point) point)))
```

There are technical problems with this solution. First, a type of the form (packof$_{nonce}$ point ...) is not allowed by the grammar, which permits only a nonce type in the position of the first occurrence of point. So the type grammar needs to be extended to allow type identifiers to fill this hole. Second, we expect that a polymorphic value with type (forall (point) ...) can be projected onto *any* type, but here the only sensible types that can be supplied for point are nonce types. So the forall-bound type identifier in this case must somehow be restricted to range over nonce types. This can be accomplished via bounded quantification (see Section 12.2.4) or by annotating forall-bound type-identifier declarations with explicit kinds (see Section 12.3.2). Thus, the problem of abstracting over nonce packages is not insurmountable, but the solution is complicated.

3. *Insufficient abstraction.* Nonce packages are sound in the sense that a well-typed program cannot encounter a run-time type error. In particular, they prevent abstraction violations in which a procedure is treated as a pair, a boolean as an integer, etc. However, there is still a form of abstraction violation that can occur with nonce packages. An example of this is shown in Figure 14.9. The make-rat-impl procedure makes a rational number imple-

```
(let ((make-rat-impl
       (abs ((b bool))
         (pack_nonce rat (pairof int int)
           (record (make-rat (abs ((n int) (d int))
                                  (up (if b (pair n d) (pair d n)))))
                   (numer (abs ((r rat))
                              (if b (fst (down r)) (snd (down r)))))
                   (denom (abs ((r rat))
                              (if b (snd (down r)) (fst (down r)))))))))))
  (let ((leftist-rat (make-rat-impl #t))
        (rightist-rat (make-rat-impl #f)))
    ((unpack_nonce rightist-rat rty rops (select numer rops))
     ((unpack_nonce leftist-rat lty lops (select make-rat lops)) 1 2))))
```

Figure 14.9   A form of abstraction violation that can occur with nonce types.

mentation, which in all cases represents a rational number as a pair of integers. However, it is abstracted over a boolean argument b that chooses one of two representations. When b is #t, the numerator is the first, or left, element of the pair and the denominator is the second, or right, element; we will call this the "leftist representation." When b is #f, a "rightist representation" is used, in which the numerator is second (on the right) and the denominator is first (on the left).

In the example, the numer procedure of the rightist representation is applied to a leftist rational with numerator 1 and denominator 2. Since nonce types are determined by static occurrences of pack_nonce and there is only one of these in the example, the two dynamic invocations of make-rat-impl yield implementations that use the same nonce type for rat. Thus, the application is well typed and at run time will return the value 2.

Thus, the nonce package system allows different implementations of a data abstraction to intermingle as long as they are represented via the same concrete type. Although this might seem reasonable in some cases, we normally expect an abstract type system to enforce the contract chosen by the designer of an abstraction. Enforcing the contract (and not just ensuring compatible representations) enables the abstraction and the clients to rely on important invariants that, among other things, ensure correctness of programs.

Exercise 14.10

a. Would the expression in Figure 14.9 be well typed if all occurrences of pack_nonce and unpack_nonce were replaced by pack_exist and unpack_exist? Explain.

b. Below are three replacements for the body of the inner `let` in the example in Figure 14.9. For each replacement, indicate whether the whole example expression would be well typed using (1) nonce packages and (2) existential packages. (Assume that pack_{nonce} in the figure is changed to pack_{exist} for the existential case.) For each case, discuss whether you think the type system does the "right thing" in that case.

   i.   `((unpack leftist-rat lty1 lops1 (select numer lops1))`
         `((unpack leftist-rat lty2 lops2 (select make-rat lops2)) 1 2))`

   ii.   `(unpack leftist-rat lty lops`
       `(unpack rightist-rat rty rops`
         `((select numer lops) ((select make-rat rops) 1 2))))`

   iii. `(unpack leftist-rat lty1 lops1`
       `(unpack leftist-rat lty2 lops2`
         `((select numer lops1) ((select make-rat lops2) 1 2))))`

Exercise 14.11 As noted above, the inability to write down nonce types is incompatible with top-level `def` declarations in FLEX/P, which require an explicit type to handle potentially recursive definitions. Design a top-level definition mechanism for FLEX/P that enables the declaration of nonrecursive global values. Illustrate how your mechanism can be used to give the global name `pair-point-npkg` to $E_{pair\text{-}point\text{-}npkg}$.

Exercise 14.12 If the abstract type name τ_{abs} in $(\text{pack}_{nonce}\ \tau_{abs}\ T_{rep}\ E_{impl})$ were required to be a globally unique name, then it could serve as a programmer-specified nonce type. Assume that type identifiers are not automatically alpha-renamed before type checking.

a. Give type rules for versions of pack_{nonce} and unpack_{nonce} that are consistent with this interpretation.

b. Describe how to modify the type-checking rules to verify the global uniqueness requirement.

c. Discuss the advantages and disadvantages of this approach to nonce types. Is it a good idea?

Exercise 14.13 Modify the syntax and type rules of FLEX/P to handle parameterized nonce types. (Compare this to Exercise 14.8 in Section 14.3.)

Exercise 14.14 In this exercise, we consider existential and nonce types in the context of type reconstruction by adding them to FLARE. You may assume a version of FLARE that supports records whose types are reconstructed using the row-type mechanism described in Section 13.5.3.

a. Nonce packages can be added to FLARE by extending it with nonce types and the single expression $(\text{pack}_{nonce}\ E_{impl})$.

   i.   Give a FLARE type rule for the modified version of pack_{nonce}.

   ii.   Describe how to extend the FLARE reconstruction algorithm to reconstruct the modified pack_{nonce}.

iii.   The unpack_{nonce} expression and packof_{nonce} type are not necessary in FLARE. Explain why.

b. Existential packages can be added to FLARE by extending it with the expressions $(\text{pack}_{exist}\ E_{impl})$ and $(\text{unpack}_{exist}\ E_{pkg}\ T_{pkg}\ I_{impl}\ E_{body})$ and the existential type $(\text{packof}_{exist}\ \tau_{abs}\ T_{impl})$. In the modified unpack_{exist}, the type T_{pkg} is the type of the expression E_{pkg}.

    i.   Give FLARE type rules for the modified pack_{exist} and unpack_{exist}.

    ii.   Describe how to extend the FLARE reconstruction algorithm to reconstruct the modified pack_{exist} and unpack_{exist} forms. Explain how the export restriction is checked.

    iii. Explain why it is necessary for a simple reconstruction system to be explicitly given the type T_{pkg} of the existential package expression E_{pkg}. Why can't it reconstruct this package type?

c. What changes would need to be made above to handle existential and nonce packages with parameterized types?

Exercise 14.15 Many languages support abstract types that can only be declared globally. Here we explore an abstract type mechanism introduced by a top-level declaration `def-cluster` that is inspired by the cluster mechanism in CLU. For simplicity, we assume that programs have the form

```
(program Ebody
   (def-cluster Iimpl₁ τabs₁ Trep₁ Eimpl₁)
      ⋮
   (def-cluster Iimplₖ τabsₖ Trepₖ Eimplₖ))
```

where all $I_{impl_1}, \ldots, I_{impl_k}$ are distinct and all $\tau_{abs_1}, \ldots, \tau_{abs_k}$ are distinct.

a. One interpretation of `def-cluster` is given by the following desugaring for `program`:

```
(let ((Iimpl₁ (packexist τabs₁ Trep₁ Eimpl₁))
         ⋮
      (Iimplₖ (packexist τabsₖ Trepₖ Eimplₖ)))
   (unpackexist Iimpl₁ τabs₁ Iimpl₁
      ·⋱
         (unpackexist Iimplₖ τabsₖ Iimplₖ
            Ebody)))
```

Would the interpretation be any different if all occurrences of pack_{exist} and unpack_{exist} were replaced by pack_{nonce} and unpack_{nonce}, respectively?

b. Give a direct type rule for the `program` construct with `def-cluster` declarations that gives the same static semantics as the above desugaring.

c. An alternative desugaring for `program` is:

$$(\text{let } ((I_{impl_1} \ (\text{pack}_{exist} \ \tau_{abs_1} \ T_{rep_1} \ E_{impl_1})))$$
$$(\text{unpack}_{exist} \ I_{impl_1} \ \tau_{abs_1} \ I_{impl_1}$$

$$\ddots$$

$$(\text{let } ((I_{impl_k} \ (\text{pack}_{exist} \ \tau_{abs_k} \ T_{rep_k} \ E_{impl_k})))$$
$$(\text{unpack}_{exist} \ I_{impl_k} \ \tau_{abs_k} \ I_{impl_k}$$
$$E_{body})))$$

What advantage does this desugaring have over the previous one? Give an example where this desugaring would be preferred.

d. It is sometimes useful for top-level `def-cluster` declarations to be mutually recursive. Write a simple example program that requires mutually recursive clusters, and give a direct type rule for mutually recursive top-level `def-cluster` declarations.

e. Suppose that we want to be able to locally define a collection of clusters anywhere in a program, as follows:

$$(\text{let-clusters } ((I_{impl} \ \tau_{abs} \ T_{rep} \ E_{impl})^*) \ E_{body})$$

Discuss the design issues involved in specifying the semantics of `let-clusters`.

14.5 Dependent Types

As we saw with existential packages, the inability to express "the type exported by *this* package" makes many programs awkward to write. Nonce package types provide a way to express this idea but suffer from other problems: they are difficult to write down explicitly, are challenging to abstract over, and can allow abstract types from different instances of the same syntactic package expression to be confused.

We now study a third approach, which exhibits the best features of the other two approaches but suffers from few of their drawbacks. The key idea is to use a structured name to represent the abstract type associated with a package. We introduce a new type construct $(\text{dtypeof } E_{pkg})$ to mean "the abstract type exported by the package denoted by E_{pkg}." The `dtypeof` construct is a safe way to track the flow of the abstract type of a package outside the scope of an `unpack` expression, so it solves the export restriction problem of existential packages. Moreover, this construct can be written by programmers, so it does not suffer from the unwritability problems of nonce types. Finally, we shall see that an abstract type system based on `dtypeof` enables abstracting over different packages having the same interface but prohibits the abstraction violations exhibited by nonce packages.

A type that contains a value expression is called a **dependent type**, because the type it represents *depends* in some sense on the value of the expression. The reader may be justifiably concerned about this unholy commingling of types and values, especially with respect to static type checking. As we shall see, dependent types raise some nettlesome issues that the language designer must address in order to reap the benefits of their expressiveness.

14.5.1   A Dependent Package System

We now explore a simple package system that uses dependent types to express abstract types. We shall use the term **dependent package** to refer to a package in this system.

The point-manipulation example in Figure 14.10 highlights three key features of the dependent package system:

1. Package types ($\texttt{packof}_{depend}$ τ_{abs} T_{impl}) are like those in the existential system. Because the abstract type is expressed via a programmer-writable type identifier τ_{abs} rather than an unwritable nonce type, it is easy to define the point interface (`point-dface`) and two point implementations satisfying this interface (`pair-point-dpkg` and `proc-point-dpkg`). Modulo name changes and the extended form for arrow types (discussed below), these three definitions are identical to the ones given earlier for existential packages.

2. The construct (`dtypeof` E_{pkg}) stands for the abstract type of the package E_{pkg}, allowing this type to be written outside the scope of an $\texttt{unpack}_{depend}$ that opens the package. For example, both `pair-point-1` and `pair-point-2` are given the type (`dtypeof pair-point-dpkg`), a programmer-writable type that can be used to track the flow of the abstract type from the package named `pair-point-dpkg`. In an existential package system, such top-level point definitions are prohibited by the export restriction, because there is no way to specify an abstract point type outside the scope of an $\texttt{unpack}_{exist}$ expression. The nonce package system does allow abstract point types to leave the scope of an $\texttt{unpack}_{nonce}$ expression, but there is no way for the programmer to declare the type of these points, which would be unwritable nonce types.

   In our dependent package system, a type is a dependent type if and only if it contains at least one occurrence of `dtypeof`, because this is the only type construct that may refer to values.

3. A procedure's return type may depend on the *values* of its parameters, as expressed in the **parameterized arrow type**[9] (-> ($(I_i \ T_i)_{i=1}^{n}$) T_{result}).

---

[9]In the literature, such types are commonly called *dependent function types*. In our terminology, "dependent arrow (or procedure) type" is *any* arrow type that is also a dependent type, regardless of whether the dependency arises from the use of the parameter names.

```
(def-type point-dface
  (packof_depend point
    (recordof (make-pt (-> ((x int) (y int)) point))
              (pt-x (-> ((p point)) int))
              (pt-y (-> ((p point)) int)))))
(def pair-point-dpkg point-dface
  (pack_depend point (pairof int int)
    (record (make-pt (abs ((x int) (y int)) (up (pair x y))))
            (pt-x (abs ((p point)) (fst (down p))))
            (pt-y (abs ((p point)) (snd (down p)))))))
(def proc-point-dpkg point-dface
  (pack_depend point (-> ((b bool)) int)
    (record (make-pt (abs ((x int) (y int))
                          (up (abs ((b bool)) (if b x y)))))
            (pt-x (abs ((p point)) ((down p) #t)))
            (pt-y (abs ((p point)) ((down p) #f))))))
(def pair-point-1 (dtypeof pair-point-dpkg)
  (unpack_depend pair-point-dpkg pt point-ops
    (with point-ops (make-pt 1 2))))
(def make-transpose (-> ((point-dpkg point-dface))
                        (-> ((p (dtypeof point-dpkg)))
                            (dtypeof point-dpkg)))
  (abs ((point-dpkg point-dface))
    (unpack_depend point-dpkg pt point-ops
      (with point-ops
        (abs ((p pt))
          (make-pt (pt-y p) (pt-x p)))))))
(def pair-point-2 (dtypeof pair-point-dpkg)
  ((make-transpose pair-point-dpkg) pair-point-1))
```

Figure 14.10 Point manipulation in the dependent package system.

An arrow type is now a binding construct in which the formal parameter names $I_1, \ldots, I_n$ stand for the actual argument values to which the procedure will be applied. T_{result} may contain dependent types of the form $(\texttt{dtypeof } E)$ where E references these names. For example, in the type of `make-transpose`,

```
(-> ((point-dpkg point-dface))
    (-> ((p (dtypeof point-dpkg)))
        (dtypeof point-dpkg)))
```

the two occurrences of (dtypeof point-dpkg) in the inner arrow type refer
to the formal parameter name point-dpkg of the outer arrow type. This type
says that the result of calling make-transpose on a dependent point package
is a procedure that maps an abstract point from that package to another
abstract point from the same package. In contrast, we have seen that the type
of make-transpose is inexpressible with existential packages because of the
export restriction and is complex to express with nonce packages.

   The syntax, dynamic semantics, and static semantics of dependent packages
are summarized in Figures 14.11–14.13. There is syntactic sugar (Figure 14.11)
for writing arrow types in the traditional way (without explicit formal parameter
names) in the common case where the result type does not refer to the parameter
names. Because types may contain expressions (in the (dtypeof E_{pkg}) type),
computing the free identifiers in an expression must be extended to analyze embedded types. Figure 14.11 extends $FrIds$ (now called $FrIds_{exp}$ for clarity) to do
this and introduces a new function, $FrIds_{ty}$, that determines the free value identifiers of a type. Since expressions contain types and types contain expressions,
these functions are mutually recursive.

   Figure 14.12 shows the new type-equivalence rules. The $[\rightarrow\text{-}\approx]$ rule allows
alpha-renaming of the formal parameter names in an arrow type, so the particular parameter names (such as the ones chosen by the -> desugaring) are
irrelevant. As in packof$_{exist}$, the type identifier τ_{abs} in packof$_{depend}$ may be
alpha-renamed ($[dpackof\text{-}\approx]$). This makes it easy to abstract over renamed versions of the same packof$_{depend}$ type — something that is very messy in the nonce
package system. The most interesting type-equivalence rule in the dependent
package system is $[dtypeof\text{-}\approx]$. This is discussed later, on page 877. For now,
assume that $E_1 \approx_{depends} E_2$ means $E_1 = E_2$.

   The type rules in Figure 14.13 are the heart of the dependent package system.
They use a restricted form of type environment (discussed later, on page 879) in
which names for any new bindings must not conflict with names already in the
environment. The [dpack] rule is exactly like the [epack] rule in the existential
package system except for explicit parameter names in the arrow types for up
and down. In contrast, the [dunpack] rule is more similar to the [nunpack] rule in
the nonce package system, because the dependent type (dtypeof E_{pkg}), which
plays the role of a nonce type, is substituted for the local type name τ_{ty} in the
body E_{body} of the unpack$_{depend}$ expression. In addition, it is substituted for the
abstract type τ_{abs} in the packof$_{depend}$ body type T_{impl}. For example, in the
definition of pair-point-1, the expression (with point-ops (make-pt 1 2))
is type-checked in an environment in which point-ops has the type

Syntax

$E ::= \ldots$ FLEX/P *expressions* $\ldots$
$\quad | \; (\text{pack}_{depend} \; \tau_{abs} \; T_{rep} \; E_{impl}) \; | \; (\text{unpack}_{depend} \; E_{pkg} \; \tau_{ty} \; I_{impl} \; E_{body})$

$T ::= \ldots$ FLEX/P *types except* $(\text{->} \; (T^*) \; T) \ldots$
$\quad | \; (\text{packof}_{depend} \; \tau_{abs} \; T_{impl})$ [PackageType]
$\quad | \; (\text{dtypeof} \; E_{pkg})$ [DependentTypeExtraction]
$\quad | \; (\text{->} \; ((I_{argName} \; T_{arg})^*) \; T_{result})$ [ParameterizedArrowType]

New Syntactic Sugar

$(\text{->} \; (T_{i=1}^n) \; T_0) \leadsto_{ds} (\text{->} \; ((I_i \; T_i)_{i=1}^n) \; T_0)$, where $I_{i=1}^n$ are fresh

Free Identifiers

$FrIds_{exp} : \text{Exp} \to \mathcal{P}(\text{Ident})$

$FrIds_{exp}[\![I]\!] = \{I\}$

$FrIds_{exp}[\![(\text{abs} \; ((I_i \; T_i)_{i=1}^n) \; E_{body})]\!]$
$\quad = (\cup_{i=1}^n FrIds_{ty}[\![T_i]\!]) \cup (FrIds_{exp}[\![E_{body}]\!] - \cup_{i=1}^n \{I_i\})$

$FrIds_{exp}[\![(\text{let} \; ((I_i \; E_i)_{i=1}^n) \; E_0)]\!]$
$\quad = (\cup_{i=1}^n FrIds_{exp}[\![E_i]\!]) \cup (FrIds_{exp}[\![E_0]\!] - \cup_{i=1}^n \{I_i\})$

$FrIds_{exp}[\![(\text{letrec} \; ((I_i \; T_i \; E_i)_{i=1}^n) \; E_0)]\!]$
$\quad = ((\cup_{i=1}^n FrIds_{ty}[\![T_i]\!]) \cup (\cup_{i=0}^n FrIds[\![E_i]\!])) - \cup_{i=1}^n \{I_i\}$

$FrIds_{exp}[\![(\text{pack}_{exist} \; \tau_{abs} \; T_{rep} \; E_{impl})]\!] = FrIds_{ty}[\![T_{rep}]\!] \cup FrIds_{exp}[\![E_{impl}]\!]$

$FrIds_{exp}[\![(\text{unpack}_{exist} \; E_{pkg} \; \tau_{ty} \; I_{impl} \; E_{body})]\!]$
$\quad = FrIds_{exp}[\![E_{pkg}]\!] \cup (FrIds_{exp}[\![E_{body}]\!] - \{I_{impl}\})$

$FrIds_{exp}[\![E]\!] = (\cup_{i=1}^n FrIds_{exp}[\![E_i]\!]) \cup (\cup_{j=1}^k FrIds_{ty}[\![T_j]\!])$ for all other expressions E,
$\quad$ where $E_{i=1}^n$ are the immediate component expressions appearing in E
$\quad$ and $T_{j=1}^k$ are the immediate component types appearing in E.

$FrIds_{ty} : \text{Type} \to \mathcal{P}(\text{Ident})$

$FrIds_{ty}[\![(\text{->} \; ((I_i \; T_i)_{i=1}^n) \; T_0)]\!] = (\cup_{i=1}^n FrIds_{ty}[\![T_i]\!]) \cup (FrIds_{ty}[\![T_0]\!] - \cup_{i=1}^n \{I_i\})$

$FrIds_{ty}[\![(\text{dtypeof} \; E)]\!] = FrIds_{exp}[\![E]\!]$

$FrIds_{ty}[\![T]\!] = \cup_{i=1}^n FrIds_{ty}[\![T_i]\!]$ for all other types T,
$\quad$ where $T_{i=1}^n$ are the immediate component types appearing in T.

$FrTyIds_{ty} : \text{Type} \to \mathcal{P}(\text{TypeId})$

$FrTyIds_{ty}[\![(\text{->} \; ((I_i \; T_i)_{i=1}^n) \; T_0)]\!] = \cup_{i=0}^n FrTyIds_{ty}[\![T_i]\!]$

$FrTyIds_{ty}[\![(\text{dtypeof} \; E_{pkg})]\!] = FrTyIds_{exp}[\![E_{pkg}]\!]$

$FrTyIds_{ty}[\![(\text{packof}_{depend} \; \tau_{abs} \; T_{impl})]\!] = FrTyIds_{ty}[\![T_{impl}]\!] - \{\tau_{abs}\}$

$FrTyIds_{exp} : \text{Exp} \to \mathcal{P}(\text{TypeId})$ is defined as for existential types in Figure 14.4 on page 850.

Figure 14.11 The essence of dependent packages in FLEX/P, Part 1.

Dynamic Semantics (via Type Erasure)

Same as for $\mathtt{pack}_{exist}/\mathtt{unpack}_{exist}$ in Figure 14.4 on page 850.

Type Equivalence

$$\frac{\forall_{i=1}^{n} \cdot (T_i \approx T_i') \quad [I_i'/I_i]_{i=1}^{n}\, T_0 \approx T_0'}{(\text{->}\ ((I_i\ \ T_i)_{i=1}^{n})\ \ T_0) \approx (\text{->}\ ((I_i'\ \ T_i')_{i=1}^{n})\ \ T_0')} \qquad [\text{->-}\approx]$$
$$\text{where}\quad \forall_{i=1}^{n} \cdot (I_i' \notin \mathit{FrIds}_{ty}[\![T_0]\!])$$

$$\frac{[\tau'/\tau]\,T \approx T'}{(\mathtt{packof}_{depend}\ \tau\ T) \approx (\mathtt{packof}_{depend}\ \tau'\ T')} \qquad [dpackof\text{-}\approx]$$

$$\frac{E_1 \approx_{depends} E_2}{(\mathtt{dtypeof}\ E_1) \approx (\mathtt{dtypeof}\ E_2)} \qquad [dtypeof\text{-}\approx]$$
$$\text{where}\ \ \approx_{depends}\ \text{is discussed in Section 14.5.2.}$$

Figure 14.12   The essence of dependent packages in FLEX/P, Part 2.

```
(recordof (make-pt (-> ((x int) (y int)) (dtypeof pair-point-dpkg)))
          (pt-x (-> ((p (dtypeof pair-point-dpkg))) int))
          (pt-y (-> ((p (dtypeof pair-point-dpkg))) int)))
```

So the type of (make-pt 1 2) and of the with expression is the dependent type
(dtypeof pair-point-dpkg). There is no export restriction, so this dependent
type is allowed to leave the scope of the $\mathtt{unpack}_{depend}$ expression.

As with existential packages, [*dpack*] and [*dunpack*] have an import restriction
that prevents the local name of the abstraction from capturing an existing type
name. As before, this restriction can be satisfied by automatically alpha-renaming
programs to make all logically distinct type identifiers unique. The [*dunpack*] rule
(as well as many of the other type rules) has an additional purity restriction that
we will discuss in more detail later, on page 880.

The [*->-intro*] rule is like the standard one (Figure 11.7 on page 644) except
that it remembers the formal parameter names in the resulting arrow type. It
is essential to declare these names in the arrow type so they can be referenced
in dependent types that occur in the result type. For example, we have seen
that the result type of make-transpose contains dependent types that refer to
the parameter name point-dpkg. These dependent types are introduced by the
$\mathtt{unpack}_{depend}$ expression that unpacks the point-dpkg parameter in the body of
the make-transpose abstraction.

The [*->-elim*] rule modifies the standard rule (Figure 11.7 on page 644) by performing a substitution $[E_i/I_i]_{i=1}^{n}$ of the operand expressions for the formal parameters in the result type T_0 of the rator's arrow type. In the dependent package sys-

Type Environments

$TE \in \text{TypeEnvironment} = \text{Ident} \rightharpoonup \text{Type}$

As usual, the notation $TE[I_1 : T_1, \ldots, I_n : T_n]$ indicates the type environment that results from extending TE with the given type assignments. As before, the identifiers $I_1, \ldots, I_n$ must be distinct. Unlike before, we further require that $dom(TE)$ and $\cup_{i=1}^{n}\{I_i\}$ must be disjoint; see page 879 for a discussion of this requirement.

Type Rules

$$\frac{TE[\text{up} : (\text{->} ((\text{x } T_{rep})) \; \tau_{abs}), \text{down} : (\text{->} ((\text{x } \tau_{abs})) \; T_{rep})] \vdash}{TE \vdash (\text{pack}_{depend} \; \tau_{abs} \; T_{rep} \; E_{impl}) : (\text{packof}_{depend} \; \tau_{abs} \; T_{impl})} \quad [dpack]$$

$$\text{where} \quad \tau_{abs} \notin \cup_{I \in FrIds[\![E_{impl}]\!]} \left(FrTyIds_{ty}[\![TE(I)]\!] \right) \quad [import\ restriction]$$

$$\frac{TE \vdash E_{pkg} : (\text{packof}_{depend} \; \tau_{abs} \; T_{impl})}{TE[I_{impl} : [(\text{dtypeof } E_{pkg})/\tau_{abs}] \; T_{impl}] \vdash} \atop {[(\text{dtypeof } E_{pkg})/\tau_{ty}] \; E_{body} : T_{body}}}{TE \vdash (\text{unpack}_{depend} \; E_{pkg} \; \tau_{ty} \; I_{impl} \; E_{body}) : T_{body}} \quad [dunpack]$$

$$\text{where} \quad \tau_{ty} \notin \cup_{I \in FrIds[\![E_{body}]\!]} \left(FrTyIds_{ty}[\![TE(I)]\!] \right) \quad [import\ restriction]$$
$$\qquad\quad E_{pkg} \text{ is pure} \qquad\qquad\qquad\qquad [purity\ restriction]$$

$$\frac{TE[I_i : T_i]_{i=1}^{n} \vdash E : T}{TE \vdash (\text{abs } ((I_i \; T_i)_{i=1}^{n}) \; E) : (\text{->} ((I_i \; T_i)_{i=1}^{n}) \; T)} \quad [\rightarrow\text{-}intro]$$

$$\frac{TE \vdash E_{rator} : (\text{->} ((I_i \; T_i)_{i=1}^{n}) \; T_0) \quad \forall_{i=1}^{n} . \; (TE \vdash E_i : T_i)}{TE \vdash (E_{rator} \; E_{i=1}^{n}) : [E_i/I_i]_{i=1}^{n} T_0} \quad [\rightarrow\text{-}elim]$$

$$\text{where} \quad \forall_{i=1}^{n} . \; E_i \text{ is pure if } (I_i \in FrIds_{ty}[\![T_0]\!]) \quad [purity\ restriction]$$

$$\frac{\forall_{i=1}^{n} . \; (TE \vdash E_i : T_i) \quad TE[I_i : T_i]_{i=1}^{n} \vdash E_0 : T_0}{TE \vdash (\text{let } ((I_i \; E_i)_{i=1}^{n}) \; E_0) : [E_i/I_i]_{i=1}^{n} T_0} \quad [let]$$

$$\text{where} \quad \forall_{i=1}^{n} . \; E_i \text{ is pure if } (I_i \in FrIds_{ty}[\![T_0]\!]) \quad [purity\ restriction]$$

$$\frac{\forall_{i=0}^{n} . \; (TE[I_i : T_i]_{i=1}^{n} \vdash E_i : T_i)}{TE \vdash (\text{letrec } ((I_i \; T_i \; E_i)_{i=1}^{n}) \; E_0) : [E_i'/I_i]_{i=1}^{n} T_0} \quad [letrec]$$

$$\text{where} \quad \forall_{i=1}^{n} . \left(E_i' = (\text{letrec } ((I_j \; T_j \; E_j)_{j=1}^{n}) \; I_i) \right)$$
$$\qquad\quad \forall_{i=1}^{n} . \; E_i' \text{ is pure if } (I_i \in FrIds_{ty}[\![T_0]\!]) \quad [purity\ restriction]$$

$$\frac{TE \vdash E_{rcd} : (\text{recordof } (I_i \; T_i)_{i=1}^{n}) \quad TE[I_i : T_i]_{i=1}^{n} \vdash E_{body} : T_{body}}{TE \vdash (\text{with } E_{rcd} \; E_{body}) : [(\text{select } I_i \; E_{rcd})/I_i]_{i=1}^{n} T_{body}} \quad [with]$$

$$\text{where} \quad E_{rcd} \text{ is pure if } (\cup_{i=1}^{n}\{I_i\} \cap FrIds_{ty}[\![T_{body}]\!]) \neq \{\} \quad [purity\ restriction]$$

All other type rules are as in FLEX/P.

Figure 14.13 The essence of dependent packages in FLEX/P, Part 3.

tem, such substitutions are critical for tracking the flow of abstract types through a program. For example, when a procedure with the type of make-transpose is called on any package (call it $E_{point\text{-}pkg}$) satisfying the point-dface interface, the result has the type

(-> ((p (dtypeof $E_{point\text{-}pkg}$))) (dtypeof $E_{point\text{-}pkg}$))

in which the operand expression $E_{point\text{-}pkg}$ has been substituted for the parameter name point-dpkg. We can now see why the definition of pair-point-2 is well typed. The type of the application (make-transpose pair-point-dpkg) is

(-> ((p (dtypeof pair-point-dpkg))) (dtypeof pair-point-dpkg))

Since pair-point-1 has the type (dtypeof pair-point-dpkg), the application ((make-transpose pair-point-dpkg) pair-point-1) also has the type (dtypeof pair-point-dpkg).

In a dependent type system, substitutions similar to those performed in [→-elim] must be performed in the type rule for any construct that declares value identifiers. Now that types refer to values, any time a value escapes the scope of a value identifier, that identifier must be replaced with an appropriate expression if it occurs free in the value's type. If this were not done, dependent types could contain free value identifiers that would be meaningless in the same way that abstract type identifiers exported by unpack$_{exist}$ are meaningless. For example, in the [let] type rule, free references to let-bound identifiers are replaced by the corresponding definition expressions in the result type of a let expression. The [letrec] rule is more complex because the definition expressions are in the scope of all the letrec-bound identifiers and must be wrapped in a letrec expression to maintain the scoping of these identifiers. In the [with] rule, each reference to a field I_i of the record E_{rcd} in the result type is replaced by the record selection expression (select I_i E_{rcd}).

It is instructive to revisit the rational-number example from Figure 14.9 on page 866 in the context of dependent types. Consider the following expressions:

```
((unpack_depend rightist-rat rty rops (select numer rops))
  ((unpack_depend leftist-rat lty lops (select make-rat lops))
    1 2))

((unpack_depend leftist-rat lty1 lops1 (select numer lops1))
  ((unpack_depend leftist-rat lty2 lops2 (select make-rat lops2))
    1 2))
```

With dependent types, the first expression is ill typed because an attempt is made to apply a procedure of type (-> ((r (dtypeof rightist-rat))) int) to a value of type (dtypeof leftist-rat). However, the second expression is

well typed since the procedure parameter and the argument point both have type
(dtypeof leftist-rat). So dependent types are able to catch the abstraction
violation in the first expression while permitting operations and values of the same
abstract type to interoperate outside of unpack$_{depend}$ in the second expression.
In contrast, neither expression is well typed with existential packages (because
of the export restriction), and both expressions are well typed with nonce types
(which cannot distinguish different instantiations of a pack$_{nonce}$ expression).

14.5.2 Design Issues with Dependent Types

Dependent types are clearly very powerful. However, care must be taken to ensure
that a dependent type system is sound. Moreover, programmers typically expect
that a statically typed language will respect the **phase distinction**: the well-
typedness of their programs will be verified in a first (terminating) type-checking
phase that runs to completion before the second (possibly nonterminating) run-
time execution phase begins [Car88a, HMM90].

In this section, we shall explore several design dimensions in systems with
dependent types. We shall also see that minor tweaks to the type rules and type-
equivalence rules can have dramatic consequences in terms of which programs
are considered well typed. We shall also see that in some designs for dependent
types the type-checking and execution phases are interleaved and type-checking
may not terminate.

Type Equivalence of Dependent Types

Perhaps the most important design dimension is equivalence on dependent types:
When is (dtypeof E_1) considered equivalent to (dtypeof E_2)? How this question is answered has a significant impact on the properties of the language.

One option is to treat types as first-class run-time entities and dependent
packages as pairs $\langle T_{rep}, V_{impl} \rangle$ of a type T_{rep} and an implementation value V_{impl}
that uses T_{rep} as the concrete representation type for the abstract type of the
package. Such pairs are known as **strong sums**,[10] because the type component
serves as a tag that can be used for dynamic dispatch. In this interpretation,
(dtypeof E_{pkg}) extracts the representation type T_{rep} from the pair $\langle T_{rep}, V_{impl} \rangle$
denoted by E_{pkg}. So (dtypeof E_1) is equivalent to (dtypeof E_2) if their representation types are type-equivalent. Since type checking and evaluation are
inextricably intertwined in this design, there is no phase distinction. Furthermore, abstraction is surrendered by making representation types transparent.

---

[10]In contrast, existential packages are sometimes called **weak sums**.

The PEBBLE language [BL84] took this approach and used a lock and key mechanism (similar to that described in Section 14.2) to support data abstraction.

Another option is to consider (dtypeof E_1) to be the same as (dtypeof E_2) if the expressions E_1 and E_2 are "equivalent" for a suitable notion of equivalence. This is the approach taken in the [dtypeof-$\approx$] rule in Figure 14.12, which is parameterized over a notion of equivalence ($\approx_{depends}$) that is not defined in the figure. There are two broad approaches to defining $\approx_{depends}$:

- *Value equivalence*: At one end of the spectrum, we can interpret two expressions to be the same under $\approx_{depends}$ if they denote the same package in the usual dynamic semantics of expressions. In the general case, this implies that type checking may require expression evaluation. As with strong sums, type checking in this approach may not terminate and may need to be performed at run time. Even worse, determining if two package values are the same in general requires comparing procedures for equality, which is uncomputable! In practice, some computable conservative approximation for procedure equality must be used. Such an approximation must necessarily distinguish some procedures that are denotationally equivalent. A common technique is to associate a unique identifier with each run-time procedure value and to say that two procedures are equal only if they have the same identifier.

- *Static equivalence*: In order to preserve the phase distinction and static type checking (with no run-time requirements and a guarantee that type checking terminates), we desire a definition of $\approx_{depends}$ that is statically computable. The easiest solution is to say that two dtypeof types are equal if their body expressions are textually identical, and this simple solution is the one that we adopt for our dependent package system.

However, any conservative approximation of expression equivalence will fail to treat as equivalent certain dependent types that the programmer knows to be equivalent. For example, all of the following dependent types are intuitively equivalent, but will be considered distinct according to our "textually identical" criterion:

```
(dtypeof pkg1)
(dtypeof (if #t pkg1 pkg2))
(dtypeof (let ((pkg pkg1)) pkg))
(dtypeof (fst (pair pkg1 pkg2)))
```

There are other choices for $\approx_{depends}$ besides textual identity. We could, for example, allow the expressions in equivalent `dtypeof`s to admit alpha-renaming. We could allow certain simple evaluation steps or substitution steps to take place. As long as the equivalence is statically computable and ensures that expressions that denote different values are not equal, the system is sound. We refer to any such system as a **static dependent type (SDT)** system.

Soundness

For a dependent type system to be sound, we need to guarantee that a value that uses a type exported from one package cannot masquerade as a value of some other type — e.g., a point from `proc-point-dpkg` cannot be passed to an operation from `pair-point-dpkg`.

One aspect of soundness is preventing a subtle form of name capture that can occur when substitutions are performed in a dependent type system. Consider the following example:

```
(let ((trans (make-transpose pair-point-dpkg))
      (pair-point-dpkg proc-point-dpkg))
  (trans (unpack_depend pair-point-dpkg point pt-ops
           (with pt-ops
             (make-pt 1 2)))))
```

If this expression is type-checked in a naive way, it will be considered well typed because `trans` has type

```
(-> ((p (dtypeof pair-point-dpkg))) (dtypeof pair-point-dpkg))
```

and the `unpack`$_{depend}$ expression has type `(dtypeof pair-point-dpkg)`. But the occurrences of `pair-point-dpkg` in the type of `trans` refer to the external definition of `pair-point-dpkg` while the occurrence of `pair-point-dpkg` in the type of the `unpack`$_{depend}$ expression refers to the `let`-bound definition of `pair-point-dpkg`, which really denotes `proc-point-dpkg`. The application of `trans` must be treated as ill typed in a sound type system.

One way to prevent this form of name capture is to add an appropriate side condition to the type rule of every construct that declares value identifiers. In our system, we have taken the simpler approach of restricting type environments (see Figure 14.13) so that a name already appearing in a type environment cannot locally be rebound. In this approach, the above expression is ill typed because `pair-point-dpkg` is already bound in the enclosing type environment. The restriction that a name cannot be shadowed in an inner scope might seem stringent, but in practice it can be satisfied by automatically alpha-renaming expression identifiers in a program so that all logically distinct variables are uniquely named.[11] As mentioned previously, alpha-renaming of type (rather than expression) identifiers is useful for implementing the import restriction in the [*dpack*] and [*dunpack*] type rules.

A second aspect of soundness is that in a dependent type ($\mathtt{dtypeof}\ E_{pkg}$), the expression E_{pkg} must be pure — i.e., it must not vary with state. This is true whether a language uses value equivalence or static equivalence to determine type equivalence. In a language with mutation, the same syntactic expression might have different meanings at different times. This purity property is important because it guarantees that different occurrences of ($\mathtt{dtypeof}\ E_{pkg}$) in the same naming context denote the same abstract type.

As an example of what can go wrong in the presence of side effects, consider the following expression:

```
(let ((c (cell pair-point-pkg)))
  (let ((q (unpack_depend (^ c) pt ops
             ((select make-pt ops) 1 2)))) 
    (begin (:= c proc-point-pkg)
           ((unpack_depend (^ c) pt ops
              (select pt-x ops)) q))))
```

When cell c contains `pair-point-pkg`, the pair point q is created and has type (`dtypeof` (^ c)). Then c is modified to contain `proc-point-pkg`, and the procedural point operation `pt-x` (with type (`-> (p (dtypeof (^ c))) int`)) is applied to q. It should be an abstraction violation to apply the procedural point operation `pt-x` to a pair point, but the type system encounters no error, because the argument type of `pt-x` and the type of q are both (`dtypeof` (^ c)). The type system does not track the fact that (^ c) refers to different packages at different times.

We address this problem by qualifying the type rules with **purity restrictions** that guarantee that every dependent type generated by the type system (as opposed to being written by the programmer) contains a pure expression. In the

---

[11] Alpha-renaming can sometimes be performed in a separate pass that precedes type checking. But this is not possible in languages with constructs that extend the current scope with bindings from a structure with named components, such as FLEX's **with** construct for records, or the **open** construct for opening modules in the FLEX/M language presented in Section 15.2. For such constructs, the type of the record/module is needed to determine the scope of names, so alpha-renaming in such constructs must be delayed until type-checking time. Renaming need be performed only on references to the named components in bodies of the **with**/**open** constructs, not within the records/modules on the named components themselves.

[*dunpack*] rule, which introduces all dependent types that are generated by the type system, the purity restriction requires that E_{pkg} be pure in (`dtypeof` E_{pkg}). The purity restrictions in the other type rules guarantee that the body of a dependent type remains a pure expression when substitutions are performed on it. Exercise 14.19 shows that the type system is sound even if the programmer writes dependent types containing impure expressions.

Of course, it is undecidable to know when an expression is pure. A simple conservative approximation is to require that E_{pkg} be a syntactic value, a notion introduced in Section 8.3.6 (page 428) and used in polymorphic types (Section 12.2, page 734) and in the type reconstruction system of FLARE (Section 13.5.1, page 816). However, we will see in Chapter 15 that this approximation prohibits many expressions we would like to write. A better alternative is to use an effect system (see Chapter 16) to conservatively approximate pure expressions.

The issue of tracking side effects can be quite subtle if an abstract type system with dependent types allows packages to be loaded from an external file system, which is a mutable storage medium. This issue is explored in Section 15.6.

Substitutions

Another design dimension involves the details of where substitutions are performed in the type rules. In the [*dunpack*] rule, substitutions are performed "on the way in" — i.e., on types and expressions appearing in the rule premises. In rules for other binding constructs, substitutions are performed "on the way out" — i.e., on the result type in the rule conclusion. In any of these rules, it is possible to change where substitutions are performed. This can affect which expressions are considered well typed.

For example, consider the following expression:

```
E_leftist =
  (let ((leftist1 (make-rat-impl #t))
        (leftist2 (make-rat-impl #t)))
    ((unpack_depend leftist1 lty1 lops1 (select numer lops1))
      ((unpack_depend leftist2 lty2 lops2 (select make-rat lops2))
        1 2)))
```

Intuitively, this expression is type safe because `leftist1` and `leftist2` both refer to the same package. But using the [*let*] type rule, the expression is ill typed because a procedure of type (`->` ((`r` (`dtypeof` `leftist1`))) `int`) is applied to a value of type (`dtypeof` `leftist2`). The problem is that the substitution that shows that both `leftist1` and `leftist2` are the same expression, (`make-rat-impl` `#t`), is performed on the way out rather than on the way in.

Performing substitutions on the way in often enables more dependent types to be considered equal. For example, consider the following variant of the $[let]$ rule, which performs substitutions on the way into `let` expressions rather than on the way out:

$$\frac{\forall_{i=1}^n \, . \, (TE \vdash E_i : T_i) \quad TE \vdash [E_i/I_i]_{i=1}^n E_0 : T_0}{TE \vdash (\texttt{let} \, ((I_i \; E_i)_{i=1}^n) \; E_0) : T_0} \quad [let\,']$$

$$\text{where} \quad \forall_{i=1}^n \, . \, E_i \text{ is pure if } (I_i \in \textit{FrIds}_{exp}[\![E_0]\!]) \quad \textit{[purity restriction]}$$

If $[let\,']$ is used in place of $[let]$, $E_{leftist}$ is well typed, because a procedure with type `(-> ((r (dtypeof (make-rat-impl #t)))) int)` is applied to a value with type `(dtypeof (make-rat-impl #t))`.

From this example, it seems that $[let\,']$ is a "better" type rule than $[let]$. Why do we use the latter rather than the former as the default type rule for `let`? The reason is that the purity restriction for $[let\,']$ is much more stringent than the one for $[let]$. The $[let\,']$ rule will not work when any definition expression whose name is used in the body performs a side effect. But we need *some* way to name the result of evaluating an impure expression, and `let` is the most convenient way to do this, so we stick with the original $[let]$ rule. Alternatively, we could adopt a more sophisticated version of the $[let\,']$ rule that substitutes only those definitions that are pure on the way into the rule.

It is also worth noting that the default $[let]$ rule nicely handles cases in which a package is computed by an impure expression. For example, suppose that E_{impure} is an impure expression that returns a package. For instance, it might choose a package based on the value of a mutable counter or by reading input from the user. Then we can still have expressions of the form

    `(let ((pkg `E_{impure}`))` E_{body}`)`

where E_{body} manipulates the value `pkg` of a particular evaluation of E_{impure}. In the type checking of E_{body}, any dependent types mentioning the package value will use the pure identifier `pkg` rather than the impure E_{impure}. There will be a problem only if there is an attempt to return a dependent type mentioning `pkg` outside the scope of the `let`. The purity restriction of the $[let]$ rule prevents this from happening. Thus, in this case the system gracefully degrades to what is essentially the export rule from existential packages.

Why does the $[dunpack]$ rule perform substitutions on the way in rather than the way out? As suggested by our study of the $[let\,']$ rule, this allows certain expressions to be treated as well typed that would not otherwise be well typed. There are issues involving impure expressions similar to those we saw with $[let\,']$, but the fact that `let` can be used to give a pure name to any impure expression lets us have our cake and eat it too. This is explored in Exercise 14.17.

Bundling Abstract Types

A final dimension involves how abstract types are bundled up into and extracted from packages. In the system we have studied so far, dependent packages have a single abstract type that is extracted via `dtypeof`; but more generally, a dependent package can have several abstract type components. These are typically named and extracted in a record-like fashion. For example, in a system in which packages can export multiple abstractions, we could write (`dselect` I E_{pkg}) to select named types from a package E_{pkg} just as we select named values from records. We will use `dselect` rather than `dtypeof` in the FLEX/M module system presented in Chapter 15.

Exercise 14.16 Dependent types permit code to be abstracted over particular implementations of a data abstraction. The type rules of this section require that such abstractions be curried by the programmer because of the scoping of parameter names in arrow types. The `make-transpose` procedure studied above is an example of such currying. In its type,

```
(-> ((point-dpkg point-dface))
  (-> ((p (dtypeof point-dpkg)))
      (dtypeof point-dpkg))),
```

the argument type of the transposition procedure refers to `point-dpkg`.

Suppose that we want to modify the type rules for a dependently typed language to implicitly curry multiple parameters — i.e., to allow the types of later parameters to refer to the names of earlier parameters. For example, in the modified system, an uncurried form of `make-transpose` could have the type

```
(def-type uncurried-make-transpose-type
  (-> ((point-dpkg point-dface) (p (dtypeof point-dpkg)))
      (dtypeof point-dpkg)))
```

a. Modify the definition of the **abs** clause of $FrIds_{exp}$ to handle implicit currying.

b. Curiously, the [$\rightarrow$-intro] rule does not need to change to support implicitly curried parameters.[12] The [$\rightarrow$-elim] rule, however, must change. Write a new [$\rightarrow$-elim] rule that supports procedure parameter types that refer to previous parameters. E.g., a procedure with type `uncurried-make-transpose-type` must be applied to two arguments where the type of the second argument depends on the value of the first.

---

[12] In a system with kinds (see Section 12.3.2), the [$\rightarrow$-intro] rule *would* change because we would need the scope to be explicit to verify that dependent types are well formed.

Exercise 14.17 Thai Ping suggests the following alternative [*dunpack'*] type rule that does dependent type substitutions on the way out of unpack_{depend} rather than on the way in.

$$
\frac{
\begin{array}{c}
TE \vdash E_{pkg} : (\texttt{packof}_{depend}\ \tau_{abs}\ T_{impl}) \\
TE[I_{impl} : [\tau_{ty}/\tau_{abs}]\,T_{impl}] \vdash E_{body} : T_{body}
\end{array}
}{
TE \vdash (\texttt{unpack}_{depend}\ E_{pkg}\ \tau_{ty}\ I_{impl}\ E_{body}) : [(\texttt{dtypeof}\ E_{pkg})/\tau_{ty}]\,T_{body}
}\quad [\textit{dunpack'}]
$$

$$
\begin{array}{ll}
\text{where} & \tau_{ty} \notin \cup_{I \in FrIds[\![E_{body}]\!]}\ \big(FrTyIds_{ty}[\![TE(I)]\!]\big)\quad\text{[import restriction]} \\
& E_{pkg}\ \text{is pure if } (\tau_{ty} \in FrTyIds_{ty}[\![T_{body}]\!])\quad\text{[purity restriction]}
\end{array}
$$

Unlike [*dunpack*], the [*dunpack'*] rule is more similar to the unpacking rule for existential packages than nonce packages.

a. Using dependent packages, redo part **b** of Exercise 14.10 in Section 14.4 using (1) the original [*dunpack*] rule and (2) Thai's [*dunpack'*] rule. Which rule do you think is better and why?

b. Thai claims that [*dunpack'*] is better than [*dunpack*] in some situations where E_{pkg} contains side effects. Write an expression that is well typed with [*dunpack'*] but not [*dunpack*].

c. For any expression that is well typed with [*dunpack'*] but not [*dunpack*], it is possible to make the expression well typed using [*dunpack*] by naming E_{pkg} with a `let`. Show this in the context of your expression from the previous part.

Exercise 14.18 Ben Bitdiddle looks at the type rules in Figure 14.13 and your solutions to Exercises 14.16 and 14.17 and complains that all the substitutions make him dizzy. He suggests leaving them all out except for those in the [$\rightarrow$-*elim*] rule. Under what assumptions is his idea sound? Write a type-safe program that type-checks under the given rules but does not type-check under Ben's.

Exercise 14.19 In all dependent types ($\texttt{dtypeof}\ E_{pkg}$) generated by the type system for a well-typed program, E_{pkg} is guaranteed to be a pure, well-typed expression that denotes a dependent package. But the programmer can write nonsensical explicit dependent types in which E_{pkg} is impure, does not denote a package, or is ill typed.

a. Show that an expression containing nonsensical dependent types can still be well typed.

b. Argue that well-typed programs containing nonsensical dependent types are still sound.

c. Describe modifications to the type system that would prevent the programmer from writing nonsensical dependent types.

Notes

Abstract types and modules (the subject of the following chapter) are intimately related: both are linguistic mechanisms to support modularity in software systems. Data abstraction is a software engineering methodology in which programs are decomposed into software modules, each implementing one or more related data structures and their associated operations [Par71, Par72]. For example, data abstraction was the guiding principle of the design of CLU [L+79, LSAS77, LZ74, LZ75], whose *cluster* mechanism provides a way to specify abstract types. CLU's clusters were also the unit of program decomposition (modules). A CLU program uses free references to cluster names in order to refer to the carrier of an abstract type. Thus CLU's type names are similar to nonce types, except that, because only one implementation of a cluster is allowed in any given program, the names are programmer-friendly.

The remainder of this section will focus on the underlying abstraction mechanisms related to this chapter. For more on data abstraction in module systems, see the notes at the end of Chapter 15 on page 940.

Reynolds observed that user-defined types and procedural data structures are complementary mechanisms for data abstraction [Rey75]. With user-defined types, the type system hides the data representation shared by a set of operations. Procedural data abstraction (like the message-passing points in Figure 14.1 on page 843) hides the data representation in the environments of one or more procedures. The decentralized nature of procedural data abstractions allows different procedures to use different representations for the same abstraction but prohibits optimizations based on the representation. Cook expands on this idea in [Coo91], where he equates procedural data abstraction with object-oriented programming.

Morris showed how to use scoping and first-class procedures to provide data abstraction via a dynamic lock and key mechanism [Mor73]. Morris referred to *sealing* and *unsealing* an object.

Existential types are due to John Mitchell and Gordon Plotkin [MP84], and there is a nice discussion in [Mit96, pp. 679–685]. [CW85] discusses existential types and compares existential types to data abstraction in ADA.

Interestingly, existential types do not actually add any power to a language with universal polymorphism, because any program written using existential types can be rewritten to an equivalent program using universal polymorphism ([Mit96, p. 701], [Pie02, Section 24.3]).

Nonce types express the idea that each instantiation of an abstract type has a unique name. A language may simply stamp each abstract type implementation with such a unique identifier and use this for testing type equality. This implementation strategy was formalized in the notion of *type generativity* in SML [MTH90]. See [Ler96] for a good discussion of type generativity.

[Mac86] uses the inability to refer to the type implemented by a value of existential type, i.e., the lack of a *witness* operator, to motivate the use of dependent types for this purpose. Luca Cardelli's QUEST language [Car89] employed first-class existential types and dependent type names to solve this problem. QUEST's dependent type expressions were limited to *structured identifiers*, i.e., sequences of one or more identifiers separated by dots (such as `m.t`) to simplify type comparison and to overcome issues of side effects.

In [Car88a], Cardelli discusses the phase distinction. He describes how to take a dependent type system and reestablish a phase distinction by using kinds and restricting dependent types. For more on the phase distinction, see [HMM90]. The central issue of type equivalence in a dependent type system is discussed in [AH05], especially pages 53–54.

The static dependent type system presented here is based on [SG90]. The dependent arrow types above are often referred to as Π types in the literature (see, for example, [Mac86] and [Mit96, Chapter 9]).

The introduction of abstraction over types leads to the question of whether the language design uses kinds (sorts, etc.) to specify the well-formedness of types. If not, then the question arises whether `type : type`. This is attractive in a language with dependent types, because then the ordinary mechanism of procedure abstraction can be used to express dependent functions. But there are some drawbacks. Girard showed that logics with `type : type` are inconsistent [Gir71]. [MR86] demonstrated that such type systems are nonnormalizing and suffer from other difficulties. See [Car86] for a summary of these issues in a language with `type : type`. [HH86] demonstrates that even without the `type : type` axiom, a language with impredicative strong existential types is logically inconsistent.

The programming language PEBBLE [BL84, LB88], on the other hand, took exactly this approach and included a completely general system of dependent types. PEBBLE included strong existential types (also known as strong sums) and dependent types that could contain any value. Type checking in PEBBLE could fail to terminate if values in dependent types looped. Interestingly, PEBBLE does not actually protect against changes in abstract type implementation, and so it uses a lock and key (they call them *passwords*) mechanism to guard the representation of abstract types. They choose this over a generative mechanism such as that used in ML.

CAYENNE [Aug98] is another language with a general system of dependent types in which type checking may not terminate.

For a somewhat different of view in which a type *is* its operation set, see the programming language RUSSELL [BDD80]. RUSSELL included syntactic constraints that guaranteed that certain expressions were pure. RUSSELL also included a notion of dependent type.

The notion of dependent types is quite general, and its study goes far beyond the constrained use we have made of it here. The idea of completing all the possible sorts of abstraction mechanism (mapping values to values, types to values, types to types, and values to types) is neatly summarized by Barendregt's *lambda cube* [Bar91]. See [Pie02, Section 30.5] for a nice summary of the general notion of dependent type with examples. [AH05] is an extensive treatment of dependent types and their associated type rules and kind rules.

A classic example of a generalized notion of dependent type is the use of an array with integer bounds. In such a language, an array-type constructor would construct a type from an element type and an integer array size. A dependent procedure to sum the elements of an array would take an integer size and an array whose type included that size; the type of the procedure's second parameter depends on the value of the first parameter. General dependent types increase the expressiveness of a language's type system and permit many useful static checks, such as array bounds checking and ensuring that operations are not performed on empty lists. These benefits have little to do with abstract types. Of course, the challenge of such systems is, as above, striking a balance among expressiveness, decidability, and complexity. Examples of such systems include the work on Dependent ML (DML) [XP98, Xi99a, XP99, Xi99b, Xi01, Xi07], whose type system solves systems of constraints on dependent type expressions. [CX05] describes the *Applied Type System (ATS)* framework for formalizing and designing advanced type systems. This extends a simple constraint solver with the capacity to accept programmer-supplied proofs of complex constraints.

15

Modules

Many the voices, one great music,
Part of me and part of you.

— Marty Haugen, "One Ohana"

15.1 An Overview of Modules and Linking

It is desirable to decompose a program, especially a large one, into modular components that can be separately written, compiled, tested, and debugged. Such components are typically called **modules** but are also known as packages, structures, units, and classes.[1] Ideally, each individual module is described by an **interface** that specifies the components required by the module from the rest of the program (the **imports**) and the components supplied by the module to the rest of the program (the **exports**). Interfaces often list the names and types of imported and exported values along with informal English descriptions of these values. Such interfaces make it possible for programmers to implement a module without having to know the implementation details of other modules. They also make it possible for a compiler to check for type consistency within a single module.

Modules support software engineering by bundling up items of related functionality that can be used (and reused) by other program components. Typically, modules are record-like entities that have both type and value components. Like records, modules support nonhierarchical scoping and name control (see Section 7.2.3).

Modules often provide the means of expressing abstract types (Chapter 14) in addition to being a mechanism for decomposing a program into parts. Abstract types allow a language to support and enforce a separation of the concerns of a module's implementer and its user (or client), and are therefore central to program modularity. The key differences between the modules discussed here and

---

[1] In many languages, such as C, files serve as de facto modules, but in general the relationship between source files and program modules can be more complex.

the packages we studied in Sections 14.3–14.5 are that (1) a single module can define bindings for multiple abstract types and values and (2) there is an expectation that modules can be written and compiled separately and later combined to form a whole program.

The process of combining modules to form a whole program is called **linking**. The specification for how to combine the modules to form a program is written in a **linking language**. Linking is typically performed in a distinct **link time** phase that is performed after all the individual modules are compiled (compile time) but before the entire program is executed (run time).

A crude form of linking involves hard-wiring the file names for imported modules within the source code for a given module. In more flexible approaches, a module is parameterized over names for the imported modules and the linking language specifies the actual modules to be used for the parameters. A good linking language should check that the interface types of the actual module arguments are consistent with those of the formal module parameters, a feature that is especially important in modern systems with dynamically loaded modules. In this case, the linking language is effectively a simply typed programming language.

Often, a linking language simply lists the modules to be combined. For example, the object files of a C program are linked by supplying a list of file names to the compiler/linker. A linking language can be made more powerful by adding other programming language features that allow more computation to be performed during the linking process. For instance, it is useful to have a function-like entity, known as a **functor**, that takes modules as arguments and/or returns a module as a result. Functors can express parameterized modules, such as a binary-search-tree module abstracted over a type that admits a total ordering.

The desire to make linking languages more expressive is often in tension with the desire to guarantee that (1) the linking process terminates and (2) mere mortals can reliably understand and use the sophisticated types that often accompany more expressive linking languages. An extreme design point is to make the linking language the same as the base language used to express the modules themselves. Such **first-class module systems** are powerful, because arbitrary modules can be created at run time and the decision of which module to import can be based on dynamic conditions. Functors need not be special: they are ordinary procedures that happen to operate on modules. These systems blur the distinction between compile time, link time, and run time,[2] and for any Turing-complete

---

[2] In fact, modern program environments include dynamically loaded shared code, even though they typically do not support first-class modules. JAVA includes a very flexible dynamic class loader.

base language, the compilation process (including type checking) and/or linking process may not terminate.

To address these problems, linking is usually specified in a different language from the base language — a language that is suitably restricted to guarantee that a terminating linking phase follows a terminating compilation phase and precedes the program execution phase. In such **second-class module systems**, modules are not first-class values that can be manipulated in the base language. It is still possible to have an expressive functor mechanism in such a system that is separate from the base language's notion of function. ADA's generic packages, CLU's parameterized clusters, and functors in many ML dialects are examples of such a mechanism.

In the rest of this chapter, we present a first-class module system that will serve as a vehicle for studying various dimensions of module-system design. Our relatively simple module system combines in an interesting way several key ideas that we have explored so far: static dependent types, sum-of-products data types and pattern matching, universal types, and subtyping. By no means a full-fledged system, it nevertheless achieves three goals essential to any module system:

- separate compilation of independently written program components that can then be linked together in a type-safe way;

- a means of expressing abstract types; and

- namespace control for values and types.

A production system would benefit from other features, such as modules with bindings for concrete (i.e., nonabstract) types, modules with macro specifications for syntactic extensions, and more flexible relationships between interfaces and modules. Section 15.7 discusses limitations of the system we present.

15.2 An Introduction to FLEX/M

We explore the design of a first-class module system in the context of FLEX/M, an extension of the explicitly typed FLEX/SP language from Section 12.2.2, which supports subtyping and universal polymorphism. FLEX/M adds the following features to FLEX/SP:

- static dependent types that guarantee a phase distinction between type checking and program execution (though not between linking and execution);

- module definitions that allow multiple abstract type constructor definitions and value definitions per module (the dependent package system in Section 14.5 allows only one abstract type per package);

- a `dselect` construct that selects type constructor components from module expressions (this generalizes the `dtypeof` construct in the dependent package system);

- sum-of-products data-type definitions for defining abstract-type constructors like `pairof`, `listof`, and `treeof` (the dependent package system supports the expression of abstract types but not abstract-type constructors);

- data-type constructor and deconstructor procedures that mediate between concrete and abstract views of data and thus play the role of the `up` and `down` procedures in the dependent package system;

- an implicit projection feature that allows omitting many explicit projections (`pcall`) of polymorphic values;

- pattern matching to simplify data-type deconstruction; and

- the ability to load first-class modules from a file system.

Though all widely used languages have second-class modules, we have chosen to explore a first-class system for two reasons:

1. It combines several features discussed in the book into a system of considerable power and flexibility (the dependent package system seen in Section 14.5, polymorphism, subtyping, and sum-of-products data types with pattern matching).

2. It forces us to address issues of dynamic linking, particularly its impact on type safety. All widely used programming systems support dynamic linking and loading, i.e., the interleaving of code linking and loading with program execution. For example, JAVA's run-time system (and users of the JAVA class loader facilities) must deal with many of the same issues we encounter when we describe module loading in Section 15.6.

Figure 15.1 presents the new expression and type syntax that FLEX/M adds to FLEX/SP. We will first explain these new constructs using informal English descriptions and examples. We will formally define their static semantics in Section 15.4 and their dynamic semantics in Section 15.5. Figure 15.2 presents the new syntactic sugar constructs.

Modified Syntax

$P \in \text{Prog} ::= (\text{flex/Mk} \ ((I_{fml} \ T_{fmlTy})^*) \ E_{body})$

$E \in \text{Exp} ::= \dots \ \textit{FLEX/SP expressions except} \ \texttt{letrec} \ \dots$
$\qquad\qquad | \ (\text{module} \ DD^* \ VD^*) \qquad\qquad [\text{ModuleCreate}]$
$\qquad\qquad | \ (\text{open} \ E_{mod} \ E_{body}) \qquad\qquad [\text{ModuleOpen}]$
$\qquad\qquad | \ (\text{load} \ Y_{fileName} \ T_{fileTy}) \ [\text{LoadFromFile}]$

$O \in \text{Primop} ::= \dots \ \textit{FLEX/SP primitives except pair and list operators} \ \dots$

$\qquad \text{ExpKwd} = \text{Keyword}_{FLEX/SP} \cup \{\texttt{load}, \texttt{match}, \texttt{module}, \texttt{mselect}, \texttt{open}\}$

$\quad I \in \text{Ident} = \text{Ident}_{FLEX/SP} - (\text{ExpKwd} \cup \text{TypeKwd} \cup \text{TyConId})$

$DD \in \text{DatatypeDefinition} ::= (\text{def-datatype} \ AT_{absTy} \ (I_{constructor} \ T_{compTy}^*)^*)$

$VD \in \text{ValueDefinition} ::= (\text{def} \ I_{name} \ T_{defTy} \ E_{def})$

$T \in \text{Type} ::= \dots \ \textit{FLEX/SP types except} \ \texttt{pairof}, \ \texttt{listof}, \ \texttt{trec}, \ \textit{and} \ \texttt{tletrec} \ \dots$
$\qquad\qquad | \ v \qquad\qquad\qquad\qquad\qquad\qquad\qquad [\text{UnificationVariable}]$
$\qquad\qquad | \ (\text{->} \ ((I_{argName} \ T_{arg})^*) \ T_{result}) \qquad [\text{ParameterizedArrowType}]$
$\qquad\qquad | \ (\text{moduleof} \ (AT_{absTy}^*) \ (I_{name} \ T_{defTy})^*) \ [\text{ModuleType}]$
$\qquad\qquad | \ (TC_{tycon} \ T_{arg}^*) \qquad\qquad\qquad\qquad [\text{TyConApp}]$

$AT \in \text{AbstractType} ::= (\theta_{tycon} \ \tau_{param}^*)$

$TC \in \text{TypeConstructor} ::= \theta_{tycon} \qquad\qquad\qquad [\text{TyConName}]$
$\qquad\qquad\qquad | \ (\text{dselect} \ \theta_{tycon} \ E_{mod}) \ [\text{DependentTyConSelection}]$

$v \in \text{UnificationVar} = \{Y \mid Y \text{ begins with ?}\} \ ; \ \textit{for implicit projection}$
$\qquad\qquad\qquad\qquad\qquad\qquad\qquad ; \ (\textit{Section 15.4.5})$

$\theta \in \text{TyConId} = \{Y \mid Y \text{ ends with of}\} - \text{TypeKwd}$

$\qquad \text{TypeKwd} = \text{BaseType}_{FLEX/SP} \cup \{\text{->}, \texttt{cellof}, \texttt{moduleof}, \texttt{oneof},$
$\qquad\qquad\qquad\qquad\qquad\qquad\qquad \texttt{prodof}, \texttt{recordof}, \texttt{seqof}\}$

$\tau \in \text{TypeId} = \text{SymLit} - (\text{TypeKwd} \cup \text{UnificationVar} \cup \text{TyConId})$

Figure 15.1 Modified syntax for FLEX/M, an extension to FLEX/SP with first-class modules.

A module is a record-like entity created by the `module` construct. It has two kinds of components: (1) abstract type components declared using the `def-datatype` declaration similar to the one in Section 13.5.4 and (2) value components declared using the `def` declaration, which includes an explicit type $T_{defnType}$ for the definition expression E_{defn}. Some module systems (such as those of SML, OCAML, and FX-91) allow both concrete and abstract type definitions in modules. Although FLEX/M could be extended to support concrete type definitions, they are omitted for simplicity.

New Syntactic Sugar

$(\text{-> } (T_{i=1}^n) \ T_0) \leadsto_{ds} (\text{-> } ((I_i \ T_i)_{i=1}^n) \ T_0)$, where $I_{i=1}^n$ are fresh

$(\text{mselect } I \ E_{mod}) \leadsto_{ds} (\text{open } E_{mod} \ I)$

$(\text{letrec } ((I_i \ T_i \ E_i)_{i=1}^n) \ E_{body}) \leadsto_{ds} (\text{open } (\text{module } (\text{def } I_i \ T_i \ E_i)_{i=1}^n) \ E_{body})$

$(\text{match } E_{disc} \ (PT \ E)^*)$ where $PT \in \text{Pattern} ::= L \mid I \mid \_ \mid (I \ PT^*)$
    The desugaring for $\texttt{match}$ is explained in Section 15.4.6.

$(\text{flex/M } ((I_h \ T_h)_{h=1}^m) \ E_{body} \ (\text{def-type } \tau_i \ T_i)_{i=1}^n \ DD_{j=1}^p \ VD_{k=1}^q)$
    $\leadsto_{ds} (\text{flex/Mk } ((I_h \ T_h)_{h=1}^m)$
            $(\text{open } (\text{load standard-library.flxm } T_{standardLib})$
                $\{Assume \ \texttt{standard-library.flxm} \ contains \ a \ module \ with\}$
                $\{standard \ bindings \ and \ T_{standardLib} \ is \ the \ type \ of \ this \ module.\}$
                $(\text{let-type* } ((\tau_i \ T_i)_{i=1}^n) \ \{Type \ definitions \ from \ program\}$
                    $(\text{open } (\text{module } DD_{j=1}^p \ VD_{k=1}^q)$
                        $E_{body}))))$

Figure 15.2   New syntactic sugar for FLEX/M, an extension to FLEX/SP with first-class modules.

In a $\texttt{module}$ expression, all value-component names and the names of all constructor and deconstructor procedures introduced by the data-type declarations are required to be distinct. The scope of all these names is all the E_{defn} expressions within the value definitions, so these definitions are mutually recursive.

As an example of a $\texttt{module}$ expression, consider $E_{listModule}$ in Figure 15.3, which implements a module defining the unary type constructor $\texttt{listof}$ and its associated operations. The $\texttt{listof}$ type constructor is declared by

```
(def-datatype (listof t)
  (null)
  (cons t (listof t)))
```

which also implicitly defines constructor and deconstructor procedures with the types given in Figure 15.4.[3]   These types are similar to those introduced for FLARE's $\texttt{def-datatype}$ in Section 13.5.4, except that in the explicitly typed FLEX/M language, polymorphism is expressed via $\texttt{forall}$ types rather than

---

[3]Like the dependent package system of Section 14.5, FLEX/M has dependent types, so it supports parameterized arrow types $(\text{-> } ((I_i \ T_i)_{i=1}^n) \ T_0)$ that allow procedure result types to depend on the values of the procedure's arguments. However, when there is no such dependency, we write the sugar form $(\text{-> } (T_{i=1}^n) \ T_0)$, which does not require explicit parameter names. For example, all arrow types in Figures 15.3 and 15.4 are sugared.

```
E_listModule =
  (module
    (def-datatype (listof t)
      (null)
      (cons t (listof t)))
    (def null? (forall (t) (-> ((listof t)) bool))
      (pabs (t)
        (abs ((xs (listof t)))
          (match xs
            ((null) #t)
            ((cons _ _) #f)))))
    (def car (forall (t) (-> ((listof t)) t))
      (pabs (t)
        (abs ((xs (listof t)))
          (match xs
            ((null) (error car-of-empty-list t))
            ((cons a _) a)))))
    (def cdr (forall (t) (-> ((listof t)) (listof t)))
      (pabs (t)
        (abs ((xs (listof t)))
          (match xs
            ((null) (error cdr-of-empty-list (listof t)))
            ((cons _ d) d)))))
  )
```

Figure 15.3 A module expression $E_{listModule}$ that has type $T_{listModule}$.

generic types.[4] Although FLEX/M data-type declarations only allow the definition of type constructors, it is an easy extension to have them define types as well (see Exercise 13.15). $E_{listModule}$ also explicitly defines the predicate procedure null? and the selector procedures car and cdr. These have polymorphic types introduced via the pabs construct that can be explicitly eliminated using the pcall construct (see Section 12.2.2).

---

[4]Another difference is that type-constructor names in FLEX/M are required to end in of (e.g., listof, pairof, tableof) and cannot be the same as type-constructor keywords (e.g., ->, moduleof, cellof). Expression identifiers must exclude all type-constructor names and keywords so that the sugar form (-> ($T_{i=1}^n$) T_0) for parameterized arrow types of the form (-> ((I_i T_i)$_{i=1}^n$) T_0) is unambiguous. Without these restrictions, examples like (-> ((foo int)) bool) would be ambiguous; (foo int) could be either an explicit parameter name and type (I_i T_i) in a parameterized arrow type or a type $T_i = (TC\ T)$ in the sugared form of an arrow type that is an application of a unary type constructor.

```
null : (forall (t) {t is the list element type}
          (-> () (listof t)))

null~ : (forall (r t) {r is the return type; t is the list element type}
          (-> ((listof t) {type of datum to deconstruct}
               (-> () r)   {type of success continuation}
               (-> () r))  {type of failure continuation}
              r))          {return type of deconstructor}

cons : (forall (t) {t is the list element type}
          (-> (t (listof t)) (listof t)))

cons~ : (forall (r t) {r is the return type; t is the list element type}
          (-> ((listof t)                  {type of datum to deconstruct}
               (-> (t (listof t)) r) {type of success continuation}
               (-> () r))            {type of failure continuation}
              r))                    {return type of deconstructor}
```

Figure 15.4 Types of the constructor and deconstructor procedures introduced by the def-datatype declaration in $E_{listModule}$.

Since it is cumbersome to eliminate forall types using the explicit projection construct pcall, FLEX/M includes an **implicit projection** feature that allows many pcalls to be omitted. In particular, if the result of projecting a polymorphic value is a procedure that is applied directly to arguments, and it is possible to determine the type of the procedure's result unambiguously from the types of the arguments, then the pcall may be omitted.

We formalize implicit projection in Section 15.4.5, but will use it liberally in the examples of this section. For instance, here is a version of a map procedure with explicit projections:

```
(def map (forall (s t) (-> ((-> (s) t) (listof s)) (listof t)))
  (pabs (s t)
    (abs ((f (-> (s) t)) (xs (listof s)))
      ((pcall cons~ s) xs
                      (abs ((y s) (ys (listof s)))
                        ((pcall cons t) (f y)
                                        ((pcall map s t) f ys)))
                      (abs () ((pcall null t)))))))
```

From the type (-> (s) t) of f and the type (listof s) of ys, it is easy to determine that the recursive call to map must be projected onto s and t and must return a result of type (listof t). So implicit projection allows ((pcall map s t) f ys) to be simplified to (map f ys). Similar reasoning al-

lows the (pcall cons t) to be simplified to cons and the (pcall cons˜ s) to
be simplified to cons˜. However, the type (listof t) for the null application
cannot be determined from its (nonexistent) arguments, so explicit projection is
still required in this case. With implicit projection, the map abstraction can be
simplified to

```
(pabs (s t)
  (abs ((f (-> (s) t)) (xs (listof s)))
    (cons˜ xs
           (abs ((y s) (ys (listof s)))
             (cons (f y) (map f ys)))
           (abs () ((pcall null t)))))))
```

Explicit deconstructor applications can be hidden using the pattern matching
construct presented in Section 10.5. Using match (as well as implicit projection),
the map abstraction can be further simplified to

```
(pabs (s t)
  (abs ((f (-> (s) t)) (xs (listof s)))
    (match xs
      ((cons y ys) (cons (f y) (map f ys)))
      ((null) ((pcall null t))))))
```

The match construct can be desugared by a process similar to the one described
in Figure 10.27 on page 603, except that the desugaring functions must take additional arguments bearing type information needed to deduce explicit types required by FLEX/M. This typed match desugaring is discussed in Section 15.4.6.

The type of a module, also known as its **signature**, is a moduleof type that
lists the abstract type constructors of a module and the types of each of the
named value components. Each type constructor has a parameter list whose
purpose is to document the number of parameters. In a well-formed moduleof
type, all type-constructor names must be distinct and all value-component names
must be distinct.

As an example of a moduleof type, Figure 15.5 presents the type $T_{listModule}$
of $E_{listModule}$. In the abstract type (listof t) at the beginning of the moduleof
type, listof is a binding occurrence of a type-constructor name, and all other
occurrences of listof in the moduleof type refer to this binding occurrence.
In contrast, the t in (listof t) is just a dummy name indicating that the
listof constructor takes one argument. It does *not* have to be the same as the
element type used in any of the forall types. Similar comments hold for the
def-datatype declaration (listof t) in $E_{listModule}$.

Because the listof type constructor and list operations can be specified in a
user-defined module, these are not kernel constructs in FLEX/M. Similarly, the

pairof type constructor and pair operations are not kernel FLEX/M constructs
(see Exercise 15.1). All recursive types in FLEX/M are specified via data-
type declarations, so there is no need for the trec or tletrec constructs from
Section 11.8.6.

The named type and value components of the module denoted by E_{mod} are
made available to a client expression E_{body} via (open E_{mod} E_{body}), which is the
module analogue of with for typed records (see Section 11.8.1). For example,
if list-module is a name for the module $E_{listModule}$ from Figure 15.3, then an
integer-list doubling procedure can be expressed as

$E_{dblProc}$ = (open list-module
          (letrec ((dbl (abs ((xs (listof int)))
                     (match xs
                       ((null) ((pcall null int)))
                       ((cons y ys)
                       (cons (* 2 y) (dbl ys)))))))
       dbl))

Opening list-module makes the listof type constructor and its associated
constructors and deconstructors available for use in the dbl abstraction.

A single value named I can be selected from a module E_{mod} via the construct
(mselect I E_{mod}), which is just syntactic sugar for (open E_{mod} I). In many
languages, this module selection is expressed via the dot notation $E_{mod}.I$.

A type constructor named θ can be selected from a module E_{mod} via the construct (dselect θ E_{mod}), which is written in many languages as $E_{mod}.\theta$. This
is a **dependent type constructor**, because it depends on the value expression
E_{mod}. Dependent type constructors naturally arise in the context of open expressions. For instance, what is the type of $E_{dblProc}$ in the open example above?
Intuitively, it has the type (-> ((listof int)) (listof int)); but this type
is exported out of (open list-module ...), where the listof type constructor
is not defined. To handle this situation, we use a dependent type constructor to
give a type to $E_{dblProc}$:

$E_{dblProc}$: (-> (((dselect listof list-module) int))
            ((dselect listof list-module) int))

For example, this type allows the type system to show that the application

($E_{dblProc}$ (open list-module
           (cons 17 ((pcall null int)))))

is well typed, because the list has type ((dselect listof list-module) int),
which matches the argument type of the procedure. (Note the use of implicit
projection for cons.)

```
T_listModule =
  (moduleof
    ((listof t))
    (null (forall (t) (-> () (listof t))))
    (null~ (forall (r t) (-> ((listof t) (-> () r) (-> () r)) r)))
    (cons (forall (t) (-> (t (listof t)) (listof t))))
    (cons~ (forall (r t)
              (-> ((listof t) (-> (t (listof t)) r) (-> () r)) r)))
    (null? (forall (t) (-> ((listof t)) bool)))
    (car (forall (t) (-> ((listof t)) t)))
    (cdr (forall (t) (-> ((listof t)) (listof t))))
    )
```

Figure 15.5 The type $T_{listModule}$ of a list module.

FLEX/M's `dselect` construct is a generalization of `dtypeof` from the dependent package system studied in Section 14.5. Whereas (`dtypeof` E_{pkg}) stands for the single abstract type of the package E_{pkg}, (`dselect` θ E_{mod}) stands for one of possibly several named abstract type constructors in the module E_{mod}. A FLEX/M type is a dependent type if and only if it contains at least one occurrence of `dselect`, because this is the only type construct that may refer to values. FLEX/M uses a conservative syntactic notion of type equivalence for dependent types to guarantee that they can be statically checked. This notion, which is like the one presented for the dependent package system in Section 14.5.2, is discussed further in Section 15.4.

The (`load` Y T) construct loads a separately compiled expression of type T from the file named Y in an external file storage system. Although any pure FLEX/M expression may be compiled into a file, modules and functors are the typical unit of compilation. For example, if $E_{listModule}$ has been compiled to the file `list.flxm`, then the expression (`load list.flxm` $T_{listModule}$) is equivalent to the expression (`the` $T_{listModule}$ $E_{listModule}$). The type specified in the `load` expression serves as an interface for the compiled expression that (in some approaches) allows type-checking the `load` expression without having the contents of the file, a feature important for separate compilation. Section 15.6 explores in detail the design and implementation challenges associated with `load`.

FLEX/M modules are first-class, so they can be named, passed to procedures as arguments, returned from procedures as results, and stored in data structures, including other modules. The expression in Figure 15.6 illustrates all of these features. The `mod-of-mods` module has two component modules: `list-module`, which defines the `listof` type constructor and its associated operations, and

```
(let ((mod-of-mods
        (module
          (def list-module T_listModule E_listModule)
          (def pair-module T_pairModule E_pairModule)))
            {assume E_pairModule has type T_pairModule (see Exercise 15.1)}
      (make-polymod
        (abs ((mm (moduleof ()
                    (list-module T_listModule)
                    (pair-module T_pairModule))))
          (open mm
            (open list-module
              (open pair-module
                (module
                  (def-datatype (polyof)
                    (poly (listof (pairof int int))))
                  (def empty (-> () (polyof))
                    (abs ()
                      (poly ((pcall null (pairof int int))))))
                  (def add-point (-> (int int (polyof)) (polyof))
                    (abs ((x int) (y int) (p (polyof)))
                      (match p
                        ((poly points)
                         (poly (cons (pair x y) points)))))))
                ))))))
  (make-polymod mod-of-mods))
```

Figure 15.6   A FLEX/M expression illustrating the first-class properties of modules.

pair-module, which defines the **pairof** type constructor and its associated operations. The **make-polymod** procedure takes any module with list and pair submodules and returns a new module in which polygons having abstract type (polyof) are represented as lists of integer pairs.

A procedure like **make-polymod** that takes modules as arguments and/or returns a module as a result is traditionally known as a functor. The ability to express functors as regular procedure enables FLEX/M to be used as the linking language for its own module system. This stands in contrast to languages like SML and OCAML, in which functors are distinct from procedures and module linking is expressed in a separate module language distinct from the core language that is used to express computation.

$$T_{envModule} = \texttt{(moduleof ((envof t))}$$
```
               (empty (forall (t) (-> () (envof t))))
                  {Creates an environment with no name/value bindings.}
               (bind (forall (t) (-> (symb t (envof t)) (envof t))))
                  {Extends an environment with a new name/value binding,
                    shadowing any existing binding with the given name.}
               (lookup (forall (t) (-> (symb (envof t)) t)))
                  {Returns the value bound to name in an environment, or
                    generates an unbound error if there is no such binding.}
               )
```

Figure 15.7 The signature for an environment module.

15.3 Module Examples: Environments and Tables

Before delving into the technical details of the FLEX/M module system, we present some examples involving the implementation of modules for environment and table data structures. These examples illustrate the abstract nature of module type constructors, information hiding in modules, and parameterized modules and linking.

Figure 15.7 presents the signature for a module that implements environments like those used for specifying denotational semantics and type checking. Abstractly, a value of type (envof t) is an environment that contains bindings of symbolic names to values of type t. Such environments can be manipulated with the polymorphic empty, bind, and lookup procedures.

Figure 15.8 shows examples of expressions abstracted over an environment module. $E_{envTest}$ takes an environment module and uses it to build some simple environments binding names to integers, then looks up values in these environments. $E_{envSwap}$ takes an environment and uses it to construct a polymorphic procedure that swaps the values bound to two names in an environment. Both expressions use FLEX/M's the construct to indicate the type of the abstraction. Note that $E_{envSwap}$ requires a parameterized arrow type to model the dependency of the envof type constructor on the parameter named envmod. Also note that implicit projection makes these expressions much more concise than they would otherwise be.

We now describe two very different ways to implement the environment module. Figure 15.9 presents an implementation that represents an environment as a list of entries, where each entry pairs a name (a symbol) with a value. The polymorphic empty procedure creates an empty list of entries. The polymorphic bind procedure prepends a new entry binding a name to a value onto the envi-

$E_{envTest}$ =
  (the (-> ($T_{envModule}$) int)
       (abs ((envmod $T_{envModule}$))
         (open envmod
           (let ((e0 ((pcall empty int)))) $\{e0 = \{\}\}$
             (let ((e1 (bind (sym a) 1 e0))) $\{e1 = \{a \mapsto 1\}\}$
               (let ((e2 (bind (sym b) 2 e1))) $\{e2 = \{a \mapsto 1, b \mapsto 2\}\}$
                 (let ((e3 (bind (sym a) 3 e2))) $\{e3 = \{a \mapsto 3, b \mapsto 2\}\}$
                   (+ (* 1000 (lookup (sym a) e3))
                     (+ (* 100 (lookup (sym b) e3))
                       (+ (* 10 (lookup (sym a) e2))
                         (lookup (sym b) e2)))) $\{Result\ is\ 3212\}$
               )))))))

$E_{envSwap}$ =
  (the (-> ((envmod $T_{envModule}$))
           (forall (t)
             (-> (symb symb ((dselect envof envmod) t))
                 ((dselect envof envmod) t))))
       (abs ((envmod $T_{envModule}$))
         (open envmod
           (pabs (t)
             (abs ((s1 symb) (s2 symb) (env (envof t)))
               (let ((v1 (lookup s1 env))
                     (v2 (lookup s2 env)))
                 (bind s1 v2 (bind s2 v1 env)))))))))

Figure 15.8 Some expressions abstracted over an environment module.

ronment's list of entries. The polymorphic `lookup` procedure uses a local `loop` procedure to find an entry with the given name, and then returns the value from this entry (or generates an `unbound` error if no such entry is found).

In these three procedures, the `list-env` constructor converts the concrete list type (`listof (entryof t)`) to the abstract type (`envof t`) and the `list-env˜` deconstructor (implicitly used in the `match` construct) converts the abstract environment type to the concrete list type. It would be a type error to use a list as an environment or vice versa. In this way, constructor and deconstructor procedures in FLEX/M serve the roles of the `up` and `down` procedures for converting between concrete and abstract types in Sections 14.2–14.5.

A signature T_{open} that describes all bindings of the module value of the `open` expression E_{open} within $E_{listEnvModule}$ is shown in Figure 15.10. This signature contains a type constructor (`entryof t`) and four procedures (`entry`,

```
E_listEnvModule = (the  T_envModule  E_open),
where E_open =
  (open list-module
    (module
      (def-datatype (entryof t)
        (entry symb t))
      (def-datatype (envof t)
        (list-env (listof (entryof t))))
      (def empty (forall (t) (-> () (envof t)))
        (pabs (t)
          (abs () (list-env ((pcall null (entryof t)))))))
      (def bind (forall (t) (-> (symb t (envof t)) (envof t)))
        (pabs (t)
          (abs ((name symb) (val t) (env (envof t)))
            (match env
              ((list-env entries)
               (list-env (cons (entry name val) entries)))))))
      (def lookup (forall (t) (-> (symb (envof t)) t))
        (pabs (t)
          (abs ((name symb) (env (envof t)))
            (match env
              ((list-env entries)
               (letrec ((loop (-> ((listof (entryof t))) t)
                          (abs ((ents (listof (entryof t))))
                            (match ents
                              ((null) (error unbound t))
                              ((cons (entry n v) rest)
                               (if (sym=? name n) v (loop rest)))))))
                 (loop entries)))))))
    ))
```

Figure 15.9   An environment module that represents environments as lists of bindings. Assume that list-module is a name for the module $E_{listModule}$ from Figure 15.3.

entry˜, list-env, and list-env˜) that do not appear in the simpler signature $T_{envModule}$. These names expose aspects of the environment implementation that are irrelevant to clients of the environment module (like $E_{envTest}$ and $E_{envSwap}$) and should remain hidden behind an abstraction barrier. A client should only be able to form an environment using empty and bind and to look up names in an environment using lookup. If the client has access to the entryof type constructor and the constructor/deconstructor procedures, the client can access information that should not be revealed, such as whether there are older bindings for a given name that are shadowed by newer ones.

```
T_open =
  (moduleof ((entryof t) (envof t))
    (entry (forall (t) (-> (symb t) (entryof t))))
    (entry~ (forall (r t)
              (-> ((entryof t) (-> (symb t) r) (-> () r)) r)))
    (list-env (forall (t)
                (-> (((dselect listof list-module) (entryof t)))
                    (envof t))))
    (list-env~ (forall (r t)
                 (-> ((envof t)
                      (-> (((dselect listof list-module) (entryof t)))
                          r)
                      (-> () r))
                     r)))
    (empty (forall (t) (-> () (envof t))))
    (bind (forall (t) (-> (symb t (envof t)) (envof t))))
    (lookup (forall (t) (-> (symb (envof t)) t)))
    )
```

Figure 15.10 A signature describing all bindings of the module value of the open expression E_{open} within $E_{listEnvModule}$.

FLEX/M uses explicit subtyping conversions expressed via the **the** construct to enforce this kind of information hiding. There is a subtyping relation on module signatures similar to the subtyping relation on record types: signature T_1 is a subtype of signature T_2 if T_1 has at least the type constructor and value names that T_2 has, and the types of the shared value names in T_1 are subtypes of the corresponding types in T_2. (We shall formalize FLEX/M subtyping in Section 15.4.3.) If T_1 is a subtype of T_2 and expression E_1 has type T_1, then the expression (**the** T_2 E_1) declares that the value of the **the** expression has type T_2. With modules, **the** can be used to hide local module bindings that should not be exported. For example, since T_{open} is a subtype of $T_{envModule}$, the expression (**the** $T_{envModule}$ E_{open}) is a well-typed expression that hides the implementation-dependent components of E_{open} and can be used wherever a value of type $T_{envModule}$ is expected. Because FLEX/M requires explicit subtyping conversions, neither abstraction in Figure 15.8 can be applied directly to E_{open}, but both abstractions can be applied to $E_{listEnvModule}$ = (**the** $T_{envModule}$ E_{open}).

A very different implementation of the environment module is presented in Figure 15.11. In this implementation, environments are represented as procedures that map symbols to values. The conversion (**the** $T_{envModule}$ ...) hides the con-

```
E_procEnvModule =
  (the  T_envModule
    (module
      (def-datatype (envof t)
        (proc-env (-> (symb) t)))
      (def empty (forall (t) (-> () (envof t)))
        (pabs (t)
          (abs ()
            (proc-env (abs ((n symb)) (error unbound t))))))
      (def bind (forall (t) (-> (symb t (envof t)) (envof t)))
        (pabs (t)
          (abs ((name symb) (val t) (env (envof t)))
            (proc-env (abs ((n symb))
                        (if (sym=? n name)
                            val
                            (lookup n env)))))))
      (def lookup (forall (t) (-> (symb (envof t)) t))
        (pabs (t)
          (abs ((name symb) (env (envof t)))
            (match env
              ((proc-env proc) (proc name))))))
      ))
```

Figure 15.11 An environment module that represents environments as procedures from symbols to values.

structor/deconstructor procedures `proc-env`/`proc-env~`, effectively erecting an abstraction barrier that makes it impossible to treat symbol-to-value procedures as environments or vice versa. Like $E_{listEnvModule}$, $E_{procEnvModule}$ can be used wherever a value of type $T_{envModule}$ is expected.

Static dependent types even allow using both environment modules in the same program. For example, the following expression picks an environment module based on a boolean `b`, uses this module to construct an environment `env`, and then uses $E_{envSwap}$ to create another environment from `env`.

```
(let ((em (if b E_listEnvModule  E_procEnvModule)))
  (let ((env (open em
              (bind (sym c) 4
                (bind (sym d) 5
                  ((pcall empty int)))))))
    ((pcall (E_envSwap em) int) (sym c) (sym d) env)))
```

Using the type rules presented in Section 15.4, we can show that `env` has type
`((dselect envof em) int)` and that `(pcall ($E_{envSwap}$ em) int)` has type

> `(-> (symb symb ((dselect envof em) int)) ((dselect envof em) int))`

so the procedure application that is the body of the inner `let` has type `((dselect envof em) int)`. Indeed, the whole expression is well typed with type

> `((dselect envof (if b $E_{listEnvModule}$ $E_{procEnvModule}$)) int)`

where the `let`-bound name `em` has been replaced by its definition in accordance with the type rules for the static dependent type system.

In contrast, here is a similar expression that is ill typed because it attempts to use the operations of one environment module on an environment constructed from another module:

```
(let ((env (open E_listEnvModule
                 (bind (sym c) 4
                   (bind (sym d) 5
                     ((pcall empty int)))))))
     ((pcall (E_envSwap E_procEnvModule) int) (sym c) (sym d) env))
```

Here, `env` has type `((dselect envof $E_{listEnvModule}$) int)` and `(pcall ($E_{envSwap}$ $E_{procEnvModule}$) int)` has type

> `(-> (symb symb ((dselect envof $E_{procEnvModule}$) int))`
> `    ((dselect envof $E_{procEnvModule}$) int))`

Because the type of `env` is not equivalent to the type of the third argument of the arrow type, the procedure application is ill typed.

The utility of functors (i.e., parameterized modules) becomes clear when generalizing environments to immutable tables, data structures that maintain bindings of keys of one type to values of another type.[5] An environment is a specialized table in which the keys are required to be symbols. Figure 15.12 presents the type $T_{makeTableModule}$ of a functor for creating a table module. This is a dependent arrow type whose argument is a key module `key-mod` specifying a key type, `(keyof)` (an application of the nullary type constructor `keyof`), and an equality procedure `key=?` on elements of this type. The return type is a generalization of the environment signature (Figure 15.7) to a table signature in which the type `symb` is abstracted over by a more general key type `((dselect keyof key-mod))` that depends on the parameter `key-mod`.

---

[5]Tables often support additional operations, such as the ability to delete a binding from the table and the ability to list all keys in the table. For simplicity, we ignore these additional operations.

```
T_makeTableModule =
  (-> ((key-mod (moduleof ((keyof))
                  (key=? (-> ((keyof) (keyof)) bool)))))
    (moduleof ((tableof t))
      (empty (forall (t) (-> () (tableof t))))
        {Creates a table with no key/value bindings.}
      (bind (forall (t) (-> (((dselect keyof key-mod)) t (tableof t))
                            (tableof t))))
        {Extends a table with a new key/value binding.}
      (lookup (forall (t) (-> (((dselect keyof key-mod)) (tableof t))
                              t)))
        {Returns the value bound to key in a table, or}
        {generates an unbound error if there is no such binding.}
      ))

E_makeTableModule =
  (the  T_makeTableModule
      (abs ((key-mod (moduleof ((keyof))
                        (key=? (-> ((keyof) (keyof)) bool)))))
        ... a copy of E_open from Figure 15.9 in which
            (1) envof is replaced by tableof and
            (2) sym=? is replaced by (open key-mod key=?) ... ))

E_symKeyMod = (module
                (def-datatype (keyof)
                  (sym->key symb))
                (def key=? (-> ((keyof) (keyof)) bool)
                  (abs ((k1 (keyof)) (k2 (keyof)))
                    (match k1
                      ((sym->key s1)
                        (match k2
                          ((sym->key s2) (sym=? s1 s2)))))))))

E_envTableTest =
  (let ((sym-key-mod E_symKeyMod))
    (let ((env-table-mod (E_makeTableModule sym-key-mod)))
      (open sym-key-mod
        (open env-table-mod
          (let ((env (bind (sym->key (sym a)) 1
                        (bind (sym->key (sym b)) 2
                          ((pcall empty int))))))
            (+ (* 10 (lookup (sym->key (sym a)) env))
               (lookup (sym->key (sym b)) env)))))))
```

Figure 15.12 $E_{makeTableModule}$ is a table-module functor that can be instantiated to an environment module that requires converting symbols to the abstract key type.

$T'_{makeTableModule} =$
```
  (forall (key)
    (-> ((-> (key key) bool))
        (moduleof ((tableof t))
          (empty (forall (t) (-> () (tableof t))))
          (bind (forall (t) (-> (key t (tableof t)) (tableof t))))
          (lookup (forall (t) (-> (key (tableof t)) t)))
          )))
```

$E'_{makeTableModule} =$
```
    (the T'makeTableModule
        (pabs (key)
          (abs ((key=? (-> (key key) bool)))
            ... a copy of Eopen from Figure 15.9 in which
              (1) envof is replaced by tableof and
              (2) sym=? is replaced by key=? ... )))
```

$E'_{envTableTest} =$
```
  (let ((env-table-mod ((pcall E'makeTableModule symb) sym=?)))
    (open env-table-mod
      (let ((env (bind (sym a) 1
                    (bind (sym b) 2
                      ((pcall empty int)))))))
        (+ (* 10 (lookup (sym a) env))
           (lookup (sym b) env)))))
```

Figure 15.13 $E'_{makeTableModule}$ is a table-module functor that can be instantiated to an environment module that uses raw symbols as keys.

$E_{makeTableModule}$ in Figure 15.12 is a functor with type $T_{makeTableModule}$. It is a parameterized version of the E_{open} implementation for environments as lists from Figure 15.9 in which (1) every occurrence of envof is replaced by tableof and (2) the single occurrence of sym=? in lookup is replaced by the more general key=? procedure from the key-mod argument of the functor.

We can create an environment-like module by applying the $E_{makeTableModule}$ functor to a module that defines symbolic keys, as in the $E_{envTableTest}$ expression in Figure 15.12. In this example, sym-key-mod is a module that implements the abstract (keyof) type as a symbol, and applying the $E_{makeTableModule}$ functor to this module yields the env-table-mod module. Because (keyof) is an abstract type, it is necessary to use sym->key from sym-key-mod to convert concrete symbols to abstract keys in the resulting module. For example, with bind and lookup, it is necessary to use (sym->key (sym a)) rather than (sym a) as a key.

The conversion between symbols and keys in this example is cumbersome. It would be preferable for environments instantiated from tables to use raw symbols as keys. Can we do this in FLEX/M? Yes, but in a way that is at odds with modularity. The functor $E'_{makeTableModule}$ in Figure 15.13 separates the key type (now called key) and key equality predicate and abstracts over them separately. Using this new functor, the $E_{envTableTest}$ test expression from Figure 15.12 can be rewritten as $E'_{envTableTest}$ in Figure 15.13. In this example, env-table-mod is created by first projecting $E'_{makeTableModule}$ on the type symb and then applying the resulting procedure to the symbol-equality procedure, sym=?. Because the key type is not abstract in this example, raw symbols can be used as keys in bind and lookup, just as in the hand-crafted environment examples we studied earlier.

Although $E'_{makeTableModule}$ is in some ways a more convenient functor than $E_{makeTableModule}$, it has a cost in terms of modularity: it separates the key type and the key-equality predicate, which are no longer glued together in a module. In FLEX/M, there is no way to achieve this result with a module. This is a consequence of our design choice that all type bindings of module signatures must be abstract, which in turn requires some means of converting between concrete representation types (like symb) and abstract types (like (keyof)). In Section 15.7.2, we shall discuss a feature of the SML module system that allows the key type and key-equality predicate to be combined in a single module without requiring such conversions.

Exercise 15.1 Pairs are not kernel constructs in FLEX/M because they can be specified in a user-defined module.

a. Define a moduleof type $T_{pairModule}$ describing a module that defines the pairof type constructor, the pair constructor, the pair~ deconstructor, and the selectors fst and snd.

b. Define a module expression $E_{pairModuleSOP}$ having type $T_{pairModule}$ in which a pair is represented as a sum-of-products datum created via a constructor introduced by def-datatype.

c. Define a module expression $E_{pairModuleChurch}$ having type $T_{pairModule}$ in which a pair is represented as a Church pair (see Section 6.6.4).

d. Define an abstraction $E_{makeSwap}$ that takes any module m of type $T_{pairModule}$ and returns a swapping procedure that takes any pair p constructed by m and returns a new pair q whose components are the swapped components of p. What is the type of $E_{makeSwap}$?

Exercise 15.2 Here is a FLEX/M signature for an immutable stack abstraction:

$T_{stackMod} =$
  (moduleof ((stackof t))
    (empty (forall (t) (-> () (stackof t))))   {*create an empty stack*}
    (empty? (forall (t) (-> ((stackof t)) bool))) {*check if stack is empty*}
    (push (forall (t)
          (-> (t (stackof t)) (stackof t))))   {*push element onto stack*}
    (pop (forall (r t) {*r is result type; t is stack element type*}
        (-> ((stackof t)   {*stack to decompose into top and rest*}
          (-> (t (stackof t)) r) {*success continuation*}
          (-> () r))   {*failure continuation*}
        r))))   {*result*}

a. Write a FLEX/M expression $E_{stackMod1}$ with type $T_{stackMod}$ that implements stacks via a data-type definition with constructors empty and push.

b. Write a FLEX/M expression $E_{stackMod2}$ with type $T_{stackMod}$ that implements stacks as lists. You will still need a data-type declaration to create constructor/deconstructor procedures that convert between stacks and lists.

c. Suppose that $T'_{stackMod}$ is just like $T_{stackMod}$, except that it includes a type binding for a stack-reversal procedure as well:

    (reverse (forall (t) (-> ((stackof t)) (stackof t))))

Write a FLEX/M functor $E_{makeReverseStack}$ with type (-> ($T_{stackMod}$) $T'_{stackMod}$) that takes any stack implementation and returns an implementation with a new reverse procedure that reverses the elements of a stack.

15.4   Static Semantics of FLEX/M Modules

15.4.1   Scoping

FLEX/M has two new binding constructs: moduleof and module. The moduleof construct declares type-constructor names whose scope is the types of the value components. For example, in

```
(moduleof ((treeof s))
  (a (moduleof ((pairof s t))
       (c (pairof (treeof int) (treeof symb)))))
  (b (pairof int (treeof bool))))
```

the pairof in the type of b is a free type-constructor name because it does not appear within the scope of a moduleof declaring pairof. In contrast, the pairof in the type of c and all occurrences of `treeof` are bound by surrounding `moduleof` declarations. It is assumed that $FrTyconIds_{ty}$ calculates the free type-constructor names of a type.

The `module` construct declares both type-constructor names and value names, including the names of constructor and deconstructor procedures. The scope of the type-constructor names is all types that appear within the `module` expression, including types within the constructor specifications of data-type declarations. The scope of the value names is the set of definition expressions that are the right-hand sides of value definitions, including expressions that appear in `dselect` types within these definition expressions. The type-constructor and value names of a module may also be used in the body of any `open` expression in which the module is opened, so there is a nonhierarchical aspect to the scope of names declared in a module as well.

15.4.2 Type Equivalence

Type equivalence for FLEX/M is defined by extending the type-equivalence rules for FLEX/SP with the rules in Figure 15.14.

Two `moduleof` types are equivalent if their abstract-type specifications and value-component types are equivalent, modulo permutation. The type identifiers $\tau_{i=1}^{n}$ in an abstract-type specification ($\theta\ \tau_{i=1}^{n}$) are dummy names and only their number matters (for indicating the number of parameters). Thus, two abstract-type specifications are equivalent if they have the same type-constructor name and the same number of dummy parameters.

Two type-constructor applications are equivalent if their type constructors are equivalent (via $\approx_{tc}$), both have the same number of type arguments, and corresponding type arguments are equivalent. Two type constructors are equivalent if they are the same type constructor name θ or the result of using `dselect` to select the same type-constructor name from equivalent (via $\approx_{depends}$) module expressions. To maintain the phase distinction between type checking and program execution, we require static dependent types — i.e., it must be possible to determine $\approx_{depends}$ at type-checking time. The simplest definition of $\approx_{depends}$ satisfying this requirement is syntactic equality, but, as discussed on page 878, more sophisticated definitions can also be used.

The type-equivalence rule for arrow types is the $[\rightarrow\text{-}\approx]$ rule from Figure 14.12 on page 874, which allows consistent renaming of the parameter names in parameterized arrow types.

15.4.3   Subtyping

Subtyping for FLEX/M is defined by extending the subtype rules for FLEX/SP with the rules in Figure 15.15. The [*moduleof-*$\sqsubseteq$] rule is similar to the [*recordof-*$\sqsubseteq$] rule in Figure 12.2 on page 703 except for two differences. Suppose T_{mod} and T'_{mod} are `moduleof` types and $T_{mod} \sqsubseteq T'_{mod}$:

1. The set of abstract types in T_{mod} may be a superset of the abstract types in T'_{mod}, allowing a supertype to hide type constructors from a subtype.

2. All free type-constructor names in T'_{mod} must also be free in T_{mod}. This restriction prevents accidental name capture of type constructors. For example, consider the following `moduleof` types:

$$T_{mod1} = \text{(moduleof ((xof s) (yof t))}$$
$$\text{(a (xof (yof int)))}$$
$$\text{(b (yof (zof bool)))}$$
$$\text{(c (wof symb)))}$$
$$T_{mod2} = \text{(moduleof ((yof t))}$$
$$\text{(a (xof (yof int))))}$$
$$T_{mod3} = \text{(moduleof ((yof t))}$$
$$\text{(b (yof (zof bool))))}$$

T_{mod1} and T_{mod2} both have components named a with type (`xof (yof int)`), but the `xof` in T_{mod1} refers to the type constructor `xof` exported by T_{mod1} while the `xof` in T_{mod2} refers to some externally declared type constructor. Since $FrTyconIds_{ty}[\![T_{mod2}]\!] = \{\text{xof}\} \not\subseteq \{\text{wof}, \text{zof}\} = FrTyconIds_{ty}[\![T_{mod1}]\!]$, the variable-capture restriction prevents T_{mod1} from being a subtype of T_{mod2}. In contrast, T_{mod1} *is* a subtype of T_{mod3} because (1) the components named b have the same type (`yof (zof bool)`), (2) the type constructor `yof` is bound in both T_{mod1} and T_{mod3}, and (3) the type constructor `zof` is free in both T_{mod1} and T_{mod3} (and so is assumed to refer to the same externally declared type constructor).

The [$\rightarrow$-$\sqsubseteq$] rule modifies the usual subtyping rule on arrow types to allow the renaming of parameters in FLEX/M's parameterized arrow types.

15.4.4   Type Rules

To simplify the type rules for FLEX/M, we will embed some machinery in the specification of type environments (see Figure 15.16). As usual, type environments are partial functions from identifiers to types. In order to prevent name

Type Equivalence

$$\frac{\forall_{j=1}^{m} \, . \, \exists h \in [1..m] \, . \, \left(AT_h \approx_{at} AT'_j\right) \quad \forall_{k=1}^{n} \, . \, \exists i \in [1..n] \, . \, ((I_i = I'_k) \wedge (T_i \approx T'_k))}{\begin{array}{c}(\texttt{moduleof} \ (AT_{h=1}^m) \ (I_i \ \ T_i)_{i=1}^n) \\ \approx (\texttt{moduleof} \ (AT'^{\,m}_{j=1}) \ (I'_k \ \ T'_k)_{k=1}^n)\end{array}} \quad [\textit{moduleof-}\approx]$$

$$\frac{TC \approx_{tc} TC' \quad \forall_{i=1}^{n} \, . \, (T_i \approx T'_i)}{(TC \ T_{i=1}^n) \approx (TC' \ T'^{\,n}_{i=1})} \quad [\textit{tyconapp-}\approx]$$

The $[\rightarrow\text{-}\approx]$ rule is the same as in Figure 14.12 on page 874. All other FLEX/M type-equivalence rules are specified in Section 11.8 and in Figure 12.9 on page 731.

Abstract-Type Equivalence

$$(\theta \ \tau_{i=1}^n) \approx_{at} (\theta \ \tau'^{\,n}_{i=1}) \quad [\approx_{at}]$$

Type-Constructor Equivalence

$$\theta \approx_{tc} \theta \quad [\textit{id-}\approx_{tc}]$$

$$\frac{E_{mod} \approx_{depends} E'_{mod}}{(\texttt{dselect} \ \theta \ E_{mod}) \approx_{tc} (\texttt{dselect} \ \theta \ E'_{mod})} \quad [\textit{dselect-}\approx_{tc}]$$

where $\approx_{depends}$ is any statically determinable equivalence on expression values (this is textual equality by default, but may be more sophisticated — see page 878).

Figure 15.14 New type-equivalence rules for FLEX/M, which inherits all the type-equivalence rules except for $[\rightarrow\text{-}\approx]$ from FLEX/SP.

$$\frac{\forall_{j=1}^{p} \, . \, \exists h \in [1..m] \, . \, \left(AT_h \approx_{at} AT'_j\right) \quad \forall_{k=1}^{q} \, . \, \exists i \in [1..n] \, . \, ((I_i = I'_k) \wedge (T_i \sqsubseteq T'_k))}{\begin{array}{c}(\texttt{moduleof} \ (AT_{h=1}^m) \ (I_i \ \ T_i)_{i=1}^n) \\ \sqsubseteq (\texttt{moduleof} \ (AT'^{\,p}_{j=1}) \ (I'_k \ \ T'_k)_{k=1}^q)\end{array}} \quad [\textit{moduleof-}\sqsubseteq]$$

$$\text{where} \quad \textit{FrTyconIds}_{ty}[\![(\texttt{moduleof} \ (AT'^{\,p}_{j=1}) \ (I'_k \ \ T'_k)_{k=1}^q)]\!]$$
$$\subseteq \textit{FrTyconIds}_{ty}[\![(\texttt{moduleof} \ (AT_{h=1}^m) \ (I_i \ \ T_i)_{i=1}^n)]\!]$$

$$\frac{\forall_{i=1}^{n} \, . \, (T'_i \sqsubseteq T_i) \quad [I'_i/I_i]_{i=1}^n \, T_{body} \sqsubseteq T'_{body}}{(\texttt{->} \ ((I_i \ \ T_i)_{i=1}^n) \ T_{body}) \sqsubseteq (\texttt{->} \ ((I'_i \ \ T'_i)_{i=1}^n) \ T'_{body})} \quad [\rightarrow\text{-}\sqsubseteq]$$
$$\text{where} \quad \forall_{i=1}^{n} \, . \, (I'_i \notin \textit{FrIds}_{ty}[\![T_{body}]\!])$$

All other FLEX/M subtype rules are specified in Figure 12.2 on page 703 and in Figure 12.9 on page 731.

Figure 15.15 New subtyping rules for FLEX/M, which inherits all the subtyping rules except for $[\rightarrow\text{-}\sqsubseteq]$ from FLEX/SP.

Type Environments

$TE \in \text{TypeEnvironment} = \text{Ident} \rightharpoonup \text{Type}$

As with dependent packages (Figure 14.13), extending a type environment via $TE[I_1 : T_1, \ldots, I_n : T_n]$ requires both that the identifiers $I_1, \ldots, I_n$ must be distinct and, further, that $dom(TE)$ and $\cup_{i=1}^{n}\{I_i\}$ must be disjoint; see page 879 for a discussion of this requirement.

The notation $TE \oplus DD$ is the same as that defined for FLARE in Figure 13.29 on page 831 *except that* (1) all occurrences of `generic` should be replaced by `forall` and (2) the type (`forall () ` T) of every constructor procedure for a nullary type constructor should be replaced by T.

$TE \oplus [DD_1, \ldots, DD_n]$ is an abbreviation for $((TE \oplus DD_1) \oplus \ldots) \oplus DD_n$.

Figure 15.16   Type environments for FLEX/M.

capture that can make a static dependent type system unsound (see page 879), FLEX/M's type environments do not permit rebinding an identifier. Automatically alpha-renaming expression identifiers satisfies this restriction with no impact on the programmer.

The notation $TE \oplus DD$ stands for the type environment that results from extending TE with type bindings for the constructor and deconstructor procedures declared by the data-type declaration DD. For example, given the declaration

```
DD_listof = (def-datatype (listof t)
               (null)
               (cons t (listof t)))
```

$TE \oplus DD$ denotes the result of extending TE with the type bindings in Figure 15.4 on page 896. As noted in Figure 15.16, the FLEX/M $\oplus$ operator has essentially the same definition as the FLARE $\oplus$ operator except for two changes. The first change (replacing `generic` by `forall`) is necessary because FLEX/M, unlike FLARE, is an explicitly typed language with explicit universal types. The second change (replacing (`forall () ` T) by T) is an optimization that eliminates unnecessary type quantification for nullary type constructors (which are isomorphic to types). The notation $TE \oplus [DD_1, \ldots, DD_n]$ is shorthand for $((TE \oplus DD_1) \oplus \ldots) \oplus DD_n$.

Figure 15.17 presents the new and modified type rules for FLEX/M (except for the type rule for `load`, which is discussed in Section 15.6).

The [*moduleof-intro*] rule specifies the `moduleof` type for a `module` expression. The abstract-type specification ($\theta_i \ \tau_{i,1} \ \ldots \ \tau_{i,k_i}$) for each data-type declaration

DD_i is simply recorded in the `moduleof` type. The identifier/type bindings of the `moduleof` type come from two sources:

1. The type bindings for the constructor and deconstructor procedures are deduced from the data-type declarations. The type environment $TE_{DD} = \{\} \oplus [DD_1, \ldots, DD_m]$ contains exactly these constructor and deconstructor bindings. The notation $(I\ TE_{DD}(I))_{I \in dom(TE_{DD})}$ stands for the result of converting all the bindings $I : T$ of TE_{DD} into a sequence of s-expression bindings of the form $(I\ T)$.

2. Each value-component definition (`def` $I\ T\ E$) gives rise to a type binding $(I\ T)$.

The rule also verifies that for each definition (`def` $I\ T_{defn}\ E_{defn}$), the expression E_{defn} has type T_{defn}. Since E_{defn} may refer to the constructor and deconstructor procedures introduced by the data-type declarations, the type environment used for this verification process must include the bindings in $TE \oplus [DD_1, \ldots, DD_m]$. Because value definitions are mutually recursive, the type environment must also include bindings for all the value definitions. In this respect, the [*moduleof-intro*] rule is like the [*letrec*] rule we have seen in other typed dialects of FL. This is why the `module` construct supplants `letrec` in FLEX/M; the latter can be expressed as sugar in terms of the former (see Figure 15.2 on page 894).

Since constructors create values with the abstract type and deconstructors decompose values with the abstract type, they play the role of `up` and `down` in the type rule for `pack`$_{depend}$ in the dependent package system (Figure 14.13 on page 875). Since the constructor/deconstructor mechanism is already present in FLEX/M for creating recursive sum-of-products data types, using it to perform conversions between concrete and abstract types avoids the need to develop a separate mechanism for this purpose. Hiding the concrete structure of sum-of-products data does have some drawbacks, however. For instance, it prevents the definition of a default structural equality test on sum-of-products data instances and a default way to display such instances in textual form. Equality procedures, pretty-printing procedures, etc., must be defined by the programmer for each representation of an abstract type.

The [*moduleof-elim*] rule specifies type checking for the (`open` $E_{mod}\ E_{body}$) construct. Like the [*record-with*] rule for opening records in FLEX (Figure 11.18 on page 678), it extends the type environment with type bindings for all value components of the module when checking the type of E_{body}. Like the [*with*] rule for opening records in a dependent package system (Figure 14.13 on page 875), it must perform substitutions on the body type (i.e., substituting (`open` $E_{mod}\ I$)

for each value name I from E_{mod}) to properly track dependencies in the dependent type system.

The [*moduleof-elim*] rule is also similar to the [*dunpack*] rule for dependent packages (Figure 14.13 on page 875) in that it substitutes a dependent type constructor (dselect θ E_{mod}) for each occurrence of an abstract-type constructor θ in the body expression E_{body} and in the types of the value components in the type environment. As discussed on pages 881–883, such substitutions enhance dependent-type equivalence.

The [*moduleof-elim*] rule has a purity restriction that guarantees that the substitutions performed in the rule are sound. As in the [*dunpack*] rule in the dependent package system, dependent types of the form (dselect θ E_{mod}) that are introduced by substituting for θ on the way into the rule require that E_{mod} be pure. As in the [*with*] rule in the dependent package system, substituting (open E_{mod} I) for each value name I in the result type T_{body} on the way out of the rule also requires that E_{mod} be pure. The easiest way to satisfy these requirements is to dictate that E_{mod} satisfies a syntactic purity test similar to the one defined for FLARE in Figure 13.25 on page 816. Although simple to state, this restriction is overly conservative because it doesn't specially handle the case where no relevant substitutions are performed on the way into or out of the rule (in which case E_{mod} need not be pure). Additionally, as discussed on page 938, this restriction also has a fundamental drawback in the presence of parameterized modules.

The [*moduleof-intro*] and [*moduleof-elim*] rules also have an import restriction like the rules for existential and dependent packages (see Figures 14.4 and 14.13), and for exactly the same reason: Local type-constructor bindings must not be allowed to capture references to type constructors with the same name in an outer scope. As before, alpha-renaming of type constructors will solve this problem.

FLEX/M does *not* have implicit subtyping via FLEX/SP's [*inclusion*] rule:

$$\frac{TE \vdash E : T' \qquad T' \sqsubseteq T}{TE \vdash E : T} \qquad \text{[\textit{inclusion}]}$$

Instead, all subtyping in FLEX/M must be specified explicitly using the, according to the following type rule:

$$\frac{TE \vdash E : T' \qquad T' \sqsubseteq T}{TE \vdash (\text{the } T\ E) : T} \qquad \text{[\textit{the-inclusion}]}$$

Requiring explicit conversions for all subtyping ensures that every FLEX/M expression has a unique type (up to alpha-renaming of arrow type parameters and forall-bound type identifiers).

Type Rules

$$\frac{\forall_{j=1}^{n} \cdot (TE \oplus [DD_1, \ldots, DD_m]) [I_h : T_h]_{h=1}^{n} \vdash E_j : T_j}{\begin{array}{l} TE \vdash (\texttt{module } DD_{i=1}^{m} \ (\texttt{def } I_j \ T_j \ E_j)_{j=1}^{n}) \\ \quad : (\texttt{moduleof } ((\theta_i \ \tau_{i,1} \ \ldots \ \tau_{i,k_i})_{i=1}^{m}) \\ \qquad (I \ \ TE_{DD}(I))_{I \in dom(TE_{DD})} \ (I_j \ \ T_j)_{j=1}^{n}) \end{array}} \quad [\textit{moduleof-intro}]$$

where $\forall_{i=1}^{m} \cdot (DD_i = (\texttt{def-datatype } (\theta_i \ \tau_{i,1} \ \ldots \ \tau_{i,k_i}) \ \ldots \ ))$
$\qquad TE_{DD} = \{\} \oplus [DD_1, \ldots, DD_m]$
$\qquad \forall_{i=1}^{m} \cdot \theta_i \notin \left(\cup_{j=1}^{n} \left(\cup_{I \in FrIds_{exp}[\![E_j]\!]} \left(FrTyconIds_{ty}[\![TE(I)]\!] \right) \right) \right)$
$\qquad\qquad\qquad\qquad\qquad\qquad [\textit{import restriction}]$

$$\frac{\begin{array}{c} TE \vdash E_{mod} : (\texttt{moduleof } ((\theta_i \ \ldots \ )_{i=1}^{n}) \ (I_j \ T_j)_{j=1}^{m}) \\ TE[I_j : (dsub \ T_j)]_{j=1}^{m} \vdash (dsub \ E_{body}) : T_{body} \end{array}}{TE \vdash (\texttt{open } E_{mod} \ E_{body}) : [(\texttt{open } E_{mod} \ I_j)/I_j]_{j=1}^{m} \ T_{body}} \quad [\textit{moduleof-elim}]$$

where $(dsub \ X) = [(\texttt{dselect } \theta_i \ E_{mod})/\theta_i]_{i=1}^{n} X$ [*dependent-type introduction*]
$\qquad E_{mod}$ is pure   [*purity restriction*]
$\qquad \forall_{i=1}^{n} \cdot \theta_i \notin \left(\cup_{I \in FrIds_{exp}[\![E_{body}]\!]} \left(FrTyconIds_{ty}[\![TE(I)]\!] \right) \right)$
$\qquad\qquad\qquad\qquad\qquad\qquad [\textit{import restriction}]$

$$\frac{TE \vdash E : T \qquad T \sqsubseteq T'}{TE \vdash (\texttt{the } T' \ E) : T'} \quad [\textit{the-inclusion}]$$

Various type rules for the `load` construct are discussed in Section 15.6. The [→-intro], [→-elim], and [let] rules for FLEX/M are the same as those for the dependent package system in Figure 14.13 on page 875. All the other type rules for FLEX/M are inherited from FLEX/SP, except for the [inclusion] rule in Figure 12.1 on page 703; implicit subtyping is not supported in FLEX/M, where all subtyping is by explicit conversion using the [the-inclusion] rule defined above.

Figure 15.17 Type rules for FLEX/M.

As seen in the examples of Section 15.3, an important use of subtyping in FLEX/M is for hiding module components. In particular, subtyping gives the programmer fine-grained control over how values of abstract type are constructed and deconstructed. If the constructors for an abstract type are hidden in a module, clients cannot create forgeries that possibly violate representation invariants. If the deconstructors for an abstract type are hidden, then clients cannot directly manipulate the concrete representation of an abstract value.

Exercise 15.3

a. Determining free value/type/type-constructor identifiers and performing substitutions in FLEX/M cannot generally be done until type-checking time. Explain why. *Hint:* Focus on the `open` construct.

To model the dependency of free-identifier and substitution functions on types, we extend their signatures to include a type environment. For example:

$FrIds_{exp}$: Exp → TypeEnvironment → $\mathcal{P}$(Ident)

$FrIds_{ty}$: Type → TypeEnvironment → $\mathcal{P}$(Ident)

$FrIds_{tycon}$: TypeConstructor → TypeEnvironment → $\mathcal{P}$(Ident)

Similar changes are made for $FrTyIds_{exp}$, $FrTyIds_{ty}$, and $FrTyIds_{tycon}$ (which return an element of $\mathcal{P}$(TypeId)) and for $FrTyconIds_{exp}$, $FrTyconIds_{ty}$, and $FrTyconIds_{tycon}$ (which return an element of $\mathcal{P}$(TyConId)).

b. Write clauses for all the free-identifier functions mentioned above to handle the new FLEX/M expressions, types, and type constructors presented in Figure 15.1.

c. Several FLEX/M type rules involve checking for free variables and performing substitutions. Since type checking depends on these operations, but these operations themselves depend on type checking, there is a question of whether the operations are well defined. For each such type rule, justify that the operations are well defined.

Exercise 15.4 What is the type of the `make-polymod` procedure in Figure 15.6 on page 900?

15.4.5   Implicit Projection

In an explicitly typed polymorphic language, it is a hassle for programmers to project polymorphic values (i.e., values with `forall` types) onto explicit type arguments using `pcall`, especially since these projections are "obvious" in many cases. Using the type reconstruction machinery from Chapter 13 to solve local type constraints, it is possible to automatically deduce the type arguments to `pcall` in many common cases, thus relieving the programmer from writing many `pcall`s. We call this feature **implicit projection**. JAVA uses a form of implicit projection for generic methods.

FLEX/M supports implicit projection in the common case where a polymorphic procedure is being applied to argument expressions and the type arguments of `pcall` can be deduced from the types of the argument expressions. We will explain how implicit projection works in the context of the following example:

```
E_implicit = (pabs (u)
              (abs ((x u))
                (let ((g (pabs (v)
                          (abs ((f (-> (u) v)))
                            (pair x f)))))
                  (g (abs ((z u)) #t)))))
```

We assume that `pair` has the type `(forall (s t) (-> (s t) (pairof s t)))`. Without implicit projection, $E_{implicit}$ is ill typed because `pair` and g are applied directly as procedures without first using `pcall` to eliminate their `forall` types.

The key idea of implicit projection is to eliminate `forall` types by projecting them onto unification variables, thus replacing `forall`-bound variables by unification variables, and then use type reconstruction to locally solve type constraints involving these unification variables.[6] For example, in `(pair x f)`, projecting the type of `pair` on the unification variables `?a` and `?b` yields the arrow type `(-> (?a ?b) (pairof ?a ?b))`. By unifying `?a` and `?b` with the actual argument types `u` (of x) and `(-> (u) v)` (of f), we see that the result of the `pair` application in this case has the type `(pairof u (-> (u) v))`. Based on this, we determine that g has type

$$T_g = \text{(forall (v)}$$
$$\qquad \text{(-> ((-> (u) v))}$$
$$\qquad\qquad \text{(pairof u (-> (u) v)))))}$$

Similarly, projecting T_g on the unification variable `?c` yields the arrow type `(-> ((-> (u) ?c)) (pairof u (-> (u) ?c)))`. Unifying `(-> (u) ?c)` with the type `(-> (u) bool)` of `(abs ((z u)) #t)` binds `?c` to `bool`, so we deduce that the result of the g application has type `(pairof u (-> (u) bool))`.

This example underscores the importance of distinguishing `pabs`-bound and `forall`-bound variables (e.g., s, t, u, and v) from the unification variables (e.g., `?a`, `?b`, and `?c`) used by the unification process. In particular, `pabs`-bound and `forall`-bound variables must be treated as constants that unify only with themselves. E.g., if `(abs ((z u)) #t)` were changed to `(abs ((z int)) #t)`, the type `(-> (u) ?c)` should *not* unify with `(-> (int) bool)` (by somehow binding u to `int`). The `(pabs (u) ...)` in $E_{implicit}$ abstracts over *any* type u, so u cannot be equated with a particular type (like `int`) within the body of this `pabs`.

The implicit projection process is formalized by the [*implicit-projection*] rule in Figure 15.18, which is a modified version of the [→-*elim*] rule from Figure 14.13 on page 875. In this rule, the rator of the application is a polymorphic procedure with type `(forall ($\tau_{j=i}^m$) (-> (($I_i$ $T_i$)$_{i=1}^n$) $T_0$))` that is not explicitly projected via `pcall`. The rule uses a type-reconstruction process that attempts to deduce bindings for the type identifiers $\tau_{j=i}^m$ that will make the parameter

---

[6]The machinery for implicit projection distinguishes two classes of type names: (1) unification variables $\upsilon \in$ UnificationVar (names that begin with ?) and (2) type identifiers $\tau \in$ TypeId (names that do not begin with ?). This distinction wasn't necessary in Chapter 13, where all type names were unification variables. However, in FLEX/M it is necessary to distinguish the `pabs`-bound and `forall`-bound type names (i.e., type identifiers) that appear in explicit types from the unification variables used by the type reconstruction process for implicit projection.

types $T_{i=1}^n$ match the rand types $T'^n_{i=1}$. If this process succeeds (the solvability restriction is satisfied), the type of the application is the body type T_0 with (1) any references to the $\tau_{j=i}^m$ replaced by the corresponding deduced types and (2) any references to the argument names $I_{i=1}^n$ replaced by the corresponding rand expressions (as in the [$\rightarrow$-elim] rule).

In the [implicit-projection] rule, type reconstruction is performed by substituting fresh unification variables $v_{j=i}^m$ for the forall-bound type identifiers $\tau_{j=i}^m$ before solving the type constraints between the declared parameter types $T_{i=1}^n$ and the actual argument types $T'^n_{i=1}$. If unification succeeds with a type substitution σ, the same substitution of unification variables for type identifiers must be performed on the result type T_0 before applying σ.

The unification algorithm presented in Figure 13.8 on page 784 must be changed to produce substitutions that map unification variables (rather than type identifiers) to types. The unification algorithm must also be extended to handle other FLEX/M types, including type-constructor applications, moduleof types, and forall types. These are straightforward except for the case of unifying two forall types. In this case, the two forall types must have the same number of parameters. We normalize the parameter names (and avoid name capture issues) by substituting the same sequence of fresh type identifiers for both type-parameter sequences, and then attempt to unify the bodies of the forall types. E.g., to unify (forall (a b) (-> (a bool) b)) and (forall (s t) (-> (s ?x) t)), we replace [a, b] and [s, t] by fresh type identifiers, say [t.173, t.174], and then unify the types (-> (t.173 bool) t.174) and (-> (t.173 ?x) t.174), which yields the substitution $\{?x \mapsto \text{bool}\}$.

The [implicit-projection] rule includes a capture restriction that prevents the variable-capture of arrow-type parameter names $I_{i=1}^n$ that happen to also appear in dependent types within $T_{i=1}^n$ or $T'^n_{i=1}$. As usual, such capture could also be avoided by suitably alpha-renaming the program.

Like the [$\rightarrow$-elim] rule, the [implicit-projection] rule has a purity restriction requiring the purity of any rand expression E_i denoted by an arrow-type parameter name I_i mentioned within a dependent type in the procedure body type T_0. Because of the variable-capture restriction, the substitution σ cannot introduce any of the names $I_{i=1}^n$ into $T'_0 = \sigma\,([v_j/\tau_j]_{j=1}^m\,T_0)$; so $I_i \in FrIds_{ty}[\![T_0]\!]$ if and only if $I_i \in FrIds_{ty}[\![T'_0]\!]$.

The [implicit-projection] rule has a locality restriction requiring that no unification variables remain after the substitution σ is performed on the result type.[7] This forces the collection and solution of all type constraints to occur within the

---

[7]Assume that $FrUniVars_{ty}$ returns the unification variables that appear in a type.

$$TE \vdash E_{rator} : (\texttt{forall} \ (\tau_{j=i}^m) \ (\texttt{->} \ ((I_i \ T_i)_{i=1}^n) \ T_0))$$
$$\frac{\forall_{i=1}^n \ . \ (TE \vdash E_i : T_i')}{TE \vdash (E_{rator} \ E_{i=1}^n) : [E_i/I_i]_{i=1}^n T_0'} \qquad \textit{[implicit-projection]}$$

where $\quad (\cup_{i=1}^n \{I_i\}) \cap (\cup_{i=1}^n (\textit{FrIds}_{ty}[\![T_i]\!] \cup \textit{FrIds}_{ty}[\![T_i']\!])) = \{\}$
$\textit{[capture restriction]}$

$\quad\quad\quad v_{j=1}^m$ are fresh unification variables
$\quad\quad\quad solve_{TCS} \ \biguplus_{i=1}^n \{[v_j/\tau_j]_{j=1}^m T_i \doteq T_i'\}_{TCS}$
$\quad\quad\quad\quad = (\text{TypeSubst} \rightarrowtail \text{UnifySoln} \ \sigma) \qquad \textit{[solvability restriction]}$
$\quad\quad\quad T_0' = \sigma \ ([v_j/\tau_j]_{j=1}^m T_0)$
$\quad\quad\quad \textit{FrUniVars}_{ty}[\![T_0']\!] = \{\} \qquad \textit{[locality restriction]}$
$\quad\quad\quad \forall_{i=1}^n \ . \ E_i$ is pure if $(I_i \in \textit{FrIds}_{ty}[\![T_0]\!]). \quad \textit{[purity restriction]}$

Figure 15.18   A type rule for implicit projection in FLEX/M.

[implicit-projection] rule, so that other FLEX/M type rules do not need to be modified to pass around type-constraint sets. A consequence of this restriction is that there are cases where implicit projection fails. For instance, in the application (null), the return type would be (listof ?t), where ?t is an unresolved unification variable. In normal type reconstruction, this could be resolved by the context in which (null) is used, but the locality restriction prevents this, forcing explicit projection to be used instead.

It is possible to extend implicit projection to handle cases like (null) if we change the other type rules to collect and propagate type constraints and solve the type constraints only for top-level programs/modules. But we must ensure that the SDT-related substitutions performed by various type rules are performed in all types that appear in the type-constraint sets. Since this would further complicate already complex type rules, we have chosen the simpler approach for FLEX/M.

You may be able to imagine other cases in which implicit projection would be useful and can be implemented. However, no matter how clever we are with implicit projections, we can't eliminate explicit projections entirely, because of the undecidability of type reconstruction for the second-order lambda calculus.

15.4.6   Typed Pattern Matching

The FLEX/M match construct has the same syntax as the match construct for FLIC+{def-data} used in Section 10.5 and also in FLARE+{def-datatype} in Section 13.5.4. However, FLEX/M cannot simply use the desugaring for `match` presented in Figure 10.27 on page 603 because the desugaring will have to generate type information that is not apparent in the `match` syntax.

For example, consider the following procedure for determining if all elements in an integer list are positive:

```
(def all-pos? (-> ((listof int)) bool)
  (abs ((xs (listof int)))
    (match xs
      ((null) #t)
      ((cons y ys) (and (> y 0) (all-pos? ys))))))
```

The desugaring process must transform the `match` expression in the body of this procedure to an expression like

```
((pcall null~ bool int)
   xs
   (abs () #t)
   (abs ()
     ((pcall cons~ bool int)
        xs
        (abs ((y int) (ys (listof int)))
          (and (> y 0) (all-pos? ys)))
        (abs () (error no-match bool)))))
```

To create the success continuation for `cons~`, the process must determine that `y` has type `int` and `ys` has type `(listof int)`. To create the failure continuation for `cons~`, the process must determine that the `error` construct has type `bool`. The process must also determine the projection types `bool` and `int` for `null~` and `cons~`, but these could be deduced by implicit projection after the type information in the success and failure continuations has been determined.

Rather than requiring the programmer to somehow specify the missing explicit types in the `match` construct, we instead modify the `match` desugaring to automatically deduce the correct explicit types. This approach, which was briefly discussed on page 742 and explored in Exercises 12.20 and 12.25, is based on the following observations. In a well-typed `match` expression, we know the type T_{disc} of the discriminant, the type T_{ret} of the whole `match` expression, and the type of any constructor mentioned in a constructor pattern. This type information is needed in two key spots of the typed `match` desugaring:

1. When the typed version of the clause-processing function $\mathcal{DS}_{clauses}$ runs out of clauses, the `no-match` error must be annotated with the explicit type T_{ret}. In the `all-pos?` example, T_{ret} is `bool`, so the error expression is (`error no-match bool`).

2. When the typed version of the pattern-processing function $\mathcal{DS}_{pat}$ encounters a constructor pattern $(I_{constr} \; PT_{j=1}^{m})$, the well-typedness of the `match` expression guarantees that the discriminant type T_{disc} has the form $(\theta \; T_{i=1}^{n})$ and the constructor I_{constr} has a type of the form

$$\texttt{(forall } (\tau_{i=1}^{n}) \; \texttt{(-> } (T'^{\,m}_{\,j=1}) \; (\theta \; \tau_{i=1}^{n})))$$

From this information, we deduce that the explicit projection for the polymorphic deconstructor is $(\texttt{pcall } I_{constr}\bowtie^{\sim} \; T_{ret} \; T_{i=1}^{n})$. In the `all-pos?` example, T_{ret} is `bool` and T_{disc} is `(listof int)`, so both `null~` and `cons~` must be projected on the types `bool` and `int`.

We also deduce that the argument types of the success continuation should be the result of substituting the types $T_{i=1}^{n}$ for the `forall`-bound type identifiers $\tau_{i=1}^{n}$ in the constructor argument types $T'^{\,m}_{\,j=1}$. E.g., since `cons` has type

$$\texttt{(forall (t) (-> (t (listof t)) (listof t)))}$$

when deconstructing a discriminant with type `(listof int)`, the success continuation for the pattern `(cons y ys)` should have the form

$$\texttt{(abs ((y } [\texttt{int/t}]\texttt{t) (ys } [\texttt{int/t}]\texttt{(listof t))) ...)}$$
$$= \texttt{(abs ((y int) (ys (listof int))) ...)}$$

In our approach, the `match` desugaring needs to know the type of the discriminant expression and the type of the whole `match` expression. Since the desugaring phase *precedes* the type-checking phase in FLEX/M, the `match` desugaring cannot be performed in the usual desugaring phase. So we perform the expansion of `match` in a separate match-expansion phase that follows type checking (though it is also possible to perform the `match` desugaring simultaneously with type checking). This implies that we need a type rule for type-checking `match`. We also need to modify the desugaring functions from Figure 10.27 on page 603 to take extra arguments with type information and use this information as sketched above. A complete description of the `match` type rule and the typed versions of the `match` desugaring functions can be found in the Web Supplement.

15.5 Dynamic Semantics of FLEX/M Modules

We now consider the dynamic semantics of FLEX/M module constructs except for `load`, whose dynamic semantics is discussed in Section 15.6. As shown in Figure 15.19, the dynamic semantics of these constructs can be defined via a type-erasure function that maps well-typed FLEX/M expressions to expressions

Dynamic Semantics (via Type Erasure)

$erase : \text{Exp}_{FLEX/M} \to \text{TypeEnvironment} \to \text{Exp}_{FLIC+\{\texttt{def-data}\}}$
$\quad (\lceil E \rceil^{TE} \text{ abbreviates } (erase\ E\ TE))$

$\lceil (\texttt{module}\ DD_{i=1}^{m}\ (\texttt{def}\ I_j\ T_j\ E_j)_{j=1}^{n}) \rceil^{TE}$
$\quad = (\texttt{recordrec}\ (I_{dd_k}\ E_{dd_k})_{k=1}^{p}\ (I_j\ \lceil E_j \rceil^{TE'})_{j=1}^{n})$
$\qquad \text{where } \mathcal{DS}_{def}[\![\lceil DD_1 \rceil_{DD}]\!] @ \cdots @ \mathcal{DS}_{def}[\![\lceil DD_m \rceil_{DD}]\!] = [(\texttt{def}\ I_{dd_k}\ E_{dd_k})_{k=1}^{p}]$
$\qquad\qquad \text{using the } \mathcal{DS}_{def} \text{ function from Figure 10.21 on page 587}$
$\qquad\qquad \text{and } TE' = TE[I_j : T_j]_{j=1}^{n}$

$\lceil (\texttt{open}\ E_{mod}\ E_{body}) \rceil^{TE} = (\texttt{with-fields}\ (I_{j=1}^{n})\ \lceil E_{mod} \rceil^{TE}\ \lceil E_{body} \rceil^{TE'}),$
$\quad \text{where } typeof\ \langle E_{mod}, TE \rangle = (\texttt{moduleof}\ (AT_{i=1}^{m})\ (I_j\ T_j)_{j=1}^{n})$
$\qquad\qquad \text{and } TE' = TE[I_j : T_j]_{j=1}^{n}$

See Section 15.6 for the dynamic semantics of `load`.

$erase_{DD} : \text{DatatypeDefinition} \to \text{Def}_{FLIC+\{\texttt{def-data}\}}$
$\quad (\lceil DD \rceil_{DD} \text{ abbreviates } (erase_{DD}\ DD))$

$\lceil (\texttt{def-datatype}\ (\theta_{tycon}\ \tau_{i=1}^{m})\ (I_{constructor_j}\ T_{j,1}\ \ldots\ T_{j,k_j})_{j=1}^{n}) \rceil_{DD}$
$\quad = (\texttt{def-data}\ I_{tycon}\ (I_{constructor_j}\ \texttt{x}_1\ \ldots\ \texttt{x}_{k_j})_{j=1}^{n}),$
$\qquad \text{where } I_{tycon} \text{ is a FLIC expression identifier with the same name as } \theta_{tycon}.$

Figure 15.19   Dynamic semantics for FLEX/M expressed via type erasure.

in FLIC+{`def-data`}, a version of the dynamically typed FLIC language that
supports records, oneofs, and sum-of-products data declarations. The type erasure of a FLEX/M expression E, written $\lceil E \rceil^{TE}$, is performed relative to a type
environment TE in which E is well typed. As we shall see, this type-environment
argument is needed for the type erasure of `open` expressions.

A `module` expression behaves like a record that has bindings for the constructor and deconstructor procedures introduced by the data-type declarations in
addition to the value bindings declared by the module. All value names declared
by the module (including constructor and deconstructor names) are bound in a
single mutually recursive scope, as indicated by the use of `recordrec` (defined in
Figure 7.17 on page 355) in the `module` type erasure. The constructor and deconstructor procedures for a FLEX/M data-type declaration DD are obtained by
using $\lceil DD \rceil_{DD}$ (defined at the bottom of Figure 15.19) to erase a data-type definition to a corresponding `def-data` declaration in FLIC+{`def-data`}, and then
using the $\mathcal{DS}_{def}$ function from Figure 10.21 on page 587 to map this `def-data`
declaration to a sequence of procedure definitions for the constructors and deconstructors.

(open E_{mod} E_{body}) evaluates E_{body} relative to the current environment extended with bindings for all the components of the record denoted by E_{mod}. The environment extension is expressed using the **with-fields** construct defined in Figure 7.17 on page 355. In a dynamically typed language, such a construct requires an explicit list of names to be extracted from the record. The type-environment argument to the type erasure function is used to find the **moduleof** type of E_{mod}, from which the names required by **with-fields** can be determined.

15.6 Loading Modules

The **load** construct supports the development and construction of large programs by allowing separately developed program modules to refer to one another. Loading files in a system with first-class modules and dependent types represents a fascinating design challenge that reinforces the relationships between static and dynamic semantics, between dependent types and side effects, and between the programming language itself and the external programming environment. Many of the challenges and tradeoffs we examine apply equally to apparently simpler and more conventional systems, such as JAVA.

First, we must establish the unit of separate compilation and loading. We insist that the unit of compilation be a single pure FLEX/M expression that has no free identifiers apart from references to the standard library, i.e., an expression whose value does not depend on the store and whose type does not depend on the context into which it is loaded. Although this expression may have any type, typically it will denote a module or functor. The requirement that the expression be pure is important for guaranteeing that **load** expressions themselves are pure and so can be used in conjunction with **dselect**. For example, if the list module discussed earlier has been compiled to the file **listmod.flxm**, then we can write (dselect listof (load listmod.flxm $T_{listModule}$)).

The compilation process performs type checking on a source expression E_Y and stores some compiled representation of this expression in the compiled file named Y. To describe a source-level dynamic semantics of the compiled expression, we assume it is possible to extract E_Y from the compiled file using the notation $fileExp(Y)^8$ even though a practical system will typically not store the source expression. To describe the static semantics of the compiled expression, we

---

[8] $fileExp(Y)$ stands for the source expression associated with the code currently in the file named Y. It is undefined if the file system does not currently have a file named Y. Note that $fileExp$ cannot be a function because it depends on the time-changing state of the file system, which is not an explicit argument.

assume it is possible to extract from the compiled file the type T_Y that the compiler determined for E_Y using the notation $fileType(Y)$. Some practical systems, e.g., JAVA, do store type information in compiled files.

At a certain level, loading a compiled file Y is not terribly complex — the static and dynamic semantics of the loaded file are the static and dynamic semantics of the source expression $fileExp(Y)$. But there are three issues that complicate matters:

1. *File-Type Coherence:* File systems are mutable, so the contents of a file, and therefore its type, may change over time. References to file contents must be carefully integrated into any statically typed language, which cannot abide expressions whose type changes over time.

2. *File-Value Coherence:* Some systems require that loading a file with a given name always have the same *value* throughout the execution of a program. A system based on static dependent types needs this for type soundness, because statically computed type constructors of the form (dselect θ (load Y T)) would be ill defined otherwise. This issue is not unique to SDT-based systems, however. For example, any reference to a JAVA class might cause the class file to be loaded, and all such references must refer to the same class object.[9]

3. *Type Soundness:* There are two distinct types associated with file loading: the static type T_{load} that the client expects from the expression (load Y T_{load}) and the dynamic type $fileType(Y)$ of the expression $fileExp(Y)$ loaded from the file Y. We expect that (load Y T_{load}) should behave like the expression (the T_{load} $fileExp(Y)$). Because of the subtyping performed by the, type soundness requires that $fileType(Y)$ must be a subtype of T_{load} at run time. We will discuss two strategies for ensuring the type soundness of load:

   (a) checking that $fileType(Y)$ is a subtype of T_{load} at load time;

   (b) checking that $fileType(Y)$ is a subtype of T_{load} at compile time, and guaranteeing that the type of the file Y does not change between compile time and load time.

   We will see that the issue of file-type coherence complicates the second strategy. We will then discuss the issue of file-value coherence, which is largely independent of the type soundness discussion.

---

[9]In addition to type soundness issues similar to those in SDT-based systems, JAVA must also address potential side effects in class initialization code that is executed when a class is loaded. To guarantee that this code is executed at most once, a class file is loaded only at the first dynamic reference. Subsequent references use a class object cached from the first load.

Static Semantics

$$TE \vdash (\texttt{load}\ \ Y\ \ T_{load}) : T_{load} \qquad\qquad [load_{LTstat}]$$

Dynamic Semantics

$$(\texttt{load}\ \ Y\ \ T_{load}) \rightsquigarrow \textbf{if}\ \ fileType(Y) \sqsubseteq T_{load}\ \ \textbf{then}\ \ fileExp(Y) \qquad [load_{LTdyn}]$$
$$\textbf{else}\ \ (\texttt{error load-type-mismatch}\ T_{load})\ \textbf{end}$$

Figure 15.20 Semantics of `load` based on load-time type comparison.

15.6.1 Type Soundness of `load` via a Load-Time Check

Perhaps the simplest strategy for guaranteeing type soundness is to check at *load time* that the type supplied by the loaded file is a subtype of the type expected by the client of the `load` expression (Figure 15.20). In this strategy, the type-checking rule for $(\texttt{load}\ \ Y\ \ T_{load})$ is trivial: the type checker simply accepts that T_{load} is the type of the loaded file and leaves verification of this fact to the run-time system. This dynamic test is expressed by the test $fileType(Y) \sqsubseteq T_{load}$ in the operational semantics rewrite rule for the `load` expression. If the test succeeds, the `load` expression has the same semantics as the source expression $fileExp(Y)$ associated with the file. If the test fails, the `load` expression produces an error indicating a load-time type mismatch.[10]

Load-time checking is easy to understand and facilitates separate compilation. The file Y mentioned in a client's `load` expression need not even exist when the client is compiled, so program files can be written and compiled (and recompiled) in any order.

However, the load-time checking strategy has two key disadvantages. First, there is time overhead associated with extracting the type $fileType(Y)$ from the compiled file and comparing it with the type T_{load} of the `load` expression.[11] The second disadvantage is more philosophical in nature: performing a dynamic type check is fundamentally at odds with the discipline of static type checking! Since the goal of static type checking is to eliminate dynamic type errors, it is disturbing that `load` can encounter a `load-type-mismatch` error.

On the other hand, as we shall see, it is difficult to statically guarantee type safety in a time-changing file storage medium, so we may be willing to treat dynamic type errors associated with file loading as acceptable. After all, since it is also necessary to check when loading a file that a file with the given name

---

[10]For simplicity, the operational semantics is assumed to be specified in terms of source-level expressions. In practice, loading a compiled file would execute compiled code whose behavior should be the same as the source-level behavior.

[11]There is also a space overhead for storing type information in the compiled file, but almost all the strategies we discuss require this overhead.

exists, it does not seem unreasonable to check that a file with the given name is
type-compatible with the executing program.

15.6.2   Type Soundness of `load` via a Compile-Time Check

A second strategy for ensuring the type soundness of `load` is to check at *compile
time* that the type supplied by the file Y to be loaded is a subtype of the type
expected by the client of the `load` expression (Figure 15.21). But there's a
problem: the type of file Y may change between the time the client is compiled
(when the type comparison is performed) and the time when the client is run
(when file Y is loaded). There are two solutions to this problem:

1. *Prevent the type of file Y from changing between compile time and run time.*
   For example, the compiler can effectively load the file at compile time by
   textually including the contents of file Y at the point of the load, as with
   C's `#include` file-inclusion declaration. (Other techniques for guaranteeing
   the immutability of file Y's type are explored in the Web Supplement.) This
   approach promises true static type checking. Since no change is allowed that
   would undermine the validity of the type equivalence proven at compile-time,
   this equivalence is guaranteed at load time, and there is no need for any load-
   time type checks.

2. *Check that the type of file Y has not changed between compile time and run
   time.* The code emitted by the compiler for (`load` Y T_{load}) can include a
   proxy for file Y's type (such as a unique file identifier, a version number, or
   a fingerprint of the file's content or type) that can be used to verify at load
   time that the type has not changed since compile time. This is really a hybrid
   strategy, since it implies some sort of load-time check in addition to the type
   check performed at compile time. This check can be much more efficient than
   the full load-time type check implied by the $[load_{LTdyn}]$ rule.

   For example, JAVA uses this hybrid strategy to load class files. Consider
   compiling a JAVA class `B` that manipulates instances of class `A`. The JAVA
   compiler uses the compile-time implementation of class `A` to determine the
   argument and result types for methods from class `A`, so these do not need to
   be explicitly specified by the programmer.[12] However, when class `B` is loaded
   (potentially on a different machine having a different file system than the one
   on which it was compiled), the JAVA class loader must find an implementation
   of class `A` and verify that this implementation satisfies the requirements on `A`
   discovered when compiling `B`.

---

[12] JAVA programmers can specify method types explicitly via so-called interface types, but
they are not required to do this.

Static Semantics

$$\frac{TE_{std} \vdash \mathit{fileExp}(Y) : T_Y \qquad T_Y \sqsubseteq T_{load}}{TE \vdash (\texttt{load } Y \ T_{load}) : T_{load}} \qquad [\mathit{load}_{CTstat}]$$

where TE_{std} has bindings for all names in the standard library.

Dynamic Semantics

$$(\texttt{load } Y \ T_{load}) \rightsquigarrow \mathit{fileExp}(Y) \qquad [\mathit{load}_{CTdyn}]$$

where the type $\mathit{fileType}(Y)$ of file Y has not changed
since type-checking time, as discussed in the text.

Figure 15.21 Semantics of `load` based on compile-time type comparison.

An important problem with any approach based on a compile-time type check
for the loaded file is that it potentially puts cumbersome constraints on program
development. If file B loads file A, then it is necessary to write and compile
A before compiling B so that the type of the code in A can be available when
type-checking B. Any change to A suggests the need to recompile B. In essence,
the `load` statements in a set of program files induces a **load dependency** graph
that constrains the compilation sequence. In particular, the dependencies must be
acyclic if there is to be a well-defined compilation order. Thus, these dependencies
are incompatible with the goal of separate compilation, and they prohibit modules
that load each other recursively.

However, in FLEX/M, this problem is far less severe than it might otherwise
seem because of the presence of first-class modules. A **functorization** technique
can be used to reestablish separate compilation for strategies based on a compile-
time type check for the loaded file. Any module that loads other modules can
be transformed into a functor that performs no loads but instead takes the modules that would have been loaded as arguments. In the functorization strategy,
functors can be supplied with their argument modules in a single top-level module that performs all loading and linking. For example, if the source code for a
`use-stack.flxm` file is

```
(open (load stack.flxm T_stackModule) E_body)
```

then we create a program `use-stack-functor.flxm` whose source code is

```
(abs ((stack-module T_stackModule))
  (open stack-module E_body))
```

Whereas compile-time checks would require `stack.flxm` to be compiled before
`use-stack.flxm`, the functor expression can be compiled before `stack.flxm` is
compiled or even written. The stack-module compilation can be delayed until it

actually becomes necessary to run the original program, which is accomplished
in the following expression:

```
((load use-stack-functor.flxm (-> (T_stackModule) T_body))
 (load stack.flxm T_stackModule))
```

Functorization can even be used to compile modules that have recursive dependencies — as long as the programmer is familiar with the Y operator (see Exercise 15.5).

15.6.3   Referential Transparency of `load` for File-Value Coherence

The rules in Figures 15.20 and 15.21 do not address the file-value coherence issue mentioned earlier. The soundness of our SDT-based type system depends critically on the referential transparency of `load` expressions. That is, every time a (`load` Y T_{load}) expression is encountered during the execution of a program, it must evaluate to the same *value*, not just have the same type. To see what can go wrong if this assumption is violated, consider the following rational-number example:

$$T_{ratMod} = \texttt{(moduleof ((ratof))}$$
$$\texttt{(make-rat (-> (int int) (ratof)))}$$
$$\texttt{(numer (-> ((ratof)) int))}$$
$$\texttt{(denom (-> ((ratof)) int)))}$$

$$E_{ratTest} = \texttt{((open (load ratFile } T_{ratMod}\texttt{) denom)}$$
$$\texttt{(open (load ratFile } T_{ratMod}\texttt{) (make-rat 3 4)))}$$

$$T_{dselectRat} = \texttt{((dselect ratof (load ratFile } T_{ratMod}\texttt{)))}$$

In FLEX/M, the expression $E_{ratTest}$ is well typed because the first **open** expression has type (-> ($T_{dselectRat}$) int) and the second **open** expression has type $T_{dselectRat}$. However, since the file system is mutable and external to FLEX/M program execution, it is possible that between the evaluation of the two **open** expressions, a programmer changes the contents of `ratFile` to be a new module that has the same type T_{ratMod} but uses a new representation for rational numbers that is incompatible with the previous one (e.g., rational numbers are represented as procedures rather than as pairs). In this case, no error would be detected by the load-time type check in the [$load_{LTdyn}$] rule, but a dynamic type error will occur when the **denom** procedure from the first representation is applied to a rational number created by **make-rat** from the second representation.

In the Web Supplement we discuss some techniques for guaranteeing the referential transparency of `load` expressions.

```
T_A = (moduleof () (f (-> (int) int)))
T_B = (moduleof () (g (-> (int) int)))
E_A = (module (def f (-> (int) int)
                (abs ((x int))
                  (if (= x 0)
                      0
                      ((open (load B.flxm T_B) g) (- x 1))))))
E_B = (module (def g (-> (int) int)
                (abs ((y int))
                  (if (= y 0)
                      1
                      (+ ((open (load A.flxm T_A) f) (- y 1))
                         (g (- y 1)))))))
E_C = (let ((amod (load A.flxm T_A))
            (bmod (load B.flxm T_B)))
        (+ (open amod (f 3)) (open bmod (g 3))))
```

Figure 15.22 Types and expressions illustrating modules that load each other recursively. Assume that expression E_A is compiled to the file `A.flxm` and E_B is compiled to the file `B.flxm`.

Exercise 15.5 The types and expressions in Figure 15.22 illustrate how FLEX/M modules can load each other recursively. Assume that expression E_A is compiled to the file `A.flxm` and E_B is compiled to the file `B.flxm`.

a. In a system that uses a load-time type check for loaded files (Figure 15.20), show that expressions E_A, E_B, and E_C are all well typed and that E_C does not encounter a `load-type-mismatch` error when executed. Is there any constraint on the order in which E_A and E_B are compiled?

b. Consider a system that uses a compile-time type check for loaded files (Figure 15.21), e.g., by using compile-time file inclusion or a load-time check of a file version number.

   i.   Explain why it is impossible to successfully compile E_A and E_B.

   ii. Using a modified version of the functorization technique, show that it is possible to transform E_A, E_B, and E_C into E'_A, E'_B, and E'_C such that (1) E'_A and E'_B can be compiled in any order before E'_C is type-checked and executed and (2) executing E'_C will return the desired result. *Hint:* It may help to review the Y operator from page 303. E'_A and E'_B should not be modules that directly load modules from particular files; instead, each should be a functor parameterized over a module-returning thunk and should reference another module by dethunking this parameter. The loading of the compiled files for E'_A and E'_B should take place in E'_C, which is also responsible for constructing the thunks expected by E'_A and E'_B and "tying the knot" of recursion.

15.7   Discussion

Unifying the programming and linking languages via `load` and first-class modules
is very powerful. As illustrated above, the creation, instantiation, and linking of
parameterized modules are easily accomplished with ordinary procedures and
application. It is also possible to conditionally choose which modules to load at
run time, as in the following procedure:

```
(abs ((data T_data))
  (open (if (sparse? data)
            (load sparse-matrix-module.flxm T_matrixModule)
            (load dense-matrix-module.flxm T_matrixModule))
    ... code performing matrix manipulations on data ...))
```

The ability to use arbitrary computation when linking program components permits idioms that are not expressible in most linking languages. Although this system guarantees static type checking during a separate compilation phase, linking
is not a separate phase from computation, and may not terminate.

Although powerful, the simple module facility described here has several
shortcomings, which are described in the remainder of this section.

15.7.1   Scoping Limitations

In a FLEX/M module value-component definition (`def` I T E), the scope of
the name I includes the expressions of all other `def` declarations in the module
but not their types. This makes it easy to define mutually recursive procedures,
but prevents the type of one component from depending on the value of another
component. To see why one might want to do this, consider the following example,
in which the definition of the `make-point` procedure opens the `pair-mod` module:

$$E_{illegal} = \text{(module ()}$$
```
        (def pair-mod (moduleof ((pairof s t))
                          (pair (forall (s t)
                                    (-> (s t) (pairof s t)))))
                      ... )
          (module (def-datatype (pairof s t) (pair s t))))
        (def make-point (-> (int int)
                            ((dselect pairof pair-mod) int int))
            (open pair-mod
              (abs ((x int) (y int))
                (pair x y)))))
```

The declared type of `make-point` is consistent with the type of the expression
(`open pair-mod ...`). However, this type uses the name `pair-mod`, which by
the scoping rules for `module` is not in scope within $T_{makePoint}$. So the FLEX/M
scoping restriction prohibits us from writing this module expression.

The scoping restriction is a consequence of our design choice that `def` declarations in a module should be mutually recursive with respect to their expressions
but should not be in the scope of their types. This choice was made to simplify
the [*moduleof-elim*] type rule.

Alternatively, we could have decided that `def` declarations should be sequential, in which case the scope of a name defined by such a declaration would include
the expressions *and* types of subsequent definitions. In this alternative approach,
$E_{illegal}$ would be a well-typed expression. However, there are drawbacks to this
approach: (1) such a system would need a separate `letrec` expression (it would
no longer be sugar for `open`ing a `module`); (2) defining mutually recursive procedures in a module would be more cumbersome; and (3) the scoping and type
rules for `module` would be more complex.

15.7.2 Lack of Transparent and Translucent Types

In FLEX/M, every type constructor is **opaque** in the sense that its implementation is abstract and can never be seen outside the module in which it is defined.
The only way to manipulate an element whose type mentions an abstract type
constructor is to use the type-converting capabilities of its associated constructor
and deconstructor procedures.

In a full-fledged module system, it is also desirable for modules and signatures
to have named type components that are specified by **transparent** type definitions, whose concrete implementations are visible to any client of the module
or its signature. For example, a signature for a module of function transformations might include transparent definitions like `intfun` for (`-> (int) int`)
and `transform` for (`-> (intfun) intfun`). Like the `let-type` sugar in FLEX,
transparent definitions allow clients to use a short name like `transform` in place
of the complex type (`-> ((-> (intfun) intfun)) (-> (intfun) intfun)`) it
abbreviates (and to which it is type-equivalent). Because the scope of transparent
definitions typically includes the rest of the signature or module in which they
appear, such abbreviations also help the implementer to significantly simplify the
types mentioned later in these constructs.

Although FLEX/M does not support transparent type definitions, it would
be easy to add them; we omitted them to simplify the module system. Indeed,
the design of FLEX/M is inspired by FX-91, a language whose module system
supports both opaque and transparent type definitions.

In FX-91, transparent and opaque type definitions are two distinct categories; once a type name is defined, its category cannot change. The SML module system uses a more flexible approach to type definitions that has important practical benefits. In an SML module, a type name may either be transparent (defined to be synonymous with a type) or opaque (having no type definition). Unlike FLEX/M's opaque types, which are always abstract, SML's opaque types are **translucent** in the sense that they can later be refined to partially or fully transparent types by a unification-like process called **signature matching** [HL94]. For instance, if a module type component initially specified as `type r` is matched against a signature with the definition `type r = s -> t`, then it acquires the latter definition. If later `s` is refined to `int` and `t` is refined to `bool`, it is as if the original specification were expanded to `type r = int -> bool`.

Signature matching facilitates expressing functors that can propagate concrete type information. Let's revisit the table-module functor from Figure 15.12 on page 907, which is parameterized over a key module having (1) a key type and (2) an equality procedure on elements of this type. In FLEX/M (as in FX-91), the fact that the key type must be abstract requires that cumbersome conversions be used between the concrete key type (such as `symb`) and the abstract key type in a table module that results from invoking the functor. When the table-module functor example is expressed in SML (see the Web Supplement for details), signature matching allows the concrete key type to be used directly in the `bind` and `lookup` procedures of the resulting table module.

With translucency, an opaque type definition in a module is not necessarily abstract; it is simply unknown, and may later be refined. Some additional mechanism must be used to specify abstract types. In SML, this is done by **sealing** a signature, which prevents the signature-matching process from further refining any opaque type names mentioned in the signature. So abstract types in modules can be specified by module signatures (the approach taken in SML) rather than by using procedures that convert between the concrete and abstract types (the approach taken in FLEX/M and FX-91).

Although translucency has significant benefits, formalizing it requires additional technical machinery beyond the scope of this book. For a high-level discussion of translucency, consult [HP05]; for a technical overview, see [HL94].

15.7.3   The Coherence Problem

In FLEX/M, it is difficult to express type relationships that must hold among modules, such as the submodules of a module or the module arguments of a functor. This is known as the **coherence problem** [HP05].

For example, consider a simple two-stage compiler that parses a string into an abstract syntax tree (AST) and then generates output code for the AST. For simplicity, we assume the output code is also represented as a string. Suppose that there are parser and code generator modules with the following types, in which (astof) is the AST type:

$$T_{parserMod} = \text{(moduleof ((astof))}$$
$$\text{(parse (-> (string) (astof))))}$$

$$T_{generatorMod} = \text{(moduleof ((astof))}$$
$$\text{(codegen (-> ((astof)) string)))}$$

Then we might expect to be able to write a functor that creates a compiler by composing a parser module and a code generator module:

$$E_{makeCompiler} = \text{(abs ((parser } T_{parserMod}\text{) (generator } T_{generatorMod}\text{))}$$
$$\text{(abs ((pgm string)) } \{compilation\ procedure\}$$
$$\text{((open generator codegen)}$$
$$\text{((open parser parse) pgm))))}$$

However, such a functor is ill typed! (open parser parse) has type

```
(-> (string) ((dselect astof parser)))
```

but (open generator codegen) has type

```
(-> (((dselect astof generator))) string)
```

Because the variable references parser and generator are not syntactically identical, the body of the functor fails to type-check.

The problem here is that there is no guarantee that the two modules use the same implementation of astof. If they do use different implementations, then it is not safe for the generator to use an AST created by the parser. So the type checker is correctly reporting a potential problem. Indeed, because all FLEX/M type constructors are opaque, two modules that happen to have the same abstract type constructor names can *never* have interoperable data values whose types mention these constructors.

However, there are situations where the programmer knows that the same AST implementation is shared by the parser and code generator. How can the programmer convey this sharing knowledge to the type checker so that the compilation functor will type check?

One approach, known as **sharing by construction**, is to reorganize the program to make the sharing explicit. For example, we can remove the parse and codegen procedures from modules and instead abstract them over an AST module described by a suitable type T_{astMod}:

$$T_{makeParser} = \texttt{(-> ((ast1 } T_{astMod}\texttt{))}$$
$$\texttt{(-> (string) ((dselect astof ast1))))}$$

$$T_{makeGenerator} = \texttt{(-> ((ast2 } T_{astMod}\texttt{))}$$
$$\texttt{(-> (((dselect astof ast2))) string))}$$

Then we can write a procedure that combines these abstracted procedures:

$$E'_{makeCompiler} = \texttt{(abs ((make-parser } T_{makeParser}\texttt{)}$$
$$\texttt{(make-generator } T_{makeGenerator}\texttt{)}$$
$$\texttt{(ast3 } T_{astMod}\texttt{))}$$
$$\texttt{(let ((parser (make-parser ast3))}$$
$$\texttt{(codegen (make-generator ast3)))}$$
$$\texttt{(abs ((pgm string)) \{\textit{compilation procedure}\}}$$
$$\texttt{(codegen (parser pgm)))))}$$

In addition to taking arguments with types $T_{makeParser}$ and $T_{makeGenerator}$, this procedure also takes an AST module `ast3` that it uses to create both the `parser` and `codegen` procedures, thus ensuring they share the same AST implementation. According to the type rule for procedure application in a dependent type system, `parser = (make-parser ast3)` has type

```
(-> (string) ((dselect astof ast3)))
```

and `codegen = (make-generator ast3)` has type

```
(-> (((dselect astof ast3))) string)
```

so these two functions can interoperate as desired.

Although sharing by construction solves the coherence problem, it requires reorganizing the program to get the right plumbing for the sharing information. Along the way, it may be necessary to break abstraction/module boundaries to expose the units of sharing. For instance, in the compiler example, it is necessary to move the the `parse` and `codegen` procedures out of modules with different (as far as the type checker is concerned) `astof` type constructors and instead parameterize them over an AST module with this constructor. The reorganization is not so bad in this example, but in an example of realistic complexity it can lead to a plumbing nightmare.

An alternative solution to the coherence problem, known as **sharing by specification**, is to allow sharing declarations that indicate relationships that hold between modules mentioned in a type. This is the approach taken in the SML module system. For example, an SML functor for combining a parser module `Parser` with a code generator module `Generator` can specify that both modules must use the same AST type `ast` via the following sharing declaration:

```
sharing type Parser.ast = Generator.ast
```

Applications of the functor are well typed only when this sharing constraint is satisfied by the argument modules. As hinted at by this example, the sharing-by-specification approach to the coherence problem is more elegant than the sharing-by-construction approach. It allows sharing to be specified by adding declarations to a program without changing its plumbing or exposing implementation details that should remain hidden; e.g., specifying that `Parser` and `Generator` have the same `ast` type in SML does not divulge *how* they share the type. Thus, sharing by specification would seem to scale more readily to large programs (see [HP05]).

In SML, the sharing-by-specification approach depends on translucent type definitions, which FLEX/M does not support. There is thus no straightforward way to add this feature to FLEX/M.

15.7.4 Purity Issues

The FLEX/M module system requires that certain expressions be pure — i.e., they cannot allocate, read, or write any store locations. In particular:

- an argument expression of a dependent procedure application must be pure if the associated parameter name appears in the result type of the application;

- a definition expression of a `let` expression must be pure if its name appears in the result type of the body expression;

- the expression denoting the module opened by `open` must be pure;

- the expression compiled to yield a `load`able file must be pure.

These restrictions guarantee that any expression E_{mod} appearing in a dependent type constructor (`dselect` θ E_{mod}) is pure. Since all occurrences of a pure module expression E_{mod} in the same environment denote the same module value, all occurrences of (`dselect` θ E_{mod}) in the same environment denote the same abstract-type constructor.

These purity restrictions can get in the way of practical programming, where it may be necessary for certain module expressions to perform side effects. For example, if each instance of a mutable-table data structure is represented as a module, then an expression $E_{newTable}$ that creates a new table will allocate one or more locations in the store. There are workarounds for these situations in FLEX/M. For example, thunking $E_{newTable}$ allows it to be compiled and loaded; every invocation of this thunk creates a new table. Although $E_{newTable}$ cannot be opened directly, it is possible to open a table instance that has been named via let because names are pure:

```
(let ((tbl E_{newTable}))
  (open tbl ...)
```

For similar reasons, many module systems have immutable module names and require type components to be selected from names (or a path of identifiers, like library.trees.bst) rather than from arbitrary module expressions.

A simple way to determine expression purity is to use the syntactic purity test defined in Figure 13.25 on page 816. However, in the presence of parameterized modules, there is a fundamental problem with using this crude test to conservatively approximate which module expressions do not touch the store. To see this, consider the following example, which uses some expressions from the table-module example in Figure 15.12 on page 907:

$$E_{escape} = \text{(let ((sym-key-mod } E_{symKeyMod}))$$
$$\text{(let ((env-table-mod (}E_{makeTableModule} \text{ sym-key-mod)))}$$
$$\text{(open sym-key-mod}$$
$$\text{(open env-table-mod}$$
$$\text{(bind (sym->key (sym a)) 1}$$
$$\text{((pcall empty int)))))))}$$

In this case, the type of the bind application and both open expressions is

```
((dselect tableof env-table-mod) int)
```

Because of the substitutions performed on the way out of the [let] rule, the inner let would have the type

```
((dselect tableof (E_{makeTableModule} sym-key-mod)) int)
```

and the outer let would have the type

```
((dselect tableof (E_{makeTableModule} E_{symKeyMode})) int)
```

The problem with the last two types is that both module expressions in the dselects are applications and therefore are not pure according to the syntactic purity test. Even though both applications do not touch the store and so are actually pure, the conservative syntactic test causes type checking to fail. This sort of failure will occur whenever an attempt is made to export a type containing an abstract type from a parameterized module outside the scope of an application of the functor creating that module.

We have seen that a syntactic purity test imposes a kind of export restriction on abstract values, thereby reducing the power of the module system. This problem can be mitigated somewhat by using `let` to introduce names for applications, as in the `let` binding of `env-table-mod`, without which the inner `open` expression would be ill typed (because ($E_{makeTableModule}$ `sym-key-mod`) is not syntactically pure). But `let` only locally increases the scope in which subexpressions are well typed and cannot remove what is effectively the same export restriction that plagues existential package systems.

Another way to address this problem is to define a class of functors — so-called **applicative functors** — whose application is necessarily pure. These stand in contrast to **generative functors**, whose application may be impure. Although different occurrences of the same generative-functor application might denote different modules, different occurrences of the same applicative functor application must denote the same module. OCAML's functors are applicative whereas SML's functors are generative.

What we really need is a more accurate way to determine the purity of an expression. This is the subject of the next chapter.

Exercise 15.6 Assume that $E_{stackMod1}$, $E_{stackMod2}$, and $E_{makeReverseStack}$ are the solutions to the parts of Exercise 15.2 on page 909. (You do not have to solve that exercise to do this one.) Consider the following FLEX/M expression context:

$$\mathbb{E}_{test} = \texttt{(let ((sm1 } E_{stackMod1}\texttt{)}$$
$$\texttt{(sm2 } E_{stackMod2}\texttt{)}$$
$$\texttt{(make-reverse-stack } E_{makeReverseStack}\texttt{))}$$
$$\texttt{(let ((rsm1 (make-reverse-stack sm1))}$$
$$\texttt{(rsm2 (make-reverse-stack sm2)))}$$
$$\square\texttt{))}$$

For each of the following expressions, indicate whether the result of filling the hole in $\mathbb{E}_{test}$ with the expression is well typed in FLEX/M. Explain your answers.

a. `(open sm1 ((pcall push int) 1 ((pcall empty int))))`

b. `((pcall (open sm1 push) int) 1 ((pcall (open sm1 empty) int)))`

c. `((pcall (open sm1 push) int) 1 ((pcall (open sm2 empty) int)))`

d. `(open rsm1 ((pcall push int) 1 ((pcall empty int))))`

e. `(open rsm1 ((pcall empty? int) ((pcall empty int))))`

f. `((pcall (open rsm1 empty?) int) ((pcall (open rsm1 empty) int)))`

g. `((pcall (open rsm1 empty?) int) ((pcall (open rsm2 empty) int)))`

h. `((pcall (open rsm1 empty?) int) ((pcall (open sm1 empty) int)))`

Notes

As mentioned in Section 14.5.2, the design of module systems is intimately related to the notion of abstract type. The interested reader should look there for additional notes related specifically to abstract types.

The module system presented in this chapter is based on the FX-91 module system [GJSO92], which supported first-class modules, static dependent types, type and effect inference, explicit and implicit polymorphism, and transparent and opaque bindings for types and descriptions of higher kind. FX-91 also supported constructors for abstract sum-of-products types and a pattern-matching facility. Implicit projection was introduced in FX-87 [GJLS87].

[HP05] discusses important issues in module design. [Mit96, pp. 692–701] shows how to formalize a module/abstract data-type system with functors using product and sum types. Sum types can be used to describe dependent types. This section ends with a theoretical discussion of the tradeoff between expressive power and static type checking.

In software engineering, there is traditionally a strong correspondence between the unit of program modularity (from the point of view of the programmer) and compilation units (from the point of view of the compiler and linker) [Ler94]. These ideas are essentially the same in our module system, as they were in Modula-2 [Wir85], CLU, and many other languages.

The CLU language tied program modules to the notion of abstract data types: every program module, called a *cluster*, defines a single, perhaps parameterized, type and its associated operations. The programmer specifies abstraction boundaries by using the cvt keyword to mark conversions between the abstract type and its representation. CLU also has a mechanism for importing a cluster and requiring that it support particular operations. For example, one can require that the type of an object inserted into a generic hash table support a comparison operation. This is essentially a kind of bounded quantification on module types.

The ML language has served as the foundation for several sophisticated module systems. The original ML module system, due to David MacQueen [Mac84, Mac88], was based on a second-class module language that was well integrated with the base language and supported type reconstruction. [Mit96] describes the ML module system in some detail. Dependent types were used to express modular structure [Mac86]. [Ler95] investigates an SML-based module system that eliminates the need for generative types (with their attendant operational character) by using applicative functors that always return compatible abstract types when applied to equivalent arguments. [CHP99] investigated how to add recursive module dependencies into the ML module system while maintaining static type checking and ensuring that the linking process terminates.

[CHD02] attempts to build a type theory that encompasses nearly all the above work. Moscow ML [RRS00] has first-class, recursive structures and higher-order functors.

Unfortunately, the initial ML module system did not readily support separate compilation. [Rus98] (especially Chapter 6) places the blame for this problem on the choice of compilation unit and proposes a coding style that permits separate compilation in most cases. [Rus98] then goes on to explore the problem of ML's lack of syntactic interfaces for some modules.

Putting type declarations into a language with type reconstruction can lead to some surprising results. For example, it is easy to make type checking undecidable. To see how inferable and noninferable types can be combined in a decidable type system, see James O'Toole's work in [OG89].

The CAYENNE language [Aug98] uses dependent types and record types to implement program modules. In CAYENNE as in PEBBLE [BL84] (which treats types as first-class, run-time entities), type checking may fail to terminate. Early attempts to understand the ML module system were based on models with dependent types. [HMM90] showed how to develop such a model in order to enforce a phase distinction between compile time and run time.

The problems of loading modules are instances of problems related to persistence in type-safe languages. [CM85], for example, discusses the need for *identifications*, which are unique handles for objects. [Har86] discusses many of these issues (including the need for persistent type information associated with a module) in the context of the ML module system. All of these problems arise in object-oriented languages like JAVA, which dynamically loads class definitions and does substantial run-time checking [GJS96] (which can result in exceptions due to linking errors). For more general information about linking, see [Lev00].

A somewhat different approach to abstraction is based on how things work in the physical world. Simulation languages, such as Simula 67 [DMN70], sought to make it convenient to represent objects in the world with state and behavior. This approach led to the modern notion of object-oriented programming, in which abstraction is achieved by encapsulating state and behavior within objects and classes.

Simulation work also motivated various approaches to concurrent programming, notably the *actor model* developed by Carl Hewitt and others [HBS73, Hew77]. An actor is a stateful process that can respond to and send messages. C. A. R. Hoare's *communicating sequential processes (CSP)* [Hoa85] took a similar approach, which was used as the basis for the OCCAM [occ95] module system. An OCCAM module is a process definition that may be instantiated multiple times and is accessed only via its designated input and output channels.

16

Effects Describe Program Behavior

Nothing exists from whose nature some effect does not follow.
— Benedict Spinoza, *Ethics, I*, proposition 36

16.1 Types, Effects, and Regions: What, How, and Where

We have seen that types are a powerful tool for reasoning about higher-order procedures (Chapter 6), naming (Chapter 7), and data (Chapter 10). Yet types do not help us reason in detail about the behavior of programs exhibiting state (Chapter 8), control (Chapter 9), or concurrency.[1] An **effect system** is a formal system for reasoning about many of the state, control, concurrency, and storage issues that arise in practical programs. An effect system produces a concise description of the observable actions of an expression, and this description is called the **effect** of the expression. Example effects include writing into a region of the store or jumping to a nonlocal label. Just as a type describes *what* an expression computes, an effect describes *how* an expression computes.

In this chapter, we introduce effect systems and explore their applications. As we shall see, effects describe a wide variety of properties of a program that are useful to programmers, compiler writers, language designers, and even to users of applications concerned about the security of those applications. Effect systems provide improvements to documentation, safety, and execution efficiency. Documentation and safety improvements include better understanding of code behavior, such as determining how modules developed by others may modify state, perform or be the target of nonlocal jumps, or use other system resources (e.g., the file system, the display console, the network). Efficiency improvements

---

[1]Consult the Web Supplement for this book for material on concurrency.

come from increased opportunities for optimization, including better expression scheduling and storage management. For example, expressions without store dependencies can be reordered or executed in parallel as long as any data dependencies are preserved.

To make effect systems more precise and more useful, we introduce the notion of **regions** that describe *where* effects are performed. In our effect system, every object in the store resides in a single region, and the type of the object is extended to describe its region. We can think of regions as colors (red, blue, green, etc.), as distinct memory banks (bank 1, bank 2, bank 3, etc.), or even as machines or network domains (`mit.edu`, `wellesley.edu`, etc.). Regions are logical locations, and may or may not correspond to physical storage locations in a given implementation. For example, control points can be associated with regions that represent locations in code as opposed to regions in the store.

When two objects are in distinct regions, mutating one of the objects cannot cause changes to the other object. This is a consequence of our invariant that an object is only in a single region. Thus, regions can be used to prove that object references do not alias one another. **Aliasing** occurs when two distinct references refer to the same object. Aliasing can inhibit important compiler optimizations such as common subexpression elimination, code motion, dead code elimination, and caching the values of mutable objects in registers.

In this chapter, we discuss a system with both effects and regions, but it is possible to have effects without regions and regions without effects. However, there is little reason to decouple effects and regions. In the absence of regions, an effect system has only a limited repertoire of broad effects and is too coarse to be useful. In the absence of an effect system, a region system alone cannot deduce when a particular region is accessed or when it becomes inaccessible.

To produce an accurate accounting of effects we include three key changes to our type system. First, the type of every mutable object includes the object's region. Second, we account for the effect of executing a procedure in the type of the procedure as a **latent effect** that is realized when the procedure is called. Latent effects communicate the effects of a procedure from the point of the procedure's definition to its points of use. Third, we introduce the idea of effect and region polymorphism to permit procedures to have effects that depend on their input parameters.

An effect system not only must produce valuable information, but programmers must also find it easy to use. We achieve this goal by reconstructing effects and regions without programmer declarations or assistance. Early experiments with effect systems[2] showed that programmers had a difficult time composing appropriate effect declarations, and thus an effect reconstruction algorithm is necessary for practical effect systems. Since procedure types include effects, effect reconstruction naturally depends upon type reconstruction and vice versa. In this chapter, we demonstrate how to reconstruct both types and effects simultaneously and fully automatically in the FLARE language from Chapter 13.

In our study of effects, we first focus on **store effects** that describe the creation, observation, and mutation of store-based state. We then discuss how effect systems can be used to analyze a wide variety of behaviors that include control transfers, lifetime-based storage management, concurrency, exceptions, program execution time, and the security of mobile code.

16.2   A Language with a Simple Effect System

We study effects in the context of FLARE/E, which extends the implicitly typed FLARE language (from Chapter 13) with store effects. The expressions of FLARE/E are exactly the same as those of FLARE, but the types of FLARE/E include effect and region information, and the type rules of FLARE must be modified to manipulate this information appropriately. We begin by discussing the structure of FLARE/E types, effects, and regions. We then present type/effect rules for FLARE/E, show how type and effect information can be automatically reconstructed for a type/effect system with these rules, and describe a way to hide local effects from the surrounding program. We conclude this section by discussing how an effect-based purity test is superior to a syntactic purity test for generalizing types but requires a considerably more complex type reconstruction algorithm.

In this section, we use store effects for concreteness, but the concepts, rules, and algorithms we introduce for FLARE/E generalize to a broad class of effects.

16.2.1   Types, Effects, and Regions

Recall that FLARE has the store operations `cell` (allocate and initialize a cell in the store), `^` (read the content of a cell), and `:=` (write the content of a cell). The FLARE/E effect system summarizes how these operations are used in an expression. For example, the expression (`cell 5`) creates a mutable cell containing an integer in an abstract region of the store that we arbitrarily call

---

[2]For example, with the FX-87 language of [GJLS87].

r1. In FLARE/E, the type of a cell includes its region as well as the type of its content, so the type of this cell is (cellof int r1). Moreover, every FLARE/E expression has an effect as well as a type. The effect of (cell 5) is (init r1), which indicates that it allocates and initializes a cell in region r1.[3] We use the notation $E : T \, ! \, F$ to indicate that expression E has type T and effect F.[4] So we can summarize the type and effect of (cell 5) as follows:

$$(\text{cell 5}) : (\text{cellof int r1}) \, ! \, (\text{init r1})$$

As another example, consider the expression

$E_{boolcell}$ = (let ((b (cell #f))) (begin (:= b #t) (^ b)))

Here are the types and effects of three subexpressions of this expression:

$$
\begin{array}{rcl}
(\text{cell \#f}) : & (\text{cellof bool r2}) \, ! & (\text{init r2}) \\
(\text{:= b \#t}) : & \text{unit} \quad\quad ! & (\text{write r2}) \\
(\text{\^{} b}) : & \text{bool} \quad\quad ! & (\text{read r2})
\end{array}
$$

These assume that r2 is the region for the new cell created by (cell #f). (:= b #t) performs a write effect on this region and (^ b) performs a read effect on the region. The type and effect of $E_{boolcell}$ combine this information:

$$E_{boolcell} : \text{bool} \, ! \, (\text{maxeff (init r2) (write r2) (read r2)})$$

where maxeff is the means of combining all the effects performed within an expression.

The structure of types, effects, and regions in FLARE/E is summarized in Figure 16.1. The simplest effects, or **base effects**, are either effect variables (typically introduced by type schemas or the type reconstruction process) or have the form (FCR R), where FCR is an effect constructor (init for cell, read for ^, and write for :=), and R is the name of a region. The effect constructors and base effects can easily be extended to model effects other than store effects. Effects are combined with maxeff, which glues together any number of effects. So any effect expression is essentially a "maxeff tree" — a tree of maxeff nodes whose leaves are base effects.

---

[3]In FLARE/E, there is only one effect constructor, init, for both allocation and initialization, because there is no way to allocate an uninitialized cell. Separate allocation and initialization effects could be used in a language in which these operations are distinct.

[4]We will see in Section 16.2.2 that this notation is part of a type/effect judgment that in general requires a type environment. For now, we use this notation informally and omit the type environment.

The FLARE/E effect system does not keep track of the ordering of effects or the number of times a particular effect is used, so an effect is treated as a set of base effects. We formalize this by defining the meaning of an effect expression (using the function $\mathcal{F}$ defined in Figure 16.1) as the set of base effects that are its leaves when it is viewed as a `maxeff` tree. The effect-equivalence relation ($\approx_e$) and subeffect relation ($\sqsubseteq_e$) are both defined in terms of this set-based interpretation. For example, we can say that $E_{boolcell}$ has the effect

$$F'_{boolcell} = \texttt{(maxeff (maxeff (read r2) (write r2))}$$
$$\texttt{(maxeff (read r2) (init r2)))}$$

because $E_{boolcell}$ has effect $F_{boolcell} = \texttt{(maxeff (init r2) (write r2) (read r2))}$ and $F_{boolcell} \approx_e F'_{boolcell}$:

$$\mathcal{F}[\![F_{boolcell}]\!] = \{\texttt{(init r2)}, \texttt{(read r2)}, \texttt{(write r2)}\} = \mathcal{F}[\![F'_{boolcell}]\!]$$

The notion of pure expressions (expressions that do not touch the store) arose in our discussion of referential transparency (Section 8.3.6) as well as in type reconstruction for FLARE in the presence of state (Section 13.5.1). To model such expressions, we treat the effect expression `pure` as syntactic sugar for `(maxeff)`, which denotes an empty set of effects.

Under the effect-equivalence relation $\approx_e$, `maxeff` induces what is known as an **ACUI algebra** because it has the following four properties (stated for the simple case in which `maxeff` combines exactly two effects):

Associative (A):	`(maxeff` F_1 `(maxeff` F_2 F_3`))`
	$\approx_e$ `(maxeff (maxeff` F_1 F_2`)` F_3`)`
Commutative (C):	`(maxeff` F_1 F_2`)` $\approx_e$ `(maxeff` F_2 F_1`)`
Unitary (U):	`(maxeff` F `pure)` $\approx_e F$
Idempotent (I):	`(maxeff` F F`)` $\approx_e F$

This just says that `maxeff` behaves like a set-union operator on effects when they are viewed as sets of base effects. Henceforth, we will implicitly treat effects as sets of base effects without explicitly invoking $\mathcal{F}$ or $\approx_e$.

FLARE/E procedure types `(->` $(T_{i=1}^n)$ F_{latent} T_{result}`)` include an effect F_{latent}, known as the **latent effect** of the procedure type. This describes the actions performed when the procedure is called. For example, consider:

$$E_{inc\text{-}c!} = \texttt{(let ((c (cell 0)))}$$
$$\texttt{(let ((inc-c! (abs ()}$$
$$\texttt{(begin (:= c (+ 1 (^ c)))}$$
$$\texttt{(^ c)))))}$$
$$\texttt{(pair (inc-c!) (inc-c!))))}$$

Here are the types and effects of four key subexpressions of $E_{inc\text{-}c!}$:

```
(cell 0)      : (cellof int r3)          ! (init r3)
(begin ... ) : int                       ! (maxeff (read r3) (write r3))
(abs () ... ) : (-> ()
                    (maxeff (read r3)
                            (write r3))
                int)                     ! pure
(inc-c!)      : int                      ! (maxeff (read r3) (write r3))
```

We assume that cell c is allocated in region r3. The begin expression in the body of the abstraction reads and writes cell c, so it has effect

$$F_{begin} = \texttt{(maxeff (read r3) (write r3))}$$

Evaluating the abstraction (abs () ...) simply creates the inc-c! procedure and does not evaluate its body; since evaluating the abstraction does not touch the store, the abstraction is pure. However, each application of inc-c! evaluates the begin expression in its body and so has the effect F_{begin}. To communicate this effect from the body of the procedure definition to the point of procedure application, the effect F_{begin} is incorporated into the type of the procedure inc-c! as its latent effect. The type and effect of $E_{inc\text{-}c!}$ are:

$$E_{inc\text{-}c!} : \texttt{(pairof int int) ! (maxeff (init r3) (read r3) (write r3))}$$

The only nontrivial type-equivalence rule in FLARE/E is [→-≈] (see Figure 16.1), which says that two procedure types are equivalent iff their argument and result types are equivalent *and* their latent effects are equivalent — i.e., they denote the same set of base effects. For example:

```
(-> () (maxeff (read r3) (write r3)) int)
≈ (-> () (maxeff (read r3) (maxeff (write r3) (read r3))) int)
```

Henceforth, we implicitly consider two types to be the same as long as any corresponding procedure types they mention have equivalent latent effects.

Procedures in FLARE/E can be polymorphic over effects and regions as well as types. Consider the following example:

```
E_twice = (let ((bools (cell (list #t #f)))
               (ints (cell (list 1 2 3)))
               (dup! (abs (c)
                       (begin (:= c (cons (car (^ c)) (^ c)))
                              (^ c))))
               (apply-twice (abs (f x) (begin (f x) (f x)))))
          (pair (apply-twice dup! bools) (apply-twice dup! ints)))
```

Syntax

$BT \in \text{BaseType} = \{\texttt{unit}, \texttt{int}, \texttt{bool}, \texttt{symb}\}$; *as in* FLARE.

$TCR \in \text{TypeConstructor} = \{\texttt{->}, \texttt{pairof}, \texttt{listof}, \texttt{cellof}\}$

$FCR \in \text{EffectConstructor} = \{\texttt{init}, \texttt{read}, \texttt{write}\}$

$\delta \in \text{DescId} = \text{SymLit} - (\text{BaseType} \cup \text{TypeConstructor} \cup \text{EffectConstructor}$
$\qquad\qquad\qquad\qquad\qquad\qquad\qquad \cup \{\texttt{maxeff}, \texttt{generic}\})$

$T \in \text{Type} ::= \delta \mid BT \mid (\texttt{->} \ (T^*) \ F \ T)$
$\qquad\qquad \mid (\texttt{pairof} \ T \ T) \mid (\texttt{listof} \ T) \mid (\texttt{cellof} \ T \ R)$

$BF \in \text{BaseEffect} ::= \delta \mid (FCR \ R)$

$F \in \text{Effect} ::= BF \mid (\texttt{maxeff} \ F^*)$

$R \in \text{Region} ::= \delta$

$D \in \text{Desc} ::= T \mid F \mid R$

$TS \in \text{TypeSchema} ::= T \mid (\texttt{generic} \ (\delta^*) \ T)$

$BFS \in \text{BaseEffectSet} = \mathcal{P}(\text{BaseEffect})$

Syntactic Sugar

$\texttt{pure} \rightsquigarrow_{ds} (\texttt{maxeff})$

Denotation of Effect Expressions

$\mathcal{F} : \text{Effect} \to \text{BaseEffectSet}$

$\mathcal{F}[\![BF]\!] = \{BF\}$

$\mathcal{F}[\![(\texttt{maxeff} \ F_{i=1}^{n})]\!] = \cup_{i=1}^{n} \mathcal{F}[\![F_i]\!]$

Effect Equivalence

$$F_1 \approx_e F_2 \quad \text{where } \mathcal{F}[\![F_1]\!] = \mathcal{F}[\![F_2]\!] \qquad\qquad [\approx_e]$$

Subeffects

$$F_1 \sqsubseteq_e F_2 \quad \text{where } \mathcal{F}[\![F_1]\!] \subseteq \mathcal{F}[\![F_2]\!] \qquad\qquad [\sqsubseteq_e]$$

$$(\text{The notation } F_2 \sqsupseteq_e F_1 \text{ means } F_1 \sqsubseteq_e F_2)$$

Type Equivalence

$$\frac{\forall_{i=0}^{n} \cdot (T_i \approx T_i') \quad F \approx_e F'}{(\texttt{->} \ (T_{i=1}^{n}) \ F \ T_0) \approx (\texttt{->} \ (T_{i=1}'^{n}) \ F' \ T_0')} \qquad [\to\text{-}\approx]$$

All other type-equivalence rules for FLARE/E are straightforward.

Figure 16.1 FLARE/E types, effects, and regions.

The `dup!` procedure takes a cell `c` containing a list, modifies it to contain a list
with the first element duplicated, and returns the new list. For maximum utility,
the `dup!` procedure should have a polymorphic type that abstracts over (1) the
type `?t` of the elements in the list in the cell `c` and (2) the region `?r` of the cell `c`.
Here is a type schema for `dup!` with the desired degree of polymorphism:

```
(generic (?t ?r)                          {?t is type of list elements}
                                          {?r is region of cell}
    (-> ((cellof (listof ?t) ?r))         {type of the argument c}
        (maxeff (read ?r) (write ?r))     {latent effect of dup!}
        (listof ?t)))                     {type of result of dup!}
```

The `apply-twice` procedure is polymorphic in the input type of `f`, the output
type of `f`, and the latent effect of `f`:

```
(generic (?t1 ?t2 ?e)       {?t1 is input type of f}
                            {?t2 is output type of f}
                            {?e is latent effect of f}
    (-> ((-> (?t1) ?e ?t2)  {type of f}
        ?t1)                {type of x}
        ?e                  {latent effect of apply-twice, inherited from f}
        ?t2))               {type of result of apply-twice}
```

In this case, the latent effect `?e` of the argument procedure `f` is inherited by
`apply-twice`. If we assume that the `bools` cell is allocated in region `r4` and the
`ints` cell is allocated in region `r5`, then we have the following instantiations for
the `generic`-bound variables in the two applications of `apply-twice`:

Variable	(apply-twice dup! bools)	(apply-twice dup! ints)
?t	bool	int
?r	r4	r5
?t1	(cellof (listof bool) r4)	(cellof (listof int) r5)
?t2	(listof bool)	(listof int)
?e	(maxeff (read r4) (write r4))	(maxeff (read r5) (write r5))

So the type and effect of E_{twice} are:

$$E_{twice} : \text{(pairof (listof bool) (listof int))}$$
$$! \text{ (maxeff (init r4) (read r4) (write r4)}$$
$$\text{(init r5) (read r5) (write r5))}$$

Types, effects, and regions together are **descriptions** — they *describe* program expressions. We saw descriptions earlier, in Section 12.3.1, where they were
used to specify the structure of type constructors. Here, effects and regions are
new kinds of descriptions for describing program behavior. In FLARE/E, a de-

scription identifier δ can name any description and supersedes FLARE's type
identifier τ, which can name only types. This allows us to treat descriptions uniformly in type schemas (as illustrated above) and allows us to define notations for
substitution and unification uniformly with types, effects, and regions. This uniformity simplifies our presentation, but can lead to ill-formed descriptions (e.g.,
a type appearing in a position where an effect is expected, or vice versa). Such
ill-formed descriptions can be avoided by using a simple kind system as discussed
in Section 12.3.2 (see Exercise 16.3).

16.2.2 Type and Effect Rules

An **effect system** is a set of rules for assigning effects to program expressions.
Figures 16.2 and 16.3 present a type and effect system that assigns both a type
and an effect to every FLARE/E expression. The system is based on type/effect
judgments of the form

$$TE \vdash E : T \mathbin{!} F$$

This is pronounced "expression E has type T and effect F in type environment
TE." As in FLARE, the type environments in this system map identifiers to type
schemas. The type/effect rules in Figure 16.3 are similar to the type rules for
the full FLARE language presented in Figures 13.3 (page 775), 13.19 (page 805),
and 13.24 (page 815), except that they determine the effects of expressions in
addition to their types.

Literals, variable references, errors, and abstractions are all pure because their
evaluation does not touch the store and so can have no store effect. Variable references would not be pure if FLARE/E included mutable variables (**set!**). The
[*genvar*] rule allows substitution of arbitrary descriptions (types, effects, regions)
for the **generic**-bound description variables in a type schema. Substituting the
wrong kind of description (e.g., substituting a type for a description variable used
as an effect) would lead to an ill-formed type expression. But this is not problematic, because descriptions in the [*genvar*] rule must be "guessed" correctly to
show that an expression is well typed. The formal parameters of **generic** can be
annotated with kind information to guarantee that all types resulting from this
substitution are well formed (see Exercise 16.3).

The rules for all compound expressions (except abstractions) use **maxeff** to
combine the effects of all subexpressions and include them in the effect of the
whole expression. The [$\rightarrow$-*intro*] and [$\rightarrow$-*elim*] rules communicate effect information from the point of procedure definition to the point of procedure application.
The [$\rightarrow$-*intro*] rule includes the effect of an abstraction's body as the latent ef-

---

Domains

$TE \in \text{TypeEnvironment} = \text{Ident} \rightharpoonup \text{TypeSchema}$

Other type and effect domains are defined in Figure 16.1.

Type Functions

$egen : \text{Type} \rightarrow \text{TypeEnvironment} \rightarrow \text{TypeSchema}$

$(egen\ T\ \ TE) = (\texttt{generic}\ (\delta_{i=1}^{n})\ \ T),$
  where $\{\delta_1, \ldots, \delta_n\} = \mathit{FrDescIds}_{ty}[\![T]\!] - (\mathit{FrDescIds}_{tyenv}\ TE)$

$egenPure_{SP} : \text{Type} \rightarrow \text{TypeEnvironment} \rightarrow \text{Exp} \rightarrow \text{TypeSchema}$

$(egenPure_{SP}\ T_{defn}\ TE\ E) = \begin{cases} (egen\ T_{defn}\ TE) & \text{if } \vdash_{pure} E, \text{ where } \vdash_{pure} \text{ is defined} \\ & \quad \text{in Figure 13.25 on page 816} \\ T_{defn} & \text{otherwise} \end{cases}$

Figure 16.2   Type/effect rules for FLARE/E, Part 1.

fect in the procedure type of the abstraction, and the [$\rightarrow$-*elim*] rule includes the latent effect of a procedure type in the effect of a procedure application. Latent effects are also propagated by the [*prim*] rule to handle the fact that the types of cell operators must now carry nontrivial latent effects. Operator types in the primitive type environment TE_{prim} must now carry latent effects, which are pure except for the cell operators. For example:

```
 cell : (generic (?t ?r) (-> (?t) (init ?r) (cellof ?t ?r)))
    ^ : (generic (?t ?r) (-> ((cellof ?t ?r)) (read ?r) ?t))
   := : (generic (?t ?r) (-> ((cellof ?t ?r) ?t) (write ?r) unit))
    + : (-> (int int) pure int)
 cons : (generic (?t) (-> (?t (listof ?t)) pure (listof ?t)))
```

The [*let*$_{SP}$] and [*letrec*$_{SP}$] rules for FLARE/E are similar to the [*let*$'_{LP}$] and [*letrec*$'_{LP}$] rules for FLARE (Figure 13.24 on page 815). One difference is that *egenPure*$_{SP}$ is defined in terms of *egen*, which generalizes over all free description variables (not just type variables) in the type T that do not appear in the type environment TE. We assume that the *FrDescIds*$_{ty}$ function returns the free type, effect, and region variables in a type and the *FrDescIds*$_{tyenv}$ function returns all of the free type, effect, and region variables in a type environment. The definitions of these functions are left as an exercise (Exercise 16.2).

The *SP* subscript, which stands for "syntactic purity," emphasizes that these rules and functions use the same syntactic test for expression purity that is used in FLARE. This seems crazy — why not use the effect system itself to deter-

Type/Effect Rules

$TE \vdash \texttt{\#u} : \texttt{unit} \,!\, \texttt{pure}$ $[unit]$ $TE \vdash N : \texttt{int} \,!\, \texttt{pure}$ $[int]$ $TE \vdash B : \texttt{bool} \,!\, \texttt{pure}$ $[bool]$

$TE \vdash (\texttt{sym } Y) : \texttt{symb} \,!\, \texttt{pure}$ $[symb]$ $TE \vdash (\texttt{error } Y) : T \,!\, \texttt{pure}$ $[error]$

$$TE \vdash I : T \,!\, \texttt{pure} \;\; \text{where } TE(I) = T \hfill [var]$$

$$TE \vdash I : ([D_i/\delta_i]_{i=1}^n) \, T_{body} \,!\, \texttt{pure} \;\; \text{where } TE(I) = (\texttt{generic } (\delta_{i=1}^n) \; T_{body}) \;\; [genvar]$$

$$\frac{TE \vdash E_{test} : \texttt{bool} \,!\, F_{test} \qquad TE \vdash E_{then} : T \,!\, F_{then} \qquad TE \vdash E_{else} : T \,!\, F_{else}}{TE \vdash (\texttt{if } E_{test} \; E_{then} \; E_{else}) : T \,!\, (\texttt{maxeff } F_{test} \; F_{then} \; F_{else})} \;\; [if]$$

$$\frac{TE[I_i : T_i]_{i=1}^n \vdash E_{body} : T_{body} \,!\, F_{body}}{TE \vdash (\texttt{abs } (I_{i=1}^n) \; E_{body}) : (\texttt{-> } (T_{i=1}^n) \; F_{body} \; T_{body}) \,!\, \texttt{pure}} \;\; [\rightarrow\text{-}intro]$$

$$\frac{TE \vdash E_0 : (\texttt{-> } (T_{i=1}^n) \; F_{latent} \; T_{res}) \,!\, F_0 \qquad \forall_{i=1}^n . \; (TE \vdash E_i : T_i \,!\, F_i)}{TE \vdash (E_0 \; E_{i=1}^n) : T_{res} \,!\, (\texttt{maxeff } F_{latent} \; F_{i=0}^n)} \;\; [\rightarrow\text{-}elim]$$

$$\frac{TE_{prim} \vdash O : (\texttt{-> } (T_{i=1}^n) \; F_{latent} \; T_{res}) \,!\, \texttt{pure} \qquad \forall_{i=1}^n . \; (TE \vdash E_i : T_i \,!\, F_i)}{TE \vdash (\texttt{prim } O \; E_{i=1}^n) : T_{res} \,!\, (\texttt{maxeff } F_{latent} \; F_{i=1}^n)} \;\; [prim]$$

$$\frac{\forall_{i=1}^n . \; (TE \vdash E_i : T_i \,!\, F_i) \qquad TE[I_i : (\texttt{egenPure}_{SP} \; T_i \; TE \; E_i)]_{i=1}^n \vdash E_0 : T_0 \,!\, F_0}{TE \vdash (\texttt{let } ((I_i \; E_i)_{i=1}^n) \; E_0) : T_0 \,!\, (\texttt{maxeff } F_{i=0}^n)} \;\; [let_{SP}]$$

$$\frac{\forall_{i=1}^n . \; \left(TE[I_j : T_j]_{j=1}^n \vdash E_i : T_i \,!\, F_i\right) \qquad TE[I_i : (\texttt{egenPure}_{SP} \; T_i \; TE \; E_i)]_{i=1}^n \vdash E_0 : T_0 \,!\, F_0}{TE \vdash (\texttt{letrec } ((I_i \; E_i)_{i=1}^n) \; E_0) : T_0 \,!\, (\texttt{maxeff } F_{i=0}^n)} \;\; [letrec_{SP}]$$

$$\frac{TE \vdash E : T \,!\, F}{TE \vdash E : T \,!\, F'} \;\;, \text{where } F \sqsubseteq_e F' \qquad [does]$$

$$\frac{\{I_i : T_i\}_{i=1}^n \vdash E_{body} : T_{body} \,!\, F_{body}}{\vdash_{prog} (\texttt{flarek } (I_{i=1}^n) \; E_{body}) : (\texttt{-> } (T_{i=1}^n) \; F_{body} \; T_{body}) \,!\, \texttt{pure}} \;\; [prog]$$

Figure 16.3 Type/effect rules for FLARE/E, Part 2.

mine purity? The reason is that an effect-based test for purity complicates the reconstruction of types and effects and the relationship between FLARE/E and FLARE. This is explored in more detail in Section 16.2.5.

Because our use of effect equivalence and type equivalence in FLARE/E type derivations is implicit, the type and effect system does not include an explicit type rule for type equivalence (e.g., the [*type-≈*] rule in Figure 11.20 on page 680). For example, consider the following FLARE/E type/effect derivation:

$$
\frac{
\begin{array}{l}
\quad\quad\quad\quad\quad\quad\quad\quad\quad\quad\quad\vdots \\
TE \vdash E_1 : \text{(-> (int) (maxeff (read r1) (write r2)) bool)} \,!\, \text{pure} \\
\\
\quad\quad\quad\quad\quad\quad\vdots \\
TE \vdash E_2 : \text{int} \,!\, \text{(maxeff (read r1) (read r2))}
\end{array}
}{
TE \vdash (E_1 \; E_2) : \text{bool} \,!\, \text{(maxeff (read r1) (read r2) (write r2))}
} \; [\text{→-}elim]
$$

This is valid because the effect

```
(maxeff (maxeff (read r1) (write r2)) pure (maxeff (read r1) (read r2)))
```

specified by the [→-*elim*] rule can be simplified to the following effect using implicit effect equivalence:

```
(maxeff (read r1) (read r2) (write r2))
```

The effect of an expression determined by our type and effect system is a conservative approximation of the actions performed by the expression at run time. Combining the effects of subexpressions with `maxeff` can lead to effects that overestimate the actual actions performed. For example, suppose that E_{pure} has effect `pure`, E_{read} has effect `(read r6)`, and E_{write} has effect `(write r6)`. Then `(if #t` E_{pure} E_{read}`)` has effect `(read r6)` even though it does not touch the store at run time, and the conditional `(if b` E_{read} E_{write}`)` has effect `(maxeff (read r6) (write r6))` even though only one of its branches is taken at run time.

It is possible to inflate the effect of an expression via the [*does*] rule, which allows an expression with effect F to be given effect F' as long as F is a subeffect of F'. In order to derive a type and effect for an expression, it is sometimes necessary to use the [*does*] rule to get the latent effects embedded in two procedure types to be the same. Consider the expression

$$E_{ifproc} \; = \; \text{(if b (abs () } E_{read}\text{) (abs () } E_{write}\text{))}$$

relative to a type environment TE in which b has type `bool`, E_{read} has type T and effect `(read r6)`, and E_{write} has type T and effect `(write r6)`. Without using the [*does*] rule, we can show:

$$TE \vdash \text{(abs () } E_{read}\text{)} : \text{(-> () (read r6) } T\text{)} \,!\, \text{pure}$$

$$TE \vdash \text{(abs () } E_{write}\text{)} : \text{(-> () (write r6) } T\text{)} \,!\, \text{pure}$$

The [*if*] rule requires that the types of the two branch expressions be the same, but in this case the procedure types are not the same because their effects differ. To show that E_{ifproc} is well typed, it is necessary to use the [*does*] rule to give the effect $F_{rw} =$ (maxeff (read r6) (write r6)) to the bodies of both procedures, resulting in the following derivation:

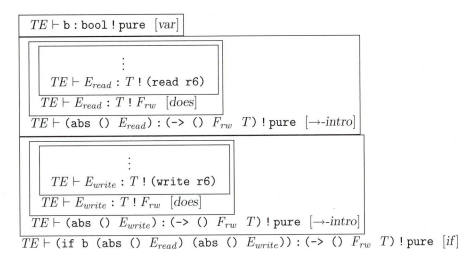

In the above example, the [*does*] rule is used to artificially inflate the effects of procedure bodies before forming procedure types so that the procedure types (and, specifically, their latent effect components) will be identical elsewhere in the type derivation. This is the key way in which the [*does*] rule is used in practice. The FLARE/E type system does not support any form of subtyping, so that there is no direct way to show that a procedure with type (-> (int) (maxeff (read r) (write r)) int) can be used in place of one with type (-> (int) (maxeff (init r) (read r) (write r)) int). However, as illustrated above, the [*does*] rule can be used in conjunction with the [→-intro] rule to inflate the base effects in the latent effect of a procedure when it is created.

The [*does*] rule permits an expression to take on many possible effects. We shall see below (on page 962 in Section 16.2.3) that there is a well-defined, indeed practically computable, notion of least effect. Henceforth, when we refer to the effect of an expression, we mean the smallest effect that can be proven by our rules. When we discuss effect reconstruction (Section 16.2.3), we will show how to automatically calculate the smallest effect allowed by the rules.

How is the FLARE/E type and effect system related to the FLARE type system studied earlier? It has exactly the same typing power as FLARE — a program is typable in FLARE if and only if it is typable in FLARE/E. This relationship is a consequence of the following theorem, which uses the notations $\lceil T \rceil^e_T$ and $\lceil TE \rceil^e_{TE}$ (see Exercise 16.4) to stand for the result of erasing effect and region information from the FLARE/E type T and FLARE/E type environment TE:

> **Theorem 16.1** $TE' \vdash E : T'$ *in the* FLARE *type system if and only if there exists a* FLARE/E *type environment TE, a* FLARE/E *type T, and an effect F such that* $\lceil TE \rceil^e_{TE} = TE'$, $\lceil T \rceil^e_T = T'$, *and* $TE \vdash E : T \,!\, F$ *in the* FLARE/E *type/effect system.*

Proving that $TE \vdash E : T \,!\, F$ implies $TE' \vdash E : T'$ is easily done by showing that erasing all effect information in the FLARE/E type/effect derivation yields a FLARE type derivation (see Exercise 16.5). The other direction ($TE' \vdash E : T'$ implies $TE \vdash E : T \,!\, F$) is proven by showing that the judgments and procedure types in a FLARE type derivation can always be extended with effect information to yield a FLARE/E type/effect derivation (Exercise 16.6).

Exercise 16.1 Consider the following program:

```
(flarek (b)
  (let ((c (prim cell 2)))
    (let ((one (abs (x) 1))
          (get (abs (y) (prim ^ y)))
          (setc! (abs (z) (let ((_ (prim := c z))) z))))
      ((abs (appc)
         ((if b setc! one) (prim + (appc get) (appc one))))
       (abs (f) (f c))))))
```

a. Give a type derivation showing that the above program is well typed in the FLARE/E type system. You will need to use the [*does*] rule to inflate some latent effects in procedure types, but use the minimal latent effect possible.

b. How would your answer to part **a** change if the subexpression

```
((abs (appc) ... ) (abs (f) (f c)))
```

were changed to

```
(let ((appc (abs (f) (f c)))) ... )?
```

Exercise 16.2 Define the following functions for determining the free description identifiers of various domains:

$$
\begin{aligned}
FrDescIds_{reg} &: \text{Region} \rightarrow \mathcal{P}(\text{DescId}) \\
FrDescIds_{eff} &: \text{Effect} \rightarrow \mathcal{P}(\text{DescId}) \\
FrDescIds_{ty} &: \text{Type} \rightarrow \mathcal{P}(\text{DescId}) \\
FrDescIds_{tysch} &: \text{TypeSchema} \rightarrow \mathcal{P}(\text{DescId}) \\
FrDescIds_{tyenv} &: \text{TypeEnvironment} \rightarrow \mathcal{P}(\text{DescId})
\end{aligned}
$$

Exercise 16.3 Intuitively, each description identifier that is a formal parameter in a FLARE/E `generic` expression denotes one of a type, an effect, or a region. For example, in the type schema

```
(generic (?a ?b ?c)
  (-> ((-> (?a) ?b ?a) (cellof ?a ?c))
      (maxeff ?b (read ?c) (write ?c))
      ?a))
```

`?a` denotes a type, `?b` denotes an effect, and `?c` denotes a region. This intuition can be formalized using a simple kind system (cf. Section 12.3.2) based on the following domains:

$$K \in \text{Kind} ::= \texttt{type} \mid \texttt{effect} \mid \texttt{region}$$
$$DK \in \text{DescIdKind} ::= (\delta \ K)$$
$$TS \in \text{TypeSchema} ::= T \mid (\texttt{generic} \ (DK^*) \ T)$$

The TypeSchema domain has been changed so that every formal parameter declared by `generic` has an explicit kind. In the modified system, the example type schema above would be rewritten to have the form

```
(generic ((?a type) (?b effect) (?c region)) ... )
```

We say that a type schema with explicitly kinded parameters is **well kinded** if each reference to the parameter in the body of the type schema is consistent with its kind. For example, the type schema above (with explicit kinds) is well kinded. However, the schema

```
(generic ((?d type) (?e region))
  (-> (?d) pure (cellof ?e ?d)))
```

is not well kinded because region `?e` is used as a type and the second occurrence of type `?d` is used as region.

a. Develop a formal deduction system for determining the well-kindedness of a type schema with explicitly kinded parameters.

b. Define variants of each of the functions in Exercise 16.2 that return an element of $\mathcal{P}(\text{DescIdKind})$ (in which each description identifier is paired with its kind) rather than an element of $\mathcal{P}(\text{DescId})$.

c. Modify the definition of the *egen* function in Figure 16.2 to use the functions from part **b** to return a type schema with explicitly kinded parameters. Under what simple conditions is the type schema guaranteed to be well kinded? Explain.

d. Modify the [*genvar*] rule to guarantee that only descriptions of the appropriate kind are substituted for `generic`-bound description parameters in the body of the type schema. Argue that the type resulting from these substitutions is always well formed.

Exercise 16.4 Define the following effect-erasure functions for FLARE/E types, type schemas, and type environments:

$$effectErase_{ty} : \text{Type}_{FLARE/E} \to \text{Type}_{FLARE}$$
$$effectErase_{tysch} : \text{TypeSchema}_{FLARE/E} \to \text{TypeSchema}_{FLARE}$$
$$effectErase_{tyenv} : \text{TypeEnvironment}_{FLARE/E} \to \text{TypeEnvironment}_{FLARE}$$

The notations $\lceil T \rceil_T^e$, $\lceil TS \rceil_{TS}^e$, and $\lceil TE \rceil_{TE}^e$ abbreviate (respectively) $(effectErase_{ty}\ T)$, $(effectErase_{tysch}\ TS)$, and $(effectErase_{tyenv}\ TE)$. Each function should erase all effect and region information from the FLARE/E entity to yield the FLARE entity. In the definition of $effectErase_{tysch}$, it is helpful (but not absolutely necessary) to assume that it is possible to determine the kind of each `generic` parameter (see Exercise 16.3).

Exercise 16.5 The notion of effect erasure from Exercise 16.4 can be extended to type/effect judgments and type/effect derivations in FLARE/E as follows:

$$effectErase_{judge} : \text{TypeJudgment}_{FLARE/E} \to \text{TypeJudgment}_{FLARE}$$
The notation $\lceil TJ \rceil_{TJ}^e$ abbreviates $(effectErase_{judge}\ TJ)$.

$$\lceil TE \vdash_{FLARE/E} E : T\ !\ F \rceil_{TJ}^e = \lceil TE \rceil_{TE}^e \vdash_{FLARE} E : \lceil T \rceil_T^e$$

$$effectErase_{deriv} : \text{TypeDerivation}_{FLARE/E} \to \text{TypeDerivation}_{FLARE}$$
The notation $\lceil TD \rceil_{TD}^e$ abbreviates $(effectErase_{deriv}\ TD)$.

$$\left\lceil \frac{TD}{TE \vdash_{FLARE/E} E : T\ !\ F'}\ [does] \right\rceil_{TD}^e = \lceil TD \rceil_{TD}^e$$

$$\left\lceil \frac{TD_1 \ldots TD_n}{TJ} \right\rceil_{TD}^e = \frac{\lceil TD_1 \rceil_{TD}^e \ldots \lceil TD_n \rceil_{TD}^e}{\lceil TJ \rceil_{TJ}^e}, \text{ for all other type derivations.}$$

Prove that $effectErase_{deriv}$ is a well-defined function. That is, if TD is a FLARE/E type derivation, then $\lceil TD \rceil_{TD}^e$ is a legal FLARE type derivation according to the type rules of FLARE. Your proof should be by induction on the structure of a type derivation TD and by case analysis on the type rule used in the root node of the type derivation tree. The well-definedness of $effectErase_{deriv}$ proves that $TE \vdash_{FLARE/E} E : T\ !\ F$ implies $\lceil TE \rceil_{TE}^e \vdash_{FLARE} E : \lceil T \rceil_T^e$ in Theorem 16.1.

Exercise 16.6 This exercise sketches a proof of the forward direction of Theorem 16.1 (i.e., that any FLARE type derivation can be annotated with appropriate effect information to yield a FLARE/E type/effect derivation) and asks you to work out the details. A simple approach is to assume that all cells are allocated in a single region (call it δ_{reg}), in which case the maximal effect is

$$F_{max} = (\texttt{maxeff (init}\ \delta_{reg})\ (\texttt{read}\ \delta_{reg})\ (\texttt{write}\ \delta_{reg}))$$

Then any FLARE type derivation can be transformed to a FLARE/E type/effect derivation by:

- changing every FLARE cell type (cellof T) to the FLARE/E cell type (cellof T δ_{reg});

- changing every nonprimitive FLARE arrow type (-> ($T_{i=1}^n$) T_0) to the FLARE/E arrow type (-> ($T_{i=1}^n$) F_{max} T_0);

- using the [*does*] rule to inflate the effect of every procedure body to F_{max} before the [$\rightarrow$-*intro*] rule is applied; and

- introducing and propagating effects as required by the FLARE/E analogues of the FLARE type rules.

a. Based on the above sketch, formally define a transformation

$$\mathcal{TD} : TypeDerivation_{FLARE} \rightarrow TypeDerivation_{FLARE/E}$$

that transforms a valid FLARE type derivation for a well-typed expression into a valid FLARE/E type/effect derivation for the same expression.

b. Suppose that TD is a FLARE type derivation for the type judgment $TE' \vdash E : T'$. Then ($\mathcal{TD}$ TD) is a FLARE/E type/effect derivation for the type/effect judgment $TE \vdash E : T \, ! \, F$. Show that $\lceil TE \rceil_{TE}^e = TE'$ and $\lceil T \rceil_T^e = T'$. This completes the proof of Theorem 16.1.

16.2.3   Reconstructing Types and Effects: Algorithm Z

Effect-Constraint Sets

We can adapt the FLARE type reconstruction algorithm (Algorithm R) from Section 13.3 to reconstruct effects as well as types. Recall that R has the signature

$$R : \text{Exp} \rightarrow \text{TypeEnvironment} \rightarrow (\text{Type} \times \text{TypeConstraintSet})$$

and is expressed via deductive-style rules involving judgments of the form

$$R[\![E]\!] \; TE \; = \; \langle T, TCS \rangle$$

Elements $TCS \in \text{TypeConstraintSet}$ are abstract sets of type-equality constraints that are collected and solved by the algorithm. The extended algorithm, which we call Algorithm Z (Figures 16.4, 16.6, 16.8, and 16.9), has the signature

$$Z : \text{Exp} \rightarrow \text{TypeEnvironment}$$
$$\rightarrow (\text{Type} \times \text{TypeConstraintSet} \times \text{Effect} \times \text{EffectConstraintSet})$$

and is expressed via deductive-style rules involving judgments of the form

$$Z[\![E]\!] \; TE \; = \; \langle T, TCS, F, FCS \rangle$$

Domains

$FC \in \text{EffectConstraint} = \text{DescId} \times \text{Effect}$
     ; (>= δ F) stands for an element $\langle \delta, F \rangle$ of EffectConstraint

$FCS \in \text{EffectConstraintSet} = FC^*$
      ; Define $dom(FCS) = \bigcup \{\delta \mid (\text{>= } \delta \ F) \in FCS\}$

$\sigma \in \text{DescSubst} = \text{DescId} \rightharpoonup \text{Desc}$

$us \in \text{UnifySoln} = \text{DescSubst} + \text{Failure}$

Other type and effect domains are defined in Figure 16.1.

Functions

$solve_{FCS} : \text{EffectConstraintSet} \rightarrow \text{DescSubst}$
$= \lambda FCS \ . \ \mathbf{fix}_{\text{DescSubst}} \left(\lambda \sigma \ . \ \left(\lambda \delta^{FCS} \ . \ (\sigma \ (\texttt{maxeff} \ \delta \ F_{i=1}^{n})_{(\text{>= } \delta \ F_i) \in FCS}) \right) \right)$
    where $\perp_{\text{DescSubst}} = \lambda \delta^{FCS} \ . \ \texttt{pure}$
    and $\lambda \delta^{FCS} \ . \ d_{body}$ stands for $\lambda \delta \ . \ \mathbf{if} \ \delta \in dom(FCS) \ \mathbf{then} \ d_{body}$
                                                 else *undefined* **end**

$solve_{TCS} : \text{TypeConstraintSet} \rightarrow \text{UnifySoln}$ is defined as in Figure 13.12 on page 790, where it is assumed that *unify* is modified in a straightforward way to handle the unification of `listof` types, `pairof` types, `cellof` types, and `->` types with latent effects (which are guaranteed to be effect variables). A successful unification now results in an element of DescSubst rather than TypeSubst because nontype description variables are encountered in the unification of `cellof` types (in which region variables are unified) and `->` types (in which effect variables are unified).

Figure 16.4   Domains and functions for the FLARE/E type and effect reconstruction algorithm.

In addition to returning the type T and type-constraint set TCS of an expression E relative to a type environment TE, Algorithm Z returns:

1. The effect F of the expression.

2. A collection $FCS \in \text{EffectConstraintSet}$ of effect *inequality* constraints having the form (>= δ F). Such a constraint means that the effect F' denoted by the effect variable δ must be at least as large as F — i.e., $F' \sqsupseteq_e F$.

What are the effect inequality constraints for? As mentioned in the discussion of the [*does*] rule beginning on page 954, the most challenging problem encountered when constructing a type/effect derivation in FLARE/E is guaranteeing that the latent effects of procedure types are identical in all situations where the rules require that two procedure types be the same. The purpose of the effect-constraint sets generated by Algorithm Z is to solve this problem. An effect constraint $(\texttt{>=}\ \delta_{lat}\ F_{body})$ is generated by Algorithm Z when a derivation in the implicit type/effect system would use the $[\textit{does}]$ rule to inflate the effect of a procedure body from F_{body} to $\delta_{lat} = F'_{body}$ in conjunction with an application of the $[\rightarrow\textit{-intro}]$ rule:

$$
\frac{\dfrac{TE[I_i : T_i]_{i=1}^{n} \vdash E_{body} : T_{body}\ !\ F_{body}}{TE[I_i : T_i]_{i=1}^{n} \vdash E_{body} : T_{body}\ !\ F'_{body}}\ [\textit{does}]}{TE \vdash (\texttt{abs}\ (I_{i=1}^{n})\ E_{body}) : (\texttt{->}\ (T_{i=1}^{n})\ F'_{body}\ T_{body})\ !\ \texttt{pure}}\ [\rightarrow\textit{-intro}]
$$

The extent to which F_{body} needs to be inflated by the $[\textit{does}]$ rule depends on how the procedure type introduced by the $[\rightarrow\textit{-intro}]$ rule flows through the rest of the type/effect derivation and is compared to other procedure types. Algorithm Z addresses this problem by introducing the description variable δ_{lat} to stand for F'_{body} and by generating an effect inequality constraint $(\texttt{>=}\ \delta_{lat}\ F_{body})$ that must later be solved. The type and effect reconstruction system handles the above derivation pattern by a single application of the $[\rightarrow\textit{-intro}_Z]$ rule:

$$
\frac{Z[\![E_{body}]\!]\ TE[I_i : \delta_i]_{i=1}^{n} = \langle T_{body}, TCS_{body}, F_{body}, FCS_{body}\rangle}{\begin{array}{c}Z[\![(\texttt{abs}\ (I_{i=1}^{n})\ E_{body})]\!]\ TE = \langle(\texttt{->}\ (\delta_{i=1}^{n})\ \delta_{lat}\ T_{body}), TCS_{body},\\ \texttt{pure}, (\texttt{>=}\ \delta_{lat}\ F_{body}) . FCS_{body}\rangle\end{array}}\ [\rightarrow\textit{-intro}_Z]
$$

This is like the $[\rightarrow\textit{-intro}_R]$ type reconstruction rule for FLARE except that: (1) it introduces the description variables $\delta_{i=1}^{n}$ for the parameters instead of type variables; (2) it specifies that abstractions have a $\texttt{pure}$ effect; and (3) it adds the effect constraint $(\texttt{>=}\ \delta_{lat}\ F_{body})$ to whatever effect constraints were generated in reconstructing the type and effect of E_{body}.

For a reason explained later, an effect-constraint set is concretely represented as a sequence of effect constraints. So $(FC . FCS)$ is the result of inserting the effect constraint FC into the effect-constraint set FCS, $FCS_1 \otimes FCS_2$ is the union of effect-constraint sets FCS_1 and FCS_2, and $\otimes_{i=1}^{n} FCS_i$ is the union of the n effect-constraint sets $FCS_1, \ldots, FCS_n$. We still use the set notation $FC \in FCS$ to indicate that effect constraint FC is an element of the effect-constraint set FCS. We define $dom(FCS)$ as the set of effect variables δ appearing in constraints of the form $(\texttt{>=}\ \delta\ F)$ within FCS.

A solution to an effect-constraint set FCS is a substitution $\sigma \in \text{DescSubst} = \text{DescId} \rightharpoonup \text{Desc}$ such that $dom(\sigma) = dom(FCS)$ and $(\sigma\ \delta) \sqsupseteq_e (\sigma\ F)$ for every effect constraint $(\texttt{>=}\ \delta\ F)$ in FCS. Although the formal signature of a solution

```
      F_i = (init r7)
      F_r = (read r7)
      F_w = (write r7)
    F_max = (maxeff F_i F_r F_w)
   FCS_ex = [(>= δ_1 pure),
             (>= δ_2 (maxeff δ_1 F_i)),
             (>= δ_3 (maxeff δ_2 F_r)),
             (>= δ_4 (maxeff δ_2 F_w)),
             (>= δ_4 δ_5),
             (>= δ_5 (maxeff δ_3 δ_4))]
```

Figure 16.5 FCS_{ex} is an example of an effect-constraint set.

substitution is DescId $\rightharpoonup$ Desc, the signature is really DescId $\rightharpoonup$ Effect since all
the description variables being solved denote effects.[5]

There are infinitely many solutions for any effect-constraint set. For example,
consider the effect-constraint set FCS_{ex} in Figure 16.5.   Below are four solutions
to FCS_{ex}:

σ	$(\sigma\ \delta_1)$	$(\sigma\ \delta_2)$	$(\sigma\ \delta_3)$	$(\sigma\ \delta_4)$	$(\sigma\ \delta_5)$
σ_{ex_1}	pure	F_i	(maxeff F_i F_r)	F_{max}	F_{max}
σ_{ex_2}	F_i	F_i	(maxeff F_i F_r)	F_{max}	F_{max}
σ_{ex_3}	F_r	(maxeff F_i F_r)	(maxeff F_i F_r)	F_{max}	F_{max}
σ_{ex_4}	F_{max}	F_{max}	F_{max}	F_{max}	F_{max}

There are also infinitely many solutions of the form σ_{ex_F} parameterized by $F \in$
Effect that map every effect variable in FCS_{ex} to (maxeff F F_{max}).

Since the Effect domain is a pointed CPO (see Sections 5.2.2 and 5.2.3) under
the $\sqsubseteq_e$ ordering, the domain DescId $\rightharpoonup$ Effect is also a pointed CPO, and so there
is a well-defined notion of a least solution to an effect-constraint set. The structure
of the CPO and the existence of a least solution depend critically on the ACUI
nature of effect combination via maxeff.

The iterative approach to finding least fixed points from Section 5.2.5 can be
used to calculate the least solution to an effect-constraint set FCS. We start with
an approximation σ_0 that maps each effect variable δ in $dom(FCS)$ to pure. For
each step j, we define a better approximation σ_j that maps each δ in $dom(FCS)$ to
an effect that combines $(\sigma_{j-1}\ \delta)$ with $(\sigma_{j-1}\ F_i)$ for each F such that (>= δ F)
is in FCS. $(\sigma_j\ \delta)$ is guaranteed to be at least as big as $(\sigma_{j-1}\ \delta)$, and so in this

---

[5]An effect constraint also typically contains description variables denoting regions, but these
will not be in $dom(\sigma)$ for a solution substitution σ.

sense is a "better" approximation. Since there are finitely many effect variables $\delta \in dom(FCS)$ and since $(\sigma_j \ \delta)$ always denotes some combination of the finite number of base effects mentioned in FCS, the iteration is guaranteed to converge to a fixed point in a finite number of steps.

For example, this process finds the least solution to FCS_{ex} in three steps (the fourth step verifies that σ_3 is a solution):

j	$(\sigma_j \ \delta_1)$	$(\sigma_j \ \delta_2)$	$(\sigma_j \ \delta_3)$	$(\sigma_j \ \delta_4)$	$(\sigma_j \ \delta_5)$
0	pure	pure	pure	pure	pure
1	pure	F_i	F_r	F_w	pure
2	pure	F_i	(maxeff F_i F_r)	(maxeff F_i F_w)	(maxeff F_r F_w)
3	pure	F_i	(maxeff F_i F_r)	F_{max}	F_{max}
4	pure	F_i	(maxeff F_i F_r)	F_{max}	F_{max}

The definition of the $solve_{FCS}$ function in Figure 16.4 formalizes this strategy for finding the least solution to an effect-constraint set. Let

$$\lambda \delta^{FCS} . \ effect\text{-}expression$$

stand for a partial function that denotes the value of *effect-expression* when $\delta \in dom(FCS)$ and is otherwise undefined. The least solution of an effect-constraint set FCS is the least fixed point of a series of solutions starting with the bottom solution $\perp_{\text{DescSubst}} = \lambda \delta^{FCS} . \ \texttt{pure}$. An approximate solution σ is transformed to a better solution σ' by mapping each effect variable $\delta \in dom(FCS)$ to $(\sigma \ (\texttt{maxeff} \ \delta \ F_1 \ \ldots \ F_n))$, where $\{F_1, \ldots, F_n\}$ is the set of all effects F_i appearing in constraints of the form $(\texttt{>=} \ \delta \ F_i)$ in FCS. Since

$$
\begin{aligned}
(\sigma' \ \delta) &= (\sigma \ (\texttt{maxeff} \ \delta \ F_1 \ \ldots \ F_n)) \\
&= (\texttt{maxeff} \ (\sigma \ \delta) \ (\sigma \ F_1) \ \ldots \ (\sigma \ F_n))
\end{aligned}
$$

clearly $(\sigma \ \delta) \sqsubseteq_e (\sigma' \ \delta)$ for each δ mentioned in FCS, so the transformation is monotonic. By the argument given above, each chain of solutions is finite, so monotonicity is sufficient to guarantee the existence of a least solution for $\textbf{fix}_{\text{DescSubst}}$.

Simple Type/Effect Reconstruction Rules

The Algorithm Z type/effect reconstruction rules for most expressions are presented in Figure 16.6. The rules for literals, errors, and nongeneric variable references are similar to the FLARE type reconstruction rules, but additionally specify a $\texttt{pure}$ effect and an empty effect-constraint set. The $[\rightarrow\text{-}intro_Z]$ rule has already been discussed above. The $[if_Z]$, $[\rightarrow\text{-}elim_Z]$, $[prim_Z]$ rules are similar to

Function Signature for Type/Effect Reconstruction of Expressions

$Z : \text{Exp} \to \text{TypeEnvironment}$
$\qquad \to (\text{Type} \times \text{TypeConstraintSet} \times \text{Effect} \times \text{EffectConstraintSet})$

Type/Effect Reconstruction Rules for Expressions

$$Z[\![\texttt{\#u}]\!]\ TE\ =\ \langle \text{unit}, \{\}_{TCS}, \text{pure}, [\,]_{FC} \rangle \qquad\qquad [unit_Z]$$
$$[bool_R],\ [int_R],\ \text{and}\ [symb_R]\ \text{are similar}$$

$$Z[\![(\texttt{error}\ Y)]\!]\ TE\ =\ \langle \delta, \{\}_{TCS}, \text{pure}, [\,]_{FC} \rangle\ \text{where}\ \delta\ \text{is fresh.} \qquad [error_Z]$$

$$Z[\![I]\!]\ TE\ =\ \langle T, \{\}_{TCS}, \text{pure}, [\,]_{FC} \rangle\ \text{where}\ TE(I)\ =\ T \qquad\qquad [var_Z]$$

$$Z[\![I]\!]\ TE\ =\ \langle \text{unit}, fail_{TCS}, \text{pure}, [\,]_{FC} \rangle\ \text{where}\ I \notin dom(TE) \qquad [var\text{-}fail_Z]$$

$$\frac{\forall_{i=1}^{3}\ .\ (Z[\![E_i]\!]\ TE\ =\ \langle T_i, TCS_i, F_i, FCS_i \rangle)}{\begin{array}{l} Z[\![(\texttt{if}\ E_1\ E_2\ E_3)]\!]\ TE\ =\ \langle T_2, \left(\uplus_{i=1}^{3} TCS_i\right) \uplus \{T_1 \doteq \text{bool}, T_2 \doteq T_3\}_{TCS}, \\ \qquad\qquad (\texttt{maxeff}\ F_{i=1}^{3}),\ @_{i=1}^{3} FCS_i \rangle \end{array}} \quad [if_Z]$$

$$\frac{Z[\![E_{body}]\!]\ TE[I_i : \delta_i]_{i=1}^{n}\ =\ \langle T_{body}, TCS_{body}, F_{body}, FCS_{body} \rangle}{\begin{array}{l} Z[\![(\texttt{abs}\ (I_{i=1}^{n})\ E_{body})]\!]\ TE\ =\ \langle (\texttt{->}\ (\delta_{i=1}^{n})\ \delta_{lat}\ T_{body}),\ TCS_{body}, \\ \qquad\qquad \text{pure},\ (\texttt{>=}\ \delta_{lat}\ F_{body})\ .\ FCS_{body} \rangle \\ \text{where}\quad \delta_{i=1}^{n}\ \text{and}\ \delta_{latent}\ \text{are fresh} \end{array}} \quad [\to\text{-}intro_Z]$$

$$\frac{\forall_{i=0}^{n}\ .\ (Z[\![E_i]\!]\ TE\ =\ \langle T_i, TCS_i, F_i, FCS_i \rangle)}{\begin{array}{l} Z[\![(E_0\ E_{i=1}^{n})]\!]\ TE \\ =\ \langle \delta_{res}, \left(\uplus_{i=0}^{n} TCS_i\right) \uplus \{T_0 \doteq (\texttt{->}\ (T_{i=1}^{n})\ \delta_{lat}\ \delta_{res})\}_{TCS}, \\ \quad (\texttt{maxeff}\ F_{i=0}^{n}\ \delta_{lat}),\ @_{i=0}^{n} FCS_i \rangle \\ \text{where}\quad \delta_{lat}\ \text{and}\ \delta_{res}\ \text{are fresh} \end{array}} \quad [\to\text{-}elim_Z]$$

$$\frac{\begin{array}{c} Z[\![O_{op}]\!]\ TE_{prim}\ =\ \langle T_{op}, TCS_0, \text{pure}, [\,]_{FC} \rangle \\ \forall_{i=1}^{n}\ .\ (Z[\![E_i]\!]\ TE\ =\ \langle T_i, TCS_i, F_i, FCS_i \rangle) \end{array}}{\begin{array}{l} Z[\![(\texttt{prim}\ O_{op}\ E_{i=1}^{n})]\!]\ TE \\ =\ \langle \delta_{res}, \left(\uplus_{i=0}^{n} TCS_i\right) \uplus \{T_{op} \doteq (\texttt{->}\ (T_{i=1}^{n})\ \delta_{lat}\ \delta_{res})\}_{TCS}, \\ \quad (\texttt{maxeff}\ F_{i=1}^{n}\ \delta_{lat}),\ @_{i=1}^{n} FCS_i \rangle \\ \text{where}\quad \delta_{lat}\ \text{and}\ \delta_{res}\ \text{are fresh} \end{array}} \quad [prim_Z]$$

Figure 16.6 The FLARE/E type/effect reconstruction algorithm for simple expressions expressed via deduction rules. For `let` polymorphism see Figure 16.8.

their FLARE type reconstruction counterparts except that they (1) combine the effects of all subexpressions (and the latent effect of the applied procedure in the case of $[\to\text{-}elim_Z]$ and $[prim_Z]$) and (2) they combine the effect-constraint sets of all subexpressions.

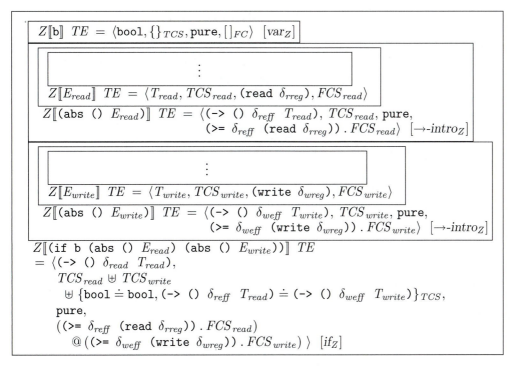

Figure 16.7 Type/effect reconstruction corresponding to the type/effect derivation of E_{ifproc} on page 955.

As an example, Figure 16.7 shows the fragment of the type/effect derivation for E_{ifproc} from page 955 expressed in the reconstruction system. Distinct effect variables δ_{reff} and δ_{weff} are introduced as the latent effects for (abs () E_{read}) and (abs () E_{write}), respectively, but these are forced to be the same by the type constraint

$$\text{(-> () } \delta_{reff} \ T_{read}) \doteq \text{(-> () } \delta_{weff} \ T_{write})$$

We assume that the unification algorithm used by the type-constraint set solver $solve_{TCS}$ is extended to unify the latent effects of two procedure types and the regions of two cellof types. The extension is straightforward, because both of these are guaranteed to be description variables: all procedure types generated by the $[\rightarrow\text{-}intro_Z]$ rule have latent effects that are description variables and all regions are description variables. Modifying the algorithm to unify arbitrary effects would be significantly more complicated, because the algorithm would need to generate a set of effect constraints in addition to a solution substitution (see [JG91] for details).

Algebraic Type Schemas for Let Polymorphism

A key difference between Algorithm Z and Algorithm R is how `let` polymorphism is handled. Recall that Algorithm R uses type schemas of the form (`generic` $(\tau_{i=1}^n)$ T) to permit a type identifier to be instantiated to different types in different contexts. For example, the identity function (`abs (x) x`) can be used on any type of input. When it is `let`-bound to an identifier, it has the type schema (`generic (?t) (-> (?t) ?t)`). The job of a type schema is to describe all of the possible types of an identifier by determining type variables that can be generalized.

In the implicit type/effect system of FLARE/E, type schemas were elaborated with effect and region variables. Reconstructing effects and regions requires us to extend type schemas further to carry along a set of constraints on the effects and regions they describe. In Algorithm Z, generic type schemas (Figure 16.8) are modified to have the form (`generic` (δ^*) T (FCS)), where FCS contains effect constraints that may involve the effect and region variables in δ^*.

We call a type schema that includes an effect-constraint set an **algebraic type schema** [JG91]. The fact that effect-constraint sets appear within algebraic type schemas that have an s-expression representation is the reason that we have chosen to represent effect constraints using the s-expression notation (`>=` δ F) and to represent effect-constraint sets as sequences of such constraints.

As a simple example, consider the algebraic type schema that the primitive type environment TE_{prim} assigns to the cell assignment operation (`:=`):

```
(generic (?t ?e ?r)
  (-> ((cellof ?t ?r)) ?e unit)   {type}
  ((>= ?e (write ?r))))           {effect constraints}
```

This type schema has three parts: (1) the description variables (`?t ?e ?r`) describe the type, effect, and region variables that can be generalized in the type schema; (2) the procedure type (`-> ((cellof ?t ?r)) ?e unit`) describes the cell assignment operation and notes that its application has effect `?e`; and (3) the effect-constraint set (`(>= ?e (write ?r))`) describes the constraints on the effect variable `?e`. In this case, the assignment operation can have any effect as long as it is larger than (`write ?r`), where `?r` specifies the region in which the cell is allocated.

A `swap` procedure that swaps the contents of two cells would have the following algebraic type schema:

$$TS_{swap} = \text{(generic (?t ?e ?r1 ?r2)}$$
```
             (-> ((cellof ?t ?r1) (cellof ?t ?r2)) ?e unit)
             ((>= ?e (maxeff (read ?r1) (write ?r1)
                            (read ?r2) (write ?r2)))))
```

Domains

$ATS \in \text{AlgebraicTypeSchema} ::= T \mid (\texttt{generic} \ (\delta^*) \ T \ (FCS))$

$TE \in \text{TypeEnvironment} = \text{Ident} \rightharpoonup \text{AlgebraicTypeSchema}$

Type Functions

$zgen : \text{Type} \rightarrow \text{TypeEnvironment} \rightarrow \text{TypeConstraintSet}$
$\qquad \rightarrow \text{EffectConstraintSet} \rightharpoonup \text{AlgebraicTypeSchema}$

$(zgen \ T \ TE \ TCS \ FCS)$

$$= \begin{cases} (\texttt{generic} \ (\delta_1 \ \ldots \ \delta_n) \ (\sigma \ T) \ ((\sigma \ FCS))), \\ \quad \text{if } solve_{TCS} \ TCS = (\text{TypeSubst} \rightarrowtail \text{UnifySoln } \sigma) \\ \quad \text{and } \{\delta_1, \ldots, \delta_n\} = (FrDescIds_{ty}[\![(\sigma \ T)]\!] \cup FrDescIds_{FCS}[\![(\sigma \ FCS)]\!]) \\ \qquad\qquad\qquad - (FrDescIds_{tyenv} \ (\sigma \ TE)) \\ undefined, \text{ otherwise} \end{cases}$$

$zgenPure_{SP} : \text{Type} \rightarrow \text{TypeEnvironment} \rightarrow \text{TypeConstraintSet}$
$\qquad \rightarrow \text{EffectConstraintSet} \rightarrow \text{Exp} \rightharpoonup \text{AlgebraicTypeSchema}$

$(zgenPure_{SP} \ T_{defn} \ TE \ TCS \ FCS \ E)$

$$= \begin{cases} (zgen \ T_{defn} \ TE \ TCS \ FCS) & \text{if } \vdash_{pure} E \text{ (defined in Figure 13.25 on page 816)} \\ T_{defn} & \text{otherwise} \end{cases}$$

Type/Effect Reconstruction Rules

$$Z[\![I]\!] \ TE = \langle ([\delta_i'/\delta_i]_{i=1}^n) \, T_{body}, \{\}_{TCS}, \texttt{pure}, ([\delta_i'/\delta_i]_{i=1}^n) FCS_{body} \rangle \qquad [\text{genvar}_Z]$$
$$\text{where} \quad TE(I) = (\texttt{generic} \ (\delta_{i=1}^n) \ T_{body} \ (FCS_{body}))$$
$$\delta_{i=1}'^n \text{ are fresh}$$

$$\frac{\begin{array}{c} \forall_{i=1}^n \ . \ (Z[\![E_i]\!] \ TE = \langle T_i, TCS_i, F_i, FCS_i \rangle) \\ Z[\![E_0]\!] \ TE[I_i : (zgenPure_{SP} \ T_i \ TE \ TCS_i \ FCS_i \ E_i)]_{i=1}^n \\ = \langle T_0, TCS_0, F_0, FCS_0 \rangle \end{array}}{\begin{array}{c} Z[\![(\texttt{let} \ ((I_i \ E_i)_{i=1}^n) \ E_0)]\!] \ TE \\ = \langle T_0, TCS_0 \uplus TCS_{defns}, (\texttt{maxeff} \ F_{i=0}^n), @_{i=0}^n FCS_i \rangle \\ \text{where} \quad TCS_{defns} = \uplus_{i=1}^n TCS_i \end{array}} \qquad [\text{let}_{SPZ}]$$

$$\frac{\begin{array}{c} \forall_{i=1}^n \ . \ \left(Z[\![E_i]\!] \ TE[I_j : \delta_j]_{j=1}^n = \langle T_i, TCS_i, F_i, FCS_i \rangle \right) \\ Z[\![E_0]\!] \ TE[I_i : (zgenPure_{SP} \ T_i \ TE \ TCS_{defns} \ FCS_{defns} \ E_i)]_{i=1}^n \\ = \langle T_0, TCS_0, F_0, FCS_0 \rangle \end{array}}{\begin{array}{c} Z[\![(\texttt{letrec} \ ((I_i \ E_i)_{i=1}^n) \ E_0)]\!] \ TE \\ = \langle T_0, TCS_0 \uplus TCS_{defns}, (\texttt{maxeff} \ F_{i=0}^n), @_{i=0}^n FCS_i \rangle \\ \text{where} \quad \delta_{i=1}^n \text{ are fresh} \\ TCS_{defns} = (\uplus_{i=1}^n TCS_i) \uplus (\uplus_{i=1}^n \{\delta_i \doteq T_i\}_{TCS}) \\ FCS_{defns} = @_{i=1}^n FCS_i \end{array}} \qquad [\text{letrec}_{SPZ}]$$

Figure 16.8 FLARE/E type/effect reconstruction for `let` polymorphism.

The effect-constraint set in this algebraic type schema constrains the latent effect of the swap procedure type to include read and write effects for the regions of both cells.

As in FLARE type reconstruction, the type/effect reconstruction system introduces type schemas in the rules for let and letrec expressions. Algebraic type schemas are created by the $zgenPure_{SP}$ and $zgen$ functions defined in Figure 16.8. These are similar to the $rgenPure$ and $rgen$ functions used in FLARE type reconstruction (as defined in Figure 13.26 on page 818), except that:

- $zgenPure_{SP}$ takes an additional argument, an effect-constraint set, and returns an algebraic type schema rather than a regular type schema. The purity of the expression argument determines whether generalization takes place, and the effect-constraint set is passed along to $zgen$. $zgenPure_{SP}$ employs the same syntactic purity test used in Algorithm R and the FLARE/E type/effect system; see Section 16.2.5 for a discussion of an alternative purity test.

- $zgen$ takes one additional argument, an effect-constraint set, which it incorporates into the algebraic type schema. Note that the schema generalizes over free description variables in the effect constraints (as well as in the type) that are not mentioned in the type environment.

As in $rgen$, the type constraints in $zgen$ must be solved before generalization can take place. Why not solve the effect constraints as well? Because effect constraints involve *inequalities* rather than equalities, they can only be solved globally, not locally. E.g., knowing that ?e is larger than (read r1) and (write r2) does not allow us to conclude that ?e = (maxeff (read r1) (write r2)), since there may be other constraints on ?e elsewhere in the program that force it to encompass more effects. So the solution of effect inequality constraints must be delayed until all effect constraints in the whole program have been collected (see the $[prog_Z]$ rule in Figure 16.9, which is discussed later). In contrast, type equality constraints can be solved eagerly as well as lazily. This is why algebraic type schemas must carry effect constraints but not type constraints.

When the type environment assigns an algebraic type schema to a variable, the $[genvar_Z]$ rule instantiates the parameters of the type schema with fresh description variables. Because different description variables are chosen for different occurences of the variable, the definitions associated with the variables may be used polymorphically. Although the variable reference itself is pure, its effect-constraint set includes instantiated versions of the algebraic type schema's effect constraints. For example, suppose that cell x is an integer cell allocated in region

Domains for Type/Effect Reconstruction of Programs

$RA \in \text{ReconAns} = \text{Type} + \text{Failure}$

$\quad \text{Failure} = \{\texttt{fail}\}$

Function Signature for Type/Effect Reconstruction of Programs

$Z_{pgm} : \text{Prog} \to \text{ReconAns}$

Type/Effect Reconstruction Rules for Programs

$$\frac{Z[\![E]\!] \ \{I_i : \delta_i\}_{i=1}^n \ = \ \langle T, TCS, F, FCS \rangle}{Z_{pgm}[\![(\texttt{flarek} \ (I_1 \ \ldots \ I_n) \ E)]\!] \ = \ RA_{pgm}} \qquad [prog_Z]$$

where $\delta_{i=1}^n$ are fresh

$$RA_{pgm} \ = \ \begin{cases} (\text{ProgType} \rightarrowtail \text{ReconAns} \ (\sigma_{FCS} \ (\sigma_{TCS} \ (\texttt{=>} \ (\delta_{i=1}^n) \ F \ T)))), \\ \quad \text{if } solve_{TCS} \ TCS = (\text{TypeSubst} \rightarrowtail \text{UnifySoln} \ \sigma_{TCS}) \\ \quad \text{and } solve_{FCS} \ (\sigma_{TCS} \ FCS) = \sigma_{FCS} \\ (\text{Failure} \rightarrowtail \text{ReconAns} \ \texttt{fail}), \text{ otherwise} \end{cases}$$

Figure 16.9 The FLARE/E type/effect reconstruction algorithm for programs expressed via a deduction rule.

$\texttt{rx}$ and and cell $\texttt{y}$ is an integer cell allocated in region $\texttt{ry}$. Then the reconstruction of $(\texttt{swap x y})$ would yield an effect-constraint set equivalent to

$$((\texttt{>= e1 (maxeff (read rx) (write rx) (read ry) (write ry))))}$$

(where $\texttt{e1}$ is the fresh description variable substituted for $\texttt{?e}$). The reconstruction of $(\texttt{swap x x})$ would yield an effect-constraint set equivalent to

$$((\texttt{>= e2 (maxeff (read rx) (write rx))))}$$

Instantiating the effect-constraint set of the algebraic type schema in the $[genvar]$ rule is consistent with the view that referencing an expression variable bound by a $\texttt{let}$ or $\texttt{letrec}$ to a pure expression E is equivalent to replacing the variable reference by E.

Reconstructing Programs

At the level of a whole program, the $[prog_Z]$ rule in Figure 16.9 models the result of successful type/effect reconstruction as a program type whose

- parameter types are the types of the program parameters;

- result type is the type of the program body; and

- latent effect is the effect of the program body.

This program type is constructed via

$$(\sigma_{FCS} \ (\sigma_{TCS} \ (\texttt{=>} \ (\delta_{i=1}^{n}) \ F_{body} \ T_{body})))$$

where

- $\delta_{i=1}^{n}$ are the description variables generated for the types of the program parameters.

- F_{body} is the effect reconstructed for the program body, E_{body}.

- T_{body} is the type reconstructed for E_{body}.

- σ_{TCS} is the description substitution that is the solution of the type constraints TCS_{body} collected in the reconstruction of E_{body}.

- σ_{FCS} is the description substitution $solve_{FCS} \ (\sigma_{TCS} \ FCS_{body})$ that is the global solution of all the effect constraints FCS_{body} collected in the reconstruction of E_{body}. Before $solve_{FCS}$ is called, the substitution σ_{TCS} must be applied to each constraint in FCS_{body} to incorporate information gleaned from unifying latent effect variables in procedure types and region variables in cell types. For a similar reason, σ_{FCS} is applied to the program type *after* σ_{TCS} has been applied. Note that the application of σ_{FCS} resolves effect variables not only in F_{body} but also in the latent effects of any procedure types that occur in T_{body}.

Algorithm Z has the Power of FLARE/E

Algorithm Z succeeds if the type constraints and effect constraints collected for the program body are solvable. We have seen from the discussion of $solve_{FCS}$ on page 963 that the effect constraints are *always* solvable, so reconstruction succeeds if and only if the type constraints are solvable.

The following theorems say that Algorithm Z is sound and complete for the FLARE/E implicit type/effect system in Figure 16.3 on page 953:

Theorem 16.2 (Soundness of Algorithm Z) *Suppose* $Z[\![E]\!] \ TE \ = \langle T, TCS, F, FCS \rangle$. *If* σ_{TCS} *is any solution of* TCS, σ_{FCS} *is any solution of* $(\sigma_{TCS} \ FCS)$, *and* $\sigma \ = \ \sigma_{FCS} \circ \sigma_{TCS}$, *then* $(\sigma \ TE) \vdash E : (\sigma \ T) \ ! \ (\sigma \ F)$.

Theorem 16.3 (Completeness of Algorithm Z) *If* $TE \vdash E : T \ ! \ F$ *then* $Z[\![E]\!] \ TE \ = \ \langle T', TCS, F', FCS \rangle$ *where there are solutions* σ_{TCS} *of* TCS *and* σ_{FCS} *of* $(\sigma_{TCS} \ FCS)$ *such that* $((\sigma_{FCS} \circ \sigma_{TCS}) \ T') \ = \ T$ *and* $((\sigma_{FCS} \circ \sigma_{TCS}) \ F') \ = \ F$.

In both of these theorems, σ_{TCS} may be less general than the most general unifier calculated by $(solve_{TCS}\ TCS)$ and σ_{FCS} may be greater than the least solution calculated by $(solve_{FCS}\ (\sigma_{TCS}\ FCS))$. In both theorems, it is necessary to apply the composition $\sigma_{FCS} \circ \sigma_{TCS}$ to both types and effects rather than just applying σ_{TCS} to types and σ_{FCS} to effects. For types, σ_{FCS} may be needed to resolve latent effect variables in procedure types that were determined when solving the effect constraints in FCS. For effects, σ_{TCS} may be needed to resolve effect and region variables that were unified as part of solving the type constraints in TCS.

Together, the soundness and completeness theorems for Algorithm Z imply a principality result similar to the one shown for Algorithm R: Any type that can be assigned to an expression in FLARE/E is a substitution instance of the type found by Algorithm Z, and any effect that can be assigned to an expression in FLARE/E is a substitution instance of the effect Algorithm Z.

Since FLARE expressions are typable in the FLARE/E implicit type/effect system if and only if they are typable in the FLARE implicit type system (by Theorem 16.1 on page 956) and expressions are typable in the FLARE implicit type system if and only if their type can be reconstructed by Algorithm R (by Theorems 13.7 and 13.8 on page 799), a consequence of Theorems 16.2 and 16.3 is that Algorithm Z and Algorithm R succeed on *exactly* the same set of FLARE expressions and programs.

Exercise 16.7

a. Write a FLARE/E abstraction $E_{swapabs}$ that swaps the contents of its two cell arguments.

b. Show the derivation for $(Z[\![E_{swapabs}]\!]\ \{\})$, the type/effect reconstruction of $E_{swapabs}$ in the empty type environment.

c. Use $zgenPure$ to create an algebraic type schema for $E_{swapabs}$, supplying the type and effect information from part **b** as arguments.

d. Is your algebraic type schema from part **c** equivalent to TS_{swap} defined on page 966? Explain any discrepancies.

Exercise 16.8 Construct an Algorithm Z type/effect derivation for the following program:

```
(flarek (a b)
  (let ((mapcell (abs (c f)
                   (let ((v (prim ^ c)))
                     (let ((_ (prim := c (f v))))
                       v)))))
    (mapcell a (abs (x) (mapcell b (abs (y) x))))))
```

Exercise 16.9 Give type/effect reconstruction derivations for the programs in part **a** and part **b** of Exercise 16.1 on page 956.

Exercise 16.10 Write a FLARE/E program whose type/effect reconstruction uses an algebraic type schema whose effect-constraint set has more than one constraint. Show this by giving the type/effect reconstruction derivation for your program.

Exercise 16.11 Modify the FLARE/E implicit type/effect system and Algorithm Z to handle mutable variables (via the `set!` construct). Begin by studying Exercise 13.11 on page 820 to get a sense for the issues involved in this extension. In particular, references to variables modified by `set!` are no longer pure — they have a `read` effect! Your system should distinguish variables modified by `set!` from those that are not; references to the latter can still be considered pure.

16.2.4   Effect Masking Hides Unobservable Effects

We now explore some variations on the FLARE/E type/effect system. The first involves **effect masking**, which allows effects to be deleted from an expression when they cannot be observed from outside of the expression. For example, consider the following procedure, which sums the elements of a list of integers:

$$E_{sumabs} = \text{(abs (ints)}$$
```
              (let ((sum (cell 0)))
                (letrec ((loop (abs (ns)
                                 (if (null? ns)
                                     (^ sum)
                                     (begin (:= sum (+ (^ sum)
                                                       (car ns)))
                                            (loop (cdr ns)))))))
                  (loop ints))))
```

Suppose that the cell named `sum` is in region `rs`. According to the effect rules we have studied thus far, the latent effect of the type for this procedure is

$$\text{(maxeff (init rs) (read rs) (write rs))}$$

Intuitively, however, the `sum` cell is completely internal to the summation procedure and cannot be observed outside the procedure. There is no experiment that a client can perform to determine whether or not the summation procedure uses cells in its implementation.

We can use the type/effect system to prove that the effects within the summation procedure are unobservable outside the procedure. We do this by showing that no cell in region `rs` can be referenced outside the `let` expression that is the body of the procedure. Region `rs` does not appear in the type (`int`) of the

$$\frac{TE \vdash E : T \mathbin{!} F}{TE \vdash E : T \mathbin{!} F'} \qquad\qquad \textit{[effect-masking]}$$

where $F' \sqsubseteq_e F$
$\forall BF \in (\mathcal{F}[\![F]\!] - \mathcal{F}[\![F']\!])$.
$\quad (\forall \delta \in FrDescIds_{eff}[\![BF]\!]$.
$\quad\quad ((\delta \notin FrDescIds_{ty}[\![T]\!])$ *[export restriction]*
$\quad\quad \wedge (\forall I \in FrIds[\![E]\!]$. $(\delta \notin FrDescIds_{ty}[\![TE(I)]\!]))))$ *[import restriction]*

Figure 16.10 An effect-masking rule for FLARE/E.

procedure body, nor does it appear in the type environment in the types of the free variables used in the procedure body (`ints`, `cell`, `^`, `:=`, `+`, `null?`, `car`, `cdr`). This shows that region `rs` is inaccessible outside the procedure body, and so cannot be observed by any client of the procedure.

We can add effect masking to FLARE/E by extending the type/effect rules with the [*effect-masking*] rule in Figure 16.10. This rule says that any base effect BF can be deleted from the effect of an expression E as long as it is purely local to E — i.e., it cannot be observed elsewhere in the program. BF is local to E if no effect and region variable δ appearing in it is mentioned in the type of any free variable used by E (the import restriction) or can escape to the rest of the program in the type of E (the export restriction). In some sense, the [*effect-masking*] rule is the opposite of the [*does*] rule, since it allows deflating the effect of an expression as opposed to inflating it.

In the case of the list summation procedure, the [*effect-masking*] rule formalizes our above reasoning about effect observability. It allows the `let` expression to be assigned the `pure` effect, making the latent effect of the procedure type for E_{sumabs} `pure` as well.

Note that the [*effect-masking*] rule does *not* allow any effects to be deleted from the `letrec` expression in the list summation procedure. Although `rs` does not appear in the type (`int`) of this expression, it does appear in the type (`cellof int rs`) of the free variable `sum` used in the expression.

Effect masking is an important tool for encapsulation. The [*effect-masking*] rule can detect that certain expressions, while internally impure, are in fact externally pure. It thus permits impure expressions to be included in otherwise stateless functional programs; expressions can take advantage of local side effects for efficiency without losing their referential transparency. As we will see in Section 16.3.1, it also allows effects that denote control transfers to be masked, indicating that an expression may perform internal control transfers that are not observable outside of the expression.

If the [*effect-masking*] rule is so important, why didn't we include it as a rule in the FLARE/E type/effect system presented in Figure 16.3 on page 953? The reason is that it complicates the story of type reconstruction. The effects computed by the $solve_{FCS}$ function in Algorithm Z are the least effects for the type/effect system presented in Figure 16.3. But they are no longer the least effects when the [*effect-masking*] rule is added, since this rule allows even smaller effects. For example, Algorithm Z would determine that the effect of the `let` expression that is the body of E_{sumabs} includes `init`, `read`, and `write` effects for the region `rs` in which the `sum` cell is allocated, but we have seen that these can be eliminated by the [*effect-masking*] rule.

Exercise 16.12 Consider the following FLARE expression:

```
(abs (a)
  (let ((b (cell 1)))
    (snd (let ((_ (:= a (^ b)))
               (c (cell 2))
               (d (cell 3)))
           (let ((_ (:= c (^ e))))  {e is a free variable}
             (pair c d))))))
```

a. Construct a FLARE/E type/effect derivation for this expression that does not use the [*effect-masking*] rule. Assume that each cell is allocated in a separate region.

b. Construct a FLARE/E type/effect derivation for this expression that uses the [*effect-masking*] rule to find the smallest allowable effect for each subexpression.

16.2.5   Effect-based Purity for Generalization

It may be surprising that the $egenPure_{SP}$ function for type generalization in the FLARE/E type rules (Figure 16.2 on page 952) determines expression purity using a syntactic test rather than using the effect system itself. Here we explore an alternative type/effect system FLARE/E$_{EP}$ that determines purity via an effect-based test rather than a syntactic test. (The EP subscript stands for "effect purity.")

The key difference between FLARE/E$_{EP}$ and FLARE/E is the new function $egenPure_{EP}$ in Figure 16.11. Like $egenPure_{SP}$, $egenPure_{EP}$ uses its third argument to determine the purity (and thus the generalizability) of an expression. However, $egenPure_{EP}$'s third argument is an effect determined from the effect system, whereas $egenPure_{SP}$'s is an expression whose effect is determined by a separate syntactic deduction system. The [let_{EP}] and [$letrec_{EP}$] rules employ effect-based purity by passing appropriate effects to $egenPure_{EP}$.

New Type Function

$egenPure_{EP}$: Type $\rightarrow$ TypeEnvironment $\rightarrow$ Effect $\rightarrow$ TypeSchema

$$(egenPure_{EP}\ T_{defn}\ TE\ F) = \begin{cases} (egen\ T_{defn}\ TE) & \text{if } F \approx_e \text{pure} \\ T_{defn} & \text{otherwise} \end{cases}$$

Modified Type/Effect Rules

$$\frac{\forall_{i=1}^{n}\ .\ (TE \vdash E_i : T_i\ !\ F_i) \quad TE[I_i : (egenPure_{EP}\ T_i\ TE\ F_i)]_{i=1}^{n} \vdash E_0 : T_0\ !\ F_0}{TE \vdash (\texttt{let}\ ((I_i\ E_i)_{i=1}^{n})\ E_0) : T_0\ !\ (\texttt{maxeff}\ F_{i=0}^{n})} \quad [let_{EP}]$$

$$\frac{\forall_{i=1}^{n}\ .\ \left(TE[I_j : T_j]_{j=1}^{n} \vdash E_i : T_i\ !\ F_i\right) \quad TE[I_i : (egenPure_{EP}\ T_i\ TE\ F_i)]_{i=1}^{n} \vdash E_0 : T_0\ !\ F_0}{TE \vdash (\texttt{letrec}\ ((I_i\ E_i)_{i=1}^{n})\ E_0) : T_0\ !\ (\texttt{maxeff}\ F_{i=0}^{n})} \quad [letrec_{EP}]$$

Figure 16.11 Modified type/effect rules for FLARE/E_{EP}, a system that uses the effect system itself rather than syntactic tests to determine purity.

The FLARE/E_{EP} type system is more powerful than the FLARE and FLARE/E systems: every expression typable in FLARE and FLARE/E is typable in FLARE/E_{EP}, but there are expressions typable in FLARE/E_{EP} that are not typable in FLARE or FLARE/E. Consider the expression:

```
E_curriedPair = (let ((cp (abs (x) (abs (y) (prim pair x y)))))
                  (let ((cp1 (cp 1)))
                    (prim pair (cp1 #u) (cp1 #t))))
```

This expression is *not* well typed in FLARE. According to the syntactic definition of purity in Figure 13.25 on page 816, the application (cp 1) is considered impure, so the type of cp1 cannot be generalized to a polymorphic type and must be a monomorphic type of the form (-> (T_y) (pairof int T_y)). Since (cp1 #u) requires T_y to be unit and (cp1 #t) requires T_y to be bool, no FLARE typing is possible. Similar reasoning shows that $E_{curriedPair}$ is not well typed in FLARE/E.

In contrast, $E_{curriedPair}$ *is* well typed in FLARE/E_{EP}, as shown by the type/effect derivation in Figure 16.12. The key difference is that the effect system can deduce that the application (cp 1) is pure, and this allows the type of cp1 to be generalized in FLARE/E_{EP}. The extra typing power of FLARE/E_{EP} derives from using the more precise purity test of the effect system itself in place of the crude syntactic purity test used in FLARE and FLARE/E.

Abbreviations

$E_{curriedPair}$ = (let ((cp E_{abs1}))
                (let ((cp1 (cp 1)))
                  (prim pair (cp1 #u) (cp1 #t)))))

E_{abs1} = (abs (x) E_{abs2})

E_{abs2} = (abs (y) (prim pair x y))

TE_1 = {cp : (generic (?x ?y)
                    (-> (?x) pure (-> (?y) pure (pairof ?x ?y))))}

TE_2 = TE_1[cp1 : (generic (?y) (-> (?y) pure (pairof int ?y)))]

T_{iu} = (pairof int unit)

T_{ib} = (pairof int bool)

Type/Effect Derivation

TE_{prim} ⊢ pair : (-> (?x ?y) pure (pairof ?x ?y)) ! pure [genvar]

{x : ?x, y : ?y} ⊢ x : ?x ! pure [var]

{x : ?x, y : ?y} ⊢ y : ?y ! pure [var]

{x : ?x, y : ?y} ⊢ (prim pair x y) : (pairof ?x ?y) ! pure [prim]

{x : ?x} ⊢ E_{abs2} : (-> (?y) pure (pairof ?x ?y)) ! pure [→-intro]

{} ⊢ E_{abs1} : (-> (?x) pure (-> (?y) pure (pairof ?x ?y))) ! pure [→-intro]

TE_1 ⊢ cp : (-> (int) pure
             (-> (?y) pure (pairof int ?y))) ! pure [genvar]

TE_1 ⊢ 1 : int ! pure [int]

TE_1 ⊢ (cp 1) : (-> (?y) pure (pairof int ?y)) ! pure [→-elim]

TE_{prim} ⊢ pair : (-> (T_{iu} T_{ib}) pure (pairof T_{iu} T_{ib})) ! pure [genvar]

TE_2 ⊢ cp1 : (-> (unit) pure (pairof int unit)) ! pure [genvar]

TE_2 ⊢ #u : unit ! pure [unit]

TE_2 ⊢ (cp1 #u) : (pairof int unit) ! pure [→-elim]

TE_2 ⊢ cp1 : (-> (bool) pure (pairof int bool)) ! pure [genvar]

TE_2 ⊢ #t : bool ! pure [bool]

TE_2 ⊢ (cp1 #t) : (pairof int bool) ! pure [→-elim]

TE_2 ⊢ (prim pair (cp1 #u) (cp1 #t)) : (pairof T_{iu} T_{ib}) ! pure [prim]

TE_1 ⊢ (let ((cp1 (cp 1)))
       (prim pair (cp1 #u) (cp1 #t))) : (pairof T_{iu} T_{ib}) ! pure [let]

{} ⊢ $E_{curriedPair}$: (pairof T_{iu} T_{ib}) ! pure [let]

Figure 16.12 Type/effect derivation for $E_{curriedPair}$ in FLARE/E_{EP}.

Given the apparent advantages of effect-based purity over syntactic purity, why did we adopt syntactic purity as the default in the FLARE/E type/effect system? The reason is that effect-based purity greatly complicates type reconstruction. With syntactic purity, the decision to generalize types in the $[let_{SPZ}]$ and $[letrec_{SPZ}]$ type reconstruction rules is independent of solving the effect constraints collected during reconstruction. With effect-based purity, type generalization may depend on the result of solving effect constraints. This introduces a fundamental dependency problem: the decision to generalize must be made when processing `let` and `letrec` expressions, but the effect constraints cannot be solved until the whole program body has been processed. One way to address this dependency problem is via backtracking (see Exercise 16.16).

Exercise 16.13 Show that the FLARE/E$_{EP}$ type/effect system can be made even more powerful by extending it with the [effect-masking] rule in Figure 16.10 on page 973. That is, give an expression that is typable in FLARE/E$_{EP}$ + [effect-masking] that is not typable in FLARE/E$_{EP}$.

Exercise 16.14 Thai Ping suggests the following subtyping rule for FLARE/E procedure types:

$$\frac{\forall_{i=1}^{n} . (T_i \sqsubseteq T'_i) \quad T'_{body} \sqsubseteq T_{body} \quad F' \sqsubseteq_e F}{(\text{->} \ (T'^{n}_{1=1}) \ F' \ T'_{body}) \sqsubseteq (\text{->} \ (T^{n}_{i=1}) \ F \ T_{body})} \qquad [\text{->-}\sqsubseteq]$$

a. Suppose that the FLARE/E$_{EP}$ type system were extended with Thai's rule as well as with a version of the [inclusion] type rule in Figure 12.1 on page 703. Give an example of an expression that is well typed in the extended system that is not well typed in the original one.

b. Suppose that the FLARE/E type system were extended with Thai's rule as well as the [inclusion] type rule. Are there any expressions that are well typed in the extended system but not well typed in the original one? Either give such an expression or show that the two systems are equivalent in terms of typing power.

Exercise 16.15 Bud Lojack thinks that a small modification to Algorithm Z can make it sound and complete for FLARE/E$_{EP}$, the version of the FLARE/E type system using effect-based purity. He modifies the reconstruction rules for `let` and `letrec` to use a new $zgenPure_{EP}$ function that performs an effect-based purity test (Figure 16.13).

Excitedly, Bud shows his modifications to Thai Ping. But Thai bursts Bud's bubble when he observes, "Your modified rules are just another way of reconstructing types and effects for FLARE/E, not for FLARE/E$_{EP}$. The problem is that the purity test in $zgenPure_{EP}$ involves effect expressions containing effect variables that may eventually be shown to be pure but are conservatively assumed to be impure when the purity test is performed."

Show that Thai is right by fleshing out the following two steps, which show that replacing the $[let_{SPZ}]/[letrec_{SPZ}]$ rules by the $[let_{EPZ}]/[letrec_{EPZ}]$ rules does not change which expressions can be reconstructed by Algorithm Z.

a. Prove the following lemma:

> **Lemma 16.4** *In Bud's modified Algorithm Z, suppose that $Z[\![E]\!]\ TE = \langle T, TCS, F, FCS \rangle$ and $(solve_{TCS}\ TCS) = (TypeSubst \mapsto UnifySoln\ \sigma_{TCS})$. Then $(\sigma_{TCS}\ F) \approx_e$ pure if and only if $(\vdash_{pure} E)$ according to the deduction system for $\vdash_{pure}$ defined in Figure 13.25 on page 816.*

> *Hint:* What is the form of every latent effect in a procedure type generated by Algorithm Z? What does this imply about the purity of procedure applications?

b. Using Lemma 16.4, show that in any type/effect derivation from Bud's modified Algorithm Z, any instances of the $[let_{EPZ}]$ and $[letrec_{EPZ}]$ rules can be replaced by the $[let_{SPZ}]$ and $[letrec_{SPZ}]$ rules without changing the validity of the derivation.

Exercise 16.16 Bud Lojack's version of Algorithm Z (see Exercise 16.15) fails to reconstruct the types and effects of some expressions that are well typed in the $\text{FLARE}/\text{E}_{EP}$ type/effect system because it doesn't "know" the purity of certain effect variables that eventually turn out to be pure. This drawback can be addressed by aggressively assuming that all effect variables are pure unless there is evidence otherwise, and backtracking in any case where the assumption is later proven to be false.

a. Design and implement a backtracking version of Bud's modified Algorithm Z based on this idea.

b. Show that your modified version of Algorithm Z can successfully reconstruct the type and effect of the expression $E_{curriedPair}$ defined on page 975.

16.3   Using Effects to Analyze Program Behavior

Thus far we have considered a system for calculating only store effects. Store effects are especially useful for guiding compiler optimizations like parallelization, common subexpression elimination, dead code elimination, and code hoisting (see Section 17.6). We now explore other kinds of effects and show how effect information can be used to reason about program behavior and guide the implementation of programs.

16.3.1   Control Transfers

Effects can be used to analyze control transfers, such as those expressed via the label and jump constructs studied in Section 9.4. Recall that (label I_{cp} E_{body}) evaluates E_{body} in an environment where I_{cp} names the control point corresponding to the continuation of the label expression, and (jump E_{cp} E_{val}) jumps to

---

New Type Function

$zgenPure_{EP}$: Type $\rightarrow$ TypeEnvironment $\rightarrow$ TypeConstraintSet
$\qquad\qquad\rightarrow$ EffectConstraintSet $\rightarrow$ Effect $\rightharpoonup$ AlgebraicTypeSchema

$(zgenPure_{EP}\ T_{defn}\ TE\ TCS\ FCS\ F)$

$= \begin{cases} (zgen\ T_{defn}\ TE\ TCS\ FCS), \\ \quad \text{if } solve_{TCS}\ TCS = (\text{TypeSubst} \rightarrowtail \text{UnifySoln } \sigma) \text{ and } (\sigma\ F) \approx_e \text{pure} \\ T_{defn}, \text{ otherwise} \end{cases}$

Modified Type/Effect Reconstruction Rules

$$\frac{\forall_{i=1}^n\ .\ (Z[\![E_i]\!]\ TE = \langle T_i, TCS_i, F_i, FCS_i\rangle) \quad Z[\![E_0]\!]\ TE[I_i : (zgenPure_{EP}\ T_i\ TE\ TCS_i\ FCS_i\ F_i)]_{i=i}^n = \langle T_0, TCS_0, F_0, FCS_0\rangle}{\begin{array}{c} Z[\![(\texttt{let}\ ((I_i\ E_i)_{i=1}^n)\ E_0)]\!]\ TE \\ = \langle T_0, TCS_0 \uplus TCS_{defns}, (\texttt{maxeff}\ F_{i=0}^n), @_{i=0}^n FCS_i\rangle \\ \text{where}\quad TCS_{defns} = \biguplus_{i=1}^n TCS_i \end{array}}\quad [\text{let}_{EPZ}]$$

$$\frac{\forall_{i=1}^n\ .\ \left(Z[\![E_i]\!]\ TE[I_j : \delta_j]_{j=1}^n = \langle T_i, TCS_i, F_i, FCS_i\rangle\right) \quad Z[\![E_0]\!]\ TE[I_i : (zgenPure_{EP}\ T_i\ TE\ TCS_{defns}\ FCS_{defns}\ F_i)]_{i=i}^n = \langle T_0, TCS_0, F_0, FCS_0\rangle}{\begin{array}{c} Z[\![(\texttt{letrec}\ ((I_i\ E_i)_{i=1}^n)\ E_0)]\!]\ TE \\ = \langle T_0, TCS_0 \uplus TCS_{defns}, (\texttt{maxeff}\ F_{i=0}^n), @_{i=0}^n FCS_i\rangle \\ \text{where}\quad \delta_{i=1}^n \text{ are fresh} \\ TCS_{defns} = (\biguplus_{i=1}^n TCS_i) \uplus (\biguplus_{i=1}^n \{\delta_i \doteq T_i\}_{TCS}) \\ FCS_{defns} = @_{i=1}^n FCS_i \end{array}}\quad [\text{letrec}_{EPZ}]$$

Figure 16.13 Bud Lojack's modified type/effect reconstruction rules for `let` and `letrec` in Algorithm Z (Exercise 16.15).

the control point denoted by E_{cp} with the value of E_{val}. Here is a simple example in a version of FLARE/E extended with these two constructs:

E_{proc1} = (abs (x y)
$\qquad\qquad$ (+ 1 (label exit
$\qquad\qquad\qquad\qquad$ (* 2 (if (< y 0) (jump exit y) x)))))

In E_{proc1}, `label` gives the name `exit` to the control point that returns the value of the `label` expression. If `y` is negative, the `jump` to `exit` returns `y` as the value of the `label` expression, and E_{proc1} returns one more than the value of `y`. Otherwise, no jump is performed, the value of the `label` expression is double the value of `x`, and E_{proc1} returns one more than double the value of `x`. (See Section 9.4 for more examples of nonlocal exits.)

$\qquad$ The control behavior of `label` and `jump` can be modeled by introducing a new type and two new effect constructors:

$$\frac{TE[I_{cp} : (\texttt{controlpointof}\ T_{body}\ R)] \vdash E_{body} : T_{body}\ !\ F_{body}}{TE \vdash (\texttt{label}\ I_{cp}\ E_{body}) : T_{body}\ !\ (\texttt{maxeff}\ (\texttt{comefrom}\ R)\ F_{body})} \quad [\textit{cp-intro}]$$

$$\frac{\begin{array}{c} TE \vdash E_{cp} : (\texttt{controlpointof}\ T_{val}\ R)\ !\ F_{cp} \\ TE \vdash E_{val} : T_{val}\ !\ F_{val} \end{array}}{TE \vdash (\texttt{jump}\ E_{cp}\ E_{val}) : T_{any}\ !\ (\texttt{maxeff}\ (\texttt{goto}\ R)\ F_{cp}\ F_{val})} \quad [\textit{cp-elim}]$$

Figure 16.14   Type/effect rules for `label` and `jump`.

$$T \in \text{Type} ::= \ldots \mid (\texttt{controlpointof}\ T\ R)$$
$$FCR \in \text{EffectConstructor} = \ldots \cup \{\texttt{goto}, \texttt{comefrom}\}$$

The type $(\texttt{controlpointof}\ T\ R)$ describes a control point in region R that expects to receive a value of type T. An expression has effect $(\texttt{goto}\ R)$ if it might jump to a control point in R, and it has effect $(\texttt{comefrom}\ R)$[6] if it creates a control point in R that could be the target of a jump. Although regions represent areas of memory in store effects, they represent sets of control points in control effects, and can have other meanings for other kinds of effects.

The FLARE/E type/effect system can be extended to handle control effects with the two rules in Figure 16.14. In the [*cp-intro*] rule, $(\texttt{label}\ I_{cp}\ E_{body})$ introduces a control point with type $(\texttt{controlpointof}\ T_{body}\ R)$ into the type environment in which E_{body} is type-checked. The type of the `label` expression must be the same whether E_{body} returns normally (without encountering a `jump`) or a `jump` is performed to the named control point. This constrains the received value type in the `controlpointof` type to be the same as the type T_{body} of E_{body}. The effect of the `label` expression includes $(\texttt{comefrom}\ R)$ to indicate that it introduces a control point in region R.

The [*cp-elim*] rule requires that in $(\texttt{jump}\ E_{cp}\ E_{val})$ the type of E_{cp} must be $(\texttt{controlpointof}\ T_{val}\ R)$, where the received value type T_{val} must match the type of the supplied value E_{val}. The effect of a `jump` expression includes $(\texttt{goto}\ R)$ to model its control-point-jumping behavior. The `jump` expression has an unconstrained type, T_{any}, that is determined by the context in which it is used. For example, in

```
(* 2 (if (< y 0) (jump exit y) x))
```

the `jump` expression has type `int` to match the type of `x`. But in

```
(* 2 (if (scor (< y 0) (jump exit x)) y x))
```

---

[6]The effect name `comefrom` is a play on the name `goto`, and was inspired by a spoof article [Cla73] on a COME FROM statement dual to a GOTO statement.

the `jump` expression must have type `bool` because it appears in a context that requires a boolean value.

Returning to our example,

E_{proc1} = (abs (x y)
            (+ 1 (label exit
                    (* 2 (if (< y 0) (jump exit y) x)))))

`exit` has type (`controlpointof int cp1`), where `cp1` is a control region. The expression (`jump exit y`) has type `int` and effect (`goto cp1`). The `label` expression has type `int` and an effect, (`maxeff (comefrom cp1) (goto cp1)`), describing that it establishes a control point in region `cp1` that is the target of `jump` that may be performed in its body.

In this simple example, the control effects (`comefrom cp1`) and (`goto cp1`) are completely local to the `label` expression. So a system that supports effect masking (Section 16.2.4) can delete them from the effect of the `label` expression and the latent effect of the abstraction, making these effects `pure`. This highlights that effect masking works for all effects, including control effects and store effects. When a control effect in region R can be masked from expression E, it means that no part of the program outside E will be subject to unexpected control transfers with respect to the continuation associated with R. Effect masking of control effects is powerful because it allows module implementers to use control transfers internally, while allowing clients of the modules to insist that these internal control transfers not alter the clients' control flow. In a system using explicit types and effects at module boundaries, a client can guarantee this invariant by ensuring that it does not call module procedures with control effects.

As an example where control effects cannot be deleted, consider:

E_{proc2} = (label exit
            (abs (y)
              (if (= y 0)
                  (jump exit (abs (z) z))
                  (+ 1 y)))))

In this example, evaluating the `label` expression returns the procedure created by (`abs (y) ...`) without peforming any jumps. This procedure behaves like an incrementing procedure when called on a nonzero argument. But applying it to 0 has the bizarre effect of returning from the `label` expression a second time with the identity procedure instead!

What are the types in this example? Let's assume that the control point for `exit` is in region `cp2`. Then (`abs (y) ...`) must have type

T_{proc2} = (-> (int) (goto cp2) int)

because it takes an integer y, returns an integer (+ 1 y), and may jump to exit. The type of exit must be (controlpointof T_{proc2} cp2), because the [*cp-intro*] rule requires the received value type of the control point to be the same as the body type. The type of (abs (z) z) must also be T_{proc2}, because the [*cp-elim*] rule requires the received value type of the control point to match the type of the value supplied to jump. Finally, the label expression has type T_{proc2} and effect (comefrom cp2), which does not include a goto effect because no jump can be performed by evaluating the label expression. Because cp2 appears in the type T_{proc2} of E_{proc2}, the (comefrom cp2) effect *cannot* be deleted from E_{proc2} via effect masking. This effect tracks the fact that the procedure resulting from E_{proc2} can jump back into E_{proc2} if it is called with the argument 0. Since the impurity of E_{proc2} is externally observable (see Exercise 16.17), the control effect cannot be deleted.

Exercise 16.17

a. Assuming E_{proc2} is the expression studied above, what is the value of the following expression?

```
(let ((g Eproc2) (h Eproc2))
  (list (g 1) (h 1) (h 0)))
```

b. Based on your answer to part **a**, argue that E_{proc2} cannot be a pure expression.

Exercise 16.18 Extend the Algorithm Z type/effect reconstruction rules to handle label and jump.

Exercise 16.19 Control effects can be used to describe the behavior of the procedure cwcc (see Section 9.4.4).

a. Give a type schema for cwcc that is as general as possible.

b. Show how your type schema for cwcc can be instantiated in the following FLARE/E expressions:

i. $E'_{proc1} =$
```
(abs (x y)
  (+ 1 (cwcc (abs (exit)
              (* 2 (if (< y 0) (exit y) x))))))
```

ii. $E'_{proc2} =$
```
(cwcc (abs (exit)
        (abs (y)
          (if (= y 0)
              (exit (abs (z) z))
              (+ 1 y)))))
```

c. Consider the following FLARE/E abstraction:

$$E'_{proc3} = \text{(abs (x y)}$$
$$\text{(+ 1 (cwcc (abs (exit)}$$
$$\text{(* 2 (if (scor (< y 0) (exit x)) (exit y) x))))))}$$

i. Explain why E'_{proc3} is ill typed in FLARE/E.

ii. In an explicitly typed dialect of FLARE/E with universal (i.e., `forall`) types, (1) give a type for `cwcc` and (2) write a well-typed version of E'_{proc3} with appropriate explicit type annotations.

iii. Convert E'_{proc3} to a well-typed FLARE/E abstraction that uses `label` and `jump` instead of `cwcc`.

iv. What feature of the `label` and `jump` type/effect rules makes the well-typedness of your converted abstraction possible?

v. Show that your converted abstraction can be given a `pure` latent effect in a version of FLARE/E with the [*effect-masking*] rule.

16.3.2 Dynamic Variables

In a dynamically scoped language (see Section 7.2.1), dynamically bound variables (i.e., the free variables of a procedure) take their meaning from where the procedure is called rather than where it is defined. References to dynamically bound variables can be tracked by an effect system in which (1) the effect of an expression is the set of dynamically bound variables it might reference and (2) procedure types are extended to have the form

$$\text{(-> } (T^*_{arg})\ ((I_{dyn}\ T_{dyn})^*)\ T_{result})$$

Each binding $(I_{dyn}\ T_{dyn})$ serves both as a kind of latent effect (each name I_{dyn} is a dynamically bound variable that may be referenced wherever the procedure is called) and as a way to check (using T_{dyn}) that the dynamically bound variable is used with the right type at every invocation of the procedure.

This sketch for how effects can be used to give types to dynamic variables is fleshed out in Exercise 16.20.

Exercise 16.20 Dinah McScoop likes both dynamic scoping and explicit types, so she creates a new language, DIFLEX, that includes both! The syntax of DIFLEX is like FLEX, except for the definition and type of procedures, which have been modified as follows:

$$E \in \text{Exp} ::= \ldots \mid \text{(abs } ((I_{fml}\ T_{fml})^*)\ ((I_{dyn}\ T_{dyn})^*)\ E_{body})$$
$$T \in \text{Type} ::= \ldots \mid \text{(-> } (T^*_{arg})\ ((I_{dyn}\ T_{dyn})^*)\ T_{result})$$

In abs, the first list of identifiers and types, $((I_{fml} \; T_{fml})^*)$, specifies the formal parameters of the procedure and their types. The second list, $((I_{dyn} \; T_{dyn})^*)$, specifies the names and types of the dynamically bound identifiers (all non-parameter identifiers) that appear in E_{body}. Procedure types include the names and types of dynamically bound identifiers in addition to the usual parameter type list and result type. As usual, in a procedure application, the procedure's parameter types must match the types of the actual arguments. Because DIFLEX is dynamically scoped, the types of the dynamically bound identifiers in the procedure type must match the types of these identifiers wherever the procedure is called, not where it is defined.

For example, the following expression is well typed in Dinah's language because the dynamically bound variable x is a boolean where procedure p is called (the fact that x is an integer where p is created is irrelevant):

```
(let ((x 1))
  (let ((p (abs ((y int)) ((x bool)) (if x y 0))))
    (let ((x #t))
      (p 1)))) {This expression evaluates to 1}
```

In contrast, the following expression is ill typed:

```
(let ((x #t))
  (let ((p (abs ((y int)) ((x bool)) (if x y 0))))
    (let ((x 1))
      (p 1)))) {x is not a boolean in this call to p}
```

Dinah realizes that uses of dynamic variables can be tracked by an effect system. Dinah extends the FLEX typing framework to employ type/use judgments of the form

$$TE \vdash E : T \,\&\, IS$$

which means "in type environment TE, E has type T and may use identifiers from the set IS." Assume $IS \in \mathrm{IdSet} = \mathcal{P}(\mathrm{Ident})$. For example, Dinah's type/use rule for variable references is:

$$TE \vdash I : TE(I) \,\&\, \{I\} \qquad\qquad\qquad \text{[var]}$$

Dinah provides the following examples of type/use judgments for her system:

$$\{x : \mathtt{int}\} \vdash (\mathtt{prim} + 1\ \mathtt{x}) : \mathtt{int} \,\&\, \{x\}$$

$$\{\} \vdash (\mathtt{let}\ ((\mathtt{x}\ 1))\ (\mathtt{prim} + 1\ \mathtt{x})) : \mathtt{int} \,\&\, \{\}$$

$$\{x : \mathtt{bool}, y : \mathtt{int}\} \vdash (\mathtt{if}\ \mathtt{x}\ \mathtt{y}\ 0) : \mathtt{int} \,\&\, \{x, y\}$$

$$\{x : \mathtt{int}\} \vdash (\mathtt{abs}\ ((\mathtt{y}\ \mathtt{int}))\ ((\mathtt{x}\ \mathtt{bool}))\ (\mathtt{if}\ \mathtt{x}\ \mathtt{y}\ 0))$$
$$: (\mathtt{->}\ (\mathtt{int})\ ((\mathtt{x}\ \mathtt{bool}))\ \mathtt{int}) \,\&\, \{\}$$

$$\{x : \mathtt{bool}, p : (\mathtt{->}\ (\mathtt{int})\ ((\mathtt{x}\ \mathtt{bool}))\ \mathtt{int})\} \vdash (\mathtt{p}\ 1) : \mathtt{int} \,\&\, \{p, x\}$$

In the final type judgment, note that the identifier set for (p 1) includes x because the procedure p has a dynamic reference to x.

a. Write type/use rules for the following constructs: let, abs, and procedure application.

b. Briefly argue that your type/use rules guarantee that in a well-typed program, an identifier can never be unbound or used with an incorrect type.

c. Dinah's friend Thai Ping observes that the following DIFLEX expression is ill typed:

```
(abs ((b bool)) ()
  (let ((f (abs ((x int)) ((c int)) (prim + x c)))
        (g (abs ((y int)) ((d int)) (prim * y d))))
    (let ((c 1) (d 2))
      ((if b f g) 3))))
```

    i.   Explain why this expression is ill typed.

   ii.   Thai suggests that expressions like this can be made well typed by extending the type/usage rules for DIFLEX with a type-inclusion rule (see Figure 12.1 on page 703). Define an appropriate notion of subtyping for DIFLEX's procedure types, and show how Thai's example is well-typed in the presence of type inclusion.

d. Based on ideas from the DIFLEX language and type system, develop an explicitly typed version of the DYNALEX language (Exercise 7.25 on page 349) named DYNAFLEX. Describe the syntax and type system of DYNAFLEX. *Hint:* Since DYNAFLEX has two namespaces — a static one and a dynamic one — the type system needs two type environments.

16.3.3 Exceptions

Recall from Section 9.6 that exception-handling mechanisms specify how to deal with abnormal conditions in a program. A type/effect system can be used to track the exceptions that might be raised when evaluating an expression. One way to do this in FLARE/E is to use new base effects with the form (raises I_{tag} T_{info}) to indicate that an expression raises an exception with tag I_{tag} and information of type T_{info}. If an expression E handles an exception with tag I_{tag}, the (raises I_{tag} T_{info}) effect can be removed from the effect set of E. Exercise 16.21 explores a specialized effect system that tracks only exceptions and not other effects.

JAVA is an example of an explicitly typed language with an effect system for exceptions. It tracks a subset of exceptions known as checked exceptions. If a checked exception is thrown (JAVA's terminology for raising an exception) in the body of a method, then it must either be explicitly handled by a try/catch statement or explicitly listed in a **throws** clause of the method specification. For example, a JAVA method that displays the first n characters of a text file might have the following specification:

```
public static void readFirst (n:int, filename:string)
  throws FileNotFoundException, EOFException;
```

The `throws` clause indicates that the `readFirst` method may not handle the case where there is no file named `filename` (in which case a `FileNotFoundException` is thrown) and might attempt to read past the end of a file (in which case an `EOFException`[7] is thrown). The `throws` clause serves as an explicit latent exception effect for the method. Any method invoking `readFirst` in its body must either handle the exceptions it throws or explicitly declare them in its own `throws` clause.

Exercise 16.21 Bud Lojack wants to add exceptions with termination semantics to FLARE. He extends the FLARE expression and type syntax as follows:

$$E \in \mathrm{Exp} ::= \dots \mid \texttt{(raise } I_{tag} \ E_{info}) \mid \texttt{(handle } I_{tag} \ E_{handler} \ E_{body})$$
$$T \in \mathrm{Type} ::= \dots \mid \texttt{(handlerof } T_{info})$$

The dynamic semantics of the `raise` and `handle` constructs is described in Section 9.6. Bud's new type (`handlerof` T_{info}) stands for an exception handler that processes exception information with type T_{info}. In Bud's new type rules, the `handlerof` type is used to communicate type information from the point of the `raise` to the point of the `handle`:

$$\frac{\begin{array}{c} TE \vdash E_{handler} : \texttt{(-> } (T_{info}) \ T_{body}) \\ TE[I_{tag} : \texttt{(handlerof } T_{info})] \vdash E_{body} : T_{body} \end{array}}{TE \vdash \texttt{(handle } I_{tag} \ E_{handler} \ E_{body}) : T_{body}} \qquad [handle]$$

$$\frac{TE \vdash I_{tag} : \texttt{(handlerof } T_{info}) \qquad TE \vdash E_{info} : T_{info}}{TE \vdash \texttt{(raise } I_{tag} \ E_{info}) : T_{raise}} \qquad [raise]$$

Note that because `raise` never returns in termination semantics, the type T_{raise} of a `raise` expression (like the type of an `error` expression) can be any type required by the surrounding context.

Bud proudly shows his new rules to type guru Thai Ping, who is unimpressed. "Your rules make the type system unsound!" exclaims Thai. "You've assumed that exception handlers are statically bound when they're actually dynamically bound."

a. Explain what Thai means. In particular, provide expressions E_{outer} and E_{inner} such that the following expression is well typed according to Bud's rules, but generates a dynamic type error:

```
(handle an-exn E_outer
   (let ((f (abs () (raise an-exn 17))))
      (handle an-exn E_inner
         (f)))))
```

Thai observes that raising an exception I_{tag} with a value of type T_{info} is similar to referencing a dynamic variable named I_{tag} bound to a handler procedure with type (`->` (T_{info}) T_{result}), where T_{result} can be different for different handlers associated with

---

[7] EOF stands for "End Of File."

I_{tag}. Since dynamic variables can be typed using an effect system (see Exercise 16.20), Thai aims to develop a similar effect system for typing exceptions. Thai's system is based on "effects" from the following domain:

$$ES \in \text{ExceptionSpec} = \text{Ident} \rightharpoonup \text{Type}$$

An **exception specification** ES is a partial function mapping the name of an exception that can be raised to the type of the information value with which it is raised. For example, representing a partial function as a set of bindings, the exception specification $\{\texttt{bounds} \mapsto \texttt{int}, \texttt{wrong} \mapsto \texttt{bool}\}$ indicates that the $\texttt{bounds}$ exception is raised with an integer and the $\texttt{wrong}$ exception is raised with a boolean. Two exception specifications can be combined via $\oplus$ or $\ominus$, which require that they agree on names for which they are both defined:

$$ES_1 \oplus ES_2 = \begin{cases} \lambda I \,.\, \textbf{if } I \in dom(ES_1) \textbf{ then } (ES_1\ I) \\ \qquad \textbf{else if } I \in dom(ES_2) \textbf{ then } (ES_2\ I) \textbf{ else } undefined \textbf{ end} \\ \qquad \textbf{end}, \\ \qquad \text{if } I \in (dom(ES_1) \cap dom(ES_2)) \text{ implies } (ES_1\ I) \approx (ES_2\ I) \\ undefined, \text{ otherwise} \end{cases}$$

$$ES_1 \ominus ES_2 = \begin{cases} \lambda I \,.\, \textbf{if } (I \in dom(ES_1)) \wedge (I \notin dom(ES_2)) \textbf{ then } (ES_1\ I) \\ \qquad \textbf{else } undefined \textbf{ end}, \\ \qquad \text{if } I \in (dom(ES_1) \cap dom(ES_2)) \text{ implies } (ES_1\ I) \approx (ES_2\ I) \\ undefined, \text{ otherwise} \end{cases}$$

In Thai's type/exception system, judgments have the form

$$TE \vdash E : T \,\#\, ES$$

which means "in type environment TE, expression E has type T and may raise exceptions as specified by ES." For example, the judgment

$$TE \vdash E_{test} : \texttt{bool} \,\#\, \{\texttt{x} \mapsto \texttt{int}, \texttt{y} \mapsto \texttt{symb}\}$$

indicates that if E_{test} returns normally, its value will be a boolean, but that evaluation of E_{test} could raise the exception $\texttt{x}$ with an integer value or the exception $\texttt{y}$ with a symbol value. Thai's system guarantees that no other exceptions can be raised by E_{test}. Thai's system also uses **exception masking** to remove exceptions from judgments when it is clear that they will be handled. E.g., the exception specification of

$$TE \vdash (\texttt{handle x (abs (z) (> z 0))}\ E_{test}) : \texttt{bool} \,\#\, \{\texttt{y} \mapsto \texttt{symb}\}$$

does not include $\texttt{x} \mapsto \texttt{int}$ from E_{test} because the exception named $\texttt{x}$ has been handled by the $\texttt{handle}$ expression.

Thai eliminates Bud's $\texttt{handlerof}$ from the FLARE type system and instead changes procedure types to carry a latent exception specification describing exceptions that might be raised *when the procedure is applied*:

$T \in \text{Type} ::= \dots \text{ FLARE } \textit{types except for } \text{-> } \dots \mid \text{(-> } (T^*_{arg}) \; ES_{lat} \; T_{res})$

Here are two of the type/exception rules from Thai's system:

$$TE \vdash N : \text{int} \# \{\} \qquad\qquad [\textit{int}]$$

$$\frac{TE \vdash E_1 : \text{bool} \# ES_1 \quad TE \vdash E_2 : T \# ES_2 \quad TE \vdash E_3 : T \# ES_3}{TE \vdash (\text{if } E_1 \; E_2 \; E_3) : T \# ES_1 \oplus ES_2 \oplus ES_3} \qquad [\textit{if}]$$

Thai seeks your help in fleshing out other parts of his type/exception system:

b. Give the type/exception rules for abs, procedure application, raise, and handle.

c. Give a type/exception derivation for the following expression, which should be well typed according to your rules:

```
(abs (n m)
  (handle e (abs (a) (not a))
    (let ((f (abs (x) (if (prim < x 0) (raise e x) (prim + x n)))))
      (prim < 0 (if (handle e (abs (y) (prim > y n))
                       (prim = m (f n)))
                    (handle e (abs (z) (if (prim = z n) (raise e #f) z))
                       (prim * 2 (f m)))
                    (handle e (raise e #t)
                       (raise e (raise e (sym beardly))))))))))
```

d. Describe how to extend Thai's type/exception system so that it tracks errors generated by the error construct as well as exceptions.

e. Discuss the technical challenges that need to be addressed in order to modify Algorithm Z to automatically reconstruct types and exception specifications for Thai's system (FLARE+{raise, handle}). For simplicity, ignore all store effects and focus solely on tracking exception specifications. What do constraints on exception specifications look like? Can they always be solved?

16.3.4 Execution Cost Analysis

It is sometimes helpful to have an estimate for the cost of evaluating an expression. A cost might measure abstract units of time or other resources (e.g., memory space, database accesses, network bandwidth) required to evaluate the expression. An effect system can estimate the cost of evaluating an expression by (1) associating a cost effect with each expression and (2) extending procedure types to have a latent cost effect that is accounted for every time a procedure is called. Exercise 16.22 explores a simple cost system based on this idea. For practical cost systems, it must be possible to express costs that depend on the size of data structures (e.g., the length of a list or dimensions of a matrix) [RG94].

Cost systems can be helpful for parallel scheduling; two noninterfering expressions should be scheduled for parallel execution only if their execution times are large enough to outweigh the overheads of the mechanism for parallelism. Cost systems also provide a simple way to conservatively determine which expressions must terminate and which might not. Cost systems can even be used to approximate the complexity of an algorithm [DJG92].

Exercise 16.22 In order to estimate the running time of FLARE programs, Sam Antics wants to develop a set of static rules that assign every expression a **cost** as well as a type. The cost of an expression is a conservative estimate of how long the expression will take to evaluate.

Sam develops a type/cost system for DISCOUNT, a variant of FLARE in which procedure types carry latent cost information:

$$T \in \text{Type} ::= \ldots \text{FLARE } \textit{types except for } \text{-> } \ldots \mid \text{(-> } (T_{arg}^*) \; C_{lat} \; T_{res})$$
$$C \in \text{Cost} ::= NT \mid \texttt{loop} \mid \texttt{(sumc } C^*) \mid \texttt{(maxc } C^*)$$
$$NT \in \text{NatLit} ::= \texttt{0} \mid \texttt{1} \mid \texttt{2} \mid \ldots$$

For example, the DISCOUNT type (-> (int int) 5 bool) is the type of a procedure that takes two integers, returns a boolean result, and costs at most 5 abstract time units every time it is called.

Sam formulates a cost analysis in DISCOUNT via type/cost judgments of the form

$$TE \vdash E : T \; \$ \; C$$

which means "in type environment TE, expression E has type T and cost C." For example, here are Sam's type/cost rules for integers and (nongeneric) variable references:

$$TE \vdash N : \texttt{int} \; \$ \; 1 \qquad\qquad\qquad [int]$$
$$TE \vdash I : TE(I) \; \$ \; 1 \qquad\qquad\qquad [var]$$

That is, Sam assigns both integers and variable references a cost of 1 abstract time unit. In addition, Sam specifies the following costs for some other DISCOUNT expressions:

- The cost of an `abs` expression is 2.

- The cost of an `if` expression is 1 more than the cost of the predicate expression plus the maximum of the costs of the two branch expressions.

- The cost of an n-argument procedure application is the sum of the cost of the operator expression, the cost of each operand expression, the latent cost of the operator, and n.

- The cost of an n-argument primitive application is the sum of the cost of each operand expression, the latent cost of the primitive operator (as specified in the primitive type environment TE_{prim}), and n. Here are some example types of primitive operators:

$$TE_{prim}(\texttt{+}) = \texttt{(-> (int int) 1 int)}$$
$$TE_{prim}(\texttt{>}) = \texttt{(-> (int int) 1 bool)}$$

Here are some example judgments that hold in Sam's system:

$\{a : \texttt{int}\} \vdash (\texttt{prim + a 7}) : \texttt{int}\,\$\,5$

$\{a : \texttt{int}, b : \texttt{int}\} \vdash (\texttt{prim > (prim + a 7) b}) : \texttt{bool}\,\$\,9$

$\{a : \texttt{int}\} \vdash (\texttt{abs (x) (prim > x a)}) : (\texttt{-> (int) 5 bool})\,\$\,2$

$\{a : \texttt{int}, gt : (\texttt{-> (int) 5 bool})\} \vdash (\texttt{gt 17}) : \texttt{bool}\,\$\,8$

$\{a : \texttt{int}, b : \texttt{int}, gt : (\texttt{-> (int) 5 bool})\} \vdash (\texttt{if (gt b) (prim + b 1) 0}) : \texttt{int}\,\$\,14$

The abstract cost `loop` is assigned to expressions that may diverge. For example, the expression

$$E_{hang} = (\texttt{letrec ((hang (abs () (hang)))) (hang)})$$

is assigned cost `loop` in DISCOUNT. Because it is undecidable whether an arbitrary expression will diverge, it is impossible to have a type/cost system in which *exactly* the diverging expressions have cost `loop`. So Sam settles for a system that makes a *conservative approximation*: every program that diverges will be assigned cost `loop`, but some programs that do not diverge will also be assigned `loop`.

The cost constructs (`sumc` C_1 ... C_n) and (`maxc` C_1 ... C_n) are used for denoting, respectively, the sum and maximum of the costs C_1 ... C_n, which may include nonnumeric costs like `loop` and cost identifiers (see part **d**). Sam's system ensures that `sumc` and `maxc` satisfy sensible cost-equivalence axioms, such as:

$$(\texttt{sumc } NT_1 \; NT_2) \approx_c NT_3, \text{ where } \mathcal{N}[\![NT_3]\!] = \mathcal{N}[\![NT_1]\!] +_{Nat} \mathcal{N}[\![NT_2]\!]$$

$$(\texttt{sumc loop } NT) \approx_c (\texttt{sumc } NT \texttt{ loop}) \approx_c (\texttt{sumc loop loop}) \approx_c \texttt{loop}$$

$$(\texttt{maxc } NT_1 \; NT_2) \approx_c NT_3, \text{ where } \mathcal{N}[\![NT_3]\!] = (\text{max } \mathcal{N}[\![NT_1]\!] \; \mathcal{N}[\![NT_2]\!])$$

$$(\texttt{maxc loop } NT) \approx_c (\texttt{maxc } NT \texttt{ loop}) \approx_c (\texttt{maxc loop loop}) \approx_c \texttt{loop}$$

In Sam's system, such cost equivalences can implicitly be used wherever costs are mentioned.

a. Give type/cost rules for `abs`, procedure application, primitive application, and `if`.

b. Sam wants the following DISCOUNT expression to be well typed:

$$E_{if} = (\texttt{if b}$$
$$\qquad (\texttt{abs (x) (prim + x x)})$$
$$\qquad (\texttt{abs (y) (prim + (prim + y y) y)}))$$

But the types of the two branches, (`-> (int) 5 int`) and (`-> (int) 9 int`), are procedure types differing in their latent costs, which causes this expression to be ill typed. To fix this problem, define (1) a sensible cost-comparison relation $\leq_c$ (2) a notion of subtyping in DISCOUNT and (3) a type/cost inclusion rule for DISCOUNT (a variant of the [*inclusion*] rule in Figure 12.1 on page 703). Show that E_{if} is well typed with your extensions.

c. Define type/cost rules for monomorphic versions of `let` and `letrec`. Show why E_{hang} must be assigned cost `loop` using your rules.

d. Define type/cost rules for polymorphic versions of `let` and `letrec` and a rule for referencing a variable whose type is a generic type schema. You may assume that the Cost domain is extended to include description variables $\delta \in \text{DescId}$ that can stand for costs. Using your rules, give a type/cost derivation showing that the following expression is well typed:

```
(let ((app5 (abs (f) (f 5))))
  (if (app5 (abs (x) (prim > x 0)))
      (app5 (abs (y) y))
      (app5 (abs (z) (prim + z 1)))))
```

e. Discuss the technical challenges that need to be addressed in order to modify Algorithm Z to automatically reconstruct types and costs for DISCOUNT. For simplicity, ignore all store effects and focus solely on calculating costs. What do cost constraints look like? Can they always be solved?

f. In Sam's DISCOUNT type/cost system, every recursive procedure has latent cost `loop`. Since DISCOUNT uses recursion to express iteration, all iterations are conservatively assigned the infinite cost `loop`. While this is sound, it is not very useful. For example, it would be nice for an iteration summing the integers from 1 to n to have a finite cost that depends on n. Design a simple iteration construct that would allow assigning finite costs to some iterations, and discuss the technical issues that arise in the context of your construct.

16.3.5 Storage Deallocation and Lifetime Analysis

In implementations of languages like FLARE/E, it is often difficult to determine statically when a cell can no longer be referenced. For this reason, cells are typically allocated in a dynamically managed storage area called the **heap**, where they are reclaimed dynamically by a garbage collector (see Chapter 18).

However, an effect system with regions enables a framework for the static allocation and deallocation of memory. The following expression illustrates the key idea:

```
(let ((my-cell (cell 1))  {assume this cell is in region rm}
      (your-cell (cell 2)))  {assume this cell is in region ry}
  (pair (^ my-cell) (abs () (^ your-cell))))
```

The region `rm` for `my-cell` is completely local to the `let` expression and can be deleted from the effect of the `let` expression. This means that the allocation and all uses of `my-cell` occur within the `let` expression, so `my-cell` may be deallocated when the `let` expression is exited. In contrast, the region `ry` for `your-cell` appears in the type `(pairof int (-> () (read ry) int))` of the

$$\frac{TE \vdash E : T \mathbin{!} F}{TE \vdash (\texttt{letregion } R \ E) : T \mathbin{!} F'} \qquad [letregion]$$

where $\mathcal{F}[\![F']\!] = \{BF \mid ((BF \in \mathcal{F}[\![F]\!]) \wedge (R \notin \mathrm{FrDescIds}_{\mathit{eff}}[\![BF]\!]))\}$

$R \notin \mathrm{FrDescIds}_{\mathit{ty}}[\![T]\!]$ *[export restriction]*

$\forall I \in \mathrm{FrIds}[\![E]\!] \,.\, (R \notin \mathrm{FrDescIds}_{\mathit{ty}}[\![TE(I)]\!])$ *[import restriction]*

$\forall BF \in \mathcal{F}[\![F']\!] \,.\, (BF \neq (\texttt{comefrom } R'))$ *[control restriction]*

Figure 16.15   The type/effect rule for region-based storage management.

`let` expression, indicating that `your-cell` must outlive the `let` expression. But if `ry` does not "escape" some enclosing expression E, it may be deallocated when E is exited.

Region-based static storage management can be formalized by extending the expressions of FLARE/E with a binding construct ($\texttt{letregion } R \ E$) that declares the region named R in the scope of the body expression E. In the dynamic semantics, this construct creates a new segment of memory named R in which cells may be allocated, evaluates E to a value V, and then deallocates the entire segment R before returning V. So memory is organized as a stack of segments such that entering `letregion` pushes a new segment onto the stack and exiting `letregion` pops its segment off the stack. We also replace the `cell` primitive by the kernel construct ($\texttt{cell } E \ R$), in which the region name R explicitly indicates in which segment the cell should be allocated. We assume that `letregion` is used only to declare cell regions and that other regions, such as regions representing control points in control effects, are handled as before.

Using the region name R in the `cell` construct is sound only if (1) it is in the lexical scope of a `letregion` expression declaring R and (2) the cell cannot outlive (i.e., escape from the scope of) the `letregion` expression declaring R. Condition 1 can be expressed by requiring that a program body contain no free cell region names — i.e., all cell regions mentioned in the program body must be bound by an enclosing `letregion`. Condition 2 is expressed by the [*letregion*] type/effect rule in Figure 16.15. This is a specialized version of the [*effect-masking*] rule in Figure 16.10 on page 973 guaranteeing that it is safe to deallocate the memory segment created by ($\texttt{letregion } R \ E$) once the evaluation of E is complete. The effect F' of ($\texttt{letregion } R \ E$) contains all base effects in the effect F of E except for those that mention R. As in the [*effect-masking*] rule, the export and import restrictions of the [*letregion*] rule guarantee that R is only used locally and may safely be excluded from F'.

In a system without control transfers, the export and import restrictions are enough to justify that it is safe to deallocate the memory segment named by R, since no cell allocated in R can be referenced again upon termination of the `letregion` expression. However, in the presence of control effects, an additional control restriction is necessary to guarantee that the rest of the program can never jump back into the `letregion` expression. If such a jump were to occur, the memory segment associated with R might be accessed after the termination of the `letregion` expression, and so deallocation of this segment would be unsafe. This possibility can be precluded by requiring that the `letregion` expression not have a `comefrom` effect, and thus cannot be the target of any control transfers.

The above cell example can be transformed to use `letregion` as follows:

```
(letregion rm
  (let ((my-cell (cell 1 rm))
        (your-cell (cell 2 ry)))   {ry is free here but is presumably}
                                   {bound by an enclosing letregion.}
    (pair (^ my-cell) (abs () (^ your-cell)))))
```

This expression is well typed, so it is safe to deallocate the region `rm` containing `my-cell` upon exiting (`letregion rm ...`). Although only one cell is allocated in a region in this example, in general arbitrarily many cells may be allocated in a single region. But an attempt to allocate `your-cell` in `rm` in this example would make the `letregion` expression ill typed because the export restriction would be violated. It is necessary to allocate `your-cell` in a separate region `ry` that is declared by some other `letregion` expression syntactically enclosing this one. In the worst case, `ry` might be declared by a top-level `letregion` that wraps the entire program body.

We have focused on the region-based storage management of cells, but any type of value — e.g., pairs, lists, procedures, and even integers and booleans — can be associated with regions of memory. In FLARE/E, all these values are immutable and so they have no effects observable by the programmer. However, even immutable values must be stored *somewhere*, and regions are useful for managing the storage of such values. In this context, effects and regions can be used to perform a static **lifetime analysis** that determines where in the program a value created at one point can still be "alive."[8] This is necessary for determining when the storage associated with the value can be deallocated. The lifetime analysis of immutable values is explored in Exercise 16.24.

A practical region-based storage management system requires a way to automatically determine the placement of `letregion` declarations and annotate `cell` expressions with region information while maintaining the well-typedness of a program. A crude approach is to wrap all `letregion`s around the program body, but a more useful (and challenging!) goal is to make the scope of every `letregion`

---

[8]A closely related analysis is an **escape analysis** that determines which values can escape the scope in which they were declared.

as small as possible. Procedures that can be polymorphic in regions are helpful for shrinking the scope of `letregions`; see Exercise 16.23.

One such region-based storage management system has been designed and implemented by Tofte and Talpin [TT97]. They developed and proved correct an algorithm for translating an implicitly typed functional language into a language with explicit `letregion` expressions, region annotations, and region-polymorphic procedures. Their system handles integers, procedures, and immutable pairs, all of which are allocated in regions, but it can easily be extended to mutable data as well.

Exercise 16.23

a. The following is a FLARE/E program in which the two `cell` expressions have been annotated with explicit regions. Add explicit `letregion` expressions declaring `r1` and `r2` so that (1) the resulting expression is well typed and (2) the scope of each `letregion` expression is as small as possible:

```
(flarek (a b)
  (let ((f (abs (x)
               (let ((p (cell (prim - x 1) r1))
                     (q (cell (prim + x 1) r2)))
                 (prim pair (prim ^ p) q)))))
    (let ((s (prim fst (f a)))
          (t (prim snd (f b))))
      (prim + s (prim ^ t)))))
```

b. Sketch an algorithm for adding `letregion` declarations and explicit `cell` regions to a well-typed FLARE/E expression E so that (1) the resulting expression E' is well typed and (2) the scope of each `letregion` expression in E' is as small as possible. You may assume that you are given the complete type derivation for E.

c. Polly Morwicz observes that tighter `letregion` scopes can often be obtained if some procedures are region-polymorphic. For example, using the `pabs` and `pcall` constructs from Figure 12.9 on page 731, she modifies the procedure `f` in the program from part **a** to abstract over region `r2`:

```
(flarek (a b)
  (let ((f (pabs (r2)
               (abs (x)
                 (let ((p (cell (prim - x 1) r1))
                       (q (cell (prim + x 1) r2)))
                   (prim pair (prim ^ p) q))))))
    (let ((s (prim fst ((pcall f r3) a)))
          (t (prim snd ((pcall f r4) b))))
      (prim + s (prim ^ t)))))
```

Add explicit `letregion` expressions to Polly's modified expression, striving to make all `letregion` scopes as small as possible.

Exercise 16.24 Thai Ping wants to use regions and effects to perform lifetime analysis and storage management for pairs and other immutable values in FLARE/E. He begins by modifying the type grammar of FLARE/E to extend a `pairof` type to include the region where it is stored:

$$T \in \text{Type} ::= \dots \text{ all types except } (\texttt{pairof } T \ T) \ \dots \ | \ (\texttt{pairof } T \ T \ R)$$

He also extends the effect grammar to include a new `access` effect constructor:

$$FCR \in \text{EffectConstructor} = \dots \cup \{\texttt{access}\}$$

Thai explains that the effect (`access` R) is a **lifetime effect** used both for allocating an immutable pair value in region R and for extracting its components.

a. Write the type schemas for `pair` and `fst` in the primitive type environment used by the FLARE/E implicit type/effect system.

b. Explain how `access` effects and the [*letregion*] rule can be used to aggressively deallocate pair p in the following expression:

```
(let ((g (abs (a b)
            (let ((p (prim pair a b)))
              (prim pair (prim snd p) (prim fst p))))))
   (g 1 2))
```

The FLARE/E `pair` primitive does not take explicit regions, but you may assume that the scope of the region R declared by (`letregion` R E) includes any `pairof` types and `access` effects that appear in the type derivation of E.

c. `access` effects are used for the lifetime analysis of immutable values and should not affect the purity of expressions. For example, the expressions (`prim pair 1 2`) and (`prim fst p`) both have effects of the form (`access` R), but should still be considered pure since they do not have store effects or control effects that could cause them to interfere with other expressions. Describe how to modify the FLARE/E notion of purity to handle lifetime effects.

d. FLARE/E lists and procedures can also be modified to support a region-based lifetime analysis similar to the one Thai developed for pairs. Describe all the changes that need to be made to the FLARE/E syntax and type rules to accomplish this.

16.3.6 Control Flow Analysis

In function-oriented languages, a **control flow analysis** tracks the flow of higher-order procedures in a program.[9] Each abstraction in a program can be annotated with a distinct label, just as each `cell` expression can be associated with a region name. Then every procedure type can be annotated with the set of labels

---

[9]Although traditionally used to track the flow of procedure values, the same analysis can easily be extended to track the flow of any kind of value.

describing the abstractions that could be the source of that type. Although these labels are not effects, such an analysis can be accomplished using the machinery of an effect system.

Consider the following FLARE expression, in which each abstraction has been annotated with an explicit integer label:

```
(let ((inc (abs 1 (x) (+ x 1)))
      (dbl (abs 2 (y) (* y 2)))
      (app3 (abs 3 (f) (f 3)))
      (app4 (abs 4 (g) (g 4))))
  (list (app3 inc) (app4 inc) (app4 dbl)))
```

The annotated type of inc would be (-> (int) {1} int) and that of dbl would be (-> (int) {2} int). A type/label system can determine that the argument g to app4 has type (-> (int) {1, 2} int) (because it might be either the inc or dbl procedure) while the argument f to app3 has type (-> (int) {1} int) (because it can only be the inc procedure). Knowing which procedures reach which call sites can guide program optimizations. For example, if only one procedure reaches a call site, the call can be replaced by an inlined version of the procedure's body. Information from a control flow analysis is particularly important for choosing procedure representations in a compiler (see Section 17.10.2).

A control flow analysis is simpler than the lifetime analysis discussed in Section 16.3.5. In lifetime analysis, the latent effect in a procedure type describes all values that might be referenced when the procedure is called (see Exercise 16.24). In a control flow analysis, the annotation on a procedure type just describes which source abstractions might flow to the expression with that type. Consult [NNH98] for an extensive discussion of control flow analysis and how it can be expressed in an effect system.

16.3.7 Concurrent Behavior

Thus far we have studied only **sequential** programs, in which execution can be visualized as the progress of a single control token that moves through the program, performing each operation it encounters along the way. The path taken by the control token is known as a **control thread**. This single thread of control can be viewed as a time line along which all operations performed by the computation are arranged in a total order. For example, a computation that sequentially performs the operations A, B, C, and D can be depicted as the following total order, where $X \to Y$ means that X is performed before Y:

$$\to A \to B \to C \to D \to$$

In a **concurrent** program, multiple control threads may be active at the same time, allowing the time relationship between operations to be a partial order rather than a total order. Here is a sample partial order that declares that A precedes B along one control thread and C precedes D along another control thread, but does not otherwise constrain the operation order:

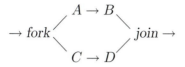

The diagram introduces two new nodes labeled *fork* and *join*. The purpose of these nodes is to split and merge control threads so that a computation has a distinguished starting edge and a distinguished ending edge. A control token reaching a *fork* node splits into two subtokens on the output edges of the node. When tokens are on both input edges of a *join* node, they merge into a single token on the output node. If only one input edge to a *join* has a token, it cannot move forward until the other edge contains a token. Any node like *join* that forces one control token to wait for another is said to **synchronize** them. There are many linguistic mechansims for specifying concurrency and synchronization, some of which are described in the Web Supplement to this book.

Suppose that on any step of a multithreaded computation, only one control token is allowed to move.[10] Then a particular execution of a concurrent program is associated with the sequence of its observable actions, which we shall call an **interleaving**. The behavior of the concurrent program is the set of all possible interleavings that can be exhibited by the program. For example, assuming that all operations (except for *fork* and *join*) are observable, then the behavior of the branching diagram above is:

$$\{ABCD,\ ACBD,\ ACDB,\ CABD,\ CADB,\ CDAB\}$$

The behavior of a concurrent program may be the empty set (no interleavings are possible), a singleton set (exactly one interleaving is possible), or a set with more than one element (many interleavings are possible). A concurrent program with more than one interleaving exhibits nondeterministic behavior. Although sequential programs can exhibit nondeterminism,[11] nondeterminism is most commonly associated with concurrent programs.

---

[10] There are concurrent models in which multiple control tokens can move in a single step, but we shall not consider these.

[11] For example, a purely sequential language can exhibit nondeterminism if operand expressions in procedure applications may be evaluated in any order or if it supports an (either E_1 E_2) construct that returns the value of one of E_1 or E_2.

In some models of concurrency, concurrently executing threads can communicate by having one thread send a value to another thread over a **channel** to which they share access. Communication establishes a timing constraint between the threads: a value sent over a channel cannot be received by the receiving thread until it has been sent by the sending thread.

We can extend FLARE/E to be a channel-based concurrent language by adding the following four constructs:

(channel) : Create and return a new channel.

(send! E_{chan} E_{val}) : First evaluate E_{chan} to the channel value V_{chan}, then evaluate E_{val} to the value V_{val}, and then send V_{val} over the channel V_{chan}. It is an error if V_{chan} is not a channel.

(receive! E_{chan}) : Evaluate E_{chan} to the channel value V_{chan} and then return the next value received from the channel V_{chan}. It is an error if V_{chan} is not a channel.

(cobegin E_1 ... E_n) : Evaluate each of E_1 ... E_n in a separate thread and return the value of E_n.

For example, here is a procedure that uses three channels to communicate between three threads:

$$E_{concabs} = \texttt{(abs (x)}$$

```
              (let ((a (channel)) (b (channel)) (c (channel)))
                (cobegin (send! c (+ 1 (receive! a)))
                         (send! c (* 2 (receive! b)))
                         (begin (send! a (- x 3))
                                (send! b (/ x 4))
                                (+ (receive! c) (receive! c)))))))
```

Since + is commutative, the order in which the values are received from channel c by the third thread does not affect the value returned by the procedure. But the returned value would depend on the order if the + were replaced by a noncommutative operator like -.

An effect system can be used to analyze the communication behavior of a channel-based concurrent program. If we interpret a region R as denoting an abstract channel, then we can model sending a value over channel R with an effect (out R) and model the receipt of a value from this channel with an effect (in R). In a simple communication-effect system (such as the one described in [JG89b]), in and out effects can be tracked just like the store and control effects studied earlier. Such a system can determine that an expression communicates on certain channels, but the ACUI nature of the `maxeff` effect combiner makes it impossible to determine any ordering on these communications. E.g., if channels a, b, and c in the above example are in regions `ra`, `rb`, and `rc`, respectively, then the body of $E_{concabs}$ has the effect

```
(maxeff (in ra) (in rb) (in rc) (out ra) (out rb) (out rc))
```

which does not indicate the relative order of the communication actions or the number of times they are performed. However, the information is sufficient to show that the communication effects are completely local to the procedure body and so can be deleted by effect masking.

In more sophisticated communication-effect systems (such as the one described in [ANN97]), the ordering of communication effects is modeled by specifying the sequential and parallel composition of effects. For example, in such a system, the effect of the `cobegin` expression in $E_{concabs}$ might be:

```
(par (seq (in ra) (out rc))
     (seq (in rb) (out rc))
     (seq (out ra) (out rb) (in rc) (in rc)))
```

where `seq` is used to combine effects for sequential execution and `par` is used to combine effects for parallel execution. This shows the ordering of channel operations in each thread and the fact that the third thread receives two values from the channel in region `rc`. Such a specification resembles the kinds of specifications used in process algebra frameworks like *Communicating Sequential Processes (CSP)* [Hoa85] and the *Calculus of Communicating Systems (CCS)* [Mil89].

16.3.8   Mobile Code Security

In modern computer systems, it is often desirable for applications on a local computer to automatically download and execute **mobile code** from remote Internet sites. But this is a dangerous prospect, since executing arbitrary mobile code might destroy or steal local information or use the local computer's resources for nefarious purposes like sending spam email, attacking Web servers, or spreading viruses.

One application of effects is to provide mobile code security by labeling primitive operations with latent effects that describe their actions. For example, all procedures that write on the local computer's disk could carry a `write-disk` latent effect. Other latent effects could be assigned to display and networking procedures. These effects create a verifiable, succinct summary of the actions of

imported mobile code. These effects can be presented to a security checker —
which might involve a user dialogue box — that accepts or rejects mobile code
on the basis of its effects.

Since mobile code is downloaded and executed on the fly, any security analysis
performed by the local computer must be relatively quick in order to be practical.
Although some properties can efficiently be deduced by analyzing the downloaded
code from scratch, other important properties are too expensive for the local
computer to reconstruct. For example, for arbitrary low-level code, it is difficult
to prove memory safety properties like the following: (1) no variable is accessed
until it is initialized; (2) no out-of-bounds access is made to an array; and (3) there
is no dereference of a pointer to a deallocated memory block.[12] This problem can
be addressed by requiring the code producer to include explicit type and effect
annotations in the mobile code that are sufficient to allow the code consumer to
rapidly verify security properties. For example, the types might encode a proof
that no array access is out of bounds, and a simple type-checking procedure by the
code consumer could verify this proof. Generating the appropriate annotations
might be expensive for the producer, but the consumer can use type and effect
rules to quickly verify that the annotations are valid.

This is an example of a technique called **proof-carrying code** [NL98, AF00],
in which mobile code carries a representation of proofs of various properties in
addition to the executable code. It is used for properties that are difficult for the
consumer to determine from raw low-level code, but are easy for the consumer to
verify if the producer of the low-level code (which presumably has access to more
information, in the form of the high-level source program) provides a proof.

Notes

Effect systems were introduced by Lucassen and Gifford in [Luc87, LG88], which
outlined the need for a new kind of static analysis for describing program behavior. Early experiments with the design and use of effect systems were performed in the context of the FX-87 programming language [GJLS87], an explicitly typed language including effects and regions. Later versions of FX incorporated region and effect inference [JG91]. Effects were used to guide standard
compiler optimizations (e.g., common subexpression elimination, dead code elimination, and code hoisting) as well as to find opportunities for parallel evaluation
[Luc87, HG88]. We explore effect-based code optimization in Section 17.6.2.

---

[12]See Chapter 18 for a discussion of memory allocation and deallocation.

The first polymorphic type/effect reconstruction system was presented in [JG91]. The improved reconstruction systems in [TJ92, TJ94a] guaranteed principal types and minimal effects. Our Algorithm Z incorporates two key features of the improved systems in a derivation-style reconstruction algorithm: It (1) allows subeffecting via the [*does*] rule to compute minimal effects and (2) requires the latent type of a procedure type to be a description variable, which simplifies the unification of procedure types and the solution of effect constraints. Without the second feature, it would be necessary to modify the unification algorithm to produce effect-equality constraints between the latent effects of two unified procedure types and to extend the effect-constraint solver to handle such equality constraints.

A wide variety of effect systems have been developed, including systems for cost accounting [DJG92, RG94, CW00], control effects [JG89a], and communication effects [JG89b]. The FX-91 programming language [GJSO92] included all of these features. Other examples of effect systems include control flow analysis [TJ94b], region-based memory management [TT97], behavior analysis for concurrency [ANN97], atomicity effects for concurrency, [FQ03], register usage analysis [Aga97, AM03], and trace effects for verifying program safety properties [SSH08]. As noted in Section 16.3.3, JAVA has a simple effect system for tracking exceptions that can be thrown by a method [GJS96]. Monadic systems for expressing state can be extended with an effect system [Wad98].

For a detailed introduction to effect systems and a summary of work done in this area, see [TJ94a], [NNH98, Chapter 5], and [ANN99].

Part IV

Pragmatics

17

Compilation

Bless thee, Bottom! bless thee! thou art translated.
   — William Shakespeare, *A Midsummer Night's Dream,* act 2, scene 1

17.1 Why Do We Study Compilation?

Compilation is the process of translating a high-level program into instructions that can be directly executed by a low-level machine, such as a microprocessor or a simple virtual machine. Our goal in this chapter is to use compilation to further our understanding of advanced programming language features, including the practical implications of language design choices. To be a good designer or user of programming languages, one must know not only how a computer carries out the instructions of a program (including how data are represented) but also the techniques by which a high-level program is converted into something that runs on an actual computer. In this chapter, we will show the relationship between the semantic tools developed earlier in the book and the practice of translating high-level language features to executable code.

Our approach to compilation is different from the approach taken in most compiler texts. We assume that the input program has already been parsed and is syntactically correct, thus ignoring issues of lexical analysis and parsing that are important in real compilers. We also assume that type and effect checking are performed by the reconstruction techniques we have already studied. Our focus will be a series of source-to-source program transformations that implement complex high-level naming, state, and control features by making them explicit in an FL-like intermediate compilation language. A key benefit of our approach is that it dispenses with traditional special-purpose compilation machinery like symbol tables, invocation frames, stacks, and basic blocks. These notions are uniformly represented as patterns in the structure of the intermediate code. The result of compilation will be a program in a restricted subset of the intermediate language that can be viewed as instructions for a simple virtual register machine. In this way we avoid details of code generation that are important when targeting a real microprocessor. Throughout the compilation process, efficiency will take a back seat to clarity, modularity, expressiveness, and demonstrable correctness.

The notion of compilation by source-to-source transformation has a rich history. Beginning with Guy Steele's RABBIT compiler ([Ste78]), there is a long line of research compilers based on this approach. (See the notes at the end of this chapter for more details.) In homage to RABBIT, we will call our compiler TORTOISE.

We study compilation for the following reasons:

- We can review many of the language features presented earlier in this book in a new light. By showing how programs can be transformed into low-level machine code, we arrive at a more concrete understanding of these features.

- We present some simple ways to implement language features by translation. These techniques can be useful in everyday programming, especially if your programming language doesn't support the features that you need.

- We will see how complex translations can be composed out of many simple passes. Although in practice these passes might be merged, we will discuss them separately for conceptual clarity.

- We will see that the inefficiencies that crop up in the compiler are a good motivation for studying static semantics. These inefficiencies can be addressed by a combination of two methods:

  - Developing smarter translation techniques that exploit information known at compile time.

  - Restricting source languages to make them more amenable to static analysis techniques.

  For example, we'll see (in Section 18.2.2) that dynamically typed languages imply a run-time overhead that can be reduced by clever techniques or eliminated by requiring the language to be statically typable.

We begin with an overview of the transformation-based architecture of TORTOISE (Section 17.2). We then discuss the details of each transformation in turn (Sections 17.3–17.12).

17.2 Tortoise Architecture

17.2.1 Overview of Tortoise

The TORTOISE compiler is organized into ten transformations that incrementally massage a source language program into code resembling register machine code (Figure 17.1). The input and output of each transformation are programs written either in dialects of FLARE or in dialects of an FL-like intermediate language named FIL that is defined later. The output of the compiler is a program in FIL_{reg}, a dialect of FIL whose constructs can be viewed as instructions for a low-level register machine. We review FLARE in this section and present the dialects of FIL later as they are needed.

We will see that dialects of FL (including FLARE) can be powerful intermediate languages for compilation. Many low-level machine details find a surprisingly convenient expression in FL-like languages. Some advantages of structuring our compiler as a series of source-to-source transformations on dialects of FL are:

- All the intermediate languages are closely related to FL, a language whose semantics we already understand well.

- When intermediate languages are closely related, compiler writers are more likely to develop modular stages and experiment with their ordering.

- The result of every transformation stage is executable source code in a dialect of FL. This facilitates reading and testing the transformation results using an interpreter (or compiler) for the dialect. Because the dialects are so similar, their interpreters are closely related. Indeed, modulo the verification of certain syntactic constraints, a single interpreter can be used for most of the dialects.

Each compiler transformation expects its input program to satisfy certain preconditions and produces output code that satisfies certain postconditions. These conditions will be stated explicitly in the formal specification of each transformation. They will help us understand the purpose of each transformation, and why the compiler is sound. A compiler is **sound** when it produces low-level code that faithfully implements the formal semantics of the compiler's source language. We will not formally prove the soundness of any of the transformations because such proofs can be very complex. Indeed, soundness proofs for some of these transformations have been the basis for Ph.D. dissertations! However, we will informally argue that the transformations are sound.

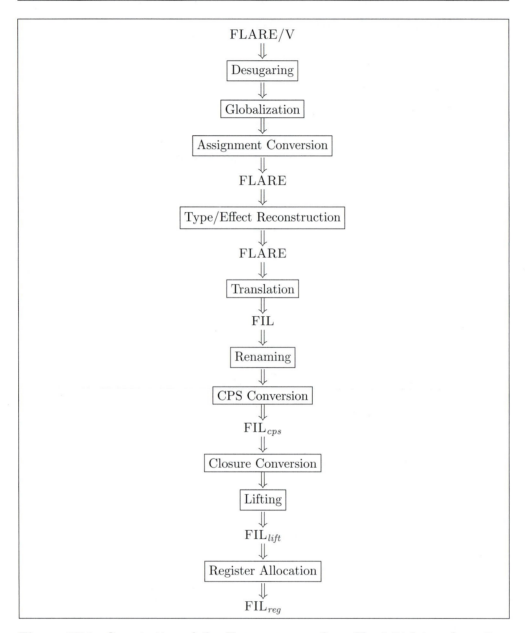

Figure 17.1 Organization of the TORTOISE compiler. The initial transformations translate the FLARE/V source program to a FLARE program. This is translated into the FIL intermediate language and is then gradually transformed into a form that resembles register machine code.

Tortoise implements each transformation as a separate pass for clarity of presentation and to allow for experimentation. Although we will apply the transformations in a particular order in this chapter, other orders are possible. Our descriptions of the transformations will explore some alternative implementations and point out how different design choices affect the efficiency and semantics of the resulting code. We generally opt for simplicity over efficiency in our presentation.

17.2.2 The Compiler Source Language: FLARE/V

The source language of the Tortoise compiler is FLARE/V, a version of the FLARE language presented in Chapter 13 extended with mutable variables (using the `set!` construct from the FLAVAR language presented in Section 8.4). We include mutable variables in the source language because they are a standard feature in many languages and we wish to show how they can be automatically transformed into mutable cells (via the assignment conversion transformation in Section 17.5).

FLARE/V is a stateful, call-by-value, statically scoped, function-oriented, and statically typed language with type reconstruction that supports mutable cells, mutable variables, pairs, and homogeneous immutable lists. For convenience, the complete syntax of FLARE/V is presented in Figures 17.2 and 17.3. This is the same as the presentation of FLARE in Figure 13.23 on page 814 except that (1) FLARE/V includes mutable variables via the `set!` construct and (2) the desugaring of a full-language program into a kernel program does *not* introduce bindings for standard identifiers like the names of primitive operations.[1] All primitive names (such as `*`, `>`, and `cons`) may still be used as free identifiers in a FLARE/V program, where they denote global procedures performing the associated primitive operations, but this is implemented by the globalization transformation presented in Section 17.4 rather than via desugaring. As before, (`prim * `E_1` `E_2`)` may be written as (`* `E_1` `E_2`)` in almost any context. We say "almost any" because these names can be assigned and locally rebound like any other names. For example, the program

```
(flare (x y)
  (let ((- +))
    (begin (set! / *) (- (/ x x) (/ y y)))))
```

calculates the sum of the squares of `x` and `y`.

---

[1] For simplicity, we reuse the program keywords `flare` and `flarek` for FLARE/V rather than introducing new ones.

Kernel Grammar

$P \in \text{Prog} ::= (\texttt{flarek}\ (I_{formal}^*)\ E_{body})$

$E \in \text{Exp} ::= L \mid I \mid (\texttt{error}\ Y_{message}) \mid (\texttt{if}\ E_{test}\ E_{then}\ E_{else}) \mid$
$\qquad\qquad \mid (\texttt{set!}\ I_{var}\ E_{val}) \mid (\texttt{prim}\ O_{primop}\ E_{arg}^*)$
$\qquad\qquad \mid (\texttt{abs}\ (I_{formal}^*)\ E_{body}) \mid (E_{rator}\ E_{rand}^*)$
$\qquad\qquad \mid (\texttt{let}\ ((I_{name}\ E_{defn})^*)\ E_{body}) \mid (\texttt{letrec}\ ((I_{name}\ E_{defn})^*)\ E_{body})$

$L \in \text{Lit} ::= \texttt{\#u} \mid B \mid N \mid (\texttt{sym}\ Y)$

$B \in \text{BoolLit} = \{\texttt{\#t}, \texttt{\#f}\}$ as in FL.

$N \in \text{IntLit} =$ as in FL and FLARE.

$Y \in \text{SymLit} =$ as in FL and FLARE.

$O \in \text{Primop} ::= \texttt{+} \mid \texttt{-} \mid \texttt{*} \mid \texttt{/} \mid \texttt{\%}$ *; arithmetic ops*
$\qquad\qquad \mid \texttt{<=} \mid \texttt{<} \mid \texttt{=} \mid \texttt{!=} \mid \texttt{>} \mid \texttt{>=} \mid \texttt{bool=?} \mid \texttt{sym=?}$ *; relational ops*
$\qquad\qquad \mid \texttt{not} \mid \texttt{and} \mid \texttt{or}$ *; logical ops*
$\qquad\qquad \mid \texttt{pair} \mid \texttt{fst} \mid \texttt{snd}$ *; pair ops*
$\qquad\qquad \mid \texttt{cons} \mid \texttt{car} \mid \texttt{cdr} \mid \texttt{null} \mid \texttt{null?}$ *; list ops*
$\qquad\qquad \mid \texttt{cell} \mid \texttt{\^{}} \mid \texttt{:=} \mid \texttt{cell=?}$ *; mutable cell ops*

$\qquad \text{Keyword} = \{\texttt{abs}, \texttt{error}, \texttt{flarek}, \texttt{if}, \texttt{let}, \texttt{letrec}, \texttt{prim}, \texttt{set!}, \texttt{sym}\}$

$\qquad \text{SugarKeyword} = \{\texttt{begin}, \texttt{cond}, \texttt{def}, \texttt{flare}, \texttt{list}, \texttt{recur}, \texttt{scand}, \texttt{scor}\}\}$

$I \in \text{Ident} = \text{SymLit} - (\{Y \mid Y\ \text{begins with}\ \texttt{@}\} \cup \text{Keyword} \cup \text{SugarKeyword})$

Figure 17.2   Kernel grammar for the FLARE/V language.

Figure 17.4 presents a contrived but compact FLARE/V program that illustrates many features of the language, such as numbers, booleans, lists, locally defined recursive procedures, higher-order procedures, tail and nontail procedure calls (see Section 17.9.1 for a discussion of tail versus nontail calls), and mutable variables. We will use it as a running example throughout the rest of this chapter.

The `revmap` procedure takes a procedure `f` and a list `elts` of elements and returns a new list that is the reversal of the list obtained by applying `f` to each element of `elts`. The accumulation of the new list `ans` is performed by a local iterative `loop` procedure that is defined using the `recur` sugar, which abbreviates the declaration and invocation of a recursive procedure. The `loop` procedure performs an iteration in a single state variable `xs` denoting the unprocessed elements of `elts`. Although `ans` could easily be made a second argument to `loop`, here it is defined externally to `loop` and updated via `set!` to illustrate the use of a mutable variable.

The example program takes two integer arguments, a and b, and returns a list of the two booleans $((7 \cdot a) > b)$ and $(a > b)$. For example, on the inputs 6 and 17, the program returns the list $\triangleleft true, false \triangleright$.

Syntactic Sugar

$(@O_{primop}\ E_{i=1}^n) \leadsto_{ds} (\texttt{prim}\ O_{primop}\ E_{i=1}^n)$

$(\texttt{cond}\ (\texttt{else}\ E_{default})) \leadsto_{ds} E_{default}$

$(\texttt{cond}\ (E_{test_1}\ E_{then_1})\ (E_{test_i}\ E_{then_i})_{i=2}^n\ (\texttt{else}\ E_{default}))$
$\quad \leadsto_{ds} (\texttt{if}\ E_{test_1}\ E_{then_1}\ (\texttt{cond}\ (E_{test_i}\ E_{then_i})_{i=2}^n\ (\texttt{else}\ E_{default})))$

$(\texttt{scand}) \leadsto_{ds}$ #t
$(\texttt{scand}\ E_{conjunct}\ E_{rest}^*) \leadsto_{ds} (\texttt{if}\ E_{conjunct}\ (\texttt{scand}\ E_{rest}^*)$ #f$)$

$(\texttt{scor}) \leadsto_{ds}$ #f
$(\texttt{scor}\ E_{disjunct}\ E_{rest}^*) \leadsto_{ds} (\texttt{if}\ E_{disjunct}$ #t $(\texttt{scor}\ E_{rest}^*))$

$(\texttt{recur}\ I_{proc}\ ((I_i\ E_i)_{i=1}^n)\ E_{body})$
$\quad \leadsto_{ds} (\texttt{letrec}\ ((I_{proc}\ (\texttt{abs}\ (I_{i=1}^n)\ E_{body})))\ (I_{proc}\ E_{i=1}^n))$

$(\texttt{begin}) \leadsto_{ds}$ #u
$(\texttt{begin}\ E) \leadsto_{ds} E$
$(\texttt{begin}\ E_1\ E_{rest}^*) \leadsto_{ds} (\texttt{let}\ ((\_\ E_1))\ (\texttt{begin}\ E_{rest}^*)),$
$\quad$ where _ is a special identifier that can never be referenced

$(\texttt{list}) \leadsto_{ds} (\texttt{prim null})$
$(\texttt{list}\ E_1\ E_{rest}^*) \leadsto_{ds} (\texttt{prim cons}\ E_1\ (\texttt{list}\ E_{rest}^*))$

$(\texttt{def}\ (I_{procName}\ I_{procFormal}^*)\ E_{procBody})$
$\quad \leadsto_{ds} (\texttt{def}\ I_{procName}\ (\texttt{abs}\ (I_{procFormal}^*)\ E_{procBody}))$

$(\texttt{flare}\ (I_{pgmFormal}^*)\ E_{pgmBody}\ (\texttt{def}\ I_{name_i}\ E_{defn_i})_{i=1}^n)$
$\quad$ {*Assume procedure defs already desugared to* $(\texttt{def}\ I\ E)$ *by the previous rule.*}
$\quad \leadsto_{ds} (\texttt{flarek}\ (I_{pgmFormal}^*)$
$\qquad$ {*Compiler handles standard identifiers via globalization, not desugaring.*}
$\qquad (\texttt{letrec}\ ((I_{name_i}\ E_{defn_i})_{i=1}^n)\ E_{pgmBody}))$

Figure 17.3 Syntactic sugar for the FLARE/V language.

```
(flare (a b)
  (let ((revmap (abs (f elts)
                  (let ((ans (null)))
                    (recur loop ((xs elts))
                      (if (null? xs)
                          ans
                          (begin (set! ans (cons (f (car xs)) ans))
                                 (loop (cdr xs)))))))))
    (revmap (abs (x) (> x b)) (list a (* a 7))))))
```

Figure 17.4 revmap program.

$$tf \in \mathit{Transform}_{FLARE/V} = \mathrm{Exp}_{FLARE/V} \to \mathrm{Exp}_{FLARE/V}$$

$$mapsub_{FLARE/V} : \mathrm{Exp}_{FLARE/V} \to \mathit{Transform}_{FLARE/V} \to \mathrm{Exp}_{FLARE/V}$$

$$mapsub_{FLARE/V}[\![L]\!] \; tf \; = \; L$$

$$mapsub_{FLARE/V}[\![I]\!] \; tf \; = \; I$$

$$mapsub_{FLARE/V}[\![(\texttt{error } Y_{msg})]\!] \; tf \; = \; (\texttt{error } Y_{msg})$$

$$mapsub_{FLARE/V}[\![(\texttt{if } E_{test} \; E_{then} \; E_{else})]\!] \; tf$$
$$= \; (\texttt{if } (tf \; E_{test}) \; (tf \; E_{then}) \; (tf \; E_{else}))$$

$$mapsub_{FLARE/V}[\![(\texttt{set! } I_{var} \; E_{val})]\!] \; tf \; = \; (\texttt{set! } I_{var} \; (tf \; E_{val}))$$

$$mapsub_{FLARE/V}[\![(\texttt{abs } (I_{i=1}^{n}) \; E_{body})]\!] \; tf \; = \; (\texttt{abs } (I_{i=1}^{n}) \; (tf \; E_{body}))$$

$$mapsub_{FLARE/V}[\![(E_{rator} \; E_{i=1}^{n})]\!] \; tf \; = \; ((tf \; E_{rator}) \; (tf \; E_i)_{i=1}^{n})$$

$$mapsub_{FLARE/V}[\![(\texttt{prim } O \; E_{i=1}^{n})]\!] \; tf \; = \; (\texttt{prim } O \; (tf \; E_i)_{i=1}^{n})$$

$$mapsub_{FLARE/V}[\![(\texttt{let } ((I_i \; E_i)_{i=1}^{n}) \; E_{body})]\!] \; tf$$
$$= \; (\texttt{let } ((I_i \; (tf \; E_i))_{i=1}^{n}) \; (tf \; E_{body}))$$

$$mapsub_{FLARE/V}[\![(\texttt{letrec } ((I_i \; E_i)_{i=1}^{n}) \; E_{body})]\!] \; tf$$
$$= \; (\texttt{letrec } ((I_i \; (tf \; E_i))_{i=1}^{n}) \; (tf \; E_{body}))$$

Figure 17.5   The $mapsub_{FLARE/V}$ function simplifies the specification of purely structural transformations.

17.2.3   Purely Structural Transformations

Most of the FLARE/V and FIL program transformations that we shall study can be described by functions that traverse the abstract syntax tree of the program and transform some of the tree nodes but leave most of the nodes unchanged. We will say that a transformation is **purely structural** for a given kind of tree node if the result of applying it to that node results in the same kind of node, in which each child node is a transformed version of the corresponding child of the original node.

We formalize this notion for FLARE/V via the $mapsub_{FLARE/V}$ function defined in Figure 17.5. This function returns a copy of the given FLARE expression whose immediate subexpressions have been transformed by a given transformation tf. A FLARE transformation is purely structural for a given kind of node if its action on that node can be written as an application of $mapsub_{FLARE/V}$.

As an example of $mapsub_{FLARE/V}$, consider a transformation $\mathcal{T}$ that rewrites every occurrence of (if (prim not E_1) E_2 E_3) to (if E_1 E_3 E_2). The fact that $\mathcal{T}$ is purely structural on all but if nodes is expressed via a single invocation of $mapsub_{FLARE/V}$ in the following definition:

$$\begin{array}{l}
subexps_{FLARE/V} : \text{Exp}_{FLARE/V} \rightarrow \text{Exp}^*_{FLARE/V} \\[4pt]
subexps_{FLARE/V}[\![L]\!] = [\,] \\[4pt]
subexps_{FLARE/V}[\![I]\!] = [\,] \\[4pt]
subexps_{FLARE/V}[\![(\texttt{error } Y_{msg})]\!] = [\,] \\[4pt]
subexps_{FLARE/V}[\![(\texttt{if } E_{test} \ E_{then} \ E_{else})]\!] = [E_{test}, E_{then}, E_{else}] \\[4pt]
subexps_{FLARE/V}[\![(\texttt{set! } I_{var} \ E_{val})]\!] = [E_{val}] \\[4pt]
subexps_{FLARE/V}[\![(\texttt{abs } (I_{i=1}^{n}) \ E_{body})]\!] = [E_{body}] \\[4pt]
subexps_{FLARE/V}[\![(E_{rator} \ E_{i=1}^{n})]\!] = [E_{rator}, E_1, \ldots, E_n] \\[4pt]
subexps_{FLARE/V}[\![(\texttt{prim } O \ E_{i=1}^{n})]\!] = [E_1, \ldots, E_n] \\[4pt]
subexps_{FLARE/V}[\![(\texttt{let } ((I_i \ E_i)_{i=1}^{n}) \ E_{body})]\!] = [E_1, \ldots, E_n, E_{body}] \\[4pt]
subexps_{FLARE/V}[\![(\texttt{letrec } ((I_i \ E_i)_{i=1}^{n}) \ E_{body})]\!] = [E_1, \ldots, E_n, E_{body}]
\end{array}$$

Figure 17.6 The $subexps_{FLARE/V}$ function returns a sequence of all immediate subexpressions of a given FLARE/V expression.

$$\begin{array}{l}
\mathcal{T} : \text{Exp}_{FLARE/V} \rightarrow \text{Exp}_{FLARE/V} \\[4pt]
\mathcal{T}[\![(\texttt{if } (\texttt{prim not } E_1) \ E_2 \ E_3)]\!] = (\texttt{if } (\mathcal{T}[\![E_1]\!]) \ (\mathcal{T}[\![E_3]\!]) \ (\mathcal{T}[\![E_2]\!])) \\[4pt]
\mathcal{T}[\![E]\!] = mapsub_{FLARE/V}[\![E]\!] \ \mathcal{T}, \text{ for all other expressions } E
\end{array}$$

When manipulating expressions, it is sometimes helpful to extract from an expression a collection of its immediate subexpressions. Figure 17.6 defines a $subexps_{FLARE/V}$ function that returns a sequence of all child expressions of a given FLARE/V expression.

17.3 Transformation 1: Desugaring

The first pass of the TORTOISE compiler performs desugaring, converting the convenient syntax of FLARE/V into a simpler kernel subset of the language. The advantage of having the first transformation desugar the program is that subsequent analyses and transforms are simpler to write and prove correct because there are fewer syntactic forms to consider. Additionally, subsequent transformations also do not require modification if the language is extended by introducing new syntactic shorthands.

We will provide preconditions and postconditions for each of the TORTOISE transformations. In the case of desugaring, these are:

Preconditions: The input to the desugaring transformation is a well-formed full FLARE/V program.

Postconditions: The output of the desugaring transformation is a well-formed kernel FLARE/V program.

We will say that a program is **well formed** in a language when it satisfies the grammar of the language — i.e., it does not contain any syntactic errors.

There is an additional postcondition that we expect for desugaring (and all other transformations we study): The output program should have the same behavior as the input program. This is a fundamental property of each compilation stage that we will not explicitly state in every postcondition. One consequence of this property is that if the input program never encounters a dynamic type error, then neither does the output program. For dialects of FLARE, we can use a notion of well-typedness to conservatively approximate which programs never encounter a dynamic type error. (Although we have not formally described a type system for full FLARE/V, it is possible to define one by extending the type system of kernel FLARE with type rules for `set!` and all the syntactic sugar constructs.) We expect that Tortoise stages transforming programs in these dialects should preserve well-typedness.

The desugaring process for FLARE/V is similar to the rewriting approach to desugaring summarized in Figures 6.6 and 6.7 on pages 232 and 233, so we will not repeat the details of the transformation process here. Figure 17.7 shows the result of desugaring the `revmap` example introduced in Figure 17.4. The (`recur loop ...`) desugars into a `letrec`, the `begin` desugars into a `let` that binds the special variable _ (which we assume is never referenced), and the `list` desugars into a `null`-terminated nested sequence of `cons`es.

17.4 Transformation 2: Globalization

In general, a program unit being compiled may contain free identifiers that reference externally defined values in standard libraries or other program units. Such free identifiers must somehow be resolved via a **name resolution** process before they are referenced during program execution. Depending on the nature of the free identifiers, name resolution can take place during compilation, during a linking phase that takes place after compilation but before execution (see Section 15.1), or during the execution of the program unit. In cases where name resolution takes place after compilation, the compiler may still require *some* information about the free identifiers, such as their types, even though their values may be unknown.

```
(flarek (a b)
  (let ((revmap
          (abs (f elts)
            (let ((ans (null)))
              (letrec ((loop
                          (abs (xs)
                            (if (null? xs)
                                ans
                                (let ((_ (set! ans
                                                (cons (f (car xs)) ans))))
                                  (loop (cdr xs)))))))
                (loop elts)))))))
    (revmap (abs (x) (> x b))
            (prim cons a (prim cons (* a 7) (prim null)))))))
```

Figure 17.7 revmap program after desugaring.

In the TORTOISE compiler, we consider a very simple form of compile-time linking that resolves free references to standard identifiers like +, <, and cons. We will call this linking stage **globalization** because it determines the meanings of global variables defined by the language. Globalization has the following specification:

Preconditions: The input to the globalization transformation is a well-formed kernel FLARE/V program.

Postconditions: The output of the globalization transformation is a well-formed kernel FLARE/V program that is *closed* — i.e., it contains no free identifiers.

Removing free identifiers from a program at an early stage simplifies later transformations, which do not need to treat them as a special case. If the input program contains unresolvable free identifiers, the globalization stage should fail.

The Wrapping Strategy

A simple approach to globalization in FLARE/V is to wrap the body of the program in a `let` that associates each standard identifier used in the program with an appropriate abstraction (see the function $\mathcal{GW}$ in Figure 17.8, which does globalization by wrapping). This **wrapping strategy** is a variant of the approach we have used thus far to handle standard identifiers when desugaring programs in the dialects of FL we have studied. The difference is that the

$$\mathcal{GW} : \mathrm{Prog}_{FLARE/V} \rightharpoonup \mathrm{Prog}_{FLARE/V}$$

$$\mathcal{GW}[\![(\texttt{flarek}\ (I_{i=1}^n)\ E_{body})]\!] = (\texttt{flarek}\ (I_{i=1}^n)\ (wrap[\![E_{body}]\!]\ (FrIds[\![E_{body}]\!])))$$

$$wrap : \mathrm{Exp}_{FLARE/V} \to \mathcal{P}(\mathrm{Ident}_{FLARE/V}) \rightharpoonup \mathrm{Exp}_{FLARE/V}$$

$$wrap[\![E]\!]\ \{\} = E$$

$$wrap[\![E]\!]\ \{I_1, \ldots, I_n\} = (\texttt{let}\ ((I_i\ \mathcal{ABS}[\![I_i]\!])_{i=1}^n)\ E),\ \text{where}\ n \geq 1.$$

$$\mathcal{ABS} : \mathrm{Ident}_{FLARE/V} \rightharpoonup \mathrm{Exp}_{FLARE/V}$$

$$\mathcal{ABS}[\![O]\!] = (\texttt{abs}\ (I_{i=1}^n)\ (\texttt{prim}\ O\ I_{i=1}^n))$$
   where $I_{i=1}^n$ are fresh and $TE_{prim}(O) = (\texttt{->}\ (T_{i=1}^n)\ T_{res})$
   or $TE_{prim}(O) = (\texttt{generic}\ (\tau_{j=1}^m)\ (\texttt{->}\ (T_{i=1}^n)\ T_{res}))$

$$\mathcal{ABS}[\![I]\!] = \textit{undefined},\ \text{where}\ I \notin \mathrm{Primop}_{FLARE/V}$$

Figure 17.8   The wrapping approach to globalization.

wrapping strategy used here includes bindings for only the standard identifiers actually used in the program rather than all those that are supported by the language. For example, the wrapping strategy transforms the program

```
(flarek (x y) (+ (* x x) (* y y)))
```

into

```
(flarek (x y)
  (let ((+ (abs (v.0 v.1) (prim + v.0 v.1)))
        (* (abs (v.2 v.3) (prim * v.2 v.3))))
    (+ (* x x) (* y y))))
```

We assume that identifiers ending in a period followed by a number (such as v.0 and v.1) are names that are freshly generated during the compilation process.

Constructing an abstraction for a primitive operator (via $\mathcal{ABS}$) requires knowing the number of arguments that it takes. In FLARE/V, this can be determined from the type of the primitive operator name in the primitive type environment, TE_{prim}. $\mathcal{ABS}$ is a partial function because it is undefined for identifiers that are not the names of primitive operators. $wrap$ is also a partial function because it is undefined if any invocation of $\mathcal{ABS}$ in its definition is undefined. Similarly, $\mathcal{GW}$ is undefined if the invocation of $wrap$ in its definition is undefined; this is how the failure of the globalization transformation is modeled in the case where a free identifier in the program is not the name of a primitive operator. The wrapping strategy can be extended to handle standard identifiers that are not the names of primitive operators (see Exercise 17.2).

The Inlining Strategy

A drawback of the wrapping strategy is that global procedures are invoked via the generic procedure-calling mechanism rather than the mechanism for invoking primitive operators (`prim`). We will see in later stages of the compiler that the latter is handled far more efficiently than the former. This suggests an alternative approach in which calls to global procedures are transformed into primitive applications. Replacing a procedure call by an instantiated version of its body is known as **inlining**, so we shall call this the **inlining strategy** for globalization. Using the inlining strategy, the sum-of-squares program is transformed into:

```
(flarek (x y) (prim + (prim * x x) (prim * y y)))
```

There are three situations that need to be handled carefully in the inlining strategy for globalization:

1. A reference to a global procedure can be converted to an instance of `prim` only if it occurs in the rator position of a procedure application. References in other positions must be handled either by wrapping or by converting them to abstractions. Consider the expression

   ```
   (cons + (cons * (null)))
   ```

   which makes a list of two procedures. The occurrences of `cons` and `null` can be transformed into `prim`s, but the `+` and `*` cannot be. They can, however, be turned into abstractions containing `prim`s:

   ```
   (prim cons (abs (v.0 v.1) (prim + v.0 v.1))
     (prim cons (abs (v.2 v.3) (prim * v.2 v.3))
       (prim null)))
   ```

   Alternatively, we can "lift" the abstractions for `+` and `*` to the top of the enclosing program and name them, as in the wrapping approach.

2. In languages like FLARE/V, where local identifiers may have the same name as global standard identifiers for primitive operators, care must be taken to distinguish references to global and local identifiers.[2] For example, in the program `(flare (x) (let ((+ *)) (- (+ 2 x) 3)))`, the invocation of `+` in `(+ 2 x)` cannot be inlined, but the invocation of `-` can be:

   ```
   (flare (x)
     (let ((+ (abs (v.0 v.1) (prim * v.0 v.1))))
       (prim - (+ 2 x) 3)))
   ```

---

[2]Many programming languages avoid this and related problems by treating primitive operator names as reserved keywords that may not be used as identifiers in declarations or assignments. This allows compiler writers to inline all primitives.

3. In FLARE/V, the values associated with global primitive identifier names can be modified by `set!`. For example, consider

```
(flarek (x y)
  (* (+ x (let ((_ (set! + -))) y))
     (+ x y)))
```

in which the first occurrence of + denotes addition and the second occurrence denotes subtraction. It would clearly be incorrect to replace the second occurrence by an inlined addition primitive. Correctly inlining addition for the first occurrence and subtraction for the second occurrence is possible in this case, but can be justified only by a sophisticated effect analysis. A simple conservative way to address this problem in the inlining strategy is to use wrapping rather than inlining for any global name that is mutated somewhere in the program. For the above example, this yields:

```
(flarek (x y)
  (let ((+ (abs (v.2 v.3) (prim + v.2 v.3))))
    (prim * (+ x (let ((_ (set! + (abs (v.0 v.1)
                                    (prim - v.0 v.1)))))
                   y))
           (+ x y))))
```

All of the above issues are handled by the definition of the inlining approach to globalization in Figure 17.9. The $\mathcal{GI}_{prog}$ function uses $MutIds_{prog}$ (defined in Figure 17.10) to determine the mutated free identifiers of a program — i.e., the free identifiers that are targets of assignments — and wraps the program body in abstractions for these. All other free identifiers should name primitives that may be inlined in call positions or expanded to abstractions (via $\mathcal{ABS}$ from Figure 17.8) in other positions. The identifier-set argument to $\mathcal{GI}_{exp}$ keeps track of the unmutated free identifiers in the program that have not been locally redeclared. Again, the undefined cases of partial functions are used to model the situations in which globalization fails.

Figure 17.11 shows our `revmap` example after the globalization stage using the inlining strategy. In this case, all references to free identifiers have been converted to primitive applications. In this and subsequent examples, we "resugar" primitive applications (`prim` O ...) to (@O ...) to make the code more concise.

Exercise 17.1 What is the result of globalizing the following program using (1) the wrapping strategy and (2) the inlining strategy?

```
(flare (* /) (+ (let ((+ *)) (- + 1))
                (let ((* -)) (* / 2))))
```

$$IS \in \text{IdSet} = \mathcal{P}(\text{Ident}_{FLARE/V})$$

$$\mathcal{GI}_{prog} : \text{Prog}_{FLARE/V} \rightharpoonup \text{Prog}_{FLARE/V}$$

$\mathcal{GI}_{prog}[\![P]\!] = (\text{flarek } (I_{i=1}^n) \; (\text{wrap}[\![\mathcal{GI}_{exp}[\![E_{body}]\!] \; IS_{unmuts}]\!] \; IS_{muts}))$
  where $P = (\text{flarek } (I_{i=1}^n) \; E_{body})$,
  $IS_{muts} = \text{MutIds}_{prog}[\![P]\!], \; IS_{unmuts} = (\text{FrIds}[\![P]\!]) - IS_{muts}$,
  wrap is defined in Figure 17.8, and MutIds_{prog} is defined in Figure 17.10

$$\mathcal{GI}_{exp} : \text{Exp}_{FLARE/V} \rightarrow \text{IdSet} \rightharpoonup \text{Exp}_{FLARE/V}$$

$\mathcal{GI}_{exp}[\![(I_{rator} \; E_{i=1}^n)]\!] \; IS$
$= \textbf{if } I_{rator} \in IS$
  $\quad \textbf{then if } I_{rator} \in \text{Primop}_{FLARE/V} \; \textbf{then } (\text{prim } I_{rator} \; (\mathcal{GI}_{exp}[\![E_i]\!] \; IS)_{i=1}^n)$
  $\qquad\qquad \textbf{else } \textit{undefined} \; \textbf{end}$
  $\quad \textbf{else } (I_{rator} \; (\mathcal{GI}_{exp}[\![E_i]\!] \; IS)_{i=1}^n) \; \textbf{end}$

$\mathcal{GI}_{exp}[\![I]\!] \; IS = \textbf{if } I \in IS \; \textbf{then } \mathcal{ABS}[\![I]\!] \; \textbf{else } I \; \textbf{end}$
  where $\mathcal{ABS}$ is defined in Figure 17.8

$\mathcal{GI}_{exp}[\![(\text{abs } (I_{i=1}^n) \; E_{body})]\!] \; IS = (\text{abs } (I_{i=1}^n) \; (\mathcal{GI}_{exp}[\![E_{body}]\!] \; (IS - \cup_{i=1}^n \{I_i\})))$

$\mathcal{GI}_{exp}[\![(\text{let } ((I_i \; E_i)_{i=1}^n) \; E_{body})]\!] \; IS$
$= (\text{let } ((I_i \; (\mathcal{GI}_{exp}[\![E_i]\!] \; IS))_{i=1}^n) \; (\mathcal{GI}_{exp}[\![E_{body}]\!] \; (IS - \cup_{i=1}^n -I_i{''})))$

$\mathcal{GI}_{exp}[\![(\text{letrec } ((I_i \; E_i)_{i=1}^n) \; E_{body})]\!] \; IS$
$= (\text{letrec } ((I_i \; (\mathcal{GI}_{exp}[\![E_i]\!] \; IS'))_{i=1}^n) \; (\mathcal{GI}_{exp}[\![E_{body}]\!] \; IS'))$
  where $IS' = IS - \cup_{i=1}^n \{I_i\}$

$\mathcal{GI}_{exp}[\![E]\!] \; IS = \text{mapsub}_{FLARE/V}[\![E]\!] \; (\lambda E_{sub} . \mathcal{GI}_{exp}[\![E_{sub}]\!] \; IS)$, otherwise.

Figure 17.9 The inlining approach to globalization.

Exercise 17.2 The globalization strategies described in this section assume that all standard identifiers name primitive procedures, but a standard library typically contains other kinds of entities. Describe how to extend globalization (both the wrapping and inlining strategies) to handle standard identifiers that name (1) literal values (e.g., `true` standing for `#t`) and (2) nonprimitive procedures (e.g., `length` and `map` from the FL standard library). Keep in mind that the nonprimitive procedures might be recursive or even mutually recursive.

17.5 Transformation 3: Assignment Conversion

Assignment conversion removes all mutable variables from a program by converting them to mutable cells. We will say that the resulting program is **assignment-free** because it contains no occurrences of the `set!` construct.

$$MutIds_{prog} : \text{Prog}_{FLARE/V} \to \mathcal{P}(\text{Ident}_{FLARE/V})$$

$$MutIds_{prog}[\![(\texttt{flarek}~(I_{i=1}^{n})~E_{body})]\!] = MutIds[\![E_{body}]\!] - \cup_{i=1}^{n}\{I_i\}$$

$$MutIds : \text{Exp}_{FLARE/V} \to \mathcal{P}(\text{Ident}_{FLARE/V})$$

$$MutIds[\![(\texttt{set!}~I~E)]\!] = \{I\} \cup MutIds[\![E]\!]$$

$$MutIds[\![(\texttt{abs}~(I_{i=1}^{n})~E_{body})]\!] = MutIds[\![E_{body}]\!] - \cup_{i=1}^{n}\{I_i\}$$

$$MutIds[\![(\texttt{let}~((I_i~E_i)_{i=1}^{n})~E_{body})]\!]$$
$$= (\cup_{i=1}^{n}MutIds[\![E_i]\!]) \cup (MutIds[\![E_{body}]\!] - \cup_{i=1}^{n}\{I_i\})$$

$$MutIds[\![(\texttt{letrec}((I_i~E_i)_{i=1}^{n})~E_{body})]\!]$$
$$= ((\cup_{i=1}^{n}MutIds[\![E_i]\!]) \cup MutIds[\![E_{body}]\!]) - \cup_{i=1}^{n}\{I_i\}$$

$$MutIds[\![E]\!] = \cup_{E' \in subexps[\![E]\!]} MutIds[\![E']\!], \text{ otherwise,}$$
(Since literals, variable references, and error expressions have
no subexpressions, they have no mutated free identifiers.)

Figure 17.10   Mutated free identifiers of FLARE/V expressions and programs.

Assignment conversion makes all mutable storage explicit and simplifies later passes by making all variable bindings immutable. After assignment conversion, all variables denote values rather than implicit cells containing values. A variable may be bound to an explicit cell value whose content varies with time, but the explicit cell value bound to the variable cannot change. As we will see later in the closure conversion stage (Section 17.10), assignment conversion is important because it allows environments to be treated as immutable data structures that can be freely shared and copied without concerns about side effects. In our compiler, assignment conversion precedes type and effect reconstruction because reconstruction is simpler in a language without mutable variables (FLARE) than one with them (FLARE/V). Additionally, in a language without mutable variables, all variable references are guaranteed to be pure, which enhances `let`-style polymorphism.

A straightforward approach to assignment conversion is to make an explicit cell for *every* variable in a given program. For example, the factorial program

```
(flarek (x)
  (let ((ans 1))
    (letrec ((loop (abs (n)
                     (if (@= n 0)
                         ans
                         (let ((_ (set! ans (@* n ans))))
                           (loop (@- n 1)))))))
      (loop x))))
```

```
(flare (a b)
  (let ((revmap
          (abs (f elts)
            (let ((ans (@null)))
              (letrec
                ((loop (abs (xs)
                         (if (@null? xs)
                             ans
                             (let ((_ (set! ans
                                            (@cons (f (@car xs)) ans))))
                               (loop (@cdr xs))))))))
                (loop elts))))))
    (revmap (abs (x) (@> x b)) (@cons a (@cons (@* a 7) (@null))))))
```

Figure 17.11 revmap example after globalization using inlining.

can be assignment-converted to

```
(flarek (x)
  (let ((x (@cell x)))
    (let ((ans (@cell 1)))
      (letrec ((loop
                 (@cell (abs (n)
                          (let ((n (@cell n)))
                            (if (@= (@^ n) 0)
                                (@^ ans)
                                (let ((_ (@:= ans (@* (@^ n)
                                                      (@^ ans)))))
                                  ((@^ loop) (@- (@^ n) 1)))))))))
        ((@^ loop) (@^ x))))))
```

In the converted program, each of the variables in the original program (x, ans, loop, n) is bound to an explicit cell. Each variable reference I in the original program is converted to a cell reference (@^ I), and each variable assignment (set! I E) in the original program is converted to a cell assignment of the form (@:= I E'), where E' is the converted E.

The code generated by the naive approach to assignment conversion can contain many unnecessary cell allocations, references, and assignments. A cleverer strategy is to make explicit cells only for those variables that are mutated in the program. Determining exactly which variables are mutated when a program executes is undecidable. We employ a simple conservative syntactic approximation that defines a variable to be mutated if it is assigned within its scope. In the

factorial example, the alternative strategy yields the following program, in which
only the `ans` variable is converted to a cell:

```
(flarek (x)
  (let ((ans (@cell 1)))
    (letrec ((loop (abs (n)
                     (if (@= n 0)
                         (@^ ans)
                         (let ((_ (@:= ans (@* n (@^ ans)))))
                           (loop (@- n 1)))))))
        (loop x))))
```

The improved approach to assignment conversion is formalized in Figure 17.12.
The $\mathcal{AC}_{prog}$ function wraps the transformed body of a FLARE/V program in
a `let` that binds each mutated program parameter (that is, each mutated free
identifier in the body) to a cell. The free identifiers syntactically assigned within
an expression are determined by the *MutIds* function defined in Figure 17.10.

Expressions are transformed by the $\mathcal{AC}_{exp}$ function, whose second argument is
the set of in-scope identifiers naming variables that have been transformed to cells.
Processing of variable references transforms such identifiers to cell references;
variable assignments are transformed to cell assignments.

The only other nontrivial cases for $\mathcal{AC}_{exp}$ are the binding constructs `abs`,
`let`, and `letrec`. All of these cases use the *partition* function to partition the
identifiers declared by these constructs into two sets: the mutated identifiers
IS_M that are assigned somewhere in the given expressions, and the unmutated
identifiers IS_U that are not assigned. In each of these cases, any subexpression
in the scope of the declared identifiers is processed by $\mathcal{AC}_{exp}$ with an identifier
set that includes IS_M but excludes IS_U. The exclusion is necessary to prevent
the conversion of local unmutated variables that have the same name as external
mutated variables. For example,

```
(flarek (x) (let ((_ (set! x (@* x 2)))))
              ((abs (x) x) x)))
```

is converted to

```
(flarek (x)
  (let ((x (@cell x)))
    (let ((_ (@:= x (@* (@^ x) 2))))
      ((abs (x) x) (@^ x)))))
```

Even though the program parameter `x` is converted to a cell, the `x` in the abstraction body is not.

$IS \in \mathrm{IdSet} = \mathcal{P}(\mathrm{Ident}_{FLARE/V})$

$\mathcal{AC}_{prog} : \mathrm{Prog}_{FLARE/V} \to \mathrm{Prog}_{FLARE}$

Preconditions: The input to $\mathcal{AC}_{prog}$ is a well-formed, closed, kernel FLARE/V program.

Postconditions: The output of $\mathcal{AC}_{prog}$ is a well-formed, closed, assignment-free, kernel FLARE program.

$\mathcal{AC}_{prog}[\![(\texttt{flarek} \ (I_{i=1}^{n}) \ E_{body})]\!]$
  $= (\texttt{flarek} \ (I_{i=1}^{n}) \ (\textit{wrap-cells} \ IS_{muts} \ (\mathcal{AC}_{exp}[\![E_{body}]\!] \ IS_{muts})))$
  where $IS_{muts} = MutIds[\![E_{body}]\!]$ and $MutIds$ is defined in Figure 17.10.

$\mathcal{AC}_{exp} : \mathrm{Exp}_{FLARE/V} \to \mathrm{IdSet} \to \mathrm{Exp}_{FLARE}$

$\mathcal{AC}_{exp}[\![I]\!] \ IS = \textbf{if} \ I \in IS \ \textbf{then} \ (\texttt{@\^{}} \ I) \ \textbf{else} \ I \ \textbf{end}$

$\mathcal{AC}_{exp}[\![(\texttt{set!} \ I \ E)]\!] \ IS = (\texttt{@:=} \ I \ (\mathcal{AC}_{exp}[\![E]\!] \ IS))$

$\mathcal{AC}_{exp}[\![(\texttt{abs} \ (I_{i=1}^{n}) \ E_{body})]\!] \ IS$
  $= \textbf{let} \ \langle IS_M, IS_U \rangle \ \textbf{be} \ (\textit{partition} \ \{I_1, \ldots, I_n\} \ [E_{body}])$
    $\textbf{in} \ (\texttt{abs} \ (I_{i=1}^{n}) \ (\textit{wrap-cells} \ IS_M \ (\mathcal{AC}_{exp}[\![E_{body}]\!] \ ((IS \cup IS_M) - IS_U))))$

$\mathcal{AC}_{exp}[\![(\texttt{let} \ ((I_i \ E_i)_{i=1}^{n}) \ E_{body})]\!] \ IS$
  $= \textbf{let} \ \langle IS_M, IS_U \rangle \ \textbf{be} \ (\textit{partition} \ \{I_1, \ldots, I_n\} \ [E_{body}])$
    $\textbf{in} \ (\texttt{let} \ ((I_i \ (\textit{maybe-cell} \ I_i \ IS_M \ (\mathcal{AC}_{exp}[\![E_i]\!] \ IS)))_{i=1}^{n})$
      $(\mathcal{AC}_{exp}[\![E_{body}]\!] \ ((IS \cup IS_M) - IS_U)))$

$\mathcal{AC}_{exp}[\![(\texttt{letrec} \ ((I_i \ E_i)_{i=1}^{n}) \ E_{body})]\!] \ IS$
  $= \textbf{let} \ \langle IS_M, IS_U \rangle \ \textbf{be} \ (\textit{partition} \ \{I_1, \ldots, I_n\} \ [E_1, \ldots, E_n, E_{body}])$
    $\textbf{in} \ (\texttt{letrec} \ ((I_i \ (\textit{maybe-cell} \ I_i \ IS_M \ (\mathcal{AC}_{exp}[\![E_i]\!] \ IS')))_{i=1}^{n})$
      $(\mathcal{AC}_{exp}[\![E_{body}]\!] \ IS')),$
  where $IS' = ((IS \cup IS_M) - IS_U)$

$\mathcal{AC}_{exp}[\![E]\!] \ IS = \textit{mapsub}_{FLARE/V}[\![E]\!] \ (\lambda E_{sub} . \mathcal{AC}_{exp}[\![E_{sub}]\!] \ IS), \ \text{otherwise}.$

$\textit{wrap-cells} : \mathrm{IdSet} \to \mathrm{Exp}_{FLARE} \to \mathrm{Exp}_{FLARE}$

$\textit{wrap-cells} \ \{\} \ E = E$

$\textit{wrap-cells} \ \{I_1 \ldots I_n\} \ E = (\texttt{let} \ ((I_i \ (\texttt{@cell} \ I_i))_{i=1}^{n}) \ E), \ \text{where} \ n \geq 1.$

$\textit{partition} : \mathrm{IdSet} \to \mathrm{Exp}_{FLARE/V}^{*} \to (\mathrm{IdSet} \times \mathrm{IdSet})$

$\textit{partition} \ IS \ [E_1 \ldots E_n] = \textbf{let} \ IS_M \ \textbf{be} \ \cup_{i=1}^{k}(MutIds[\![E_i]\!]) \ \textbf{in} \ \langle IS \cap IS_M, IS - IS_M \rangle$

$\textit{maybe-cell} : \mathrm{Ident} \to \mathrm{IdSet} \to \mathrm{Exp}_{FLARE/V}$

$\textit{maybe-cell} \ I \ IS \ E = \textbf{if} \ I \in IS \ \textbf{then} \ (\texttt{@cell} \ E) \ \textbf{else} \ E \ \textbf{end}$

Figure 17.12 An assignment-conversion transformation that converts only those variables that are syntactically assigned in the program.

Abstractions are processed like programs in that the transformed abstraction body is wrapped in a `let` that binds each mutated identifier to a cell. This preserves the call-by-value semantics of FLARE, since an assignment to the formal parameter of an abstraction is transformed to a cell assignment that modifies the content of a cell that is allocated locally within the abstraction. The transformation can be modified to instead implement a call-by-reference semantics (see page 436), in which a formal parameter assignment is transformed to an assignment of a cell passed into the abstraction from the point of application (Exercise 17.5).

In processing `let` and `letrec`, *maybe-cell* is used to wrap the binding expressions for mutated identifiers in applications of the `cell` primitive. These two forms are processed similarly except for scoping differences in their declared names.

Figure 17.13 shows our `revmap` example after the assignment-conversion stage. The only variable assigned in the input program is `ans`, and this is converted to a cell.

Intuitively, consistently converting a mutated variable along with its references and assignments into explicit cell operations should not change the observable behavior of a program. So we expect that assignment conversion should preserve both the type safety and the meaning of a program. However, formally proving such intuitions can be challenging. See [WS97] for a proof that a version of assignment conversion for SCHEME is a meaning-preserving transformation.

Exercise 17.3 Show the result of assignment-converting the following programs using $\mathcal{AC}_{prog}$:

```
(flarek (a b c)
  (let ((_ (set! a (@+ a c))))
    (abs (a d)
      (let ((_ (set! c (@* a b))))
        (set! d (@+ c d))))))
(flarek (x)
  (letrec ((f (abs (y) (@pair y (g (@- y 1)))))
           (g (abs (z)
                (let ((_ (set! g (abs (w) w))))
                  (f z)))))
    (f x)))
```

Exercise 17.4 Can assignment conversion be performed before globalization? Explain.

Exercise 17.5 Suppose that FLARE/V had a call-by-reference semantics rather than a call-by-value semantics for mutable variables (see Section 8.4). Modify the definition of assignment conversion so that it implements call-by-reference semantics. (Compare to Exercise 8.22 on page 439.)

```
(flare (a b)
  (let ((revmap
          (abs (f elts)
            (let ((ans (@cell (@null))))
              (letrec
                ((loop (abs (xs)
                         (if (@null? xs)
                             (@^ ans)
                             (let ((_ (@:= ans (@cons (f (@car xs))
                                                      (@^ ans)))))
                               (loop (@cdr xs)))))))
                (loop elts))))))
    (revmap (abs (x) (@> x b)) (@cons a (@cons (@* a 7) (@null))))))
```

Figure 17.13 `revmap` program after assignment conversion.

Exercise 17.6 A straightforward implementation of the $\mathcal{AC}_{prog}$ and $\mathcal{AC}_{exp}$ functions in Figure 17.12 is inefficient because (1) it traverses the AST of every declaration node at least twice: once to determine the free mutated identifiers, and once to transform the node; and (2) it may recalculate the free mutated identifiers for the same expression many times. Describe how to modify the assignment-conversion algorithm so that it works in a single traversal of the program AST and calculates the free mutated identifiers only once at every node. Note: You may need to modify the information stored in the nodes of a FLARE/V AST.

17.6 Transformation 4: Type/Effect Reconstruction

The fourth stage of the TORTOISE compiler is type and effect reconstruction. Only well-typed FLARE programs are allowed to proceed through the rest of the compiler. The details of how types and effects are reconstructed were described earlier, in Section 16.2.3. Note that assignment conversion *must* precede this stage because type and effect reconstruction was defined for the FLARE language, which does not include `set!`.

> **Preconditions:** The input to type/effect reconstruction is a well-formed, closed kernel FLARE program that is assignment-free.
>
> **Postconditions:** The output of type/effect reconstruction is a valid, closed kernel FLARE program that is assignment-free. We will use the term **valid** to describe a program or expression that is well formed and is guaranteed not to encounter a dynamic type error.

17.6.1   Propagating Type and Effect Information

Although neither FLARE nor FIL (the intermediate language to be used from the next compilation stage on) has explicit types or effects, this does not mean that the type and effect information generated by the FLARE type/effect reconstruction phase is thrown away. This information can be passed through the compiler stages via a separate channel, where it is appropriately transformed by each pass. In an actual implementation, this information might be stored in abstract syntax tree nodes for FLARE and FIL expressions, in symbol tables mapping variable names to their types, or in explicit type/effect derivation trees. We assume that this type and effect information is available for later stages, where it can be used to guide the compilation process. Similarly, the results from other static analyses, such as flow information [NNH98, DWM+01], could be computed at this stage and passed along to other compiler stages.

An alternative approach used in many modern research compilers is to use so-called **typed intermediate languages (TILs)** that carry explicit type information (possibly including effect, flow, and other analysis information) through all stages of the compiler. In these systems, program transformations effectively transform type derivations of programs. The fact that each program manipulated by a TIL-based compiler is well typed has several advantages. The compiler can avoid generating code to check for run-time type errors, because these are provably impossible. The explicit type information carried by a TIL can be inspected to guide compilation (e.g., determining clever representations for certain types) and to implement run-time operations (such as tag-free garbage collection and checking safety properties of dynamically linked code). It also serves as an important tool for debugging a compiler implementation: if the output of a transformation doesn't type-check, the transformation must have a bug.

The reason that we do not use TILs in our presentation is to keep our compiler simple. TILs typically require a sophisticated type system with universal and existential types. Specifying each compiler stage becomes more complicated because it transforms not only expressions but their types. The explicit type information is often larger than the code it describes, which makes it impractical to show the result of compilation of even relatively simple expressions. See [MWCG99] for a presentation of using TILs to translate a high-level language all the way down into a typed assembly language.

17.6.2   Effect-based Code Optimization

The effect information reconstructed for a FLARE program is important for enabling many standard code optimizations performed by a compiler. We now discuss some of these in the context of the TORTOISE compiler.

Many program transformations require knowledge about expression interference (see Section 8.3.6). In our system, two expressions interfere if they both `write` to the same region or if one has a `read` effect on a region the other has an `init` or `write` effect on. A `pure` expression does not interfere with any other expression because it does not depend on the store in any way. For example, if two expressions interfere, it is unsafe to reorder them relative to each other, since this could change the order of operations on the store locations manipulated by both expressions. But if two expressions do not interfere, then it may be possible to reorder them, execute them in parallel, or perform other improvements.

As a simple example of how effects can enable code optimizations, we demonstrate how the following FLARE abstraction can be improved if certain effect information is known.

```
(abs (n)
  (letrec ((loop (abs (i)
                   (if (@= i 0)
                       (@^ x)
                       (begin (h (f i) (g i))
                              (@:= x (k (g (f i))))
                              (@:= x (h (g i) (k n)))
                              (loop (@- i 1)))))))
    (loop n)))
```

Assume that this abstraction appears in a scope where x is a cell in region rx and f, g, h, and k are procedures with the following latent effects:

Procedure	Latent Effect
f	(read rx)
g	(maxeff (read ry) (write ry))
h	(maxeff (read rz) (write rz))
k	pure

Since the latent effects of f and g do not overlap, (f i) and (g i) do not interfere, and may be executed in **parallel**. This means that in a computer with multiple processing units, the expressions can be executed at the same time on different processing units. This is an improvement because it allows (f i) and (g i) to be executed in the maximum of the execution times for the two expressions rather than the sum of their times.[3] If FLARE is extended with a `letpar` binding construct whose binding definition expressions are executed in parallel, then the `begin` expression in our example can be transformed to:

---

[3]In practice, there is often an additional overhead associated with parallel execution; the individual execution times must be big enough to justify this overhead.

```
(letpar ((a (f i)) (b (g i)))
   (begin (h a b)
          (@:= x (k (g (f i))))
          (@:= x (h (g i) (k n)))
          (loop (@- i 1))))
```

Extending FLARE with mutable arrays, each of which has an associated region, would further expand opportunities for parallelism. For example, given two arrays in distinct regions, loops to sum their elements could be executed in parallel.

If an expression occurs more than once and it does not interfere with itself or any intervening expressions, then the result of the first occurrence can be named and the name can be used for the subsequent occurrences. This is known as **common subexpression elimination**. For example, the only effect of (f i) is (read rx), so it does not interfere with the invocations of f, g, and h (none of which has a (write rx) effect) that appear before the second occurrence. Since the first occurrence of (f i) already has the name a, the second occurrence of (f i) can be replaced by a:

```
(letpar ((a (f i)) (b (g i)))
   (begin (h a b)
          (@:= x (k (g a)))  {(f i) replaced by a}
          (@:= x (h (g i) (k n)))
          (loop (@- i 1))))
```

Although (g i) also appears twice, its second occurrence *cannot* be eliminated because it interferes with the first occurrence as well as with (g a). Because g both reads and writes region ry, the second (g i) may have a different value than the first one.

When an expression does not contribute to a program in its value or its effect, it may be removed via a process known as **dead code elimination**. For example, the second assignment expression, (@:= x (h (g i) (k n))), does not read rx before writing it, so the first assignment to x, in (@:= x (k (g a))), is unnecessary. This leaves (k (g a)), which cannot be entirely eliminated because (g a) writes to region ry, which is read later by (g i). But the invocation of k *can* be eliminated because it is pure and its result is not used:

```
(letpar ((a (f i)) (b (g i)))
   (begin (h a b)
          (g a)  {assignment to x and call to k eliminated}
          (@:= x (h (g i) (k n)))
          (loop (@- i 1))))
```

It might seem unlikely that a programmer would ever write dead code, but it occurs in practice for a variety of reasons. For example, the assumptions in place when the code is originally written may no longer hold when the code is later modified. In our example, perhaps g and/or h initially had a latent (read rx) effect justifying the first assignment to x, but the procedures were later changed to remove this effect, and the programmer neglected to remove the first assignment to x. Perhaps the dead code was not written by a human but was created by an automatic program generator or was the result of transforming another program. Generators and transformers can be simpler to build when they are allowed to produce code that contains inefficiencies (such as common subexpressions and dead code) that are cleaned up by later optimization phases.

When an expression in the body of a procedure or loop is guaranteed to have the same value for every invocation of the procedure or loop, it may be lifted out of the body via a transformation called **code hoisting**. In our example, since k is a pure procedure and n is an immutable variable defined outside the loop procedure, the invocation (k n) in the body of loop always has the same value. We can hoist it outside the definition of loop so that it is calculated only once rather than for every invocation of loop:

```
(abs (n)
  (let ((c (k n))) {(k n) has been hoisted outside loop}
    (letrec ((loop (abs (i)
                     (if (@= i 0)
                         (@^ x)
                         (letpar ((a (f i)) (b (g i)))
                           (begin (h a b)
                                  (g a)
                                  (@:= x (h (g i) c)) {c replaces (k n)}
                                  (loop (@- i 1)))))))))
      (loop n))))
```

Note that if the k in (k n) were replaced by f or g, the expression could *not* be hoisted. The loop body writes to regions (rx and ry) that are read by these procedures, so (f n) and (g n) are not guaranteed to be loop-invariant.

In each of the optimizations we have mentioned, effect information is critical for justifying the optimization. Without any effect information, we would need to conservatively assume that all invocations of f, g, h, and k are impure and interfere with each other and with the assignments to x. With these conservative assumptions, *none* of the optimizations we performed on our example would be permissible!

17.7   Transformation 5: Translation

In this transformation, a kernel FLARE program is translated into the FIL intermediate language. All subsequent transformations are performed on FIL programs. We first present the FIL language and then describe how to transform FLARE to FIL.

17.7.1   The Compiler Intermediate Language: FIL

The intermediate language of the main stages of our transformation-based compiler uses a language that we call FIL, for **F**unctional **I**ntermediate **L**anguage. Like FLARE, FIL is a stateful, call-by-value, statically scoped, function-oriented language. However, FIL is simpler than FLARE in two important ways:

1. FIL supports fewer features than FLARE. It does not have a recursion construct (`letrec`) or an assignment construct (`set!`), and it represents both cells and pairs with a single form of mutable product. So specifying FIL transformations requires fewer cases than FLARE transformations.

2. Unlike FLARE, FIL does not have a formal type system and does not support type reconstruction. Although all of the remaining transformations *can* be expressed in a typed framework, the type systems and transformations are rather complex to describe. Specifying these transformations in FIL is much simpler. However, we will not completely disregard type and effect information. As discussed later (page 1035), we will assume that certain type and effect information is preserved by FIL programs, but will not formally describe how this is accomplished.

The Syntax of FIL

The syntax of FIL is specified in Figure 17.14. FIL is similar to many of the stateful variants of FL that we have studied. Some notable features of FIL are:

- As in FLARE, multiargument abstractions and applications are hardwired into the kernel rather than being treated as syntactic sugar, and the abstraction keyword is `abs`. Unlike in FLARE, FIL applications have an explicit `app` keyword.

- As in FLARE, multibinding `let` expressions are considered kernel expressions rather than sugar for applications of explicit abstractions.

Kernel Grammar

$P \in \mathrm{Prog}_{FIL} ::= (\texttt{fil} \ (I^*_{formal}) \ E_{body})$

$E \in \mathrm{Exp}_{FIL} ::= L \mid I \mid (\texttt{error} \ Y_{message})$
$\qquad\qquad\quad \mid (\texttt{if} \ E_{test} \ E_{then} \ E_{else}) \mid (\texttt{prim} \ O_{primop} \ E^*_{arg})$
$\qquad\qquad\quad \mid (\texttt{abs} \ (I^*_{formal}) \ E_{body}) \mid (\texttt{app} \ E_{rator} \ E^*_{rand})$
$\qquad\qquad\quad \mid (\texttt{let} \ ((I_{name} \ E_{defn})^*) \ E_{body})$

$L \in \mathrm{Lit}_{FIL} ::= \texttt{\#u} \mid B \mid N \mid (\texttt{sym} \ Y)$

$B \in \mathrm{BoolLit} = \{\texttt{\#t}, \texttt{\#f}\}$ as in FLARE/V.

$N \in \mathrm{IntLit} = $ as in FLARE/V.

$J \in \mathrm{PosLit} = \{1, 2, 3, \ldots\}$

$Y \in \mathrm{SymLit} = $ as in FLARE/V.

$O \in \mathrm{Primop}_{FIL} ::= \texttt{+} \mid \texttt{-} \mid \texttt{*} \mid \texttt{/} \mid \texttt{\%}$ *; arithmetic ops*
$\qquad\qquad\quad \mid \texttt{<=} \mid \texttt{<} \mid \texttt{=} \mid \texttt{!=} \mid \texttt{>} \mid \texttt{>=} \ \texttt{bool=?} \mid \texttt{sym=?}$ *; relational ops*
$\qquad\qquad\quad \mid \texttt{not} \mid \texttt{and} \mid \texttt{or}$ *; logical ops*
$\qquad\qquad\quad \mid \texttt{cons} \mid \texttt{car} \mid \texttt{cdr} \mid \texttt{null} \mid \texttt{null?}$ *; list ops*
$\qquad\qquad\quad \mid \texttt{mprod} \mid (\texttt{mget} \ J) \mid (\texttt{mset!} \ J) \mid \texttt{mprod=?}$ *; mut. prod. ops*
$\qquad\qquad\quad \mid \ldots$ *other primitives will be added as needed* $\ldots$

$\qquad \mathrm{Keyword}_{FIL} = \{\texttt{abs}, \texttt{app}, \texttt{error}, \texttt{fil}, \texttt{if}, \texttt{let}, \texttt{let*}, \texttt{prim}, \texttt{sym}\}$

$I \in \mathrm{Ident}_{FIL} = \mathrm{SymLit} - (\{Y \mid Y \ \text{begins with} \ \texttt{@}\} \cup \mathrm{Keyword}_{FIL})$

Syntactic Sugar

$(\texttt{@mget} \ J \ E_{mprod}) \leadsto_{ds} (\texttt{prim} \ (\texttt{mget} \ J) \ E_{mprod})$
$(\texttt{@mset!} \ J \ E_{mprod} \ E_{new}) \leadsto_{ds} (\texttt{prim} \ (\texttt{mset!} \ J) \ E_{mprod} \ E_{new})$
$(\texttt{@}O_{op} \ E^n_{i=1}) \leadsto_{ds} (\texttt{prim} \ O_{op} \ E^n_{i=1})$, where $O_{op} \notin \{(\texttt{mget} \ J), (\texttt{mset!} \ J)\}$

$(\texttt{let*} \ () \ E_{body}) \leadsto_{ds} E_{body}$
$(\texttt{let*} \ ((I_1 \ E_1) \ (I_{rest} \ E_{rest})^*) \ E_{body})$
$\quad \leadsto_{ds} (\texttt{let} \ ((I_1 \ E_1)) \ (\texttt{let*} \ ((I_{rest} \ E_{rest})^*) \ E_{body}))$

Figure 17.14 Syntax of FIL, the TORTOISE compiler intermediate language.

- Unlike FLARE/V, FIL does not have mutable variables (i.e., no `set!`). But FIL does have mutable products (also known as mutable tuples), which are created via `mprod`, whose component slots are accessed via `mget` and changed via `mset!`, and which are tested for equality (i.e., same location in the store) via `mprod=?`. We treat `mget` and `mset!` as "indexed primitives" $(\texttt{mget} \ J_{index})$ and $(\texttt{mset!} \ J_{index})$ in which the primitive operator includes the index J_{index} of the manipulated component slot. If we wrote $(\texttt{prim} \ \texttt{mget} \ E_{index} \ E_{mp})$, this would imply that the index could be calculated by an arbitrary expression E_{index} when in fact it must be a positive integer literal J_{index}. So we instead write (prim (mget J_{index}) E_{mp}) (and similarly for mset!). Treating mget and mset! as primitives rather than as kernel constructs simplifies the definition of several transformations.

- Unlike FLARE, FIL does not include cells and pairs; both are implemented as mutable products.[4]

- Unlike FLARE, FIL does not have any explicit kernel expression form (such as letrec) for recursive definitions. It is assumed that the "knot-tying" of recursion is instead performed by setting the components of mutable products. This is the approach taken in the translation from FLARE to FIL.

- Other data include integers, booleans, symbols, and immutable lists, all of which are in FLARE.

- Unlike FLARE, FIL does not support globally bound standard identifiers for procedures like +, <, and cons. This means that all valid FIL programs must be closed (i.e., have no free variables).

To improve the readability of FIL programs, we will use the syntactic sugar specified in Figure 17.14. The @ notation is a more concise way of writing primitive applications. E.g., (@+ 1 2) abbreviates (prim + 1 2) and (@mget 1 t) abbreviates (prim (mget 1) t). The let* construct abbreviates a sequence of nested single-binding let expressions. Throughout the rest of this chapter, we will "resugar" expressions using these abbreviations in all code examples to make them more readable.

The readability of FIL programs is further enhanced if we assume that the syntactic simplifications in Figure 17.15 are performed when FIL ASTs are constructed. These simplifications automatically remove some of the silly inefficiencies that can be introduced by transformations. In transformation-based compilers, such simplifications are typically performed via a separate simplifying transformation, which may be called several times in the compilation process. However, building the simplifications into the AST constructors is an easy way to guarantee that the inefficient forms are never constructed in the first place. The conciseness and readability of the FIL examples in this chapter is due in large part to these simplifications. Putting all the simplifications in one place means that individual transformations do not need to implement any simplifications, so this also simplifies the specification of transformations.

---

[4]To model the immutability of pairs, Tortoise could be extended with immutable products. We have chosen to have only a single kind of product, for simplicity.

$$(\texttt{let ()}\ E_{body}) \xrightarrow{simp} E_{body} \qquad\qquad [\textit{empty-let}]$$

$$(\texttt{app (abs}\ (I_{i=1}^{n})\ E_{body})\ E_{i=1}^{n}) \xrightarrow{simp} (\texttt{let}\ ((I_i\ E_i)_{i=1}^{n})\ E_{body}) \quad [\textit{implicit-let}]$$

$$(\texttt{abs}\ (I_{i=1}^{n})\ (\texttt{app}\ E_{rator}\ I_{i=1}^{n})) \xrightarrow{simp} E_{rator} \qquad\qquad [\textit{eta}]$$
$$\text{where}\ \ E_{rator}\ \text{is a variable or abstraction}$$
$$\text{and}\ \textit{FrIds}[\![E_{rator}]\!]\ \cap \{I_1, \dots, I_n\}\ =\ \{\}$$

$$(\texttt{let}\ ((I\ I'))\ E_{body}) \xrightarrow{simp} [I'/I]E_{body} \qquad\qquad [\textit{copy-prop}]$$

Figure 17.15 Simplifications performed when constructing FIL ASTs.

The [*empty-let*] rule removes trivial instances of `let`. This rule eliminates the need for special cases (like the cases in the *wrap* function in Figure 17.8 and the *wrap-cells* function in Figure 17.12) in FIL transformations that might introduce an empty `let`.

The [*implicit-let*] rule treats an application of an explicit `abs` as a `let` expression. The [*eta*] rule performs **eta reduction** on an abstraction. The requirement that E_{rator} be a variable or abstraction is a simple syntactic constraint guaranteeing that E_{rator} is pure. If E_{rator} is impure, the simplification is unsafe because it could change the order of side effects in (and thus the meaning of) the program. For example, it is safe to simplify (`abs (a b) (app f a b)`) to `f`, but it is not safe to simplify

```
(abs (a b)
  (app (let ((_ (@mset! 1 c (@* 2 (@mget 1 c))))) f)
       a b))
```

to (`let ((_ (@mset! 1 c (@* 2 (@mget 1 c))))) f`) because the latter performs the `mset!` once rather than every time the procedure is called. Also, an `abs` cannot be eliminated by [*eta*] if E_{rator} mentions one of its formal parameters, as in (`abs (a) (app (abs (b) (@+ a b)) a)`).

The [*copy-prop*] rule performs a **copy propagation** simplification that is an important optimization in traditional compilers. This simplification removes a `let` that simply introduces one variable to rename the value of another. Recall that $[I'/I]E$ denotes the *capture-free* substitution of I' for I in E, renaming bound variables as necessary to prevent variable capture. In a language with mutable variables, the [*copy-prop*] simplification can be unsafe in the presence of assignments involving I or I' (see Exercise 17.7). However, this is not an issue in FIL because it does not have mutable variables.

The [*empty-let*], [*implicit-let*], and [*copy-prop*] simplifications are easy to perform in any context. The [*eta*] rule requires information about the free identifiers of subexpressions. It can be efficiently performed in practice if each AST node is annotated with its free identifiers.

If the simplification rules in Figure 17.15 can be performed in any order, there is a problem. The rules are not confluent, so applying the rules in different orders can lead to different results. For example, consider the expression

$$E_{ambig} = (\texttt{app } (\texttt{abs } (I) \ (\texttt{app } I_{rator} \ I)) \ E)$$

where $I \neq I_{rator}$. Here are two simplifications involving E_{ambig}:

$$E_{ambig} \xrightarrow{simp} (\texttt{let } ((I \ E)) \ (\texttt{app } I_{rator} \ I)) = E_{let} \text{ (via [\textit{implicit-let}] on outer \texttt{app})}$$

$$E_{ambig} \xrightarrow{simp} (\texttt{app } I_{rator} \ E) = E_{app} \qquad\qquad \text{(via [\textit{eta}] on \texttt{abs})}$$

If E is not an identifier (in which case E_{let} can simplify to E_{app} by applying the [*copy-prop*] rule), there is no way to simplify E_{let} and E_{app} to the same expression. It is possible to restore confluence by adding another simplification rule, but this has undesirable consequences for other stages of our compiler (see Exercise 17.8). Instead, we avoid ambiguity by requiring that the simplification rules be applied in a bottom-up fashion. That is, a simplification rule can be applied to an expression only if no simplification rules can be applied to any of its subexpressions. Using this bottom-up strategy, E_{ambig} unambiguously simplifies to E_{app} (assuming E cannot be simplified further); the [*implicit-let*] rule cannot be applied to the outer **app** because its rator can be simplified.

Finally, we assume the existence of functions $mapsub_{FIL}$ and $subexps_{FIL}$ that are analogous to the $mapsub_{FLARE/V}$ and $subexps_{FLARE/V}$ functions defined in Figures 17.5 and 17.6 (Section 17.2.3).

Exercise 17.7 Although the [*copy-prop*] rule is always safe in FIL (which does not have mutable variables), it is not always safe in a language with mutable variables, such as FLARE. Consider the following FLARE program skeleton:

```
(flare (a)
  (let ((f Efun))
    (let ((b a)) Ebody)))
```

For each of the following scenarios, develop an example in which applying the [*copy-prop*] simplification rule to (`let ((b a))` E_{body}) is unsafe:

a. E_{body} contains an assignment to **a** (but not **b**).

b. E_{body} contains an assignment to **b** (but not **a**).

c. E_{body} contains no assignments to **a** or **b**, but E_{fun} contains an assignment to **a**.

Exercise 17.8

a. Show that the simplification system in Figure 17.15 can be made confluent by adding the following rule:

$$(\text{let } ((I_i \ E_i)_{i=1}^{n}) \ (\text{app } E_{rator} \ I_{i=1}^{n})) \xrightarrow{simp} (\text{app } E_{rator} \ E_{i=1}^{n}) \qquad [\textit{eta-let}]$$
$$\text{where} \quad E_{rator} \text{ is a variable or abstraction}$$
$$\text{and } \textit{FrIds}[\![E_{rator}]\!] \cap \{I_1, \dots, I_n\} = \{\}$$

b. Unfortunately, the [*eta-let*] rule is problematic for dialects of FIL used in later stages of the compiler. For example, the kernel grammar in Figure 17.22 on page 1046 describes FIL_{cps}, a restricted subset of FIL that is the result of the CPS conversion stage of the compiler. Show that applying the [*eta-let*] rule to a FIL_{cps} expression can yield an expression that is not in FIL_{cps}.

c. Modify the [*eta-let*] rule so that it always simplifies FIL_{cps} expressions to FIL_{cps} expressions. Is the simplification system with your modified [*eta-let*] rule confluent?

The Semantics of FIL

FIL is a statically scoped, call-by-value language. Since FIL is stateful, the order of expression evaluation matters: the subexpressions of an `app`, arguments of a `prim`, and definition expressions of a `let` are evaluated from left to right. All FIL constructs have been studied before, so we will not repeat their dynamic semantics here.

In the interests of pedagogical simplicity, our FIL intermediate language does *not* have a formal type system. The FLARE program that is the input to the Translation stage is well typed, so it is necessarily valid (see page 1025) — i.e., it cannot encounter a dynamic type error. Intuitively, we expect that the Translation stage preserves behavior, so the program resulting from this stage should be valid as well. But we do not have a formal type system to prove this fact. We will assume that each subsequent compiler stage also preserves validity.

We would need a *very* sophisticated type system to show formally that well-typedness is preserved by the FIL transformations. Moreover, since the types in such a system could not all be reconstructed, many FIL expressions would have to be annotated with explicit types. If FIL had explicit types, it would be necessary for the compiler stages to transform these types as well as the expressions. (This could be done using a typed intermediate language — see page 1026.) Not only would this make the stages more difficult to specify, but the types for many sample programs would become so large that they would be nearly impossible to read. To justify the preservation of well-typedness, we would have to argue that each stage essentially transforms not just programs but valid type derivations of programs. Clearly, focusing on types in FIL would make the intermediate language more complex and would be at odds with our goal of making the compiler conceptually simple.

Although FIL has no formal type system, we will still assume that the stages of the TORTOISE compiler do not introduce any dynamic type errors. Since the input to the Translation stage is well typed, we will assume that the program resulting from Translation and every subsequent stage cannot encounter any dynamic type errors. In later stages, we will use this assumption to avoid handling certain cases. E.g., when processing (if E_1 0 (@+ E_2 E_3)), there is no question that E_1 denotes a boolean value and E_2 and E_3 denote integers. There is no need to handle cases where these expressions might have other types.

17.7.2   Translating FLARE to FIL

The translation from FLARE to FIL is performed by the $\mathcal{T}_{\mathrm{prog}}$ and $\mathcal{T}_{\mathrm{exp}}$ functions presented in Figure 17.16. Because the source and target languages are so similar, the translation has the flavor of a transformation that is purely structural except that (1) $\mathcal{T}_{\mathrm{prog}}$ changes the program keyword from flarek to fil; (2) $\mathcal{T}_{\mathrm{exp}}$ adds app to applications; (3) $\mathcal{T}_{\mathrm{exp}}$ transforms each letrec into a let that binds each variable to a cell (represented as a one-slot mutable product); and (4) $\mathcal{T}_{\mathrm{exp}}$ translates FLARE cell and immutable pair operations to FIL mutable product operations. We do not give the details of the other cases because they are straightforward. Note that we cannot use the $mapsub_{FLARE/V}$ or $mapsub_{FIL}$ functions to formally specify these cases because these functions transform an expression in a language (FLARE/V or FIL) to another expression in the *same* language. But $\mathcal{T}_{\mathrm{exp}}$ translates a FLARE expression to a FIL expression.

The translation of letrec effectively performs three conceptually distinct transformations in one pass: (1) the following letrec desugaring from FLAVAR,

```
(letrec ((I₁ E₁) ... (Iₙ Eₙ)) E_body)
  ⤳_ds (let ((I₁ #u) ... (Iₙ #u))
          (begin (set! I₁ E₁) ... (set! Iₙ Eₙ) E_body))
```

(2) the assignment conversion of the mutable variables $I_1, \ldots, I_n$ to cells; and (3) the translation of these cells into single-slot mutable products. These steps could have been performed in three separate compiler stages, but we have combined them to reduce the number of stages. Note that the first step cannot be performed as a FLARE/V-to-FLARE/V transformation because it does not preserve well-typedness: A variable holding #u cannot be assigned the value of an arbitrary definition expression. It is possible, but messy and inefficient, to rephrase the desugaring in a type-safe way using lists or oneofs (see Exercise 17.9). This is

$\mathcal{T}_{\text{prog}} : \text{Prog}_{\text{FLARE}} \to \text{Prog}_{FIL}$

Preconditions: The input to $\mathcal{T}_{\text{prog}}$ is a valid, closed, assignment-free, kernel FLARE program

Postconditions: The output of $\mathcal{T}_{\text{prog}}$ is a valid kernel FIL program.

$\mathcal{T}_{\text{prog}}[\![(\texttt{flarek}\ (I_{i=1}^n)\ E_{body})]\!] = (\texttt{fil}\ (I_{i=1}^n)\ (\mathcal{T}_{\text{exp}}[\![E_{body}]\!]))$

$\mathcal{T}_{\text{exp}} : \text{Exp}_{\text{FLARE}} \to \text{Exp}_{FIL}$

$\mathcal{T}_{\text{exp}}[\![(E_{rator}\ E_{i=1}^n)]\!] = (\texttt{app}\ \mathcal{T}_{\text{exp}}[\![E_{rator}]\!]\ (\mathcal{T}_{\text{exp}}[\![E_i]\!])_{i=1}^n)$

$\mathcal{T}_{\text{exp}}[\![(\texttt{letrec}\ ((I_i\ E_i)_{i=1}^n)\ E_{body})]\!]$
$\quad = (\texttt{let}\ ((I_i\ (\texttt{prim mprod \#u}))_{i=1}^n)$
$\qquad (\texttt{let*}\ ((\_\ (\texttt{prim (mset! 1)}\ I_i\ (msubst\ \mathcal{T}_{\text{exp}}[\![E_i]\!])))_{i=1}^n)$
$\qquad\quad (msubst\ \mathcal{T}_{\text{exp}}[\![E_{body}]\!]))),$
$\qquad\qquad \text{where}\ (msubst\ E) = ([(\texttt{prim (mget 1)}\ I_i)/I_i]_{i=1}^n)E$

$\mathcal{T}_{\text{exp}}[\![(\texttt{prim cell}\ E_1)]\!] = (\texttt{prim mprod}\ \mathcal{T}_{\text{exp}}[\![E_1]\!])$

$\mathcal{T}_{\text{exp}}[\![(\texttt{prim \^{}}\ E_{cell})]\!] = (\texttt{prim (mget 1)}\ \mathcal{T}_{\text{exp}}[\![E_{cell}]\!])$

$\mathcal{T}_{\text{exp}}[\![(\texttt{prim :=}\ E_{cell}\ E_{new})]\!] = (\texttt{prim (mset! 1)}\ \mathcal{T}_{\text{exp}}[\![E_{cell}]\!]\ \mathcal{T}_{\text{exp}}[\![E_{new}]\!])$

$\mathcal{T}_{\text{exp}}[\![(\texttt{prim cell=?}\ E_1\ E_2)]\!] = (\texttt{prim mprod=?}\ \mathcal{T}_{\text{exp}}[\![E_1]\!]\ \mathcal{T}_{\text{exp}}[\![E_2]\!])$

$\mathcal{T}_{\text{exp}}[\![(\texttt{prim pair}\ E_1\ E_2)]\!] = (\texttt{prim mprod}\ \mathcal{T}_{\text{exp}}[\![E_1]\!]\ \mathcal{T}_{\text{exp}}[\![E_2]\!])$

$\mathcal{T}_{\text{exp}}[\![(\texttt{prim fst}\ E_{pair})]\!] = (\texttt{prim (mget 1)}\ \mathcal{T}_{\text{exp}}[\![E_{pair}]\!])$

$\mathcal{T}_{\text{exp}}[\![(\texttt{prim snd}\ E_{pair})]\!] = (\texttt{prim (mget 2)}\ \mathcal{T}_{\text{exp}}[\![E_{pair}]\!])$

All other cases of $\mathcal{T}_{\text{exp}}$ are purely structural.

Figure 17.16 Translating FLARE to FIL.

the first of several cases we will encounter of a transformation that is simpler to express without the constraints of a formal type system, which is the main reason we use FIL rather than variants of FLARE or FLEX in the remainder of the compiler.

The precondition for $\mathcal{T}_{\text{prog}}$ requires a closed FLARE program. This simplifies the transformation by making it unnecessary to translate global free identifiers like + and cons. We assume that such free identifiers have already been eliminated by performing globalization. The postcondition does not explicitly mention a closed program because all valid FIL programs are necessarily closed.

Figure 17.17 shows our revmap example after the translation stage. In this and subsequent code presentations, we shall "resugar" a nested sequence of let expressions into a let* expression and use the @ abbreviation for primops to improve the readability of the code. Note how ans and loop are treated similarly in the example: `ans` was converted from a mutable variable to a mutable cell by the assignment-conversion stage, while `loop` was converted to a mutable cell by the `letrec`-handling code of the translation stage. After translation, both cells are represented as single-slot mutable products.

Exercise 17.9 Consider the language FLARE_{sum} that is just like FLARE except that it supports oneofs (see Section 10.2) via the following syntax:

$$E ::= \ldots$$
$$\mid \text{(one } I_{tag}\ E_{payload}) \qquad\qquad\qquad\qquad\quad \text{[OneofIntro]}$$
$$\mid \text{(tagcase } E_{disc}\ I_{payload}\ (I_{tag}\ E_{body})^*\ \text{(else } E_{else})^?) \ \text{[OneofElim]}$$

Assume that the FLARE_{sum} type reconstruction algorithm is "smart enough" to determine the type of the **one** construct without any explicit type annotations (see Exercise 13.13).

a. Using oneofs, write a version of the FLAVAR `letrec` desugaring for FLARE_{sum} that preserves well-typedness. The key idea is to transform each `letrec`-bound variable into a mutable cell that holds a oneof that is either (1) the unit value or (2) the value of the corresponding definition expression. Argue that the expression that is the result of the desugaring is indeed well typed.

b. After studying your solution to part **a**, Abby Stracksen remarks, "You can write a type-safe desugaring of `letrec` in regular FLARE, without oneofs, using empty and nonempty lists." Show what Abby means by writing a type-safe desugaring of `letrec` in FLARE.

Exercise 17.10 Consider the language FIL_{sum} that is just like FIL except:

- it does not have the boolean literals `#t` and `#f`;

- it has no `if` expressions;

- it does not have the list operators `cons`, `car`, `cdr`, `null`, or `null?`;

- it supports oneofs (see Section 10.2) via the same syntax used in Exercise 17.9.

Show how to translate FLARE boolean literals, `if` expressions, and list operations into FIL_{sum}.

17.8   Transformation 6: Renaming

A program fragment is **uniquely named** if no two logically distinct variables appearing in the fragment have the same name. For example, the following two expressions have the same structure and meaning, but the second is uniquely named while the first is not:

```
(fil (a b)
  (let ((revmap
          (abs (f elts)
            (let* ((ans (@mprod (@null)))
                   (loop (@mprod #u))
                   (_ (@mset! 1 loop
                         (abs (xs)
                            (if (@null? xs)
                                (@mget 1 ans)
                                (let ((_ (@mset 1 ans
                                              (@cons (app f (@car xs))
                                                     (@mget 1 ans)))))
                                   (app (@mget 1 loop) (@cdr xs)))))))
                (app (@mget 1 loop) elts)))))
    (app revmap
         (abs (x) (@> x b))
         (@cons a (@cons (@* a 7) (@null))))))
```

Figure 17.17   revmap program after translation.

```
((abs (x) (x w)) (abs (x) (let ((x (* x 2))) (+ x 1))))

((abs (x) (x w)) (abs (y) (let ((z (* y 2))) (+ z 1))))
```

Some of the subsequent program transformations we will study require that programs are uniquely named to avoid problems with variable capture or otherwise simplify the transformation. Here we describe a renaming transformation whose output program is a uniquely named version of the input program.

The renaming transformation is presented in Figure 17.18. In this transformation, every bound identifier in the program is replaced by a fresh identifier. Fresh names are introduced in all declaration constructs: the fil program construct and abs and let expressions. Renaming environments in the domain *RenEnv* are used to associate these fresh names with the original names and communicate the renamings to all variable references. Renaming is a purely structural transformation for all other nodes.

As in many other transformations, we gloss over the mechanism for generating fresh identifiers. This mechanism can be formally specified and implemented by threading some sort of name-generation state through the transformation. For example, this state could be a natural number that is initially 0 and is incremented every time a fresh name is generated. The fresh name can combine the original name and the number in some fashion. In our examples, we assume that renamed

---

Renaming Environments

$re \in RenEnv = \text{Ident} \rightarrow \text{Ident}$

$rbind : \text{Ident} \rightarrow \text{Ident} \rightarrow RenEnv \rightarrow RenEnv$
$\quad = \lambda I_{old}\ I_{new}\ re\ .\ \lambda I_{key}\ .\ \textbf{if } I_{key} = I_{old} \textbf{ then } I_{new} \textbf{ else } (re\ I_{key})\,\textbf{end}$

$\quad (rbind\ I_{old}\ I_{new}\ re)$ is abbreviated as $[I_{old}{\mapsto}I_{new}]re$; this notation associates
$\quad$ to the right. I.e., $[I_1{\mapsto}I_1'][I_2{\mapsto}I_2']re = [I_1{\mapsto}I_1']([I_2 \mapsto I_2']re)$

Renaming Transformation

$\mathcal{R}_{\text{prog}} : \text{Prog}_{FIL} \rightarrow \text{Prog}_{FIL}$

$\quad$ **Preconditions:** The input to $\mathcal{R}_{\text{prog}}$ is a valid kernel FIL program.

$\quad$ **Postconditions:** The output of $\mathcal{R}_{\text{prog}}$ is a valid and uniquely named kernel FIL
$\quad\quad$ program.

$\mathcal{R}_{\text{prog}}[\![(\texttt{fil}\ (I_{i=1}'^{n})\ E_{body})]\!]$
$= (\texttt{fil}\ (I_{i=1}'^{n})\ (\mathcal{R}_{\text{exp}}[\![E_{body}]\!]\ ([I_1 \mapsto I_1']\ldots[I_n \mapsto I_n'](\lambda I\ .\ I)))),$
$\quad$ where $I_{i=1}'^{n}$ are fresh.

$\mathcal{R}_{\text{exp}} : \text{Exp}_{FIL} \rightarrow RenEnv \rightarrow \text{Exp}_{FIL}$

$\mathcal{R}_{\text{exp}}[\![I]\!]\ re = (re\ I)$

$\mathcal{R}_{\text{exp}}[\![(\texttt{abs}\ (I_{i=1}^{n})\ E_{body})]\!]\ re$
$= (\texttt{abs}\ (I_{i=1}'^{n})\ (\mathcal{R}_{\text{exp}}[\![E_{body}]\!]\ ([I_1 \mapsto I_1']\ldots[I_n \mapsto I_n']re))),$ where $I_{i=1}'^{n}$ are fresh.

$\mathcal{R}_{\text{exp}}[\![(\texttt{let}\ ((I_i\ E_i)_{i=1}^{n})\ E_{body})]\!]\ re$
$= (\texttt{let}\ ((I_i'\ (\mathcal{R}_{\text{exp}}[\![E_i]\!]\ re))_{i=1}^{n})$
$\quad\quad (\mathcal{R}_{\text{exp}}[\![E_{body}]\!]\ ([I_1 \mapsto I_1']\ldots[I_n \mapsto I_n']re))),$ where $I_{i=1}'^{n}$ are fresh.

$\mathcal{R}_{\text{exp}}[\![E]\!]\ re = \text{mapsub}_{FIL}[\![E]\!]\ (\lambda E_{sub}\ .\ \mathcal{R}_{\text{exp}}[\![E_{sub}]\!]\ re),$ otherwise.

Figure 17.18   Renaming transformation.

identifiers have the form *prefix.number*, where *prefix* is the original identifier,
number is the current name-generator state value, and "." is a special character
that may appear in compiler-generated names but not in user-specified names.[5]
Later compiler stages may rename generated names from previous stages; we
assume that only the prefix of the old generated name is used as the prefix for
the new generated name. For example, x can be renamed to x.17, and x.17 can
be renamed to x.42 (not x.17.42). Figure 17.19 shows our running example
after the renaming stage.

Exercise 17.11 What changes need to be made to $\mathcal{R}_{\text{exp}}$ to handle the FIL_{sum} language
(see Exercise 17.10)?

---

[5]*prefix* is not really necessary, since *number* itself is unique. But maintaining the original
names helps human readers track variables through the compiler transformations.

```
(fil (a.0 b.1)
 (let ((revmap.2
        (abs (f.3 elts.4)
          (let* ((ans.5 (@mprod (@null)))
                 (loop.6 (@mprod #u))
                 (_ (@mset! 1 loop.6
                      (abs (xs.7)
                        (if (@null? xs.7)
                            (@mget 1 ans.5)
                            (let ((_ (@mset! 1 ans.5
                                       (@cons (app f.3 (@car xs.7))
                                              (@mget 1 ans.5)))))
                                (app (@mget 1 loop.6) (@cdr xs.7)))))))))
            (app (@mget 1 loop.6) elts.4)))))
   (app revmap.2
        (abs (x.8) (@> x.8 b.1))
        (@cons a.0 (@cons (@* a.0 7) (@null))))))))
```

Figure 17.19 revmap program after renaming.

Exercise 17.12 This exercise explores ways to formalize the generation of fresh names in the renaming transformation. Assume that *rename* is a function that renames variables according to the conventions described above. E.g., (*rename* x 17) = x.17 and (*rename* x.17 42) = x.42.

a. Suppose that the signature of $\mathcal{R}_{\text{exp}}$ is changed to accept and return a natural number that represents the state of the fresh name generator:

$$\mathcal{R}_{\text{exp}} : \text{Exp}_{FIL} \rightarrow RenEnv \rightarrow Nat \rightarrow (\text{Exp}_{FIL} \times Nat)$$

Give modified definitions of $\mathcal{R}_{\text{prog}}$ and $\mathcal{R}_{\text{exp}}$ in which *rename* is used to generate all fresh names uniquely. Define any auxiliary functions you find helpful.

b. An alternative way to thread the name-generation state through the renaming transformation is to use continuations. Suppose the signature of $\mathcal{R}_{\text{exp}}$ is changed as follows:

$$\mathcal{R}_{\text{exp}} : \text{Exp}_{FIL} \rightarrow RenEnv \rightarrow RenameCont \rightarrow Nat \rightarrow \text{Exp}_{FIL}$$

RenameCont is a renaming continuation defined as follows:

$$rc \in RenameCont = \text{Exp}_{FIL} \rightarrow Nat \rightarrow \text{Exp}_{FIL}$$

Give modified definitions of $\mathcal{R}_{\text{prog}}$ and $\mathcal{R}_{\text{exp}}$ in which *rename* is used to generate all fresh names uniquely. Define any auxiliary functions you find helpful.

c. The *mapsub*$_{FIL}$ function cannot be used in the above two parts because it does not thread the name-generation state through the processing of subexpressions. Develop modified versions of *mapsub*$_{FIL}$ that would handle the purely structural cases in the above parts.

17.9   Transformation 7: CPS Conversion

Did he ever return, no he never returned
And his fate is still unlearned
> — Bess Hawes and Jacqueline Steiner, "Charley on the MTA"

In Chapter 9, we saw that continuations are a powerful mathematical tool for modeling sophisticated control features like nonlocal exits, unrestricted jumps, coroutines, backtracking, and exceptions. Section 9.2 showed how such features can be simulated in any language supporting first-class procedures. The key idea in these simulations is to represent a possible future of the current computation as an explicit procedure, called a **continuation**. The continuation takes as its single parameter the value of the current computation. When invoked, the continuation proceeds with the rest of the computation. In these simulations, procedures no longer return to their caller when invoked. Rather, they are transformed so that they take one or more explicit continuations as arguments and invoke one of these continuations on their result instead of returning the result. A program in which every procedure invokes an explicit continuation parameter in place of returning is said to be written in **continuation-passing style (CPS)**.

As an example of CPS, consider the FIL expression E_{sos} in Figure 17.20. It defines a squaring procedure sqr and a sum-of-squares procedure sos and applies the latter to 3 and 4. E_{sos}^{cps} is the result of transforming E_{sos} into CPS form. In E_{sos}^{cps}, each of the two procedures sqr and sos has been extended with a continuation parameter, which by our convention will come last in the parameter list and begin with the letter k. The sqr_{cps} procedure invokes its continuation ksqr on the square of its input. The sos_{cps} procedure first calls sqr_{cps} on a with a continuation that names the result asqr. This continuation then calls sqr_{cps} on b with a second continuation that names the second result bsqr. Finally, sos_{cps} invokes its continuation ksos on the sum of these two results. The initial call (sos 3 4) must also be converted. We assume that klet* names a continuation that proceeds with the rest of the computation given the value of the let* expression.

The process of transforming a program into CPS form is called **CPS conversion**. Here we shall study CPS conversion as a stage in the TORTOISE compiler. Whereas globalization makes explicit the meaning of standard identifiers, and assignment conversion makes explicit the implicit cells of mutable variables, CPS conversion makes explicit all control flow in a program. In addition to transforming every procedure to use an explicit continuation, our compiler's CPS transformation also makes explicit the order in which primitive operations are executed.

E_{sos} = (let* ((sqr (abs (x) (@* x x)))
    (sos (abs (a b) (@+ (app sqr a) (app sqr b)))))
  (app sos 3 4))

E_{sos}^{cps} = (let* ((sqr$_{cps}$ (abs (x ksqr) (app ksqr (@* x x))))
    (sos$_{cps}$ (abs (a b ksos)
       (app sqr$_{cps}$ a
        (abs (asqr)
         (app sqr$_{cps}$ b
          (abs (bsqr)
           (app ksos (@+ asqr bsqr)))))))))))
  (app sos$_{cps}$ 3 4 klet*))

Figure 17.20 E_{sos}^{cps} is a CPS version of E_{sos}.

Performing CPS conversion as a compiler stage has several benefits:

- *Procedure-calling mechanism*: A compiler must implement the mechanism for calling a procedure, which specifies: how arguments and control are passed from the caller to the procedure when it is called; how the procedure's result value and control are passed from the procedure back to the caller when the procedure returns; and how values needed by the caller after the procedure call are preserved during the procedure's execution.

  Continuations are an explicit representation of the stack of procedure-call invocation frames used in traditional compilers to implement the call/return mechanism of procedures. In CPS-converted code, a continuation (such as (abs (asqr) ...) above) corresponds to a pair of (1) an invocation frame that saves variables needed after the call (i.e., the free variables of the continuation, which are b and ksos in the case of (abs (asqr) ...)) and (2) a return address (i.e., a specification of the code to be executed after the call). Since CPS procedures never return, every procedure call in a CPS-converted program can be viewed as an assembly code jump that passes arguments. In particular, invoking a continuation corresponds in assembly code to jumping to a return address with a return value in a distinguished return register.

- *Code linearization*: CPS conversion makes explicit the order in which subexpressions are evaluated, yielding code that linearizes basic computation steps in a way similar to assembly code. For example, the body of sos$_{cps}$ makes it clear that the square of a is calculated before the square of b. We shall see that our CPS transformation also linearizes nested primitive applications. For instance, CPS-converting the expression (@* (@+ c d) (@- c 1)) yields code in which it is clear that the addition is performed first, followed by the subtraction, and then the multiplication.

- *Sophisticated control features*: Representing control explicitly in the form of continuations facilitates the implementation of advanced control features (such as nonlocal exits, exceptions, and backtracking) that can be challenging to implement in traditional stack-based approaches.

- *Uniformity*: Representing control features via procedures keeps intermediate program representations simple and flexible. Moreover, any optimizations that improve procedures will work on continuations as well. But this uniformity also has a drawback: because of the liberal use of procedures, the efficiency of procedure calls in CPS code is of the utmost importance, making certain optimizations almost mandatory.

We present the TORTOISE CPS transformation in four stages. The structure of the CPS code produced by the CPS transformation is formalized in Section 17.9.1. A straightforward approach to CPS conversion that is easy to understand but leads to intolerable inefficiencies in the converted code is described in Section 17.9.2. Section 17.9.3 presents a more complex but considerably more efficient CPS transformation that is used in TORTOISE. Finally, we consider the CPS conversion of advanced control constructs in Section 17.9.4.

17.9.1   The Structure of Tortoise CPS Code

All procedure applications can be classified according to their relationship to the innermost enclosing procedure declaration (or program). A procedure application is a **tail call** if its implicit continuation is the same as that of its enclosing procedure. In other words, no computational work is done between the termination of the inner tail call and the termination of its enclosing procedure. These two events can be viewed as happening simultaneously. All other procedure applications are **nontail calls**. These are characterized by pending computations that must take place between the termination of the nontail call and the termination of a call to its enclosing procedure. The notion of a tail call is important in CPS conversion because every procedure call in CPS code must be a tail call. Otherwise, it would have to return to perform a pending computation.

As concrete examples of tail versus nontail calls, consider the FIL abstractions in Figure 17.21.

- In E_{abs1}, the call to g is a tail call because a call to E_{abs1} returns a value v when g returns v. But both calls to f are nontail calls because the results of these calls must be passed to g before E_{abs1} returns.

```
E_abs1 = (abs (f g x) (app g (app f x) (app f (@+ x 1))))

E_abs2 = (abs (p q r s y)
           (let ((a (app p (app q y))))
             (app r a (app s a))))

E_abs3 = (abs (filter pred base zs)
           (if (@null? zs)
               (app base zs)
               (if (app pred (@car zs))
                   (@cons (@car zs) (app filter pred base (@cdr zs)))
                   (app filter pred base (@cdr zs)))))
```

Figure 17.21 Sample abstractions for understanding tail versus nontail calls.

- In E_{abs2}, only the call to r is a tail call. The results of the calls to p, q, and s must be further processed before E_{abs2} returns.

- In E_{abs3}, there are two tail calls: the call to base, and the second call to filter. The result of the first call to filter must be processed by @cons before E_{abs3} returns, so this is a nontail call. The result of pred must be checked by the if, so this is a nontail call as well. In this example, we see that (1) a procedure body may have multiple tail calls and (2) the same procedure can be invoked in both tail calls and nontail calls within the same expression.

Tail and nontail calls can be characterized syntactically. The FIL expression contexts in which tail calls can appear are defined by $\mathbb{TC}$ in the following grammar:

$$\mathbb{TC} \in \text{TailCallContext} ::= \square$$
$$| \ (\text{if } E_{test} \ \mathbb{TC} \ E)$$
$$| \ (\text{if } E_{test} \ E \ \mathbb{TC})$$
$$| \ (\text{let } ((I \ E)^*) \ \mathbb{TC})$$
$$| \ (\text{abs } (I^*) \ \mathbb{TC})$$

In FIL, an application expression E_{app} = (app E E^*) is a tail call if and only if the enclosing program can be expressed in the form (fil (I^*) $\mathbb{TC}\{E_{app}\}$) — i.e., as the result of filling a tail context in the program body with E_{app}. Any application that does not appear in a tail context is a nontail call. In particular, applications occurring in (but not wrapped by abs in) if tests, let definition expressions, and app and prim arguments are nontail calls.

$P \in \text{Prog}_{cps} ::= (\texttt{fil} \ (I^*_{formal}) \ E_{body})$

$E \in \text{Exp}_{cps} ::= (\texttt{app} \ I_{rator} \ V^*_{rand}) \ | \ (\texttt{if} \ V_{test} \ E_{then} \ E_{else})$
$\qquad\qquad\quad | \ (\texttt{let} \ ((I_{name} \ LE_{defn})) \ E_{body}) \ | \ (\texttt{error} \ Y_{message})$

$V \in \text{ValueExp}_{cps} ::= L \ | \ I$

$LE \in \text{LetableExp}_{cps} ::= L \ | \ (\texttt{abs} \ (I^*_{formal}) \ E_{body}) \ | \ (\texttt{prim} \ O_{primop} \ V^*_{arg})$

$L \in \text{Lit} \ = \ \textit{as in full} \ \text{FIL}$

$Y \in \text{SymLit} \ = \ \textit{as in full} \ \text{FIL}$

$O \in \text{Primop} \ = \ \textit{as in full} \ \text{FIL}$

$I \in \text{Ident} \ = \ \textit{as in full} \ \text{FIL}$

Figure 17.22 Kernel grammar for FIL_{cps}, the subset of FIL in CPS form. The result of CPS conversion is a FIL_{cps} program.

Understanding tail calls is essential for studying the structure of TORTOISE CPS code, which is defined by the grammar for FIL_{cps}, a restricted dialect of FIL presented in Figure 17.22. The FIL_{cps} grammar requires specialized component expressions for many constructs that can have arbitrary component expressions in FIL: the rator of an `app` must be an identifier; the rands of an `app`, arguments of a `prim`, and test of an `if` must be literals or identifiers; and the definition expression of a `let` must be a literal, abstraction, or primitive application. As explained below, these restrictions guarantee that all FIL_{cps} procedure calls are tail calls, that all procedure calls and primitive applications are linearized, and that FIL_{cps} code resembles assembly code in many ways:

- The definition of Exp_{cps} in FIL_{cps} guarantees that `app` expressions appear precisely in the tail contexts $\mathbb{TC}$ discussed above. So every call in a FIL_{cps} program is guaranteed to be a tail call. In a continuation-based denotational semantics (see Section 9.3) of a FIL_{cps} program, the expression continuation k for every `app` expression is exactly the same: the top-level continuation of the program. We say that procedure calls in a CPS program "never return" because no procedure call establishes a new control point to which a value can be returned. This explains why calls in a CPS program can be viewed as assembly-language jumps (that happen to additionally pass arguments).

- Operands of `app` and `prim` must be literals or variables, so one application (of a procedure or a primitive) may not be nested within another. The test subexpression of an `if` must also be a literal or variable. The definition subexpression of a `let` can only be one of a restricted number of simple "letable expressions" that does not include apps, ifs, or other lets. These restrictions impose the straight-line nature of assembly code on the bodies of FIL abstractions and programs, which must be elements of Exp_{cps}. The only violation of the straight-line property is the if expression, which has an element of Exp_{cps} for each branch. This branching code would need to be linearized elsewhere in order to generate assembly language (see Exercise 17.16 on page 1056).

- The grammar effectively requires specifying the order of evaluation of primitive applications by forcing the result of every primitive application to be named by a let. So the CPS transformation of an expression containing nested primitive applications uses a sequence of nested single-binding let expressions to introduce names for the intermediate results returned by the primitives. For example, CPS-converting the expression

```
(@+ (@- 0 (@* b b)) (@* 4 (@* a c)))
```

in the context of an initial continuation ktop.0 yields:[6]

```
(let* ((t.3 (@* b b))
       (t.2 (@- 0 t.3))
       (t.5 (@* a c))
       (t.4 (@* 4 t.5))
       (t.1 (@+ t.2 t.4)))
  (app ktop.0 t.1)))
```

The let-bound names represent abstract registers in assembly code. Mapping these abstract registers to the actual registers of a real machine (a process known as register allocation — see Section 17.12) must be performed by a later compilation stage.

- The operator of an app must be an identifier. In classical CPS conversion, the operator of an app may be an abstraction as well. However, we require that all abstractions be named in a let binding so that certain properties of the FIL_{cps} structure are preserved by later TORTOISE transformations. In particular, the subsequent closure-conversion stage will transform abstractions into applications of the mprod primitive. Such applications cannot appear in the context of CPS values V, but can appear in "letable expressions" LE.

- Every execution path through an abstraction or program body E_{body} must end in either an app or an error. The Exp_{cps} grammar does not include literals, identifiers, and abstractions, because these would allow procedures and

---

[6]The particular let-bound names used are irrelevant. Here and below, we show the results of CPS conversion using our implementation of the transformation described in Section 17.9.3.

```
(let* ((sqr_FILcps (abs (x ksqr)
                    (let ((t1 (@* x x)))
                      (app ksqr t1))))
       (sos_FILcps (abs (a b ksos)
                    (let ((k1 (abs (asqr)
                               (let ((k2 (abs (bsqr)
                                          (let ((t2 (@+ asqr bsqr)))
                                            (app ksos t2)))))
                                 (app sqr_FILcps b k2)))))
                      (app sqr_FILcps a k1))))))
  (app sos_FILcps 3 4 klet*))
```

Figure 17.23   A CPS version of E_{sos} expressed in FIL_{cps}.

programs to return values. But FIL_{cps} procedures and programs never return, so the last action in procedure or program body must be to call a procedure or signal an error. Moreover, apps and errors can appear only as the final expressions executed in such bodies — they cannot appear in let definitions, procedure or primitive operands, or if tests. Modulo the branching allowed by if, program and abstraction bodies in FIL_{cps} are similar in structure to **basic blocks** in traditional compilers. A basic block is a sequence of statements such that the only control transfers into the block are at the beginning and the only control transfers out of the block are at the end.

The fact that ValueExp_{cps} does not include abstractions or primitive applications means that E_{sos}^{cps} in Figure 17.20 is not a legal FIL_{cps} expression. A FIL_{cps} version of the E_{sos} expression is presented in Figure 17.23. To satisfy the syntactic constraints of FIL_{cps}, let-bound names must be introduced to name abstractions (the continuations k1 and k2) and the results of primitive applications (t1 and t2). Note that some calls (to sqr_{FILcps} and sos_{FILcps}) are to transformed versions of procedures in the original E_{sos} expression. These correspond to the jump-to-subroutine idiom in assembly code. The other calls (to ksqr and ksos) are to continuation procedures introduced by CPS conversion. These model the return-from-subroutine idiom in assembly code.

We will assume that the grammar for FIL_{cps} in Figure 17.22 describes the structure of CPS code *after* the standard FIL simplifications in Figure 17.15 have been performed. The CPS conversion functions we study below sometimes generate expressions that are illegal according to the FIL_{cps} grammar before such simplifications are performed. However, in all these cases, simplification yields a legal FIL_{cps} expression. For example, CPS conversion might generate (let ((a.2 b.1)) (app k.0 a.2)), which is not a FIL_{cps} expression because the variable reference b.1 is not an element of the domain Letable-Exp_{cps}. However, applying the [*copy-prop*] simplification to this expression yields (app k.0 b.1), which is indeed a FIL_{cps} expression.

The next two sections present two different CPS transforms, each of which converts every procedure call in the program into a tail call:

Preconditions: The input to CPS conversion is a valid, uniquely named kernel FIL program.

Postconditions: The output of CPS conversion is a valid, uniquely named kernel FIL_{cps} program.

17.9.2 A Simple CPS Transformation

The first transformation we will examine, $\mathcal{SCPS}$ (for *Simple* CPS conversion), is easier to explain, but generates code that is much less efficient than that produced by the second transformation.

The $\mathcal{SCPS}$ transformation is defined in Figure 17.24. $\mathcal{SCPS}_{exp}$ transforms any given expression E to an abstraction (abs (I_k) E') that expects as its argument I_k an explicit continuation for E and eventually calls this continuation on the value of E within E'. This explicit continuation is immediately invoked to pass along (or "return") the values of literals, identifiers, and abstractions. Each abstraction is transformed to take as a new additional final parameter a continuation I_{kcall} that is passed as the explicit continuation to its transformed body. Because the grammar of FIL_{cps} does not allow abstractions to appear directly as app arguments, it is also necessary to name the transformed abstraction in a let using a fresh identifier I_{abs}.

In the transformation of an app expression (app E_0 E_1 ... E_n), explicit continuations specify that the rator E_0 and rands E_1 ... E_n are evaluated in left-to-right order before the invocation takes place. The fresh variables I_0 ... I_n are introduced to name the values of the subexpressions. Since every procedure has been transformed to expect an explicit continuation as its final argument, the transformed app must supply its continuation I_k as the final rand. The let transformation is similar, except that the let-bound names are used in place of fresh names for naming the values of the definition expressions. The unique naming requirement on input programs to $\mathcal{SCPS}$ guarantees that no variable capture can take place in the let transformation (see Exercise 17.15).

The transformation of `prim` expressions is similar to that for `app` and `let`. The syntactic constraints of FIL_{cps} require that a fresh variable (here named I_{ans}) be introduced to name the result of a `prim` expression before passing it to the continuation.

In a transformed `if` expression, a fresh name I_{test} names the result of the test expression and the same continuation I_k is supplied to both transformed branches. This is the only place in $\mathcal{SCPS}$ where the explicit continuation I_k is referenced more than once in the transformed expression. The transformed `error` construct is the only place where the continuation is never referenced. All other constructs use I_k in a linear fashion — i.e., they reference it exactly once. This makes intuitive sense for regular control flow, which has only one possible "path" out of every expression other than `if` and `error`. Even in the `if` case, only one branch can be taken in a dynamic execution even though the continuation is mentioned twice. In Section 17.9.4 we will see how CPS conversion exposes the nonlinear nature of some sophisticated control features.

FIL programs are converted to CPS form by $\mathcal{SCPS}_{prog}$, which adds an additional parameter I_{ktop} that is an explicit top-level continuation for the program. It is assumed that the mechanism for program invocation will supply an appropriate procedure for this argument. For example, an operating system might construct a top-level continuation that displays the result of the program on the standard output stream or in a window within a graphical user interface.

The clauses for $\mathcal{SCPS}_{exp}$ contain numerous instances of the pattern

$$\texttt{(app } (\mathcal{SCPS}_{exp}[\![E_1]\!]) \ E_2)$$

where E_2 is an abstraction or variable reference. But $\mathcal{SCPS}_{exp}$ is guaranteed to return an `abs` expression, and the FIL_{cps} grammar does not allow any subexpression of an `app` to be an `abs`. Doesn't this yield an illegal FIL_{cps} expression? The result of $\mathcal{SCPS}_{exp}$ *would* be illegal were it not for the [*implicit-let*] simplification, which transforms every `app` of the form

$$\texttt{(app (abs } (I_k) \ E_1') \ E_2)$$

to the expression

$$\texttt{(let } ((I_k \ E_2)) \ E_1')$$

Since the grammar for letable expressions LE permits definition expressions that are abstractions, the result of $\mathcal{SCPS}_{exp}$ is guaranteed to be a legal FIL_{cps} expression when E_2 is an abstraction. When E_2 is a variable, the [*copy-prop*] simplification will also be performed, eliminating the `let` expression.

$\mathcal{SCPS}_{prog} : \text{Prog}_{FIL} \rightarrow \text{Prog}_{cps}$

$\mathcal{SCPS}_{prog}[\![(\texttt{fil}\ (I_{i=1}^n)\ E_{body})]\!] = (\texttt{fil}\ (I_{i=1}^n\ I_{ktop})\ ;\ I_{ktop}\ \text{fresh}$
$\qquad\qquad\qquad\qquad\qquad\qquad (\texttt{app}\ (\mathcal{SCPS}_{exp}[\![E_{body}]\!])\ I_{ktop}))$

$\mathcal{SCPS}_{exp} : \text{Exp}_{FIL} \rightarrow \text{Exp}_{cps}$

$\mathcal{SCPS}_{exp}[\![L]\!] = (\texttt{abs}\ (I_k)\ (\texttt{app}\ I_k\ L))\ ;\ I_k\ \text{fresh}$

$\mathcal{SCPS}_{exp}[\![I]\!] = (\texttt{abs}\ (I_k)\ (\texttt{app}\ I_k\ I))\ ;\ I_k\ \text{fresh}$

$\mathcal{SCPS}_{exp}[\![(\texttt{abs}\ (I_{i=1}^n)\ E_{body})]\!] = (\texttt{abs}\ (I_k)\ ;\ I_k\ \text{fresh}$
$\qquad\qquad\qquad\qquad\qquad (\texttt{let}\ ((I_{abs}\ ;\ I_{abs}\ \text{fresh}$
$\qquad\qquad\qquad\qquad\qquad\qquad\quad (\texttt{abs}\ (I_{i=1}^n\ I_{kcall})\ ;\ I_{kcall}\ \text{fresh}$
$\qquad\qquad\qquad\qquad\qquad\qquad\qquad (\texttt{app}\ (\mathcal{SCPS}_{exp}[\![E_{body}]\!])\ I_{kcall}))))$
$\qquad\qquad\qquad\qquad\qquad\quad (\texttt{app}\ I_k\ I_{abs})))$

$\mathcal{SCPS}_{exp}[\![(\texttt{app}\ E_{i=0}^n)]\!] = (\texttt{abs}\ (I_k)\ ;\ I_k\ \text{fresh}$
$\qquad\qquad\qquad\qquad\quad (\texttt{app}\ (\mathcal{SCPS}_{exp}[\![E_0]\!])$
$\qquad\qquad\qquad\qquad\qquad\quad (\texttt{abs}\ (I_0)\ ;\ I_0\ \text{fresh}$
$\qquad\qquad\qquad\qquad\qquad\qquad\qquad \cdot\cdot\cdot$
$\qquad\qquad\qquad\qquad\qquad\qquad (\texttt{app}\ (\mathcal{SCPS}_{exp}[\![E_n]\!])$
$\qquad\qquad\qquad\qquad\qquad\qquad\quad (\texttt{abs}\ (I_n)\ ;\ I_n\ \text{fresh}$
$\qquad\qquad\qquad\qquad\qquad\qquad\qquad (\texttt{app}\ I_{i=0}^n\ I_k)))\ \ldots\ )))$

$\mathcal{SCPS}_{exp}[\![(\texttt{let}\ ((I_i\ E_i)_{i=1}^n)\ E_{body})]\!]$
$= (\texttt{abs}\ (I_k)\ ;\ I_k\ \text{fresh}$
$\quad\ (\texttt{app}\ (\mathcal{SCPS}_{exp}[\![E_1]\!])$
$\qquad\quad (\texttt{abs}\ (I_1)$
$\qquad\qquad \cdot\cdot\cdot$
$\qquad\qquad\quad (\texttt{app}\ (\mathcal{SCPS}_{exp}[\![E_n]\!])$
$\qquad\qquad\qquad (\texttt{abs}\ (I_n)\ (\texttt{app}\ (\mathcal{SCPS}_{exp}[\![E_{body}]\!])\ I_k)))\ \ldots\ )))$

$\mathcal{SCPS}_{exp}[\![(\texttt{prim}\ O\ E_{i=1}^n)]\!]$
$= (\texttt{abs}\ (I_k)\ ;\ I_k\ \text{fresh}$
$\quad\ (\texttt{app}\ (\mathcal{SCPS}_{exp}[\![E_1]\!])$
$\qquad\quad (\texttt{abs}\ (I_1)\ ;\ I_1\ \text{fresh}$
$\qquad\qquad \cdot\cdot\cdot$
$\qquad\qquad\quad (\texttt{app}\ (\mathcal{SCPS}_{exp}[\![E_n]\!])$
$\qquad\qquad\qquad (\texttt{abs}\ (I_n)\ ;\ I_n\ \text{fresh}$
$\qquad\qquad\qquad\quad (\texttt{let}\ ((I_{ans}\ (\texttt{prim}\ O\ I_{i=1}^n)))\ ;\ I_{ans}\ \text{fresh}$
$\qquad\qquad\qquad\qquad (\texttt{app}\ I_k\ I_{ans}))))\ \ldots\ )))$

$\mathcal{SCPS}_{exp}[\![(\texttt{if}\ E_{test}\ E_{then}\ E_{else})]\!]$
$= (\texttt{abs}\ (I_k)\ ;\ I_k\ \text{fresh}$
$\quad\ (\texttt{app}\ (\mathcal{SCPS}_{exp}[\![E_{test}]\!])$
$\qquad\quad (\texttt{abs}\ (I_{test})\ ;\ I_{test}\ \text{fresh}$
$\qquad\qquad (\texttt{if}\ I_{test}$
$\qquad\qquad\qquad (\texttt{app}\ (\mathcal{SCPS}_{exp}[\![E_{then}]\!])\ I_k)$
$\qquad\qquad\qquad (\texttt{app}\ (\mathcal{SCPS}_{exp}[\![E_{else}]\!])\ I_k)))))$

$\mathcal{SCPS}_{exp}[\![(\texttt{error}\ Y_{msg})]\!] = (\texttt{abs}\ (I_k)\ (\texttt{error}\ Y_{msg}))\ ;\ I_k\ \text{fresh}$

Figure 17.24   A simple CPS transformation.

As a simple example of $\mathcal{SCPS}$, consider the CPS conversion of the incrementing program $P_{inc} = $ (fil (a) (@+ a 1)). Before any simplifications are performed, $\mathcal{SCPS}_{prog}[\![P_{inc}]\!]$ yields

```
(fil (a ktop.0)
  (app (abs (k.2)
          (app (abs (k.6) (app k.6 a))
              (abs (t.3)
                  (app (abs (k.5) (app k.5 1))
                      (abs (t.4)
                          (let ((t.1 (@+ t.3 t.4)))
                            (app k.2 t.1)))))))
        ktop.0))
```

Three applications of [*implicit-let*] simplify this code to

```
(fil (a ktop.0)
  (let ((k.2 ktop.0))
    (let ((k.6 (abs (t.3)
                  (let ((k.5 (abs (t.4)
                                (let ((t.1 (@+ t.3 t.4)))
                                  (app k.2 t.1)))))
                    (app k.5 1)))))
      (app k.6 a))))
```

A single [*copy-prop*] replaces k.2 by ktop.0 to yield the final result P'_{inc}:

```
(fil (a ktop.0)
  (let ((k.6 (abs (t.3)
                (let ((k.5 (abs (t.4)
                              (let ((t.1 (@+ t.3 t.4)))
                                (app ktop.0 t.1)))))
                  (app k.5 1)))))
    (app k.6 a)))
```

P'_{inc} is a legal FIL$_{cps}$ program — go ahead and check! Its convoluted nature makes it a bit tricky to read. Here is one way to read this program:

> The program is given an input a and top-level continuation ktop.0. First evaluate a and pass its value to continuation k.6, which gives it the name t.3. Then evaluate 1 and pass it to continuation k.5, which gives it the name t.4. Next, calculate the sum of t.3 and t.4 and name the result t.1. Finally, return this answer as the result of the program by invoking ktop.0 on t.1.

This is a lot of work to increment a number! Even though the [*implicit-let*] and [*copy-prop*] rules have simplified the program, it could still be simpler: the continuations k.5 and k.6 merely rename the values of a and 1 to t.3 and t.4, which is unnecessary.

In larger programs, the extent of these undesirable inefficiencies becomes more apparent. For example, Figure 17.25 shows the result of using $\mathcal{SCPS}$ to transform a numerical program P_{quad} with several nested subexpressions. Try to read the transformed program as we did with P'_{inc}. Along the way you will notice numerous unnecessary continuations and renamings. The result of performing $\mathcal{SCPS}$ on our revmap example is so large that it would require several pages to display. The desugared revmap program has an abstract syntax tree with 46 nodes; transforming it with $\mathcal{SCPS}_{prog}$ yields a result with 314 nodes. And this is after simplification — the unsimplified transformed program has 406 nodes!

Can anything be done to automatically eliminate the inefficiencies introduced by $\mathcal{SCPS}$? Yes! It is possible to define additional simplification rules that will make the CPS-converted code much more reasonable. For example, in (let ((I E_{defn})) E_{body}), if E_{defn} is a literal or abstraction, it is possible to replace the let by the substitution of E_{defn} for I in E_{body}. This simplification is traditionally called **constant propagation** and (when followed by [implicit-let]) is called **inlining** for abstractions. For example, two applications of inlining on P'_{inc} yield

```
(fil (a ktop.0)
  (let ((t.3 a))
    (let ((t.4 1))
      (let ((t.1 (@+ t.3 t.4)))
        (app ktop.0 t.1)))))
```

and then copy propagation and constant propagation simplify the program to

```
(fil (a ktop.0)
  (let ((t.1 (@+ a 1)))
    (app ktop.0 t.1)))
```

Performing these additional simplifications on P'_{quad} in Figure 17.25 gives the following *much* improved CPS code:

```
(fil (a b c ktop.0)
  (let* ((t.20 (@* b b))
         (t.16 (@- 0 t.20))
         (t.9 (@* a c))
         (t.5 (@* 4 t.9))
         (t.1 (@* t.16 t.5)))
    (app ktop.0 t.1)))
```

These examples underscore the inefficiency of the code generated by $\mathcal{SCPS}$.

Why don't we just modify FIL to include the constant propagation and inlining simplifications? Constant propagation of literals is not problematic,[7] but inlining is a delicate transformation. In FIL_{cps}, it is legal to copy an abstraction only to certain positions (such as the rator of an app, where it can be removed by [*implicit-let*]). When a named abstraction is used more than once in the body of a let, copying the abstraction multiple times makes the program bigger. Unrestricted inlining can lead to **code bloat**, a dramatic increase in the size of a program. In the presence of recursive procedures, special care must often be taken to avoid infinitely unwinding a recursive definition. Since we insist that FIL simplifications be straightforward to implement, we do not include inlining as a simplification. Inlining issues are further explored in Exercise 17.17.

Does that mean we are stuck with an inefficient CPS transformation? No! In the next section, we study a cleverer approach to CPS conversion that avoids generating unnecessary code in the first place.

Exercise 17.13 Consider the FIL program $P = $ (fil (x y) (@* (@+ x y) (@- x y))).

a. Show the result P_1 generated by $\mathcal{SCPS}_{prog}[\![P]\!]$ without performing any simplifications.

b. Show the result P_2 of simplifying P_1 using the standard FIL simplifications (including [*implicit-let*] and [*copy-prop*]).

c. Show the result P_3 of further simplifying P_2 using inlining in addition to the standard FIL simplifications.

Exercise 17.14

a. Suppose that begin, scand, scor, and cond (from FLARE/V) were kernel FIL constructs. Give the $\mathcal{SCPS}_{exp}$ clauses for these four constructs.

b. Suppose that FIL_{cps} were extended to include mutable variables by adding the assignment construct (set! I E) as an element of LE. Give the $\mathcal{SCPS}_{exp}$ clause for set!.

Exercise 17.15

a. Give a concrete example of how variable capture can take place in the let clause of $\mathcal{SCPS}_{exp}$ if the initial program is not uniquely named.

b. Modify the let clause of $\mathcal{SCPS}_{exp}$ so that it works properly even if the initial program is not uniquely named.

---

[7]Nevertheless, we do not include constant propagation in our list of standard simplifications because we don't want constants to be copied when we get to the register-allocation stage of our compiler.

```
P_quad = (fil (a b c) (@+ (@- 0 (@* b b)) (@* 4 (@* a c))))

SCPS_prog[[P_quad]] = P'_quad,
   where P'_quad =
     (fil (a b c ktop.0)
       (let* ((k.17
                (abs (t.3)
                  (let* ((k.6
                           (abs (t.4)
                             (let ((t.1 (@+ t.3 t.4)))
                               (app ktop.0 t.1)))))
                         (k.15
                          (abs (t.7)
                            (let* ((k.10 (abs (t.8)
                                          (let ((t.5 (@* t.7 t.8)))
                                            (app k.6 t.5))))
                                   (k.14
                                    (abs (t.11)
                                      (let ((k.13
                                              (abs (t.12)
                                                (let ((t.9 (@* t.11 t.12)))
                                                  (app k.10 t.9)))))
                                        (app k.13 c)))))
                              (app k.14 a)))))
                    (app k.15 4))))
              (k.26
               (abs (t.18)
                 (let* ((k.21 (abs (t.19)
                               (let ((t.16 (@- t.18 t.19)))
                                 (app k.17 t.16))))
                        (k.25 (abs (t.22)
                               (let ((k.24 (abs (t.23)
                                             (let ((t.20 (@* t.22 t.23)))
                                               (app k.21 t.20)))))
                                 (app k.24 b)))))
                   (app k.25 b)))))
         (app k.26 0)))
```

Figure 17.25 Simple CPS conversion of a numeric program.

Exercise 17.16 Control branches in linear assembly language code are usually provided via branch instructions that perform a jump if a certain condition holds but "drop through" to the next instruction if the condition does not hold. We can model assembly-style branch instructions in FIL_{cps} by restricting if expressions to the form

$$(\text{if } V_{test} \ (\text{app } V_{rator} \ V_{rand}^*) \ E_{else})$$

which immediately performs a subroutine jump (via **app**) if the test is true and otherwise drops through to E_{else}. Modify the $\mathcal{SCPS}_{exp}$ clause for if so that all transformed ifs have this restricted form.

Exercise 17.17 This exercise explores procedure inlining. Consider the following [*copy-abs*] simplification rule, where AB ranges over FIL abstractions:

$$(\text{let } ((I \ AB)) \ E_{body}) \xrightarrow{simp} [AB/I]E_{body} \qquad\qquad [\textit{copy-abs}]$$

Together, [*copy-abs*] and the standard FIL [*implicit-let*] and [*copy-prop*] rules implement a form of procedure inlining. For example

```
(let ((inc (abs (x) (@+ x 1))))
  (@* (app inc a) (app inc b)))
```

can be simplified via [*copy-abs*] to

```
(@* (app (abs (x) (@+ x 1)) a)
    (app (abs (x) (@+ x 1)) b))
```

Two applications of [*implicit-let*] give

```
(@* (let ((x a)) (@+ x 1))
    (let ((x b)) (@+ x 1)))
```

and two applications of [*copy-prop*] yield the inlined code

```
(@* (@+ a 1) (@+ b 1))
```

a. Use inlining to remove all calls to sqr in the following FIL expression. How many multiplications does the resulting expression contain?

```
(let ((sqr (abs (x) (@* x x))))
  (app sqr (app sqr (app sqr a))))
```

b. Use inlining to remove all calls to sqr, quad, and oct in the following FIL expression. How many multiplications does the resulting expression contain?

```
(let* ((sqr (abs (x) (@* x x)))
       (quad (abs (y) (@* (app sqr y) (app sqr y))))
       (oct (abs (z) (@* (app quad z) (app quad z)))))
  (@* (app oct a) (app oct b)))
```

c. What happens if inlining is used to simplify the following FIL expression?

```
(let ((f (abs (g) (app g g))))
  (app f f))
```

d. Can expressions like the one in part **c** ever arise in the compilation of a FLARE/V program? Explain.

e. Using only standard FIL simplifications, the result of $\mathcal{SCPS}_{prog}$ is guaranteed to be uniquely named if the input is uniquely named. This property does not hold in the presence of inlining. Write an example program P_{nun} such that the result of simplifying $\mathcal{SCPS}_{prog}[\![P_{nun}]\!]$ via inlining is not uniquely named. *Hint:* Where can duplication occur in a CPS-converted program?

f. Inlining multiple copies of an abstraction can lead to code bloat. Develop an example FIL program P_{bloat} where performing inlining on the result of $\mathcal{SCPS}_{prog}[\![P_{bloat}]\!]$ yields a *larger* transformed program rather than a smaller one. *Hint:* Where can duplication occur in a CPS-converted program?

Exercise 17.18 Emil P. Mentor wants to modify the CPS transformation to add a little bit of profiling information. Specifically, the modified CPS transformation should produce code that keeps a count of user procedure (not continuation) applications. Users will be able to access this information with the new construct (app-count), which is added to the grammar of kernel FIL_{cps} expressions:

$$E \in \text{Exp} ::= \dots \mid \texttt{(app-count)}$$

Emil gives the following example (where he uses the notation $\langle x, y \rangle$ normally used for pair values to represent mutable products with two components):

```
(let ((f (abs (x) (prim mprod x (app-count))))
      (id (abs (y) y))
      (twice (abs (g) (abs (z) (app g (app g z)))))))
  (prim mprod (app f (app-count))
              (prim mprod (app id (app f (app id (app-count))))
                          (app f (app (app (app twice twice) id)
                                      (app-count))))))
```
$\xrightarrow[FIL]{} \langle\langle 0, 1 \rangle, \langle\langle 1, 3 \rangle, \langle 4, 16 \rangle\rangle\rangle$

In the modified $\mathcal{SCPS}$ transformation, all procedures (including continuations) should take as an extra argument the number of user procedure applications made so far. For example, here are Emil's new $\mathcal{SCPS}$ clauses for program, literals, and conditionals:

$\mathcal{SCPS}_{prog}[\![(\texttt{fil}\ (I_{i=1}^n)\ E_{body})]\!]$
$\quad = \quad (\texttt{fil}\ (I_{i=1}^n\ I_{ktop})\ ;\ I_{ktop}\ \textit{fresh}$
$\qquad\quad (\texttt{app}\ (\mathcal{SCPS}_{exp}[\![E_{body}]\!])\ 0\ I_{ktop}))$

$\mathcal{SCPS}_{exp}[\![L]\!]\ =\ (\texttt{abs}\ (I_n\ I_k)\ ;\ I_n\ \textit{(app count)}\ \text{and}\ I_k\ \textit{(continuation)}\ \textit{fresh}$
$\qquad\qquad\qquad (\texttt{app}\ I_k\ I_n\ L))$

$\mathcal{SCPS}_{exp}[\![(\texttt{if}\ E_{test}\ E_{then}\ E_{else})]\!]$
$\quad = (\texttt{abs}\ (I_{n0}\ I_k)\ ;\ I_{n0}\ \text{and}\ I_k\ \textit{fresh}$
$\qquad (\texttt{app}\ (\mathcal{SCPS}_{exp}[\![E_{test}]\!])$
$\qquad\qquad I_{n0}$
$\qquad\qquad (\texttt{abs}\ (I_{n1}\ I_{test})\ ;\ I_{n1}\ \text{and}\ I_{test}\ \textit{fresh}$
$\qquad\qquad\quad (\texttt{if}\ I_{test}$
$\qquad\qquad\qquad\quad (\texttt{app}\ (\mathcal{SCPS}_{exp}[\![E_{then}]\!])\ I_{n1}\ I_k)$
$\qquad\qquad\qquad\quad (\texttt{app}\ (\mathcal{SCPS}_{exp}[\![E_{else}]\!])\ I_{n1}\ I_k)))))$

Write the modified $\mathcal{SCPS}$ clauses for abs, app, let, and app-count.

17.9.3   A More Efficient CPS Transformation

Reconsider the result of $\mathcal{SCPS}$ on the program (fil (a) (@+ a 1)):

```
(fil (a ktop.0)
  (let ((k.6 (abs (t.3)
                  (let ((k.5 (abs (t.4)
                                  (let ((t.1 (@+ t.3 t.4)))
                                    (app ktop.0 t.1)))))
                    (app k.5 1)))))
    (app k.6 a)))
```

The inefficient code we eliminated by inlining in the last section is shown in gray. Our goal in developing a more efficient CPS transformation is to perform these simplifications as part of CPS conversion itself rather than waiting to do them later. Instead of eliminating unsightly gray code as an afterthought, we want to avoid generating it in the first place!

Our approach is based on a diabolically simple shift of perspective: we view the gray code as part of the metalanguage specification of the transformation rather than as part of the FIL code being transformed. If we change the gray FIL lets, abss, and apps to metalanguage lets, λs, and applications, our example becomes:

```
(fil (a ktop.0)
```
  let k_6 be (λV_3 .

              let k_5 be (λV_4 .

```
                      (let ((t.1 (@+ V_3 V_4)))
                        (app ktop.0 t.1)))
```
              in (k_5 1))

  in (k_6 a))

To enhance readability, we will keep the metalanguage notation in gray and the FIL_{cps} code in black teletype font. Note that k_5 and k_6 name metalanguage functions whose parameters (V_3 and V_4) must be pieces of FIL_{cps} syntax — in particular, FIL_{cps} value expressions (i.e., literals and variable references). Indeed, k_5 is applied to the FIL_{cps} literal 1 and k_6 is applied to the FIL_{cps} identifier a. The result of evaluating the gray metalanguage expressions in our example yields

```
(fil (a ktop.0)
  (let ((t.1 (@+ a 1)))
    (app ktop.0 t.1)))
```

which is exactly the simplified result we want!

We have taken computation that would have been performed when executing the code generated by CPS conversion and instead performed it when the code is generated. The output of CPS conversion can now be viewed as code that is executed in two stages: the gray code is the code that can be executed as part of CPS conversion, while the black code is the **residual code** that can only be executed later at run time. This notion of **staged computation** is the key idea of an approach to optimization known as **partial evaluation**. The goal of partial evaluation is to evaluate at compile time all static expressions — i.e., those expressions that do not depend on information known only at run time — and leave behind a residual dynamic program that is executed at run time. In our case, the static expressions are the gray metalanguage code that is executed "for free" as part of CPS conversion, and the dynamic expressions are the black FIL_{cps} code.

Our improved approach to CPS conversion will make heavy use of gray abstractions of the form $(\lambda V . \ldots)$ that map FIL_{cps} value expressions (i.e., literals and variable references) to other FIL_{cps} expressions. Because these abstractions play the role of continuations at the metalanguage level, we call them **metacontinuations**. In the above example, k_5 and k_6 are examples of metacontinuations.

A metacontinuation can be viewed as a metalanguage representation of a special kind of context: a FIL_{cps} expression with named holes that can be filled only with FIL_{cps} value expressions. Such contexts may contain more than one hole, but a hole with a given name can appear only once. For example, here are metacontinuations that will arise in the CPS conversion of the incrementing program:

Context Notation	Metalanguage Notation
(app ktop.0 $\square_1$)	$\lambda V_1 .$ (app ktop.0 V_1)
(let ((t.1 (@+ $\square_3$ $\square_4$))) (app ktop.0 t.1))	$\lambda V_4 .$ (let ((t.1 (@+ V_3 V_4))) ; V_3 is free (app ktop.0 t.1))
(let ((t.1 (@+ $\square_3$ 1))) (app ktop.0 t.1))	$\lambda V_3 .$ (let ((t.1 (@+ V_3 1))) (app ktop.0 t.1))

Figures 17.26 and 17.27 present an efficient version of CPS conversion that is based on the notions of staged computation and metacontinuations. We call this transformation $\mathcal{MCPS}$ (for *meta*CPS conversion). The metavariable m ranges over metacontinuations in the domain *MetaCont*, which consists of functions that map FIL_{cps} value expressions to FIL_{cps} expressions.

The $\mathcal{MCPS}$ functions in Figures 17.26 and 17.27 are similar to the $\mathcal{SCPS}$ functions in Figure 17.24 (page 1051). Indeed, except for the let and if clauses, the $\mathcal{MCPS}$ clauses can be derived automatically from the $\mathcal{SCPS}$ clauses by the following transformation process:

Domain

$m \in MetaCont = \text{ValueExp}_{cps} \to \text{Exp}_{cps}$

Conversion Functions

$mc{\to}exp : MetaCont \to \text{Exp}_{cps} = (\lambda m . \ (\text{abs} \ (I_{temp}) \ (m \ I_{temp}))) \ ; I_{temp} \ \text{fresh}$

$id{\to}mc : \text{Ident} \to MetaCont = (\lambda I . \ (\lambda V . \ (\text{app} \ I \ V)))$

MetaCPS Program Transformation

$\mathcal{MCPS}_{prog} : \text{Prog}_{FIL} \to \text{Prog}_{cps}$

$\mathcal{MCPS}_{prog}[\![(\text{fil} \ (I_{i=1}^n) \ E_{body})]\!] = (\text{fil} \ (I_{i=1}^n \ I_{ktop}) \ ; I_{ktop} \ \text{fresh}$
$\qquad\qquad\qquad\qquad\qquad\qquad\qquad (\mathcal{MCPS}_{exp}[\![E_{body}]\!] \ (id{\to}mc \ I_{ktop})))$

Figure 17.26   An efficient CPS transformation based on metacontinuations, Part 1.

- Transform every continuation-accepting FIL_{cps} abstraction $(\text{abs} \ (I_k) \ \dots)$ into a metacontinuation-accepting metalanguage abstraction $(\lambda m . \ \dots)$.

- Transform every FIL_{cps} application $(\text{app} \ I_k \ V)$ in which I_k denotes a continuation to a **metacall** (i.e., metalanguage function call) of the form $(m \ V)$, where m is the metacontinuation that corresponds to I_k. This makes sense because the metacontinuation m is a metalanguage function that expects a value expression V as its argument.

- Transform every FIL_{cps} application $(\text{app} \ (\mathcal{SCPS}_{exp}[\![E]\!]) \ (\text{abs} \ (I) \ \dots))$ to a metacall $(\mathcal{MCPS}_{exp}[\![E]\!] \ (\lambda V . \ \dots))$. This transforms every FIL_{cps} continuation of the form $(\text{abs} \ (I) \ \dots)$ into a metacontinuation of the form $(\lambda V . \ \dots)$, thus providing the metacontinuation-accepting function returned by $\mathcal{MCPS}_{exp}[\![E]\!]$ with the metacontinuation it expects.

- Transform every FIL_{cps} application $(\text{app} \ (\mathcal{SCPS}_{exp}[\![E]\!]) \ I_k)$ in which I_k has not already been transformed to m to a metacall $(\mathcal{MCPS}_{exp}[\![E]\!] \ (id{\to}mc \ I_k))$, where $id{\to}mc$ converts a FIL_{cps} identifier I_k denoting an unknown continuation to a metacontinuation $(\lambda V . \ (\text{app} \ I_k \ V))$. This conversion is necessary to provide the metacontinuation-accepting function returned by $\mathcal{MCPS}_{exp}[\![E]\!]$ with the metacontinuation it expects.

- Transform every FIL_{cps} application $(\text{app} \ I_{i=0}^n \ I_k)$ in which $I_0, \dots, I_n$ are the bound variables of continuations and I_k denotes the continuation bound by an $\mathcal{SCPS}_{exp}$ clause to $(\text{let} \ ((I_k' \ (mc{\to}exp \ m))) \ (\text{app} \ V_{i=0}^n \ I_k'))$, where

  - I_k' is a fresh name;

  - $V_0, \dots, V_n$ are the bound variables of the metacontinuations that correspond to the continuations binding $I_0, \dots, I_n$;

MetaCPS Expression Transformation

$\mathcal{MCPS}_{exp} : \text{Exp}_{FIL} \to MetaCont \to \text{Exp}_{cps}$

$\mathcal{MCPS}_{exp}[\![L]\!] = (\lambda m \, . \, (m \; L))$

$\mathcal{MCPS}_{exp}[\![I]\!] = (\lambda m \, . \, (m \; I))$

$\mathcal{MCPS}_{exp}[\![(\texttt{abs} \; (I_{i=1}^{n}) \; E_{body})]\!]$
$= (\lambda m \, . \, (\texttt{let} \; ((I_{abs} \; ; I_{abs} \text{ fresh}$
$\qquad\qquad\qquad (\texttt{abs} \; (I_{i=1}^{n} \; I_{kcall}) \; ; I_{kcall} \text{ fresh}$
$\qquad\qquad\qquad\qquad (\mathcal{MCPS}_{exp}[\![E_{body}]\!] \; (\text{id}{\to}\text{mc} \; I_{kcall})))))$
$\qquad\quad (m \; I_{abs})))$

$\mathcal{MCPS}_{exp}[\![(\texttt{app} \; E_{i=0}^{n})]\!]$
$= (\lambda m \, . \, (\mathcal{MCPS}_{exp}[\![E_0]\!]$
$\qquad\quad (\lambda V_0 \, .$
$\qquad\qquad\qquad \ddots$
$\qquad\qquad\qquad (\mathcal{MCPS}_{exp}[\![E_n]\!]$
$\qquad\qquad\qquad\quad (\lambda V_n \, . \, (\texttt{let} \; ((I_k \; (\text{mc}{\to}\text{exp} \; m))) \; ; I_k \text{ fresh}$
$\qquad\qquad\qquad\qquad\qquad (\texttt{app} \; V_{i=0}^{n} \; I_k))) \; \dots \;)))$

$\mathcal{MCPS}_{exp}[\![(\texttt{let} \; ((I_i \; E_i)_{i=1}^{n}) \; E_{body})]\!]$
$= (\lambda m \, . \, (\mathcal{MCPS}_{exp}[\![E_1]\!]$
$\qquad\quad (\lambda V_1 \, .$
$\qquad\qquad\qquad \ddots$
$\qquad\qquad\qquad (\mathcal{MCPS}_{exp}[\![E_n]\!]$
$\qquad\qquad\qquad\quad (\lambda V_n \, . \, (\texttt{let*} \; ((I_i \; V_i)_{i=1}^{n})$
$\qquad\qquad\qquad\qquad\qquad (\mathcal{MCPS}_{exp}[\![E_{body}]\!] \; m))) \; \dots \;)))$

$\mathcal{MCPS}_{exp}[\![(\texttt{prim} \; O \; E_{i=1}^{n})]\!]$
$= (\lambda m \, . \, (\mathcal{MCPS}_{exp}[\![E_1]\!]$
$\qquad\quad (\lambda V_1 \, .$
$\qquad\qquad\qquad \ddots$
$\qquad\qquad\qquad (\mathcal{MCPS}_{exp}[\![E_n]\!]$
$\qquad\qquad\qquad\quad (\lambda V_n \, . \, (\texttt{let} \; ((I_{ans} \; (\texttt{prim} \; O \; V_{i=1}^{n}))) \; ; I_{ans} \text{ fresh}$
$\qquad\qquad\qquad\qquad\qquad (m \; I_{ans}))) \; \dots \;)))$

$\mathcal{MCPS}_{exp}[\![(\texttt{if} \; E_{test} \; E_{then} \; E_{else})]\!]$
$= (\lambda m \, . \, (\mathcal{MCPS}_{exp}[\![E_{test}]\!]$
$\qquad\quad (\lambda V_{test} \, . \, (\texttt{let} \; ((I_{kif} \; (\text{mc}{\to}\text{exp} \; m))) \; ; I_{kif} \text{ fresh}$
$\qquad\qquad\qquad (\texttt{if} \; V_{test}$
$\qquad\qquad\qquad\qquad (\mathcal{MCPS}_{exp}[\![E_{then}]\!] \; (\text{id}{\to}\text{mc} \; I_{kif}))$
$\qquad\qquad\qquad\qquad (\mathcal{MCPS}_{exp}[\![E_{else}]\!] \; (\text{id}{\to}\text{mc} \; I_{kif}))))))$

$\mathcal{MCPS}_{exp}[\![(\texttt{error} \; Y_{msg})]\!] = (\lambda m \, . \, (\texttt{error} \; Y_{msg}))$

Figure 17.27 An efficient CPS transformation based on metacontinuations, Part 2.

- m is the metacontinuation variable bound by the $\mathcal{MCPS}_{exp}$ clause corresponding to the $\mathcal{SCPS}_{exp}$ clause that binds the continuation variable I_k; and

- $mc{\rightarrow}exp$ is a function that converts a metacontinuation m to a FIL_{cps} continuation (abs (I) $(m\ I)$). For example:

  $(mc{\rightarrow}exp\ (\lambda V_3\ .\ $ (let (($\mathtt{t.1}$ (@+ V_3 1))) (app ktop.0 t.1))))
  = (abs (t.2) (let ((t.1 (@+ t.2 1))) (app ktop.0 t.1)))

In this case, there is no metacontinuation-accepting function to process the metacontinuation m, so $mc{\rightarrow}exp$ is necessary to convert the gray m into a black residual FIL_{cps} abstraction. The FIL_{cps} grammar forces this abstraction to be named, which is the purpose of the (let ((I_k' ...)) ...).

The $\mathcal{MCPS}$ clauses for let and if are based on the above transformations, but also contain some special-purpose code. The let clause contains additional code to construct a residual let* expression binding the original let-bound identifiers. To avoid potential duplication involving the metacontinuation m, the if clause gives the name I_{kif} to a residual version of m and uses $(id{\rightarrow}mc\ I_{kif})$ in place of m for the two branches.

The key benefit of the metacontinuation approach to CPS conversion is that many beta reductions that would be left as residual run-time code in the simple approach are performed at compile time. The $\mathcal{MCPS}$ functions are carefully designed so that every metacontinuation-accepting function $(\lambda m\ .\ \dots\ )$ that arises in the conversion process is applied to a metacontinuation of the form $(\lambda V_{formal}\ .\ M)$, where M is a metalanguage expression denoting a FIL_{cps} expression. Observe that in each $(\lambda m\ .\ M')$ that appears in the $\mathcal{MCPS}$ definition, the metacontinuation m is referenced at most once in M'. If m is referenced zero times in M', then the metacall $((\lambda m\ .\ M')\ (\lambda V_{formal}\ .\ M))$ simply reduces to M'. If m is referenced once in M', then M' can be written as $\mathbb{M}\{m\}$, where $\mathbb{M}$ is a one-holed metalanguage expression context. By the usual metalanguage beta-reduction rule, each metacall of the form

$$((\lambda m\ .\ \mathbb{M}\{m\})\ (\lambda V_{formal}\ .\ M))$$

can be reduced to

$$\mathbb{M}\{(\lambda V_{formal}\ .\ M)\}$$

In the case where m is applied to a value expression within M', the metacall

$$((\lambda m\ .\ \mathbb{M}\{(m\ V_{actual})\})\ (\lambda V_{formal}\ .\ M))$$

reduces to

$$\mathbb{M}\{[V_{actual}/V_{formal}]M\}$$

via two beta reductions. Since $\mathcal{MCPS}_{exp}[\![V_{actual}]\!] = (\lambda m \,.\, (m\ V_{actual}))$, meta-calls of the form

$$(\mathcal{MCPS}_{exp}[\![V_{actual}]\!]\ (\lambda V_{formal} \,.\, M))$$

are special cases of this pattern that can be reduced to

$$[V_{actual}/V_{formal}]M$$

The fact that m is referenced at most once in every function that accepts a metacontinuation guarantees that reducing a metacall makes the metalanguage expression smaller, and so the metacall reduction process eventually terminates. At this point, no gray code remains since all metacalls have been eliminated and there is no way other than a metacall to include gray code in an element of Exp_{cps}. So all that remains is a black residual FIL_{cps} program. Another consequence of the fact that m is referenced at most once in every metacontinuation-accepting function is that there is no specter of duplication-induced code bloat that haunts more general inlining optimizations. Using $mc{\rightarrow}exp$ to convert m to a FIL_{cps} abstraction named I_{kif} in the if clause of $\mathcal{MCPS}_{exp}$ is essential for avoiding code duplication.

We illustrate compile-time beta reductions in Figure 17.28, which shows the CPS conversion of the expression (app f (@* x (if (app g y) 2 3))) relative to an initial continuation named k. The example illustrates how $\mathcal{MCPS}$ effectively turns the input expression "inside out." In the input expression, the call to f is the outermost call, and (app g y) is the innermost call. But in the CPS-converted result, the call to g is the outermost call and the call to f is nested deep inside. This reorganization is necessary to make explicit the order in which operations are performed:

1. first, g is applied to y;

2. then the result t.5 of the g application is tested by if;

3. the test determines which of 2 or 3 will be named t.3 and multiplied by x;

4. then f is invoked on the result t.1 of the multiplication;

5. finally, the result of the f application is supplied to the continuation k.

Variables such as t.1, t.3, t.5 can be viewed as registers that hold the results of intermediate computations.

The example assumes that $(mc{\rightarrow}exp\ (id{\rightarrow}mc\ \mathtt{k}))$ can be simplified to $\mathtt{k}$.[8] To see why, observe that

$$
\begin{aligned}
&(mc{\rightarrow}exp\ (id{\rightarrow}mc\ \mathtt{k})) \\
&= ((\lambda m\,.\ (\mathtt{abs}\ (I_{temp})\ (m\ I_{temp})))\ (\lambda V\,.\ (\mathtt{app}\ \mathtt{k}\ V))) \\
&= (\mathtt{abs}\ (I_{temp})\ ((\lambda V\,.\ (\mathtt{app}\ \mathtt{k}\ V))\ I_{temp})) \\
&= (\mathtt{abs}\ (I_{temp})\ (\mathtt{app}\ \mathtt{k}\ I_{temp}))
\end{aligned}
$$

The final expression can be simplified to $\mathtt{k}$ by the [*eta*] rule. This eta reduction eliminates an abstraction in cases where the CPS transformation would have generated a trivial continuation that simply passed its argument along to another continuation with no additional processing. This simplification is sometimes called the **tail-call optimization** because it guarantees that tail calls in the source program require no additional control storage in the compiled program. In particular, there is no need to push an invocation frame corresponding to a trivial continuation onto the procedure-call stack. This allows tail calls to compile to assembly code jumps that pass arguments.

A language is said to be **properly tail recursive** if implementations are required to compile source tail calls into jumps. Our FIL mini-language is properly tail recursive, as is the real language SCHEME. Such languages can leave out iteration constructs (like `while` and `for` loops) and still express the constant-control-space iterative computations specified by such constructs using recursive procedures that invoke themselves via tail calls.

Figure 17.29 shows the result of using $\mathcal{MCPS}$ to CPS-convert our `revmap` example. Observe that the output of CPS conversion looks much closer to assembly language code than the input (Figure 17.19 on page 1041). You should study the code to convince yourself that this program has the same behavior as the original program. CPS conversion has introduced only one nontrivial continuation abstraction: `k.41` names the continuation of the call to `f` (now called `f.3`) in the body of the loop. Each input abstraction has been extended with a final argument naming its continuation: `revmap` (which has been renamed to `abs.10`) takes continuation argument `k.20`; the looping procedure (`abs.25`) takes continuation argument `k.29`; and the greater-than-b procedure (`abs.11`) takes continuation `k.18`. Note that the looping procedure (which is not only named `abs.25` but is also named `t.26` and `t.37` when it is extracted from the first slot of the mutable product `t.23`) is always invoked with the same continuation as the enclosing abstraction (`k.20` when it is named `t.26` and `k.29` when it is named `t.37`). So it requires only constant control space and is thus truly iterative like loops in traditional languages.

---

[8]Subsequently, $(\mathtt{let}\ ((\mathtt{t.0}\ \mathtt{k}))\ (\mathtt{app}\ V_1\ V_2\ \mathtt{t.0}))$ is simplified to $(\mathtt{app}\ V_1\ V_2\ \mathtt{k})$ by an application of [*copy-prop*].

$(\mathcal{MCPS}_{exp}[\![\,(\text{app f } (\text{@* x } (\text{if } (\text{app g y}) \ 2 \ 3)))\,]\!] \ (id{\rightarrow}mc \ \text{k}))$

$= ((\lambda m \ . \ (\mathcal{MCPS}_{exp}[\![\text{f}]\!] \ (\lambda V_1 \ . \ (\mathcal{MCPS}_{exp}[\![\,(\text{@* x } (\text{if } (\text{app g y}) \ 2 \ 3))\,]\!]$
$\qquad\qquad\qquad\qquad\qquad (\lambda V_2 \ . \ (\text{let } ((\text{t.0 } (mc{\rightarrow}exp \ m)))$
$\qquad\qquad\qquad\qquad\qquad\qquad\qquad (\text{app } V_1 \ V_2 \ \text{t.0})))))))$
$\qquad (id{\rightarrow}mc \ \text{k}))$

$= (\mathcal{MCPS}_{exp}[\![\text{f}]\!] \ (\lambda V_1 \ . \ (\mathcal{MCPS}_{exp}[\![\,(\text{@* x } (\text{if } (\text{app g y}) \ 2 \ 3))\,]\!]$
$\qquad\qquad\qquad\qquad\qquad (\lambda V_2 \ . \ (\text{let } ((\text{t.0 } (mc{\rightarrow}exp \ (id{\rightarrow}mc \ \text{k}))))$
$\qquad\qquad\qquad\qquad\qquad\qquad (\text{app } V_1 \ V_2 \ \text{t.0})))))$

$= (\mathcal{MCPS}_{exp}[\![\,(\text{@* x } (\text{if } (\text{app g y}) \ 2 \ 3))\,]\!] \ (\lambda V_2 \ . \ (\text{app f } V_2 \ \text{k})))$

$= ((\lambda m \ . \ (\mathcal{MCPS}_{exp}[\![\text{x}]\!]$
$\qquad\qquad (\lambda V_3 \ . \ (\mathcal{MCPS}_{exp}[\![\,(\text{if } (\text{app g y}) \ 2 \ 3)\,]\!]$
$\qquad\qquad\qquad (\lambda V_4 \ . \ (\text{let } ((\text{t.1 } (\text{@* } \ V_3 \ V_4))) \ (m \ \text{t.1})))))))$
$\qquad (\lambda V_2 \ . \ (\text{app f } V_2 \ \text{k})))$

$= (\mathcal{MCPS}_{exp}[\![\text{x}]\!]$
$\qquad (\lambda V_3 \ . \ (\mathcal{MCPS}_{exp}[\![\,(\text{if } (\text{app g y}) \ 2 \ 3)\,]\!]$
$\qquad\qquad (\lambda V_4 \ . \ (\text{let } ((\text{t.1 } (\text{@* } \ V_3 \ V_4))) \ (\text{app f t.1 k})))))$

$= (\mathcal{MCPS}_{exp}[\![\,(\text{if } (\text{app g y}) \ 2 \ 3)\,]\!]$
$\qquad (\lambda V_4 \ . \ (\text{let } ((\text{t.1 } (\text{@* x } \ V_4))) \ (\text{app f t.1 k}))))$

$= ((\lambda m \ . \ (\mathcal{MCPS}_{exp}[\![\,(\text{app g y})\,]\!]$
$\qquad\qquad (\lambda V_5 \ . \ (\text{let } ((\text{kif.2 } (mc{\rightarrow}exp \ m)))$
$\qquad\qquad\qquad (\text{if } V_5 \ (\mathcal{MCPS}_{exp}[\![\text{2}]\!] \ (id{\rightarrow}mc \ \text{kif.2}))$
$\qquad\qquad\qquad\qquad (\mathcal{MCPS}_{exp}[\![\text{3}]\!] \ (id{\rightarrow}mc \ \text{kif.2})))))))$
$\qquad (\lambda V_4 \ . \ (\text{let } ((\text{t.1 } (\text{@* x } \ V_4))) \ (\text{app f t.1 k}))))$

$= (\mathcal{MCPS}_{exp}[\![\,(\text{app g y})\,]\!]$
$\qquad (\lambda V_5 \ . \ (\text{let } ((\text{kif.2 } (\text{abs } (\text{t.3})$
$\qquad\qquad\qquad\qquad\qquad (\text{let } ((\text{t.1 } (\text{@* x t.3}))) \ (\text{app f t.1 k})))))$
$\qquad\qquad (\text{if } V_5 \ (\mathcal{MCPS}_{exp}[\![\text{2}]\!] \ (\lambda V_6 \ . \ (\text{app kif.2 } V_6)))$
$\qquad\qquad\qquad (\mathcal{MCPS}_{exp}[\![\text{3}]\!] \ (\lambda V_7 \ . \ (\text{app kif.2 } V_7)))))))$

$= ((\lambda m \ . \ (\mathcal{MCPS}_{exp}[\![\text{g}]\!]$
$\qquad\qquad (\lambda V_8 \ . \ (\mathcal{MCPS}_{exp}[\![\text{y}]\!]$
$\qquad\qquad\qquad (\lambda V_9 \ . \ (\text{let } ((\text{t.4 } (mc{\rightarrow}exp \ m))) \ (\text{app } V_8 \ V_9 \ \text{t.4}))))))))$
$\qquad (\lambda V_5 \ . \ (\text{let } ((\text{kif.2 } (\text{abs } (\text{t.3})$
$\qquad\qquad\qquad\qquad\qquad (\text{let } ((\text{t.1 } (\text{@* x t.3}))) \ (\text{app f t.1 k})))))$
$\qquad\qquad (\text{if } V_5 \ (\text{app kif.2 2}) \ (\text{app kif.2 3})))))$

$= (\text{let } ((\text{t.4 } (\text{abs } (\text{t.5}) \ ; \ (\text{abs } (\text{t.5}) \ \dots \ ) = (mc{\rightarrow}exp \ (\lambda V_5 \ . \ \dots \ )))$
$\qquad\qquad\qquad (\text{let } ((\text{kif.2 } (\text{abs } (\text{t.3})$
$\qquad\qquad\qquad\qquad\qquad\qquad (\text{let } ((\text{t.1 } (\text{@* x t.3}))) \ (\text{app f t.1 k})))))$
$\qquad\qquad\qquad (\text{if t.5 } (\text{app kif.2 2}) \ (\text{app kif.2 3}))))))$
$\qquad (\text{app g y t.4})) \ ; \ \text{substituted g for } V_8 \ \text{and y for } V_9 \ \text{in } (\text{app } V_8 \ V_9 \ \text{t.4})$

Figure 17.28 An example of CPS conversion using metacontinuations.

Note that the looping procedure (abs.25) is the only nontrivial value ever stored in the first slot of the mutable product named t.23, so that all references to this slot (i.e., the values named by t.26 and t.37) denote the looping procedure. In the case of t.26, this fact can be automatically discovered by a simple **peephole optimization** (a local code optimization that transforms small sequences of instructions) on let* bindings:

$$(\texttt{let*} \; (\ldots \; (I_1 \; (\texttt{@mset!} \; J \; I_{mprod} \; V)) \; (I_2 \; (\texttt{@mget} \; J \; I_{mprod})) \; \ldots) \; E_{body})$$
$$\xrightarrow{simp} (\texttt{let*} \; (\ldots \; (I_1 \; (\texttt{@mset!} \; J \; I_{mprod} \; V)) \; (I_2 \; V) \; \ldots \;) \; E_{body})$$

In conjunction with the [copy-prop] simplification, this peephole optimization can justify simplifying

```
(let* ( ... (t.24 (@mset! 1 t.23 abs.25)) (t.26 (@mget 1 t.23)))
   (app t.26 elts.4 k.20))
```

to

```
(let* ( ... (t.24 (@mset! 1 t.23 abs.25)))
   (app abs.25 elts.4 k.20))
```

in the CPS-converted revmap code. A much more sophisticated analysis would be necessary to determine that t.37 denotes the looping procedure. However, even this knowledge cannot be used to replace t.37 by abs.25 because abs.25 is a let-bound variable whose scope does not include the body of the abstraction (abs (xs.7 k.29) ...).

The conciseness of the code in Figure 17.29 is a combination of the simplifications performed by reducing metacalls at compile time *and* the standard FIL_{cps} simplifications. To underscore the importance of the latter, Figure 17.30 shows the result of $\mathcal{MCPS}$ before any FIL_{cps} simplifications are performed. Nine applications of the [copy-prop] rule and four applications of the [eta] rule are used to simplify the code in Figure 17.30 to the code in Figure 17.29. In addition to making the code shorter, these simplifications are essential for performing the tail-call optimization. For example, the call (app t.37 t.38 k.40) in Figure 17.30 uses the trivial continuation k.40 = (abs (t.39) (app kif.30 t.39)), which itself uses the trivial continuation kif.30 = (abs (t.43) (app k.29 t.43)). This call is transformed to the new call (app t.37 t.38 k.29) by using two applications of the [eta] rule (simplifying (abs (t.43) (app k.29 t.43)) to k.29 and (abs (t.39) (app kif.30 t.39)) to kif.30) and two applications of the [copy-prop] rule (replacing kif.30 and k.40 by k.29).

A drawback of the [copy-prop] simplifications is that they rename some of the identifiers from the input, making it harder for programmers to compare the

```
(fil (a.0 b.1 ktop.9)
 (let* ((abs.10
          (abs (f.3 elts.4 k.20)
           (let* ((t.22 (@null))
                  (t.21 (@mprod t.22))
                  (t.23 (@mprod #u))
                  (abs.25
                   (abs (xs.7 k.29)
                    (let ((t.31 (@null? xs.7)))
                     (if t.31
                          (let ((t.42 (@mget 1 t.21)))
                            (app k.29 t.42))
                          (let* ((t.34 (@car xs.7))
                                 (k.41
                                   (abs (t.35)
                                    (let* ((t.36 (@mget 1 t.21))
                                           (t.33 (@cons t.35 t.36))
                                           (t.32 (@mset! 1 t.21 t.33))
                                           (t.37 (@mget 1 t.23))
                                           (t.38 (@cdr xs.7)))
                                      (app t.37 t.38 k.29)))))
                            (app f.3 t.34 k.41))))))
                  (t.24 (@mset! 1 t.23 abs.25))
                  (t.26 (@mget 1 t.23)))
            (app t.26 elts.4 k.20))))
        (abs.11 (abs (x.8 k.18)
                  (let ((t.19 (@> x.8 b.1)))
                    (app k.18 t.19))))
        (t.14 (@* a.0 7))
        (t.15 (@null))
        (t.13 (@cons t.14 t.15))
        (t.12 (@cons a.0 t.13)))
   (app abs.10 abs.11 t.12 ktop.9)))
```

Figure 17.29   revmap program after metaCPS conversion (with simplifications).

input and output of CPS conversion. In the **revmap** example, [*copy-prop*] changes
ans.5 to **t.21** and **loop.6** to **t.23** and also replaces two occurrences of **_** (by
t.32 and **t.24**). Since techniques to avoid such renamings are complex, and the
particular names used don't affect the correctness of the resulting code, we opt
to accept such renamings without complaint.

```
(fil (a.0 b.1 ktop.9)
 (let* ((abs.10
          (abs (f.3 elts.4 k.20)
            (let* ((t.22 (@null))
                   (t.21 (@mprod t.22))
                   (ans.5 t.21)
                   (t.23 (@mprod #u))
                   (loop.6 t.23)
                   (abs.25
                     (abs (xs.7 k.29)
                       (let* ((kif.30 (abs (t.43) (app k.29 t.43)))
                              (t.31 (@null? xs.7)))
                         (if t.31
                             (let ((t.42 (@mget 1 ans.5)))
                               (app kif.30 t.42))
                             (let* ((t.34 (@car xs.7))
                                    (k.41
                                      (abs (t.35)
                                        (let* ((t.36 (@mget 1 ans.5))
                                               (t.33 (@cons t.35 t.36))
                                               (t.32 (@mset! 1 ans.5 t.33))
                                               (_ t.32)
                                               (t.37 (@mget 1 loop.6))
                                               (t.38 (@cdr xs.7))
                                               (k.40 (abs (t.39)
                                                         (app kif.30 t.39))))
                                          (app t.37 t.38 k.40)))))
                               (app f.3 t.34 k.41))))))
                   (t.24 (@mset! 1 loop.6 abs.25))
                   (_ t.24)
                   (t.26 (@mget 1 loop.6))
                   (k.28 (abs (t.27) (app k.20 t.27))))
              (app t.26 elts.4 k.28))))
        (revmap.2 abs.10)
        (abs.11 (abs (x.8 k.18)
                  (let ((t.19 (@> x.8 b.1)))
                    (app k.18 t.19))))
        (t.14 (@* a.0 7))
        (t.15 (@null))
        (t.13 (@cons t.14 t.15))
        (t.12 (@cons a.0 t.13))
        (k.17 (abs (t.16) (app ktop.9 t.16))))
   (app revmap.2 abs.11 t.12 k.17)))
```

Figure 17.30   revmap program after metaCPS conversion (without simplifications).

Exercise 17.19 Use $\mathcal{MCPS}_{exp}$ to CPS-convert the following FIL expressions relative to an initial metacontinuation $(id{\rightarrow}mc\ \mathbf{k})$.

a. `(abs (f) (@+ 1 (app f 2)))`

b. `(abs (g x) (@+ 1 (app g (@* 2 x))))`

c. `(abs (f g h x) (app f (app g x) (app h x)))`

d. `(abs (f) (@* (if (app f 1) 2 3) (if (app f 4) 5 6)))`

Exercise 17.20 Use $\mathcal{MCPS}_{prog}$ to CPS-convert the following FIL programs:

a. The program P_{quad} from Figure 17.25 (page 1055).

b.
```
(fil (x)
   (let ((fact (@mprod #u))
         (_ (@mset! 1 fact
              (abs (n)
                 (if (@= n 0)
                     1
                     (@* n (app (@mget 1 fact) (@- n 1)))))))))
      (app (@mget 1 fact) x)))
```

c.
```
(fil (x)
   (let ((fib (@mprod #u))
         (_ (@mset! 1 fib
              (abs (n)
                 (if (@<= n 1)
                     n
                     (@+ (app (@mget 1 fib) (@- n 1))
                         (app (@mget 1 fib) (@- n 2))))))))
      (app (@mget 1 fib) x)))
```

Exercise 17.21 Do Exercise 17.14 part **a** (page 1054), giving $\mathcal{MCPS}_{exp}$ clauses instead of $\mathcal{SCPS}_{exp}$ clauses.

Exercise 17.22 The unique naming prerequisite on programs is essential for the correctness of $\mathcal{MCPS}_{prog}$. To demonstrate this, show that the output of $\mathcal{MCPS}_{prog}[\![P_{mnun}]\!]$ has a different behavior from P_{mnun}, where P_{mnun} is:

   `(fil (a b) (@+ (let ((a (@* b b))) a) a))`

Exercise 17.23 Suppose that both FIL and FIL_{cps} were extended to include mutable variables by adding the assignment construct $(\mathtt{set!}\ I\ E)$ as an element of E for FIL and $(\mathtt{set!}\ I\ V)$ as an element of LE for FIL_{cps}.

a. Give the $\mathcal{MCPS}_{exp}$ clause for `set!`.

$$\mathcal{MCPS}_{exp}[\![(\texttt{label}\ I_{ctrlPt}\ E_{body})]\!] =$$
$$(\lambda m\ .\ (\texttt{let}\ ((I_{ctrlPt}\ (\text{mc}{\rightarrow}\text{exp}\ m)))$$
$$(\mathcal{MCPS}_{exp}[\![E_{body}]\!]\ (\text{id}{\rightarrow}\text{mc}\ I_{ctrlPt}))))$$

$$\mathcal{MCPS}_{exp}[\![(\texttt{jump}\ E_{ctrlPt}\ E_{val})]\!] =$$
$$(\lambda m\ .\ (\mathcal{MCPS}_{exp}[\![E_{ctrlPt}]\!]$$
$$(\lambda V_{ctrlPt}\ .\ (\mathcal{MCPS}_{exp}[\![E_{val}]\!]$$
$$(\lambda V_{val}\ .\ (\texttt{app}\ V_{ctrlPt}\ V_{val}))))))$$

Figure 17.31   CPS conversion of the `label` and `jump` constructs.

b. Show the result of using $\mathcal{MCPS}_{exp}$ to convert the following program $P_{set!}$:

```
(fil (a b)
  (let ((_ (set! a (set! b (@+ a b)))))
    (@mprod a b)))
```

c. In the TORTOISE compiler, assignment conversion is performed before CPS conversion. Show the result of $\mathcal{MCPS}_{prog}[\![\mathcal{AC}_{prog}[\![P_{set!}]\!]]\!]$.

d. It is possible to perform assignment conversion *after* CPS conversion. Show the result of $\mathcal{AC}_{prog}[\![\mathcal{MCPS}_{prog}[\![P_{set!}]\!]]\!]$. Is the result a valid FIL$_{cps}$ program?

e. Describe how to modify assignment conversion to guarantee that if its input is a valid FIL$_{cps}$ program then its output is also a valid FIL$_{cps}$ program.

17.9.4   CPS-Converting Control Constructs

A key benefit of CPS conversion is that it enables seemingly complex control constructs to be compiled simply. The continuations made explicit by CPS conversion can be manipulated to implement the advanced control features studied in Chapter 9, such as nonlocal jumps, exception handling, coroutines, and backtracking.

For example, Figure 17.31 gives the $\mathcal{MCPS}_{exp}$ clauses for the `label` and `jump` constructs presented in Section 9.4. The expression (`label` I_{ctrlPt} E_{body}) is translated to a `let` expression that evaluates the translation of E_{body} in a context where I_{ctrlPt} names a FIL abstraction,

$$(\text{mc}{\rightarrow}\text{exp}\ m) = (\texttt{abs}\ (I)\ (m\ I))$$

that is an explicit representation of the current continuation. The metacontinuation for converting E_{body},

$$(\text{id}{\rightarrow}\text{mc}\ I_{ctrlPt}) = (\lambda V\ .\ (\texttt{app}\ I_{ctrlPt}\ V))$$

is equivalent to m but avoids code bloat by referring to the name I_{ctrlPt} rather than duplicating the code it names (see Exercise 17.25). (jump E_{ctrlPt} E_{val}) is translated to an expression that simply applies the continuation value of E_{ctrlPt} to the value of E_{val}.

Figure 17.32 shows that CPS-converting the FIL expression

```
(@+ 1 (label exit (@* 2 (if b 3 (jump exit 4)))))
```

relative to the initial continuation k yields the FIL_{cps} expression

```
(let* ((exit (abs (t.2) (let ((t.1 (@+ 1 t.2))) (app k t.1))))
       (k.4 (abs (t.5) (let ((t.3 (@* 2 t.5))) (app exit t.3)))))
  (if b (app k.4 3) (app exit 4)))
```

The label-bound name exit names the abstraction

```
(abs (t.2) (let ((t.1 (@+ 1 t.2))) (app k t.1)))
```

which is a continuation representing the evaluation context (app k (@+ 1 □)) in which the label expression is encountered. The identifier k.4 names the abstraction

```
(abs (t.5) (let ((t.3 (@* 2 t.5))) (app exit t.3)))
```

which is the normal continuation representing the evaluation context

```
(@+ 1 (label exit (@* 2 □)))
```

in which the if expression appears. This continuation eventually invokes the exit continuation to return a value from the label expression in which the (@* 2 ...) appears. The 3 in the then arm of the if translates to (app k.4 3), which passes 3 to the normal continuation k.4. The (jump exit 4) in the else arm of the if translates to (app exit 4); in this case, the normal continuation k.4 is ignored because the body of the metalanguage abstraction $(\lambda m \ . \ \ldots)$ that is the result of translating (jump exit 4) never mentions the metacontinuation m that corresponds to the normal continuation. The fact that different continuations are taken from the two if branches underscores the nonlinear nature of nonlocal exits. Naming a continuation with label allows it to be copied and used to replace the normal continuation elsewhere in the program.

If the normal continuation replaced by a jump is not mentioned elsewhere, it will not appear in the CPS-converted code. For example, if the if expression in Figure 17.32 were replaced by (jump exit 3), the result of CPS conversion would be

```
(let ((exit (abs (t.2) (let ((t.1 (@+ 1 t.2))) (app k t.1)))))
  (app exit 3))
```

Note that the continuation corresponding to the context (app exit (@* 2 □)) is eliminated because the clause for jump never uses its metacontinuation m.

Exercise 17.24 Use $\mathcal{MCPS}_{exp}$ to CPS-convert the following FIL+{label, jump} expressions relative to an initial metacontinuation $(id{\to}mc\ \text{k})$:

a. `(@+ 1 (label a (@* 2 (label b (@- (jump b 3) (jump a 4))))))`

b. `(@+ 1 (label a (@* 2 (label b (@- (jump a 3) (jump b 4))))))`

c. ```
(label exit
   (abs (y)
      (if (@= y 0)
          (jump exit (abs (z) z))
          (@+ 1 y))))
```

d. ```
(abs (ints)
   (label return
      (let* ((product (@mprod #u))
             (_ (@mset! 1 product
                  (abs (ns)
                     (if (@null? ns)
                         1
                         (if (@= (@car ns) 0)
                             (jump return 0)
                             (@* (@car ns)
                                 (app (@mget 1 product) (@cdr ns)))))))))
         (app (@mget 1 product) ints))))
```

Exercise 17.25 Bud Lojack suggests that $(id{\to}mc\ I_{ctrlPt})$ be replaced by m in the $\mathcal{MCPS}_{exp}$ clause for label. Discuss the ramifications of Bud's change. For example, how would Bud's CPS conversions of the following examples differ from the conversions shown above?

```
(@+ 1 (label exit (@* 2 (if b 3 (jump exit 4)))))
(@+ 1 (label exit (@* 2 (jump exit 3))))
```

Exercise 17.26 Suppose that the FIL kernel is extended with the cwcc feature introduced in Section 9.4.4:

$$E \in \text{Exp} ::= \dots \mid (\text{cwcc } E_{receiver})$$

a. Write an $\mathcal{SCPS}_{exp}$ clause for cwcc.

b. Write an $\mathcal{MCPS}_{exp}$ clause for cwcc. Be careful to avoid code duplication.

Exercise 17.27 Sam Antics wants to explore the implementation of dynamically scoped exceptions with termination semantics (see Section 9.6). He extends FIL with two new constructs:

$$E \in \text{Exp} ::= \dots \mid (\text{throw } E_{info}) \mid (\text{catch } E_{handler}\ E_{body})$$

$(\mathcal{MCPS}_{exp}[\![(@+ \ 1 \ (\texttt{label exit} \ (@* \ 2 \ (\texttt{if b 3 (jump exit 4)})))))]\!] \ (id{\rightarrow}mc \ \texttt{k}))$

$= ((\lambda m \ . \ (\mathcal{MCPS}_{exp}[\![1]\!]$
$\qquad\qquad (\lambda V_1 \ . \ (\mathcal{MCPS}_{exp}[\![(\texttt{label exit} \ (@* \ 2 \ (\texttt{if b 3 (jump exit 4)})))]\!]$
$\qquad\qquad\qquad (\lambda V_2 \ . \ (\texttt{let ((t.1 (@+} \ V_1 \ V_2 \texttt{)))} \ (m \ \texttt{t.1)))))))$
$\quad (\lambda V_3 \ . \ (\texttt{app k} \ V_3)))$

$= (\mathcal{MCPS}_{exp}[\![(\texttt{label exit} \ (@* \ 2 \ (\texttt{if b 3 (jump exit 4)})))]\!]$
$\quad (\lambda V_2 \ . \ (\texttt{let ((t.1 (@+ 1} \ V_2 \texttt{)))} \ (\texttt{app k t.1}))))$

$= ((\lambda m \ . \ (\texttt{let ((exit} \ (mc{\rightarrow}exp \ m) \texttt{))}$
$\qquad\qquad (\mathcal{MCPS}_{exp}[\![(@* \ 2 \ (\texttt{if b 3 (jump exit 4)}))]\!] \ (id{\rightarrow}mc \ \texttt{exit})))$
$\quad (\lambda V_2 \ . \ (\texttt{let ((t.1 (@+ 1} \ V_2 \texttt{)))} \ (\texttt{app k t.1}))))$

$= (\texttt{let ((exit (abs (t.2) (let ((t.1 (@+ 1 t.2))) (app k t.1)))))}$
$\quad (\mathcal{MCPS}_{exp}[\![(@* \ 2 \ (\texttt{if b 3 (jump exit 4)}))]\!]$
$\quad (\lambda V_4 \ . \ (\texttt{app exit} \ V_4))))$

$= (\texttt{let ((exit (abs (t.2) (let ((t.1 (@+ 1 t.2))) (app k t.1)))))}$
$\quad ((\lambda m \ . \ (\mathcal{MCPS}_{exp}[\![2]\!]$
$\qquad\qquad (\lambda V_5 \ . \ (\mathcal{MCPS}_{exp}[\![(\texttt{if b 3 (jump exit 4)})]\!]$
$\qquad\qquad\qquad (\lambda V_6 \ . \ (\texttt{let ((t.3 (@*} \ V_5 \ V_6 \texttt{)))} \ (m \ \texttt{t.3)))))))$
$\quad (\lambda V_4 \ . \ (\texttt{app exit} \ V_4))))$

$= (\texttt{let ((exit (abs (t.2) (let ((t.1 (@+ 1 t.2))) (app k t.1)))))}$
$\quad (\mathcal{MCPS}_{exp}[\![(\texttt{if b 3 (jump exit 4)})]\!]$
$\quad (\lambda V_6 \ . \ (\texttt{let ((t.3 (@* 2} \ V_6 \texttt{)))} \ (\texttt{app exit t.3})))))$

$= (\texttt{let ((exit (abs (t.2) (let ((t.1 (@+ 1 t.2))) (app k t.1)))))}$
$\quad ((\lambda m \ . \ (\mathcal{MCPS}_{exp}[\![\texttt{b}]\!]$
$\qquad\qquad (\lambda V_7 \ . \ (\texttt{let ((k.4} \ (mc{\rightarrow}exp \ m) \texttt{))}$
$\qquad\qquad\qquad (\texttt{if} \ V_7$
$\qquad\qquad\qquad\qquad (\mathcal{MCPS}_{exp}[\![3]\!] \ (id{\rightarrow}mc \ \texttt{k.4}))$
$\qquad\qquad\qquad\qquad (\mathcal{MCPS}_{exp}[\![(\texttt{jump exit 4})]\!] \ (id{\rightarrow}mc \ \texttt{k.4}))))))$
$\quad (\lambda V_6 \ . \ (\texttt{let ((t.3 (@* 2} \ V_6 \texttt{)))} \ (\texttt{app exit t.3})))))$

$= (\texttt{let* ((exit (abs (t.2) (let ((t.1 (@+ 1 t.2))) (app k t.1))))}$
$\qquad\quad (\texttt{k.4 (abs (t.5) (let ((t.3 (@* 2 t.5))) (app exit t.3))))))$
$\quad (\texttt{if b}$
$\qquad (\texttt{app k.4 3})$
$\qquad ((\lambda m \ . \ (\mathcal{MCPS}_{exp}[\![\texttt{exit}]\!]$; m *not used in this metacontinuation body*
$\qquad\qquad\qquad (\lambda V_8 \ . \ (\mathcal{MCPS}_{exp}[\![4]\!] \ (\lambda V_9 \ . \ (\texttt{app} \ V_8 \ V_9)))))))$
$\qquad\qquad (id{\rightarrow}mc \ \texttt{k.4})))) $

$= (\texttt{let* ((exit (abs (t.2) (let ((t.1 (@+ 1 t.2))) (app k t.1))))}$
$\qquad\quad (\texttt{k.4 (abs (t.5) (let ((t.3 (@* 2 t.5))) (app exit t.3))))))$
$\quad (\texttt{if b (app k.4 3) (app exit 4)}))$

Figure 17.32 An example of CPS-converting `label` and `jump` using metacontinuations.

Sam's `throw` and `catch` constructs are simplified versions of the `raise` and `handle` constructs from Section 9.6. Exception tags are unnecessary because there is only one possible kind of exception:

(`throw` E_{info}) evaluates E_{info} to a value V_{info} and transfers control with information V_{info} to the nearest dynamically enclosing `catch` handler. It is an error if there is no dynamically enclosing `catch` handler.

(`catch` $E_{handler}$ E_{body}) first evaluates $E_{handler}$ to a unary exception-handling procedure $V_{handler}$. (It is an error if $E_{handler}$ does not denote a procedure.) Then E_{body} is evaluated. If no exception is thrown in the evaluation of E_{body}, its value is the value of the `catch` expression. If an exception with information V_{info} is thrown and not handled within E_{body}, the value of the `catch` expression is the result of applying $V_{handler}$ to V_{info}.

Sam gives the following examples of his constructs in action:

$$E_{catchabs} = \text{(abs (n)}$$
$$\text{(catch (abs (x) (@+ x 1))}$$
$$\text{(let ((f (abs (y) (if (@> y n) y (throw y)))))}$$
$$\text{(@- (f 5) (catch (abs (z) (@* 2 z)) (f 3))))))}$$

(app $E_{catchabs}$ 0) $\xrightarrow[\overline{FIL}]{}$ 2 $\{5 - 3 = 2\}$

(app $E_{catchabs}$ 4) $\xrightarrow[\overline{FIL}]{}$ -1 $\{5 - (2*3) = -1\}$

(app $E_{catchabs}$ 8) $\xrightarrow[\overline{FIL}]{}$ 6 $\{5 + 1 = 6\}$

a. Sam modifies the standard $\mathcal{SCPS}$ conversion clauses to translate every expression into a procedure taking two continuations: an exception continuation and a normal continuation. Sam's $\mathcal{SCPS}$ conversion clauses for programs, literals, and conditionals are:

$$\mathcal{SCPS}_{prog}[\![(\text{fil } (I_{i=1}^{n})\ E_{body})]\!]$$
$$= \quad (\text{fil } (I_{i=1}^{n}\ I_{kntop})\ ;\ I_{kntop}\ \textit{fresh}$$
$$\qquad (\text{let } ((I_{ketop}\ (\text{abs } (I_{info})\ ;\ I_{ketop}\ \textit{and}\ I_{info}\ \textit{fresh}$$
$$\qquad\qquad\qquad (\text{error uncaught-exception)))})$$
$$\qquad\quad (\text{app } (\mathcal{SCPS}_{exp}[\![E_{body}]\!])\ I_{ketop}\ I_{kntop})))$$

$$\mathcal{SCPS}_{exp}[\![L]\!] = (\text{abs } (I_{ke}\ I_{kn})\ ;\ I_{ke}\ \textit{(exception cont.) and}\ I_{kn}\ \textit{(normal cont.) fresh}$$
$$\qquad\qquad (\text{app } I_{kn}\ L))$$

$$\mathcal{SCPS}_{exp}[\![(\text{if } E_{test}\ E_{then}\ E_{else})]\!]$$
$$= (\text{abs } (I_{ke}\ I_{kn})\ ;\ I_{ke}\ \textit{and}\ I_{kn}\ \textit{fresh}$$
$$\qquad (\text{app } (\mathcal{SCPS}_{exp}[\![E_{test}]\!])$$
$$\qquad\qquad I_{ke}$$
$$\qquad\qquad (\text{abs } (I_{test})\ ;\ I_{test}\ \textit{fresh}$$
$$\qquad\qquad\quad (\text{if } I_{test}$$
$$\qquad\qquad\qquad\quad (\text{app } (\mathcal{SCPS}_{exp}[\![E_{then}]\!])\ I_{ke}\ I_{kn})$$
$$\qquad\qquad\qquad\quad (\text{app } (\mathcal{SCPS}_{exp}[\![E_{else}]\!])\ I_{ke}\ I_{kn})))))$$

Write the $\mathcal{SCPS}_{exp}$ clauses for `abs`, `app`, `throw`, and `catch`.

b. For $\mathcal{MCPS}$, Sam modifies $\mathcal{MCPS}_{exp}$ to take an additional argument (an identifier naming the current exception continuation) before the metacontinuation argument. For example:

$$\mathcal{MCPS}_{prog}[\![(\texttt{fil } (I_{i=1}^{n}) \ E_{body})]\!]$$
$$= (\texttt{fil } (I_{i=1}^{n} \ I_{kntop}) \ ; I_{kntop} \text{ fresh}$$
$$\quad (\texttt{let } ((I_{ketop} \ (\texttt{abs } (I_{info}) \ ; I_{ketop} \text{ and } I_{info} \text{ fresh}$$
$$\quad\quad\quad\quad\quad\quad (\texttt{error uncaught-exception}))))$$
$$\quad\quad (\mathcal{MCPS}_{exp}[\![E_{body}]\!] \ I_{ketop} \ (id{\rightarrow}\text{mc } I_{kntop}))))$$

$$\mathcal{MCPS}_{exp} : \text{Exp}_{FIL} \rightarrow \text{Ident} \rightarrow MetaCont \rightarrow \text{Exp}_{cps}$$

$$\mathcal{MCPS}_{exp}[\![L]\!] = (\lambda I_{ke} \ m \ . \ (m \ L))$$

$$\mathcal{MCPS}_{exp}[\![(\texttt{if } E_{test} \ E_{then} \ E_{else})]\!]$$
$$= (\lambda I_{ke} \ m \ . \ (\mathcal{MCPS}_{exp}[\![E_{test}]\!] \ I_{ke}$$
$$\quad\quad (\lambda V_{test} \ . \ (\texttt{let } ((I_{kif} \ (\text{mc}{\rightarrow}\text{exp } m))) \ ; I_{kif} \text{ fresh}$$
$$\quad\quad\quad\quad (\texttt{if } V_{test}$$
$$\quad\quad\quad\quad\quad\quad (\mathcal{MCPS}_{exp}[\![E_{then}]\!] \ I_{ke} \ (id{\rightarrow}\text{mc } I_{kif}))$$
$$\quad\quad\quad\quad\quad\quad (\mathcal{MCPS}_{exp}[\![E_{else}]\!] \ I_{ke} \ (id{\rightarrow}\text{mc } I_{kif}))))))$$

Write the $\mathcal{MCPS}_{exp}$ clauses for abs, app, throw, and catch.

c. Based on the metaCPS conversion of FIL+{throw, catch} explain how to perform metaCPS conversion for FIL+{raise, handle}.

17.10 Transformation 8: Closure Conversion

In a block-structured language, code can refer to variables declared outside the current block (i.e., in an outer procedure or class declaration). As we have seen in Chapters 6–7, the meaning of such free variable references is often explained in terms of environments. Traditional interpreters and compilers have special-purpose machinery to manage environments.

The TORTOISE compiler avoids such machinery by making all environments explicit in the intermediate language. Each procedure is transformed into an abstract pair of code and environment, where the code explicitly accesses the environment to retrieve values formerly referenced by free variables. The resulting abstract pair is known as a **closure** because its code component is closed—i.e., it contains no free variables. The process of transforming all procedures into closures is traditionally called **closure conversion**. Because it makes all environments explicit, **environment conversion** is another name for this transformation.

Closure conversion transforms a program that may contain higher-order procedures into one that contains only first-order procedures: rather than passing a procedure as a parameter or returning one as a result, a transformed program passes or returns a closure data structure. This technique is not only useful as a compiler transformation, but programmers may also apply it manually to simulate higher-order procedures in languages that support only first-order procedures (such as C, PASCAL, and ADA) or objects with methods (such as SMALLTALK, JAVA, C++, and C#). All one needs is a way to embed a procedure value (or a reference to a procedure) in a data structure (or object).

In the TORTOISE compiler, closure conversion has the following specification:

Preconditions: The input to closure conversion is a valid kernel FIL program.

Postconditions: The output of closure conversion is a valid kernel FIL program in which all abstractions are closed.

Other properties: If the input program is in FIL$_{cps}$, so is the output program.

In the TORTOISE compiler, the closure conversion stage follows the renaming and CPS conversion stages, but closure conversion can be performed on any FIL program, even ones that are not uniquely named or in FIL$_{cps}$. The reason that TORTOISE performs closure conversion *after* CPS conversion is so that closure conversion will be performed on the continuation procedures introduced by CPS conversion as well as on the user-defined procedures already in the program. The TORTOISE closure conversion specification requires that any FIL$_{cps}$ program will be tranformed to another FIL$_{cps}$ program, so the output of the closure conversion stage of the compiler is guaranteed to be in FIL$_{cps}$.

There are numerous approaches to closure conversion that differ in their representations of environments and closures. We shall focus on one class of representations, **flat closures**, and then briefly discuss some alternatives.

17.10.1   Flat Closures

Consider the following example:

```
(let ((linear (abs (a b)
                (abs (x)
                  (@+ (@* a x) b)))))
  (let ((f (app linear 4 5))
        (g (app linear 6 7)))
    (@+ (app f 8) (app g 9))))
```

Given a and b, the linear procedure returns a procedural representation of a line with slope a and y-intercept b. The f and g procedures represent two such lines, each of which is associated with the abstraction (abs (x) ...), which has free variables a and b. In the case of f, these variables have the bindings 4 and 5, respectively, while for g they have the bindings 6 and 7.

We will convert this example by hand and then develop an automatic closure conversion transformation. One way to represent f and g as closed procedures is shown below:

```
(let ((fg_code (abs (env x)
                (let ((a (@mget 1 env))
                      (b (@mget 2 env)))
                  (@+ (@* a x) b))))
      (f_env (@mprod 4 5))
      (g_env (@mprod 6 7)))
  (let ((f_clopair (@mprod fg_code f_env))
        (g_clopair (@mprod fg_code g_env)))
    (@+ (app (@mget 1 f_clopair) (@mget 2 f_clopair) 8)
        (app (@mget 1 g_clopair) (@mget 2 g_clopair) 9))))
```

In this approach, the two procedures share the same code component, fg_{code}, which takes an explicit environment argument env in addition to the original argument x. The env argument is assumed to be a tuple (product) whose two components are the values of the former free variables a and b. These values are extracted from the environment and given their former names in a wrapper around the body expression (@+ (@* a x) b). Note that fg_{code} has no free variables and so is a closed procedure. The environments f_{env} and g_{env} are tuples holding the free variable values. The closures $f_{clopair}$ and $g_{clopair}$ are formed by making explicit **code/environment pairs**, each combining the shared code component with a specific environment for the closure. To handle the change in procedure representation, each call of the form (app f E) must be transformed to (app (@mget 1 $f_{clopair}$) (@mget 2 $f_{clopair}$) E) (and similarly for g) in order to pass the environment component as the first argument to the code component.

Closure conversion can be viewed as an exercise in abstract data type implementation. The abstraction being considered is the procedure, whose interface has two operations: abs, which creates procedures, and app, which applies procedures. The goal of closure conversion is to find an implementation of this interface that behaves the same, but in which procedure creation requires no free variables. As in traditional data structure problems, we're keen to design correct implementations that are as efficient as possible.

```
(let ((linear
        (@mprod {this closure (clo.1) has only a code component}
          (abs (clo.1 a b) {the parameter clo.1 is not referenced}
            (@mprod {this closure (clo.2) has code + vars {a, b}}
              (abs (clo.2 x)
                (let ((a (@mget 2 clo.2))
                      (b (@mget 3 clo.2)))
                  (@+ (@* a x) b)))
              a b)) {vars used by clo.2 = {a, b}}
          ))) {clo.1 has no vars}
  (let ((f (app (@mget 1 linear) linear 4 5))
        (g (app (@mget 1 linear) linear 6 7)))
    (@+ (app (@mget 1 f) f 8)
        (app (@mget 1 g) g 9)))))
```

Figure 17.33   Result of closure-converting the linear example.

For example, a more efficient approach to using explicit code/environment
pairs is to collect the code and free variable values into a single tuple, as shown
below:

```
(let ((fg'_code (abs (clo x)
                  (let ((a (@mget 2 clo))
                        (b (@mget 3 clo)))
                    (@+ (@* a x) b)))))
  (let ((f_clo (@mprod fg'_code 4 5))
        (g_clo (@mprod fg'_code 6 7)))
    (@+ (app (@mget 1 f_clo) f_clo 8)
        (app (@mget 1 g_clo) g_clo 9))))
```

This approach, known as **closure-passing style**, avoids creating a separate environment tuple every time a closure is created, and avoids extracting this tuple
from the code/environment pair every time the closure is invoked.

If we systematically use closure-passing style to transform every abstraction
and application site in the original linear example, we get the result shown in
Figure 17.33. The inner abs has been transformed into a tuple that combines
fg_{code} with the values of the free variables a and b from the outer abs. For
consistency, the outer abs has also been transformed; its tuple has only a code
component since the original abs has no free variables. By convention, we will
refer to a closure tuple by the name of the first argument of its code component.
In this example, the code comments refer to the outer closure tuple as clo.1 and
the inner closure tuple as clo.2.

Figure 17.34 shows an example involving nested open procedures and un-referenced variables. In the unconverted `clotest`, the outermost abstraction, (`abs` (`c d`) ...), is closed; the middle abstraction, (`abs` (`r s t`) ...), has `c` as its only free variable (`d` is never used); and the innermost abstraction, (`abs` (`y`) ...), has $\{c, r, t\}$ as its free variables (`d` and `s` are never used). In the converted `clotest`, each abstraction has been transformed into a tuple that combines a closed code component with all the free variables of the original abstraction. The resulting tuples are called **flat closures** because all the environment information has been condensed into a single tuple that does not reflect any of the original nesting structure. Note that unreferenced variables from an enclosing scope are ignored. For example, the innermost body does not reference `d` and `s`, so these variables are not extracted from `clo.3` and are not included in the innermost closure tuple.

A formal specification of the flat closure conversion transformation is presented in Figure 17.35. The transformation is specified via the $\mathcal{CL}_{exp}$ function on FIL expressions. The only nontrivial cases for $\mathcal{CL}_{exp}$ are `abs` and `app`. $\mathcal{CL}_{exp}$ converts an `abs` to a tuple containing a closed code component and all the free variables of the abstraction. The code component is derived from the original `abs` by adding a closure argument I_{clo} and extracting the free variables from this argument in a wrapper around the body. The order of the free variables is irrelevant as long as it is consistent between tuple creation and projection. An `app` is converted to another `app` that applies the code component of the converted rator closure to the closure and the converted operands.

Certain parts of the $\mathcal{CL}_{exp}$ definition are written in a somewhat unnatural way to guarantee that an input expression in FIL_{cps} will be translated to an output expression in FIL_{cps}. This is the purpose of the separate clause for converting an `abs` that occurs in a `let` binding and of the `let*` bindings in the `app` and `abs` conversions. We will ignore these details in our informal examples of closure conversion.

Note that the unique naming property is *not* preserved by $\mathcal{CL}_{exp}$. The names I_{fv_i} declared in the body of the closed abstraction stand for variables that are logically distinct from variables with the same names in the `mprod` application that creates the closure tuple.

Figure 17.36 shows the `revmap` example after closure conversion. In addition to transforming procedures present in the original code in Figure 17.4 on page 1011 (`clo.56` is `revmap`, `clo.52` is `loop`, and `clo.60` is the greater-than-b procedure), closure conversion also transforms the continuation procedures introduced by CPS conversion (`clo.48` is the continuation for the `f` call—compare Figure 17.29 on page 1067). The free variables in converted continuations corre-

Unconverted Expression
```
(let ((clotest
        (abs (c d)
          (abs (r s t)
            (abs (y)
              (@+ (@/ (@* r y) t) (@- r c))))))))
  (let ((p (app clotest 4 5)))
    (let ((q1 (app p 6 7 8))
          (q2 (app p 9 10 11)))
      (@+ (app q1 12) (app q2 13)))))
```
Converted Expression
```
(let ((clotest
        (@mprod {this closure (clo.1) has only a code component}
          (abs (clo.1 c d) {the parameter clo.1 is never referenced}
            (@mprod {this closure (clo.2) has code + var {c}}
              (abs (clo.2 r s t)
                (let ((c (@mget 2 clo.2)))
                  (@mprod {this closure (clo.3) has code + vars {c, r, t}}
                    (abs (clo.3 y)
                      (let ((c (@mget 2 clo.3))
                            (r (@mget 3 clo.3))
                            (t (@mget 4 clo.3)))
                        (@+ (@/ (@* r y) t) (@- r c))))
                    c r t))) {vars used by clo.3 = {c, r, t}}
                c)) {vars used by clo.2 = {c}}
            ))) {clo.1 has no vars}
  (let ((p (app (@mget 1 clotest) clotest 4 5)))
    (let ((q1 (app (@mget 1 p) p 6 7 8))
          (q2 (app (@mget 1 p) p 9 10 11)))
      (@+ (app (@mget 1 q1) q1 12) (app (@mget 1 q2) q2 13)))))
```

Figure 17.34   Flat closure conversion on an example with nested open procedures.

spond to the caller-saved register values that a traditional implementation would save on the stack during a subroutine call that returns to the control point represented by the continuation. In the TORTOISE compiler, this saving behavior is automatically implemented by performing closure conversion after CPS conversion, but the saved values are stored in the continuation closure rather than on an explicit stack. For example, continuation closure clo.48 includes the values needed by the loop after a call to f: the cell t.21 resulting from the assignment

$$\mathcal{CL}_{exp} : \text{Exp}_{FIL} \to \text{Exp}_{FIL}$$

$\mathcal{CL}_{exp}[\![(\text{abs } (I_{i=1}^n) \ E_{body})]\!]$
  = **let** $\{I_{fv_1}, \ldots, I_{fv_k}\}$ **be** $FrIds[\![(\text{abs } (I_{i=1}^n) \ E_{body})]\!]$
        ; *assume an appropriate definition of FrIds for FIL*
    in $(\text{@mprod } (\text{abs } (I_{clo} \ I_{i=1}^n) \ ; I_{clo} \ fresh$
                $(\text{let* } ((I_{fv_j} \ (\text{@mget } \overline{j+1} \ I_{clo})))_{j=1}^k); \mathcal{N}[\![\overline{n}]\!] = n \ \text{for } n \in Nat$
              $\mathcal{CL}_{exp}[\![E_{body}]\!]))$
        $I_{fv_1} \ \ldots \ I_{fv_k})$

$\mathcal{CL}_{exp}[\![(\text{let } ((I_{abs} \ (\text{abs } (I_{i=1}^n) \ E_{absbody}))) \ E_{letbody})]\!]$
  ; *special case of* **abs** *conversion that preserves* FIL_{cps}
  = **let** $(\text{@mprod } E_{code} \ I_{fv_1} \ \ldots \ I_{fv_k})$ **be** $\mathcal{CL}_{exp}[\![(\text{abs } (I_{i=1}^n) \ E_{absbody})]\!]$
    in $(\text{let* } ((I_{code} \ E_{code}) \ ; I_{code} \ fresh$
              $(I_{abs} \ (\text{@mprod } I_{code} \ I_{fv_1} \ \ldots \ I_{fv_k})))$
        $\mathcal{CL}_{exp}[\![E_{letbody}]\!])$

$\mathcal{CL}_{exp}[\![(\text{app } E_{rator} \ E_{i=1}^n)]\!]$
  = $(\text{let* } ((I_{clo} \ \mathcal{CL}_{exp}[\![E_{rator}]\!]) \ ; I_{clo} \ fresh$
            $(I_{code} \ (\text{@mget } 1 \ I_{clo}))) \ ; I_{code} \ fresh$
      $(\text{app } I_{code} \ I_{clo} \ \mathcal{CL}_{exp}[\![E_i]\!]_{i=1}^n))$

$\mathcal{CL}_{exp}[\![E]\!] = \text{mapsub}_{FIL}[\![E]\!] \ \mathcal{CL}_{exp}$, *otherwise.*

Figure 17.35 The flat closure conversion transformation $\mathcal{CL}_{exp}$.

conversion of **ans**, the cell holding the looping procedure **t.23**, the loop state variable **xs.7**, and the end-of-loop continuation **k.29**.

In Figure 17.36, we assume that the top-level continuation **ktop.9** supplied by the operating system is consistent with the calling convention used by the closure-converted code. I.e., **ktop.9** must be a closure tuple whose first slot contains an abstraction with two parameters: (1) the closure tuple and (2) the argument expected by the system's unary continuation procedure. Alternatively, for the case where closure conversion is known to follow CPS conversion, we could define a special program-level closure conversion function $\mathcal{CL}_{prog}$ that assumes that the final argument in the input FIL_{cps} program is an unconverted unary continuation procedure (see Exercise 17.30).

In order to work properly, $\mathcal{CL}_{exp}$ requires that the input expression contain no assignments (**set!**). This is necessarily true in FIL, which does not support **set!**, but would be an issue in extensions to FIL that include **set!** (e.g., see Exercises 17.14 and 17.23 in Sections 17.9.2 and 17.9.3). The reason for this restriction is that the copying of free variable values by $\mathcal{CL}_{exp}$ in the **abs** clause does not preserve the semantics of mutable variables. Consider the following example of a nullary procedure that increments a counter every time it is called in FIL+{set!}:

```
(let ((count 0))
  (abs ()
    (let* ((new-count (@+ count 1))
           (_ (set! count new-count)))
      new-count)))
```

Closure-converting this example yields:

```
(let ((count 0))
  (@mprod (abs (clo)
            (let* ((count (@mget 2 clo)))
              (let* ((new-count (@+ count 1))
                     (_ (set! count new-count)))
                new-count)))
          count))
```

The set! in the transformed code changes the local variable count within the abstraction, which is always initially bound to the value 0. So the closure-converted procedure always returns 1, which is not the correct behavior. Performing assignment conversion before closure conversion fixes this problem, since count will then name a sharable mutable cell rather than a number, and the set! will be transformed to an mset! on this cell.

The interaction between mutable variables and closure conversion arises in practice in JAVA. JAVA's *anonymous inner classes* allow the programmer to create an instance of an unnamed class (the inner class) within the method of another class (the outer class). Because it is possible for the inner class instance to refer to parameters and local variables of the enclosing method, the inner class instance is effectively a closure over these variables. For example, Figure 17.37 shows how an inner class can be used to express the linear example from page 1076 in JAVA. The IntFun interface is a specification for a class providing an app method that takes a single integer argument and returns an integer result. The linear method of the Linear class takes integers a and b and returns an instance of an anonymous class satisfying the IntFun specification whose app method maps an argument x to the result (a*x)+b. This instance corresponds to the first-class procedure (abs (x) (+ (* a x) b)) in FIL. JAVA requires any enclosing local variables mentioned in the inner class (a and b in this example) to be declared immutable (using the keyword final). This restriction allows the JAVA compiler to copy the values of these variables into instance variables of the anonymous inner class instance rather than attempting to share the locations of these variables (which would require some form of assignment conversion).

```
(fil (a.0 b.1 ktop.9)
 (let* ((code.57 {code of clo.56}
          (abs (clo.56 f.3 elts.4 k.20)
            (let* ((t.22 (@null))
                   (t.21 (@mprod t.22))
                   (t.23 (@mprod #u))
                   (code.53 {code of clo.52}
                    (abs (clo.52 xs.7 k.29)
                       (let* ((t.21 (@mget 2 clo.52))
                              (t.23 (@mget 3 clo.52))
                              (f.3  (@mget 4 clo.52))
                              (t.31 (@null? xs.7)))
                         (if t.31
                             (let* ((t.42 (@mget 1 t.21))
                                    (code.44 (@mget 1 k.29)))
                               (app code.44 k.29 t.42))
                             (let* ((t.34 (@car xs.7))
                                    (code.49 {code of clo.48}
                                     (abs (clo.48 t.35)
                                        (let* ((t.21 (@mget 2 clo.48))
                                               (t.23 (@mget 3 clo.48))
                                               (xs.7 (@mget 4 clo.48))
                                               (k.29 (@mget 5 clo.48))
                                               (t.36 (@mget 1 t.21))
                                               (t.33 (@cons t.35 t.36))
                                               (t.32 (@mset! 1 t.21 t.33))
                                               (t.37 (@mget 1 t.23))
                                               (t.38 (@cdr xs.7))
                                               (code.46 (@mget 1 t.37)))
                                          (app code.46 t.37 t.38 k.29))))
                                    (k.41
                                      (@mprod code.49 t.21 t.23 xs.7 k.29)) {clo.48}
                                    (code.50 (@mget 1 f.3)))
                               (app code.50 f.3 t.34 k.41))))))
                   (abs.25 (@mprod code.53 t.21 t.23 f.3)) {clo.52}
                   (t.24 (@mset! 1 t.23 abs.25))
                   (t.26 (@mget 1 t.23))
                   (code.54 (@mget 1 t.26)))
              (app code.54 t.26 elts.4 k.20))))
        (abs.10 (@mprod code.57)) {clo.56}
        (code.61 (abs (clo.60 x.8 k.18) {code of clo.60}
                   (let* ((b.1 (@mget 2 clo.60))
                          (t.19 (@> x.8 b.1))
                          (code.58 (@mget 1 k.18)))
                     (app code.58 k.18 t.19))))
        (abs.11 (@mprod code.61 b.1)) {clo.60}
        (t.14 (@* a.0 7))
        (t.15 (@null))
        (t.13 (@cons t.14 t.15))
        (t.12 (@cons a.0 t.13))
        (code.62 (@mget 1 abs.10)))
   (app code.62 abs.10 abs.11 t.12 ktop.9)))
```

Figure 17.36 revmap program after closure conversion.

Exercise 17.28

a. A function f is **idempotent** iff $(f \ (f \ x)) = (f \ x)$ for all $x \in dom(f)$. $\mathcal{CL}_{exp}$ is not idempotent. Explain why. Can any closure conversion transformation be idempotent?

b. In the abs clause for $\mathcal{CL}_{exp}$, suppose $FrIds[\![(\text{abs} \ (I_{i=1}^n) \ E_{body})]\!]$ is replaced by the set of all variables in scope at that point. Is this a meaning-preserving change? What are the advantages and disadvantages of such a change?

c. In a FIL-based compiler, $\mathcal{CL}_{exp}$ must necessarily be performed after an assignment conversion pass. Could we perform it before a renaming pass? A globalization pass? A CPS-conversion pass? Explain.

Exercise 17.29 In the abs clause, the $\mathcal{CL}_{exp}$ function uses a **wrapping strategy** to wrap the body of the original abs in a let* that extracts and names each free variable value in the closure. An alternative **substitution strategy** is to replace each free reference in the original abs by a closure access. Here is a modified version of the clo.2 code component from Figure 17.33 that uses the substitution strategy:

```
(abs (clo.2 x) (@+ (@* (@mget 2 clo.2) x) (@mget 3 clo.2)))
```

Neither strategy is best in all situations. Describe situations in which the wrapping strategy is superior and in which the substitution strategy is superior. State all of the assumptions of your argument.

Exercise 17.30

a. Define a program-level closure conversion function $\mathcal{CL}_{prog}$ that expects a FIL_{cps} program:

$$\mathcal{CL}_{prog} : \text{Prog}_{cps} \to \text{Prog}_{cps}$$

In both the input and output programs, the final program argument I_{ktop} is expected to be the top-level unary continuation procedure. $\mathcal{CL}_{prog}$ must handle I_{ktop} specially so that it is applied directly to its single argument rather than via the closure application convention. It is not necessary to modify $\mathcal{CL}_{exp}$.

b. Show the result of using your $\mathcal{CL}_{prog}$ function to closure-convert the following program:

```
(fil (a b ktop)
  (let ((add-a (abs (x k)
                  (let ((t (@+ x a)))
                    (app k t)))))
    (if b (app add-a a ktop) (app ktop a))))
```

Exercise 17.31 Using anonymous inner classes, complete the following translation of the clotest example from Figure 17.34 into JAVA by filling in the hole in the following code with a single JAVA expression:

```
interface IntFun { public int app (int x); }

public class Linear {

  public static IntFun linear (final int a, final int b) {
    return new IntFun() { public int app (int x) {return (a*x)+b;} };
  }

  public static int example () {
    IntFun f = linear(4,5);
    IntFun g = linear(6,7);
    return f.app(8) + g.app(9);
  }
}
```

Figure 17.37 Using anonymous inner classes to express the `linear` example from page 1076 in JAVA.

```
interface IntFun1 { public int app (int x); }
interface IntFun2 { public IntFun3 app (int x, int y); }
interface IntFun3 { public IntFun1 app (int x, int y, int z); }

public class Clotest {

  public static int example () {
    IntFun2 clotest = □;
    IntFun3 p = clotest.app(4,5);
    IntFun1 q1 = p.app(6,7,8);
    IntFun1 q2 = p.app(9,10,11);
    return q1.app(12) + q2.app(13);
  }
}
```

17.10.2 Variations on Flat Closure Conversion

Now we consider several variations on flat closure conversion. We begin with an optimization to $\mathcal{CL}_{exp}$. Why does $\mathcal{CL}_{exp}$ transform an already closed `abs` into a closure tuple? This strategy simplifies the transformation by enabling all procedure applications to be transformed uniformly to "expect" such a tuple. But it is also possible to use nonuniform transformations on abstractions and applications as long as the correct behavior is maintained. Given a **control flow analysis** (see page 995) that indicates which procedures flow to which call sites (application expressions that use the procedures in their rator positions), we can do a better job via so-called **selective closure conversion** [WS94].

```
(let ((linear
        (abs (a b) {this closed abstraction is not transformed}
            (@mprod {this is the closure tuple for an open abstraction}
                (abs (clo.2 x)
                    (let* ((a (@mget 2 clo.2))
                           (b (@mget 3 clo.2)))
                       (@+ (@* a x) b)))
                    a b)))) {free vars of clo.2}
   (let ((f (app linear 4 5)) {this application is not transformed}
         (g (app linear 6 7))) {this application is not transformed}
      (@+ (app (@mget 1 f) f 8)
          (app (@mget 1 g) g 9)))))
```

Figure 17.38   Result of selective closure conversion in the `linear` example.

In this approach, originally closed procedures that flow only to call sites where only originally closed procedures are called are left unchanged by the closure conversion process, as are their call sites. This avoids unnecessary tuple creation and projection. The result of selective closure conversion for the `linear` example is presented in Figure 17.38 (compare Figure 17.33 on page 1078). Because the `linear` procedure is closed, its abstraction and the calls to `linear` are not transformed. But the procedure returned by invoking `linear` has free variables (a and b), and so must be converted to a closure tuple.

In selective closure conversion, a closed procedure p_{closed} cannot be optimized when it is called at the same call site s as an open procedure p_{open} in the original program. The call site must be transformed to expect for its rator a closure tuple for p_{open}, and so p_{closed} must also be represented as a closure tuple since it flows to the rator position of s. This representation constraint can similarly force other closed procedures that share call sites with p_{closed} to be converted, leading to a contagious phenomenon called **representation pollution** [DWM$^+$01].

In the following example, although f is closed, selective closure conversion must still convert f to a closure tuple because it flows to the same call site (app (if b f g) 3) as the open procedure g:

$$E_{polluted} = \text{(abs (b c)}$$
```
               (let ((f (abs (x) (@+ x 1)))
                     (g (let ((a (if b 4 5)))
                            (abs (y) (@+ (@* a y) c)))))
                  (@+ (app f 2)
                      (app (if b f g) 3))))
```

Representation pollution can sometimes be avoided by duplicating a closed procedure and using different representations for the two copies. For instance, if we split f in $E_{polluted}$ into two copies, then the copy that flows to the call site (app f 2) need not be converted to a tuple in the closure-converted code:

```
(abs (b c) {assume the outer abstraction need not be converted to a tuple}
  (let ((f1 (abs (x) (@+ x 1))) {this copy is not converted to a tuple}
        (f2 (@mprod (abs (clo.1 x) (@+ x 1))))
             {this copy is converted to a tuple}
        (g (let ((a (if b 4 5)))
             (@mprod (abs (clo.2 y) {this must be converted to a tuple}
                       (let ((a (@mget 1 clo.2))
                             (c (@mget 2 clo.2)))
                         (@+ (@* a y) c)))
                     a c))))
    (@+ (app f1 2) {this is an unconverted call site}
        (let ((clo.3 (if b f2 g))) {this is a converted call site}
          (app (@mget 1 clo.3) clo.3 3)))))
```

When closed and open procedures flow to the same call site (e.g., f2 and g above), we can force the closed procedure to have the same representation as the open one (i.e., a closure tuple). Another way to handle heterogeneous procedure representations is to affix tags to procedures to indicate their representation. Call sites where different representations flow together perform a dynamic dispatch on the tagged value. For example, using the oneof notation introduced in Section 10.2, we can use code to tag a closed procedure and closure to tag a closure tuple, as in the following conversion of $E_{polluted}$:

```
(abs (b c) {assume the outer abstraction need not be converted to a tuple}
  (let ((f1 (abs (x) (@+ x 1))) {this copy is not converted to a tuple}
        (f2 (one code (abs (x) (@+ x 1)))) {tagged as a closed procedure}
        (g (let ((a (if b 4 5)))
             (one closure {tagged as a closure}
               (@mprod (abs (clo y)
                         (let ((a (@mget 2 clo))
                               (c (@mget 3 clo)))
                           (@+ (@* a y) c)))
                       a c)))))
    (@+ (app f1 2) {this is an unconverted call site}
        (app-generic (if b f2 g) 3))))
```

Here, (app-generic E_{rator} $E_{i=1}^{n}$) is assumed to desugar to

```
(let ((I_i E_i)_{i=1}^{n}) ; I_{i=1}^{n} are fresh
  (tagcase E_rator I_rator
    (code (app I_rator I_{i=1}^{n}))
    (closure (app (@mget 1 I_rator) I_rator I_{i=1}^{n}))))
```

This tagging strategy is not necessarily a good idea. Analyzing and converting programs to handle tags is complex, and the overhead of tag manipulation can offset the gains made by reducing representation pollution [DWM$^+$01].

In an extreme version of the tagging strategy, all procedures that flow to a given call site are viewed as members of a sum-of-products data type. Each element in this data type is a tagged environment tuple. The tag indicates which abstraction created the procedure, and the environment tuple holds the free variable values of the procedure. A procedure call can then be converted to a dispatch on the environment tag that calls an associated closed procedure. Using this strategy on $E_{polluted}$ yields

```
(abs (b c)
  (let ((fcode (abs (x) (@+ x 1)))  {code for f}
        (fenv (one abs1 (@mprod)))  {tagged environment for f}
        (gcode (abs (y a c) (@+ (@* a y) c)))  {code for g}
        (genv (let ((a (if b 4 5)))
                (one abs2 (@mprod a c)))))  {tagged environment for g}
    (@+ (app fcode 2)
        (app-env (if b fenv genv) 3))))
```

where (app-env E_{env} E_{rand}) is an abbreviation for

```
(let (($I_{rand}$ $E_{rand}$))
  (tagcase $E_{env}$ $I_{env}$
    (abs1 (app fcode $I_{rand}$))
    (abs2 (app gcode $I_{rand}$ (@mget 1 $I_{env}$) (@mget 2 $I_{env}$)))))
```

The procedure call overhead in the dispatch can often be reduced by an inlining process that replaces some calls by appropriately rewritten copies of their bodies. E.g., app-env could be rewritten as

```
(let (($I_{rand}$ $E_1$))
  (tagcase $E_{env}$ $I_{env}$
    (abs1 (@+ $I_{rand}$ 1))
    (abs2 (@+ (@* (@mget 1 $I_{env}$) $I_{rand}$) (@mget 2 $I_{env}$)))))
```

This example uses only a single app-env procedure, but in the worst case a different environment application procedure might be needed at every call site.

This environment-tagging strategy is known as **defunctionalization** [Rey72] because it removes all higher-order functions from a program. Defunctionalization is an important closure conversion technique for languages (such as ADA and PASCAL) in which function pointers cannot be stored in data structures — a feature required in all the previous techniques we have studied. Some drawbacks of defunctionalization are that it requires the whole program (it cannot be performed on individual modules) and that environment application procedures like app-env might need to dispatch on all abstractions in the entire program. In practice, type and control flow information can be used to significantly narrow the set of abstractions that need to be considered at a given call site, making defunctionalization a surprisingly efficient approach to closure conversion [CJW00].

A closure need not carry with it the value of a free variable if that variable is available in all contexts where the closure is invoked. This observation is the key idea behind so-called **lightweight closure conversion** [WS94, SW97], which can decrease the number of free variables in a procedure by adding extra arguments to the procedure if those arguments are always dynamically available at all call sites for the procedure. In our example, the lightweight optimization is realized by rewriting the $E_{polluted}$ as follows before performing other closure conversion techniques:

```
(abs (b c)
  (let ((f (abs (x c) (@+ x 1))) {(3) By 2, need param c here.}
        (g (let ((a (if b 4 5)))
             (abs (y c) (@+ (@* a y) c))))) {(1) Add c as param.}
    (@+ (app f 2 c) {(4) By 3, must add c as an arg here, too.}
        (app (if b f g) 3 c)))) {(2) By 1, need arg c here.}
```

Since g's free variable c is available at the one site where g is called, we should be able to pass it as an argument at the site rather than storing it in the closure for g. But representation constraints also force us to add c as an argument to f, since f shares a call site with g. If f were called in some context outside the scope of c, this fact would invalidate the proposed optimization. This example only hints at the sophistication of the analysis required to perform lightweight closure conversion in practice.

Exercise 17.32 Consider the following FIL abstraction E_{abs}:

```
(abs (b)
  (let ((f (abs (x) (@+ x 1)))
        (g (abs (y) (@* y 2)))
        (h (abs (a) (abs (z) (@/ z a))))
        (p (abs (r) (app r 3))))
    (@+ (app (if b f g) 4)
        (@* (app p (app h 5)) (app p (app h 6))))))
```

a. Show the result of applying flat closure conversion to E_{abs}.

b. The transformation can be improved if we use selective closure conversion instead. Show the result of selective closure conversion on E_{abs}.

c. Suppose we replace (app h 6) by g in E_{abs} to give E'_{abs}. Then selective closure conversion on E'_{abs} does not yield an improvement over regular closure conversion on E'_{abs} Explain why.

d. Describe a simple meaning-preserving change to E'_{abs} after which selective closure conversion will be an improvement over regular closure conversion.

Exercise 17.33 Using the flat closure conversion techniques presented so far, translate the following FIL program into C, JAVA, and PASCAL. The program has the property that equality, remainder, division, and subtraction operations are performed only when p is called, not when q is called. Your translated programs should also have this property

```
(fil (n)
  (let* ((p (abs (w)
              (if (@= 0 w)
                  (abs (x) x)
                  (if (@= 0 (@% w 2))
                      (let ((p1 (p (@/ w 2))))
                        (abs (y) (@* 2 (app p1 y))))
                      (let ((p2 (p (@- w 1))))
                        (abs (z) (@+ 1 (app p2 z))))))))))
        (let ((q (app p n)))
          (@+ (app q 1) (app q n)))))
```

17.10.3   Linked Environments

Thus far we have assumed that all free variable values of a procedure are stored in a single flat environment or closure. This strategy minimizes the information carried in a particular closure. However, it is often the case that a free variable is referenced by several closures. Setting aside a slot for (a pointer to) the value of this variable in several closures/environments increases the space requirements of the program. For example, in the flat `clotest` example of Figure 17.34, closures p, q1, and q2 all contain a slot for the value of free variable c.

An alternative approach is to structure closures to enhance sharing and reduce copying. In a code/environment model, a high degree of sharing is achieved when every call site bundles the environment of the called procedure (the **parent environment**) together with the argument values to create the environment for the body of the called procedure. In this approach, each closed abstraction takes a single argument, its environment, and all variables are accessed through this environment. This is called a **linked environment** approach because environments are represented as chains of linked components called **frames**.

Figure 17.39 shows this approach for the `clotest` example. Note that the first slot of environment frames env1, env2, and env3 contains (a pointer to) its parent frame. Variables declared by the closest enclosing `abs` are accessed directly from the current frame, but variables declared in outer abstractions require one or more indirections through parent frames. For instance, in the body of the innermost `abs`, variable y, which is the first argument of the current frame, env3, is accessed via (@mget 2 env3); the variable r, which is the first argument one frame back, is accessed via (@mget 2 (@mget 1 env3)); and the variable c, which is the first argument two frames back, is accessed via (@mget 2 (@mget 1 (@mget 1 env3))).

```
(let ((clotest
       (@mprod
         (abs (env1) {env1 = ⟨env0, c, d⟩}
           (@mprod
             (abs (env2) {env2 = ⟨env1, r, s, t⟩}
               (@mprod
                 (abs (env3) {env3 = ⟨env2, y⟩}
                   (@+ (@/ (@* (@mget 2 (@mget 1 env3)) {get r}
                               (@mget 2 env3)) {get y}
                           (@mget 4 (@mget 1 env3))) {get t}
                       (@- (@mget 2 (@mget 1 env3)) {get r}
                           (@mget 2 (@mget 1 (@mget 1 env3)))))))) {get c}
                 env2))
             env1))
         (@mprod)))) {This is env0 = the empty environment}
      (let ((p (app (@mget 1 clotest) (@mprod (@mget 2 clotest) 4 5))))
        (let ((q1 (app (@mget 1 p) (@mprod (@mget 2 p) 6 7 8)))
              (q2 (app (@mget 1 p) (@mprod (@mget 2 p) 9 10 11))))
          (@+ (app (@mget 1 q1) (@mprod (@mget 2 q1) 12))
              (app (@mget 1 q2) (@mprod (@mget 2 q2) 13)))))))
```

Figure 17.39 A version of the clotest example with linked environments.

In general, each variable has a **lexical address** $\langle back, over \rangle$, where $back$ indicates how many frames back the variable is located and $over$ indicates its position in the resulting frame. A variable with lexical address $\langle b, o \rangle$[9] is translated to (@mget o (@mget^b 1 e)), where e is the current lexical environment frame and (@mget^b 1 e) stands for the b-fold composition of the first projection starting with e. Traditional compilers often use such lexical addresses to locate variables on a stack, where so-called **static links** are used to model chains of frames stored on the stack. Linked environments are also commonly used in interpreters for block-structured languages. For example, the environment model interpreter in [ASS96] represents procedures as closures whose environments are linked frames.

Figure 17.40 depicts the shared environment structure in the clotest example with linked environments. Note how the environment of p is shared as the parent environment of q1's environment and q2's environment. In contrast with the flat environment case, p, q1, and q2 all share the same slot holding c, so less slot space is needed for c. Another advantage of sharing is that the linked environment approach to closure conversion can support set! directly without the need for assignment conversion (see Exercise 17.35).

---

[9]Assume that $back$ indices b start at 0 and $over$ indices o start at 2.

However, there are several downsides to linked environments. First, variable access is slower than for flat closures because of the indirections through parent environment links. Second, environment slots hold values (such as d and s) that are never referenced, so space is wasted on these slots. A final subtle point is that shared slots can hold onto values longer than they are actually needed by a program, leading to space leaks in the storage manager (see Section 18.1). Some of these points and some alternative linked strategies are explored in the exercises.

Exercise 17.34

a. In the context of closure-converting the following FIL expression, discuss the issues involved in converting let expressions in the linked environment approach described above:

```
(abs (a)
  (let ((b (@+ a 1))
        (c (@* a a)))
    (let ((f (abs (d) (@+ a (@* c d)))))
      (@mprod (app f b) (app f c)))))
```

let-bound names (such as b and f) that do not appear as the free variables of an abstraction should not be put in environment frames.

b. Formally define a closure conversion transformation on FIL expressions that implements the linked environment approach. Do not worry about preserving the CPS form of input programs.

Exercise 17.35 Use the linked environment approach to closure-convert the following FIL+{set!} expression. A set! in the input expression should be converted to an mset! on an environment tuple in the converted expression.

```
(let ((r (abs (x)
           (abs (y)
             (let ((z (@+ x y)))
               (let ((_ (set! x z)))
                 z))))))
  (let ((s1 (app r 1))
        (s2 (app r 2)))
    (@mprod (app s1 3) (app s2 4) (app s1 5))))
```

Exercise 17.36 The linked environment approach illustrated by the code in Figure 17.39 constructs a mutable tuple representing an environment frame at every call site. An alternative approach, which we shall call the **code/linked-env** representation, is to construct new linked environment frames only when building the closure tuple. This way, the procedure calling convention looks exactly like that for code/environment pairs; the only difference from the code/environment approach studied earlier is that the environments are not flat but are composed of linked frames.

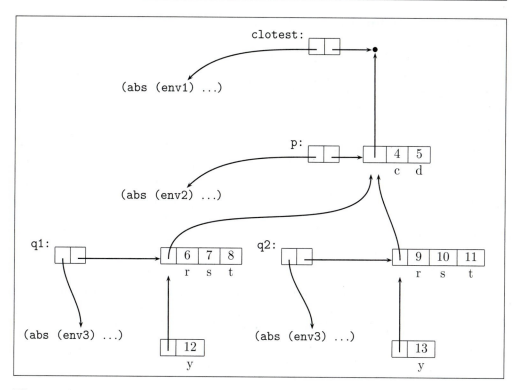

Figure 17.40 Depiction of the links in the linked `clotest` example.

a. Show the code/linked-env approach for the `clotest` example by fleshing out the hole in the following code:

```
(let ((clotest □))
  (let ((p (app (@mget 1 clotest) (@mget 2 clotest) 4 5)))
    (let ((q1 (app (@mget 1 p) (@mget 2 p) 6 7 8))
          (q2 (app (@mget 1 p) (@mget 2 p) 9 10 11)))
      (@+ (app (@mget 1 q1) (@mget 2 q1) 12)
          (app (@mget 1 q2) (@mget 2 q2) 13)))))
```

b. Compare the code/linked-env approach with the linked environment approach discussed in the text on the following points: number of tuples created, efficiency of accessing variables, omitting variables from environment frames, converting `let` expressions, and handling `set!`.

c. Formally define a closure conversion transformation on FIL expressions that implements the code/linked-env strategy. Do not worry about preserving the CPS form of input programs.

17.11   Transformation 9: Lifting

Programmers nest procedures when an inner procedure needs to use variables that are declared in an outer procedure. The free variables in such an inner procedure are bound by the outer procedure. We have seen that closure conversion eliminates free variables in every procedure. However, because it leaves abstractions in place, it does not eliminate procedure nesting.

A procedure is **global** when it is declared at **top level** — i.e., in the outermost scope of a program. **Lifting** (also called **lambda lifting**[10]) is the process of eliminating procedure nesting by collecting all procedure abstractions and declaring them as global procedures. All procedure abstractions must be closed before lifting is performed — otherwise, lifting them to top level would break the fundamental connection between free variable references and their associated declarations. Once all of the procedures in a program are declared at top level, each one can be compiled into straight-line code (modulo branches for any `if` expressions in its body) and given a global name.[11] In the analogy with assembly code, such a name corresponds to an assembly code label for the first instruction in the subroutine corresponding to the procedure.

In the TORTOISE compiler, the result of the lifting phase is a program in FIL_{lift} (Figure 17.41), a variant of the FIL_{cps} language. The key difference between FIL_{lift} and FIL_{cps} is that abstractions may appear only at the top level of a program in new declaration constructs having the form (`def` S AB), where AB is an abstraction and S is special kind of identifier called a **subroutine name**. Each subroutine name `subr0`, `subr1`, `subr2`, ... is the concatenation of the name `subr` and a natural number literal. For $n \in Nat$, we use both subr_n and $\text{subr} \bowtie n$ to stand for the result of concatenating the name `subr` with the digits of the numeral for n. E.g., $\text{subr}_{17} = \text{subr} \bowtie 17 = \text{subr17}$. The definition of Prog_{lift} requires that `subr0` be used for the first subroutine, `subr1` be used for the second subroutine, etc. This requirement makes it possible to refer to procedures by number rather than by name. Every subroutine name is a legal identifier and so may be used as a variable reference elsewhere in a program. As in

---

[10]In the literature on compiling functional programming languages (e.g., [Joh85, Pey87]), "lambda lifting" often refers to a process that not only lifts all functions to top level, but also serves as a closure conversion transformation in which closures are represented as partially applied curried functions.

[11]It is possible to compile a procedure with nested internal procedures directly to assembly code by placing unconditional branch instructions around the code for the internal procedures. Avoiding unnecessary unconditional branches is important for modern processors with instruction caches, instruction prefetching, and pipelined architectures.

$$P \in \text{Prog}_{lift} ::= (\texttt{fil} \ (I^*_{formal}) \ E_{body} \ (\texttt{def} \ \texttt{subr}_i \ AB_i)^n_{i=0})$$

$$AB \in \text{Abstraction}_{lift} ::= (\texttt{abs} \ (I^*_{formal}) \ E_{body})$$

$$E \in \text{Exp}_{lift} ::= (\texttt{app} \ I_{rator} \ V^*_{rand}) \ | \ (\texttt{if} \ V_{test} \ E_{then} \ E_{else})$$
$$| \ (\texttt{let} \ ((I_{name} \ LE_{defn})) \ E_{body}) \ | \ (\texttt{error} \ Y_{message})$$

$$V \in \text{ValueExp}_{lift} ::= L \ | \ I$$

$$LE \in \text{LetableExp}_{lift} ::= L \ | \ (\texttt{prim} \ O_{primop} \ V^*_{arg})$$

$$L \in \text{Lit} = \textit{as in full FIL}$$

$$Y \in \text{SymLit} = \textit{as in full FIL}$$

$$O \in \text{Primop} = \textit{as in full FIL}$$

$$\text{Keyword}_{lift} = \{\texttt{abs}, \texttt{app}, \texttt{def}, \texttt{error}, \texttt{fil}, \texttt{if}, \texttt{let}, \texttt{let*}, \texttt{prim}, \texttt{sym}\}$$

$$I \in \text{Ident}_{lift} = \text{SymLit} - (\{Y \mid Y \text{ begins with @}\} \cup \text{Keyword}_{lift})$$

$$NT \in \text{NatLit} = \{0, 1, 2, \ldots\}$$

$$S \in \text{Subr} = \textit{identifiers of the form } \texttt{subr} \bowtie n \ ; \ \texttt{subr}_n \textit{ is shorthand for } \texttt{subr} \bowtie n$$
$$; \textit{ For } n \in Nat, \textit{ the notation } I \bowtie n \textit{ stands for the identifier that}$$
$$; \textit{ results from concatenating the characters of the name } I \textit{ with}$$
$$; \textit{ the digit characters of the numeral in NatLit that denotes } n.$$

Figure 17.41 Grammar for FIL_{lift}, the result of the TORTOISE lifting stage.

other FL-like languages we have studied, the names declared by `def` have global scope — they may be referenced in all expressions in the program, including the bodies of all `def` declarations.

The TORTOISE lifting transformation $\mathcal{LI}_{prog}$ has the following specification:

Preconditions: The input to $\mathcal{LI}_{prog}$ is a valid kernel FIL_{cps} program in which every abstraction is closed.

Postconditions: The output of $\mathcal{LI}_{prog}$ is a program in which every abstraction is globally defined via `def` at the top level of a program, as specified in the FIL_{lift} grammar in Figure 17.41. The free identifiers in each abstraction must be a subset of the subroutine names bound by `def`s in the program.

Although abstractions are required to be closed before lifting, abstractions after lifting are not necessarily closed. This is because each nested abstraction is replaced by a `def`-bound subroutine name that is necessarily free in the immediately enclosing abstraction. But the `def`-bound subroutine names are the only names that can be free in the abstractions that result from the lifting transformation.

Here is a sketch of the algorithm employed by $\mathcal{LI}_{prog}$ for a program containing n abstractions:

1. Associate with each abstraction AB_i $(0 \leq i \leq n)$ in the program the subroutine name $\mathtt{subr}_i$.

2. Replace the abstraction AB_i in the program by a reference to its associated name, $\mathtt{subr}_i$.

3. Return a program of the form

$$(\mathtt{fil}\ (I^*_{fml})\ E'_{body}\ (\mathtt{def\ subr}_0\ AB'_0)\ \ldots\ (\mathtt{def\ subr}_n\ AB'_n))$$

where $AB'_0, \ldots, AB'_n$ are the transformed versions of all the abstractions AB_0, ..., AB_n in the original program, and E'_{body} is the transformed body.

For example, Figure 17.42 shows the $\mathtt{revmap}$ example after lambda lifting. $\mathtt{subr0}$ is the code for the $\mathtt{revmap}$ procedure, $\mathtt{subr1}$ is the code for the $\mathtt{loop}$ procedure, $\mathtt{subr2}$ is the code for the continuation of the call to $\mathtt{f}$ within the body of the $\mathtt{loop}$ procedure, and $\mathtt{subr3}$ is the code for the greater-than-b procedure. The example shows how replacing each abstraction with its unique subroutine name can introduce free variables into otherwise closed abstractions. For instance, the body of the abstraction named $\mathtt{subr0}$ contains a reference to $\mathtt{subr1}$ and the body of the abstraction named $\mathtt{subr1}$ contains a reference to $\mathtt{subr2}$.

In the $\mathtt{revmap}$ example, $\mathtt{code.62}$ always denotes the subroutine named $\mathtt{subr0}$, $\mathtt{code.46}$ and $\mathtt{code.54}$ always denote $\mathtt{subr1}$, $\mathtt{code.58}$ always denotes $\mathtt{subr2}$, and $\mathtt{code.50}$ always denotes $\mathtt{subr3}$. In all these cases, it would be safe to replace these code references (and eliminate their associated $(\mathtt{mget\ 1})$ operations) by the subroutine names. In assembly code, this optimization corresponds to replacing an indirect jump to a subroutine by a direct jump. It is possible for the compiler to perform this optimization automatically, but a sophisticated analysis that tracks control-flow and store-effect information would be required to determine when the optimization can be safely applied.

Exercise 17.37 Formally define the $\mathcal{LI}_{prog}$ function sketched above. You will also need to define appropriate functions on other FIL_{cps} syntactic domains. For simplicity, you may assume that fresh subroutine names are generated in the order $\mathtt{subr0}$, $\mathtt{subr1}$, ...; i.e., you need not thread a subroutine name counter through your functions.

```
(fil (a.0 b.1 ktop.9)
  (let* ((abs.10 (@mprod subr0))
         (abs.11 (@mprod subr3 b.1))
         (t.14 (@* a.0 7))
         (t.15 (@null))
         (t.13 (@cons t.14 t.15))
         (t.12 (@cons a.0 t.13))
         (code.62 (@mget 1 abs.10)))
    (app code.62 abs.10 abs.11 t.12 ktop.9))
  (def subr0 (abs (clo.56 f.3 elts.4 k.20)
                  (let* ((t.22 (@null))
                         (t.21 (@mprod t.22))
                         (t.23 (@mprod #u))
                         (abs.25 (@mprod subr1 t.21 t.23 f.3))
                         (t.24 (@mset! 1 t.23 abs.25))
                         (t.26 (@mget 1 t.23))
                         (code.54 (@mget 1 t.26)))
                    (app code.54 t.26 elts.4 k.20))))
  (def subr1 (abs (clo.52 xs.7 k.29)
                  (let* ((t.21 (@mget 2 clo.52))
                         (t.23 (@mget 3 clo.52))
                         (f.3 (@mget 4 clo.52))
                         (t.31 (@null? xs.7)))
                    (if t.31
                        (let* ((t.42 (@mget 1 t.21))
                               (code.44 (@mget 1 k.29)))
                          (app code.44 k.29 t.42))
                        (let* ((t.34 (@car xs.7))
                               (k.41 (@mprod subr2 t.21 t.23 xs.7 k.29))
                               (code.50 (@mget 1 f.3)))
                          (app code.50 f.3 t.34 k.41))))))
  (def subr2 (abs (clo.48 t.35)
                  (let* ((t.21 (@mget 2 clo.48))
                         (t.23 (@mget 3 clo.48))
                         (xs.7 (@mget 4 clo.48))
                         (k.29 (@mget 5 clo.48))
                         (t.36 (@mget 1 t.21))
                         (t.33 (@cons t.35 t.36))
                         (t.32 (@mset! 1 t.21 t.33))
                         (t.37 (@mget 1 t.23))
                         (t.38 (@cdr xs.7))
                         (code.46 (@mget 1 t.37)))
                    (app code.46 t.37 t.38 k.29))))
  (def subr3 (abs (clo.60 x.8 k.18)
                  (let* ((b.1 (@mget 2 clo.60))
                         (t.19 (@> x.8 b.1))
                         (code.58 (@mget 1 k.18)))
                    (app code.58 k.18 t.19)))))
```

Figure 17.42   revmap program after lambda lifting.

17.12   Transformation 10: Register Allocation

The goal of the TORTOISE compiler is to translate high-level programs to code that can be executed on a register machine. A register machine provides two kinds of storage locations for values: a small number of registers with fast access times and a large number of memory locations with slow access times. It typically has instructions for loading values into registers from memory, storing values from registers to memory, and performing operations whose arguments and results are in registers.

The code generated by the Lifting stage of the TORTOISE compiler resembles assembly code for a register machine except for its handling of variable names. Intuitively, each identifier in a FIL_{lift} program that is not a subroutine name can be viewed as an abstract register. Because fresh identifiers are introduced by many transformations, there is no bound on the number of abstract registers that a program may use. But any register machine executing the program employs a relatively small number of actual registers. The process of mapping the abstract registers of a program to the actual registers of a register machine is known as **register allocation**. Register allocation makes the storage locations represented by variable names explicit. TORTOISE also uses registers to pass procedure arguments, so register allocation makes the argument-passing mechanism explicit.

We will study a simple approach to register allocation in the context of transforming FIL_{lift} to FIL_{reg}, the target language of the TORTOISE compiler. In Section 17.12.1, we describe FIL_{reg} and explain how to view it as the instruction set for a register machine. We then describe how to convert FIL_{lift} to FIL_{reg} in Sections 17.12.2–17.12.5.

17.12.1   The FIL_{reg} Language

FIL_{reg} (Figure 17.43) is a language that is designed to be viewed in two very different ways:

1. FIL_{reg} is basically a restricted subset of FIL_{lift}. A FIL_{reg} program can be executed like any other FIL_{lift} program.

2. FIL_{reg} is the instruction set for a simple register machine. This machine, FRM, is discussed in Section 18.2.

Remarkably, FIL_{reg} programs have the same behavior whether we view them as FIL_{lift} programs or as register machine programs. This section summarizes the features of the syntax of FIL$_{reg}$ and describes how to view FIL$_{reg}$ programs and expressions in terms of the underlying register machine operations they are intended to represent. Later (Section 18.2) we will sketch how FIL$_{reg}$ programs are executed on the FRM register machine. (A full description of FRM program execution can be found in the Web Supplement.)

The general identifiers of FIL$_{lift}$ have been replaced by a restricted domain Ident$_{reg}$ containing only (1) subroutine names S (as in FIL$_{lift}$) and (2) register names R (new in FIL$_{reg}$). Each register name r0, r1, r2, ... is the concatenation of the name r and a numeral for a natural number between 0 and n_{max}, where $n_{max} + 1$ is the number n_{reg} of registers in the machine. For $n \in Nat$, we use $\mathbf{r}_n$ to stand for r⋈n.

In FIL$_{reg}$, the formal parameter sequences of programs and abstractions and the operand sequences of applications must be prefixes RS of the register sequence $[\mathbf{r0}, \mathbf{r1}, \mathbf{r2}, \ldots, \mathbf{r}_{n_{max}}]$. That is, abstractions and applications must have the following form:

Number of params/rands	Abstraction	Application
0	(abs () E)	(app I)
1	(abs (r0) E)	(app I r0)
2	(abs (r0 r1) E)	(app I r0 r1)
3	(abs (r0 r1 r2) E)	(app I r0 r1 r2)
$\vdots$	$\vdots$	$\vdots$

These restricted forms represent a decision to pass program and procedure arguments in specific registers: the first argument is always passed in register r0, the second argument is always passed in register r1, etc. An abstraction definition (def S (abs (RS) E)) represents the entry point to a subroutine; an application (app S RS) represents a direct jump to the subroutine labeled S; and an application of the form (app R RS) is an indirect jump to the subroutine whose label (address) is stored in register R. From the register machine's point of view, the formal parameter names and argument names are superfluous: The arguments are in the registers and both the caller and the callee know how many arguments there are. The names appear in the syntax so that we can continue to interpret our code from the FIL perspective as well.

In FIL$_{reg}$, all if tests must be register names. (if R E_{then} E_{else}) is thus an instruction that tests the content of register R and continues with the instructions in E_{then} if R contains true and with the instructions in E_{else} if R contains false.

The FIL$_{reg}$ expression (error Y_{msg}) terminates program execution in an error state that includes the error message Y_{msg}. The new (halt NT R) expression terminates program execution with a return code specified by NT; for some return codes, the result of the program is the value in register R. This expression is used in the register-machine implementation of FIL_{reg} (see the Web Supplement for details).

The FIL_{reg} expression (let ((R_{dst} LE)) E) loads the value of LE into the destination register R_{dst} and then proceeds with the instructions in E. The nature of this load depends on the structure of the letable expression LE:

- The case where LE is a literal corresponds to loading the literal value into R_{dst}.

- The case where LE is a primitive application (prim O_{op} R^*_{src}) corresponds to code that performs an operation on the contents of the source registers R^*_{src} and stores the result in the destination register R_{dst}. Note that the operand registers of primitive applications, unlike those of procedure applications, needn't be a specific sequence, because register machines let you specify arbitrary registers for primitive operations.

- The case where LE is an application (prim copy R_{src}) of the new primitive operator copy, which acts as an identity, represents code that copies the content of register R_{src} to the register R_{dst}. This cannot be accomplished by just having a register R_{src} as the letable expression, because the [copy-prop] rule will always eliminate a let expression of the form (let ((R_1 R_2)) E) by substituting R_2 for R_1 in E.

- The case where LE is the new letable expression (addr S) represents a load of a subroutine address into R_{dst}. This cannot be accomplished by just using a subroutine name S as the letable expression, because the [copy-prop] rule will always eliminate a let expression of the form (let ((R S)) E) by substituting S for R in E. This case is slightly different from the copy case above: addr, which acts like the identity on subroutine names, cannot be a primitive operator, because all prim operands must be register names, and S is not a register name.

Registers are used to store values that are needed later in the computation. Sometimes the number of values needed by the rest of the computation exceeds the number of registers. In this case, the extra values must be stored in the register machine's memory, a process known as **spilling**. The spget and spset! primitives are used for spilling. They are explained in Section 17.12.5.

To model the simplicity of register operations and facilitate spilling, all FIL_{reg} primitive operators take zero, one, or two arguments. The one primitive in pre-

Kernel Grammar

$P \in \text{Prog}_{reg} ::= (\text{fil } (RS_{formals}) \ E_{body} \ (\text{def subr}_i \ AB_i)_{i=0}^{n})$

$AB \in \text{Abstraction}_{reg} ::= (\text{abs } (RS_{formals}) \ E_{body})$

$E \in \text{Exp}_{reg} ::= (\text{app } I_{rator} \ RS_{rands}) \mid (\text{if } R_{test} \ E_{then} \ E_{else})$
$\phantom{E \in \text{Exp}_{reg} ::=} \mid (\text{let } ((R_{dst} \ LE_{defn})) \ E_{body})$
$\phantom{E \in \text{Exp}_{reg} ::=} \mid (\text{error } Y_{message}) \mid (\text{halt } NT_{returnCode} \ R_{result})$

$I \in \text{Ident}_{reg} ::= R \mid S$

$LE \in \text{LetableExp}_{reg} ::= L \mid (\text{addr } S) \mid (\text{prim } O_{primop} \ R_{src}^{*})$

$L \in \text{Lit} = \text{as in full FIL}$

$Y \in \text{SymLit} = \text{as in full FIL}$

$O \in \text{Primop}_{reg} ::= \ldots \text{FIL } \textit{primops except } \texttt{mprod} \ldots$
$\phantom{O \in \text{Primop}_{reg} ::=} \mid \texttt{copy} \qquad\qquad\qquad\qquad\quad \textit{; register copy}$
$\phantom{O \in \text{Primop}_{reg} ::=} \mid (\texttt{mnew } NT) \qquad\qquad\qquad \textit{; mutable tuple allocation}$
$\phantom{O \in \text{Primop}_{reg} ::=} \mid (\texttt{spget } NT) \mid (\texttt{spset! } NT) \quad \textit{; spill get and set}$

$NT \in \text{NatLit} = \{0, 1, 2, \ldots\}$

$R \in \text{Reg} = \{\texttt{r0}, \texttt{r1}, \ldots, \texttt{r}_{n_{max}}\} \ ; \ \texttt{r}_n \ \textit{is shorthand for } \texttt{r}{\bowtie}n$

$RS \in \text{RegSeq} = \textit{any prefix of } [\texttt{r0}, \texttt{r1}, \ldots, \texttt{r}_{n_{max}}] \ ; \ n_{max} + 1 = n_{reg}$

$S \in \text{Subr} = \textit{identifiers of the form } \texttt{subr}{\bowtie}n \ ; \ \texttt{subr}_n \ \textit{is shorthand for } \texttt{subr}{\bowtie}n$
$\phantom{S \in \text{Subr} =} \textit{; For } n \in \text{Nat}, \textit{ the notation } I{\bowtie}n \textit{ stands for the identifier that}$
$\phantom{S \in \text{Subr} =} \textit{; results from concatenating the characters of the name } I \textit{ with}$
$\phantom{S \in \text{Subr} =} \textit{; the digit characters of the numeral in NatLit that denotes } n.$

New Syntactic Sugar

$(\texttt{@mnew } NT) \rightsquigarrow_{ds} (\texttt{prim } (\texttt{mnew } NT))$

$(\texttt{@spget } NT) \rightsquigarrow_{ds} (\texttt{prim } (\texttt{spget } NT))$

$(\texttt{@spset! } NT \ R) \rightsquigarrow_{ds} (\texttt{prim } (\texttt{spset! } NT) \ R)$

Figure 17.43 Grammar for FIL$_{reg}$, the result of the register allocation transformation and the language of FRM, the virtual register machine discussed in Section 18.2.

vious FIL dialects that took an arbitrary number of arguments — `mprod` — is replaced by a combination of the new primitive operator (`mnew` NT) (which creates a mutable tuple with $\mathcal{N}[\![NT]\!]$ slots) and a sequence of `mset!` operations for filling the slots. For example, the FIL$_{lift}$ expression

$$(\texttt{let } ((I_{mprod} \ (\texttt{@mprod } S \ I_{arg1} \ 17))) \ E_{body})$$

can be expressed in FIL$_{reg}$ as follows (where R_{temp}, R_{mprod}, and R_{arg1} are three distinct registers):

```
(let* ((R_mprod (@mnew 3))
       (R_temp (addr S))
       (R_temp (@mset! 1 R_mprod R_temp))
       (R_temp (@mset! 2 R_mprod R_arg1)) {assume R_arg1 corresponds to I_arg1}
       (R_temp 17)
       (R_temp (@mset! 3 R_mprod R_temp)))
  E'_body) {the translation of E_body, in which R_mprod corresponds to I_mprod}
```

Because the operands of a primitive application must be register names, the integer literal 17 and the subroutine label (addr S) must be stored in temporary registers before they can be used in applications of the primitive operator mset!.

17.12.2   A Register Allocation Algorithm

The TORTOISE register allocation transformation $\mathcal{RA}_{prog}$ has the following specification:

> **Preconditions:** The input to $\mathcal{RA}_{prog}$ is a valid kernel FIL$_{lift}$ program in which the only free identifiers of any abstraction are subroutine names.
>
> **Postconditions:** The output of $\mathcal{RA}_{prog}$ is a valid kernel FIL$_{reg}$ program in which the only free identifiers of any abstraction are subroutine names.

Register allocation is largely the process of renaming fil-bound, abs-bound, and let-bound identifiers in FIL$_{lift}$ to the register names r0, ... , r$_{n_{max}}$ in FIL$_{reg}$. In TORTOISE, register allocation must also ensure that the resulting program respects the other syntactic restrictions of FIL$_{reg}$ by naming literals and subroutine names and expanding each mprod into mnew followed by a sequence of mset!s.

Register allocation has been studied intensively, and it is the subject of many elegant and efficient algorithms. (The notes at the end of this chapter provide some references.) TORTOISE uses a simple register allocation algorithm that is not particularly efficient but is easy to describe. The algorithm has three phases:

1. The **expansion phase** takes a FIL$_{lift}$ program, ensures that all literals and subroutine names are bound to identifiers in a let before they are used, and converts instances of mprod into sequences of mnew and mset!s. The output is in a language called FIL$_{regId}$, a version of FIL$_{reg}$ in which $R \in$ Reg is redefined to be any nonsubroutine identifier and $RS \in$ RegSeq is redefined to be any sequence of nonsubroutine identifiers.

Domains

Prog_{lift} = *as defined in Figure 17.41*

Prog_{regId} = *programs in* FIL_{regId}, *a version of* FIL_{reg} *in which nonsubroutine identifiers are used in place of registers*

$\text{Prog}_{reg\infty}$ = *programs in* $\text{FIL}_{reg\infty}$, *a version of* FIL_{reg} *supporting an unbounded number of registers*

Prog_{reg} = *as defined in Figure 17.43*

Register Allocation Functions

$\mathcal{EX}_{prog} : \text{Prog}_{lift} \to \text{Prog}_{regId}$; *described in Section 17.12.3*

$\mathcal{RC}_{prog} : \text{Prog}_{regId} \to \text{Prog}_{reg\infty}$; *described in Section 17.12.4*

$\mathcal{SP}_{prog} : \text{Prog}_{reg\infty} \to \text{Prog}_{reg}$; *described in Section 17.12.5*

$\mathcal{RA}_{prog} : \text{Prog}_{lift} \to \text{Prog}_{reg}$

$\mathcal{RA}_{prog}[\![P]\!] = \mathcal{SP}_{prog}[\![\mathcal{RC}_{prog}[\![\mathcal{EX}_{prog}[\![P]\!]]\!]]\!]$

Figure 17.44 The TORTOISE register allocation transformation $\mathcal{RA}_{prog}$ is the composition of the expansion transformation $\mathcal{EX}_{prog}$, the register conversion transformation $\mathcal{RC}_{prog}$, and the spilling transformation $\mathcal{SP}_{prog}$.

2. The **register conversion phase** takes a FIL_{regId} program, renames all nonsubroutine identifiers to be register names, and ensures that all formal parameter sequences and operand sequences of procedure applications are prefixes of $[\text{r0}, \text{r1}, \text{r2}, \ldots]$. It introduces appropriate register moves (via the `copy` primitive) to satisfy this requirement. The output is in a language called $\text{FIL}_{reg\infty}$, a version of FIL_{reg} in which $R \in \text{Reg}$ is redefined to include an unbounded number of register names of the form r_n. This phase greedily reuses register names in an attempt to reduce the number of registers needed by the program, but that number may still exceed the fixed number n_{reg} of registers provided by the register machine.

3. The **spilling phase** guarantees that only n_{reg} registers are used in the final code by moving the contents of some registers to memory if necessary.

Figure 17.44 shows how these three phases are composed to implement the register allocation function $\mathcal{RA}_{prog}$. In the following three sections, we sketch each of these phases by providing an English description of how they work along with some examples. The formal details of each phase are fleshed out in the Web Supplement.

17.12.3   The Expansion Phase

The expansion phase of the TORTOISE register allocator converts FIL_{lift} programs to FIL_{regId} programs by performing two transformations:

1. It introduces `let`-bound names for all literals and subroutine names that appear in `if` tests and in the operands of procedure and primitive applications.

2. It expands each primitive application of `mprod` into a primitive application of `mnew` to allocate the mutable tuple followed by a sequence of primitive applications of `mset!` to fill the slots of the new tuple.

   Figure 17.45 illustrates the expansion phase on the body of the `revmap` program after the Lifting stage. Both `mprod`s in the input are expanded to the `mnew`/`mset!` idiom, and new `let`s are introduced to name the literals and subroutine names in the input.

17.12.4   The Register Conversion Phase

The register conversion phase of the TORTOISE register allocator converts FIL_{regId} programs to $\text{FIL}_{reg\infty}$ programs by performing three transformations:

1. It converts every formal parameter sequence $I_{i=0}^{n}$ of the program or its abstractions to an ordered register sequence $\mathbf{r}_{i=0}^{n}$.

2. It renames every `let`-bound name to a register name.

3. It guarantees that the operand sequence $I_{i=0}^{n}$ of every `app` expression is an ordered register sequence $\mathbf{r}_{i=0}^{n}$.

   We will illustrate each of these transformations in the context of register-converting the following abstraction:

```
AB₀ = (abs (clo.7 x.8 k.9)
          (let* ((t.10 (@mget 2 clo.7))
                 (t.11 (@mget 3 clo.7))
                 (t.12 (@* x.8 x.8))
                 (t.13 (@* t.11 t.12))
                 (t.14 (@+ x.8 t.12))
                 (code.15 (@mget 1 t.10)))
            (app code.15 t.10 t.14 t.13 t.11 k.9)))
```

The first transformation renames the formal parameters `clo.7`, `x.8`, and `k.9` to `r0`, `r1`, and `r2`, respectively:

```
Body of Lifted revmap Before Expansion Phase
  (let* ((abs.10 (@mprod subr0))
         (abs.11 (@mprod subr3 b.1))
         (t.14 (@* a.0 7))
         (t.15 (@null))
         (t.13 (@cons t.14 t.15))
         (t.12 (@cons a.0 t.13))
         (code.62 (@mget 1 abs.10)))
    (app code.62 abs.10 abs.11 t.12 ktop.9))
Body of revmap After Expansion Phase
  (let* ((abs.10 (@mnew 1))
         (t.79 (addr subr0))
         (t.78 (@mset! 1 abs.10 t.79))
         (abs.11 (@mnew 2))
         (t.82 (addr subr3))
         (t.80 (@mset! 1 abs.11 t.82))
         (t.81 (@mset! 2 abs.11 b.1))
         (t.83 7)
         (t.14 (@* a.0 t.83))
         (t.15 (@null))
         (t.13 (@cons t.14 t.15))
         (t.12 (@cons a.0 t.13))
         (code.62 (@mget 1 abs.10)))
    (app code.62 abs.10 abs.11 t.12 ktop.9))
```

Figure 17.45 Illustration of the expansion phase on the body of the lifted revmap program.

$$AB_1 = \text{(abs (r0 r1 r2)}$$
```
             (let* ((t.10 (@mget 2 r0))
                    (t.11 (@mget 3 r0))
                    (t.12 (@* r1 r1))
                    (t.13 (@* t.11 t.12))
                    (t.14 (@+ r1 t.12))
                    (code.15 (@mget 1 t.10)))
               (app code.15 t.10 t.14 t.13 t.11 r2)))
```

We assume that there are enough registers to handle the longest formal parameter sequence. The later spilling phase will handle the case where this assumption is false.

The second transformation renames each identifier I declared in a let expression to a register name R that does not appear free in the body of the let expression. Although it would be safe to use any nonfree register name, the algorithm chooses the "least" one according to the order $r_i \leq r_j$ if and only if $i \leq j$. This greedy strategy attempts to reduce register usage by reusing low-numbered registers whose values are no longer needed. For example, renaming let-bound identifiers transforms AB_1 to

$AB_2 =$
```
(abs (r0 r1 r2)
   (let* ((r3 (@mget 2 r0))    {r0,r1,r2 used later, so use r3 for t.10}
          (r0 (@mget 3 r0))    {r0=clo.7 not used later, so reuse r0 for t.11}
          (r4 (@* r1 r1))      {r0-r3 used later, so use r4 for t.12}
          (r5 (@* r0 r4))      {r0-r4 used later, so use r5 for t.13}
          (r1 (@+ r1 r4))      {r1=x.8 not used later, so reuse r1 for t.14}
          (r4 (@mget 1 r3)))   {r4=t.12 not used later, so reuse r4 for code.15}
      (app r4 r3 r1 r5 r0 r2)))
```

Note how r0, r1 and r4 are reused when they are no longer mentioned in the rest of the computation.

After the first two transformations are performed, the program satisfies the grammar of $\text{FIL}_{reg\infty}$ *except* for app expressions (app I_{rator} $R_{i=0}^{n-1}$). Although the first two transformations guarantee that all app operands are registers, they are not necessarily the sequence $r_{i=0}^{n-1}$ required by the $\text{FIL}_{reg\infty}$ grammar. This form can be achieved by a **register shuffling** process that uses a sequence of copy applications to move the contents of the registers in the source operand sequence $R_{i=0}^{n-1}$ to the corresponding registers in the destination operand sequence $r_{i=0}^{n-1}$. For example, (app subr5 r2 r0) can be transformed to

```
(let* ((r1 (@copy r0))
       (r0 (@copy r2)))
  (app subr5 r0 r1))
```

A simple but very inefficient implementation of shuffling would first copy the n operands to n fresh registers not mentioned in $\left(\bigcup_{i=0}^{n-1}\{r_i\}\right) \cup \left(\bigcup_{i=0}^{n-1}\{R_i\}\right) \cup \{I_{rator}\}$, and then copy the operands from the fresh registers to $r_{i=0}^{n-1}$. This is expensive both in the number of additional registers used (n) and the number of copy operations performed ($2n$). Using more registers also increases the need for spilling.

We now sketch a register shuffling algorithm that uses at most two registers in addition to the ones already mentioned in the source and destination register sets. (See the Web Supplement for full details.) The register shuffling algorithm begins by testing whether the operator of the app is a register in the difference of the destination and source register sets. If so, it must be renamed to a name not in the union of these sets to avoid blocking later `copy` operations. This is the first additional register that the algorithm may use. For example, in the application (`app r4 r3 r1 r5 r0 r2`) of AB_2, the operator `r4` is a destination register not mentioned in the source registers, and so is renamed to the least register not appearing in either set (`r6`):

```
(let ((r6 (@copy r4)))
  (app r6 r3 r1 r5 r0 r2))
```

The rest of the register shuffling algorithm transforms a FIL_{regId} application $E_{app} = (\text{app } I_{rator} \ R_{i=0}^{n-1})$ to a $\text{FIL}_{reg\infty}$ expression of the form

```
(let* ((R'_dst_j  (@copy  R'_src_j))_{j=1}^k)
  (app I'_rator  r_{i=0}^{n-1}))
```

that has the same meaning as E_{app}. This transformation is guided by a **register dependence graph (RDG)** that keeps track of the `copy` operations that still need to be performed. An RDG is a set of edges, where each edge is a pair of register names, written $R_{dst} \dashrightarrow R_{src}$, that associates a **destination register** R_{dst} with a **source register** R_{src}. Such an edge indicates that the value in R_{src} must be moved into R_{dst}, and so corresponds to the `let` binding (R_{dst} (`@copy` R_{src})). The direction of the arrow indicates that the final content of the R_{dst} depends on the current content of R_{src}. For the application (`app r6 r3 r1 r5 r0 r2`), this graph can be depicted as

$$\text{r4} \dashrightarrow \text{r2} \dashrightarrow \text{r5} \quad \text{r0} \dashrightarrow \text{r3}$$

There is no edge involving `r1` because it is already in the correct position. There are two connected components in this graph: the acyclic component involving `r4`, `r2`, and `r5`, and the cyclic component involving `r0` and `r3`.

The `copy` associated with the edge $\text{r}_{dst} \dashrightarrow \text{r}_{src}$ can be performed only if the destination register r_{dst} will not be the source of a later `copy` operation — i.e., only if there is no edge of the form $R \dashrightarrow \text{r}_{dst}$ in the RDG. Another way of phrasing this condition is that the number of directed edges going into vertex r_{dst} (its **in-degree**) must be 0. We will call an edge $\text{r}_{dst} \dashrightarrow \text{r}_{src}$ a **root edge** of an RDG if the in-degree of r_{dst} is 0. A root edge appears as an initial edge of an acyclic component of the RDG.

The fundamental strategy of the register shuffling algorithm is to find a root edge $EG_{root} = \text{r}_{dst} \dashrightarrow \text{r}_{src}$ in the RDG (there may be more than one) and perform its corresponding `copy` operation via the `let` binding (r_{dst} (`@copy` r_{src})). The shuffling process then continues after removing EG_{root} from the RDG because r_{dst} now contains its final value. For example, processing the first two root

edges in the RDG r4 $\dashrightarrow$ r2 $\dashrightarrow$ r5   r0 $\dashrightarrow$ r3 for (app r6 r3 r1 r5 r0 r2) yields

```
(let* ((r4 (@copy r2))   {move r2 to r4 in (app r6 r3 r1 r5 r0 r2)}
       (r2 (@copy r5)))  {move r5 to r2 in (app r6 r3 r1 r5 r0 r4)}
  (app r6 r3 r1 r2 r0 r4))
```

When processing root edge r_{dst} $\dashrightarrow$ r_{src}, if the operator is named r_{src}, it is necessary to rename it to r_{dst}. This does not happen in our example.

The RDG for the residual application (app r6 r3 r1 r2 r0 r4) is the cyclic

graph r0 $\dashrightarrow$ r3, which contains no root edge. To handle this situation, a temporary register R_{temp} is used to break one of the cycles, converting it to an acyclic component. An arbitrary edge EG_{arb} = r_{dst} $\dashrightarrow$ r_{src} is chosen from one of the cyclic components, and the content of r_{src} is stored in R_{temp} by the let binding (R_{temp} (@copy r_{src})). Replacing EG_{arb} in the RDG by r_{dst} $\dashrightarrow$ R_{temp} yields an acyclic component r_{src} $\dashrightarrow$ ... $\dashrightarrow$ r_{dst} $\dashrightarrow$ R_{temp} that allows the root-edge-finding strategy of the algorithm to proceed. The temporary register R_{temp} can be the least register that is different from I_{rator} and is not a member of the final destination registers. In the case where an RDG contains multiple cyclic components, a single temporary register can be used to break all of the components. This is the second of the two registers that may be required to perform the register shuffling. (The first additional register was used for potentially renaming the operator of an application.)

In our example, suppose the edge r0 $\dashrightarrow$ r3 is chosen to break the cycle

r0 $\dashrightarrow$ r3. Since r0 through r4 are reserved for the final operands and the operator is r6, r5 is chosen as the temporary register. The residual application (app r6 r3 r1 r2 r0 r4) is now transformed to

```
(let* ((r5 (@copy r3)))   {break cycle in (app r6 r3 r1 r2 r0 r4) with r5}
  (app r6 r5 r1 r2 r0 r4))
```

where the new RDG r3 $\dashrightarrow$ r0 $\dashrightarrow$ r5 consists of a single acyclic component. Processing the remaining two edges leads to two more let bindings:

```
(let* ((r3 (@copy r0))   {move r0 to r3 in (app r6 r5 r1 r2 r0 r4)}
       (r0 (@copy r5)))  {move r5 to r0 in (app r6 r5 r1 r2 r3 r4)}
  (app r6 r0 r1 r2 r3 r4))
```

So the final abstraction AB_3 that results from applying our register shuffling
algorithm to AB_2 is:

```
AB₃ = (abs (r0 r1 r2)
           (let* ((r3 (@mget 2 r0))
                  (r0 (@mget 3 r0))
                  (r4 (@* r1 r1))
                  (r5 (@* r0 r4))
                  (r1 (@+ r1 r4))
                  (r4 (@mget 1 r3))
                  (r6 (@copy r4))
                  (r4 (@copy r2))
                  (r2 (@copy r5))
                  (r5 (@copy r3))
                  (r3 (@copy r0))
                  (r0 (@copy r5)))
             (app r6 r0 r1 r2 r3 r4)))
```

Applying the expansion and register conversion phases to the `revmap` example
yields the $\mathrm{FIL}_{reg\infty}$ program in Figure 17.46.   Such a program is clearly very
close to register machine language; it leaves very little to the imagination! The
program uses eight registers (`r0` through `r7`), so no spilling is required as long as
the number of machine registers n_{reg} is at least eight.

Although our algorithm is simple and tends to use a small number of registers,
it can use more registers and/or perform more `copy` operations than necessary.
For example, here is a register-converted version of AB_0 that uses only five
registers and one copy operation:

```
(abs (r0 r1 r2)
   (let* ((r4 (@copy r2))    {moving r2 to r4 right away frees up r2.}
          (r3 (@mget 3 r0))
          (r0 (@mget 2 r0)) {this @mget moved later so r0 free for result.}
          (r5 (@* r1 r1))
          (r2 (@* r3 r5))
          (r1 (@+ r1 r5))
          (r5 (@mget 1 r0)))
     (app r5 r0 r1 r2 r3 r4)))
```

This version avoids many `copy` operations by (1) storing results in registers chosen
according to their operand position in the `app` expression and (2) reordering the
`(@mget 2 r0)` and `(@mget 3 r0)` bindings so that the result of `(@mget 2 r0)`
can be stored directly in `r0`.

Code using fewer registers or register moves (i.e., `copy` operations) than our
algorithm can be obtained with other register allocation algorithms from the

```
(fil (r0 r1 r2)                          {continued from left column}
  (let* ((r3 (@mnew 1))                    (def subr1
         (r4 (addr subr0))                   (abs (r0 r1 r2)
         (r4 (@mset! 1 r3 r4))                 (let* ((r3 (@mget 2 r0))
         (r4 (@mnew 2))                               (r4 (@mget 3 r0))
         (r5 (addr subr3))                            (r0 (@mget 4 r0))
         (r5 (@mset! 1 r4 r5))                        (r5 (@null? r1)))
         (r1 (@mset! 2 r4 r1))                   (if r5
         (r1 7)                                      (let* ((r0 (@mget 1 r3))
         (r1 (@* r0 r1))                                    (r1 (@mget 1 r2))
         (r5 (@null))                                       (r3 (@copy r1))
         (r1 (@cons r1 r5))                                 (r1 (@copy r0))
         (r0 (@cons r0 r1))                                 (r0 (@copy r2)))
         (r1 (@mget 1 r3))                            (app r3 r0 r1))
         (r5 (@copy r1))                           (let* ((r5 (@car r1))
         (r1 (@copy r4))                                  (r6 (@mnew 5))
         (r4 (@copy r3))                                  (r7 (addr subr2))
         (r3 (@copy r2))                                  (r7 (@mset! 1 r6 r7))
         (r2 (@copy r0))                                  (r3 (@mset! 2 r6 r3))
         (r0 (@copy r4)))                                 (r3 (@mset! 3 r6 r4))
    (app r5 r0 r1 r2 r3))                                 (r1 (@mset! 4 r6 r1))
  (def subr0                                              (r1 (@mset! 5 r6 r2))
    (abs (r0 r1 r2 r3)                                    (r1 (@mget 1 r0))
      (let* ((r0 (@null))                                 (r3 (@copy r1))
             (r4 (@mnew 1))                               (r1 (@copy r5))
             (r0 (@mset! 1 r4 r0))                        (r2 (@copy r6)))
             (r0 (@mnew 1))                          (app r3 r0 r1 r2)))))))
             (r5 #u)                          (def subr2
             (r5 (@mset! 1 r0 r5))              (abs (r0 r1)
             (r5 (@mnew 4))                       (let* ((r2 (@mget 2 r0))
             (r6 (addr subr1))                           (r3 (@mget 3 r0))
             (r6 (@mset! 1 r5 r6))                       (r4 (@mget 4 r0))
             (r4 (@mset! 2 r5 r4))                       (r0 (@mget 5 r0))
             (r4 (@mset! 3 r5 r0))                       (r5 (@mget 1 r2))
             (r1 (@mset! 4 r5 r1))                       (r1 (@cons r1 r5))
             (r1 (@mset! 1 r0 r5))                       (r1 (@mset! 1 r2 r1))
             (r0 (@mget 1 r0))                           (r1 (@mget 1 r3))
             (r1 (@mget 1 r0))                           (r2 (@cdr r4))
             (r4 (@copy r1))                             (r3 (@mget 1 r1))
             (r1 (@copy r2))                             (r4 (@copy r1))
             (r2 (@copy r3)))                            (r1 (@copy r2))
        (app r4 r0 r1 r2))))                             (r2 (@copy r0))
  {continued in right column}                            (r0 (@copy r4)))
                                                    (app r3 r0 r1 r2))))
                                          (def subr3
                                            (abs (r0 r1 r2)
                                              (let* ((r0 (@mget 2 r0))
                                                     (r0 (@> r1 r0))
                                                     (r1 (@mget 1 r2))
                                                     (r3 (@copy r1))
                                                     (r1 (@copy r0))
                                                     (r0 (@copy r2)))
                                                (app r3 r0 r1)))))
```

Figure 17.46   revmap program after expansion and register conversion.

literature. Many of these are based on a classic register-coloring algorithm that uses registers to "color" an interference graph whose vertices are abstract register names and whose edges connect vertices that cannot be the same actual register [CAC+81, Cha82]. These algorithms can be adapted to pass procedure arguments in registers, as required by our approach.

The assumption that all n-argument procedures take their arguments in registers $r_{i=0}^{n-1}$ simplifies our algorithm, but is too restrictive. Algorithms for **interprocedural register allocation** (e.g., [BWD95]) can reduce the number of copy operations by using different argument registers for different procedures. For example, before register shuffling is performed, the top-level call to the revmap procedure is transformed to (app r1 r3 r4 r0 r2). Since this is the only call to revmap in the program, the register shuffling operations that transform the operand sequence $[r3, r4, r0, r2]$ to $[r0, r1, r2, r3]$ can be eliminated if the subroutine corresponding to the revmap procedure (subr0) is simply modified to expect its arguments in the unshuffled registers:

```
(def subr0 (abs (r3 r4 r0 r2) ... ))
```

Of course, in order to use specialized argument registers for a particular procedure, the compiler must have access to its definition and all its calls.

Exercise 17.38

a. Write a six-operand application (app I_{rator} $R_{i=0}^5$) whose RDG has two cyclic components, one acyclic component, and one vertex with in-degree 2.

b. Show the result of using the register shuffling algorithm described in the text on your example.

Exercise 17.39 For an application with n operands, what is the number of copy operations needed by the register shuffling algorithm described in the text in the best case? In the worst case? Write a six-operand application (app I_{rator} $R_{i=0}^5$) that requires the worst-case number of copies.

Exercise 17.40

a. Consider the following abstraction AB_a:

```
(abs (clo.0 a.1 b.2 k.3)
  (let* ((t.4 (@mget 2 clo.0))
         (t.5 (@mget 3 clo.0))
         (t.6 (@- a.1 t.4))
         (t.7 (@/ b.2 t.4))
         (code.8 (@mget 1 t.5)))
    (app code.8 t.5 t.6 t.7 k.3)))
```

What is the result of register-converting this abstraction using the algorithm described in the text?

b. Consider the abstraction AB_b obtained from AB_a by changing the application expression to

   (app code.8 t.5 t.4 t.6 t.7 k.3) {*new argument t.4 added before t.6*}

   What is the result of register-converting AB_b?

c. Consider the abstraction AB_c obtained from AB_b by changing the application expression to

   (app code.8 t.5 t.4 t.4 t.6 t.7 k.3) {*second t.4 added before t.6*}

   What is the result of register-converting AB_c?

d. The results of part **b** and part **c** use more registers and copy operations than necessary. Show this by register-converting AB_b and AB_c to $\text{FIL}_{reg\infty}$ abstractions by hand to use both the minimal number of registers and the minimal number of copy operations. You may reorder let bindings and interleave copy bindings with the existing let bindings as long as you do not change the meaning of the abstractions.

17.12.5   The Spilling Phase

A $\text{FIL}_{reg\infty}$ register is **live** if its current value may be accessed from the register later in the computation. When the number of live $\text{FIL}_{reg\infty}$ registers exceeds the number n_{reg} of registers in the machine, some of the register values must be stored elsewhere in memory. The process of moving values that would otherwise be stored in registers to memory is called **spilling**.

In the TORTOISE compiler, we use the name **spill memory** for the area of memory used to store spilled values. We treat spill memory like a zero-indexed mutable array of slots manipulated via two FIL_{reg} primitive operations:

- (prim (spset! NT) R) stores the content of R in the slot at index $\mathcal{N}[\![NT]\!]$ in spill memory and returns #u. This is abbreviated (@spset! NT R).

- (prim (spget NT)) returns the value stored in the slot at index $\mathcal{N}[\![NT]\!]$ in spill memory. This is abbreviated (@spget NT).

TORTOISE uses a simple spilling algorithm that assumes $n_{reg} \geq 2$. Given a $\text{FIL}_{reg\infty}$ program P, the algorithm first determines the largest register $\mathbf{r}_{top}$ used in P. If $top < n_{reg}$, then P is already a FIL_{reg} program, so it is returned. But if $top \geq n_{reg}$, then all references to registers of the form $\mathbf{r}_i$ such that $i \geq n_{reg}$ must be eliminated to convert the program to FIL_{reg}. This is accomplished by dedicating the top two registers, $\mathbf{r}_{sp} = \mathbf{r}_{(n_{reg}-2)}$ and $\mathbf{r}_{(sp+1)} = \mathbf{r}_{(n_{reg}-1)}$, to the spilling process and storing the content of every register $\mathbf{r}_j$ as follows:

- If $j < sp$, the content of $\mathbf{r}_j$ continues to be stored in register $\mathbf{r}_j$.

- If $j \geq sp$, the content of $\mathbf{r}_j$ is stored in slot $(j - sp)$ of spill memory. In this case we say that $\mathbf{r}_j$ is a **spilled register**.

We assume that spill memory is large enough to hold the values of all spilled registers.

   The spilling phase performs the following spill conversion transformations on the $\mathrm{FIL}_{reg\infty}$ program, which are illustrated in Figure 17.47.

- The program formal parameter sequence, all abstraction formal parameter sequences, and all application operand sequences are truncated to contain no register larger than $\mathbf{r}_{(sp-1)}$. This is because we pass the first sp arguments in registers and any arguments beyond this in spill memory. We assume that the program-invoking mechanism of the operating system "knows" that any arguments beyond those mentioned in the program formal parameters must be passed in spill memory.

- A `let` expression (`let` ((R_{dst} LE)) E_{body}) in which $\mathbf{r}_{dst}$ is a spilled register is converted to

   ```
   (let* ((r_sp LE')
          (r_(sp+1) (@spset! dst − sp r_sp)))
     E'_body)
   ```

   where LE' is the spill-converted version of LE, E'_{body} is the spill-converted version of E_{body}, and $\overline{dst - sp}$ is a natural number literal NT such that $\mathcal{N}[\![NT]\!]$ $= (dst - sp)$. This takes the value that would have been stored in $\mathbf{r}_{dst}$ and instead (1) stores it in the dedicated register $\mathbf{r}_{sp}$ and (2) uses `spset!` to move it from $\mathbf{r}_{sp}$ to spill memory at index $(dst - sp)$. Storing the unit value resulting from `spset!` in $\mathbf{r}_{(sp+1)}$ rather than in $\mathbf{r}_{sp}$ allows the value in $\mathbf{r}_{sp}$ to be used later in improved versions of the spilling algorithm.

- Any reference to a spilled register $\mathbf{r}_{src}$ that appears as a conditional test, as an operator of a procedure application, or as the first argument of a primitive application is converted to a reference to $\mathbf{r}_{sp}$ in a context where $\mathbf{r}_{sp}$ is `let`-bound to (`@spget` $\overline{src - sp}$). This takes the value that would have been retrieved directly from $\mathbf{r}_{src}$, and instead (1) uses `spget` to retrieve it from spill memory at index $(src - sp)$, (2) stores it in the dedicated register $\mathbf{r}_{sp}$, and (3) retrieves it from $\mathbf{r}_{sp}$. Similarly, any reference to a spilled register $\mathbf{r}_{src}$ that appears as the second argument of a primitive application is converted to a reference to $\mathbf{r}_{(sp+1)}$ in a context where $\mathbf{r}_{(sp+1)}$ is `let`-bound to (`@spget` $\overline{src - sp}$). A spilled register in the second argument position is stored in a different register than one in the first position to handle the case where both argument registers are spilled registers.

In the spilling example in Figure 17.47, where $sp = 2$, the formal parameter registers r2, r3, and r4 of the abstraction are stored in spill memory and are accessed via (@spget 0), (@spget 1), and (@spget 2), respectively. The global spill conversion transformation guarantees that any invocation of this (or any other) five-parameter subroutine will use spset! to store the third, fourth, and fifth operands in spill memory locations 0, 1, and 2 before control is passed to the subroutine. The example illustrates this parameter spilling for subroutine calls in the application of the six-parameter subroutine stored in r1. The converted code uses spset! to store the value of parameters r2 and r5 in spill memory locations 0 and 3. No explicit spset!s are needed for spilling r3 and r4 to locations 1 and 2 because these values were already placed in spill memory by the caller of the converted abstraction and are not changed in its body.

Our simple spilling algorithm can generate code with some obvious inefficiencies. For example, if $sp = 2$, it transforms

```
(let* ((r2 (@* r4 r4))
       (r3 (@< r1 r2)))
  (if r3 (app r1 r0) (error wrong)))
```

to

```
(let* ((r2 (@spget 2))      {move content of spilled r4 into r2}
       (r3 (@spget 2))      {move content of spilled r4 into r3}
       (r2 (@* r2 r3))      {calculate spilled r4 times spilled r4}
       (r3 (@spset! 0 r2))  {store content of spilled r2 into memory}
       (r2 (@spget 0))      {move content of spilled r2 into r2}
       (r2 (@< r1 r2))      {calculate r1 less than spilled r2}
       (r3 (@spset! 1 r2))  {move content of spilled r3 into memory}
       (r2 (@spget 1)))     {move content of spilled r3 into r2}
  (if r2 (app r1 r0) (error wrong)))
```

when the following much simpler code would work:

```
(let* ((r2 (@spget 2)) {move content of spilled r4 into r2}
       (r2 (@* r2 r2)) {use r2 for both args and for result; no need to}
                       { spill r2 to memory since only used in next binding}
       (r3 (@< r1 r2)));{use r2 directly and store result directly in r3; no need}
                       { to spill r3 to memory since only used in if test}
  (if r3 (app r1 r0) (error wrong))) {use r3 directly}
```

The Web Supplement explores these inefficiencies and how they can be eliminated. Some of the simplifications can be made by a peephole optimization

---

Abstraction before Spilling
```
(abs (r0 r1 r2 r3 r4)
  (let* ((r5 (@< r4 r2))
         (r0 (@+ r0 r4)))
    (if r5
        (app r3 r0 r1 r2)
        (let ((r2 (@* r0 r0)))
          (app r1 r0 r1 r2 r3 r4 r5)))))
```

Abstraction after Spilling (where $sp = 2$**)**
```
(abs (r0 r1)                        {truncate formal parameters}
  (let* ((r2 (@spget 2))            {move content of spilled r4 into r2}
         (r3 (@spget 0))            {move content of spilled r2 into r3}
         (r2 (@< r2 r3))            {calculate spilled r4 less than spilled r2}
         (r3 (@spset! 3 r2))        {store content of spilled r5 into memory}
         (r3 (@spget 2))            {move content of spilled r4 into r3}
         (r0 (@+ r0 r3))            {use r3 for spilled r4}
         (r2 (@spget 3)))           {move content of spilled r5 into r2}
    (if r2                          {use r2 for spilled r5}
        (let ((r2 (@spget 1)))      {move content of spilled r3 into r2}
          (app r2 r0 r1))           {use r2 for spilled r3 and truncate operands}
        (let* ((r2 (@* r0 r0))      {calculate content of spilled r2}
               (r3 (@spset! 0 r2))) {store content of spilled r2 into memory}
          (app r1 r0 r1)))))        {truncate operands}
```

Figure 17.47   A spilling example.

phase that performs local transformations on the result of the spilling phase. Other improvements require modifying the spilling algorithm itself.

Any approach to spilling based purely on an index threshold is rather crude.[12] It would be better to estimate the frequency of register usage and spill the less frequently used registers.

---

[12]But index thresholds for spilling have an interesting precedent. All machines in the IBM 360 line executed uniform machine code assuming the same number of virtual registers. Since hardware registers were expensive, cheaper machines in the line used a small number of hardware registers for the low-numbered virtual registers and main memory locations for high-numbered virtual registers. These machines employed a threshold-based spilling mechanism implemented in hardware!

Notes

The literature on traditional compiler technology is vast. A classic text is the "Dragon book" [ASU86]. More modern treatments are provided by Cooper and Torczon [CT03] and by Appel's textbooks [App98b, App98a, AP02]. Comprehensive coverage of advanced compilation topics, especially optimizations, can be found in Muchnick's text [Muc97]. Inlining is a particularly important but subtle optimization — see especially [CHT91, ASG97, DC00, JM02]. Issues in functional-language compilation are considered by Peyton Jones in [Pey87].

Compiling programs via transformations on an intermediate, lambda calculus-based language was pioneered in the SCHEME community through a series of compilers that started with Steele's RABBIT [Ste78] and was followed by many others [Roz84, KKR⁺86, Cli84, KH89, FL92, CH94]. An extreme version of this idea is the *nanopass compiler* for SCHEME, which is composed of fifty simple transformation stages [SWD04]. The idea (embodied in FIL_{reg}) that the final intermediate-language program can also be interpreted directly as a register-machine program is due to Kelsey [Kel89, KH89]. He showed that realistic compiler features like register allocation, instruction selection, and stack-based allocation could be modeled in such a framework and demonstrated that the transformational technique was viable for compiling traditional languages like PASCAL and BASIC.

The next major innovation along these lines was developing transformation-oriented compilers based on explicitly typed intermediate languages (e.g., [Mor95, TMC⁺96, Pey96, PM97, Sha97, BKR98, TO98, MWCG99, FKR⁺00, CJW00, DWM⁺01]. The type information guides program analyses and transformations, supports run-time operations such as garbage collection, and is an important debugging aid in the compiler development process. In [TMC⁺96], Tarditi and others explored how to express classical optimizations within a typed intermediate language framework. In some compilers (e.g., [MWCG99]) type information is carried all the way through to a typed assembly language, where types can be used to verify certain safety properties of the code. The notion that untrusted low-level code should carry information that allows safety properties to be verified is the main idea behind *proof-carrying code* [NL98, AF00].

Early transformation-based compilers typically included a stage converting the program to CPS form. The view that procedure calls can be viewed as jumps that pass arguments was championed by Steele, who observed that a stack discipline in compilation is not implied by the procedure-call mechanism but rather by the evaluation of nested subexpressions [SS76, Ste77].

The TORTOISE $\mathcal{MCPS}$ transformation is based on a study of CPS conversion by Danvy and Filinski [DF92]. They distinguish so-called *static continuations* (what we call "metacontinuations") from *dynamic continuations* and used these notions to derive an efficient form of CPS conversion from the simple but inefficient definition. Appel studied the use of continuations for compiler optimizations in [App92].

In [FSDF93], Flanagan et al. argued that explicit CPS form was not necessary for such optimizations. They showed that transformations performed on CPS code could be expressed directly in a non-CPS form they called *A-normal form*. Although modern transformation-based compilers tend to use something like A-normal form, we adopted a CPS form in the TORTOISE compiler. It is an important illustration of the theme of making implicit structures explicit, and it simplifies the compilation of complex control constructs like nonlocal exits, exceptions, and backtracking. The observation that these constructs use continuations in a nonlinear way is discussed in [Baw93].

Closure conversion is an important stage in a transformation-based compiler. Johnsson's lambda-lifting transformation [Joh85] lifts abstractions to top level after they have been extended with initial parameters for free variables. It uses curried functions that are partially applied to these initial parameters to represent closures. This closure representation is standard in compilers for combinator reduction machines [Hug82, Pey87]. The TORTOISE lifting stage also lifts closed abstractions to top level, but uses a different representation for closures: the closure-passing style invented by Appel and Jim in [AJ88]. Defunctionalization (a notion due to Reynolds [Rey72]) has been used as the basis for closure conversion in some ML compilers [TO98, CJW00]. Selective and lightweight closure conversion were studied by Steckler and Wand [WS94, SW97]. The notion of representation pollution was studied by Dimock et al. [DWM+01] in a compiler that chooses the representation of a closure depending on how it is used in a program. Sophisticated closure conversion systems rely on a control flow analysis to determine how procedures are used in a program. In [NNH98], Nielson, Nielson, and Hankin provide excellent coverage of control flow analysis and other program analyses.

[BCT94] summarizes work on register allocation and spilling. The classic approach to register allocation and spilling involves graph-coloring algorithms [CAC+81, Cha82]. See [BWD95] for one approach to managing registers across procedure calls.

18

Garbage Collection

Be you the mean hombre that's a-hankerin' for a heap of trouble, stranger?
Well, be ya?

— Yosemite Sam, in "Hare Trigger"

18.1 Why Garbage Collection?

Programming without some form of automatic memory management is dangerous
and may lead to run-time type errors. Here is why: A programmer forced to
manage memory manually may inadvertently release a block of memory for reuse,
yet retain the ability to access the block by holding on to a pointer to the block
(a so-called **dangling pointer**). When this memory block is reused by the
system, the value in it will be accessible by two independent pointers, perhaps
even under two independent types (the type expected by the logically invalid
pointer and that expected by the new pointer). Modifying the value via one
pointer will unexpectedly cause the value accessible via the other to be changed
as well, leading to insidious bugs that are notoriously difficult to catch. The
program is incorrect, and in some cases, type safety can be lost![1]

Thus a critical run-time service in type-safe programming language implementations is the safe allocation and deallocation of memory for compound values
such as tuples, arrays, lists, and oneofs. Such values are stored in units called
blocks in a region of memory called the **heap**. As described in Chapter 17,
the TORTOISE complier generates FIL_{reg} code for a simple register machine that
uses the primitive operator `mnew` to allocate a mutable product value and the
primitives `mget` and `mset!` to manipulate the contents of such products. The job
of this chapter is to demonstrate how to implement primitives like these.

This chapter describes a safe storage management system based on a technique for automatic heap deallocation called garbage collection. The implementa-

---

[1]The same problem arises in languages that do not do array bounds checking, a deficiency
exploited by countless security attacks.

tions of almost all type-safe languages (e.g., JAVA, C#, LISP, SMALLTALK, ML, HASKELL) use garbage collection. In a system with manual heap deallocation, where programmers must explicitly declare when heap blocks may be reused, it is possible for a sophisticated type checker that models the state of memory to guarantee that there are no dangling pointers [ZX05]. But any such type system necessarily limits expressiveness by rejecting some programs that are actually safe. In contrast, garbage collection guarantees value integrity and type safety without limiting expressiveness.

Garbage collection (GC) is a process that identifies memory blocks that will not be used again and makes their storage available for reuse. A heap block is **live** in a program state if it will be accessed later in the program execution, and otherwise the block is **dead**. It is not in general possible to prove which blocks are live in a program state, and thus a garbage collector must identify and reuse only blocks that it can prove are dead. The engineering challenge is to design a garbage collector that efficiently preserves live memory blocks and a minimum of dead blocks.

Garbage collection also reduces **memory leaks** that arise when a programmer does not deallocate dead blocks so they can be used for something else. Memory leaks can cause a program to abort with an out-of-memory error that could have been avoided if the dead blocks were reused. It is in fact common for long-running programs to crash because of slow memory leaks that exhaust available storage. Memory leaks are notoriously difficult to find and fix, especially in a large and complex program like an operating system. Garbage collectors can also exhibit memory leaks, but they are better equipped than human beings to reason about block liveness, and typically do a better job of efficiently reclaiming dead blocks.

In manual deallocation systems, the programmer is caught between two dangers: Deallocating blocks too early creates dangling pointers, whereas deallocating them too late causes memory leaks. Yet it is often difficult, if not impossible, for the programmer to know when a heap-allocated data structure can no longer be accessed by the program. For example, consider a graphics application in which two-dimensional points are represented as pairs of x and y coordinates and lines are represented as pairs of points. A single point might be shared by many lines. When a line is deleted by the application, it may be safe to deallocate the pair associated with the line, but it is not safe to deallocate the pairs associated with the line's endpoints, since these might be shared by other lines. Without explicitly tracking how many lines a point participates in, the programmer has no idea when to deallocate a point in such a system. In contrast, because a garbage collector "knows" the exact pointer wiring structure for heap blocks in memory, it can determine properties that are difficult for a programmer to keep track of, such as how many references there are to a particular point. If the answer is 0, the point may be reclaimed.

Manual deallocation also complicates the implementation of data structures and data abstractions. When a compound data structure becomes dead, many of its components become dead as well. The programmer must carefully free all dead components (often recursively) before freeing the storage for the compound structure itself. Manual deallocation complicates data abstractions because allocation and deallocation responsibilities must become part of the interface. Implementers of an abstraction must often provide a mechanism for deallocating abstract data structures. C++ provides this functionality for objects via a **destructor function** that is called whenever the storage for the object is deallocated. A destructor function typically deallocates storage for components of the object. But the problem is more complex still: Only the client of the data abstraction knows when abstract data values and many of the components used to create them are dead; but only the implementer knows the actual structure of abstract values, including their components, data-sharing properties, and invariants. Choreographing allocations and deallocations for even relatively simple and common abstractions, such as generic linked lists, can prove extremely complex and error-prone.

In the mid-1990s garbage collection came into the mainstream when the implementers of the first widely adopted type-safe programming language, JAVA, chose to use garbage collection for their implementation of safe storage. Although garbage collection has a rich history in languages like LISP and SMALLTALK, until recently it was considered too inefficient to support in mainstream programming languages like C, PASCAL, and ADA, which opted for manual storage deallocation instead. (In fact, the ADA specification allows implementations to perform garbage collection but does not require it: Programmers are effectively required to manually deallocate storage in the many implementations that do not support garbage collection.) JAVA's type safety was sufficient inducement for programmers to accept a system that uses garbage collection.

The remainder of this chapter explores garbage collection in the context of FRM, the **FIL Register Machine** that executes the FIL_{reg} code generated by the TORTOISE compiler presented in the previous chapter. FRM allocates heap blocks for mutable tuples, list nodes, and symbols, and garbage collection will allow reuse of such blocks when it determines that they will never be accessed again. Section 18.2 presents the relevant details of FRM, especially how compound values are laid out in memory. Section 18.3 discusses approximations for block liveness. Section 18.4 lays out a complete design for an FRM garbage collector. Section 18.5 sketches some other approaches to garbage collection, including a *conservative GC* technique that can be used for languages that traditionally rely on manual deallocation. Garbage collection is a dynamic approach to automatic heap deallocation; Section 18.6 briefly discusses some static approaches to automatic heap deallocation.

To keep our discussions at a high level, we will explain implementation issues and algorithms using a combination of English and pictures. A complete metalanguage formalization of FRM and several heap management strategies can be found in the Web Supplement.

18.2   FRM: The FIL Register Machine

In order to explain heap management strategies for FRM, we first need to give an overview of the FRM architecture and explain how FRM values are represented.

18.2.1   The FRM Architecture

The fundamental unit of information is the *binary digit*, commonly called a **bit**. A bit can be one of two values, 0 or 1. Every FRM value is encoded as a single **word**, which is a fixed-size sequence of bits. A value that is too big to fit into a single word (such as a mutable tuple, nonempty list node, or symbol) is represented as a single **address word** (or **pointer**) that is the address of a **block** of words in the heap.

Uniformly representing all values in a single-sized word datum greatly simplifies many aspects of the FRM implementation. For example, a word-sized register can hold any value, the ith component of any heap block can be stored in its ith word, and polymorphic functions require no special implementation techniques. Many practical language implementations use nonuniform value sizes (e.g., single-precision floating point numbers requiring one word and double-precision floating point numbers requiring two words) for efficiency reasons, but they would create needless complexity here.

The state of a program running on FRM has four components:

1. The current FIL_{reg} expression E being executed. As noted in Section 17.12.1, each FIL_{reg} expression can be viewed as a register machine instruction whose execution updates the state of the machine and specifies the next instruction. (See the Web Supplement for an SOS that specifies the action of each FIL_{reg} expression as an FRM instruction.) This component corresponds to the **program counter**, the address of the currently executing instruction, in traditional architectures. An FRM program executes until it terminates with a `halt` or `error` expression.

2. The **subroutine memory** S, where the definitions of all the program's subroutines are stored. This is the **code segment** in a traditional architecture. Rather than worry about the address of the start of a subroutine in memory, we will simply refer to each subroutine by an integer index. That is, subroutine i stands for E_{body} in the definition (`def subr`$_n$ `(abs` (RS) E_{body}`))` in the FIL_{reg} program being executed. As observed on page 1099, FRM can ignore the register parameters in an abstraction, because the actual argument values are passed in the registers of the machine.

3. The **register memory** R, where the contents of the FRM registers are stored. As in FIL_{reg}, we assume that there are n_{reg} registers. Each register holds one word. The notation $R[n]$ stands for the word stored in register $\mathtt{r}_n$.

4. The **heap memory** H, where the contents of memory blocks are stored. We assume that the heap is a part of **main memory**, an array M of words indexed by addresses that are natural numbers. The notation $M[n_{addr}]$ denotes the word stored at address n_{addr} in M. Some of the main memory may be reserved for purposes other than the heap, such as a program's subroutine and/or spill memory.[2] We assume that the portion of main memory reserved for the heap uses indices in the range $[0..(n_{size} - 1)]$, where n_{size} is the number of words reserved for the heap.

18.2.2 FRM Descriptors

We have seen that all FRM values are single words, where some words are pointers to blocks of words in the heap. We will now explore how to represent words and blocks on a typical register machine. This allows us to discuss some of the low-level representation choices that are important in programming language implementations.

A word is represented as an n-tuple of bits. We can define FRM for a machine of any word size, but for concreteness we shall assume that all words consist of 32 bits. Suppose B ranges over bits. Then we abbreviate the word tuple $\langle B_1, B_2, \ldots, B_{31}, B_{32} \rangle$ by the juxtaposition $B_1 B_2 \cdots B_{31} B_{32}$ of its bits. The notation B^n represents n consecutive copies of B. For example, $0^{20} 10101^8$ stands for the word that has 20 0s followed by 1010 followed by eight 1s.

There are standard ways to represent natural numbers and signed integers using bits, and standard ways to perform arithmetic on these representations. For more information, consult the Web Supplement.

---

[2] The FRM SOS in the Web Supplement shows how to handle spill memory, which we ignore here.

Each FRM value can be represented as a single 32-bit word, which we shall call its **descriptor**. A value is said to be **unboxed** when all information about the value fits into the descriptor, in which case its descriptor is said to be **immediate**. A value is said to be **boxed** when some of its information is stored in a heap block, in which case its descriptor contains the address of the block and is said to be **nonimmediate**. We assume that word addresses are specified by 30 bits. This is consistent with the word-alignment restrictions in many 32-bit architectures.[3]

Descriptors with Type Tags

Each FRM value is encoded as a single word with an unambiguous representation. This unambiguous representation encodes both the type of the value and the value itself. Thus, we can examine the FRM value stored in a register and decode its type and value without additional information. Such explicit type information is necessary for descriptor representations in a dynamically typed language, where it is necessary to check the type of a value at run time. Such type information can also be helpful in a statically typed language, where it can be used by run-time processes (such as garbage collectors, debuggers, and value displayers) to parse memory into values.

The left-hand column of Figure 18.1 shows the way we have chosen to encode type and value information in a descriptor. A descriptor is divided into a **type tag** — the lower-order bits that specify the type of the value — and the **value representation** — the remaining bits that distinguish values of a given type. In this particular representation, the lowest-order bit is 0 for immediate values and 1 for nonimmediate values. Since nonimmediate values have only 30 bits of address information, the next-to-last bit is arbitrary; we assume that it is 0. So all pointers have a 30-bit address followed by the type tag 01. For immediate values, the next-to-last bit distinguishes integers (0) from nonintegers (1). This leaves 30 bits of information to represent a signed integer. For simplicity, we will assume that FRM supports only 30-bit signed integers in this representation. It is possible to represent integers with more bits if we box them in a heap block.[4] The third-to-last bit distinguishes subroutine indices (for which this bit is 0) from other values (for which this bit is 1). This leaves 29 bits available to express the subroutine index itself (as an unsigned integer). Two additional type bits are used to distinguish the remaining four types of immediate values: unit (00), null

---

[3]In many 32-bit architectures, a 32-bit address word specifies a byte address. But data one word wide must be aligned to a *word boundary*, i.e., its address must have 00 as its lowermost bits. So the information content of a word address is limited to its upper 30 bits.

[4]This technique can be used to represent arbitrary-sized integers, known as **bignums**.

Descriptor with type tags		Value	Descriptor with GC tags only	
[30-bit signed integer]	00	integer	[31-bit signed integer]	0
[29-bit subroutine index]	010	subroutine	[31-bit subroutine index]	0
0^{27}	00110	unit	0^{31}	0
0^{27}	01110	null	0^{31}	0
$0^{26}0$	10110	false	$0^{30}0$	0
$0^{26}1$	10110	true	$0^{30}1$	0
0^{19} [8-bit ASCII code]	11110	character	0^{23} [8-bit ASCII code]	0
[30-bit address]	01	pointer	[30-bit address]	01

Figure 18.1 Two layouts for FRM descriptors: one with full type tags and one with garbage collection (GC) tags.

list (01), boolean (10), and character[5] (11). The unit and null list types have only one value each, so the remaining 27 bits are arbitrary; we assume they are all 0. The boolean type has two values, which are distinguished by the 27th bit: 0 for false and 1 for true. In a character descriptor, the remaining 27 bits can be used to encode the particular character — e.g., as an 8-bit ASCII code or a 16-bit unicode representation.

From the perspective of encoding words as bits, the placement and content of the type tags are arbitrary. For example, we could have put the type tags in the leftmost bits rather than the rightmost bits, and we could have made the integer type tag 01 and the pointer type tag 00. However, the particular choices made for type tags in Figure 18.1 have practical benefits on real architectures:

- Using a rightmost tag of 00 for integers simplifies integer arithmetic. Each 30-bit signed integer i is represented by a word that denotes $4i$. Addition,

---

[5]Although FIL does not have character literals, FRM uses character values to represent symbols as boxed values whose components are characters.

subtraction, and remainder can be performed on these descriptors simply using the standard 32-bit arithmetic operations without using any other bit-level operations, because these operations preserve the rightmost 00 bits. Multiplication and division take slightly more work: one of the multiplication operands must be shifted right (arithmetically) by two bits to eliminate its 00 tag before performing the multiplication; and the result of division must be shifted left by two bits to add the 00 tag. Arithmetic would require more work if leftmost tags were used or a rightmost tag other than 00 were used (see Exercise 18.1).

- Using a nonzero rightmost tag for pointers is efficient on most architectures via an offset addressing mode, which allows direct access to memory at a fixed offset (a small signed integer) from a 32-bit byte address stored in a register or memory location. An address with a 01 pointer tag can effectively be converted into a word-aligned byte address by specifying a −1 offset.

Exercise 18.1 Assuming the following alternative placement and/or content of type tags, describe how to perform (1) integer arithmetic (+, −, ×, ÷, and %) and (2) accesses for memory addresses.

a. Type tags are the rightmost two bits of a descriptor, 11 is the integer type tag, and 00 is the pointer type tag.

b. Type tags are the leftmost two bits of a descriptor, 00 is the integer type tag, and 01 is the pointer type tag.

c. Type tags are the leftmost two bits of a descriptor, 01 is the integer type tag, and 00 is the pointer type tag.

Descriptors with Garbage Collection (GC) Tags

In the run-time system for a statically typed language, descriptors need not carry complete type information, because dynamic type checking is unnecessary. This is true for FIL_{reg} programs that are produced by the TORTOISE compiler.

However, it is still helpful for descriptors to carry information that aids other run-time services, like garbage collection. As we shall see later, a garbage collector needs to distinguish between pointers and nonpointers. This can be accomplished with a one-bit **GC tag**. The right-hand column of Figure 18.1 shows a descriptor layout that uses the low-order bit as the GC tag. A 0 indicates a nonpointer, a 1 indicates a pointer. Since pointers have only 30 bits of address information, we will use a two-bit 01 tag for pointers, reserving the 11 tag for for header words in heap blocks (see Section 18.2.3).

The choice of the placement and values of the GC tags is guided by the same logic used for type tags. Using a rightmost 0 bit for immediate descriptors

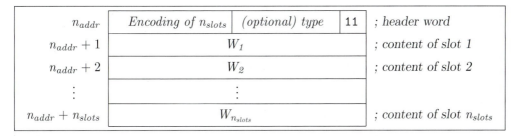

Figure 18.2 The layout of a heap block with contents $W_1, \ldots, W_{n_{slots}}$ at word address n_{addr}.

simplifies integer arithmetic, and the 01 pointer tag can be processed at little or no cost by offset addressing. This layout yields an extra bit of integer precision. Note that because immediate descriptors do not include distinguishing type bits, many different values can have the same bit pattern. For example, the bit pattern 0^{32} is used for the integer 0, the unit value, the null list, the boolean *false*, and the character whose ASCII code is 0.

Tagless Descriptors

Implementations can support garbage collection without using GC tags in descriptors. In these *tag-free GC* systems (Section 18.5.2), descriptors need not carry any type or GC tags, so all bits can be used for the value representation. For example, a 32-bit descriptor can encode a 32-bit integer or a 32-bit byte address. Tagless descriptors are essential in *conservative GC* systems (Section 18.5.3) for languages like C/C++ and PASCAL, which cannot tolerate GC bits in their descriptors.

18.2.3 FRM Blocks

FRM blocks are allocated from the heap, an area of main memory that is indexed by 30-bit addresses. An FRM block is described by a single word FRM descriptor that includes its 30-bit address. This address n_{addr} points to the **header word** of the FRM block, which is followed in memory by a variable number of slots, each of which can hold a single word (Figure 18.2). The header word at address n_{addr} indicates the size of the block in words (excluding the header word itself) and possibly the type of the block. To aid in parsing the heap into blocks, header words have a two-bit tag of 11, which distinguishes them from immediate and nonimmediate descriptors (see Figure 18.1). This tag is not strictly necessary, but convenient. The words at addresses $[(n_{addr} + 1) .. (n_{addr} + n_{slots})]$ are the descriptors for the contents of the n_{slots} slots of the block.

Header with type and size	Header Type	Header with size only
[28-bit size] 0011	mutable tuple	[30-bit size] 11
$0^{26}10$ 0111	list node (size 2)	$0^{28}10$ 11
[28-bit size] 1011	symbol	[30-bit size] 11
[28-bit size] 1111	closure	[30-bit size] 11

Figure 18.3 Two layouts for FRM header words: one with size and type information and one with size information only.

For a statically typed language with garbage collection (the right-hand column of Figure 18.3), the type of every block is statically known, but the garbage collector needs to know the size of each block. The first 30 bits of the header are used to encode this size.

For a dynamically typed language, the header may encode type information in addition to size information. The choices in the left-hand column of Figure 18.3 indicate that there are four types of FIL_{reg} values represented as blocks: mutable tuples (created by mnew), nonempty list nodes, symbols, and closures.[6] The types of these four values can be distinguished by two type bits in addition to the 11 header tag. More type bits would be needed if FIL_{reg} were extended to support additional compound values, such as strings and arrays.

For example, here are two heap block representations for the result of compiling and executing the FLARE/V expression (@pair #t 42):

Block with type info			Block with GC info	
$0^{26}10$ 0011	mutable tuple header		$0^{28}10$ 11	
$0^{26}1$ 10110	true		$0^{30}1$ 0	
$0^{24}101010$ 00	42		$0^{25}101010$ 0	

In this block representation, accessing or changing slot i (1-indexed) of a block at 30-bit address n_{addr} with n_{slots} slots simply manipulates the location at address

---

[6]Although closures are represented as mutable tuples in FIL_{reg}, it is helpful to distinguish the types of closure tuples from the types of other mutable tuples. In a compiler that maintains implicit type annotations for all expressions, closure types would be introduced by the closure conversion stage.

$n_{addr} + i$ in main memory. In the case where the block size is not known at compile time (e.g., for an array of unknown size) it is first necessary to check at run time that $0 < i \leq n_{slots}$, where n_{slots} is determined from the header word at address n_{addr}. Failure to pass this check leads to an out-of-bounds index error. But for data whose size is known statically (e.g., FIL's mutable products), no dynamic index check is necessary.

The simple heap-block layout depicted in Figure 18.2 does not make efficient use of space for heap-allocated products with a small, statically known number of components (in FIL_{reg}, list nodes and tuples/closures with a small number of components). Using a header word to encode the size (and possibly type) of these products has a high space overhead. One way to avoid the header word in these cases is to encode the size/type of the block in the pointer to the block rather than in the block itself. For example, reserving three right-hand bits of the pointer next to the 01 tag for this purpose would allow distinguishing eight size/type possibilities, one of which would indicate the standard block-with-header but the other seven of which would indicate headerless blocks. In addition to eliminating the header word for small blocks, this technique allows the type of a block in a dynamically typed system to be tested without a potentially expensive memory access. An obvious drawback of this approach is that the extra size/type bits reduce the range of the address space that can be expressed with the remaining address bits. Moreover, extra bit-diddling is required to turn these modified pointers into recognizable memory addresses.

Size/type information can be encoded in the pointer without these drawbacks using the **Big Bag of Pages (BIBOP)** scheme. This is based on decomposing memory into **pages** by viewing the higher-order bits of a word address as a page address and the lower-order bits of a word address as a location within a particular page. In BIBOP, all blocks allocated on a page must have the same size/type information. In the simplest incarnation of BIBOP, each type of object is stored in its own single (large) page. In this case, the page address *is* the block type tag. It is also possible to decompose memory into many smaller pages and store the size/type information in a table indexed by the page address. BIBOP saves space by effectively using a single header per page rather than per block.

There are other inefficiencies that can be addressed with clever block layouts. For example, the straightforward way to represent an n-character symbol or string as a block is to have a header word with size/type information followed by n character words. But using a 32-bit word to represent a single 8-bit ASCII character or 16-bit unicode character is wasteful of space. It is possible to employ **packed representations** in which 4 ASCII characters or 2 unicode characters are stored in a 32-bit word within a block.

Exercise 18.2 C. Hacker doesn't like reserving a bit of every FRM descriptor for a GC tag because then it isn't possible to have full 32-bit integers. Observing that every descriptor is either in the heap or in a register, he proposes an alternative way to store GC tags:

- In a heap block, the header word is followed by one or more GC-tag words that precede the content words of the block and store the GC tags of these content words. For example, the ith bit (1-indexed) of the first GC-tag word is the GC tag of the ith content word, where $1 \leq i \leq 32$; the ith bit of the second GC-tag word is the GC tag of the $(32 + i)$th content word; and so on.

- For every 32 registers, a 32-bit GC-tag register is reserved to store the GC tags of the register contents.

a. Describe the benefits and drawbacks of C. Hacker's idea.

b. If FRM were extended to include homogeneous arrays, what would be an efficient way to extend C. Hacker's approach to store the GC tags for the array components?

18.3   A Block Is Dead if It Is Unreachable

A storage system may reuse any dead block. Recall that a heap block is live in an FRM state if it will be accessed later in the program execution and is dead if it will not be accessed later. Unfortunately, this property is uncomputable in general, since there is no way to prove whether a program will or will not use a pointer to an arbitrary memory block. Therefore, a garbage collector must approximate liveness by reusing only *provably* dead blocks.

A sound garbage collector may classify a dead block as live, but not vice versa. The worst sound approximation is that all blocks are live, in which case GC degenerates to a simple heap manager that allocates blocks but never deallocates them, an approach viable for programs with small storage needs but not suitable for serious programming.

Intuitively, a block is dead if it cannot be reached by following a chain of pointers from the data values currently accessible to the program. Since there is no way the program can access the block, it is provably dead. (This assumes that programs cannot generate new pointers themselves by, for example, performing arbitrary pointer arithmetic.) As we shall see, there are different algorithms for determining which blocks are reachable.

GC algorithms are evaluated over many dimensions: the accuracy of their identification of live and dead blocks, how much time and space they require, whether they maintain locality (i.e., keep blocks that refer to each other close together in memory), whether they can be performed in a separate thread from the executing program, and how long a pause may be needed to perform GC. Real-time computer systems often cannot tolerate long GC-induced pauses, and thus require incremental GC algorithms that perform only a small amount of work every time the garbage collector is invoked.

18.3.1 Reference Counting

One day a student came to Moon and said: "I understand how to make a better garbage collector. We must keep a reference count of the pointers to each cons." Moon patiently told the student the following story:

> *"One day a student came to Moon and said: 'I understand how to make a better garbage collector...' "*

— MIT AI Koan about David Moon, attributed to Danny Hillis

There are two basic techniques for approximating the liveness of a block. The first is **reference counting**, in which each block has associated with it a **reference count** that indicates the number of pointers pointing to the block. When the reference count falls to zero, the block is provably dead and can be immediately reclaimed, e.g., by inserting it into a **free list** of blocks used for allocation.

Reference counting is conceptually simple and is easy to adapt to an incremental algorithm suitable for real-time systems. However, it suffers from numerous drawbacks. The run-time system executing a program must carefully increment a block's reference count whenever a pointer to it is copied and decrement its reference count whenever a register or memory slot containing a pointer to it is overwritten, and the time overhead for this bookkeeping can be substantial. Storage must be set aside for the reference counts; e.g., a certain number of bits in the block header word can be reserved for this purpose. When reference counts are modeled by a fixed number of bits, the maximal count must be treated as "infinity" — incrementing or decrementing this count must yield the same count, and blocks with this count can never be reclaimed even when they are actually dead. Dead cyclic structures can never be deallocated by reference counting alone, since each element in the structure has at least one pointer to it.

Like any heap manager that maintains a free list of blocks (regardless of whether it uses manual or automatic deallocation), reference-counting garbage collectors can suffer from **memory fragmentation**, where unallocated storage consists of many small blocks, none of which are contiguous. This happens when the heap manager reuses the storage of a deallocated block, but needs only part of it. Although a fragmented memory may contain a large amount of unallocated storage, the largest block that can be allocated may be small, causing programs to abort prematurely because of out-of-memory errors. Fragmentation can be fixed by **memory compaction**, a process that moves all live blocks to the beginning of memory to yield a single large unallocated block. Compaction requires rewiring pointers and may change the contents of registers as well as the contents of heap blocks. We shall study a form of compaction in the context of the stop-and-copy garbage collection algorithm presented in Section 18.4.

Reference counting is used in practice in the allocation and deallocation of disk blocks in Unix-like operating systems (including Linux). File deletion actually just removes a pointer, or **hard link**, and the operating system eventually collects all blocks with zero reference counts. Users are not permitted to make hard links to a directory in these systems, because this can create unreclaimable, cyclic structures on disk.

18.3.2   Memory Tracing

The second basic technique for approximating the liveness of a block is **memory tracing**, in which a block is considered live if it can be reached by a sequence of pointer-following steps from a **root set** of descriptors. In FRM, the root set for any machine state consists of the set of live registers (i.e., the registers that are mentioned in the current expression).[7] In a given machine state, any block that is not reachable from the root set can not be accessed in a future state and thus is dead and may be safely collected as garbage. If we imagine that pointers to heap blocks are strings connecting physical boxes, then tracing-based GC may be viewed as a process in which the root-set descriptors are anchored down while a vacuum cleaner is applied to the heap. Any blocks that are not connected by some sequence of strings to the root set are untethered and will be sucked up by the vacuum cleaner. Memory tracing is a better approximation to reachability than reference counting, because it classifies cyclic structures unreachable from the root set as garbage. Memory tracing can also collect blocks that a reference counting scheme with fixed-size counts would render uncollectible with a count of "infinity."

Tracing-based GC imposes two requirements on a language implementation. In order to traverse all reachable blocks, it must be possible at run time to (1) distinguish block pointers from nonpointers (to know which descriptors to follow)

---

[7]The root set also includes spill memory, which we are ignoring here (but see the Web Supplement for details). In language implementations with a run-time stack of procedure invocation frames, all descriptors in the stack are also in the root set. FRM does not have a run-time stack; instead, stack frames are encoded as heap-based continuation closures.

and (2) determine the size of a block (in order to process its components). In the FRM implementation we have discussed, the GC tag of a descriptor satisfies requirement 1, and the size information in a block header word satisfies requirement 2. But there are other ways to satisfy these requirements. For example, the discussion starting on page 1129 shows ways to encode size information in the pointer word itself, and Exercise 18.4 on page 1138 explores how a single header bit per word can be used to encode the size of a heap block without a header word. Some systems specially mark blocks containing no pointers so that GC does not have to examine the components of such a block.

18.4 Stop-and-copy GC

Memory tracing is the basis for a wide variety of GC strategies, including a relatively simple and effective one known as **stop-and-copy**. The essential idea is familiar to anyone who has moved from one dwelling to another: put everything you want to keep into a moving van, and anything not on the van at the end is garbage. Stop-and-copy garbage collection reclaims memory by copying all live data to a new area of memory and declaring everything left in the old memory space to be garbage. We will first sketch the stop-and-copy algorithm and then describe the details for FRM below.

To distinguish new and old memory spaces, a heap memory of size n_{size} is divided into two equal-sized areas called **semispaces**: a lower semispace covering addresses in the range $[0..((n_{size} \div 2) - 1)]$ and an upper semispace covering addresses in the range $[(n_{size} \div 2)..(n_{size} - 1)]$.[8] At any time, one semispace is active and the other is inactive.

The active semispace is used for all allocations, using the simplest possible strategy: Allocations start at the beginning (or symmetrically the end) of the active semispace, and each successive allocation request is satisfied with the memory block after the last one allocated. This continues until there is an allocation request for more memory than remains in the active semispace. The inactive semispace is like a field lying fallow; it contains no live blocks and is not used for allocation.

When a request is made to allocate a block that cannot fit at the top of the active space, the program is stopped and the garbage collector is invoked. At this point, the active semispace is called **from-space** and the inactive semispace is called **to-space**. Garbage collection begins by copying the root set (the contents of the registers) to the bottom of to-space. It then enters a **copy phase** in which

---

[8]For simplicity, assume that n_{size} is even.

it copies into to-space all blocks in from-space that are reachable from the root set. It must preserve the pointer relationships between blocks, so that the graph structure of the copied blocks is isomorphic to the original one. It must also update any pointers in the root set to point to the appropriate copied blocks in to-space.

Once the copy phase is complete, all live blocks are in to-space, and the algorithm installs the updated root-set descriptors in the machine state (because all pointers have moved to to-space). At this point, the semispaces are **flipped**: to-space becomes the new active semispace and from-space becomes the new inactive semispace. An attempt is now made to retry the failed allocation request in the new active space: if it succeeds, the program continues normally; otherwise, program execution fails with an out-of-memory error.

A Stop-and-copy GC for FRM

Implementing the allocation strategy above requires only a **free pointer** n_{free}, which points to the first free word in the active semispace. If the lower semispace is active first, n_{free} is initially 0, and the semispace is completely full when $n_{free} = (n_{size} \div 2)$.

If the addresses of the active semispace are in the range $[n_{lo}..n_{hi}]$, then the free pointer partitions the active semispace into two parts: allocated blocks stored in the address range $[n_{lo}..(n_{free} - 1)]$ and free memory available for future allocation in the address range $[n_{free}..n_{hi}]$.

A request to allocate an n-slot block is handled as follows:

1. Calculate $n'_{free} = n_{free} + n + 1$ (the 1 accounts for the header word).

2. If there is enough room to allocate the block (i.e., if $n'_{free} \leq n_{hi} + 1$):

   (a) store a header word for size n in slot $\mathcal{M}[n_{free}]$;

   (b) save the value of n_{free} as n_{result};

   (c) update the free pointer n_{free} to n'_{free}; and

   (d) indicate that allocation has succeeded and that n_{result} is the address of the newly allocated block.

   If there is not enough room to perform the allocation, then do a garbage collection (see below) and attempt the allocation again. If it fails a second time, then fail with an out-of-memory error.

In FRM, the copy-phase algorithm is an iteration in three state variables: (1) a **scan pointer** n_{scan} that keeps track of the blocks that need to be copied

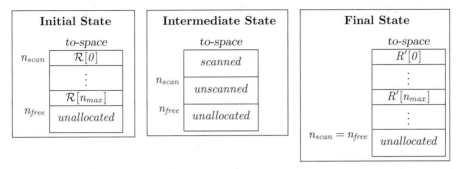

Figure 18.4 Depictions of initial, intermediate, and final states of the copy phase iteration in the stop-and-copy garbage collection algorithm.

from from-space to to-space; (2) a **free pointer** n_{free} used to allocate storage in to-space for blocks being copied from from-space; and (3) the main memory $\mathcal{M}$ whose heap component is partitioned into from-space and to-space. Figure 18.4 shows initial, intermediate, and final states of the copy phase. The copy phase begins by installing the root set (the contents of all the registers)[9] into the first $n_{reg} = n_{max} + 1$ slots of to-space, setting n_{scan} to point to the first slot of the root set, and setting n_{free} to point to the first slot after the root set.

If to-space spans the memory addresses $[n_{lo}..n_{hi}]$, then every step of the copy-phase iteration maintains the following invariant:

$$n_{lo} \leq n_{scan} \leq n_{free} \leq n_{hi} + 1 \quad (18.1)$$

Indeed, the n_{scan} and n_{free} pointers partition to-space into three regions:

- The bottom region of to-space, occupying the address range $[n_{lo}..(n_{scan} - 1)]$, is the **scanned region**, which contains words that have been successfully processed by the copy phase, so that pointers in the scanned region point to blocks in to-space.

- The middle region of to-space, occupying the address range $[n_{scan}..(n_{free} - 1)]$, is the **unscanned region**, which contains words still to be processed by the copy phase. This region effectively serves as a first-in first-out queue of words to be processed by the copy phase; when a word at the bottom of this region is processed, new words may be added to the top of this region.

---

[9]For simplicity, the algorithm includes all registers in the root set. A more precise tracing-based approximation to block liveness would be achieved by including only the *live* registers — i.e., those registers actually mentioned in the current expression of the FRM state. See Exercise 18.3.

- The top region of to-space, occupying the address range $[n_{free}..n_{hi}]$, is the **unallocated region** into which blocks from from-space will be copied.

Two additional invariants hold at each step of the copy-phase iteration:

$$\textit{Pointers in the scanned region point to blocks in to-space} \qquad (18.2)$$

$$\textit{Pointers in the unscanned region point to blocks in from-space} \quad (18.3)$$

The copy-phase invariants hold in the initial state of the copy phase iteration: invariant (18.1) clearly holds; the scanned region is initially empty, so invariant (18.2) trivially holds; and the unscanned region initially contains the root set, whose pointers all point to from-space, so invariant (18.3) holds.

Each step of the copy phase is described by one of the pictorial rewrite rules in Figure 18.5. Each rule processes the word at n_{scan}, increments n_{scan} to yield n'_{scan}, and updates n_{free} to yield n'_{free}. The rules are distinguished by the type of the first element (the element at n_{scan}) in the queue of unscanned words. If this word is a nonpointer — i.e, it is an immediate descriptor or a header word — then the iteration simply skips it and moves on to the next word in the queue. If the descriptor is a pointer word, by invariant (18.3) it must specify an address n_{from} of a from-space block. The first time the copy phase visits the block, it copies the contents of the block (including its header word) into to-space starting at address n_{free} and updates the free pointer accordingly; since all pointers in the block refer to from-space, invariant (18.3) is preserved for the next iteration. It also changes the descriptor at n_{scan} to point to the new to-space address (n_{free}) rather than the old from-space address (n_{from}), thus preserving invariant (18.2) for the next iteration. Finally, it replaces the header word of the original from-space block with its **forwarding address**, the new to-space address (n_{free}) of the block, to indicate that the block has already been moved to to-space. If the copy phase encounters a from-space block with a forwarding address n_{fwd} (distinguishable from a block header by having a tag of 01 instead of 11), it means that the block has already been copied to to-space, and it is only necessary to convert the block pointer to its forwarding address (in order to preserve invariant (18.2)).

The copy phase eventually processes all block pointers that can be reached from the root set, thus performing a memory trace that approximates liveness by reachability from the root set. Because new blocks are copied to the end of the queue in the unscanned region, blocks are traversed in a breadth-first manner. The copy phase ends when the unscanned region queue becomes empty — i.e., when the scan pointer catches up to the free pointer. At this point, all objects reachable from the root set have been copied from from-space to to-space, and invariant (18.2) guarantees that all pointer descriptors in to-space now point into to-space.

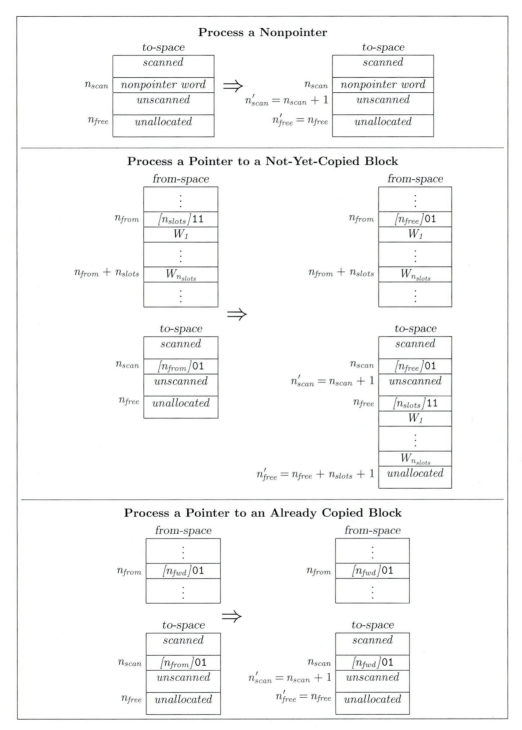

Figure 18.5 A pictorial description of the stop-and-copy garbage collection algorithm.

At the termination of the copy phase, the updated register contents in the first n_{reg} slots of to-space are copied back into the registers, yielding the new register memory $\mathcal{R}'$. Additionally, a semispace flip is performed by making to-space the new active semispace. Subsequent allocations then take place starting at n_{free} in this new active semispace.

The stop-and-copy algorithm has several nice properties. Unlike reference counting, it can collect cyclic garbage. Stop-and-copy GC compacts live blocks at the bottom of to-space; this avoids memory fragmentation and simplifies block allocation. The time to perform a stop-and-copy GC is proportional to the total size of reachable blocks, so if most of from-space is garbage, very little work is needed to perform a stop-and-copy GC.

However, stop-and-copy has some serious drawbacks as well. Reserving half of heap memory for the inactive semispace wastes a large chunk of potential storage space. The breadth-first nature of the memory trace performed by stop-and-copy does not preserve the locality of blocks, which can seriously degrade memory performance. The block movement of the copy phase causes significantly more memory traffic than in-place approaches like reference counting and the mark-sweep strategy discussed below.

Exercise 18.3 The stop-and-copy GC algorithm presented above has a root set that includes the contents of all registers. However, if a dead register (one that is not in the free variables of the currently executing expression) contains a pointer to a block, then this block will be treated as live by any tracing-based GC algorithm, even though it may be provably dead. Because of this, GC may not collect as much garbage as it could. Fix this problem by making a simple change to the GC algorithm that prevents it from following pointers stored in dead registers.

Exercise 18.4 In a system that requires only GC information (not types), Ben Bitdiddle thinks that encoding the size of a block in a header word wastes too much space. He observes that it is possible to dispense with all block header words if an additional bit (which he calls the *header bit*) is reserved in every descriptor to indicate whether it is the first word of a block in the heap. So two tag bits are necessary in every descriptor: the header bit and the GC tag. Here is one possible tag encoding:

00	immediate descriptor that is not the first word in a heap block
10	immediate descriptor that is the first word in a heap block
01	nonimmediate descriptor that is not the first word in a heap block
11	nonimmediate descriptor that is the first word in a heap block

The header bit should be 1 only for descriptors stored in the first word of a block in the heap. Any other descriptor (including those stored in registers) should have a header bit of 0.

a. Modify the stop-and-copy GC algorithm to work with Ben's representation.

b. What are the advantages and drawbacks of Ben's approach?

Exercise 18.5 Suppose that the first 20 words of main memory $\mathcal{M}$ in an executing FRM program have the contents shown below. (Assume the FRM GC-tag-only descriptor and size-only block representations presented in Sections 18.2.2 and 18.2.3 are being used. The number to the left of each slot is its address. In each slot, a bracketed decimal integer followed by tag bits stands for the binary representation of the integer concatenated with the tag bits.)

0	[5]01	5	[1]11	10	[3]11	15	[2]01
1	[5]0	6	[10]01	11	[3]0	16	[7]01
2	[2]11	7	[2]11	12	[5]01	17	[2]11
3	[7]01	8	[2]0	13	[14]01	18	[10]01
4	[2]01	9	[2]01	14	[2]11	19	[5]01

Suppose that the program uses only the first two registers (i.e., $n_{reg} = 2$), where $\mathcal{R}[0] = [17]01$ and $\mathcal{R}[1] = [14]01$, and the program does not spill any registers. Finally, suppose that the currently executing FIL_{reg} expression has the form

```
(let* ((r0 0)              {Set register 0 to 0}
       (r0 (@mnew NT)))    {Set register 0 to the address of a new block with NT slots}
   E_rest)
```

where $FrIds[\![E_{rest}]\!] = \{r0, r1\}$ (i.e., it refers to both registers).

a. Draw a box-and-pointer diagram depicting the two registers and all the heap blocks in $\mathcal{M}$. You should draw a register as a one-slot box. You should draw a heap block with n content slots as an n-slot box. A slot containing an immediate value should show that value. A slot containing an address should be the source of an arrow that points at the box representing the heap block at that address.

b. Based on your diagram in part **a**, indicate which heap blocks are live and which are dead when the mnew primitive is executed.

c. Assume that heap memory has 40 slots (so that the first 20 fill one semispace). Show the contents of heap memory after performing the stop-and-copy GC algorithm initiated when the mnew primitive is executed. What is the largest value of NT for which the program will not encounter an out-of-memory error?

Exercise 18.6 Ben Bitdiddle has been hired by the Analog Equipment Corporation to consult on a memory management problem. Analog uses Balsa, a programming language in which heap storage is explicitly managed by programmers using the following two expression constructs:

(malloc E): If the value of E is a positive integer n, returns a pointer to a block of storage that is $n + 1$ words long. The first word of the returned block is a size header; the other n words are uninitialized. An out-of-memory error is generated if there is insufficient storage to allocate a block of the requested size. An error is generated if the value of E is not a positive integer.

(free E): If the value of E is a pointer to a block of storage, deallocates the storage of that block (allowing it to be reused by malloc) and returns *unit*. Otherwise, an error is generated.

Analog is having problems with a very large Balsa application (dubbed *The Titanic* by the development staff) that eventually either mysteriously crashes or runs out of heap space. Ben suspects that the programmers who wrote the application are not properly deallocating storage.

In order to debug Analog's problem, Ben decides to implement a standard stop-and-copy garbage collector for Balsa. He modifies malloc and free to keep track of the total amount of "busy" storage — malloc increments a global *busy* counter with the number of words in the block it creates and free decrements the *busy* counter by the number of words in the block it frees. In Ben's system, free just decrements the *busy* counter and does not actually free any storage. Instead, when storage is exhausted, the garbage collector runs and copies live storage from the old active semispace into the new one.

a. Let *live* be the number of words copied during a garbage collection and *busy* be the value of the *busy* counter at the time of the garbage collection. In each of the following situations encountered while executing a Balsa program in Ben's system *with* garbage collection, describe the implications for executing the same program in the original system *without* garbage collection:

i. *live* < *busy*

ii. *live* > *busy*

iii. *live* = *busy*

b. How can Ben modify his garbage collector to detect dangling pointers?

c. Ben tests his garbage collector on another very large AEC program called *The Brittanic*.[10] The program uses malloc and free for explicit memory management and works fine with one megabyte of available memory. Ben installs enough extra memory to support two semispaces, each of which has one megabyte of storage beyond the space needed for the garbage collector itself. Ben turns on the garbage collector, and, full of hope, runs the program. To his surprise, *The Brittanic* encounters an out-of-memory error.

i. How can you explain this behavior?

ii. How can Ben fix the problem?

---

[10]The *Brittanic* (1914–1916) was an identical sister ship of the *Titanic*.

18.5 Garbage Collection Variants

Stop-and-copy is just one of many approaches to garbage collection. Here we review some other approaches.

18.5.1 Mark-sweep GC

Another popular tracing-based GC algorithm is **mark-sweep**, an approach to GC that takes place in two phases. First, the **mark phase** traverses memory from the root set, marking each reachable block along the way (e.g., by setting a mark bit associated with each block it visits). Then the **sweep phase** linearly scans through memory and collects all unmarked blocks into a free list. The mark-sweep collector is invoked whenever an allocation request is made and the free list does not have a big enough block.

Mark-sweep has several benefits compared to stop-and-copy. Unlike stop-and-copy, which uses only half of heap memory for allocating blocks, mark-sweep can allocate blocks in all of heap memory. Like reference counting, mark-sweep is an **in-place** algorithm that does not move blocks, and so it can be used in situations (such as conservative GC, discussed later) where blocks cannot be moved. In-placeness also helps to preserve block locality and reduce memory traffic during GC. But in-placeness has a big downside as well — it implies using a free list for allocation, which leads to memory fragmentation.

There are other drawbacks to mark-sweep. There is space overhead for the mark bits and time overhead for manipulating them. There is also space overhead for controlling the mark-phase traversal, although this can be eliminated using the clever pointer-reversal technique described in [SW67]. Finally, the sweep phase takes time proportional to the size of the heap rather than to the size of live memory. In contrast, stop-and-copy GC takes time proportional to the size of live memory.

18.5.2 Tag-free GC

A GC algorithm is said to be **tag-free** if GC descriptors do not require tags. For a statically typed language, it is possible to implement a tag-free GC that can also eliminate header words for blocks whose sizes are statically known. The basic idea is to design the implementation so that the garbage collector is provided with (or can find) run-time type information for every word in the root set. This type information can be used as a "map" that guides GC by distinguishing pointers from nonpointers and indicating the sizes of blocks whose size is statically known.

(Size-bearing header words are still necessary for blocks whose size is known only dynamically, such as arrays.)

For example, a descriptor with type (prodof int bool (listof int)) is a pointer to a block with three slots, the first two of which are nonpointers, but the third of which (if nonnull) is a pointer to a two-slot block with one nonpointer and one pointer. Because it has compact descriptions for complex specifications (e.g., (listof int) describes the layout of integer lists of any length), such a type "map" generally requires far less storage than that needed to explicitly annotate every word and block with GC information. But tag-free GC complicates the compiler (which must supply type information to the run-time system), the run-time system (which must preserve the type information), and the GC algorithm (which must find and follow the type "map").

18.5.3   Conservative GC

In a tracing-based GC, it is never sound to treat a pointer as a nonpointer, since this could result in classifying a live block as dead. However, it is sound to treat some nonpointers as pointers. For example, in a system where words do not carry GC tags, if an integer in a register happens to have the same bit pattern as a pointer to a heap block, it's OK to consider that block reachable; the only downside is that this block may now cause a memory leak. But if the probability of misinterpreting an integer as a block pointer is low, then this sort of memory leak may not be any worse than leaks due to other liveness approximations.

This is the key idea behind a tag-free approach known as **conservative GC** [BW88], which can be used for garbage collection in implementations of languages (e.g., C/C++ and Pascal) that cannot tolerate GC tags in their word representations. There are clever techniques for efficiently determining whether an arbitrary word is a possible heap-block address and, if so, for determining the size of the block. Conservative GC must use an in-place algorithm (like mark-sweep) to collect dead blocks because there is no reliable way to distinguish integers from pointers when performing the pointer rewiring required by copying techniques. Empirically, conservative GC appears to work well in many situations, and it is the only GC technique available for many languages.

18.5.4   Other Variations

There are many other variations on the garbage collection approaches that we have discussed. Based on the observation that most blocks in some systems are short-lived, so-called **generational collectors** partition the heap into regions based on block lifetimes; recently allocated blocks are put in regions where collection is performed frequently, and older blocks migrate to regions where collection is performed less frequently. There are numerous incremental versions of many approaches that reduce the length of GC pauses or bound them so that GC can be used in real-time systems. There are also many concurrent GC algorithms that can run in a thread separate from the one(s) used for program execution; the challenging problem these algorithms must address is how to handle the fact that some threads are changing the graph of blocks while GC is being performed in a separate thread. Even more challenging is performing garbage collection in distributed environments, where memory is distributed over processing nodes connected by a communication network with an arbitrary topology.

In practice, choosing a garbage collector depends critically on numerous details, such as the typical lifetimes of blocks of particular sizes, the tolerance for memory leaks, the frequency of cyclic data, the acceptability of GC pauses, the necessity of keeping blocks in place, the importance of memory locality, the cost of memory traffic, and various other issues involving time and space resources. Finding a good heap manager can require implementing several solutions, comparing them empirically, and fine-tuning the one that performs best in typical situations. Sometimes it is a good idea to combine several of the strategies we have discussed. For example, a system might require certain blocks to be deallocated manually and use reference counts to automatically deallocate other blocks, relying on a periodic stop-and-copy GC to compact and collect cyclic garbage from the reference-counted storage.

Exercise 18.7 This exercise continues the scenario started in Exercise 18.5 on page 1139.

a. Assume that heap memory has just 20 slots, containing the values shown in Exercise 18.5. Show the contents of heap memory after performing the mark-sweep GC algorithm initiated when the `mnew` primitive is executed. Assume that one bit of each header word is reserved for the mark bit and that reclaimed blocks are stored in a free list that is used for allocation. Assume that the free list is stored in a special register R_{free} initially containing 0 (denoting the empty list) and that a block of size n_{slots} is added to the free list by first setting the first content slot of the block to contain the content of R_{free} and then setting R_{free} to the address of the block. What is the largest value of NT for which the program will not encounter an out-of-memory error?

b. Again assume that heap memory has just 20 slots and that memory is allocated from a free list as described in part **a** (where R_{free} is initially the empty list). Assume that a reference-counting garbage collector is used, where 3 bits of each header word are reserved for a reference count. Show the contents of heap memory and R_{free} (1) after performing the instruction that sets R_0 to 0 and (2) after performing the `mnew` primitive. What is the largest value of NT for which the program will not encounter an out-of-memory error?

Exercise 18.8 Consider the following FLARE/V program P:

```
(flare (n)
  (recur loop ((p (pair 0 0)))
    (let ((s (snd p)))
      (if (= s n)
          (fst p)
          (loop (pair s (+ s 1)))))))
```

a. Explain what this program does.

b. Suppose that P is compiled by TORTOISE and executed in a version of FRM using a simple heap manager that allocates blocks but never deallocates them. On the ith iteration of the loop, how many pair blocks are live and how many are dead?

c. Suppose that we extend FLARE/V and FIL with a manual deallocation construct (free E). If E denotes a compound value, then free indicates that the heap block representing this value may be reclaimed; otherwise free generates an error. Modify P to a program P' that uses free in such a way that it will not abort with an out-of-memory error for any natural number input when executed using a heap of reasonable size.

d. Remark on the suitability of each of the following approaches to garbage collection for executing P: (1) stop-and-copy; (2) mark-sweep; and (3) reference counting.

e. Suppose that P is translated to C, where pair is replaced by a call to malloc, C's memory allocator, and loop is replaced by a while loop. What, if any, garbage collection techniques can prevent the program from running out of memory?

18.6   Static Approaches to Automatic Deallocation

We have studied dynamic approaches to automatic deallocation, but there are static approaches as well.

In a language implementation with a run-time stack of frames that store information (e.g., arguments, local variables, return addresses) associated with procedure invocations, popping a frame on procedure exit can reclaim a large chunk of storage with low cost (resetting the stack pointer). Languages like C/C++, PASCAL, and ADA permit (indeed, encourage) the programmer to allocate data blocks on the stack by declaring compound values that are local to a procedure; these are implicitly deallocated when the procedure returns. PASCAL and ADA do not allow creating pointers to stack-allocated data that can outlive the stack frame for the procedure invocation in which they were allocated, so stack deallocation cannot give rise to dangling pointers in these languages. In contrast, C and C++ *do* allow pointers to stack-allocated data to outlive the stack frame in which they were allocated, providing yet another way to generate dangling pointers in these languages.

An alternative approach is to rely on a system that statically determines (e.g., using the lifetime analysis in Section 16.3.5) which blocks can safely be allocated on the stack. For example, in the TORTOISE compiler, such a system would be able to determine automatically that all closures for continuation procedures introduced by the CPS stage can be stack-allocated — an expected result, since they correspond to traditional stack frames.[11]

The region-based approach to memory management sketched in Section 16.3.5 generalizes this idea by statically allocating each program value within a particular region of a stack of abstract regions associated with an automatically placed `let-region` construct. This allows an entire region to be deallocated when the `let-region` that introduced it is exited.

Notes

A wealth of information about modern garbage collection techniques can be found in the surveys [Wil92] and [Jon99]. Earlier work is surveyed in [Coh81].

Mark-sweep collection was invented by McCarthy in the first version of LISP [McC60]. The idea of copying garbage collection originated with Minsky [Min63], who wrote live data to disk and read it back into main memory. Fenichel and Yochelson developed a two-semispace algorithm for list memory in which live list nodes were scanned recursively [FY69]. The recursion implies extra storage for a recursion stack, but this can be eliminated by the pointer-reversal technique described in [SW67]. The iterative scanning algorithm we describe, which uses constant control space for scanning, is due to Cheney [Che70]. There are incremental versions of this algorithm that can limit the duration of a GC pause (e.g., [HGB78, AEL88, NOPH92, NO93, NOG93]).

[App89] sketches how static typing can eliminate the need for almost all tag bits in a garbage-collected language. Many of the details of tag-free GC were worked out in [Gol91]. Determining the types of tagless objects in a statically typed language with polymorphism is a problem. One solution is to dynamically reconstruct the types at run time [AFH94]. Another is to modify the compiler and

---

[11]This is true only because FLARE/V does not include constructs that capture control points, such as `label`/`jump` or `cwcc`. Also, note that stack allocation of continuation closures can be performed without sophisticated analysis. For example, Rozas's Liar compiler for SCHEME [Roz84] achieved this result by performing a pre-CPS closure-conversion pass that allocated closures on the heap and a post-CPS closure conversion pass that allocated closures on the stack.

run-time system to explicitly pass the types onto which polymorphic functions are projected [Tol94]. Conservative GC [BW88] is a variant of tag-free GC suitable for languages whose data representations cannot contain GC tag bits.

An operational framework for reasoning formally about memory management is presented in [MFH95]. Interestingly, type reconstruction in this system can be used to identify values that, though reachable, will never actually be referenced, and so can be reclaimed as garbage. So-called *linear types*, which track the number of times a value is used, can be used in such a framework to eagerly reclaim values after their last use [IK00].

Many techniques have been developed to reduce dangling pointer errors in languages with manual heap deallocation. One approach is to insert additional run-time checks before memory operations to guarantee memory safety [NMW02, JMG⁺02]. Another approach is to prove statically that no dangling pointers can be encountered in a running program. Although this is undecidable in general, it can be done for certain kinds of programs with a sufficiently sophisticated analysis (e.g., [DKAL03, ZX05, Zhu06]).

Heap management is only one of many services provided by the run-time system for a programming language implementation. For a discussion of a more full-featured run-time system, see [App90], which provides an overview of data layout and run-time services (including garbage collection, module loading, input/output, foreign function calls, and execution profiling) for an ML implementation.

Appendix A

A Metalanguage

Man acts as though he were the shaper and master of language, while in fact language remains the master of man.

— Martin Heidegger, "Building Dwelling Thinking," *Poetry, Language, Thought* (1971)

This book explores many aspects of programming languages, including their form and their meaning. But we need some language in which to carry out these discussions. A language used for describing other languages is called a **metalanguage**. This appendix introduces the metalanguage used in the body of the text.

The most obvious choice for a metalanguage is a natural language, such as English, that we use in our everyday lives. When it comes to talking about programming languages, natural language is certainly useful for describing features, explaining concepts at a high level, expressing intuitions, and conveying the big picture. But natural language is too bulky and imprecise to adequately treat the details and subtleties that characterize programming languages. For these we require the precision and conciseness of a mathematical language.

We present our metalanguage as follows. We begin by reviewing the basic mathematics upon which the metalanguage is founded. Next, we explore two concepts at the core of the metalanguage: functions and domains. We conclude with a summary of the metalanguage notation.

A.1   The Basics

The metalanguage we will use is based on set theory. Since set theory serves as the foundation for much of popular mathematics, you are probably already familiar with many of the basics described in this section. However, since some of our notation is nonstandard, we recommend that you at least skim this section in order to familiarize yourself with our conventions.

A.1.1   Sets

A **set** is an unordered collection of elements. Sets with a finite number of elements
are written by enclosing the written representations of the elements within braces
and separating them by commas. So $\{2, 3, 5\}$ denotes the set of the first three
primes. Order and duplication don't matter within set notation, so $\{3, 5, 2\}$ and
$\{3, 2, 5, 5, 2, 2\}$ also denote the set of the first three primes. A set containing one
element, such as $\{19\}$, is called a **singleton**. The set containing no elements is
called the **empty set** and is written $\{\}$.

We will assume the existence of certain sets:

$Unit\ =\ \{unit\}$; *standard singleton set*
$Bool\ =\ \{true, false\}$; *truth values*
$Int\ =\ \{\ldots, -2, -1, 0, 1, 2, \ldots\}$; *integers*
$Pos\ =\ \{1, 2, 3, \ldots\}$; *positive integers*
$Neg\ =\ \{-1, -2, -3, \ldots\}$; *negative integers*
$Nat\ =\ \{0, 1, 2, \ldots\}$; *natural numbers*
$Rat\ =\ \{0, 1, -1, \frac{1}{2}, -\frac{1}{2}, 2, -2, \frac{1}{3}, -\frac{1}{3}, \frac{2}{3}, -\frac{2}{3}, 3, -3, \frac{3}{2}, -\frac{3}{2}, \ldots\}$; *rationals*
$Char\ =\ \{\text{'a', 'b'}, \ldots, \text{'A', 'B'}, \ldots, \text{'1', '2'}, \ldots, \text{'.', ',',} \ldots\}$; *text characters*
$String\ =\ \{\text{"", "a", "b"}, \ldots, \text{"foo"}, \ldots \text{"a string"}, \ldots\}$; *all character strings*

(The text in *slanted font* following the semicolon is just a comment and is not a
part of the definition. This is one of two commenting styles used in this book.
In the other commenting style, the comments are written in slanted font and are
delimited by braces. However, the braces would be confusing in the presence
of set notation, so we use the semicolon style in some cases.) The *Unit* set is
the canonical singleton set; its single element is named *unit*. *Bool* is the set of
the boolean truth values *true* and *false*. *Int*, *Pos*, *Neg*, *Nat*, and *Rat* (which
contains all ratios of integers) are standard sets of numbers. *String* is the set of
all character strings. *Unit* and *Bool* are finite sets, but the other examples are
infinite. Since it is impossible to write down all elements of an infinite set, we
use ellipses ("...") to stand for the missing elements in standard sets where it is
clear what the remaining elements are.

We consider the *unit* value, truth values, numbers, and characters to be **primitive** elements that cannot be broken down into subparts. Character strings are
not primitive because they can be decomposed into their component characters.

Sets can contain any structure, including other sets. For example, the set
$\{Int, Nat, \{2, 3, \{4, 5\}, 6\}\}$ contains three elements: the set of integers, the set
of natural numbers, and a set of four elements (one of which is itself a set of
two numbers). Here the names *Int* and *Nat* are used as synonyms for the set
structures they denote.

Set membership is specified by the symbol $\in$ (pronounced "element of" or "in"). The notation $e \in S$ asserts that e is an **element** of the set S, while $e \notin S$ asserts that e is not an element of S. (In general, a slash through a symbol indicates the negation of the property denoted by that symbol.) For example,

$$0 \in Nat$$
$$0 \notin Neg$$
$$Int \in \{Int, Nat, \{2, 3, \{4, 5\}, 6\}\}$$
$$Neg \notin \{Int, Nat, \{2, 3, \{4, 5\}, 6\}\}$$
$$2 \notin \{Int, Nat, \{2, 3, \{4, 5\}, 6\}\}$$

In the last example, 2 is not an element of the given set even though it is an element of one of that set's elements.

A set A is a **subset** of a set B (written $A \subseteq B$) if every element of A is also an element of B. Every set is a subset of itself, and the empty set is trivially a subset of every set. E.g.,

$$\{\} \subseteq \{1, 2, 3\} \subseteq Pos \subseteq Nat \subseteq Int \subseteq Rat$$
$$Nat \subseteq Nat$$
$$Nat \not\subseteq Pos$$

Two sets A and B are **equal** (written $A = B$) if they contain the same elements, i.e., if every element of one is an element of the other. Note that $A = B$ if and only if $A \subseteq B$ and $B \subseteq A$. A is said to be a **proper subset** of B (written $A \subset B$) if $A \subseteq B$ and $A \neq B$.

Sets are often specified by describing a defining property of their elements. The **set builder** notation $\{x \mid P_x\}$ (pronounced "the set of all x such that P_x") designates the set of all elements x such that the property P_x is true of x. For example, Nat could be defined as $\{n \mid n \in Int \text{ and } n \geq 0\}$. The sets described by set builder notation are not always well defined. For example, $\{s \mid s \notin s\}$, (the set of all sets that are not elements of themselves) is a famous nonsensical description known as **Russell's paradox**.

We will use $[lo..hi]$ (pronounced "the integers between lo and hi, inclusive") as an abbreviation for $\{n \mid n \in Int \text{ and } lo \leq n \leq hi\}$; if $lo > hi$, then $[lo..hi]$ denotes the empty set.

Some common binary operations on sets are defined below using set builder notation:

$$A \cup B = \{x \mid x \in A \text{ or } x \in B\} \quad ; union$$
$$A \cap B = \{x \mid x \in A \text{ and } x \in B\} \quad ; intersection$$
$$A - B = \{x \mid x \in A \text{ and } x \notin B\} \quad ; difference$$

The notions of union and intersection can be extended to (potentially infinite) collections of sets. If A is a set of sets, then $\bigcup A$ denotes the union of all of the component sets of A. That is,

$$\bigcup A = \{x \mid \text{there exists an } a \in A \text{ such that } x \in a\}$$

If A_i is a family of sets indexed by elements i of some given index set I, then

$$\bigcup_{i \in I} A_i = \bigcup \{A_i \mid i \in I\}$$

denotes the union of all the sets A_i as i ranges over I. Intersections of collections of sets are defined in a similar fashion.

Two sets B and C are said to be **disjoint** if and only if $B \cap C = \{\}$. A set of sets $A = \{A_i \mid i \in I\}$ is said to be **pairwise disjoint** if and only if A_i and A_j are disjoint for any distinct i and j in I. A is said to **partition** (or **be a partition of**) a set S if and only if $S = \bigcup_{i \in I} A_i$ and A is pairwise disjoint.

The **cardinality** of a set A (written $|A|$) is the number of elements in A. The cardinality of an infinite set is said to be infinite. Thus $|Int|$ is infinite, but $|\{Int, Nat, \{2, 3, \{4, 5\}, 6\}\}| = 3$. Still, there are distinctions between infinities. Informally, two sets are said to be in a **one-to-one correspondence** if it is possible to pair every element of one set with a unique and distinct element in the other set without having any elements left over. Any set that is either finite or in a one-to-one correspondence with Nat is said to be **countable**. For instance, the set Int is countable because every nonnegative element n in Int can be paired with $2n$ in Nat and every negative element n in Int can be paired with $1 - 2 \cdot (n + 1)$. Clearly $Unit$, $Bool$, Pos, Neg, and $Char$ are also countable. It can be shown that Rat and $String$ are countable as well. Informally, all countably infinite sets "have the same size." On the other hand, any infinite set that is not in a one-to-one correspondence with Int is said to be **uncountable**. Cantor's celebrated diagonalization proof shows that the real numbers are uncountable.[1] Informally, the size of the reals is a much "bigger" infinity than the size of the integers.

The **powerset** of a set A (written $\mathcal{P}(A)$) is the set of all subsets of A. For example,

$$\mathcal{P}(\{1, 2, 3\}) = \{\{\}, \{1\}, \{2\}, \{3\}, \{1, 2\}, \{1, 3\}, \{2, 3\}, \{1, 2, 3\}\}$$

The cardinality of the powerset of a finite set is given by:

$$|\mathcal{P}(A)| = 2^{|A|}$$

---

[1] A description of Cantor's method can be found in many books on mathematical analysis and computability. We particularly recommend [Hof80].

In the above example, the powerset has size $2^3 = 8$. The set of all subsets of the integers, $\mathcal{P}(Int)$, is an uncountable set.

A.1.2 Boolean Operators and Predicates

In our metalanguage, we will often employ standard operators to manipulate expressions that denote the boolean truth values, *true* and *false*. Suppose that p, q, and r are any expressions that stand for boolean truth values. Then:

- $\neg p$, the **logical negation** of p, is *false* if p is *true* and is *true* if p is *false*. The notation $\neg p$ is pronounced "not p." Note that $\neg(\neg p) = p$.

- $p \wedge q$, the **logical conjunction** of p and q, is *true* only if both p and q are *true*; otherwise it is *false*. The notation $p \wedge q$ is pronounced "p and q." It is commutative ($p \wedge q = q \wedge p$) and associative (($p \wedge q) \wedge r = p \wedge (q \wedge r)$).

- $p \vee q$, the **logical disjunction** of p and q, is *false* only if both p and q are *false*; otherwise it is *true*. The notation $p \vee q$ is pronounced "p or q." It is commutative and associative.

- The **logical implication** statements "p implies q,"[2] "if p then q," and "p only if q" are synonymous, and are *true* only when p is *false* or q is *true*; otherwise, they are *false*. So these statements are equivalent to $(\neg p) \vee q$. When p is *false*, these statements are said to be **vacuously true**.

- The **contrapositive** of "p implies q" is "not q implies not p." This is logically equivalent to "p implies q," which we can see because $(\neg(\neg q)) \vee (\neg p)$ can be simplified to $(\neg p) \vee q$.

- The statement "p if q" is equivalent to "if q then p" and thus to $p \vee (\neg q)$.

- The statement "p if and only if q," usually abbreviated "p iff q," is *true* only if both "p implies q" and its **converse**, "q implies p," are *true*; otherwise it is *false*. It is equivalent to $((\neg p) \vee q) \wedge (p \vee (\neg q))$.

For our purposes, a **predicate** is a metalanguage expression, usually containing variables, that may denote either *true* or *false* when the variables are instantiated with values. Some examples are $n \in Pos$, $A \subseteq B$, and $x > y$. The first of these examples is a **unary predicate**, a predicate that mentions one variable (in this case, n).

---

[2] "p implies q" is traditionally written as $p \rightarrow q$ or $p \Rightarrow q$. However, the arrows $\rightarrow$ and $\Rightarrow$ are used for other purposes in this book. To avoid confusion, we will always express logical implication in English.

We have already seen predicates in set builder notation; the expression to the right of the | symbol is a predicate over the variables mentioned in the expression to the right. For example, the notation

$$\{x \mid x \in \mathit{Int} \text{ and } (x \geq 0 \text{ or } x \leq 5)\}$$

denotes the set of integers between 0 and 5, inclusive. In this case, the predicate after the | symbol is built out of three smaller predicates, and we could rewrite it using boolean operators as

$$(x \in \mathit{Int}) \wedge (x \geq 0 \vee x \leq 5)$$

Suppose that S is a set and $P(x)$ is a unary predicate over the variable x. Then the **universal quantification** statement $\forall_{x \in S} . P(x)$, pronounced "for all x in S, $P(x)$," is *true* iff P is *true* when x is instantiated to any member of S. If there is some element for which the predicate is *false*, the universal quantification statement is *false*. If S is empty, $\forall_{x \in S} . P(x)$ is *true* for any predicate $P(x)$; in this case, the statement is said to be **vacuously true**. We use the notation $\forall_{i=lo}^{hi} . P(i)$ as an abbreviation for $\forall_{i \in [lo..hi]} . P(i)$, where $[lo..hi]$ is the set of all integers i such that $lo \leq i \leq hi$.

The **existential quantification** statement $\exists_{x \in S} . P(x)$, pronounced "there exists an x in S such that $P(x)$," is *true* iff there is at least one element $x_{witness}$ in S such that $P(x)$ is *true* when x is instantiated to $x_{witness}$. If there is no element for which the predicate is *true*, the existential quantification statement is *false*. The element $x_{witness}$ (if it exists) is called a **witness** for the existential quantification because it provides the evidence that the statement is *true*.

A.1.3 Tuples

A **tuple** is an ordered collection of elements. A tuple of length n, called an n-tuple, can be envisioned as a structure with n slots arranged in a row, each of which is filled by an element. Tuples with a finite length are written by writing the slot values down in order, separated by commas, and enclosing the result in angle brackets. Thus $\langle 2, 3, 5 \rangle$ is a tuple of the first three primes. The number and order of elements in a tuple matter, so $\langle 2, 3, 5 \rangle$, $\langle 3, 2, 5 \rangle$, and $\langle 3, 2, 5, 5, 2, 2 \rangle$ denote three distinct tuples. Tuples of size 2 through 5 are called, respectively, **pairs**, **triples**, **quadruples**, and **quintuples**. The 0-tuple, $\langle \rangle$, and 1-tuples also exist.

The element of the ith slot of a tuple t can be obtained by **projection**, written $t \downarrow i$. For example, if s is the triple $\langle 2, 3, 5 \rangle$, then $s \downarrow 1 = 2$, $s \downarrow 2 = 3$, and $s \downarrow 3 = 5$. The notation $t \downarrow i$ is well formed only when t is an n-tuple and

$1 \leq i \leq n$. Two tuples s and t are **equal** if they have the same length n and $s \downarrow i$ $= t \downarrow i$ for all $1 \leq i \leq n$.

As with sets, tuples may contain other tuples; e.g., $\langle\langle 2, 3, 5, 7\rangle, 11, \langle 13, 17\rangle\rangle$ is a tuple of three elements: a quadruple, an integer, and a pair. Moreover, tuples may contain sets and sets may contain tuples. For instance, $\langle\langle 2, 3, 5\rangle, \textit{Int},$ $\{\{2, 3, 5\}, \langle 7, 11\rangle\}\rangle$ is a well-formed tuple.

If A and B are sets, then their **Cartesian product** (written $A \times B$) is the set of all pairs whose first slot holds an element from A and whose second slot holds an element from B. This can be expressed using set builder notation as:

$$A \times B = \{\langle a, b\rangle \mid a \in A \text{ and } b \in B\}$$

For example:

$$\{2, 3, 5\} \times \{7, 11\} = \{\langle 2, 7\rangle, \langle 2, 11\rangle, \langle 3, 7\rangle, \langle 3, 11\rangle, \langle 5, 7\rangle, \langle 5, 11\rangle\}$$
$$\textit{Nat} \times \textit{Bool} = \{\langle 0, \textit{false}\rangle, \langle 1, \textit{false}\rangle, \langle 2, \textit{false}\rangle, \ldots, \langle 0, \textit{true}\rangle, \langle 1, \textit{true}\rangle, \langle 2, \textit{true}\rangle, \ldots\}$$

If A and B are finite, then $|A \times B| = |A| \cdot |B|$.

The product notion extends to families of sets. If $A_1, \ldots, A_n$ is a family of sets, then their product (written $A_1 \times A_2 \times \ldots \times A_n$ or $\prod_{i=1}^{n} A_i$) is the set of all n-tuples $\langle a_1, a_2, \ldots, a_n\rangle$ such that $a_i \in A_i$. The notation A^n $(= \prod_{i=1}^{n} A)$ stands for the n-fold product of the set A.

A.1.4 Relations

A **binary relation** on A is a subset of $A \times A$.[3] For example, the less-than relation, $<_{Nat}$, on natural numbers is the subset of $\textit{Nat} \times \textit{Nat}$ consisting of all pairs of natural numbers $\langle n, m\rangle$ such that n is less than m:

$$<_{Nat} = \{\langle 0, 1\rangle, \langle 0, 2\rangle, \langle 0, 3\rangle, \ldots, \langle 1, 2\rangle, \langle 1, 3\rangle, \ldots, \langle 2, 3\rangle, \ldots\}$$

For a binary relation R on A, the notation $a_1 \ R \ a_2$ is shorthand for $\langle a_1, a_2\rangle \in R$. Similarly, the notation $a_1 \ \cancel{R} \ a_2$ means that $\langle a_1, a_2\rangle \notin R$. Thus, $1 <_{Nat} 2$ is really just another way of saying $\langle 1, 2\rangle \in <_{Nat}$, and $3 \not<_{Nat} 2$ is another way of saying $\langle 3, 2\rangle \notin <_{Nat}$.

For any set A, the equality relation $=_A$ on A is defined as $\{\langle a, a\rangle \mid a \in A\}$. If N is one of the standard numerical sets (*Nat, Int, Pos, Neg, Rat*, etc.), then $<_N$, $\leq_N$, $\geq_N$, and $>_N$ denote the standard binary numerical relations on N. The subscripts in these relations may be omitted when they are clear from context.

---

[3]The notion of a relation can be generalized to arbitrary products: an *n*-**ary relation** on the sets $A_1, \ldots, A_n$ is a subset of $A_1 \times \ldots \times A_n$. However, binary relations on a single set are sufficient for most of our purposes.

Binary relations are often classified by certain properties. Let R be a binary relation on a set A. Then:

- R is **reflexive** if, for all $a \in A$, $a \, R \, a$.

- R is **symmetric** if, for all $a_1, a_2 \in A$, $a_1 \, R \, a_2$ implies $a_2 \, R \, a_1$.

- R is **antisymmetric** if, for all $a_1, a_2 \in A$, $a_1 \, R \, a_2$ and $a_2 \, R \, a_1$ implies $a_1 =_A a_2$.

- R is **transitive** if, for all $a_1, a_2, a_3 \in A$, $a_1 \, R \, a_2$ and $a_2 \, R \, a_3$ imply $a_1 \, R \, a_3$.

For example:

- The $=_{Nat}$ relation has all four properties: it is reflexive, symmetric, antisymmetric, and transitive.

- The "has the same remainder modulo 3" relation on natural numbers (which we shall call $=_{mod3}$) is reflexive, symmetric, and transitive, but is not antisymmetric (why?).

- The $\leq_{Nat}$ relation and the "is a divisor of" relation on natural numbers are reflexive, antisymmetric, and transitive, but not symmetric.

- The $<_{Nat}$ relation is antisymmetric and transitive but not reflexive or symmetric. (It is antisymmetric because the premise $a_1 <_{Nat} a_2$ and $a_2 <_{Nat} a_1$ doesn't hold for any two natural numbers a_1 and a_2, so the property is vacuously true.)

- The following *isOneLess* relation on *Int* is (vacuously) antisymmetric, but not reflexive, symmetric, or transitive:

$$isOneLess = \{\langle i, (i+1) \rangle \mid i \in Int\}$$

A binary relation that is reflexive, symmetric, and transitive is called an **equivalence relation**. An equivalence relation R on A uniquely **partitions** the elements of A into disjoint **equivalence classes** A_i whose union is A and that satisfy the following: $a_1 \, R \, a_2$ if and only if a_1 and a_2 are elements of the same A_i. For example, it's easy to show that the $=_{mod3}$ relation introduced above satisfies the criteria for an equivalence relation. It partitions *Nat* into three equivalence classes:

$$
\begin{aligned}
Nat_0 &= \{0, 3, 6, 9, \ldots\} \\
Nat_1 &= \{1, 4, 7, 10, \ldots\} \\
Nat_2 &= \{2, 5, 8, 11, \ldots\}
\end{aligned}
$$

The **quotient** of a set A by an equivalence relation R (written A/R) is the set of equivalence classes into which R partitions A. Thus, $(Nat/=_{mod3})=\{Nat_0, Nat_1, Nat_2\}$. $= \{\,[\bar{0}]\,,\,[\bar{1}]\,,\,[\bar{2}]\,\}$

A binary relation that is reflexive, antisymmetric, and transitive is called a **partial order**. We study partial orders in more detail in Chapter 5.

There are several operations on binary relations that produce new relations. For $n \in Nat$, the **n-fold composition** of a binary relation R, written R^n, is the unique relation such that $a_{left} \; R^n \; a_{right}$ if and only if there exist a_i, $1 \leq i \leq n+1$, such that $a_1 = a_{left}$, $a_{n+1} = a_{right}$, and $a_j \; R \; a_{j+1}$ for each j such that $1 \leq j \leq n$. For example, n-fold composition of the *isOneLess* relation introduced above yields:

$$isOneLess^n = \{\langle i, (i+n)\rangle \mid i \in Int\}$$

Note that R^0 is the equality relation $=_A$ and R^1 is the same relation as R.

The **reflexive transitive closure** of a binary relation R on A, written R^*, is defined as:

$$R^* = \{\langle a_{left}, a_{right}\rangle \mid a_{left} \; R^n \; a_{right} \text{ for some natural number } n\}$$

If we instead require $n \geq 1$ in this definition, we obtain the **transitive closure** of R, written R^+. For example, *isOneLess** is the same relation as $\leq_{Int}$ and *isOneLess*$^+$ is the same relation as $<_{Int}$.

Exercise A.1 Let P be the set $\{reflexive, symmetric, antisymmetric, transitive\}$ of the names of four properties that relations can have. Let X be the three-element set $\{a, b, c\}$. For each set $S \in \mathcal{P}(P)$, either

- define a binary relation on X (i.e., as a set of pairs in $X \times X$) that has all the properties in S but none of the properties in $P - S$; or

- explain why no such relation can be defined.

Note that there are 16 subsets of P. For example, for $S_{st} = \{symmetric, transitive\}$, one answer is the binary relation $R_{st} = \{\langle a, b\rangle, \langle b, a\rangle, \langle a, a\rangle, \langle b, b\rangle\}$. R_{st} is symmetric and transitive, but it isn't reflexive (since it's missing $\langle c, c\rangle$) and it isn't antisymmetric (since $a \; R_{st} \; b$ and $b \; R_{st} \; a$ but $a \neq_X b$). Keep in mind that a relation can be vacuously symmetric, antisymmetric, or transitive — i.e., if the premises in the definition of one of these properties are never true, the property vacuously holds.

A.2 Functions

Functions are crucial elements of our metalanguage. Here we carefully explain what they are in the context of sets (**set-theoretic functions**) and develop notations to express them.

A.2.1   What Is a Function?

Informally, a function is a mapping from an **argument** to a **result**. More formally, a **function** f is a triple of three components:[4]

1. The **source** S of the function, written $src(f)$ — the set from which the argument is taken.

2. The **target** T of the function, written $tgt(f)$ — the set from which the result is taken.

3. The **graph** of a function, written $gph(f)$ — a subset G of $S \times T$ such that each $s \in S$ appears as the first component in no more than one pair $\langle s, t \rangle \in G$.

For example, the increment function inc_{Int} on the integers can be defined as

$$inc_{Int} = \langle Int, Int, G_{inc} \rangle$$

where G_{inc} is the set of all pairs $\langle i, i+1 \rangle$ such that $i \in Int$. That is,

$$G_{inc} = \{\ldots, \langle -3, -2 \rangle, \langle -2, -1 \rangle, \langle -1, 0 \rangle, \langle 0, 1 \rangle, \langle 1, 2 \rangle, \langle 2, 3 \rangle, \ldots\}$$

Note that $src(inc_{Int}) = Int$, $tgt(inc_{Int}) = Int$, and $gph(inc_{Int}) = G_{inc}$.

A **total function** is one that is defined for all elements of its source — that is, one for which $\{s \mid \langle s, t \rangle \in gph(f)\} = src(f)$. If there are source elements for which the function is undefined, the function is said to be **partial**. Most familiar numerical functions are total, but some are partial. The reciprocal function on rationals is partial because it is not defined at 0. And a square-root function defined as

$$sqrt = \langle Nat, Nat, \{\langle n^2, n \rangle \mid n \in Nat\} \rangle$$

is partial because it is defined only at perfect squares.

For any function f, we use the notation $dom(f)$ to stand for its **domain of definition**, the source elements at which f is defined. That is,

$$dom(f) = \{s \mid \langle s, t \rangle \in gph(f)\}$$

For example, $dom(sqrt)$ is the set of perfect squares. A function f is total if $dom(f) = src(f)$ and otherwise is partial.

---

[4]What we call source and target are commonly called **domain** and **codomain**, respectively. We use different names so as not to cause confusion with the meaning of the term **domain** introduced in Section A.3.

It is always possible to turn a partial function into a total function by adding a distinguished element to the target that represents the undefined case, and altering the graph to map all previously unmapped members of the source to this element. By convention, this element is called **bottom** and is written $\bot$. Using this element, we can define a total reciprocal function whose source is Rat, whose target is $Rat \cup \{\bot\}$, and whose graph is

$$\{\langle 0, \bot \rangle\} \cup \{\langle q, \tfrac{1}{q} \rangle \mid q \in Rat \text{ and } q \neq 0\}$$

Bottom plays a crucial role in the explanation of fixed points in Chapter 5.

The notation $S \to T$ stands for the set of all total functions with source S and target T, while the notation $S \rightharpoonup T$ stands for the set of all partial functions with source S and target T. The notation $f : S \to T$ declares that $f \in (S \to T)$; in this case, we say that $S \to T$ is the **signature** of the function.[5] In a function signature, the arrow $\to$ can be replaced by $\rightharpoonup$ to indicate a partial function.

Two functions are **equal** if they are equal as triples — i.e., if their sources, targets, and graphs are respectively equal. In particular, it is not sufficient for their graphs to be equal — they must have the same signature as well. For example, consider the two functions $abs_1 = \langle Int, Int, G_{abs} \rangle$ and $abs_2 = \langle Int, Nat, G_{abs} \rangle$, where G_{abs} is the set of all pairs $\langle i, i_{abs} \rangle$ such that i is an integer and i_{abs} is the absolute value of i. Then even though abs_1 and abs_2 have the same graph, they are not equal as functions because the signature of abs_1, $Int \to Int$, is different from the signature of abs_2, $Int \to Nat$.

Many programming languages use the term "function" to refer to a kind of subroutine. To avoid confusion, we will use the term **procedure** for a programming language subroutine, and will reserve the term **function** for the mathematical notion. We wish to carefully distinguish them because they differ in some important respects:

- We often think of procedures as methods, or sometimes even agents, for computing an output (result) from an input (argument). A function doesn't use any method or perform any computation; it doesn't *do* anything. It simply *is* a structure that contains the source, the target, and all input/output pairs.

- We typically view procedures as taking multiple arguments or returning multiple results. But a function always has exactly one argument and exactly one result. However, we will see shortly how these procedural notions can be simulated with functions.

---

[5]The signature of a function is also called its **type**. In Section A.3, we will generalize the notion of type to describe the well-formedness of arbitrary metalanguage expressions.

- In addition to returning a value, procedures often have a side effect — e.g., changing the state of the computer's memory or display screen. There is no equivalent notion of side effect for a function. However, we will see in Chapter 8 how to use functions to model side effects in a programming language.

- When viewed in terms of their input/output behavior, procedures can specify only a subset of functions known as the **computable functions** — i.e., those functions whose results can be determined by executing a computational process on their arguments. The most famous example of an uncomputable function is the halting function, which maps the text of a program to a boolean that indicates whether or not the program will halt when executed.

The above points do not necessarily apply to the procedural entities in all languages. In particular, the subroutines in so-called functional programming languages are very close in spirit to mathematical functions.

A.2.2   Application

The primary operation involving a function is the **application** of the function to an **argument**, an element in its source. The function is called the **operator** of the application, while the argument is called the **operand** of the application. The result of applying an operator f to an operand s is the unique element t in the target of f such that $\langle s, t \rangle$ is in the graph of f. If there is no pair $\langle s, t \rangle$ in the graph of f, then the result of the application of f to s is said to be **undefined**.

We use the juxtaposition $f\ s$ to denote the application of a function f to an argument s.[6] For instance, the increment of 3 is written inc_{Int} 3. Parentheses are used to structure nested applications. Thus, inc_{Int} (inc_{Int} 3) expresses the increment of the increment of 3. In the metalanguage, parentheses that don't affect the application structure can always be added without changing the meaning of an expression.[7] For example, ((inc_{Int}) (inc_{Int} (3))) is equivalent to the above application. Function application associates to the left, so that the expression $a\ b\ c\ d$ parses as ((($a\ b$) c) d).

---

[6]The reader may find it strange that we depart from the more traditional notation for application, which is written $f(s)$ for single arguments, and $f(s_1, s_2, \ldots, s_n)$ for multiple arguments. The reason is that in the traditional notation, f is usually restricted to be a *function name*, whereas we will want to allow the function position of an application to be any metalanguage expression that stands for a function. Application by juxtaposition is a superior notation for handling this more general case because it visually distinguishes less between the function position and the argument position.

[7]This contrasts with s-expression grammars (see Section 2.3), as in LISP-like programming languages, in which no parentheses are optional.

If f is a partial function and $s \in src(f)$ but $s \notin dom(f)$, then $f\ s$ is undefined. We sometimes write $f\ s = undefined$ to indicate this situation; in this notation, *undefined* does *not* denote an element of $tgt(f)$. For example, $sqrt\ 4 = 2$ but $sqrt\ 5 = undefined$.

The application notation $f\ s$ is well formed only when $f : S \to T$ and $s \in S$. For example, $(sqrt\ -3)$ is an invalid application because $-3 \notin Nat$ and $(1\ 2)$ is an invalid application because 1 is not a function.

A.2.3 More Function Terminology

For any set A, there is an **identity** function $id_A : A \to A$ that maps every element of A to itself:

$$id_A = \langle A, A, \{\langle a, a\rangle \mid a \in A\}\rangle$$

Given sets A and B, for each element $b \in B$, there is a **constant** function $const_{A,B,b}$ that maps every element of A to b:

$$const_{A,B,b} = \langle A, B, \{\langle a, b\rangle \mid a \in A\}\rangle$$

If $f : A \to B$ and $g : B \to C$, then the **composition** of g and f, written $g \circ f$, is a function with signature $A \to C$ defined as follows:

$$(g \circ f)\ a = (g\ (f\ a)), \text{ for all } a \in A$$

The composition function[8] is associative, so that

$$f \circ g \circ h = (f \circ g) \circ h = f \circ (g \circ h)$$

If $f : A \to A$ then the **n-fold composition** of f, written f^n, is

$$\underbrace{f \circ f \circ \ldots \circ f}_{n \text{ times}}$$

f^0 is defined to be the identity function on A. Because of the associativity of composition, $f^n \circ f^m = f^{n+m}$.

For any set B such that $B \subseteq A$, there is an **inclusion** function $B \hookrightarrow A$ that maps every element of B to the same element in the larger set:

$$B \hookrightarrow A = \langle B, A, \{\langle b, b\rangle \mid b \in B\}\rangle$$

---

[8]There is not a single composition function, but really a family of composition functions indexed by the sets A, B, and C used in its definition.

Inclusion functions are handy for satisfying the constraints imposed by function signatures. For example, if $inc : Int \to Int$ and $square : Int \to Nat$, then the composition $inc \circ square$ is ill defined because the target set of $square$ is not the same as the source set of inc. Using an inclusion function leads to the well-formed composition $inc \circ (Nat \hookrightarrow Int \circ square)$.

The **image** of a function is that subset of the target to which the function actually maps all source elements. That is, for $f : S \to T$, the image of f is

$$img(f) = \{t \mid \text{there exists an } s \text{ such that } (f\ s) = t\}$$

A function f is **injective** when no two elements of the source map to the same target element, i.e., when $(f\ s_1) = (f\ s_2)$ implies $s_1 = s_2$. A function f is **surjective** when every element in the target is the result of some application, i.e., when $img(f) = tgt(f)$. A function is **bijective** if it is both injective and surjective. Two sets A and B are said to be **isomorphic** or in a **one-to-one correspondence** if there exists a bijective function with signature $A \to B$; such a function is called an **isomorphism** between A and B.

For any $n \in Nat$, an isomorphism with signature $[1..n] \to [1..n]$ is called a **permutation**. By convention, we will use π to range over permutations, and will write the application of π to k as $\pi(k)$. We will use permutations to formally express that phrases indexed by numbers in the range $[1..n]$ can be reordered.

A.2.4   Higher-order Functions

The sources and targets of functions are not limited to familiar sets like numbers, but may be sets of sets, sets of tuples, or even sets of functions. Functions whose sources or targets themselves include functions are called **higher-order functions**. We make extensive use of higher-order functions throughout this book.

As a natural example of a function that returns a function, consider a function *make-expt* that, given a power, returns a function that raises numbers to that power. The signature of *make-expt* is $Nat \to (Nat \to Nat)$. That is, the source of *make-ext* is Nat, and the target of *make-expt* is the set of all functions with signature $Nat \to Nat$. The graph of *make-expt* is:

$$
\begin{aligned}
&\{\langle 0, \langle Nat, Nat, \{\langle 0,1\rangle, \langle 1,1\rangle, \langle 2,1\rangle, \langle 3,1\rangle, \langle 4,1\rangle, \ldots\}\rangle\rangle, \\
&\ \langle 1, \langle Nat, Nat, \{\langle 0,0\rangle, \langle 1,1\rangle, \langle 2,2\rangle, \langle 3,3\rangle, \langle 4,4\rangle, \ldots\}\rangle\rangle, \\
&\ \langle 2, \langle Nat, Nat, \{\langle 0,0\rangle, \langle 1,1\rangle, \langle 2,4\rangle, \langle 3,9\rangle, \langle 4,16\rangle, \ldots\}\rangle\rangle, \\
&\ \langle 3, \langle Nat, Nat, \{\langle 0,0\rangle, \langle 1,1\rangle, \langle 2,8\rangle, \langle 3,27\rangle, \langle 4,64\rangle, \ldots\}\rangle\rangle, \\
&\ \ldots\}
\end{aligned}
$$

That is, (*make-expt* 0) denotes a function that maps every natural number to 1, (*make-expt* 1) denotes the identity function on natural numbers, (*make-expt* 2) denotes the squaring function, (*make-expt* 3) denotes the cubing function, and so on.

As an example of a function that takes functions as arguments, consider the function *apply-to-five* that takes a function between natural numbers and returns the value of this function applied to 5. The signature of *apply-to-five* is $(Nat \rightarrow Nat) \rightarrow Nat$ and its graph is:

$$\{\langle id_{Nat}, 5 \rangle, \langle inc_{Nat}, 6 \rangle, \langle dec_{Nat}, 4 \rangle, \langle square_{Nat}, 25 \rangle, \langle cube_{Nat}, 125 \rangle,$$
$$\ldots, \langle \langle Nat, Nat, \{\ldots, \langle 5, n \rangle, \ldots\} \rangle, n \rangle, \ldots\}$$

where inc_{Nat}, dec_{Nat}, $square_{Nat}$, and $cube_{Nat}$ denote, respectively, the incrementing function, decrementing function, squaring function, and cubing function on natural numbers.

A.2.5 Multiple Arguments and Results

We noted before that every mathematical function has a single argument and a single result. Yet, as programmers, we are used to thinking that many familiar procedures, like addition and multiplication, have multiple arguments. Sometimes we think of procedures as returning multiple results; for instance, a division procedure can profitably be viewed as returning both a quotient and a remainder. How can we translate these programming language notions into the world of mathematical functions?

Multiple Arguments

There are two common approaches for handling multiple arguments:

1. In the first approach, called **tupling**, the multiple arguments can be boxed up into a single argument tuple. For instance, under this approach, the binary addition function $+_{Nat}$ on natural numbers would have signature $(Nat \times Nat) \rightarrow Nat$ and would have the following graph:

$$\{\langle \langle 0,0 \rangle, 0 \rangle, \langle \langle 0,1 \rangle, 1 \rangle, \langle \langle 0,2 \rangle, 2 \rangle, \langle \langle 0,3 \rangle, 3 \rangle, \ldots,$$
$$\langle \langle 1,0 \rangle, 1 \rangle, \langle \langle 1,1 \rangle, 2 \rangle, \langle \langle 1,2 \rangle, 3 \rangle, \langle \langle 1,3 \rangle, 4 \rangle, \ldots,$$
$$\langle \langle 2,0 \rangle, 2 \rangle, \langle \langle 2,1 \rangle, 3 \rangle, \langle \langle 2,2 \rangle, 4 \rangle, \langle \langle 2,3 \rangle, 5 \rangle, \ldots,$$
$$\ldots\}$$

Then an application of the addition function to 3 and 5, say, would be written as $(+_{Nat} \langle 3, 5 \rangle)$.

2. A function of multiple arguments can be represented as a higher-order function that takes the first argument and returns a function that takes the rest of the arguments. This approach is named **currying**, after its inventor, Haskell Curry. Under this approach, the binary addition function $+_{Nat}$ on natural numbers would have signature $Nat \rightarrow (Nat \rightarrow Nat)$ and would have the following graph:

$$\{\langle 0, \langle Nat, Nat, \{\langle 0,0 \rangle, \langle 1,1 \rangle, \langle 2,2 \rangle, \langle 3,3 \rangle, \ldots\}\rangle\rangle,$$
$$\langle 1, \langle Nat, Nat, \{\langle 0,1 \rangle, \langle 1,2 \rangle, \langle 2,3 \rangle, \langle 3,4 \rangle, \ldots\}\rangle\rangle,$$
$$\langle 2, \langle Nat, Nat, \{\langle 0,2 \rangle, \langle 1,3 \rangle, \langle 2,4 \rangle, \langle 3,5 \rangle, \ldots\}\rangle\rangle,$$
$$\ldots\}$$

When $+_{Nat}$ is applied to n, the resulting value is the increment-by-n function. So, given 0, it returns the identity function on natural numbers; given 1, it returns the increment-by-one function; given 2, it returns the increment-by-two function; and so on. With currying, the application of $+_{Nat}$ to 3 and 5 is written as $((+_{Nat}\ 3)\ 5)$ or, relying on the left-associativity of application, as $(+_{Nat}\ 3\ 5)$.

In the currying approach, functions like $+_{Nat}$ or *make-expt* can be viewed differently according to the context in which they are used. Sometimes, we may like to think of them as functions that "take two arguments." Other times, it is helpful to view them as functions that take a single argument and return a function. Of course, they are exactly the same function in both cases; the only difference is the glasses through which we're viewing them.

Throughout this book, we will use the second approach, currying, as our standard method of handling multiple arguments.

Now that we have a way to express functions of multiple arguments, we will describe some standard functions that we will use throughout the book. For example, we can view the logical negation ($\neg : Bool \rightarrow Bool$), conjunction ($\wedge : Bool \rightarrow (Bool \rightarrow Bool)$), and disjunction ($\vee : Bool \rightarrow (Bool \rightarrow Bool)$) operators as functions with the following graphs:

$$gph(\neg) = \{\langle false, true \rangle, \langle true, false \rangle\}$$

$$gph(\wedge) = \{\langle false, \langle Bool, Bool, \{\langle false, false \rangle, \langle true, false \rangle\}\rangle\rangle,$$
$$\langle true, \langle Bool, Bool, \{\langle false, false \rangle, \langle true, true \rangle\}\rangle\rangle\}$$

$$gph(\vee) = \{\langle false, \langle Bool, Bool, \{\langle false, false \rangle, \langle true, true \rangle\}\rangle\rangle,$$
$$\langle true, \langle Bool, Bool, \{\langle false, true \rangle, \langle true, true \rangle\}\rangle\rangle\}$$

Suppose that N is a numerical set (*Nat*, *Int*, *Rat*, etc.). The standard binary numerical operator names $+_N$ (addition), $-_N$ (subtraction),[9] and $\times_N$ (multiplication) denote curried functions with signature $N \to (N \to N)$. So, $+_{Nat}$ is addition on the naturals, $-_{Int}$ is subtraction on the integers, and $(\times_{Rat} 2)$ denotes a doubling function on rationals.

The absolute value function on integers, $abs_{Int} : Int \to Int$, returns i for $i \geq 0$ and $(-_{Int} 0\ i)$ for $i < 0$. We abbreviate $(abs_{Int}\ i)$ as $|i|$.

The division function for rationals is $\div_{Rat} : Rat \to (Rat \rightharpoonup Rat)$; the second arrow signifies a partial function because division by zero is undefined. If N is *Nat* or *Int*, the functions $\div_N$ and $\%_N$ have the signature $N \to (N \rightharpoonup N)$ and denote, respectively, quotient and remainder functions on N. Given a numerator $n \in N$ and denominator $d \in N$ such that $d \neq 0$, these calculate the unique quotient q and remainder r (where $0 \leq r < |d|$ if $n \geq 0$ and $-|d| < r \leq 0$ if $n < 0$) such that $n = (+_N\ (\times_N\ q\ d)\ r)$. For example,

n	d	q	r
17	5	3	2
-17	5	-3	-2
17	-5	-3	2
-17	-5	3	-2

We will assume that the standard binary numerical relation names, such as $<_N$, $\leq_N$, $=_N$, $\neq_N$, $\geq_N$, and $>_N$ can be used not only as relations but as curried functions with signature $N \to (N \to Bool)$, where N is a numerical set. Functions that return boolean values are called **predicate functions**. When a binary relation name R is used as a predicate, $(R\ n_1\ n_2)$ denotes *true* if $n_1\ R\ n_2$ and denotes *false* otherwise. E.g., $(<_{Nat}\ 1\ 2) = true$ and $(>_{Nat}\ 1\ 2) = false$.

Since infix notation for standard binary functions is so much more familiar than the curried prefix form, we will typically use infix notation when both arguments are present. Thus, the expression $(b_1 \wedge b_2)$ is synonymous with $(\wedge\ b_1\ b_2)$, $(i_1 +_{Int} i_2)$ is synonymous with $(+_{Int}\ i_1\ i_2)$, and $(n_1 <_{Nat} n_2)$ is synonymous with $(<_{Nat}\ n_1\ n_2)$.

We will often omit the subscript on a function name when it is clear from context. For example, by the domain variable convention on page 1172, i_1 and i_2 are known to be integers, so $(i_1 + i_2)$ is assumed to mean $(i_1 +_{Int} i_2)$.

---

[9]The *Nat* subtraction $(-_{Nat}\ n_1\ n_2)$ is defined to be 0 if $n_1 \leq_{Nat} n_2$; otherwise it is the n_3 such that $(+_{Nat}\ n_2\ n_3) = n_1$. Since *Pos* does not contain 0, the *Pos* subtraction $(-_{Pos}\ n_1\ n_2)$ is undefined if $n_1 \leq_{Pos} n_2$; $-_{Pos}$ is a partial function with signature $Pos \to (Pos \rightharpoonup Pos)$. Corresponding remarks hold for *Neg*.

Conditionals are expressed via a family of curried three-argument functions if_S, indexed by a set S, with signatures $Bool \to (S \to (S \to S))$.[10] These return the second argument if the first argument is $true$, and return the third argument if the first argument is $false$. E.g.,

$$(if_{Nat}\ (1\ =_{Nat}\ 1)\ 3\ 4) = 3$$
$$(if_{Nat}\ (1\ =_{Nat}\ 2)\ 3\ 4) = 4$$

Multiple Results

The handling of multiple results parallels the handling of multiple arguments. Again, there are two common approaches:

1. Return a tuple of the results. Under this approach, a quotient-and-remainder function $quot\&rem$ on natural numbers would have the signature

$$Nat \to (Nat \rightharpoonup (Nat \times Nat))$$

Some sample applications using this approach:

$$(quot\&rem\ 17\ 4) = \langle 4, 1 \rangle$$
$$(quot\&rem\ 17\ 5) = \langle 3, 2 \rangle$$
$$(quot\&rem\ 17\ 0) = undefined$$

2. Suppose the goal is to define a function f of k arguments that "returns" n results. Instead define a function f' that accepts the k arguments that f would, but in addition also takes a special extra argument called a **receiver**. The value returned by f' is the result of applying the receiver to the n values we want f to return. The receiver indicates how the n returned values can be combined into a single value. For example:

$$(quot\&rem\ 14\ 4\ -_{Int}) = (3 -_{Int} 2) = 1$$
$$(quot\&rem\ 14\ 4\ \times_{Int}) = (3 \times_{Int} 2) = 6$$

In these examples the signature of $quot\&rem$ is

$$Nat \to (Nat \rightharpoonup ((Nat \to (Nat \to Nat)) \to Nat))$$

In general, the notation $(f'\ a_1\ \ldots\ a_k\ r)$ can be pronounced "Apply receiver r to the n results of the application of f to $a_1 \ldots a_k$." Note how this pronunciation mentions the f upon which f' is based.

---

[10]We use these conditional functions until they are superseded by the **if** notation introduced on page 1190.

We will use both of these approaches for returning multiple values. The second approach probably seems obscure and bizarre at first reading, but it will prove to be a surprisingly useful technique in many situations. In fact, it is just a special case of a more general technique called continuation-passing style that we will study in Sections 9.2 and 17.9.

A.2.6 Lambda Notation

Up to this point, the only notation we've had to express new functions is a combination of tuple notation and set builder notation. For example, the squaring function on natural numbers can be expressed by the notation:

$$square = \langle Nat, Nat, \{\langle n, n^2\rangle \mid n \in Nat\}\rangle$$

This notation is cumbersome for all but the simplest of functions.

For our metalanguage, we will instead adopt **lambda notation** as a more compact and direct notation for expressing functions. The lambda notation version of the above *square* function is:

$$square : Nat \rightarrow Nat = \lambda n \,.\, (n \times_{Nat} n)$$

Here, the source and target of the function are encoded in the signature that is attached to the function name. The Greek lambda symbol, λ, introduces an **abstraction** that specifies the graph of the function, i.e., how the function maps its argument to a result. An abstraction has the form λ *formal.body* where *formal* is a **formal parameter** variable that ranges over the source of the function, and *body* is a metalanguage expression, possibly referring to the formal parameter, that specifies a result in the target of the function. The abstraction λ *formal.body* is pronounced "A function that maps *formal* to *body*."

For a function with signature $A \rightarrow B$, an abstraction defines the graph of the function to be the following subset of $A \times B$:

$$\{\langle a, b\rangle \mid a \in A \text{ and } body \text{ denotes an element } b \in B \text{ when each}$$
$$\text{occurrence of } formal \text{ in } body \text{ is replaced by } a\}$$

(The notion of replacing each occurrence of a name in an expression that may contain other abstractions is fraught with subtle problems. These are discussed in Section 6.3.5.) For example, the abstraction $\lambda n \,.\, (n \times_{Nat} n)$ specifies the graph $\{\langle n, n^2\rangle \mid n \in Nat\}$. In the case of a partial function, *body* may not be defined at all elements of the source set. For example, consider a reciprocal function defined as:

$$recip : Rat \rightarrow Rat \ = \ \lambda q \,.\, (1 \div q)$$

The graph of *recip* defined by the abstraction contains no pair of the form $\langle 0, q_0 \rangle$ because $(1 \div_{Rat} 0)$ is undefined.

An abstraction for a function with signature $A \rightarrow B$ is well formed only when its body expression is well formed and denotes an element of B (or is undefined, in the case of a partial functions) when each occurrence of its formal parameter is replaced by any element of A. For example, the abstraction $\lambda n \,.\, 0$ is not a well-formed abstraction for a function with signature $Nat \rightarrow Pos$ because the returned value 0 is not an element of the target, Pos. However, the very same abstraction is well formed for a function with signature $Nat \rightarrow Nat$. As another example, the definition

$$dec : Nat \rightarrow Nat \ = \ \lambda n \,.\, (-1 +_{Nat} n)$$

is not well formed because in the body of the abstraction $+_{Nat}$ is applied to an argument, -1, that is not in the set Nat. Issues of well-formedness involving abstractions can be explained in terms of a notion of type that is introduced in Section A.3.

An important feature of lambda notation is that it facilitates the expression of higher-order functions. For example, suppose that *expt* is a binary exponentiation function on natural numbers such that $(expt \ n_{base} \ n_{power})$ is the result of raising n_{base} to n_{power}. Then the *make-expt* function from Section A.2.4 can be expressed succinctly as:

$$make\text{-}expt : Nat \rightarrow (Nat \rightarrow Nat) \ = \ \lambda n_1 \,.\, (\lambda n_2 \,.\, (expt \ n_2 \ n_1))$$

The abstraction $\lambda n_1 \,.\, \ldots$ can be read as "The function that maps n_1 to an exponentiating function that raises its argument to the n_1 power." Similarly, the *apply-to-five* function can be concisely written as:

$$apply\text{-}to\text{-}five : (Nat \rightarrow Nat) \rightarrow Nat \ = \ \lambda f \,.\, (f \ 5)$$

By the signature of *apply-to-five*, the argument f is constrained to range over functions with the signature $Nat \rightarrow Nat$. The lambda notation says that the *apply-to-five* function maps a given f to the result of applying f to 5.

An abstraction for a function with signature $S \rightarrow T$ can appear anywhere that a function with signature $S \rightarrow T$ can be used. For example, an application of the squaring function to the result of adding 2 and 3 can be written:

$$(\lambda n \,.\, (n \times_{Nat} n)) \ (2 +_{Nat} 3)$$

Such an application can be simplified by any manipulation that maintains the meaning of the expression. For instance:

$$
\begin{aligned}
&(\lambda n \,.\, (n \times_{Nat} n)) \ (2 +_{Nat} 3) \\
&= (\lambda n \,.\, (n \times_{Nat} n)) \ 5 \\
&= 5 \times_{Nat} 5 \\
&= 25
\end{aligned}
$$

In the next-to-last step above, the number 5 was substituted for the formal parameter n in the body expression $n \times_{Nat} n$. This step is justified by the meaning of application in conjunction with the function graph specified by the abstraction. As another sample application, consider:

$$
\begin{aligned}
&\textit{make-expt}\ 3 \\
&= (\lambda n_1 \,.\, (\lambda n_2 \,.\, (\textit{expt}\ n_2\ n_1)))\ 3 \\
&= \lambda n_2 \,.\, (\textit{expt}\ n_2\ 3)
\end{aligned}
$$

In this case, the result of the application is a cubing function.

Often the same abstraction can be used to define many different functions. For example, the abstraction $\lambda a . a$ can be used to define the graph of any identity or inclusion function. Because the variable a ranges over the source, though, the resulting graphs are different for each source. A family of functions defined by the same abstraction is said to be a **polymorphic function**. We will often parameterize such functions over a set or sets to take advantage of their common structure. Thus, we can define the polymorphic identity function as

$$
id_A : A \to A = \lambda a . a
$$

where the subscript A means that id_A defines a family of functions indexed by the type A. We specify a particular member of the family by fixing the subscript to be a known type. So id_{Int} is the identity function on integers, and id_{Bool} is the identity function on booleans. As another example of a polymorphic function, consider the following polymorphic version of the *apply-to-five* function studied above:

$$
\textit{apply-to-five}_T : (Nat \to T) \to T = \lambda f . (f\ 5)
$$

The family of functions *apply-to-five*$_T$ is parameterized over the target set T of the function parameter f. As a final example, we can define a polymorphic function composition function *compose*$_{A,B,C}$ with signature $(B \to C) \to ((A \to B) \to (A \to C))$ using the abstraction $\lambda f . (\lambda g . (\lambda a . (f\ (g\ a))))$.

There are several conventions for making lambda notation more compact:

- It is common to abbreviate nested abstractions by collecting all the formal parameters and putting them between a single λ and dot. Thus,

$$\lambda a_1 . \lambda a_2 . \ldots \lambda a_n . \, body$$

can also be written as

$$\lambda a_1 a_2 \ldots a_n . \, body$$

This abbreviation promotes the view that curried functions accept "multiple arguments": $\lambda a_1 a_2 \ldots a_n . \, body$ can be considered a specification for a function that "takes n arguments."

- Formal parameter names are almost always single characters, perhaps annotated with a subscript or prime. This means that whitespace separating such names can be removed without resulting in any ambiguity. In combination with the left-associativity of application, these conventions allow $\lambda a \ b \ c \, . \, ((b \ c) \ \ a)$ to be written as $\lambda abc.bca$. In situations where formal parameter names contain multiple characters, whitespace will be used to separate the names. E.g., if bc is a single name, then we would write $\lambda a \ bc \, . \, (bc \ a)$ instead of $\lambda abc \, . \, bca$.

- Nested abstractions are potentially ambiguous since it's not always apparent where the body of each abstraction ends. For example, the abstraction $\lambda x \, . \, \lambda y \, . \, yx$ could be parsed either as $\lambda x \, . \, \lambda y \, . \, (yx)$ or as $\lambda x \, . \, (\lambda y \, . \, y)x$. Traditionally, the following disambiguating convention is used in such cases: the body of an abstraction is assumed to extend as far right as explicit parentheses allow. By this convention, $\lambda x \, . \, \lambda y \, . \, yx$ means $\lambda x \, . \, (\lambda y \, . \, (yx))$. We will tend to use explicit parentheses to clarify the extent of an abstraction.

A.2.7   Recursion

Using lambda notation, it is possible to write **recursive** function specifications: functions that are directly or indirectly defined in terms of themselves. For example, the factorial function *fact* on natural numbers can be defined as:

$$fact : Nat \to Nat = \lambda n \, . \, (if_{Nat} \ (n =_{Nat} 0) \ 1 \ (n \times_{Nat} (fact \ (n -_{Nat} 1))))$$

We can argue that *fact* is defined on all natural numbers based on the principle of mathematical induction. That is, for the base case of an argument equal to 0, the definition clearly specifies the value of *fact* to be 1. For the inductive case, assume that *fact* is defined for the argument m. Then, according to the definition, the value of $(fact \ (m + 1))$ is $((m + 1) \times_{Nat} (fact \ m))$. But by the assumption that $(fact \ m)$ is defined, this expression has a clear meaning. So $(fact \ (m + 1))$ is also defined. By induction, *fact* is defined on every element of *Nat*, so the above definition determines a unique total function.

There are many recursive definitions for which the above kind of inductive argument fails. Consider the definition of the *strange* function given below:

$$strange : Nat \to Nat = \lambda n \, . \, (if_{Nat} \ (even?_{Nat} \ n) \ 0 \ (strange \ (n +_{Nat} 2)))$$

(Assume that $even?_{Nat}$ is a predicate function that tests whether its argument is even.) Clearly the function *strange* maps every even number to 0. But what does it map odd numbers to? Induction does not help us because the argument never gets smaller. If we think in terms of function graphs, then we see that for any natural number c, the above definition is consistent with a graph of the form

$$\{\langle 2n, 0\rangle \mid n \in Nat\} \cup \{\langle 2n + 1, c\rangle \mid n \in Nat\}$$

So the specification for *strange* is ambiguous; it designates any of an infinite number of function graphs!

The *strange* example illustrates that recursive definitions need to be handled with extreme care. For now, we will assume that the only case in which a recursive definition has a well-defined meaning is one for which it is possible to construct an inductive argument of the sort used for *fact*. Chapter 5 presents a technique for determining the meaning of a broad class of recursive definitions that includes functions like *strange*.

A.2.8 Lambda Notation Is Not Lisp!

Those familiar with a dialect of the LISP programming language may notice a variety of similarities between lambda notation and LISP. (Those unfamiliar with LISP may safely skip this section.) Although LISP is in many ways related to our metalanguage, we emphasize that there are some crucial differences:

- Our metalanguage requires that signatures declaring source and target sets must be specified for every abstraction. Most dialects of LISP, on the other hand, provide no mechanism for specifying the signatures of procedures.[11]

- Most LISP-like languages support procedures that handle multiple arguments. Because abstractions specify mathematical functions, they always take a single argument. However, we have seen that the notion of multiple arguments can be simulated by currying or tupling.

---

[11] The FX language [GJSO92] is a notable exception.

- Every parenthesis in a LISP expression is required, but parentheses are strictly necessary in our lambda notation only to override the default way in which a metalanguage expression is parsed. Of course, extra parentheses may be added to clarify a metalanguage expression.

- LISP dialects are characterized by evaluation strategies that determine details like which subexpressions of a conditional are evaluated and when argument expressions are evaluated relative to the evaluation of a procedure body. Our metalanguage, on the other hand, is not associated with any notion of a dynamic evaluation strategy. Rather, it is just a notation to describe the graph of a function, i.e., a set of argument/result pairs. Any reasoning about an abstraction is based on the structure of the graph it denotes.

For example, compare the metalanguage abstraction

$$\lambda a \, . \, (if_{Nat} \; (even?_{Nat} \; a) \; (a +_{Nat} 1) \; (a \times_{Nat} 2))$$

with the similar LISP expression

```
(lambda (a) (if (even? a) (+ a 1) (* a 2)))
```

In the case of LISP, only one branch of the conditional is evaluated for any given argument a; if a is even, then `(+ a 1)` is evaluated, and if it's odd, `(* a 2)` is evaluated. In the case of the metalanguage, the value of the function for any argument a is the result of applying the if_{Nat} function to the three arguments $(even?_{Nat} \; a)$, $(a +_{Nat} 1)$, and $(a \times_{Nat} 2)$. Here there is no notion of evaluation, no notion that some event does or does not happen, and no notion of time. The expression simply designates the mathematical function:

$$\langle Nat, Nat, \{\langle 0, 1 \rangle, \langle 1, 2 \rangle, \langle 2, 3 \rangle, \langle 3, 6 \rangle, \langle 4, 5 \rangle, \langle 5, 10 \rangle, \ldots \} \rangle$$

In fact, a metalanguage abstraction can be viewed as simply a structured name for a particular function.

Although there are many differences between LISP and lambda notation, the two obviously share some important similarities. Some functional programming languages have features that are even more closely patterned after lambda notation. (The FL language presented in Chapter 6 is an example.) However, our purpose for introducing lambda notation here is to have a convenient notation for expressing mathematical functions, not for writing programs. The relationship between mathematical functions and programs is the essence of semantics, which is studied in the main text of the book.

A.3   Domains

A.3.1   Motivation

Sets and set-theoretic functions have too simple a structure to model some important aspects of the semantics of programming languages. Yet, we would like to proceed with the simplifying assumption that sets are adequate for our purposes until the need for more structure arises. And when we do augment sets with more structure (see Chapter 5), we would prefer not to throw away all of the concepts and notations developed up to that point and start from scratch.

To protect against such a disaster, we will use the same technique that good programmers use to guarantee that their code can be easily modified: **abstraction**.[12] The essence of abstraction is constructing an **abstraction barrier** or **interface** that clearly separates behavior from implementation. In programming, an interface usually consists of a collection of procedures that manipulate elements of an abstract data type. The data type is abstract in the sense that it can be manipulated only by the procedures in the interface; its internal representation details are hidden. The power of abstraction is that changes to the representation of a data type are limited to the implementation side of the barrier; as long as the interface specification is maintained, no client of the abstraction needs to be modified.

We introduce an abstract structure called a **domain** that will serve as our basic entity for modeling programming languages. Domains are set-like structures that have constituent elements, but may have other structure as well. In our initial naive implementation, domains are just sets. In Chapter 5, however, we change this implementation by considering sets whose elements are ordered by information content; the additional ordering structure is essential for defining recursive functions and domains.

The simplest kind of domain is a **primitive domain**, whose elements are treated as indecomposable entities. Examples of primitive domains include *Unit*, *Nat*, *Int*, and *Rat*.[13] **Domain constructors** build more complex domains from simpler ones. Elements of the resulting **compound domains** can be **constructed** out of the elements of simpler domains and can be **deconstructed** into the elements from which they were constructed. We will study four domain constructors, $\times$, $+$, *, and $\rightarrow$, and their associated means for constructing

---

[12]Note that this use of the term "abstraction" is different from that used in the previous section, where it meant a metalanguage expression that begins with a λ.

[13]For purposes of examples, we will also often treat *Bool* and *Char* as primitive domains, but we shall see in Section A.3.4 that they can be constructed as sum domains. We shall always treat *Rat* as a primitive domain rather than as a product of *Int* domains.

and deconstructing compound elements. Together, primitive domain names and domain constructors define a simple language of **domain expressions**. In our presentation of domains, we will typically use D (possibly subscripted) to stand for an arbitrary domain expression, and d (possibly subscripted) to stand for an arbitrary **element expression** that stands for the element of some domain.

A.3.2   Types

If an element expression d can be assigned a domain D such that d denotes an element of D, this domain D is called the **type** of d. We write $d : D$ (pronounced "d has type D") to declare that the element expression d has type D. If an element expression can be assigned a type, it is **well typed**; otherwise it is **ill typed**. In our presentation of domains, we shall describe (using a combination of English and metalanguage) the well-typedness conditions for each kind of domain expression. See Chapter 11 for a more formal way to describe the well-typedness conditions of a language via type rules.

The elements of many primitive domains have an obvious type. For example, $unit : Unit$, $true : Bool$, 'a' $: Char$, and $\frac{2}{3} : Rat$. However, the types of some elements are ambiguous; e.g., 3 could have type Nat, Int, or Rat. When the type of such an element is not clear from context, we will write it explicitly, as in $3 : Int$.

The type of applications of standard unary and binary operators is straightforward. For example, $(1 +_{Nat} 2) : Nat$ and $(3 <_{Int} 4) : Bool$. It is clear from context that 1 and 2 are being used with type Nat and 3 and 4 are being used with type Int.

To enhance the readability of element expressions, we adopt a convention in which each domain of interest has associated with it a **domain variable** that ranges over elements of the domain. Suppose v ranges over domain variable names. Then the notation $v \in D$ indicates that v is the domain variable for the domain D. For example, we use the following conventions throughout the text:

$b \in Bool$
$h \in Char$
$n \in Nat$
$z \in Pos$
$i \in Int$
$q \in Rat$

Domain variables, possibly in subscripted or primed form, are used in metalanguage expressions to indicate that they denote only entities from their associated domain. So $(n +_{Nat} 1)$, $(n_1 -_{Nat} n_2)$, and $(n' \times_{Nat} n'')$ are all well-typed element expressions having type Nat. However, the expressions $(i +_{Nat} 1)$, $(n -_{Int} 2)$, and $(i \times_{Int} q)$ are all ill typed. In some cases, inclusion functions (see Section A.2.3) can be used to turn an ill-typed expression into a well-typed one. E.g., $((Nat \hookrightarrow Int\ n) -_{Int} 2)$ is a well-typed expression.

A.3.3 Product Domains

The product of domains D_1 and D_2, written $D_1 \times D_2$, is the domain version of a Cartesian product. Elements of a compound domain are created by an appropriate **constructor function**. In the case of products, the constructor function $tuple_{D_1,D_2} : D_1 \to (D_2 \to (D_1 \times D_2))$ creates elements of the product domain $D_1 \times D_2$, which are called **tuples**. If $d_1 : D_1$ and $d_2 : D_2$ then $\left(tuple_{D_1,D_2}\ d_1\ d_2\right) : (D_1 \times D_2)$. The domain subscripts on $tuple_{D_1,D_2}$ emphasize that it is really a family of functions indexed by the domains D_1 and D_2. For example, $tuple_{Nat,Bool}$ and $tuple_{Int,Int}$ both serve to pair elements, but the fact that they have different sources, targets, and graphs makes them different functions.

We will abbreviate $\left(tuple_{D_1,D_2}\ d_1\ d_2\right)$ as $\langle d_1,\ d_2 \rangle_{D_1,D_2}$, and will drop the domain subscripts when they are clear from context. For example, the product of Nat and $Bool$ technically is

$$Nat \times Bool =$$
$$\{\left(tuple_{Nat,Bool}\ 0\ false\right),\ \left(tuple_{Nat,Bool}\ 1\ false\right),\ \left(tuple_{Nat,Bool}\ 2\ false\right),\ \ldots,$$
$$\left(tuple_{Nat,Bool}\ 0\ true\right),\ \left(tuple_{Nat,Bool}\ 1\ true\right),\ \left(tuple_{Nat,Bool}\ 2\ true\right),\ \ldots\}$$

but we will usually write it as

$$Nat \times Bool = \{\langle 0, false \rangle,\ \langle 1, false \rangle,\ \langle 2, false \rangle,\ \ldots,$$
$$\langle 0, true \rangle,\ \langle 1, true \rangle,\ \langle 2, true \rangle,\ \ldots\}$$

Domains of n-tuples (known as n-ary products) are written

$$\textstyle\prod_{j=1}^{n} D_j = D_1 \times D_2 \times \cdots \times D_n$$

and elements of this domain are constructed via $tuple_{D_1,D_2,\ldots,D_n}$, which is a function with signature $D_1 \to \left(D_2 \to \ldots \left(D_n \to \prod_{j=1}^{n} D_j\right) \ldots \right)$. The application $\left(tuple_{D_1,D_2,\ldots,D_n}\ d_1\ d_2\ \ldots\ d_n\right)$ is abbreviated $\langle d_1,\ d_2,\ \ldots,\ d_n \rangle_{D_1,D_2,\ldots,D_n}$, where the domain subscripts D_i can be dropped if they are understood from context. The well-typedness condition for tuples is: if $\forall_{j=1}^{n}\ .\ d_j : D_j$, then $\langle d_1,\ \ldots,\ d_n \rangle_{D_1,\ldots,D_n} : \prod_{j=1}^{n} D_j$. The notation D^n stands for the product of n copies of D.

Deconstruction of tuples in the product domain $\prod_{j=1}^{n} D_j$ is performed via n **projection functions** of the form

$$Proj\,k_{D_1,\ldots,D_n} : (D_1 \times \ldots \times D_n) \to D_k,$$

where k is in the range $[1..n]$. $Proj\,k_{D_1,\ldots,D_n}$ extracts the kth element from an n-tuple:

$$Proj\,k_{D_1,\ldots,D_n} \,\langle d_1,\ldots,d_n\rangle_{D_1,\ldots,D_n} = d_k, \text{ if } k \in [1..n]$$

For example,

$$Proj\,1_{Nat,Bool} \,\langle 19,\ true\rangle = 19$$
$$Proj\,2_{Nat,Bool} \,\langle 19,\ true\rangle = true$$

Again, the domain subscripts indicate that for each k, $Proj\,k$ is a family of functions indexed by the component domains of the tuple being operated on. They will be omitted when they are clear from context. The well-typedness condition for $Proj\,k_{D_1,\ldots,D_n}$ is: if $d : \prod_{j=1}^{n} D_j$ and $k \in [1..n]$, then $\big(Proj\,k_{D_1,\ldots,D_n}\ d\big) : D_k$.

Notice that we have overloaded the notation $\langle\ldots\rangle$, which may now denote either a set-theoretic tuple or a domain-theoretic one. We have done this because in the simple implementation of domains as sets, product domains simply *are* set-theoretic Cartesian products, and set-theoretic tuples *are* tuples. However, thinking in terms of a concrete implementation for domains can be somewhat dangerous. Product domains are really defined only by the behavior of *tuple* and *Proj\,k*, which must satisfy the following two properties:

1. $Proj\,k_{D_1,\ldots,D_n}\ \big(tuple_{D_1,\ldots,D_n}\ d_1 \ \ldots \ d_n\big) = d_k,$ if $k \in [1..n]$ — not necessary in order

2. $tuple_{D_1,\ldots,D_n}\ \big(Proj\,1_{D_1,\ldots,D_n}\ d\big) \ \ldots \ \big(Proj\,n_{D_1,\ldots,D_n}\ d\big) = d,$ if $d : \prod_{j=1}^{n} D_j$

Any implementation of *tuple* and *Proj\,k* that satisfies these two properties is a valid implementation of products for domains. For example, it's perfectly legitimate to define $tuple_{Nat,Bool}$ by

$$tuple_{Nat,Bool}\ n\ b = \langle b, n\rangle,$$

where the order of elements in the concrete (set-theoretic) representation is reversed, as long as $Proj\,k_{Nat,Bool}$ is defined consistently:

$$Proj\,1_{Nat,Bool} \,\langle b, n\rangle = n$$
$$Proj\,2_{Nat,Bool} \,\langle b, n\rangle = b$$

From here on, and in the body of the text, the $\langle \ldots \rangle$ notation will by default denote domain-theoretic tuples rather than set-theoretic tuples.

Since writing out compound domains in full can be cumbersome, it is common to introduce synonyms for them via a **domain definition** of the form

$$v \in \textit{domain-name} = \textit{domain-description}$$

where the domain variable declaration "$v \in$" is optional. For example, the domain definitions

$$\textit{Vector} = \textit{Int} \times \textit{Int}$$
$$c \in \textit{Circle} = \textit{Vector} \times \textit{Int} \times \textit{Bool}$$

introduce the name *Vector* as a synonym for a domain of pairs of integers and the name *Circle* as a synonym for a domain of triples whose components represent the state of a graphical circle object: the position of its center (a pair of integers), its radius (an integer), and a flag indicating whether or not it is filled (a boolean). The domain variable c ranges over elements of *Circle*, but no domain variable is declared for the *Vector* domain.

Domain definitions are often used merely to introduce more mnemonic names for domains. The following set of domain definitions is equivalent to the set above:

$$\textit{Vector} = \textit{X-coord} \times \textit{Y-coord}$$
$$\textit{X-coord} = \textit{Int}$$
$$\textit{Y-coord} = \textit{Int}$$
$$c \in \textit{Circle} = \textit{Position} \times \textit{Radius} \times \textit{Filled?}$$
$$\textit{Position} = \textit{Vector}$$
$$\textit{Radius} = \textit{Int}$$
$$\textit{Filled?} = \textit{Bool}$$

Domain equality is purely structural and has nothing to do with names. Thus, the assertion $\textit{Position} = (\textit{Int} \times \textit{Int})$ is true because both descriptions designate the domain of pairs of integers.[14]

---

[14] It may seem confusing that the equality symbol, $=$, is used both to test domains for equality and to define new domain names. But this confusion is standard in mathematics. In the first case, it is assumed that the meaning of all names is known, and $=$ asserts that the left- and right-hand sides are equal. In the second case, it is assumed that the meaning of the left-hand names are unknown, and the equations are solved to make the $=$ assertions true. In the circle examples above, the equations are trivial to solve, but domain equations with recursion can be difficult to solve (see Chapter 5).

A.3.4   Sum Domains

Sum domains are analogous to variant records and unions in programming languages. The sum of two domains, written $D_1 + D_2$, is a domain that is the **disjoint union** of the two domains. A disjoint union differs from the usual set union in that each element of the union is effectively "tagged" to indicate which component set it comes from. An element of a sum domain, which we will call a **oneof**, is constructed by an **injection function**

$$Inj\,k_{D_1,D_2} : D_k \rightarrow (D_1 + D_2)$$

Here, k, which can be either 1 or 2, indicates which component domain the element is from.

Intuitively, $\left(Inj\,k_{D_1,D_2}\ d_k\right)$ (where d_k is an element of D_k) can be viewed as a pair $\langle k, d_k \rangle$ whose first component k serves as a tag that indicates which domain the second component is from (see Exercise A.2). The tag is essential for interpreting the meaning of d_k when D_1 and D_2 are the same or their elements overlap. For example, if $D_1 = Nat$ and $D_2 = Int$, then $\left(Inj\,1_{Nat,Int}\ 5\right)$ (which can be viewed as the tagged pair $\langle 1, 5 \rangle$) designates the natural number 5 while $\left(Inj\,2_{Nat,Int}\ 5\right)$ (which can be viewed as the tagged pair $\langle 2, 5 \rangle$) designates the integer 5.

It is often the case that the tag indicates information that cannot be deduced from the untagged value. Consider a system for representing geometric figures that are either squares or equilateral triangles, where side lengths are natural numbers. A figure can be represented as an element of the sum domain $Nat + Nat$, where $\left(Inj\,1_{Nat,Nat}\ n\right)$ represents a square with side length n and $\left(Inj\,2_{Nat,Nat}\ n\right)$ represents an equilateral triangle with side length n. In this case, the tag indicates the kind of figure (1 for square, 2 for equilateral triangle), while the natural number indicates a property of the figure (its side length).

A sum domain contains all oneofs that can be constructed from its component domains. For example,

$$Nat + Int = \{\left(Inj\,1_{Nat,Int}\ 0\right), \left(Inj\,1_{Nat,Int}\ 1\right), \left(Inj\,1_{Nat,Int}\ 2\right), \ldots,$$
$$\ldots, \left(Inj\,2_{Nat,Int}\ -1\right), \left(Inj\,2_{Nat,Int}\ 0\right), \left(Inj\,2_{Nat,Int}\ 1\right), \ldots\}$$

If the familiar set-theoretic union were performed on the domains Nat and Int, it would be impossible to determine the source domain for any $n \geq 0$ in the union.

The notion of sum naturally extends to n-ary sums, which are constructed via the notation

$$\sum_{k=1}^{n} D_k = D_1 + \ldots + D_n = \{\left(Inj\,k_{D_1,\ldots,D_n}\ d_k\right) \mid (k \in [1..n]) \wedge (d_k : D_k)\}$$

where, for each k in $[1..n]$, the injection function $Inj\,k_{D_1,...,D_n}$ has the signature $D_k \to \sum_{j=1}^{n} D_j$. For example, for geometric figures that are either squares, rectangles, or triangles (not necessarily equilateral), we can define a *Figure* domain as a sum of three domains:

$f \in Figure = Square + Rectangle + Triangle$
$s \in Square = Nat$; *side length of square*
$r \in Rectangle = Nat \times Nat$; *two side lengths of rectangle*
$t \in Triangle = Nat \times Nat \times Nat$; *three side lengths of triangle*

When $D_{sum} = \sum_{j=1}^{n} D_j$ and all the domain names D_j are distinct, we write $D_k \rightarrowtail D_{sum}$ as a synonym for $Inj\,k_{D_1,...,D_n}$. For example, $Rectangle \rightarrowtail Figure$ is a synonym for $Inj\,2_{Square,Rectangle,Triangle}$. Note that since the *Bool* domain contains only two elements, we can define it as the sum of two *Unit* domains:

$Bool = True + False$
$True = Unit$
$False = Unit$

Then the value *true* is a synonym for $(True \rightarrowtail Bool\ unit)$ and the value *false* is a synonym for $(False \rightarrowtail Bool\ unit)$.

A key benefit of the mnemonic injection functions $D_k \rightarrowtail D_{sum}$ is that they use domain names rather than positions to indicate the intended injection. Unlike the positional notation, the mnemonic notation remains the same if the order of summands is changed; we can still write $True \rightarrowtail Bool$ whether *Bool* is defined as *True + False* or as *False + True*. However, this also means that the mnemonic injection notation is one place in domain expressions where the name, rather than the structure, of a domain matters. Even though $True = Unit = False$, the injection function $True \rightarrowtail Bool$ is *not* the same as $False \rightarrowtail Bool$. And if *Bool* were instead described as the sum *Unit + Unit*, the mnemonic injection functions could not be used because the name $Unit \rightarrowtail Bool$ would be ambiguous.

Generalizing the definition of *Bool*, we can construct any finite domain (such as *Char*) with n elements as an n-ary sum of n copies of the *Unit* domain.

Oneofs are deconstructed by a case analysis construct that performs a dispatch based on the tag of the oneof. We will introduce this construct in the context of a concrete example and then discuss its general form. Our concrete example is a function that calculates the perimeter of an element $f \in Figure$:

$perim : Figure \to Nat$
$= \lambda f .\ \mathbf{cases}\ _{Figure,Nat}\ f$
$\quad \rhd (Square \rightarrowtail Figure\ s) [\![4 \times_{Nat} s$
$\quad \rhd (Rectangle \rightarrowtail Figure\ r) [\![2 \times_{Nat} ((Proj\,1_{Nat,Nat}\ r) +_{Nat} (Proj\,2_{Nat,Nat}\ r))$
$\quad \rhd (Triangle \rightarrowtail Figure\ t) [\![(Proj\,1_{Nat,Nat,Nat}\ t) +_{Nat}$
$\qquad\qquad (Proj\,2_{Nat,Nat,Nat}\ t) +_{Nat} (Proj\,3_{Nat,Nat,Nat}\ t)$
$\quad \mathbf{end}$

The construct **cases**$_{Figure,Nat}$ performs a case analysis on a **discriminant** value in *Figure* (in this case, f) and returns an element in *Nat*. The perimeter calculation depends on which kind of figure f is, so there is one clause for each of the three kind of figures. Each clause has the form $\triangleright$ *head* $\parallel$ *body*, where the head $(D \rightarrowtail$ *Figure v*) can be viewed as a pattern that can "match" one of the three forms of a figure value (i.e., D is one of *Square*, *Rectangle*, or *Triangle*). The v appearing in the head stands for a metavariable that ranges over elements of D. For example, in the clause head (*Rectangle* $\rightarrowtail$ *Figure r*), r is a metavariable ranging over elements of *Rectangle* $=$ *Nat* $\times$ *Nat*.

The discriminant value matches the clause head $(D \rightarrowtail$ *Figure v*) if it can be expressed as $(D \rightarrowtail$ *Figure d*) for some element d in D. In this case, the value of the **cases** construct is the result of evaluating the clause body after replacing each occurrence of the variable v by d. For example, if f is (*Rectangle* $\rightarrowtail$ *Figure* $\langle 3, 4 \rangle$), then it matches the second clause of the **cases** in *perim*, and the value of this clause body after replacing r by $\langle 3, 4 \rangle$ is

$$2 \times_{Nat} \left(\left(\text{Proj } 1_{Nat,Nat} \ \langle 3, 4 \rangle \right) +_{Nat} \left(\text{Proj } 2_{Nat,Nat} \ \langle 3, 4 \rangle \right) \right)$$
$$= 2 \times_{Nat} (3 +_{Nat} 4) = 14$$

Here are examples involving the other two kinds of figures:

$$(\text{perim} \ (Square \rightarrowtail Figure \ 6)) = 4 \times_{Nat} 6 = 24$$

$$(\text{perim} \ (Triangle \rightarrowtail Figure \ \langle 8, 2, 1 \rangle))$$
$$= \left(\text{Proj } 1_{Nat,Nat,Nat} \ \langle 8, 2, 1 \rangle \right)$$
$$+_{Nat} \left(\text{Proj } 2_{Nat,Nat,Nat} \ \langle 8, 2, 1 \rangle \right) +_{Nat} \left(\text{Proj } 3_{Nat,Nat,Nat} \ \langle 8, 2, 1 \rangle \right)$$
$$= 8 +_{Nat} 2 +_{Nat} 1 = 11$$

Suppose $D_{sum} = \sum_{j=1}^{n} D_j$. Then the general **cases**$_{D_{sum},D_{res}}$ construct has the form

$$
\begin{aligned}
&\textbf{cases} \ _{D_{sum}, D_{res}} \ d_{disc} \\
&\triangleright (D_1 \rightarrowtail D_{sum} \ v_1) \parallel d_{res_1} \\
&\triangleright (D_2 \rightarrowtail D_{sum} \ v_2) \parallel d_{res_2} \\
&\quad \vdots \\
&\triangleright (D_n \rightarrowtail D_{sum} \ v_n) \parallel d_{res_n} \\
&\textbf{end}
\end{aligned}
$$

This construct describes how to map the value of the discriminant expression d_{disc}, which must be an element of D_{sum}, into an element of the result domain D_{res}. The domain subscripts on **cases** will be omitted when they are clear from context. The discriminant value must be expressible as $(D_i \rightarrowtail D_{sum}\ d_i)$ for some summand D_i of D_{sum} and some element d_i of D_i. The **cases** construct dispatches on this discriminant value to the unique matching clause,

$$\rhd\, (D_i \rightarrowtail D_{sum}\ v_i) [\!] \ d_{res_i}$$

and evaluates the body expression d_{res_i} after replacing every occurrence of v_i by d_i. The value of this body expression, which must have type D_{res}, is the value of the **cases** construct.

For example, the value of

$$
\begin{aligned}
&\textbf{cases}\ _{Nat+Int,Int}\ ((Nat \rightarrowtail Nat\ +\ Int)\ 3)\\
&\rhd\, ((Nat \rightarrowtail Nat\ +\ Int)\ n)\ [\!]\ (Nat \hookrightarrow Int\ \ (n +_{Nat} 1))\\
&\rhd\, ((Int \rightarrowtail Nat\ +\ Int)\ i)\ [\!]\ i \times_{Int} i\\
&\textbf{end}
\end{aligned}
$$

is 4, because the discriminant $((Nat \rightarrowtail Nat\ +\ Int)\ 3)$ matches the head of the first clause, $((Nat \rightarrowtail Nat\ +\ Int)\ n)$, and when n is 3, the value of $n +_{Nat} 1$ is 4. Similarly,

$$
\begin{aligned}
&\textbf{cases}\ _{Nat+Int,Int}\ ((Int \rightarrowtail Nat\ +\ Int)\ 3)\\
&\rhd\, ((Nat \rightarrowtail Nat\ +\ Int)\ n)\ [\!]\ (Nat \hookrightarrow Int\ \ (n +_{Nat} 1))\\
&\rhd\, ((Int \rightarrowtail Nat\ +\ Int)\ i)\ [\!]\ i \times_{Int} i\\
&\textbf{end}
\end{aligned}
$$

has the value 9 because $((Int \rightarrowtail Nat\ +\ Int)\ 3)$ matches the head $((Int \rightarrowtail Nat\ +\ Int)\ i)$ of the second clause, and the value of $i \times_{Int} i$ is 9 when i is 3. The inclusion function $Nat \hookrightarrow Int$ is necessary to guarantee that the body expression of the first clause has type Int. The domain variable names n and i in the clause heads have been chosen to reflect the type of value being injected ($n : Nat$ and $i : Int$).

Because the **cases** clauses use mnemonic injection functions, the order of the clauses does not matter, so they can be reordered without changing the meaning of the expression. E.g,

$$
\begin{aligned}
&\textbf{cases}\ _{Nat+Int,Int}\ ((Nat \rightarrowtail Nat\ +\ Int)\ 3)\\
&\rhd\, ((Int \rightarrowtail Nat\ +\ Int)\ i)\ [\!]\ i \times_{Int} i\\
&\rhd\, ((Nat \rightarrowtail Nat\ +\ Int)\ n)\ [\!]\ (Nat \hookrightarrow Int\ \ (n +_{Nat} 1))\\
&\textbf{end}
\end{aligned}
$$

is a well-formed **cases** expression with the value 4. So the most general form of a **cases** expression is really

$$\textbf{cases}_{D_{sum}, D_{res}} \; d_{disc}$$
$$\triangleright \, (D_{\pi(1)} \rightarrowtail D_{sum} \; v_{\pi(1)}) \parallel d_{res_{\pi(1)}}$$
$$\vdots$$
$$\triangleright \, (D_{\pi(n)} \rightarrowtail D_{sum} \; v_{\pi(n)}) \parallel d_{res_{\pi(n)}}$$
$$\textbf{end}$$

where π is a permutation on the integer range $[1..n]$ (see page 1160). This expression is well typed with type D_{res} iff $D_{sum} = \sum_{j=1}^{n} D_j$, $d_{disc} : D_{sum}$, and for each $k \in [1..n]$, $d_{res_k} : D_{res}$ under the assumption that $v_k : D_k$. The $\textbf{cases}_{Nat+Int, Int}$ expressions above are all well typed with type Int.

When the expression d_{test} has type $Bool$ the notation

$$\textbf{if}_{\, D} \; d_{test} \; \textbf{then} \; d_{then} \; \textbf{else} \; d_{else} \; \textbf{end}$$

is an abbreviation for the $\textbf{cases}$ expression

$$\textbf{cases}_{Bool, D} \; d_{test}$$
$$\triangleright \, (\mathit{True} \rightarrowtail Bool \; v_{ignore}) \parallel d_{then}$$
$$\triangleright \, (\mathit{False} \rightarrowtail Bool \; v_{ignore}) \parallel d_{else}$$
$$\textbf{end}$$

This abbreviation treats the $Bool$ domain as the sum of two $Unit$ domains (see page 1177). The $\textbf{if}$ is subscripted with the domain D of the result, but we will omit it when it is clear from context. Here, the domain variable v_{ignore} should be a name that does not appear in either d_{then} or d_{else}.[15]

Since a $\textbf{cases}$ expression has one clause for each summand, there is exactly one clause that matches the discriminant. However, for convenience, the distinguished clause head $\textbf{else}$ may be used as a catch-all to handle all tags unmatched by previous clauses. Since an $\textbf{else}$ clause does not mention a domain variable, it can be used only in situations where the injected element is irrelevant. For example, the expansion of the $\textbf{if}_{\, D}$ expression from above could also be written

$$\textbf{cases}_{Bool, D} \; d_{test}$$
$$\triangleright \, (\mathit{True} \rightarrowtail Bool \; v_{ignore}) \parallel d_{then}$$
$$\triangleright \, \textbf{else} \; d_{else}$$
$$\textbf{end}$$

Like products, sums are defined only by their abstract behavior — in this case, the behavior of the injection functions and the $\textbf{cases}$ construct. In particular, these must satisfy the following two properties:

---

[15]This restriction prevents the variable capture problems discussed in Section 6.3.

1.
$$
\boxed{
\begin{array}{l}
\textbf{cases}\ _{D_{sum},D_k}\ (D_k \rightarrowtail D_{sum}\ d_k) \\
\triangleright (D_k \rightarrowtail D_{sum}\ v_k) \parallel v_k \\
\triangleright \textbf{else}\ d'_k \\
\textbf{end}
\end{array}
}
= d_k, \text{ for all } k \in [1..n], \text{ where } d'_k
$$
is an arbitrary element expression
such that $d'_k : D_k$

2.
$$
\boxed{
\begin{array}{l}
\textbf{cases}\ _{D_{sum},D_{sum}}\ d \\
\triangleright (D_1 \rightarrowtail D_{sum}\ v_1) \parallel (D_1 \rightarrowtail D_{sum}\ v_1) \\
\qquad \vdots \\
\triangleright (D_n \rightarrowtail D_{sum}\ v_n) \parallel (D_n \rightarrowtail D_{sum}\ v_n) \\
\textbf{end}
\end{array}
}
= d
$$

In the first property, the requirement that the arbitrary expression d'_k have type D_k is needed to ensure that the $\textbf{cases}_{D_{sum},D_k}$ expression is well typed with type D_k. Any implementation of sums in which the injection functions and $\textbf{cases}$ satisfy these two properties is a legal implementation of sums for domains.

Exercise A.2 It is natural to represent a oneof in $\sum_{i=1}^{n} D_i$ as a set-theoretic pair containing the tag i and an element d_i of D_i:

$$
\left(Inj\, i_{D_1,\ldots,D_n}\ d_i \right) = \langle i, d_i \rangle
$$

Assuming that oneofs are represented as pairs, use lambda notation to construct a set-theoretic function of a oneof argument $s \in S = D_1 + D_2$ that has the same meaning as the following $\textbf{cases}$ expression:

$$
\begin{array}{l}
\textbf{cases}\ _{S,D_{res}}\ s \\
\triangleright (D_1 \rightarrowtail S\ v_1) \parallel d_{res_1} \\
\triangleright (D_2 \rightarrowtail S\ v_2) \parallel d_{res_2} \\
\textbf{end}
\end{array}
$$

(Assume d_{res_1} and d_{res_2} each have type D_{res}. Use the three-argument $if_{D_{res}}$ function on page 1164 rather than the **if** abbreviation on page 1180, which itself is implemented in terms of a $\textbf{cases}$ expression.)

A.3.5   Sequence Domains

Sequence domains model finite sequences of elements all taken from the same domain. They are built by the * domain constructor; a sequence domain whose sequences contain elements from domain D is written D^*. An element of a sequence domain is simply called a **sequence**. A sequence is characterized by its length n and its ordered elements, which are indexed from 1 to n. E.g., Int^* contains all finite-length sequences with integer elements and $Char^*$ contains all finite-length sequences with character elements. We will use the convention that if v is a variable ranging over the domain D, v^* is a variable ranging over the domain D^*.

A length-n sequence over the domain D is constructed by the function

$$sequence_{n,D} : D^n \rightarrow D^*$$

Thus $sequence_{3,Int}\langle -5, 7, -3 \rangle$ is a sequence of length three with -5 at index 1, 7 at index 2, and -3 at index 3. We will abbreviate $\big(sequence_{n,D} \ \langle d_1, \ \ldots, d_n \rangle\big)$ as $[d_1, \ldots, d_n]_D$. So the sample sequence above could also be written $[-5, 7, -3]_{Int}$, and the empty sequence of integers would be written $[\,]_{Int}$.[16] As elsewhere, we will omit the domain subscripts when they can be inferred from context. Observe that $Char^*$ is isomorphic to the $String$ domain introduced in Section A.1.1, so that a character sequence (such as $sequence_{3,Char}\langle \text{`c'}, \text{`a'}, \text{`t'} \rangle$) can be viewed as another way of writing a string (in this case, "cat").

Every sequence domain D^* is equipped with the following functions:

- $cons_D : D \rightarrow (D^* \rightarrow D^*)$
  Suppose that $d : D$, $d^* : D^*$, and d^* is a length-n sequence. Then $(cons_D \ d \ s)$ is a length-$(n + 1)$ sequence whose first element is d and whose kth element (for $k \in [2..n + 1]$) is the $(k - 1)$th element of d^*. Using $cons_D$, if $n > 0$, the notation $\big(sequence_{n,D} \ \langle d_1, \ \ldots, d_n \rangle\big)$ can be interpreted as an abbreviation for the nested $cons$ applications $(cons_D \ d_1 \ \ldots (cons_D \ d_n \ [\,]_D) \ldots)$.

- $empty?_D : D^* \rightarrow Bool$
  $\big(empty?_D \ d^*\big)$ is $true$ if $d^* = [\,]_D$ and $false$ otherwise.

- $head_D : D^* \rightharpoonup D$
  If $d^* : D^*$ is nonempty, $(head_D \ d^*)$ is the first element of d^*. $head_D$ is a partial function because it is undefined on an empty sequence. (An alternative approach would be to treat $head_D$ as a total function and define $(head_D \ [\,]_D)$ as a particular element of D.)

- $tail_D : D^* \rightarrow D^*$
  If $d^* : D^*$ is nonempty, $(tail_D \ d^*)$ is the subsequence of the sequence d^* that consists of all elements but the first element. If d^* is empty, $(tail_D \ d^*)$ is defined as $[\,]_D$; so $tail_D$, unlike $head_D$, is a total function. We could have instead made $tail_D$ a partial function, but treating $(tail_D \ [\,]_D)$ as $[\,]_D$ is helpful in many situations.

---

[16]The empty sequence is created using a 0-tuple.

Other useful functions can be defined in terms of the above functions:

$$length_D : D* \to Nat$$
$$= \lambda d* . \; \textbf{if} \left(empty?_D \; d*\right) \; \textbf{then} \; 0 \; \textbf{else} \left(1 +_{Nat} \left(length_D \; \left(tail_D \; d*\right)\right)\right) \; \textbf{end}$$

$$nth_D : Pos \to (D* \to D)$$
$$= \lambda z d* . \; \textbf{if} \left(z =_{Pos} 1\right) \; \textbf{then} \left(head_D \; d*\right) \; \textbf{else} \left(nth_D \; \left(z -_{Pos} 1\right) \; \left(tail_D \; d*\right)\right) \; \textbf{end}$$

$$append_D : D* \to (D* \to D*)$$
$$= \lambda d_1* d_2* . \; \textbf{if} \left(empty?_D \; d_1*\right) \; \textbf{then} \; d_2*$$
$$\textbf{else} \left(cons_D \; \left(head_D \; d_1*\right) \; \left(append_D \; \left(tail_D \; d_1*\right) \; d_2*\right)\right) \; \textbf{end}$$

$$map_{D_1,D_2} : (D_1 \to D_2) \to (D_1* \to D_2*)$$
$$= \lambda f d* . \; \textbf{if} \left(empty?_{D_1} \; d*\right) \; \textbf{then} \; [\,]_{D_2}$$
$$\textbf{else} \left(cons_{D_2} \; \left(f \; \left(head_{D_1} \; d*\right)\right) \; \left(map_{D_1,D_2} \; f \; \left(tail_{D_1} \; d*\right)\right)\right) \; \textbf{end}$$

$length_D$ returns the length of a sequence. nth_D returns the element of the given sequence at the given index, which must be a positive integer. $append_D$ concatenates a length-m sequence and a length-n sequence to form a length-$(m + n)$ sequence. Given a function $f : (D_1 \to D_2)$ and a length-n sequence of D_1 elements $[d_1, \ldots, d_n]$, map_{D_1,D_2} returns a length-n sequence of D_2 elements $[(f \; d_1), \ldots, (f \; d_n)]$.

All of the above function definitions exhibit a simple form of recursion in which the size of the first argument is reduced at every recursive call. By the principle of mathematical induction, all of the functions are therefore well defined.

The *cons* and *append* functions are common enough to warrant some convenient abbreviations:

- $d . d*$ is an abbreviation of $(cons \; d \; d*)$. The dot ("$.$") is an infix binary function that naturally associates to the right. Thus, $d_1 . d_2 . d*$ is parsed as $d_1 . (d_2 . d*)$.

- $d_1* @ d_2*$ is an abbreviation of $(append \; d_1* \; d_2*)$. The at sign, $@$, is an associative infix binary operator.

As with products and sums, sequences are defined purely in terms of their abstract behavior. A legal implementation of sequence domains is one that satisfies the following properties for all domains D, all $d : D$, and all $d* : D*$:

1. $\left(empty?_D \; [\,]_D\right) \; = \; true$

2. $\left(empty?_D \; (d . d*)\right) \; = \; false$

3. $(head_D \ (d.d^*)) \ = \ d$

4. $(head_D \ []_D) \ = \ undefined$

5. $(tail_D \ (d.d^*)) \ = \ d^*$

6. $(tail_D \ []_D) \ = \ []_D$

7. $(cons_D \ (head_D \ d^*) \ (tail_D \ d^*)) \ = \ d^* \ \ if \ \ \neg(empty?_D \ d^*)$

A.3.6   Function Domains

The final constructor we will consider is the binary infix function-domain constructor, $\rightarrow$. In the naive implementation of domains as sets, $D_1 \rightarrow D_2$ is the domain of all total functions with D_1 as their source and D_2 as their target. Elements of a function domain are called **functions**. As with tuples, there is the possibility for confusion between set-theoretic functions and domain-theoretic functions. These are the same in the naive implementation, but differ when we change the implementation of domains. In the body of the text, "function" means domain-theoretic function; we explicitly refer to "set-theoretic functions" when necessary. The same holds for arrow notation, which refers to the function-domain constructor unless otherwise specified.

The arrow and type notations mesh nicely with the use of arrows and signatures already familiar from set-theoretic functions (Section A.2.1). Thus, the notation $f : Int \rightarrow Bool$ can now be interpreted as "f is an element of the function domain $Int \rightarrow Bool$." Elements of this domain are predicates on the integers, such as functions for testing whether an integer is even or odd, or for testing whether an integer is positive or negative. Similarly, the domain $Int \rightarrow (Int \rightarrow Int)$ is the domain of functions on two (curried) integer arguments that return an integer. The binary integer functions $+_{Int}$, $-_{Int}$, and $\times_{Int}$ are elements of this domain.

As before, the application of a function f to an argument d is written with the juxtaposition notation $f \ d$. Such an application is well typed with type D_{res} (written $(f \ d) : D_{res}$) iff $d : D_{arg}$ and $f : (D_{arg} \rightarrow D_{res})$.

The $\rightarrow$ constructor is right-associative:

$$D_1 \rightarrow D_2 \rightarrow \cdots \rightarrow D_{n-1} \rightarrow D_n \ \ means \ \ (D_1 \rightarrow (D_2 \rightarrow (\cdots (D_{n-1} \rightarrow D_n) \cdots)))$$

The right-associativity of $\rightarrow$ interacts nicely with the left associativity of application. That is, if $a : A$, $b : B$, and $f : (A \rightarrow B \rightarrow C)$, then $(f \ a) : B \rightarrow C$, so that $(f \ a \ b) : C \ = \ ((f \ a) \ b) : C$, just as we'd like.

We write particular elements of a function domain using lambda notation. Thus $(\lambda n \, . \, (n \times_{Nat} n)) : Nat \to Nat$ is the squaring function on natural numbers, and $(\lambda i \, . \, (i >_{Int} 0)) : Int \to Bool$ is a predicate function for testing whether an integer is positive.

When the formal parameter of an abstraction is the domain variable v (possibly in subscripted or primed form) associated with a domain D, we will assume that the abstraction argument must have type D. Thus $(\lambda b \, . \, b)$ and $(\lambda b_1 \, . \, b_1)$ both unambiguously denote the identity function in the domain $Bool \to Bool$, and $(\lambda n \, . \, n)$ and $(\lambda n' \, . \, n')$ both denote the identity function in the domain $Nat \to Nat$. Given the domain definition

$$p \in NatPred \; = \; Nat \to Bool$$

the abstraction $(\lambda p \, . \, p)$ denotes the identity function in the domain

$$NatPred \to NatPred \; = \; (Nat \to Bool) \to (Nat \to Bool)$$

and the abstraction $(\lambda n \, . \, \lambda p \, . \, (p \; n))$ is an element of the function domain

$$Nat \to NatPred \to Bool = Nat \to (Nat \to Bool) \to Bool$$

The well-typedness condition for an abstraction is $(\lambda v \, . \, d) : (D_{arg} \to D_{res})$ iff $d : D_{res}$ under the assumption that $v : D_{arg}$. As seen above, the type of the formal parameter v will usually be apparent from its name. But when v is not a domain variable for a particular domain, its type can be determined from an explicit function signature. So $(\lambda x \, . \, x) : Int \to Int$ specifies the identity function on integers, while $(\lambda x \, . \, x) : Bool \to Bool$ specifies the identity function on booleans. We have already used this convention in the definition of the sequence functions on page 1183. For example, in the defining abstraction $(\lambda f d^* \ldots)$ for the map_{D_1, D_2} function, the types of f and d^* are not apparent from their names. But since this function has the type $(D_1 \to D_2) \to (D_1{}^* \to D_2{}^*)$, we know that $f : (D_1 \to D_2)$ and $d^* : D_1{}^*$.

Our description of function domains in this section has a different flavor than the description of product, sum, and sequence domains. With the other domains, elements of the compound domain were abstractly defined by constructor functions that had to satisfy certain properties with respect to deconstructor functions. But with function domains, we concretely specify the elements as set-theoretic functions designated by lambda notation. Is there a more abstract approach to defining function domains? Yes, but it is rather abstract and not important to our current line of development; see Exercise A.3.

Exercise A.3 This exercise explores some further properties of function domains. Consider the following two functions:

- $apply_{A,B} : ((A \to B) \times A) \to B$
  If $f : A \to B$ and $a : A$, then $\left(apply_{A,B}\ \langle f, a \rangle \right)$ denotes the result of applying f to a.

- $curry_{A,B,C} : ((A \times B) \to C) \to (A \to (B \to C))$
  If $f : (A \times B) \to C$, then $\left(curry_{A,B,C}\ f \right)$ denotes a curried version of f — i.e., it denotes a function g such that $(g\ a\ b) = (f\ \langle a, b \rangle)$ for all $a \in A$ and $b \in B$.

a. Use lambda notation to define set-theoretic versions of *apply* and *curry*.

b. Using your definitions from above, show that if $f : (A \times B) \to C$, then

$$f = apply_{B,C} \circ \left((curry_{A,B,C}\ f) \times id_B \right)$$

Recall that id_B is the identity function on the domain B. The meaning of $\times$ on functions is defined as follows: if $f : A \to B$, $g : C \to D$, $a : A$, and $c : C$, then $(f \times g) : (A \times C) \to (B \times D)$ is defined by

$$((f \times g)\ \langle a, c \rangle) = \langle (f\ a), (g\ c) \rangle$$

c. Using your definitions from above, show that if $g : A \to (B \to C)$, then

$$g = \left(curry_{A,B,C}\ \left(apply_{B,C} \circ (g \times id_B) \right) \right)$$

It turns out that any domain implementation with an *apply* and a *curry* function that satisfy the properties in part **b** and part **c** is a valid implementation of a function domain. This is the abstract view of function domains alluded to above.

A.4   Metalanguage Summary

So far we've introduced many pieces of the metalanguage. The goal of this section is to put all of the pieces together. We'll summarize the metalanguage notation introduced so far and introduce a few more handy notations.

In the study of programming languages, it is often useful to break up the description of a language into two parts: the core of the language, called the **kernel**, and various extensions that can be expressed in terms of the core, called the **syntactic sugar**. We shall use this approach to summarize the metalanguage. (See Section 6.2 for an example of using this approach to specify a programming language.)

A.4.1   The Metalanguage Kernel

The entities manipulated by the metalanguage are domains and their elements. Domains are either primitive, in which case they can be viewed as sets of unstructured elements, or compound, in which case they are built out of component domains. Domains are denoted by **domain expressions**. Domain expressions are either domain names (such as *Bool*, *Nat*, etc.) or are the application of the domain operators $\times$, $+$, *, and $\rightarrow$ to other domain expressions. So if D_1 and D_2 are any valid domain expressions, the following are also valid domain expressions: $(D_1 \times D_2)$, $(D_1 + D_2)$, D_1*, and $(D_1 \rightarrow D_2)$. New names can be given to domains via **domain definitions** of the form

$$v \in \textit{domain-name} = \textit{domain-description}$$

where the optional declaration "$v \in$" introduces a domain variable v that ranges over the elements of the domain named by *domain-name*.

Domain elements are denoted by **element expressions**. The kernel element expressions are summarized in Figure A.1. Every well-formed domain expression d must be well typed with some type D, written $d : D$, which indicates that the element denoted by d is in the domain D. Constants are names for particular domain elements; these include numbers, booleans, and functions. We will assume that the type of every constant is evident from context. Variables are introduced as formal parameters in abstractions, names in the heads of a **cases** clauses, or as the domain variable of a definition. Every variable ranges over a particular domain. If a variable is the domain variable introduced by some domain definition having the declaration $v \in D$, it is assumed that v (possibly with subscripts or primes) has type D. Otherwise, it must be possible to determine the type of the variable from its context; variables with an ambiguous type are not permitted.

Applications are compound expressions in which an operator d_{fun} is applied to an operand d_{arg}. The operator expression must denote an element of a function domain $D_{arg} \rightarrow D_{res}$, and the operand expression must denote an element of the domain D_{arg}; in this case, the application denotes an element of the domain D_{res}. Applications with multiple operands are usually expressed by currying. Elements of primitive domains are often the operands to functions (such as arithmetic and logical functions) associated with the domain. Elements of product, sum, and sequence domains can be built by the application of constructor functions ($tuple_{D_1,\ldots,D_n}$, $Inj\,k_{D_1,\ldots,D_n}$, or $sequence_{n,D}$, respectively) to the appropriate arguments. Compound domains are equipped with many other useful functions that operate on elements of the domain.

Abstractions are compound expressions that denote the elements of function domains. Structurally, an abstraction $(\lambda v_{fml} . d_{body})$ consists of a formal parameter variable v_{fml} and a body element expression d_{body}. The type of the abstraction should either be given explicitly or should be inferable from the structure of the parts of the abstraction. If v_{fml} is assumed to have type D_{fml}, then d_{body} should be well typed with some type D_{body}. In this case, the abstraction is well typed with type $D_{fml} \rightarrow D_{body}$, and it denotes a function whose source is the domain D_{fml}, whose target is the domain D_{body}, and whose graph is a set of all pairs $\langle d_{src}, d_{tgt} \rangle$ where d_{src} ranges over D_{fml} and d_{tgt} is the element of D_{body} obtained by evaluating the body expression d_{body} after replacing each occurrence of v_{fml} by d_{src}.

While products and sequences are deconstructed into their component parts by function application, elements of a sum domain are deconstructed by the **cases** construct. A **cases**$_{D_{sum}, D_{res}}$ expression consists of a discriminant d_{disc} that must have a sum type $D_{sum} = \sum_{j=1}^{n} D_j$ and a set of clauses, each of which has a head of the form $(D_j \rightarrowtail D_{sum} \; v_j)$ and a body element expression d_{res_j}. There must be one clause to handle each summand in the domain D_{sum}. A clause with the keyword **else** as its head handles all cases not handled by other clauses. All body expressions d_{res_j} — which may contain v_j, the untagged value of d_{disc} from D_j — must denote elements of the same result domain D_{res} so that the domain D_{res} of the value denoted by the **cases** expression is well defined.

Element expressions can be used in the following **element definition** form to define a named domain element:

$$name : D = d_{defn}$$

Here, $name$ is the name of the element being defined, D is a domain expression denoting the type of the element, and d_{defn} is an element expression that specifies the element. For example:

$$five : Nat = ((+_{Nat} \; 2) \; 3)$$
$$origin : Int \times Int = ((tuple_{Int,Int} \; 0) \; 0)$$
$$inc : Int \rightarrow Int = (+_{Int} \; 1)$$
$$app5_D : (Int \rightarrow D) \rightarrow D = (\lambda f \; . \; (f \; 5))$$

Element definitions may be recursive only in the case where it can be shown that d_{defn} defines a unique element in the domain D. One way to do this is to use induction; another way is to use the iterative fixed point technique developed in Chapter 5.

A.4.2   The Metalanguage Sugar

It is *possible* to write all element expressions using kernel element expressions, but it is not always *convenient* to do so. We have introduced various notational conventions to make the metalanguage more readable and concise. We review those notations here, and introduce a few more.

---

constants: E.g., $true : Bool$, $-1 : Int$, $\vee : Bool \to Bool$,
$+_{Nat} : Nat \to (Nat \to Nat)$, $<_{Int} : Int \to (Int \to Bool)$,
$tuple_{Nat,Bool} : Nat \to (Bool \to (Nat \times Bool))$,
$Proj 1_{Nat,Bool} : (Nat \times Bool) \to Nat$,
$Inj 2_{Nat,Bool} : Bool \to (Nat + Bool)$,
$sequence_{3,Int} : (Int \times Int \times Int) \to Int^*$,
$cons_{Nat} : Nat \to (Nat^* \to Nat^*)$.

variables: $v : D$. E.g., $b : Bool$, $n : Nat$, $i : Int$.

applications: $(d_{fun}\ d_{arg}) : D_{res}$ iff $d_{fun} : (D_{arg} \to D_{res})$ and $d_{arg} : D_{arg}$.
   E.g, $(\neg\ b) : Bool$, $(<_{Int}\ 1) : Int \to Bool$, $((+_{Nat}\ 2)\ 3) : Nat$, $((\lambda i\,.\,i)\ 4) : Int$.

abstractions:
   $(\lambda v_{fml}\,.\,d_{body}) : D_{fml} \to D_{body}$ iff $d_{body} : D_{body}$ assuming that $v_{fml} : D_{fml}$.
   E.g., $(\lambda n\,.\,n) : Nat \to Nat$, $(\lambda i\,.\,i) : Int \to Int$,
      $(\lambda n\,.\,((>_{Nat}\ n)\ 5)) : Nat \to Bool$,
      $(\lambda i\,.\,(\lambda f\,.\,(\neg\ (f\ i)))) : Int \to ((Int \to Bool) \to Bool)$.

case analysis: $\textbf{cases}_{D_{sum},D_{res}}\ d_{disc}$ or $\textbf{cases}_{D_{sum},D_{res}}\ d_{disc}$
   $\rhd (D_1 \rightarrowtail D_{sum}\ v_1)\ \|\ d_{res_1}$
   $\rhd (D_2 \rightarrowtail D_{sum}\ v_2)\ \|\ d_{res_2}$
   $\vdots$ *some subset of clauses*
   $\rhd (D_n \rightarrowtail D_{sum}\ v_n)\ \|\ d_{res_n}$
   end $\vdots$
                  $\rhd \textbf{else}\ \|\ d_{res_{else}}$
                  end

   These $\textbf{cases}_{D_{sum},D_{res}}$ expressions are well typed with type D_{res} iff $D_{sum} = \sum_{j=1}^{n} D_j$, $d_{disc} : D_{sum}$, and, for each j in $[1..n]$, $d_{res_j} : D_{res}$ assuming $v_j : D_j$.

Figure A.1   The kernel element expressions and well-typedness conditions.

Figure A.2 gives examples of the syntactic sugar for element expressions. Applications and abstractions are simplified by various conventions. The default left-associativity of application simplifies the expression of multiargument applications; thus, $(expt\ 2\ 5)$ is an abbreviation for $((expt\ 2)\ 5)$. This default can be overridden by explicit parenthesization. Applications of familiar binary functions like $+_{Nat}$ are often written in infix style to enhance readability. For example, $2 +_{Nat} 3$ is an abbreviation for $((+_{Nat}\ 2)\ 3)$. The formal parameters of nested abstractions are often coalesced into a single abstraction. For instance, $\lambda abc.(c\ a)$ is shorthand for $\lambda a\,.\,\lambda b\,.\,\lambda c\,.\,(c\ a)$.

The construction of elements in product, sum, and sequence domains is aided by special notation. Thus,

$$\langle 1, true \rangle \quad \text{is shorthand for} \quad (tuple_{Nat,Bool} \ 1 \ true)$$

$$((Nat \rightarrowtail Nat + Int) \ 3) \quad \text{is shorthand for} \quad (Inj \ 1_{Nat,Int} \ 3)$$

$$[5, 3, 2, 7] \quad \text{is shorthand for} \quad sequence_{4,Nat} \ \langle 5, 3, 2, 7 \rangle$$

(We have assumed in all these examples that the numbers are elements of *Nat* rather than of some other numerical domain.) The notations $d \cdot d^*$ and $d_1^* \ @ \ d_2^*$ are abbreviations for $(cons \ d \ d^*)$ and $(append \ d_1^* \ d_2^*)$ respectively, so that the following notations all denote the same sequence of natural numbers:

$$[5, 3, 2, 7] = 5 \cdot [3, 2, 7] = [5, 3] \ @ \ [2, 7]$$

The **if** conditional expression

$$\textbf{if} \ d_{test} \ \textbf{then} \ d_{then} \ \textbf{else} \ d_{else} \ \textbf{end}$$

is an abbreviation for the case analysis

$$\begin{aligned}
&\textbf{cases} \ _{Bool,D_{res}} \ d_{test} \\
&\triangleright (True \rightarrowtail Bool \ v_{ignore}) \ [\![\ d_{then} \\
&\triangleright (False \rightarrowtail Bool \ v_{ignore}) \ [\![\ d_{else} \\
&\textbf{end}
\end{aligned}$$

where d_{test} is an expression that denotes an element of the domain *Bool* and d_{then} and d_{else} denote elements of a result domain D_{res}. The variable v_{ignore} can be any variable that does not appear in d_{then} or d_{else}. This notation assumes that the *Bool* domain is represented as a sum of two synonyms for the *Unit* domain named *True* and *False*. We will use this **if** notation in preference to the $if_{D_{res}}$ conditional function from page 1163.

The **match** expression is an extension to the **cases** notation that simplifies deconstructing tuples and sequences in addition to oneofs. It is inspired by pattern-matching constructs that enhance program readability and conciseness in programming languages like ML and HASKELL. We use a different keyword (**match** instead of **cases**) to emphasize that **match** is syntactic sugar. Since **match** subsumes **cases**, we will use **match** rather than **cases** throughout the main text.

A **match** expression has the form:

$$\begin{aligned}
&\textbf{match} \ _{D_{disc},D_{res}} \ d_{disc} \\
&\triangleright p_1 \ [\![\ d_{res_1} \\
&\triangleright p_2 \ [\![\ d_{res_2} \\
&\quad \vdots \\
&\triangleright p_n \ [\![\ d_{res_n} \\
&\textbf{end}
\end{aligned}$$

applications: E.g., $(expt\ 2\ 5)$, $(2 +_{Nat} 3)$.

abstractions: $\lambda p_1 \ldots p_n\ .\ d_{body}$, where here and below p ranges over metalanguage patterns (see Figure A.3). E.g., $\lambda abc\ .\ (c\ a)$, $\lambda \langle n_1, n_2\ .\ n_{rest}^* \rangle\ .\ \langle n_1 +_{Nat} n_2, n_{rest}^* \rangle$.

tuples: E.g., $\langle 1, true \rangle$.

oneofs: E.g., $((Nat \rightarrowtail Nat + Int)\ 3)$.

sequences: E.g., $[5, 3, 2, 7]$, $5 . [3, 2, 7]$, $[5, 3]\ @\ [2, 7]$.

if: **if** d_{test} **then** d_{then} **else** d_{else} **end**

match: **match** $_{D_{disc}, D_{res}}$ d_{disc} or   **match** $_{D_{disc}, D_{res}}$ d_{disc}

        $\triangleright p_1\ [\![\ d_{res_1}$

        $\triangleright p_2\ [\![\ d_{res_2}$ $\vdots$

                           some subset of clauses

        $\vdots$

        $\triangleright p_n\ [\![\ d_{res_n}$ $\vdots$

        end $\triangleright$ **else** $[\![\ d_{res_{else}}$

                            end

let: **let** p_1 **be** d_1 **and**

        p_2 **be** d_2 **and**

        $\vdots$

        p_n **be** d_n

     in d_{body}

Figure A.2   Sugar for element expressions.

As in **cases**, a **match** expression consists of a discriminant and a number of clauses, and the domain subscripts on **match** will be omitted when they are clear from context. The two parts of a **match** clause are called the **pattern** and the **body**. A pattern (indicated by the metavariable p) is more general than the head of a **cases** clause and can be composed of constants, variables, sum injections, and tuple and sequence constructors (see Figure A.3). For example, the following are typical patterns:

$$n$$
$$\langle n, 1 \rangle$$
$$((Nat \rightarrowtail Nat + Int)\ n)$$
$$[i_1, -17, i_3]$$
$$n . n^*$$
$$\langle b, \langle n_1, 1 \rangle, ((Nat \rightarrowtail Nat + Int)\ n_2), [i_1, -17, i_3] \rangle$$

We require that the same variable cannot appear more than once in a pattern.

---

constant patterns: E.g., *true*, *17*, *−1*

variable patterns: E.g., *b*, *n*, *i*

tuple patterns: E.g., $\langle b, 17, \langle \mathit{false}, i \rangle \rangle$

oneof patterns: E.g., $((\mathit{Nat} \rightarrowtail \mathit{Nat} + \mathit{Int})\ n)$

sequence patterns: E.g., $[i_1, \text{-}17, i_3]$, $n . n^*$

Figure A.3   Structure of metalanguage patterns.

A pattern is said to **match** a value d_{val} if it is possible to assign values to the variables appearing in the pattern such that the pattern would denote d_{val} if it were interpreted as an element expression with the assignments in effect. Thus, the pattern $\langle n, 1 \rangle$ matches the value $\langle 2, 1 \rangle$ with $n = 2$, but it does not match the values $\langle 3, 4 \rangle$ or $\langle 2, 1, 3 \rangle$. Similarly, $n . n^*$ matches $[3, 7, 4]$ with $n = 3$ and $n^* = [7, 4]$, but it does not match $[\,]$.

The value of the **match** expression, which has type D_{res}, is determined by the first clause (reading top down) whose pattern matches the discriminant. In this case, the value of the **match** expression is the value of the clause body in a context where each variable introduced by the pattern denotes the value determined by the match. For example, consider the following **match** expression, where the discriminant expression d_{disc} is assumed to have type $(\mathit{Nat} + \mathit{Bool}) \times \mathit{Nat}$:

$$
\begin{aligned}
&\textbf{match}\ _{(\mathit{Nat}+\mathit{Bool})\times\mathit{Nat},\mathit{Nat}}\ d_{disc} \\
&\quad \triangleright\ \langle ((\mathit{Bool} \rightarrowtail \mathit{Nat} + \mathit{Bool})\ b), n_2 \rangle\ [\![\ \textbf{if}\ b\ \textbf{then}\ n_2\ \textbf{else}\ n_2 \times_{\mathit{Nat}} 2\ \textbf{end} \\
&\quad \triangleright\ \langle ((\mathit{Nat} \rightarrowtail \mathit{Nat} + \mathit{Bool})\ n_1), 1 \rangle\ [\![\ n_1 +_{\mathit{Nat}} 1 \\
&\quad \triangleright\ \langle ((\mathit{Nat} \rightarrowtail \mathit{Nat} + \mathit{Bool})\ n_1), 2 \rangle\ [\![\ n_1 \times_{\mathit{Nat}} n_1 \\
&\quad \triangleright\ \langle ((\mathit{Nat} \rightarrowtail \mathit{Nat} + \mathit{Bool})\ n_1), n_2 \rangle\ [\![\ n_1 +_{\mathit{Nat}} n_2 \\
&\textbf{end}
\end{aligned}
$$

If the first component of d_{disc} is a boolean b, then the second component (a natural number n_2) is returned if b is *true* and twice n_2 is returned if b is *false*. Otherwise, the first component of d_{disc} must be a natural number n_1. If the second component is 1, then the result is one more than n_1; if the second component is 2, then the result is n_1 squared; and otherwise the result is the sum of the two numerical components.

A **match** expression can always be rewritten in terms of **cases**, conditional expressions (which themselves are shorthand for **cases**), and explicit component extraction functions. For example, the above **match** expression is equivalent to:

$$\textbf{cases}_{(Nat+Bool)\times Nat,Nat}\left(\text{Proj 1}_{(Nat+Bool),Nat}\ d_{disc}\right)$$
$$\triangleright\ ((Bool\rightarrowtail Nat\ +\ Bool)\ \ b)$$
$$\|\ (\lambda n_2\ .\ \textbf{if}\ b\ \textbf{then}\ n_2\ \textbf{else}\ n_2\ \times_{Nat}\ 2\ \textbf{end})\ \left(\text{Proj 2}_{(Nat+Bool),Nat}\ d_{disc}\right)$$
$$\triangleright\ ((Nat\rightarrowtail Nat\ +\ Bool)\ \ n_1)$$
$$\|\ \textbf{if}\ \left(\text{Proj 2}_{(Nat+Bool),Nat}\ d_{disc}\right)=_{Nat}\ 1$$
$$\textbf{then}\ n_1\ +_{Nat}\ 1$$
$$\textbf{else if}\ \left(\text{Proj 2}_{(Nat+Bool),Nat}\ d_{disc}\right)=_{Nat}\ 2$$
$$\textbf{then}\ n_1\ \times_{Nat}\ n_1$$
$$\textbf{else}\ (\lambda n_2\ .\ n_1\ +_{Nat}\ n_2)\ \left(\text{Proj 2}_{(Nat+Bool),Nat}\ d_{disc}\right)$$
$$\textbf{end}$$
$$\textbf{end}$$
$$\textbf{end}$$

In most cases, the **match** expression is more concise and more readable than the desugared form.

As a more compelling example, we can use **match** to simplify the *perim* function definition from page 1177 by eliminating all projection-function invocations:

$$perim : Figure \rightarrow Nat$$
$$= \lambda f\ .\ \textbf{match}_{Figure,Nat}\ f$$
$$\triangleright\ (Square\rightarrowtail Figure\ \ n)\ \|\ 4\times_{Nat} n$$
$$\triangleright\ (Rectangle\rightarrowtail Figure\ \ \langle n_1,n_2\rangle)\ \|\ 2\times_{Nat}(n_1+_{Nat}n_2)$$
$$\triangleright\ (Triangle\rightarrowtail Figure\ \ \langle n_1,n_2,n_3\rangle)\ \|\ n_1+_{Nat}n_2+_{Nat}n_3$$
$$\textbf{end}$$

As in **cases**, the last clause of the **match** expression can have an **else** pattern that handles any discriminant that did not successfully match the preceding patterns. The value of a **match** expression is undefined if no pattern matches the discriminant.

For the **match** expression in Figure A.2, the well-typedness conditions are as follows:

- The discriminant d_{disc} must have the type D_{disc};

- For each j in $[1..n]$, assume that the pattern p_j contains variables $v_{j,1}$, ..., v_{j,k_j}. Then it must be possible to assign the types $D_{j,1}$, ..., D_{j,k_j} to these variables, respectively, such that, with these assignments:

  - The pattern p_j has the type D_{disc} when interpreted as an element expression; and

  - The body expression d_{res_j} has the type D_{res}.

Since pattern matching is such a useful technique, we shall extend some of our other notations to use implicit pattern matching in contexts where variables are introduced. For example, we shall allow formal parameters to an abstraction to be patterns rather than just variables. The abstraction

$$\lambda p_1 \ldots p_n . d_{body}$$

is shorthand for

$$\lambda v_1 \ldots v_n . \ \textbf{match} \ \langle v_1, \ldots, v_n \rangle$$
$$\triangleright \langle p_1, \ldots, p_n \rangle \ [\!] \ d_{body}$$
$$\textbf{end}$$

For example, the abstraction $(\lambda \langle n_1, n_2 \rangle . \ n_1 +_{Nat} n_2)$ specifies a function with type $(Nat \times Nat) \rightarrow Nat$ that is shorthand for

$$\lambda v . \ \textbf{match} \ v$$
$$\triangleright \langle n_1, n_2 \rangle \ [\!] \ (n_1 +_{Nat} n_2)$$
$$\textbf{end}$$

where v is assumed to range over $Nat \times Nat$.

Throughout the book, we will often avoid a very long (even multipage) **match** construct by using patterns to define a function by cases. For example, we can define a function *stringLength* that maps a sequence of characters to its length as follows:

$$stringLength : Char^* \rightarrow Nat$$
$$stringLength \ [\,]_{Char} = 0$$
$$stringLength \ (h_{first} . h^*_{rest}) = 1 +_{Nat} (stringLength \ h^*_{rest})$$

This is equivalent to:

$$stringLength : Char^* \rightarrow Nat$$
$$= \lambda h^* . \ \textbf{match} \ h^*$$
$$\triangleright [\,]_{Char} \ [\!] \ 0$$
$$\triangleright h_{first} . h^*_{rest} \ [\!] \ 1 +_{Nat} (stringLength \ h^*_{rest})$$
$$\textbf{end}$$

The definition-by-cases notation is especially helpful when we define functions that operate over programs, where each clause defines the function for a particular type of program expression.

Our last piece of metalanguage sugar is the **let** expression, whose form is:

$$\textbf{let } p_1 \textbf{ be } d_1 \textbf{ and}$$
$$p_2 \textbf{ be } d_2 \textbf{ and}$$
$$\vdots$$
$$p_n \textbf{ be } d_n$$
$$\textbf{in } d_{body}$$

This is pronounced "Let p_1 match the value of d_1 and p_2 match the value of d_2 ... and p_n match the value of d_n in the expression d_{body}." The **let** expression is used to name (parts of) intermediate results that can then be referenced by name in the body expression. The value of a **let** expression is the value of its body expression d_{body} in a context where the variable assignments specified by the pattern matches are in effect. For example, if $point_1$ and $point_2$ are two-dimensional points with integer coordinates, then the vector sum of these two points can be written

$$\textbf{let } \langle i_x, i_y \rangle \textbf{ be } point_1 \textbf{ and}$$
$$\langle i'_x, i'_y \rangle \textbf{ be } point_2$$
$$\textbf{in } \langle i_x +_{Int} i'_x, i_y +_{Int} i'_y \rangle$$

The general **let** expression above is just a more readable form of the following application of an abstraction:

$$((\lambda p_1 p_2 \ldots p_n \,.\, d_{body}) \ d_1 \ d_2 \ \ldots \ d_n)$$

This expansion makes it clear that none of the expressions $d_1 \ldots d_n$ can refer to any of the variables introduced by the patterns $p_1 \ldots p_n$. For example, the expression

$$\textbf{let } n_x \textbf{ be } 3 \textbf{ and}$$
$$n_y \textbf{ be } 4 \textbf{ and}$$
$$\textbf{in } \textbf{let } n_x \textbf{ be } n_x +_{Nat} n_y$$
$$n_y \textbf{ be } n_x \times_{Nat} n_y$$
$$\textbf{in } \langle n_x, n_y \rangle$$

has the value $\langle 7, 12 \rangle$ rather than $\langle 7, 28 \rangle$ because the n_x in $n_x \times_{Nat} n_y$ refers to the one declared by the outer **let**, not the inner **let**. The region of an expression in which a variable can be referenced is called its **scope**. So we can say that the scope of the variables introduced in the **let** patterns $p_1 \ldots p_n$ includes d_{body} but not $d_1 \ldots d_n$. See Section 6.3.1 for an in-depth discussion of the notion of variable scope, which plays an important role in programming language design.

Notes

The concept of domains introduced in this appendix is refined in Chapter 5. See the references on page 204 for reading on domain theory.

Defining products, sums, and functions in an abstract way is at the heart of *category theory*. [Pie91] and [BW90] are accessible introductions to category theory aimed at computer scientists.

For coverage of computability issues, we recommend [Min67, HU79, Hof80, Sip06].

Appendix B

Our Pedagogical Languages

Language name	Mnemonic	Where defined
EL	**E**xpression **L**anguage	Sections 2.1 and 4.2
ELM	**EL** **M**inus	Sections 3.2.5 and 4.2.2
ELMM	**EL** **M**inus **M**inus	Sections 3.2.6 and 4.2.3
FL	**F**unctional **L**anguage	Chapter 6
FLIC	**FL** **I**ncluding mutable **C**ells	Section 8.3
FLAVAR	**FL** **A**nd mutable **VAR**iables	Section 8.4
FLEX	**FL** with **EX**plicit types	Sections 11.4 and 11.8
FLEX/S	**FLEX** with **S**ubtyping	Section 12.1
FLEX/SP	**FLEX/S** with **P**olymorphism	Section 12.2
FLEX/P	**FLEX** with **P**olymorphism	Section 12.2
FLEX/SPD	**FLEX/SP** with **D**escriptions	Section 12.3.1
FLEX/SPDK	**FLEX/SPD** with **K**inds	Section 12.3.2
FLARE	**FL** **A**nd type **RE**construction	Sections 13.2 and 13.5
FLEX/M	**FLEX/SP** with **M**odules	Section 15.2
FLARE/E	**FLARE** with **E**ffects	Section 16.2
FLARE/V	**FLARE** with mutable **V**ariables	Section 17.2.2
FIL	**F**unctional **I**ntermediate **L**anguage	Section 17.7
HOOPLA	**H**umble **O**bject-**O**riented **P**rogramming **LA**nguage	Section 7.3
PostFix		Section 1.4

References

[AA+85]   Hal Abelson, Norman Adams, et al. Revised revised report on Scheme, or an Uncommon Lisp. Technical Report AIM-848, MIT Artificial Intelligence Laboratory, August 1985.

[AB97]   Zena M. Ariola and Stefan Blom. Cyclic lambda calculi. In *Theoretical Aspects of Computer Software*, pages 77–106, 1997.

[AC96]   Martìn Abadi and Luca Cardelli. *A Theory of Objects*. Springer-Verlag, 1996.

[AEL88]   Andrew W. Appel, John R. Ellis, and Kai Li. Real-time concurrent collection on stock multiprocessors. In *PLDI '88: Proceedings of the ACM SIGPLAN 1988 Conference on Programming Language Design and Implementation*, pages 11–20. ACM, 1988.

[AF00]   Andrew W. Appel and Amy Felty. A semantic model of types and machine instructions for proof-carrying code. In *POPL '00: Proceedings of the 27th ACM SIGACT-SIGPLAN Symposium on Principles of Programming Languages*, pages 243–253, Boston, January 2000.

[AFH94]   Shail Aditya, Christine H. Flood, and James E. Hicks. Garbage collection for strongly-typed languages using run-time type reconstruction. In *LFP 94: Proceedings of the 1994 ACM SIGPLAN Conference on Lisp and Functional Programming*, pages 12–23. ACM, 1994.

[Aga97]   Johan Agat. Types for register allocation. In Chris Clack, Kevin Hammond, and Antony J. T. Davie, editors, *IFL '97: Implementation of Functional Languages, 9th International Workshop, Selected Papers*, volume 1467 of *Lecture Notes in Computer Science*, pages 92–111, 1997.

[Agh86]   Gul Agha. *Actors: A Model of Concurrent Computation in Distributed Systems*. MIT Press, 1986.

[AH05]   David Aspinall and Martin Hofmann. Dependent types. In Benjamin C. Pierce, editor, *Advanced Topics in Types and Programming Languages*. MIT Press, 2005.

[AJ88]   Andrew W. Appel and Trevor Jim. Continuation-passing, closure-passing style. Technical Report CS-TR-183-88, Princeton University Department of Computer Science, July (revised September) 1988.

[AM03]   Torben Amtoft and Robert Muller. Inferring annotated types for interprocedural register allocation with constructor flattening. In *TLDI '03: The 2003 ACM SIGPLAN International Workshop on Types in Language Design and Implementation*, pages 86–97, January 2003.

[Ame91]   Pierre America. Designing an object-oriented programming language with behavioural subtyping. In *Proceedings of the REX School/Workshop on Foundations of Object-Oriented Languages*, pages 60–90, London, UK, 1991. Springer-Verlag.

[AMO⁺95]   Zena M. Ariola, John Maraist, Martin Odersky, Matthias Felleisen, and Philip Wadler. A call-by-need lambda calculus. In *POPL '95: Proceedings of the 22nd ACM SIGACT-SIGPLAN Symposium on Principles of Programming Languages*, pages 233–246. ACM, 1995.

[Amt93]   Torben Amtoft. Minimal thunkification. In *WSA '93: Proceedings of the 3rd International Workshop on Static Analysis*, volume 724 of *Lecture Notes in Computer Science*, pages 218–229. Springer-Verlag, September 1993.

[ANN97]   Torben Amtoft, Flemming Nielson, and Hanne Riis Nielson. Type and behaviour reconstruction for higher-order concurrent programs. *Journal of Functional Programming*, 7(3):321–347, May 1997.

[ANN99]   Torben Amtoft, Flemming Nielson, and Hanne Riis Nielson. *Type and Effect Systems: Behaviors for Concurrency*. Imperial College Press, 1999.

[AP02]   Andrew Appel and Jens Palsberg. *Modern Compiler Implementation in Java*. Cambridge University Press, second edition, 2002.

[App89]   Andrew W. Appel. Runtime tags aren't necessary. *Lisp and Symbolic Computation*, 2:153–162, 1989.

[App90]   Andrew W. Appel. A runtime system. *Lisp and Symbolic Computation*, 3:343–380, 1990.

[App92]   Andrew W. Appel. *Compiling with Continuations*. Cambridge University Press, 1992.

[App98a]   Andrew Appel. *Modern Compiler Implementation In C*. Cambridge University Press, 1998.

[App98b]   Andrew Appel. *Modern Compiler Implementation In ML*. Cambridge University Press, 1998.

[AR88]   Norman Adams and Jonathan Rees. Object-oriented programming in Scheme. In *LFP '88: Proceedings of the 1988 ACM Conference on LISP and Functional Programming*, pages 277–288. ACM, 1988.

[ASG97]   Andrew Ayers, Richard Schooler, and Robert Gottlieb. Aggressive inlining. In *PLDI '97: Proceedings of the ACM SIGPLAN Conference on Programming Language Design and Implementation*, June 1997.

[ASS96]   Harold Abelson, Gerald Jay Sussman, and Julie Sussman. *Structure and Interpretation of Computer Programs*. MIT Press and McGraw-Hill, second edition, 1996.

[ASU86]   Alfred V. Aho, Ravi Sethi, and Jeffrey D. Ullman. *Compilers: Principles, Techniques, and Tools*. Addison-Wesley, 1986.

[Aug85]   Lennart Augustsson. Compiling pattern matching. In *FPCA '85: Functional Programming Languages and Computer Architecture*, volume 201 of *Lecture Notes in Computer Science*, pages 368–381, September 1985.

[Aug98]   Lennart Augustsson. Cayenne — a language with dependent types. In *ICFP '98: Proceedings of the Third ACM SIGPLAN International Conference on Functional Programming*, pages 239–250. ACM, 1998.

[AWL94]   Alexander Aiken, Edward L. Wimmers, and T. K. Lakshman. Soft typing with conditional types. In *POPL '94: Proceedings of the 21st ACM SIGPLAN-SIGACT Symposium on Principles of Programming Languages*, pages 163–173. ACM, 1994.

[AZ02]   Davide Ancona and Elena Zucca. A calculus of module systems. *Journal of Functional Programming*, 12(2):91–132, 2002.

[Bac78]   John Backus. Can programming be liberated from the von Neumann style? A functional style and its algebra of programs. *Communications of the ACM*, 21(8):245–264, August 1978.

[Bar84]   H. P. Barendregt. *The Lambda-Calculus: Its Syntax and Semantics*. North-Holland, 1984.

[Bar91]   Henk Barendregt. Introduction to generalized type systems. *Journal of Functional Programming*, 1(2):125–154, 1991.

[Bar92]   Henk Barendregt. Lambda calculi with types. In S. Abramsky, D. M. Gabbay, and T. S. E. Maibaum, editors, *Handbook of Logic in Computer Science*, volume 2, chapter 2, pages 117–309. Oxford University Press, 1992.

[Baw93]   Alan Bawden. *Implementing Distributed Systems Using Linear Naming*. PhD thesis, MIT EECS, March 1993. Available as MIT AI Lab Technical Report AITR-1627.

[BBG+63]   J. W. Backus, F. L. Bauer, J. Green, C. Katz, J. McCarthy, A. J. Perlis, H. Rutishauser, K. Samelson, B. Vauquois, J. H. Wegstein, A. van Wijngaarden, and M. Woodger. Revised report on the algorithmic language ALGOL 60. *Communications of the ACM*, 6(1):1–17, 1963.

[BCT94]   P. Briggs, K. D. Cooper, and L. Torczon. Improvements to graph coloring register allocation. *ACM Transactions on Programming Languages and Systems*, 16(3):428–455, May 1994.

[BDD80]   H. Boehm, A. Demers, and J. Donahue. An informal description of Russell. Technical Report TR80-430, Cornell University, Department of Computer Science, 1980.

[BdM96]   Richard Bird and Ooge de Moor. *The Algebra of Programming*. Prentice Hall, 1996.

[Bir98]   Richard Bird. *Introduction to Functional Programming Using Haskell*. Prentice Hall, second edition, 1998.

[BKR98]   Nick Benton, Andrew Kennedy, and George Russell. Compiling Standard ML to Java bytecodes. In *ICFP '98: Proceedings of the Third ACM SIGPLAN International Conference on Functional Programming*, pages 129–140, 1998.

[BL84]   R. Burstall and B. W. Lampson. *A Kernel Language for Abstract Data Types and Modules*, volume 173 of *Lecture Notes in Computer Science*. Springer-Verlag, 1984.

[BL92]   Gilad Bracha and Gary Lindstrom. Modularity meets inheritance. In *Proceedings of the IEEE Computer Society International Conference on Computer Languages*, pages 282–290, Washington, DC, 1992. IEEE Computer Society.

[Ble90]   Guy E. Blelloch. *Vector Models for Data-Parallel Computing*. MIT Press, 1990.

[BM85]   Marianne Baudinet and David MacQueen. Tree pattern matching for ML, 1985. Unpublished paper. Available at `http://www.smlnj.org/compiler-notes/85-note-baudinet.ps`.

[BN98]   Franz Baader and Tobias Nipkow. *Term Rewriting and All That*. Cambridge University Press, 1998.

[BOSW98]   Gilad Bracha, Martin Odersky, David Stoutamire, and Philip Wadler. Making the future safe for the past: Adding genericity to the Java programming language. In *OOPSLA '98: Conference Proceedings on Object-oriented Programming Systems, Languages and Applications*, pages 183–200. ACM, 1998.

[BR88]   Alan Bawden and Jonathan Rees. Syntactic closures. In *LFP '88: Proceedings of the 1988 ACM Conference on LISP and Functional Programming*, pages 86–95. ACM, 1988.

[BR03]   Didier Le Botlan and Didier Rémy. ML^F: Raising ML to the power of system F. In *ICFP '03: Proceedings of the Eighth ACM SIGPLAN International Conference on Functional Programming*, pages 27–38. ACM, 2003.

[Bru02]   Kim B. Bruce. *Foundations of Object-Oriented Languages*. The MIT Press, 2002.

[BW88]   Hans-Juergen Boehm and Mark Weiser. Garbage collection in an uncooperative environment. *Software — Practice and Experience*, 18(9):807–820, September 1988.

[BW90]   Michael Barr and Charles Wells. *Category Theory for Computer Scientists*. Prentice-Hall, 1990.

[BWD95]   Robert G. Burger, Oscar Waddell, and R. Kent Dybvig. Register allocation using lazy saves, eager restores, and greedy shuffling. In *PLDI '95: Proceedings of the ACM SIGPLAN Conference on Programming Language Design and Implementation*. ACM SIGPLAN, June 1995.

[BWW+89] J. Backus, J. H. Williams, E. L. Wimmers, P. Lucas, and A. Aiken. FL language manual, parts 1 and 2. Technical Report RJ 7100 (67163), IBM Research, 1989.

[BWW90] J. Backus, J. H. Williams, and E. L. Wimmers. An introduction to the programming language FL. In D. A. Turner, editor, *Research Topics in Functional Programming*, pages 219–249. Addison-Wesley, Reading, MA, 1990.

[BZ02] Gérard Boudol and Pascal Zimmer. Recursion in the call-by-value lambda-calculus. In Zoltán Ésik and Anna Ingólfsdóttir, editors, *FICS*, volume NS-02-2 of *BRICS Notes Series*, pages 61–66. University of Aarhus, 2002.

[CAC+81] G. Chaitin, M. A. Auslander, A. K. Chandra, J. Cocke, M. E. Hopkins, and P. W. Markstein. Register allocation via coloring. *Computer Languages*, 6(1):47–57, January 1981.

[Car86] Luca Cardelli. A polymorphic λ-calculus with Type:Type. Technical Report 10, Digital Equipment Corporation Systems Research Center, Palo Alto, CA, May 1986.

[Car87] Luca Cardelli. Basic polymorphic typechecking. *Science of Computer Programming*, 8(2):147–172, April 1987.

[Car88a] Luca Cardelli. Phase distinctions in type theory. Manuscript, 1988.

[Car88b] Luca Cardelli. A semantics of multiple inheritance. *Information and Computation*, 76(2-3):138–164, 1988.

[Car89] Luca Cardelli. Typeful programming. In *IFIP Advanced Seminar on Formal Description of Programming Concepts*, 1989.

[CC77] P. Cousot and R. Cousot. Abstract interpretation: A unified lattice model for static analysis of programs by construction or approximation of fixpoints. In *POPL '77: Proceedings of the 4th ACM SIGACT-SIGPLAN Symposium on Principles of Programming Languages*, pages 238–252, Los Angeles, California, 1977. ACM.

[CC91] Felice Cardone and Mario Coppo. Type inference with recursive types: Syntax and semantics. *Information and Computation*, 92(1):48–80, 1991.

[CCH+89] Peter Canning, William Cook, Walter Hill, Walter Olthoff, and John C. Mitchell. F-bounded polymorphism for object-oriented programming. In *FPCA '89: Proceedings of the Fourth International Conference on Functional Programming and Computer Architecture*, pages 273–280. ACM Press, 1989.

[CF58] H. B. Curry and R. Feys. *Combinatory Logic I*. Studies in Logic and the Foundations of Mathematics. North-Holland, Amsterdam, 1958.

[CF91] Robert Cartwright and Mike Fagan. Soft typing. In *PLDI '91: Proceedings of the ACM SIGPLAN Conference on Programming Language Design and Implementation*, pages 278–292. ACM Press, 1991.

[CF98]   Robert Cartwright and Matthias Felleisen. Program verification through soft typing. *ACM Computing Surveys*, 28(2):349–351, June 1998.

[CH94]   William D. Clinger and Lars Thomas Hansen. Lambda, the Ultimate Label, or a simple optimizing compiler for Scheme. In *LFP '94: Proceedings of the 1994 ACM Conference on LISP and Functional Programming*, pages 128 – 139. ACM, 1994.

[Cha82]   G. J. Chaitin. Register allocation & spilling via graph coloring. In *SIGPLAN '82: Proceedings of the 1982 SIGPLAN Symposium on Compiler Construction*, pages 98–105, 1982.

[Cha92]   Craig Chambers. Object-oriented multi-methods in Cecil. In *ECOOP '92: Proceedings of the European Conference on Object-oriented Programming*, pages 33–56, London, UK, 1992. Springer-Verlag.

[CHC90]   William R. Cook, Walter Hill, and Peter S. Canning. Inheritance is not subtyping. In *POPL '90: Proceedings of the 17th ACM SIGPLAN-SIGACT Symposium on Principles of Programming Languages*, pages 125–135. ACM Press, 1990. Reprinted in [GM94].

[CHD02]   K. Crary, R. Harper, and D. Dreyer. A type system for higher-order modules. In *POPL '02: Proceedings of the 29th ACM SIGACT-SIGPLAN Symposium on Principles of Programming Languages*, 2002.

[Che70]   C. J. Cheney. A nonrecursive list compacting algorithm. *Communications of the ACM*, 13(11):677–678, 1970.

[CHP99]   Karl Crary, Robert Robert Harper, and Sidd Puri. What is a recursive module? In *PLDI '99: Proceedings of the ACM SIGPLAN Conference on Programming Language Design and Implementation*, June 1999.

[CHS72]   Haskell Brooks Curry, J. Roger Hindley, and Jonathan P. Seldin. *Combinatory Logic*, volume 2. North-Holland, 1972.

[CHT91]   Kenneth Cooper, Mary W. Hall, and Linda Torczon. An experiment with inline substitution. *Software — Practice and Experience*, 21(6):581–601, June 1991.

[Chu32]   Alonzo Church. A set of postulates for the foundation of logic. *Annals of Mathematics*, 33(2):346–366, April 1932. A second part of this paper including revisions was published as [Chu33].

[Chu33]   Alonzo Church. A set of postulates for the foundation of logic (second paper). *Annals of Mathematics*, 34(4):839–864, October 1933.

[Chu36]   Alonzo Church. An unsolvable problem of elementary number theory. *American Journal of Mathematics*, 58(2):345–363, April 1936.

[Chu40]   Alonzo Church. A formulation of the simple theory of types. *The Journal of Symbolic Logic*, 5:56–68, 1940.

[Chu41]   Alonzo Church. *The Calculi of Lambda-Conversion*. Princeton University Press, 1941.

[CJW00]   Henry Cejtin, Suresh Jagannathan, and Stephen Weeks. Flow-directed closure conversion for typed languages. In *ESOP '00: Proceedings of the 9th European Symposium on Programming*, pages 56–71, Berlin, Germany, March 2000.

[Cla73]   R. Lawrence Clark. A linguistic contribution to GOTO-less programming. *Datamation*, December 1973. Reprinted in Communications of the ACM, April 1984.

[Cli84]   William Clinger. The Scheme 311 compiler: An exercise in denotational semantics. In *LFP '84: Proceedings of the 1984 ACM Symposium on LISP and Functional Programming*, pages 356–364. ACM, 1984.

[CM85]   Luca Cardelli and David MacQueen. Persistence and type abstraction. In *Proceedings of the Persistence and Data Types Workshop*, Appin, Scotland, August 1985.

[CM91]   Luca Cardelli and John C. Mitchell. Operations on records. *Mathematical Structures in Computer Science*, 1(1):3–48, March 1991. Reprinted in [GM94].

[CM98]   Guy Cousineau and Michel Mauny. *The Functional Approach to Programming*. Cambridge University Press, Secaucus, NJ, USA, 1998.

[CMMS94] Luca Cardelli, Simone Martini, John C. Mitchell, and Andre Scedrov. An extension of system F with subtyping. *Information and Computation*, 109(1/2):4–56, 1994.

[Coh81]   Jacques Cohen. Garbage collection of linked data structures. *Computing Surveys*, 13(3):341–367, September 1981.

[Con63]   Melvin E. Conway. Design of a separable transition-diagram compiler. *Communications of the ACM*, 6(7):396–408, 1963.

[Coo89]   W. R. Cook. A proposal for making Eiffel type-safe. *The Computer Journal*, 32(4):305–311, 1989.

[Coo91]   William R. Cook. Object-oriented programming versus abstract data types. In *Proceedings of the REX School/Workshop on Foundations of Object-Oriented Languages*, pages 151–178, London, UK, 1991. Springer-Verlag.

[Coo92]   William R. Cook. Interfaces and specifications for the Smalltalk-80 collection classes. In *OOPSLA '92: Conference Proceedings on Object-oriented Programming Systems, Languages, and Applications*, pages 1–15. ACM, 1992.

[Cou90]   Bruno Courcelle. Graph rewriting: An algebraic and logic approach. In J. van Leeuwen, editor, *Handbook of Theoretical Computer Science, Volume B: Formal Models and Semantics*, pages 193–242. MIT Press/Elsevier, 1990.

[CR91]   William Clinger and Jonathan Rees. Macros that work. In *POPL '91: Proceedings of the 18th ACM SIGACT-SIGPLAN Symposium on Principles of Programming Languages*, pages 155–162. ACM, 1991.

[CT03]   Keith D. Cooper and Linda Torczon. *Engineering a Compiler.* Morgan Kaufmann, 2003.

[CW85]   Luca Cardelli and Peter Wegner. On understanding types, data abstraction, and polymorphism. *ACM Computing Surveys*, 17(4):471–522, 1985.

[CW00]   Karl Crary and Stephnie Weirich. Resource bound certification. In *POPL '00: Proceedings of the 27th ACM SIGPLAN-SIGACT symposium on Principles of programming languages*, pages 184–198. ACM, 2000.

[CX05]   Chiyan Chen and Hongwei Xi. Combining programming with theorm proving. In *ICFP '05: Proceedings of the 10th ACM SIGPLAN International Conference on Functional Programming.* ACM, 2005.

[DC00]   Julian Dolby and Andrew Chien. An automatic object inlining optimization and its evaluation. In *PLDI '00: Proceedings of the ACM SIGPLAN 2000 Conference on Programming Language Design and Implementation*, pages 345–357. ACM, 2000.

[DF92]   Olivier Danvy and Andrzej Filinski. Representing control: A study of the CPS transformation. *Mathematical Structures in Computer Science*, 2:361–391, 1992.

[DG87]   Linda G. DeMichiel and Richard P. Gabriel. The Common Lisp Object System: An overview. In *European Conference on Object-oriented Programming (ECOOP) '87*, pages 151–170, London, UK, 1987. Springer-Verlag.

[DG08]   Jeffrey Dean and Sanjay Ghemawat. MapReduce: Simplified data processing on large clusters. *Communications of the ACM*, 51(1):107–113, 2008.

[Dic92]   Ken Dickey. Scheming with objects. *AI Expert*, 7(10):24–33, 1992. Available from `ftp://ftp.cs.indiana.edu/pub/scheme-repository/doc/pubs/swob.txt`.

[DJ90]   Nachum Dershowitz and Jean-Pierre Jouannaud. Rewrite systems. In J. van Leeuwen, editor, *Handbook of Theoretical Computer Science, Volume B: Formal Models and Semantics*, pages 243–320. MIT Press/Elsevier, 1990.

[DJG92]   V. Dornic, P. Jouvelot, and D. Gifford. Polymorphic time systems for estimating program complexity. *ACM Letters on Programming Languages and Systems*, 1:33–45, 1992.

[DKAL03]   Dinakar Dhurjati, Sumant Kowshik, Vikram Adve, and Chris Lattner. Memory safety without runtime checks or garbage collection. In *Proceedings of the 2003 ACM SIGPLAN Conference on Language, Compiler, and Tool Support for Embedded Systems*, pages 69–80. ACM, 2003.

[DM82]   Luís Damas and Robin Milner. Principal type schemes for functional programs. In *POPL '82: Proceedings of the 9th ACM SIGACT-SIGPLAN Symposium on Principles of Programming Languages*, pages 207–212, 1982.

[DMN70]   O.-J. Dahl, B. Myhrhaug, and K. Nygaard. SIMULA67 common base language. Technical Report S-22, Norwegian Computing Centre, Oslo, 1970.

[DWM+01] Allyn Dimock, Ian Westmacott, Robert Muller, Franklyn Turbak, and J. B. Wells. Functioning without closure: Type-safe customized function representations for Standard ML. In *ICFP '01: Proceedings of the Sixth ACM SIGPLAN International Conference on Functional Programming*, pages 14–25, Firenze, Italy, September 2001. ACM.

[ECM99] ECMA, Geneva, Switzerland. *ECMAScript Language Specification*, third edition, December 1999.

[EH97] Conal Elliott and Paul Hudak. Functional reactive animation. In *ICFP '97: Proceedings of the Second ACM SIGPLAN International Conference on Functional Programming*, pages 263–273. ACM, 1997.

[FD01] Darrell Ferguson and Dwight Deugo. Call with current continuation patterns. In *8th Conference on Pattern Languages of Programs*, September 2001.

[FF86] Matthias Felleisen and Daniel Friedman. Control operators, the SECD-machine, and the λ-calculus. In M. Wirsing, editor, *Formal Description of Programming Concepts — III*, pages 193–219. North-Holland, 1986.

[FFF] Matthias Felleisen, Robby Findler, and Matthew Flatt. *Modeling Programming Languages: Semantics Engineering with Redex*. MIT Press. To be published. Extended version of an earlier monograph, "Programming Languages and Lambda Calculi," by Felleisen and Flatt, 2006.

[FH92] Matthias Felleisen and Robert Hieb. The revised report on the syntactic theories of sequential control and state. *Theoretical Computer Science*, 102:235–271, 1992.

[FHK84] Daniel P. Friedman, Christopher T. Haynes, and Eugene E. Kohlbecker. Programming with continuations. In P. Pepper, editor, *Program Transformation and Programming Environments*, pages 263–274. Springer-Verlag, 1984.

[FKR+00] Robert Fitzgerald, Todd B. Knoblock, Erik Ruf, Bjarne Steensgaard, and David Tarditi. Marmot: An optimizing compiler for Java. *Software — Practice and Experience*, 30(3):199–232, 2000.

[FL92] Marc Feeley and Guy Lapalme. Closure generation based on viewing lambda as epsilon plus compile. *Computer Languages*, 17(4):251–267, 1992.

[FQ03] Cormac Flanagan and Shaz Qadeer. A type and effect system for atomicity. In *PLDI '03: Proceedings of the ACM SIGPLAN 2003 Conference on Programming Language Design and Implementation*, pages 338–349, 2003.

[FSDF93] Cormac Flanagan, Amr Sabry, Bruce F. Duba, and Matthias Felleisen. The essence of compiling with continuations. In *PLDI '93: Proceedings of the ACM SIGPLAN Conference on Programming Language Design and Implementation*, pages 238–247. ACM, 1993.

[FWH01] Daniel P. Friedman, Mitchell Wand, and Christopher T. Haynes. *Essentials of Programming Languages*. MIT Press, second edition, 2001.

[FY69]   Robert R. Fenichel and Jerome C. Yochelson. A LISP garbage-collector for virtual-memory computer systems. *Commununications of the ACM*, 12(11):611–612, 1969.

[Gar04]   Jacques Garrigue. Relaxing the value restriction. In Yukiyoshi Kameyama and Peter J. Stuckey, editors, *FLOPS '04: Proceedings of the 7th International Symposium on Functional and Logic Programming*, volume 2998 of *Lecture Notes in Computer Science*, pages 196–213. Springer, 2004.

[GdM03]   Jeremy Gibbons and Oege de Moor, editors. *The Fun of Programming*. Palgrave Macmillan, 2003.

[GG00]   Ralph E. Griswold and Madge T. Griswold. *The ICON programming Language*. Coriolis Group Books, third edition, 2000.

[GH75]   Irene Greif and Carl Hewitt. Actor semantics of PLANNER-73. In *POPL '75: Proceedings of the 2nd ACM SIGPLAN-SIGACT Symposium on Principles of Programming Languages*, pages 67–77. ACM, 1975.

[Gib94]   Jeremy Gibbons. An introduction to the Bird-Meertens Formalism. Presented at *New Zealand Formal Program Development Colloquium*, Hamilton, November 1994, November 1994.

[Gir71]   J.-Y. Girard. Une extension de l'interpretation de Gödel à l'analyse, et son application à l'élimination des coupures dans l'analyse et la théorie des types. In J. E. Fenstad, editor, *Proceedings of the Second Scandinavian Logic Symposium*, pages 63–92. North-Holland, 1971.

[Gir90]   Jean-Yves Girard. The system F of variable types, fifteen years later. In Huet [Hue90], pages 87–126.

[GJLS87]   David K. Gifford, Pierre Jouvelot, John M. Lucassen, and Mark A. Sheldon. FX-87 reference manual. Technical Report MIT/LCS/TR-407, MIT Laboratory for Computer Science, September 1987.

[GJS96]   James Gosling, Bill Joy, and Guy Steele. *The Java Language Specification*. Addison-Wesley, 1996.

[GJSO92]   David Gifford, Pierre Jouvelot, Mark A. Sheldon, and James O'Toole. Report on the FX-91 programming language. Technical Report MIT/LCS/TR-531, MIT Laboratory for Computer Science, February 1992.

[GLP00]   Vladimir Gapayev, Michael Y. Levin, and Benjamin C. Pierce. Recursive subtyping revealed. In *ICFP '00: Proceedings of the Fifth ACM SIGPLAN International Conference on Functional Programming*, pages 221–231, 2000.

[GM94]   Carl A. Gunter and John C. Mitchell, editors. *Theoretical Aspects of Object-Oriented Programming: Types, Semantics, and Language Design*. MIT Press, 1994.

[Gol91]   Benjamin Goldberg. Tag-free garbage collection for strongly typed programming languages. In *PLDI '91: Proceedings of the ACM SIGPLAN 1991 Conference on Programming Language Design and Implementation*, pages 165–176. ACM, 1991.

[Gor79]   Michael J. C. Gordon. *The Denotational Description of Programming Languages*. Springer-Verlag, 1979.

[GR83]   Adele Goldberg and David Robson. *Smalltalk-80: The Language and Its Implemenation*. Addison Wesley, 1983.

[GR99]   Jacques Garrigue and Didier Rémy. Semi-explicit first-class polymorphism for ML. *Information and Computation*, 155(1-2):134–169, 1999.

[Gri87]   David Gries. *The Science of Programming*. Springer-Verlag New York, Inc., Secaucus, NJ, USA, 1987.

[GS90]   C. A. Gunter and D. S. Scott. Semantic domains. In J. van Leeuwen, editor, *Handbook of Theoretical Computer Science, Volume B: Formal Models and Semantics*, pages 633–674. MIT Press/Elsevier, 1990.

[Gun92]   Carl A. Gunter. *Semantics of Programming Languages: Structures and Techniques*. MIT Press, 1992.

[Har86]   Robert Harper. Modules and persistence in Standard ML. Technical Report ECS-LFCS-86-11, University of Edinburgh, Laboratory for Foundations of Computer Science, September 1986.

[HBS73]   Carl Hewitt, Peter Bishop, and Richard Steiger. A universal modular AC-TOR formalism for artificial intelligence. In *Third International Joint Conference on Artificial Intelligence*, pages 235–245, Stanform, California, August 1973.

[HCNP03]   Paul Hudak, Antony Courtney, Henrik Nilsson, and John Peterson. Arrows, robots, and functional reactive programming. In *Summer School on Advanced Functional Programming 2002, Oxford University*, volume 2638 of *Lecture Notes in Computer Science*, pages 159–187. Springer-Verlag, 2003.

[Hen80]   Peter Henderson. *Functional Programming: Application and Implementation*. Prentice Hall, 1980.

[Hew77]   Carl Hewitt. Viewing control structures as patterns of passing messages. *Artificial Intelligence*, pages 323–364, 1977.

[HF87]   Christopher T. Haynes and Daniel P. Friedman. Abstracting timed preemption with engines. *Computer Languages*, 12(2):109–121, 1987.

[HFW86]   Christopher T Haynes, Daniel P Friedman, and Mitchell Wand. Obtaining coroutines with continuations. *Computer Languages*, 11(3-4):143–153, 1986.

[HG88]   R. T. Hammel and D. K. Gifford. FX-87 performance measurements: Dataflow implementation. Technical Report MIT-LCS-TR-421, MIT Laboratory for Computer Science, Cambridge, MA, USA, September 1988.

[HGB78]   Jr. Henry G. Baker. List processing in real time on a serial computer. *Communications of the ACM*, 21(4):280–294, 1978.

[HH86]   James G. Hook and Douglas J. Howe. Impredicative strong existential equivalent to type:type. Technical Report TR 86-760, Department of Computer Science, Cornell University, Ithaca, New York, June 1986.

[Hic08]   Jason Hickey. *Introduction to Objective Caml*. Cambridge University Press, 2008.

[Hin97]   J. Roger Hindley. *Basic Simple Type Theory*, volume 42 of *Cambridge Tracts in Theoretical Computer Science*. Cambridge University Press, 1997.

[HL94]   Robert Harper and Mark Lillibridge. A type-theoretic approach to higher-order modules with sharing. In *POPL '94: Proceedings of the 21st ACM SIGACT-SIGPLAN Symposium on Principles of Programming Languages*, pages 123–137. ACM Press, January 1994.

[HLW03]   Tom Hirschowitz, Xavier Leroy, and J. B. Wells. Compilation of extended recursion in call-by-value functional languages. In *PPDP '03: Proceedings of the 5th ACM SIGPLAN International Conference on Principles and Practice of Declarative Programming*, pages 160–171. ACM, 2003.

[HMM90]   Robert Harper, John C. Mitchell, and Eugenio Moggi. Higher-order modules and the phase distinction. In *Converence Record of the Seventeenth Annual ACM Symposium on Principles of Programming Languages*, pages 341–354, San Francisco, CA, January 1990.

[Hoa85]   C.A.R. Hoare. *Communicating Sequential Processes*. Prentice-Hall, 1985.

[Hof80]   Douglas R. Hofstadter. *Gödel, Escher, Bach: An Eternal Golden Braid*. Vintage Books, 1980.

[HP05]   Robert Harper and Benjamin C. Pierce. Design considerations for ML-style module systems. In Benjamin C. Pierce, editor, *Advanced Topics in Types and Programming Languages*, pages 293–345. MIT Press, 2005.

[HPW+92]   Paul Hudak, Simon Peyton Jones, Philip Wadler, et al. Report on the programming language Haskell, version 1.2. *ACM SIGPLAN Notices*, 27(5), May 1992.

[HS86a]   W. Daniel Hillis and Guy L. Steele Jr. Data parallel algorithms. *Communications of the ACM*, 29(12), 1986.

[HS86b]   J. Roger Hindley and Jonathan P. Seldin. *Introduction to Combinators and λ-calculus*. Cambridge University Press, 1986.

[HU79]   John E. Hopcroft and Jeffrey Ullman. *Introduction to Automata Theory, Languages, and Computation*. Addison-Wesley, 1979.

[Hud89]   Paul Hudak. Conception, evolution, and application of functional programming languages. *ACM Computing Surveys*, 21(3):359–411, 1989.

[Hud00]   Paul Hudak. *The Haskell School of Expression: Learning Functional Programming Through Multimedia*. Cambridge University Press, 2000.

[Hue90]   Gerard Huet, editor. *Logical Foundations of Functional Programming*. Addison-Wesley, 1990.

[Hug82]   R. J. M. Hughes. Super-combinators: A new implementation technique for applicative languages. In *LFP '82: Proceedings of the 1982 ACM Symposium on Lisp and Functional Programming*, pages 1–10. ACM Press, August 1982.

[Hug89]   John Hughes. Why functional programming matters. *Computer Journal*, 32(2):98–107, 1989. Reprinted in [Tur90], pp. 17–42.

[HW04]   Christian Haack and J. B. Wells. Type error slicing in implicitly typed higher-order languages. *Science of Computer Programming*, 50(1–3):189–224, March 2004.

[IK00]   Atsushi Igarashi and Naoki Kobayashi. Garbage collection based on a linear type system. Technical Report CMU-CS-00-161, Carnegie Mellon University, 2000.

[Ing61]   P. Z. Ingerman. Thunks: A way of compiling procedure statements with some comments on procedure declarations. *Communications of the ACM*, 4(1):55–58, January 1961.

[Ing81]   Daniel H. H. Ingalls. Design principles behind Smalltalk. *Byte*, 6(8):286–298, August 1981.

[IPW01]   Atsushi Igarashi, Benjamin C. Pierce, and Philip Wadler. Featherweight Java: A minimal core calculus for Java and GJ. *ACM Transactions on Programming Languages and Systems*, 23(3):396–450, 2001.

[JG89a]   P. Jouvelot and D. Gifford. Reasoning about continuations with control effects. In *PLDI '89: Proceedings of the ACM SIGPLAN Conference on Programming Language Design and Implementation*, pages 218–226, 1989.

[JG89b]   Pierre Jouvelot and David K. Gifford. Communication effects for message-based concurrency. Technical Report MIT/LCS/TM-386, MIT Laboratory for Computer Science, February 1989.

[JG91]   Pierre Jouvelot and David K. Gifford. Algebraic reconstruction of types and effects. In *POPL '91: Proceedings of the 18th ACM SIGACT-SIGPLAN Symposium on Principles of Programming Languages*, pages 303–310. ACM Press, 1991.

[Jim96]   Trevor Jim. What are principal typings and what are they good for? In *POPL '96: Proceedings of the 23rd ACM SIGPLAN-SIGACT Symposium on Principles of Programming Languages*, pages 42–53. ACM, 1996.

[JM02]   Simon Peyton Jones and Simon Marlow. Secrets of the Glasgow Haskell Compiler inliner. *Journal of Functional Programming*, 12(4+5):393–434, 2002.

[JMG+02]   T. Jim, G. Morrisett, D. Grossman, M. Hicks, J. Cheney, and Y. Wang. Cyclone: A safe dialect of C. In *Proceedings of the 2002 USENIX Annual Technical Conference*, pages 275–288, 2002.

[JN95]   Neil D. Jones and Flemming Nielson. Abstract interpretation: A semantic-based tool for program analysis. In Samson Abramsky, T. S. Maibaum, and Dov M. Gabbay, editors, *Handbook of Logic in Computer Science: Volume 4: Semantic Modelling*, pages 527–636. Clarendon Press, Oxford, 1995.

[Joh75]   S. C. Johnson. Yacc — yet another compiler compiler. Computing Science Technical Report 32, Bell Laboratories, Murray Hill, N.J., 1975.

[Joh85]   Thomas Johnsson. Lambda lifting: Transforming programs to recursive equations. In *FPCA '85: Functional Programming Languages and Computer Architecture*, volume 201 of *Lecture Notes in Computer Science*, pages 190–203, September 1985.

[Jon99]   Richard Jones. *Garbage Collection: Algorithms for Automatic Dynamic Memory Management*. John Wiley and Sons, 1999.

[JP99]   Mark Jones and Simon Peyton Jones. Lightweight extensible records for Haskell. In *Proceedings of the 1999 Haskell Workshop*, September 1999. Available from University of Utrecht Computer Science Departmentas Technical Report UU-CS-1999-28.

[JVWS07]   Simon Peyton Jones, Dimitrios Vytiniotis, Stephanie Weirich, and Mark Shields. Practical type inference for arbitrary-rank types. *Journal of Functional Programming*, 17(1):1–82, 2007.

[Kah87]   Gilles Kahn. Natural semantics. In *Proceedings of STACS '87, 4th Annual Symposium on Theoretical Aspects of Computer Science*, volume 247 of *Lecture Notes in Computer Science*, pages 22–39. Springer-Verlag, 1987.

[KBO⁺05]   Benjamin A. Kuperman, Carla E. Brodley, Hilmi Ozdoganoglu, T.N Vijaykumar, and Ankit Jalote. Detection and prevention of stack buffer overflow attacks. *Communications of the ACM*, 48(11):51–56, November 2005.

[KCR⁺98]   Richard Kelsey, William Clinger, Jonathan Rees, et al. Revised[5] report on the algorithmic language Scheme. *Higher-Order and Symbolic Computation*, 11(1):7–105, August 1998.

[Kel89]   Richard Kelsey. *Compilation by Program Transformation*. PhD thesis, Yale University, 1989.

[KFFD86]   Eugene Kohlbecker, Daniel P. Friedman, Matthias Felleisen, and Bruce Duba. Hygienic macro expansion. In *LFP '86: Proceedings of the 1986 ACM Conference on LISP and Functional Programming*, pages 151–161. ACM, 1986.

[KG77]   Alan Kay and Adele Goldberg. Personal dynamic media. *Computer*, 10(3):31–41, March 1977.

[KH89]   Richard Kelsey and Paul Hudak. Realistic compilation by program transformation. In *POPL '89: Proceedings of the 16th ACM SIGACT-SIGPLAN Symposium on Principles of Programming Languages*, pages 281–292. ACM, 1989.

[KKR⁺86]   David Kranz, Richard Kelsey, Jonathan A. Rees, Paul Hudak, James Philbin, and Norman I. Adams. Orbit: An optimizing compiler for Scheme. In *Proceedings of the SIGPLAN '86 Symposium on Compiler Construction*, pages 219–233. ACM, June 1986.

[KM89]   Tsung-Min Kuo and Prateek Mishra. Strictness analysis: A new perspective baed on type inference. In *FPCA '89: Proceedings of the Fourth Interna-

tional Conference on Functional Programming and Computer Architecture, pages 260–272, 1989.

[Kni89]   Kevin Knight. Unification: A multidisciplinary survey. *ACM Computing Surveys*, 21(1):93–124, 1989.

[Kow79]   Robert Kowalski. Algorithm = logic + control. *Communications of the ACM*, 22(7):424–436, 1979.

[KPS93]   Dexter Kozen, Jens Palsberg, and Michael I. Schwartzbach. Efficient recursive subtyping. In *POPL '93: Proceedings of the 20th ACM SIGACT-SIGPLAN Symposium on Principles of Programming Languages*, pages 419–428, 1993.

[KTU93]   A. J. Kfoury, J. Tiuryn, and P. Urzyczyn. Type reconstruction in the presence of polymorphic recursion. *ACM Transactions on Programming Languages and Systems*, 15(2):290–311, 1993.

[KW87]   E. E. Kohlbecker and M. Wand. Macro-by-example: Deriving syntactic transformations from their specifications. In *POPL '87: Proceedings of the 14th ACM SIGACT-SIGPLAN Symposium on Principles of Programming Languages*, pages 77–84. ACM, 1987.

[KW95]   A. J. Kfoury and J. B. Wells. New notions of reduction and non-semantic proofs of strong β-normalization in typed λ-calculi. In *IEEE Symposium on Logic in Computer Science*, pages 311–321, 1995.

[L$^+$79]   Barbara Liskov et al. CLU reference manual. Technical Report MIT/LCS/TR-225, MIT Laboratory for Computer Science, October 1979.

[Lan64]   P. J. Landin. The mechanical evaluation of expressions. *The Computer Journal*, pages 308–320, January 1964.

[Lan65a]   P. J. Landin. A correspondence between ALGOL 60 and Church's lambda-notation, Part I. *Communications of the ACM*, 8(2):89–101, February 1965.

[Lan65b]   P. J. Landin. A correspondence between ALGOL 60 and Church's lambda-notation, Part II. *Communications of the ACM*, 8(3):158–165, March 1965.

[Lan66]   P. J. Landin. The next 700 programming languages. *Communications of the ACM*, 9(3):157–166, March 1966.

[Lan98]   Peter J. Landin. A generalization of jumps and labels. *Higher-Order and Symbolic Computation*, 11(2):125–143, 1998. Reprint of a UNIVAC Systems Programming Research Report from August, 1965.

[Lau93]   John Launchbury. A natural semantics for lazy evaluation. In *POPL '93: Proceedings of the 20th ACM SIGACT-SIGPLAN Symposium on Principles of Programming Languages*, pages 144–154. ACM, 1993.

[LB88]   B. Lampson and R. Burstall. Pebble, a kernel language for modules and abstract data types. *Information and Compututation*, 76(2–3):278–346, 1988.

[Ler94]   Xavier Leroy. Manifest types, modules, and separate compilation. In *21st Symposium on Principles of Programming Languages*, pages 109–122. ACM, 1994.

[Ler95]   Xavier Leroy. Applicative functors and fully transparent higher-order modules. In *POPL '95: Proceedings of the 22nd ACM SIGACT-SIGPLAN Symposium on Principles of Programming Languages*. ACM, 1995.

[Ler96]   Xavier Leroy. A syntactic theory of type generativity and sharing. *Journal of Functional Programming*, 6(5):1–32, September 1996.

[Les75]   M. E. Lesk. Lex — a lexical analyzer generator. Computing Science Technical Report 39, Bell Laboratories, Murray Hill, N.J., 1975.

[Lev00]   John R. Levine. *Linkers & Loaders*. Morgan Kaufmann, 2000.

[LG88]   John M. Lucassen and David K. Gifford. Polymorphic effect systems. In *POPL '88: Proceedings of the 15th ACM SIGACT-SIGPLAN Symposium on Principles of Programming Languages*, pages 47–57, 1988.

[LHL+77]   B. W. Lampson, J. J. Horning, R. L. London, J. G. Mitchell, and G. J. Popek. Report on the programming language Euclid. *SIGPLAN Notices*, 12(2):1–79, 1977.

[Lie86]   Henry Lieberman. Using prototypical objects to implement shared behavior in object-oriented systems. In *OOPSLA '86: Conference proceedings on Object-Oriented Programming Systems, Languages and Applications*, pages 214–223. ACM, 1986.

[LJ95]   John Launchbury and Simon L. Peyton Jones. State in Haskell. *Lisp and Symbolic Computation*, 8(4):293–341, 1995.

[LLMS00]   Jeffrey R. Lewis, John Launchbury, Erik Meijer, and Mark B. Shields. Implicit parameters: Dynamic scoping with static types. In *POPL '00: Proceedings of the 27th ACM SIGACT-SIGPLAN Symposium on Principles of Programming Languages*, pages 108–118. ACM, 2000.

[LSAS77]   Barbara Liskov, Alan Snyder, Russell Atkinson, and Craig Schaffert. Abstraction mechanisms in CLU. *Communications of the ACM*, 20(8):564–576, August 1977.

[LTU]   Lambda the Ultimate: The programming languages web log. `http://lambda-the-ultimate.org/`.

[Luc87]   John M. Lucassen. *Types and Effects: Towards the Integration of Functional and Imperative Programming*. PhD thesis, MIT, 1987.

[LY98]   Oukseh Lee and Kwangkeun Yi. Proofs about a folklore let-polymorphic type inference algorithm. *ACM Transactions on Programming Languages and Systems*, 20(4):707–723, July 1998.

[LZ74]   Barbara Liskov and Stephen Zilles. Programming with abstract data types. In *Procedings of the ACM SIGPLAN Conference on Very High Level Languages*, volume 9 of *SIGPLAN Notices*. ACM, 1974.

[LZ75]   Barbara Liskov and Stephen Zilles. Specification techniques for data abstractions. *IEEE Transactions on Software Engingineering*, pages 7–19, March 1975.

[Mac84]   David MacQueen. Modules for standard ML. In *LFP '84: Proceedings of the 1984 ACM Symposium on LISP and Functional Programming*, 1984.

[Mac86]   D. B. MacQueen. Using dependent types to express modular structure. In *POPL '86: Proceedings of the 13th ACM SIGACT-SIGPLAN Symposium on Principles of Programming Languages*. ACM, 1986.

[Mac88]   David MacQueen. An implementation of standard ML modules. Part of the SMLNJ Distribution, March 1988.

[Mac02]   Elena L. Machkasova. *Computational Soundness of Non-Confluent Calculi with Applications to Modules and Linking*. PhD thesis, Boston Univ., 2002.

[McC60]   John McCarthy. Recursive functions of symbolic expressions and their computation by machine, part I. *Communications of the ACM*, 3(4):184–195, 1960.

[McC62]   John McCarthy. Towards a mathematical science of computation. In *Information Processing*, pages 21–28, Amsterdam, 1962. North Holland.

[McC67]   John McCarthy. A basis for a mathematical theory of computation. In P. Braffort and D. Hirschberg, editors, *Computer Programming and Formal Systems*. North-Holland, Amsterdam, 1967.

[McC79]   Nancy Jean McCracken. *An Investigation of a Programming Language with a Polymorphic Type Structure*. PhD thesis, Syracuse University School of Computer and Information Science, June 1979.

[MCG+99]   Greg Morrisett, Karl Crary, Neil Glew, Dan Grossman, Richard Samuels, Frederick Smith, David Walker, Stephanie Weirich, and Steve Zdancewic. TALx86: A realistic typed assembly language. In *ACM SIGPLAN Workshop on Compiler Support for System Software*, pages 25–35, May 1999.

[Mey92]   Bertrand Meyer. *Eiffel: The Language*. Prentice-Hall, Inc., Upper Saddle River, NJ, USA, 1992.

[Mey97]   Bertrand Meyer. *Object-Oriented Software Construction*. Prentice Hall, 1997.

[MFH95]   Greg Morrisett, Matthias Felleisen, and Robert Harper. Abstract models of memory management. In *FPCA '95: Proceedings of the Seventh International Conference on Functional Programming Languages and Computer Architecture*, pages 66–77. ACM, 1995.

[MFP91]   Erik Meijer, Maarten Fokkinga, and Ross Paterson. Functional programming with bananas, lenses, envelopes and barbed wire. In *FPCA '91: Proceedings of the 5th ACM Conference on Functional Programming Languages and Computer Architecture*, pages 124–144, New York, NY, USA, 1991. Springer-Verlag New York, Inc.

[Mil77]   Robin Milner. Fully abstract models of typed λ-calculi. *Theoretical Computer Science*, 4(1):1–22, February 1977.

[Mil78]   Robin Milner. A theory of type polymorphism in programming. *Journal of Computer and System Sciences*, pages 348–375, 1978.

[Mil89]   Robin Milner. *Communication and Concurrency*. Prentice-Hall, 1989.

[Min63]   Marvin Minsky. A LISP garbage collector algorithm using secondary storage. A.I. Memo 58, MIT Project MAC, 1963.

[Min67]   Marvin Minsky. *Finite and Infinite Machines*. Prentice-Hall, 1967.

[Mit96]   John C. Mitchell. *Foundations for Programming Languages*. MIT Press, Cambridge, Massachusetts, 1996.

[Mit03]   John C. Mitchell. *Concepts in Programming Languages*. Cambridge University Press, 2003.

[Mog89]   Eugenio Moggi. Computational lambda-calculus and monads. In *IEEE Symposium on Logic in Computer Science*, pages 14–23, Washington, DC, 1989. IEEE Computer Society Press.

[Mog91]   Eugenio Moggi. Notions of computation and monads. *Information and Computation*, 93(1):55–92, 1991.

[Moo86]   David A. Moon. Object-oriented programming with Flavors. In *OOPSLA '86: Conference proceedings on Object-oriented programming systems, languages and applications*, pages 1–8. ACM, 1986.

[Mor73]   James H. Morris Jr. Protection in programming languages. *Communications of the ACM*, 16(1):15–21, January 1973.

[Mor82]   James H. Morris. Real programming in functional languages. In *Functional Programming and Its Applications: An Advanced Course*, pages 129–176. Cambridge University Press, New York, NY, USA, 1982.

[Mor95]   Greg Morrisett. *Compiling with Types*. PhD thesis, Carnegie Mellon University, 1995.

[Mor98]   Luc Moreau. A syntactic theory of dynamic binding. *Higher-Order and Symbolic Computation*, 11(3):233–279, December 1998.

[Mos70]   Joel Moses. The function of FUNCTION in LISP or why the FUNARG problem should be called the environment problem. *SIGSAM Bulletin*, pages 13–27, July 1970.

[Mos90]   Peter Mosses. Denotational semantics. In J. van Leeuwen, editor, *Handbook of Theoretical Computer Science, Volume B: Formal Models and Semantics*, pages 575–631. MIT Press/Elsevier, 1990.

[MOSS96]   Stephan Murer, Stephen Omohundro, David Stoutamire, and Clemens Szyperski. Iteration abstraction in Sather. *ACM Transactions on Programming Languages and Systems*, 18(1):1–15, 1996.

[MP84]   John C. Mitchell and Gordon D. Plotkin. Abstract types have existential type. In *POPL '84: Proceedings of the 11th ACM SIGACT-SIGPLAN Symposium on Principles of Programming Languages*, pages 37–51. ACM, 1984.

[MR86]   Albert R. Meyer and Mark B. Reinhold. "Type" is not a type. In *POPL '86: Proceedings of the 13th ACM SIGACT-SIGPLAN symposium on Principles of programming languages*, pages 287–295, New York, NY, USA, 1986. ACM.

[MS76]   Robert Milne and Christopher Strachey. *A Theory of Programming Language Semantics*. Chapman and Hall, 1976. Two volumes.

[MT91a]   Ian A. Mason and Carolyn L. Talcott. Equivalence in functional languages with effects. *Journal of Functional Programming*, 1(3):287–327, 1991.

[MT91b]   Robin Milner and Mads Tofte. *Commentary on Standard ML*. MIT Press, Cambridge, MA, 1991.

[MT00]   Elena Machkasova and Franklyn A. Turbak. A calculus for link-time compilation. In *ESOP 2000: 9th European Symposium on Programming*, volume 1782 of *Lecture Notes in Computer Science*, pages 260–274, 2000.

[MTH90]   Robin Milner, Mads Tofte, and Robert Harper. *The Definition of Standard ML*. MIT Press, Cambridge, MA, 1990.

[MTHM97]   Robin Milner, Mads Tofte, Robert Harper, and David MacQueen. *The Definition of Standard ML (Revised)*. MIT Press, Cambridge, MA, 1997.

[Muc97]   Steven S. Muchnick. *Advanced Compiler Design and Implementation*. Morgan Kaufmann, 1997.

[MWCG99]   Greg Morrisett, David Walker, Karl Crary, and Neil Glew. From System F to typed assembly language. *ACM Transactions on Programming Languages and Systems*, 21(3):528–569, May 1999.

[Myc80]   Alan Mycroft. The theory and practice of transforming call-by-need into call-by-value. In *Proceedings of the Fourth International Symposium on Programming*, pages 269–281, 1980.

[ND81]   Kristen Nygaard and Ole-Johan Dahl. The development of the SIMULA languages. In *History of Programming Languages I*, pages 439–480. ACM, New York, NY, USA, 1981.

[NL98]   George C. Necula and Peter Lee. The design and implementation of a certifying compiler. In *PLDI '98: Proceedings of the ACM SIGPLAN Conference on Programming Language Design and Implementation*, pages 333–344, Montreal, June 1998. ACM.

[NMW02]   George C. Necula, Scott McPeak, and Westley Weimer. CCured: Type-safe retrofitting of legacy code. In *POPL '02: Proceedings of the 29th ACM SIGPLAN-SIGACT Symposium on Principles of Programming Languages*, pages 128–139. ACM Press, 2002.

[NNH98]   Flemming Nielson, Hanne Riis Nielson, and Chris Hankin. *Principles of Program Analysis*. Springer, 1998.

[NO93]   Scott M. Nettles and James W. O'Toole. Real-time replication garbage collection. In *PLDI '93: Proceedings of the ACM SIGPLAN Conference on Programming Language Design and Implementation*. ACM, June 1993.

[NOG93]   Scott Nettles, James O'Toole, and David Gifford. Concurrent garbage collection of persistent heaps. Technical Report MIT/LCS/TR-569, MIT Laboratory for Computer Science, June 1993.

[NOPH92] Scott M. Nettles, James W. O'Toole, David Pierce, and Nicholas Haines. Replication-based incremental copying collection. In *Proceedings of the SIGPLAN International Workshop on Memory Management*, pages 357–364. ACM, Springer-Verlag, September 1992.

[NW06]   Maurice Naftalin and Philip Wadler. *Java Generics and Collections*. O'Reilly, 2006.

[occ95]   *occam 2.1 reference manual*. SGS-Thomson Microeclectronics Limited, May 1995.

[OG89]   James William O'Toole, Jr. and David K. Gifford. Type reconstruction with first-class polymorphic values. In *PLDI '89: Proceedings of the ACM SIGPLAN Conference on Programming Language Design and Implementation*, pages 207–217, Portland, Oregon, June 1989. ACM.

[OJ97]   Robert O'Callahan and Daniel Jackson. Lackwit: A program understanding tool based on type inference. In *ICSE '97: Proceedings of the 19th International Conference on Software Engineering*, pages 338–348. ACM, 1997.

[Oka98]   Chris Okasaki. *Purely Functional Data Structures*. Cambridge University Press, New York, NY, USA, 1998.

[OL96]   Martin Odersky and Konstantin Läufer. Putting type annotations to work. In *POPL '96: Proceedings of the 23rd ACM SIGPLAN-SIGACT Symposium on Principles of Programming Languages*, pages 54–67. ACM, 1996.

[Par71]   David Parnas. Information distribution aspects of design methodology. In *Proceedings of IFIP Congress*. North Holland, 1971.

[Par72]   David Parnas. On the criteria to be used in decomposing systems into modules. *Communications of the ACM*, 15(12), December 1972.

[Pau96]   Larry C. Paulson. *ML for the Working Programmer*. Cambridge University Press, second edition, 1996.

[Pey87]   Simon L. Peyton Jones. *The Implementation of Functional Programming Languages*. Prentice-Hall, 1987.

[Pey96]   Simon Peyton Jones. Compiling Haskell by program transformation: A report from the trenches. In *ESOP '96: Proceedings of the European Symposium on Programming*. Springer, 1996.

[Pie91]   Benjamin C. Pierce. *Basic Category Theory for Computer Scientists*. MIT Press, 1991.

[Pie02]   Benjamin C. Pierce. *Types and Programming Languages*. MIT Press, Cambridge, Massachusetts, 2002.

[Pie05]   Benjamin C. Pierce, editor. *Advanced Topics in Types and Programming Languages*. MIT Press, 2005.

[Plo75]   Gordon D. Plotkin. Call-by-name, call-by-value and the lambda calculus. *Theoretical Computer Science*, 1:125–159, 1975.

[Plo77]   Gordon D. Plotkin. LCF considered as a programming language. *Theoretical Computer Science*, 5(3):223–255, December 1977.

[Plo81]   Gordon D. Plotkin. A structural approach to operational semantics. Technical Report DAIMI FN-19, Aarhus University Computer Science Department, September 1981.

[Plu02]   Mike Plusch. *Water: Simplified Web Services and XML Programming*. John Wiley & Sons, Hoboken, NJ, December 2002.

[PM97]   Simon Peyton Jones and Erik Meijer. Henk: A typed intermediate language. In *TIC '97: Proceedings of the 1997 ACM SIGPLAN Workshop on Types in Compilation*, Amsterdam, The Netherlands, June 1997. Boston College Computer Science Department Technical Report BCCS-97-03.

[Por92]   Harry H. Porter, III. Separating the subtype hierarchy from the inheritance of implementation. *Journal of Object-Oriented Programming*, 4(6):20–29, 1992.

[PR05]   Franccois Pottier and Didier Rèmy. The essence of ML type inference. In Benjamin C. Pierce, editor, *Advanced Topics in Types and Programming Languages*, pages 389–489. MIT Press, 2005.

[PW93]   Simon Peyton Jones and Philip Wadler. Imperative functional programming. In *POPL '93: Proceedings of the 20th ACM SIGACT-SIGPLAN Symposium on Principles of Programming Languages*. ACM, 1993.

[Que93]   Christian Queinnec. A library of high level control operators. *SIGPLAN Lisp Pointers*, VI(4):11–26, 1993.

[Que04]   Christian Queinnec. Continuations and web servers. *Higher-Order and Symbolic Computation*, 17(4):277–295, 2004.

[Ree01]   Jonathan Rees. JAR on object-oriented, December 2001. Message posted on the Lightweight Languages mailing list at MIT. Available at http://mumble.net/~jar/articles/oo.html.

[Rém94]   Didier Rémy. Type inference for records in natural extension of ML. In Gunter and Mitchell [GM94], pages 67–95.

[Rém05]   Didier Rémy. Simple, partial type-inference for System F based on type-containment. In *ICFP '05: Proceedings of the Tenth ACM SIGPLAN International Conference on Functional Programming*, pages 130–143. ACM, 2005.

[Rey72]   John Reynolds. Definitional interpreters for higher-order programming languages. In *ACM Annual Conference*, pages 717–740, 1972. Republished as [Rey98].

[Rey74]   J. C. Reynolds. Towards a theory of type structure. In *Proceedings, Colloque sur la Programmation*, volume 19 of *Lecture Notes in Computer Science*, pages 408–425. Springer-Verlag, 1974.

[Rey75]   John C. Reynolds. User-defined types and procedural data structures as complementary approaches to type abstraction. In S. A. Schuman, editor, *New Directions in Algorithmic Languages*, pages 157–168. INRIA, Rocquencourt, 1975. Reprinted in [GM94], pp. 13–23.

[Rey90]   John C. Reynolds. Introduction to part II. In Huet [Hue90], pages 77–86.

[Rey93]   John C. Reynolds. The discoveries of continuations. *Lisp and Symbolic Computation*, 6:233–247, 1993.

[Rey98]   John Reynolds. Definitional interpreters for higher-order programming languages. *Higher-Order and Symbolic Computation*, 11(4):363–397, December 1998. A republished version of [Rey72].

[RG94]   Brian Reistad and David K. Gifford. Static dependent costs for estimating execution time. In *LFP '94: Proceedings of the 1994 ACM Symposium on LISP and Functional Programming*, pages 65–78. ACM, June 1994.

[RH04]   Peter Van Roy and Seif Haridi. *Concepts, Techniques, and Models of Computer Programming*. MIT Press, 2004.

[RKDB92] Robert Hieb R. Kent Dybvig and Carl Bruggeman. Syntactic abstraction in Scheme. *Lisp and Symbolic Computation*, 5(4):295–326, December 1992.

[Rob65]   J. A. Robinson. A machine-oriented logic based on the resolution principle. *Journal of the ACM*, 12(1):23–41, 1965.

[Ros92]   J. P. Rosen. What orientation should Ada objects take? *Communications of the ACM*, 35(11):71–76, November 1992.

[Roz84]   Guillermo J. Rozas. Liar, an Algol-like compiler for Scheme. Master's thesis, EECS Department, MIT, January 1984.

[RRS00]   Segei Romanenko, Claudio Russo, and Peter Sestoft. Moscow ML owner's manual, version 2.00. `http://www.dina.kvl.dk/~sestoft/mosml.html`, June 2000.

[Rus98]   Claudio V. Russo. *Types for Modules*. PhD thesis, The University of Edinburgh, 1998.

[RV98]   Didier Rémy and Jérôme Vouillon. Objective ML: An effective object-oriented extension to ML. *Theory and Practice of Object Systems*, 4(1):27–50, 1998.

[RW89]   Erik Ruf and Daniel Weise. Nondeterminism and unification in LogScheme: integrating logic and functional programming. In *FPCA '89: Proceedings of the Fourth International Conference on Functional Programming Languages and Computer Architecture*, pages 327–339. ACM, 1989.

[Sab88]   Gary W. Sabot. *The Paralation Model*. MIT Press, 1988.

[Sch86]   David Schmidt. *Denotational Semantics: A Methodology for Language Development*. Allyn and Bacon, 1986.

[Sch94]   David Schmidt. *The Structure of Typed Programming Languages*. MIT Press, 1994.

[Sco73]   Dana Scott. Models for various type-free calculi. In Patrick Suppes, Leon Henkin, Athanase Joja, and G. C. Moisil, editors, *Logic, Methodology, and Philosophy of Science IV*, pages 157–187, Amsterdam, 1973. North-Holland.

[Sco76]   Dana Scott. Data stypes as lattices. *SIAM Journal on Computing*, 5(3):522–567, 1976.

[Sco77]   Dana S. Scott. Logic and programming languages. *Communications of the ACM*, 20(9):634–641, September 1977. Turing Award Lecture.

[Ses96]   Peter Sestoft. ML pattern match compilation and partial evaluation. In Olivier Danvy, Robert Glück, and Peter Thiemann, editors, *Dagstuhl Seminar on Partial Evaluation*, volume 1110 of *Lecture Notes in Computer Science*, pages 446–464. Springer, 1996.

[SF89]   George Springer and Daniel Friedman. *Scheme and the Art of Programming*. McGraw Hill/MIT Press, 1989.

[SF93]   Amr Sabry and Matthias Felleisen.   Reasoning about programs in continuation-passing style. *Lisp and Symbolic Computation*, 6(3–4):289–360, 1993.

[SG90]   Mark A. Sheldon and David K. Gifford. Static dependent types for first class modules. In *LFP '90: Proceedings of the 1990 ACM Conference on LISP and Functional Programming*, pages 29–29. ACM, 1990.

[Sha96]   Andrew Shalit. *The Dylan Reference Manual: The Definitive Guide to the New Object-oriented Dynamic Language*. Addison Wesley Longman Publishing Co., Inc., Redwood City, CA, USA, 1996.

[Sha97]   Zhong Shao. An overview of the FLINT/ML compiler. In *TIC '97: Proceedings of the 1997 ACM SIGPLAN Workshop on Types in Compilation*, Amsterdam, The Netherlands, 1997.

[Sip06]   Michael Sipser. *Introduction to the Theory of Computation*. Thomson Course Technology, second edition, 2006.

[Sny86]   Alan Snyder. Encapsulation and inheritance in object-oriented programming languages. In *OOPLSA '86: Conference Proceedings on Object-oriented Programming Systems, Languages and Applications*, pages 38–45. ACM, 1986.

[SS71]   Dana Scott and Christopher Strachey. Toward a mathematical semantics for computer languages. In J. Fox, editor, *Proceedings of the Symposium on Computers and Automata*, pages 19–46, New York, 1971. Polytechnic

Institute of Brooklyn Press. Also published as Technical Monograph PRG-6, Programming Research Group, University of Oxford.

[SS75]   Gerald Jay Sussman and Guy L. Steele Jr. Scheme: An interpreter for extended lambda calculus. Technical Report AIM-349, MIT Artificial Intelligence Laboratory, December 1975.

[SS76]   Guy L. Steele Jr. and Gerald Jay Sussman. LAMBDA: The Ultimate Imperative. Technical Report AIM-353, MIT Artificial Intelligence Laboratory, March 1976.

[SS78]   Guy L. Steele Jr. and Gerald Jay Sussman. The art of the interpreter, or, the modularity complex (parts zero, one, and two). Technical Report AIM-453, MIT Artificial Intelligence Laboratory, May 1978.

[SSH08]   Christian Skalka, Scott Smith, and David Van Horn. Types and trace effects of higher order programs. *Journal of Functional Programming*, 18(2):179–249, March 2008.

[Ste76]   Guy L. Steele Jr. LAMBDA: The Ultimate Declarative. Technical Report AIM-379, MIT Artificial Intelligence Laboratory, November 1976.

[Ste77]   Guy L. Steele Jr. Debunking the "expensive procedure call" myth, or procedure call implementations considered harmful, or LAMBDA, the Ultimate Goto. Technical Report AIM-443, MIT Artificial Intelligence Laboratory, October 1977.

[Ste78]   Guy Lewis Steele Jr. Rabbit: A compiler for Scheme. MIT AI Memo 474, Massachusetts Institute of Technology, Cambridge, Mass., May 1978.

[Sto85]   Joseph E. Stoy. *Denotational Semantics: The Scott-Strachey Approach to Programming Language Theory*. MIT Press, 1985.

[Str86]   Bjarne Stroustrup. *The C++ Programming Language*. Addison-Wesley, 1986.

[Str00]   Christopher Strachey. Fundamental concepts in programming languages. *Higher-Order and Symbolic Computation*, 13(1/2):11–49, 2000.

[SU06]   Morten Heine Sørensen and Pawel Urzyczyn. *Lectures on the Curry-Howard Isomorphism, Volume 149 (Studies in Logic and the Foundations of Mathematics)*. Elsevier Science Inc., New York, NY, USA, 2006.

[SW67]   H. Schorr and W. Waite. An efficient machine-independent procedure for garbage collection in various list structures. *Communications of the ACM*, 10(8):481–492, August 1967.

[SW74]   Christopher Strachey and Christopher P. Wadsworth. Continuations: A mathematical semantics which can deal with full jumps. Monograph PRG-11, Oxford University Computing Laboratory, Programming Research Group, Oxford, UK, 1974. Reprinted in [SW00].

[SW94]   Paul Steckler and Mitch Wand. Selective thunkification. In Baudouin Le Charlier, editor, *Proceedings of the 1st International Static Analysis Sym-*

posium, volume 864 of *Lecture Notes in Computer Science*, pages 162–178. Springer-Verlag, September 1994.

[SW97] Paul Steckler and Mitchell Wand. Lightweight closure conversion. *ACM Transactions on Programming Languages and Systems*, 19(1):48–86, January 1997.

[SW00] Christopher Strachey and Christopher P. Wadsworth. Continuations: A mathematical semantics which can deal with full jumps. *Higher-Order and Symbolic Computation*, 13(1–2):135–152, 2000. Reprint of [SW74].

[SWD04] Dipanwita Sarkar, Oscar Waddell, and R. Kent Dybvig. A nanopass infrastructure for compiler education. In *ICFP '04: Proceedings of the Ninth ACM SIGPLAN International Conference on Functional Programming*, pages 201–212, New York, NY, USA, 2004. ACM.

[Tai67] William W. Tait. Intensional interpretations of functionals of finite type I. *Journal of Symbolic Logic*, 32(2):198–212, June 1967.

[Ten76] R. D. Tennent. The denotational semantics of programming languages. *Communications of the ACM*, 19(8):437–453, August 1976.

[Tho99] Simon Thompson. *Haskell: The Craft of Functional Programming*. Addison-Wesley, second edition, 1999.

[Tiu90] Jerzy Tiuryn. Type inference problems: A survey. In B. Rovan, editor, *Mathematical Foundations of Computer Science (MFCS '90)*, volume 452 of *Lecture Notes in Computer Science*, pages 105–120. Springer-Verlag, 1990.

[TJ92] Jean-Pierre Talpin and Pierre Jouvelot. Polymorphic type, region, and effect inference. *Journal of Functional Programming*, 2(3):245–271, 1992.

[TJ94a] Jean-Pierre Talpin and Pierre Jouvelot. The type and effect discipline. *Information and Computation*, 111(1):245–296, 1994.

[TJ94b] Yan Mei Tang and Pierre Jouvelot. Separate abstract interpretation for control-flow analysis. In *TACS '94: Proceedings of the International Conference on Theoretical Aspects of Computer Software*, pages 224–243, London, UK, 1994. Springer-Verlag.

[TMC+96] D. Tarditi, G. Morrisett, P. Cheng, C. Stone, R. Harper, and P. Lee. TIL: A type-directed optimizing compiler for ML. In *PLDI '96: Proceedings of the ACM SIGPLAN Conference on Programming Language Design and Implementation*. ACM, 1996.

[TO98] Andrew P. Tolmach and Dino Oliva. From ML to Ada: Strongly-typed language interoperability via source translation. *Journal of Functional Programming*, 8(4):367–412, 1998.

[Tol94] Andrew Tolmach. Tag-free garbage collection using explicit type parameters. In *LFP 94: Proceedings of the 1994 ACM SIGPLAN Conference on Lisp and Functional Programming*, pages 1–11. ACM, 1994.

[TT97]   Mads Tofte and Jean-Pierre Talpin. Region-based memory management. *Information and Computation*, 1997.

[Tur85]   D. A. Turner. Miranda: A non-strict functional language with polymorphic types. In *FPCA '85: Functional Programming Languages and Computer Architecture*, volume 201 of *Lecture Notes in Computer Science*, pages 1–16, 1985.

[Tur90]   David Turner, editor. *Research Topics in Functional Programming*. Addison Wesley, 1990.

[Ull97]   Jeffrey Ullman. *Elements of ML Programming*. Prentice-Hall, 1997.

[US87]   David Ungar and Randall B. Smith. Self: The power of simplicity. In *OOPSLA '87: Conference Proceedings on Object-oriented Programming Systems, Languages and Applications*, pages 227–242, New York, NY, USA, 1987. ACM.

[vS]   Anton van Straaten. RE: What's so cool about Scheme? Email sent to Guy Steele on June 4, 2003. Available from `http://people.csail.mit.edu/gregs/ll1-discuss-archive-html/msg03277.html`.

[Wada]   Philip Wadler. Efficient compilation of pattern-matching. Chapter 5 in [Pey87], pp. 78–103.

[Wadb]   Philip Wadler. Functional programming in the real world. List maintained on the web page `http://homepages.inf.ed.ac.uk/wadler/realworld/`.

[Wad87]   Philip Wadler. Views: A way for pattern matching to cohabit with data abstraction. In *POPL '87: Proceedings of the 14th ACM SIGACT-SIGPLAN Symposium on Principles of Programming Languages*, pages 307–313. ACM, 1987.

[Wad92]   Philip Wadler. The essence of functional programming. In *POPL '92: Proceedings of the 19th ACM SIGACT-SIGPLAN Symposium on Principles of Programming Languages*, pages 1–14. ACM, 1992.

[Wad95]   Philip Wadler. Monads for functional programming. In J. Jeuring and E Meijer, editors, *Advanced Functional Programming*, volume 925 of *Lecture Notes in Computer Science*. Springer-Verlag, 1995.

[Wad98]   Philip Wadler. The marriage of effects and monads. In *ICFP '98: Proceedings of the Third ACM SIGPLAN International Conference on Functional Programming*, pages 63–74. ACM, 1998.

[Wad03]   Philip Wadler. Call-by-value is dual to call-by-name. In *ICFP '03: Proceedings of the Eighth ACM SIGPLAN International Conference on Functional Programming*, pages 189–201. ACM, 2003.

[Wad05]   Philip Wadler. Call-by-value is dual to call-by-name, reloaded. In *RTA '05: Proceedings of the 16th International Conference on Term Rewriting and Applications*, volume 3467 of *Lecture Notes in Computer Science*, pages 185–203. Springer, 2005.

[Wan80]   Mitchell Wand. Continuation-based multiprocessing. In *LFP '80: Proceedings of the 1980 ACM Conference on LISP and Functional Programming*, pages 19–28. ACM, 1980.

[Wan91]   Mitchell Wand. Type inference for record concatenation and multiple inheritance. *Information and Computation*, 93:1–15, 1991.

[WD94]   A. Wright and B. Duba. Pattern matching for Scheme. Technical report, Rice University, February 1994.

[Weg87]   Peter Wegner. Dimensions of object-based language design. *SIGPLAN Notices*, 22(12):168–182, 1987.

[Weg90]   Peter Wegner. Concepts and paradigms of object-oriented programming. *SIGPLAN OOPS Messenger*, 1(1):7–87, 1990.

[Wel99]   J. B. Wells. Typability and type checking in System F are equivalent and undecidable. *Annals of Pure and Applied Logic*, 98(1–3):111–156, 1999.

[Wel02]   J. B. Wells. The essence of principal typings. In *ICALP '02: Proceedings of the 29th International Colloquium on Automata, Languages and Programming*, pages 913–925, London, UK, 2002. Springer-Verlag.

[WF94]   Andrew K. Wright and Matthias Felleisen. A syntactic approach to type soundness. *Information and Computation*, 115(1):38–94, June 1994.

[Wil92]   Paul R. Wilson. Uniprocessor garbage collection techniques. In *International Workshop on Memory Management*, volume 637 of *Lecture Notes in Computer Science*, St. Malo, France, September 1992. An expanded version of this workshop paper was made available as a University of Texas technical report in 1994.

[Win93]   Glynn Winskel. *The Formal Semantics of Programming Languages: An Introduction.* MIT Press, 1993.

[Wir85]   Niklaus Wirth. *Programming in MODULA-2.* Springer Verlag, 1985.

[WJ98]   Andrew Wright and Suresh Jagannathan. Polymorphic splitting: An effective polyvariant flow analysis. *ACM Transactions on Programming Languages and Systems*, 20(1):166–207, January 1998.

[WPP77]   David H D Warren, Luis M. Pereira, and Fernando Pereira. Prolog — the language and its implementation compared with Lisp. In *Proceedings of the 1977 Symposium on Artificial Intelligence and Programming Languages*, pages 109–115. ACM, 1977.

[Wri95]   Andrew K. Wright. Simple imperative polymorphism. *Lisp and Symbolic Computation*, 8(4):343–355, 1995.

[WS94]   Mitchell Wand and Paul Steckler. Selective and lightweight closure conversion. In *POPL '94: Proceedings of the 21st ACM SIGACT-SIGPLAN Symposium on Principles of Programming Languages*, pages 435–445, January 1994.

[WS97]   Mitchell Wand and Gregory T. Sullivan. Denotational semantics using an operationally-based term model. In *POPL '97: Proceedings of the 24th ACM SIGACT-SIGPLAN Symposium on Principles of Programming Languages*, pages 386–399, 1997.

[WSD02]   Oscar Waddell, Dipanwita Sarkar, and R. Kent Dybvig. Robust and effective transformation of letrec. In *Workshop on Scheme and Functional Programming (2002)*, October 2002.

[WV04]   Mitchell Wand and Dale Vaillancourt. Relating models of backtracking. In *ICFP '04: Proceedings of the Ninth ACM SIGPLAN International Conference on Functional Programming*, pages 54–65. ACM, 2004.

[Xi99a]   Hongwei Xi. Dead code elimination through dependent types. In *The First International Workshop on Practical Aspects of Declarative Languages*, pages 228–242, San Antonio, January 1999. Springer-Verlag LNCS vol. 1551.

[Xi99b]   Hongwei Xi. Dependently typed data structures. In *Proceedings of Workshop of Algorithmic Aspects of Advanced Programming Languages (WAAAPL '99)*, pages 17–32, Paris, September 1999.

[Xi01]   Hongwei Xi. Dependent types for program termination verification. In *Proceedings of 16th IEEE Symposium on Logic in Computer Science*, pages 231–242, Boston, June 2001.

[Xi07]   Hongewei Xi. Dependent ML: An approach to practical programming with dependent types. *Journal of Functional Programming*, 17:215–286, 2007.

[XP98]   Hongwei Xi and Frank Pfenning. Eliminating array bound checking through dependent types. In *Proceedings of ACM SIGPLAN Conference on Programming Language Design and Implementation*, pages 249–257, Montreal, June 1998.

[XP99]   Hongwei Xi and Frank Pfenning. Dependent types in practical programming. In *Proceedings of the 26th ACM SIGPLAN Symposium on Principles of Programming Languages*, pages 214–227, San Antonio, January 1999.

[You81]   Richard M. Young. The machine inside the machine: Users' models of pocket calculators. *International Journal of Man-Machine Studies*, 15:51–85, 1981.

[Zhu06]   Dengping Zhu. *To Memory Safety Through Proofs*. PhD thesis, Department of Computer Science, Boston University, April 2006.

[ZMC87]   Ramin Zabih, David A. McAllester, and David Chapman. Non-deterministic Lisp with dependency-directed backtracking. In *AAAI '87: Proceedings of the Sixth National Conference on Artificial Intelligence*, pages 59–65, 1987.

[ZX05]   Dengping Zhu and Hongwei Xi. Safe programming with pointers through stateful views. In *Proceedings of the 7th International Symposium on Practical Aspects of Declarative Langauges (PADL'05)*, pages 83–97, January 2005. Springer Verlag LNCS vol. 3350.

Index

$X_{i=j}^{k}$ (indexed sequence), 34

f^{n} (n-fold function composition), 1159

$\circ$ (function composition), 1159

$\overline{n}$ (Church numeral), 298, *see also* Church numeral

$\xrightarrow[L]{V_1,\ldots,V_n}$ (program execution with arguments V in language L), 9, 217

$\mathcal{P}(\ldots)$ (powerset), 1150

: (POSTFIX2 command composition), 39, 40, 41

_ (wildcard pattern/variable), 516
  desugaring in `match`, 597–598
  `match` pattern, 590

? (type reconstruction variable prefix), 770

~ (tilde or "twiddle") in deconstructor name, 584

[[ ]], 35–36

[$lo..hi$] (integer range notation), 1149

[0; 1] (unit interval), 167

! ("bang," suffix for state-changing functions), 385

! (has effect), 946

: (has type), 643

$ (has cost), 989

$ (special name prefix in HOOK), 363

(sequence size), 546

(nonce type prefix), 860, 861

#f (false literal), 209, 211, 465

#t (true literal), 209, 211, 212, 465

#u (unit literal), 209, 211, 212

. (infix prepend), 34, 1183

@ (infix append), 34, 1183

@$\cdots$ (FL primitive application sugar), 218, 219
  desugaring in FL, 220, 233
  primitive operator vs. standard library procedure, 451

resugaring in TORTOISE examples, 1018, 1032, 1037

$\bowtie$ (denotational soundness agreement relation), 151

$\bowtie$ (name concatenation), 586, 1094, 1095, 1101

$\downarrow$ (tuple/sequence projection), 546, 1152

->, *see* Arrow type

->>, *see* Arrow kind

=>, *see* Program type

$\rightarrow$ (total function arrow), 1157

$\rightarrow$ (function-domain constructor), 1184

$\rightharpoonup$ (partial function arrow), 1157

$\twoheadrightarrow$ (BOS evaluation relation), 75

$\rightarrowtail$ (injection into sum domain), 1177

$\hookrightarrow$ (set-inclusion function), 1159

$\rightarrow$ (SOS simplification step relation), 271, *see also* Simplification step relation

$\xrightarrow{simp}$ (simplification relation)
  in FIL, 1033
  in POSTFIX, 90

$\xrightarrow[n.o.]{}$ (lambda calculus normalization step relation), 292–295

$\circ\!\!\xrightarrow[n.o.]{}$ (lambda calculus nonnormalization step relation), 292, 294

$\rightsquigarrow$ (context-based SOS reduction relation), 72, *see also* Reduction relation

$\overset{s}{\rightsquigarrow}$ (context-based SOS stateful reduction relation)
  in FLICK, 407, 409
  single-threading, 407

$\rightsquigarrow_{ds}$ (one-step desugaring relation), 233

$\Rightarrow_{ds}$ (desugaring transition relation), 233

$\circ\!\!\Rightarrow$ (SOS nonevaluation step relation), 271

$\Rightarrow$ (SOS one-step transition relation), 49,
    see also Rewrite rule; Transition
    relation
$\stackrel{*}{\Rightarrow}$ (SOS multistep transition relation), 50
$\stackrel{n}{\Rightarrow}$ (SOS n-step transition relation), 50
$\stackrel{\infty}{\Rightarrow}$ (SOS looping configuration), 50
∞ (looping outcome in SOS), 50, 212
$\not\Rightarrow$ (SOS irreducible configuration), 50
+ (EL/FL addition primitive), 25, 213
    FL standard library binding for, 236
    in EL dialects DS, 121
    in FLK DS, 285
    in restricted ELMM DS, 118
    type in μFLEX, 643
- (EL/FL subtraction primitive), 25, 213
    type in μFLEX, 643
* (EL/FL multiplication primitive), 25,
    213
    type in μFLEX, 643
* ("star," prefix for single-threading state
    functions), 392
/ (EL/FL division primitive), 25, 213
    in EL dialects DS, 121
    type in μFLEX, 643
% (EL/FL remainder primitive), 25, 213
    type in μFLEX, 643
^ (FLIC mutable cell content), 398
    in FLICK DS, 417
    in FLICK SOS, 409
    in FLICK standard DS, 477
    informal semantics, 398
    type rule in FLEX, 681
; metalanguage comment style 1, 1148
{metalanguage comment style 2}, 1148
{mini-language comment style}, 9, 212
:= (FLIC mutable cell assignment), 398,
    966
    in FLICK DS, 417
    in FLICK SOS, 409
    in FLICK standard DS, 477
    informal semantics, 398
    set! vs., 431
    type rule in FLEX, 681

$\perp$ (bottom), 150, 172, 176, 1157
    representing nontermination, 185, 275,
    280
$\top$ (top), 176
$\vdash$
    kind judgment, 760
    type/cost judgment, 989
    type/effect judgment, 951
    type/exception judgment, 987
    type judgment, 645
$\vdash_{pure}$ (syntactic purity judgment),
    816–817, see also Syntactic purity
    judgment
    in type/effect system, 952
    variable assignments and, 821
... (ellipsis notation), 33
$\langle \ldots \rangle$ (tuple notation), 1152
[...] (sequence notation), 1182
'...' (symbolic outcome in FL), 212
$\langle \cdots, \cdots \rangle$ (pair outcome in FL), 212
$\lceil T \rceil^e_T$ (effect/region erasure), 956, 959
$\lceil TE \rceil^e_{TE}$ (effect/region erasure), 956, 959
$\lceil E \rceil$, 772, 774, see also Type erasure
$\lceil P \rceil_{pgm}$, 772, 774, see also Type erasure
$\lceil TD \rceil_{TD}$, 776, see also Type erasure
$\lceil TJ \rceil_{TJ}$, 776, see also Type erasure
$[\alpha]$ (lambda calculus alpha reduction),
    295
$[\beta$-value] (CBV FLK reduction), 310
$[\beta]$, see also Beta reduction
    in CBN FLK SOS, 259, 261, 310
    in μFLARE SOS, 778
    in μFLEX SOS, 662, 664
    in lambda calculus SOS, 292
$[\eta]$ (lambda calculus eta reduction), 295
α reduction (alpha reduction), 295
α-equivalence (alpha-equivalence),
    250–251
α-renaming, 251, see also
    Alpha-renaming
$\alpha \in AssignedVal$, 412
β reduction, see Beta reduction
$\delta \in DescId$, 753, 949
$\theta \in TyConId$, 831, 893

η expansion (eta expansion), 295
  in DS clause, 526
η reduction (eta reduction), 295
  FIL simplification, 1033
  in DS clause, 478
λ (function abstraction), 1165
Λ (polymorphic abstraction), 730
$\underline{\lambda}$ (strict function abstraction), 200
μFLARE, *see* entry before FLARE
μFLEX, *see* entry before FLEX
$\nu \in$ NonceType, 861
$\prod_{i=1}^{n} D_i$ (product of set family/domains),
  1153, 1173
$\sigma \in$ DescSubst, *see* DescSubst
$\sigma \in$ TypeSubst, *see* TypeSubst
$\sigma \in$ *Storable*, 412
$\sum_{i=1}^{n} D_i$ (sum of domains), 1176
$\tau \in$ TypeId, *see* TypeId; Type identifier
$\upsilon \in$ UnificationVar, 893
$\wedge$ (logical conjunction), 1151, 1162
$\vee$ (logical disjunction), 1151, 1162
$\neg$ (logical negation), 1151, 1162
$\forall$, *see* Universal quantification
$\exists$, *see* Existential quantification
$+$ (numerical addition), 1163
$+$ (sum-domain constructor), 1176–1181
$-$ (numerical subtraction), 1163
$-$ (set difference), 1149
$*$ (sequence-domain constructor), 1181
$\times$ (numerical multiplication), 1163
$\times$ (product-domain constructor),
  1173–1175
$\times$ (set product), 1153
$\div$ (numerical division), 1163
$/$ (set quotient), 1155
$\%$ (numerical remainder), 1163
$\succeq$ ("at least as general" operator on
  substitutions), 785
$<$ (less-than relation), 1153, 1163
$\leq$ (less-than-or-equal-to relation), 1153,
  1163
$=$, *see* Equality relation
$=_S$ (equality relation on elements of
  set/domain S), 1153

$=_\alpha$ (alpha-equivalence), 250–251
$=_{obs}$, 91, *see also* Observational
  equivalence
$=$ (domain definition), 1175, 1187
$\doteq$, *see* Type constraint
$\neq$ (inequality relation), 1163
$>$ (greater-than relation), 1153, 1163
$\geq$ (greater-than-or-equal-to relation),
  1153, 1163
$<$-$>$ (named subpattern in `match`), 604
$<$ (EL/FL less-than primitive), 25, 213
  in FLK DS, 285
  type in μFLEX, 643
$<=$ (FL less-than-or-equal-to primitive),
  213
  type in μFLEX, 643
$<=$ (in bounded quantification), 745
$=$ (EL/FL equality primitive), 25, 213
  type in μFLEX, 643
$!=$ (FL inequality primitive), 213
  type in μFLEX, 643
$>=$ (FL greater-than-or-equal-to
  primitive), 213
  type in μFLEX, 643
$>=$ (effect inequality constraint), 960, 961
$>$ (EL/FL greater-than primitive), 25,
  213
  type in μFLEX, 643
$\{\ldots\}$ (set notation), 1148
$\{\}$ (empty type environment), 643
$\{\}$ (empty set), 1148
$\{\}_{TCS}$ (empty type-constraint set), *see*
  empty$_{TCS}$
$\{x \mid P_x\}$ (set builder notation), 1149
$\mid$ (such that), 1149
$\mid \mid$ (absolute value), 1163
$\mid \mid$ (cardinality of set), 1150
$\in$ (element of set), 1149
$\notin$ (not element of set), 1149
$\oplus$ (extend type environment with
  data-type definitions), 830
  in FLEX/M, 914

⊎ (environment merge), 277

⊎ (type-constraint set union), *see* $union_{TCS}$

∪ (set union), 1149

∩ (set intersection), 1149

⊆ (subset), 1149

⊂ (proper subset), 1149

⊑ (subtype), 702, 703, 707
type equivalence and, 708

$\sqsubseteq_{AS}$ (subtype), 707

$\sqsubseteq_e$ (subeffect), 947, 949, 954

$\sqsupseteq_e$ (supereffect), 949

$[E/I]$ (substitute E for I), 253, 254, 637, 639, *see also* Substitution

$[E_i/I_i]_{i=1}^n$ (simultaneous substitution), 256

$[T/\tau]$ (substitute T for τ), 637, *see also* Substitution

$\sim_{SA}$ (POSTFIX stack-answer equivalence), 94

$\sim_S$ (POSTFIX stack equivalence), 94

$\sim_Q$ (POSTFIX transform equivalence), 93

$\sim_V$ (POSTFIX value equivalence), 94

$\approx_{at}$ (abstract-type equivalence), 913

$\approx_e$ (effect equivalence), 947, 949

$\approx_{tc}$ (type-constructor equivalence), 913

$\approx_{depends}$ (dependent type equivalence), 872, 874, 877–879, 911

$\approx$ (type equivalence), 679, 708, *see also* Type equivalence

$[\approx_{at}]$ (abstract-type-equivalence rule), 913

[+] (FLK SOS reduction), 259

[/] (FLK SOS reduction), 259

[<] (FLK SOS reduction), 259

[^] (FLICK SOS stateful reduction), 407, 409

[:=] (FLICK SOS stateful reduction), 407, 409

[∀-⊑] (FLEX/SP subtype rule), 731

[∀-$\approx_{BQ}$] (FLEX/SP type rule), 747

[∀-$\approx$] (FLEX/SP equivalence rule), 731

[∀-$elim_{BQ}$] (FLEX/SP type rule), 747

[∀-*elim*]
FLEX/SP type rule, 730, 731
FLEX/SPDK type rule, 763

[∀-$intro_{BQ}$] (FLEX/SP type rule), 747

[∀-*intro*]
FLEX/SP type rule, 730, 731, 732, 734
FLEX/SPDK type rule, 763

[→-⊑] (subtype rule)
in FLEX/M, 912, 913
in FLEX/S, 703, 704

[→-$\approx$] (type-equivalence rule)
for dependent procedures, 874
FLARE/E, 949
in FLEX, 679, 680

[→-*elim-inclusion*] (FLEX/S type rule), 715, 716

[→-*elim*] (type rule), 644
for dependent procedures, 875
μFLARE, 775
FLARE/E type/effect rule, 951, 952, 953
μFLEX, 646

[→-*intro*] (type rule), 644
for dependent procedures, 875
μFLARE, 774, 775
FLARE/E type/effect rule, 951, 953, 955, 961
μFLEX, 646
FLEX/SPDK, 763

[→] (FLEX/SPDK kind rule), 760

[->>-*elim*] (FLEX/SPDK kind rule), 760

[->>-*intro*] (FLEX/SPDK kind rule), 760

[→$elim_R$] (μFLARE type reconstruction rule), 793, 794

[→$intro_R$] (μFLARE type reconstruction rule), 793

[→-$elim_Z$] (FLARE/E type/effect reconstruction rule), 963, 964

[→-$intro_Z$] (FLARE/E type/effect reconstruction rule), 961, 964, 965

$A \in \text{AnsExp}$, *see* AnsExp

$A \in \text{ArithmeticOperator}$, 25

$\mathcal{A}$ (arithmetic operator meaning function)
   in EL dialects, 121
   in PostFix, definition, 137
   in PostFix, signature, 135
   in restricted ELMM, 118

$a \in \text{Answer}$, *see* Answer

$AB \in \text{Abstraction}$, 321, 1095

Abadi, Martín, 381

`abort!` (a transaction), 423–425

$\mathcal{ABS}$ (abstraction collecting function), 1016

`abs` (multiabstraction), 219, *see also* λ; `lam`
   desugaring in FL, 220, 233
   desugaring in HOOK, 369, 375
   free identifiers of, 638
   in DIFLEX, 983
   in FIL_{cps}, 1046
   in FIL kernel, 1030
   in FIL_{lift}, 1095
   in FIL_{reg}, 1101
   in FL, 218–221
   in μFLARE/FLARE kernel, 772
   in μFLEX/FLEX kernel, 628, 631, 632
   in μFLEX SOS, 664
   in lambda calculus, 291
   in metaCPS conversion, 1061
   in simple CPS conversion, 1051
   substitution, in μFLEX, 639
   tuple-based desugaring, 257
   type rule in dependent type system, 875
   type rule in μFLEX, 644
   type rule in FLEX/SPDK, 763
   with latent exception, 987

abs_{Int} (absolute value), 1163

Absolute value (abs_{Int}, $|\ |$), 1163

[*abs-pure*] (FLARE syntactic purity axiom), 816

Abstract class in Java, 724

Abstract data type (ADT), *see* Abstract type

Abstract grammar, 20

Abstract interpretation, 699

Abstraction, 1187, *see also* λ; `abs`; `lam`
   abstraction barrier, 1171
   body of, 1165
   Captain, 212
   data, *see* Abstract type; Data abstraction
   formal parameter of, 1165
   lambda (λ), 291, 1165
   in object-oriented programming, 379
   procedural, 841
   views in pattern-matching, 607–610

Abstraction (syntactic domain)
   in CBV recursion, 321
   in FIL_{lift}, 1095

Abstraction barrier, 402, 839, *see also* Interface

Abstraction violation, 357, 402, 841

Abstract machine, 47

Abstract syntax, 20–21, 42

Abstract syntax DAG, 248–250

Abstract syntax tree (AST), 20, 42, 115
   in interpreters and translators, 116

Abstract type, 839–887, *see also* Data abstraction
   as static lock and key, 848
   closure as example of, 1077
   controlling complexity with, 333
   dependent type, 869–884, *see also* Dependent Type
   environment example, 901–906
   existential type, 847–859, *see also* Existential Type
   export of, 847
   in FLEX/M, 914, 915
   generativity, 886
   nonce type, 859–869, *see also* Nonce Type
   point example, 851, 861, 871
   sealing/unsealing, 885, 934
   table example, 906–909

AbstractType (domain), 893

$\mathcal{AC}$ (assignment conversion transform), 1023

access (POSTHEAP command), 110

Acrobatics, notational, 57

Action in monadic style, 394

Activation frame, *see* Procedure call frame

Actor language, 378, 380, 537, 941

Actual parameter, of procedure application, 214, *see also* Argument

ACUI (associative, commutative, unitary, idempotent), 947, 962, 999

ADA

    array, as homogeneous product, 548

    as explicitly typed language, 625

    as imperative language, 384

    as statically typed language, 623

    closure conversion via defunctionalization, 1088

    command, 472

    dangling pointers, lack of, 1144

    data abstraction, 885

    garbage collection in (or not), 1121

    second-class modules, 891

    simulating higher-order procedures, 1076

    type conversion, 716

    type safety, 622

    valueless procedure, 385

    value-returning function, 385

add (POSTFIX command), 8, 40, *see also* Arithmetic operator

    informal semantics, 10

    POSTFIX DS, 137

add (extended number addition), 568

Addition function ($+$), 1163, *see also* +; add; Arithmetic operator

    on Church numerals, 299

addr (FIL$_{reg}$ subroutine label), 1101

Address, lexical, 1091

Address word, 1122

Adequacy of denotational semantics, 147, 157–159

    of EL, 158

    of POSTFIX, 158

Ad hoc polymorphism, 748–750, *see also* Polymorphism

after (FL monadic action sequencing), 395

Agre, Phil, 269

Agreement relation in denotational soundness ($\ltimes$), 151

Algebra, semantic and syntactic, 115

Algebraic data type, *see* Sum of products

Algebraic type schema, 966–969

AlgebraicTypeSchema (domain), 967

ALGOL 60

    Backus-Naur form originating with, 43

    call-by-name parameter passing, 309

ALGOL 68

    as explicitly typed language, 625

Algorithm $\mathcal{M}$ (type reconstruction), 836

Algorithm R (type reconstruction), *see* R

Algorithm $\mathcal{W}$ (type reconstruction), 836

Algorithm Z (type/effect reconstruction), *see* Z

Aliasing, 437, 944

    optimization inhibited by, 944

allocate (POSTHEAP command), 110

allocating (computation function), 415

    in CBL product DS, 557

    with continuation, 485

Allocation effect, 946

Allocation of memory, *see* Heap allocation

Alpha-equivalence ($=_\alpha$), 250–251

    alpha-equivalence class, 250

Alpha reduction, 295

Alpha-renaming, 251

    dependent types and, 872, 879–880

    import restriction and, 853, 858, 874, 880, 920

    in [*copy-prop*], 1066

    in HOOK-to-FL translation, 373

    in TORTOISE compiler, 1038–1041

    of arrow type parameters, 916

    of expression identifiers, 269, 914

    of type constructors, 916

    of type identifiers, 732, 735

alts (list procedure), 240, 242

amb (nondeterministic choice), 538

$AN \in$ Assumption, 692, 707

Analysis time, 617

AND (on Church booleans), 301

and (EL/FL boolean conjunction), 25, 213

  in FLK DS, 285

  type in μFLEX, 643

[and] (FLK SOS reduction), 259

Anonymous inner class, *see* Inner class

A-normal form, 1117

AnsExp (SOS answer semantic domain)

  in CBL product SOS, 553

  in CBN product SOS, 552

  in CBV named sum SOS, 572

  in CBV product SOS, 543

  in μFLARE, 778

  in μFLEX, 664

  in FLICK+{label, jump} SOS, 503

  in FLICK SOS, 406

  in FLK, 259

Answer (semantic domain)

  in EL dialects DS, 121

  in ELM DS, 124, 126

  in ELMM DS, 120

  in FLICK continuation-based DS, 474

  in FLICK standard DS, 473

  in FLK, 275, 276

  in POSTFIX DS, 132

Answer compatibility for μFLEX type soundness, 667

Answer domain, *see also* AnsExp; *Answer*

  of continuation-based DS, 474

  of DS, 115

  of restricted ELMM, 117

  of SOS, 48, 49

Antecedent of rewrite rule, 54

Antisymmetric relation, 1154

  partial order as example of, 174

  subtyping as example of, 702

API (Application Programming Interface), 235, 839, *see also* Interface

APL

  compositional programming, 613

  dynamically typed language, 623

  dynamic scoping, 338

  matrix-manipulation libraries, 239

app (FLK application), 211, 214, *see also* Multiapplication

  actual parameter (argument) of, 214

  continuations as procedure-call stack in CPS, 1043

  in CBD DS, 328

  in CBL FLAVARK DS, 435

  in CBN vs. CBV DS, 317

  in CBN vs. CBV parameter passing, 316

  in CBN vs. CBV SOS, 310

  in CBN FLAVARK DS, 434

  in CBN FLK SOS, 259

  in CBR FLAVARK DS, 435

  in CBVC DS, 565

  in CBV FLAVARK DS, 434

  in FIL_{cps}, 1046

  in FIL_{lift}, 1095

  in FIL_{reg}, 1101

  in FLAVARK DS, 431

  in FLICK standard DS, 477

  in FLICK standard DS for exceptions, 520, 521

  in FLK DS, 283, 286

  in lambda calculus, 291, 292

  in metaCPS conversion, 1061

  in simple CPS conversion, 1051

  in static vs. dynamic scope, 335

  kernel multiapplication in FIL, 1030

  nontail call, 1044–1049

  operand (rand) of, 214

  operator (rator) of, 214

  procedure-calling mechanism in CPS conversion, 1043

  procedure call not returning in CPS, 1043, 1046

  single-threaded store in CBV FLICK app clause, 418

  tail call, 1044–1049

Appel, Andrew, 1116, 1117

append (metalanguage sequence
    function), 34, 1183

`append` (procedure), 237, 238

Application, *see also* Multiapplication
    of description, 753
    of function, 1158–1159, 1187
    of procedure, *see* `app`

Application Programming Interface
    (API), 235, 839, *see also* Interface

Applicative functor, 939

Applicative language, 305

Applicative-order reduction, 377

Applied type system (ATS), 887

apply-to-five (higher-order function),
    1161, 1166, 1167

`apply-twice` (type/effect example), 950

`arg` (EL/ELM argument reference), 25,
    67
    in ELM and EL DS, 126
    expression constructor, 585

`arg˜` (ELM expression deconstructor),
    585

Argument
    of function, 1156, 1158
    of procedure, 214
    of program, 217
    simulating multiple function/procedure
        arguments, 214, 1161–1164

Arithmetic module, 358

Arithmetic operation, *see also* Primitive
        application
    in EL dialects DS, 121
    in ELMM DS, 65
    in POSTFIX DS, 55
    in restricted ELMM DS, 118

Arithmetic operator, *see also* Primitive
        operator
    in EL dialects, 25
    in EL dialects DS, 121
    in ELMM DS, 65
    in FL dialects, 213
    in metalanguage, 1162

in POSTFIX DS, 55, 137
in POSTFIX grammar, 40
in POSTFIX informal semantics, 10
in restricted ELMM DS, 118
on Church numerals, 298–300

ArithmeticOperator (EL domain), 25

`arithop` (ELM expression constructor),
    585

`arithop` (POSTFIX2 command), 41

arithop (function in POSTFIX DS)
    definition, 143, 144
    specification, 133

[*arithop*]
    ELM BOS rule, 77
    ELMM BOS rule, 75
    ELMM SOS rule, 65
    POSTFIX SOS rule, 55

`arithop˜` (ELM expression
    deconstructor), 585

Array, 540
    bounds check, 542
    indexing, *see* Product indexing
    mutable, 548
    sequence vs., 544

Arrow kind (`->>`), 759
    in FLEX/SPDK, 759
    kind checking in FLEX/SPDK, 760
    of type constructor, 760

Arrow type (`->`), 630
    desugaring in FLEX/M, 894
    inclusion rule for implicit argument
        subtyping, 716
    kind checking in FLEX/SPDK, 760
    parameterized, 870, 873
    subtyping, 704
    subtyping in FLEX/M, 913
    subtyping in FLEX/S, 703
    type constructor, 630
    type equivalence, 680

$AS \in$ AssumptionSet, 692, 707

assign (store function), 412

[*assign*] (FLEX type rule), 681

AssignedVal (DS stored binding domain),
    411, 412

Assignment (SOS assignment domain)
    in CBL product SOS, 553
    in FLICK SOS, 406
Assignment conversion, 430, 439, 820
    in CBR language, 1024
    closure conversion and, 1082
    letrec-bound variables in
        FLARE-to-FIL translation, 1036
    in TORTOISE compiler, 1019–1025
Assignment-free program, 1019
Assignment of variable, 430–439, *see also*
        Mutable cell; Mutable variable
Association list, 540, 550
Associative operator, 41
[*assumed*] (FLEX/S subtype rule), 706,
        707
Assumption/AssumptionSet (domains for
        comparing equirecursive types), 691,
        692, 707
AST, *see* Abstract syntax tree
$AT \in$ AbstractType, 893
$ATS \in$ AlgebraicTypeSchema, 967
Autoboxing/autounboxing in JAVA, 750
Automata-based type comparison
    equirecursive subtyping, 707, 767
    equirecursive type equivalence, 691
Automatic heap deallocation, 1119, *see
        also* Garbage collection (GC)
Automatic storage management, *see*
        Garbage collection (GC)
Axiom, 54–58
Axiomatic semantics, 441

$B \in$ BoolLit, 25, 211
$\mathcal{B}$ (boolean literal meaning function), 283
$b \in Bool$, 129, 132, 276, 1148
Backtracking, 422, 445
    in extended FLICK, 422
    nondeterminism and, 538
    stream and, 612
    success/failure continuations and, 612
    with continuations, 465–471
    with generate-and-test using iterator,
        512

Backus, John, 613
    Backus-Naur form (BNF), 43
    FL and FP languages, 207
    Turing award paper, 305
balance (bank account procedure)
    implementation, 402
    specification, 384
Bang (!) suffix for state-changing
        functions, 385
Bank account
    in imperative style, 401–403
    with message-passing objects, 403
    in stateless language, 384–389, 392–396
Barendregt, Henk, 887
Base effect, 946
BaseEffect (domain), 949
BaseEffectSet (domain), 949
Base kind environment, 761
[*base-tycon*] (FLEX/SPDK kind rule),
        760
Base type, 629
BaseType (base type domain in typed
        FL dialects)
    in μFLARE, 775
    in FLARE, 815
    in FLARE/E, 949
    in μFLEX, 628
[*base-type*] (FLEX/SPDK kind rule),
        760
BaseTypeConstructor (domain)
    in FLEX/SPD, 753
BASIC, lack of passable procedures, 320
Basic block, 1005, 1048
BdIds (bound identifier function)
    in FLK, 247
    ill-defined on alpha-equivalence class,
        251
$BE \in$ BoolExp, 25
$\mathcal{BE}$ (EL boolean expression meaning
        function), 129
Beardly, 988
begin (FLICK sequencing construct),
        386
    desugaring in FLEX, 681

begin (*continued*)
  desugaring of in FLIC, 401
  extended sequencing sugar, 399
  in CBR FLAVARK DS, 435
  in FLARE, 813
  in FLICK DS, 386, 416, 418
  in FLICK SOS, 386, 409
  in FLICK standard DS, 477
  in simple CPS conversion, 1054
  nonkernel version, 410
  type rule in FLEX, 681
[begin] (FLICK SOS reduction), 409
[*begin*] (FLEX type rule), 681
begin-transaction!, 423–425
beh (behavior of SOS), 51
beh$_{det}$ (deterministic behavior of SOS),
    51, 91
  denotational behavior and, 151
  in language *L*, *see L*, SOS
Behavioral equivalence, 90, *see also*
    Observational equivalence
Behavior of program, 50–52
  of concurrent program, 997
  deterministic, 51
  nondeterministic, 51, 997
  observational equivalence and, 91
Bekić expansion, 229, 327
Beta-redex, 261
Beta reduction, 261
  in CBN FLK SOS, 259, 261, 310
  in CBV FLK SOS, 310
  in μFLARE SOS, 778
  in μFLEX SOS, 662, 664
  in lambda calculus SOS, 292
  in metaCPS conversion, 1062
  in type application, 730
between (iterator example), 509
BF ∈ BaseEffect, 949
BF ∈ BooleanFormula, 465
BFS ∈ BaseEffectSet, 949
Big Bag of Pages (BIBOP), 1129
Bignum, 1124
Big-step operational semantics (BOS),
    75–79

  error, 76
  evaluation relation ($\longrightarrow$), 75
  evaluation tree, 75
  of EL, 79
  of ELM, 76–77
  of ELMM, 75–76
  of FLK, 269
  of POSTFIX, 77–78
  small-step semantics vs., 78
Bijective function, 1160
Binary relation, 1153
Binary tree
  example sum-of-products type, 750
  example types, 694
  multiple-value return examples,
    450–453
  procedures for manipulating, 451
  type abstraction in make-node, 751
  type specified with trec, 688
  view example, 607–610
bind (POSTLISP command), 109
bind (environment procedure in
    FLEX/M), 901
  list representation, 903
  procedure representation, 905
bind (environment binding function), 322
bind-exit (DYLAN nonlocal exit
    construct), 505
Binding
  in FLK DS, 276
  local type binding expression, *see* trec;
    tletrec
  local value binding expression, *see* let;
    letrec; let*; recur
  of a variable, 245
  of formal parameter to argument, 209,
    214
  in standard library, 235, 236, 237
  top-level, 235
Binding construct, 122, 144, 244, 334
  defined with higher-order function, 124
  in FL, 334
  in FLK, 307
Binding occurrence of identifier, 245

BindingValue (binding value semantic
    domain), 276
bindtypeof (μFLEX type-binding
    construct), 660
Bit, 1122
Bizarre, *see* Beardly
Block, *see* Heap block
block (exit point declaration in
    COMMON LISP), 348
Block structure, 337, 1075
    environment machinery for, 1075
    in SCHEME, 378
Blotation of code, 1054
    lack of in metaCPS conversion, 1063
BNF (Backus-Naur form), 43
Body
    of function, 1165
    of pattern-matching clause, 590, 1191
    of procedure, 214
    of program, 209
Body clause/expression of tagcase, 570
Bool (boolean set & semantic domain),
    129, 132, 276, 1148
bool (boolean type), 628, 629
[*bool*]
    μFLARE type axiom, 775
    FLARE/E type/effect axiom, 953
    μFLEX type axiom, 644
bool=? (FL boolean equality), 213
    type in μFLEX, 643
bool? (FL boolean type predicate), 213
BoolAnswer (EL semantic domain), 129
Boolean, *see also* *Bool*; BoolLit
    Church booleans in lambda calculus,
        300
    message-passing HOOK object, 365
    message-passing SMALLTALK object,
        365
boolean-cont (standard DS function),
    473, 475
BooleanFormula (domain), 465
Boolean formula satisfiability, 466
Boolean operator, *see also* Logical
    operator

in metalanguage, 1151
BoolExp (EL domain), 25
BoolLit (boolean syntactic domain)
    in EL dialects, 25
    in FL dialects, 211
[*bool$_R$*] (μFLARE type reconstruction
    axiom), 793
BOS, *see* Big-step operational semantics
Bottom ($\bot$), 150, 172, 176, 1157
    representing nontermination, 185, 275,
        280
Bounded quantification, 745–746
Bound identifier, 246, *see also* BdIds
Bound occurrence of identifier, 245
Bounds check, 542
Bound variable, 246, *see also* BdIds
Boxed value, 1124
Boxing/unboxing in JAVA, 750
Branch, *see* Conditional expression; Jump
break (loop termination), 488–490
    in C/JAVA, 445, 490
    as sugar in FLIC+{label, jump}, 501
Bronte, Charlotte (quoted), 843
$BT \in$ BaseType, 628, 775, 815, 949
$BTCR \in$ BaseTypeConstructor, 753
Buffer overflow exploit, 542
Built-in value, 235
Bureaucracy, as model for computation,
    269

$\mathcal{C}$ (POSTFIX command meaning
    function), 135, 136–138
C
    answer domain, 474
    array, as homogeneous product, 548
    array, as mutable sequence, 561
    array subscripting notation, 561
    as call-by-value language, 309
    as explicitly typed language, 625
    as imperative language, 384
    as language without block structure,
        337
    as monomorphic language, 629, 658
    as statically typed language, 623

C (*continued*)

  bounds checking, lack of, 542
  call-by-value-copy of structures, 566
  call-by-value-sharing of arrays, 566
  compile-time inclusion of files, 928
  conservative GC, 1127, 1142
  dangling pointer, 1144
  defining macros with #define, 330
  downcast, 723
  files as de facto modules, 889
  garbage collection, lack of, 1121
  libraries of numerical methods, 239
  linking, 890
  mutable string, 548
  mutable variable, 430
  named product (struct), 353, 550,
      561, 568, 580
  nonlocal exits (setjmp/longjmp), 506
  perim definition using struct and
      union, 582
  pointer variable, as mutable cell, 397
  program arguments as string array, 217
  return/break/continue, 445
  simulating higher-order procedures,
      1076
  strict application, 215
  sum (union), 567, 568, 580
  type coercion, 718
  type conversion, 716
  type loophole, 567, 580–583, 621–622
  void expression as command, 472
  void type, 209
  void vs. value-returning function, 385
C++
  array, as mutable sequence, 561
  array subscripting notation, 561
  as explicitly typed language, 625
  as language without block structure,
      337
  as object-oriented language, 362
  as stateful language, 384
  as statically typed language, 623
  bounds checking, lack of, 542
  conservative GC, 1127, 1142

  constructor method, 366
  dangling pointer, 1144
  destructor function, 1121
  integers and booleans as nonobjects,
      365, 379
  iterator, 507, 512
  libraries, 239
  multiple inheritance, 380
  non-object-oriented features, 379
  overloading, 748
  simulating higher-order procedures,
      1076
  standard library API, 235
  sum-of-products data via objects, 579
  template, 748
  type coercion, 718
  type conversion, 716
  void expression as command, 472
C#
  as object-oriented language, 362
  as stateful language, 384
  garbage collection, 1120
  integers and booleans as nonobjects,
      365
  simulating higher-order procedures,
      1076
calculate, 57
Calculator language, 61–62
Calculus of Communicating Systems
      (CCS), 999
Call, procedure, *see* app
call/cc, *see* cwcc;
      call-with-current-continuation
Call-by-denotation (CBD) parameter
      passing, 328–332
Call-by-lazy (CBL), *see* Call-by-need
Call-by-name (CBN)
  CBN/CBV relationship, 311–314
  CBN and CBV in NAVAL, 327
  CBV vs., in μFLEX SOS, 662, 672
  CBV vs., in stateful language, 425–426
  dragging tail and, 316
  duality with CBV, 378
  either (sum), 574

inefficiencies of, 312–314, 433
mutable variable DS, 433, 434
normal-order reduction vs., 293, 377
pair, 318–320
parameter passing, 309, 331, 433, 434
parameter-passing DS, 316–318
parameter-passing SOS, 310–316
positional sum, 576
problems with in stateful language,
    425–426, 433
product, 551–552
side effects and, 312
simulation in CBV, 325, 378
Call-by-need (CBL)
    lambda calculus, 440
    mutable variable DS, 435
    parameter passing, 434–436
    product, 552–555
Call-by-reference (CBR)
    assignment conversion and, 1024
    for mutable tuples, 566
    for obtaining result of valueless
        procedure, 437
    mutable variable DS, 435
    parameter passing, 436–438
    with mutable products, 566
Call-by-value (CBV)
    applicative-order reduction vs., 377
    assignment conversion and, 1024
    CBN vs., in μFLEX SOS, 662, 672
    CBN/CBV relationship, 311–314
    CBN and CBV in NAVAL, 327
    CBN vs., in stateful language, 425–426
    duality with CBN, 378
    either (sum), 573
    FLARE semantics, 813
    imperative features in FLEX, 682, 696
    lambda calculus, 378
    letrec desugaring in FLAVAR, 432
    mutable variable DS, 433, 434
    named sum, 569–576
    pair, 318–320
    parameter passing, 309, 331, 397, 433,
        434

parameter-passing DS, 316–318
parameter-passing SOS, 310–316
positional sum, 576
product, 541–550
recursion and, 378, 484–487
recursion in FLICK DS, 417
recursion in FLICK SOS, 408–410
recursion in FLK, 320–324
simulation in CBV, 378
Call-by-value-copy (CBVC), 564–566
Call-by-value-sharing (CBVS), 563–566
Caller-saves register, correspondence with
    free variable in closure conversion,
    1080
Call frame, see Procedure call frame
Call site, 1085
call-with-current-continuation
    (control-point-capturing construct in
    SCHEME), 505–506, 538, see also
    CWCC
Cantor, Georg, 1150
Captain Abstraction, 212
Capture of a variable, see Variable
    capture
Capture restriction, 920, 921
capturing-cont (control-point duplicating
    function), 498, 500
car (list head), 236
    definition in FLEX/M, 895
    definition in FLEX/SPD, 754
    polymorphic type of, 728
    sum-of-products data version, 586
    type in FLEX/M list module, 899
    type rule in FLEX, 686
[car] (FLEX type rule), 686
Cardelli, Luca, 381, 698, 768, 886
Cardinality of set (| |), 1150
Cartesian product (×), 1153, 1173
cases (metalanguage oneof
    deconstructor), 1177–1181, 1188,
    1189, see also match
Cast, see Type cast; Type coercion; Type
    conversion

catch (exception construct)
  control operator in SCHEME, 537
  in COMMON LISP, 506, 514
  in FIL, 1072
  in JAVA, 514, 985
Category theory, 1196
  duality of sums and products, 571, 613
CAYENNE, dependent types, 886, 941
CBD, *see* Call-by-denotation
CBL, *see* Call-by-need
CBN, *see* Call-by-name
CBR, *see* Call-by-reference
CBV, *see* Call-by-value
CBVC, *see* Call-by-value-copy
[*CBV*-rec] (FLICK SOS stateless
  reduction), 409, 410
CBVS, *see* Call-by-value-sharing
CCS (Calculus of Communicating
  Systems), 999
cdr (list tail), 236
  definition in FLEX/M, 895
  polymorphic type of, 728
  sum-of-products data version, 586
  type in FLEX/M list module, 899
  type rule in FLEX, 686
[*cdr*] (FLEX type rule), 686
CECIL
  multimethods, 380
  prototype-based objects, 380
cell (FLICK cell value), 406, 407
Cell, *see* cell; Mutable cell
cell (FLIC mutable cell creation), 398
  in FLARE, 813
  in FLICK DS, 416, 418
  in FLICK SOS, 409
  in FLICK standard DS, 477
  informal semantics, 398
  type rule in FLEX, 681
[cell] (FLICK SOS stateful reduction),
  407, 409
cell=? (FLIC mutable cell equality
  predicate), 398
  in FLICK DS, 417
  in FLICK SOS, 409

  in FLICK standard DS, 477
  informal semantics of, 399
  type rule in FLEX, 681
[cell=?-*F*] (FLICK SOS stateless
  reduction), 409
[cell=?-*T*] (FLICK SOS stateless
  reduction), 409
[cell?-*F*] (FLICK SOS stateless
  reduction), 409
[cell?-*T*] (FLICK SOS stateless
  reduction), 409
cell? (FLIC mutable cell type
  predicate), 398
  in FLICK DS, 417
  in FLICK SOS, 409
  in FLICK standard DS, 477
  informal semantics of, 399
cellans (SOS cell outcome token), 406
[*cell-eq*] (FLEX type rule), 681
cellof (type constructor), 681, 682
  in FLARE, 813
  invariant subtyping in FLEX/S,
    704–706, 710
  kind checking in FLEX/SPDK, 760
  type equivalence, 681
[*cellof-≈*] (type-equivalence rule)
  in FLEX, 681, 682
  in FLEX/S, 705
[*cellof-elim*] (FLEX type rule), 681, 682
[*cellof-eq*] (FLEX type rule), 682
[*cellof-intro*] (FLEX type rule), 681, 682
[*cell-set*] (FLEX type rule), 681, 682
CF (SOS configuration), 49
  in language *L*, *see* *L*, SOS
  state component, in FLICK SOS, 407
$\mathcal{CF}$ (POSTFIX configuration meaning
  function), 153
cf ∈ *CF*, 49
Chain
  in a partial order, 177
  strictly decreasing, 104
channel (channel creation), 998
Channel, for concurrency, 998

Char (character set & semantic domain), 1148

Character, of symbol in FRM, 1125

check-... (computation function), 417, 473, 475

Checked exception in JAVA, 985

`check-quota` (quota construct), 492–493

`choice`, `choose` (nondeterministic choice constructs), 538

Church, Alonzo, 298, 305, 699

Church booleans (*TRUE* and *FALSE*), 300

Church conditional (*IF*), 300

`church-fst`, in FLEX/SP, 737

Church numeral ($\overline{n}$), 298
   arithmetic on, 298–300, 302, 303
   pictorial representation of, 298

Church pair, 302, 320, 737

`church-pair`, in FLEX/SP, 737

Church-Rosser (CR) property, 82, *see also* Confluence

`church-snd`, in FLEX/SP, 737

Church tuple, 225, 302

$\mathcal{CL}$ (flat closure conversion transform), 1081

`class` (HOOPLA class sugar), 369

Class, equivalence, 1154

Classification, *see also classify*
   of FLK expression, 272
   objectification of *ness*ness, 362
   preservation of, by FLK nonevaluation step, 273

classify (FLK expression classification function), 273

Class methods, 362

Class of object, 362
   controlling complexity with, 333
   representing in HOOK, 366
   simulated in prototype-based system, 366
   subclass, 366, 723–725
   superclass, 366

Class variable, 362

Clause
   cases clause, 1178

function definition by clauses, 35
   match clause (metalanguage), 1191
   `match` clause (FL), 590
   `tagcase` body clause, 570

Client
   of data abstraction, 839
   of module, 352

CLOS
   multimethods, 380
   multiple inheritance, 380

Closed expression, 246

Closed procedure, *see* Closure

Closed program, 247, 1015

Closure, 290, 378, 1075
   as abstract data type, 1077
   actor and, 378
   code/environment pair, 1077
   code/linked-environment pair, 1092
   flat, 1076–1085
   as heap block in FRM, 1128
   objects as poor man's closures, 441
   in SCHEME, 378

Closure conversion, 441, 1075–1093, 1117
   closure-passing style, 1078, 1117
   code/environment pair, 1077
   code/linked-environment pair, 1092
   control-flow analysis in, 1085–1090
   correspondence of free variable to caller-saves register, 1080
   defunctionalization, 1088, 1117
   JAVA inner classes and, 441, 1082
   lightweight, 1089, 1117
   linked environment, 1090–1093
   mutable variable and, 1081–1082, 1092
   ordering of CPS conversion in TORTOISE, 1076
   representation pollution, 1086
   selective, 1085, 1117
   substitution strategy for, 1084
   with flat closures, 1076–1085
   wrapping strategy for, 1084

Closure of relation
   reflexive transitive, 196, 1155
   transitive, 1155

Closure-passing style, 1078, 1117
CLU
　　1-based indexing, 562
　　array, as dynamically sized mutable
　　　　sequence, 562
　　array, as mutable sequence, 561
　　cluster, 885, 940
　　data abstraction, 885
　　exception handling via
　　　　signal/except when, 514
　　explicit resignaling of exceptions, 514
　　immutable string, 548
　　immutable updatable sequence, 548
　　iterator, 506
　　mutable and immutable data types, 563
　　second-class modules, 891
　　separate compilation, 940
　　sum values, 568
　　updatable sequence, 545
Cluster in CLU, 885, 940
Cmdcont (standard DS domain), 473
Coalesced sum, 186
cobegin (concurrent evaluation), 998
COBOL, as imperative language, 384
Code, residual, in metaCPS conversion,
　　1059
Code/environment pair, 1077
Code/linked-environment pair, 1092
Code bloat, 1054
　　lack of in metaCPS conversion, 1063
Code component of a configuration, 47
　　in FLICK SOS, 407
Code hoisting, 1029
Code linearization, in CPS conversion,
　　1042, 1043, 1047
Code motion, inhibited by aliasing, 944
Code optimization, see Optimization
Code segment, 1123
Codomain (target) of function, 1156
Coercion of types, see Type coercion
Coercion semantics of subtyping, 718
Coherence
　　file-type coherence, 926
　　file-value coherence, 926

modules and, 934–937
Column-major order, 547
Combination, see Application
Combinator, 291
　　S and K combinators, 296
comefrom (control effect), 979
Command, 472
　　in POSTFIX, 8
Command continuation, 472–474
Comment
　　in metalanguage, 1148
　　in mini-language, 9
Commingling, unholy, 870
commit! (a transaction), 423–425
COMMON LISP, see also LISP
　　as dynamically typed language, 623
　　as mostly functional language, 384
　　as object-oriented language, 362
　　defstruct, 590
　　dynamic scoping via special, 348
　　exception handling via throw/catch,
　　　　514
　　implicit resignaling of exceptions, 514
　　multimethods, 380
　　multiple namespaces, 348
　　nonlocal exits via block and
　　　　return-from, 348
　　nonlocal exits via throw/catch, 506
　　tagbody and go, 347–348
　　unsafe features, 622
Common subexpression elimination, 1028
　　inhibited by aliasing, 944
Communicating Sequential Processes
　　(CSP), 941, 999
Communication, between threads via
　　channel, 997
Communication effect, 998–999, 1001
Comp (computation semantic domain)
　　equality laws, in
　　　　FLICK+{label, jump} continuation
　　　　semantics, 500
　　equality laws, in FLICK standard
　　　　semantics, 476
　　equality laws, in FLK, 282

equality laws, on store-based
  computations in FLICK, 416
functions on, in FLICK, 415
functions on, in FLK, 281
in exception semantics, 524, 525
in FLICK, 413–416, 418
in FLICK continuation semantics,
  482–484
in FLK, 275, 276, 279
Compaction of memory, 1132
compare, 57
Compatibility with a type, 667
Compilation, 7, 1005–1117, *see also*
  TORTOISE compiler; Translation
A-normal form, 1117
optimization in, *see* Optimization
type and effect information, 1026
via source-to-source transformation,
  1005–1009, 1116
Compile time, 617, 890
Completeness, of type reconstruction
  algorithm, 799
Complete partial order (CPO), 182–184
Complete row type, 823
Completion of a set, 184
Component (semantic domain)
  to model pair components, 320
Component value, 319–320
compose (HOOK object composition),
  363, 365
translation to FL, 371
Composition
  of functions (∘), 1159
  of functions, *n*-fold (f^n), 1159, *see also*
    Church numeral
  of relations, 1155
Compositionality
  of compiler transforms, 1006
  of denotational semantics, 116
  of stack transforms, 135
Compound domain, 1171
  syntactic, 25
Compound expression, 20
Compound phrase, 26
Computable function, 199, 1158

Computation, 275, *see also Comp*
  as abstraction for simplifying DS, 275,
    279
  pending, circumventing with
    continuation, 455–457, 494–495, 522
  pending, representing with
    continuation, 453
  in stateful language, 413–416
Computational universality, *see* Universal
  programming language
Computation-based DS
  of exceptions, 524–527
  of FLICK, 411–420
  of FLICK, continuation-based,
    482–493
  of FLK, 275–290
  of label and jump, 498, 500
Computation laws, *see Comp*, equality
  laws
conceal (record-field hiding), 353, 354,
  550
DS, 357
Concrete syntax, 22–23
Concurrency, 996–999
  behavior analysis, 998–999, 1001
  channel for, 998
  interleaving, 997
  in object-oriented programming, 379
  parallelism, 1027
  synchronization, 997
cond (FL *n*-way conditional), 219, 222
  desugaring in FL, 220, 233
  in simple CPS conversion, 1054
Conditional expression (if)
  elseless if sugar in FLICK, 399, 401
  in assembly language, 1056
  in EL, 20
  in EL dialects, 21, 25
  in FL dialects, 211, 214
  in FLK DS, 282
  in FLK SOS, 259, 261
  in lambda calculus, 300
  n-way (cond), 222
  via message-passing in HOOK, 365
Conditional function (if_S), 1164

Configuration of SOS ($cf \in CF$), 47, 49
  code component, 47
  context component, *see* Configuration
    of SOS, state component
  final, 50
  initial, 47
  in language L, *see* L, SOS
  irreducible ($\not\Rightarrow$), 50
  looping ($\overset{\infty}{\Rightarrow}$), 50
  normal form, 50
  reducible, 50
  state component, 47
  state component, in FLICK SOS, 407
  stuck, 50
Confluence, 82
  of FLK simplification ($\rightarrow$), 273
  in ISWIM, 306
  of lambda calculus simplification, 292
  one-step, 82
Congruence, 679
Conjunction, logical ($\wedge$), 1151, 1162
cons (list prepend), 236
  definition in FLEX/M, 895
  definition in FLEX/SPD, 754
  generic type of list constructor, 827
  pattern example, 592
  pattern-matching view, 607
  polymorphic type of, 728
  sum-of-products data version, 586
  type in FLEX/M list module, 896, 899
  type rule in FLEX, 686
cons (metalanguage sequence prepend),
    34, 1182–1184, 1189
[*cons*] (FLEX type rule), 686
cons˜ (list deconstructor)
  generic type of, 827
  type in FLEX/M list module, 896, 899
Consequent of rewrite rule, 54
Conservative approximation to
    undecidable property, 618
Conservative GC, 1127, 1142
cons-stream (SCHEME stream
    constructor), 561
const$_{A,B,b}$ (constant function), 1159
Constant, 1187

Constant declaration, 430
Constant function, 1159
Constant pattern, in metalanguage, 1192
Constant propagation, 1053
Constraint
  effect inequality constraint, 960
  type equality constraint, *see* Type
    constraint
Construction of a domain element, 1171
Constructor
  for domain, 1171, 1173, 1187
  for sum-of-products value, *see*
    Constructor procedure
  type constructor, *see* Type constructor
Constructor application pattern, 590
  desugaring in match, 599–601
Constructor method, 366
Constructor procedure, 583, 599
  deconstructor, 584, 590, *see also*
    Deconstructor procedure
  from def-data desugaring, 587, 588
  from def-datatype desugaring, 740
  type schema for, 827–833, 894, 896, 914
Consumer/producer coroutine, 457–461
Contagious error value, 60
Content of a mutable cell, 397
Context, 71
  control context, 443–446
  desugaring context ($\mathbb{DC}$), *see*
    DesugaringContext
  evaluation context ($\mathbb{E}$), 71, *see also*
    EvalContext
  filling hole in, 71
  hole in, 71
  naming context, 443
  naming context for referential
    transparency, 389
  normalization context ($\mathbb{NC}$), *see*
    NormContext
  observational equivalence and, 91
  POSTFIX command sequence context,
    91
  POSTFIX evaluation context, 73
  POSTFIX program context, 91
  program context, 91

simplification context (S), *see*
 SimpContext
state context, 443
tail-call context, 1045
Context-based SOS semantics, 71–73
Context component of configuration, *see*
 Configuration of SOS, state
 component
Context domain
 continuation in FLICK standard DS,
  476
 in DS, 115
 in ELM DS, 124, 128
 environment in FLK DS, 280
 flow of in program, 128
 store in FLICK DS, 413
Context-free grammar, 26, 43
Continuation, 445–538
 command continuation, 472–474
 control point vs., 493
 in CPS conversion, 1042–1075
 domain, 472
 duplication of, in `label`, 498
 dynamic, 1117
 exception, 1074
 expression continuation, 474
 expression list continuation, 474
 failure, *see* Failure continuation
 for backtracking, 465–471
 for coroutine, 457–461
 for multiple-value return, 450–455
 for nonlocal exit, 455–457
 for pending computation, 453, 457
 iteration and, 447–449
 normal, 446
 as procedure, 446–471
 procedure-call stack representation in
  CPS, 1043
 receiver, *see* Receiver
  function/procedure
 static, 1117
 success, *see* Success continuation
Continuation-based denotational
 semantics, 471–493

Continuation-passing style (CPS), 124,
 449–450, 480, 538, 1042, 1116, 1165
 continuations as call stack, 450, 1043
 evaluation order, 1042, 1043, 1047
 metaCPS conversion ($\mathcal{MCPS}$),
  1058–1070
 procedure-calling mechanism explicit
  in, 1043
 procedure call not returning, 1043,
  1046
 representing advanced control features
  in, 1070–1075
 simple CPS conversion ($\mathcal{SCPS}$),
  1049–1057
 simplification in FIL and, 1048, 1064
 structure of CPS code, 1044–1049
`continue` (loop continuation), 488–490
 in C/Java, 445, 490
 as sugar in FLIC+{`label`, `jump`}, 501
Continuous function, 187
Contract, 839, *see also* Interface
Contrapositive, 1151
Contravariant subtyping, 704
Control, 443–538
 branch, *see* Conditional expression
 continuation-based DS, 471–493
 control context, 443–446
 coroutine via iterator, 506–513
 exception handling, 513–537
 iteration/looping, *see* Iteration
 jump, *see* Jump
 modeling with procedures, 446–471
 nonlocal exit, 493–506
 recursion, *see* Recursion
 representing in CPS, 1070–1075
 thread, *see* Thread of control
Control effect, 978–983, 1001
Control flow analysis, 995–996, 1001,
 1117, *see also* Control
 closure conversion and, 1085–1090
Control point, 493
 continuation vs., 493
 as first-class continuation value, 493,
  495–496

ControlPoint (semantic domain), 497

controlpointof (type constructor), 979
in μFLARE, 800
in μFLEX, 658–659

Control restriction, in [*letregion*] rule, 992

Control space, 449

Control transfer analysis, 978–983

Converse, 1151

Cooper, Keith, 1116

copy (FIL$_{reg}$ register move), 1101
reducing number of, 1109

Copy phase, 1133

[*copy-prop*] (FIL simplification), 1033
mutable variables and, 1034
renaming in, 1066

Copy propagation, *see* [*copy-prop*]

Coroutine, 445, 457–461
between scanner and parser, 457
in compiler organization, 538

Cost system, 988–991
latent cost effect, 988, 989

Countable set, 1150

Covariant subtyping, 703, 704

cp (control point value in
FLICK+{label, jump} SOS), 503

controlpointans (SOS control point
outcome token), 503

[*cp-elim*] (control point type/effect rule),
980

[*cp-intro*] (control point type/effect rule),
980

CPO (Complete partial order), 182–184

CPS, *see* Continuation-passing style

CPS conversion, 1042–1075, 1117
continuation in, 1049
metacontinuation in, 1059
metaCPS conversion ($\mathcal{MCPS}$),
1058–1070
of cwcc, 1072
of exceptions, 1072
of label and jump, 1070–1075
ordering of closure conversion in
Tortoise, 1076

simple CPS conversion ($\mathcal{SCPS}$),
1049–1057

CR (Church-Rosser) property, 82, *see
also* Confluence

CSP (Communicating Sequential
Processes), 941, 999

cummings, e e (quoted), 19

Curry, Haskell, 699, 835, 1162

Curry-Howard isomorphism, 700

Currying, 672
of dependently typed procedures, 883
of FL procedures, 214, 219
lambda notation for, 1168
Lisp's lack of, 221, 1169
simulation of multiple arguments, 214,
1162, 1168

cwcc (FLIC control-point-capturing
construct), 505–506, *see also*
call-with-current-continuation
denotational valuation clause for, 506
in FLEX/SP, 737
label/jump and, 505, 506
in metaCPS conversion, 1072
type and effect for, 982
type rule, 717

Cyclic lambda calculus, 440

Cyclic unification and recursive types,
836

$D \in Def$, *see* Def

$D \in Desc$, 753, 759, 949

dabs (description abstraction), 753
in FLEX/SPD, 752
in FLEX/SPDK, 759
kind checking in FLEX/SPDK, 760

[*dabs-α-$\approx$*] (FLEX/SPD equivalence
rule), 756

[*dabs-β-$\approx$*] (FLEX/SPD equivalence
rule), 756

[*dabs-η-$\approx$*] (FLEX/SPD equivalence
rule), 756

DAG (directed acyclic graph) for abstract
syntax, 248–250

Damas, Luis, 835

Dangling pointer, 1119

Danvy, Olivier, 1117

[*dapply-≈*] (FLEX/SPD equivalence rule), 756

Data abstraction, 839–842
  abstraction barrier, 402, 839, *see also* Interface
  API, 839, *see also* Interface
  client, 839
  compromised by inheritance, 767
  contract, 839
  controlling complexity with, 333
  implementer, 839
  interface, 839, *see also* Interface
  invariant of, 402, 842
  in object-oriented programming, 379
  point example, 840–841, 842, 844, 851, 861, 871
  secure, 842
  via abstract type, *see* Abstract type
  via dynamic lock and key, 843–847
  via message-passing procedure, 403, 842, 885
  violation, 402, 841

Data declaration (def-data), 583–590

Data dependency, 391

Data flow, single-threaded, 392–394

Data safety, *see* Data abstraction

Data security, *see* Data abstraction

Data space, 449

Data type, *see* Abstract type; Data abstraction; Sum of products

Data type declaration, *see* def-data; def-datatype

DatatypeDefinition (domain)
  in FLARE, 831
  in FLEX/M, 893

$\mathbb{DC} \in$ DesugaringContext, 232

$DD \in$ DatatypeDefinition, 831, 893

Dead code elimination, 1028
  inhibited by aliasing, 944

Dead heap block, 1120, 1130–1133

Deallocation of memory, *see* Garbage collection (GC)

Death $\neq$ parenthesis, 19

Declaration of variable, 244

Decomposition of a programming language, 207

decon (deconstructor accessor), 611

Deconstruction of a domain element, 1171

Deconstructor procedure, 584, 590, *see also* Constructor procedure
  alternative declaration, 611
  from def-data desugaring, 587, 588
  from def-datatype desugaring, 740
  type schema for, 827–833, 894, 896, 914
  user-defined view, 605–612

decorate (FLIC tree procedure), 405

deepCopying (computation function), 565

Deep copy of mutable data, 565

Def (definition domain)
  in FL, 219
  in FLIC+{def-data}, 587
  in HOOK, 363

def (definition), 219, 893
  desugaring in FL, 230, 231, 233
  desugaring in μFLEX, 634
  in FIL$_{lift}$, 1095
  in FIL$_{reg}$, 1101
  in FLEX/M, 893
  in FLEX/SPD program, 754
  POSTTEXT command, 106, 141

default-handlers (exception-handling environment), 519, 521, 525

def-constructor, 611

def-data (sum-of-products declaration), 583–590
  desugaring, 587
  desugaring into predicates and selectors, 589

def-datatype (typed sum-of-products declaration), 739, 740, 893
  desugaring in FLEX/SP, 741
  dynamic semantics in FLEX/M, 924
  in FLEX/M, 893
  in type-reconstructed language, 828, 831

def-desc (description definition), 754

Deferred class in EIFFEL, 724
#define (*C* macro-definition), 330
Definition, in program, *see also* def; Def
    in FL, 230–232
    in μFLEX, 634
defstruct (COMMON LISP data
    declaration), 590
Defunctionalization, 1088, 1117
delay (delay evaluation), 560
Delayed evaluation, 324, *see also* Thunk
    delay and force, 560
    freeze and thaw, 228
    wrap and unwrap, 315
Delayed value, 560
Delegation, in object-oriented
    programming, 379
Denotational reasoning, 145–150
Denotational semantics (DS), 15, 113–162
    adequacy of, 147, 157–159
    answer domain, 115
    applications of, 116
    basic framework, 115–116
    compositionality of, 116
    computation-based continuation DS of
        FLICK, 482–493
    computation-based DS of exceptions,
        524–527
    computation-based DS of label and
        jump, 498, 500
    context domain, 115
    continuation-based DS, 471–493
    direct semantics, 444, 471
    equational reasoning/proof, 119
    error-hiding functions, 122, 142, 144
    game board, 116
    how to read, 136–138, 142–145,
        280–282, 417–420, 474, 476–479
    importance of studying domains and
        signatures, 128, 134–135
    meaning function, 115
    of CBL parameter-passing, 435
    of CBL parameter-passing with
        mutable variables, 434–436
    of CBL product, 555
    of CBN parameter-passing with
        mutable variables, 433
    of CBN product, 552
    of CBN vs. CBV parameter passing,
        316–318
    of CBR parameter-passing, 435
    of CBR parameter-passing with
        mutable variables, 436–438
    of CBVC parameter-passing, 565
    of CBV named sums, 573–576
    of CBV parameter-passing with
        mutable variables, 433, 434
    of CBV product, 543
    of CBV recursion in FLK, 320–324
    of CBVS parameter-passing, 564
    of EL, 127–128, 129
    of ELM, 124–126
    of ELMM, 120–124
    of FLICK, 411–420
    of FLK, 275–290
    of lambda calculus, 296–297
    of mutable variables, 431–439
    of POSTFIX, 131–145
    of POSTFIX2, 141
    of restricted ELMM, 117–120
    of static vs. dynamic scope, 335
    of strict vs. nonstrict pair, 318–320
    operational semantics related to,
        150–160
    operational semantics vs., 161–162
    overview of, 113–117
    phrase denoting a meaning, 115
    program vs., 128
    reasoning with, 145–150
    semantic algebra, 115
    soundness of, *see* Denotational
        soundness
    standard DS, 471
    standard DS for exceptions, 519–524
    standard DS of FLICK, 472–480
    standard DS of label and jump,
        497–498
    syntactic algebra, 115
    valuation function, 115

Denotational soundness, 151–156
  of EL, 156
  of POSTFIX, 151–156
Dependency, data, 391
Dependent description, 765
Dependent package, 870
Dependent type, 627, 765, 869–884
  definition of, 869
  dependent arrow/function type, 870
  dependent package, 870
  equivalence, 877–879, 911
  name-capture restriction, 875, 879
  soundness of, 879–881, 882, 883
  specified by structured identifier, 886
  static, 879, 891, 905, 911
  substitutions in, 881–883
Dependent type constructor, 898
deposit! (bank account procedure)
  *deposit! (single-threaded), 392
  implementation, 402
  specification, 384
Dereference a mutable variable, 432
Derivation, see also Proof tree
  of SOS transition, 64
  of type judgment, 648–650
derivative (example of procedure with
    implicit parameter), 344
Desc (description domain)
  in FLARE/E, 949
  in FLEX/SPD, 753
  in FLEX/SPDK, 759
DescId (description identifier domain)
  in FLARE/E, 949
  in FLEX/SPD, 753
DescIdKind (description identifier
    declaration)
  in FLARE/E, 957
[desc-inclusion] (FLEX/SPDK type
    rule), 763
DescKeyword (FLEX/SPD description
    keyword domain), 753
Description, 750–758
  application of, 753
  dependent, 765

equivalence, 756
  higher-order description operator, 755
  including effects and regions, 950
Descriptor in FRM, 1124
DescSubst (description substitution
    domain), 960
Destination register, 1107
Destructor function for storage
    deallocation in C++, 1121
Desugaring, 208, 218–234, see also
    Syntactic sugar
  desugaring-function (DS) approach to,
    218–232
  in TORTOISE compiler, 1013–1014
  of def-data, 587
  of def-datatype in FLEX/SP, 741
  of definition in FL, 230–234
  of definition in μFLEX, 634
  of expression in FL, 218–229, 232–234
  of expression in μFLEX, 634
  of letrec in FLARE-to-FIL
    translation, 1036
  of letrec preserving well-typedness,
    1038
  of match, 594–605
  of match, final version, 603
  of match, first cut, 597
  of match, optimization of, 605
  of nullary abstraction/application, 228
  of program in FL, 230–234
  of program in μFLEX, 634
  of raise, handle, and trap, 527–529
  rewriting-based (⤳_{ds}) approach to,
    232–234
DesugaringContext (domain), 232
Deterministic language, 80
Deterministic program behavior, 51, 79
  in EL, 80–84
  in ELMM, 76
  in POSTFIX, 58
Deterministic transition relation, 50, 51,
    58
Dethunk, 325, see also Thunk
Diabolically simple, 1058

Diagonalization, 1150
Diamond property, *see* Confluence
Dictionary, in POSTTEXT, 106
Difference
    of records, 550
    of sets (−), 1149
Differences, programming by, 366
DIFLEX (with dynamic and lexical
        scoping), 984, 985
Dimock, Allyn, 1117
Direct denotational semantics, 444, 471
Directed acyclic graph (DAG) for
        abstract syntax, 248–250
`direction` (sample HOOPLA class), 371
DISCOUNT (language with cost system),
        989
Discrete partial order, 175
Discriminant, 1178
    of `match`, 590
    of `tagcase`, 570
    of `sumcase`, 576
Discriminated union, *see* Sum
Disjoint sets, 1150
Disjoint union, 1176
Disjunction, logical (∨), 1151, 1162
Dismissal semantics of exceptions, 522,
        528–530
`div` (POSTFIX command), 8, 40, *see also*
        Arithmetic operator
    informal semantics, 10
    POSTFIX DS, 137
Divergence, *see also* Nontermination
    in CBV vs. CBN parameter passing,
        denotational view, 316–318
    in CBV vs. CBN parameter passing,
        operational view, 310
    in strict vs. nonstrict pairs, 319
    making observationally equivalent to
        error, 427
    represented by bottom (⊥), 185
Division function (÷), 1163, *see also* `/`;
        Arithmetic operator; `div`
$DK \in \text{DescIdKind}$, 957
$DK \in \text{DescKeyword}$, 753

`dlet` (FLEX/SPD description binding),
        751, 753, 754
    opaque version, 757
`dletrec` (recursive description binding),
        753
    decidability of kind checking and, 761
    kind checking in FLEX/SPDK, 760
[*dletrec*] (FLEX/SPDK kind rule), 760
DML (Dependent ML), 887
`do` (monadic style sequencing), 396
[*does*] (FLARE/E type/effect rule), 953,
        954–955, 1001
    [*effect-masking*] vs., 973
    inflation of latent effect, 955, 956, 959,
        960–961
dom (function domain of definition), 1156
Domain, 1171–1186
    answer domain, *see* Answer domain
    as type, 1172–1173
    compound domain, 1171
    constructor for, 1171, 1173, 1187
    context domain, *see* Context domain
    element expression, 1172, 1187
    equality of, 1175
    function (→) domain, *see* Function
        domain
    lifted domain, 176
    primitive domain, 1171
    product (×) domain, *see* Product
        domain
    reflexive domain, 201–202
    semantic domain, 115
    sequence (*) domain, *see* Sequence
        domain
    sum (+) domain, *see* Sum domain
    syntactic domain, 24
Domain (source) of function, 1156
Domain definition, 1175, 1187
Domain element
    construction of, 1171
    deconstruction of, 1171
Domain equation, 1175, 1187
    recursion, 132, 150, 161, 201–202
Domain expression, 1172, 1187

Domain of definition (*dom*), 1156
Domain variable, 25, 26, 33, 1172
Dorough, Bob (quoted), 539
Dot notation, 550, 898
down (convert to concrete type), 844–845
   existential type without, 859
   in dependent type system, 875
   in existential type system, 849, 850
   in nonce type system, 861, 862
   not necessary in FLEX/M, 902
Downcast, 721
   in *C*, 723
   in JAVA, 723
[*downcast*] (FLEX/S type rule), 722
[*downcast-fail*] (FLEX/S reduction rule),
   722
[*downcast-succeed*] (FLEX/S reduction
   rule), 722
Downward type conversion, 721–723
Doyle, Sir Arthur Conan, 769
[*dpack*] (dependent package type rule),
   875
[*dpackof-≈*] (type-equivalence rule), 874
Dragging tail, 316
Dragon book, 1116
drec (recursive description binding), 753
DS, *see* Denotational semantics
DS (desugaring function), 220, 231
   of def-data, 587
   match desugaring, final version, 603
   match desugaring, first cut, 597
   well-definedness of, 229
dselect (dependent type selection), 892,
   893, 898, 899, 916
   type constructor equivalence, 913
[*dselect-≈$_{tc}$*] (type-constructor
   equivalence rule), 913
dtypeof (dependent type), 869–870
   type equivalence, 874
   type rules involving, 875
[*dtypeof-≈*] (type-equivalence rule), 874
Duality
   between CBN and CBV, 378

between recordof and oneof
   subtyping, 704
between sums and products, 571, 573,
   613
[*dunpack*] (dependent package type rule),
   875
   dependent type substitution, 872,
     881–883
   dependent type substitution,
     alternative, 884
   import restriction, 874, 880
   purity restriction, 881
dup (PostFix command), 101–102
dup! (generic type of including effects
   and regions), 950
dyabs (dynamic variable abstraction),
   349
DYLAN
   multimethods, 380
   nonlocal exits (bind-exit), 505
   object-oriented language, 362
   overloading, 748
dylet (dynamic variable binding), 349,
   528
DYNAFLEX, 985
DYNALEX (with statically and
   dynamically scoped variables), 349
Dynamically typed language, 623, *see
   also* Dynamic type checking
Dynamic bounds check, 542
Dynamic continuation, 1117
Dynamic correspondence theorem
   (μFLEX/μFLARE), 781
Dynamic environment, 341
Dynamic nontype error, 661
Dynamic property, 617–620
Dynamic scope, 334, 338, 378
   dynamic environment, 341
   exception handling and, 343, 519–520,
     527–529
   FUNARG problem, 378
   implicit parameter and, 343, 379
   program execution tree and, 338
   side effects and, 378

Dynamic scope (*continued*)
 simulating in stateful language with
  `fluid-let`, 438
 static scope vs., 335, 339–344
 by translation to static scope, 346
Dynamic semantics, 16
 static semantics vs., 617–620
 of X, *see* X, BOS; X, DS; X, SOS
Dynamic type checking, 623
 in FLK, 260, 263
 in FLK DS, 279, 284, 318
 in FLK primitive application, 213
 in POSTFIX DS, 136
 languages with, 623
 of positional product, 548
 static type checking vs., 623–625
 sums and, 568–572
 type reconstruction and, 837
Dynamic type error, 661
 invalid program/expression in
  TORTOISE, 1025
 lack of in FIL, 1035–1036
Dynamic type system, *see* Dynamic type
  checking
Dynamic variable analysis, 983–985
`dyref` (dynamic variable reference), 349,
  528
Dysfunctional programming language,
  207

$\mathbb{E} \in$ ElmEvalContext, 74
$\mathbb{E} \in$ ElmmEvalContext, 72
$\mathbb{E} \in$ EvalContext, *see* EvalContext
$E \in$ Exp, *see* Exp
$\mathcal{E}$ (expression meaning function)
 in CBD DS, 328
 in CBL FLAVARK DS, 435
 in CBL product DS, 557
 in CBN FLAVARK DS, 434
 in CBN product DS, 552
 in CBN vs. CBV parameter passing,
  317
 in CBR FLAVARK DS, 435
 in CBVC DS, 565
 in CBV FLAVARK DS, 434

 in CBV named sum DS, 575
 in CBV product DS, 543
 in CBVS DS, 564
 in computation-based exception DS,
  525
 in FLAVARK DS, 431
 in FLICK, 418
 in FLICK standard DS, 476–480
 in FLICK standard DS for exceptions,
  520, 521
 in FLK, 279, 280–289
 in lambda calculus, 296–297
 in static vs. dynamic scope, 335
 in strict vs. nonstrict pair DS, 319
$\mathcal{E}^*$ (expression sequence meaning
  function)
 in FLICK standard DS, 477
 in FLICK standard DS for exceptions,
  520
 in FLK, 283
Early termination, 445, 455–457
`ecase` (either case analysis), 574
ECMASCRIPT, 380, *see also*
  JAVASCRIPT
Effect, 308, 385, 943–1001
 allocation effect, 946
 base effect, 946
 CBN parameter passing and, 312
 communication effect, 998–999, 1001
 compilation, use in, 1026
 conservative approximation to, 954
 control effect, 978–983, 1001
 denotation of, 947
 as description, 752
 dynamic scope and, 378
 equivalence ($\approx_e$), 947, 949
 of expression, 943
 for code optimization, 1026–1029
 for concurrency analysis, 996–999
 for control flow analysis, 995–996, 1001
 for cost analysis, 988–991
 for dynamic variable analysis, 983–985
 for exception analysis, 985–988
 for lifetime/storage analysis, 991–995,
  1001

for mobile code security, 999–1000
inequality constraint, 960
initialization effect, 946
latent, *see* Latent effect
lifetime, 995
masking, 972–974
masking for control effects, 981
masking for exceptions, 987
of procedure call, 385
purity, *see* Pure expression; `pure`
reconstruction, 959–972, 1000, 1001
reconstruction, in TORTOISE compiler,
    1025–1029
region of, *see* Region
store effect, 427–428, *see also* Store
    effect
subeffect ($\sqsubseteq_e$), 947, 949, 954
supereffect ($\sqsupseteq_e$), 949
system, *see* Effect system
Effect (domain), 949
Effect/region erasure, 956, 959
Effect/type judgment, 951
EffectConstraint (domain), 960
Effect-constraint set, 959–963
    solution, 961, 968
EffectConstraintSet (domain), 960
EffectConstructor (domain), 949
    extended with control effects, 979
effectErase, 958
[*effect-masking*] (type/effect rule), 973,
    974
Effect system, 627, 817, 943–963, *see also*
    Effect
    alias detection, 944
    code optimization with, 1000,
        1026–1029
    utility of, 943–944
Efficiency, *see also* Optimization
    of CBL parameter-passing, 434
    of code generated by TORTOISE
        compiler, 1006
    in heap block representation, 1129
    inefficiencies of CBN parameter
        passing, 312–314, 433

egen (type/effect generalization), 952
egenPure (type/effect/region
    generalization), 952, 974, 975
EIFFEL
    deferred class, 724
    multiple inheritance, 380
    object-oriented language, 362, 379
    procedure subtyping, 709
    SATHER as dialect of, 507
Either, 574
    call-by-name (CBN), 574
    call-by-value (CBV), 573
    sum, 567
`either` (ELMM choice construct), 83
EL (expression mini-language), 20–39
    abstract grammar, 21
    adequacy of, 158
    BOS, 79
    context-based SOS, 73
    denotational soundness of, 156
    deterministic behavior, 80–84
    DS, 127–128, 129
    expression evaluation in, 62–63
    full abstraction of, 159
    observational uniqueness of, 158
    SOS, 67
    syntax, 21, 25, 29, 31
    termination, 89
`el` (program keyword), 25
    in EL DS, 129
`elect` (election construct), 490–492
Element definition, 1188
Element expression, 1172, 1187
Element of ($\in$), 1149
ELM (EL with numerical expressions),
    67
    algebraic simplifier, 595
    BOS, 76–77
    context-based SOS, 73, 74
    DS, 124–126
    Fahrenheit-to-Celsius conversion
        example, 578
    interpreter for, 241–242, 243
    SOS, 67

`elm` (program keyword), 67
  in ELM DS, 126
`elm-eval` (ELM interpreter)
  using explicit deconstructors, 585
  using `match`, 594
  using records and oneofs, 578
  using s-expressions, 241, 243
ElmEvalContext (domain), 74
`elm-exp` (data declaration), 585
ELM expression, as sum of products,
    577, 578, 585
ELMM (ELM without arguments),
    63–67
  BOS, 75–76
  context-based SOS, 72–73
  deterministic behavior, 76, 80–84
  DS, 120–124
  error propagation in DS, 120–124
  modeling errors in DS, 120
  restricted ELMM DS, 117–120
  SOS, 63–67
  syntax, 63
  translation to POSTFIX, 100
`elmm` (program keyword)
  in ELMM DS, 121
  in restricted ELMM DS, 118
ElmmEvalContext (domain), 72
ElmmRedex (domain), 72
ElmRedex (domain), 74
`else` (`tagcase` default clause), 570
Else expression of conditional, 20
Emerson, Ralph Waldo (quoted), 207
`empty` (environment in FLEX/M), 901
  list representation, 903
  procedure representation, 905
empty? (metalanguage sequence
    predicate), 1182–1184
empty-env (empty environment), 277
[*empty-let*] (FIL simplification), 1032,
    1033
Empty set, 1148
empty-store (store constant), 412
empty$_{TCS}$ (empty type-constraint set),
    788, 789, 790

empty-tenv (empty tag environment)
  in CBV named sum DS, 575
Encapsulation of behavior/state, *see also*
    Data abstraction; Object-oriented
    programming
  compromised by inheritance, 767
  in object-oriented programming, 403
Energy of a POSTFIX configuration,
    84–85
ensure-. . . (computation function), 473,
    475
Env (environment domain), 275, 276
  in lambda calculus, 296, 297
  operations on, 277–278
Envelope, as model for value, 269
`env-empty` (empty environment),
    461–464
  using exceptions, 517
`env-extend` (environment extension),
    461–464
Environment, 275, 1075, *see also Env*
  binding names to locations, 431
  call-time environment, 338
  dynamic environment, 338, 341
  dynamic handler environment for
    exceptions, 519
  error-handling example, 461–464,
    517–518
  kind environment, 760
  lexical environment, 341
  linked, 1090–1093
  making explicit in TORTOISE, 1075
  module example, 901–906
  parent environment, 1090
  as product, 540
  tag environment, 573
  type environment, 643–644
  value environment, 643
  as virtual substitution, 280
Environment conversion, 1075, *see also*
    Closure conversion
Environment diagram, 341, 378
Environment frame, 1090

env-lookup (environment lookup),
461–464
env-merge (environment merging),
461–464
using exceptions, 517
envof (type constructor), 901
list representation, 903
procedure representation, 905
env-test1, 462
using exceptions, 518
env-test2, 464
using exceptions, 518
[epack] (existential type rule), 850
[epackof-≈] (type-equivalence rule), 850
Epictetus (quoted), 113
EQ ∈ PostfixEvalSequenceContext, 74
eq (POSTFIX command), 8, 40, *see also*
Relational operator
informal semantics, 10
POSTFIX DS, 137
equal?, 237, 238
Equality relation (=), 1163, *see also* =;
eq; Relational operator
on functions, 1157
on set elements, 1153
on sets, 1149
on tuples, 1153
$equal_L$ (equality test in match
desugaring), 596
Equational proof, 119
hierarchical structuring of, 139
Equational reasoning, 119
Equipotent, 228
Equirecursive type equivalence, 690, 699,
761
[equiv-⊑] (FLEX/S subtype rule), 702,
703, 708
Equivalence
behavioral, *see* Observational
equivalence
of descriptions, 756
observational, *see* Observational
equivalence
stack-answer equivalence ($\sim_{SA}$), 94

stack equivalence ($\sim_S$), 94
transform equivalence ($\sim_Q$), 93, *see
also* Transform equivalence
type equivalence, *see* Type equivalence
value equivalence ($\sim_V$), 94
Equivalence class, 1154
Equivalence relation, 250, 1154
type equality as example of, 679
Eratosthenes, sieve of, 558
ERLANG
as dynamically typed language, 623
as function-oriented language, 209
Error, *see also* Exception
as $\perp_{Fcn}$ in lambda calculus DS, 296
as "contagious" error token in
POSTFIX SOS, 60
as error token in BOS, 76
as error token in BOS for ELMM,
ELM, and POSTFIX, 79
as error token in ELMM DS, 120
as error token in FLK DS, 280, 282
as error token in FLK SOS, 268
as error token in SOS, 52
as stuck state in μFLARE SOS, 780
as stuck state in μFLEX SOS, 666
as stuck state in FLK SOS, 264, 266
as stuck state in SOS, 48, 52, 58
error-hiding functions in DS, 122, 142,
144
errors in POSTFIX DS, 131–132, 134,
136
handling with continuations, 461–464
in CBV vs. CBN parameter passing,
denotational view, 316–318
in CBV vs. CBN parameter passing,
operational view, 310
in FLK DS, 275
in FLK primitive application, 213
in POSTFIX SOS, 52–53
in strict vs. nonstrict pairs, 319
making observationally equivalent to
divergence, 427
modeling in direct semantics, 444–445
nontype error, *see* Nontype error

Error (*continued*)
  propagation of in ELMM DS, 120–124
  type error, *see* Type error
  user-generated (`error`), 213
Error (semantic domain)
  in EL dialects DS, 121
  in FLK, 276
  in POSTFIX DS, 132
Error (domain in POSTFIX), 52
`error`, 211, 213
  in FIL$_{cps}$, 1046
  in FIL$_{lift}$, 1095
  in FIL$_{reg}$, 1101
  in μFLEX, 628, 632
  in FLICK standard DS, 477
  in FLK DS, 282, 283
  in metaCPS conversion, 1061
  in simple CPS conversion, 1051
  SOS error token, 52
  type rule in μFLEX, 644
  type rule in FLEX/SPDK, 763
[*error*]
  μFLARE type axiom, 774, 775
  FLARE/E type/effect axiom, 953
  μFLEX type axiom, 644
  FLEX/SPDK type rule, 763
error:··· (error outcome in FL
    semantics), 212, 213
errorAnswer (in POSTFIX DS)
  definition, 143
  specification, 133
error-cont (standard DS continuation),
    473, 475
[*error-pure*] (FLARE syntactic purity
    axiom), 816
[*error$_R$*] (μFLARE type reconstruction
    axiom), 793, 794
errorResult (in POSTFIX DS)
  definition, 143
  specification, 133
ErrorStack (domain), 93
`errorStack`, 93
errorStack (in POSTFIX DS), 114, 131
  definition, 143

specification, 133
errorTransform (in POSTFIX DS)
  definition, 143
  specification, 133
[*error$_Z$*] (FLARE/E type/effect
    reconstruction axiom), 964
err-to-comp (computation function), 414
  for exception handling, 525
  in FLK, 279, 281
  with continuation, 483, 485, 525
  with store in FLICK, 414
$ES \in$ ExceptionSpec, 987
`escape` (Reynolds's control operator), 537
Escape analysis, 993
Escape procedure, 505
[*eta*] (FIL simplification), 1033
Eta expansion, 295
  in DS clause, 526
Eta reduction, 295
  in DS clause, 478
  FIL simplification, 1033
EUCLID, as essentially a functional
    language, 440
[*eunpack*] (existential type rule), 850
EvalContext (SOS evaluation context)
  in CBL product SOS, 553
  in CBN product SOS, 552
  in CBN vs. CBV parameter passing,
    310
  in CBV named sum SOS, 572
  in CBV product SOS, 543
  in μFLARE, 778
  in μFLEX, 664
  in FLEX/SP, 731
  in FLICK+{`label`, `jump`} SOS, 503
  in FLICK SOS, 409
  in FLK, 259, 260, 272
  in strict vs. nonstrict pair SOS, 319
Evaluation, *see also* Interpreter
  delayed, *see* Delayed evaluation
  rule, *see* Rewrite rule of SOS;
      Valuation function
  static type checking as kind of, 641–643

Evaluation context, 71, *see also* EvalContext
Evaluation order, *see also* Reduction strategy
  explicit, in CPS, 1042, 1043, 1047
  in FLK, 284
Evaluation relation
  in BOS ($\twoheadrightarrow$), 75
  in FLK ($\Rightarrow$), 260
Evaluation tree of BOS, 75
even? (mutual recursion example)
  in FL, 224–226, 230
  in FLEX, 636
  in lambda calculus, 304
  in recursive record, 354
evens (infinite stream), 558
Exception, 445, 506, 513–537, *see also* Error
  checked exception in JAVA, 985
  dismissal semantics of, 522, 528–530
  exception-handling procedure, 515
  handling, 514
  handling, and dynamic scope, 343, 519–520, 527–529
  information, 515
  latent exception effect, 986, 987
  metaCPS conversion, 1072
  nondismissal semantics of, 522, 528–530
  raising, 514
  resignaling, 514
  resumption semantics, 514, 515, 520
  signaling, 514
  tag, 515
  termination semantics, 514, 515, 520
Exception analysis, 985–988
Exception continuation, 1074
Exception masking, 987
ExceptionSpec (domain), 987
Exception specification, 987
except when (CLU exception construct), 514
exec (POSTFIX command), 8, 40
  informal semantics, 10
  POSTFIX DS, 137
  POSTFIX SOS, 55

[exec] (POSTFIX BOS rule), 78
[exec-done] (POSTFIX SOS rule), 69
[exec-prog] (POSTFIX SOS rule), 69
execs (POSTSAVE command), 105
executable (POSTFIX outcome), 92, 99
Executable sequence, 8, 40
  informal semantics, 10
  in POSTFIX2, 39
  in POSTFIX DS, 137
  in POSTFIX SOS, 55
[execute] (POSTFIX SOS rule), 55
Execution cost analysis, 988–991
Execution frame, 338, *see also* Procedure call frame
Execution of program in SOS, 58–62
Execution tree, 338
Existential package, 849
Existential quantification ($\exists$), 849, 1152
  witness, 886, 1152
Existential type, 627, 847–859, 885
  definition of, 849
  dynamic and static semantics, 850
  existential package, 853
  export restriction, 853–856, 858
  import restriction, 853, 858
  universal type equivalent to, 885
exists? (higher-order list procedure), 239, 241
Exp (expression domain)
  in dependent type system, 873
  in existential type system, 850
  in FIL, 1031
  in FIL_{cps}, 1046
  in FIL_{lift}, 1095
  in FIL_{reg}, 1101
  in FL, 219
  in μFLARE, 773
  in FLARE, 814
  in FLARE/V, 1010
  in μFLEX, 628
  in FLEX, 697
  in FLIC, 401
  in FLICK, 398
  in FLICK SOS, 406, 407
  in FLK, 211

Exp (*continued*)
  in FLEX/M, 893
  in FLEX/SP, 731
  in FLEX/SP with bounded
    quantification, 747
  in FLEX/SPD, 753
  in HOOK, 363
  in nonce type system, 861
Expansion phase of TORTOISE register
  allocator, 1102, 1104
Expcont (standard DS domain), 473
Explicit subtyping, 713–717
Explicit type, 625–627, *see also* Static
  type checking
  μFLEX as language with, 628
  used in type checking, 632, 769
Explicit type projection, *see* Polymorphic
  value projection, explicit
Explistcont (standard DS domain), 473
Export
  of abstract type, 847
  of module bindings, 333, 352, 889
Export restriction
  in [*effect-masking*] rule, 973
  in existential types, 853–856, 858
  in [*letregion*] rule, 992
  in nonce types, lack of, 860, 862
Expressible (semantic domain)
  Nameable vs., 278
  in FLK, 275, 276
Expressible value, 275, *see also*
  Expressible
Expression, *see also* Exp
  closed, 246
  of domain, 1172
  in FL, 218–227
  in FLK, 209–217
  interference, 427, 1027–1029
  jump as valueless, 498
  open, 246
  structured name, 307
  valid, in TORTOISE, 1025
Expression continuation, 474
Expression evaluation, in EL 62–63

Expression list continuation, 474
Expressive power, 471, 619, 727
Expressive type system, 627–628, 802
expr-to-comp (computation function),
  414
extend (environment, $[I \mapsto n]e$), 277
*extend** (environment with bindings), 277
Extended-number arithmetic, 568–571
  using explicit tags, 569
  using oneofs, 571
extend-handlers (exception handling),
  519, 521, 525
extending-handlers (computation
  function), 525
extend-tenv (tag environment extension)
  in CBV named sum DS, 575
*extend-tenv** (tag environment extension)
  in CBV named sum DS, 575
Extensionality, 119
External variable capture, 252
extract-value, 322
  in CBV recursion of FLK, 322

$F \in$ Effect, 949
$\mathcal{F}$ (denotation of effect), 947, 949
#f (false literal), 209, 211, 465
Factorial
  assignment conversion example,
    1020–1022
  CPS conversion example, 1069
  CPS version, 449
  examples with procedural
    continuations, 447–449
  illustrating rec semantics, 409
  in FL, 226
  in FLK, 216
  in lambda calculus, via iterators, 302
  in lambda calculus, via Y operator, 303
  in metalanguage, 1168
  iterative imperative version, 400
  iterative stateless version, 400
  in POSTFIX+{dup}, 102
  recur example, 227
  using label and jump, 496, 501

Fahrenheit-to-Celsius formula
  constructor representation, 585
  ELM expression, 578
  sum-of-products encoding, 579
  XML representation, 581
fail (nondeterministic choice), 538
failsoln for type unification, 784
fail$_{TCS}$ (type-constraint set), 788, 789,
  790
Failure (domain)
  in FLARE/E, 969
  in type reconstruction, 791, 792
  in type unification, 784
Failure continuation
  for backtracking, 465–470, 612
  for error handling, 461–464
  for iterator, 513
  for pattern matching, 584, 600, 601
Failure thunk in match desugaring, 595
FALSE (Church boolean), 300
false (boolean literal)
  in EL, 25
  in EL DS, 129
  FL standard library binding, 236
false (false value outcome in FLK), 212
false (false value of *Bool*), 1148
FC, *see* Final configuration of SOS
FC ∈ EffectConstraint, 960
Fcn (lambda calculus function domain),
  296–297
FCR ∈ EffectConstructor, 949
FCS ∈ EffectConstraintSet, 960
FEATHERWEIGHT JAVA (FJ), 768
Felleisen, Matthias, 112, 699
Fenichel, Robert R., 1145
fetch (store function), 412
fetching (computation function), 415
  in CBL product DS, 557
  with continuation, 485
FEXPR (MACLISP abstraction), 330
Fibonacci number
  CPS conversion example, 1069
  infinite stream, 558
  in POSTFIX+{dup}, 102

with self construct, 488
Field of a record, 353
FIL (TORTOISE compiler intermediate
  language), 1030–1036
  lack of dynamic type errors in,
    1035–1036
  semantics, 1035–1036
  simplification, 1032–1034
  syntactic sugar, 1031
  syntax, 1030–1034
  translation from FLARE, 1036–1038
fil (program keyword)
  in FIL, 1031
  in FIL$_{cps}$, 1046
  in FIL$_{lift}$, 1095
  in FIL$_{reg}$, 1101
FIL$_{cps}$ (TORTOISE compiler CPS
  intermediate language), 1046
File-type coherence, 926
File-value coherence, 926
Filinski, Andrzej, 1117
FIL$_{lift}$ (TORTOISE compiler intermediate
  language), 1095
Filling hole in context, 71
FIL$_{reg}$ (TORTOISE compiler target
  language), 1007, 1098–1102
  syntax, 1101
FIL$_{sum}$ (FIL plus oneofs), 1038
filter (higher-order list procedure), 239,
  241
Final configuration of SOS (*FC*), 48, 50
  in language *L*, *see L*, SOS
finally (exception construct), 532–533
FinalStack (POSTFIX domain), 53
Finite set, 1150
first-bigger-than (stream procedure),
  558–559
First-class continuation, 493
First-class procedure, 130, 209, 214–215,
  see also Higher-order function;
    Higher-order procedure
  modeling in DS, 275
  modeling in SOS, 262
  representing message-passing objects
    with, 402

First-class value, 349

first-fresh (store function), 412

First-order procedure
  in C, PASCAL, and ADA, 1076
  closure conversion from higher-order,
    1075
  in FL^{--}, 349

Fischer, Michael, 537

fix$_D$ (least fixed point of domain D), 191
  in FLK DS of **rec**, 286

Fixed point, 167, 190, 277, 321, 413
  examples, 191–195
  game board, 171
  iterative technique for finding, 168–173
  least, 173
  solution to effect constraint set, 962
  theorem of least, 190

Fixed-point combinator, *see* Y operator

FJ (FEATHERWEIGHT JAVA), 768

FL (Backus's applicative language), 207

FL (functional mini-language), 207–306,
    see also FLK
  binding constructs, 307
  definition in, 230–232
  denotational semantics, 290
  example procedures/programs, 239–242
  kernel syntax, 211
  list as chain of pairs, 221
  list procedures, 236, 237
  overview of, 208–242
  primitive operators, 213
  program in, 230–232
  scheme syntax vs. FL syntax, 210
  simplification, in proof of CBN/CBV
    relationship, 312
  simulating state in, 390–397
  standard library, 235–239
  as stateless language, 384–389
  syntactic sugar, 218–234
  syntactic sugar for record constructs,
    355
  translation from HOOK, 370–373

fl (program keyword), 219
  desugaring, 230, 231, 233

FL^{--}, 349

Flanagan, Cormac, 1117

μFLARE (subset of FLARE), 772–813
  dynamic semantics (SOS), 778–781
  lack of unique types, 776
  monomorphism of, 801
  static semantics, 774–778
  syntax, 773
  type reconstruction, 781–800
  type rules, 775
  type soundness of, 780

μFLARE$_{LP}$ (with let polymorphism),
    803–813
  less expressive than FLEX/SP, 806
  type reconstruction, 808–812
  type rules, 805

FLARE (FL with implicit types),
    813–819
  CBV semantics, 813
  dynamic semantics, 813
  pattern matching and sum-of-products
    data, 831
  static semantics, 813–817
  syntactic purity, 816
  syntactic sugar, 814
  syntax, 813, 814
  translation to FIL, 1036–1038
  type reconstruction, 817
  type rules, 815
  type system less powerful than
    FLARE/E$_{EP}$'s, 975

flare (program keyword), 773
  desugaring in FLARE, 814
  desugaring in FLARE/V, 1011

FLARE/E, 945–978
  syntax, 949
  type/effect reconstruction rules,
    963–970
  type system as powerful as FLARE's,
    955
  type system less powerful than
    FLARE/E$_{EP}$'s, 975

FLARE/E$_{EP}$, 974–978
  type system more powerful than
    FLARE's and FLARE/E's, 975

FLARE/V (TORTOISE compiler source language), 1009–1013
  syntactic sugar, 1011
  syntax, 1010
flarek (program keyword), 773, 814
  extended with pattern matching and sum-of-products data, 831
FLARE$_{sum}$ (FLARE plus oneofs), 1038
FLAT (language with only closed procedures), 344
Flat closure, 1076–1085
  conversion using control-flow analysis, 1085–1090
Flat partial order, 176
FLAVAR (FLIC with mutable variables), 429–439
FLAVARK (FLAVAR kernel), 430
  CBL DS, 434–436
  CBN DS, 433
  CBR DS, 436–438
  CBV DS, 433
  mutable variable DS, 431
FLAVORS
  generic functions, 380
  multiple inheritance, 380
  Vanilla base type, 380
μFLEX (subset of FLEX), 628–673
  CBN vs. CBV SOS, 662, 672
  free identifiers, 636–640
  monomorphic type system, 629, 655–660
  programs, 634–636
  SOS, 662–667
  static semantics, 681
  substitution, 636–640
  syntactic sugar, 634–636
  syntax, 628, 629–640
  type rules, 645–648
  type soundness, 667–673
  type system, 640–660
FLEX (FL with explicit types), 675–698
  CBV semantics, 682, 696
  syntax, 697
  type system, 675–698

flex (program keyword), 635, 647
  desugaring in μFLEX, 634
FLEX/M, 891–900
  constructors and deconstructors, 915
  data-type declarations, 915
  dynamic semantics, 923–925
  first-class modules, 899
  scoping, 910–911
  static semantics, 910–923
  subtyping, 912, 913
  syntax, 893
  type constructors in, 915
  type environments, 914
  type equivalence, 911, 913
  type rules, 912–918
flex/M (program keyword), 894
flex/Mk (program keyword), 893
FLEX/P (FLEX with polymorphism), 727, 848
FLEX/S (FLEX with subtyping), 702–725
  recursive subtype rules, 707
  subtype rules, 703
  type rule, 703
FLEX/SP (FLEX with subtyping and polymorphism), 727–750
  syntax, 731
  type and subtype rules, 731
  with bounded quantification, 747
flex/SP (program keyword), 741
FLEX/SPD (FLEX with subtyping, polymorphism, and descriptions)
  free identifiers and substitution, 758
  syntax, 753
FLEX/SPDK (FLEX with subtyping, polymorphism, descriptions, and kinds), 758–767
  kind checking, 760–763
  syntax, 759
  type-checking rules, 763
flexk (program keyword), 628
  type rule in μFLEX, 644
FLIC (FL with mutable cells), 397–428
  example programs, 400–404
  iterators in, 507–513

FLIC (*continued*)
  syntactic sugar, 399, 401
  syntax, 398, 401
flic (program keyword), 399
  desugaring, 401
FLICK (FLIC kernel), 397–399
  answer domain in continuation-based
    DS, 474
  command as expression, 472
  computation-based continuation DS,
    482–493
  continuation-based semantics, 471–493
  DS, 411–420
  exception handling with raise,
    handle, and trap, 515–532
  nonlocal exits with label and jump,
    494–506
  SOS, 405–411
  standard DS, 472–480
  syntax, 398
flick (program keyword), 398
  standard DS, 477
  standard DS for exceptions, 524
FLIC# (FLIC extension), 492–493
Flipping of GC semispaces, 1134
FLK (FL kernel), *see also* FL
  BOS, 269
  CBN vs. CBV parameter passing,
    denotational view, 316–318
  CBN vs. CBV parameter passing,
    operational view, 310–316
  denotational semantics, 275–290
  evaluation, 258–269
  evaluation order, 284
  evaluation reduction relation ($\rightsquigarrow$), 259
  evaluation SOS, 258
  evaluation step relation ($\Rightarrow$), 259
  expression in, 209–210
  free and bound identifiers, 247
  informal semantics, 210–217
  lambda calculus vs., 291–294
  list as chain of pairs, 215
  nonstrict application, 215
  nonstrict pair, 216
  overview of, 209–217

  primitive operators, 213
  program in, 209, 217
  safe transformation in, 270–274
  scheme syntax vs. FLK syntax, 210
  semantic algebra, 275–280
  semantic domains, 276
  s-expressions as program inputs, 259
  simplification, 270–274
  simplification step relation ($\circ\!\!\Rightarrow$), 271
  substitution, 254
  syntax, 209–210, 211
  valuation functions, 280–289
  value in, 210–212
flk (program keyword), 209, 211
  in FLK DS, 283
  free and bound identifiers, 247
Flow, *see* Control flow analysis; Data flow
FLUID (dynamically scoped CBV FL),
  345
fluid-let (dynamic scope in statically
  scoped language), 379, 438
foldr (higher-order list procedure), 240,
  241
  to express other higher-order list
    procedures, 240
for
  desugaring into loop in FLIC, 489
  PostLoop command, 103, 141
forall (polymorphic type), 728, 729
  in FLEX/M, 914
  in FLEX/SPDK, 759
  generic vs., 802–804
  kind checking in FLEX/SPDK, 760
  type rules involving, 731
  type rules involving, in bounded
    quantification, 747
[*forall*] (FLEX/SPDK kind rule), 760
forall? (higher-order list procedure),
  239, 241
[*forall-$\sqsubseteq_{BQ}$*] (FLEX/SP subtype rule),
  747
force (undelay evaluation), 560
fork (of control threads), 997
For loop, control context in, 443

Formal parameter
   of abstraction, 214, 244
   of function, 1165
   of method, 363
   of program, 209
   of program, scope of, 230
FORTH, as stack language, 8
FORTRAN
   1-based indexing, 562
   array, as mutable sequence, 561
   as imperative language, 384
   as language without block structure,
      337
   as monomorphic language, 629
   as statically typed language, 623
   call-by-reference parameter passing,
      436
   command, 472
   lack of passable procedures, 320
   libraries of numerical methods, 239
   mutable variable, 430
   nameable and expressible values, 278
   valueless procedure, 385
   value-returning function, 385
Forwarding address in GC, 1136
FP (Backus's applicative language), 207
Fragmentation of memory, 1131
Frame
   environment, 1090
   procedure call, 1005
   procedure call, continuation
      representing, 445, 448, 1043, 1132
Frank, Michael, 102
FrDescIds (free description identifiers),
      756, 952
   in FLEX/SPD, 758
Free identifier, 246, 389, *see also FrIds*
Free list, 1131
Free occurrence of identifier, 245
Free pointer in GC, 1134, 1135
Free variable, 246, *see also FrIds*
   capture of, 251–252, *see also* Variable
      capture
   substituting for, 253
freeze (delay evaluation), 228

Fresh identifier, 221, 255
   in letrec desugaring, 225
   mechanism for generating, 1039–1041
   to avoid name capture in macro
      systems, 331
fresh-loc (store function), 412
FrIds (free identifiers)
   in dependent type system, 873
   in existential type system, 850
   in μFLEX, 636, 638
   in FLK, 247
   in FLEX/SP, 731
   in FLEX/SP with bounded
      quantification, 747
   in FLEX/SPD, 758
   in nonce type system, 861
   well-defined on alpha-equivalence class,
      251
Friedman, Dan, 112
FRM (FIL register machine), 1121,
      1122–1130
   architecture, 1122–1123
   descriptor, 1123–1124
   heap block, 1127–1130
   program state, 1122
from (iterator/stream example), 509, 556
From-space in GC, 1133
Frost, Robert (quoted), 443
FrTyIds (free type identifiers)
   in dependent type system, 873
   in existential type system, 850
   in μFLARE$_{LP}$, 805, 806
   in μFLEX, 637, 638
   in FLEX/SP, 731
   in FLEX/SP with bounded
      quantification, 747
   in nonce type system, 861
FST (first element of Church pair), 302
fst (pair primitive), 213, 215
   in FLK DS, 285
   generic type for in FLARE, 813
   POSTFIX command, 102, 141
   sum-of-products data version, 586
   type rule in FLEX, 675
[fst] (FLK SOS reduction), 259

Full abstraction, 159–160
  of EL, 159
  lack of for POSTFIX, 160
Full language, 208
FUNARG problem, 378
Function, 1155–1170, *see also* Procedure
  abstraction (λ), 1165
  application of, *see* Function application
  argument of, 1156, 1158
  as element of function domain, 1184
  bijective, 1160
  binding construct defined with, 124
  codomain of, 1156
  composition of ($\circ$), 1159
  computable, 199, 1158
  constant function, 1159
  definition of, 1156
  domain of, 1156
  domain of definition of (*dom*), 1156
  equality ($=$) on, 1157
  extensionality, 119
  graph of (*gph*), 1156
  higher-order, 1160–1161, 1166
  identity function, 1159, 1167
  image of (*img*), 1160
  inclusion function ($\hookrightarrow$), 1159
  injective, 1160
  lambda notation, 1165–1170
  multiple arguments via currying, 1168
  n-fold composition of (f^n), 1159
  nonstrict, 199
  one-to-one, 1160
  partial function, 1156
  polymorphic, 1167
  predicate function, 1163
  procedure vs., 209, 1157–1158
  recursive, 1168–1169
  result of, 1156
  set theoretic, 1155–1170
  signature, 1157
  simulating multiple arguments,
    1161–1164
  simulating multiple results, 1164–1165
  source of (*src*), 1156
  strict, 199
  surjective, 1160
  on syntactic domain, 35–36
  target of (*tgt*), 1156
  total function, 1156
  type of, 1157, 1166
  uncomputable, 199, 1158
Functional language, *see*
    Function-oriented programming
Function application, 1158–1159
  operand of, 1158
  operator of, 1158
  parentheses and, 1158
Function domain, 1184–1186
  partial order on, 178–179
Function-oriented programming, 207,
    1158, 1170
  expressing denotational-style
    interpreter, 128
  in real-world languages, 304
Function type, *see* Arrow type
Functor, 890
  applicative, 939
  generative, 939
  table example, 906–909
Functorization, 929
Fundamental tension, 619
FX
  as implicitly typed language, 626
  as LISP dialect with procedure
    signatures, 1169
  HDM type reconstruction, 836
FX-87
  early experiments with effects, 1000
  explicit effect declarations, 945
  implicit type projection, 940
FX-91
  modules with abstract and concrete
    type definitions, 893, 934
  module system, 940

Game board
  of denotational semantics, 116
  of fixed points, 171
  of operational semantics, 48

Garbage collection (GC), 438, 991,
    1119–1146
  conservative, 1127, 1142
  from-space, 1133
  generational, 1142
  heap, *see* Heap allocation; Heap
    memory
  in-place, 1141
  mark-sweep, 1141
  memory tracing, 1132–1133
  reference counting, 1131–1132
  stop-and-copy, 1133–1140
  tag-free, 1127, 1141–1142, 1145
  to-space, 1133
GC tag, 1126
gen (FLARE type generalization), 805,
    806
Generating function, 167
Generational garbage collection, 1142
Generative functor, 939
Generator (procedure/iterator in Icon),
    507
generic (type schema)
  in FLARE/E, 949, 966
  in μFLARE$_{LP}$, 802, 803
  forall vs., 802–804
Generic function in object-oriented
    programming, 380
Generic type in Java, 749, 768
genPure (FLARE type generalization),
    815, 816
gensym (Lisp fresh identifier generator),
    331
[*genvar*] (FLARE/E type/effect axiom),
    951, 953
[*genvar$_{LP}$*] (μFLARE$_{LP}$ type axiom),
    804, 805
[*genvar$_{LPR}$*] (μFLARE$_{LP}$ type
    reconstruction axiom), 809
[*genvar$_Z$*] (FLARE/E type/effect
    reconstruction axiom), 967, 968, 969
Geometric shape, as sum of products,
    577, 583–584
get (PostFix extension command), 102
get (tuple projection), 541

type reconstruction, 825
type rule in FLEX, 676
[*get*] (stateless reduction rule), 541, 543
get (store accessing function), 405, 406
  in CBL product SOS, 553
get-age (subtyping example), 701, 702,
    715, 716, 719
get-handler (exception-handling
    environment lookup), 519, 521, 525
getting-handler (computation function),
    525
$\mathcal{GI}$ (globalization inlining transform),
    1019
Gifford, David K., 1000
Girard, Jean-Yves, 768, 886
GJ (Java with generics), 768
Glück, Louise (quoted), 839
Globalization, 1015
  inlining strategy for, 1017–1019
  in Tortoise compiler, 1014–1019
  wrapping strategy for, 1015–1016
Global procedure, 1094
Global scope, 346, 352, 1095
go (goto construct in Common Lisp),
    348
goto (control effect), 979
goto (unrestricted jump construct), 497
gph (function graph), 1156
Grammar, 20, *see also* Syntax
  abstract, 20
  context-free, 26, 43
  s-expression, *see* S-expression grammar
Graph coloring for register allocation,
    1117
Graphics abstract class in Java, 724
Graph of function (*gph*), 1156
Graph reduction, 315
  for lazy evaluation, 314, 440
Graph rewriting system, 112
Greater-than-or-equal-to relation (>),
    1163, *see also* >=; Relational
    operator
Greater-than relation (>), 1163, *see also*
    >; gt; Relational operator
Greatest lower bound (glb), 176

gt (POSTFIX command), 8, 40, *see also*
     Relational operator
  informal semantics, 10
  POSTFIX DS, 137
$\mathcal{GW}$ (globalization wrapping transform),
     1016
Gymnastics, mental, 446

halt (program termination)
  in FIL_{reg}, 1101
  in FLICK extension, 501
Halting problem, 618, *see also*
     Undecidability
  halting function, 198, 1158
  halting theorem, 49
Hamming numbers, 560
handle (FLIC exception-handling
     construct), 515–532
  computation-based DS, 524–527
  desugaring-based implementation,
     527–529
  metaCPS conversion, 1072
  standard DS, 519–524
  termination semantics, 515, 520
  in type/effect system, 986–988
handle (SML exception construct), 514
[*handle*] (unsound type/effect rule), 986
Handle an exception, 514
HandlerEnv (exception handler domain),
     519, 521, 525
Handler environment for exceptions, 519
handlerof (exception handler type),
     986–988
Hankin, Chris, 1117
Hard link, 1132
Hash (PERL record), 353
HASKELL
  array, as updatable sequence, 545
  array indexing, 548
  as block-structured language, 337
  as implicitly typed language, 626
  as purely functional language, 384
  as purely functional lazy language, 209
  as statically typed language, 623

currying of constructor arguments,
     588–589
  extensible records, 767
  garbage collection, 1120
  HDM type reconstruction, 836
  heterogeneous tuple, 548
  immutable string, 548
  immutable updatable sequence, 548
  implicit parameter, 379
  lack of abstraction in pattern
     matching, 607–610
  list-manipulation libraries, 239
  monadic style and do notation, 396
  nonstrict application, 215
  nonstrict product, 551
  pattern matching, 590, 605–610, 768,
     829
  sum (Either), 568
  sum-of-products data, 579, 829
  type reconstruction, 812
  universal polymorphism, 627
  unsafe features, 622
  user-defined data-type declaration,
     588–589
Hasse diagram for partial order, 174
Haugen, Marty (quoted), 889
Hawes, Bess (quoted), 1042
HDM type reconstruction, 812, 836
head (SCHEME stream head), 561
head (metalanguage sequence function),
     1182–1184
Header word in FRM block, 1127
Heap allocation
  in active semispace of stop-and-copy
     GC, 1133–1134
  of FRM block, 1127
  in POSTHEAP, 110
Heap block, 1119, 1122, *see also* FRM
  live or dead, 1120, 1130–1133
  stack allocation of, 1144
Heap deallocation, *see* Garbage collection
     (GC)
Heap memory, 438, 991, 1119, 1123
  in POSTHEAP, 110

Heidegger, Martin (quoted), 1147

Heterogeneous list, 686

Heterogeneous product, 548, 677

Hewitt, Carl, 941

Hewlett Packard stack calculator, 8

Hiding names, 333, 901

Hierarchical scope, 334–347, 352

Higher-order function, 1160–1161, *see also* First-class procedure; Higher-order procedure

  binding construct defined with, 124

  lambda notation and, 1166

  to simulate multiple arguments (currying), 1162

Higher-order polymorphic lambda calculus, 765

Higher-order procedure, 214–215, *see also* First-class procedure; Higher-order function

  closure conversion to simulate with first-order procedure, 1075

  list procedure, 239–240

  perspectives on, 305

Higher-order type, 750–767

  description, 750–758

  kind, 758–767

Hindley, J. Roger, 835

Hindley-Damas-Milner (HDM) type reconstruction, 812, 836

Hoare, C. A. R., 941

Hole

  in context, 71

  in scope of a variable, 245, 337

Holmes, Sherlock (quoted), 769

Homogeneous list, 686

Homogeneous product, 548, 677

Homomorphism, 115

HOOK (Humble Object-Oriented Kernel), 362–368, *see also* HOOPLA

  class, simulating with prototype object, 366

  prototype-based language, 380

  semantics, 370–373

static scope, 366

  syntax, 363

  translation to FL, 370–373

hook (HOOK program keyword), 363

HOOPLA (Humble Object-Oriented Programming Language), 362, 368–370, *see also* HOOK

  extending with state, 403

  namespaces, 376

  sample classes, 371

hoopla (HOOPLA program keyword), 369

Horace (quoted), 163

Horizontal style for type derivation, 648–650

HTML, sum-of-products data via markups, 580

Hudak, Paul, 305

Hughes, R. J. M., 305

Hygienic macros, 331, 379

$I \in$ Ident, *see* Ident

$I \in$ Inputs, *see* Inputs

$i \in Int$, *see* Int

IBM 360, register spilling, 1115

Ice cream, inspiration for mixin, 380

Icon generators, 507

$[id\text{-}\approx_{tc}]$ (type-constructor equivalence axiom), 913

id_A (identity function), 1159, 1167

Idempotence, 1084

Ident (identifier domain)

  in $\text{FIL}_{reg}(\text{Ident}_{reg})$, 1099

  in FL dialects, 211

  in FLEX/M, 893

  in HOOK, 363

Identification (unique object handle), 941

Identifier, 244, 334, *see also* Variable; Variable reference

  binding occurrence of, 245

  bound, 246

  bound occurrence of, 245

  in FLK, 210

  free, 246, 389

Identifier (*continued*)
  free occurrence of, 245
  fresh, 221, 225, 255, 331
  primitive name, 307
  structured, 886
  variable vs., 244
Identifier pattern, 590
  desugaring in `match`, 598
Identity element of an operator, 40
Identity function, 1159, 1167
Identity of an object, 383
  state and, 383–384
Identity substitution, 782
$id{\rightarrow}mc$ (metaCPS function), 1060
IdSet (identifier set domain), 1019
$\mathcal{IE}$ (input expression meaning function), 283
IF (Church conditional), 300
IF (SOS input function), *see* Input function of SOS
if (metalanguage conditional), 1180, 1190, 1191
if (EL/FL conditional)
  desugaring in HOOK, 369
  elseless if sugar in FLICK, 399, 401
  in EL dialects, 25
  in EL DS, 129
  in FIL$_{cps}$, 1046
  in FIL$_{lift}$, 1095
  in FIL$_{reg}$, 1101
  in FL dialects, 211, 214
  in FLICK standard DS, 477
  in FLK DS, 282, 283
  in FLK SOS, 259, 261
  in metaCPS conversion, 1061
  in simple CPS conversion, 1051
  as primitive operator, 267
  type rule in μFLEX, 644
if_S (conditional function), 1164
[*if*]
  μFLARE type rule, 775
  FLARE/E type/effect rule, 953, 955
  μFLEX type rule, 644, 646
  type/exception rule, 988
[`if`-*F*] (FLK SOS reduction), 259, 261

iff (if and only if), 1151
[*if-pure*] (FLARE syntactic purity rule), 816
[*if$_R$*] (μFLARE type reconstruction rule), 793
[`if`-*T*] (FLK SOS reduction), 259, 261
[*if$_Z$*] (FLARE/E type/effect reconstruction rule), 963, 964
Ill-typed expression, 641, 645, 770
  `match` expression, 593
  metalanguage expression, 1172
Image of function (*img*), 1160
Immediate component expression, 1013
Immediate descriptor, 1124
Immediate subexpression, 1013
Immutable data, 397
  named product, 353–359, 549–550, 677–678, 821–826
  positional product, 541–549, 676–677
  sequence, 544–545, 677
  string, 548
  tuple, 541–542, 676–677
  updatable sequence, 545–547, 548
`impeach` (election construct), 490–492
Imperative programming, 384, 397, *see also* Stateful language
  essence, 397
  examples, 400–404
Imperative type variable, 837
Implementation language, 7
[*implicit-let*] (FIL simplification), 1033
Implicit parameter, 343, 344
  in HASKELL, 379
[*implicit-projection*] (FLEX/M type rule), 921
Implicit subtyping, 713–717
Implicit type, 625–627, 774, *see also* Type reconstruction
Implicit type projection, *see* Polymorphic value projection, implicit
Import of module bindings, 333, 352, 889
Import restriction, 916
  in [*effect-masking*] rule, 973
  in existential types, 853, 858
  in [*letregion*] rule, 992

in nonce types, lack of, 862
in universal polymorphism, 731, 732
Impredicative type system, 735
    of FLEX/SP, 804
in (communication effect), 998
in (input function of DS), 151
inc$_{Int}$ (metalanguage incrementing
    function), 1156
[*inclusion*] (FLEX/S type rule), 702, 703,
    719
Inclusion function ($\hookrightarrow$), 1159
Inclusion on types, *see* Subtyping
Incomparable elements in partial order,
    175
Incomplete row type, 823
In-degree of graph vertex, 1107
Indexing, *see* Product indexing
Induction, 1168, *see also* Structural
    induction
Inequality relation ($\neq$), 1163, *see also*
    !=; Relational operator
+inf, -inf (extended integer), 568
Inference of types, *see* Type
    reconstruction
Inference rule for type judgment, 645
Infinite data, *see also* Lazy (CBL)
    product; Nonstrictness; Stream
    in CBN FL, 217, 324
    coroutine producer value sequence, 459
    thunk implementation in CBV FL, 325
Infinite loop, *see* Divergence;
    Nontermination
Infinite set, 1150
Information, of exception, 515
Information hiding, 901
Ingalls, Daniel H. H. (quoted), 362
Inheritance, 362, 366–367, 379
    hierarchy, 362
    multiple, 380
    subtyping vs., 723–725, 767
init (initialization effect in FLARE/E),
    946, 949
Initial configuration of SOS, 47
Initialization effect, 946

inj (positional sum injection), 576
Injection, into sum value, 570
Injection function, 1176, 1189
Injective function, 1160
Inj k (metalanguage oneof injection),
    1176, 1189
inleft (either injection), 574
Inlining, 1017, 1053, 1056, 1088, 1116
    inlining strategy for globalization,
    1017–1019
Inner class in JAVA, 338
    closure conversion and, 441, 1082
[*input*] (ELM BOS rule), 77
InputExp (input value domain)
    in μFLARE, 778
    in μFLEX, 664
    in FLK, 258, 259–260
Input function of SOS (*IF*), 47, 50
    in FLICK, 407
    in language L, *see* L, SOS
Inputs (program inputs domain), 49, *see*
    also InputExp
    in EL, 152
    in POSTFIX, 53, 152
inright (either injection), 574
install-cont (control-point invoking
    function), 498, 500
Instance method, 362
    representing in HOOK, 366
Instance of class, 362
    representing in HOOK, 366
Instance variable, 362
    representing in HOOK, 366
Instantiation of type by substitution, 783
Int (integer set & semantic domain), 1148
    in EL DS, 118
    in POSTFIX DS, 132
int (POSTFIX2 command), 41
int (extended integer conversion), 568
int (integer type), 628, 629
[*int*]
    μFLARE type axiom, 775
    FLARE/E type/effect axiom, 953
    μFLEX type axiom, 644
    type/exception axiom, 988

int? (FL integer type predicate), 213
  in FLK DS, 285
intAt (function in POSTFIX DS)
  definition, 143
  specification, 133
Integer, *see also Int*; IntLit; *Nat*; NatLit;
      Neg; *Pos*; PosLit
  message-passing HOOK object, 364
  message-passing SMALLTALK object,
      365
  numeral vs., 57
Integer arithmetic module, 358
Integer range notation ([*lo..hi*]), 1149
Interface, 235, 333, 839, 889, 1171, *see
      also* Abstraction barrier; API
  in dependent type system, 870
  in existential type system, 856
  in JAVA, 724
  of module, 352
Interference between expressions, 427
  code optimization and, 1027–1029
interleave (list interleaving view), 607
Interleaving of observable actions, 997
Internal variable capture, 252
Interpreter, 7
  ASTs processed by, 116
  denotational semantics vs. program to
      specify, 128
  for ELM, 241–242, 243
  interpreted language, 623
  metacircular, for FL, 242
Interprocedural register allocation, 1111
Intersection
  of records, 550
  of sets (∩), 1149
[int?-F] (FLK SOS reduction), 259
intlist (integer list data type)
  def-datatype declaration in FLARE,
      833, 834
  def-datatype declaration in
      FLEX/SP, 738, 739
IntLit (integer syntactic domain)
  in EL dialects, 25
  in FL dialects, 211

[*int_R*] (μFLARE type reconstruction
      axiom), 793
[int?-*T*] (FLK SOS reduction), 259
int-tree (integer tree data type)
  declared by def-data, 609
  example sum-of-products type, 750
  example types, 694
  type specified with trec, 688
Invariant
  loop-invariant expressions and code
      hoisting, 1029
  of representation, 402, 842
Invariant subtyping, 704–706
Inverse limit construction, 202
Invocation, procedure, *see* app
Invocation frame, *see* Procedure call
      frame
Irreducible (SOS configurations), 50
Irreducible SOS configuration ($\not\to$), 50
IS ∈ IdSet, 1019
Isomorphism, 1160
  isomorphic sets, 1160
Isorecursive type equivalence, 689, 699,
      761
ISWIM (Landin's *If You See What I
      Mean* language), 305
  CBN variant, 378
  CBV lambda calculus and, 378
Iter (iterator in SATHER), 507
Iterating procedure, 507
Iteration, 390, *see also* Iterator; Loop
  Church numeral expressing, 298
  continuations and, 447–449
  factorial as example of, 400–401
  in FL, 226
  in FLIC via for, 489
  in FLIC via loop, 488–490
  in FLIC via repeat, 420, 489
  in POSTLOOP via for/repeat, 103,
      141
  via label and jump, 496
  looping constructs, 449
  simulating state with, 390–391
  tail recursion and, 1064

using `recur`, 227

`while` sugar, 399, 401

Iterative fixed point technique, 168–173

Iterative procedure, 449

Iterator, *see also* Iteration

    in C++, 507, 512

    in CLU, 506

    in FLIC, 507–513

    in Java, 507, 512

    stream vs., 556, 612

    with success and failure continuations, 513

`iterator` (FLIC iterator construct), 507

`J` (Landin's control operator), 537

JAVA

    abstract class, 724

    answer domain, 474

    array, as fixed-length mutable sequence, 561

    array, as homogeneous product, 548

    array subscripting notation, 561

    as call-by-value language, 309

    as explicitly typed language, 625

    as language without block structure, 337

    as monomorphic language, 658

    as object-oriented language, 362

    as stateful language, 384

    autoboxing/autounboxing, 750

    call-by-value-sharing of mutable products, 563

    constructor method, 366

    covariant array subtyping, 709

    downcast, 723

    dynamic and static type checking, 624

    dynamic loading, 890, 892, 928, 941

    dynamic loading and side effects, 926

    effect system for tracking exceptions, 1001

    exception handling with `throw`/`try...catch`, 514, 985

    explicit typing example, 626

    file-value coherence, 926

garbage collection, 1120, 1121

generic types, 749, 768

immutable string, 548

implicit projection for generic methods, 918

inner class and closure conversion, 441, 1082

inner class as limited form of block structure, 338

integers and booleans as nonobjects, 365, 379

interface, 724

iterator, 507, 512

lack of universal polymorphism, 749–750

libraries, 239

object, 550

overloading, 748

program arguments as string array, 217

resignaling of exceptions, 514

`return`/`break`/`continue`, 445, 490

simulating higher-order procedures, 1076

standard library API, 235

strict application, 215

sum-of-products data via objects, 579

`this` as receiver parameter, 363

`throws` to specify exceptions, 514, 985

type coercion, 718

type conversion, 716

type information in compiled files, 926

type vs. class, 723

universal polymorphism, lack of, 627

vector, as dynamically sized mutable sequence, 561, 562

vector, as heterogeneous product, 562

`void` expression as command, 472

`void` type, 209

`void` vs. value-returning method, 385

JAVASCRIPT

    as dynamically typed language, 623

    as object-oriented language, 362

    prototype-based objects, 380

Jim, Trevor, 1117

Johnsson, Thomas, 1117
`join` (list joining view), 607
join (of control threads), 997
Judgment
    kind, 760
    syntactic purity, *see* Syntactic purity
        judgment
    type, 645
    type/cost, 989
    type/effect, 951
    type/exception, 987
Jump, *see also* `break`; `continue`; `goto`;
    `jump`
    in assembly language, 1056
    to represent procedure call, 1043, 1046,
        1064
`jump`, 494–506, 717
    computation-based DS for, 500
    control effects and, 978–983
    in μFLARE, 800
    in μFLEX, 658–659
    in FLICK SOS, 503–504
    in metaCPS conversion, 1070–1075
    in standard DS, 497
    as sugar for `cwcc`, 506
    as valueless expression, 498
[*jump*] (SOS transition rule), 503

K (lambda calculus combinator), 296
$K \in$ Kind, 759
Kahn, Gilles, 112
Kelsey, Richard, 1116
Kernel of programming language, 207,
    1186
Key/lock for data abstraction, 843–847
Keyword (keyword domain), 211
    in language L, *see* L, syntax
Keyword, reserved, 210
Kind, 758–767
    well-kinded description, 760
Kind (kind domain)
    in FLARE/E, 957
    in FLEX/SPDK, 759
Kind assignment, 761

Kind checking, 760–763
    decidability of, 761
    interactions with type checking, 762
Kind environment, 760
    base kind environment, 761
Kind judgment, 760
`knull` (alternative to `null`), 611
`kons` (alternative to `cons`), 611

$L \in$ Lit, *see* Lit
$L \in$ LogicalOperator, 25
$\mathcal{L}$ (literal meaning function)
    in EL, 129
    in FLK, 283
$l \in$ *Location*, 412
`label` (control point), 494–506
    computation-based DS for, 500
    control effects and, 978–983
    duplication of continuation, 498
    in μFLARE, 800
    in μFLEX, 658–659
    in FLICK SOS, 503–504
    in metaCPS conversion, 1070–1075
    in standard DS, 497
    as sugar for `cwcc`, 506
[*label*] (SOS transition rule), 503
`lam` (FLK abstraction), 211, 214
    free and bound identifiers, 247
    in CBN vs. CBV SOS, 310
    in FLICK standard DS, 477
    in FLICK standard DS for exceptions,
        520, 521
    in FLK DS, 283, 286
    in FLK ValueExp domain, 258
    in lambda calculus, 291
    in static vs. dynamic scope, 335
    scope, 245
    substitution, in FLK, 254
Lambda abstraction, 1165
Lambda calculus (LC), 290–304
    Church boolean, 300–301
    Church conditional, 300–301
    Church numeral, 298–300
    Church pair, 302

Church tuple, 225

combinator as program, 291

denotational semantics, 296–297

FLK vs., 291–294

higher-order polymorphic, 765

history, 305

normalization, 292–295

operational semantics, 291–296

polymorphic, 764, 768

recursion (Y operator), 303–304

second-order, 764

simplification, 291

simply typed, 674, 699, 764

syntactic sugar, 291

syntax, 291

untyped, 622

Lambda cube, 887

Lambda lifting, 1094–1096, 1117

Lambda notation, 1165–1170

   for curried function, 1168

   LISP vs., 1169–1170

   recursion, 1168–1169

Landin, Peter, 42, 112, 162, 305, 378, 537

lastStack (POSTFIX function), 93

   alternative definitions of, 98

Latent effect (of a procedure), 944, 947

   in control flow analysis, 996

   inflating with [*does*], 955

   latent control effect example, 981

   latent cost effect, 988, 989

   latent exception effect, 986, 987

   latent store effect examples, 952

   in security analysis, 999

   unifying in reconstruction, 965

Latently typed language, *see*

      Dynamically typed language

Laziness, *see also* Nonstrictness

   graph reduction and, 314, 440

   lazy evaluation, 434, *see also*

      Call-by-need; Lazy (CBL) product

   lazy language, 209

   lazy list, *see* Stream

   lazy parameter passing, 434, *see*

      Call-by-need

modularity of, 440, 559, 612

Lazy (CBL) product, 552–555

   denotational semantics of, 555

   SOS, 553–555

$LC \in$ Location, 406

LC, *see* Lambda calculus

leaf (tree constructor), 608, 609

   generic type of, 832

leaf? (tree predicate), 451, 608

leaf~ (tree deconstructor)

   generic type of, 832

least (extended FL construct), 267

Least fixed point, 173, 190

   in FLK DS of rec, 286

   solution to effect constraint set, 962

Least Fixed Point Theorem, 190

Least upper bound (lub), 176

leaves (iterator example), 509

left (tree selector), 451, 608

Left-hand side (LHS) of transition, 50

length (procedure), 236, 238

length (metalanguage sequence function),

   1183

Length of transition path, 50

Less-than-or-equal-to relation ($\leq$), 1163,

   see also <=; Relational operator

Less-than relation ($<$), 1163, *see also* <;

   Relational operator; lt

let (metalanguage binding), 1191,

   1194–1195

let (FL local binding), 219, 223

   desugaring in FL, 220, 223, 233

   desugaring in HOOK, 369

   free identifiers, in μFLEX, 638

   in FIL, 1030

   in FIL$_{cps}$, 1046

   in FIL$_{lift}$, 1095

   in FIL$_{reg}$, 1101

   in μFLARE/FLARE kernel, 772

   in μFLEX/FLEX kernel, 628, 631, 632

   in μFLEX SOS, 664

   in metaCPS conversion, 1061

   in simple CPS conversion, 1051

   letrec equipotent with, 228

let (*continued*)

polymorphic type reconstruction, 808, 815

scope, 245

substitution, in μFLEX, 639

type rule in dependent type system, 875

type rule in μFLEX, 644

[*let*]

μFLARE SOS reduction, 778

μFLARE type rule, 775

μFLEX SOS reduction, 663, 664

μFLEX type rule, 644, 646

type rule with dependent types, 875

type rule with dependent types, alternative, 882

[*let'$_{LP}$*] (FLARE type rule), 815

purity required for generalization, 816

[*let'$_{LPR}$*] (FLARE type reconstruction rule), 818

let* (local sequential binding), 227

FIL sugar, 1031, 1032

LetableExp (domain), 1046, 1047

in FIL$_{lift}$, 1095

in FIL$_{reg}$, 1101

[*let$_{EP}$*] (FLARE/E$_{EP}$ type/effect rule), 974, 975

[*let$_{EPZ}$*] (proposed by Bud Lojack), 979

[*let$_{LP}$*] (μFLARE$_{LP}$ type rule), 805, 806

[*let$_{LPR}$*] (μFLARE$_{LP}$ type reconstruction rule), 809

letpar (parallel binding construct), 1027

Let polymorphism, 801–813

[*let-pure*] (FLARE syntactic purity rule), 816

[*let$_R$*] (μFLARE type reconstruction rule), 793, 794

letrec (mutual recursion), 219

alternative desugaring, 229, 267

Bekić expansion for desugaring, 229, 327

CBV desugaring, 326

desugaring in CBN FL, 224–226

desugaring in CBV FLAVAR, 432

desugaring in FL, 220, 233

desugaring in FLARE-to-FIL translation, 1036

desugaring in FLEX/M, 894

free identifiers, in μFLEX, 638

in μFLARE/FLARE kernel, 772

in μFLEX/FLEX kernel, 628, 631, 632

in μFLEX SOS, 664

let equipotent with, 228

polymorphic type reconstruction, 808, 815

scope, 245

substitution, in μFLEX, 639

type rule in μFLEX, 644

type rule in dependent type system, 875

type rule in FLEX/SPDK, 763

well-typedness preserving desugaring, 1038

[*letrec*]

μFLARE SOS reduction, 778

μFLARE type rule, 774, 775

μFLEX SOS reduction, 663, 664

μFLEX type rule, 644, 646

FLEX/SPDK type rule, 763

type rule with dependent types, 875

[*letrec'$_{LP}$*] (FLARE type rule), 815

purity required for generalization, 816

[*letrec'$_{LPR}$*] (FLARE type reconstruction rule), 818

[*letrec$_{EP}$*] (FLARE/E$_{EP}$ type/effect rule), 974, 975

[*letrec$_{EPZ}$*] (proposed by Bud Lojack), 979

[*letrec$_{LP}$*] (μFLARE$_{LP}$ type rule), 805, 806

[*letrec$_{LPR}$*] (μFLARE$_{LP}$ type reconstruction rule), 809

[*letrec-pure*] (FLARE syntactic purity rule), 816

[*letrec$_R$*] (μFLARE type reconstruction rule), 793

[*letrec$_{SP}$*] (FLARE/E type/effect rule), 952, 953

[*letrec*$_{SPZ}$] (FLARE/E type/effect reconstruction rule), 967

letregion (region-based storage management), 992, 994

[*letregion*] (type/effect rule), 992

[*let*$_{SP}$] (FLARE/E type/effect rule), 952, 953

[*let*$_{SPZ}$] (FLARE/E type/effect reconstruction rule), 967

let-type (type binding), 634, 635

let-type* (type binding), 634, 635

Lex (scanner generator), 43

Lexical address, 342, 1091

Lexical environment, 341

Lexical scope, *see* Static scope

Lexicographic order, 104

lget (CBL product projection), 552–555
    DS, 555, 557
    SOS, 553–555

[*lget*] (stateful reduction rule), 553

[*lget-progress*] (evaluation rule), 553

LHS (left-hand side) of transition, 50

$\mathcal{LI}$ (TORTOISE lifting transform), 1095

Liar compiler for SCHEME, 1145

Life $\neq$ paragraph, 19

Lifetime analysis, 991–995, 1145

Lifetime effect, 995

Lifted domain, 176

Lifting compiler transformation, *see* Lambda lifting

Lightweight closure conversion, 1089, 1117

Linearization of code, in CPS conversion, 1042, 1043, 1047

Linear type, 1146

Linked environment, 1090–1093

Linking, 890–891, 1014, *see also* Globalization; Loading modules

Linking language, 890

Link time, 890

Linux, reference counts in file system, 1132

LISP, *see also* COMMON LISP; SCHEME
    association list, 550

avoiding variable capture in macros with gensym, 331

compositional programming, 613

currying, lack of, 221, 1169

dynamic scoping, 338

encoding sums, 567

evaluation strategy, 1170

FL syntax vs. LISP syntax, 210

FUNARG problem, 378

garbage collection, 1120, 1121

generic functions, 380

lambda notation vs., 1169–1170

list-manipulation libraries, 239

macros, 379

mutable one-slot cell, 397

object-oriented dialects, 362

parentheses required, 1158, 1170

procedure signatures, lack of, 1169

s-expression notation, 43

sum-of-products data via s-expressions, 580

value-returning function, 385

LISP MACHINE LISP, generic functions, 380

List, 540
    association list, 540, 550
    chain of pairs, 221
    heterogeneous vs. homogeneous, 686
    higher-order list procedure, 239–240
    list node as heap block in FRM, 1128
    stream vs., 559
    sum of products, 577
    typed, 685–688

list, 219, 221
    desugaring in FL, 220, 233
    in FLARE, 813
    in FLEX, 686
    match pattern, 603
    need for type in, 686–687

list? (type predicate), 236, 238

list-data (data declaration), 586

list-map (higher-order description example), 755

list-module (FLEX/M example), 898

listof (type constructor), 685–688
  covariant subtyping in FLEX/S, 703
  definition in FLEX/M, 895
  definition in FLEX/SPD, 754
  in FLARE, 813
  in FLEX/M list module type, 899
  kinding of, in FLEX/SPDK, 761–762
  type equivalence, 686
[*listof*-≈] (type-equivalence rule), 686
[*listof*-⊑] (FLEX/S subtype rule), 703
Lit (literal domain in FL dialects), 211
  in FLK DS, 282
  in metaCPS conversion, 1061
  in simple CPS conversion, 1051
lit (ELM expression constructor), 585
lit~ (ELM expression deconstructor),
  585
Literal, *see also* Lit
  in FLICK standard DS, 477
  in FLK, 209
  in FLK DS, 282, 283
  primitive name, 307
  translation of HOOK message-passing
    literals to FL, 371
  type rule in μFLEX, 644
Literal pattern, 590
  desugaring in match, 596
[*lit-pure*] (FLARE syntactic purity
    axiom), 816
Live heap block, 1120, 1130–1133
Live register, 1112
load (module load), 893, 899, 925–931
  referential transparency in, 930
  semantics with compile-time
    comparison, 929
  semantics with load-time comparison,
    927
  type soundness of, 926, 927–931
[*load*$_{CTdyn}$] (FLEX/M reduction), 929
[*load*$_{CTstat}$] (FLEX/M type axiom), 929
[*load*$_{LTdyn}$] (FLEX/M reduction), 927
[*load*$_{LTstat}$] (FLEX/M type axiom), 927
Load dependency, 929
Loading modules, 899, 925–931

Local binding, *see* let; letrec; let*;
    recur
Locality restriction of implicit projection,
    920, 921
Location, 397
  in CBL product, 553
  in mutable product, 563
  in POSTHEAP, 110
  in SOS, 405
Location (domain), 412
Location (SOS domain), 406
lock (data sealing), 843–847
Lock/key for data abstraction, 843–847
logapp (boolean operation), 260
Logical operator, *see also* Primitive
    operator
  on Church booleans, 301
  conjunction (∧), 1151, 1162
  contrapositive, 1151
  disjunction (∨), 1151, 1162
  existential quantification (∃), *see*
    Existential quantification
  implication, 1151
  in EL dialects, 25
  in EL DS, 129
  in FL dialects, 213
  in metalanguage, 1151–1152
  negation (¬), 1151, 1162
  short-circuit, 222, *see also* scand; scor
  universal quantification (∀), *see*
    Universal quantification
LogicalOperator (domain), 25
Logical relations, 699
Logic programming, 445, 538, 612
login! (quota construct), 492–493
LOGO, as dynamically typed language,
    623
logout! (quota construct), 492–493
longjmp/setjmp (*C* nonlocal exit), 506
lookup (POSTLISP command), 109
lookup (environment procedure in
    FLEX/M), 901
  list representation, 903
  procedure representation, 905

lookup (environment lookup), 277
Loop, *see also* Iteration
  Church numeral, 298
  early termination of, 445
  infinite, *see* Divergence;
    Nontermination
  `while` sugar, 399, 401
`loop` (POSTFIX command), 68
`loop` (looping construct), 488–490
  as sugar in FLIC+{`label`, `jump`}, 501
[*loop*] (POSTFIX SOS rule), 68
Loophole, type, *see* Type loophole
Looping SOS configuration ($\stackrel{\infty}{\Rightarrow}$), 50
`loopout` (looping token in SOS), 50
Lower bound, 176
LProd (CBL product domain), 557
`lprod` (CBL product creation), 552–555
  DS, 555, 557
  SOS, 553–555
[*lprod*] (stateful reduction rule), 553
`*lprod*` (CBL product value), 553
`lt` (POSTFIX command), 8, 40, *see also*
  Relational operator
  informal semantics, 10
  POSTFIX DS, 137
lub (least upper bound), 176
Lucassen, John M., 1000
$\mathcal{LV}$ (L-Value meaning function)
  CBR DS for mutable tuples, 566
  CBR FLAVARK DS, 435
L-value
  of expression, 436
  of mutable variable, 432

$\mathcal{M}$ (type reconstruction algorithm), 836
Machine language (typeless), 622
MacLisp, FEXPR construct, 330
MacQueen, David, 940
Macro, 330, 379
  dynamic scoping in macro systems, 338
  high-level language for, 379
  hygienic, 331, 379
  in POSTMAC, 107
Main memory, 1123

`make-account` (procedure)
  implementation, 402
  specification, 384
make-expt (higher-order function), 1160,
  1166
`make-pt`
  dependent type implementation, 871
  dynamic type implementation, 840
  existentially typed object
    implementation, 857
  existential type implementation,
    848–849
  message-passing implementation
    (`make-pair-point`,
    `make-proc-point`), 843
  nonce type implementation, 860–861
  using dynamic lock and key, 844
make$_{TCS}$ (type-constraint set), 788, 789,
  790
Mann, Thomas (quoted), 3
Manual heap deallocation, 1120
`map` (list procedure), 239, 241
  polymorphic, 726, 730
map (metalanguage sequence function),
  1183
`mapperof` (higher-order description), 755
MapReduce model, 613
mapsub, 1012, 1034
Mark-sweep GC, 1141
Match
  clause, 590
  expansion phase, 923
  of pattern and value, 1192
  s-expression pattern, 27
match (extension to **cases**), 590,
  1190–1194
`match` (FL pattern matching), 590–612
  body, 590
  clause, 590
  desugaring, 594–605
  desugaring, final version, 603
  desugaring, first cut, 597
  desugaring, optimization of, 605
  discriminant, 590

match (*continued*)
   failure thunk in match desugaring, 595
   free identifiers, 602
   in FLARE, 831
   in FLEX/M, 894, 921–923
   in FLEX/SP, 742
   informal semantics, 590
   pattern, 590
   success expression in desugaring, 596
   well-typed vs. ill-typed, 593
match-prod (pattern-based tuple access)
   type reconstruction, 825
Matrix module, 360, 361
max (procedure), 236
maxeff (combine effects), 946, 947, 949
maybe-cell (assignment conversion
     function), 1023, 1024
McCarthy, John, 42, 43, 1145
mc→exp (metaCPS function), 1060
$\mathcal{MCPS}$ (metaCPS), 1058–1070
Meaning
   of phrase in DS, 115
   of whole from meaning of parts, 116
meaning (function), 151
Meaning function, 115, *see also* Valuation
     function
   operational behavior and, 151
member?, 237, 238
Memo (domain), 435
   in CBL product DS, 555, 557
Memoization, 314, 555
   in CBL parameter passing, 434
   in CBL product, 555
   for nonstrict parameter passing, 314
Memory allocation, *see* Heap allocation
Memory compaction, 1132
Memory fragmentation, 1131
Memory leak, 1120
Memory management, *see* Garbage
     collection (GC)
Memory page, 1129
Memory tracing for GC, 1132–1133
Mental gymnastics, 446
merge (list procedure), 240, 242
merge (environment merge, ⊎), 277

merge-sort, 240, 242
Message (HOOK domain), 362, 363
Message-passing object, *see also* Object
   in object-oriented programming, 362
   procedural representation of, 403, 842,
     885
Metacall, 1060
Metacircular interpreter for FL, 242
MetaCont (domain), 1060
Metacontinuation, 1059
MetaCPS conversion, 1058–1070
   beta reduction in, 1062
   of cwcc, 1072
   of exceptions, 1072
   of label and jump, 1070–1075
Metalanguage, 7, 16, 1147–1196
   boolean operator, 1151
   commenting convention, 1148
   conditional function (if_S), 1164
   domain, 1171–1186
   function, 1155–1170
   function domain, 1184–1186
   kernel, 1186–1188
   lambda notation, 1165–1170
   logical operator, 1151–1152
   predicate, 1151–1152
   product domain, 1173–1175
   recursion, 1168–1169
   relation, 1153–1155
   sequence domain, 1181–1184
   set, 1148–1151
   sum domain, 1176–1181
   syntactic sugar, 1188–1195
   tuple, 1152–1153
Metaprogramming, 7
Method
   class method, 362
   constructor method, 366
   controlling complexity with, 333
   in HOOK/HOOPLA, 363–370
   instance method, 362
method (HOOK object constructor), 363
   translation to FL, 371
mfst (mutable pair selector), 421

mget (mutable product projection), 562, 1031
  CBR DS for mutable tuples, 566
  CBVS DS, 564
  desugaring with mutable cell, 563
mgu (most general unifier), 785
Milner, Robin, 835, 836
min (procedure), 236
Mini-language, 7
Minsky, Marvin, 1145
MIRANDA
  as implicitly typed language, 626
  as purely functional language, 384
  as purely functional lazy language, 209
  HDM type reconstruction, 836
Mitchell, John, 885
Mixin, 367–368, 380
ML, see also OCAML; SML
  as block-structured language, 337
  as call-by-value language, 309
  as function-oriented language, 209
  as implicitly typed language, 626
  as mostly functional language, 384
  as statically typed language, 623
  constraint-based type reconstruction
    for, 836
  dependent types in DML, 887
  first-class control point, 497
  garbage collection, 1120
  implicit resignaling of exceptions, 514
  implicit typing example, 626
  list-manipulation libraries, 239
  module system, 940
  mutable cell ref, 397
  pattern matching, 590, 605–610, 612,
    768, 829
  polymorphism, 768
  second-class modules, 891
  strict application, 215
  sum-of-products data, 579, 829
  type reconstruction, 812
  universal polymorphism, 627
  unsafe features, 622
  value restriction, 817

ML-style type reconstruction, 812
$mm \in Memo$, 435
mnew (mutable product allocation), 1101
Mobile code, security of, 999–1000
MODULA-2, separate compilation, 940
Modularity
  of laziness, 440, 559, 612
  polymorphism and, 727
  of state in imperative program, 397,
    404, 440
Module, 352, 540, 889–941, see also
    Record
  arithmetic module example, 358
  client, 352
  coherence problem, 934–937
  controlling complexity with, 333
  dot notation, 898
  dynamic semantics, 381, 923–925
  environment example, 901–906
  examples of, 356–359
  exports, 333, 889
  first-class, 890
  imports, 333, 352, 889
  interface of, 352
  linking, 890–891
  loading, 899, 925–931
  matrix module example, 360, 361
  multiple bindings in, 890
  record vs., 353
  scoping in FLEX/M, 910–911
  second-class, 891
  separate compilation of, 890
  signature of, 897
  static dependent types and, 891, 911
  static semantics of FLEX/M, 910–923
  subtyping, 912, 913
  table example, 906–909
  type, 627, see also moduleof
  type equivalence and, 911, 913
  type rules for FLEX/M, 912–918
module, 893–895, 914
  dynamic semantics in FLEX/M, 924
  static semantics in FLEX/M, 917

moduleof (type), 893, 897, 914
  subtyping in FLEX/M, 913
  type equivalence, 913
  type rules involving, in FLEX/M, 917
[*moduleof*-≈] (type-equivalence rule), 913
[*moduleof*-⊑] (FLEX/M subtype rule),
  912, 913
[*moduleof-elim*] (FLEX/M type rule),
  917
[*moduleof-intro*] (FLEX/M type rule),
  917
Moggi, Eugenio, 440
Monad, 396, 440
Monadic style, 124, 394–396, 414, 417
  via after and return in FL, 394
  do notation in HASKELL, 396
  effects and, 1001
  lack of modularity, 404, 440
  to hide state plumbing, 395, 414
  to simulate stateful features, 440
Monomorphism, 655–660, 725, *see also*
  Simple type system
  of FLEX type system, 629
Monotonic function, 187
Morris, F. Lockwood, 537
Morris, James, 537
Mortis, rigor, 57
Moscow ML, 941
Moses, Joel, 378
Most general unifier (mgu), 785
Mostly functional language, 384, *see also*
  Function-oriented programming
mpair (mutable pair), 421
MProd (mutable tuple domain)
  in CBVC DS of mutable tuples, 565
  in CBVS DS of mutable tuples, 564
mprod (mutable product), 562, 1031
  CBVS DS, 564
  desugaring with mutable cell, 563
mprod=? (mutable product equality),
  1031
mselect (module selection), 898
  desugaring in FLEX/M, 894

mset! (mutable product assignment),
  562, 1031
  CBVS DS, 564
  desugaring with mutable cell, 563
msnd (mutable pair selector), 421
Muchnick, Steven, 1116
mul (POSTFIX command), 8, 40, *see also*
  Arithmetic operator
  informal semantics, 10
  POSTFIX DS, 137
Multiabstraction, *see* abs
Multiapplication, *see also* app,
  Application
  desugaring in FL, 220, 233
  desugaring in HOOK, 369
  in FL, 218–221
  in μFLARE/FLARE kernel, 772
  in μFLEX/FLEX kernel, 628, 632
  in μFLEX SOS, 664
  in lambda calculus, 291
  kernel construct (app) in FIL, 1030
  tuple-based desugaring, 257
  type rule in dependent type system,
  875
  type rule in μFLEX, 644
Multiple arguments
  of function, 1161–1164
  of procedure, 214
Multiple inheritance, 380
Multiple-value return, 450–455
  via result and result-bind, 710–712
  simulating with receiver procedure,
  394, 451–453, 1164–1165
Multiplication function (×), 1163, *see
  also* *; Arithmetic operator; mul
  on Church numerals, 300
Multistep SOS transition relation ($\overset{*}{\Rightarrow}$), 50
Multithreaded computation, 997
Mutable cell, 397–399
  assignment conversion from mutable
  variable, 1019
  content of, 397
  as getter/setter procedures, 710
  for mutable data, 563

mutable variable in CBR vs., 437
operations on, 398–399
typed, 681–682
type reconstruction and, 837
Mutable data, 397
  array, 548
  cell, *see* Mutable cell
  deep copy, 565
  invariant subtyping of, 704–706
  mutable tuple, 562–566, 1031, 1101, 1104, 1128
  pair, 421
  parameter passing of mutable products, 563–566
  product, 561–566, 1031, 1101, 1104, 1128
  sequence, 561–562
  shallow copy, 565
  string, 548
  using mutable cell, 563
Mutable variable, 429–430
  assignment conversion to mutable cell, 1019
  closure conversion and, 1081–1082, 1092
  copy propagation and, 1034
  dereferencing, 432
  in CBL FLAVARK DS, 434–436
  in CBN FLAVARK DS, 433
  in CBR FLAVARK DS, 436–438
  in CBV FLAVARK DS, 433
  in FLARE/V, 1009
  in FLAVAR, 430–439
  in FLAVARK DS, 431
  L-value, 432
  mutable cell vs., in CBR, 437
  R-value, 432, 436
  type reconstruction, 820–821, 837
Mutation, 385, *see also* Effect
MutIds (mutated free identifiers function), 1018, 1020, 1022
Mutual recursion, *see also* Recursion, mutual
  as single recursive definition, 163

in FL, 224–226, *see also* letrec
in FLEX type, 688, *see also* tletrec
in lambda calculus, 304

$N \in$ IntLit, 25, 211
$\mathcal{N}$ (numeral meaning function)
  in EL dialects, 118
  in FLK, 283
  in PostFix, definition, 137
  in PostFix, signature, 135
  in restricted ELMM, 118
$\overline{n}$ (Church numeral), 298, *see also* Church numeral
Name, *see* Identifier; Variable
Nameable (domain)
  Expressible vs., 278
  in CBD, 328
  in CBN vs. CBV, 316, 317
  in FLAVARK, 431
  in FLICK, 416, 418
  in FLICK standard DS, 473
  in FLK, 276, 278
Nameable value, 275, 308, 319–320, *see also Nameable*
Name capture, *see* Variable capture
Name control, 308, 332–359, 891
  modules and, 889
Named product, 353–359, 549–550
  typed, 677–678, 821–826
Named sum
  DS, 573–576
  SOS, 572
Name equivalence of types, 864
Name hiding, 333, 901
Name resolution, 1014, *see also* Linking
Namespace, 308, 347–351, 891
  in HOOPLA, 376
  multiple, 347, 635, 636
  multiple, in Common Lisp, 348
Naming, 307–381
  binding construct, 307, *see also* Binding construct
  cognitive issues with, 332–333
  engineering issues with, 333

Naming (*continued*)
  expression as structured name, 307, 869
  import of module bindings, 333, 352,
      889
  in POSTLISP, 109
  in POSTTEXT, 106
  literals and identifiers as primitive
      names, 307
  name control, *see* Name control
  name hiding, 333, 901
  parameter passing, *see* Parameter
      passing
  renaming, *see* Alpha-renaming
  scope, *see* Scope of a variable
  unique, *see* Unique naming
Naming context, 443
  for referential transparency, 389
nam-to-comp (computation function)
  in FLICK, 414
  in FLK, 279, 281
Nanopass compiler for SCHEME, 1116
n-ary relation, 1153
Nat, 1148
NatLit (natural numeral domain), 406
nats (infinite stream), 558
Natural semantics, 75, *see also* Big-step
      operational semantics (BOS)
NAVAL (CBN and CBV language), 327
$\mathbb{NC} \in$ NormContext, 292
$NE \in$ NumExp, 25
$\mathcal{NE}$ (numerical-expression meaning
      function), 129
  in ELM, 126
  in ELMM, 121
  in restricted ELMM, 117, 118
Neg (set & domain), 1148
Negation, logical ($\neg$), 1151, 1162
*ness*ness, 362
new (HOOK instance creation), 366
$new-\cdots$ (HOOK literal), 372, 373
new-key (sealing key generator), 843–847
next-location (store function), 412
$NF \in$ NormalForm, 292

n-fold composition
  of functions (f^n), 1159, *see also*
      Church numeral
  of relations, 1155
nget
  CBN product projection, 551–552
  POSTFIX command, 8, 40
  POSTFIX DS for, 137
  POSTFIX informal semantics for, 10
  POSTFIX SOS for, 55
[*nget*]
  POSTFIX SOS rule, 55
  stateless reduction rule, 552
Nielson, Flemming, 1117
Nielson, Hanne Riis, 1117
nil (empty list value), 236
  sum-of-products data version, 586
nlam (NAVAL CBN abstraction), 327
$\mathbb{NLNC} \in$ NonLambdaNormContext, 292
NLNF $\in$ NonLambdaNormalForm, 292
node (tree constructor), 451, 608, 609
  generic type of, 832
node~ (tree deconstructor)
  generic type of, 832
non-boolean (dynamic type error), 473
NonceType (domain), 861
Nonce type, 859–869
  difficulties with, 863–866
  dynamic and static semantics, 861
  import/export restrictions, lack of, 860,
      862
  nonce package, 860
  type generativity in SML and, 886
Nondeterministic, 51, 445, 997
  BOS, 76
  either construct in ELMM, 83
  logic programming, 538
  transition relation, 50, 51
Nondismissal semantics of exceptions,
      522, 528–530
Nonevaluation step relation ($\rightarrowtail$), 271,
      272
  preservation of classification, 273
[*non-exec*] (POSTFIX BOS rule), 78

Nonhierarchical scope, 352–359, 889

Nonimmediate descriptor, 1124

noninteger (exception tag), 516

NonLambdaNormalForm (domain), 292

NonLambdaNormContext (domain), 292

Nonlocal exit, 445, 455–457, 493–506

Nonnormalization step ($\circ_{\overline{n.o.}}$), 294

Nonstrictness, 267, *see also* Laziness; Strictness

  CBN parameter passing, 310, 316

  if as primitive operator in FLK, 267

  inefficiencies associated with, 262, 263

  modeling with envelopes, 269

  nonstrict function, 199

  nonstrict pair, 216–217, 266, 269, 318–320

  nonstrict parameter passing, *see* Call-by-name (CBN); Call-by-need (CBL)

  nonstrict procedure, 215, 262

  nonstrict product, 551–561, *see also* Call-by-name (CBN), product; Lazy (CBL) product; Stream

Nontail call, 1044–1049

Nontermination

  in FLK, 263

  in lambda calculus, 293

  in POSTFIX+{dup}, 101

  represented by $\perp_{Comp}$ in FLK, 275, 280

  represented by $\perp_{Fcn}$ in lambda calculus DS, 296

  represented by bottom ($\perp$), 185

  universality and, 79–80, 100

Nontype error, 661

  stuck at, 666, 780

Normal continuation, 446

Normal form, 50

  of FLK simplification ($\rightarrow$), 272, 273

  in lambda calculus, 292

  weak head, in lambda calculus, 378

NormalForm (domain), 292

Normalization

  in lambda calculus, 292–295

  strong, *see* Strong normalization

Normal-order reduction strategy, 293–295, 309, 377

NormContext (domain), 292

NOT (on Church booleans), 301

not (FL boolean negation), 213

  FL standard library binding for, 236

  in FLK DS, 285

  type in μFLEX, 643

not-a-$\cdots$ (dynamic type error), 281, 473, 479, 480

Notational acrobatics, 57

[not-F] (FLK SOS reduction), 259

[not-T] (FLK SOS reduction), 259

[$npack$] (nonce type rule), 861

[$npackof$-$\approx$] (type-equivalence rule), 861

NProd (CBN product domain), 552

nprod (CBN product creation), 551–552

n-step SOS transition relation ($\overset{n}{\Longrightarrow}$), 50

$NT \in$ NatLit, 406

nth (list indexing procedure), 236, 238

  in letrec desugaring, 224

  variable capture in letrec desugaring, 257

nth (metalanguage sequence function), 1183

n-tuple, 1152

null (empty list procedure), 236

  definition in FLEX/M, 895

  definition in FLEX/SPD, 754

  generic type of list constructor null, 827

  need for type in, 686–687

  pattern example, 592

  polymorphic type of, 728

  sum-of-products data version, 586

  type in FLEX/M list module, 896, 899

  type rule in FLEX, 686

[$null$] (FLEX type rule), 686

null? (empty list predicate), 236

  definition in FLEX/SPD, 754

  polymorphic type of, 728

  type in FLEX/M list module, 899

  type rule in FLEX, 686

[$null?$] (FLEX type rule), 686

null~ (list deconstructor)
  generic type of, 827
  type in FLEX/M list module, 896, 899
Nullary procedure, 221, 228
null-object (HOOK empty object),
    363, 368
Null pointer, in sum-of-products
    encoding, 579
[*num*]
  ELM BOS rule, 77
  ELMM BOS rule, 75
  POSTFIX SOS rule, 54–56
Numeral
  integer vs., 57
  semantics of, 118, 131
NumExp (EL domain), 25
[*nunpack*] (nonce type rule), 861
n-way conditional (cond), 222

O ∈ Primop, *see* Primop
𝒪 (primitive operator meaning function)
  in FLICK, 419
  in FLICK standard DS, 477
  in FLK, 285
o ∈ Outcome, 50
Object, 362, 379
  dot notation, 550
  dynamic semantics, 381
  in HOOK/HOOPLA, 363–370
  in JAVA, 550
  notion of state and, 383–384
  as poor man's closure, 441
  special syntax, 549–550
object (HOOPLA object sugar), 369
Objectification of *ness*ness, 362
Object-oriented programming (OOP),
    362–377, *see also* Stateful language
  class, simulating in prototype-based
    system, 366
  class-based, 362, 366, 379–380
  design dimensions, 379
  generic-function, 380
  inheritance, 366–367
  mixin, 367–368, 380

multimethod, 380
procedural representation of
    message-passing object, 403
programming by differences, 366
prototype-based, 380
sigma calculus, 381
state and, 403, 441
stateful programming and, 384
type-based, 381, 768
Observable properties, 389
Observational equivalence (=_{obs}), 90, 91
  adequacy and, 157
  full abstraction and, 159
  in ISWIM, 306
  in POSTFIX, 89–100
  POSTFIX transform equivalence and,
    96–98
Observational uniqueness, 157
  of EL, 158
  of POSTFIX, 158
OCAML
  applicative functors, 939
  functors distinct from procedures, 900
  modules with abstract and concrete
    type definitions, 893
  object-oriented language, 362
  pattern-based tuple access, 825
  row variables with object types, 836
  unique record field names, 822
OCCAM module system, 941
Occurs check, 785, 786
  removing to reconstruct recursive
    types, 836
odd? (mutual recursion example)
  in FL, 224–226, 230
  in FLEX, 636
  in lambda calculus, 304
  in recursive record, 354
OF (SOS output function), *see* Output
    function of SOS
one (sum creation), 569, 570
  CBV named sum DS, 575
  CBV named sum SOS, 572
  match pattern, 602

type reconstruction, 826

type rule in FLEX, 684

type rule in FLEX/SPDK, 763

one-arg (standard DS function), 473, 475

Oneof, 568, 570, *see also* Sum

injection function (*Inj k*), 1176, 1189

metalanguage sum value, 1176

sum, 567

Oneof (named sum semantic domain), 573, 575

oneof (sum type constructor), 682–685

in FLEX/S, 704

kind checking in FLEX/SPDK, 760

subtyping in FLEX/S, 703

type equivalence, 684

[*oneof-≈*] (type-equivalence rule), 684, 685

[*oneof-⊑*] (FLEX/S subtype rule), 703, 704

[*oneof-elim1*] (FLEX type rule), 684

[*oneof-elim2*] (FLEX type rule), 684, 685

[*oneof-intro*]

FLEX/SPDK type rule, 763

FLEX type rule, 683, 684

Oneof pattern, in metalanguage, 1192

One-step confluence, 82

One-step SOS transition relation (⇒), 49

One-to-one correspondence, 1150, 1160

OOP, *see* Object-oriented programming

Opaque type, 757, 933, 934

open (module open), 893, 898, 915, 916

dynamic semantics in FLEX/M, 924

static semantics in FLEX/M, 917

Open expression, 246

Operand of application, 214, 1158, 1187

Operation, pending, *see* Computation, pending

Operational execution, 58–62

Operational reasoning, 79–100

Operational semantics, 15, 45–112

behavior, 50–52, *see also* Behavior of program

big-step, *see* Big-step operational semantics (BOS)

denotational semantics related to, 150–160

denotational semantics vs., 161–162

drawbacks of, 113

game board, 48

natural, *see* Big-step operational semantics (BOS)

reasoning with, 79–100

small-step, *see* Small-step operational semantics (SOS)

of *X*, *see* *X*, BOS; *X*, SOS

Operator of application, 214, 1158, 1187

Optimization, *see also* Efficiency

aliasing inhibits, 944

code hoisting, 1029

common subexpression elimination, 1028

constant propagation, 1053

copy propagation, 1033

dead code elimination, 1028

def-data desugaring, 587

of descriptor encoding, 1126–1127

effect-based, 1026–1029

eta reduction, 1033

of heap block representation, 1129

of match desugaring, 605

memoization, 434

parallelization, 1027

peephole optimization, 1066

procedure inlining, 1053, 1056, 1088, 1116

of sum-of-products encoding, 578

tail-call optimization, 1064

OR (on Church booleans), 301

or (EL/FL boolean disjunction), 25, 213

type in *μ*FLEX, 643

Order of evaluation, *see* Evaluation order; Reduction strategy

out (communication effect), 998

Outcome (outcome domain of SOS), 50

Output function of SOS (*OF*), 48, 50

in CBL product SOS, 553

in CBN product SOS, 552

in CBV named sum SOS, 572

Output function of SOS (*continued*)
  in CBV product SOS, 543
  in μFLARE, 779
  in μFLEX, 664
  in FLICK, 407
  in FLICK+{label, jump} SOS, 503
  in FLK, 260
Overloading, 748
override (record combination), 353, 354, 550
  DS, 357

$\mathbb{P} \in$ PostfixProgContext, 91
$P \in$ Prog, *see* Prog
$\mathcal{P}$ (program meaning function)
  in EL, 129
  in ELM, 126
  in ELMM, 121
  in FLICK, 419
  in FLICK standard DS, 477
  in FLICK standard DS for exceptions, 524
  in FLK, 283, 289
  in PostFix, definition, 137
  in PostFix, signature, 135
  in restricted ELMM, 117, 118
pabs (polymorphic abstraction in FLEX/SP), 728, 729, 730
  as compile-type fiction, 734
  dynamic semantics, 731, 736, 747
  in bounded quantification, 745, 747
  in FLEX/SPD, 752
  in FLEX/SPDK, 759, 763
  static semantics, 731, 747, 763
pack (data abstraction creation)
  in dependent type system, 873, 875
  in existential type system, 850
  in nonce type system, 861
Package, 848
  dependent package, 870
  existential package, 849
  nonce package, 860
package (STACKFIX command), 105
Packed representation of data, 1129

packof (data abstraction type)
  in dependent type system, 873, 874, 875
  in existential type system, 850
  in nonce type system, 861
Page of memory, 1129
PAIR (Church pair constructor), 302
Pair, 1152, *see also* Church pair; pair; Product
  mutable, 421
  positional product, 541
  strict vs. nonstrict, 318–320
  sum represented as, 567
  typed, 675–676
Pair (semantic domain)
  in FLICK, 418
  in FLK, 276
  in strict vs. nonstrict pair DS, 319
pair (FL pairing expression), 211, 215–216
  generic constructor type of, 832
  generic type for in FLARE, 813
  in FLARE, 813
  in FLICK standard DS, 477
  in FLK DS, 282, 283
  in FLK InputExp domain, 258
  in FLK ValueExp domain, 258
  PostFix command, 102, 141
  as primitive operator, 268
  strict vs. nonstrict semantics, 319
  sum-of-products data version, 586
  type rule in FLEX, 675
  as user-defined procedure, 268
pair? (FL pair type predicate), 213
pair~, generic deconstructor type of, 832
pairans (SOS pair outcome token), 258, 260, 319
  meaning in FLK SOS, 266
pair-data (pair data declaration), 586
pairof (type constructor), 675–676
  covariant subtyping in FLEX/S, 703
  definition in FLEX/SPD, 754
  in FLARE, 813
  type equivalence, 680

[*pairof*] (FLEX/S subtype rule), 707

[*pairof-≈*] (type-equivalence rule), 679, 680

[*pairof-⊑*] (FLEX/S subtype rule), 702, 703

[*pairof-elim-fst*] (FLEX type rule), 675, 676

[*pairof-elim-snd*] (FLEX type rule), 675

[*pairof-intro*] (FLEX type rule), 675

`pair-point-impl` (pair implementation of points), 840

Pair tree, 217, 259
    partridge not in a, 217

Pairwise disjoint, 1150

Paragraph ≠ life, 19

Parallelism, 1027, *see also* Concurrency

Parameter
    actual, of procedure, 214
    formal, of abstraction, 244
    formal, of function, 1165
    formal, of method, 363
    formal, of procedure, 214
    formal, of program, 209
    formal, of program, scope of, 230

Parameterized arrow/procedure type, 870, 873

Parameter passing, 308, 309–332, *see also* Reduction strategy
    call-by-denotation (CBD), 328–332
    call-by-name (CBN), 309, 310–328, 377
    call-by-name (CBN) with mutable variables, 433
    call-by-need (CBL), 434–436
    call-by-reference (CBR), 436–438
    call-by-value (CBV), 309, 310–328, 377, 378
    call-by-value (CBV) with mutable variables, 433
    call-by-value-copy (CBVC), 564–566
    call-by-value-sharing (CBVS), 563–566
    mutable products and, 563–566
    mutable variables and, 432–439

Parametric polymorphism, *see* Universal polymorphism

Parent environment, 1090

Parentheses
    ≠ death, 19
    in lambda notation, 1168
    in LISP vs. metalanguage, 1170
    in metalanguage, 1158
    in s-expression, 24

Parser generator, 43
    semantic actions and DS, 116

Partial evaluation, 1059

Partial function ($\rightharpoonup$), 1156, 1157
    lambda (λ) abstraction and, 1165

Partial order, 174–182, 1155
    complete, 182–184
    discrete, 175
    flat, 176
    pointed, 185–187, 321

Partition, 250, 1150
    of set by equivalence relation, 1154

`partition` (list partitioning view), 610

partition (assignment conversion function), 1022, 1023

Partridge, not in a `pair` tree, 217

PASCAL
    answer domain, 474
    array, as homogeneous product, 548
    array, as mutable sequence, 561
    array indexing, 547, 548
    array length in array type, 627
    as block-structured language, 337
    as call-by-value language, 309
    as explicitly typed language, 625
    as imperative language, 384
    as monomorphic language, 629, 658
    as statically typed language, 623
    call-by-reference parameter passing, 436
    call-by-value-copy of arrays and records, 566
    closure conversion via defunctionalization, 1088
    command, 472
    conservative GC, 1127, 1142
    dangling pointers, lack of, 1144

PASCAL (*continued*)
  enumerations as indices, 562
  function vs. procedure, 209
  garbage collection, lack of, 1121
  limitations on passable procedures, 320
  mutable variable, 430
  pointer variable, as mutable cell, 397
  record, 353, 550, 561
  simulating higher-order procedures,
    1076
  strict application, 215
  sum (variant record), 567, 583
  type conversion, 716
  type loophole, 567, 583, 621
  unstorability of procedures, 412
  valueless procedure, 385
  value-returning function, 385
Passable (semantic domain)
  to model parameter passing, 320
Passable value, 319–320
Password data abstraction mechanism in
  PEBBLE, 886
Pattern, 590
  in abstraction parameter, 1194
  constructor application pattern, 590
  identifier pattern, 590
  informal matching rules, 591
  in **let** expression, 1194
  in **match** clause, 1191
  `list` pattern, 603
  literal pattern, 590
  metalanguage constant pattern, 1192
  metalanguage oneof pattern, 1192
  metalanguage tuple pattern, 1192
  metalanguage variable pattern, 1192
  named subpattern (`<->`), 604
  record and oneof patterns, 602
  sequence pattern, 31–32, 1192
  s-expression pattern, 26–32, *see also*
    S-expression pattern
  wildcard pattern (`_`), 590
Pattern (syntactic domain), 590
Pattern for s-expression, 26

Pattern matching, 124, 590–612
  desugaring of `match`, 594–605
  desugaring of `match`, final version, 603
  desugaring of `match`, first cut, 597
  efficient, in SML, 601
  in ML, 612
  optimizing `match` desugaring, 605
  typed, *see* Typed pattern matching
  view, 605–612
Payload of a sum, 567
`pcall` (polymorphic projection in
  FLEX/SP), 728, 729, 730
  as compile-time fiction, 734
  dynamic semantics, 731, 736, 747
  in bounded quantification, 747
  in FLEX/SPDK, 763
  static semantics, 731, 747, 763
PCF (Programming Computable
  Functions), 699
PD ∈ ProgDesc, 753
PEBBLE
  dependent types, 886
  first-class types, 941
  language with `type : type`, 768
  password data abstraction mechanism,
    886
Peephole optimization, 1066, 1114
`perim` (shape procedure)
  using explicit deconstructors, 584
  using `match`, 592
  using predicates and selectors, 589
  using record and oneof patterns, 602
  using records and oneofs, 578
  using `struct` and `union` in C, 582
  using typed sums and products, 683
PERL
  as dynamically typed language, 623
  record, 353
  type markers, 625
Permutation, 1160
Persistence, in object-oriented
  programming, 379
Peyton Jones, Simon, 1116

Phase distinction, 877, 878, 886

Phrase tag, 30

Phrase type in s-expression production, 26

Pierce, Benjamin C., 699

Pivot of a partition, 610

plet (FL^{--} procedure binding), 349

plet (polymorphic binding), 751, 753, 754

  opaque version, 757

pletrec (recursive polymorphic binding), 753, 754

Plotkin, Gordon, 112, 305, 378, 885

Plumbing

  of continuations, 490

  of exception handler environment, 524

  of sharing information in modules, 936

  of state, hiding with monadic style, 395, 414

point (sample HOOPLA class), 371

Pointed partial order, 185–187, 321, 413

Pointer, 1122

  in PostHeap, 110

Pointer variable in C/Pascal, as mutable cell, 397

Pollution, in closure conversion, 1086

Polymorphic function, 1167

Polymorphic lambda calculus, 764, 768

  undecidability of type reconstruction, 837

[polymorphic projection] (FLEX/SP type rule), 731

[polymorphic projection$_{BQ}$] (FLEX/SP type rule), 747

Polymorphic type, 701, 725–750, see also Universal polymorphism

  in second-order lambda calculus, 764

Polymorphic value, 725, 728

  in second-order lambda calculus, 764

Polymorphic value projection

  explicit, 728, 729, 730, 731, 736, 738, 804

  implicit, 730, 896, 918–921

  implicit, in FX-87 and FX-91, 768

  implicit, in type-reconstructed language, 804

  locality restriction of, 920, 921

  in second-order lambda calculus, 764

Polymorphism, 701–768, see also Polymorphic type; Polymorphic value; Subtyping

  ad hoc, 748–750

  bounded quantification, 745–746

  parametric, see Universal polymorphism

  in type reconstruction, 772, 801–813

  universal, see Universal polymorphism

pop (PostFix command), 8, 40

  informal semantics, 10

  PostFix DS, 137

  PostFix SOS, 55

pop (function in PostFix DS)

  definition, 143, 144

  specification, 133

[pop] (PostFix SOS rule), 55

Porter, Cole (quoted), 567

Pos (positive number set & semantic domain), 1148

Positional product, 541–549

  fixed-length, 541–545

  immutable sequence, 544–545

  immutable tuple, 541–542

  size, 544

  typed, 676–677

  type reconstruction, 825

  updatable sequence, 545–547

  variable-length, 545–547

Positional sum, 576

  call-by-name (CBN), 576

  call-by-value (CBV), 576

PosLit (positive numeral domain), 1031

Postcondition of transformation, 1013

PostFix (stack mini-language), 8–15

  $\perp$ in recursive domains, 150

  adequacy of, 158

  BOS, 77–78

POSTFIX (*continued*)

  command specification, 10

  compositionality of stack transforms in DS, 135

  configuration energy in, 84–85

  context-based SOS, 73, 74

  denotational soundness of, 151–156

  deterministic behavior, 58

  DS, 131–145

  error, 52–53, 60

  error, as stuck state, 58

  informal semantics, 9–12

  lack of full abstraction of, 160

  meaning function, 134–145

  observational equivalence in, 89–100

  observational uniqueness of, 158

  program, 8

  safe transformation in, 89–100

  safe transformation in, using DS, 147, 150

  semantic algebra, 131–134

  semantic domains, 131–132

  SOS, 52–54

  SOS, with one-component configurations, 70

  syntax, 8–9, 39–42

  termination, 84–89

  transform equivalence, 92–100

  translation from ELMM, 100

  valuation functions, 134–145

postfix (POSTFIX program keyword), 8

  in POSTFIX DS, 137

  in POSTFIX SOS, 53

POSTFIX+{dup}, 101–102

  expressing recursion in, 102–103

  POSTSAFE and, 104

  type system for, 654–655

  universality, 102, 112

POSTFIX2 (POSTFIX with alternative syntax), 39–42

  DS, 141

  SOS, 60

  termination, 87

Postfix calculator language, 61

PostfixEvalSequenceContext (domain), 74

PostfixProgContext (domain), 91

PostFixRedex (domain), 74

PostfixSequenceContext (domain), 91

POSTHEAP (POSTFIX plus a heap), 110

POSTLISP (POSTFIX plus name stacks), 109

POSTLOOP (POSTFIX plus looping), 103

POSTMAC (POSTFIX plus macros), 107

POSTSAFE (POSTFIX plus safe duplication), 104

POSTSAVE (POSTFIX plus stack save/restore), 105

POSTSCRIPT

  as call-by-value language, 309

  as stack language, 8

POSTTEXT (POSTFIX plus dictionaries), 106

Powerdomain, 182

  partial order on, 182

Powerset $(\mathcal{P}(\ldots))$, 1150

Pragmatics, 4, 6

Precondition of transformation, 1013

Predicate

  in def-datatype sugar, 589

  in metalanguage, 1151–1152, 1163

Predicative type system, 735

  of μFLARE, 804

prefix (iterator example), 509

prefix (stream prefix), 556

Prefix ordering on sequence domain, 179

Preservation theorem for type soundness

  in μFLARE, 780

  in μFLEX, 662

prim (FL primitive application), 211, 212

  in FIL_{cps}, 1046

  in FIL_{lift}, 1095

  in FIL_{reg}, 1101

  in FLICK standard DS, 477

  in FLK DS, 282, 283

  in FLK SOS, 259, 260–261

  in metaCPS conversion, 1061

  in simple CPS conversion, 1051

  optionality in FL programs, 230–231

  type rule in μFLEX, 644

[*prim*]
  μFLARE type rule, 775
  FLARE/E type/effect rule, 952, 953
  μFLEX type rule, 644, 647
primes (infinite stream), 558
Primitive application, *see also* Arithmetic
    operation; Relational operation
  error in, 213
  explicit order of, in CPS, 1042, 1043,
    1047
  FL sugar for (@), 218
  in FIL_{reg}, 1100
  in FLK SOS, 260–261
Primitive domain, 1171
Primitive operator, 20, *see also*
    Arithmetic operator; Logical
    operator; Relational operator
  extending language with new operator,
    235
  number of arguments in FIL_{reg}, 1100
  in EL dialects, 25
  in FLK DS, 285
  in FLK SOS, 259
  in FL standard library, 213, 236
  top-level binding for, 236
  type assignment in μFLEX, 643
Primitive set elements, 1148
Primitive syntactic domain, 25
Primitive type environment (TE_{prim}),
    643, 647
Primop (primitive operator domain)
  in FLEX/M, 893
  in FIL, 1031
  in FIL_{reg}, 1101
  in FLARE, 814
  in FLARE-to-FIL translation, 1037
  in FLARE/V, 1010
  in FL dialects, 211
  in μFLEX, 628
  in FLICK, 398
  in wrapping-based globalization, 1016
[*prim-pure*] (FLARE syntactic purity
    rule), 816
[$prim_R$] (μFLARE type reconstruction
    rule), 793, 794

[$prim_Z$] (FLARE/E type/effect
    reconstruction rule), 964
[$prim_Z$]FLARE/E type/effect
    reconstruction rule, 963, 964
Principal type, 796
  property, 836, 971
  for type reconstruction algorithm, 799
Principal typing property, 836
Private Data, *see* Captain Abstraction;
    Data abstraction
Proc (procedure semantic domain)
  in CBV recursion, 321
  in computation-based exception DS,
    524, 525
  in FLICK, 418
  in FLICK DS, 418–419
  in FLICK standard DS, 473, 474–475
  in FLICK standard DS for exceptions,
    520, 521
  in FLK, 276, 278
  in static vs. dynamic scope, 335
proc? (FL procedure type predicate), 213
procans (SOS procedure outcome token),
    258, 260
Procedural abstraction, 841
Procedure, 209, *see also* Function
  closure, 378
  as continuation, 446–471
  controlling complexity with, 333
  early termination of, 445, 455–457
  exception-handling procedure, 515
  first-class, 214–215
  first-class vs. second-class, 349
  first-order, in FL^{--}, 349
  function vs., 209, 1157–1158
  higher-order, 214–215, 239–240, 305
  higher-order to first-order conversion,
    1075
  iterating procedure, 507
  iterative, 449
  simulating multiple arguments via
    currying, 214
  virtual, *see* Method
  yielding procedure, 507

procedure (procedure outcome in FL),
    212
Procedure application, *see* `app`
Procedure body, 214
Procedure call, *see* `app`
Procedure call frame, 338, 1005
    continuation representing, 445, 448,
        1043, 1132
    deallocation, 1144
procedure-cont (standard DS function),
    473, 475
Procedure inlining, *see* Inlining
Procedure invocation, *see* `app`
Procedure type, 630, *see also* Arrow type
`proc-point-impl` (procedural
        implementation of points), 840
Prod (product semantic domain)
    in CBV product DS, 542, 543
`prod` (tuple creation), 541
    type reconstruction, 825
    type rule in FLEX, 676
`prodof` (tuple type constructor), 676–677
    covariant subtyping in FLEX/S, 703
    kind checking in FLEX/SPDK, 760
    type equivalence, 680
    type reconstruction, 825
[*prodof-≈*] (type-equivalence rule), 679,
    680
[*prodof-⊑*] (FLEX/S subtype rule), 703
[*prodof-elim*] (FLEX type rule), 676, 677
[*prodof-intro*] (FLEX type rule), 676
Producer/consumer coroutine, 457–461
Product, 319, 539–566
    call-by-name (CBN), 551–552
    call-by-value, 551
    Church pair, 302
    Church tuple, 225
    of domains ($\times$), 1173–1175
    fixed-length, 541–545
    heterogeneous, 548, 677
    homogeneous, 548, 677
    immutable, 541–561
    lazy (CBL), 552–555
    mutable, 561–566, 1031, 1101, 1104,
        1128

named, 549–550, 677–678
nonstrict, 551–561
positional, 541–549, *see also* Positional
    product
projection, *see* Projection of product
of set family ($\prod_{i=1}^{n} A_i$), 1153
of sets ($\times$), 1153
special syntax, 548–549
strict (CBV), 541–550
sum as dual of, 571, 573, 613
type as dimension, 548
typed, *see* Typed product
variable-length, 545–547
Product domain, 539, 1173–1175
    partial order on, 177–178
Product indexing, 547
    0- vs. 1-based indexing, 547
    calculated name, 550
    calculated position, 544
    literal name, 549
    literal position, 541
    PASCAL array indexing, 547
Production rule, 24
    production, 26
Profiling, 1057
Prog (program domain)
    in EL, 25
    in FIL, 1031
    in FIL$_{cps}$, 1046
    in FIL$_{lift}$, 1095
    in FIL$_{reg}$, 1101
    in μFLARE, 773
    in FLARE, 814
    in FLARE/V, 1010
    in μFLEX, 628
    in FLEX, 697
    in FLIC, 401
    in FLICK, 398
    in FLK, 211
    in FLEX/M, 893
    in FLEX/SP, 741
    in FLEX/SPD, 753
    in HOOK, 363

[*prog*]
  ELM BOS rule, 77
  ELMM BOS rule, 75
  µFLARE type rule, 774, 775
  FLARE/E type/effect rule, 953
  µFLEX type rule, 644, 647
  POSTFIX BOS rule, 78
ProgDesc (program description in
      FLEX/SPD), 753
[*prog-left*] (ELMM SOS rule), 65
[*prog_R*] (µFLARE type reconstruction
      rule), 793, 794
  extended to support pattern matching,
      831
Program, *see also* Prog
  arguments in FLK, 217
  assignment-free, 1019
  denotational semantics vs., 128
  execution in SOS, 58–62
  in FL, 230–232
  in FLK, 209, 217
  of language *L*, *see* Prog (program
      domain), in *L*
  reasoning about, *see* Denotational
      reasoning; Operational reasoning
  valid, in TORTOISE, 1025
Program context, 91
Program counter, 1122
Program equality
  proving via DS, 145–147
  in SOS, *see* Observational equivalence
Programming by differences, 366
Programming language
  actor, *see* Actor language
  applicative language, 305
  block-structured, 337, *see also* Block
      structure
  decomposition, 207
  dynamically scoped, 334, *see also*
      Dynamic scope
  dynamically typed, *see* Dynamic type
      checking
  expressive power, 471, 619, 727
  extending with new primitive
      operators, 235

full, 208
functional, *see* Function-oriented
      programming
imperative, *see* Imperative
      programming; Stateful language
interpreted, 623
kernel of, 207, 1186
logic-oriented, 445
machine language, 622
object-oriented, *see* Object-oriented
      programming
polymorphic, *see* Polymorphism
reasoning about, *see* Denotational
      reasoning; Operational reasoning
scope, *see* Scope
simply typed, *see* Simple type system
standard library of, 208, 235
stateful, *see* Imperative programming;
      Object-oriented programming;
      Stateful language
stateless, *see* Stateless language
statically scoped, 334, *see also* Static
      scope
statically typed, *see* Static type
      checking
syntactic sugar, 208, 218, *see also*
      Desugaring; Syntactic sugar
typed, *see* Dynamic type checking;
      Static type checking
typeless, 622
universal, *see* Universal programming
      language
von Neumann language, 305
Programming paradigm, 16
Program optimization, *see* Optimization
Program transformation, *see also*
      Compilation; Optimization; Safe
      transformation; Simplification;
      Translation
  alpha-renaming, 1038–1041, *see also*
      Alpha-renaming
  assignment conversion, 430, 439,
      1019–1025
  closure conversion, 441, 1075–1093,
      1117, *see also* Closure conversion

Program transformation (*continued*)
  CPS conversion, 1042–1075, *see also*
    CPS conversion
  defunctionalization, 1117
  desugaring, 1013–1014, *see also*
    Desugaring
  globalization, 1014–1019
  lambda lifting, 1094–1096, 1117
  preconditions and postconditions, 1013
  purely structural, 1012
  register allocation, 1098–1115, 1117,
    see also register allocation
  translation, in TORTOISE compiler,
    1030–1038
  type/effect reconstruction, 1025–1029
Program type (=>), 630, *see also*
    ProgType
  example, 636
  introduced by [*prog*] rule in μFLEX,
    647
Progress rule, 54, 62–71
  proof tree, 64
  structure restriction, 68
Progress theorem for type soundness
  in μFLARE, 780
  in μFLEX, 662
[*prog-right*] (ELMM SOS rule), 65
ProgType (program type domain in
    typed FL dialects)
  in μFLARE, 775
  in FLARE, 815
  in μFLEX, 628
  in FLEX, 697
[*prog_Z*] (FLARE/E type/effect
    reconstruction rule), 968, 969
Projection of polymorphic value on type,
    see Polymorphic value projection
  implicit, 896, 918–921
Projection of product
  CBL tuple (lget), 552–555
  CBN tuple (nget), 551
  immutable sequence (seq-get), 544,
    677
  metalanguage tuple, 1152, 1174, 1189

mutable tuple (mget), 562, 1031
named product (select), 353, 549, 678
named product (select-sym), 550
named product (with), 678
named product (with-fields), 355
named product, dot notation, 550
pair (fst, snd), 213, 675
positional product (get), 541, 676
updatable sequence (useq-get), 545
Proj k (metalanguage tuple projection),
    1174, 1189
PROLOG
  backtracking, 445
  as logic programming language, 538
  pattern matching, 590
Promise, 324, 560, *see also* Delayed
    evaluation
Proof-carrying code, 1000, 1116
Proof tree, 65, *see also* Derivation
  for BOS evaluation step, 75
  linearization of, 66
  for SOS transition, 64
Proper subset ($\subset$), 1149
Proper tail recursion, 1064
Prototype-based object-oriented
    programming, 366
Prototype object, 380
  used to simulate class, 366
Proverbs (quoted), 307
$PT \in$ Pattern, 590
$PT \in$ ProgType, 628, 697, 775, 815
pt-x/pt-y
  dependent type implementation, 871
  dynamic type implementation, 840
  existentially typed object
    implementation, 857
  existential type implementation,
    848–849
  nonce type implementation, 860–861
  using dynamic lock and key, 844
pure (effect in FLARE/E), 947, 949
Pure expression, 428, 880, 947, 973, *see
    also* Purity restriction
  purity test, effect-based, 974–978

purity test, syntactic, *see* Syntactic
purity
referential transparency and, 428
required for type generalization, 815,
816
Purely functional language, 209, 384, *see
also* Function-oriented programming;
Stateless language
monadic style to simulate state,
394–396, 440
Purely structural rewrite rule, 69
Purely structural transformation, 1012
Purely structural type rule, 647
Purity restriction, *see also* Pure
expression
in dependent type system, 875,
880–881, 882, 883
in eta reduction ([*eta*]), 1033
in FLEX/M implicit type projection,
920, 921
in `let` polymorphism, 815
in module system with dependent
types, 916, 917, 937–939
in universal polymorphism, 731, 734,
735
value restriction in SML, 817, 837
push (function in POSTFIX DS)
definition, 143, 144
specification, 133
`put` (POSTFIX extension command), 102
PYTHON, as dynamically typed language,
623

$\mathbb{Q} \in$ PostfixSequenceContext, 91
$\mathcal{Q}$ (POSTFIX command sequence meaning
function), 135–136, 137
Quadruple, 1152
Quantification, *see* Existential
quantification ($\exists$); Universal
quantification ($\forall$)
QUEST, first-class existential types in, 886
Quota for store, 492–493
`quote` (FL s-expression sugar), 219, 222
desugaring in FL, 220, 233

Quotient (/), 1155
Quux, The Great, *see* Steele, Guy Lewis
Jr.

$\mathcal{R} \in$ ElmmRedex, 72
$\mathcal{R} \in$ ElmRedex, 74
$\mathcal{R} \in$ PostFixRedex, 74
R (type reconstruction function), 836
completeness of, 799
deduction-style specification, 791, 794,
795, 836
for data-type definitions, 831
for μFLARE, 790–800
for FLARE, 818
for μFLARE$_{LP}$, 809
for positional products, 825
for records, 823–824
for recursive sum-of-products types,
835
for sums, 826
function-style specification, 794
principal types for, 799
soundness of, 799
$R \in$ Region, 949
$R \in$ RelationalOperator, 25
$\mathcal{R}$ (renaming transform), 1040
$\mathcal{R}$ (relational operator meaning function)
in EL, 129
in POSTFIX, definition, 137
in POSTFIX, signature, 135
$r \in$ *Result*, 132
$RA \in$ ReconAns, *see* ReconAns
Rabbit compiler, 1006, 1116
`raise` (FLIC exception-generating
construct), 515–532
computation-based DS, 524–527
desugaring-based implementation,
527–529
metaCPS conversion, 1072
standard DS, 519–524
in type/effect system, 986–988
`raise` (SML exception construct), 514
[*raise*] (unsound type/effect rule), 986
Raise an exception, 514

raise-quota! (quota construct), 493
raises (exception base effect), 985
raises (exception construct), 532–533
Rand of application, 20, 214
Range notation ($[lo..hi]$), 1149
Range of function, *see* Target of function
Rat (rational number set & semantic
    domain), 1148
Rational arithmetic module, 358
Rator of application, 20, 214
rbind (renaming environment binding
    function), 1040
RDG (register dependence graph), 1107
$re \in RenEnv$, 1040
read (effect in FLARE/E), 946, 949
Reasoning
    aliasing complicates, 437
    denotational, 145–150, *see also Comp*,
        equality laws
    equational, 119
    operational, 79–100
    referential transparency simplifies, 389,
        427
    state complicates, 397, 400, 408, 430,
        440
rec (FL local recursive binding), 211,
    216–217
    free and bound identifiers, 247
    in CBN FLK DS, 283, 286–289, 321
    in CBN FLK SOS, 259
    in CBV continuation-based DS,
        484–487
    in CBV FLICK DS, 417, 418
    in CBV FLICK SOS, 408–410
    in CBV FLK DS, 320–323
    in CBV FLK SOS, 320
    in CBV FLK SOS, alternative, 323
    in CBV language, 378
    substitution, in FLK, 254
[rec] (FLK SOS reduction), 259, 263
receive! (channel reception), 998
Receiver function/procedure, to simulate
    multiple-value return, 394, 451–453,
    1164

Receiver of message, 363
Receiver parameter (self/this), 363
ReconAns (type reconstruction answer)
    in μFLARE, 791, 792
    in FLARE/E, 969
Reconstruction of types, *see* Type
    reconstruction
Record, 353–359, 540, 549, *see also*
    Module
    arithmetic module example, 358
    difference, 550
    dot notation, 550
    dynamic semantics, 381
    examples of, 356–359
    field, 353
    in PASCAL, 561
    intersection, 550
    matrix module example, 360, 361
    module vs., 353
    named product, 549–550
    nonhierarchical scope of, 353
    in PASCAL, 353, 550
    special syntax, 549–550
    subtyping, 701–702, 703–704
    subtyping of, and object-oriented
        programming, 768
    typed, 677–678, 821–826
    variant, 1176, *see also* Sum
    variant, in PASCAL, 567, 583
Record (semantic domain), 357
record (record creation), 353, 549
    DS, 357
    match pattern, 602
    type reconstruction, 823
    type rule in FLEX, 678
record-delete, 550
record-insert, 550
recordof (record type constructor),
    677–678
    kind checking in FLEX/SPDK, 760
    subtyping in FLEX/S, 703
    subtyping rule, alternative, 720
    type equivalence, 680

[*recordof-≈*] (type-equivalence rule), 679, 680

[*recordof-⊑*] (FLEX/S subtype rule), 703

[*recordof-elim*] (FLEX type rule), 677, 678

[*recordof-elim*$_R$] (type reconstruction rule), 823

[*recordof-intro*] (FLEX type rule), 678

[*recordof-intro*$_R$] (type reconstruction rule), 823

[*recordof-with*] (FLEX type rule), 678

recordrec (recursive record), 354, 355

record-size, 550

rectangle (shape constructor), 583–584
from shape desugaring, 588

rectangle~ (shape deconstructor), 584
from shape desugaring, 588

recur (FL local recursion), 219, 226
desugaring in FL, 220, 233

Recursion
in CBN FLK rec, 216–217
in CBV FLICK continuation-based DS, 484–487
in CBV FLICK DS, 417
in CBV FLICK SOS, 408–410
in CBV FLK, 320–324
in CBV language, 378
in domain equations, 132, 150, 161, 201–202
induction and, 1168
in lambda calculus (Y operator), 303–304
in metalanguage, 1168–1169
letrec desugaring in CBN FL, 224–226
letrec desugaring in CBV FLAVAR, 432
mutual, *see* letrec; Mutual recursion; tletrec
type recursion, *see* tletrec; trec
unwinding, 263
value recursion, *see* letrec; rec; recur

Recursive definition, 163, 1168–1169
solution to, 164

Recursive domain equations, 132, 150, 161, 201–202

Recursive type, 688–696
canonical form, 690–691
equirecursive equivalence of, 690, 699, 761
equirecursive subtyping of, 699, 707
finite automata and, 691
isorecursive equivalence of, 689, 699, 761
isorecursive subtyping of, 699
strong normalization and, 688
subtyping of, 706–707, 767
type equivalence, 688–692

Redex, 71, 83

Reducible (SOS configurations), 50

reducible (expression classification), 272

Reduct, 73

Reduction relation (⤳), 72
in CBN vs. CBV parameter passing, 310
in ELM, 74
in ELMM, 72
in μFLARE, 778
in μFLEX, 664
in FLK, 259, 260
in PostFix, 74
stateful reduction in FLICK ($\overset{s}{\leadsto}$), 407, 409
stateless reduction in FLICK, 407, 409

Reduction strategy, *see also* Evaluation order; Parameter passing
applicative-order, 377
normal-order, 293–295, 309, 377

reelect (election construct), 490–492

Rees, Jonathan, 362, 380, 612

ref (PostText command), 106, 141

Reference (ref, ML mutable cell), 397,
see also Mutable cell

Reference counting for GC, 1131–1132

Reference to variable, *see* Variable reference

Referential transparency, 79, 389, 427–428
  effect masking and, 973
  lack of in stateful language, 427
  in module loading, 930
  of polymorphic value, 734
  purity and, 428
[*reflexive-≈*] (type-equivalence rule), 679, 680
[*reflexive-⊑*] (FLEX/S subtype rule), 708
Reflexive domain, 201–202
Reflexive relation, 1154
  partial order as example of, 174
  subtyping as example of, 702
  type equality as example of, 679
Reflexive transitive closure, 196, 1155
Region (domain), 949
`region` (control delimiter), 501–502
Region (of effect), 944, 945–951
  as channel in communication effect, 998–999
  in control effect, 980–982
  effect masking and, 972–974
  in mutable cell type, 945
Region-based concurrency analysis, 998
Region-based storage management, 991–995, 1001, 1145
Register
  argument passing in, 1099
  caller-saves, correspondence with free variable in closure conversion, 1080
  destination register, 1107
  live, 1112
  source register, 1107
  spilled register, 1113
  usage analysis, 1001
Register allocation, 1047, 1098–1115, 1117, *see also* Spilling
  conversion phase, 1103, 1104–1112
  expansion phase, 1102, 1104
  interprocedural, 1111
  register shuffling, 1106–1112
  spilling phase, 1103, 1112–1115
Register caching and aliasing, 944

Register conversion phase of TORTOISE register allocator, 1103, 1104–1112
Register dependence graph (RDG), 1107
Register machine, 1098
Register memory, 1123
Register move, using `copy`, 1100
  reducing number of, 1109
Register shuffling, 1106–1112
Regular tree, 690, 761
relapp (relational operation on boolean literals), 260
Relation, 1153–1155
  antisymmetric, 1154
  binary, 1153
  equivalence relation, 1154
  n-ary, 1153
  n-fold composition of, 1155
  partial order, 1155
  reflexive, 1154
  reflexive transitive closure of, 1155
  symmetric, 1154
  transitive, 1154, *see also* Transitive relation
  transitive closure of, 1155
Relational operation
  in EL DS, 129
  in POSTFIX DS, 55
Relational operator, *see also* Primitive operator
  in EL dialects, 25
  in EL DS, 129
  in FL dialects, 213
  in metalanguage, 1153, 1163
  in POSTFIX DS, 55, 137
  in POSTFIX grammar, 40
  in POSTFIX informal semantics, 10
RelationalOperator (EL domain), 25
`relop` (POSTFIX2 command), 41
[*relop-false*] (POSTFIX SOS rule), 55
[*relop-true*] (POSTFIX SOS rule), 55
`rem` (POSTFIX command), 8, 40, *see also* Arithmetic operator
  informal semantics, 10
  POSTFIX DS, 137

Remainder function (%), 1163, *see also* %;
    Arithmetic operator; `rem`
`rename` (record-field renaming), 355, 356
Renaming a variable, *see* Alpha-renaming
RenEnv (renaming environment), 1040
`repeat` (FLIC looping construct), 420
    desugaring into `loop`, 489
`repeat` (PostLoop command), 103, 141
Representation conversion, 718
Representation invariant, 402, 842
Representation pollution, in closure
    conversion, 1086
Reserved keyword, 210
Residual code, in metaCPS conversion,
    1059
Resignaling of exception, 514
resToAns (function in PostFix DS)
    definition, 143
    specification, 133
`restrict` (record-field restriction), 355,
    356
Restricted ELMM, 117
    DS, 117–120
Resugaring
    of `let` expressions in Tortoise, 1037
    of primitive applications in Tortoise,
        1018, 1032
Result
    of function, 1156
    of procedure application, 214
    of procedure application, simulating
        with call-by-reference, 437
    of program execution, 209
    simulating multiple results, 1164–1165
Result (semantic domain)
    in PostFix DS, 132
`resume` (exception construct), 534
Resumption semantics of exceptions, 514,
    515, 520
Resumption thunk, 508
`return` (FL monadic action return), 395
`return` (procedure/loop termination in
    C/Java), 445
Return code, 514

`return-from` (block-exiting construct in
    Common Lisp), 348
Return of multiple values, *see*
    Multiple-value return
`reverse` (procedure), 238
    iterative version, 390
    recursive version, 237
`revmap` (Tortoise compiler example
    program), 1009
    0. initial, 1011
    1. after desugaring, 1015
    2. after globalization, 1021
    3. after assignment conversion, 1025
    4. after type/effect reconstruction,
        1025
    5. after translation, 1039
    6. after renaming, 1041
    7. after CPS conversion, 1067
    7′. after CPS conversion (without
        simplifications), 1068
    8. after closure conversion, 1083
    9. after lambda lifting, 1097
    10. after register allocation, 1110
Rewrite rule of SOS, 49, 54–58, *see also*
    ⇒; Transition relation
    antecedent, 54
    axiom, 54–58
    consequent, 54
    progress rule, 54, 62–71
    purely structural, 69
    side condition, 57
    transition pattern, 54
Reynolds, John, 537, 768, 1117
rgen (μFLARE$_{LP}$ type reconstruction
    generalization function), 808, 809
rgenPure (FLARE type generalization
    function), 817, 818
RHS (right-hand side) of transition, 50
`right` (tree selector), 451, 608
Right-hand side (RHS) of transition, 50
Rigor mortis, 57
Robinson, J. A., 836
Root edge of RDG, 1107
Root set of GC, 1132

Rose tree, 833

rot (PostFix command), 59

Row-major order, 547

Row type
  complete, 823
  incomplete, 823
  for reconstructing product types, 822
  for reconstructing sum types, 826
  for reconstructing tuple types, 824
  unification, 823

Row variable
  in ML, 836
  in object-oriented language, 836
  for reconstructing product types, 822

RPN (stack calculator language), 61

Run time, 617, 890

Russell, type as operation set, 887

Russell's paradox, 1149

R-value of mutable variable, 432, 436

S (lambda calculus combinator), 296

$S \in$ Stack, see Stack

$\mathbb{S} \in$ SimpContext, 271

$S \in$ Store, 406

$\mathcal{S}$ (stack meaning function), 153

$s \in Stack$, 132

$s \in Store$, 412–413

SA_{error} (StackAnswer error value), 93

Safe transformation, 79, see also
      Compilation; Optimization; Program
      transformation; Simplification;
      Translation
  in FLK, 270–274
  in PostFix, 89–100
  in PostFix, using DS, 147–150
  in stateful language, 427–428
  interference and, 427, 1027–1029
  observational equivalence of divergence
      and errors, 427
  safety of FLK simplification ($\rightarrow$), 274

Safety
  of data, see Data abstraction
  of typed language, see Type safety

Safety property analysis, 1001

Sather iters, 507

Satisfiable boolean formula, 466

satisfy (boolean formula satisfaction
      procedure), 466–470

scale (shape procedure, using typed
      sums and products), 683

scand (FL short-circuit and), 219, 222
  desugaring in FL, 220, 233
  in simple CPS conversion, 1054

Scanned region of stop-and-copy GC,
      1135

Scanner generator, 43

Scan pointer in GC, 1134

scar (stream head), 556

scdr (stream tail), 556

Schema, see Type schema

Scheme, see also Lisp
  as block-structured language, 337, 378
  as call-by-value language, 309
  as dynamically typed language, 623
  as function-oriented language, 209
  as mostly functional language, 384
  call-by-value-sharing of mutable
      products, 563
  call-with-current-continuation,
      505, 538
  catch construct, 537
  dynamic scope simulated via
      fluid-let, 379
  first-class control point, 497
  FL syntax vs. Scheme syntax, 210
  hygienic macros, 331, 379
  mutable string, 548
  mutable variable, 430
  pair, 561
  static scope, 378
  stream, 560–561
  strict application, 215
  vector, as heterogeneous product, 562
  vector, as mutable sequence, 561

scons (stream constructor), 556

Scope of a variable, 223, 245, 308, 334
  block structure, see Block structure
  dynamic, see Dynamic scope

global, *see* Global scope

hierarchical, *see* Hierarchical scope

hole in, 245, 337

lexical, *see* Static scope

in metalanguage, 1195

nonhierarchical, *see* Nonhierarchical scope

shadowing, 231

static, *see* Static scope

scor (FL short-circuit or), 219, 222

desugaring in FL, 220, 233

in simple CPS conversion, 1054

Scott, Dana, 161, 162

$\mathcal{SCPS}$ (simple CPS conversion), 1049–1057

SDT, 879, *see also* Static dependent type

sdup (POSTSAFE command), 104

Sealing an abstract type, 885, 934

SECD machine, 112

Second-class procedure, 349

Second-order lambda calculus, 764

Security

of data, *see* Data abstraction

of mobile code, 999–1000

sel (POSTFIX command), 8, 40

informal semantics, 10

POSTFIX DS, 137

POSTFIX SOS, 55

select (record-field selection), 353, 354, 549

DS, 357

type reconstruction, 821, 822, 823

type rule in FLEX, 678

Selective closure conversion, 1085, 1117

Selector, in def-datatype sugar, 589

select-sym (record selection with calculated field), 550

SELF, prototype-based objects, 380

self (FLIC recursive procedure call), 488

self (receiver parameter)

in HOOK, 366

in SELFISH, 376

in SMALLTALK, 363

[sel-false] (POSTFIX SOS rule), 55

SELFISH (HOOK variant with self), 376

Self-reference, *see* Self-reference

[sel-true] (POSTFIX SOS rule), 55, 57

Semantic action in parser generator, 116

Semantic algebra, 115

in FLK DS, 275–280

how to read, 142–145

importance of studying signatures, 134

of language L, *see* L, DS

Semantic domain, 115

for FLICK standard DS, 473

for FLK, 276

importance of studying, 128

Semantics, 4, 5–6

axiomatic, 441

coercion semantics for subtyping, 718

denotational, *see* Denotational semantics

dynamic semantics, *see* Axiomatic semantics; Denotational semantics; Operational semantics

dynamic semantics of X, *see* X, BOS; X, DS; X, SOS

informal, pitfalls of, 14–15

operational, *see* Operational semantics

static semantics, *see* Effect; Effect system; Type; Type System

static semantics of X, *see* X, static semantics; X type rule; X, type system

subset semantics for subtyping, 718

Semispace in GC, 1133

send (HOOK message send), 363, 364

translation to FL, 371

send! (channel transmission), 998

seq (POSTFIX2 command), 41

seq (sequence creation), 544

type rule in FLEX, 677

[seq] (POSTFIX SOS rule), 55

seq-get (sequence projection), 544

type rule in FLEX, 677

seq-map (higher-order description example), 755

seqof (type constructor), 677
   covariant subtyping in FLEX/S, 703
   kind checking in FLEX/SPDK, 760
   type equivalence, 680
[seqof-≈] (type-equivalence rule), 679, 680
[seqof-⊑] (FLEX/S subtype rule), 703
[seqof-elim] (FLEX type rule), 677
[seqof-intro] (FLEX type rule), 677
[seqof-size] (FLEX type rule), 677
seq-size (sequence size), 544
   type rule in FLEX, 677
Sequence, 540, 544
   array vs., 544
   immutable fixed-length positional
      product, 544–545
   immutable updatable, 548
   strictly decreasing, 70
   typed, 677
   updatable, 545–547
sequence (computation function), 415
   with continuation, 485
sequence (metalanguage sequence
      constructor), 1182, 1189
Sequence domain, 1181–1184
   partial order on, 179–180
   prefix ordering on, 179
   sum-of-products ordering on, 180
Sequence notation, 34–35
Sequence pattern
   in metalanguage, 1192
   in s-expression, 31–32
Sequential program, 996
Sergeant Spaghetticode, 333, 497, see also
      Captain Abstraction
Set, 1148–1151
   builder notation ($\{x \mid P_x\}$), 1149
   cardinality (| |), 1150
   completion of, 184
   countable, 1150
   difference (−), 1149
   disjoint, 1150
   element of (∈), 1149
   empty ({}), 1148
   equality (=), 1149
   finite, 1150

function, 1155–1170
   infinite, 1150
   intersection (∩), 1149
   isomorphism, 1160
   not element of (∉), 1149
   one-to-one correspondence, 1150, 1160
   pairwise disjoint, 1150
   partition, 1150, 1154
   powerset of ($\mathcal{P}(\ldots)$), 1150
   primitive element, 1148
   product (×), 1153
   product of set family ($\prod_{i=1}^{n} A_i$), 1153
   proper subset (⊂), 1149
   quotient (/), 1155
   singleton, 1148
   subset (⊆), 1149
   uncountable, 1150
   union (∪), 1149
set! (variable assignment in FLAVAR
      and FLARE/V), 430
   := vs., 431
   assignment conversion to mutable cell,
      1019–1025
   closure conversion and, 1081–1082,
      1092
   FLAVARK DS, 431–432
   in simple CPS conversion, 1054
   type reconstruction and, 820
   type rule in FLEX, 681
set-car! (SCHEME pair procedure), 561
set-cdr! (SCHEME pair procedure), 561
setjmp/longjmp (C nonlocal exit
      constructs), 506
set-mfst! (mutable pair assigner), 421
set-msnd! (mutable pair assigner), 421
Set theory, 1147
SExp (s-expression domain), 219
S-expression (symbolic expression), 23–24
   abstract syntax tree as, 210, 222, 580
   FLK program input, 259
   in LISP, 43
   quote sugar for, 222
S-expression grammar, 15, 23–39
   concise form, 29
   sum-of-products interpretation, 36–38

S-expression pattern, 26
  matching, 27
  sequence pattern, 31–32
`sfilter` (stream filtering), 559
Shadowing of a name, 231
Shakespeare, William (quoted), 185, 1005
Shallow copy of mutable data, 565
`shape` (data declaration), 583–584
Shape, as sum of products, 577, 583–584
Sharing
  by construction, 935
  by specification, 936
Shelley, Percy Bysshe (quoted), 383
Short-circuit logical operator, 222, *see
    also* `scand`; `scor`
Side condition of rewrite rule, 57
Side effect, *see* Effect
Sieve of Eratosthenes, 558
Sigma calculus, 381
`signal` (CLU exception construct), 514
Signal an exception, 514
Signature
  of function, 1157
  of module, 897
Signature matching of module, 934
`simp` (algebraic simplifier for ELM), 595
SimpContext (SOS simplification
    context)
  in FLK, 271
  in lambda calculus, 292
[*simple*-$\sqsubseteq_{AS}$] (FLEX/S subtype rule),
    707
Simple CPS conversion ($\mathcal{SCPS}$),
    1049–1057
Simple type system, 617–700
Simplification
  algebraic simplifier for ELM, 595
  confluence of, in FLK, 273
  confluence of, in lambda calculus, 292
  constant propagation, 1053
  copy propagation, 1033
  eta reduction, 1033
  in FIL, 1032–1034
  in FIL, and CPS code, 1048, 1064

  in FIL, making confluent, 1035
  in FIL, nonconfluence of, 1034
  in FLK, 270–274
  in lambda calculus, 291, 292
  safety of, in FLK, 274
  standardization of, in FLK, 274
  standardization of, in lambda calculus,
    295
  tail-call optimization, 1064
Simplification step relation ($\rightarrow$)
  confluence of, 273, 292
  in FLK, 271
  in lambda calculus, 291, 292
  safety of, 274
  standardization of, 274
Simplification strategy, *see* Reduction
    strategy
Simply typed lambda calculus, 674, 699,
    764
SIMULA 67
  abstraction, 941
  first object-oriented language, 362, 379
Simulation
  of CBN lambda calculus in CBV, 378
  of CBN parameter passing in CBV, 325
  of CBV lambda calculus in CBN, 378
  of class in prototype-based object
    system, 366
  of dynamic scope in static scope with
    `fluid-let`, 438
  of higher-order procedures with
    first-order procedures via closure
    conversion, 1076
  of message-passing object with
    procedure, 403, 842, 885
  of multiple function/procedure
    arguments, 214, 1161–1164
  of multiple function/procedure results,
    394, 451–453, 1164–1165
  of procedure result(s) with
    call-by-reference, 437
  of state in a stateless language, 390–397
  of state with monadic style, 394–396,
    440

Simultaneous substitution ($[E_i/I_i]_{i=1}^n$),
   256
Single-threaded store, 392–394, 411, 471
  global store, 408, 440
  in CBV FLICK app clause, 418
  in FLICK SOS, 408
  lack of modularity with, 404, 440
Singleton set, 1148
skip (POSTFIX2 command), 39, 40, 41
Skolem constant, 862
Small-step operational semantics (SOS),
   49–73
  answer, 48
  axiom, 54
  behavior, 50–52
  big-step semantics vs., 78
  CBN vs. CBV parameter passing,
   310–316
  CBV recursion, alternative rule, 323
  configuration ($cf \in CF$), 47, 49, see
   also Configuration of SOS
  drawbacks of, 113
  error, 52–53, 58, 60
  final configuration (FC), 48, 50
  game board, 48
  initial configuration, 47
  input function (IF), 47, 50, see also
   Input function of SOS
  multistep transition relation ($\overset{*}{\Rightarrow}$), 50
  n-step transition relation ($\overset{n}{\Rightarrow}$), 50
  of CBL product, 553–555
  of CBN/CBV recursion in FLK, 320
  of CBN product, 552
  of CBV named sums, 572
  of CBV product, 543
  of EL, 67
  of ELM, 67
  of ELMM, 63–67
  of μFLARE, 778–781
  of μFLEX, 662–667
  of FLICK, 405–411
  of FLK, 258–274
  of FLK evaluation, 258–269
  of FLK simplification, 270–274

  of label and jump, 503–504
  of lambda calculus normalization, 292
  of lambda calculus simplification, 292
  of POSTFIX, 52–54
  of POSTFIX, with one-component
   configurations, 70
  of POSTFIX2, 60
  of static vs. dynamic scope, 335
  of strict vs. nonstrict pair, 318–320
  one-step transition relation ($\Rightarrow$), see
   Transition relation
  output function (OF), 48, 50, see also
   Output function of SOS
  program execution, 58–62
  progress rule, 54, 62–71
  rewrite rule, 49, 54–58
  stuck state, 48, 50
  transition path, 50
  transition relation ($\Rightarrow$), see Transition
   relation
SMALLTALK
  as call-by-value language, 309
  as dynamically typed language, 623
  as stateful language, 384
  garbage collection, 1120, 1121
  integers and booleans as
   message-passing objects, 365, 379
  purely object-oriented language, 362,
   379
  self as receiver parameter, 363
  simulating higher-order procedures,
   1076
  sum-of-products data via objects, 579
smap (stream mapping), 559
Smash sequence, 187
Smash sum, 186
SML (STANDARD ML)
  efficient pattern matching, 601
  exception handling via raise/handle,
   514
  functors distinct from procedures, 900
  generative functors, 939
  heterogeneous tuple, 548
  immutable string, 548

implicit-typing example, 626
lack of abstraction in pattern
    matching, 607–610
making type reconstruction practical,
    835
modules with abstract and concrete
    type definitions, 893
mutable variables, 837
record syntax, 549, 550
sharing, 936
signature sealing, 934
simulating mutable products, 563
translucent types, 934
tuple syntax, 548
tupling of constructor arguments, 588
type generativity, 886
user-defined data-type declaration,
    588–589
value restriction, 837
vector, as updatable sequence, 545
SND (second element of Church pair),
    302
snd (pair primitive), 213, 215
    generic type for in FLARE, 813
    POSTFIX command, 102, 141
    sum-of-products data version, 586
    type rule in FLEX, 675
[snd] (FLK SOS reduction), 259
snil (empty stream), 556
SNOBOL4, dynamic scoping in, 338
snoc (list postpending view), 606, 607
snoc~ (list view deconstructor), 606
snull? (empty stream predicate), 556
Soft typing, 624, 837
Solvability restriction, 920, 921
solve$_{FCS}$ (effect constraint solver), 960,
    963
solve$_{TCS}$ (type constraint solver), 788,
    789, 790, 969
    extended to handle effects, 965
Sort ("type" of a kind), 765
Sorting (merge sort), 240
SOS (small-step (or structural)
    operational semantics), *see*
    Small-step operational semantics

Soundness
    of compiler, 1007
    of denotational semantics, 151–156
    of dependent types, 879–881
    of subtyping in FLEX/S, 708–713
    of type reconstruction algorithm, 799
    of type system, *see* Type soundness
Sound with respect to (wrt), 151
Source (domain) of function (*src*), 1156
Source language, 7
Source register, 1107
Source-to-source transformation,
    1005–1009, 1116, *see also* Desugaring
Spaghetticode, Sergeant, 333, 497, *see*
    also Captain Abstraction
special (dynamically scoped variable in
    COMMON LISP), 348
spget (FIL$_{reg}$ spill register get), 1101,
    1112
Spilling, 1100, 1112, 1117
    in IBM 360, 1115
    spilled register, 1113
    spilling phase of TORTOISE register
        allocator, 1103, 1112–1115
    spill memory, 1112
Spinoza, Benedict (quoted), 943
split (list splitting view), 607
spset! (FIL$_{reg}$ spill register set), 1101,
    1112
sqrt (metalanguage square root partial
    function), 1156
square (shape constructor), 583–584
    from shape desugaring, 588
square~ (shape deconstructor), 584
    from shape desugaring, 588
src (function source), 1156
Stack
    CPS continuations as procedure-call
        stack, 448, 450, 453, 1043
    first-class value in STACKFIX, 105
    name stack in POSTLISP, 109
    stack of procedure-call frames, 1005,
        1144
Stack (POSTFIX domain), 53

Stack (POSTFIX DS domain), 132
StackAnswer (domain), 93
Stack-answer equivalence ($\sim_{SA}$), 94
Stack calculator language, 61
Stack equivalence ($\sim_S$), 94
STACKFIX (POSTFIX plus first-class
   stacks), 105
Stack frame, *see* Procedure call frame
Stack smashing, *see* Buffer overflow
   exploit
Stack transform, *see also StackTransform*
  compositionality of, 135
  in POSTFIX DS, 113, 132
StackTransform (POSTFIX DS domain),
   132
Stack value equivalence ($\sim_V$), 94
Staged computation, 1059
Standard DS, 471
  how to read, 476–479
  of exceptions, 519–524
  of FLICK, 472–480
  of `label` and `jump`, 497–498
Standard identifier, 230
  in FL, 236, 237
  in FLARE/V, 1009
Standardization
  of FLK simplification ($\rightarrow$), 274
  in ISWIM, 306
  of lambda calculus simplification ($\rightarrow$),
   295
Standard library, 208, 230, 235
  built-in value, 235
  in FL, 235–239
  top-level value, 235
STANDARD ML, *see* SML
STANDARD ML OF NEW JERSEY, *see
   also* SML
  `callcc` construct, 505
Standard path, 274
Star (∗) prefix for single-threading state
   functions, 392
State, 383–441
  analysis of, *see* Effect
  identity and, 383–384

iteration state variable, 390
lack of referential transparency with,
   389
monadic style to hide plumbing of, 395,
   414
in object-oriented programming, 403,
   441
philosophy of, 383–384, 440
problems with CBN in the presence of,
   425–426, 433
simulating dynamic scope with
   `fluid-let`, 438
threading of, 78, 392–394
time and, 383–384
State component of a configuration, 47
  in FLICK SOS, 407
State context, 443
Stateful language, 384, *see also*
   Imperative programming,
   Object-oriented programming
  lack of referential transparency, 389,
   397, 427
  modularity advantages, 397, 404, 440
  problems with CBN, 425–426, 433
  simulating dynamic scope with
   `fluid-let`, 438
  time-based bugs, 400
Stateless language, 384–389
  lack of modularity, 404, 440
  monadic style to simulate state,
   394–396, 440
  referential transparency and, 389
  simulating state in, 390–397
Statement, 472, *see also* Command
State variable of iteration, 390
Statically typed language, *see also* Static
   type checking
Static analysis, 39, 79
  alias analysis, 944
  concurrent behavior analysis, 998–999
  control flow analysis, 995–996
  control transfer analysis, 978–983
  dynamic variable analysis, 983–985
  effect system, 943

escape analysis, 993
exception analysis, 985–988
execution cost analysis, 988–991
free variables, 247
lifetime analysis, 991–995
security analysis, 999–1000
static type checking, 623
store effect analysis, 943–978
termination analysis, 618
undecidability and, 618–619
Static checkability, 79, *see also* Static
    analysis
Static continuation, 1117
Static correspondence theorem in
    μFLEX/μFLARE, 776
Static dependent type, 879
modules and, 891, 905, 911
Static link, 1091
Static property, 617–620, *see also*
    Analysis time; Compile time; Static
    analysis
Static scope, 334, 336–338
block structure, 337
closure, 378
dynamic scope vs., 335, 339–344
environment diagram, 341
in HOOK, 366
lexical addressing, 342
lexical environment, 341
Static semantics, 16, 617–620
dynamic semantics vs., 617–620
effect system, *see* Effect; Effect system
type system, *see* Static type checking;
    Type; Type system
of X, *see* X, static semantics; X type
    rule; X, type system
Static type checking, 623, *see also* Static
    semantics
dynamic type checking vs., 623–625
as evaluation, 641–643
explicit type annotations, 632, 769
in μFLEX, 640–660
languages with, 623

of list, 685–688
of positional product, 548, 676–677
of record, 677–678
of sequence, 677
of sum, 682–685
of sum of products, 738–745
of X, *see* X, static semantics; X, type
    rule; X, type system
statically typed language, 623
strong normalization and, 673–674, 699
syntax-directed, 648, 713, 714
type reconstruction, *see* Type
    reconstruction
Static type system, 619, *see also* Static
    type checking
Steckler, Paul, 1117
Steele, Guy Lewis Jr., 1006, 1116
    (quoted), 397, 577
Steiner, Jacqueline (quoted), 1042
Stop-and-copy garbage collection,
    1133–1140
Storable (DS storable value domain), 412
in CBL FLAVARK DS, 435
in CBL product DS, 555, 557
in CBN FLAVARK DS, 434
in CBR FLAVARK DS, 435
in CBV FLAVARK DS, 434
in FLICK, 416, 418
in FLICK standard DS, 473
Storage management, *see* Garbage
    collection (GC)
Store, 397
alternative implementation of, 413
in DS, 411–413
global, via single-threading, 408, 440
implementation of, 408
quota, 492–493
single-threaded, 471, *see also*
    Single-threaded store
in SOS, 405–408
Store (DS store domain), 412–413
Store (SOS store domain), 406, 407
store (PostHeap command), 110

Store effect, 945
  allocation effect, 946
  analysis of, 943–978
  combination of, 946
  initialization effect, 946
  pure effect, 947
  read effect, 946
  write effect, 946
Stoy, Joseph, 249
Stoy diagram, 249–253, 337, 389
Strachey, Christopher, 162
Stream, 555–561, *see also* Lazy (CBL)
    product
  for backtracking, 612
  examples of, 558
  iterator vs., 556, 612
  strict list vs., 559
strict (strict function), 200
Strictly decreasing chain, 104
Strictly decreasing sequence, 70
Strictness, *see also* Nonstrictness
  parameter passing, 199
  strict (CBV) pair, 318–320
  strict (CBV) product, 541–550
  strict function, 199
  strict list vs. stream, 559
  strictness analysis, 314
  strict parameter passing, *see also*
    Call-by-value
  strict procedure, 215
String, 540, 548
  immutable, 548
  mutable, 548
String (string set & semantic domain),
    1148
Strong normalization, 52, 79, 84, *see also*
    Termination
  POSTFIX programs, 84–89
  recursive types and, 688
  static type checking and, 673–674, 699
  type/kind system, 761
Strong sum, 877
struct (C named product), 353, 550,
    561, 568, 580

Structural equivalence of types, 864
Structural induction, 88
  in ELMM determinism proof, 80–81
  in POSTFIX termination proof, 88–89
  in Postfix Transform Equivalence
    proof, 96
Structural operational semantics (SOS),
    49, 69, *see also* Small-step
    operational semantics
Structure (example of product), 540, *see*
    also **struct** (*C* named product)
Structured identifier, 886
Structured name, 869
Structured programming, 497
Structure restriction, 68
Stuck (stuck states in SOS), 50
stuck (expression classification), 272
stuck (stuck outcome in SOS), 50
stuckout (stuck token in SOS), 50
Stuck state of SOS, 48, 50
  example of in POSTFIX, 58
  in μFLARE, 779
  in FLK, 264, 266
  in POSTFIX, 52
  stuck at a nontype error, 666, 780
  stuck at a type error, 666, 780
stuffit (unsound cell subtyping
    example), 705
sub (POSTFIX command), 8, 40, *see also*
    Arithmetic operator
  informal semantics, 10
  POSTFIX DS, 137
Subclass, 366
  inheritance vs. subtyping, 723–725
Subeffect ($\sqsubseteq_e$), 947, 949, 954
subexps$_{FLARE/V}$ (function), 1013
subexps$_{FIL}$ (function), 1034
Subject reduction theorem for type
    soundness, 662
Subr (subroutine name domain in
    FIL$_{lift}$), 1095, 1101
Subroutine, **addr** as address of, 1100
Subroutine memory, 1123
Subroutine name, 1094

Subset ($\subseteq$, $\subset$), 1149

Subset semantics of subtyping, 718

subst (expression substitution), *see also*
　　Substitution
　in μFLEX, 639
　in FLK, 254

Substitution ($[E_1/I]E_2$), 253–257
　capture-free, in closed expression, 269
　environment as virtual, 280
　in μFLEX, 637, 639
　in FLK, 254
　in FLEX/SPD, 758
　of type in expression or type ($[T/\tau]$),
　　in μFLEX, 641
　simultaneous ($[E_i/I_i]_{i=1}^n$), 256
　type substitution (σ) in reconstruction,
　　see Type substitution

Substitution strategy for closure
　　conversion, 1084

substTy (type substitution), 641, *see also*
　　Substitution

Subtraction function ($-$), 1163, *see also*
　　-; Arithmetic operator; sub
　on Church numerals, 302

Subtyping, 627, 701–725, *see also*
　　FLEX/S; Polymorphism
　of arrow types, 704
　automata-based approach, 707
　in bounded quantification, 747
　coercion semantics, 718
　contravariant, 704
　covariant, 703, 704
　dimensions of, 713–725
　downward conversion, 721–723
　explicit vs. implicit, 713–717
　inheritance vs., 723–725, 767, *see also*
　　Subclass
　invariant subtyping of mutable
　　structure, 704–706
　modules and, 912, 913
　of record types, 701–702, 703–704
　of recursive types, 706–707, 767

reflexivity, 702

semantics (subset vs. coercion),
　　718–721

soundness of in FLEX/S, 708–713, 719

subset semantics, 718

type checking and, 714, 715

type equivalence and, 708

unsoundness of covariant subtyping for
　　procedure arguments, 710

upward conversion, 714

Success continuation
　for backtracking, 465–470, 612
　for error handling, 461–464
　for iterator, 513
　for pattern matching, 584, 606

Success expression, in match desugaring,
　　596

Sugar (syntactic), *see* Syntactic sugar

Sum, 567–576
　discriminant of, 570, 576
　dynamic typing and, 568–572
　extended-number arithmetic example,
　　568–571
　named, 567–576
　named sum DS, 573–576
　named sum SOS, 572
　pair vs., 567
　payload, 567
　positional, 576
　product as dual of, 571, 573, 613
　strong, 877
　tag, 567
　typed, 682–685, *see also* Typed sum
　weak, 877

sum
　iterator example, 507
　rec example in FLK DS, 286
　tree summation procedure, 608, 609

sumcase (positional sum case analysis),
　　576

Sum domain, 568, 1176–1181
　partial order on, 178

Sum of products, 577–583
  constructor procedure, *see* Constructor
    procedure
  declaration, *see* def-data;
    def-datatype
  deconstructor procedure, *see*
    Deconstructor procedure
  ELM expression example, 577, 585
  list, 577
  optimization of encoding, 578
  shape example, 577, 583–584
  typed, *see* Typed sum of products
  typed pattern matching, *see* Typed
    pattern matching
Sum-of-products interpretation of
    s-expression grammar, 36–38
Sum-of-products ordering on a sequence
    domain, 180
Superclass, 366
Supereffect ($\sqsupseteq_e$), 949
Supertype, 702, 714
Surjective function, 1160
Suspension, 325, 560, *see also* Delayed
    evaluation
swap (POSTFIX command), 8, 40
  informal semantics, 10
  POSTFIX DS, 137
  POSTFIX SOS, 55
swap (cell-swapping example)
  algebraic type schema for, 966, 968
  solving effect constraints for, 969
[*swap*] (POSTFIX SOS rule), 55
Sweep phase of mark-sweep GC, 1141
switch (STACKFIX command), 105
switch (exception construct), 534–537
SWITCHEROO (FLIC extension), 534–537
$SX \in$ SExp, 219
Sym (symbol semantic domain)
  in FLK, 276
sym (FL symbolic literal), 209, 211, 212
  type rule in μFLEX, 644
sym=? (FL symbol equality), 213
  type in μFLEX, 643
sym? (FL symbol type predicate), 213

symb (symbol type), 628, 629
[*symb*]
  μFLARE type axiom, 775
  FLARE/E type/effect axiom, 953
  μFLEX type axiom, 644
Symbol
  as block of characters in FRM, 1125,
    1128
  FL value, 209
  message-passing HOOK object, 365
Symbolic expression, *see* S-expression
Symbolic token, s-expression leaf, 23
Symbol table, 1005
[*symb$_R$*] (μFLARE type reconstruction
    axiom), 793
SymLit (symbol syntactic domain)
  in FL dialects, 211
[*symmetric-$\approx$*] (type-equivalence rule),
    679, 680
Symmetric relation, 1154
  type equality as example of, 679
Synchronization, 997
Syntactic algebra, 115
Syntactic domain, 24
  compound, 25
  primitive, 25
Syntactic function, 35–36
Syntactic purity, 428, *see also* Pure
    expression
  deduction system for testing, 816–817
  in module system with dependent
    types, 916, 938
  syntactic value, *see* Syntactic value
  in type/effect system, 952, 968
  variable assignments and, 821
Syntactic purity judgment ($\vdash_{pure}$),
    816–817
  in type/effect system, 952
  variable assignments and, 821
Syntactic sugar, 208, 218–234, 1186, *see
    also* Desugaring; Resugaring
  in FL, 218–234
  user-defined, *see* Macro

Syntactic value, 428, 816, *see also* Syntactic purity
  in `let` polymorphism, 817, 837
  in dependent type rules, 881
  in universal type rule, 734
Syntax, 4–5, 19–43
  abstract, 20–21
  concrete, 22–23
  named product syntax, 549–550
  of language L, *see L*, syntax
  product syntax, 548–549
  s-expression grammar, 23–39
Syntax-directed type system, 648, 713, 714
System F, 764, *see also* Polymorphic lambda calculus
System F_2, F_i, F_ω, 764–765

T, prototype-based objects, 380
$\mathcal{T}$ (FLARE-to-FIL translation), 1037
$\mathcal{T}$ (HOOK-to-FL translation), 372
$T \in Type$, *see* Type
$t \in StackTransform$, 132
`#t` (true literal), 209, 211, 212, 465
Table
  module example, 906–909
  as product, 540
`tabulate` (sequence constructor), 545
Tag
  of exception, 515
  GC tag, 1126
  phrase tag, 30
  of sum, 567
  type tag, 1124
`tagbody` (COMMON LISP goto label), 347–348
`tagcase` (sum case analysis), 569, 570
  body clause, 570
  body expression, 570
  CBV named sum DS, 575
  CBV named sum SOS, 572
  `else`, 570
  type reconstruction, 826
  type rule in FLEX, 684

[*tagcase*] (stateless reduction rule), 572
[*tagcase-else*] (stateless reduction rule), 572
TagEnv (sum tag environment), 575
Tag environment, 573
Tag-free GC, 1127, 1141–1142, 1145
Tagged sum, *see* Sum
Tagged union, *see* Sum
`tail` (SCHEME stream tail), 561
tail (metalanguage sequence function), 1182–1184
Tail call, 1044–1049
  optimization, 1064
TailCallContext (context domain), 1045
Tail recursion, proper, 1064
Talpin, Jean-Pierre, 994
Tarditi, David, 1116
Target (codomain) of function (*tgt*), 1156
Target language, 7
`tbind` (local type abbreviation), 640
$\mathbb{TC} \in$ TailCallContext, 1045
$TC \in$ TypeConstraint, 784
$TCR \in$ TypeConstructor, 893, 949
$TE \in$ TypeEnvironment, 643, 775, 815, 875, 914, 952
Template, in C++, 748
Term (lambda calculus expression), 291
Terminating language/SOS, 52, *see also* Strong normalization
Termination, *see also* Strong normalization
  early termination of procedures/loops, 445, 455–457
  of POSTFIX programs, 84–89
  of POSTLOOP, 103
  of POSTSAFE, 104
Termination analysis, 618
Termination semantics of exceptions, 514, 515, 520
Term rewriting system, 112
Test expression of conditional, 20
tgt (function target), 1156
`thaw` (undelay evaluation), 228

the (μFLEX type ascription), 628, 633
  in μFLEX SOS, 664
  inclusion rule for explicit subtyping,
    715
  static semantics in FLEX/M, 917
  type rule in μFLEX, 644
  upward type conversion in FLEX/M,
    904, 916, 926
  upward type conversion in FLEX/S,
    714
[*the*]
  μFLEX SOS reduction, 664
  μFLEX type rule, 644, 647
[*the-inclusion*] (type rule)
  in FLEX/M, 916, 917
  in FLEX/S, 714, 715
  in FLEX/S, alternative, 716
Then expression of conditional, 20
this (JAVA receiver parameter), 363
Thoreau, Henry David (quoted), 701
Threading of state, 78, 392–394, *see also*
    Single-threaded store
Thread of control, 996
  communication by channel, 997
  interleaving, 997
  synchronization, 997
throws (JAVA exception-handling
    specification), 514, 985
Thunk, 324–328, *see also* Delayed
    evaluation
  failure thunk in match desugaring, 595
  in producer/consumer coroutine, 461
  resumption thunk, in iterator, 508
  to implement infinite data in a CBV
    language, 325
  to simulate CBN parameter passing in
    a CBV language, 325
Tilde (~), deconstructor suffix, 584
Time
  bugs due to time-based nature of
    stateful programming, 400
  data dependency and, 391
  state and, 383–384
tletrec (recursive type), 688

Tofte, Mads, 994
Token, s-expression leaf, 23
to-list (iterator example), 508
to-list (stream-to-list conversion), 556
top (top type in FLEX/SP with
    bounded quantification), 746, 747
top (function in POSTFIX DS)
  definition, 143
  specification, 133
Top ($\top$), 176
[*top-$\sqsubseteq_{BQ}$*] (FLEX/SP subtype rule), 747
top-level-cont (standard DS
    continuation), 473, 475
Top level of program, 1094
Top-level values, 235
Torczon, Linda, 1116
TORTOISE compiler, 1006
  alpha-renaming, 1038–1041
  assignment conversion, 1019–1025
  closure conversion, 1075–1093
  CPS conversion, 1042–1075
  desugaring, 1013–1014
  FLARE-to-FIL translation, 1030–1038
  globalization, 1014–1019
  lambda lifting, 1094–1096
  preconditions and postconditions for
    transformations, 1013
  register allocation, 1098–1115
  source language (FLARE/V),
    1009–1013
  structure of CPS code, 1044–1049
  target language (FIL$_{reg}$), 1007,
    1098–1102
  transformation-based architecture,
    1007–1009
  type/effect reconstruction, 1025–1029
  well-formed program, 1014
To-space in GC, 1133
Total function ($\rightarrow$), 1156, 1157
Total order, 175
Transaction, 423
transform (function in POSTFIX DS)
  definition, 143
  specification, 133

Transformation, *see* Program transformation; Safe transformation; Source-to-source transformation; Translation

Transform equivalence ($\sim_Q$), 93
  in EL, 99
  in POSTFIX, 92–100
  in POSTFIX, observational equivalence and, 96–98

Transition path of SOS, 50
  length, 50

Transition pattern of rewrite rule, 54

Transition relation, 49, *see also* Rewrite rule of SOS
  confluence of, 82
  in context-based SOS, 71
  deterministic, 50, 51, 58
  evaluation context, 71
  in ELMM, 65
  in μFLARE, 778
  in μFLEX, 664
  in FLICK, 407, 409
  in FLK, 259, 260
  in POSTFIX, 55
  left-hand side (LHS), 50
  multistep ($\stackrel{*}{\Rightarrow}$), 50
  nondeterministic, 50, 51
  n-step ($\stackrel{n}{\Rightarrow}$), 50
  one-step ($\Rightarrow$), 49
  redex, 71, 83
  right-hand side (RHS), 50

[*transitive-$\approx$*] (type-equivalence rule), 679, 680

[*transitive-$\sqsubseteq$*] (FLEX/S subtype rule), 703

Transitive closure, 1155

Transitive relation, 1154
  partial order as example of, 174
  subtyping as example of, 702
  type equality as example of, 679

Translation, 7, *see also* Compilation
  ASTs processed by, 116
  between exception-handling languages, 534
  of ELMM to POSTFIX, 100
  of FLARE to FIL, 1036–1038
  of FLARE/V to FLARE (assignment conversion), 1019–1025
  of HOOK to FL, 370–373
  type-directed, 720

Translucent type, 934

Transparent type, 933

Transparent type bindings, 757

`trap` (FLIC exception-handling construct), 515–532
  computation-based DS, 524–527
  desugaring-based implementation, 527–529
  resumption semantics, 515, 520
  standard DS, 519–524

`trec` (recursive type), 688
  subtyping in FLEX/S, 706–707
  type equivalence, 688–692
  unsound subtyping rule, 713

[*trec-α*] (type-equivalence rule), 689

[*trec-β*] (type-equivalence rule), 689

[*trec-left*] (FLEX/S subtype rule), 707

[*trec-right*] (FLEX/S subtype rule), 707

Tree, *see* Abstract syntax tree; Binary tree; S-expression

Tree decoration, as imperative programming example, 404

`treeof` (example type constructor), 752

`tree-product` (nonlocal exit example), 455–457, 480
  CPS version, 456
  CPS version with nonlocal exit, 456
  non-CPS version with nonlocal exit, 457
  simple recursive version, 456
  version using `cwcc`, 505
  version using `label` and `jump`, 495

`triangle` (shape constructor), 583–584
  from `shape` desugaring, 588

`triangle~` (shape deconstructor), 584
  from `shape` desugaring, 588

Triple, 1152

TRUE (Church boolean), 300

true (boolean literal)
    in EL, 25
    in EL DS, 129
    FL standard library binding, 236
true (true value outcome in FLK), 212
true (true value of *Bool*), 1148
try (FLIC backtracking construct), 422
try...catch (JAVA exception-handling
        construct), 514, 985
$TS \in$ TypeSchema, *see* TypeSchema
Tuple, 540
    equality (=), 1153
    heterogeneous product in SML and
        HASKELL, 548
    immutable fixed-length positional
        product, 541–542
    metalanguage product value,
        1152–1153, 1173
    mutable tuple, 562–566, 1031, 1101,
        1104, 1128
    pair, 1152
    projection function (*Proj k*), 1174, 1189
    projection of ($\downarrow$), 1152
    quadruple, 1152
    to simulate multiple arguments
        (tupling), 1161
    to simulate multiple results, 1164
    triple, 1152
    typed, 676–677
    type reconstruction, 825
tuple (metalanguage tuple constructor),
        1173, 1189
Tuple notation ($\langle \ldots \rangle$), 1152
Tuple pattern, in metalanguage, 1192
turtle (sample HOOPLA class), 371
Twiddle (~), deconstructor suffix, 584
two-args (standard DS function), 473, 475
twos (infinite list/stream)
    in CBN FL, 324
    stream implementation, 558
    thunk implementation in CBV FL, 325
[*tyconapp-*≈] (type-equivalence rule), 913
TyConId (type constructor name), 831
    in FLARE, 831
    in FLEX/M, 893

Type, 16, 620–622
    abstract type, *see* Abstract type
    arrow type, *see* Arrow type
    as abstract description of value, 620
    as approximate value, 621, 641, 699
    as data dimension, 548
    as formula, 700
    as partial value, 621
    as set, 621
    base type, 629
    compilation, use in, 1026
    dependent, *see* Dependent type
    dimensions of, 622–628, 698
    domain as, 1172–1173
    dynamic, *see* Dynamic type checking
    dynamic vs. static, 623–625
    existential, *see* Existential type
    explicit, *see* Explicit type
    explicit vs. implicit, 625–627
    expressive vs. simple, 627–628
    of function, 1157, 1166
    generativity, 886
    generic, *see* generic
    ill-typed expression, *see* Ill-typed
        expression
    implicit, *see* Implicit type
    implicit vs. explicit, 625–627
    linear, 1146
    monomorphic, *see* Monomorphism
    nonce, *see* Nonce type
    in object-oriented programming, 379,
        381, 768
    opaque, 933, 934
    polymorphic, *see* Polymorphic type
    principal type, 796, 799
    principal type property, 836, 971
    principal typing property, 836
    of procedure, *see* Arrow type
    product, *see* Typed product
    of program, *see* Program type
    recursive, *see* Recursive type
    simple, 617–700
    simple vs. expressive, 627–628
    static, *see* Static type checking
    static vs. dynamic, 623–625

subtype, *see* Subtyping

sum, *see* Typed sum

sum-of-products, *see* Typed sum of products

supertype, 702, 714

translucent, 934

transparent, 933

typed data, *see* Typed data

union type, *see* Typed sum

universal, *see* Universal quantification

well-typed expression, *see* Well-typed expression

Type (domain)

  extended with control points, 979

  in dependent type system, 873

  in existential type system, 850

  in μFLARE, 775

  in FLARE, 815

  in FLARE/E, 949

  in μFLEX, 628

  in FLEX, 697

  in FLEX/M, 893

  in FLEX/SP, 731

  in FLEX/SP with bounded quantification, 747

  in nonce type system, 861

  with type constructor applications in FLARE, 831

Type/cost judgment, 989

Type/effect judgment, 951

Type/exception judgment, 987

Type/kind judgment, 762

type : type, 886

[*type-≈*] (type-equivalence rule), 679, 680

  in FLEX/S, 708

Type assignment, 643

Type cast, 717, *see also* Type coercion; Type conversion

  downcast, 721

  upcast, 721

Type checking

  dynamic, *see* Dynamic type checking

  explicit type annotations, 632, 769

  interactions with kind checking, 762

soft, 837

static, *see* Static type checking

subtyping and, 714, 715

Type coercion, 718, *see also* Type cast; Type conversion

  in C/C++/Java, 718

TypeConstraint (domain), 784

Type constraint ($\doteq$), 770, 771

  solution to, 781, 783

Type-constraint set, 787–790

TypeConstraintSet (domain), 787–790

Type constructor, 630, 752

  arrow kind (->>) of, 760

  arrow type (->) as, 630

  dependent, 898

  as description in FLEX/SPD, 751–755

TypeConstructor (domain)

  in FLARE/E, 949

  in FLEX/M, 893

Type conversion, 633, *see also* Type cast; Type coercion

  in C/C++/Java, 716

  downward, 721

  upward, 714

Typed assembly language, 1026, 1116

Typed data, 675–698, *see also* Typed mutable data; Typed product; Typed sum; Typed sum of products

Type derivation, 648–650

  horizontal style, 648–650

  vertical style, 648–650, 699

TypeDerivation (domain)

  in μFLEX, 776

  in μFLARE, 776

Typed intermediate language, 1026, 1116

Type-directed translation, 720

Typed lambda calculus

  higher-order polymorphic, 765

  polymorphic, 764, 768

  second-order, 764

  simply typed, 674, 699, 764

Typed list, 685–688

Typed mutable data, 681–682

  type reconstruction and, 837

Typed pair, 675–676

Typed pattern matching, 742–745, 894–897, 921–923

Typed product, 675–679
  pair, 675–676
  record, 677–678
  sequence, 677
  tuple, 676–677
  type reconstruction, 821–826

Typed record, 677–678

Typed sequence, 677

Typed sum, 682–685
  type reconstruction, 821–826

Typed sum of products, 738–745, 766–767, 894–897
  pattern matching, 742–745, 894–897, 921–923
  typed list, 685–688
  type reconstruction, 826–835

Typed tuple, 676–677

Type environment, 643–644
  empty type environment, 643
  extending, 644
  extending with data-type definitions, 830, 831, 832, 912–914
  in FLEX/M, 914
  name-capture restriction in dependent type system, 875, 879
  primitive (TE_{prim}), 643, 647

TypeEnvironment (domain), 643
  in dependent type system, 875
  in μFLARE, 775
  in FLARE, 815
  in FLARE/E, 952, 967
  in μFLARE$_{LP}$, 805
  in FLEX/M, 914

Type equivalence ($\approx$), 679–680
  automata-based approach, 691
  equirecursive, 690, 699, 761
  isorecursive, 689, 699, 761
  name equivalence, 864
  of dependent types, 872, 874, 877–879, 911
  of existential types, 850

of modules with dependent types, 911, 913
  of nonce types, 861, 864
  structural equivalence, 864
  subtyping and, 708

typeErase (function), μFLEX to μFLARE, 774, 776

Type erasure, 734, 772–774
  μFLEX to μFLARE, 774
  in FLEX/M, 923–925
  of type derivation, 775
  of type judgment, 775

Type error, 621, 661
  stuck at, 666, 780

Type-error slicing, 837

TypeId (type identifier domain)
  in μFLARE, 775
  in FLARE, 815
  in μFLEX, 628, 630, 635
  in FLEX/M, 893

Type identifier (τ), 630, see also TypeId
  for type reconstruction (?t), 770
  unconstrained, 772

Type inclusion, see Subtyping

Type inference, see Type reconstruction

$type_{inp}$ (program input type)
  in μFLARE, 779
  in μFLEX, 665

Type judgment, 645

TypeJudgment (domain)
  in μFLEX, 776
  in μFLARE, 776

Typeless language, 622

Type loophole, 567, 580–583, 621–622, 633, 723, see also Type safety

typeof (function), 656

Type operator, 752, see also Type constructor

Type polymorphism, see Polymorphism

Type projection, see Polymorphic value projection

Type reconstruction, 16, 626, 769–837
  completeness of, 799
  for μFLARE, 781–800

for FLARE, 817

for μFLARE$_{LP}$, 808–812

Hindley-Damas-Milner (HDM), 812, 836

in dynamically typed language, 837

in TORTOISE compiler, 1025–1029

ML-style, 812

of mutable variable, 820–821

of positional product, 825

of typed product, 821–826

of typed sum, 821–826

of typed sum of product, 826–835

pinpointing type errors, 837

principal types for, 799

soundness of, 799

undecidability for polymorphic recursion, 806

undecidability for universal types, 808

undecidability in System F, 837

with type annotations, 837

Type rule, 645

  axiom, 645

  inference rule, 645

  purely structural, 647

  for X, see X, static semantics; X, type rule; X, type system

Type safety, 621, 624, 702, 709, see also Type loophole

Type schema, 802, 805, 806, 966–971

  algebraic, 966–969

  in μFLARE$_{LP}$, 803

  in type environment, 804

TypeSchema (domain)

  in FLARE, 815

  in FLARE/E, 949, 957

  in μFLARE$_{LP}$, 803, 805

Type soundness, 661–673, 699

  of dynamic loading, 926, 927–931

  of μFLARE, 780

  preservation theorem, 662, 780

  progress theorem, 662, 780

  subject reduction theorem, 662

TypeSubst (type substitution domain), 781, 784

Type substitution (σ), 781–783, see also Substitution

  in dependent type, 881–883

  identity substitution, 782

  instantiation of type by, 783

  substitution instance, 783, 804

Type system, 621, see also Type checking; Type reconstruction; Type rule

  expressive, 627–628

  μFLEX, 640–660

  FLEX, 675–698

  monomorphic, see Monomorphism

  polymorphic, see Polymorphism

  simple, see Simple type system

  static, 619, see also Static type checking

  strongly normalizing, 761

  strong normalization and, 673–674, 699

  syntax-directed, 648, 713, 714

  for X, see X, static semantics; X, type rule; X, type system

Type tag, 1124

Type variable, see also Type identifier

  imperative type variable, 837

Typing, see Type checking; Type derivation; Type rule

#u (unit literal), 209, 211, 212

Unallocated region of stop-and-copy GC, 1136

Unary predicate, 1151

Unassigned (unassigned location domain), 412

unassigned, 412

unassigned-location (FLICK error), 485

unbind (POSTLISP command), 109

Unbound (unbound name domain), 276

unbound, 276

unbound-var (unbound variable error), 280, 281

unbound-variable (exception tag), 517

Unbound variable error, 247, 282

Unboxed value, 1124

Uncomputable function, 199, 1158

Uncountable set, 1150

Undecidability, *see also* Halting problem
    static analysis and, 618–619
    of variable mutation, 1021

undef (extended integer), 568

Undefined (function result), 1158

Underscore variable, *see* Wildcard
    pattern/variable

Unholy commingling, 870

Unification, 781, 783–787
    in implicit projection, 919–921
    most general unifier (mgu), 785
    recursive types and, 836
    of row types, 822–824
    signature matching and, 934
    unifier, 784

UnificationVar (domain), 893

Unification variable, 919, *see also* Type
    identifier

unify (function), 784, 785

unifyLoop (function), 784, 785–787

UnifySoln (domain), 784
    in FLARE/E, 960

Union
    disjoint, 1176
    of domains, 1176
    of sets ($\cup$), 1149
    sum value, 568
    tagged, *see* Sum

union (C sum), 567, 568, 580

$union_{TCS}$ (type-constraint set union),
    788, 789, 790

Union type, *see* Typed sum

Union value, *see* Sum

Unique naming, 1038, *see also*
    Alpha-renaming
    metaCPS conversion and, 1069
    not preserved by closure conversion,
        1079
    variable capture and, in CPS
        conversion, 1054

Unique types, lack of in μFLARE, 776

Unit (singleton set/domain), 1148

unit (unit type), 628, 629

unit (unit value outcome in FLK), 212

unit (only value of *Unit*), 1148

[*unit*]
    μFLARE type axiom, 775
    FLARE/E type/effect axiom, 953
    μFLEX type axiom, 644

unit? (FL unit type predicate), 213

Unit interval, $[0; 1]$, 167

[$unit_R$] (μFLARE type reconstruction
    axiom), 793

[$unit_Z$] (FLARE/E type/effect
    reconstruction axiom), 964

Universal polymorphism, 627, 727–738,
    see also Polymorphism
    dynamic semantics, 736–738
    static semantics, 730–736

Universal programming language, 49, 79,
    101, 102, 110, 390
    lambda calculus as example of, 290
    nontermination and, 79–80, 100

Universal quantification ($\forall$), 1152
    equivalent to existential type, 885
    universal type, 728, 735, *see also*
        forall

Unix, reference counts in file system, 1132

unless (FL conditional construct)
    in CBN FL, 324
    in NAVAL, 327
    thunk implementation in CBV FL, 325

unlock (data unsealing), 843–847

unmatched-tagcase-tag (error
    message), 575

unpack (data abstraction use)
    in dependent type system, 873, 875
    in dependent type system, alternative
        version, 883
    in existential type system, 850
    in nonce type system, 861

unpackage (STACKFIX command), 105

Unscanned region of stop-and-copy GC,
    1135

Unsealing an abstract type, 885

[*unsound-cellof-*⊑*], 705

Untyped lambda calculus, 290–304, 622, *see also* Lambda calculus (LC)

Unwinding a recursion, 263

unwrap (undelay evaluation), 315

up (convert to abstract type), 844–845
  existential type without, 859
  in dependent type system, 875
  in existential type system, 849, 850
  in nonce type system, 861, 862
  not necessary in FLEX/M, 902

Upcast, 721

Updatable sequence, 545–547
  immutable, 548

update (computation function), 415
  with continuation, 485

Upper bound, 175

Upward type conversion, 714

us ∈ UnifySoln, 784, 960

useq... (updatable sequence procedure), 545–546

User-defined data type, *see* Sum of products

V ∈ Value, *see* Value

$\mathcal{V}$ (stack value meaning function), 153

v ∈ *Value*, *see* *Value*

Vacuously true, 1151, 1152, 1154, 1155

Valid program or expression, 1025

Valid type judgment, 645

val-to-comp (computation function), 414
  in computation-based exception DS, 525
  in FLICK, 414
  in FLICK computation-based continuation DS, 483, 485
  in FLK, 279, 281

val-to-storable (value function)
  in CBL FLAVARK DS, 435
  in CBN FLAVARK DS, 434
  in CBR FLAVARK DS, 435
  in CBV FLAVARK DS, 434
  signature of, in FLAVARK DS, 431

Valuation clause, in FLICK, 416–420

Valuation function, 115, 134, *see also* Meaning function
  in FLICK standard DS, 476–480
  in FLK, 280–289
  how to read, in FLICK, 417–420
  how to read, in FLK, 280–282
  how to read, in POSTFIX, 136–138
  importance of studying signatures, 128, 134–135
  of X, *see* X, DS

Value (POSTFIX domain), 53

Value (semantic domain)
  in CBL product DS, 557
  in CBN product DS, 552
  in CBVC DS of mutable tuples, 565
  in CBV named sum DS, 573, 575
  in CBV product DS, 542, 543
  in CBVS DS of mutable tuples, 564
  in FLICK, 414, 415, 416, 418
  in FLICK+{**label**, **jump**} standard DS, 497
  in FLK, 275, 276
  in POSTFIX DS, 132
  in record DS, 357

value (expression classification), 272

Value, syntactic, *see* Syntactic value

Value constructor procedure, 583, *see also* Constructor procedure
  from **def-data** desugaring, 587, 588

ValueDefinition (domain), 893

Value environment, 643

Value equivalence ($\sim_V$), 94

ValueExp (SOS value domain)
  in CBL product SOS, 553
  in CBN product SOS, 552
  in CBV named sum SOS, 572
  in CBV parameter passing, 310
  in CBV product SOS, 543
  in FIL$_{cps}$, 1046, 1048
  in FIL$_{lift}$, 1095
  in FIL$_{reg}$, 1101
  in μFLARE, 778
  in μFLEX, 664
  in FLICK+{**label**, **jump**} SOS, 503

ValueExp (*continued*)
    in FLICK SOS, 406, 407
    in FLK, 258–260
    in FLEX/SP, 731
    in FLEX/SP with bounded
        quantification, 747
    in strict vs. nonstrict pair SOS, 319
Value representation in FRM, 1124
Value restriction, 817, 837, *see also*
        Purity restriction; Syntactic value
Vanilla (base type in FLAVORS), 380
van Wijngaarden, Adriaan, 537
[*var*]
    μFLARE type axiom, 775
    FLARE/E type/effect axiom, 953
    μFLEX type axiom, 644
    FLEX/SPDK kind rule, 760
[*var-fail$_{LPR}$*] (μFLARE$_{LP}$ type
        reconstruction axiom), 809
[*var-fail$_R$*] (μFLARE type reconstruction
        axiom), 793
[*var-fail$_Z$*] (FLARE/E type/effect
        reconstruction axiom), 964
Variable, 244, 334, 1187, *see also*
        Identifier
    alpha-renaming, *see* Alpha-renaming
    assignment, 430–439, *see also* Mutable
        cell; Mutable variable
    binding, 245
    bound, 246
    capture, *see* Variable capture
    class variable, 362
    declaration of, 244, 334, 389
    dereferencing, 432
    domain variable, 25, 26, 33, 1172
    free, 246, *see also* Free variable
    identifier vs., 244
    instance variable, 362
    lexical address of, 342
    mutable, *see* Mutable variable
    pointer variable in *C*/PASCAL, as
        mutable cell, 397
    reference to, *see* Variable reference
    renaming, *see* Alpha-renaming

scope, *see* Scope of a variable
    shadowing, 231
    state variable in iteration, 390
    unbound, *see* Unbound variable error
Variable capture, 251–252, 308, 732
    alpha-renaming to avoid, *see*
        Alpha-renaming
    avoiding in dependent type system,
        875, 879
    in call-by-denotation, 329, 330
    in desugaring, 330
    external, 252
    import restriction to avoid, *see* Import
        restriction
    internal, 252
    lack of in closed expression, 269
    in macro systems, 330, 331, 379
    unique naming and, in CPS conversion,
        1054
Variable pattern, in metalanguage, 1192
Variable reference, 244, 334
    bound, 245
    free, 245
    handling in syntactic function, 246
    in CBD DS, 328
    in CBL FLAVARK DS, 435
    in CBN FLAVARK DS, 434
    in CBR FLAVARK DS, 435
    in CBV FLAVARK DS, 434
    in FIL$_{cps}$, 1046
    in FLAVARK DS, 431
    in FLICK standard DS, 477
    in FLK DS, 282, 283
    in lambda calculus, 291
    in metaCPS conversion, 1061
    in simple CPS conversion, 1051
    in Stoy diagram, 249
    substituting for free, 253
    type rule in μFLEX, 644
Variant, *see* Sum
Variant record, 1176, *see also* Sum
    in PASCAL, 567, 583
[*var$_{LP}$*] (μFLARE$_{LP}$ type axiom), 804,
        805

[var_{LPR}] (μFLARE$_{LP}$ type reconstruction axiom), 809

[var-$pure$] (FLARE syntactic purity axiom), 816

[var_R] (μFLARE type reconstruction axiom), 793, 794

[var_Z] (FLARE/E type/effect reconstruction axiom), 964

$VD \in$ ValueDefinition, 893

Vector, 540

Vertical style for type derivation, 648–650, 699

View in pattern matching, 605–612
abstraction in pattern-matching, 607–610
list views, 607

Violation of abstraction, *see* Abstraction violation

Virtual procedure, *see* Method

vlam (NAVAL CBV abstraction), 327

vlet (FL^{--} value binding), 349

void (base type)
as bottom type, 717
in C and Java, 209, 385, 472

von Neumann language, 305

$\mathcal{W}$ (type reconstruction algorithm), 836

Wadler, Philip, 378, 440

Wadsworth, Chris, 537

Wand, Mitchell, 836, 1117

Weak head normal form, 378

Weak sum, 877

Wegner, Peter, 379, 698, 768

Well-formed program, 1014

Well-kinded description, 760

Well-kinded type schema, 957

Wells, J. B., 837

Well-typed expression, 640–642, 645, 713, 714, 770
match expression, 593
metalanguage expression, 1172

Well-typed program, 623

while (FLIC loop sugar), 399, 401, 420, 487, 489

While loop, control context in, 443

Whitespace, 8, 24, 210

Wildcard pattern/variable (_), 516
desugaring in match, 597–598
match pattern, 590

with (FLEX record opening), 678
type rule in dependent type system, 875
type rule in FLEX, 678
with-fields vs., 678

[$with$] (type rule with dependent types), 875

with-...-and-checked-index (computation function), 542, 543, 552, 557

with-...-comp (computation function), 500
in FLICK, 414
in FLK, 279, 281

with-...-val (computation function)
in FLICK, 414
in FLK, 279, 281

withdraw! (bank account procedure)
implementation, 402
specification, 384

with-fields (FL record opening), 355
with vs., 678

with-int (error-hiding function in ELMM DS), 122

with-int&stack (error-hiding function in PostFix DS), 142, 144

with-nameable (computation function)
in FLK, 281

with-stack-values (error-hiding function in PostFix DS), 142, 144

with-val&stack (error-hiding function in PostFix DS), 142, 144

with-value (computation function)
in computation-based exception DS, 525
in FLICK, 414
in FLICK computation-based continuation DS, 483, 485
in FLK, 279, 281

with-values (computation function)
in FLICK, 414
in FLK, 279, 281

Witness
    of abstract type, 886
    of existential quantifier, 1152
Witty, Carl, 102
Word, 1122
Wordsworth, William (quoted), 45, 617
wrap (delay evaluation), 315
wrap-cells (assignment conversion
        function), 1023
Wrapping strategy
    for closure conversion, 1084
    for globalization, 1015–1016
Wright, Andrew K., 699
Wright, Steven (quoted), 383
write (effect in FLARE/E), 946, 949
write-disk (effect), 999
wrong-number-of-args (error), 258, 283,
        289, 473, 477
wrt (with respect to), 151

XML, 581
    Fahrenheit-to-Celsius conversion
        example, 581
    sum-of-products data via markups, 580

$Y \in$ SymLit, *see* SymLit
Yacc (parser generator), 43
Yielding procedure, 507
Yochelson, Jerome C., 1145
Y operator (lambda calculus fixed-point
        combinator), 303, 930, 931
Yosemite Sam (quoted), 1119

$Z \in$ Assignment, 406
Z (type/effect reconstruction function),
        959, 960, 961, 963–972
    completeness of, 970
    R vs., 966, 971
    soundness of, 970
zgen (type/effect/region generalization),
        967, 968
zgenPure (type/effect/region
        generalization), 967, 968
    proposed by Bud Lojack, 979